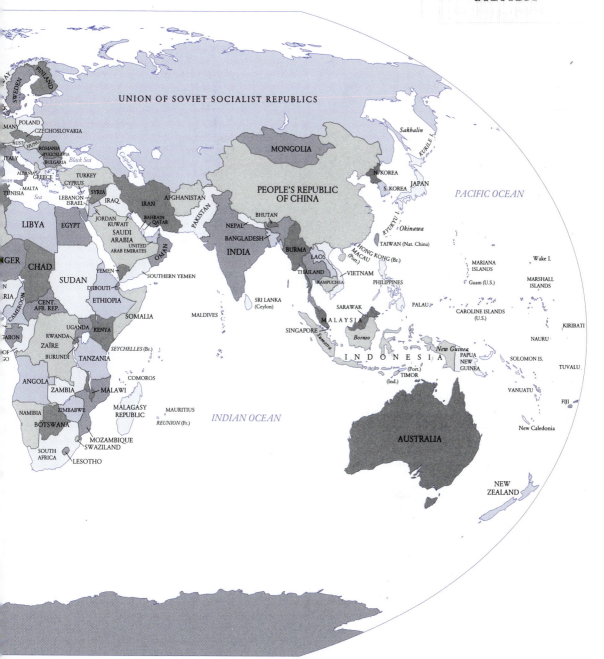

UNION OF SOVIET SOCIALIST REPUBLICS

PACIFIC OCEAN

MONGOLIA

PEOPLE'S REPUBLIC
OF CHINA

Sakhalin

N. KOREA

S. KOREA JAPAN

RYUKYU I.

Okinawa

TAIWAN (Nat. China)

HONG KONG (Br.)
MACAU
(Port.)

Wake I.

MARIANA
ISLANDS

Guam (U.S.)

MARSHALL
ISLANDS

FINLAND

SWEDEN

POLAND
CZECHOSLOVAKIA
AUST. HUNG.
ROMANIA
YUGOSLAVIA
BULGARIA   *Black Sea*
ALBANIA GREECE   TURKEY
CYPRUS
MALTA   SYRIA
TUNISIA   LEBANON
Sea   ISRAEL   IRAQ
JORDAN   KUWAIT
BAHRAIN
QATAR
LIBYA   EGYPT   SAUDI
ARABIA
UNITED
ARAB EMIRATES
OMAN

AFGHANISTAN

IRAN

PAKISTAN

BHUTAN

NEPAL

BANGLADESH

INDIA   BURMA

LAOS

VIETNAM

THAILAND

KAMPUCHEA

PHILIPPINES

PALAU

CAROLINE ISLANDS
(U.S.)

KIRIBATI

NAURU

ITALY

NIGER   CHAD

SUDAN

YEMEN

SOUTHERN YEMEN

DJIBOUTI

ETHIOPIA

SOMALIA

CENT.
AFR. REP.

CAMEROON

UGANDA   KENYA

RWANDA
ZAÏRE
BURUNDI

TANZANIA

SRI LANKA
(Ceylon)

MALDIVES

SEYCHELLES (Br.)

SINGAPORE

MALAYSIA

SARAWAK

Borneo

I N D O N E S I A

New Guinea

PAPUA
NEW
GUINEA

SOLOMON IS.

TUVALU

ANGOLA

ZAMBIA   MALAWI

NAMIBIA   ZIMBABWE

BOTSWANA

MALAGASY
REPUBLIC

COMOROS

MAURITIUS

REUNION (Fr.)

INDIAN OCEAN

(Port.)
TIMOR
(Ind.)

VANUATU

FIJI

New Caledonia

SOUTH
AFRICA

MOZAMBIQUE
SWAZILAND

LESOTHO

AUSTRALIA

NEW
ZEALAND

Caspian Sea

KURILE I.

SEVENTH EDITION

POLITICS AMONG NATIONS
The Struggle for Power and Peace

Hans J. Morgenthau
*Late Albert A. Michelson Distinguished Service
Professor of Political Science and Modern History
at the University of Chicago
and Late Director of the Center for the
Study of American Foreign Policy at the University of Chicago*

Revised by
Kenneth W. Thompson
*Director, Miller Center of Public Affairs
University of Virginia*

and
W. David Clinton
*Associate Professor of Political Science
Tulane University*

Boston   Burr Ridge, IL   Dubuque, IA   Madison, WI   New York   San Francisco   St. Louis
Bangkok   Bogotá   Caracas   Kuala Lumpur   Lisbon   London   Madrid   Mexico City
Milan   Montreal   New Delhi   Santiago   Seoul   Singapore   Sydney   Taipei   Toronto

The **McGraw·Hill** Companies

 Higher Education

POLITICS AMONG NATIONS, 7/e

Published by McGraw-Hill/Irwin, a business unit of The McGraw-Hill Companies, Inc., 1221
Avenue of the Americas, New York, NY, 10020. Copyright © 2006, 1985, 1978, 1973, 1967, 1960,
1954, 1948 by The McGraw-Hill Companies, Inc. All rights reserved. No part of this publication may
be reproduced or distributed in any form or by any means, or stored in a database or retrieval system,
without the prior written consent of The McGraw-Hill Companies, Inc., including, but not limited
to, in any network or other electronic storage or transmission, or broadcast for distance learning.

Some ancillaries, including electronic and print components, may not be available to customers
outside the United States.

This book is printed on acid-free paper.

1 2 3 4 5 6 7 8 9 0 FGR/FGR 0 9 8 7 6 5

ISBN 0-07-289539-X

Vice president and Editor-in-chief: *Emily Barrosse*
Publisher: *Lyn Uhl*
Senior sponsoring editor: *Monica Eckman*
Development editor: *Margaret Manos*
Marketing manager: *Katherine Bates*
Media producer: *Sean Crowley*
Production editor: *Mel Valentin*
Design manager: *Violeta Diaz*
Cover and interior designer: *Susan Breitbard*
Art editor: *Ayelet Arbel*
Senior production supervisor: *Rich DeVitto*
Typeface: *10/12 Garamond BE Regular*
Compositor/CSR: *International Typesetting and Composition*
Printer: *Quebecor World Fairfield Inc.*

Library of Congress Cataloging-in-Publication Data

Morgenthau, Hans Joachim, 1904–1980
    Politics among nations : the struggle for power and peace / Hans J. Morgenthau.–7th ed.
    / revised by Kenneth W. Thompson and W. David Clinton.
        p. cm.
    Includes bibliographical references and index.
    ISBN 0-07-289539-X (alk. paper)
        1. International relations–Textbooks. I. Thompson, Kenneth W., 1921– II. Clinton, W.
David. III. Title.
JZ1242.M68 2005
327–dc22   2005041520

www.mhhe.com

Preface

For over five decades *Politics Among Nations* has been considered by many the premier text in international politics. Now appearing in its seventh edition, its main themes, including national interest, power, and diplomacy, are commonplace among practitioners of foreign policy. At the same time, its value for a wider public is beginning to be felt, especially when assertions are heard that "9/11 has changed everything." Certainly, circumstances have altered since 2001, and even more since the appearance of the sixth edition in 1985. But it was Professor Morgenthau's conviction that, beneath the rapid succession of events, certain basic characteristics of international politics remained that were essential to understanding the ebb and flow of contemporary international life.

Our agreement with this conviction led to the two complementary decisions made early on in the preparation of this edition. First, we have preserved essentially intact the entire text of the sixth edition. Professor Morgenthau believed that his classic text, as it moved through successive editions during his lifetime, should retain unaltered the core elements of his philosophy of international relations: a realist theory, politics as a struggle for power, the foreign policies of the major powers, nationalism, national power, diplomacy, and the possibilities for a world state. The sixth edition (the first posthumous edition) itself consciously kept to a minimum the changes it made to Professor Morgenthau's fifth edition, confining them to the updating of factual material and some brief excisions of material such as that on judicial settlement, which had been considered in an earlier section of the book on international law. In preparing the sixth edition, Professor Thompson— with the able assistance of Mr. Peter Gellman, and relying on Professor Morgenthau's papers, made available at Alderman Library at the University of Virginia through the cooperation of his children, Susanna and Matthew—sought to emulate the approach of Morgenthau, who had written in his preface to the fifth edition that it had continued "in an organic and almost inevitable fashion the work of the preceding editions." In a like spirit we have decided to let the seventh edition speak for itself. We should note that throughout the manuscript the male pronoun predominates, as was customary at the time the book was first published. In the sixth edition, and therefore in the seventh edition, the decision was made not to alter the original language. We would hope that we might be understood as referring to men and women wherever appropriate in our use of the male pronoun.

Nevertheless, the march of events since 1985 cannot be ignored—hence our second editorial decision. As part of our effort to suggest the continuing relevance of Professor Morgenthau's thought even in the vastly changed circumstances of contemporary international life, we have made two additions to this classic text. The first is found at the beginning of the book; it is an introductory essay in which we set out the timeless insights of the realist approach to international politics with which he is so closely associated, note some underappreciated aspects of his thought as revealed in *Politics Among Nations,* and speak to several current problems at the beginning of the twenty-first century. The second addition may be found at the conclusion of the book. It consists of several essays by recognized scholars of varying traditions of international thought, in which they respond to Professor Morgenthau's realism from within those other traditions, as well as an essay by Admiral William Crowe, speaking from within the realist tradition and applying it to issues of war and peace facing the United States in the contemporary world. Timely essays in current events by General Brent-Scowcroft and Ambassador David Newsom have also been included. In approaching the opportunity of bringing Professor Morgenthau's wisdom to a new generation of students and citizens in this way, we believe that we are acting on the best authority—the example set by Morgenthau himself in his editing, along with Professor Thompson, of another classic work—*Principles and Problems of International Politics: Selected Readings* (New York: Alfred A. Knopf, 1950).

For most students of international relations, *Politics Among Nations* requires no introduction. It has become an intellectual staple for faculty and graduate students and for thousands of undergraduate students. It is our hope that the present edition will serve to broaden its audience even further, reaching new readers and serving the changing needs of a new era in higher education and public affairs.

Kenneth W. Thompson
W. David Clinton

Contents

MAPS

CHARTS

Foreword

The Continuing Relevance of Politics Among Nations

"If our discipline [of international relations] has any founding father, it is [Hans] Morgenthau," states one contemporary scholar who is neither an acolyte of Morgenthau's realism nor an inconsiderable scholarly figure in his own right.[1] At the outset of the twenty-first century, who would disagree with this assessment of either Morgenthau or his most famous work, *Politics Among Nations*? More than fifty years after the appearance of such a path-breaking analysis, its admirers attempt to build on its insights even as its critics feel obliged to begin their arguments with an effort to demonstrate its inadequacies. It remains the single most influential text on international relations and has guided the intellectual development of more than one generation of American students.

In one sense, then, the task of stating the relevance of *Politics Among Nations* is very simple; it is attested to in practically every introductory international relations class as instructors respond to its arguments, either explicitly or implicitly. In another sense, however, championing this classic book more than twenty years after the death of its eminent author is quite difficult because of its very absorption into the bloodstream of the discipline. Those parts of it with which contemporary scholars agree, they often simply appropriate as part of the generally understood background conditions of international life. "Everyone knows that" is the watchword, with the implication that Morgenthau need no more be cited than Isaac Newton be quoted when one observes that an apple has fallen to the ground. (What this causal transformation of the contentions of *Politics Among Nations* into "common sense" forgets is that, at the time of its initial publication, many of these arguments were thought extremely contentious!) At the same time, those of Morgenthau's arguments with which there is disagreement receive the attention, frequently with the observation that, whatever their worth in the days of the Cold War, they are certainly not valid today.

Our task, therefore, in explaining why a new edition of *Politics Among Nations* is a worthwhile contribution is a threefold one. First, this introductory essay will, in a fairly summary form, note certain fundamental observations about international life, identified with realism as Morgenthau understood it, that remain valid in the aftermath of the Cold War and in the midst of the War on Terrorism. These points are closely connected with a classical realist view of the world and thus need not be discussed at length, except to note that their acuteness did not desert them with the collapse of the Soviet Union. Second, we shall present a case for considering a concern with the ethical deterioration of the international system as equally an inheritance from Morgenthau; the greater detail in this section is necessitated by the often-encountered assumption that ethics was not his concern. Third, the essay will conclude by applying Morgenthau's ideas to contemporary events, in a *tour d'horizon* of the international scene, with all its elements that he could not have imagined in his lifetime but that nonetheless he could powerfully have grasped using the intellectual framework found in his great work. The argument here, in other words, moves from familiar principles, to an unfamiliar principle, to the application of those principles.

REALISM AND THE PERENNIAL PRESENCE OF CONFLICT

Realists have always been fascinated by conflict. While not condoning it, they have never followed the irenic call that conflict, even only violent conflict, can be removed root and branch from international life. To say that international conflict has continued to occur following the Cold War, just as it did prior to that struggle, is to note a truism. Still, Morgenthau would not have been surprised by the refusal of the world to become a peaceful, cooperative place simply because the Soviet Union ceased to exist.

Realism, then, expects to find conflict as the usual pattern of interaction in international politics. Differences in circumstances and views create different definitions of self-interest, and these interests clash. The energy of self-interest as a motor or motive force, and the weakness of the moral or institutional brake, drives us into contests the outcomes of which are largely determined by relative power.

The relish that realists sometimes evince in noting the ubiquity of conflict can be connected to their debunking predilections, as they seek to puncture the assertions by their intellectual opponents that harmony has been achieved, or readily can be, through the comparatively simple application of rationality, morality, or institutional adjustment. To the extent that the roots of conflict are found in human nature, the belief that strife is an inevitable part of political life fits well with the tragic line of realist descent. Morgenthau freely conceded that his view of human nature was a bleak one.

In fact, it could be argued that realists, in advocating reliance on touchstones such as *raison d'état* and the balance of power, endeavor to break out of this grim and repetitive cycle and place statesmanship on the more promising footing of calculable self-interest.[2] Even here, nonetheless, the furthest that the realist can be persuaded to go is the moderation, limitation, and channeling of conflict, not its abolition. Even if their prescriptions are adopted, these prudent calculators do not allow their hopes to be raised so high. Contests, threats, and counterthreats are still the norm, even if they are veiled in caution and diplomatic protocol. No realists expect the lion and the lamb to lie down together, any more than they anticipate two lions ceasing to contend for preeminence. If the contest can be settled through growls and menacing body language without recourse to sanguinary combat, so much the better, but in the end one will has prevailed over the other. In such a conflict-ridden environment, if one does not behave somewhat aggressively, one will only be taken advantage of. In other words, prudence encompasses not just a sense of how safe it is to rely on the pacifying effects of international society but also a shrewdness in wielding the instruments of power effectively. The mutually beneficial balance rests on the assumption of the subtle pursuit of self-interest by the major players; overall stability relies on restrained, but nevertheless real, conflict.

Thus, in the well-publicized disputes between the United States and some of its European allies—disputes that the end of the Cold War and the disappearance of a common enemy permitted to emerge in full force—it was sometimes overlooked that, along with their reluctance to employ military force against *Iraq,* the Europeans were willing (or at least stated that they were willing) to employ economic coercion by granting or withholding access to their markets depending on *Iran's* cooperation with international inspection of its nuclear program. As Reinhold Niebuhr pointed out, coercion involves the infliction of pain, whether through military strikes or through economic sanctions, and political life almost always operates through the medium of coercion. Even if one adopts a narrower definition of coercion that restricts it to military action, there is the example of China's armed demonstrations to assert its claims to the potentially oil-rich Spratly Islands chain. If Vietnam, Taiwan, Malaysia, Brunei, or the Philippines wished to contest these claims, they would also have to be prepared to back up their positions with force, either their own or that of an outside power prepared to support them, such as the United States.[3] Conflict in the twenty-first century might occur over religious fundamentalism or over natural resources, but conflict, it seemed, there would be; and realism claimed to impart the necessary tough-mindedness to accept the reality of conflict, wage it, and prevail in it. Even a stalemate would rest on the unwillingness of any party to press its claims too far, for fear of provoking coercive action by the others; the avoidance of open conflict would be achieved through conflict at one remove. Players would be willing to resort to diplomacy because they counted the costs of confronting other states that had demonstrated that they were prepared to engage in conflict. Without that anticipation of counteraction, however, the shadow of the future would not deter present coercive actions. Into this side of international life, realism gives the clearest insights.

To the extent that they are not shocked to find conflict a part of the international system (because they do not *discover* this is so, they *assume* it), realists may be inoculated against overreacting to it. This is another way of saying that they would wish to confront the phenomenon of conflict with prudence. It will do a people who have suffered a severe injury no good to allow their justifiable anger to cause them to strike out wildly without considering coolly how to attain their military objectives. No state has unlimited resources, and all may confront multiple dangers. It is precisely the recognition that another conflict lurks in the distance that warns a state against, in all but the most desperate circumstances, unwisely overinvesting in the present one.

The ideological battle that was an important part of the Cold War has, of course, been superseded. A world in which the members of international society are not bitterly divided over the proper domestic organization of states and societies is a world in which one significant cause of war has been removed. More generally, the realist tradition would be inclined to search out motives of power and interest behind publicly professed ideological aspirations as the true reasons for collisions among any repositories of power, and would see the discrediting of Communism not only as the defeat of a tyranny but also as a desirable occasion for clearing away the underbrush of slogans that had obscured underlying suspicions relating to resources, prestige, and control. But has this conflict only been replaced by a new quasi-ideological confrontation between the West and Muslim fundamentalism?

An appreciation for the careful attention that realists have paid to conflict carries with it the implication, naturally enough, that they have less to say about cooperation. Certainly, selfless dedication to a common goal is not the primary preoccupation of realists, many of whom lived through eras of widespread international and domestic disorder, if not of systemic collapse. Rivalry, suspicion, confrontation—these are the relations that realists find most illuminating about international politics. Accommodation, amity, cooperation—these, for realists, are always more tentative and less fundamental, more of an overlay softening and concealing but never abolishing the relations of power underneath. This is not to say that such lineaments of international society as the diplomatic system are unknown to realists—Morgenthau, for one, discusses them at length, as we shall see below—but in his work one always finds the reminder that these practices are not a substitute for power politics. Instead, they are a way of guiding power in ways that all sides find useful, as well as a path toward the development of shared norms that will allow the competition for power to go on in less ferocious ways than were seen, for instance, during the Cold War.

The question then arises whether trust and collaboration have flourished in the post–Cold War period in such profusion as to create substantial areas of international life in which realist assumptions are out of sync with actual diplomatic, economic, or strategic practice. Without doubt, relations between the two former centers of power in the Cold War system have improved, the unprecedented experiment in regional integration and the creation of supranational institutions in Europe has continued, and international financial institutions such as the World Trade Organization have been granted increased scope and authority. The allying of Russia and China in an effort to balance the power of the United States, long predicted by many neorealists, has yet to occur. Still, one may wonder whether these developments constitute a remolding of the presuppositions at the heart of the system. It is possible to argue that enmity between Washington and Moscow has diminished almost to the vanishing point because the latter is no longer an active rival to the former—and even here certain European capitals would like to maintain NATO as an insurance policy against a renewal of the power and the ambitions of the Russian state. The rounds of negotiations under the aegis of the WTO remain very much encounters in which the players jealously guard and seek to advance their economic interests. A Sino-Russian bloc balancing the United States has not emerged, but a Franco-German one, atop the new power bloc represented by the European Union, is at least conceivable. The point is that a concern for relative power appears to be alive and well in the international politics of a post–Cold War, post-9/11 world. By and large, realists have not maintained that international cooperation is impossible but only that, in order to be successful, efforts at international cooperation must accommodate themselves to the realities of power, rather than vainly attempting to suppress the desire for power or ignoring the pattern of relative influence that the current distribution of power creates. Realism may well be usefully supplemented by other traditions in an effort to understand eras of relative calm and strengthened international society, but that is well short of saying that realism has lost all or even most of its relevance, if the world is indeed entering one of those eras.

REALISM AND THE IMPOSSIBILITY OF IGNORING POWER

The international system has, in the post–Cold War period, arrived at a greater concentration of power than existed at any point during Morgenthau's lifetime. How should the United States employ this power? Realists seem as one in urging restraint, cautioning that the possession of great power does not exempt the leaders of a dominant state from the lust for domination, the misguided confidence, or the irrational passions that have in the past led states to disaster. At the same time, no realist would counsel the United States to abdicate responsibility by following a passive foreign policy. The danger of dirty hands is not one that realists find compelling.

For the realist attitude toward power is in fact complex and at the least bifurcated. Stemming from their understanding of human nature and their reading of history, realists hold such respect for the destructiveness of power and such fear that it will be misused that they are convinced that it must be *controlled*. Realism is little inclined toward trust—except in its resigned acceptance that human can generally be trusted to seek to advance their own interests over those of anyone else. Without the internal control supplied by conscience, one must fall back on external controls, which in the case of the international arena leads to the well-known expedient of the balance of power. Greater or lesser claims have been made for the beneficent effects of a proper distribution of power, but at bottom the rationale for a close and abiding attention to "the power situation"[4] has been that only if power is checked and countered by sufficient opposing power will the danger of its misuse for the exploitation of others be minimized. Even the skillful application of a policy of balancing power may not preserve peace, but the very willingness to accept war as a mechanism for preserving or restoring a "safe" distribution of power illustrates the price that realists have been willing to pay for (that is, the value that they have placed upon) an equilibrium of power that does not expect safety from uncertain self-restraint but instead rests on the solid ground of actual or potential coercion by those holding sufficient power resources to make their threats credible. No person or collective entity could be trusted to hold unchecked, uncontrolled power. Realists from Burke to Morgenthau have long contended against those who claimed that the desirability of their objectives and the purity of their motives meant that they could be trusted with unrestrained power. Power uncontrolled was dangerous, unaccountable power, and this unhappy state of affairs existed not because of the imperfections in one person or set of institutions but because of the flawed psychology or soul of all humans, which infected all institutions operated by humans. Thus the determination that power must be controlled has a particular hold on the imagination of realists.

A second, and at least on the surface not entirely compatible, realist attitude toward power is that it must be *used*. True, power ought to be prominently labeled "Hazardous Material" and not left unattended, that is, left unchecked. It is, nevertheless, a fact of life, and realists place great importance in accommodation to the facts of life. The phenomenon of power cannot be wished away; the only result of an attempt by one group to divest itself of its power will be that the power of other, competing groups will be left unchecked, and therefore probably abused. The fact that the exercise of power inevitably leads one to do evil does not excuse one from the power game, for justice is likely to suffer if some players are more concerned with refraining from dirtying their hands than with protecting the legitimate interests of their people. Realism has little patience with pacifism or with schemes for replacing power-competitive politics with power-neutral administration. Morgenthau would have argued that such as unfounded hope exemplifies the illusions of "scientific man." To say that power cannot avoid being employed is necessarily to imply a concern for using it as wisely or as nondestructively as possible—hence the advice that power must be used is particularly attractive to realists. How can it be brought to bear with greatest effect? How may it be wielded so as to provoke the least countervailing opposition? To what degree is its use compatible with the development of rules and norms among its holders?

The advent and evolution of the post–Cold War world does not seem to have rendered obsolete concerns about either the control or the use of power. Rarely has the safety of concentrations of power been more widely debated than in a unipolar era. Whatever opinion one may hold on the abstract desirability of an international system characterized by the existence of one great center of power, however, the reality of American power exists. It must be taken account of. It can be frittered away, but it cannot be wished away. Discussions of its proper employment are in some measure a continuation of Morgenthau's reminders of the ubiquity of power.

REALISM AS TRUTH SERUM

Realism has continuing relevance for the contribution it makes as a "debunking" approach to political life. As a habit of mind, it is particularly sharp-eyed in seeing the self-interest and hypocrisy that underlie all human (and therefore all collective) actions. Pride and self-interest have not been cleansed from human behavior, nor have government propaganda machines ceased operation since Morgenthau's life-time. When President Charles Taylor speaks to reporters of his abiding concern for the people of Liberia, whose livelihoods he has ruined for years, this skepticism seems fully justified. Some pretensions may have disappeared in the post–Cold War era (those of the former Soviet Union to its self-proclaimed role of defender of the world's downtrodden, for example), but others have become more inflated due to the peculiar circumstances of contemporary international politics (the self-image of the United States as a wholly disinterested or altruistic indispensable nation, or the attribution to the United Nations of a status as something more than the site of interaction of its member states—perhaps the idea of idea of "the world's conscience").

The tragic side of realism is naturally predisposed to look beneath the benev-olent surface and find selfish motivations. Morgenthau's warning against the ten-dency to take the interests of our own group and make them into the moral law of the universe has never been more timely than in an age in which liberal states earnestly debate the degree to which they should tolerate the existence of polities founded on any other basis.[5] The delight that we can take in the domination we exercise over others, or even the pain we cause them, helps to make comprehen-sible the many human rights abuses that disfigure so much of the international landscape. One reason sovereignty is under attack, and political, legal, and moral reasons for humanitarian intervention are being sought, is the sheer number of occasions for such outside interference in the systematic misgoverning of a peo-ple by its own rulers.

So, too, the prudent side of realism discerns advantage in seeing things as they really are, undistorted by self-congratulations or illusions. In all realist argu-ments lies the conviction that an unnecessarily inaccurate picture of the world is an obstacle to the effective exercise of political power, and in a dangerous setting the inability to employ power for one's chosen ends constitutes a potentially fatal handicap. Misconceptions must be debunked, not only because it is desirable to know the truth of things for its own sake but also because the safety of the regime may depend on the correspondence of its policies to the circumstances they are intended to address.

MORAL VALUES AND THE NATIONAL INTEREST

In a world of states the question of the relation between moral values and the national interest is one of the most troubling and difficult ones that statesmen and scholars ponder. It has proved particularly thorny in the realist tradition, not least because that tradition has so often been misunderstood as denying any connec-tion between moral principles and the practical responsibilities of statecraft. At no realist has the charge been leveled more often than Morgenthau. Yet Morgenthau illuminated the possibilities for combining a concern for moral principles with a dedication to the national interest, ironically, by arguing that in his own time the two had been divorced to a historically unprecedented degree. His description of the means by which they could still be brought together remains an insightful and provocative challenge to all who seek to understand international society. It may be approached through his observation in *Politics Among Nations* that "the national interest, as created by the character of modern war, and the possibility of satisfying that interest, as presented by the modern technology of warfare, have had a deteriorating effect upon the moral limitations of international politics."[6]

As well as any twentieth-century realist, Morgenthau balanced the two counterweights of national interests and moral principles in the realist scale. He did so, in *Politics Among Nations* and other works of the period, by contending that the international environment confronting states was composed not only of the distribution of power but also of the climate of ideas. A "tamed" national interest would be restrained by an internationally accepted set of ideas (including moral values) that limited the expression of the power drives of individual states.

To be sure, the Morgenthau of the 1940s and early 1950s can be quoted as an adherent of more than one side. At times he could adopt the tragic stance of condemning all states for the partial, limited view they take in defining their interests. In 1952, when he described as "jingoist whitewash" declarations that historically American foreign policy had been based on moral principles, and termed it "ruthless" instead, he added, "We know that this is the way all nations are when their interests are at stake—so cruel, so faithless, so cunning."[7] Recognizing that in this matter one's own country could be as great a sinner as others was necessary to the acceptance of "the tragic sense of life, the awareness of unresolvable discord" that underlay the conclusion of *Scientific Man*.[8] And he declared that "any black-white pattern, conceived in moral and intellectual terms, is virtually by definition inadequate to do justice to a political situation in which on either side good and evil, wisdom and error, are inextricably blended and intertwined."[9]

More often, he insisted that politics was an autonomous realm in which power was at least the immediate end, just as material well-being was the concern of economics and lawful conduct the concern of law.[10] Within the political sphere, then, it could be said that "the political actor, has, beyond the general moral duties, a special moral responsibility to act wisely, that is, in accordance with the rules of the political act; and for him expediency becomes a moral duty."[11] The consequences of unwise actions, even those with good intentions, went far beyond the political decision maker to his country and his fellow citizens, and "they are indeed blameworthy who in their moralistic disdain for the laws of politics endanger the interests of the nationals in their care."[12] Therefore, "there can be no political morality without prudence, that is, without consideration of the political consequences of seemingly moral action," and "there is no other standard of action and of judgment, moral and intellectual, to which a great nation can repair, than the national interest."[13] When Morgenthau discerned "a profound and neglected truth hidden in Hobbes's extreme dictum that the state creates morality as well as law and that there is neither morality nor law outside the state," he seemingly appeared adamantly amoral: "Between these two conceptions of foreign policy, the national interest and moral principles, there can be no compromise."[14]

Nevertheless, Morgenthau did strive for a compromise between the two. He did so by asserting that, as the leaders of states sought to make out their national interests, they were much influenced by the international set of ideas and opinions within which they worked. The powerful force exerted by "international society," as the English School would put it, made itself felt in even the most materially minded of statesmen, precisely because it was so pervasive that it escaped notice. It was particularly potent in restraining leaders from claiming as much under the rubric of national interest as they might otherwise have done.

Morgenthau could discern this flexibility in national interests because of his two-part definition of this term, which was so central to his thought. The "irreducible minimum" of a state's national interest, "the necessary element of its interests vis-à-vis other units," could be stated simply as its "survival . . . in its identity"—that is, "the integrity of the nation's territory, of its political institutions, and of its culture."[15] National interest considered in this way—as national security—was the hard core that guaranteed the political unit its continued existence, "which diplomacy must defend without compromise and even at the risk of war."[16] Here was the area in which national self-assertion was absolutely necessary and wholly justifiable. No other authority was available to look out for these manifestations of security on behalf of the state, and it was required by this international vacuum to adopt the Hobbesian rule in considering power and not other values its end. The size of the stakes when one was responsible *for* a national society, and the call of moral duty when one was responsible *to* all one's fellow citizens, demanded the ruthlessness to which Morgenthau referred—when national interest understood as national survival was at issue.

When he moved beyond the triad of territory, institutions, and culture, however, Morgenthau opened the way for a more nuanced, even sinuous, approach to protecting one's self-interest, because of the multiplicity of ends that might be considered among the variable part of national interest. "The goals that might be pursued by nations in their foreign policy can run the whole gamut of objectives any nation has ever pursued or might possibly pursue."[17] Here one left the realm of Hobbesian necessity and entered the realm of diplomatic choice.

In choosing the goals that they would pursue under the variable portion of the national interest, statesmen would consider the moral values of the people they represented; to do otherwise would be to undermine the national culture that was central to the unchanging core of national interest. They would consider the interests of other states and the likelihood of conflict over such objectives; "prudence, that is, . . . consideration of the political consequences of seemingly moral actions," demanded a calculation of the costs to one's power of advancing these secondary goals.[18]

What they might not consciously consider, but what could nonetheless powerfully shape their thinking, was an international code of conduct that set limits on both the objectives that states might pursue and the means that they might employ to pursue them. Morgenthau was no materialist; he made it quite clear that, while it was utopian to believe that stability and peace could be achieved by rationality alone (a conviction that is often taken to be the whole of his contribution), it was no more realistic to believe that stability and peace could be achieved by power alone.[19] The intangible influence of an international set of moral principles could, in other words, not only act to restrain policies based on national interests but also serve to define those interests.

Such moral values were so fundamental that they set the contours of practical political action: "Common moral standards are part of the political reality itself which goes into the making of government—nay, its very foundation."[20] True, states determined their policies based on their interests, but certain values were powerful enough to determine what could be considered an interest:

> For although . . . states are moved in their international actions by regard for their own interests and will observe the rules of international law only as long as they serve these interests, the violation of the fundamental rights of other states has generally been held within certain bounds by a few moral principles to which the law of nations as well as Western civilization as a whole owe their existence. The contradiction between these two statements is only illusory; for these moral principles have been so powerful as to exclude from the sphere of political interests, such aims which could only be pursued by violation of those fundamental rights. These moral principles delimited not so much the international actions in pursuit of political interests as the sphere of possible political interests itself, so that it did not even enter the mind of statesmen to regard as [a] possible political interest what could only be accomplished in violation of those fundamental rights.[21]

This was true of international law, which owed "its existence to identical or complementary interests of states, backed by power as a last resort." "Where there is neither community of interests nor balance of power, there is no international law," but national interests—at least those beyond the core interests of survival—drew their meaning and their force as guides to action from "a body of principles which incorporate the guiding ideas of justice and order to be expounded by the rules of law."[22] It was true also of the other practices that, Morgenthau contended, created and then reflected the shared norms, rules, and practices of international society. It was true of "the community-building processes of diplomacy." It was true of the balance of power, which, he argued, rested on an "awareness of an intellectual and moral unity . . . [that] makes its beneficial operations possible."[23] The solution to the problem of attaining international peace—"temporary and ever precarious solution" though it was—depended on three things: "social pressure which is able to contain the selfish tendencies of human nature within socially tolerable bounds," a social equilibrium, and "a moral climate" that promised at least an approximation of justice.[24]

In all these references we see the role of moral values in shaping national interests. Even the most pragmatic of leaders would, without realizing it, be strongly influenced by a set of assumptions about what a possible interest was, and the power of the assumptions was demonstrated in the fact that they remained always unspoken—the background to any specific decision, without ever being discussed as part of the decision-making process. The ideas shaping diplomacy were as significant as the material stakes over which diplomacy was conducted.

This role of moral values was both limiting and limited. It was limiting in that it took certain objectives off the table, making them impossible even to consider as potential interests to be asserted. It lessened the stakes of international politics, squeezing interests down to a manageable size that could be negotiated and compromised. It opened a (welcome) gap between what was physically within man's grasp and what was normatively conceivable for him to grasp for:

> [I]f we ask ourselves what statesmen and diplomats are capable of doing to further the power objectives of their respective nations and what they actually do, we realize that they do less than they probably could and less than they actually did in other periods of history. They refuse to consider certain ends and to use certain means, either altogether or under certain conditions, not because in the light of expediency they appear impractical or unwise, but because certain moral rules interpose an absolute barrier. Moral rules do not permit certain policies to be considered at all from the point of view of expediency.[25]

The autonomy of the political sphere was thus breached; ends other than power entered into the calculations of the political actor, making some steps—which would be useful if the sole criterion was gaining power—almost literally unthinkable.

The role of moral values was limited in that it did not end conflict and self-assertion but only moderated them. When Morgenthau called it "a requirement of political morality" that "the national interest of a nation which is conscious not only of its own interests but also of that of other nations must be defined in terms compatible with the latter," he specifically denied "presuming that the uniformly enlightened pursuit of their self-interest by all individuals, as by all nations, will of itself be conducive to a peaceful and harmonious society." Rather, he assumed "continuous conflict and threat of war, to be minimized through the continuous adjustment of conflicting interests by diplomatic action"; this assumption was made necessary by the fact that one could *not* assume that "all nations at all times conceived of their national interest only in terms of their survival and, in turn, defined their interest in survival in restrictive and rational terms."[26] The power-political realm did not cease to be political because of a diplomatic accommodation, and "[t]hat this conciliation is nothing more than a *modus vivendi*, uneasy, precarious, and even paradoxical, can disappoint only those who prefer to gloss over and to distort the tragic contradictions of human existence with the soothing logic of specious concord."[27]

A "tamed" national interest (for all Morgenthau's skepticism regarding the place of rationality or science in politics, he sometimes referred to a "rational" or a "scientific" one[28]) would be restrained by an internationally accepted set of ideas that limited the expression of the power drives of individual states. These preconceptions prevented states from pressing too far and straining the fabric of international society. Morgenthau not only acknowledged that states had to act in furtherance of their national interests but insisted that they so act, arguing that in the dangerous circumstances of international politics they were both obliged and obligated to look after their own well-being, because no one else would do so. Simultaneously, he recognized the limited, partial view that all states, including his own, had of justice in international affairs, and he advocated placing them all on the same plane of seekers after their own interests. Accepting that "all nations stand under the judgment of God, inscrutable to the human mind," he took to heart the caution against "[t]he light-hearted equation between a particular nationalism and the counsels of Providence." National interest limited by an unspoken consensus on moral values provided the vehicle for introducing this humility into action:

> [I]t is exactly the concept of interest defined in terms of power that saves us from both . . . moral excess and . . . political folly. For if we look at all nations, our own included, as political entities pursuing their respective interests defined in terms of power, we are able to do justice to all of them. And we are able to do justice to all of them in a dual sense: We are able to judge other nations as we judge our own and, having judged them in this fashion, we are then capable of pursuing policies that respect the interests of other nations, while protecting and promoting those of our own. Moderation in policy cannot fail to reflect the moderation of moral judgment.[29]

By restraining the claims of national interests and therefore circumscribing the areas of overlap and conflict between the interests of competing states, moral values would open the way for modesty of policy, diplomacy, and peace.

"THE CENTRE CANNOT HOLD"

What is striking about Morgenthau's treatment of the effect of moral values in limiting what would otherwise become dangerously expansive definitions of national interest is that it is phrased in the past tense. His primary fear for the international politics of the twentieth century was that it had lost these moral values, so that national interests had become unlimited and uncompromising. This state of affairs increased the chances of collisions between nations' interests—a political condition that combined dangerously with the simultaneous vast increase in the destructive technologies available to states.

The "Old Regime"

Morgenthau found the older set of ideas in the values of Christendom—*moral* beliefs that supplied a common framework for political contests and made it "possible for us to refer to the Western world as not merely a geographic unit but a cultural and moral entity."[30] These norms constituted a "framework of shared beliefs and common values, which impose[d] effective limitations upon the ends and means of [states'] struggle for power."[31] Although less than universal, in that they were the heritage only of the *European* states-system, they encompassed all the great powers with which the system of sovereign states was concerned. He described "the restraining influence of the moral climate" in this way:

> There were quarrels within that family of nations, as there are quarrels in all kinds of families. Yet there was something stronger than all those conflicts, something that kept the ambitions and rivalries of nations within certain bounds, and that was the consciousness of a unity, overriding all disruptive tendencies: the unity of Western civilization itself. All the members of that "family of nations" took the continuing existence of that common framework of values and conduct for granted. Their aspirations and policies with regard to each other would go only as far as was compatible with the continuing existence of that common framework. Foreign policy was a limited means to a limited end.[32]

Nationalistic Universalism

"Of this political and moral system little is left today," Morgenthau tells us.[33] Changes in the climate of ideas have destroyed it. Among these changes was the growth of nationalism, "the result partly of the almost divine prestige which the nation enjoys in our time." As the influence over popular thinking of religion declined–and, indeed, "[o]rganized religion tended to identify itself with the national state rather than to transcend it"–and as local or provincial attachments were weakened by the centralizing pull of national loyalty, "the nation became the ultimate point of reference for the allegiance of the individual."[34]

Still psychologically in need of a universal set of beliefs, humans did not replace the old international society with a competition among states based solely on the struggle for power, as dangerous as that would have been. Rather, they took an even more dangerous course, adopting the belief that the ideas or the ideology of one's own nation were the ideas that should govern the entire earth. Thus "[t]his fragmentation of a formerly cohesive international society into a multiplicity of morally self-sufficient national communities, which have ceased to operate within a common framework of moral precepts, is but the outward symptom of the profound change that in recent times has transformed the relations between universal moral precepts and the particular systems of national ethics."[35] One's own national interest was privileged or superior, and states' interests no longer met on a ground of equality: "Compromise, the virtue of the old diplomacy, becomes the treason of the new; for the mutual accommodation of conflicting claims, possible or legitimate within a common framework of moral standards, amounts to surrender when the moral standards themselves are the stakes of the conflict."[36] In each nationalistic capital there appeared an ideological, uncompromising, crusading foreign policy. Nationalism "[n]ot only . . . fatally weakened, if not destroyed, the restraints which [had] come down to us from previous ages, it . . . also supplied the aspirations for power of individual nations with a good conscience and a pseudo-religious fervor. . . . [and] inspired them with a thirst and a strength for universal dominion."[37] Both because of its consequences (leading to more conflicts, which meant more human suffering) and because of its hubris, the triumph of this nationalistic universalism was a moral tragedy.

In such an intellectual and moral climate, the tamed or rational national interest that was a practical possibility under the old international moral society became obsolete. At the very time that optimists were proclaiming the unprecedented application of rational analysis to the problems of international life, nationalistic universalism in fact liberated the power drives of states from the restraints of rationality:

> [O]ur age was destined to experience a decisive change in the proportional part which reason, on the one hand, and interests and emotions, on the other, have in determining social action. . . . The revival of religious wars in the form of warfare between political ideologies, with the concomitant torture, punishment, and extermination of the dissenters, illuminates the degree to which that change has taken place in our time.[38]

As morality and rationality receded, the simple, unadorned contest for power loomed ever larger; in that sense international relations became increasingly overtly "political" and therefore ruthless. Writing in early 1939, Morgenthau summed up the trends of the interwar years and foretold the new war that would begin a few months hence:

> These ethico-legal delimitations of the political sphere itself . . . have been swept away by the totalitarian political philosophies and practices of recent years. The political sphere has now become limitless; there is no longer any human value which cannot and in the long run will not, of necessity, be subjected to political aspirations. This moral revolution in which universal moral principles are superseded by particular political philosophies cannot but deeply affect the validity and effectiveness of the law of nations.

As "the ethico-legal principles of non-intervention, independence, and equality as well as the legal distinction between peace and war" were replaced by the "new politico-moral tendencies[–] . . . superior politico-military power and a far-reaching war-machine, particularly fit for the support of boundless political aspirations"–"one may understand the dread of nations."[39] Well might this destruction of an international community of moral principles and conduct be called a "moral revolution."

The Road Back

As much as it was a demonstration to its American and Western readers of the serious pass to which they had come, *Politics Among Nations* was an explanation of the steps to be taken to reduce the dangers facing the world in the second half of the twentieth century. Of prime importance, of course, was a diminution in the malign influence of nationalistic universalism and its replacement with some contemporary counterpart of the traditional international society. With his unflinching examination of the political impulse, Morgenthau had justified the first part of the subtitle of the book (*The Struggle for Power*); with his exhortation to institute ways of restraining this power drive, he would justify the second (*and Peace*).

The cake of custom had been broken; one could not go back to the Age of Faith after Darwin, Nietzsche, and Freud. Therefore what once might be said to have existed by nature had now to be created through art. What Morgenthau prescribed was a skillful and humane diplomacy that would establish the idea that give-and-take among states did *not* amount to treason. In fact, the act of compromising nonvital interests was, in and of itself, a good thing, because of the habit of mind to which it led—one that accepted the legitimacy of the other players in the game and, still more important, accepted that there was a *game*—a contest, but a limited one, with definite and well-understood rules and less-than-ultimate stakes. Diplomacy, in short, was to provide the modern substitute for the traditional restraints created by religion and chivalry.

The diplomatic approach would turn the very lack of a moral consensus to the advantage of stability and self-control. True enough, at the end of a century and half during which the rise of nationalistic universalism had done its destructive work, there were no supranational moral principles concrete enough to give guidance to states in particular circumstances, nor any enforcement agency to sanction violators if such principles had existed. Given this very thin veneer of international society, what states had to rely on instead was "that relativistic philosophy and tolerance of other political systems and policies based on different moral principles, which is the concomitant of policies based upon the national interest, and the precondition of a number of nations living side by side."[40]

Such was the way to ease over the dangers of the Cold War, for example—not by a fight to the death between Communism and liberal democracy, certainly, but not by thinking that reason and good will alone could resolve that conflict, either. Rather, accepting their divergence in moral outlook as a fact of life, the two superpowers should find ways of coexisting according to common rules that could manage and tamp down their contest. "Thus, while technologically speaking this is potentially one world, morally and politically speaking we live in a world which is separated by a deep and wide abyss from the other world behind the Iron Curtain," Morgenthau readily asserted. "It therefore follows that, despite the profound [technological] changes which have occurred in the world, it still remains true, as it has always been true, that a nation confronted with the hostile aspirations of other nations has one prime obligation—to take care of its own interests."[41] But its interests, as we have seen, should be understood as he wished them to be—as rational, limited claims that, beyond the core of national security, could and should be the subject of bargaining with other states possessing their own legitimate interests.

Morgenthau therefore wished no opportunity to be missed for the practice of diplomacy. (This included the United Nations, as long as that organization was used for quiet discussions and not "as a platform from which to make propaganda speeches, as a stage on which to strike poses for the home audience, as a kind of theater prop with which to strike ineffectually at the enemy."[42] It also included a willingness to set up spheres of influence in an arrangement with the Soviet Union; he approvingly quoted Arnold Toynbee's suggestion that the superpowers "would say to each other, 'You take Manchuria, and we will take the rest of China' and so forth around the globe."[43]) The decline of the old moral consensus had rendered traditional diplomacy—the expression of a limited contest among players recognizing one another's legitimacy—obsolete. Yet the practice of something like traditional diplomacy could help to reestablish a moral consensus. When Morgenthau noted, "A situation of fact favorable to a negotiated settlement consists of two elements: strength and conflicting interests capable of reconciliation," he was referring to both the requisite elements.[44] Attention to the national interest, particularly the core survival interests, would preserve the necessary strength; moral values would be found in the moderation and pluralism characteristic of a diplomatic system that allowed for negotiation and reconciliation of interests.

Morgenthau would have every statesman recognize that in pursuing his country's interests he was in fact pursuing, not disinterested justice or an untainted moral ideal, but a practical, self-interested increment of power (as necessary and justifiable as that might be from the point of view of his responsibilities to his constituents), just as other statesmen were following similarly limited and egotistical policies. Morgenthau's statesman would have a sharp eye for the realities of power and would bargain very hard for his country's interests, even while staying within the rules of the contest. While it would not rest on a re-created moral consensus, in its probable results and in its modesty this renewed international society would represent a far more moral outcome than any likely to be achieved in a world governed by nationalistic universalism. The rest could be left to the unknown future.

That future has since arrived, of course, with the fall of the Soviet system and the end of the Cold War. For all these changes, however, Morgenthau's dissection of the relationship between national interests and moral values remains both pertinent and highly valuable, because it meets the challenge that he himself suggested might be beyond the wit of man: "If a nation is able to escape the Scylla of national suicide, the threat of which is ever present in the emphasis upon moral principles to the neglect of the national interest, it is likely to fall into the Charybdis of the crusading spirit which is the great destroyer of morality among nations."[45] His critique of and proposed alternative to nationalistic universalism did illuminate a way to avoid both Scylla and Charybdis. Rationality and restraint that limited the statesman's operating definition of the national interest to the objectives truly necessary to national security would help him avoid the crusading spirit of a political religion and open the way for diplomacy to inculcate the habits of tolerance and compromise, while at the same time enabling him to fulfill his responsibility to his fellow citizens of safeguarding their national life. Moreover, it looks very much like a forerunner, both of the contemporary efforts by Barry Buzan and others to marry the insights of realism and the English School,[46] and the debate over the efforts of the reflectivists to challenge the dominance of neorealism.[47] And it does so while remaining true to the insights of classical realism noted in the first section of this essay.

CONTEMPORARY ISSUES

How are all these insights reflected in the current state of international politics? America confronts unprecedented challenges resulting from the horrific events of September 11, 2001. One challenge threatens national security at home and abroad; another, democracy and an open society. While the former requires new systems for homeland security, the other calls for defensive and offensive actions around the globe. Both demand eternal vigilance lest human rights and fundamental freedoms be abridged. Claims of clarity and decisiveness aside, nothing about this enterprise is simple. As recently as the Clinton administration, the subject of terrorism received only passing attention from the public; the *New York Times* described the 1995 World Trade Center attack as a one-time event of only limited success. With the passing of this false sense of security, a host of pertinent questions have surfaced: Are there any conditions under which terrorism can be morally justified? What are the credible distinctions between freedom fighters and terrorists? In what ways has terrorism remade American politics now that evaluating terrorism has become part of daily American news broadcasts? In what way do the personal predilections of presidents shape public policy? Is it true that every president has to balance national security interests against the liberties of the people? What do the data reveal about reactions to the USA Patriot Act and other recent legislation in different parts of the country and diverse American communities? Which of our values are most threatened? What segment of the American public has followed the president's advice to go about their daily lives without being too constrained by security concerns? What, if anything, are we being asked to sacrifice for the War on Terror? Has the Bush administration called for personal sacrifice in forthright language?

We are bound to assume that if Professor Morgenthau were to return to the scene of public discourse he would be addressing issues such as these. It is wrong to conclude that he was concerned only with foreign policy, for many of his writings were centered precisely on such questions as democracy, civil rights, and threats to human freedom. A major part of his work dealt with presidents past and present and their domestic and foreign policies.[48] No doubt he would have much to say about George W. Bush and his policies, some of which merit praise and others critical examination.

Almost surely Morgenthau would begin by reviewing the dynamics of terrorism. What are its wellsprings and underlying sources? To what extent is it a worldwide movement drawing strength from conditions within particular regions and individual states? To what degree is the movement empowered by nationalism or ethnicity around the world, and how much of its power results from other political and cultural factors? What are the differences between our interests in

Iraq and in Afghanistan? Which should be viewed as the primary concerns in American foreign policy? Is our mission in the world since 9/11 to resist terrorists and terrorism everywhere, or will our policy be determined by the answer we gave to the question "Who is the enemy?"? To what extent would Morgenthau have looked at the threat as coming from al-Qaeda and Osama bin Laden, and to what extent would he see the threats as a result of the actions of others? If Iraq has become the central front in the War on Terror, what does that mean for its comparison with other threats? Does the importance of democracy and freedom in the Middle East outweigh for the United States and the world the importance of al-Qaeda?

The complexities derive from leadership as well as ideology, and Morgenthau, in his discussion of the elements of power in *Politics Among Nations,* provides insights into both. His lively awareness of the decisive role that perceptive or even ruthless individuals can play in advancing their interests in power competition reminds us of the general importance of leadership. But one quality to which he points in particular is the ability to prod organizations, which often tend to slip into routine mimesis, out of their lethargy and into imaginative responses to changing conditions. No observation could be more topical at a time when the danger is great that loosely organized terrorist groups, inspired by videotapes of a charismatic figure like bin Laden, can slip like quicksilver through the fingers of ponderous state intelligence and security bureaucracies. To Morgenthau's reference to the Prussian army at the Battle of Jena and the French general staff behind the Maginot Line as examples of uncreative leadership may someday be added the cautionary instance of the FBI and the CIA in falling behind the rapidly evolving threat from al-Qaeda.

Looking back, we remember Morgenthau as the foremost American critic of the war in Vietnam. As the historical record has become clearer with regard to both Morgenthau's opposition to our policy in Vietnam and the continuing results of that policy, what are its lessons for us today? Following this line of reasoning, what are the parallels between Vietnam and Iraq for American foreign policy, and what are the primary differences? If it is true that generals tend to fight the current war using the plans and strategies of the previous war as their guide, are we repeating past policy in Vietnam by our actions in Iraq? Or is our approach in Iraq radically different from that employed in Vietnam? Whatever the lessons from Vietnam, are they still relevant, or to what extent are they misplaced as a guide to policy in Iraq or Afghanistan?

As to democracy, what was Morgenthau's vision of the future of democracy in the Middle East? Did he expect that countries like Iraq (or earlier the Soviet Union and China) could fairly easily become democratic? For him, who were the principal actors in the Middle East, and what was their cultural and political legacy? How rational is it to argue that change, if it were to occur in Iraq, would spread to other nations in the region? Which country is most capable of influencing others, and which countries are unlikely to follow foreign examples in adopting democracy? To what extent is Israel and not Iraq the leading democracy in the region, and is this state of affairs likely to change? Is Iraq destined, given our policy, to acquire the stature to serve as a model for the rest of the area? Finally, are we missing the point of the present world crisis if we believe that change in one society in the Middle East can bring about change in all the rest and in other developing countries?

Here we would do well to bear in mind Morgenthau's discussion of national character. While avoiding crude stereotypes and granting that the concept was necessarily "elusive," he nevertheless pointed to the long-lasting and often decisive effect of the fact that "certain qualities of intellect and character occur more frequently and are more highly valued in one nation than in another." Any effort to export the values necessary to make a liberal democratic polity work must take account of these variations in the thinking of those who would receive such complex institutions and practices. Morgenthau might well have asked whether democracy is so naturally contagious that it can, through conscious effort, be transmitted not only from the United States to the highly dissimilar society of Iraq, but then to its regional neighbors, with all their variety of history, culture, and religion.

We should hasten to point out that what we have written about the present crisis might have seemed to Morgenthau to be "putting the cart before the horse." Morgenthau argued not so much for specific policies as for concepts and theories regarding conflict, coercion, and the prospects for moderating the systemic forces that lead to these forms of political interaction. If conflict is indeed perennial, then our task is to increase our influence, if not by combining with our next most powerful allies, as in the Second World War, then by finding the most effective ways of concentrating our power and influence. It will not be enough to settle for weaker coalitions of the willing or to stretch ourselves thin and unaided around the world. Regardless of our actions, certain deficits of power will always remain, because the potential goals that could ideally be sought by any foreign policy will in all cases exceed the finite resources available to even the strongest power. Hence the necessity for choice. What Morgenthau would expect of our political leadership is a rational calculation in making that choice, beginning with the time-honored precept of first determining our own national interest and our power to achieve and defend it. Particularly in regions torn by conflict, have we gone on to assess the interests of opposing forces or states and their ability to realize those interests and to thwart our own? Not only is power–especially the purely material aspect of power–seldom fungible today, but countries divided by religion and ethnicity may be virtually beyond the capacity of any form of norms or power to achieve fundamental change, especially in the short run: witness Iraq. Change is hindered there by regional rivalries, factionalism, and deep religious and political controversies and divisions.

Most serious of all, a single-gauged plan that concentrates primarily, if not exclusively, on military action will overlook and neglect certain inevitable problems of occupation and reconstruction. Morgenthau's most pointed warning against such a "utopian, non-political approach" was voiced in a book he published in 1951, between the first and second editions of *Politics Among Nations*. *In Defense of the National Interest* warns against rigidity in the international arena. Morgenthau decried "a conception of international affairs which denies that the struggle for power never ends and instead asserts that it consists of an unconnected number of mere 'criminal disturbances'"–a conception that is overly simplistic but nonetheless gives rise to a prescription that has traditionally been attractive to Americans: "Crush the enemy; force him into unconditional surrender; reeducate him in the ways of democratic, peace-loving nations; and with democracy estab-lished everywhere, peace and good will among nations will be assured." To this counsel, which Morgenthau charged had mistakenly been followed both in World War II and in the Cold War, he offered a more politically minded approach, which recognized "that the business of war does not end with military victory but only with the establishment of a viable distribution of power, the groundwork for which must be laid while the war is still in progress."[49] Half a century on, such a comprehensive understanding of the relation between military strategy and polit-ical objectives appears as worthy as ever of being a part of the ongoing discussion of American policy in a world in which the abolition of armed conflict seems, sadly, as distant as ever.

Whatever history's judgment on America's actions in Iraq or elsewhere, the real test will reside in whether areas in conflict can find new avenues for the pur-suit of peace that complement the agencies for war. As for Morgenthau, what stands out is the fact that he has become a household name written about in nearly every treatise on diplomacy. In Britain, G. R. Berridge cites him in *Diplomacy: Theory and Practice* and observes in *Diplomatic Theory from Machiavelli to Kissinger* that the Florentine would no doubt have agreed with "his famous twentieth-century follower, Hans Morgenthau, that first-class diplomacy can magnify the material power of a state."[50] This connection between Morgenthau–often mistak-enly characterized as a one-dimensional thinker whose view of international poli-tics went no further than the clashes of states based on military power–and the contributions of a nuanced diplomacy becomes far less surprising when one returns to *Politics Among Nations* to see the number of references to Richelieu and the Cambon brothers in France, or to Castlereagh and Canning in Great Britain, or to Americans such as Thomas Jefferson and John Quincy Adams–diplomatists all. The road to peace in *Politics Among Nations*, as Morgenthau sees it, is a long and winding road, but it lies through diplomacy for the here and now. Ultimately, a world state may come into being, but its beginning depends on the comity, restraint, and sense of common interest nurtured through the practice of diplo-macy. It is no accident that, after demonstrating the inadequacies of competing prescriptions for achieving lasting peace, Morgenthau concludes his study by pointing to the centrality of diplomacy. He first evaluates the four tasks of diplo-macy and the reasons for its contemporary decline, and then in his final chapter examines the future of diplomacy and the means by which it can be restored. His intention is clear, though seemingly paradoxical: to find in the tentative compro-mises of the ancient institution of diplomacy the foundation for a dramatic (though extremely long-term) political transformation–the replacement of the sys-tem of independent sovereign states by a global political authority, and the con-sequent taming of the age-old practice of war through the softening of interna-tional politics into something like what we know as domestic politics.

All this persuades us that the lessons of history for Morgenthau depend on the quality of the relationship between power and peace. For him the two are inserparable. Too often we view the two in watertight compartments, but both must be considered together—not least by all who in holding positions of authority must confront terrorism and other global crises. The world must confront weapons of mass destruction, the conditions that may at times make "regime change" necessary, and the gathering storm symbolized by a nuclear mushroom cloud; neither can it afford to neglect the old and new diplomacy, contemporary forms of mediation and conflict resolution, and meetings at the summit. Inasmuch as Morgenthau gives equal weight to the two in the subtitle, as in the text, of *Politics Among Nations,* it would seem that his is a voice well deserving a hearing today. That leaves us with the task of looking more carefully at policies and debates that would have preoccupied the author if he were alive. Through his entire corpus of scholarly work and commentary, and particularly through this seminal work, his voice does remain with us. In rereading it, we have the opportunity and the obligation to heed its warnings, confront its assertions, and grasp its promise in our own time and for the generation to come.

Kenneth W. Thompson
W. David Clinton

Endnotes

[1] Stanley Hoffmann, *Janus and Minerva: Essays in the Theory and Practice of International Politics* (Boulder, CO: Westview Press, 1987), p. 6.

[2] See Albert O. Hirschman, *The Passions and the Interest: Political Arguments for Capitalism Before Its Triumph* (Princeton, NJ: Princeton University Press, 1977).

[3] See Michael T. Klare, *Resource Wars: The New Landscape of Global Conflict* (New York: Henry Holt, 2001).

[4] See Inis Claude, *Power and International Relations* (New York: Random House, 1962).

[5] See John Rawls, *The Law of Peoples* (Cambridge, MA: Harvard University Press, 1999); Kenneth Minogue, "Religion, Reason and Conflict in the 21st Century," *The National Interest,* Vol. 72 (Summer 2003), pp. 127–37.

[6] *Politics Among Nations: The Struggle for Power and Peace* (New York: Alfred A. Knopf, 1948), p. 182. Morgenthau's thought evolved over time, not least in response to changing circumstances in the international and domestic realms. (See Jaap W. Nobel, "Morgenthau's Struggle with Power: The Theory of Power Politics and the Cold War," *Review of International Studies,* Vol. 21 [January 1995], pp. 61–85.) Because this essay is occasioned by the appearance of a new edition of *Politics Among Nations,* we have limited the exegesis in this section to the work that appeared in the years surrounding the publication of that volume—that is, from Morgenthau's early articles after his arrival in the United States, beginning in the late 1930s, to the publication of the second edition of *Politics Among Nations* (hereinafter *PAN*), the first to contain the "six principles of political realism," in 1954. For comparisons of Morgenthau's writings during the interwar years, while he still lived in Europe, with the works that appeared after he came to the United States, see Christoph Frei, *Hans J. Morgenthau: An Intellectual Biography* (Baton Rouge: Louisiana State

University Press, 2001); Niels Amstrup, "The 'Early' Morgenthau: A Comment on the Intellectual Origins of Realism," *Cooperation and Conflict: Nordic Journal of International Politics,* No. 3 (1978), pp. 163–75; Greg Russell, *Hans J. Morgenthau and the Ethics of American Statecraft* (Baton Rouge: Louisiana State University Press, 1990), esp. Chapters 2 and 3.

[7]"Another 'Great Debate': The National Interest of the United States," *American Political Science Review,* Vol. XLVI (December 1952), pp. 970–71.

[8]*Scientific Man vs. Power Politics* (Chicago: University of Chicago Press, 1946; reprint ed. 1974), pp. 206.

[9]"The Moral Dilemma in Foreign Policy," in The London Institute of World Affairs, *The Year Book of World Affairs, 1951,* edited by George W. Keeton and Georg Schwarzenberger (London: Stevens and Sons, 1951), p. 13.

[10]See *PAN,* 2nd ed (New York: Alfred A. Knopf, 1954), pp. 5, 9, 10–11.

[11]*Scientific Man,* p. 186.

[12]*In Defense of the National Interest: A Critical Examination of American Foreign Policy* (New York: Alfred A. Knopf, 1951), p. 33.

[13]"Another 'Great Debate'," p. 986; "What Is the National Interest of the United States?" *Annals of the American Academy of Political and Social Science,* Vol. 282 (July 1952), p. 7.

[14]*In Defense of the National Interest,* p. 34; "The Primacy of the National Interest," *The American Scholar,* Vol. 18 (Spring 1949), p. 212. For Morgenthau's defense against the charge that he had accepted Hobbesian prudentialism uncritically, see "Another 'Great Debate'," p. 983.

[15]"Another 'Great Debate'," p. 973.

[16]*PAN,* 1st ed., p. 440.

[17]*PAN,* 2nd ed., p. 8.

[18]"Another 'Great Debate'," p. 986.

[19]"The Machiavellian Utopia," *Ethics,* Vol. LV (January 1945), p. 145.

[20]Ibid., p. 147.

[21]"The Problem of Neutrality," *University of Kansas City Law Review,* Vol. VII (February 1939), pp. 125–26.

[22]"Positivism, Functionalism, and International Law," *American Journal of International Law,* Vol. 34 (April 1940), pp. 275, 268.

[23]*PAN,* 1st ed., pp. 445, 160.

[24]*Scientific Man,* p. 217.

[25]*PAN,* 1st ed., pp. 174–75.

[26]"Another 'Great Debate'," pp. 977–78.

[27]*Scientific Man,* p. 203.

[28]Ibid., pp. 172, 213; "The Machiavellian Utopia," p. 145; "Positivism, Functionalism, and International Law," p. 268; "Another 'Great Debate'," p. 973.

[29]*PAN,* 2nd ed., p. 10.

[30]*In Defense of the National Interest,* p. 60.

[31]*PAN,* 1st ed., p. 193.

[32]*In Defense of the National Interest,* pp. 60–61.

[33]Ibid., p. 61.

[34]*PAN,* 1st ed., pp. 190–91.

[35]Ibid., p. 191.

[36]Ibid., p. 193.

[37]Ibid., p. 268. See also *Scientific Man,* pp. 67, 197.

[38]*Scientific Man,* p. 213. Cf. "Morgenthau's Struggle with Power," pp. 64–66.

[39]"The Problem of Neutrality," p. 126.

[40]"The Primacy of the National Interest," p. 211.

[41]"What Is the National Interest of the United States?" p. 4.

[42]"The Yardstick of National Interest," *The Annals of the American Academy of Political and Social Science* (November 1954), p. 84.

[43]*In Defense of the National Interest,* pp. 155–56. See also "Morgenthau's Struggle with Power," pp. 67–68.

[44]*In Defense of the National Interest,* p. 149. See also pp. 133–35.

[45]"The Primacy of the National Interest," p. 211.

[46]See Barry Buzan, Charles Jones, and Richard Little, *The Logic of Anarchy: Neorealism to Structural Realism* (New York: Columbia University Press, 1993).

[47]See Alexander Wendt, "Anarchy Is What States Make of It: The Social Construction of Power Politics," *International Organization,* Vol. 46 (Spring 1992); Judith Goldstein and Robert Keohane, editors, *Ideas and Foreign Policy: Beliefs, Institutions, and Political Change* (Ithaca, NY: Cornell University Press, 1993).

[48]See Hans Morgenthau, *The Purpose of American Politics* (New York: Alfred A. Knopf, 1960); Morgenthau, *Truth and Power: Essays of a Decade, 1960–70* (New York: Praeger, 1970).

[49]*In Defense of the National Interest,* pp. 94–96.

[50]G. R. Berridge, *Diplomacy: Theory and Practice,* 2nd ed. (New York: Palgrave, 2002), p. 218; Berridge, Maurice Keens-Soper, and T. G. Otte, editors, *Diplomatic Theory from Machiavelli to Kissinger* (New York: Palgrave, 2001), p. 20.

PART ONE

THEORY AND PRACTICE OF INTERNATIONAL POLITICS

1 A Realist Theory of International Politics

This book purports to present a theory of international politics. The test by which such a theory must be judged is not a priori and abstract but empirical and pragmatic. The theory, in other words, must be judged not by some preconceived abstract principle or concept unrelated to reality, but by its purpose: to bring order and meaning to a mass of phenomena that without it would remain disconnected and unintelligible. It must meet a dual test, an empirical and a logical one: do the facts as they actually are lend themselves to the interpretation the theory has put upon them, and do the conclusions at which the theory arrives follow with logical necessity from its premises? In short, is the theory consistent with the facts and within itself?

The issue this theory raises concerns the nature of all politics. The history of modern political thought is the story of a contest between two schools that differ fundamentally in their conceptions of the nature of man, society, and politics. One believes that a rational and moral political order, derived from universally valid abstract principles, can be achieved here and now. It assumes the essential goodness and infinite malleability of human nature, and blames the failure of the social order to measure up to the rational standards on lack of knowledge and understanding, obsolescent social institutions, or the depravity of certain isolated individuals or groups. It trusts in education, reform, and the sporadic use of force to remedy these defects.

The other school believes that the world, imperfect as it is from the rational point of view, is the result of forces inherent in human nature. To improve the world one must work with those forces, not against them. This being inherently a world of opposing interests and of conflict among them, moral principles can never be fully realized but must at best be approximated through the ever temporary balancing of interests and the ever precarious settlement of conflicts. This school, then, sees in a system of checks and balances a universal principle for all pluralist societies. It appeals to historical precedent rather than to abstract principles and aims at the realization of the lesser evil rather than of the absolute good.

This theoretical concern with human nature as it actually is, and with the historical processes as they actually take place, has earned for the theory presented here the name of *realism*. What are the tenets of political realism? No systematic exposition of the philosophy of political realism can be attempted here; it will suffice to single out six fundamental principles, which have frequently been misunderstood.

SIX PRINCIPLES OF POLITICAL REALISM

1. Political realism believes that politics, like society in general, is governed by objective laws that have their roots in human nature. In order to improve society it is first necessary to understand the laws by which society lives. The operation of these laws being impervious to our preferences, men will challenge them only at the risk of failure.

Realism, believing as it does in the objectivity of the laws of politics, must also believe in the possibility of developing a rational theory that reflects, however imperfectly and one-sidedly, these objective laws. It believes also, then, in the possibility of distinguishing in politics between truth and opinion—between what is true objectively and rationally, supported by evidence and illuminated by reason, and what is only a subjective judgment, divorced from the facts as they are and informed by prejudice and wishful thinking.

Human nature, in which the laws of politics have their roots, has not changed since the classical philosophies of China, India, and Greece endeavored to discover these laws. Hence, novelty is not necessarily a virtue in political theory, nor is old age a defect. The fact that a theory of politics, if there be such a theory, has never been heard of before tends to create a presumption against, rather than in favor of, its soundness. Conversely, the fact that a theory of politics was developed hundreds or even thousands of years ago—as was the theory of the balance of power—does not create a presumption that it must be outmoded and obsolete. A theory of politics must be subjected to the dual test of reason and experience. To dismiss such a theory because it had its flowering in centuries past is to present not a rational argument but a modernistic prejudice that takes for granted the superiority of the present over the past. To dispose of the revival of such a theory as a "fashion" or "fad" is tantamount to assuming that in matters political we can have opinions but no truths.

For realism, theory consists in ascertaining facts and giving them meaning through reason. It assumes that the character of a foreign policy can be ascertained only through the examination of the political acts performed and of the foreseeable consequences of these acts. Thus we can find out what statesmen have actually done, and from the foreseeable consequences of their acts we can surmise what their objectives might have been.

Yet examination of the facts is not enough. To give meaning to the factual raw material of foreign policy, we must approach political reality with a kind of rational outline, a map that suggests to us the possible meanings of foreign policy.

In other words, we put ourselves in the position of a statesman who must meet a certain problem of foreign policy under certain circumstances, and we ask ourselves what the rational alternatives are from which a statesman may choose who must meet this problem under these circumstances (presuming always that he acts in a rational manner), and which of these rational alternatives this particular statesman, acting under these circumstances, is likely to choose. It is the testing of this rational hypothesis against the actual facts and their consequences that gives theoretical meaning to the facts of international politics.

2. The main signpost that helps political realism to find its way through the landscape of international politics is the concept of interest defined in terms of power. This concept provides the link between reason trying to understand international politics and the facts to be understood. It sets politics as an autonomous sphere of action and understanding apart from other spheres, such as economics (understood in terms of interest defined as wealth), ethics, aesthetics, or religion. Without such a concept a theory of politics, international or domestic, would be altogether impossible, for without it we could not distinguish between political and nonpolitical facts, nor could we bring at least a measure of systemic order to the political sphere.

We assume that statesmen think and act in terms of interest defined as power, and the evidence of history bears that assumption out. That assumption allows us to retrace and anticipate, as it were, the steps a statesman—past, present, or future—has taken or will take on the political scene. We look over his shoulder when he writes his dispatches; we listen in on his conversations with other statesmen; we read and anticipate his very thoughts. Thinking in terms of interest defined as power, we think as he does, and as disinterested observers we understand his thoughts and actions perhaps better than he, the actor on the political scene, does himself.

The concept of interest defined as power imposes intellectual discipline upon the observer, infuses rational order into the subject matter of politics, and thus makes the theoretical understanding of politics possible. On the side of the actor, it provides for rational discipline in action and creates that astounding continuity in foreign policy which makes American, British, or Russian foreign policy appear as in intelligible, rational continuum, by and large consistent within itself, regardless of the different motives, preferences, and intellectual and moral qualities of successive statesmen. A realist theory of international politics, then, will guard against two popular fallacies: the concern with motives and the concern with ideological preferences.

To search for the clue to foreign policy exclusively in the motives of statesmen is both futile and deceptive. It is futile because motives are the most illusive of psychological data, distorted as they are, frequently beyond recognition, by the interests and emotions of actor and observer alike. Do we really know what our own motives are? And what do we know of the motives of others?

Yet even if we had access to the real motives of statesmen, that knowledge would help us little in understanding foreign policies and might well lead us astray. It is true that the knowledge of the statesman's motives may give us one among many clues as to what the direction of his foreign policy might be. It cannot give us, however, the one clue by which to predict his foreign policies. History shows no exact and necessary correlation between the quality of motives and the quality of foreign policy. This is true in both moral and political terms.

We cannot conclude from the good intentions of a statesman that his foreign policies will be either morally praiseworthy or politically successful. Judging his motives, we can say that he will not intentionally pursue policies that are morally wrong, but we can say nothing about the probability of their success. If we want to know the moral and political qualities of his actions, we must know them, not his motives. How often have statesmen been motivated by the desire to improve the world and ended by making it worse? And how often have they sought one goal, and ended by achieving something they neither expected nor desired?

Neville Chamberlain's politics of appeasement were, as far as we can judge, inspired by good motives; he was probably less motivated by considerations of personal power than were many other British prime ministers, and he sought to preserve peace and to assure the happiness of all concerned. Yet his policies helped to make the Second World War inevitable and to bring untold miseries to millions of people. Sir Winston Churchill's motives, on the other hand, were much less universal in scope and much more narrowly directed toward personal and national power, yet the foreign policies that sprang from these inferior motives were certainly superior in moral and political quality to those pursued by his predecessor. Judged by his motives, Robespierre was one of the most virtuous men who ever lived. Yet it was the utopian radicalism of that very virtue that made him kill those less virtuous than himself, brought him to the scaffold, and destroyed the revolution of which he was a leader.

Good motives give assurance against deliberately bad policies; they do not guarantee the moral goodness and political success of the policies they inspire. What is important to know, if one wants to understand foreign policy, is not primarily the motives of a statesman but his intellectual ability to comprehend the essentials of foreign policy, as well as his political ability to translate what he has comprehended into successful political action. It follows that, while ethics in the abstract judges the moral qualities of motives, political theory must judge the political qualities of intellect, will, and action.

A realist theory of international politics will also avoid the other popular fallacy of equating the foreign policies of a statesman with his philosophic or political sympathies, and of deducing the former from the latter. Statesmen, especially under contemporary conditions, may well make a habit of presenting their foreign policies in terms of their philosophic and political sympathies in order to gain popular support for them. Yet they will distinguish with Lincoln between their "*official* duty," which is to think and act in terms of the national interest, and their "*personal* wish," which is to see their own moral values and political principles realized throughout the world. Political realism does not require, nor does it condone, indifference to political ideals and moral principles, but it requires indeed a sharp distinction between the desirable and the possible—between what is desirable everywhere and at all times and what is possible under the concrete circumstances of time and place.

It stands to reason that not all foreign policies have always followed so rational, objective, and unemotional a course. The contingent elements of personality, prejudice, and subjective preference, and of all the weaknesses of intellect and will that flesh is heir to, are bound to deflect foreign policies from their rational course. Especially where foreign policy is conducted under the conditions of democratic control, the need to marshal popular emotions to the support of foreign policy cannot fail to impair the rationality of foreign policy itself. Yet a theory of foreign policy that aims at rationality must for the time being, as it were, abstract from these irrational elements and seek to paint a picture of foreign policy that presents the rational essence to be found in experience, without the contingent deviations from rationality that are also found in experience.

Deviations from rationality that are not the result of the personal whim or the personal psychopathology of the policymaker may appear contingent only from the vantage point of rationality but may themselves be elements in a coherent system of irrationality. The possibility of constructing, as it were, a counter-theory of irrational politics is worth exploring.

When one reflects upon the development of American thinking on foreign policy, one is struck by the persistence of mistaken attitudes that have survived—under whatever guises—both intellectual argument and political experience. Once that wonder, in true Aristotelian fashion, has been transformed into the quest for rational understanding, the quest yields a conclusion both comforting and disturbing: we are here in the presence of intellectual defects shared by all of us in different ways and degrees. Together they provide the outline of a kind of pathology of international politics. When the human mind approaches reality with the purpose of taking action, of which the political encounter is one of the outstanding instances, it is often led astray by any of four common mental phenomena: residues of formerly adequate modes of thought and action now rendered obsolete by a new social reality; demonological interpretations of reality that substitute a fictitious reality—peopled by evil persons rather than seemingly intractable issues—for the actual one; refusal to come to terms with a threatening state of affairs by denying it through illusory verbalization; or reliance upon the infinite malleability of a seemingly obstreperous reality.

Man responds to social situations with repetitive patterns. The same situation, recognized in its identity with previous situations, evokes the same response. The mind, as it were, holds in readiness a number of patterns appropriate for different situations; it then requires only the identification of a particular case to apply to it the preformed pattern appropriate to it. Thus the human mind follows the principle of economy of effort, obviating an examination *de novo* of each individual situation and the pattern of thought and action appropriate to it. Yet when matters are subject to dynamic change, traditional patterns are no longer appropriate; they must be replaced by new ones reflecting such change. Otherwise a gap will open between traditional patterns and new realities, and thought and action will be misguided.

On the international plane it is no exaggeration to say that the very structure of international relations—as reflected in political institutions, diplomatic procedures, and legal arrangements–has tended to become at variance with, and in large measure irrelevant to, the reality of international politics. While the former assumes the "sovereign equality" of all nations, the latter is dominated by an extreme inequality of nations, two of which are called superpowers because they hold in their hands the unprecedented power of total destruction, and many of which are called "ministates" because their power is minuscule even compared with that of the traditional nation-states. It is this contrast and incompatibility between the reality of international politics and the concepts, institutions, and procedures designed to make intelligible and control the former that have caused, at least below the great-power level, the unmanageability of international relations, which borders on anarchy. International terrorism and the different government reactions to it, the involvement of foreign governments in the Lebanese civil war, the military operations of the United States in Southeast Asia, and the military intervention of the Soviet Union in Eastern Europe cannot be explained or justified by reference to traditional concepts, institutions, and procedures.

All these situations have one characteristic in common. The modern fact of interdependence requires a political order that takes that fact into account, while in reality the legal and institutional superstructure, harking back to the nineteenth century, assumes the existence of a multiplicity of self-sufficient, impenetrable, sovereign nation-states. These residues of an obsolescent legal and institutional order not only stand in the way of a rational transformation of international relations in light of the inequality of power and the interdependence of interests, but they also render precarious, if not impossible, more rational policies within the defective framework of such a system.

It is a characteristic of primitive thinking to personalize social problems. That tendency is particularly strong when the problem appears not to be susceptible to rational understanding and successful manipulation. When a particular person or group of persons is identified with the recalcitrant difficulty, that may seem to render the problem both intellectually accessible and susceptible to solution. Thus belief in Satan as the source of evil makes us "understand" the nature of evil by focusing the search for its origin and control upon a particular person whose physical existence we assume. The complexity of political conflict precludes such simple solutions. Natural catastrophes will not be prevented by burning witches; the threat of a powerful Germany to establish hegemony over Europe will not be averted by getting rid of a succession of German leaders. But by identifying the issue with certain persons over whom we have–or hope to have–control we reduce the problem, both intellectually and pragmatically, to manageable proportions. Once we have identified certain individuals and groups of individuals as the source of evil, we appear to have understood the causal nexus that leads from the individuals to the social problem; that apparent understanding suggests the apparent solution: eliminate the individuals "responsible" for it, and you have solved the problem.

Superstition still holds sway over our relations within society. The demonological pattern of thought and action has now been transferred to other fields of human action closed to the kind of rational enquiry and action that have driven superstition from our relations with nature. As William Graham Sumner put it, "The amount of superstition is not much changed, but it now attaches to politics, not to religion."[1] The numerous failures of the United States to recognize and respond to the polycentric nature of Communism is a prime example of this defect. The corollary of this indiscriminate opposition to Communism is the indiscriminate support of governments and movements that profess and practice anti-Communism. American policies in Asia and Latin America have derived from this simplistic position. The Vietnam War and our inability to come to terms with mainland China find here their rationale. So do the theory and practice of counterinsurgency, including large-scale assassinations under the Phoenix program in Vietnam and the actual or attempted assassinations of individual statesmen. Signs of a similar approach have been evident more recently in Central America.

The demonological approach to foreign policy strengthens another pathological tendency, which is the refusal to acknowledge and cope effectively with a threatening reality. The demonological approach has shifted our attention and concern toward the adherents of Communism—individuals at home and abroad, political movements, foreign governments—and away from the real threat: the power of states, Communist or not. McCarthyism not only provided the most pervasive American example of the demonological approach but was also one of the most extreme examples of this kind of misjudgment: it substituted the largely illusory threat of domestic subversion for the real threat of Russian power.

Finally, it is part of this approach to politics to believe that no problems—however hopeless they may appear—are really insoluble, given well-meaning, well-financed, and competent efforts. I have tried elsewhere to lay bare the intellectual and historical roots of this belief;[2] here I limit myself to pointing out its persistent strength despite much experience to the contrary, such as the Vietnam War and the general decline of American power. This preference for economic solutions to political and military problems is powerfully reinforced by the interests of potential recipients of economic support, who prefer the obviously profitable transfer of economic advantages to painful and risky diplomatic bargaining.

The difference between international politics as it actually is and a rational theory derived from it is like the difference between a photograph and a painted portrait. The photograph shows everything that can be seen by the naked eye; the painted portrait does not show everything that can be seen by the naked eye, but it shows, or at least seeks to show, one thing that the naked eye cannot see: the human essence of the person portrayed.

Political realism contains not only a theoretical but also a normative element. It knows that political reality is replete with contingencies and systemic irrationalities, and points to the typical influences they exert upon foreign policy. Yet it shares with all social theory the need, for the sake of theoretical understanding, to stress the rational elements of political reality; for it is these rational elements

---

[1]"Mores of the Present and Future," in *War and Other Essays* (New Haven, CT: Yale University Press, 1911), p. 159.
[2]*Scientific Man Versus Power Politics* (Chicago: University of Chicago Press, 1946).

that make reality intelligible for theory. Political realism presents the theoretical construct of a rational foreign policy that experience can never completely achieve.

At the same time political realism considers a rational foreign policy to be good foreign policy; for only a rational foreign policy minimizes risks and maximizes benefits and, hence, complies with both the moral precept of prudence and the political requirement of success. Political realism wants the photographic picture of the political world to resemble as much as possible its painted portrait. Aware of the inevitable gap between good—that is, rational—foreign policy and foreign policy as it actually is, political realism maintains not only that theory must focus upon the rational elements of political reality but also that foreign policy ought to be rational in view of its own moral and practical purposes.

Hence, it is no argument against the theory here presented that actual foreign policy does not or cannot live up to it. That argument misunderstands the intention of this book, which is to present not an indiscriminate description of political reality but a rational theory of international politics. Far from being invalidated by the fact that, for instance, a perfect balance of power policy will scarcely be found in reality, it assumes that reality, being deficient in this respect, must be understood and evaluated as an approximation to an ideal system of balance of power.

3. Realism assumes that its key concept of interest defined as power is an objective category that is universally valid, but it does not endow that concept with a meaning that is fixed once and for all. The idea of interest is indeed of the essence of politics and is unaffected by the circumstances of time and place. Thucydides' statement, born of the experiences of ancient Greece, that "identity of interests is the surest of bonds whether between states or individuals" was taken up in the nineteenth century by Lord Salisbury's remark that "the only bond of union that endures" among nations is "the absence of all clashing interests." It was erected into a general principle of government by George Washington:

> A small knowledge of human nature will convince us, that, with far the greatest part of mankind, interest is the governing principle; and that almost every man is more or less, under its influence. Motives of public virtue may for a time, or in particular instances, actuate men to the observance of a conduct purely disinterested; but they are not of themselves sufficient to produce preserving conformity to the refined dictates and obligations of social duty. Few men are capable of making a continual sacrifice of all views of private interest, or advantage, to the common good. It is vain to exclaim against the depravity of human nature on this account; the fact is so, the experience of every age and nation has proved it and we must in a great measure, change the constitution of man, before we can make it otherwise. No institution, not built on the presumptive truth of these maxims can succeed.[3]

---

[3] *The Writings of George Washington*, edited by John C. Fitzpatrick (Washington, DC: United States Printing Office, 1931–44), Vol. X, p. 363.

It was echoed and enlarged upon in the twentieth century by Max Weber's observation:

> Interests (material and ideal), not ideas, dominate directly the actions of men. Yet the "images of the world" created by these ideas have very often served as switches determining the tracks on which the dynamism of interests kept actions moving.[4]

Yet the kind of interest determining political action in a particular period of history depends upon the political and cultural context within which foreign policy is formulated. The goals that might be pursued by nations in their foreign policy can run the whole gamut of objectives any nation has ever pursued or might possibly pursue.

The same observations apply to the concept of power. Its content and the manner of its use are determined by the political and cultural environment. Power may comprise anything that establishes and maintains the control of man over man. Thus power covers all social relationships that serve that end, from physical violence to the most subtle psychological ties by which one mind controls another. Power covers the domination of man by man, both when it is disciplined by moral ends and controlled by constitutional safeguards, as in Western democracies, and when it is that untamed and barbaric force that finds its laws in nothing but its own strength and its sole justification in its aggrandizement.

Political realism does not assume that the contemporary conditions under which foreign policy operates, with their extreme instability and the ever-present threat of large-scale violence, cannot be changed. The balance of power, for instance, is indeed a perennial element of all pluralistic societies, as the authors of *The Federalist* papers well knew; yet it is capable of operating, as it does in the United States, under the conditions of relative stability and peaceful conflict. If the factors that have given rise to these conditions can be duplicated on the international scene, similar conditions of stability and peace will then prevail there, as they have over long stretches of history among certain nations.

What is true of the general character of international relations is also true of the nation-state as the ultimate point of reference of contemporary foreign policy. While the realist indeed believes that interest is the perennial standard by which political action must be judged and directed, the contemporary connection between interest and the nation-state is a product of history and is therefore bound to disappear in the course of history. Nothing in the realist position militates against the assumption that the present division of the political world into nation-states will be replaced by larger units of a quite different character, more in keeping with the technical potentialities and the moral requirements of the contemporary world.

The realist parts company with other schools of thought before the all-important question of how the contemporary world is to be transformed. The realist is persuaded that this transformation can be achieved only through the workmanlike

---

[4]Marianne Weber, *Max Weber* (Tübingen: J.C.B. Mohr, 1926), pp. 347–48. See also Max Weber, *Gesammelte Aufsätze zur Religionssoziologie* (Tübingen: J.C.B. Mohr, 1920), p. 252.

manipulation of the perennial forces that have shaped the past as they will the future. The realist cannot be persuaded that we can bring about that transformation by confronting a political reality that has its own laws with an abstract ideal that refuses to take those laws into account.

4. Political realism is aware of the moral significance of political action. It is also aware of the ineluctable tension between the moral command and the requirements of successful political action. And it is unwilling to gloss over and obliterate that tension and thus to obfuscate both the moral and the political issues by making it appear as though the stark facts of politics were morally more satisfying than they actually are, and the moral law less exacting that it actually is.

Realism maintains that universal moral principles cannot be applied to the actions of states in their abstract universal formulation but that they must be filtered through the concrete circumstances of time and place. The individual may say for himself, "*Fiat justitia, pereat mundus* (Let justice be done, even if the world perish)," but the state has no right to say so in the name of those who are in its care. Both individual and state must judge political action by universal moral principles, such as that of liberty. Yet while the individual has a moral right to sacrifice himself in defense of such a moral principle, the state has no right to let its moral disapprobation of the infringement of liberty get in the way of successful political action, itself inspired by the moral principle of national survival. There can be no political morality without prudence, that is, without consideration of the political consequences of seemingly moral action. Realism, then, considers prudence–the weighing of the consequences of alternative political actions–to be the supreme virtue in politics. Ethics in the abstract judges action by its conformity with the moral law; political ethics judges action by its political consequences. Classical and medieval philosophy knew this, and so did Lincoln when he said:

> I do the very best I know how, the very best I can, and I mean to keep doing so until the end. If the end brings me out all right, what is said against me won't amount to anything. If the end brings me out wrong, ten angels swearing I was right would make no difference.

5. Political realism refuses to identify the moral aspirations of a particular nation with the moral laws that govern the universe. As it distinguishes between truth and opinion, so it distinguishes between truth and idolatry. All nations are tempted–and few have been able to resist the temptation for long–to clothe their own particular aspirations and actions in the moral purposes of the universe. To know that nations are subject to the moral law is one thing, while to pretend to know with certainty what is good and evil in the relations among nations is quite another. There is a world of difference between the belief that all nations stand under the judgment of God, inscrutable to the human mind, and the blasphemous conviction that God is always on one's side and that what one wills oneself cannot fail to be willed by God also.

The lighthearted equation between a particular nationalism and the counsels of Providence is morally indefensible, for it is that very sin of pride against which the Greek tragedians and the biblical prophets have warned rulers and ruled. That equation is also politically pernicious, for it is liable to engender the distortion in judgment that, in the blindness of crusading frenzy, destroys nations and civilizations—in the name of moral principle, ideal, or God himself.

On the other hand, it is exactly the concept of interest defined in terms of power that saves us from both that moral excess and that political folly. For if we look at all nations, our own included, as political entities pursuing their respective interests defined in terms of power, we are able to do justice to all of them. And we are able to do justice to all of them in a dual sense: we are able to judge other nations as we judge our own and, having judged them in this fashion, we are then capable of pursuing policies that respect the interests of other nations while protecting and promoting those of our own. Moderation in policy cannot fail to reflect the moderation of moral judgment.

6. The difference, then, between political realism and other schools of thought is real, and it is profound. However much of the theory of political realism may have been misunderstood and misinterpreted, there is no gainsaying its distinctive intellectual and moral attitude to matters political.

Intellectually, the political realist maintains the autonomy of the political sphere, as the economist, the lawyer, the moralist maintain theirs. He thinks in terms of interest defined as power, as the economist thinks in terms of interest defined as wealth; the lawyer, of the conformity of action with legal rules; the moralist, of the conformity of action with moral principles. The economist asks: "How does this policy affect the wealth of society, or a segment of it?" The lawyer asks: "Is this policy in accord with the rules of law?" The moralist asks: "Is this policy in accord with moral principles?" And the political realist asks: "How does this policy affect the power of the nation?" (Or of the federal government, of Congress, of the party, of agriculture, as the case may be.)

The political realist is not unaware of the existence and the relevance of standards of thought other than political ones. As political realist he cannot but subordinate these other standards to those of politics. And he parts company with other schools when they impose standards of thought appropriate to other spheres upon the political spheres. It is here that political realism takes issue with the "legalistic-moralistic approach" to international politics. That this issue is not, as has been contended, a mere figment of the imagination but goes to the very core of the controversy can be shown from many historical examples. Three will suffice to make the point.[5]

In 1939 the Soviet Union attacked Finland. This action confronted France and Great Britain with two issues, one legal, the other political. Did that action violate the Covenant of the League of Nations, and, if it did, what countermeasures

---

[5]See the other examples discussed in Hans J. Morgenthau, "Another 'Great Debate': The National Interest of the United States," *The American Political Science Review,* Vol. XLVI (December 1952), pp. 979 ff. See also Hans J. Morgenthau, *Politics in the 20th Century,* Vol. 1, *The Decline of Democratic Politics* (Chicago: University of Chicago Press, 1962), pp. 79 ff; and abridged edition (Chicago: University of Chicago Press, 1971), pp. 204 ff.

should France and Great Britain take? The legal question could easily be answered in the affirmative, for obviously the Soviet Union had done what was prohibited by the Covenant. The answer to the political question depends, first, upon the manner in which the Russian action affected the interests of France and Great Britain; second, upon the existing distribution of power between France and Great Britain, on the one hand, and the Soviet Union and other potentially hostile nations, especially Germany, on the other; and, third, upon the influence that the countermeasures were likely to have upon the interests of France and Great Britain and the future distribution of power. France and Great Britain, as the leading members of the League of Nations, saw to it that the Soviet Union was expelled from the League, and they were prevented from joining Finland in the war against the Soviet Union only by Sweden's refusal to allow their troops to pass through Swedish territory on their way to Finland. If this refusal by Sweden had not saved them, France and Great Britain would shortly have found themselves at war with the Soviet Union and Germany at the same time.

The policy of France and Great Britain was a classic example of legalism in that they allowed the answer to the legal question, legitimate within its sphere, to determine their political actions. Instead of asking both questions, that of law and that of power, they asked only the question of law; and the answer they received could have no bearing on the issue that their very existence might have depended upon.

The second example illustrates the "moralistic approach" to international politics. It concerns the international status of the Communist government of China. The rise of that government confronted the Western world with two issues, one moral, the other political. Were the nature and policies of that government in accord with the moral principles of the Western world? Should the Western world deal with such a government? The answer to the first question could not fail to be in the negative. Yet it did not follow with necessity that the answer to the second question should also be in the negative. The standard of thought applied to the first—the moral—question was simply to test the nature and the policies of the Communist government of China by the principles of Western morality. On the other hand, the second—the political—question had to be subjected to the complicated test of the interests involved and the power available on either side, and of the bearing of one or the other course of action upon these interests and power. The application of this test could well have led to the conclusion that it would be wiser not to deal with the Communist government of China. To arrive at this conclusion by neglecting this test altogether and answering the political question in terms of the moral issue was indeed a classic example of the "moralistic approach" to international politics.

The third case illustrates strikingly the contrast between realism and the legalistic-moralistic approach to foreign policy. Great Britain, as one of the guarantors of the neutrality of Belgium, went to war with Germany in August 1914 because Germany had violated the neutrality of Belgium. The British action could be justified in either realistic or in legalistic-moralistic terms. That is to say, one could argue realistically that for centuries it had been axiomatic for British foreign policy to prevent the control of the Low Countries by a hostile power. It was then not so much the violation of Belgium's neutrality per se as the hostile intentions of the violator that provided the rationale for British intervention. If the violator had been another nation but Germany, Great Britain might well have refrained from intervening. This is the position taken by Sir Edward Grey, British foreign secretary during that period. Undersecretary for Foreign Affairs Hardinge remarked to him in 1908: "If France violated Belgian neutrality in a war against Germany, it is doubtful whether England or Russia would move a finger to maintain Belgian neutrality, while if the neutrality of Belgium was violated by Germany, it is probable that the converse would be the case." Whereupon Sir Edward Grey replied: "This is to the point." Yet one could also take the legalistic and moralistic position that the violation of Belgium's neutrality per se, because of its legal and moral defects and regardless of the interests at stake and of the identity of the violator, justified British and, for that matter, American intervention. This was the position that Theodore Roosevelt took in his letter to Sir Edward Grey of January 22, 1915:

> To me the crux of the situation has been Belgium. If England or France had acted toward Belgium as Germany has acted I should have opposed them, exactly as I now oppose Germany. I have emphatically approved your action as a model for what should be done by those who believe that treaties should be observed in good faith and that there is such a thing as international morality. I take this position as an American who is no more an Englishman than he is a German, who endeavors loyally to serve the interests of his own country, but who also endeavors to do what he can for justice and decency as regards mankind at large, and who therefore feels obliged to judge all other nations by their conduct on any given occasion.

This realist defense of the autonomy of the political sphere against its subversion by other modes of thought does not imply disregard for the existence and importance of these other modes of thought. It rather implies that each should be assigned its proper sphere and function. Political realism is based upon a pluralistic conception of human nature. Real man is a composite of "economic man," "political man," "moral man," "religious man," etc. A man who was nothing but "political man" would be a beast, for he would be completely lacking in moral restraints. A man who was nothing but "moral man" would be a fool, for he would be completely lacking in prudence. A man who was nothing but "religious man" would be a saint, for he would be completely lacking in worldly desires.

Recognizing that these different facets of human nature exist, political realism also recognizes that in order to understand one of them one has to deal with it on its own terms. That is to say, if I want to understand "religious man," I must for the time being abstract from the other aspects of human nature and deal with its religious aspect as if it were the only one. Furthermore, I must apply to the religious sphere the standards of thought appropriate to it, always remaining aware of the existence of other standards and their actual influence upon the religious qualities of man. What is true of this facet of human nature is true of all the others. No modern economist, for instance, would conceive of his science and its relations to other sciences of man in any other way. It is exactly through such a process of emancipation from other standards of thought, and the development of one appropriate to its subject matter, that economics has developed as an autonomous theory of the economic activities of man. To contribute to a similar development in the field of politics is indeed the purpose of political realism.

It is in the nature of things that a theory of politics that is based upon such principles will not meet with unanimous approval—nor does, for that matter, such a foreign policy. For theory and policy alike run counter to two trends in our culture that are not able to reconcile themselves to the assumptions and results of a rational, objective theory of politics. One of these trends disparages the role of power in society on grounds that stem from the experience and philosophy of the nineteenth century; we shall address ourselves to this tendency later in greater detail.[6] The other trend, opposed to the realist theory and practice of politics, stems from the very relationship that exists, and must exist, between the human mind and the political sphere. For reasons that we shall discuss later,[7] the human mind in its day-by-day operations cannot bear to look the truth of politics straight in the face. It must disguise, distort, belittle, and embellish the truth—the more so, the more the individual is actively involved in the processes of politics, and particularly in those of international politics. For only by deceiving himself about the nature of politics and the role he plays on the political scene is man able to live contentedly as a political animal with himself and his fellow men.

Thus it is inevitable that a theory that tries to understand international politics as it actually is and as it ought to be in view of its intrinsic nature, rather than as people would like to see it, must overcome a psychological resistance that most other branches of learning need not face. A book devoted to the theoretical understanding of international politics therefore requires a special explanation and justification.

[6]See pages 37 ff.
[7]See pages 101 ff.

2 The Science of International Politics

UNDERSTANDING INTERNATIONAL POLITICS

Different Approaches

This book has two purposes. The first is to detect and understand the forces that determine political relations among nations, and to comprehend the ways in which those forces act upon one another and upon international political relations and institutions. In most other branches of the social sciences, this purpose would be taken for granted, because the natural aim of all scientific undertakings is to discover the forces underlying social phenomena and the mode of their operation. In approaching the study of international politics, one cannot take this purpose for granted; it therefore requires special emphasis. As Dr. Grayson Kirk has put it:

> Until recent times the study of international relations in the United States has been dominated largely by persons who have taken one of three approaches. First there have been the historians who have considered international relations merely as recent history, in which the student is handicapped by the absence of an adequate amount of available data. A second group, the international lawyers, have properly concerned themselves primarily with the legal aspects of interstate relations, but they have seldom made a serious effort to inquire into the fundamental reasons for the continuing incompleteness and inadequacy of this legal nexus. Finally, there have been those who have been less concerned with international relations as they are than with the more perfect system which these idealists would like to build. Only recently—and belatedly—have students undertaken to examine the fundamental and persistent forces of world politics, and the institutions which embody them, not with a view to praise or to condemn, but merely in an effort to provide a better understanding of these basic drives which determine the

foreign policies of states. Thus the political scientist is moving into the international field at last.[1]

Professor Charles E. Martin has taken up Dr. Kirk's theme by pointing to

the problem which faces the students and the teachers of international relations more than any other, namely, that dualism we have to face in moving in two different and opposite areas. I mean the area of institutions of peace which are related to the adjustment of disputes and the area of power politics and war. Yet, it must be so. There is no escape from it. . . . I think probably one of the greatest indictments of our attitude in teaching in the last twenty years has been to write off glibly the institution of war and to write off the books the influence of power politics. I think political scientists make a great mistake in doing so. We should be the very ones who are studying power politics and its implications and the situations growing out of it, and we should be the ones who study the institution of war.[2]

Defined in such terms, international politics as an academic discipline is distinct from recent history and current events, international law, and political reform.

International politics embraces more than recent history and current events. The observer is surrounded by the contemporary scene with its ever-shifting emphasis and changing perspectives. He cannot find solid ground on which to stand, or objective standards of evaluation, without getting down to fundamentals that are revealed only by the correlation of recent events with the more distant past and the perennial qualities of human nature underlying both.

International politics cannot be reduced to legal rules and institutions. International politics operates within the framework of such rules and through the instrumentality of such institutions. But it is no more identical with them than American politics on the national level is identical with the American Constitution, the federal laws, and the agencies of the federal government.

Concerning attempts to reform international politics before making an effort to understand what international politics is about, we share William Graham Sumner's view:

The worst vice in political discussions is that dogmatism which takes its stand on great principles or assumptions, instead of standing on an exact examination of things as they are and human nature as it is. . . . An ideal is formed of some higher or better state of things than now exists, and almost unconsciously the ideal is assumed as already existing and made the basis of speculations which have no root. . . . The whole method of abstract speculation on political topics is vicious. It is popular because it is easy; it is easier to imagine a new world than to learn to know this one; it is easier to embark on speculations based on a few broad assumptions than it is to study the history of

---

[1] *American Journal of International Law*, Vol. 39 (1945), pp. 369–70.
[2] *Proceedings of the Eighth Conference of Teachers of International Law and Related Subjects* (Washington, DC: Carnegie Endowment for International Peace, 1946), p. 66.

states and institutions; it is easier to catch up a popular dogma than it is to analyze it to see whether it is true or not. All this leads to confusion, to the admission of phrases and platitudes, to much disputing but little gain in the prosperity of nations.[3]

Limitations to Understanding

The most formidable difficulty facing a theoretical inquiry into the nature and ways of international politics is the ambiguity of the material with which the observer has to deal. The events he must try to understand are, on the one hand, unique occurrences: they happened in this way only once and never before or since. On the other hand, they are similar, for they are manifestations of social forces. Social forces are the product of human nature in action. Therefore, under similar conditions, they will manifest themselves in a similar manner. But where is the line to be drawn between the similar and the unique?

This ambiguity of the events to be understood by a theory of international politics—it may be pointed out in passing—is but a special instance of a general impediment to human understanding. "As no event and no shape," observes Montaigne, "is entirely like another, so also is there none entirely different from another: *an ingenious mixture on the part of Nature. If there were no similarity in our faces, we could not distinguish man from beast; if there were no dissimilarity, we could not distinguish one man from another.* All things hold together by some similarity; every example is halting, and the comparison that is derived from experience is always defective and imperfect. And yet one links up the comparisons at some corner. And so do laws become serviceable and adapt themselves to every one of our affairs by some wrested, forced, and biased interpretation."[4] It is against such "wrested, forced, and biased interpretation" of political events that a theory of international politics must be continuously on guard.

We learn what the principles of international politics are from comparisons between such events. A certain political situation evokes the formulation and execution of a certain foreign policy. Dealing with a different political situation, we ask ourselves: how does this situation differ from the preceding one, and how is it similar? Do the similarities reaffirm the policy developed previously? Or does the blending of similarities and differences allow the essence of that policy to be retained while, in some aspects, it is to be modified? Or do the differences vitiate the analogy altogether and make the previous policy inapplicable? If one wants to understand international politics, grasp the meaning of contemporary events, and foresee and influence the future, one must be able to perform the dual intellectual task implicit in these questions. One must be able to distinguish between the similarities and differences in two political situations. Furthermore, one must be able to assess the import of these

---

[3]"Democracy and Responsible Government," *The Challenge of Facts and Other Essays* (New Haven, CT: Yale University Press, 1914), pp. 245–46.
[4]*The Essays of Michel de Montaigne,* edited and translated by Jacob Zeitlin (New York: Alfred A. Knopf, 1936), Vol. III, p. 270; Montaigne's italics.

similarities and differences for alternative foreign policies. Three series of events, taken at random, will illustrate the problem and its difficulties.

On September 17, 1796, George Washington made a speech in which he bade farewell to the nation, outlining the principles of American foreign policy in terms of abstention from European affairs. On December 2, 1823, President Monroe sent a message to Congress in which he formulated the principles of American foreign policy in similar terms. In 1917, the United States joined France and Great Britain against Germany, which threatened the independence of both. In 1941, the United States followed a similar course of action. On March 12, 1947, President Truman, in a message to Congress, reformulated the principles of American foreign policy in terms of the worldwide containment of Communism.

In 1512, Henry VIII of England made an alliance with the Hapsburgs against France. In 1515, he made an alliance with France against the Hapsburgs. In 1522 and 1542, he joined the Hapsburgs against France. In 1756, Great Britain allied itself with Prussia against the Hapsburgs and France. In 1793, Great Britain, Prussia, and the Hapsburgs were allied against Napoleon. In 1914, Great Britain joined with France and Russia against Austria and Germany, and in 1939 with France and Poland against Germany.

Napoleon, Wilhelm II, and Hitler tried to conquer the continent of Europe and failed.

Are there within each of these three series of events similarities that allow us to formulate a principle of foreign policy for each series? Or is each event so different from the others in the series that each would require a different policy? The difficulty in making this decision is the measure of the difficulty in making correct judgments in foreign policy, in charting the future wisely, and in doing the right thing in the right way and at the right time.

Should the foreign policy in Washington's Farewell Address be considered a general principle of American foreign policy, or did it stem from temporary conditions and was its validity therefore limited to them? Are the foreign policies of Washington's and Monroe's messages compatible with the Truman Doctrine? To state the problem another way, is the Truman Doctrine a mere modification of a general principle underlying Washington's and Monroe's conception of foreign affairs, or does the Truman Doctrine constitute a radical departure from the traditions of American foreign policy? If it does, is it justified in the light of changed conditions? Generally speaking, do the differences in the international position of the United States in 1796, 1823, 1917, 1941, and 1947 justify the different foreign policies formulated and executed with regard to these different political situations? What are the similarities and differences in the situations with which Europe confronted the United States in 1917, 1941, and 1947, and to what extent do they require similar or different foreign policies on the part of the United States?

What is the meaning of those shifts in British foreign policy? Have they grown from the whim and perfidy of princes and statesmen? Or are they inspired by the accumulated wisdom of a people mindful of the permanent forces, transcending any particular alignment, that determine their relations to the continent of Europe?

Are the disasters that followed in the wake of the three attempts at continental conquest so many accidents due to disparate causes? Or does the similarity in results point to similarities in the overall political situation, similarities that convey a lesson to be pondered by those who might want to try again? More particularly, were the policies the Soviet Union pursued in the aftermath of the Second World War similar to those of Napoleon, Wilhelm II, and Hitler? If they were, did they call for policies on the part of the United States similar to those pursued in 1917 and 1941?

Sometimes, as in the case of the changes in British foreign policy, the answer seems to be clear: that policy proceeded from wisdom rather than from whim. Most of the time, however, and especially when we deal with the present and the future, the answer is bound to be tentative and subject to qualifications. The facts from which the answer must derive are essentially ambiguous and subject to continuous change. To those men who would have it otherwise, history has taught nothing but false analogies. When such men have been responsible for the foreign policies of their countries, they have achieved only disaster. Wilhelm II and Hitler learned nothing from Napoleon's fate, for they thought it could teach them nothing. Those who have erected Washington's advice into a dogma to be followed slavishly have erred no less than those who would dismiss it altogether.

The Munich settlement of 1938 is another case in point. In retrospect, of course, we all know from practical experience that it was a failure, and from that experience we have developed the theoretical categories that demonstrate that it was bound to be a failure. But I remember very well the consensus with which the Munich settlement was approved at the time of its conclusion by theoreticians and practitioners of foreign policy and by the man in the street as well. The Munich settlement was then generally regarded as a great act of statesmanship, a concession made to a would-be conqueror for the sake of peace. E. H. Carr so regarded it then, and A.J.P. Taylor so regards it now. The flaw in that reasoning, which few people were—and perhaps could be—aware of at the time, was again the neglect of the contingencies inherent in political prediction. That which reveals itself as a simple truth in retrospect either was completely unknown in prospect or else could not be determined by anything but an uncertain hunch.

Take finally the contemporary issue of nuclear war. From time to time American policymakers speak openly about "prevailing" in a nuclear war. In this they mirror comments made by Russian military leaders—although not by Soviet political leaders such as Brezhnev, who more than once warned that a thermonuclear war would be suicidal for both superpowers. Particularly in the 1980s, as Cold War tensions mounted again, voices in both countries echoed the belief that victory in a nuclear war was not unthinkable, provided augmented strategic forces were formed through vastly increased defense expenditures. It is possible to develop a theory of nuclear war that assumes nuclear war to be just another kind of violence, greater in magnitude but not different in kind from the types of violence with which history has acquainted us. It follows from this assumption that nuclear war is going to be much more terrible than conventional war, but not necessarily intolerable, provided we take the measures that will enable at least some of us to survive it. In other words, once one starts with this theoretical assumption of the nature and the consequences of nuclear war, one can logically arrive at the conclusion that the foreign policy of the United States does not need to limit itself to trying to avoid nuclear war but that the United States must also prepare to survive it. And then it becomes perfectly legitimate to raise the question, provided 100 million Americans were to be killed in a nuclear war and nine-tenths of the economic capacity of the United States were to be destroyed, of how we enable the surviving Americans to rebuild the United States with the remaining one-tenth of economic capacity.

The contingent element in this theory of nuclear war is its utter uncertainty, and this uncertainty is typical of all levels of theoretical analysis and prediction in the field of politics, domestic and international. Even if one were to accept all its estimates of deaths and material destruction and of the rate of material recovery, this theory would have to be uncertain about the human reactions to the kind of human and material devastation that nuclear war is likely to bring about. Obviously, if a highly complex human society could be visualized to operate like a primitive ant society, its recuperative ability could be taken for granted. If one-half of the ants of one anthill have been destroyed together with nine-tenths of the material of the anthill, it is safe to conclude that the remaining ants will start all over again, building up the anthill and reproducing until the next catastrophe forces them to start all over again.

But a human society does not have this type of mechanical recuperative ability. Societies have a breaking point as do individuals, and there is a point beyond which human endurance does not carry human initiative in the face of such unprecedented massive devastation. Once that point is reached, civilization itself will collapse. The exact location of that point in the scale of human reactions is beyond theoretical understanding. What we are left with are hunches that may or may not be confirmed by experience.

The first lesson the student of international politics must learn and never forget is that the complexities of international affairs make simple solutions and trustworthy prophecies impossible. Here the scholar and the charlatan part company. Knowledge of the forces that determine politics among nations, and of the ways by which their political relations unfold, reveals the ambiguity of the facts of international politics. In every political situation contradictory tendencies are at play. One of these tendencies is more likely to prevail under certain conditions. But which tendency actually will prevail is anybody's guess. The best the scholar can do, then, is to trace the different tendencies that, as potentialities, are inherent in a "certain" international situation. He can point out the different conditions that make it more likely for one tendency to prevail than for another and, finally, assess the probabilities for the different conditions and tendencies to prevail in actuality.

Thus world affairs have surprises in store for whoever tries to read the future from his knowledge of the past and from the signs of the present. In 1776, Washington declared that "the Fate of our Country depends in all human probability, on the Exertion of a Few Weeks." Yet it was not until seven years later that the War of Independence came to an end. In February 1792, British prime minister Pitt justified the reduction of military expenditures (particularly a drastic decrease in the personnel of the British navy) and held out hope for more reductions to come by declaring: "Unquestionably there never was a time in the history of this country when from the situation of Europe we might more reasonably expect fifteen years of peace than at the present moment." Only two months later the continent of Europe was engulfed in war. Less than a year later Great Britain was involved. Thus was initiated a period of almost continuous warfare that lasted nearly a quarter of a century. When Lord Granville became British foreign secretary in 1870, he was informed by the permanent undersecretary that "he had never, during his long experience, known so great a lull in foreign affairs, and that he was not aware of any important question that he [Lord Granville] should have to deal with." On that same day Prince Leopold of Hohenzollern-Sigmaringen accepted the crown of Spain, an event that three weeks later led to the outbreak of the Franco-Prussian War. Six weeks before the Russian Revolution of March 1917, Lenin told a group of young socialists in Zurich: "We old people will probably not live to see the decisive battles of the coming revolution." Less than a year later, the decisive battles of the Russian Revolution began under his leadership.

When the prophecies of great statesmen fare so ill, what can we expect from the predictions of lesser minds? In how many books written on international affairs before the First World War, when common opinion held great wars to be impossible or at least of short duration, was there even an inkling of what was to come? Was any book written in the period between the two world wars that could have helped one anticipate what international politics would be like in the ninth decade of the century? Who could have guessed at the beginning of World War II what the political world would be like at its end? Who could have known in 1945 what the world would be like in 1955, or in 1960 what it would be like in 1970 or 1980? What trust then shall we place in those who today would tell us what tomorrow and the day after will bring or what the year 2000 will be like?[5]

In 1979 the intelligence community, and more particularly the Central Intelligence Agency, were criticized for their failure to warn American policymakers of the upheavals that culminated in the Shah of Iran's ouster. President Carter himself took the unprecedented step of publicly reprimanding the highest authorities in the intelligence field for their lack of foresight.

What accounts for this failure of foresight on the part of otherwise intelligent and responsible people? The answer lies in the nature of the empirical material with which these individuals had to deal. The observer is confronted with a multitude of factors, the totality of which shape the future. In order to foresee the

---

[5]The fallibility of prophecies in international affairs is strikingly demonstrated by the fantastic errors committed by the experts who have tried to forecast the nature of the next war. The history of these forecasts, from Machiavelli to General J.F.C. Fuller, is the story of logical deductions, plausible in themselves, that had no connection with the contingencies of the actual historical development. General Fuller, for instance, foresaw in 1923 that the decisive weapon of the Second World War would be gas! See *The Reformation of War* (New York. E. P. Dutton, 1923).

future, the observer would have to know all these factors, their dynamics, their mutual actions and reactions, and so forth. What he actually knows and can know is but a small fragment of the total. He must guess—and only the future will show who chose rightly among the many possible guesses.

Thus, with regard to Iran the intelligence community guessed wrong. Instead of blaming it indiscriminately, one ought to ask oneself two questions: Could one have pinpointed in time the outbreak of popular discontent? If the answer is in the affirmative, what could the United States have done about it? The answer to the second question is, at best: very little. This is probably why the intelligence community paid less attention to Iran than it might have done in the first place.

It is sobering to note that the science of economics, presumed to be the most precise of the social sciences because its central concept, wealth, is quantitative by definition, is similarly incapable of reliable prediction. An examination of a large number of forecasts of year-to-year changes in the American GNP for the years 1953–63 established an average error of about 40 percent.[6] In October 1966 the Prudential Life Insurance Company predicted that in 1967 consumer expenditures would rise by 31 billion dollars and inventory investments would amount to 7.5 billion dollars. In October 1967 it scaled its estimate of consumer expenditures down to 27 billion dollars, an error of almost 15 percent, assuming the correctness of the revised estimate; it reduced its estimate of inventory investments to 7 billion dollars. The Council of Economic Advisors overestimated the growth of the GNP for the same year by about 12 percent.

UNDERSTANDING THE PROBLEM OF INTERNATIONAL PEACE

These questions lead us to the secondary purpose of this book. No study of politics, and certainly no study of international politics in the final decades of the twentieth century, can be disinterested in the sense that it is able to divorce knowledge from action and to pursue knowledge for its own sake. International politics is no longer, as it was for the United States during most of its history, a series of incidents, costly or rewarding, but hardly calling into question the nation's very existence and destiny. The existence and destiny of the United States were more deeply affected by the domestic events of the Civil War than by the international policies leading up to, and evolving from, the Mexican War, the Spanish-American War, and the Roosevelt corollary to the Monroe Doctrine.[7]

---

[6]Viktor Zarnowitz, *An Appraisal of Short-Term Economic Forecasts* (New York: National Bureau of Economic Research, 1967).

[7]This corollary is found in the message of Theodore Roosevelt to Congress on December 6, 1904. In that message he proclaimed the right of the United States to intervene in the domestic affairs of the Latin American countries. For the text, see Ruhl J. Bartlett, editor, *The Record of American Diplomacy: Documents and Readings in the History of American Foreign Relations*, 4th ed. (New York: Alfred A. Knopf, 1964), p. 539.

Two facts peculiar to our time have completely reversed the relative importance of domestic and international policies for the United States. First of all, the United States is at the moment of this writing one of the two most powerful nations on earth. Yet, in comparison with its actual and potential competitors, it is not so powerful that it can afford to ignore the effect of its policies upon its position among the nations. From the end of the Civil War to the beginning of the Second World War, it mattered little what policies the United States pursued with regard to its Latin American neighbors, China, or Spain. The self-sufficiency of its own strength, in conjunction with the operation of the balance of power, made the United States immune to the boundless ambition born of success and the fear and frustration that goes with failure. The United States could take success and failure in stride without being unduly tempted or afraid. Now it stands outside the enclosures of its continental citadel, taking on the whole of the political world as friend or foe. It has become dangerous and vulnerable, feared and afraid.

The risk of being very powerful, but not omnipotent, is aggravated by the second fact: a threefold revolution in the political structure of the world. First, the multiple-state system of the past, whose center was in Europe, has been replaced by a worldwide, bipolar system whose centers lie outside Europe. Furthermore, the moral unity of the political world, which has distinguished Western civilization during most of its history, has been split into two incompatible systems of thought and action, competing everywhere for the allegiance of men. Finally, modern technology has made possible total war resulting in universal destruction. The preponderance of these three new elements in contemporary international politics has not only made the preservation of world peace extremely difficult but has also increased the risks inherent in war to the point where all-out nuclear war becomes a self-defeating absurdity. Since in this world situation the United States holds a position of predominant power, and hence of foremost responsibility, the understanding of the forces that mold international politics and of the factors that determine its course has become for the United States more than an interesting intellectual occupation. It has become a vital necessity.

To reflect on international politics from the vantage point of the contemporary United States, then, is to reflect upon the vital problems that confront American foreign policy in our time. While at all times the promotion of the national interests of the United States as a power among powers has been the main concern of American foreign policy, in an age that has seen two world wars and has learned how to wage total war with nuclear weapons, the preservation of peace has become the prime concern of all nations.

It is for this reason that this book is planned around the two concepts of power and peace. These two concepts are central to a discussion of world politics in the final decades of the twentieth century, when an unprecedented accumulation of destructive power gives to the problem of peace an urgency it has never had before. In a world whose moving force is the aspiration of sovereign nations for power, peace can be maintained only by two devices. One is the self-regulatory mechanism of the social forces, which manifests itself in the struggle for power on the international scene—that is, the balance of power. The other consists of normative limitations upon that struggle, in the form of international law, international morality, and world public opinion. Since neither of these devices, as they operate today, is likely to keep the struggle for power indefinitely within peaceful bounds, three further questions must be asked and answered: What is the value of the main current proposals for the maintenance of international peace? More particularly, what is the value of the proposal for transforming the international society of sovereign nations into a supranational organization, such as a world state? And, finally, what must a program for action be like that is mindful of the lessons of the past and endeavors to adapt them to the problems of the present?

PART TWO

INTERNATIONAL POLITICS AS A STRUGGLE FOR POWER

3 Political Power

WHAT IS POLITICAL POWER?[1]

As Means to the Nation's Ends

International politics, like all politics, is a struggle for power. Whatever the ultimate aims of international politics, power is always the immediate aim. Statesmen and peoples may ultimately seek freedom, security, prosperity, or power itself. They may define their goals in terms of a religious, philosophic, economic, or social ideal. They may hope that this ideal will materialize through its own inner force, through divine intervention, or through the natural development of human affairs. They may also try to further its realization through nonpolitical means, such as technical cooperation with other nations or international organizations. But whenever they strive to realize their goal by means of international politics, they do so by striving for power. The Crusaders wanted to free the holy places from domination by the Infidels; Woodrow Wilson wanted to make the world safe for democracy; the Nazis wanted to open Eastern Europe to German colonization, to dominate Europe, and to conquer the world. Since they all chose power to achieve these ends, they were actors on the scene of international politics.[2]

Two conclusions follow from this concept of international politics. First, not every action that a nation performs with respect to another nation is of a political

---

[1]The concept of political power poses one of the most difficult and controversial problems of political science. The value of any concept used in political science is determined by its ability to explain a maximum of the phenomena that are conventionally considered to belong to a certain sphere of political activity. Thus the coverage of a concept of political power, to be useful for the understanding of international politics, must be broader than the coverage of one adopted to operate in the field of municipal politics. The political means employed in the latter are much more narrowly circumscribed than are those employed in international politics.

[2]For some significant remarks on power in relation to international politics, see Lionel Robbins, *The Economic Causes of War* (London: Jonathan Cape, 1939), pp. 63 ff.

nature. Many such activities are normally undertaken without any consideration of power, nor do they normally affect the power of the nation undertaking them. Many legal, economic, humanitarian, and cultural activities are of this kind. Thus a nation is not normally engaged in international politics when it concludes an extradition treaty with another nation, when it exchanges goods and services with other nations, when it cooperates with other nations in providing relief from natural catastrophes, and when it promotes the distribution of cultural achievements throughout the world. In other words, the involvement of a nation in international politics is but one among many types of activities in which a nation can participate on the international scene.

Second, not all nations are at all times to the same extent involved in international politics. The degree of their involvement may run all the way from the maximum at present attained by the United States and the Soviet Union; through the minimum involvement of such countries as Switzerland, Luxembourg, or Venezuela; to the complete noninvolvement of Liechtenstein and Monaco. Similar extremes can be noticed in the history of particular countries. Spain in the sixteenth and seventeenth centuries was one of the main active participants in the struggle for power on the international scene but plays today only a marginal role in it. The same is true of such countries as Austria, Sweden, and Switzerland. On the other hand, nations such as the United States, the Soviet Union, and China are today much more deeply involved in international politics than they were fifty or even twenty years ago. In short, the relation of nations to international politics has a dynamic quality. It changes with the vicissitudes of power, which may push a nation into the forefront of the power struggle or may deprive a nation of the ability to participate actively in it. It may also change under the impact of cultural transformations, which may make a nation prefer other pursuits, for instance commerce, to those of power. The tendency of countries to be involved to a greater or lesser extent in the struggle for power prompted Arnold Wolfers to observe that they occupied positions at opposite extremes of a spectrum extending from what he called the pole of power to the pole of indifference.

Its Nature: Four Distinctions

When we speak of power in the context of this book, we have in mind not man's power over nature; or over an artistic medium, such as language, speech, sound, or color; or over the means of production or consumption; or over himself in the sense of self-control. When we speak of power, we mean man's control over the minds and actions of other men. By political power we refer to the mutual relations of control among the holders of public authority and between the latter and the people at large.

Political power is a psychological relation between those who exercise it and those over whom it is exercised. It gives the former control over certain actions of the latter through the effect that the former has on the latter's minds. That effect derives from three sources: the expectation of benefits, the fear of disadvantages, and the respect or love for men or institutions. It may be exerted through orders, threats, the authority or charisma of a man or of an office, or a combination of any of these.

In view of this definition, four distinctions must be made: between power and influence, between power and force, between usable and unusable power, and between legitimate and illegitimate power.

The secretary of state who advises the president of the United States on the conduct of American foreign policy has influence if the president follows his advice. But he has no power over the president; for he has none of the means at his disposal with which to impose his will upon that of the president. He can persuade but he cannot compel. The president, on the other hand, has power over the secretary of state; for he can impose his will upon the latter by virtue of the authority of his office, the promise of benefits, and the threat of disadvantages.

Political power must be distinguished from force in the sense of the actual exercise of physical violence. The threat of physical violence in the form of police action, imprisonment, capital punishment, or war is an intrinsic element of politics. When violence becomes an actuality, it signifies the abdication of political power in favor of military or pseudomilitary power. In international politics in particular, armed strength as a threat or a potentiality is the most important material factor making for the political power of a nation. If it becomes an actuality in war, it signifies the substitution of military for political power. The actual exercise of physical violence substitutes for the psychological relation between two minds, which is of the essence of political power, the physical relation between two bodies, one of which is strong enough to dominate the other's movements. It is for this reason that in the exercise of physical violence the psychological element of the political relationship is lost and that we must distinguish between military and political power.

The availability of nuclear weapons makes it necessary to distinguish between usable and unusable power. It is one of the paradoxes of the nuclear age that, in contrast to the experience of all of prenuclear history, an increase in military power is no longer necessarily conducive to an increase in political power. The threat of all-out nuclear violence implies the threat of total destruction. As such, it can still be a suitable instrument of foreign policy when addressed to a nation that cannot reply in kind. The nation armed with nuclear weapons can assert power over the other nation by saying: "Either you do as I say, or I will destroy you." The situation is different if the nation so threatened can respond by saying: "If you destroy me with nuclear weapons, you will be destroyed in turn." Here the mutual threats cancel each other out. Since the nuclear destruction of one nation would call forth the nuclear destruction of the other, both nations can afford to disregard the threat on the assumption that both will act rationally.

It is only on the assumption that the nations concerned might act irrationally by destroying each other in an all-out nuclear war that the threat of nuclear war is credible and has indeed been used by the United States and the Soviet Union against each other, for instance by the Soviet Union during the Suez Crisis of 1956, by the United States during the Berlin Crisis of 1961, and by both during the Arab-Israeli War of 1973. Yet while here the threat of force can be used as a rational instrument of foreign policy, the actual use of that force remains irrational; for the threatened force would be used not for the political purpose of influencing the will of the other side but for the irrational purpose of destroying the other side with the attendant assurance of one's own destruction.

Thus the magnitude of its destructiveness, as compared with the limited character of the political purposes that are the proper object of foreign policy, renders nuclear force unusable as an instrument of foreign policy. It can be rational under certain conditions to threaten the other side with destruction through the use of nuclear force in order to change the other side's will; it would be irrational to actually destroy the other side, thereby inviting one's own destruction. In contrast, conventional force is usable as an instrument of foreign policy; for by inflicting limited damage with commensurate risks to oneself, one can use it indeed as a suitable instrument for changing the other side's will.

Finally, legitimate power—that is, power whose exercise is morally or legally justified—must be distinguished from illegitimate power. Power exercised with moral or legal authority must be distinguished from naked power. The power of the police officer who searches me by virtue of a search warrant is qualitatively different from the power of a robber who performs the same action by virtue of his holding a gun. The distinction is not only philosophically valid but also relevant for the conduct of foreign policy. Legitimate power, which can invoke a moral or legal justification for its exercise, is likely to be more effective than equivalent illegitimate power, which cannot be so justified. That is to say, legitimate power has a better chance to influence the will of its objects than equivalent illegitimate power. Power exercised in self-defense or in the name of the United Nations has a better chance to succeed than does equivalent power exercised by an "aggressor" nation or in violation of international law. Political ideologies, as we shall see, serve the purpose of endowing foreign policies with the appearance of legitimacy.

While it is generally recognized that the interplay of the expectation of benefits, the fear of disadvantages, and the respect or love for men or institutions, in ever-changing combinations, forms the basis of all domestic politics, the importance of these factors for international politics is less obvious but no less real. There has been a tendency to reduce political power to the actual application of force, or at least to equate it with successful threats of force and with persuasion, to the neglect of charisma. That neglect, as we shall see,[3] accounts in good measure for the neglect of prestige as an independent element in international politics. Yet without taking into account the charisma of a man, such as Napoleon or Hitler, or of an institution, such as the government or the United States Constitution, evoking trust and love through which the wills of men submit themselves to the will of such a man or institution, it is impossible to understand certain phenomena of international politics that have been particularly prominent in modern times.

---

[3]See Chapter 6.

The importance that charismatic leadership and the response to it as love of the subject for the leader has for international politics is clearly revealed in a letter that John Durie, Scotch Presbyterian and worker for Protestant unity, wrote in 1632 to the British Ambassador Thomas Roe, explaining the decline of the power of Gustavus Adolphus of Sweden, then fighting for the Protestant cause in Germany:

> The increase of his authority is the ground of his abode; and love is the ground of his authority; it must be through love; for it cannot be through power; for his power is not in his own subjects but in strangers; not in his money, but in theirs; not in their good will, but in mere necessity as things stand now betwixt him and them; therefore if the necessity be not so urgent as it is; or if any other means be shown by God (who is able to do as much by another man as by him) to avoid this necessity; the money and the power and the assistance which it yieldeth unto him will fall from him and so his authority is lost, and his abode will be no longer: for the Love which was at first is gone. . . .[4]

The president of the United States exerts political power over the executive branch of the government so long as his orders are obeyed by the members of that branch. The leader of the party has political power so long as he is able to mold the actions of the members of the party according to his will. We refer to the political power of an industrialist, a labor leader, or a lobbyist in so far as his preferences influence the actions of public officials. The United States exerts political power over Puerto Rico so long as the laws of the United States are observed by the citizens of that island. When we speak of the political power of the United States in Central America, we have in mind the conformity of the actions of Central American governments with the wishes of the government of the United States.[5] Thus the statement that A has or wants political power over B signifies always that A is able, or wants to be able, to control certain actions of B through influencing B's mind.

Whatever the material objectives of a foreign policy, such as the acquisition of sources of raw materials, the control of sea lanes, or territorial changes, they always entail control of the actions of others through influence over their minds. The Rhine frontier as a century-old objective of French foreign policy points to the political objective to destroy the desire of Germany to attack France by making it physically difficult or impossible for Germany to do so. Great Britain owed its predominant position in world politics throughout the nineteenth century to the calculated policy of making it either too dangerous (because Great Britain was

---

[4]Gunnar Westin, *Negotiations About Church Unity, 1628–1634* (Upsala: Almquist and Wiksells, 1932), p. 208. The spelling has been modernized.
[5]The examples in the text illustrate also the distinction between political power as mere social fact, as in the case of the lobbyist, and political power in the sense of legitimate authority, that is, the president of the United States. Both the president of the United States and the lobbyist exercise political power, however different its source and nature may be.

too strong) or unnecessary (because it strength was used with moderation) for other nations to oppose it.

The political objective of military preparations of any kind is to deter other nations from using military force by making it too risky for them to do so. The political aim of military preparations is, in other words, to make the actual application of military force unnecessary by inducing the prospective enemy to desist from the use of military force. The political objective of war itself is not per se the conquest of territory and the annihilation of enemy armies but a change in the mind of the enemy that will make him yield to the will of the victor.

Therefore, whenever economic, financial, territorial, or military policies are under discussion in international affairs, it is necessary to distinguish between, say, economic policies that are undertaken for their own sake and economic policies that are the instruments of a political policy—a policy, that is, whose economic purpose is but the means to the end of controlling the policies of another nation. The export policy of Switzerland with regard to the United States falls into the first category. The economic policies of the Soviet Union with regard to the nations of Eastern Europe fall into the latter category. So do many economic policies of the United States in Latin America, Asia, and Europe. The distinction is of great practical importance, and the failure to make it has led to much confusion in policy and public opinion.

An economic, financial, territorial, or military policy undertaken for its own sake is subject to evaluation in its own terms. Is it economically or financially advantageous? What effects has acquisition of territory upon the population and the economy of the nation acquiring it? What are the consequences of a change in a military policy for education, population, and the domestic political system? The decisions with respect to these policies are made exclusively in terms of such intrinsic considerations.

When, however, the objectives of these policies serve to increase the power of the nation pursuing them with regard to other nations, these policies and their objectives must be judged primarily from the point of view of their contribution to national power. An economic policy that cannot be justified in purely economic terms might nevertheless be undertaken in view of the political policy pursued. The insecure and unprofitable character of a loan to a foreign nation may be a valid argument against it on purely financial grounds. But the argument is irrelevant if the loan, however unwise it may be from a banker's point of view, serves the political policies of the nation. It may of course be that the economic or financial losses involved in such policies will weaken the nation in its international position to such an extent as to outweigh the political advantages to be expected. On these grounds such policies might be rejected. In such a case, what decides the issue is not purely economic and financial considerations but a comparison of the political chances and risks involved—that is, the probable effect of these policies upon the power of the nation.

When the United States provides loans or assistance to countries such as Poland that lie in the shadow of the Red Army, the purpose is not primarily economic or financial. It is rather to enable such countries to move toward a degree of independence of the influence and power of the Soviet Union. If the repayment of loans to American agencies or financial institutions is postponed with U.S. government approval, this is not for humanitarian or charitable reasons alone. Rather, it is American policy to keep open certain options for the government of Poland, options that prevent its total dependence on the Soviet Union. Such actions in the economic sphere are based on political objectives that in the long run may assure the survival of Poland as a sovereign state—however much its geographic and political position may force it to accept the position of a satellite within the sphere of the Soviet Union at least in the short run. In a word, the aim of American economic policy toward Poland is to limit Soviet influence and power in Central and Eastern Europe while increasing the leverage of the United States in the area.

THE DEPRECIATION OF POLITICAL POWER

The aspiration for power being the distinguishing element of international politics, as of all politics, international politics is of necessity power politics. While this fact is generally recognized in the practice of international affairs, it is frequently denied in the pronouncements of scholars, publicists, and even statesmen. Since the end of the Napoleonic Wars, ever larger groups in the Western world have been persuaded that the struggle for power on the international scene is a temporary phenomenon, a historical accident that is bound to disappear once the peculiar historic conditions that have given rise to it have been eliminated. Thus Jeremy Bentham believed that the competition for colonies was at the root of all international conflicts. "Emancipate your colonies!" was his advice to the governments, and international conflict and war would of necessity disappear.[6] Adherents of free trade such as Cobden[7] and Proudhon[8] were convinced that the removal of trade barriers was the only condition for the establishment of permanent harmony among nations and might even lead to the disappearance of international politics altogether. "At some future election," said Cobden, "we may probably see the test 'no foreign politics' applied to those who offer to become the representatives of free constituencies."[9] For Marx and his followers, capitalism is at the root of international discord and war. They maintain that international socialism will do away with the struggle for power on the international scene and

---

[6]*Emancipate Your Colonies* (London: Robert Heward, 1830).

[7]"Free trade! What is it? Why, breaking down the barriers that separate nations; those barriers, behind which nestle the feelings of pride, revenge, hatred, and jealousy, which every now and then burst their bounds, and deluge whole countries with blood." "Free trade is the international law of the Almighty," and free trade and peace seem to be "one and the same cause." See *Speeches by Richard Cobden* (London: Macmillan, 1870), Vol. I, p. 79; *Political Writings* (New York: D. Appleton, 1867), Vol. II, p. 110; letter of April 12, 1842, to Henry Ashworth, quoted in John Morley, *Life of Richard Cobden* (Boston: Roberts Brothers, 1881), p. 154.

[8]"Let us suppress the tariffs, and the alliance of the peoples will thus be declared, their solidarity recognized, their equality proclaimed." *Oeuvres completes* (Paris, 1867), Vol. I, p. 248.

[9]Quoted in A.C.F. Beales, *A Short History of English Liberalism*, p. 195.

will bring about permanent peace. During the nineteenth century liberals everywhere shared the conviction that power politics and war were residues of an obsolete system of government and that the victory of democracy and constitutional government over absolutism and autocracy would assure the victory of international harmony and permanent peace over power politics and war. Of this liberal school of thought, Woodrow Wilson was the most eloquent and most influential spokesman.

In recent times the conviction that the struggle for power can be eliminated from the international scene has been connected with the great attempts at organizing the world, such as the League of Nations and the United Nations. Thus Cordell Hull, then U.S. secretary of state, declared in 1943 on his return from the Moscow Conference, which laid the groundwork for the United Nations, that the new international organization would mean the end of power politics and usher in a new era of international collaboration.[10] Mr. Philip Noel-Baker, then British minister of state, declared in 1946 in the House of Commons that the British government was "determined to use the institutions of the United Nations to kill power politics, in order that, by the methods of democracy, the will of the people shall prevail."[11]

While we shall have more to say later about these theories and the expectations derived from them,[12] it is sufficient to state that the struggle for power is universal in time and space and is an undeniable fact of experience. It cannot be denied that throughout historical time, regardless of social, economic, and political conditions, states have met each other in contests for power. Even though anthropologists have shown that certain primitive peoples seem to be free from the desire for power, nobody has yet shown how their state of mind and the conditions under which they live can be re-created on a worldwide scale so as to eliminate the struggle for power from the international scene.[13] It would be useless and even self-destructive to free one or the other of the peoples of the earth from the desire for power while leaving it extant in others. If the desire for power cannot be abolished everywhere in the world, those who might be cured would simply fall victims to the power of others.

The position taken here might be criticized on the ground that conclusions drawn from the past are unconvincing and that to draw such conclusions has always been the main stock in trade of the enemies of progress and reform. Though it is true that certain social arrangements and institutions have always existed in the past, it does not necessarily follow that they must always exist in the future. The situation is, however, different when we deal not with social arrangements and institutions created by man but with those elemental biopsychological drives by which in turn society is created. The drives to live, to propagate, and

---

[10]*New York Times*, November 19, 1943, p. 1.
[11]*House of Commons Debates* (Fifth Series, 1946), Vol. 419, p. 1262.
[12]See Part Eight.
[13]For an illuminating discussion of this problem, see Malcolm Sharp, "Aggression: A Study of Values and Law," *Ethics*, Vol. 57, No. 4, Part II (July 1947).

to dominate are common to all men.[14] Their relative strength is dependent upon social conditions that may favor one drive and tend to repress another or that may withhold social approval from certain manifestations of these drives while they encourage others. Thus, to take examples only from the sphere of power, most societies condemn killing as a means of attaining power within society, but all societies encourage the killing of enemies in that struggle for power that is called war. Dictators look askance at the aspirations for political power among their fellow citizens, but democracies consider active participation in the competition for political power a civic duty. Where a monopolistic organization of economic activities exists, competition for economic power is absent, and in competitive economic systems certain manifestations of the struggle for economic power are outlawed while others are encouraged. Ostrogorsky, invoking the authority of Tocqueville, states that "the passions of the American people are not of a political, but of a commercial, nature. In that world awaiting cultivation, the love of power aims less at men than at things."[15]

Regardless of particular social conditions, the decisive argument against the opinion that the struggle for power on the international scene is a mere historical accident must be derived from the nature of domestic politics. The essence of international politics is identical with its domestic counterpart. Both domestic and international politics are a struggle for power, modified only by the different conditions under which this struggle takes place in the domestic and in the international spheres.

The tendency to dominate, in particular, is an element of all human associations, from the family, through fraternal and professional associations and local political organizations, to the state. On the family level, the typical conflict between the mother-in-law and her child's spouse is in its essence a struggle for power, the defense of an established power position against the attempt to establish a new one. As such it foreshadows the conflict on the international scene between the policies of the status quo and the policies of imperialism. Social clubs, fraternities, faculties, and business organizations are scenes of continuous struggles for power between groups that either want to keep what power they already have or seek to attain greater power. Competitive contests between business enterprises, as well as labor disputes between employers and employees, are frequently fought not only, and sometimes not even primarily, for economic advantages but for control over each other and over others—that is, for power. Finally, the whole political life of a nation, particularly of a democratic nation, from the local to the national level, is a continuous struggle for power. In periodic elections, in voting in legislative assemblies, in lawsuits

---

[14]Zoologists have tried to show that the drive to dominate is found even in animals, such as chickens and monkeys, who create social hierarchies on the basis of will and the ability to dominate. See, e.g., Warder Allee, *Animal Life and Social Growth* (Baltimore: Williams and Wilkens, 1932), and *The Social Life of Animals* (New York: W. W. Norton, 1938). Cf. also the theories of Konrad Lorenz and the controversies concerning them.

[15]M. Ostrogorsky, *Democracy and the Organization of Political Parties* (New York: Macmillan, 1902), Vol. II, p. 592.

before courts, in administrative decisions and executive measures—in all these activities men try to maintain or to establish their power over other men. The processes by which legislative, judicial, executive, and administrative decisions are reached are subject to pressures and counterpressures by "pressure groups" trying to defend and expand their positions of power. As one of the Dead Sea Scrolls puts it:

> What nation likes to be oppressed by a stronger power? Or who wants his property plundered unjustly? Yet, is there a single nation that has not oppressed its neighbour? Or where in the world will you find a people that has not plundered the property of another? Where indeed?

"Of the gods we know," to quote Thucydides, "and of men we believe, that it is a necessary law of their nature that they rule wherever they can."[16] Or, as Tolstoy put it, "the very process of dominating another's will was in itself a pleasure, a habit, and a necessity to Dólokhov."[17]

And in the words of John of Salisbury:

> Though it is not given to all men to seize princely or royal power, yet the man who is wholly untainted by tyranny is rare or nonexistent. In common speech the tyrant is one who oppresses a whole people by a rulership based on force; and yet it is not over a people as a whole that a man can play the tyrant, but he can do so if he will even in the meanest station. For if not over the whole body of the people, still each man will lord it as far as his power extends.[18]

In view of this ubiquity of the struggle for power in all social relations and on all levels of social organization, is it surprising that international politics is of necessity power politics? And would it not be rather surprising if the struggle for power were but an accidental and ephemeral attribute of international politics when it is a permanent and necessary element of all branches of domestic politics?

TWO ROOTS OF THE DEPRECIATION OF POLITICAL POWER

The depreciation of the role power plays on the international scene grows from two roots. One is the philosophy of international relations that dominated the better part of the nineteenth century and still holds sway over much of our thinking on international affairs. The other is the particular political and intellectual circumstances that have determined the relations of the United States of America to the rest of the world.

---

[16]Thucydides, Book V, § 105.
[17]Leo Tolstoy, *War and Peace*, Book Eight, Chapter XI.
[18]John of Salisbury, *Policraticus*, translated by John Dickinson (New York: Alfred A. Knopf, 1927), Vol. VII, p. 17.

Nineteenth-Century Philosophy

The nineteenth century was led to its depreciation of power politics by its domestic experience. The distinctive characteristic of this experience was the domination of the middle classes by the aristocracy. By identifying this domination with political domination of any kind, the political philosophy of the nineteenth century came to identify the opposition to aristocratic politics with hostility to any kind of politics. After the defeat of aristocratic government, the middle classes developed a system of indirect domination. They replaced the traditional division into the governing and the governed classes, and the military method of open violence characteristic of aristocratic rule, with the invisible chains of economic dependence. This economic system operated through a network of seemingly equalitarian legal rules that concealed the very existence of power relations. The nineteenth century was unable to see the political nature of these legalized relations. They seemed to be essentially different from what had gone, so far, under the name of politics. Therefore politics in its aristocratic—that is, open and violent—form was identified with politics as such. The struggle, then, for political power—in domestic as well as in international affairs—appeared to be only a historical accident, coincident with autocratic government and bound to disappear with the disappearance of autocratic government.

The American Experience

This identification of power politics with aristocratic government found support in the American experience. It can be traced to three elements in that experience: the uniqueness of the American experiment, the actual isolation of the American continent from centers of the world conflict during the nineteenth century, and the humanitarian pacifism and anti-imperialism of American political ideology.

That the severance of constitutional ties with the British Crown was meant to signify the initiation of an American foreign policy distinct from what went under the name of foreign policy in Europe is clearly stated in Washington's Farewell Address: "Europe has a set of primary interests, which to us have none, or a very remote relation. Hence she must be engaged in frequent controversies, the causes of which are essentially foreign to our concerns. Hence, therefore, it must be unwise in us to implicate ourselves, by artificial ties, in the ordinary vicissitudes of her politics, or the ordinary combinations and collisions of her friendships or enmities." In 1796, European politics and power politics were identical; there was no other power politics but the one engaged in by the princes of Europe. "The toils of European ambition, rivalship, interest, humor or caprice" were the only manifestations of the international struggle for power before the eyes of America. The retreat from European politics, as proclaimed by Washington, could, therefore, be taken to mean retreat from power politics as such.

Yet American aloofness from the European tradition of power politics was more than a political program. Certain sporadic exceptions notwithstanding, it was an established political fact until the end of the nineteenth century. This fact was a result of deliberate choice, as well as of the objective conditions of geography. Popular writers might see in the uniqueness of America's geographic position the hand of God, which had unalterably prescribed the course of American expansion as well as isolation. But more responsible observers, from Washington on, have been careful to emphasize the conjunction of geographic conditions and a foreign policy choosing its ends in the light of geography, using geographic conditions to attain those ends. Washington referred to "our detached and distant situation" and asked: "Why forego the advantages of so peculiar a situation?" When this period of American foreign policy drew to a close, John Bright wrote to Alfred Love: "On your continent we may hope your growing millions may henceforth know nothing of war. None can assail you; and you are anxious to abstain from mingling with the quarrels of other nations."[19]

From the shores of the North American continent, the citizens of the New World watched the strange spectacle of the international struggle for power unfolding on the distant shores of Europe, Africa, and Asia. Since for the better part of the nineteenth century their foreign policy enabled them to retain the role of spectators, what was actually the result of a passing historical constellation appeared to Americans as a permanent condition, self-chosen as well as naturally ordained. At worst they would continue to watch the game of power politics played by others. At best the time was close at hand when, with democracy established everywhere, the final curtain would fall and the game of power politics would no longer be played.

To aid in the achievement of this goal was conceived to be part of America's mission. Throughout the nation's history the national destiny of the United States has been understood in antimilitaristic, libertarian terms. Where that national mission finds a nonaggressive, abstentionist formulation, as in the political philosophy of John C. Calhoun, it is conceived as the promotion of domestic liberty. Thus we may "do more to extend liberty by our example over this continent and the world generally, than would be done by a thousand victories." When the United States, in the wake of the Spanish-American War, seemed to desert this anti-imperialist and democratic ideal, William Graham Sumner restated its essence: "Expansion and imperialism are a grand onslaught on democracy . . . expansion and imperialism are at war with the best traditions, principles, and interests of the American people."[20] Comparing the tendencies of European power politics with the ideals of the American tradition, Sumner thought with George Washington that they were incompatible. Yet, as a prophet of things to come, he saw that the settlement of the Spanish-American War irrevocably committed America to the same course that was engulfing Europe in revolution and war.

---

[19]Quoted in Merle Curti, *Peace and War: The American Struggle 1636–1936* (New York: W. W. Norton, Company, 1936), p. 122.
[20]"The Conquest of the United States by Spain," *Essays of William Graham Sumner* (New Haven, CT: Yale University Press, 1940), Vol. II, p. 295.

Thus the general conception the nineteenth century had formed of the nature of foreign affairs combined with specific elements in the American experience to create the belief that involvement in power politics is not inevitable but only a historical accident, and that nations have a choice between power politics and other kinds of foreign policy not tainted by the desire for power.

THE SCIENCE OF PEACE: CONTEMPORARY UTOPIANISM

A word should be said about a school of thought—still influential in political and intellectual circles today—that proffers a "scientific" alternative to the "perennial wisdom" of a rationalist approach to international politics. This school of thought we may call "scientific utopianism" for lack of a better term; like the sources of self-deception as to the persistence of political power discussed above, the scientific interpretation has strong roots in nineteenth-century experience, both in Europe and in America. In this case, however, neither the relations of class domination nor geographical accident gave rise to utopian hopes for a "science of peace." Instead, the fantastic progress of the natural sciences led various thinkers to assume that the same kinds of methods, applied to individual and collective human behavior, could yield progress toward what Herbert Marcuse and others have called "the pacification of human existence."

The modern science of peace starts from the assumption that the world is thoroughly accessible to science and reason and that it contains in itself all the elements necessary for the harmonious cooperation of all mankind. It is for science to detect those elements, variously defined as harmony of interests, laws of economics, free trade, and modern communications; it is for law to apply them where they do not prevail spontaneously; and it is for negotiation and compromise to discover them under the surface of apparent conflict.

For such rationalism it is the atavism of power politics that conceals and distorts the harmony of interests that is the true nature of international relations. Adam Smith, a founding father of classical liberalism, as well as of classical economics, discovered such a fundamental harmony of interests lying beneath the surface manifestations of self-regarding, competitive economic behavior. Selfish pursuits led to greater wealth for all through the workings of an "invisible hand." Governed by an inner logic, the free market operates to dispose all for the best. Nineteenth-century liberalism had no use for even such residual traces of the miraculous in its search for a means to establish harmonious relations among states. Only strictly rational principles would do; all international conflicts were considered capable of satisfactory solutions, either through compromise or arbitration. Since all men partake of reason, they must sooner or later meet on that common ground, discovering that their conflicts are apparent rather than real and can all be solved by a rational formula acceptable to all. Were all nations at all times fully aware of their real interests, they would realize that apparently opposing interests are actually identical, that what is good for one country is of necessity good for all other countries, and that conflict is merely the product of ignorance and error.

Conflicts among nations are due, then, to maladjustments arising from lack of understanding and to the influence of political passions. Except for ignorance and emotion, reason would solve international conflicts as easily and as rationally as it has solved so many problems in the natural sciences. Proudhon was among the first to glorify the blessings of science in the international field:

> Truth is everywhere identical with itself: science represents the unity of mankind. If therefore science, instead of religion or authority, is taken in each country as social norm, the sovereign arbiter of interests, with the government amounting to nothing, all the laws of the universe will be in harmony. Nationality or fatherland will no longer exist in the political meaning of the term; there will only be birthplaces. Man, of whatever race or colour he may be, will actually be a native of the Universe; the right of citizenship he will acquire everywhere. In the same way in which in a certain district of the national territory the municipality represents the nation and exercises its authority, each nation of the globe will represent humanity and in its natural boundaries act for it. Harmony will reign among the nations, without diplomacy nor council; nothing shall from now on disturb it.[21]

"The duty of the pacifist," according to C.E.M. Joad, "is above all things to be reasonable. He should, that is to say, rely on the use of his own reason in making his appeal and he should assume that other men may be brought to use theirs. . . . Truth, in fact, will win out, if people are only given a sufficient chance to find it."[22] It was with the same confidence in the power of reason that Clarence Streit asserted in 1941 that "the really big men in the United States Senate and British Parliament will champion the Union [of the two countries], once they understand it."[23]

Political history, then, becomes a succession of scientific problems capable of scientific solution—but most unreasonably handled by an ignorant and impassioned humanity. Even for so realistic an observer as Homer Lea, the problem of international affairs resolved itself into a problem of knowledge; if the "valour of ignorance" is replaced by the knowledge of the pertinent facts, man will be able to act successfully on the international scene. "The time can and will come," wrote the famous pacifist Bertha von Suttner, "when the science of politics will have replaced present-day statecraft, when only those will have legislative and political power . . . who sincerely seek only the truth and through the truth strive to attain only the good—the universal good comprehending all civilized nations."

---

[21]"Idée générale de la révolution au dix-neuvième siècle," *Oeuvres complètes*, IX (1868), p. 300; see also Proudhon, *La Guerre et la paix* (Paris: E. Dentu, 1861).
[22]"Pacifism: Its Personal and Social Implications," in G. P. Gooch, *In Pursuit of Peace* (London: Methuen, 1933), pp. 61, 63.
[23]*Union Now with Britain* (New York: Harper and Brothers, 1941), p. 197.

The time Suttner spoke of has already arrived as far as the mere posses-sion of knowledge is concerned, according to Robert S. Lynd. "The diagnosis," he wrote,

> is already fairly complete, thanks to a long list of competent studies of nationalism, imperialism, international finance and trade, and other factors within our culture that encourage war. The problem of war, more than most others, has engaged the attention of scientists from several disciplines, and the dissection has proceeded to the point where fairly unequivocal knowl-edge exists. The causes of war are known and accepted by a wide group of thoughtful students. But the statement of what is to be done languishes because social science shrinks from resolving the austere findings of scholarly monographs into a bold programme for action. . . . In the case of an issue like this, where the problem does not arise from lack of knowledge, what social science appears to need is the will to mass its findings so that the truth they hold will not continue to trickle away as disparate bits of scholarship. We know enough about war and its causes to present these findings, point their meanings, and propose action in a way that will hold this damaging evidence steadily and authoritatively before the eyes of the humblest citizen.[24]

It was for this Age of Reason to replace the old methods of power politics, secret diplomacy, and war by a new, scientific approach. Territorial claims, sover-eignty over national minorities, the distribution of raw materials, the struggle for markets, disarmament, the relation between the "haves" and the "have-nots," peaceful change, and the peaceful organization of the world in general—these are not "political" problems, to be solved temporarily and always precariously accord-ing to the distribution of power among quarreling nations and its possible bal-ance. They are "technical" problems for which reason will find the one correct solution in each case.

Thus the nineteenth century developed a "science of peace" as a separate branch of scientific knowledge. Scores of books were published bearing this title. One even received first prize in a scholarly competition.[25] The concept of a "nat-ural frontier"—which had had a strategical and political, but not a scientific, connotation in the sixteenth and seventeenth centuries—was construed by the French revolutionaries and Napoleon in the sense of a geographically "correct" frontier. In the seventies and eighties of the nineteenth century, public opinion in Great Britain discussed seriously the problem of the "scientific frontier," that is, a frontier that corresponds to reason and that, consequently, makes all other frontiers in this geographical region scientifically incorrect. In his speech at Mansion House on November 9, 1878, Disraeli justified the Second Afghan War by saying that the frontier of India was "a haphazard and not a scientific one."

---

[24]*Knowledge for What?* (Princeton: Princeton University Press, 1939), p. 241.
[25]Louis Bara, *La Science de la paix* (1872).

The search for such a "scientific" frontier started in the second half of the eighteenth century when, on the occasion of partitions and annexations of territory, the relative value of the pieces of territory to be distributed was determined on the basis of certain "objective" standards, such as fertility, number and quality of population, and the like. Following this trend the Congress of Vienna, upon the suggestion of Metternich, appointed a special statistical commission; it was charged with evaluating the territories under discussion by the "objective" standard of number, quality, and type of populations.[26] The delimitation of territory thus became a kind of mathematical exercise. The idea of the "good frontier," developed in the last decades of the nineteenth century in Germany with regard to Russia's territorial aspirations, had a somewhat similar connotation. The idea of the "scientific tariff" attempted to introduce science into foreign trade, building in part upon ideas put forth in the early nineteenth century by Friedrich List. The theory and practice of international plebiscites are also typical manifestations of the rationalist approach to international problems; here the will of the majority is the scientific test according to which sovereignty over territory is to be determined. In the thirties, Major Lefebure advanced his theories on "scientific disarmament." "Geopolitics" endeavoured to put foreign policy as a whole on a scientific basis.

It was only after the First World War that this tendency to reduce political problems to scientific propositions won general acceptance. "Reason is at last becoming an independent agency," wrote Lord Allen of Hartwood, "influencing the conduct of men. This is due to the coming of science. . . . Feeling himself now to be the master of nature, his mind is beginning to work rationally instead of superstitiously. When forming an opinion he observes the phenomena around him and draws his conclusions. From that moment mind begins to be an independent agency of influence. It can now therefore be considered as a political force, whereas that has never previously been possible in the history of civilization. During the last thirty years this has begun to influence public opinion."[27]

Thus began what can properly be called the age of the scientific approach to international affairs, and the end is not yet in sight. Preceded by the Hague Conferences and hundreds of smaller peace congresses, governments themselves embarked on a program of feverish activity unprecedented in recorded history, with the purpose of solving all international problems through scientific methods. The governments, the League of Nations, and private groups vied with one another in organizing international conferences, in encouraging teaching and research, and in publishing hundreds of volumes to cure the ills of humanity in a scientific way. We have recently witnessed widespread efforts to find a scientific solution for the problems of the postwar world. These are

[26]For details see Charles Dupuis, *Le Principe d'équilibre et le Concert Européen* (Paris: Perrin et Cie, 1909), pp. 38 ff, 60 ff.
[27]"Pacifism: Its Meaning and Its Task," in *Pursuit of Peace*, pp. 22, 23.

the latest, but probably not the last, manifestation of this modern intellectual trend.[28]

Our age is forever searching for the philosophers' stone, the magic formula, which, mechanically applied, will produce the desired result and thus substitute for the uncertainties and risks of political action the certitude of rational calculation. However, what the seekers after the magic formula want is simple, rational, mechanical; what they have to deal with is complicated, irrational, incalculable. As a consequence they are compelled, in order to present at least the semblance of scientific solutions, to simplify the reality of international politics and to rely upon what one might call the "method of the single cause."

The abolition of war is obviously the fundamental problem confronting international thought. To solve the problem one must clearly first determine its cause or causes. What makes a solution appear so difficult for the nonrationalist mind is the *variety* of causes involved–causes that have their roots in the innermost recesses of the human heart. Were it possible to reduce all those multiple, complex factors to a single cause–one capable of rational formulation–the solution of the problem of war would no longer seem impossible. This is what liberal foreign policy has been trying to do since its very inception; and since the heyday of the League of Nations most people would take it for lack of creative thought if a statesman or a political thinker did not have a "constructive" plan as a remedy for the "single cause."

Are not the remnants of feudalism the great single cause making for war in this world? Let us do away with aristocratic government everywhere, the classical liberals would say, and we will have peace. In practical politics this general proposition was frequently narrowed down to more special remedies intended to meet particular situations. Thus, as we have seen, Bentham and the Benthamites pointed to the struggle for colonies as the main cause for war; they advocated abstention from colonial policy as a remedy for war. For others tariffs were the source of all evils in the international sphere; to them free trade was the source of all good. Others would abolish secret treaties and secret diplomacy in general and, through popular control of international policies, secure peace. Is not modern war an outgrowth of imperialism, which, in turn, is a result of the contradictions of monopoly capitalism? Hence, let us do away with capitalism, the Marxists would say, and we will no longer have war: socialism is peace.

---

[28]Cf. Charles A. Beard, *A Foreign Policy for America* (New York: Alfred A. Knopf, 1940), pp. 98–99: "In line with the new interests, the study of international law and diplomacy was encouraged in institutions of learning. Old-fashioned courses on diplomacy–cold, scholarly performances–were supplemented by courses on international relations, in which emphasis was laid on world peace and the means of promoting it. Books, pamphlets, and articles on pacification were written, published, and widely circulated, often with the aid of subventions from peace funds. International peace conferences were organized and provided opportunities for travel and extended discourses. Seldom had college presidents, professors, clergymen, and leaders among women enjoyed such privileges and received such marked consideration at the hands of the general public. It looked as if a new era of usefulness and distinction had been opened for them in the field of great affairs, and they made the most of its opportunities."

The same one-track mode of thought is found also in domestic politics. All social evils stem from our ignorance of the laws of economics; the "single tax" takes account of those laws and will solve all social problems. Our economic system is out of joint because the government spends more than it collects; balance the budget and our economic problems will be solved. Bad linguistic habits are at the root of our social evils; with the acquisition of good linguistic habits our social problems will be solved. Emerson, in "New England Reformers," thus described this kind of thinking:

> One apostle thought all men should go to farming; and another, that no man should buy or sell; that the use of money was the cardinal evil; another, that the mischief was in our diet, that we eat and drink damnation. These made unleavened bread, and were foes to the death to fermentation. . . . Others attacked the system of agriculture; the use of animal manures in farming; and the tyranny of man over brute nature; these abuses polluted his food. . . .
> Even the insect world was to be defended–that had been too long neglected and a society for the protection of ground worms, slugs, and mosquitoes was to be incorporated without delay. With these appeared the adepts of homeopathy; of hydropathy, of mesmerism, of phrenology, and their wonderful theories of the Christian miracles! Others assailed particular vocations, as that of the lawyer, that of the merchant, of the manufacturer, of the clergyman, of the scholar. Others attacked the institution of marriage as the fountain of social evils. Others devoted themselves to the worrying of churches and meetings for public worship; and the fertile forms of antinomianism among the elder puritans, seemed to have their match in the plenty of the new harvest of reform.[29]

In the domestic field, however, the "method of the single cause" has been of rather limited theoretical and practical importance; for here, except in periods of collective insanity, immediate personal experience reveals the absurdity of the approach; and the pressure of the affected interests prevents the quack from being mistaken for the savior.

The utopian internationalist, on the other hand, has no direct contact with the international scene. His thought, if it is sufficiently general, can roam over the globe without ever risking collision with the stark facts of politics. He who would proclaim the Four Freedoms for the United States itself would soon learn from personal experience the enormity of the social and political problems entailed by any attempt at realizing those great principles. By contrast, proclamation of the Four Freedoms "everywhere in the world" is sufficiently general to avoid contact with historical realities and political facts.

The reformer without responsibility finds in the armory of modern international thought what he is looking for. That one panacea is frequently inconsistent with another need not trouble him. For since the "single cause" is an arbitrary abstraction from a multitude of actual causes, one abstraction, and hence one

---

[29]Ralph Waldo Emerson, *Essays: Second Series* (Boston: Houghton Mifflin, 1899), pp. 204–5.

"single cause," is as good as the next one. Since, furthermore, the hunt for the "single cause" derives from a vague desire to contribute something to the betterment of human affairs rather than from a fixed resolve to intervene in a definite political situation in a definite way, virtually any general explanation of the ills of the world and any general plan to remedy them will satisfy the psychic need involved.

Hence, the great hunting ground for the "single cause" and the "scientific formula" to remedy it has been the international scene, while their great season was the two decades between the world wars.[30] International society is not organized; thus "international organization"—in its abstract rationality a kind of legal counterpart to the utopian systems of eighteenth- and nineteenth-century philosophy—became the scientific formula that, since the leading pacifist and Nobel Prize winner A. H. Fried propounded it at the beginning of the century, has been the credo of a whole school of thought. Others would look to material remedies. Are not wars being fought with arms? Let us prohibit or at least reduce armaments, and war will no longer be possible or at least will be less likely. Others, again, would combine different remedies, defending the combination—"on scientific grounds"—as the only appropriate one. Thus the French Radical-Socialist Party advocated "security, arbitration, disarmament" as logical successive steps for the establishment of permanent peace; whereas the French Socialists reversed the sequence and swore to the exclusive scientific value of the formula "security through arbitration and disarmament." French foreign policy has been especially productive in abstract schemes that, like the "plan Briand," the "plan Laval," the "plan Tardieux," the "plan Herriot," or the "plan Paul-Boncour," pretended to give in one legal formula a scientific solution to the problems of European security.

In other quarters, especially since the crisis of 1929, the "single cause" of international unrest has been found in the economic field. Restrictions on international trade, the lack of raw materials, and insufficient international purchasing power drive nations to war, so the argument ran. Then let us find a scientific formula for reciprocal trade agreements, for the redistribution of raw materials, and for the floating of international loans—and there will be peace. Faced by the imperialistic aspirations of the thirties, it was reasoned that whenever nations cannot change the status quo peacefully they will try to change it by war; thus peaceful change, scientifically defined, would make war unnecessary. Since bankers' fears for their investments were responsible for our involvement in the First World War, let us outlaw loans to belligerents: we shall thus escape participation in the next one. More recently, it has been "discovered" that national sovereignty is responsible for war; it follows that the pooling of national sovereignties in a world federation or at least in a federation of the democracies is a scientific solution to the problem of war and peace. Thus our era is always in search of the scientific formula, but an obstinate reality again and again makes the solution of today the fallacy of tomorrow.

---

[30]See Kenneth W. Thompson, *Ethics, Functionalism and Power in International Politics: The Crisis in Values* (Baton Rouge: Louisiana State University Press, 1979), pp. 35–45.

The "scientific" era of international relations resulted in the substitution of supposedly scientific standards for genuine political evaluations; in some cases this went so far as to impede, if not entirely destroy, the ability to make any intelligent political decisions at all. Power, however limited and qualified, is the value that international politics recognizes as supreme. The test to which international political decisions must be subject refers, therefore, to the measure in which those decisions affect the distribution of power. The question that Richelieu, Hamilton (no less than Jefferson, for that matter), or Disraeli would ask before they acted on the international scene was: does this decision increase or decrease the power of this and other nations? The question of the international "scientist" is different. Since for him the history of international affairs amounts to a succession of scientific problems, correctly or incorrectly handled by informed or misinformed officials, the supreme value is not power but truth. The quest for and the defense of power then become aberrations from the scientific attitude, which looks for causes and remedies. If we do not like the way things are, let us look for the cause and change things by changing the cause. There is essentially nothing to fight for; there is always something to analyze, to understand, and to reform.

How was it possible for the modern mind to make the belief in the all-embracing powers of science the *controlling force* of its foreign policy? Here again, the answer is to be found in the general premises of rationalistic philosophy, seemingly verified in its universal assumptions by domestic experience. The victory of liberalism in the domestic field led to a peculiar narrowing of the political, and a corresponding widening of the nonpolitical, sphere; and thus the latter was open to detached rational examination. Objectives that formerly had been seen as the prize in the struggle for political power were now approached in a dispassionate, matter-of-fact way and mastered in accordance with the specific techniques of economics, administration, or law. First the natural sciences and religion had freed themselves from political domination and had established their autonomy. Then liberalism, by conquering the state, freed an ever-increasing domain from direct political domination; finally, liberalism seemed to expel even politics from the realm of the state and to make statecraft itself a science. Commerce and industry were the first to win their autonomy under reason. That which for the physiocrats was still a political program, unsuccessfully suggested to the political powers of the day, was for Adam Smith already a system of scientific truths verified by experience, the practical implications of which no reasonable man could escape. Political tribunals were replaced by independent courts composed of judges trained to render justice according to the principles of legal science. Antiquated and arbitrary election systems favoring certain political groups made way for scientific devices that would secure full and equal representation for all citizens. The civil service system put the selection of government personnel on an objective, nonpolitical basis. Today legislative reforms are increasingly prepared by committees of experts who seem to be influenced largely by scientific instead of political considerations. Taxation, administration, and insurance become "scientific" in approach; and, finally, there is no field of governmental activity that would not be regarded as a proper area for the application of "political science."

The use of the scientific method in politics, to which the modern mind was led by its perception of the liberal experience, was and is a political fallacy in domestic affairs. There, however, the refined mechanism of political pressure and self-interest serves as an automatic check on doctrinaire excess. In the international field such a mechanism, acting directly upon the individual, does not exist. It is here, therefore, that the belief in the limitless power of the scientific formula has become particularly prolific—and particularly ineffective. For it is here that the panaceas engendered by this belief have no connection whatsoever with the forces that determine the actual course of events. Events will, therefore, either follow their course as though all those proposals by international commissions of experts and other rationalist-utopian devices had never been invented. Or those devices will be applied in an exceptional instance and will then produce effects unforeseen by their promoters and frequently disastrous to them—such as the sanctions against Italy during the Italo-Ethiopian War. Yet, as a supreme irony, this school of thought attempts to monopolize for itself the virtue of being "practical"; it treats with disdain the rare attempts to base international action on a genuine understanding of the forces determining political reality rather than on the ideal postulates of abstract reason.[31]

---

[31]As far back as 1877, James Lorimer could write in "Le Problème final du droit international," *Revue du droit international et de legislation comparèe*, IX (1877), p. 184: "Strangely enough, however, these speculations of English utilitarianism, taken as a whole, are of all the dissertations on the subject I know the least useful from the practical point of view." Cf. also Beard, *A Foreign Policy in America,* p. 129: "Nearly every evil that was inconceivable in internationalist ideology in 1919 came to pass within the span of twenty years. It would seem then that this scheme of thought had been based upon some misconceptions respecting the nature and propensities of men and nations or, if this explanation is invalid, that internationalists had not adopted the correct 'approach' to the goal they had set before themselves. Their image of the world had not corresponded with sufficient exactness to its realities or their methods had been deficient in points of technique. They could, and some of them did, ascribe their defeats to the madness of men and nations, but this was a confession that their former premises and actions had been founded upon errors of calculation. In any event the verdict was the same, unless all the blame was to be laid on Americans as the world's greatest scapegoats."

4 The Struggle for Power: Policy of the Status Quo

Domestic and international politics are but two different manifestations of the same phenomenon: the struggle for power. Its manifestations differ in the two different spheres because different moral, political, and social conditions prevail in each. Western national societies show a much greater degree of social cohesion within themselves than among themselves. Cultural uniformity, technological unification, external pressure, and, above all, a hierarchic political organization combine to make the national society an integrated whole set apart from other national societies. In consequence the domestic political order is, for instance, more stable and less subject to violent change than is the international order.

All history shows that nations active in international politics are continuously preparing for, actively involved in, or recovering from organized violence in the form of war. In the domestic politics of Western democracies, on the other hand, organized violence as an instrument of political action on an extensive scale has become a rare exception. Yet as a potentiality it exists here, too, and at times the fear of it in the form of revolution has exerted an important influence upon political thought and action.[1] The difference between domestic and international politics in this respect is one of degree and not of kind.

All politics, domestic and international, reveals three basic patterns; that is, all political phenomena can be reduced to one of three basic types. A political policy seeks either to keep power, to increase power, or to demonstrate power.

To these three typical patterns of politics, three typical international policies correspond. A nation whose foreign policy tends toward keeping power and not toward changing the distribution of power in its favor pursues a policy of the status quo. A nation whose foreign policy aims at acquiring more power than it actually has, through a reversal of existing power relations—whose foreign policy, in other

---

[1]This is true especially of the nineteenth century, as Guglielmo Ferrero has pointed out in *The Principles of Power* (New York: G. P. Putnam's Sons, 1942).

words, seeks a favorable change in power status—pursues a policy of imperialism. A nation whose foreign policy seeks to demonstrate the power it has, either for the purpose of maintaining or increasing it, pursues a policy of prestige.[2] It should be noted that these formulations are of a provisional nature and are subject to further refinement.[3]

The concept "status quo" is derived from *status quo ante bellum,* a diplomatic term referring to the usual clauses in peace treaties that provide for the evacuation of territory by enemy troops and its restoration to the prewar sovereignty. Thus the peace treaties with Italy[4] and Bulgaria[5] terminating the Second World War provide that "all armed forces of the Allied and Associated Powers shall be withdrawn" from the territory of the particular nation "as soon as possible and in any case not later than ninety days from the coming into force of the present Treaty." That is, within this time limit the *status quo ante bellum* shall be reestablished with regard to this territory.[6]

The policy of the status quo aims at the maintenance of the distribution of power that exists at a particular moment in history. One might say that the policy of the status quo fulfills the same function for international politics that a conservative policy performs for domestic affairs. The particular moment in history that serves as point of reference for a policy of the status quo is frequently the end of a war, when the distribution of power has been codified in a treaty of peace. This is so because the main purpose of peace treaties is to formulate in legal terms the shift in power that victory and defeat in the preceding war have brought about and to insure the stability of the new distribution of power by means of legal stipulations. Thus it is typical for a status quo policy to appear as defense of the peace

---

[2]It is not a departure from this threefold pattern of international politics when sometimes a nation gives up power without being physically compelled to do so, as Great Britain did with regard to India in 1947 and as the United States has done on several occasions with regard to Latin American countries. In such cases a nation acts as a military commander who may retreat under certain circumstances, because his front is overextended or his lines of communication are threatened or because he wants to concentrate his forces for an attack. Similarly, a nation may retreat from an exposed power position it cannot hope to hold very long. Or it may exchange one kind of control for another kind, e.g., military for political control, political for economic control, or vice versa (the substitution of the Good Neighbor policy for the policy of the "big stick" is a case in point). Or a change in the objectives of its foreign policy may require concentration of effort at another point. In any case, the fact that it gives up power voluntarily cannot be taken to mean that it is not interested in power, any more than the retreat of a military commander proves that he is not interested in military victory.

[3]It must especially be pointed out that these different patterns of international policies do not of necessity correspond to conscious motivations in the minds of statesmen or supporters of the respective foreign policies. Statesmen and supporters may not even be aware of the actual character of the policies they pursue and support. More particularly, a nation may intend to pursue a policy of the status quo, while actually, without being aware of it, it is embarking upon a policy of imperialism. Thus it has been said of the British that they acquired their empire in a "fit of absent-mindedness." In what follows on this point in the text, we are exclusively concerned with the actual character of the policies pursued and not with the motives of those who pursue them.

[4]See Article 73, *The New York Times,* January 18, 1947, p. 26.

[5]See Article 20, ibid., p. 32.

[6]For a great number of older examples, see Coleman Phillipson, *Termination of War and Treaties of Peace* (New York: E. P. Dutton, 1916), pp. 223 ff.

settlement that terminated the last general war. The European governments and political parties that pursued a policy of the status quo from 1815 to 1848 did so in defense of the peace settlement of 1815, which terminated the Napoleonic Wars. The main purpose of the Holy Alliance, which these governments concluded in 1815, was the maintenance of the status quo as it existed at the conclusion of the Napoleonic Wars. In consequence it functioned mainly as a guarantor of the peace treaty, that is, the Treaty of Paris of 1815.

In this respect the relation between the policy in defense of the status quo of 1815, the Treaty of Paris, and the Holy Alliance is similar to the relation between the policy in favor of the status quo of 1918, the peace treaties of 1919, and the League of Nations. The distribution of power as it existed at the end of the First World War found its legal expression in the peace treaties of 1919. It became the main purpose of the League of Nations to maintain peace by preserving the status quo of 1918 as it had been formulated in the peace treaties of 1919. Article 10 of the Covenant of the League, obligating its members "to respect and preserve as against external aggression the territorial integrity and existing political independence of all members of the League," recognized as one of the purposes of the League the maintenance of the territorial status quo as established by the peace treaties of 1919. Consequently, in the period between the two world wars, the struggle for and against the status quo was in the main fought either by defending or by opposing the territorial provisions of the Treaty of Versailles and their guarantee in Article 10 of the Covenant of the League. It was, therefore, only consistent from their point of view that the nations chiefly opposed to the status quo established in 1919 should sever their connections with the League of Nations–Japan in 1932, Germany in 1933, Italy in 1937.

It is not only in peace treaties and international organizations supporting them that the policy of the status quo manifests itself. Nations desiring to maintain a certain distribution of power may use as their instrument special treaties, such as "The Nine Power Treaty relating to Principles and Policies to be followed in Matters concerning China," signed in Washington, February 6, 1922,[7] and the "Treaty of Mutual Guarantee between Germany, Belgium, France, Great Britain, and Italy," signed in Locarno, October 16, 1925.[8]

The Nine Power Treaty transformed the American policy of the "open door" in China into a multilateral policy that the nations mostly interested in trade with China, as well as China itself, pledged themselves to uphold. Its main purpose was to stabilize the distribution of power with regard to China that existed at the time between the contracting nations. This meant that the special rights that certain nations, especially Great Britain and Japan, had acquired in certain parts of Chinese territory, such as Manchuria and various ports, should not only remain intact but no new special rights should be ceded by China to any of the contracting parties.

---

[7]United States *Treaty Series*, No. 671 (Washington, 1923).
[8]*American Journal of International Law*, Vol. 20 (1926), Supplement, p. 22.

The Locarno Treaty of mutual guarantee endeavored to supplement the general guarantee of the territorial status quo of 1918, contained in Article 10 of the Covenant of the League, with a special one with respect to the western frontiers of Germany. Article I of the Treaty expressly referred to the guarantee of "the maintenance of the territorial status quo resulting from the frontiers between Germany and Belgium and between Germany and France."

Alliance treaties, in particular, frequently have the function of preserving the status quo in certain respects. Thus, after the victorious conclusion of the war against France, and the foundation of the German Empire in 1871, Bismarck tried to protect the newly won dominant position of Germany in Europe by alliances intended to prevent a war of revenge on the part of France. In 1879, Germany and Austria concluded an alliance for mutual defense against Russia, and in 1894, France and Russia entered into a defensive alliance against the German-Austrian combination. The mutual fear lest the other alliance be intent upon changing the status quo while professing to maintain it was one of the main factors in bringing about the general conflagration of the First World War.

The alliance treaties that France concluded with the Soviet Union, Poland, Czechoslovakia, and Rumania in the period between the two world wars were intended to maintain the status quo, mainly in view of possible German attempts to change it. Similar treaties between Czechoslovakia, Yugoslavia, and Rumania, and the treaty between Czechoslovakia and the Soviet Union, had the same purpose. The ineffectiveness of these alliances when they were put to the test from 1935 to 1939 was one of the reasons for Germany's attack on Poland in 1939. The British-Polish Alliance of April 5, 1939, was the last attempt before the outbreak of hostilities to preserve at least the territorial status quo on the eastern German frontier. Today the alliances that the Soviet Union has concluded with the countries of Eastern Europe and those that the countries of Western Europe have concluded among themselves and with the United States aim similarly at the maintenance of the status quo as it was established in these respective European regions by the distribution of power at the end of the Second World War.

The manifestation of the policy of the status quo that has had the greatest importance for the United States and has been the cornerstone of its foreign relations in the Monroe Doctrine. A unilateral declaration made by President Monroe in his annual message to Congress on December 2, 1823, the Doctrine lays down the two essential principles of any status quo policy. On the one hand, it stipulates respect on the part of the United States for the existing distribution of power in the Western Hemisphere: "With the existing colonies or dependencies of any European power we have not interfered and shall not interfere." On the other hand, it proclaims resistance on the part of the United States to any change of the existing distribution of power by any non-American nation: "But with the governments who have declared their independence, and maintain it . . . we could not view any interposition for the purpose of oppressing them, or controlling in any other manner their destiny, by any European power, in any other light than as the manifestation of an unfriendly disposition towards the United States." As President Franklin D. Roosevelt expressed it in an address before the governing body of the Pan-American Union on April 12, 1933: "It [the Monroe Doctrine] was aimed and is aimed against the acquisition in any manner of the control of additional territory in this hemisphere by any non-American power.[9]

We have said that the policy of the status quo aims at the maintenance of the distribution of power as it exists at a particular moment in history. This does not mean that the policy of the status quo is necessarily opposed to any change whatsoever. While it is not opposed to change as such, it is opposed to any change that would amount to a reversal of the power relations among two or more nations, reducing, for instance, A from a first-rate to a second-rate power and raising B to the eminent position A formerly held. Minor adjustments in the distribution of power, however, that leave intact the relative power positions of the nations concerned are fully compatible with a policy of the status quo. For instance, the purchase of the territory of Alaska by the United States in 1867 did not then affect the status quo between the United States and Russia, since, in view of the technology of communications and warfare at the time, the acquisition by the United States of this then inaccessible territory did not affect to any appreciable extent the distribution of power between the United States and Russia.

Similarly, by acquiring the Virgin Islands from Denmark in 1917, the United States did not embark upon a policy aiming at a change of the status quo with regard to the Central American republics. While the acquisition of the Virgin Islands greatly improved the strategic position of the United States insofar as the defense of the approaches to the Panama Canal was concerned, it did not change the relative power positions of the United States and the Central American republics. The acquisition of the Virgin Islands may have strengthened the already dominant position of the United States in the Caribbean, yet it did not create it and, therefore, was compatible with a policy of the status quo. One might even say that, by strengthening the preponderance of the United States over the Central American republics, it actually reinforced the existing distribution of power and thus served the purposes of a policy of the status quo.

Beginning in 1962, the Soviet Union undertook to extend its influence significantly through the emplacement of missiles on Cuba. The Kennedy administration weighed the possible alternative courses of action it might take to remove the missiles, including an air strike; eventually it chose a policy of blockade and quarantine. The Soviets withdrew their missiles as the result of a Kennedy-Khrushchev agreement but continued to support the Castro regime with massive economic and military assistance. Meanwhile Cuba sought to increase its own ideological influence in the Caribbean and in Central America. By the 1980s, Cuban and Soviet military assistance and military personnel were identified in countries such as Grenada and Nicaragua. Leaving aside the question of popular support for Cuban intervention in these countries, the question that confronted

---

[9]*Roosevelt's Foreign Policy, 1933–41. F.D.R.'s Unedited Speeches and Messages* (New York: Wilfred Funk, 1942), p. 4.

American policymakers was the extent to which the status quo was threatened. Did independent Cuban intervention threaten the status quo? Was Cuban action as a surrogate for the Soviets the real threat? Was Soviet involvement a violation of the Monroe Doctrine and the Kennedy-Khrushchev agreement and itself a threat to the status quo? Successive administrations, beginning with that of John F. Kennedy, were forced to address this question. On October 25, 1983, the Reagan administration invaded Grenada—ostensibly to protect the lives of about 1,000 Americans on the island but actually because Grenada was seen as an arsenal for military action masterminded by the Cubans and by Soviet advisors there and elsewhere in the Caribbean. Observers continued to ask whether Cuban and Soviet activities had constituted a true threat to the status quo in the region; conflicting answers were put forth in Europe and the United States as President Reagan's policy came under critical scrutiny. The standard for judging Cuban-Soviet involvement and for determining the response of American policymakers was whether an important shift in the distribution of power was taking place, and hence in the status quo.

5 The Struggle for Power: Imperialism

WHAT IMPERIALISM IS NOT

An objective analysis of the acquisition of the Virgin Islands by the United States might show that it was part of a policy of the status quo in that region. Nevertheless, these and similar moves toward strengthening the position of the United States in the Caribbean have been decried as imperialistic by many observers. Such observers have used the term "imperialistic" not for the purpose of characterizing objectively a particular type of foreign policy but as a term of opprobrium by which a policy to which the observer is opposed can be discredited. This arbitrary use of the term for polemical purposes has become so widespread that today "imperialism" and "imperialistic" are indiscriminately applied to any foreign policy, regardless of its actual character, to which the user happens to be opposed.

Anglophobes will refer to British imperialism as an actuality in 1980, as they did in 1940 or in 1914. Russophobes will call imperialistic whatever the Russians do in foreign affairs. The Soviet Union considered all participants in the Second World War as waging an imperialistic war until it was attacked by Germany in 1941; the war it then had to fight became anti-imperialistic by definition. To enemies and critics of the United States everywhere, "American imperialism" is a standard term. To add to the confusion, certain economic and political systems and economic groups, such as bankers and industrialists, are indiscriminately identified with imperialistic foreign policies.

In this process of indiscriminate usage, the term "imperialism" has lost all concrete meaning. Everybody is an imperialist to someone who happens to take exception to his foreign policies. Under such circumstances it becomes the task of theoretical analysis to break with popular usage in order to give the term an ethically neutral, objective, and definable meaning that at the same time is useful for the theory and practice of international politics.[1]

Before we ask what imperialism actually is, let us ask first what imperialism is not but is most often supposed to be. The three most popular misconceptions require our attention.

1. Not every foreign policy aiming at an increase in the power of a nation is necessarily a manifestation of imperialism. We have already disposed of this misconception in our discussion of the policy of the status quo.[2] We defined imperialism as a policy that aims at the overthrow of the status quo, at a reversal of the power relations between two or more nations. A policy seeking only adjustment, leaving the essence of these power relations intact, still operates within the general framework of a policy of the status quo.

The view that imperialism and any purposeful increase in power are identical is held mainly by two distinct groups. Those who are opposed on principle to a particular nation and its policies, such as Anglophobes, Russophobes, and anti-Americans, regard the very existence of the object of their phobia as a threat to the world. Whenever a country thus feared sets out to increase its power, those who fear it must view the increase in power as a stepping-stone to world conquest—that is, as manifestation of an imperialistic policy. On the other hand, those who, as heirs of the political philosophy of the nineteenth century, consider any active foreign policy an evil bound to disappear in the foreseeable future, will condemn a foreign policy that seeks an increase in power. They will identify that foreign policy with what is for them the paradigm of evil—imperialism.

2. Not every foreign policy aiming at the preservation of an empire that already exists is imperialism. It is widely believed that whatever a nation, such as Great Britain, China, the Soviet Union, or the United States, does in order to maintain its preponderant position in certain regions is imperialistic. Thus imperialism becomes identified with the maintenance, defense, and stabilization of an empire already in existence rather than with the dynamic process of acquiring one. Yet, while it may make sense to apply the term "imperialism" to the domestic policies of an existing empire, it is confusing and misleading to apply the term to international policies of an essentially static and conservative character; for in international politics imperialism is contrasted with the policy of the status quo, and hence has a dynamic connotation. The history of what is commonly called "British imperialism" is instructive in this regard.

The idea of British imperialism had its origin in Great Britain itself. It was used for the first time by the Conservatives under Disraeli in the campaign for the elections of 1874. The idea of British imperialism, as conceived by Disraeli and

---

[1]The term is frequently used as synonymous with any kind of colonial expansion, as, for instance, in Parker Thomas Moon, *Imperialism and World Politics* (New York: Macmillan, 1926). Such use is unobjectionable from a theoretical point of view, so long as it implies no general theory of the nature of expansionist policies as such. Since in the text we are concerned with the general characteristics of international policies of expansion, it is obvious that a concept limited to the phenomenon of colonial expansion is too narrow for our purposes.

[2]On this point see the discussion in Chapter 4.

developed later by Joseph Chamberlain and Winston Churchill, was opposed to what the Conservatives called the cosmopolitanism and internationalism of the Liberals. It found its concrete expression in the political program of "imperial federation." The most important points of this program were (1) the unification and integration of Great Britain and its possessions into a unified empire with the aid of protective tariffs, (2) the reservation of free colonial land to Englishmen, (3) unified armed forces, and (4) a central representative organ in London.

When this "imperialistic" program was postulated and put into effect, the territorial expansion of Great Britain had in the main come to an end. The program of British "imperialism" was, therefore, essentially a program of consolidation, not of expansion. It sought to secure and exploit what had already been appropriated. It endeavored to stabilize the distribution of power that had been brought about by the creation of the British Empire.

When Kipling justified British imperialism as "the white man's burden," the burden was already shouldered. Since the 1870s, British "imperialism"—that is, British foreign policy with regard to Britain's overseas possessions—was in the main a policy of the status quo and not imperialistic at all in the exact meaning of the term. Yet the anti-imperialists in Great Britain and elsewhere, accepting the imperialistic slogans of Disraeli and Chamberlain at face value and mistaking the effects of imperialism for imperialism itself, opposed the British policy of exploitation and consolidation, especially in Africa and India, as "imperialistic." In fact, when Churchill refused in 1942 "to preside over the liquidation of the British Empire," he was speaking not as an imperialist but as a conservative in foreign affairs, a defender of the status quo of empire.

British "imperialism" and its opponents are the outstanding examples of the confusion between the consolidation and defense of empire, on the one hand, and imperialism, on the other. But they are not the only examples. When we speak of the Roman Empire and of Roman imperialism, we think naturally of the period of Roman history that starts with Augustus, the first emperor governing what was then called for the first time *imperium Romanum*. Yet, when Augustus gave Rome and its possessions the constitution of an empire, the expansion of Rome had essentially come to an end. The foreign policy of the Republic, from the Punic Wars to its overthrow by Julius Caesar, had indeed been imperialistic in the exact meaning of the term. In that period the political face of the earth had been changed and made Roman. The foreign policy of the emperors and their perpetual wars served the main purpose of securing and protecting what had been conquered before. Not unlike the "imperialistic" policies of Great Britain from the time of Disraeli to Churchill, Roman foreign policy was one of conservation, of the status quo. When there were conquests, as under Trajan, for instance, these policies served to make the empire and Roman supremacy secure.

The same is essentially true of the territorial aspects of American "imperialism" from the beginning of the twentieth century to the Second World War. The great debate for and against American imperialism that raged during the first decades of the century followed the great imperialistic expansion of the nineteenth century. The policy that was the subject of that debate was essentially a policy of consolidation, of protection, of exploration—that is, a policy of the status quo. When William Graham Sumner, in 1898, referred to the American policy of territorial expansion as "the conquest of the United States by Spain,"[3] he referred to a policy that was already consummated. When Senator Albert J. Beveridge declared that "God has made us adepts in government that we may administer government among savage and senile peoples,"[4] he endeavored to justify dominion already established rather than to support expansion planned for the future.

Thus, in both Great Britain and the United States, much of the modern debate on imperialism follows after the process of imperialistic expansion, condemning or justifying it in retrospect. In terms of actual policies to be pursued in the future, the debate is concerned primarily with the result of imperialistic policies—that is, the administration and safeguarding of empire. The explanation is not hard to find. The great debate started in Great Britain with the Conservative exaltation of the British Empire, a kind of British counterpart to the nationalism of the Continent. The British Empire was a colonial empire, and as such, it became the prototype of modern empire. In consequence, the acquisition and exploitation of colonies became synonymous with empire, which thus received primarily, if not exclusively, an economic connotation. This economic connotation gave rise to the most extensive, most systematic, and also most popular body of thought which has sought to explain imperialism in modern times: the economic theories of imperialism. Here we find the third of the misconceptions that have obscured the true nature of imperialism.

ECONOMIC THEORIES OF IMPERIALISM

The Marxist, Liberal, and "Devil" Theories of Imperialism

The economic theories of imperialism have been developed in three different schools of thought: the Marxist, the liberal, and one that has aptly been called the "devil" theory[5] of imperialism.

The Marxist theory of imperialism rests upon the conviction, which is the foundation of all Marxist thought, that all political phenomena are the reflection of economic forces. Consequently, the political phenomenon of imperialism is the product of the economic system in which it originates—that is, capitalism. Capitalist societies, according to the Marxist theory, are unable to find within themselves sufficient markets for their products and sufficient investments for their capital. They have, therefore, a tendency to enslave even larger noncapitalist and, ultimately, even capitalist areas in order to transform them into markets for their surplus products and to give their surplus capital opportunities for investment.

---

[3]See previous quotation, page 40, note 20.
[4]Speech in the Senate, January 9, 1900, reprinted in Ruhl J. Bartlett, *The Record of American Diplomacy*, 4th ed. (New York: Alfred A. Knopf, 1964), p. 385.
[5]Charles A. Beard, *The Devil Theory of War* (New York: Vanguard Press, 1936); see also *The New Republic*, Vol. 86 (March 4, 11, 18, 1936).

The moderate Marxists, such as Kautsky and Hilferding, believed that imperialism was a policy of capitalism and that, therefore, an imperialistic policy was a matter of choice toward which capitalism might be more or less inclined according to circumstances. Lenin[6] and his followers, especially Bukharin,[7] on the other hand, identified imperialism and capitalism outright. Imperialism is identical with capitalism in its last—that is, monopoly—stage of development. According to Lenin, "Imperialism is capitalism in that phase of its development in which the domination of monopolies and finance-capital has established itself; in which the export of capital has acquired very great importance; in which the division of the world among the big international trusts has begun; in which the partition of all the territory of the earth amongst the great capitalist powers has been completed."[8]

In the eyes of the Marxists, capitalism is the main evil and imperialism only its necessary or probable manifestation. The liberal school, of which John A. Hobson[9] is the chief representative, is mainly concerned with imperialism in which it finds the result, not of capitalism as such, but of certain maladjustments within the capitalist system. In conformity with Marxism, the liberal school diagnoses as the root of imperialism the surplus of goods and capital that seek outlets in foreign markets. Yet, according to Hobson and his school, imperialist expansion is not the inevitable and not even the most rational method of disposing of these surpluses. Since the surpluses are the result of the maldistribution of purchasing power, the remedy lies in the expansion of the home market through economic reforms, such as increase in purchasing power and elimination of oversavings. It is this belief in a domestic alternative to imperialism that in the main distinguishes the liberal school from Marxism.

The "devil" theory of imperialism operates on a much lower intellectual level than do its two companion theories. It is widely held by pacifists and has become a stock-in-trade of Communist propaganda. It may be said to have been the official philosophy of the Nye Committee, which in 1934–36 investigated on behalf of the United States Senate the influence of financial and industrial interests on the intervention of the United States in the First World War. The publicity that the proceedings of this committee received made the "devil" theory of imperialism for a time the most popular explanation of foreign affairs in the United States. The simplicity of the theory contributed much to its popularity. It identified certain groups that obviously profited from war, such as manufacturers of war matériel (the so-called munitions makers), international bankers ("Wall Street"), and the like. Since they profited from war, they must be interested in having war. Thus the war profiteers transform themselves into the "war mongers," the "devils" who plan wars in order to enrich themselves.

[6]*Collected Works* (New York: International Publishers, 1927), Vol. XVIII; *Selected Works* (New York: International Publishers, 1935), Vol. V.

[7]*Imperialism and World Economy* (New York: International Publishers, 1929). Of the writers who, aside from those mentioned in the text, have particularly influenced the development of the Marxist theory of imperialism, Rosa Luxemburg and Fritz Sternberg ought to be mentioned; cf. the latter's *The Coming Crisis* (New York: John Day, 1946).

[8]*Imperialism, the Highest Stage of Capitalism* (New York: International Publishers, 1933), p. 72.

[9]*Imperialism* (London: G. Allen and Unwin, 1938).

While the extreme Marxists equate capitalism and imperialism, and while the moderate Marxists and the disciples of Hobson see in imperialism the result of maladjustments within the capitalist system, for the adherents of the "devil" theory, imperialism and war in general amount to nothing but a conspiracy of evil capitalists for the purpose of private gain.

Criticism of These Theories

All economic explanations of imperialism, the refined as well as the primitive, fail the test of historical experience. The economic interpretation of imperialism erects a limited historical experience, based on a few isolated cases, into a universal law of history. It is indeed true that in the late nineteenth and twentieth centuries a small number of wars were waged primarily, if not exclusively, for economic objectives. The classic examples are the Boer War of 1899–1902 and the Chaco War between Bolivia and Paraguay in 1932–35. The main responsibility of British gold-mining interests for the Boer War can hardly be doubted. The Chaco War is considered by some to have been primarily a war between two oil companies for the control of oil fields.

But during the entire period of mature capitalism, no war, with the exception of the Boer War, was waged by major powers exclusively or even predominantly for economic objectives. The Austro-Prussian War of 1866 and the Franco-German War of 1870, for instance, had no economic objectives of any importance. They were political wars, indeed imperialistic wars, fought for the purpose of establishing a new distribution of power, first in favor of Prussia within Germany and then in favor of Germany within the European state system. The Crimean War of 1854–56, the Spanish-American War of 1898, the Russo-Japanese War of 1904–05, the Turko-Italian War of 1911–12, and the several Balkan Wars show economic objectives only in a subordinate role, if they show them at all. The two world wars were certainly political wars, whose stake was the domination of Europe, if not of the world. Naturally, victory in these wars brought economic advantages and, more particularly, defeat brought in its wake economic losses. But these effects were not the real issue; they were only by-products of the political consequences of victory and defeat. Still less were these economic effects the motives that determined in the minds of the responsible statesmen the issue of war and peace.

The economic theories of imperialism are thus not supported by the experience of that historical period that they suppose to be intimately connected, if not identical, with imperialism—that is, the period of capitalism. Furthermore, the main period of colonial expansion that the economic theories tend to identify with imperialism precedes the age of mature capitalism and cannot be attributed to the inner contradictions of the decaying capitalist system. In comparison with those of the sixteenth, seventeenth, and eighteenth centuries, the colonial acquisitions of the nineteenth and twentieth centuries are small. The latest phase of capitalism even witnesses the liquidation of empire on a large scale in the form of the retreat from Asia and Africa of Great Britain, France, Portugal, and The Netherlands.

The evidence of history is still more unfavorable to the contentions of the economic theories if one tests the theories against the evidence presented by the precapitalist processes of empire building. The policies that in ancient times led to the foundation of the Egyptian, Assyrian, and Persian empires were imperialistic in the political sense. So were the conquests of Alexander the Great and the policies of Rome in the last century before the Christian era. The Arabian expansion in the seventh and eighth centuries showed all the earmarks of imperialism. Pope Urban II used the typical ideological arguments in support of an imperialistic policy when, in 1095, he expressed to the Council of Clermont the reasons for the First Crusade in these words: "For this land which you inhabit, shut in on all sides by the seas and surrounded by the mountain peaks, is too narrow for your large population; nor does it abound in wealth, and it furnishes scarcely food enough for its cultivators. Hence it is that you murder and devour one another, that you wage war, and that very many among you perish in civil strife."[10] Louis XIV, Peter the Great, and Napoleon I were the great imperialists of the modern precapitalist age.

All these imperialisms of precapitalist times share with those of the capitalist period the tendency to overthrow the established power relations and put in their stead the dominance of the imperialistic power. Yet those two periods of imperialism share also the subordination of economic objectives to political considerations.

Alexander the Great and Napoleon I did not embark, any more than did Adolf Hitler, on imperialistic policies for the purpose of personal gain or in order to escape the maladjustment of their economic systems. What they aimed at was exactly the same thing the captain of industry is aiming at when he tries to establish an industrial "empire" by adding enterprise to enterprise until he dominates his industry in a monopolistic or quasimonopolistic manner. What the precapitalist imperialist, the capitalist imperialist, and the "imperialistic" capitalist want is power, not economic gain. The captain of industry is no more driven toward his "imperialistic" goal by economic necessity or personal greed than was Napoleon I. Personal gain and the solution of economic problems through imperialistic expansion are for all of them a pleasant afterthought, a welcome by-product, but not the goal by which the imperialistic urge is attracted.

We have seen that imperialism is not determined by economics, capitalist or otherwise. We shall see now that capitalists per se are not imperialists. According to the economic theories and, more particularly, the "devil" theory, capitalists use governments as their tools in instigating imperialistic policies. Yet the investigation of historical instances cited in support of the economic interpretation shows that in most cases the reverse relationship actually existed between statesmen and capitalists. Imperialistic policies were generally conceived by the governments who summoned the capitalists to support these policies. Thus historical evidence points to the primacy of politics over economics, and "the rule of the financier . . . over

---

[10]F. A. Ogg, editor, *A Source Book of Medieval History* (New York: American Book Company, 1907), p. 286.

international politics" is indeed, in the words of Professor Schumpeter, "a newspaper fairytale, almost ludicrously at variance with facts."[11]

Yet, far from being the instigators, capitalists as a group—aside from certain individual capitalists—were not even enthusiastic supporters of imperialistic policies. The literature and policies of the groups and political parties representing the capitalist element in modern societies are a testimony to the traditional opposition of the merchant and manufacturing classes to any foreign policy that, like imperialism, might lead to war. As Professor Viner has stated:

> It was for the most part the middle classes who were the supporters of pacifism, of internationalism, of international conciliation and compromise of disputes, of disarmament—in so far as these had supporters. It was for the most part aristocrats, agrarians, often the urban working classes, who were the expansionists, the imperialists, the jingoes. In the British Parliament it was spokesmen for the "moneyed interests," for the emerging middle classes in the northern manufacturing districts and for the "City" in London, who were the appeasers during the Napoleonic Wars, during the Crimean War, during the Boer War, and during the period from the rise of Hitler to the German invasion of Poland. In our own country it was largely from business circles that the important opposition came to the American Revolution, to the War of 1812, to the imperialism of 1898, and to the anti-Nazi policy of the Roosevelt administration prior to Pearl Harbor.[12]

From Sir Andrew Freeport in the *Spectator* at the beginning of the eighteenth century to Norman Angell's *The Great Illusion* in our time, it has been the conviction of the capitalists as a class and of most capitalists as individuals that "war does not pay," that war is incompatible with an industrial society, that the interests of capitalism require peace and not war. For only peace permits those rational calculations upon which capitalist actions are based. War carries with it an element of irrationality and chaos that is alien to the very spirit of capitalism. Imperialism, however, as the attempt to overthrow the existing power relations, carries with it the inevitable risk of war. As a group, then, capitalists were opposed to war; they did not initiate, and only supported with misgivings and under pressure, imperialistic policies that might lead, and many times actually did lead, to war.

How was it possible that a body of doctrine, such as the economic theories of imperialism, which is so completely at variance with the facts of experience, could hold sway over the public mind? Two factors are responsible for the success

---

[11]Joseph Schumpeter, *Business Cycles* (New York and London: McGraw-Hill, 1939), Vol. 1, p. 495, n. 1.
[12]Jacob Viner, "Peace as an Economic Problem," *International Economics* (Glencoe: Free Press, 1951), p. 255. Cf. Philip S. Foner, *Business and Slavery: The New York Merchants and the Irrepressible Conflict* (Chapel Hill: University of North Carolina Press, 1941), on the opposition of New York and New England merchants to the Civil War, and Disraeli's statement to Lord Salisbury of September 26, 1876: "All the monied and commercial classes in all countries are against war. . . ." Also significant in this respect is the report that the British Ambassador to Germany sent on the eve of the First World War, June 30, 1914, to his Foreign Office: "I hear in fact from all sides that the financial and industrial classes are dead against a war in any shape. . . ." *British Documents on the Origin of the War, 1898–1914* (London: His Majesty's Stationery Office, 1926), Vol. XI, p. 361.

of that doctrine: the climate of opinion in the Western world and the character of the doctrine itself. We have already pointed to the general tendency of the age to reduce political problems to economic ones.[13] The capitalists and their critics are equally guilty of this fundamental error. The former expected from the development of capitalism, freed from the atavistic fetters of the precapitalist age and following only its own inherent laws, general prosperity and peace. The latter were convinced that these aims could be achieved only through reform or the abolition of the capitalist system. Both camps looked to economic remedies for political problems. Bentham advocated the emancipation of the colonies as the means of doing away with the imperialistic conflicts that lead to war. Proudhon, Cobden, and their disciples saw in tariffs the sole source of international conflicts and reasoned that peace lay in extending free trade.[14]

In our own time we have heard it said that since German, Italian, and Japanese imperialism was born of economic needs, these countries would have refrained from imperialistic policies had they received loans, colonies, and access to raw materials. Poor nations will go to war, so the argument runs, in order to escape economic distress; if the rich nations alleviate their economic afflictions, they will have no reason to go to war. In the classic age of capitalism both the adherents and the opponents of the capitalist system believed that the economic motives that seemed to determine the actions of businessmen were guiding the actions of all men.

The other reason for the ready acceptance of the economic interpretation of imperialism lies in its plausibility. What Professor Schumpeter has said of the Marxist theory of imperialism holds generally true: "A series of vital facts of our time seems to be perfectly accounted for. The whole maze of international politics seems to be cleared up by a single powerful stroke of analysis."[15] The mystery of so threatening, inhuman, and often murderous a historical force as imperialism, the theoretical problem of defining it as a distinctive type of international politics, the practical difficulty, above all, of recognizing it in a concrete situation and of counteracting it with adequate means—all this is reduced to either the inherent tendencies or the abuses of the capitalist system. Whenever the phenomenon of imperialism presents itself for either theoretical understanding or practical action, the simple scheme will provide an almost automatic answer that puts the mind at ease.

DIFFERENT TYPES OF IMPERIALISM

The true nature of imperialism as a policy devised to overthrow the status quo can best be explained by a consideration of certain typical situations that favor imperialistic policies and that, given the subjective and objective conditions

---

[13]See pages 34 ff. See also Hans J. Morgenthau, *Scientific Man vs. Power Politics* (Chicago: University of Chicago Press, 1946; Phoenix Edition, 1965), pp. 75 ff.
[14]See page 35.
[15]Joseph Schumpeter, *Capitalism, Socialism, and Democracy* (New York and London: Harper and Brothers, 1947), p. 51.

necessary for an active foreign policy, will almost inevitably produce a policy of imperialism.

Three Inducements to Imperialism

Victorious War

When a nation is engaged in war with another nation, it is very likely that the nation that anticipates victory will pursue a policy that seeks a permanent change of the power relations with the defeated enemy. The nation will pursue this policy regardless of what the objectives were at the outbreak of the war. It is the objective of this policy of change to transform the relation between victor and vanquished that happens to exist at the end of the war into the new status quo of the peace settlement. Thus a war that was started by the victor as a defensive war–for the maintenance of the prewar status quo–transforms itself with the approaching victory into an imperialistic war, that is, for a permanent change in the status quo.

The "Carthaginian Peace," by which the Romans changed their power relations with the Carthaginians permanently in their favor, has become the byword for the kind of peace settlement that tends to perpetuate the relation between victor and vanquished as it exists at the conclusion of hostilities. The Treaty of Versailles and its companion treaties, terminating the First World War, had in the eyes of many observers a similar character. The expansion of the Soviet sphere of influence into Eastern Europe after World War II, especially as recognized in the Helsinki Accords, is a further example. A policy that aims at a peace settlement of this kind must, according to our definition, be called imperialistic. It is imperialistic because it tries to replace the prewar status quo, when approximately equal or at least not thoroughly unequal powers oppose each other, with a postwar status quo where the victor becomes the permanent master of the vanquished.

Lost War

This very status of subordination, intended for permanency, may easily engender in the vanquished a desire to turn the scales on the victor, to overthrow the status quo created by his victory, and to change places with him in the hierarchy of power. In other words, the policy of imperialism pursued by the victor in anticipation of his victory is likely to call forth a policy of imperialism on the part of the vanquished. If he is not forever ruined or else won over to the cause of the victor, the vanquished will want to regain what he has lost and, if possible, gain more.

The typical example of imperialism conceived as a reaction against the successful imperialism of others is German imperialism from 1935 to the end of the Second World War. The European status quo of 1914 was characterized by a concert of great powers, consisting of Austria, France, Germany, Great Britain, Italy, and Russia. The victory of the Allies and the subsequent peace treaties created a new status quo that was the fruition of the imperialistic policies of France. This new status quo established the hegemony of France, exercised in alliance with most of the newly created nations of Eastern and Central Europe.

German foreign policy from 1919 to 1935 operated seemingly within the framework of that status quo, while secretly preparing for its overthrow. It tried to win concessions for Germany, but it nevertheless accepted, at least for the time being and with mental reservations, the power relations established by the Treaty of Versailles. It did not openly challenge these power relations; rather, it aimed at adjustments that left their essence intact. Such was particularly the character of the "policy of fulfillment"–that is, fulfillment of the Treaty of Versailles–which the Republic of Weimar pursued. It was this attempt to improve the international position of Germany while accepting at least temporarily the status quo of Versailles that aroused the violent opposition of nationalists and National Socialists. After the National Socialists had come to power in 1933 and stabilized their regime domestically, they abrogated in 1935 the disarmament provisions of the Treaty of Versailles. In 1936, in violation of the same treaty, they occupied the Rhineland and declared void the demilitarization of the German territory adjacent to the German-French frontier. With these moves the foreign policy of National Socialist Germany became openly imperialistic; for these were the first in a series of moves that expressed Germany's resolution no longer to accept the status quo of Versailles as basis for its foreign policy but to work for the overthrow of that status quo.

Weakness

Another typical situation that favors imperialistic policies is the existence of weak states or of politically empty spaces, which are attractive and accessible to a strong state. This is the situation out of which colonial imperialism grew. It is also the situation that made possible the transformation of the original federation of thirteen American states into a continental power. Napoleon's as well as Hitler's imperialism had partly this character, the latter's particularly in the period of the "blitzkrieg" of 1940. During the closing phase of the Second World War and the decade following it, imperialism growing out of the relations between strong and weak nations was exemplified by the relations between the Soviet Union and the nations of Eastern Europe. The attractiveness of power vacuums as an incentive to imperialism is at least a potential threat to the survival of many of the new nations of Asia and Africa, deficient as they are in the most important elements of power.

Three Goals of Imperialism

As imperialism grows out of three typical situations, so imperialism moves toward three typical objectives. The objective of imperialism can be the domination of the whole politically organized globe–that is, a world empire. Or it can be an empire or hegemony of approximately continental dimensions. Or it can be a strictly localized preponderance of power. In other words, the imperialistic policy may have no limits but those set by the power of resistance of the prospective victims, or it may have geographically determined limits, such as the geographical boundaries of a continent, or it may be limited by the localized aims of the imperialistic power itself.

World Empire

The outstanding historical examples of unlimited imperialism are the expansionist policies of Alexander the Great, Rome, the Arabs in the seventh and eighth centuries, Napoleon I, and Hitler. They all have in common an urge toward expansion that knows no rational limits, feeds on its own successes, and, if not stopped by a superior force, will go on to the confines of the political world.[16] This urge will not be satisfied so long as there remains anywhere a possible object of domination—a politically organized group of men that by its very independence challenges the conqueror's lust for power. It is, as we shall see, exactly the lack of moderation, the aspiration to conquer all that lends itself to conquest, characteristic of unlimited imperialism, which in the past has been the undoing of the imperialistic policies of this kind. The only exception is Rome, for reasons that will be discussed later.[17]

Continental Empire

The type of geographically determined imperialism is most clearly presented in the policies of European powers to gain a predominant position on the European continent. Louis XIV, Napoleon III, and Wilhelm II are cases in point. The kingdom of Piedmont under Cavour seeking the domination of the Italian peninsula in the 1850s, the different participants in the Balkan Wars of 1912 and 1913 aspiring to hegemony in the Balkans, Mussolini trying to make the Mediterranean an Italian lake—these are examples of geographically determined imperialism on a less than continental basis. The American policy of the nineteenth century, consisting in the gradual expansion of American rule over the better part of the North American continent, is primarily, but not exclusively, determined by the geographic limits of a continent; for the United States has not attempted to bring Canada and Mexico under its domination, although it would have been able to do so. Continental imperialism is here modified by its limitation to a localized section of the continent.

---

[16]Hobbes has given the classical analysis of this unlimited desire for power in the *Leviathan*, Chapter XI (Everyman's Library), pp. 49 ff. "So that in the first place, I put for a generall inclination of all mankind, a perpetuall and restlesse desire of Power after power, that ceaseth only in Death. And the cause of this, is not always that a man hopes for a more intensive delight, that he has already attained to; or that he cannot be content with a moderate power: but because he cannot assure the power and means to live well, which he hath present, without the acquisition of more. And from hence it is, that Kings, whose power is greatest, turn their endeavours to the assuring it at home by Lawes, or abroad by Wars: and when that is done, there succeedeth a new desire; in some, of Fame from new conquest; in others, of ease and sensuall pleasure; in others, of admiration, or being flattered from excellence in some art, or other ability of the mind."
[17]See pages 517 ff.

The same mixed type of imperialism constitutes the essence of American foreign policy toward the Western Hemisphere as a whole. The Monroe Doctrine, by postulating for the Western Hemisphere a policy of the status quo with regard to non-American powers, erected a protective shield behind which the United States could establish its predominance within that geographic region. Within these geographic limits, however, American policy was not always uniformly imperialistic. Toward the Central American republics and certain countries of South America, it was at times frankly imperialistic, but in its dealings with some other countries, such as Argentina and Brazil, it sought only to maintain the existing superiority of the United States, which was the result of a kind of natural process rather than of a deliberate American policy. Even though the United States has had the power to impose its superiority upon these countries in the form of actual hegemony, it chose not to do so. Here again we find a localized imperialism within the general framework of a geographically limited policy.

Local Preponderance

The prototype of localized imperialism is to be found in the monarchical policies of the eighteenth and nineteenth centuries. In the eighteenth century Frederick the Great, Louis XV, Maria Theresa, Peter the Great, and Catherine II were the moving forces of this kind of foreign policy. In the nineteenth century Bismarck was the master of this imperialistic policy, which seeks to overthrow the status quo and to establish political preponderance within self-chosen limits. The difference between such a localized imperialistic policy, continental imperialism, and unlimited imperialism is the difference between the foreign policies of Bismarck, Wilhelm II, and Hitler. Bismarck wanted to establish Germany's preponderance in Central Europe; Wilhelm II, in all of Europe; Hitler, in the whole world. The traditional objectives of Russian imperialism, such as control of Finland, Eastern Europe, the Balkans, the Dardanelles, and Iran, are also of a localized nature.

The limits of this type of imperialism are not, as in the case of the geographically limited type, primarily a product of the objective facts of nature beyond which it would be either technically difficult or politically unwise to go. On the contrary, they are primarily the result of a free choice among several alternatives, one of which might be a policy of the status quo, another continental imperialism, a third localized imperialism. In the eighteenth century the third alternative recommended itself because the existing concert of powers, each of about the same strength, discouraged any attempt at continental imperialism. The experience of Louis XIV showed how hazardous such an attempt could be. Furthermore, eighteenth-century imperialism was motivated mainly by considerations of monarchical power and glory, not by the mass emotions of modern nationalism. These considerations operated within a common framework of monarchical traditions and European civilization that imposed upon the actors on the political scene a moral restraint necessarily absent in periods of religious or nationalistic crusades.

In the nineteenth century the element of choice characteristic of the policy of localized imperialism is paramount in the history of Bismarck's foreign policy.

First, he had to overcome the opposition of the Prussian conservatives who favored a policy of the status quo for Prussia over Bismarck's policy of localized imperialism aiming at hegemony within Germany. When victorious wars had made Bismarck's policy feasible, it had to be defended against those who now wanted to go beyond the limits Bismarck had set for Prussian and later German hegemony. The dismissal of Bismarck by Wilhelm II in 1890 marked the end of localized and the beginning of at least a tendency toward continental imperialism as the foreign policy of Germany.

Three Methods of Imperialism

Just as there are three types of imperialism with respect to the situations from which imperialism typically arises, and three types of imperialism in view of its objectives, so a triple distinction is to be made regarding the typical means employed by imperialistic policies. Accordingly, we must distinguish between military, economic, and cultural imperialism. A widespread popular misconception confuses these three methods with the objectives of imperialism, as though economic imperialism, for instance, aimed at nothing but economic exploitation of other peoples. This misconception has its origin in the economic theories of imperialism, as well as in the neglect of the power element in international relations, referred to above.[18] In truth, military imperialism seeks military conquest; economic imperialism, economic exploitation of other peoples; cultural imperialism, the displacement of one culture by another–but always as means to the same imperialistic end. That end is always the overthrow of the status quo–that is, the reversal of the power relations between the imperialist nation and its prospective victims. This immutable end is served by military, economic, and cultural means, either alone or in combination. It is with these means that we are here concerned.

Military Imperialism

The most obvious, the most ancient, and also the crudest form of imperialism is military conquest. The great conquerors of all times have also been the great imperialists. The advantage of this method, from the point of view of the imperialistic nation, lies in the fact that the new power relations resulting from military conquest can as a rule be changed only by another war instigated by the vanquished nation, with the odds normally against the latter. Napoleon I might have relied upon the sole power of the ideas of the French Revolution to establish the hegemony of France in Europe and in the world; that is, he might have chosen cultural imperialism instead of military conquest. On the other hand, if he could make and hold military conquests, he would reach his imperialistic goal more quickly and derive from the process of conquering that maximum of personal satisfaction that victory in combat gives to the victor. Yet the very condition under

---

[18]See pages 29 ff.

which this statement is alone correct indicates the great drawback of military conquest as a method of imperialism: war is a gamble; it may be lost as well as won. The nation that starts war for imperialistic ends may gain an empire and keep it, as Rome did. Or it may gain it and, in the process of trying to gain still more, lose it, as in Napoleon's case. Or it may gain it, lose it, and fall victim to the imperialism of others, as in the case of National Socialist Germany and of Japan. Military imperialism is a gamble played for the highest stakes.

Economic Imperialism

Economic imperialism is less obtrusive and also generally less effective than the military variety and is, as a rational method of gaining power, a product of modern times. As such, it is a concomitant of the age of mercantilist and capitalist expansion. Its outstanding modern example is what is called "dollar diplomacy." It has also played an important role in the history of British and French imperialism. British influence in Portugal since the beginning of the eighteenth century has been powerfully supported by economic control. British supremacy in the Arab world was the result of economic policies for which the term "oil diplomacy" is not misplaced. Similarly, the Arab discovery of the political uses of oil has given the oil-producing Arab nations unprecedented power over the industrial nations importing Arab oil. The predominant influence France exercised in countries such as Rumania in the period between the two world wars was to a considerable extent based upon economic factors.

The common characteristic of the policies we call economic imperialism is their tendency, on the one hand, to overthrow the status quo by changing the power relations between the imperialist nation and others and, on the other hand, to do so not through the conquest of territory but by way of economic control. If a nation cannot or will not conquer territory for the purpose of establishing its mastery over other nations, it can try to achieve the same end by establishing its control over those who control the territory. The Central American republics, for instance, are all sovereign states; they possess all the attributes of sovereignty and display the paraphernalia of sovereignty. But, their economic life being almost completely dependent upon exports to the United States, these nations, unless they receive significant support from another source, are unable to pursue for any length of time policies of any kind, domestic or foreign, to which the United States would object.

The nature of economic imperialism as an unobtrusive, indirect, but fairly effective method of gaining and maintaining domination over other nations is particularly striking where two rival imperialisms compete with economic means for control over the same government. The century-old competition between Great Britain and Russia for control of Iran, though carried on for a long time predominantly by military means, may serve as an example. Professor P. E. Roberts described this situation in Iran, then called Persia, before the First World War:

> Russia presses on her from the north, Great Britain from the south, though the influence of the two powers is very different. Great Britain holds in her

hands the bulk of the foreign trade of southern Persia, and claims a general control of the whole Asiatic coastline from Aden eastwards to Baluchistan. . . . Great Britain has never coveted territorial possessions. . . . The development of navigation of the Volga and the construction of the Transcaspian railway have given to Russia the bulk of the trade with northern Persia. But the commercial weapons of Russia are a monopoly and prohibition. She has laid an interdict upon the making of railroads in Persian territory, and has often opposed measures which might regenerate the country.[19]

Only "the commercial and political rivalry of Great Britain" seemed to bar the way to the complete absorption of Iran into the Russian orbit.

During the period of economic and political rivalry between Great Britain and Russia in that region, the foreign policies, and frequently also the domestic policies, of the Iranian government faithfully reflected the intensity of the economic, and sometimes military, pressures that the rival powers brought to bear. When Russia promised or granted economic advantages that Great Britain failed to match, or when Russia threatened to withdraw advantages it had granted, Russian influence increased, and vice versa. Russia did not dare realize its territorial ambitions with regard to Iran. Great Britain had none. But both tried to control the Iranian government, which in turn controls oil fields as well as the road to India.

Cultural Imperialism[20]

What we suggest calling cultural imperialism is the most subtle and, if it were ever to succeed by itself alone, the most successful of imperialistic policies. It aims not at the conquest of territory or at the control of economic life but at the conquest and control of the minds of men as an instrument for changing the power relations between two nations. If one could imagine the culture and, more particularly, the political ideology, with all its concrete imperialistic objectives, of State A conquering the minds of all the citizens determining the policies of State B, State A would have won a more complete victory and would have founded its supremacy on more stable grounds than any military conqueror or economic master. State A would not need to threaten or employ military force or use economic pressure in order to achieve its ends; for that end, the subservience of State B to its will, would have already been realized by the persuasiveness of a superior culture and a more attractive political philosophy.

---

[19]*Cambridge Modern History* (New York: Macmillan, 1910), Vol. XII, p. 491.

[20]What is described under this heading goes frequently by the name of ideological imperialism, the term "ideological" referring particularly to the contest of political philosophies. Two reasons, however, seem to make it advisable to use the term "cultural" instead. On the one hand, the term "cultural" comprises all kinds of intellectual influences, political and otherwise, that serve as means for imperialistic ends. On the other hand, we are using the term "ideological" in Chapter 7 in its specific sociological sense, and it would only make for confusion if we used the same term here in its general popular meaning.

This is, however, a hypothetical case. Cultural imperialism generally falls short of a victory so complete as to make other methods of imperialism superfluous. The typical role cultural imperialism plays in modern times is subsidiary to the other methods. It softens up the enemy, it prepares the ground for military conquest or economic penetration. Its typical modern manifestation is the fifth column, and one of its two outstanding modern successes is to be found in the operations of the National Socialist fifth columns in Europe before the outbreak and at the beginning of the Second World War. Its success was most spectacular in Austria, where in 1938 a pro–National Socialist government invited the German troops to occupy the country. Its success was considerable in France, where a number of influential citizens, inside and outside the government, had been converted to the National Socialist philosophy and its international objectives. It is hardly an exaggeration to say that these countries were already partly conquered by means of cultural imperialism before military conquest finished the task. Great Britain, by interning at the outbreak of the Second World War all known National Socialists and their sympathizers within its borders, paid tribute to the danger that cultural penetration presented for the prospective victims of German imperialism.

The other outstanding example of cultural imperialism in our time, antedating and surviving the National Socialist fifth column, is the Communist International. In its heyday, directed from Moscow, it guided and controlled the Communist parties in all countries and saw to it that the policies pursued by the national Communist parties were in accord with the foreign policy of the Soviet Union. To the extent that Communist parties gained influence in particular nations, the influence of the Soviet Union over these nations increased, and where Communist parties gained control of national governments, the Russian government, controlling the Communist parties, controlled these national governments.

The technique used by the Soviet Union for establishing its control over the countries of Eastern Europe provides a classic example of the organic interconnectedness between cultural imperialism and the other forms of imperialistic conquest. In those countries the promotion of Communism through Communist parties, directed from Moscow, was a mere means to the end of Russian domination and was coordinated with other means serving the same end. Thus military conquest was the foundation for the Russian domination of Eastern Europe. Supporting and in part supplanting it was Russian control over the economic life of Eastern Europe, and the consequent economic dependence of Eastern Europe upon the Soviet Union. Finally, the Soviet Union endeavored to substitute loyalty to Communism and, in consequence, to the Soviet Union for the loyalties the peoples of Eastern Europe have traditionally felt to their respective nations, religions, and parties, endeavoring thus to make them willing tools of Russian policies.

The competition between the Soviet Union and China for the domination of the world Communist movement and for predominant influence in the uncommitted nations, too, uses primarily the instruments of cultural imperialism. The two major Communist nations derive their claim to dominant influence from the assertion that each of them is the true heir of Marx and Lenin, while the other is a heretic supporting the enemies of Communism. Wherever governments and political movements adhere to Communist doctrine, this argument is a source of power for the one of the two major Communist nations that can make the argument credible.

The cultural imperialism of totalitarian governments is well disciplined and highly organized; for these governments are able, because of their totalitarian character, to exert strict control and guiding influence over the thoughts and actions of their citizens and foreign sympathizers. While the technique of cultural imperialism has been perfected by the totalitarians and has been forged into the effective political weapon of the fifth column, the use of cultural sympathy and political affinities as weapons of imperialism is almost as old as imperialism itself. The histories of ancient Greece and Renaissance Italy are replete with episodes in which imperialistic policies were executed through association with political sympathizers in the enemy ranks rather than through military conquests. In modern times religious organizations, associated or identified with governments, have played an important role in imperialistic policies of a cultural character. Typical in this respect are the imperialistic policies of Czarist Russia, which used the dual position of the czar as head of the Russian government and of the Orthodox Church for the purpose of extending the power of Russia to the followers of the Orthodox faith in foreign countries. That Russia was able in the nineteenth century to succeed Turkey as the preponderant power in the Balkans is largely due to the cultural imperialism that used the Orthodox Church as a weapon of Russian foreign policy.

In the secular field, *la mission civilisatrice* of France has been a potent weapon of French imperialism. The deliberate use of the attractive qualities of French civilization for the purposes of French foreign policy was one of the cornerstones of French imperialism in the countries adjacent to the eastern Mediterranean before the First World War. The wave of public sympathy throughout the world, which came to the aid of France in both world wars, was the fruit of cultural imperialism, which in turn strengthened the French military imperialism of the later, victorious years of both world wars. Cultural imperialism in the form of the diffusion of a national culture is incomparably less mechanical and disciplinary, but not necessarily less effective, than the totalitarian kind. While the latter makes use primarily of the affinities of political philosophy, the former impresses the intellectually influential groups of a foreign country with the attractive qualities of a civilization until these groups tend to find the political objectives and methods of that civilization equally attractive.

We have already pointed out that cultural imperialism generally plays a role subsidiary to the military and economic varieties. Similarly, while economic imperialism sometimes stands by itself, it frequently supports military policies. On the other hand, while military imperialism is able to conquer without the support of nonmilitary methods, no dominion can last that is founded upon nothing but military force. Thus the conqueror will not only prepare for military conquests by economic and cultural penetration. He will also found his empire not upon military force alone but primarily upon the control of the livelihood of the conquered and upon the domination of their minds. And it is in that most subtle yet most important task that, with the exception of Rome, all the great imperialists, from Alexander to Napoleon and Hitler, have failed. Their failure to conquer the minds of those whom they had conquered otherwise proved to be the undoing of their empires. The ever-renewed coalitions against Napoleon, the revolts of the Poles against the Russians throughout the nineteenth century, the struggle of the underground against Hitler, and the fights of Ireland and India for freedom from British rule are the classic examples in modern times of that ultimate problem which few imperialistic policies have been able to solve.

The share of economic and cultural imperialism in the overall international activities of governments has greatly increased since the Second World War. It has done so for two reasons. On the one hand, military imperialism pursued openly and on a large scale is no longer a rational instrument of foreign policy since it carries within itself the risk of escalation into a self-destructive nuclear war. Thus a nation bent upon the imperialistic expansion of its power will often substitute economic and cultural methods for military ones. On the other hand, the disintegration of the colonial empires into a great number of weak states, many of which must rely for their very survival upon outside assistance, opens up new opportunities for imperialistic nations to expand their power by economic and cultural means. Thus China, the Soviet Union, and the United States use their economic and cultural resources in order to compete with each other for the expansion of their respective power into the so-called uncommitted third of the world or at least for preventing the other nations from expanding theirs. The weakness of the new nations offers them the opportunity, and the unacceptable risk of nuclear war has transformed that opportunity into a rational necessity.

HOW TO DETECT AND COUNTER AN IMPERIALISTIC POLICY

The preceding considerations lead to the fundamental question that confronts the public officials responsible for the conduct of foreign policy, as well as citizens trying to form an intelligent opinion on international issues. This question concerns the character of the foreign policy pursued by another nation and, in consequence, the kind of foreign policy that ought to be adopted with regard to it. Is the foreign policy of the other nation imperialistic, or is it not? In other words, does it seek to overthrow the existing distribution of power, or does it only contemplate adjustments within the general framework of the existing status quo? The answer to that question has determined the fate of nations, and the wrong answer has often meant deadly peril or actual destruction; for upon the correctness of that answer depends the success of the foreign policy derived from it. While it would be fatal to counter imperialistic designs with measures appropriate to a policy of the status quo, it would be only a little less risky to deal with a policy seeking adjustments within the status quo as though it were imperialistic. The classic example of the former error is the appeasement of Germany in the late thirties.

The other error had a decisive influence upon the foreign policies of the great European powers in the decades before the outbreak of the First World War.

The Problem of Policy: Containment, Appeasement, Fear

As the policies of imperialism and the status quo are fundamentally different in nature, so must the policies designed to counter them be fundamentally different. A policy adequate to counter a policy of the status quo cannot be sufficient to meet a policy of imperialism. A policy of the status quo that seeks adjustments within the existing overall distribution of power can be dealt with by a policy of give-and-take, of balance, of compromise: a policy, in short, that makes use of the techniques of adjustment within a given overall distribution of power in order to gain a maximum of advantage and to get by with a minimum of loss. Imperialism, which seeks to overthrow the existing distribution of power, must at the very least be countered by a policy of containment that, in defense of the existing distribution of power, calls a halt to further aggression, expansion, or other disturbances of the status quo on the part of the imperialistic nation. The policy of containment erects a wall, either a real one, such as the Great Wall of China or the French Maginot Line, or an imaginary one, such as the line of military demarcation drawn in 1945 between the Soviet orbit and the Western world. It says in effect to the imperialistic nation, "This far and no farther," warning it that a step beyond the line entails the virtual certainty of war.

Appeasement is a foreign policy that attempts to meet the threat of imperialism with methods appropriate to a policy of the status quo. Appeasement tries to deal with imperialism as though it were a policy of the status quo. It errs in transferring a policy of compromise from a political environment favorable to the preservation of the status quo, where it belongs, to an environment exposed to imperialistic attack, where it does not belong. One might say that appeasement is a corrupted policy of compromise, made erroneous by mistaking a policy of imperialism for a policy of the status quo.

It is important to note, in view of the contemporary tendency to use the term "appeasement" indiscriminately as a term of opprobrium, that appeasement and imperialism are logically correlated. In other words, a policy of appeasement on the one side presupposes a policy of imperialism on the other side. If we say that State A pursues with respect to State B a policy of appeasement, we are at the same time saying that State B pursues with respect to State A a policy of imperialism. If the latter statement is incorrect, the former is meaningless.

The appeaser sees in the successive demands of the imperialistic power rationally limited objectives that in themselves are compatible with the maintenance of the status quo and must be disposed of either on their intrinsic merits or by way of compromise. His error lies is not seeing that the successive demands, far from being self-contained and growing from specific grievances, are but the links of a chain at the end of which stands the overthrow of the status quo. The conciliation of antagonistic policies on the basis of legal or moral principles or through a diplomatic bargain is indeed the great task of a diplomacy that operates on both sides within the recognized limits of the status quo. Since both sides accept the existing distribution of power, both sides can afford to settle their differences either on the basis of principle or through compromise; for whatever the settlement may be, it will not affect the basic distribution of power between them.

The situation is, however, different when one or both sides have imperialistic designs—that is, when they seek a fundamental change in the existing distribution of power. Then the settlement of the respective demands on the basis of legal or moral principles or through bargaining methods, in disregard of the influence the settlement might have upon the distribution of power, amounts to a piecemeal change in the power relations in favor of the imperialistic nation. For the latter will always be favored by compromise and will be careful in choosing the grounds for its demands so that principle will favor it, too. Ultimately, these piecemeal changes will add up to the reversal of the power relations in favor of the imperialistic nation. The imperialistic nation will have won a bloodless, yet decisive, victory over an opponent who did not know the difference between compromise and appeasement.

Germany stated its imperialistic policies openly in 1935 with the repudiation of the disarmament provisions of the Treaty of Versailles, pointing to the failure of the other nations to disarm and to the increase in French and Russian armaments. Taken by itself and in disregard of an ulterior objective, the argument was not without merit in the light of the legal principle of equality. Apart from paper protests and paper alliances, the only tangible reaction to this first German step on the road to empire was the conclusion three months later of the Anglo-German Naval Agreement, in which Great Britain conceded to Germany a naval force of not more than 35 percent that of Great Britain. Both the reoccupation of the Rhineland by Germany in 1936 and its denunciation of the international control of its waterways later in the same year found support in the legal principle of equality, if one accepted the professed rational limits of the demands as the actual ones. The annexation of Austria in 1938 could easily be defended by the principle of national self-determination, which had also been one of the professed war aims of the Allied powers in the First World War.

Later in 1938, Germany demanded the German parts of Czechoslovakia. The Munich settlement granted the German demands. When Hitler, shortly before the settlement of Munich, declared that the German parts of Czechoslovakia were the last territorial demands Germany had to make in Europe, he was really saying that the annexation of these territories was an end in itself, self-contained within its own rational limits. He pretended that German policy operated within the general framework of the European status quo and was not intent upon overthrowing it, and that the other European powers ought to view German foreign policy in that light and deal with it correspondingly. It was only by the end of March 1939, five months before the outbreak of the Second World War, that the annexation of the whole of Czechoslovakia and the territorial demands on Poland convinced the Western powers that what had appeared to be a policy of the status quo had really been from the beginning a policy of imperialism, of continental, if not world, dimensions.

At that moment, the distribution of power in Europe was already changed in favor of Germany. It was changed to such an extent that a further increase in German power could not be prevented short of war. Germany had become strong enough to challenge openly the status quo of Versailles, and the prestige—that is, the reputation for power—of the nations identified with the order of Versailles had sunk so low that they were unable to defend what was left of the status quo by mere diplomatic means. They could either surrender or go to war. Thus the appeasers of 1938 became either the quislings (if they deemed resistance to German imperialism hopeless) or the heroes of 1939–45 (if they thought that resistance was morally required regardless of the outcome or that it had even a chance to succeed). The final catastrophe, and the tragic choices with which the catastrophe confronted the actors on the international scene, were predetermined by that initial error that responded to a policy of imperialism as though it were a policy of the status quo.

Once a policy of containment has succeeded in checking a policy of imperialism, or the latter has run its course either because it has reached its objective or has exhausted itself, containment (a policy of uncompromising resistance) might well give way to compromise (a policy of give and take). Such a policy, nefarious when it seeks to appease imperialism, becomes a virtue when it aims at accommodating a policy of the status quo that has left its imperialistic aspiration behind. It was this distinction to which Sir Winston Churchill referred when he said on December 14, 1950, in the House of Commons:

> The declaration of the Prime Minister that there will be no appeasement also commands almost universal support. It is a good slogan for the country. It seems to me, however, that in this House it requires to be more precisely defined. What we really mean, I think, is no appeasement through weakness or fear. Appeasement in itself may be good or bad according to the circumstances. Appeasement from weakness and fear is alike futile and fatal. Appeasement from strength is magnanimous and noble and might be the surest and perhaps the only path to world peace.

The other fundamental error into which those responsible for the conduct of foreign affairs are most likely to fall is the reverse of the one thus far discussed. It mistakes a policy of the status quo for a policy of imperialism. By doing so, State A resorts to certain measures defensive in intent, such as armaments, bases, and alliances, with respect to State B. The latter, in turn, resorts to countermeasures, for it now sees State A embarking upon a policy of imperialism. These countermeasures strengthen the initial misapprehension, on the part of State A, of State B's policies, and so forth. Ultimately, either both countries correct their errors with regard to their respective policies or else the ever-increasing mutual suspicions, feeding upon each other, end in war. Out of an initial error there develops a vicious circle. Two or more nations, each seeking only to preserve the status quo, but each convinced of the imperialistic designs of the others, find support for their own errors of judgment and action in the errors of the others. In such a situation nothing but an almost superhuman effort will deflect the trend of events from a catastrophic denouement.

The history of European diplomacy between the Franco-German War of 1870 and the outbreak of the First World War in 1914 illustrates this situation. After the victorious conclusion of the War of 1870 and the foundation of the German Empire, German foreign policy was mainly defensive. It was concerned with the maintenance of the position Germany had acquired in Europe and with the danger, Bismarck's famous *cauchemar des coalitions,* that a hostile coalition, especially between France and Russia, might challenge that position. The Triple Alliance between Germany, Austria, and Italy was the instrument of that defensive policy. It was served also by the Reinsurance Treaty with Russia in which Russia and Germany pledged each other neutrality if either became involved in war with a third power.

After the dismissal of Bismarck in 1890, Wilhelm II decided to let the Reinsurance Treaty lapse, primarily because of the fear that its continuation might alienate Austria and thus destroy the Triple Alliance. Russia then (in 1891 and 1894) entered into agreements with France that were defensive in character and obviously inspired by fear of the intentions of the Triple Alliance. The provisions of the Military Convention of 1894, in particular, anticipated the possible transformation of the Triple Alliance from a defensive into an imperialistic instrument. Thus the Convention was to remain a force as long as the Triple Alliance. The main provisions of the Convention made the following stipulations: if France were attacked by Germany or by Italy supported by Germany, Russia would give military aid to France. France would do the same in respect to Russia if the latter were attacked by Germany or by Austria supported by Germany. In case of the mobilization of the forces of the Triple Alliance, France and Russia would mobilize their forces without delay.

First, the fear of hostile alliances led to the formation of the Triple Alliance. Then, the fear of the latter's dissolution led to the severance by Germany of the friendly relations with Russia. Finally, the fear of the intentions of the Triple Alliance brought about the Franco-Russian Alliance. It was the mutual fears of these two defensive alliances, and the general insecurity created by the erratic character of the imperialistic utterances of Wilhelm II, that inspired the diplomatic maneuvers during the two decades before the First World War. These maneuvers sought either new combinations destructive of existing alignments or the support of powers, thus far aloof, for the existing alliances. In the end, the general conflagration in 1914 was made inevitable by the fear that the other side would change the power relations decisively in its favor if not forestalled by such a change in one's own favor. In the two antagonistic blocs, Russia and Austria especially were animated by this fear. The fear of the other's suspected imperialism bred imperialism in reaction, which, in turn, gave substance to the original fear.

The distorting effects of mutual fear are particularly pronounced when antagonistic foreign policies are overlaid with world-embracing ideologies[21] to which the foreign policies actually pursued may or may not correspond. Thus the

---

[21]For the explanation of the concept, see Chapter 7.

Communist ideology of world revolution and of the communization of the world creates in non-Communist nations the fear that the foreign policies of Communist nations are of necessity at the service of a worldwide imperialism. In consequence, every move a country such as the Soviet Union or China makes on the chessboard of international politics is not judged on its own merits but in terms of imperialistic ideology. On the other hand, since Communist philosophy assumes that capitalistic nations are by nature warlike and "imperialistic," Western professions of dedication to law and order and opposition to aggression and subversion are interpreted by Communist nations as mere ideological disguises of imperialistic policies.

This mythological perception of reality on both sides calls forth policies seeking to contain the imperialism of the other side, and these policies confirm in the minds of all concerned the original mythological interpretation. The great powers are thus trapped in a vicious circle. First, fear makes them interpret reality in terms of an ideology on which that fear can feed. Then, the measures they take to protect themselves from what may be an imaginary danger confirm the other side in its fears and misinterpretation of reality. Then, countermeasures are taken against these measures, carrying a similar confirmation, and so forth. Thus the fear of one side sustains the fear of the other, and vice versa. Enmeshed in mutual fear and engaged in an arms race that seeks to still those fears, neither side is capable of putting the original assumption of imperialism to the test of actual experience. What was originally a mythological perception of reality has now become a self-fulfilling prophecy: the policies engendered by mutual fear appear to provide empirical evidence for the correctness of the original assumption.[22]

The Problem of Detection

Appeasement, which is the attempt to compromise with an imperialism not recognized as such, and the fear that creates imperialism where there is none—these are the two wrong answers, the two fatal mistakes an intelligent foreign policy must try to avoid. Such an intelligent foreign policy, which recognizes imperialism where it exists and determines its specific nature, is confronted with five difficulties, and they are all of a formidable character.

The first and most fundamental difficulty was pointed out by Bukharin, the foremost exponent of the Communist doctrine from Lenin's death to the great purges in the mid-thirties. Arguing against the noneconomic explanation of imperialism, he summarized it thus: "Imperialism is a policy of conquest. But not every policy of conquest is imperialism."[23] The statement is indeed correct and squares with what we have said previously about the distinction between a policy of conquest operating within the existing status quo and one seeking to overthrow it.[24]

---

[22]Cf. John H. Kautsky, "Myth, Self-Fulfilling Prophecy, and Symbolic Reassurance in the East West Conflict," *The Journal of Conflict Resolution,* Vol. IX, No. 1 (March 1965), pp. 1 ff.
[23]N. I. Bukharin, *Imperialism and World Economy* (New York: International Publishers, 1929), p. 114.
[24]See pages 00 ff.

To make this distinction in a concrete situation presents a formidable difficulty. How was one to know with any degree of certainty what Hitler's ultimate objectives were? From 1935 on, he made demand after demand, each of which in itself could be fully reconciled with a policy of the status quo, yet each of which might be a stepping-stone on the road to empire. The individual steps in themselves were ambiguous and, therefore, did not reveal the actual nature of the policy of which they formed the elements. Where could one, then, have found an answer to our question?

One might have found it, however tentative and open to doubt, in two of the three typical situations that we pointed out as favoring imperialistic policies. The desire to overthrow the status quo of the Treaty of Versailles had been from the very beginning one of the main points of the National Socialist program, which in 1933 became the official program of the German government. In view of this objective, one might have been able to foresee that the German government would pursue a foreign policy seeking its realization as soon as it had a chance to do so—that is, as soon as the nations identified with the status quo of the Treaty of Versailles were no longer able or willing to defend that status quo effectively.

This initial and fundamental difficulty is aggravated by the fact that a policy which starts out seeking adjustments within the existing distribution of power may change its character either in the course of its success or in the process of its frustration. In other words, the ease with which the original objectives are reached within the established distribution of power may suggest to the expanding nation that it is dealing with weak or irresolute antagonists and that a change in the existing power relations can be achieved without great effort or risk. Thus the appetite may come with the eating, and a successful policy of expansion within the status quo may overnight transform itself into a policy of imperialism. The same may be true of an unsuccessful policy of expansion within the status quo. A nation frustrated in its limited objectives, which do not seem to be attainable within the existing power relations, concludes that it must change these power relations if it is to make sure that it gets what it wants.

Where a policy is couched in purely territorial terms, the nature of the territorial objectives will sometimes indicate the nature of the policy pursued. The objective may, for instance, be a strategic point, the acquisition of which may in itself change the power relations in that particular region. No such help can be expected and, therefore, an additional difficulty must be met where a foreign policy uses mainly the vehicles of economic or cultural penetration. These methods, too, are ambiguous in view of the character of the policy they serve, but their ambiguity is much greater than that of the military method, which has defined territorial objectives. Economic and cultural expansion are generally without a clearly defined locale. They address themselves to a wide variety of ill-defined persons. And, furthermore, they are practiced on a wide scale by an indefinite number of nations. To identify economic or cultural expansion as instruments of imperialism in contrast to identical policies that have no hidden power objective beyond the explicit cultural and economic ones and, hence, are not imperialistic, is indeed a difficult task. Here again reference to the typical situations favorable to imperialistic policies will be of help.

The active economic policies Switzerland has been pursuing in the international sphere have never had an imperialistic tinge. British foreign trade policies at times have had an imperialistic character with respect to certain countries. Today their end is in the main purely economic; that is, they try to obtain for the inhabitants of the British Isles the necessities of life. They aim at economic survival through favorable trade balances, not at the maintenance or acquisition of political power over foreign nations. It is only with regard to certain strategic regions, such as Egypt and Iran, that since the end of the Second World War British economic policies have at times been subordinated to political considerations. Some of these considerations might have acquired, or under certain conditions will acquire, an imperialistic character.

The cultural penetration of Latin America by Spain was generally bound to be without imperialistic significance, for the military weakness of Spain in relation to the United States forbade any thought of changing the power relations in Latin America in Spain's favor. The cultural mission of France has been in certain countries and at certain times an end in itself. Under different circumstances and in other countries, it has been subordinated to imperialistic aims. Here, too, the character of economic and cultural expansion may change with a change in the political situation. When the opportunity beckons, the "reservoir of good will" or a preponderant position in the foreign trade of another country, which a nation has acquired as ends in themselves, may suddenly become sources of political power and potent instruments in the struggle for power. But when circumstances change again, they may lose that quality just as suddenly.

When all these difficulties have been overcome and a foreign policy has been correctly identified as imperialistic, yet another difficulty presents itself. It concerns the kind of imperialism with which one has to deal. A successful localized imperialism may find in its success an incentive to spread wider and wider until it becomes continental or worldwide. More particularly, a country may find it necessary, in order to stabilize and secure a local preponderance, to acquire preponderance of power on an even greater scale, and it may feel fully secure only in a worldwide empire. There is frequently in imperialism a dynamic force, rationalized in aggressive or defensive terms, that proceeds from a limited region to a continent and from there to the world. The Macedonian Empire under Philip and Alexander and Napoleonic imperialism were of this kind. On the other hand, a policy of worldwide imperialism, opposed by superior force, may retreat to a geographically determined region or be satisfied with local preponderance. Or it may lose its imperialistic tendencies altogether and transform itself into a policy of the status quo. The development from geographically determined to localized imperialism and from there to the permanent loss of imperialistic tendencies altogether can be traced in the history of Swedish imperialism in the seventeenth and eighteenth centuries.

Thus the evaluation of imperialistic tendencies and, consequently, of the policies countering them is never definitive. Both policies and counterpolicies are ever subject to reevaluation and reformulation. But the framers of foreign policy are always exposed to the temptation to take a particular pattern of imperialistic expansion or of any other type of foreign policy as permanent and to pursue a foreign policy adapted to that pattern even when the pattern has changed. A worldwide imperialism requires countermeasures different from those that are adequate for one that is localized, and a nation that counters the latter with measures appropriate to the former will bring on the very dangers it tries to avoid. In this necessity to recognize quickly a change in the imperialistic policy of another nation lies another difficulty and, in the failure to adapt one's own foreign policy quickly to such change, another source of error.

Finally, imperialism poses a problem that it shares with all foreign policy— presenting it, however, in a particularly acute manner. This is the problem of detecting the true nature of a foreign policy behind its ideological disguises. The actors on the international scene rarely present the foreign policy they are pursuing for what it is, and a policy of imperialism almost never reveals its true face in the pronouncements of those who pursue it. The true nature of the policies pursued disappears behind a veil of ideological disguises. The reasons this must be so and the typical shapes these ideologies take will be discussed in Chapter 7 of this book. How difficult it is to distinguish between the appearance of a foreign policy and its essence will become apparent in the course of that discussion.

6 The Struggle for Power: Policy of Prestige

The policy of prestige has rarely been recognized in modern political literature for what it is: the third of the basic manifestations of the struggle for power on the international scene. The reasons for this neglect are threefold. The policy of prestige shares this neglect with the subtle and intangible relation the understanding of which, as we have seen,[1] has suffered from the predominant theoretical and practical concern with the material aspect of power in the form of force, actual or threatened. Furthermore, the policy of prestige has used as one of its main vehicles the aristocratic forms of social intercourse practiced in the diplomatic world. That world, with its ceremonial rules, its quarrels about rank and precedence, and its empty formalisms, is the very antithesis of the democratic way of life. Even those not fully persuaded that power politics is nothing but an elitist atavism have been inclined to see in the policy of prestige as practiced by diplomats an anachronistic game, frivolous and farcical and devoid of any organic connection with the business of international politics.

Finally, prestige, in contrast to the maintenance and acquisition of power, is but rarely an end in itself. More frequently, the policy of prestige is one of the instrumentalities through which the policies of the status quo and of imperialism try to achieve their ends. This makes it easy to conclude that the policy of prestige is not important and does not deserve systematic discussion.

Actually, the policy of prestige, however exaggerated and absurd its uses may have been at times, is as intrinsic an element of the relations between nations as the desire for prestige is of the relations between individuals. Here again it becomes obvious that international and domestic politics are but different manifestations of one and the same social fact. In both spheres, the desire for social recognition is a potent dynamic force determining social relations and creating social institutions. The individual seeks confirmation, on the part of his fellows, of the evaluation he puts upon himself. It is only in the tribute others pay to his goodness, intelligence,

---

[1]See page 31.

and power that he becomes fully aware of, and can fully enjoy, what he deems to be his superior qualities. It is only through his reputation for excellence that he can gain the measure of security, wealth, and power he regards to be his due. Thus, in the struggle for existence and power—which is, as it were, the raw material of the social world—what others think about us is as important as what we actually are. The image in the mirror of our fellows' minds (that is, our prestige), rather than the original, of which the image in the mirror may be but the distorted reflection, determines what we are as members of society.

It is, then, a necessary and important task to see to it that the mental picture other people form of one's position in society at least represents faithfully the actual situation, if it does not excel it. This is exactly what the policy of prestige is about. Its purpose is to impress other nations with the power one's own nation actually possesses, or with the power it believes, or wants the other nations to believe, it possesses. Two specific instrumentalities serve this purpose: diplomatic ceremonial in the widest meaning of the term, and the display of military force.[2]

DIPLOMATIC CEREMONIAL

Two episodes from the life of Napoleon show clearly the symbols through which the power position of a ruler, representing a nation, expresses itself in ceremonial forms. One shows Napoleon at the summit of his power; the other indicates that he had left that summit behind.

In 1804, when Napoleon was about to be crowned emperor by the pope, each of the two rulers had a vital interest in demonstrating his superiority over the other. Napoleon was successful in asserting his superiority, not only by putting the crown on his head with his own hands instead of letting the pope do it but also by a ceremonial device that the Duke of Rovigo, one of Napoleon's generals and minister of police, reports in his memoirs:

> He went to meet the Pope on the road to Nemours. To avoid ceremony, the pretext of a hunting-party was assumed; the attendants, with his equipages, were in the forest. The Emperor came on horseback and in a hunting-dress, with his retinue. It was at the half-moon on the top of the hill that the meeting took place. There the Pope's carriage drew up; he got out at the left door in his white costume: the ground was dirty; he did not like to step upon it with his white silk shoes, but was obliged to do so at last.
>
> Napoleon alighted to receive him. They embraced; and the Emperor's carriage, which had been purposely driven up, was advanced a few paces, as if from the carelessness of the driver; but men were posted to hold the two doors open: at the moment of getting in, the Emperor took the right door, and an

---

[2]See also pages 339 ff. for the discussion of propaganda, which serves in good measure as an instrument of the policy of prestige.

officer of the court handed the Pope to the left, so that they entered the carriage by the two doors at the same time. The Emperor naturally seated himself on the right; and this first step decided without negotiation upon the etiquette to be observed during the whole time that the Pope was to remain at Paris.[3]

The other episode occurred in 1813 in Dresden, after the defeat in Russia, when Napoleon was threatened by a coalition of all of Europe, a coalition that shortly afterward would inflict upon him the disastrous defeat of Leipzig. In an interview lasting nine hours, Napoleon tried to restrain the Austrian chancellor, Metternich, from joining the coalition against him. Metternich treated Napoleon as a doomed man, while Napoleon acted like the master of Europe, which he had been for a decade. After a particularly stormy exchange, Napoleon, as if to test his superiority, dropped his hat, expecting the spokesman of the hostile coalition to pick it up. When Metternich feigned not to see it, it must have become clear to both men that a decisive change had occurred in the prestige and power of the victor of Austerlitz and Wagram. Metternich summed up the situation when he told Napoleon at the end of the discussion that he was sure Napoleon was lost.

The relations between diplomats lend themselves naturally as instruments for a policy of prestige, for diplomats are the symbolic representatives of their respective countries.[4] The respect shown them is really shown their countries; the respect shown by them is really shown by their countries; the insult they give or receive is really given or received by their countries. History abounds with examples illustrating these points and the importance attributed to them in international politics.

In most courts it was the custom to have foreign ambassadors introduced to the sovereign by ordinary officials while royal ambassadors were introduced by princes. When in 1698 Louis XIV had the ambassador of the Republic of Venice introduced by the prince of Lorraine, the Grand Council of Venice asked the French ambassador to assure the king that the Republic of Venice would be forever grateful for that honor, and the Council sent a special letter of thanks to Louis XIV. Through that gesture France indicated that it regarded the Republic of Venice to be as powerful as a kingdom, and it was for that new prestige that Venice showed its gratitude. At the papal court the pope used to receive the diplomatic representatives of different types of states in different halls. Ambassadors of crowned heads and of Venice were received in the *Sala Reggia,* the representatives of other princes and of republics in the *Sala Ducale.* The Republic of Genoa is said to have offered the Pope millions in order to have its representatives received in the *Sala Reggia* instead of in the *Sala Ducale.* The Pope, however, refused to grant the request because of the opposition of Venice, which did not want Genoa to be treated on equal terms with herself. Equality of treatment would have meant equality of prestige—that is, reputation for power—and to this the state superior in prestige could not consent.

---

[3] *Memoirs of the Duke of Rovigo* (London, 1828), Vol. 1, Part II, p. 73.
[4] For the different functions of diplomats, see Chapter 31.

At the end of the eighteenth century, it was still the custom at the court of Constantinople that ambassadors and members of their suites who presented themselves to the sultan were grabbed by the arms by court officials and their heads bent down. After the customary exchange of speeches between ambassador and prime minister, the court officials exclaimed: "Praise be to the Eternal that the infidels must come and give homage to our gloriously brilliant sceptre." The humiliation of the representatives of foreign countries was intended to symbolize the inferiority in power of the countries they represented.

Under President Theodore Roosevelt, all diplomatic representatives were received together on the first of January in order to present their congratulations to the president. President Taft changed the arrangement and ordered that ambassadors and ministers be received separately. When the Spanish minister, who had not been informed of this change, appeared on January 1, 1910, at the White House for the reception of the ambassadors, he was refused admission. Whereupon the Spanish government recalled the minister and protested to the government of the United States. A nation that had just lost its empire and passed to the rank of a third-rate power insisted at least upon the prestige commensurate with its former greatness.

In 1946, when the foreign minister of the Soviet Union was seated at a victory celebration in Paris in the second row, while the representatives of other great powers sat in the first, he left the meeting in protest. A nation that for long had been a pariah in the international community had attained the unquestioned position of a great power and insisted upon the prestige due to its new status. At the Potsdam Conference of 1945, Churchill, Stalin, and Truman were unable to agree on who should enter the conference room first; finally, they entered through three different doors at the same time. These three political leaders symbolized the respective power of their nations. Consequently, the precedence accorded to one of them would have given his nation a prestige of superiority over the other two which the latter were not willing to concede. Since they claimed equality of power, they were bound to be concerned with upholding the prestige in which that equality found its symbolic expression.

To cite two recent examples: France, since "de Gaulle" opposed the supranational tendencies of the European Communities, objected

> to the traditional style—striped pants, morning coat and champagne—in which Dr. Walter Hallstein, president of the Common Market Commission, has been receiving ambassadors presenting their credentials.
>
> Paris feels that such a ceremony creates the impression that Dr. Hallstein is equal in rank, for the purpose of receiving ambassadors' credentials, to a chief of state, such as President de Gaulle.
>
> The French contend that the commission is not a government and the ceremony should be toned down. This is one aspect of French opposition to the so-called supra-national features of the European communities. France views them as groups of sovereign states.[5]

---

[5] *New York Times*, May 4, 1966, p. 16.

The peace negotiations among the United States, the South and North Vietnam governments, and the National Liberation Front (Viet Cong) that were supposed to have started in November 1968 were delayed for ten weeks because of a dispute over the shape of the conference table. North Vietnam proposed a square table, or four tables arranged in a circular or diamond pattern, or a plain round table forming a complete unbroken circle. The United States, on the other hand, proposed two half-oval tables placed against each other to form a broken oval, or two half-circular tables to form a broken circle, or two half-circular tables, separated somewhat from each other, with two rectangular tables for secretaries between them. As concerns the last proposal, the United States made the concession that the two half-circular tables could be pushed together to adjoin the secretarial tables between them. However, the secretarial tables would have to just out a few inches on either side from the curved tables.[6] Finally, a circular table without nameplates, flags, or markings was agreed upon. Two rectangular tables, measuring about 3 feet by $4^1/_2$ feet, were to be placed 18 inches from the circular table at opposite sides.

What lay behind these seemingly absurd proceedings? North Vietnam insisted upon the recognition of the Viet Cong as an independent negotiating party. The United States wanted the recognition of its assumption, basic to its long-held conception of the war, that the Viet Cong were a mere extension of the North Vietnamese regime. Thus the controversy over the shape of the table was a symbolic manifestation of the substance of the conflict. Was the Vietnam War the result of the aggression of the North Vietnamese, using the Viet Cong as its instrument, or were the Viet Cong a genuine popular force, aided and abetted but not created by the North Vietnamese? The shape of the table, one way or other, would have prejudged that substantive issue. The shape finally agreed upon appeared to leave that issue in abeyance.

The political importance of the entertainment in which all diplomats vie with each other is well illustrated by these excerpts from an article dealing with the Washington social scene:

> Now the question of whether foreign embassies actually *buy* anything for their countries with all this entertainment is naturally moot. There is no check on it. But most ambassadors pursue their social rounds with dead seriousness and regard it as one of the most important and productive aspects of their job. They are probably right.
>
> After all, propriety severely constricts the activities of an ambassador in the capital to which he is accredited. Certainly an ambassador doesn't want to be seen on the Hill, mingling with Congressmen or publicly registering reaction to the tone and tenor of legislative debates. Yet he must get about enough to receive accurate impressions of American affairs and officials, and in turn leave some impress of his own and his country's character on the public mind. For this, the social avenue is almost his only approach, and unless he is attractive and adept in the salon, he will not be of much use to his country in the chancery. . . .

---

[6] *New York Times,* December 14, 1968, p. 2.

Because the Latin Americans throw the biggest and most expensive parties in Washington, and appear to profit the least thereby, there is a tendency to write them off as mere playboys. That is a mistake. What the Latinos are striving for, above all, is prestige, a place of equality in the family of American nations; and who can say that by parading not only their wealth but their good manners and bright, zestful minds in a series of unrivaled entertainments they are not accomplishing something toward that end?[7]

The policy of prestige as the policy of demonstrating the power a nation has or thinks it has, or wants other nations to believe it has, finds a particularly fruitful field in the choice of a locality for international meetings. When many antagonistic claims compete with each other and cannot be reconciled through compromise, the meeting place is frequently chosen in a country that does not participate in the competition for prestige. For this reason, The Hague in the Netherlands and Geneva in Switzerland have been favored meeting places for international conferences. Frequently, the shift from one favorite meeting place to another symbolizes a shift in the preponderance of power. During the better part of the nineteenth century, most international conferences were held in Paris. But the Congress of Berlin of 1878, held in the capital of the reestablished German Empire after its victory over France, demonstrated to all the world Germany's new prestige of being the preponderant power on the European continent. Originally, the Soviet Union opposed the choice of Geneva as headquarters of the United Nations; for Geneva, the former headquarters of the League of Nations, was symbolic of the low point in Russian prestige in the period between the two world wars. When the distribution of power within the United Nations, meeting in New York in the aftermath of the Second World War, showed the Soviet Union in what appeared to be a permanent minority, confronted with a majority under American leadership, it advocated the transfer of the headquarters of the United Nations to Geneva, which carried no symbolic reference to American supremacy. That in 1972 President Nixon met the Chinese prime minister, Chou En-lai, in Peking and not in Washington or at some neutral place has a symbolic significance for the shifts that the nations concerned believe to have occurred in the distribution of power in Asia and in the world.

Normally, a nation that has a preponderance of power in a particular field or region insists that international conferences dealing with matters concerning that field or region meet within, or at least close to, its territory. Thus most international conferences dealing with maritime questions have been held in London. International conferences concerned with Japan have met either in Washington or in Tokyo. Most international conferences concerned with the future of Europe after the Second World War have been held either on Russian territory, such as Moscow and Yalta, or in territory occupied by the Soviet Union, such as Potsdam, or in the proximity of Russian territory, such as Teheran. Yet, by the end of 1947,

---

[7]"R.S.V. Politics," *Fortune*, February 1952, p. 120. (Used by permission of *Fortune*. Copyright Time Inc., 1952.)

the political situation had changed to such an extent that President Truman could declare with considerable emphasis that he would meet Stalin nowhere but in Washington.[8]

DISPLAY OF MILITARY FORCE

Besides the practices of diplomacy, the policy of prestige uses military demonstrations as means to achieve its purpose. Since military strength is the obvious measure of a nation's power, its demonstration serves to impress the others with that nation's power. Military representatives of foreign nations are, for instance, invited to peacetime army and navy maneuvers, not in order to let them in on military secrets but to impress them and their governments with the military preparedness of the particular nation. The invitation of foreign observers to the two atomic bomb tests in the Pacific in 1946 was intended to fulfill a similar purpose. The foreign observer was, on the one hand, to be impressed by the naval might of the United States and with American technological achievements. "Twenty-one observers from the United Nations Atomic Energy Control Commission," reported the *New York Times*, ". . . agreed today that the United States was bombing a group of ships larger than many of the world's navies."[9] On the other hand, the foreign observer was to see for himself what the atomic bomb could do above and under water and how superior in military strength a nation that had the monopoly of the atomic bomb was bound to be in comparison with nations that did not have it.

Because of the high mobility of navies, which are able to bring the flag and the power of a nation to the four corners of the globe, and because of the great impressiveness of their appearance, naval demonstrations have in the past been a favorite instrument of the policy of prestige. The visit in 1891 of the French fleet to the Russian port of Kronstadt and the return visit in 1893 of the Russian fleet to the French port of Toulon mark a turning point in the political history of the world; for these mutual visits demonstrated to the world a political and military solidarity between France and Russia that was not long in crystallizing into a political and military alliance. The periodical dispatch, on the part of the great maritime powers, of naval squadrons to the ports of the Far East demonstrated to the peoples of that region the superiority of Western power. The United States has from time to time sent warships to Latin American ports in order to remind the nations concerned that in the Western Hemisphere American naval power is supreme.

Whenever the claims of a maritime power were challenged in colonial or semicolonial regions either by the natives or by competing powers, these nations would dispatch warships to the region as symbolic representatives of the power of

---

[8]*New York Times*, December 19, 1947, p. 1; July 27, 1948, p. 1; February 4, 1949, p. 1.
[9]Ibid., July 1, 1946, p. 3.

the country. A famous example of this kind of policy of prestige is the visit Wilhelm II paid in 1905 on board a German warship to Tangier, a port of Morocco, for the purpose of counteracting French claims on that state. The Mediterranean cruises American naval squadrons have been making since the Second World War to Italian, Greek, and Turkish ports are the unmistakable reply to Russian aspirations in that region. The selection of the most exposed regions of Western Europe for maneuvers by the combined forces of the Western allies is intended to demonstrate to the Soviet Union and to the allies themselves the military power of the Atlantic Alliance and the resolution to use this power in defense of the status quo in Western Europe.

The most drastic form of the military type of the policy of prestige is partial or total mobilization. Mobilization as an instrument of the policy of prestige may be obsolete today, since the war of the future will in all probability require total preparedness at all times. In the past, however, and as late as 1938 and 1939, the calling to the colors either of certain classes of the reserves or of all those subject to military service has been a potent instrument of the policy of prestige. When, for instance, in July 1914, Russia mobilized its army, followed by the mobilization of the Austrian, German, and French forces, and when France and Czechoslovakia mobilized their armies in September 1938, and France its army again in March and September 1939, the purpose was always to demonstrate to friend and foe alike one's own military strength and one's resolution to use that strength in support of one's political ends.

Here prestige—reputation for power—is employed both as a deterrent to and as preparation for war. It is hoped that the prestige of one's own nation will be great enough to deter the other nations from going to war. At the same time it is hoped that, if this policy of prestige should fail, the mobilization of the armed forces before the actual outbreak of war will put one's own nation in the most advantageous military position possible under the circumstances. At that point, political and military policy tend to merge and become two different aspects of one and the same policy. We shall have further occasion to point to the intimate relations between foreign and military policy in times of peace as well as of war.[10]

TWO OBJECTIVES OF THE POLICY OF PRESTIGE

The policy of prestige has two possible ultimate objectives: prestige for its own sake or, much more frequently, prestige in support of a policy of the status quo or of imperialism. While in national societies prestige is frequently sought for its own sake, it is rarely the primary objective of foreign policy. Prestige is at most the pleasant by-product of foreign policies whose ultimate objectives are not the reputation for power but the substance of power. The individual members of a national society, protected as they are in their existence and social position by an

---

[10]See Chapters 9, 23, 32.

integrated system of social institutions and rules of conduct, can afford to indulge in the competition for prestige as a kind of harmless social game. But nations, which as members of the international society must in the main rely upon their own power for the protection of their existence and power position, can hardly neglect the effect that a gain or loss of prestige will have upon their power position on the international scene.

It is therefore not by accident that, as we have already pointed out, observers of international affairs who underrate the importance of power tend to take questions of prestige lightly. And it is likewise not by accident that only foolhardy egocentrics are inclined to pursue a policy of prestige for its own sake. In modern times William II and Mussolini are cases in point. Intoxicated with newly acquired domestic power, they regarded international politics as a kind of personal sport where in the exaltation of one's own nation and in the humiliation of others one enjoyed one's own personal superiority. By doing so, however, they confused the international with the domestic scene. At home the demonstration of their power, or at least of its appearance, would be at worst nothing more than harmless foolishness. Abroad such a demonstration is a play with fire that will consume the player who does not have the power commensurate with his belief or his pretense. One-man governments—that is, absolute monarchies or dictatorships—tend to identify the personal glory of the ruler with the political interests of the nation. In view of the successful conduct of foreign policy, this identification is a serious weakness, for it leads to a policy of prestige for its own sake, neglectful of the national interests at stake and of the power available to support them. American policy in Indochina from 1965 to 1975 could well be seen in the light of this analysis.

The function the policy of prestige fulfills for the policies of the status quo and of imperialism grows out of the very nature of international politics. The foreign policy of a nation is always the result of an estimate of the power relations as they exist among different nations at a certain moment of history and as they are likely to develop in the immediate and distant future. The foreign policy of the United States, for instance, is based upon an evaluation of the power of the United States in relation to, let us say, the power of Great Britain, the Soviet Union, and Argentina, and of the probable future development of the power of these different nations. Likewise, the foreign policies of Great Britain, the Soviet Union, and Argentina are based upon similar evaluations, which are constantly subjected to review for the purpose of bringing them up to date.

It is the primary function of the policy of prestige to influence these evaluations. If, for instance, the United States could impress its power upon the Latin American nations to such an extent as to convince them that its predominance in the Western Hemisphere was unchallengeable, its policy of the status quo in the Western Hemisphere would not be likely to be challenged, and its success would thus be assured. The relative political stability Europe enjoyed during the twenties and in the beginning of the thirties was due mainly to the prestige of France as the strongest military power in the world. German imperialism owes its triumphs in the late thirties mainly to a successful policy of prestige. This policy was able to convince the nations interested in the maintenance of the status quo of Germany's superiority, if not invincibility. For instance, the showing of documentary films of the blitzkrieg in Poland and France to foreign audiences composed preferably of military and political leaders clearly served this purpose. Whatever the ultimate objectives of a nation's foreign policy, its prestige—its reputation for power—is always an important and sometimes a decisive factor in determining success or failure of its foreign policy. A policy of prestige is, therefore, an indispensable element of a rational foreign policy.

The Cold War, which dominated the relations of the Western world and the Soviet bloc during the two decades following the Second World War, was fought primarily with the weapons of prestige. The United States and the Soviet Union endeavored to impress each other with their military might, technological achievements, economic potential, and political principles in order to weaken each other's morale and deter each other from taking an irrevocable step toward war. Similarly, they tried to impress their allies, the members of the hostile alliance, and the uncommitted nations with these same qualities. Their aim was to keep the allegiance of their own allies, weaken the unity of the hostile coalition, and win the support of the uncommitted nations.

Prestige has become particularly important as a political weapon in an age in which the struggle for power is fought not only with the traditional methods of political pressure and military force but in large measure as a struggle for the minds of men. In wide areas of Asia, the Middle East, Africa, and Latin America, the Cold War has been fought primarily in terms of competition between two rival political philosophies, economic systems, and ways of life. This is another way of saying that in these regions prestige—reputation for performance and power—has become the main stake for which political warfare is waged. The chief instruments of this struggle are propaganda, which seeks to increase the prestige of one's own side and deflate that of the enemy, and foreign aid, which intends to impress the recipient nation with the economic and technological proficiency of the aid's provider.

A policy of prestige attains its very triumph when it gives the nation pursuing it such a reputation for powers as to enable it to forgo the actual employment of the instrument of power. Two factors make that triumph possible: reputation for unchallengeable power and reputation for self-restraint in using it. Of this rare combination the Roman and the British empires and the Good Neighbor policy of the United States, when it prevailed, are the classic examples.

The longevity of the Roman Empire, in contrast to the fate of quick dissolution that generally befalls imperial structures of similar dimensions, was due primarily to the profound respect in which the name of a Roman was held within its confines. Rome was superior in political acumen and military strength to any one of the component parts of the Empire. By making the burden of its superiority as easy as possible to bear, it deprived its subject peoples of the incentive to rid themselves of Roman domination. At worst one or the other of the subject peoples might revolt, but there was never incentive enough for the formation of a coalition sufficiently strong to challenge Rome. Isolated revolts would be dealt with swiftly and efficiently by preponderant Roman power, thus increasing Rome's prestige for power. The contrast between the dismal fate of those who dared to challenge Rome and the peaceful and prosperous existence, under the protection of the Roman law, of those who remained loyal increased Rome's reputation for moderation in the exercise of its power.

The same reputation for power tempered by self-restraint was one of the foundation stones of the British Empire. Observers have marveled at the ability of a few thousand British officials to dominate hundreds of millions of Indians, not to speak of the voluntary ties of loyalty that kept the self-governing dominions united in the Empire. But the ignominious defeats Great Britain suffered in the Second World War at the hands of Japan shattered forever its reputation for unchallengeable power. And the cry for national liberation, raised by the subject races throughout Asia, drowned out the memory of a tolerant rule mellowed by age and wisdom. When that two-fold prestige was gone and the resources to maintain the Empire by sheer force had become unavailable, the Asiatic part of the British Empire did not for long survive the prestige of Britain.

During the era of the Good Neighbor policy, the hegemony of the United States in the Western Hemisphere reposed likewise upon the reputation for unchallengeable power rather than upon its actual exercise. The superiority of the United States in the Western Hemisphere was so obvious and overwhelming that prestige alone was sufficient to assure the United States the position among the American republics commensurate with its power. The United States even at times could afford to forgo insistence upon the prestige that was its due, because the self-restraint thus manifested made its hegemony more tolerable to its neighbors to the south. Thus the United States made a point, from the inauguration of the Good Neighbor policy, to have Pan American conferences meet in Latin American countries rather than in the United States. Since in the Western Hemisphere the United States had the substance of unchallengeable power, it deemed it the better part of wisdom not to insist upon all the manifestations of the prestige that go with such overwhelming power and to allow some other country in the Western Hemisphere to enjoy at least the appearances of power in the form of prestige. Only with the decline of the Organization of American States and a shift in American policy did this outlook begin to change.

THREE CORRUPTIONS OF THE POLICY OF PRESTIGE

For a nation to pursue a policy of prestige is, however, not enough. It can do too much or too little in this respect, and in either case it will run the risk of failure. It does too much when, insecure in the awareness of its power, it invests a particular move with a measure of prestige out of all proportion to its actual importance. The prestige of a nation is not determined by the success or failure of a particular move at a particular moment in history. Quite to the contrary, it reflects the sum total of a nation's qualities and actions, of its successes and failures, of its historical memories and aspirations. The prestige of a nation is very much like the credit of a bank. A bank with large, proven resources and a record of successes can afford what a small and frequently unsuccessful competitor cannot: to make a mistake or suffer a setback. Its known power is big enough for its prestige to survive such reverses. The same is true of nations.

The pages of history are full of instances of nations that, secure in their possession of great power and recognized as such by their peers, have suffered defeat or retreated from exposed positions without suffering a loss in prestige. When was the prestige of France higher: when it fought wars in Indochina and Algeria that it could neither win nor thought it could afford to lose, or after it had liquidated these losing enterprises? And how much, in the long run, did American prestige suffer from the debacle of the Bay of Pigs in 1962? When France demonstrated the wisdom and courage to liquidate two losing enterprises on which it had staked its "honor," its prestige rose to heights it had not attained since the beginning of the Second World War, and the Bay of Pigs has weighed little in the scales of American prestige, heavy as they are with power and successes. Nations must take care not to confound ephemeral fluctuations of public opinion with the lasting foundations of national power and prestige. Prestige in a particular instance, then, like the power it mirrors, must be seen in the context of a nation's overall power and prestige. The greatness of the latter is reflected in the former, and the deficiences of the former are compensated for by the latter.

A nation also does too much when it paints an exaggerated picture of its power and thus attempts to gain a reputation for power that exceeds the power it actually possesses. In that case it builds its prestige upon the appearances of power rather than upon its substance. Here the policy of prestige transforms itself into a policy of bluff. Its outstanding example in recent history in the policy of Italy from the Ethiopian War of 1935 to the African campaign of 1942. Embarking upon a policy of imperialistic expansion with the purpose of making the Mediterranean an Italian lake, Italy during the Ethiopian War and the Spanish Civil War of 1936–39 dared defy Great Britain, then the foremost naval power on earth and the predominant power in the Mediterranean. It did so by creating the impression that it was a military power of the first order. Italy was successful in this policy so long as no other nation dared to put its pretense of power to the actual test. When this test came, it revealed the contrast between Italy's reputation for power, deliberately created by a number of propagandistic devices, and its actual power. It unmasked its policy of prestige as a policy of bluff.

The essence of a policy of bluff is well illustrated in the theater device of letting a score of extras, dressed as soldiers, walk about the stage, disappear behind the scenery, and come back again and again, thus creating the illusion of a great number of marching men. While the ignorant and the gullible will easily be deceived by this appearance of armed might, the informed and detached observer will not fall victim to the deception. And if the stage directions require that the "army" give battle to another "army" the bluff becomes patent to anyone. Here the policy of bluff is reduced to its essentials, and its mechanics are demonstrated in elemental form. It is easy for the policy of bluff to succeed in the short run, but in the long run it can succeed only if it is able to postpone forever the test of actual performance, and this even the highest quality of statecraft cannot assure.

The best that luck and political wisdom can do is to use the initial success of a policy of bluff for the purpose of bringing the actual power of one's nation up to its reputed quality. While the other nations are bluffed into giving that power undeserved consideration, time is gained for bringing prestige and actual power into harmony. A nation, therefore, that has fallen behind in the competition for power, especially in the field of armaments, might try to conceal its weakness behind a policy of bluff while at the same time endeavoring to overcome its handicap. When Great Britain, in the autumn and winter of 1940–41, was actually open to invasion, its prestige, far exceeding at that time its actual military strength, was probably the most important single factor deterring the Germans from the attempt to invade its territory. Subsequently, while maintaining the appearance of its defensive strength, it was able to acquire actual defensive strength. It must, however, be noted that luck came to the assistance of that policy of bluff in the form of Hitler's military mistakes and that this policy was not so much freely chosen by Great Britain as forced upon it as a desperate last resort by an almost irresistible necessity.[11]

While it thus remains true that it is generally a mistake in international politics to engage in a policy of bluff, it is no less a mistake to go to the other extreme and be satisfied with a reputation for power that is inferior to the actual power possessed. The outstanding examples of this "negative policy of prestige" are the United States and the Soviet Union in the period between the two world wars and, more particularly, in the first years of the Second World War.

At the outbreak of the Second World War, the United States was already potentially the most powerful nation on earth, and it had openly declared its opposition to the imperialism of Germany and Japan. Nevertheless, Germany and Japan proceeded very much as though the United States as a first-rate power did not exist at all. The significance of the attack on Pearl Harbor in view of this discussion lies in the implied expression of contempt for the military strength of the United States. The reputation for power of the United States—that is, its prestige—was so low that Japan could base its war plans upon the assumption that American military strength would not recover from the blow of Pearl Harbor in time to influence the outcome of the war. American prestige was so low that Germany and Italy, instead of trying to keep the United States out of the European war, seemed almost eager to bring it in by declaring war against it

---

[11]One can safely say that in the two most critical periods of its history Great Britain owed its salvation, at least in part, to its prestige. When in 1797 all of Europe was at Napoleon's feet and France concentrated all its efforts upon the destruction of Great Britain, a mutiny broke out in the British fleet. For a time two loyal ships were all that stood between the continent and the British Isles. In the winter of 1940–41, Great Britain was, for however different reasons, similarly helpless. In both situations, the awe in which the British name was held was one of the factors deterring its enemies from an attack that the distribution of material power greatly favored.

on December 10, 1941. Hitler is quoted as having declared in 1934: "The American is no soldier. The inferiority and decadence of this allegedly New World is evident in its military inefficiency."[12]

So enormous a depreciation was primarily due to what can almost be called the absence of an American policy of prestige insofar as reputation for military power is concerned. Far from demonstrating to the other nations what the human and material potentialities of the United States could mean in terms of military power, the United States seemed almost anxious to prove to the world its unwillingness, if not inability, to transform those enormous potentialities into actual instruments of war. Thus the United States invited neglect and attack from its enemies, failure for its policies, mortal danger to its vital interests.

The Soviet Union had to cope with similar results not because it neglected, but because it failed in, its policy of prestige. Throughout the period between the two world wars, the reputation of the Soviet Union for power was low. While Germany, France, and Great Britain at times tried to secure Russian support for their foreign policies, no nation had a sufficiently high opinion of the power of the Soviet Union to overcome the aversion to Russian political ideology and the fear of its spreading through the rest of Europe. When, for instance, during the Czechoslovakian crisis of 1938 France and Great Britain were confronted with the alternative of either approving the imperialistic expansion of Germany or trying to check it with the aid of the Soviet Union, the latter's prestige was so low that the Western European powers rejected its proffered cooperation without much hesitation. The military prestige of the Soviet Union reached its lowest point during the campaign against Finland in 1939–40, when little Finland seemed able to hold its own against the Russian giant. That lack of prestige was one of the factors that convinced the German general staff, as well as the general staffs of the Allied nations, that the Soviet Union would be unable to withstand a German attack.

For a wise foreign policy, however, such discrepancy between prestige and actual power ought not to be a matter of indifference. For if the Soviet Union had appeared to be as powerful in 1938 or 1939 or 1941 as it actually was—that is, if its prestige had then been commensurate with its power—the policies of the other nations with respect to the Soviet Union might easily have been different, and the destiny of the Soviet Union and of the world might have been different as well. Whether today the Soviet Union is as strong as it seems to be, or stronger, or weaker, is a question of fundamental importance for both the Soviet Union and the rest of the world. The same is true of the United States and of any other nation playing an active role in international politics. To demonstrate to the rest of the world the power one's own nation possesses, revealing neither too much nor too little, is the task of a wisely conceived policy of prestige.

---

[12]Hermann Rauschning, *The Voice of Destruction* (New York: G. P. Putnam's Sons, 1940), p. 71.

7 The Ideological Element in International Policies

THE NATURE OF POLITICAL IDEOLOGIES[1]

It is a characteristic aspect of all politics, domestic as well as international, that frequently its basic manifestations do not appear as what they actually are—manifestations of a struggle for power. Rather, the element of power as the immediate goal of the policy pursued is explained and justified in ethical, legal, or biological terms. That is to say, the true nature of the policy is concealed by ideological justifications and rationalizations.

The deeper the individual is involved in the power struggle, the less likely he is to see the power struggle for what it is. The words that Hamlet addresses to his mother might be addressed with equal lack of success to all hungry for power:

> . . . Mother, for love of grace,
> Lay not that flattering unction to your soul,
> That not your trespass, but my madness speaks.

Or, as Tolstoy puts it in *War and Peace:*

> When a man acts alone, he always carries within him a certain series of considerations, that have, as he supposes, directed his past conduct, and that serve to justify to him his present action, and to lead him to make projects for his future activity.

---

[1]The concept of ideology is frequently used in the general sense of philosophic, political, and moral convictions; we are dealing with the subject matter referred to by this general concept of ideology in later parts of this book. The concept of ideology used in this chapter corresponds to what Karl Mannheim has called "particular ideology." See Mannheim, *Ideology and Utopia* (New York: Harcourt, Brace, 1936), p. 49: "The particular conception of ideology is implied when the term denotes that we are sceptical of the ideas and representations advanced by our opponent. They are regarded as more or less conscious disguises of the real nature of a situation, the true recognition of which would not be in accord with his interests. These distortions range all the way from conscious lies to half-conscious and unwitting disguises; from calculated attempts to dupe others to self-deception." See also p. 238: "The study of ideologies has made it its task to unmask the more or less conscious deceptions and disguises of human interest groups, particularly those of political parties."

Assemblies of men act in the same way, only leaving to those who do not take direct part in the action to invent consideration, justifications, and projects concerning their combined activity.

For causes, known or unknown to us, the French began to chop and hack at each other. And to match the event, it is accompanied by its justification in the expressed wills of certain men, who declare it essential for the good of France, for the cause of freedom, of equality. Men cease slaughtering one another, and that event is accompanied by the justification of the necessity of centralisation of power, of resistance to Europe, and so on. Men march from west to east, killing their fellow-creatures, and this event is accompanied by phrases about the glory of France, the baseness of England, and so on. History teaches us that those justifications for the event are devoid of all common sense, that they are inconsistent with one another, as, for instance, the murder of a man as a result of the declaration of his rights, and the murder of millions in Russia for the abasement of England. But those justifications have an incontestable value in their own day.

They remove moral responsibility from those men who produce the events. At the time they do the work of brooms, that go in front to clear the rails for the train: they clear the path of men's moral responsibility. Apart from those justifications, no solution could be found for the most obvious question that occurs to one at once on examining any historical event; that is, How did millions of men come to combine to commit crimes, murders, wars, and so on?[2]

The actor on the political scene cannot help "playing an act" by concealing the true nature of his political actions behind the mask of a political ideology. The more removed the individual is from a particular power struggle, the more likely he is to understand its true nature. So it is not by accident that foreigners have often a better understanding of the politics of a particular country than have the natives and that scholars are better equipped than politicians to understand what politics is all about. On the other hand, politicians have an ineradicable tendency to deceive themselves about what they are doing by referring to their policies not in terms of power but in terms of either ethical and legal principles or biological necessities. In other words, while all politics is necessarily pursuit of power, ideologies render involvement in that contest for power psychologically and morally acceptable to the actors and their audience.

These legal and ethical principles and biological necessities fulfill a dual function in the sphere of international politics. They are either the ultimate goals of political action, of which we have spoken before[3]—that is, those ultimate objectives for the realization of which political power is sought—or they are the pretexts and false fronts behind which the element of power, inherent in all politics, is concealed. These principles and necessities may fulfill one or the other function, or they may fulfill them both at the same time. A legal and ethical principle, such as justice,

[2]Epilogue, Part II, Chapter VII.
[3]See pages 29 ff.

for example, or a biological necessity, such as an adequate standard of living, may be the goal of a foreign policy, or it may be an ideology, or it may be both at the same time. Since we are not concerned here with the ultimate goals of international politics, we shall deal with ethical and legal principles and biological necessities only insofar as they perform the function of ideologies.

These ideologies are not the accidental outgrowth of the hypocrisy of certain individuals who need only to be replaced by other, more honest individuals in order to make the conduct of foreign affairs more decent. Disappointment always follows such expectations. The members of the opposition who were most vocal in exposing the deviousness of Franklin D. Roosevelt's or Churchill's foreign policies shocked their followers, once they had become responsible for the conduct of foreign affairs, by their own use of ideological disguises. It is the very nature of politics to compel the actor on the political scene to use ideologies in order to disguise the immediate goal of his action. The immediate goal of political action is power, and political power is power over the minds and actions of men. Yet those who have been chosen as the prospective object of the power of others are themselves intent upon gaining power over others. Thus the actor on the political scene is always at the same time a prospective master and a prospective subject. While he seeks power over others, others seek power over him.

To this ambivalence of man as a political being corresponds the ambivalence of his moral evaluation of this condition. He will consider his own desire for power as just and will condemn as unjust the desire of others to gain power over him. Since the end of the Second World War, the Russians have found their own designs for power justified by considerations of their own security. But they have condemned as "imperialistic" and preparatory to world conquest the expansion of American power. The United States has put a similar stigma on Russian aspirations, while it views its own international objectives as necessities of national defense. As John Adams put it:

> Power always thinks it has a great soul and vast views beyond the comprehension of the weak and that it is doing God's service when it is violating all His laws. Our passions, ambitions, avarice, love and resentment, etc., possess so much metaphysical subtlety and so much overpowering eloquence that they insinuate themselves into the understanding and the conscience and convert both to their party.

The ambivalence of this evaluation, characteristic of the approach of all nations to the problem of power, is again inherent in the very nature of international politics. The nation that dispensed with ideologies and frankly stated that it wanted power and would, therefore, oppose similar aspirations of other nations, would at once find itself at a great and perhaps decisive disadvantage in the struggle for power. That frank admission would, on the one hand, unite the other nations in fierce resistance to a foreign policy so unequivocally stated and would thereby compel the nation pursuing it to employ more power than would otherwise be necessary. On the other hand, that admission is tantamount to flouting openly the universally accepted moral standards of the international community and would thereby put the particular nation in a position where it would be likely to pursue its foreign policy halfheartedly and with a bad conscience. To rally a people behind the government's foreign policy and to marshal all the national energies and resources to its support, the spokesman of the nation must appeal to biological necessities, such as national existence, and to moral principles, such as justice, rather than to power. This is the only way a nation can attain the enthusiasm and willingness to sacrifice without which no foreign policy can pass the ultimate test of strength.

Such are the psychological forces that inevitably engender the ideologies of international policies and make them weapons in the struggle for power on the international scene. A government whose foreign policy appeals to the intellectual convictions and moral valuations of its own people has gained an incalculable advantage over an opponent who has not succeeded in choosing goals that have such appeal or in making the chosen goals appear to have it. Ideologies, like all ideas, are weapons that may raise the national morale and, with it, the power of one nation and, in the very act of doing so, may lower the morale of the opponent. The enormous contribution Woodrow Wilson's Fourteen Points made to the victory of the Allies in the First World War by strengthening the morale of the Allies and weakening the morale of the Central Powers is the classic example of the importance of the moral factor for international politics.[4]

TYPICAL IDEOLOGIES OF FOREIGN POLICIES

It follows from the nature of international politics that imperialistic policies resort practically always to ideological disguises, whereas status quo policies more frequently can be presented as what they actually are. It also follows from this nature that certain types of ideologies are coordinated with certain types of international policies.

Ideologies of the Status Quo

A policy of the status quo can often afford to reveal its true nature and dispense with ideological disguises, because the status quo has already, by virtue of its very existence, acquired a certain moral legitimacy. What exists must have something in its favor; otherwise it would not exist. As Demosthenes put it:

> For no one would go to war as readily for aggrandizement as for the defense of his own possessions; but while all men fight desperately to keep what they are in danger of losing, it is not so with aggrandizement; men make it, indeed, their aim, but if prevented, they do not feel they have suffered any injustice from their opponents.[5]

---

[4]On the problem of national morale in general, see pages 153 ff.
[5]Demosthenes, *For the Liberty of the Rhodians,* Sections 10–11.

Since a nation that pursues a policy of the status quo seeks the preservation of the power it already has, it may avoid the need to allay the resentment of other nations and its own scruples. This is especially so when the preservation of the territorial status quo is not open to moral or legal attack and when national power has by tradition been exclusively used for the preservation of this status quo. Such nations as Switzerland, Denmark, Norway, and Sweden do not need to hesitate to define their foreign policies in terms of the maintenance of the status quo, since this status quo is generally recognized as legitimate. Other nations, such as Great Britain, France, Yugoslavia, Czechoslovakia, and Rumania, which in the period between the two world wars in the main pursued a policy of the status quo, could not afford simply to declare that their foreign policies aimed at the defense of their possessions. Since the legitimacy of the status quo of 1919 was itself being challenged within and without these nations, they had to invoke moral principles able to meet that challenge. Peace and international law fulfilled that purpose.

Peace and international law are eminently qualified to serve as ideologies for a policy of the status quo. Since imperialistic policies, by disturbing the status quo, frequently lead to war and must always take the possibility of war into account, a foreign policy that proclaims pacifism as its guiding principle is by the same token anti-imperialistic and supports the maintenance of the status quo. By expressing in pacifist terms the objectives of the policy of the status quo, a statesman puts the stigma of war-mongering upon his imperialistic opponents, clears his and his countrymen's conscience of moral scruples, and can hope to win the support of all countries interested in the maintenance of the status quo.[6]

International law fulfills a similar ideological function for policies of the status quo. Any legal order tends to be primarily a static social force. It defines a certain distribution of power and offers standards and processes to ascertain and maintain it in concrete situations. Domestic law, through a highly developed system of legislation, judicial decisions, and law enforcement, allows for adaptions and sometimes even considerable changes within the general distribution of power. International law, in the absence of such a system making for lawful change, is, as will be shown later,[7] not only primarily but essentially, by dint of its very nature, a static force. The invocation of international law, of "order under law," of "ordinary legal processes" in support of a particular foreign policy, therefore, always indicates the ideological disguise of a policy of the status quo. More particularly, when an international organization, such as the League of Nations, has been established for the purpose of maintaining a particular status quo, support of that organization becomes tantamount to support of that particular status quo.

Since the end of the First World War, it has become rather common to make use of such legalistic ideologies in justification of a policy of the status quo. While the alliances of former periods of history have not disappeared, they tend to become "regional arrangements" within an overall legal organization. The "maintenance of

---

[6]See pages 106 and 107, on the recent transformation of the ideology of peace; see also pages 248 and 275 ff.
[7]See Chapter 26.

the status quo" yields to the "maintenance of international peace and security." A number of states that have the same interest in the maintenance of the status quo will be likely to protect their common interests against a threat from a particular source not by a "Holy Alliance" but by a "system of collective security" or a "treaty of mutual assistance." Since changes in the status quo are frequently brought about at the expense of small nations, defense of the rights of small nations, such as of Belgium in 1914 and Finland and Poland in 1939, becomes under appropriate conditions another ideology of the policy of the status quo.

Ideologies of Imperialism

A policy of imperialism is always in need of an ideology; for, in contrast to a policy of the status quo, imperialism always has the burden of proof. It must prove that the status quo it seeks to overthrow deserves to be overthrown and that the moral legitimacy that in the minds of many attaches to things as they are ought to yield to a higher principle of morality calling for a new distribution of power. Thus, in the words of Gibbon: "For every war a motive of safety or revenge, of honor or zeal, of right or convenience, may be readily found in the jurisprudence of conquerors."[8]

Insofar as the typical ideologies of imperialism make use of legal concepts, they cannot well refer to positive international law, that is, to international law as it actually is. As we have seen, the static character of international law, makes it the natural ideological ally of the status quo. The dynamic quality of imperialism requires dynamic ideologies. In the domain of law it is the doctrine of natural law—that is, of the law as it ought to be—that fits the ideological needs of imperialism. Against the injustices of international law as it exists, symbolizing the status quo, the imperialistic nation will invoke a higher law that corresponds to the requirements of justice. Thus National Socialist Germany based its demands for the revision of the status quo of Versailles primarily upon the principle of equality that the Treaty of Versailles was said to have violated. The demand for colonies, for instance, of which the Treaty of Versailles had deprived Germany completely, and the demand for the revision of that treaty's provisions for unilateral disarmament, were derived from the same principle.

When the imperialistic policy is not directed against a particular status quo resulting from a lost war but grows from a power vacuum inviting conquest, moral ideologies that make it an unavoidable duty to conquer take the place of the appeal to a just natural law against an unjust positive law. Then to conquer weak peoples appears as "the white man's burden," the "national mission," "manifest destiny," a "sacred trust," a "Christian duty." Colonial imperialism, in particular, has frequently been disguised by ideological slogans of this kind, such as the "blessings of Western civilization," which it was the mission of the conqueror to bring to the colored races of the earth. The Japanese ideology of the East Asiatic "coprosperity zone" carries the similar connotation of a humanitarian mission. Whenever a political philosophy, held with the fervor of a religious faith, coincides with an imperialistic policy, it

[8]*The Decline and Fall of the Roman Empire* (Modern Library Edition), Vol. II, p. 1235.

becomes a ready instrument of ideological disguise. Arab imperialism during the period of Arab expansion justified itself as the fulfillment of religious duty. Napoleonic imperialism swept over Europe under the banner of "Liberty, Equality, Fraternity." Russian imperialism, especially in its aspirations for Constantinople and the Dardanelles, has successively or simultaneously made use of the Orthodox faith, Pan-Slavism, world revolution, and defense from capitalist encirclement.

In modern times, especially under the influence of the social philosophies of Darwin and Spencer, the ideologies of imperialism have preferred biological arguments. Transferred to international politics, the philosophy of the survival of the fittest sees in the military superiority of a strong nation over a weak one a natural phenomenon that makes the latter the preordained object of the former's power. According to this philosophy, it would be contrary to nature if the strong did not dominate the weak and if the weak tried to be the equal of the strong. The strong nation has a right to a "place in the sun"; it is the "salt of the earth." As the famous German sociologist Werner Sombart discovered in the First World War, the Germanic "hero" must necessarily win out over the British "shopkeeper." That the inferior races should serve the master race is a law of nature that only villains and fools will oppose; slavery and extermination are the latter's just desert.

Communism, fascism, and Nazism, as well as Japanese imperialism, have given these biological ideologies a revolutionary turn. The nations that nature has appointed to be the masters of the earth are kept in inferiority by the trickery and violence of the naturally inferior nations. The vigorous but poor "have-nots" are cut off from the riches of the earth by the wealthy but decadent "haves." The proletarian nations, inspired by ideals, must fight the capitalist nations defending their moneybags. The ideology of overpopulation found particular favor with Germany, Italy, and Japan before the Second World War. The Germans are a "people without space" who, if they cannot obtain "living space," must "suffocate" and, if they cannot obtain sources of raw materials, must "starve." With different variations this ideology was used in the thirties also by Italy and Japan to justify their expansionist policies and to disguise their imperialistic goals.[9]

---

[9]The purely ideological character of the claim for colonies, justified in the period between the two world wars by Germany, Italy, and Japan with population pressure and economic distress, is clearly demonstrated by the relevant population and economic statistics. The four African colonies of Germany covered 930,000 square miles and had, in 1914, a population of almost twelve million, of which only 20,000 were white. It was pointed out at that time that more Germans were living in the city of Paris than in all of Germany's colonies combined. After Eritrea had been an Italian colony for fifty years, the 2,000 square miles of territory most suitable for settlement contained about 400 Italian inhabitants. The Japanese colonies of Korea and Formosa absorbed within a period of forty years less than one year's increase of the Japanese population.

As for the economic importance of colonies to their mother countries, the figures are eloquent in the case of Germany and Italy. The imports from, and the exports to, the German colonies amounted in 1913 to 0.5 percent of the total German imports and exports. In 1933 the imports from the Italian colonies were 1.6 percent of the total imports, and the exports to them were 7.2 percent of all the exports from Italy; a considerable portion of the latter must have consisted of war material. Only for Japan were its colonies of paramount economic importance, its trade with them in 1934 amounting to almost 25 percent of its total trade (23.1 percent of the total imports, 22 percent of the total exports). See Royal Institute of International Affairs, *The Colonial Problem* (London, New York, Toronto: Oxford University Press, 1937), especially p. 287.

The most widely practiced disguise and justification of imperialism has, however, always been the ideology of anti-imperialism.[10] It is so widely used because it is the most effective of all ideologies of imperialism. As, according to Huey Long, fascism will come to the United States in the guise of antifascism, so imperialism has come to many a country in the guise of anti-imperialism. In 1914 as well as in 1939, both sides went to war in order to defend themselves against the imperialism of the other side. Germany attacked the Soviet Union in 1941 in order to forestall the latter's imperialistic designs. Since the end of the Second World War, American and British as well as Russian and Chinese foreign policy has been justified by the imperialistic objectives of other nations. By thus presenting one's own foreign policy, regardless of its actual character, as anti-imperialistic—that is, defensive and protective of the status quo—one gives one's own people that good conscience and confidence in the justice of their own cause without which no people can support its foreign policy wholeheartedly and fight successfully for it. At the same time one may confound the enemy who, ideologically less well prepared, may no longer be certain on which side justice is to be found.

The economic demands that the nations of the Third World have presented contain a strong ideological element. The responsibility for the economic distress of many of these nations, which must be attributed to a variety of reasons, such as natural poverty, irrational economic policies, corruption, and incompetence, is typically laid at the door of the developed rich and industrial nations. One stark and disquieting fact gives the concept of North-South confrontation a semblance of plausibility: the extreme differences in the standard of living between the industrial nations and those of the Third World. From that supposed causal responsibility follows the moral responsibility to make amends for the evils previously wrought and to contribute to a more equal future distribution of the world's wealth. The most salient case in point is the unequal distribution of food, causing excess and gluttony in the industrial nations and chronic undernourishment and even famine in many countries of the Third World. However, both the causal and the moral nexus between abundance in the industrial world and want in the Third World are open to serious question.

Throughout history mankind has been divided by drastic differences in standards of living. What sets the present situation apart is the awareness of these differences by the advantaged and disadvantaged members of mankind owing to the modern technologies of communication. That awareness coincides with the ascendancy of the principle of equality, both of opportunity and condition, throughout the world. Hence the aspirations of the disadvantaged to a narrowing of the gap between the rich and the poor—and the moral embarrassment of the rich in the face of these aspirations.

It goes without saying that these aspirations and the attendant moral embarrassment—both incapable of satisfaction or relief on a worldwide scale—are

---

[10]A variant of the ideology of anti-imperialism is the ideology of anti–power politics. According to this ideology, other nations are motivated in their policies by aspirations for power, while one's own nation, free from such base motives, pursues purely ideal objectives.

extensively used as ideological justifications and rationalizations for specific political aims in the service of concrete national interests. These aims are naturally directed toward changes in the status quo at the expense of the rich and in favor of the poor. The former, aware of the existing extreme inequality, and persuaded by the moral principle that condemns it, are at an obvious disadvantage in defining and promoting their own interests; they must do so, as it were, with a bad conscience, no longer fully convinced of the rightness of their case. Faced with the claim to economic equality, they are in a morally helpless position, one similar to that in which the Western democracies found themselves in 1938 when confronted with the German claim to a part of Czechoslovakia, advanced in the name of the moral principle of national self-determination.

The moral argument in favor of the equalization of the standard of living throughout the world appears as a special application of the general argument in support of humanitarian aid to nations in distress. The United States has accepted this obligation in theory and practice. However, the situation providing a moral justification for humanitarian aid differs fundamentally from the one calling for equalization of the standard of living throughout the world. Humanitarian aid is justified by a sudden natural catastrophe, the consequences of which the affected country finds hard to remedy with its own resources alone. The worldwide differences in the standard of living are the result of a complex of natural, cultural, economic, and political factors. Outside intervention may be able to modify such differences in specific instances, but it cannot expect to eliminate them through-out the world. It is this impossibility to achieve—even with the best of intentions and the most extensive commitment of resources—what is presumed to be morally required that negates the moral obligation. The principle of Roman law *ultra vires nemo obligatur* (beyond his ability nobody is obligated) applies also to presumed moral obligations.

The supposed moral obligation for the industrialized, rich nations to raise the standard of living of the nonindustrialized, poor nations throughout the world is grounded in the causal relationship that is presumed to exist between the policies and the high standard of living of the former and the low standard of living of the latter. However, the assumption of a simple causal relationship of this kind is a myth. The colonialists, imperialists, and capitalists perform here the function of the devil to whom the evils of underdevelopment can be traced. In truth, these evils have multiple causes, of which colonialism, imperialism, and capitalism are, at best, only one.

The elimination of inequalities in food supply is, then, not only—and not even primarily—a matter of agricultural technology and collective generosity but of political interest and will. In many societies the perpetuation of poverty, of which the scarcity of food is a striking manifestation, is not just another unfortunate accident to be remedied by technological reform but the result of deliberate social, economic, and political choices. If one wants to rid the world of hunger, one has to rid these societies of the arrangements that have caused it. More likely than not, that means radical reform—if not revolution. Whether the political elites of Third World nations are willing to follow their own rhetoric is a matter of controversy.

Thus the terms in which the so-called North-South conflict is fought out between the have and the have-not nations of the world in good measure conceal and at the same time justify a conflict between the traditionally powerful and the new politically weak nations whose main real object is exactly a new distribution of power.

Ambiguous Ideologies

The ideology of anti-imperialism draws its effectiveness from its ambiguity. It confounds the observer, who cannot always be sure whether he is dealing with an ideology of imperialism or with the true expression of a policy of the status quo. This confounding effect is present whenever an ideology is not made to order, as it were, for a particular type of policy but can be worn by the defenders of the status quo, as well as by the promoters of imperialism. Traditionally, and more particularly in the eighteenth and nineteenth centuries, the balance of power has been used as an ideological weapon by the defenders of the status quo and the promoters of imperialism.[11] In our time the ideologies of national self-determination and of the United Nations have performed a similar function. Since the beginning of the Cold War, they have been joined to an ever-increasing extent by the ideologies of peace, relaxation of tensions, and détente.

The principle of national self-determination, as conceived by Woodrow Wilson, justified the liberation of the Central and Eastern European nationalities from foreign domination. Theoretically, it was opposed not only to the status quo of empire but also to imperialism of any kind, either on the part of the old imperial powers—Germany, Austria, and Russia—or on the part of the liberated small nations. Yet the destruction of the old imperial order at once called forth, still in the name of self-determination, new imperialisms. Those of Poland, Czechoslovakia, Rumania, and Yugoslavia are as outstanding as they were inevitable; for the power vacuum left by the breakdown of the old imperial order had to be filled and the newly liberated nations were there to fill it. As soon as they had installed themselves in power, they invoked the self-same principle of national self-determination in defense of the new status quo. This principle was their most potent ideological weapon from the end of the First to the end of the Second World War.

It was by a stroke of propagandistic genius that Hitler hit upon the principle of national self-determination in order to disguise and justify his policies of territorial expansion. The German minorities of Czechoslovakia and Poland, under the banner of national self-determination, were now to play the same role in undermining the national existence of Czechoslovakia and Poland that the Czech, Slovak, and Polish nationalities, under the same ideological banner, had played in undermining the national existence of the Austrian-Hungarian Empire. With their own ideological weapon turned against them, the benefactors of the status quo of Versailles had no ideology, except the one of law and order, with

---

[11]See, for discussion in greater detail, pages 222 ff.

which to defend that status quo. Thus Austria and Czechoslovakia were surrendered, and Poland was exposed to mortal danger. After the settlement of Munich granted the German demands with regard to Czechoslovakia, the London *Times*, making the German ideology its own, declared: "Self-determination, the professed principle of the Treaty of Versailles, has been invoked by Herr Hitler against its written text, and his appeal has been allowed."[12] Rarely, if ever, has modern history offered a more striking example of the importance of ideologies in international politics and of the confounding effect of an ambiguous ideology aptly employed.

The ideology of national self-determination also plays a crucial part in the conflict between Israel and the Arab states. The Arab claims of national self-determination, in order to do them justice, must be put in the political context from which they have risen and within which they are supposed to operate. Arab claims for Palestinian self-determination must be seen in the context of the continuous opposition of most Arabs to the existence not only of the state of Israel but of Jewish settlements within the territory of Palestine. In other words, recognition of Israel as a state is incompatible with the claim to national self-determination of the Palestinian Arabs. For their claim is based not only upon the West Bank of the Jordan but—as innumerable pronouncements of the Palestine Liberation Organization (PLO) claim—upon the whole territory on which the state of Israel has been erected. Thus the principle of national self-determination on behalf of the Palestinian Arabs reveals itself as an ideological disguise for the unchanging aspiration of Arabs to destroy the state of Israel and establish an Arab state in its place. When Francis I of France was asked why he always made war against Charles V of Hapsburg, he replied: "Because both of us want the same thing, Italy." The same reply, substituting Palestine for Italy, could be given by the leaders of Israel and the PLO.

The United Nations was intended at its inception to serve as an instrument of China, France, Great Britain, the Soviet Union, and the United States, and of their allies, for maintaining the status quo as established by the victory of these nations in the Second World War. But in the years immediately following the conclusion of the Second World War, this status quo proved to be only provisional and subject to contradictory interpretations and claims by the different nations. The ideology of the United Nations is, therefore, used by these different nations for the purpose of justifying their particular interpretations and disguising their particular claims. All nations appear as the champions of the United Nations and quote its Charter in support of the particular policies they are pursuing. These policies being contradictory, the reference to the United Nations and its Charter becomes an ideological device justifying one's own policy in the light of generally accepted principles and at the same time concealing its true character. Its ambiguity makes this ideology a weapon with which to confound one's enemies and strengthen one's friends.

---

[12]London *Times*, September 28, 1938.

Since the end of the Second World War, the ideologies of peace, relaxation of tensions, and détente have to an ever increasing extent come to perform a similar function. In view of the general fear of a third world war, fought with the modern weapons of mass destruction, no government can expect to gain support for its foreign policies from its own and other peoples if it cannot convince them of its peaceful intentions. Thus "peace congresses," "peace offensives," and "peace crusades" have become standard weapons of propaganda in the Cold War. These well-nigh universal professions of peaceful intentions are meaningless as references to the actual foreign policies pursued, since it can well be taken for granted that, in view of the incalculable destructiveness of modern war, all nations would rather pursue their aims by peaceful means than by war. Yet by the same token these professions perform two important political functions. They tend to conceal the actual policies pursued behind a veil of professed peaceful purposes. They also tend to attract support of men of good will everywhere for these policies, whatever they may actually be, since they are presented as aiming at the preservation of peace, a goal that men of good will everywhere ardently desire.

Similar considerations apply to the well-nigh universal commitment to disarmament, especially in its "general and complete" form. An end to the armaments race is widely considered desirable on humanitarian, political, and economic grounds. But it is obvious from the experience of the last two decades that the political conditions of the world make disarmament impossible.[13] When, in view of this complete failure of all attempts at disarmament of any kind, governments declare as their policy "general and complete" disarmament, they are actually making an ideological appeal to the nations of the world yearning for peace and relief from the burdens of competitive armaments. This appeal serves the purpose of making the foreign policies actually pursued more acceptable to the other nations than they might otherwise be.

THE PROBLEM OF RECOGNITION

To see through these ideological disguises and grasp behind them the actual political forces and phenomena is, then, one of the most important and most difficult tasks for the student of international politics. This task is important because, unless it is done, it is impossible to determine correctly the character of the foreign policy with which one happens to deal. The recognition of imperialistic tendencies and of their particular character depends upon a clear distinction between the ideological pretense that generally disavows imperialistic aspirations altogether and the actual objectives of the policies pursued. To make this distinction correctly is difficult because of the general difficulty of detecting the true meaning of any human action apart from what the actor believes or feigns it to mean. This general problem is aggravated by two other difficulties peculiar, at least in their generality,

---

[13]See for an extensive discussion of the reasons for the failure of disarmament below, Chapter 23.

to international politics. One is to distinguish a boast or bluff indicative of a policy of prestige from an ideological disguise of actual imperialism. The other is to discover behind an ideology of the status quo or of localized imperialism the true meaning of the policy actually pursued.

We have already had occasion to refer to the foreign policy of William II, which conveyed through its language and manifestations the impression of being openly imperialistic while it was actually a strange mixture of imperialistic designs and neurotic boastfulness. Conversely, the true imperialistic essence of the foreign policies of Hitler and Mussolini was not generally recognized up to the late thirties, being explained away as mere bluff and boastfulness for home consumption. To determine the true character of a foreign policy behind its deliberate or unconscious ideological disguise becomes particularly difficult when the ideologies of the status quo are used as a disguise. The period following the Second World War offers striking examples of this difficulty in the foreign policies of the United States and the Soviet Union.

Both nations have expressed the objectives of their foreign policies in the almost identical terms of status quo ideologies. Both the Soviet Union and the United States have proclaimed that they have no territorial ambitions beyond the line of military demarcation that was established by the agreements of Teheran, Yalta, and Potsdam and through understandings among the military commanders at the end of the war; that they want to see free and democratic governments established everywhere; that they are guided by considerations of security and national defense; and that it is the capitalist or Communist imperialism of the other side against which they are compelled, in spite of their own wishes, to defend themselves.

Most Americans and most Russians are obviously convinced that these statements are a faithful expression of the true character of their countries' foreign policy. Yet they cannot both be right, while one or the other or both may be wrong. For it may be that the Soviet Union misunderstands the foreign policy of the United States or that the United States misunderstands the foreign policy of the Soviet Union, or that both misunderstand each other. The solution of this riddle upon which the fate of the world may well depend is not to be sought in the character of the ideologies alone but in the sum total of the factors determining the foreign policy of a nation. Of this, more will be said later.[14]

---

[14]See Part Ten.

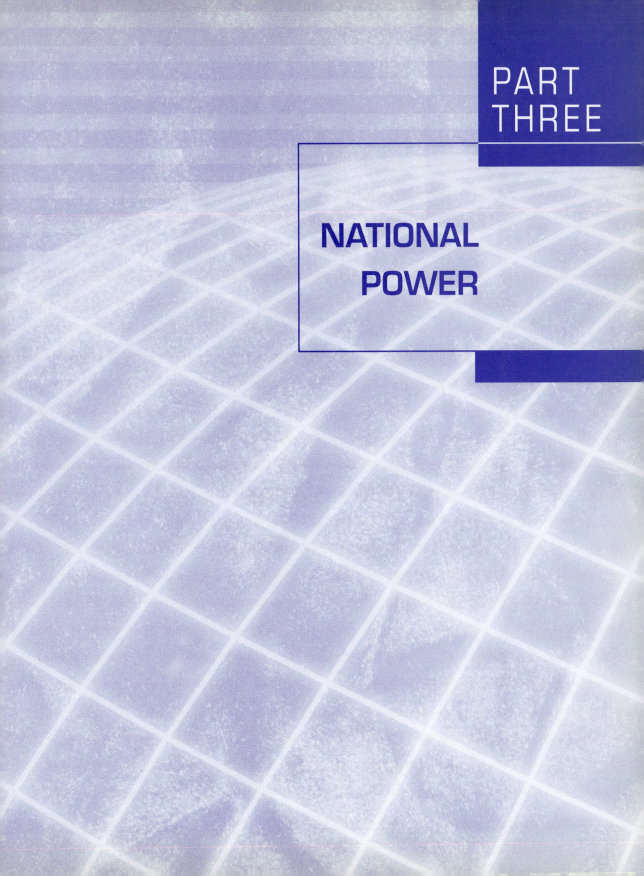

PART
THREE

NATIONAL
POWER

8 The Essence of National Power

WHAT IS NATIONAL POWER?

We have said that by power we mean the power of man over the minds and actions of other men, a phenomenon to be found whenever human beings live in social contact with one another. We have spoken of the "power of a nation" or of "national power" as though the concept were self-evident and sufficiently explained by what we have said about power in general. Yet, while it can be easily understood that individuals seek power, how are we to explain the aspirations for power in the collectivities called nations? What is a nation? What do we mean when we attribute to a nation aspirations and actions?

A nation as such is obviously not an empirical thing. A nation as such cannot be seen. What can be empirically observed are only the individuals who belong to a nation. Hence, a nation is an abstraction from a number of individuals who have certain characteristics in common, and it is these characteristics that make them members of the same nation. Besides being a member of a nation and thinking, feeling, and acting in that capacity, the individual may belong to a church, a social or an economic class, a political party, a family and may think, feel, and act in these capacities. Apart from being a member of all these social groups, he is also a human being pure and simple, and thinks, feels, and acts in that capacity. Therefore, when we speak in empirical terms of the power or of the foreign policy of a certain nation, we can mean only the power or the foreign policy of certain individuals who belong to the same nation. As Marcel Proust put it: "The life of nations merely repeats, on a larger scale, the lives of their component cells; and he who is incapable of understanding the mystery, the reactions, the laws that determine the movements of the individual can never hope to say anything worth listening to about the struggles of nations."

Yet this poses another difficulty. The power or the foreign policy of the United States is obviously not the power or the foreign policy of all the individuals who belong to the nation called the United States of America. The fact that the

United States emerged from the Second World War as the most powerful nation on earth has not affected the power of the great mass of individual Americans. It has, however, affected the power of all those individuals who administer the foreign affairs of the United States and, more particularly, speak for and represent the United States on the international scene. For a nation pursues foreign policies as a legal organization called a state, whose agents act as the representatives of the nation in international affairs. They speak for it, negotiate treaties in its name, define its objectives, choose the means for achieving them, and try to maintain, increase, and demonstrate its power. They are the individuals who, when they appear as representatives of their nation on the international scene, wield the power and pursue the policies of their nation. It is to them that we refer when we speak in empirical terms of the power and of the foreign policy of a nation.

How, then, does it come about that the great mass of the individual members of a nation, whose individual power is not affected by the vicissitudes of national power, identify themselves with the power and the foreign policies of their nation, experience this power and these policies as their own, and do so with an emotional intensity often surpassing the emotional attachment to their individual aspirations for power? By asking this question, we are posing the problem of modern nationalism. In preceding periods of history, the collectivity with whose power and aspirations for power the individual identified himself was determined by ties of blood, of religion, or of common loyalty to a feudal lord or prince. In our time the identification with the power and policies of the nation has largely superseded or, in any case, overshadows those older identifications. How is this phenomenon of modern nationalism to be explained?

We have learned from our discussion of the ideologies of foreign policies that in the mind of the individual the power aspirations of others bear the stigma of immorality. While this attitude has one of its roots in the desire of the prospective victim of the power of others to defend his freedom against this threat, the other root grows from the attempt of society as a whole to suppress and keep in bounds individual aspirations for power. Society has established a network of rules of conduct and institutional devices for controlling individual power drives. These rules and devices either divert individual power drives into channels where they cannot endanger society, or else they weaken them or suppress them altogether. Law, ethics, and mores, innumerable social institutions and arrangements—such as competitive examinations, election contests, sports, social clubs, and fraternal organizations—all serve that purpose.

In consequence, most people are unable to satisfy their desire for power within the national community. Within that community only a relatively small group permanently wields power over great numbers of people without being subject to extensive limitations by others. The great mass of the population is to a much greater extent the object of power than it is its wielder. Not being able to find full satisfaction of their desire for power within the national boundaries, the people project those unsatisfied aspirations onto the international scene. There they find vicarious satisfaction in identification with the power drives of the nation. When the citizen of the United States thinks of the power of his country, he experiences the same kind of exaltation the citizen of Rome must have felt when, identifying himself with Rome and its power and by the same token contrasting himself with the stranger, he would say: *"Civis Romanus sum."* When we are conscious of being members of a very powerful nation, the nation whose industrial capacity and material wealth are unsurpassed, we flatter ourselves and feel a great pride. It is as though we all, not as individuals but collectively, as members of the same nation, owned and controlled so magnificent a power. The power our representatives wield on the international scene becomes our own, and the frustrations we experience within the national community are compensated for by the vicarious enjoyment of the power of the nation.

These psychological trends, operating within the individual members of a nation, find support in the rules of conduct and in the institutions of society itself. Society restrains aspirations for individual power within the national community and puts the mark of opprobrium upon certain power drives pointing toward individual aggrandizement. But it encourages and glorifies the tendencies of the great mass of the population, frustrated in its individual power drives, to identify itself with the nation's struggle for power on the international scene. Power pursued by the individual for his own sake is considered an evil to be tolerated only within certain bounds and in certain manifestations. Power disguised by ideologies and pursued in the name and for the sake of the nation becomes a good for which all citizens must strive. The national symbols, especially insofar as they have reference to the armed forces and the relations with other nations, are instruments of that identification of the individual with the power of the nation. The ethics and mores of society tend to make that identification attractive by holding out rewards and threatening punishments.

Thus it is not by accident that certain groups of the population are either the most militant supporters of the national aspirations for power in the international field, or else refuse to have anything to do with them at all. These are the groups that are primarily the object of the power of others and are most thoroughly deprived of outlets for their own power drives or are most insecure in the possession of whatever power they may have within the national community. The lower middle classes especially, such as the white-collar workers, but also the main bulk of the laboring masses,[1] identify themselves completely with the national aspirations for power. Or else—and here the main example is the revolutionary proletariat in the heyday of Marxism, particularly in Europe—they do not identify themselves with national aspirations at all. While the latter group has thus far been of small concern for the foreign policies of the United States, the former has taken on ever greater importance.

It is here, then, that one must seek the roots of modern nationalism and the explanation for the increasing ferocity with which foreign policies are pursued in modern times. The growing insecurity of the individual in Western societies,

---

[1]They have, in terms of power, less to lose and more to gain from nationalistic foreign policies than any other group of the population, with the exception of the military.

especially in the lower strata, and the atomization of Western society in general have magnified enormously the frustration of individual power drives. This, in turn, has given rise to an increased desire for compensatory identification with the collective national aspirations for power. These increases have been quantitative as well as qualitative.

ROOTS OF MODERN NATIONALISM

Until the time of the Napoleonic Wars, only very small groups of the population identified themselves with the foreign policies of their nation. Foreign policies were truly not national but dynastic policies, and the identification was with the power and the policies of the individual monarch rather than with the power and the policies of a collectivity, such as the nation. As Goethe put it in a significant passage of his autobiography: "We all felt for Frederick [the Great], but what did we care for Prussia?"

"These [scientific] societies," wrote Thomas Jefferson to John Hollins on February 19, 1809, "are always at peace, however their nations may be at war. Like the republic of letters, they form a great fraternity spreading over the whole earth, and their correspondence is never interrupted by any civilized nation."

With the Napoleonic Wars began the period of national foreign policies and wars—that is, the identification of the great masses of the citizens of a nation with national power and national policies, replacing identification with dynastic interests. Talleyrand pointed to that change when he said to Czar Alexander in 1808: "The Rhine, the Alps, and the Pyrenées are the conquests of France; the rest, of the Emperor; they mean nothing to France." Up to the First World War it was doubtful to what degree the members of the European socialist parties identified themselves with the power and policies of their respective nations. Yet the full participation in that war of the main bulk of the workers in all belligerent countries demonstrated the identification of practically the whole population with the power and policies of their respective nations.

Retreat from Nationalism: Apparent and Real

The Second World War has, however, brought about a certain retrogression from that maximum of identification that the First World War witnessed. That retrogression took place on the top and at the base of the social pyramid. On the one hand, small yet powerful profascist groups of intellectual, political, and military leaders in Great Britain and France either refused to identify themselves with their countries or even preferred to identify themselves with the national enemy. The leaders who felt this way were insecure in their power positions, especially in view of the initial political and military weakness of their countries, and the enemy alone seemed to be able to assure them their positions on top of the social pyramid. On the other hand, the French Communists, owing allegiance to both France and the Soviet Union, were able to identify themselves fully with their nation only after the German attack on the Soviet Union in 1941 had brought both allegiances into play. The German attack on France alone was unable to rouse them to active opposition to the invader. But the German attack on the Soviet Union made France and the Soviet Union allies in a common cause and allowed the French Communists to oppose in the German invaders of France the common enemy of France and the Soviet Union alike. The identification of the French Communists with French national policies was predicated upon the identity of those policies with Russian interests and policies. This Communist allegiance to foreign interests and policies, to take precedence over the national ones, was a universal phenomenon that, as such, was a challenge to the cohesion of the nation-state and to its very existence.[2]

This disintegration of national solidarity can hardly be called a retreat from nationalism, for it exchanges loyalty to a foreign nation for loyalty to one's own. The Communist Frenchman, as it were, transformed himself into a Russian nationalist who supports the policies of the Soviet Union. What is new in this nationalism is its inconsistency in demanding identification with one–foreign–nation while denying the claims of other nations to the loyalty of their citizens.

It testifies to the strength of national solidarity that even this transfer of loyalty from one's own nation to another one, which is the fountainhead of a worldwide political movement, has proven to be an ephemeral interlude. For we are witnessing the revival of national solidarity in Communist governments and movements, which have begun in differing degrees to put their respective national interests ahead of the interests of the Soviet Union. The monolithic world Communist movement, directed by, and at the service of, the Soviet Union, has been replaced by "polycentrism," in which national loyalties and interests take precedence over the affinities of political philosophy.

However, the aftermath of the Second World War has brought into being a genuine retrogression from nationalism in the form of a movement toward the unification of Western Europe. This movement has thus far to its credit several concrete achievements in terms of working supranational organizations, including the European Coal and Steel Community, the Common Market (European Economic Community), and Euratom (European Atomic Energy Community).[3] Two experiences have given birth to the movement toward European unification: the destructiveness of the Second World War and the political, military, and economic decline of Europe in its aftermath. The supporters of this movement cannot help concluding from these experiences that, in Western Europe at least, the nation state is an obsolescent principle of political organization that, far from assuring the security and power of its members, condemns them to impotence and ultimate extinction either by each other or by their more powerful neighbors. Only the future will show whether this acute sense of insecurity, not only of the individuals but also of the national societies to which they belong, will lead to

---

[2]See also Chapter 30.
[3]See, on these and similar organizations, pages 532 ff.

political creativity in the form of the political, military, and economic unification of Europe, or to political impotence in the form of a retreat into "neutralism"– that is, the renunciation of an active foreign policy altogether–or to political desperation in the form of a more intense identification with the individual nations.

A force that runs counter to the revival of nationalism is the growing recognition by statesmen, intellectuals, and technical experts that certain fundamental problems posed by the modern technologies of transportation, communications, and warfare transcend the interests and the ability to solve of any single nation, however powerful. The control of nuclear energy, the protection and restoration of the natural environment, and the supply of food and raw materials are problems of this kind. They cannot be solved by an individual nation competing with other nations for national advantage. All nations, or a considerable number of them, have a common interest in the solution of these problems, which interest ought to be reflected in common policies transcending particular national interests. While some small elites have become aware of this novel element in world politics and are trying to come intellectually to terms with it, the actual conduct of national foreign policies has hardly been affected by it. To the contrary, it testifies to the undiminished strength of nationalism that organizations, such as the United Nations and its specialized agencies, created for the purpose of realizing the common interests of the nations of the world, have been seized by competing nationalisms for the purpose of serving competing national interests.[4]

Personal Insecurity and Social Disintegration

Qualitatively, the emotional intensity of the identification of the individual with his nation stands in inverse proportion to the stability of the particular society as reflected in the sense of security of its members. The greater the stability of society and the sense of security of its members, the smaller are the chances for collective emotions to seek an outlet in aggressive nationalism, and vice versa.[5] The revolutionary wars of France in the last decade of the eighteenth century and the wars of liberation against Napoleon in 1812–15 are the first examples in modern times of mass insecurity, induced by the instability of domestic societies and leading to emotional outbursts in the form of fervent mass identifications with aggressive foreign policies and wars. Social instability became acute in Western civilization during the nineteenth century. It became permanent in the twentieth century as a result of the emancipation of the individual from the ties of tradition, especially in the form of religion, of the increased rationalization of life and work, and of cyclical economic crises. The insecurity of the groups affected by these factors found an emotional outlet in fixed and emotionally accentuated nationalistic identifications. As Western society became ever more unstable, the sense of insecurity deepened and the emotional attachment to the nation as

---

[4]See also the discussion below, pages 526 ff.
[5]These collective emotions may, of course, seek an outlet in aggressiveness within the nation as well—that is, in the form of class struggle, revolution, and civil war.

the symbolic substitute for the individual became ever stronger. Under the impact of the world wars, revolutions, concentration of economic, political, and military power, and the economic crises of the twentieth century it reached the fervor of a secular religion. Contests for power now took on the ideological aspects of struggles between good and evil. Foreign policies transformed themselves into sacred missions. Wars were fought as crusades, for the purpose of bringing the true political religion to the rest of the world.

This relation between social disintegration, personal insecurity, and the ferocity of modern nationalistic power drives can be studied to particular advantage in German fascism, where these three elements were more highly developed than anywhere else. The general tendencies of the modern age toward social disintegration were driven to extremes in Germany by a conjunction of certain elements in the national character favoring the extremes rather than mediating and compromising positions, and by three events that weakened the social fabric of Germany to such an extent as to make it an easy prey for the consuming fire of National Socialism.

The first of these events was the defeat in the First World War, coinciding with a revolution that was held responsible not only for the destruction of traditional political values and institutions but for the loss of the war itself. The revolution naturally brought loss of power and insecurity in social status to those who had been at or near the top of the social hierarchy under the monarchy. Yet the social situation of large masses of the population was similarly affected by the impact of the idea that defeat and revolution were both the result of treacherous machinations of domestic and foreign enemies working for the destruction of Germany. Thus it was widely held not only that Germany was "encircled" by foreign enemies but that its own body politic was shot through with invisible hostile organisms, sapping its strength and bent upon destroying it.

The second event was the inflation of the early twenties, which proletarized economically large sectors of the middle classes and weakened, if not destroyed, in the people at large the traditional moral principles of honesty and fair dealing. The middle classes, in protest against their economic proletarization, embraced the most antiproletarian and nationalistic ideologies available. The lower strata of the middle classes especially had always derived at least a limited satisfaction from their superiority to the proletariat. When they viewed the social pyramid as a whole, they had always to look up much farther than they were able to look down. Yet, while they were not actually at the bottom of the social pyramid, they were uncomfortably close to it. Hence their frustrations and insecurity and their predisposition for the nationalistic identification. Now inflation pushed them down to the bottom, and in the desperate struggle to escape social and political identification with the amorphous mass of the proletariat, they found succor in the theory and practice of National Socialism. For National Socialism offered them lower races to look down upon and foreign enemies to feel superior to and conquer.

Finally, the economic crisis of 1929 brought all the different groups of the German people in different ways face to face with the actual or threatened loss of social status and intellectual, moral, and economic insecurity. The workers were faced with actual or threatened permanent unemployment. Those groups of the middle classes who had recovered from the economic devastation of inflation were losing what they had regained. The industrialists had to cope with increased social obligations and were haunted by the fear of revolution. National Socialism focused all those fears, insecurities, and frustrations upon two foreign enemies: the Treaty of Versailles and bolshevism, and their alleged domestic supporters. It channeled all those thwarted emotions into one mighty stream of nationalistic fanaticism. Thus National Socialism was able to identify in a truly totalitarian fashion the aspirations of the individual German with the power objectives of the German nation. Nowhere in modern history has that identification been more complete. Nowhere has that sphere in which the individual pursues his aspirations for power for their own sake been smaller. Nor has the force of the emotional impetus with which that identification transformed itself into aggressiveness on the international scene been equaled in modern civilization.

While the transformation of individual frustrations into collective identification with the nation has never in modern history been more comprehensive and intensive then it was in National Socialist Germany, nevertheless the German variety of modern nationalism differs in degree rather than in kind from the nationalism of other great powers, such as that of the Soviet Union or of the United States. In the Soviet Union the great mass of the population has no opportunity to satisfy its power drives within the domestic society. The average Russian worker and peasant has nobody to look down upon, and his insecurity is intensified by the practices of the police state as well as by a low standard of living. Here, too, a totalitarian regime projects these frustrations, insecurities, and fears onto the international scene where the individual Russian finds in the identification with "the most progressive country in the world," "the fatherland of socialism" vicarious satisfaction for his aspirations for power. The conviction, seemingly supported by historical experience, that the nation with which he identifies himself is constantly menaced by capitalist enemies serves to elevate his personal fears and insecurities onto the collective plane. His personal fears are thus transformed into anxiety for the nation. Identification with the nation thus serves the dual function of satisfying individual power drives and alleviating individual fears by projecting both onto the international scene.

In the United States the process by which national power is appropriated by the individual and experienced as his own resembles by and large the typical pattern as it developed in Western civilization during the nineteenth century. This is to say, the identification of the individual with the power and the foreign policies of the nation proceeds largely in terms of the typical frustrations and insecurities of the middle class. Yet American society is to a much greater extent a middle-class society than any other society in Western civilization. More importantly, whatever class distinctions there may be tend to be mitigated, if not resolved, in American society by the common denominator of middle-class values and aspirations. The identification of the individual with the nation in terms of middle-class frustrations and aspirations is, therefore, almost as predominant and typical in American society as the proletarian identification is in the Soviet Union. On the other hand, the relatively great mobility of American society opens to the great masses of the population avenues for social and economic improvement. These opportunities have in the past, at least in normal times, tended to keep rather low the emotional intensity of that identification as compared with the corresponding situations in the Soviet Union and in National Socialist Germany.[6]

New factors have, however, arisen in recent times with the increasing atomization of society, the threat of world revolution as symbolized by international Communism, the relative disappearance of geographical isolation, and the danger of nuclear war. Thus, in the last quarter of the twentieth century, intensified individual frustrations and anxieties have called forth a more intensive identification, on the part of the individual, with the power and the foreign policies of the nation. If, therefore, the present trend toward ever-increasing domestic frustration and international instability is not reversed, the United States is likely to partake to a growing extent in those tendencies in modern culture that have found their most extreme manifestations in Soviet Russia and National Socialist Germany, tendencies that make for an ever more complete and intensive identification of the individual with the nation. In this completeness and intensity of identification we have one of the roots of the ferocity and ruthlessness of modern foreign policies where national aspirations for power clash with each other, supported by virtually total populations with an unqualified dedication and intensity of feeling, which in former periods of history only the issues of religion could command.

---

[6]Intense nationalistic identification in the United States has been associated in the past mainly with antagonism, on the part of the most insecure sector of the middle class, against certain ethnic groups, such as the Negro or the latest wave of proletarian immigrants.

9 Elements of National Power

What are the factors that make for the power of a nation vis-à-vis other nations? What are the components of what we call national power? If we want to determine the power of a nation, what factors are we to take into consideration? Two groups of elements have to be distinguished: those that are relatively stable and those that are subject to constant change.

GEOGRAPHY

The most stable factor upon which the power of a nation depends is obviously geography. For instance, the fact that the continental territory of the United States is separated from other continents by bodies of water three thousand miles wide to the east and more than six thousand miles wide to the west is a permanent factor that determines the position of the United States in the world. It is a truism to say that the importance of this factor today is not what it was in the times of George Washington or President McKinley. But it is fallacious to assume, as is frequently done, that the technical development of transportation, communications, and warfare has eliminated altogether the isolating factor of the oceans. This factor is certainly much less important today than it was fifty or a hundred years ago, but from the point of view of the power position of the United States, it still makes a great deal of difference that the United States is separated from the continents of Europe and Asia by wide expanses of water instead of bordering directly on, let us say, France, China, or Russia. In other words, the geographical location of the United States remains a fundamental factor of permanent importance that the foreign policies of all nations must take into account, however different its bearing upon political decisions might be today from what it was in other periods of history.

Similarly, the separation of Great Britain from the European continent by a small body of water, the English Channel, is a factor that Julius Caesar could no more afford to overlook than could William the Conqueror, Philip II, Napoleon, or Hitler. However much other factors may have altered its importance throughout the course of history, what was important two thousand years ago is still important today, and all those concerned with the conduct of foreign affairs must take it into account.

What is true of the insular location of Great Britain is true of the geographic position of Italy. The Italian peninsula is separated from the rest of Europe by the high mountain massif of the Alps, and while the valleys of the Alps descend gradually southward toward the north Italian plain, they precipitate abruptly toward the north. This geographical situation has been an important element in the political and military considerations of Italy and of other nations with regard to Italy. For, under all conditions of warfare of which we know, this geographical situation has made it extremely difficult to invade Central Europe from Italy, while it has made it much less difficult to invade Italy from the north. In consequence, invasions of Italy have been much more frequent than invasions by Italy. From Hannibal in the Punic Wars to General Clark in the Second World War, this permanent geographical factor has determined political and military strategy.

The Pyrenees have fulfilled for the international position of Spain a somewhat different, but no less permanent, function. It has been said that Europe ends at the Pyrenees. The Pyrenees, by making Spain difficult of access to the outside world, have indeed functioned as a barrier shutting Spain off from the mainstream of the intellectual, social, economic, and political developments that transformed the rest of Europe. Spain has also been bypassed by most of the great political and military conflagrations of continental Europe. This position on the sidelines of continental politics is at least partially the result of that geographical seclusion provided by the mountain barrier of the Pyrenees.

Finally, let us consider the geographical situation of the Soviet Union. The Soviet Union constitutes an enormous land mass that extends over one-seventh of the land area of the earth and is two and one-half times as large as the territory of the United States. While it is about five thousand miles by air from the Bearing Straits to Koenigsberg, the capital of what was formerly East Prussia, now called Kaliningrad, it is half that distance from Murmansk at the Barents Sea to Ashkhabad at the northern frontier of Iran. This territorial extension is a permanent source of great strength that has thus far frustrated all attempts at military conquest from the outside. This enormous land mass dwarfed the territory conquered by foreign invaders in comparison with what still remained to be conquered.

Conquest of a considerable portion of a country without prospects for speedy recovery usually breaks the will to resist of the conquered people. This is, as we have seen, the political purpose of military conquests. Similar conquests—especially if, as under Napoleon and Hitler, they did not have a limited objective but aimed at the very existence of Russia as a nation—had a rather stimulating effect upon Russian resistance. For not only were the conquered parts of Russia small in comparison with those which were left in Russian hands, but the task of the invader became more difficult with every step he advanced. He had to keep an ever greater number of troops supplied over ever lengthening lines of communication deep in a hostile country. Thus geography has made the conquest of Russian territory, as soon as the objectives of such conquest became ill defined and tended to become unlimited, a liability for the conqueror rather than an asset.

Instead of the conqueror's swallowing the territory and gaining strength from it, it is rather the territory that swallows the conqueror, sapping his strength.

The possibility of nuclear war has enhanced the importance of the size of territory as a source of national power. In order to make a nuclear threat credible, a nation requires a territory large enough to disperse its industrial and population centers as well as its nuclear installations. The conjunction between the large radius of nuclear destruction and the relatively small size of their territories imposes a severe handicap upon the ability of the traditional nation-states, such as Great Britain and France, to make a nuclear threat credible. Thus it is the quasi-continental size of their territory that allows nations, such as the United States, the Soviet Union, and China, to play the role of major nuclear powers.

Another geographical factor, however, constitutes at the same time a weakness and as asset for the international position of the Soviet Union. We are referring to the fact that neither high mountains nor broad streams separate the Soviet Union from its western neighbors and that the plains of Poland and Eastern Germany form a natural continuation of the Russian plain. There exists, then, no natural obstacle to invasion on the western frontier of Russia, either on the part of the Soviet Union or on the part of the Soviet Union's western neighbors. Thus, from the fourteenth century to the present, White Russia and the westernmost part of Russia proper have been the scene of continuous thrusts and counterthrusts and a field of battle where Russia and its western neighbors met. The lack of a natural frontier—that is, of a frontier predetermined, like the Italian or the Spanish, by geographical factors—has been a permanent source of conflict between Russia and the West. Similarly, yet for the opposite reason, the possibility of such a frontier between France and Germany in the form of the Rhine, to which France always aspired and which it had rarely the strength to attain, has been a permanent source of conflict between those two countries since the times of the Romans. As concerns Russia, the bolshevist foreign minister Vishinsky summed up the transcendent importance of geography when he said, upon being reproached for following a czarist policy on the Dardanelles: "If a warship has to sail from the Mediterranean to the Black Sea, it must pass through the Dardanelles whether the government in Moscow is Czarist or Communist."[1]

NATURAL RESOURCES

Another relatively stable factor that exerts an important influence upon the power of a nation with respect to other nations is natural resources.

Food

To start with the most elemental of these resources, food: a country that is self-sufficient, or nearly self-sufficient, has a great advantage over a nation that is not

---

[1]Quoted after Denis Healey, *Neutrality* (London: Ampersand, 1955), p. 36.

and must be able to import the foodstuffs it does not grow, or else starve. It is for this reason that the power and, in times of war, the very existence of Great Britain, which before the Second World War grew only 30 percent of the food consumed in the British Isles, has always been dependent upon its ability to keep the sea-lanes open over which the vital food supplies had to be shipped in. Whenever its ability to import food was challenged, as in the two world wars through submarine warfare and air attacks, the very power of Great Britain was challenged, and its survival as a nation put in jeopardy.

For the same reason, Germany, though to a much smaller extent deficient in foodstuffs than was Great Britain, in order to survive a war was bound to pursue three principal goals, either severally or in combination: first, the avoidance of a long war through a speedy victory before its food reserves were exhausted; second, the conquest of the great food-producing areas of eastern Europe; and third, the destruction of British sea power, which cut Germany off from access to overseas sources of food. In both world wars Germany was unable to attain the first and third objectives. It reached the second goal in the First World War too late to be of decisive effect. Thus the Allied blockade, by imposing upon the German people privations that sapped their will to resist, was one of the essential factors in the victory of the Allies. In the Second World War, Germany became virtually self-sufficient with regard to food, not primarily through conquest, but through the deliberate starvation and the outright killing of millions of people in conquered territories.

A deficiency in home-grown food has thus been a permanent source of weakness for Great Britain and Germany that they must somehow overcome or face the loss of their status as great powers. A country enjoying self-sufficiency, such as the United States, need not divert its national energies and foreign policies from its primary objectives in order to make sure that its population will not starve in war. Since such countries are reasonably free from worry on that count, they have been able to pursue much more forceful and single-minded policies than otherwise would have been possible. Self-sufficiency in food has thus always been a source of great strength.

Conversely, permanent scarcity of food is a source of permanent weakness in international politics. Of the truth of this observation, India was the prime example before the so-called green revolution drastically increased its food supply. The scarcity of food from which India suffered was the result of two factors: the increase in population, outstripping the supply of food, and the insufficiency of exports to pay for the import of the food necessary to make up the deficit. This dual imbalance, which made the ever-present threat of mass starvation one of the main concerns of government, put an insuperable handicap upon any active foreign policy India might have wanted to pursue. Regardless of the other assets of national power that were at its disposal, the deficiencies in food compelled it to act in its foreign policy from weakness rather than from strength. The same observation applies with particular force to the nations of the Third World that continuously live under the threat of famine and the actuality of undernourishment without many of the other assets that go into the making of national power. These are the so-called basket cases that are limited to hoping that international generosity will help them to survive the next famine.

Self-sufficiency in food, or lack of it, is a relatively stable factor in national power, but it is sometimes, as the example of contemporary India shows, subject to decisive changes. There may be changes in the consumption of food brought about by changing conceptions of nutrition. There may be changes in the technique of agriculture that may increase or decrease the output of agricultural products. The outstanding examples of the influence of changes in the agricultural output upon national power are, however, to be found in the disappearance of the Near East and of North Africa as power centers and in the descent of Spain from a world power to a third-rate power.

The agricultural systems of the Near East and North Africa were all founded upon irrigation. Even though it can hardly be proved that the decline in the national power of Babylon, of Egypt, and of the Arabs was concomitant with the disorganization of their irrigation systems, this much is certain: the decay of their systems of agriculture made irreparable the decline of their national power, for the disappearance of regulated irrigation transformed the better part of the arable land of these regions into deserts. It was only in Egypt that the natural irrigation of the Nile preserved a certain measure of fertility even after artificial irrigation had broken down.

As for Spain, while one dates the decline of its power from the destruction of the Armada by Great Britain in 1588, its political downfall became definite only after misrule in the seventeenth and eighteenth centuries had destroyed considerable sections of its arable land through large-scale deforestation. In consequence, wide regions of northern and central Spain were transformed into virtual deserts.

Raw Materials

What holds true of food is of course also true of those natural resources that are important for industrial production and, more particularly, for the waging of war. The absolute and relative importance natural resources in the form of raw materials have for the power of a nation depends necessarily upon the technology of the warfare practiced in a particular period of history. Before the large-scale mechanization of warfare, when hand-to-hand fighting was the prevalent military technique, other factors, such as the personal qualities of the individual soldier, were more important than the availability of the raw materials with which his weapons were made. In that period of history which extends from the beginning of historical time well into the nineteenth century, natural resources played a subordinate role in determining the power of a nation. With the increasing mechanization of warfare, which since the industrial revolution has proceeded at a faster pace than in all preceding history, national power has become more and more dependent upon the control of raw materials in peace and war. It is not by accident that the two most powerful nations today, the United States and the Soviet Union, come closest to being self-sufficient in the raw materials necessary for modern industrial production and control at least the access to the sources of those raw materials that they do not themselves produce.

As the absolute importance of the control of raw materials for national power has increased in proportion to the mechanization of warfare, so certain raw materials have gained in importance over others. This has happened whenever fundamental changes in technology have called for the use of new materials or the increased use of old ones. In 1936 a statistician rated the share of a number of basic minerals in industrial production for military purposes and assigned them the following values: coal, 40; oil, 20; iron, 15; copper, lead, manganese, sulphur, 4 each; zinc, aluminum, nickel, 2 each.[2] Half a century before, the share of coal would certainly have been considerably greater, since as a source of energy it had at that time only small competition from water and wood and none from oil. The same would have been true of iron, which then had no competition from light metals and such substitutes as plastics. Great Britain, which was self-sufficient in coal and iron, was the one great world power of the nineteenth century.

The influence the control of raw materials can exert upon national power and the shifts in the distribution of power it can bring about are demonstrated in our own day most strikingly by the case of uranium. Only a few years ago the control or lack of control of uranium deposits was entirely irrelevant for the power of a nation. The author we have quoted above,[3] writing in 1936, did not even mention this mineral in his evaluation of the relative military importance of minerals. The release of atomic energy from the uranium atom and the use of that energy for warfare have at once modified the actual and potential hierarchy of nations in view of their relative power. Nations that control deposits of uranium, such as Canada, Czechoslovakia, the Soviet Union, the Union of South Africa, and the United States, have risen in the power calculations. Others that neither possess nor have access to deposits of that mineral have fallen in terms of relative power.

The Power of Oil

Since the First World War, oil as a source of energy has become more and more important for industry and war. Most mechanized weapons and vehicles are driven by oil; consequently, countries that possess considerable deposits of oil have acquired an influence in international affairs that in some cases can be attributed primarily, if not exclusively, to that possession. "One drop of oil," said Clemenceau during the First World War, "is worth one drop of blood of our soldiers." The emergence of oil as an indispensable raw material has brought about a shift in the relative power of the politically leading nations. The Soviet Union has become more powerful since it is self-sufficient in this respect, while Japan has grown considerably weaker, since it is completely lacking in oil deposits.

---

[2]Ferdinand Friedensburg, *Die mineralischen Bodenschätze als weltpolitische und militärische Machtfaktoren* (Stuttgart: F. Enke, 1936), p. 175.
[3]See preceding note.

Aside from its location as the land bridge of three continents, the Near East is strategically important because of the oil deposits of the Arabian peninsula. Control over them traditionally has been an important factor in the distribution of power, in the sense that whoever is able to add them to his other sources of raw materials adds that much strength to his own resources and deprives his competitors proportionately. It is for this reason that Great Britain, the United States, and, for a time, France embarked in the Near East upon what has aptly been called "oil diplomacy"–that is, the establishment of spheres of influence giving them exclusive access to the oil deposits in certain regions.

Yet oil is no longer one of many raw materials important in the measurement of a nation's power. It is now a material factor whose very possession threatens to overturn centuries-old patterns of international politics. The embargo on oil by the oil-producing states in the winter of 1973–74, together with the drastic rise in the price of oil, suddenly clarified certain basic aspects of world politics that we might have understood theoretically but that were brought home in earnest by the drastic change in power relations brought on by the new politics of oil.

Traditionally, a functional relationship has existed between political, military, and economic power. That is to say, political power has been throughout history a function of military and–in recent times more particularly–of economic power. Take for instance the expansion of Europe into what later became the colonial areas of the Western Hemisphere, Africa, and Asia. That expansion was primarily due to a technological gap between the colonial powers and the colonized nations. In other words, the conquest of India by Great Britain (much inferior in manpower and in many other aspects of national power) was largely made possible by Great Britain's possession of a higher technology that, when transformed into military power, the Indian states could not resist.

Those relationships of a functional nature between technology and economic power, on the one hand, and political and military power, on the other, have been disturbed–one might even say destroyed–by the recent use of oil as a political weapon. Many of those oil-producing states are states only by way of what might be called semantic courtesy. Measured in terms of natural resources, they have nothing but sand and oil. But it is the oil that seemingly overnight has made those small plots on the map that we call states important and even powerful factors in world politics. In other words, a state that has nothing to go on by way of power, that is lacking in all the elements that traditionally have gone into the making of national power, suddenly becomes a powerful factor in world politics because it has one important asset–oil. This is indeed an event that is of revolutionary importance for world politics.

Two basic factors in our period of history have made possible this divorce of political power from military and industrial-technological power. (1) Free trade between the private producers and consumers of certain raw materials and monopolistically controlled trade through colonial and semicolonial arrangements by the consumer governments have been replaced by monopolistic or quasi-monopolistic controls on the part of the producer governments acting in concert. Formerly, the consumers could keep the price low through colonial arrangements and the control of consumption; now the producers can keep the price high by controlling production. (2) Formerly, producers and consumers of raw materials were tied together by complementary interests, the balance of which favored the consumer. The latter's needs were limited as compared with the number of potential producers and the quantity of raw materials available. The consumer had, accordingly, a choice among several producers to buy from, and also of the quantity to buy from the several producers chosen. Today, what was once a buyer's market has become a seller's market. The consumption of raw materials has enormously increased, not only in absolute terms—between 1760 and 1913 imports of food and raw materials to Great Britain increased seventy-fold—but also relative to available resources. Thus oil has become the lifeblood of industrially advanced nations, many of which are completely (Japan) or in considerable measure (the nations of Western Europe) dependent upon imports from other nations.

The power that oil bestows is, first of all, the result of the technological development of modern industrial nations. Twenty or fifty years ago oil did not bestow such power upon producing nations because the use of oil as the lifeblood of modern industry was limited. When nations that have large deposits of oil are able to cooperate and coordinate policies, as the oil-exporting states were during the fall of 1973, they can apply a stranglehold to the consuming nations; they can impose political conditions that the consuming nations can refuse to meet only at the risk of enormous political, economic, and social dislocations.

A state that is powerless in all other respects, that is not a major force in terms of traditional power, can exert enormous—and under certain conditions even decisive—power over nations that have all the implements of power at their disposal except one—deposits of oil. Thus a nation like Japan, one of the foremost industrial nations of the world and potentially a great power, is completely dependent upon the supply of oil from abroad. If for some reason the oil-producing nations were to impose a total embargo upon Japan, they could destroy her political, economic, and social fabric, and if they were to connect that threat of a total embargo with political conditions, they could impose their will upon Japan. They could reduce Japan to the status of satellite, a dependency of the oil-producing nations. To a certain extent those nations have already tasted that power. During the Middle Eastern war of October 1973, they forced Japan and the nations of Western Europe (which are only partially dependent on the import of oil) to take certain political steps that they would not have taken on their own initiative but that they felt they had to take under the circumstances because otherwise they would have risked political, social, and economic ruin.

It is not only the quasi-monopoly that the oil-producing nations acting in concert have on the supply of oil that has caused such dislocation. It is particularly, and in the long run more importantly, the control (whether actual or potential) they exert over the price of oil that has become one of the main factors of instability in the world economy and one of the main sources of inflation. The inflationary tendencies that were already at work in the industrial nations of the world were greatly aggravated by the fourfold increase in the price of oil in 1973 and the further doubling of the wellhead price in 1978.

It is important to note that this situation is potentially of a permanent nature. As long as the oil-producing nations cooperate against the consuming nations, as long as there is no competition among them for markets or for economic or political advantages, they will be able to impose virtually any conditions on the oil-consuming nations, just as they did in the wake of the 1973 war. In the case of a country like Japan, it would be suicide to refuse such conditions. In the case of other nations, such as the United States, whose main sources of energy are domestic, it would mean severe discomfort of the kind already experienced in 1973. The nations of Western Europe, for example, West Germany, whose main sources of petroleum come from abroad, would face catastrophe if they attempted to defy those nations upon whom they depend for oil.

While there is no way of destroying this stranglehold short of war, there is a way of mitigating its results. It lies in weakening the monopolistic or quasi-monopolistic position of the oil-producing nations by strengthening the position of the oil-consuming ones. The latter fall into two categories: those such as Japan, who are utterly dependent upon the importation of oil, and for whom therefore the access to foreign oil is a matter of life and death; and those such as the United States, who, by virtue of domestic sources of energy, can be inconvenienced and harmed, but not mortally wounded, by the political manipulation of oil. The latter are able to protect themselves from the more severe consequences of such manipulation by limiting the importation of oil, by restricting its domestic use, by stockpiling reserves, and by embarking upon a crash program, after the model of the Manhattan Project for the discovery of nuclear fission, to develop alternative sources of energy. The very existence of such a four-pronged policy would have a salutary effect upon all concerned. It would strengthen the morale of the oil consumers and give pause to the producers.

Such a policy would also lay the psychological and material groundwork for a policy of sharing between those consumers who possess considerable domestic sources of energy and those who lack them. For the oil producers are able to strike at a consumer, such as the United States, not only directly by cutting off its supply but also indirectly by bringing its principal allies, such as Germany and Japan, to their knees. Thus the United States is doubly vulnerable to the political manipulation of oil, and it must meet that dual threat by making itself as quickly and as much as possible independent of foreign oil supplies and by making a fraction of its domestic resources available to its most endangered allies.

Finally, if one looks at this situation created by the political use of oil from an overall point of view, one realizes that it is the specific result of what we identified earlier as the main characteristic of contemporary world politics: the disjunction between the organizational structures and political processes through which we act on the world scene, on the one hand, and the objective conditions under which humanity lives, on the other. Thus one is struck by the utter irrationality of leaving the control of nuclear power, which can destroy mankind, to sovereign nation-states. The same applies to entrusting the control of oil—which can destroy in a different way (less dramatically but almost as thoroughly) the civilization of the highly developed industrial nations—to so-called nation-states that are sovereign only in a very limited sense. The states belonging to the "nuclear club" are no longer, and the oil-producing states have never been, capable of performing the functions for which government is established in the first place, that is, to protect and promote the life, liberty, and happiness of its citizens. Their power is essentially destructive.

INDUSTRIAL CAPACITY

The example of uranium illustrates, however, the importance of another factor for the power of a nation—industrial capacity. The Congo has vast deposits of high-grade uranium. Yet, while this fact has increased the value of that country as a prize of war and, therefore, its importance from the point of view of military strategy, it has not affected the power of the Congo in relation to other nations. For the Congo does not have the industrial plant to put the uranium deposits to industrial and military use. On the other hand, for Great Britain, Canada, and the United States, as for Czechoslovakia and the Soviet Union, the possession of uranium signifies an enormous increase in power. In these countries the industrial plants exist or can be built, or they can easily be used in a neighboring country, where uranium can be transformed into energy to be employed in peace and war.

The same situation can be exemplified by coal and iron. The United States and the Soviet Union have drawn a good deal of their national strength from the possession of vast amounts of these two raw materials because they possess also industrial plants that can transform them into industrial products. The Soviet Union has built its plant, and is still in the process of building it, at enormous human and material sacrifices. It is willing to make the sacrifices because it recognizes that without the industrial plant it cannot build and maintain a military establishment commensurate with its foreign policy. Without this plant the Soviet Union cannot play the important part in international politics which it intends to play.

India follows the United States and the Soviet Union closely as a depository of coal and iron. Its reserves of iron ore in the two provinces of Bihar and Orissa alone are estimated at 2.7 billion tons. Furthermore, India's output of manganese, which is indispensable for the production of steel, was a million tons as early as 1939, topped only by the output of the Soviet Union. But despite these riches in raw materials, without which no nation can attain first rank in modern times, India cannot be classified today as a first-rate power even faintly comparable to the United States and the Soviet Union. The reason for this lag between the potentialities and actualities of power, which concerns us in the context of this discussion (others will be mentioned later), is the lack of an industrial establishment commensurate with the abundance of raw materials. While India can boast of a number of steel mills, such as the Tata Iron Works, which are among the most modern in existence, it has no per capita productive capacity, especially for finished products, that can be compared with even one of the second-rate industrial nations. In 1980 fewer than six million Indians—less than 1 percent of the total population—were employed in industry. So we see that India possesses, in the abundance of some of the key raw materials, one of the elements that go into the making of national power, and to that extent it may be regarded as a potentially great power. Actually, however, it will not become a great power so long as it is lacking in other factors without which no nation in modern times can attain the status of a great power. Of these factors industrial capacity is one of the most important.

The technology of modern warfare transportation and communications has made the overall development of heavy industries an indispensable element of national power. Since victory in modern war depends upon the number and quality of highways, railroads, trucks, ships, airplanes, tanks, and equipment and weapons of all kinds, from mosquito nets and automatic rifles to oxygen masks and guided missiles, the competition among nations for power transforms itself largely into competition for the production of bigger, better, and more implements of war. The quality and productive capacity of the industrial plant, the know-how of the working man, the skill of the engineer, the inventive genius of the scientist, the managerial organization—all these are factors upon which the industrial capacity of a nation and, hence, its power depend.

Thus it is inevitable that the leading industrial nations should be identical with the great powers, and a change in industrial rank, for better or for worse, should be accompanied or followed by a corresponding change in the hierarchy of power. So long as Great Britain as an industrial nation had no equal, it was the most powerful nation on earth, the only one that deserved to be called a world power. The decline of France as a power in comparison with Germany, which was unmistakable after 1870 and was only seemingly and temporarily arrested during the decade following the First World War, was in part but the political and military manifestation of the industrial backwardness of France and of the industrial predominance of Germany on the European continent.

The Soviet Union, while having been potentially always a great power, became one in fact only when it entered the ranks of the foremost industrial powers in the thirties, and it became the rival of the United States as the other superpower only when it acquired in the fifties the industrial capacity for waging nuclear war. Similarly, the potential of China as a great power will only be realized if and when it acquires a similar industrial capacity. When the United States was at the height of its power in the forties, the *Economist* of London related that power to American economic strength by saying:

> In any comparison of potential resources of the Great Powers the United States, even before Hitler's war, far outstripped every other nation in the world in material strength, in scale of industrialization, in weight of resources, in standards of living, by every index of output and consumption. And the war, which all but doubled the American national income while it either ruined or severely weakened every other Great Power, has enormously increased the scale upon which the United States now towers above its fellows. Like mice in the cage of an elephant, they follow with apprehension the movements of the

mammoth. What chance would they stand if it were to begin to throw its weight about, they who are in some danger even if it only decides to sit down?[4]

This drastic increase in the importance of industrial capacity for national power has also accentuated the traditional distinction between great and small powers. The very term "superpower" points to an unprecedented accumulation of power in the hands of a few nations, which sets these nations apart not only from the small ones but from the traditional great powers as well. What distinguishes the superpowers from all other nations, aside from their ability to wage all-out nuclear war and absorb a less than all-out nuclear attack, is their virtual industrial self-sufficiency and their technological capacity to stay abreast of the other nations. By the same token, the dependence of the nations of the third and fourth rank upon the nations of the first rank, which we can call superpowers, has also drastically increased. The military power of the former depends to a sometimes decisive extent upon the willingness of the latter to supply them with modern weapons and the implements of modern communications and transportation. Without this supply many of them would be helpless in confrontation with an enemy thus supplied.

MILITARY PREPAREDNESS

What gives the factors of geography, natural resources, and industrial capacity their actual importance for the power of a nation is military preparedness. The dependence of national power upon military preparedness is too obvious to need much elaboration. Military preparedness requires a military establishment capable of supporting the foreign policies pursued. Such ability derives from a number of factors of which the most significant, from the point of view of our discussion, are technological innovations, leadership, and the quantity and quality of the armed forces.

Technology

The fate of nations and of civilizations has often been determined by a differential in the technology of warfare for which the inferior side was unable to compensate in other ways. Europe, in the period of its expansion from the fifteenth through the nineteenth century, carried its power on the vehicle of a technology of warfare superior to that of the Western Hemisphere, Africa, and the Near and Far East. The addition of infantry, firearms, and artillery to the traditional weapons in the fourteenth and fifteenth centuries spelled a momentous shift in the distribution of power in favor of those who used those weapons before their enemies did. The feudal lords and independent cities, who in the face of these new

---

[4]*Economist*, May 24, 1947, p. 785. (Reprinted by permission.)

weapons continued to rely upon cavalry and the castles that until then had been practically immune against direct attack, now found themselves suddenly dislodged from their position of preponderance.

Two events illustrate dramatically this shift in power that politically and militarily marks the end of the Middle Ages and the beginning of the modern era of history. First, in the battles of Morgarten in 1315 and of Laupen in 1339, armies composed of Swiss infantry inflicted disastrous defeats upon feudal cavalry, demonstrating that food soldiers recruited from the common people were superior to an aristocratic and expensive army of equestrians. The second is the invasion of Italy in 1494 by Charles VIII of France. With infantry and artillery, Charles VIII broke the power of the proud Italian city-states, until then secure behind their walls. The seemingly irresistible destructiveness of these new techniques of warfare made an indelible impression upon contemporaries, some of which is reflected in the writings of Machiavelli and other Florentine writers of the time.[5]

The twentieth century has thus far witnessed four major innovations in the technique of warfare. They gave at least a temporary advantage to the side that used them before the opponent did, or before he was able to protect himself against them. First, the submarine was used in the First World War by Germany primarily against British shipping and seemed to be capable of deciding the war in favor of Germany until Great Britain found in the convoy an answer to that menace. Second, the tank was used in considerable and concentrated numbers by the British, but not by the Germans, in the closing phase of the First World War, giving the Allies one of their assets for victory. Third, strategic and tactical coordination of the air force with the land and naval forces contributed greatly to the German and Japanese superiority in the initial stages of the Second World War. Pearl Harbor and the disastrous defeats that the British and the Dutch suffered at the hands of the Japanese on land and at sea in 1941 and 1942 were the penalties to be paid for technological backwardness in the face of a more progressive enemy. If one reads the somber review of British defeats that Churchill gave in the secret session of Parliament on April 23, 1942,[6] one is struck by the fact that all these defeats on land, on the sea, and in the air have one common denominator: the disregard or misunderstanding of the change in the technology of warfare brought about by air power. Finally, nations that possess nuclear weapons and the means to deliver them have an enormous technological advantage over their competitors.

However, the availability of nuclear weapons also results in two extraordinary paradoxes, referred to above, as concerns its bearing upon national power. Both paradoxes stem from the enormous destructiveness of nuclear weapons. It is by virtue of that destructiveness that a quantitative increase in nuclear weapons, in contrast to conventional ones, does not of necessity signify a corresponding increase in national power. Once a nation possesses all the nuclear weapons necessary to destroy all the enemy targets it has chosen for destruction, taking all possible

---

[5]See the account by Felix Gilbert, "Machiavelli: The Renaissance of the Art of War," in *Makers of Modern Strategy*, edited by Edward Mead Earle (Princeton: Princeton University Press, 1944), pp. 8, 9.
[6]*Winston Churchill's Secret Session Speeches* (New York: Simon and Schuster, 1946), pp. 53 ff.

contingencies, such as a first strike by the enemy, into consideration, additional nuclear weapons will not increase that nation's power.[7]

The other paradox lies in the inverse relationship between the degree of destructiveness of nuclear weapons and their rational usability. High-yield nuclear weapons are instruments of indiscriminate mass destruction and can therefore not be used for rational military purposes. They can be used to deter a war by threatening total destruction; but they cannot be used to fight a war in a rational manner. A nation armed with nothing but high-yield nuclear weapons could draw very little political power from its military posture; for it would have no military means by which to impose its will upon another nation, aside from threatening it with total destruction.

If such a nation has a second-strike nuclear capability, it will threaten total destruction in return, and then the two threats either will cancel each other out or will lead to the mutual destruction of the belligerents. If the threatened nation has no nuclear means of retaliation, it will either suffer total destruction or surrender unconditionally as did Japan in 1945 after Hiroshima and Nagasaki had been destroyed by nuclear bombs. In other words, the threatening nation could wipe the nonnuclear nation off the face of the earth, either piecemeal, city by city, or in one devastating blow, but it could not subtly adapt the degree of military pressure to be used to the degree of psychological resistance to be overcome. The absence of conventional weapons, susceptible to such subtle adaptations, and the sole reliance upon high-yield nuclear weapons would make a nation less powerful than it would be if it possessed a combination of high-yield nuclear weapons for the purpose of deterrence and an armory of conventional weapons usable for the ordinary purposes of warfare. Hence the paradox that in order to make nuclear weapons usable one must reduce their yield to approximate that of conventional weapons.

Leadership

Aside from the timely use of technological innovations, the quality of military leadership has always exerted a decisive influence upon national power. The power of Prussia in the eighteenth century was primarily a reflection of the military genius of Frederick the Great and of the strategic and tactical innovations introduced by him. The art of warfare had changed between the death of Frederick the Great in 1786 and the battle of Jena in 1806 when Napoleon destroyed the Prussian army, which in itself was then as good and strong as it had been twenty years before. But, what was more important, military genius was lacking in its leaders, who were fighting the battles of Frederick the Great all over again. On the other side military genius was in command, employing new ideas in strategy and tactics. This factor decided the issue in favor of France.

The Maginot Line psychology of the French general staff in the period between the two world wars has become a byword for faulty strategic thinking.

---

[7]Cf. below, pages 423 ff.

While the tendencies of modern technology, especially its trend toward mechanization of transportation and of communications, pointed toward the probability of a war of movement, the French general staff continued to think in terms of the trench warfare of the First World War. The German general staff, on the other hand, fully alive to the strategic potentialities of mechanized warfare, planned its campaigns in terms of unprecedented mobility. The conflagration of these two conceptions, not only in France but also in Poland and the Soviet Union, produced in the blitzkrieg a superiority of German power that brought Germany close to final victory. The intellectual shock and the military and political devastation caused by the onslaught of Hitler's panzers and dive bombers upon the Polish cavalry in 1939 and upon the immobile French army in 1940 ushered in a new period of military history, similar to the one initiated by Charles VIII's invasion of Italy in 1494. But, while the Italian states had nobody to fall back on in order to recover their strength, in the Second World War the superior technology of the United States and the superior manpower of the Soviet Union turned Hitler's innovations to his destruction.

Quantity and Quality of Armed Forces

The power of a nation in military terms is also dependent upon the quantity of men and arms and their distribution among the different branches of the military establishment. A nation may have a good grasp of technological innovations in warfare. Its military leaders may excel in the strategy and tactics appropriate to the new techniques of war. Yet such a nation may be militarily and, in consequence, also politically weak if it does not possess a military establishment that in its overall strength and in the strength of its component parts is neither too large nor too small in view of the tasks it may be called upon to perform. Must a nation, in order to be strong, possess a large army, or is its power not impaired by having, at least in peacetime, only small land forces, composed of highly trained, heavily armed specialized units? Have battle-ready forces-in-being become more important than trained reserves? Have large surface navies become obsolete, or do aircraft carriers still fulfill a useful purpose? How large a military establishment can a nation afford in view of its resources and commitments? Does concern for national power require large-scale peacetime production of aircraft and other mechanized weapons, or should a nation, in view of rapid changes in technology, spend its resources on research and on the production of limited quantities of improved types of weapons?

Whether a nation gives the right or the wrong answer to such questions of a quantitative character has obviously a direct bearing upon national power. Can decision in war be forced by one new weapon, such as artillery, as was thought at the turn of the fifteenth century, or the submarine, as the Germans thought in the First World War, or the airplane, as was widely believed in the period between the two world wars, or the intercontinental guided missiles, as many believe today? The wrong answers given to some of these questions by Great Britain and France in the period between the two world wars preserved for them the semblance of power in terms of the traditional military conceptions. But those errors brought them to the brink of final defeat in the course of the Second World War, whose military technique required different answers to those questions. Upon the quality of the answers we give to these and similar questions today will depend the future power of the United States in relation to other nations.

POPULATION

When we turn from material factors and those compounded of material and human elements to the purely human factors that determine the power of a nation, we have to distinguish quantitative and qualitative components. While among the latter we count national character, national morale, and the quality of diplomacy and of government in general, the former needs to be discussed in terms of size of population.

Distribution

It would, of course, not be correct to say that the larger the population of a country the greater the power of that country. For if such an unqualified correlation existed between size of population and national power, China, whose population is estimated as being over 1 billion people,[8] would be the most powerful nation on earth, followed by India with about 730 million. The Soviet Union with about 272 million and the United States with 234 million would run third and fourth, respectively. Though one is not justified in considering a country to be very powerful because its population is greater than that of most other countries, it is still true that no country can remain or become a first-rate power that does not belong to the more populous nations of the earth. Without a large population it is impossible to establish and keep going the industrial plant necessary for the successful conduct of modern war; to put into the field the large number of combat groups to fight on land, on the sea, and in the air; and, finally, to fill the cadres of the troops, considerably more numerous than the combat troops, that must supply the latter with food, means of transportation and communication, ammunition, and weapons. It is for this reason that imperialistic countries stimulate population growth with all kinds of incentives, as did Nazi Germany and Fascist Italy, and then use that growth as an ideological pretext for imperialistic expansion.

A comparison between the population of the United States and that of Australia and Canada will make clear the relation between size of population and national power. Australia has today, in an area of somewhat less than three million square miles, a population of about 15 million, while the Canadian population, in an area of close to 3.5 million square miles, amounts to 24.5 million. The

---

[8]All population figures, unless indicated otherwise, are derived from the information reported in the U.S. Census Bureau Report for mid-June 1983, *New York Times*, September 4, 1983, p. A9.

United States, on the other hand, in an area between that of Australia and Canada, has a population of 234 million, more than fifteen times larger than Australia's and nearly ten times larger than Canada's. With the population of either Australia or Canada, the United States could never have become the most powerful nation on earth. The waves of mass immigration in the nineteenth and the first two decades of the twentieth centuries brought to the United States this element of national power. Had the Immigration Law of 1924, limiting immigration to the United States to 150,000 persons a year, been enacted a hundred or even fifty years earlier, 36 or 27 million people, respectively, would have been prevented from settling in the United States, and they and their descendants would have been lost to the United States.

In 1824 the population of the United States amounted to close to 11 million. By 1874 it had risen to 44 million; by 1924, to 114 million. During that century the share of immigration in the growth of the American population was on the average close to 30 percent, approaching 40 percent in the period from 1880 to 1910. In other words, the most spectacular rise in American population coincides with the absolute and relative peaks of immigration. Free immigration from 1824 and, more particularly, from 1874 to 1924 is mainly responsible for the abundance of manpower that has meant so much for the national power of the United States in war and peace. Without this immigration it is unlikely that the population of the United States would amount to more than half of what it actually is today. In consequence, the national power of the United States would be inferior to what 234 million people make it today.

Since size of population is one of the factors upon which national power rests, and since the power of one nation is always relative to the power of others, relative size of the population of countries competing for power and, especially, the relative rate of their growth deserve careful attention. A country inferior in size of population to its competitor will view with alarm a declining rate of growth if the population of its competitor tends to increase more rapidly. Such has been the situation of France with regard to Germany between 1870 and 1940. During that period the population of France increased by 4 million, whereas Germany registered a gain of 27 million. While in 1800 every seventh European was a Frenchman, in 1930 only every thirteenth was a Frenchman. In 1940, Germany had at its disposal about 15 million men fit for military service, whereas France had only 5 million.

On the other hand, ever since the unification in 1870, Germany has viewed, sometimes with alarm and always with respect, the Russian population figures, which show a greater rate of increase than Germany's. Looking at the situation as it existed at the outbreak of the First World War solely from the point of view of population trends, Germany could feel that time was on Russia's side, and France could feel that time was on the side of Germany, while both Austria and Russia, for other reasons already alluded to,[9] could believe that postponement of the conflict would favor the opponent. Thus all the protagonists, with the exception of

[9]See pages 77 and 78.

Great Britain, had reasons of their own to prefer a war in 1914 to a peaceful settlement that they could not regard as definite but only as a breathing spell before the unavoidable settling of accounts.

As the shifts in the distribution of power within Europe in recent history have been roughly duplicated by the changes in population trends, so the emergence of the United States as the great power center of the West, taking the place of Western and Central Europe, can be read in the population figures of the respective countries. In 1870 the population of France as well as of Germany exceeded that of the United States. Yet in 1940 the population of the United States had increased by 100 million while the combined increase in the populations of France and Germany in the same period amounted to only 31 million.

It is thus obvious that a nation cannot be in the first rank without a population sufficiently large to create and apply the material implements of national power. On the other hand, it has become obvious only in recent times that a large population can also exert a drastically negative influence upon national power. This has happened in so-called underdeveloped nations, such as India and Egypt, whose populations have greatly increased, by virtue of a decrease in the mortality rates, while their food supply did not keep pace with the increase in population. These countries were continually faced with the threat of famine and with the need to take care of large masses of undernourished and diseased people. They had to divert scarce resources from the development of their national power to the feeding and care of their populations. The largeness of their population, far from being an asset for their national power, is an obstacle to its development. For such nations, to bring the number of their population into harmony with their resources is a necessity, and if resources cannot be increased, population control is a precondition of national power.[10]

Trends

It is obvious from what has been said thus far that in trying to assess the future distribution of power the prediction of population trends plays an important role. All other factors remaining approximately equal, a considerable decline in the manpower of a nation in comparison with its competitors on the international scene spells a decline in national power, and a considerable increase, under similar conditions, amounts to a gain in national strength. When, toward the end of the nineteenth century, the British Empire was the only world power in existence, its population amounted to about 400 million—that is, approximately one-fourth of the total population of the world. In 1946 it came close to 550 million. Since India's population was then estimated at 400 million, these figures illustrate the enormous loss in national power, in terms of size of population alone, that Great Britain suffered in the loss of India.

From the point of view of population, the position of the United States will continue to show considerable strength in comparison with Western Europe

[10]Cf. above page 124.

because of the latter's anticipated small increases. But compared with the population trend in Latin America, the position of the United States is well on its way to deterioration. Latin America shows the greatest rate of increase of any major region in the world. In 1900, Latin America had an estimated 63 million inhabitants to 75 million for the United States. The population of Argentina alone more than doubled between 1914 and 1965 and is now almost 28 million. In the same period the population of the United States has only risen from 99 to 234 million.

It is, however, not sufficient to know the overall population figures of different countries in order to assess correctly the influence of the population factor upon national power. The age distribution within a given population is an important element in power calculations. All other things being equal, a nation with a relatively large population of maximum potential usefulness for military and productive purposes (roughly between twenty and forty years of age) will have an edge in power over a nation in whose population the older age groups predominate.

It must be pointed out, however, that the projection of population trends is hazardous even without the interference of war or natural catastrophes. The estimates of population trends that were made in the forties painted a rather pessimistic picture of the increase of the American population as compared with that of the Soviet Union. Yet today the population of the United States exceeds by a wide margin the number that some population experts of great repute expected it to reach by 1975. Even in a field whose scientific accuracy appears to be relatively high, the prediction of national power is beset with uncertainties. But these uncertainties do not affect the importance of population trends for the development of national power. Nor can they diminish the active concern of statesmen with the population trends of their own nations.

Echoing Augustus and his successors on the throne of the Roman Empire, Sir Winston Churchill, as British prime minister, expressed this concern when he said in his radio address of March 22, 1943:

> One of the most somber anxieties which beset those who look thirty, or forty, or fifty years ahead, and in this field one can see ahead only too clearly, is the dwindling birth-rate. In thirty years, unless present trends alter, a smaller working and fighting population will have to support and protect nearly twice as many old people; in fifty years the position will be worse still. If this country is to keep its high place in the leadership of the world, and to survive as a great power that can hold its own against external pressures, our people must be encouraged by every means to have larger families.

NATIONAL CHARACTER

Its Existence

Of the three human factors of a qualitative nature that have a bearing on national power, national character and national morale stand out both for their elusiveness from the point of view of rational prognosis and for their permanent and often decisive influence upon the weight a nation is able to put into the scales of international politics. We are not concerned here with the question of what factors are responsible for the development of a national character. We are interested only in the fact—contested but (it seems to us) incontestable, especially in view of the anthropological concept of the "culture pattern"—that certain qualities of intellect and character occur more frequently and are more highly valued in one nation than in another. To quote Coleridge:

> But that there is an invisible spirit that breathes through a whole people, and is participated by all, though not by all alike; a spirit which gives a color and character both to their virtues and vices, so that the same action, such I mean as are expressed by the same words, are yet not the same in a Spaniard as they would be in a Frenchman, I hold for an undeniable truth, without the admission of which all history would be a riddle. I hold likewise that the difference of nations, their relative grandeur and meanness, all, in short, which they are or do,—(not indeed at one particular time, under the accidental influence of a single great man, as the Carthaginians under the great Xantippus, and afterwards under their own Hannibal,) but all in which they persevere, as a nation, through successions of changing individuals, are the result of this spirit . . .[11]

These qualities set one nation apart from others, and they show a high degree of resiliency to change. A few examples, taken at random, will illustrate the point.

Is it not an incontestable fact that, as John Dewey[12] and many others have pointed out, Kant and Hegel are as typical of the philosophic tradition of Germany as Descartes and Voltaire are of the French mind, as Locke and Burke are of the political thought of Great Britain, as William James and John Dewey are of the American approach to intellectual problems? And can it be denied that these philosophic differences are but expressions, on the highest level of abstraction and systematization, of fundamental intellectual and moral traits that reveal themselves on all levels of thought and action and that give each nation its unmistakable distinctiveness? The mechanistic rationality and the systematic perfection of Descartes' philosophy reappear in the tragedies of Corneille and Racine no less than in the rationalistic fury of Jacobin reform. They reappear in the sterility of the academic formalism that characterizes much of the contemporary intellectual life of France. They reappear in the scores of peace plans, logically perfect but impracticable, in which French statecraft excelled in the period between the two world wars. On the other hand, the trait of intellectual curiosity that Julius Caesar detected in the Gauls has remained throughout the ages a distinctive characteristic of the French mind.

Locke's philosophy is as much a manifestation of British individualism as the Magna Carta, due process of law, or Protestant sectarianism. In Edmund Burke, with his undogmatic combination of moral principle and political expediency, the

---

[11]Samuel Taylor Coleridge, *Essays on His Own Times* (London: William Pickering, 1850), Vol. II, pp. 668–69.
[12]*German Philosophy and Politics* (New York: G. P. Putnam's Sons, 1942), passim.

political genius of the British people reveals itself as much as in the Reform Acts of the nineteenth century or the balance-of-power policies of Cardinal Wolsey and Canning. What Tacitus said of the destructive political and military propensities of the Germanic tribes fitted the armies of Frederick Barbarossa no less than those of Wilhelm II and of Hitler. It fits, too, the traditional rudeness and clumsy deviousness of German diplomacy. The authoritarianism, collectivism, and state worship of German philosophy have their counterpart in the tradition of autocratic government, in servile acceptance of any authority so long as it seems to have the will and force to prevail, and, concomitant with it, the lack of civil courage, the disregard of individual rights, and the absence of a tradition of political liberty. The description of the American national character, as it emerges from Tocqueville's *Democracy in America*, has not been deprived of its timeliness by the intervention of more than a century. The indecision of American pragmatism between an implicit dogmatic idealism and reliance upon success as a measure of truth is reflected in the vacillations of American diplomacy between the Four Freedoms and the Atlantic Charter, on the one hand, and "dollar diplomacy," on the other.

The Russian National Character

As for Russia, the juxtaposition of two experiences, almost a century apart, will provide striking proof of the persistence of certain intellectual and moral qualities.
Bismarck wrote in his memories:

> At the time of my first stay in St. Petersburg, in 1859, I had an example of another Russian peculiarity. During the first spring days it was then the custom for everyone connected with the court to promenade in the Summer Garden between Paul's Palace and the Neva. There the Emperor had noticed a sentry standing in the middle of a grass plot; in reply to the question why he was standing there, the soldier could only answer, "Those are my orders." The Emperor therefore sent one of his adjutants to the guardroom to make inquiries; but no explanation was forthcoming except that a sentry had to stand there winter and summer. The source of the original order could no longer be discovered. The matter was talked of at court, and reached the ears of the servants. One of them, an older pensioner, came forward and stated that his father had once said to him as they passed the sentry in the Summer Garden: "There he is, still standing to guard the flower, on that spot the Empress Catherine once noticed a snowdrop in bloom unusually early, and gave orders that it was not to be plucked." This command had been carried out by placing a sentry on the spot, and ever since then one had stood there all the year round. Stories of this sort excite our amusement and criticism, but they are an expression of the elementary force and persistence on which the strength of the Russian nature depends in its attitude towards the rest of Europe. It reminds us of the sentinels in the flood at St. Petersburg in 1825, and in the Shipka Pass in 1877; not

being relieved, the former were drowned, the latter frozen to death at their posts.[13]

Time magazine of April 21, 1947, contains the following report:

Down Potsdam's slushy Berlinerstrasse stumbled twelve haggard men. . . . Their faces had the pale, creased look of prisoners. Behind them trudged a stubby, broad-faced Russian soldier, Tommy gun crooked in his right arm, the wide Ukrainian steppe in his blue eyes.

Approaching the Stadtbahn station, the group met a stream of men and women hurrying home from work.

An angular, middle-aged woman suddenly sighted the twelve men. She stopped in her tracks, stared wide-eyed at them for a full minute. Then she dropped her threadbare market bag, flew across the street in front of a lumbering charcoal-burning truck and threw herself with a gasping cry upon the third prisoner. Prisoners and passers-by paused and gaped dumbly at the two Rodinesque figures fingering the backs of each other's rough coats and mumbling hysterically; *"Wohin?" ". . . weiss nicht." "Warum?" ". . . weiss nicht."*

Slowly the Russian walked around his charges and approached the couple. Slowly a grin covered his face. He tapped the woman on the back. She shuddered. Rigid apprehension spread over the faces of the onlookers, but the Russian rumbled soothingly: *"Keine Angst. Keine Angst."* (No fear. No fear.) Then he waved the muzzle of his Tommy gun toward the prisoner, who instinctively recoiled a step, and asked: *"Dein Mann?"*

"Ja," replied the woman, tears streaming down her cheeks.

"Gu-ut" grunted the Russian, wrinkling his nose, *"Nimm mit,"* and he gave the bewildered prisoner a gentle shove toward the sidewalk.

The spectators exhaled a mass sigh of relief as the couple stumbled off deliriously, hand in hand. Eleven prisoners, muttering to each other, pushed on down the street past the muttering crowd: "Unpredictable Russians . . . incredible . . . I can't understand . . . I don't understand the Russians."

The Russian shuffled along stoically, gripping a long papirosa between yellow stained teeth as he fished in a pocket for matches. Suddenly his face clouded. He hitched the Tommy gun higher under his arm, took a dirty piece of paper from the wide, ragged sleeve of his shinel, and scowled at it. After a few steps he stuffed the paper back carefully, stared for a moment at the bent backs of the prisoners, then searched the strained faces of a new load of commuters just leaving the station.

With no fuss, the Russian stepped up to a youngish man with a briefcase under his arm and a dirty brown felt hat pulled over his ears, and commanded: *"Eeh, Dul Komm!"* The German froze, casting a terrified glance over his shoulder at the frightened stream of men and women who were trying not to see or

---

[13] *Bismarck, the Man and Statesman, Being the Reflections and Reminiscences of Otto, Prince von Bismarck*, translated under the supervision of A. J. Butler (New York and London: Harper and Brothers, 1899), Vol. I, p. 250.

hear. The Russian waved his Tommy gun and curled his lip. *"Komm!"* He pushed his petrified recruit roughly into the gutter.

Again the prisoners were twelve. The Russian's face relaxed. With a third sputtering match he lighted his papirosa and placidly blew smoke toward the tense Germans scurrying home through the gathering dusk.[14]

Between these two episodes a great revolution intervened, interrupting the historical continuity on practically all levels of national life. Yet the traits of the Russian national character emerged intact from the holocaust of that revolution. Even so thorough a change in the social and economic structure, in political leadership and institutions, in the ways of life and thought has not been able to affect the "elementary force and persistence" of the Russian character that Bismarck found revealed in his experience and that reveal themselves in the Russian soldier of Potsdam as well.

To illustrate the same continuity of the national character, let us consider the following excerpts from diplomatic dispatches sent by an American diplomat from Russia to the Department of State:

> During the last year it has been evident that the policy of Russia toward foreigners and their entrance into the empire was becoming more and more stringent.
>
> I heard of several Americans last summer who were unable to procure visas. . . . This arises mainly from political considerations and a fear of foreign influence upon the popular mind. To this it may be added that there is a strong anti-foreign party in Russia whose policy would exclude all foreigners except for mere purposes of transient commerce. . . .
>
> The position of a minister here is far from being pleasant. The opinion prevails that no communication, at least of a public nature, is safe in the post office but is opened and inspected as a matter of course. . . . The opinion also prevails that ministers are constantly subjected to a system of espionage and that even their servants are made to disclose what passed in their households, their conversations, associations, etc. . . .
>
> Secrecy and mystery characterize everything. Nothing is made public that is worth knowing.
>
> A strange superstition prevails among the Russians that they are destined to conquer the world. Appeals to the soldiery founded on this idea of fatality and its glorious rewards are seldom made in vain. To a feeling of this sort has been attributed that remarkable patience and endurance which distinguish the Russian soldier in the midst of the greatest privations.
>
> . . . Nothing is more striking to an American on his first arrival here than the rigor of the police.

---

[14] *Time*, April 21, 1947, p. 32. (Used by permission of *Time*. Copyright Time, Inc., 1947.)

These impressions were gathered, not, as one might expect, in recent years by Ambassadors Kennan, Bohlen, or Thompson, but in 1851–52 by Neill S. Brown, then United States minister to Russia.

National Character and National Power

National character cannot fail to influence national power. For those who act for the nation in peace and war; formulate, execute, and support its policies; elect and are elected; mold public opinion; produce and consume—all bear to a greater or lesser degree the imprint of those intellectual and moral qualities that make up the national character. The "elementary force and persistence" of the Russians, the individual initiative and inventiveness of the Americans, the undogmatic common sense of the British, and the discipline and thoroughness of the Germans are some of the qualities that will manifest themselves, for better or for worse, in all the individual and collective activities in which the members of a nation may engage. In consequence of the differences in national character, the German and Russian governments, for instance, have been able to embark upon foreign policies that the American and British governments would have been incapable of pursuing, and vice versa. Antimilitarism and aversion to standing armies and to compulsory military service are permanent traits of the American and British national character. Yet the same institutions and activities have for centuries stood high in the hierarchy of values of Prussia, from where their prestige spread over all of Germany. In Russia the tradition of obedience to the authority of the government and the traditional fear of the foreigner have made large, permanent military establishments acceptable to the population.

Thus the national character has given Germany and Russia an initial advantage in the struggle for power, since they could transform in peacetime a greater portion of their national resources into instruments of war. On the other hand, the reluctance of the American and British peoples to consider such a transformation, especially on a large scale and with respect to manpower, except in an obvious national emergency, has imposed a severe handicap upon American and British foreign policy. Governments of militaristic nations are able to plan, prepare, and wage war at the moment of their choosing. They can, more particularly, start a preventive war whenever it seems to be most propitious for their cause. Governments of pacifist nations, of which the United States was the outstanding example until the end of the Second World War, are in this respect in a much more difficult situation and have much less freedom of action. Restrained as they are by the innate antimilitarism of their peoples, they must pursue a more cautious course in foreign affairs. Frequently, the military strength actually at their disposal will not be commensurate with the political commitments that their concern for the national interest imposes upon them. In other words, they will not have the armed might sufficient to back up their policies. When they go to war, they may well do so on the terms of their enemies. In the past they have had to rely upon other traits in the national character and upon other compensating factors, such as geographical location and industrial potential, to carry them over the initial period of weakness and inferiority to ultimate victory. Such can be the effects, for good or evil, of the character of a nation.

The observer of the international scene who attempts to assess the relative strength of different nations must take national character into account, however difficult it may be to assess correctly so elusive and intangible a factor. Failure to do so will lead to errors in judgment and policies, such as the depreciation of the recuperative force of Germany after the First World War and the underestimation of Russian staying power in 1941–42. The Treaty of Versailles could restrict Germany in all the other implements of national power, such as territory, sources of raw materials, industrial capacity, and military establishment. But it could not deprive Germany of all those qualities of intellect and character that enabled it within a period of two decades to rebuild what it had lost and to emerge as the strongest single military power in the world. The virtually unanimous opinion of the military experts who in 1942 gave the Russian army only a few more months of resistance may have been correct in purely military terms, such as military strategy, mobility, industrial resources, and the like. Yet this expert opinion was obviously mistaken in underrating that factor of "elementary force and persistence" that better judgment has recognized as the great source of Russian strength in its dealings with Europe. The pessimism that in 1940 denied Great Britain a chance for survival had its roots in a similar neglect or misreading of the national character of the British people.

We have already mentioned in another context the contempt in which American power was held by the German leaders before the Second World War.[15] It is interesting to note that exactly the same mistake, and for the same reason, was made by the German leaders during the First World War. Thus, in October 1916, the German secretary of the navy estimated the significance of the United States joining the Allies to be "zero," and another German minister of that period declared in a parliamentary speech, after the United States had actually entered the war on the side of the Allies: "The Americans cannot swim and they cannot fly, the Americans will never come." In both cases the German leaders underestimated American power by paying attention exclusively to the quality of the military establishment at a particular moment, to the antimilitarism of the American character, and to the factor of geographical distance. They disregarded completely the qualities of the American character, such as individual initiative, a gift for improvisation, and technical skill, that together with the other material factor and under favorable conditions might more than outweigh the disadvantages of geographical remoteness and of a dilapidated military establishment.

On the other hand, the belief of many experts, at least until the battle of Stalingrad in 1943, in the invincibility of Germany drew its strength from the material factors, as well as from certain aspects of the German national character, that seemed to favor total victory. These experts neglected other aspects of the national character of the German people, in particular their lack of moderation.

---

[15]See page 95.

From the emperors of the Middle Ages and the princes fighting the Thirty Years' War to Wilhelm II and Hitler, this lack of moderation has proved to be the one fatal weakness of the German national character. Unable to restrain goal and action within the limits of the possible, the Germans have time and again squandered and ultimately destroyed the national power of Germany built upon other material and human factors.

NATIONAL MORALE

More elusive and less stable, but no less important than all the other factors in its bearing upon national power, is what we propose to call national morale. National morale is the degree of determination with which a nation supports the foreign policies of its government in peace or war. It permeates all activities of a nation, its agricultural and industrial production as well as its military establishment and diplomatic service. In the form of public opinion, it provides an intangible factor without whose support no government, democratic or autocratic, is able to pursue its policies with full effectiveness, if it is able to pursue them at all. Its presence or absence and its qualities reveal themselves particularly in times of national crisis, when either the existence of the nation is at stake or else a decision of fundamental importance must be made upon which the survival of the nation might well depend.

Its Instability

While certain traits of the national character may easily manifest themselves in the national morale of the people at a certain moment of history, such as the common sense of the British, the individualism of the French, or the tenacity of the Russians, no conclusion can be drawn from the character of a nation as to what the morale of that nation might be under certain contingencies. Their national character seems to qualify the American people to a particular degree for playing the role of a first-rate power under the conditions of the twentieth century. Yet nobody can foresee with any degree of certainty what the national morale of the American people would be like under the conditions of hardship and disintegration that prevailed in the different belligerent countries of Europe and Asia during certain phases of the Second World War and of the postwar years. Nor is there a way of anticipating the reactions of the British people to a repetition of the experiences of the Second World War. They stood up under the "blitz" and V-weapons once. Could they stand up under them a second time? And what about nuclear weapons? Similar questions can be asked of all nations, and no rational answers are forthcoming.

American national morale, in particular, has been in recent years the object of searching speculation at home and abroad; for American foreign policy and, through it, the weight of American power in international affairs are to a peculiar degree dependent upon the moods of American public opinion, as they express themselves in the votes of Congress, election results, polls, and the like. Would the United States join the United Nations and stay with it despite disappointments? Would Congress support the economic and military assistance program for Europe, and for how long would it vote billions for foreign aid throughout the world? How far were the American people willing to go in supporting South Korea, and under what conditions would they continue to do so? Would they be willing to cope indefinitely with the liabilities, risks, and frustrations attributed to the Soviet Union, without either relaxing their efforts or trying to end it all by drastic action? The main factor upon which the answers to these questions depended or depend is the state of national morale at the decisive moment.

The national morale of any people will obviously break at a certain point. The breaking point is different for different peoples and under different circumstances. Some peoples will be brought close to the breaking point by tremendous and useless losses in war, such as the French after the Nivelle offensive in 1917 in the Champagne. One great defeat will suffice to undermine the national morale of others, such as the defeat the Italians suffered in 1917 at Caporetto, which cost them three hundred thousand men in prisoners and the same number in deserters. The morale of others, such as the Russians in 1917, will break under the impact of a combination of tremendous war losses in men and territory and the mismanagement of an autocratic government. The morale of others will only slowly decline and, as it were, corrode at the edges—not break at all in one sudden collapse, even when exposed to a rare combination of governmental mismanagement, devastation, invasion, and a hopeless war situation. Such was the case of the Germans in the last stage of the Second World War, when a number of military leaders and former high officials gave up the lost cause while the masses of the people fought on until practically the moment of Hitler's suicide. The persistence of German morale in 1945 under most unfavorable circumstances illustrates dramatically the unpredictability of such collective reactions. Under much less severe circumstances the national morale of Germany collapsed in November 1918, a precedent that should have presaged a similar collapse of German morale some time in the summer of 1944, after the Allied invasion of France. Tolstoy gives in *War and Peace* a vivid analysis of the independent importance of morale for military success:

> Military science assumes that the relative strength of forces is identical with their numerical proportions. Military science maintains that the greater the number of soldiers, the greater their strength. *Les gros bataillons ont toujours raison.*
>
> To say this is as though one were in mechanics to say that forces were equal or unequal simply because the masses of the moving bodies were equal or unequal.
>
> Force (the volume of motion) is the product of the mass into the velocity.
>
> In warfare the force of armies is the product of the mass multiplied by something else, an unknown *x*.

Military science, seeing in history an immense number of examples in which the mass of an army does not correspond with its force, and in which small numbers conquer large ones, vaguely recognizes the existence of this unknown factor, and tries to find it sometimes in some geometrical disposition of the troops, sometimes in the superiority of the weapons, and most often in the genius of the leaders. But none of those factors yield results that agree with the historical facts.

One has but to renounce the false view that glorifies the effect of the activity of the heroes of history in warfare in order to discover this unknown quantity, x.

X is the spirit of the army, the greater or less desire to fight and to face dangers on the part of all men composing the army, which is quite apart from the question whether they are fighting under leaders of genius or not, with cudgels or with guns that fire thirty times a minute. The men who have the greater desire to fight always put themselves, too, in the more advantageous position for fighting. The spirit of the army is the factor which multiplied by the mass gives the product of the force. To define and express the significance of this unknown factor, the spirit of the army, is the problem of science.

This problem can only be solved when we cease arbitrarily substituting for that unknown factor x the conditions under which the force is manifested, such as the plans of the general, the arming of the men and so on, and recognize this unknown factor in its entirety as the greater or less desire to fight and face danger. Then only by expressing known historical facts in equations can one hope from comparison of the relative value of this unknown factor to approach its definition. Ten men, or battalions or divisions are victorious fighting with fifteen men or battalions or divisions, that is, they kill or take prisoner all of them while losing four of their own side, so that the loss has been four on one side and fifteen on the other. Consequently, four on one side have been equivalent to fifteen on the other, and consequently $4x = 15y$. Consequently $x/y = 15/4$ This equation does not give us the value of the unknown factors, but it does give us the ratio between their values. And from the reduction to such equations of various historical units (battles, campaigns, periods of warfare) a series of numbers are obtained, in which there must be and may be discovered historical laws.[16]

The Quality of Society and Government as Decisive Factors

While national morale is subjected to its ultimate test in war, it is important whenever a nation's power is brought to bear on an international problem. It is important partly because of the anticipated effects of national morale upon military strength, partly because national morale influences the determination with which the government pursues its foreign policies. Any segment of the population that feels itself permanently deprived of its rights and of full participation in the life of the nation will tend to have a lower national morale, to be less "patriotic" than

---

[16]Leo Tolstoy, *War and Peace*, Part XIV, Chapter II.

those who do not suffer from such disabilities. The same is likely to be true of those whose vital aspirations diverge from the permanent policies pursued by the majority or by the government. Whenever deep dissensions tear a people apart, the popular support that can be mustered for a foreign policy will always be precarious and will be actually small if the success or failure of the foreign policy has a direct bearing upon the issue of the domestic struggle.

Autocratic governments, which in the formulation of their policies do not take the wishes of the people into account, cannot rely upon much popular support for their foreign policies. Such was the case in countries like Czarist Russia and the Austrian monarchy. The example of Austria is particularly instructive. Many of the foreign policies of that country, especially with respect to the Slavic nations, aimed at weakening the latter in order better to be able to keep in check the Slavic nationalities living under Austrian rule. In consequence, these Slavic nationalities tended to be at best indifferent to the foreign policies of their own government and at worst to support actively the policies of Slavic governments directed against their own. Thus it is not surprising that during the First World War whole Slavic units of the Austro-Hungarian army went over to the Russians. The government dared to use other such units only against non-Slavic enemies, such as the Italians. For similar reasons, during the First World War the German army used Alsatian units against the Russians, and Polish units against the French.

The Soviet Union had a similar experience of lack of morale during the Second World War when large contingents composed in the main of Ukrainians and Tartars deserted to the Germans. Great Britain had the same experience with India, whose national energies supported but unwillingly and with reservations the foreign policies of its alien master—if they did not, like Bose and his followers during the Second World War, come to the assistance of the alien master's enemy. Napoleon and Hitler had to learn to their dismay that among the spoils of foreign conquest popular support of the conqueror's policies is not necessarily to be found. The amount and strength of the support Hitler, for instance, found among the conquered peoples of Europe was in inverse ratio to the quality of the national morale of the particular people.

Any country with deep and unbridgeable class divisions will find its national morale in a precarious state. French power ever since the thirties has suffered from this weakness. From the time of Hitler's ascent to power, the vacillating foreign policies of the French governments, following each other in rapid succession and concealing their impotence behind the ideologies of a status quo they were unwilling and incapable of defending, had already weakened the national morale of the French people as a whole. The crises of 1938–39, with the ever renewed threat of war and general mobilizations to meet it, followed by Hitler's successes, demobilizations, and an increasingly precarious peace, had contributed powerfully to the general decay of French morale. While there was decay everywhere, there was actual collapse only in two important sectors of French society. On the one hand, faced with social legislation limiting their powers, considerable groups of the French upper classes rallied to the cry "Rather Hitler [the enemy dictator] than Blum [the French Socialist]!" Although Hitler threatened the position of France in Europe and its very existence as a nation, these groups were unable to give wholehearted support to the French foreign policy opposing Hitler. After the conquest of France they favored the domination of France by Hitler rather than its liberation from the foreign dictator. On the other hand, the Communists, for different reasons, undermined the national morale of France so long as Hitler fought only the capitalists of the West. It was only after he had attacked the Soviet Union that they contributed new strength to French national morale by fighting in the forefront of the resistance against the invader.

However unpredictable the quality of national morale, especially at a moment of great crisis, there are obvious situations in which national morale is likely to be high, while under certain different conditions the odds are in favor of a low state of national morale. One can say, in general, that the more closely identified a people are with the actions and objectives of their government—especially, of course, in foreign affairs—the better are the chances for national morale to be high, and vice versa. Thus it can surprise only those who mistakenly think of the modern totalitarian state in terms of the autocracies of the eighteenth and nineteenth centuries that in Nazi Germany national morale was high almost to the last. It declined slowly rather than breaking in one sudden collapse as it did in November 1918. The great bulk of the Russian people, despite the greatest hardships in war and peace, have consistently shown a high degree of national morale.

The modern totalitarian state has been able to fill the gap between government and people, a gap that was typical of the monarchies of the eighteenth and nineteenth centuries, through the use of democratic symbols, totalitarian control of public opinion, and policies actually or seemingly benefiting the people. Practically all national energies flow into the channels chosen by the government, and the identification of the individual with the state, which we have recognized as one of the characteristics of modern politics,[17] reaches under the stimulation of totalitarianism the intensity of religious fervor. Therefore, so long as totalitarian governments are or seem to be successful, or can at least hold out hope for success, they can count upon the determined support of their peoples for the foreign policies they pursue.

What totalitarianism can achieve only by force, fraud, and deification of the state, democracy must try to accomplish through the free interplay of popular forces, guided by a wise and responsible government. Where the government is unable to prevent the degeneration of this interplay into class, racial, or religious conflicts, tending to split the national community into warring groups, national morale is likely to be low, at least among the victimized groups if not among the people as a whole. The policies of France before and during the Second World War illustrate this point. So does the weakness of the foreign policies in peace and war of countries where feudal aristocracies or autocratic dictators control the government and oppress the people. The governments of such nations can never choose and pursue their foreign objectives with any degree of determination, even at the risk of war, because they can never be sure of the support of their peoples. They constantly fear lest the domestic opposition exploit difficulties and reverses in the

---

[17]See pages 114 ff.

international field for the purpose of overthrowing the regime. Where, however, a government speaks as the mouthpiece, and acts as the executor, of the popular will, national morale is likely to reflect the real identity between popular aspirations and governmental actions. The national morale of Denmark under the German occupation from 1940 to the end of the Second World War illustrates this point no less strikingly than did the national morale of Germany until the defeat at Stalingrad.

In the last analysis, then, the power of a nation, in view of its national morale, resides in the quality of its government. A government that is truly representative, not only in the sense of parliamentary majorities, but above all in the sense of being able to translate the inarticulate convictions and aspirations of the people into international objectives and policies, has the best chance to marshal the national energies in support of those objectives and policies. The adage that free men fight better than slaves can be amplified into the proposition that nations well governed are likely to have a higher national morale than nations poorly governed. The quality of government is patently a source of strength or weakness with respect to most of the factors upon which national power depends, especially in view of the influence the government exerts upon natural resources, industrial capacity, and military preparedness. For the quality of national morale, the quality of government takes on a special importance. Whereas it operates upon the other elements of national power as one among several influences, all more or less manageable by human action, it is the only tangible factor among intangibles that accounts for the quality of national morale. Without national morale national power is either nothing but material force or else a potentiality that awaits its realization in vain. Yet the only means of deliberately improving national morale lies in the improvement of the quality of government. All else is a matter of chance.

THE QUALITY OF DIPLOMACY[18]

Of all the factors that make for the power of a nation, the most important, however unstable, is the quality of diplomacy. All the other factors that determine national power are, as it were, the raw material out of which the power of a nation is fashioned. The quality of a nation's diplomacy combines those different factors into an integrated whole, gives them direction and weight, and awakens their slumbering potentialities by giving them the breath of actual power. The conduct of a nation's foreign affairs by its diplomats is for national power in peace what military strategy and tactics by its military leaders are for national power in war. It is the art of bringing the different elements of the national power to bear with maximum effect upon those points in the international situation that concern the national interest most directly.

---

[18]By the term "diplomacy," as used in the following pages, we refer to the formation and execution of foreign policy on all levels, the highest as well as the subordinate. On the subject matter discussed here, see also Part Ten.

Diplomacy, one might say, is the brains of national power, as national morale is its soul. If its vision is blurred, its judgment defective, and its determination feeble, all the advantages of geographical location, of self-sufficiency in food, raw materials, and industrial production, of military preparedness, of size and quality of population will in the long run avail a nation little. A nation that can boast of all these advantages but not of a diplomacy commensurate with them may achieve temporary successes through the sheer weight of its natural assets. In the long run it is likely to squander the natural assets by activating them incompletely, haltingly, and wastefully for the nation's international objectives.

In the long run such a nation must yield to one whose diplomacy is prepared to make the most of whatever other elements of power are at its disposal, thus making up through its own excellence for deficiencies in other fields. By using the power potentialities of a nation to best advantage, a competent diplomacy can increase the power of a nation beyond what one would expect it to be in view of all the other factors combined. Often in history the Goliath without brains or soul has been smitten and slain by the David who had both. Diplomacy of high quality will bring the ends and means of foreign policy into harmony with the available resources of national power. It will tap the hidden sources of national strength and transform them fully and securely into political realities. By giving direction to the national effort, it will in turn increase the independent weight of certain factors, such as industrial potential, military preparedness, national character, and morale. It is for this reason that national power is apt to rise to its height fulfilling all its potentialities, particularly in times of war, when ends and means of policy are clearly laid out.

The United States, in the period between the two world wars, furnishes a striking example of a potentially powerful nation playing a minor role in world affairs because its foreign policy refused to bring the full weight of its potential strength to bear upon international problems. As far as the power of the United States on the international scene was concerned, the advantages of geography, natural resources, industrial potential, and size and quality of population might as well have not existed at all, for American diplomacy proceeded as though they did not exist.

The transformation American foreign policy has undergone since the end of the Second World War seemed to have answered definitively the question of whether, and to what extent, American diplomacy is willing and able to transform the potentialities of national power into political actualities. Yet at the beginning of that period, in an article significantly entitled "Imperialism or Indifference," the London *Economist* still doubted the answer. After enumerating the factors that, taken by themselves, would make the United States the most powerful nation on earth, the *Economist* continued:

> But though these things are essential ingredients, they are not all that it takes to make a Great Power. There must also be the willingness, and the ability, to use economic resources in support of national policy. The rulers of Soviet Russia . . . are not likely, at least for a generation to come, to have nearly as

good cards in their hands as the Americans. But the nature of their system of concentrated power and iron censorship enables them to play a forcing game. The Americans' hand is all trumps; but will any of them ever be played? And for what purpose?[19]

The classic example of a country that, while in other respects hopelessly outclassed, returned to the heights of power chiefly by virtue of its brilliant diplomacy is France in the period from 1890 to 1914. After its defeat in 1870 at the hands of Germany, France was a second-rate power, and Bismarck's statecraft, by isolating it, kept it in that position. With Bismarck's dismissal in 1890, Germany's foreign policy turned away from Russia and was unwilling to alleviate Great Britain's suspicion. French diplomacy took full advantage of those mistakes of German foreign policy. In 1894, France added a military alliance to the political understanding reached with Russia in 1891; in 1904 and 1912, it entered into informal agreements with Great Britain. The configuration of 1914, which found France aided by potent allies and Germany deserted by one (Italy) and burdened with the weakness of the others (Austria-Hungary, Bulgaria, Turkey), was in the main the work of a galaxy of brilliant French diplomatists: Camille Barrère, ambassador to Italy; Jules Cambon, ambassador to Germany; Paul Cambon, ambassador to Great Britain; and Maurice Paléologue, ambassador to Russia.

In the period between the two world wars, Rumania owed its ability to play a role in international affairs much superior to its actual resources chiefly to the personality of one man, its Foreign Minister Titulescu. Similarly, so small and precariously located a country as Belgium owed a great deal of the power it was able to exercise during the nineteenth century to two shrewd and active kings, Leopold I and Leopold II. Spanish diplomacy in the seventeenth and Turkish diplomacy in the nineteenth century were able for a time to compensate for the decline of national power in other respects. The ups and downs of British power are closely connected with changes in the quality of British diplomacy. Cardinal Wolsey, Castlereagh, and Canning signify the summits of British diplomacy as well as of British power, while Lord North and Neville Chamberlain stand for the decline of both. What would the power of France have been without the statecraft of Richelieu, Mazarin, and Talleyrand? What would Germany's power have been without Bismarck? Italy's without Cavour? And what did the power of the young American republic not owe to Franklin, Jefferson, Madison, Jay, the Adamses, its ambassadors and secretaries of state?

Nations must rely upon the quality of their diplomacy to act as a catalyst for the different factors that constitute their power. In other words, these different factors, as they are brought to bear upon an international problem by diplomacy, are what is called a nation's power. Therefore it is of the utmost importance that the good quality of the diplomatic service be constant. And constant quality is best assured by dependence upon tradition and institutions rather than upon the sporadic appearance of outstanding individuals. It is to tradition that Great Britain

---

[19]*Economist*, May 24, 1947, p. 785. (Reprinted by permission.)

owes the relative constancy of its power from Henry VIII to the First World War. Whatever the whims and shortcomings of its kings and ministers may have been, the traditions of its ruling class and, in recent times, its professional foreign service were able, a few notable exceptions notwithstanding, to mold the prerequisites of national power, with which Great Britain was endowed, into the greatness of its actual power. It is no accident that when, owing to the diplomacy of Stanley Baldwin and Neville Chamberlain, British power reached its lowest point in centuries, the professionals of the Foreign Office had little influence upon the conduct of British foreign policy and that the two men mainly responsible for it were, in terms of family tradition, businessmen and newcomers to the aristocracy that for centuries had ruled Great Britain. In Winston Churchill, the scion of a ruling family, the aristocratic traditions were again brought to bear upon the national power of Great Britain. Today the institutional excellence of the British foreign service reveals itself in the skill with which Great Britain has brought its commitments all over the world into harmony with the reduced resources of its national power.

On the other hand, Germany owed its power to the demoniac genius of two men, Bismarck and Hitler. Since Bismarck's personality and policies made it impossible for traditions and institutions to develop that might have been able to perpetuate the intelligent conduct of Germany's foreign policy, his disappearance from the political scene in 1890 was the signal for a deep and permanent drop in the quality of German diplomacy. The consequent deterioration of Germany's international position culminated in the military predicament with which the First World War confronted it. In the case of Hitler, the strength and weakness of German diplomacy lay in the mind of the Führer himself. The victories German diplomacy won from 1933 to 1940 were the victories of one man's mind, and the deterioration of that mind was a direct cause of the disasters that marked the last years of the Nazi regime. The national suicide of Germany in the last months of the Second World War, when military resistance had become a futile gesture paid for in hundreds of thousands of lives and the ruin of cities, and Hitler's suicide in the last stage of the war—the self-extinction, in other words, of Germany's national power and of the life of its leader—were both the work of one man. That man was unfettered by those traditions and institutional safeguards by which healthy political systems try to provide for continuity in the quality of diplomacy and thus tend to inhibit the spectacular successes of genius as well as the abysmal blunders of madmen.

So far as continuity in the quality of the conduct of foreign affairs is concerned, the United States stands between the continuous high quality of British diplomacy and the traditional low quality, interrupted by short-lived triumphs, of German foreign policy. With an unchallengeable superiority in material and human resources at its disposal, American diplomacy in the Western Hemisphere could not fail to be successful in some measure, regardless of the quality of its foreign policy. The same has been true to a lesser degree in the relations between the United States and the rest of the world. The "big stick" in the form of the material superiority of the United States spoke its own language, regardless of whether American diplomacy spoke in a soft or loud voice, in articulate or confused terms, with or without a clearly conceived purpose. The brilliance of the first decades of American diplomacy was followed by a long period of mediocrity, if not ineptitude, interrupted under the impact of great crises by three brief periods of great achievements under Woodrow Wilson, Franklin D. Roosevelt, and Harry Truman. While American diplomacy was thus lacking in the institutional excellence of the British, it had the benefit of material conditions that even poor statecraft could hardly dissipate. Furthermore, it could draw upon a national tradition, formulated in Washington's Farewell Address and, more particularly, in the Monroe Doctrine. The guidance of this tradition would protect a poor diplomacy from catastrophic blunders and make a mediocre diplomacy look better than it actually was. Unanswered is the question of whether such a tradition can save American diplomacy from a crusading ideological approach.

THE QUALITY OF GOVERNMENT

The best-conceived and most expertly executed foreign policy, drawing upon an abundance of material and human resources, must come to naught if it cannot draw also upon good government. Good government, viewed as an independent requirement of national power,[20] means three things: balance between, on the one hand, the material and human resources that go into the making of national power and, on the other, the foreign policy to be pursued; balance among those resources; and popular support for the foreign policies to be pursued.

The Problem of Balance Between Resources and Policy

Good government, then, must start by performing two different intellectual operations. First, it must choose the objectives and methods of its foreign policy in view of the power available to support them with a maximum chance of success. A nation that sets its sights too low, forgoing foreign policies well within the reach of its power, abdicates its rightful role in the council of nations; the United States fell into that error in the interwar period. A nation may also set its sights too high and pursue policies that cannot be successfully executed with the available power; this was the error the United States committed during the peace negotiations in 1919. As Lloyd George put it: "The Americans appeared to assume responsibility for the sole guardianship of the Ten Commandments and for the Sermon on the Mount; yet, when it came to a practical question of assistance and responsibility, they absolutely refused to accept it." A nation may try to play the role of a great power without having the prerequisites for doing so, and will court disaster, as Poland did in the interwar period. Or, being a great power, it may embark upon a policy of unlimited conquest, overtaxing its strength; the unsuccessful world conquerors, from Alexander to Hitler, illustrate that point.

---

[20]We have already spoken of the quality of government as a requirement of national morale; see pages 149 ff.

Thus the national power available determines the limits of foreign policy. There is only one exception to that rule, and that is when the very existence of the nation is at stake. Then the policy of national survival overrides the rational considerations of national power, and the emergency reverses the normal relationship between policy and considerations of power, establishing the primacy of the former. A nation is then called upon to subordinate all other interests to that of survival and to make a national effort that rationally could not have been expected of it. This is what Great Britain did in the fall and winter of 1940–41.

The Problem of Balance Among Resources

Once a government has brought its foreign policy into balance with the power available to it, it must bring the different elements of national power into balance with one another. A nation does not necessarily attain the maximum of national power because it is very rich in natural resources, possesses a very large population, or has built an enormous industrial and military establishment. It attains that maximum when it has at its disposal a sufficient quantity and quality, in the right admixture, of those resources of power that will allow it to pursue a given foreign policy with a maximum chance of success. Great Britain, when it was at the summit of its power, was deficient in many of the elements of national power, such as natural resources, size of population, and ground troops. Yet it had developed to unchallengeable supremacy that one element of national power, the navy, which was a perfect instrument for the British policy of overseas expansion, and at the same time assured the uninterrupted flow from abroad of those raw materials and foodstuffs without which Great Britain could not have survived. In view of this policy, of the available natural resources, and of the geographic location, a large population and a standing army would have been for Great Britain a handicap rather than an asset. On the other hand, had Great Britain continued to pursue a policy of continental expansion, as it did during the better part of the Middle Ages, it would have been in need of both.

A large population is a source of weakness rather than of strength, as the example of India has shown us,[21] if it cannot be adequately fed with the available resources. The hasty building of great industrial and military establishments by totalitarian methods creates certain elements of national power, but in its very process destroys others, such as national morale and the physical resilience of the population; the developments in the Soviet satellites of Eastern Europe are a case in point. To plan for a military establishment that is too big to be supported by the available industrial capacity, and hence can be built and maintained only at the price of galloping inflation, economic crisis, and deterioration of morale, is to plan for national weakness rather than for power. In a national emergency, when the very existence of the nation is at stake, the American government, for instance, can and must offer the people guns instead of butter; if it cannot make a case for such an emergency, it must strike a balance between military and civilian requirements by allocating a fair share of the economic product for civilian consumption.

---

[21]See pages 124, 125, 126.

Another government, such as the Chinese or Korean, might not need to take such considerations of civilian welfare into account. In other words, a government in its building of national power cannot be oblivious to the character of the nation it governs. One nation will revolt against hardships that another nation will take patiently in its stride, and sometimes a nation will surprise the world and itself by the sacrifices it willingly makes for the defense of its interests and its existence.

The Problem of Popular Support

A contemporary government, especially one subject to democratic control, has only performed part of its task when it has established the two types of balances that we have discussed above. Another task, perhaps the most difficult of all, still lies ahead of it. It must secure the approval of its own people for its foreign policies and the domestic ones designed to mobilize the elements of national power in support of them. That task is difficult because the conditions under which popular support can be obtained for a foreign policy are not necessarily identical with the conditions under which a foreign policy can be successfully pursued. As Tocqueville put it, with special reference to the United States:

> Foreign politics demand scarcely any of those qualities which are peculiar to a democracy; they require, on the contrary, the perfect use of almost all those in which it is deficient. Democracy is favorable to the increase of the internal resources of a state; it diffuses wealth and comfort, promotes public spirit, and fortifies the respect for law in all classes of society: all these are advantages which have only an indirect influence over the relations which one people bears to another. But a democracy can only with great difficulty regulate the details of an important undertaking, persevere in a fixed design, and work out its execution in spite of serious obstacles. It cannot combine its measures with secrecy or await their consequences with patience. . . .
>
> The propensity that induces democracies to obey impulse rather than prudence, and to abandon mature design for the gratification of a momentary passion, was clearly seen in America on the breaking out of the French Revolution. It was then as evident to the simplest capacity as it is at the present time that the interest of the Americans forbade them to take any part in the contest which was about to deluge Europe with blood, but which could not injure their own country. But the sympathies of the people declared themselves with so much violence in favor of France that nothing but the inflexible character of Washington and the immense popularity which he enjoyed could have prevented the Americans from declaring war against England. And even then, the exertions which the austere reason of that great man made to repress the generous but imprudent passions of his fellow citizens nearly deprived him of the sole recompense which he ever claimed, that of his country's love. The majority reprobated his policy, but it was afterwards approved by the whole nation.[22]

---

[22]Alexis de Tocqueville, *Democracy in America* (New York: Alfred A. Knopf, 1945), Vol. I, pp. 234–35.

Thinking required for the successful conduct of foreign policy can be diametrically opposed to the rhetoric and action by which the masses and their representatives are likely to be moved. The peculiar qualities of the statesman's mind are not always likely to find a favorable response in the popular mind. The statesman must think in terms of the national interest, conceived as power among other powers. The popular mind, unaware of the fine distinctions of the statesman's thinking, reasons more often than not in the simple moralistic and legalistic terms of absolute good and absolute evil. The statesman must take the long view, proceeding slowly and by detours, paying with small losses for great advantage; he must be able to temporize, to compromise, to bide his time. The popular mind wants quick results; it will sacrifice tomorrow's real benefit for today's apparent advantage.

If Tocqueville's point is well taken, the kind of thinking required for the successful conduct of foreign policy will at times be opposed to considerations by which people are moved. A foreign policy that is passionately and overwhelmingly supported by public opinion cannot be assumed for that reason alone to be good foreign policy. On the contrary, the harmony between foreign policy and public opinion may well have been achieved at the price of surrendering the principles of good foreign policy to the unsound preferences of public opinion.

In the American case these inherent difficulties are aggravated by the fact that the United States is almost continuously recovering from the last election or preparing for the next one. Especially in the latter case, the temptation is overwhelming for an administration to seek to gain electoral advantage by catering to the preferences of public opinion, regardless of foreign policy. Thus one requirement of the statesman's art is to steer a middle course between respect for the perennial principles of sound foreign policy and the fickle preferences of public opinion.

These considerations shed an illuminating light upon the apparent paradox of President Jimmy Carter, who emerged from the Democratic primaries in 1980 as virtually unbeatable in his appeal to the electorate, yet under his leadership the United States had suffered a string of humiliating defeats in its relations with other nations. The most spectacular of these defeats was the continuing captivity of fifty-two hostages in Iran. By foreswearing from the outset any form of violence in response to this outrage, Carter deprived himself of any leverage against Iran. The disadvantages he was able to threaten Iran with, primarily economic sanctions, were bound to be ineffective. The advantages he could offer (such as economic and military aid) did not outweigh, in the eyes of the Iranians, the risks and liabilities American largesse would entail. Thus the United States stood helpless—in a situation that in most other periods of American history would have called forth swift action to settle the issue, even at the risk of some American lives.

But the president, by putting the emphasis on saving American lives by peaceful means, hit upon a sympathetic chord in American public opinion. Carter did what Wilson had allegedly done before: "He kept us out of war." He did so without abandoning the most visible and sentimental American objective: saving those fifty-two American lives. It apparently did not occur to public opinion or to the president that the leader responsible for American foreign policy has a duty not only to preserve lives but also to preserve the long-term interests of the nation.

The same mixture of rhetorical commitment and political inaction has secured public support for our policies toward the Soviet Union and assured their ineffectiveness at the same time. Regardless of one's interpretation of the significance of the Soviet military takeover of Afghanistan, the belligerent verbal reaction of the president was out of all proportion to the actual measures taken in response to that takeover.

Yet while that belligerence may have surprised the Russians, the absence of action commensurate with that rhetoric did nothing to induce a change in their policies. The Russians will go as far as they can without provoking the United States into a nuclear confrontation. Positive cases in point are the Cuban missile crisis and the successive Berlin crises; a negative confirmation of this thesis is the continuing military occupation of Afghanistan.

However, the president's belligerent stance appeared to be a great success in domestic politics. The president who had declared his intention to make the protection and promotion of human rights the cornerstone of his foreign policy spoke to the Soviet Union in the language of John Foster Dulles. Public opinion polls registered overwhelming popular approval; once again, a futile foreign policy was compensated for by domestic triumph. Here, however, Carter encountered another dilemma, superimposed upon the one between foreign policy and domestic politics. It evolved from the rational unacceptability of nuclear confrontation.

The need of great powers to defend and promote their interests by the use of force as a last resort implies in the case of the United States and the Soviet Union the possibility of using nuclear weapons as an instrument of force. Yet the use of nuclear weapons not as a single, isolated demonstration, as at Hiroshima and Nagasaki, but as normal instruments of warfare would mean the destruction of all the belligerents as viable societies. Nuclear weapons thus used—in contrast to conventional weapons—would not be a rational means to the rational ends of foreign policy but instruments of desperation denoting suicide and genocide. This was the second fundamental dilemma Carter faced.

The anarchic character of the international system forced him, following a convention coterminous with history, to contemplate resort to physical violence as the ultimate factor in the settlement of international issues. Yet the irrationality of the all-out use of such violence made him shrink from the use even of conventional violence lest it escalate into nuclear war. Thus in an international crisis today the president acts with utmost caution, if he acts at all, and he compensates for the lack of effective action with belligerent talk. In this tendency President Carter did not stand alone.

Popular support is the precondition of the president's stewardship of foreign policy. The creation of a public opinion supporting him, even at the sacrifice of some elements of foreign policy, is a task that a president can only shun at the risk of losing office and, with it, his ability to pursue any foreign policy at all. The question to which Carter's conduct gave rise concerned not the need of a compromise between the requirements of a sound foreign policy and the demands of public opinion but the point at which the compromise was to be made. Aside from faulting him for ignorance and incompetence, the critics maintained that he surrendered too many principles of a sound foreign policy to the demands of public opinion. The issue was not whether the president ought to pursue the national interest regardless of the possibility of nuclear war but where to draw the line between concern for the national interest and fear of nuclear war. The question was whether Carter, in his anxiety to stay as far away as possible from nuclear war, had not needlessly sacrificed important national interests.

Confronted with this dilemma between a good foreign policy and a bad one that public opinion demands, a government must avoid two pitfalls. It must resist the temptation to sacrifice what it considers good policy upon the altar of public opinion, abdicating leadership and exchanging short-lived political advantage for the permanent interests of the country. It must also avoid widening the unavoidable gap between the requirements of good foreign policy and the preferences of public opinion. It widens that gap if, shunning tolerable compromise with the preferences of public opinion, it sticks in every detail to a foreign policy it considers to be right, and sacrifices public support to the stubborn pursuit of that policy.

Instead, the government, to be successful in its foreign and domestic policies alike, must comply with three basic requirements. It must recognize that the conflict between the requirements of good foreign policy and the preferences of public opinion is in the nature of things and, hence, unavoidable and that it can perhaps be narrowed, but it can never be bridged, by concessions to the domestic opposition. Second, the government must realize that it is the leader and not the slave of public opinion; that public opinion is not a static thing to be discovered and classified by public opinion polls as plants are by botanists but that it is a dynamic, ever-changing entity to be continuously created and re-created by informed and responsible leadership; that it is the historical mission of the government to assert that leadership lest it be the demagogue who asserts it.[23] Third, it must distinguish between what is desirable in its foreign policy and what is essential, and while it may be willing to compromise with public opinion on nonessentials, it must fight, even at the risk of its own fortunes, for what it regards to be the irreducible minimum of good foreign policy.

A government may have a correct understanding of the requirements of foreign policy and of the domestic politics to support them, but if it fails in marshaling public opinion behind these policies, its labors will be in vain, and all the other assets of national power of which the nation can boast will not be used to

---

[23]Lord Norwich, who as Mr. Duff Cooper occupied in the interwar period important cabinet posts and other government positions, puts his finger on the common misunderstanding of public opinion and the government's relation to it when he says in his memoirs (*Old Men Forget* [London: Hart-Davis, 1953]) of Neville Chamberlain: "The Prime Minister's main mistake seems to me to be two. He believes public opinion is what the 'Times' tells him it is—and he believes Conservative opinion is what the Chief Whip says it is." Unfortunately, this passive acceptance of what somebody says public opinion wants has become—and not only in the England of the interwar period—one of the main obstacles to good foreign policy.

best advantage. Of this truth the policies of contemporary democratic governments, including those of the United States, offer abundant proof.[24]

Domestic Government and Foreign Policy

It is not enough, however, for a government to marshal national public opinion
behind its foreign policies. It must also gain the support of the public opinion of
other nations for its foreign and domestic policies. This requirement is a reflection
of the changes that have occurred in recent times in the character of foreign policy. As shall be shown later in greater detail,[25] foreign policy is being pursued in
our time not only with the traditional weapons of diplomacy and military might
but also with the novel weapon of propaganda. For the struggle for power on the
international scene is today not only a struggle for military supremacy and political domination but in a specific sense a struggle for the minds of men. The power
of a nation, then, depends not only upon the skill of its diplomacy and the
strength of its armed forces but also upon the attractiveness for other nations of
its political philosophy, political institutions, and political policies. This is true in
particular of the United States and the Soviet Union, who compete with each
other not only as the two political and military superpowers but also as the foremost representatives of two different political philosophies, systems of government, and ways of life.

Thus whatever these superpowers—and this is true also, in a lesser degree, of
other nations—do or do not do, achieve or fail to achieve, in their domestic and
foreign policies has a direct bearing upon their standing as these representatives
and, hence, upon their power. A nation, for instance, that embarked upon a policy of racial discrimination could not help losing the struggle for the minds of the
colored nations of the earth. An underdeveloped nation that could increase in a
spectacular fashion the health, literacy, and standard of living of its people would
thereby have achieved a considerable increase in its power in other underdeveloped regions of the world.

At this point, then, as at others to be mentioned later,[26] the traditional distinction between foreign and domestic policies tends to break down. One might
almost be tempted to say that there are no longer any purely domestic affairs, for
whatever a nation does or does not do is held for or against it as a reflection of its
political philosophy, system of government, and way of life. A domestic achievement that is intelligible to other nations in terms of their aspirations cannot fail
to increase the power of the nation; a domestic failure, equally intelligible, is
bound to decrease it.

---

[24]This theme has been elaborated in Hans J. Morgenthau, "The Conduct of Foreign Policy," in
Aspects of American Government, edited by Sydney Bailey (London: The Hansard Society, 1950),
pp. 99 ff.; and *In Defense of the National Interest* (New York: Alfred A. Knopf, 1951; Washington, DC:
University Press of America, 1982), pp. 221 ff.
[25]See pages 339 ff.
[26]See pages 338 ff.

10 Evaluation of National Power

THE TASK OF EVALUATION

It is the task of those responsible for the foreign policy of a nation and of those who mold public opinion with regard to international affairs to evaluate correctly the bearing of these factors upon the power of their own nation and of other nations as well, and this task must be performed for both the present and the future. What is the influence of the unification of the armed services upon the quality of the military establishment of the United States? What effect will the use of nuclear energy have upon the industrial capacity of the United States and of other nations? How will the industrial capacity, military strength, and national morale of China develop after Deng's death? How has the hostility of China and Pakistan influenced the national morale of India? What is the significance of the revival of a German army for the national power of Germany? Has reeducation changed the national character of Germany and Japan? How has the national character of the people of Argentina reacted upon the political philosophies, methods, and objectives of successive military and civilian regimes? In what ways does the advancement of the Russian sphere of influence to the Elbe River affect the geographical position of the Soviet Union? Will this or that reorganization or change in the personnel of the State Department strengthen or weaken the quality of American diplomacy? These are some of the questions that must be answered correctly if a nation's foreign policy is to be successful.

Yet these questions referring to changes in one particular factor are not the most difficult to answer. There are others that concern the influence of changes in one factor upon other factors, and here the difficulties increase and the pitfalls multiply. What is, for instance, the import of the modern technology of warfare for the geographical position of the United States? How, in other words, do guided missiles and supersonic planes affect the geographical isolation of the United States from other continents? To what degree will the United States lose, and to what degree will it retain, its traditional inviolability to overseas attack?

What do the same technological developments mean in view of the geography of Russian territory? To what extent have these factors reduced the protective function of the wide expanses of the Russian plains? And what, in this context, of the protection the Channel has afforded Great Britain since the beginning of British history? What will the industrialization of Brazil, China, and India signify for the military strength of these countries? What is the relative importance of the American army, navy, and air force in view of changes in the technology of warfare? What does the anticipated rate of increase of the American population in the next two decades and the more rapid increase of the populations of Latin America, India, and China portend for the industrial capacity and military strength of the respective nations? How will fluctuations in industrial production affect the national morale of the United States, the Soviet Union, Germany, Great Britain, and France? Will the British national character preserve its traditional qualities under the impact of the fundamental changes that the industrial capacity, the economic organization, the military strength, and the geographical isolation of Great Britain are undergoing?

The task of the analyst of national power does not, however, stop here. He must yet try to answer another group of questions of a still higher order of difficulty. These questions concern the comparison of one power factor in one nation with the same or another power factor in another nation. In other words, they concern the relative weight of changes in the individual components of the power of different nations for the overall power relations of these different nations. If one considers, for instance, the relative power of the United States and the Soviet Union at a particular moment, let us say in 1985, the question arises of how the different power factors on either side add up and to which side, and in what respects, they give a superiority in power. To what extent does the quantitatively and qualitatively superior industrial capacity of the United States compensate for the probable inferiority of its land forces? What are the respective strengths and weaknesses of the highly concentrated American industrial and population centers, with their great vulnerability to air attack and their great ease of communication, and of the dispersed Russian centers, partly secret in location and character, yet faced with great difficulties in transportation? What power does the Soviet Union derive from the exposure of Western Europe to ideological and military penetration from the East? What weakness does it suffer from its exposure to air and naval attack from the Pacific? What is the significance, in terms of the respective power positions, of the pluralistic operation in the United States of groups subservient to Soviet foreign policy and of the enforced homogeneity of Soviet public opinion? What is the impact upon the national power of the United States of a democratic form of government and of a nontotalitarian economic system in comparison with the totalitarian political and economic organization of the Soviet Union?

These and similar questions must be asked and answered with regard to all nations that play an active role on the international scene. The relative influence of the different factors upon national power must be determined with regard to all nations that compete with one another in the field of international politics.

Thus one ought to know whether France is stronger than Italy and in what respects. One ought to know what the assets and liabilities in terms of the different power factors of India or China are with respect to the Soviet Union, of Japan with regard to the United States, of Argentina with regard to Chile, and so on.

The task of power computation is still not completed. In order to gain at least an approximately true picture of the distribution of power among several nations, the power relations, as they seem to exist at a particular moment in history, must be projected into the future. To achieve this it is not enough to ask oneself: what are the power relations between the United States and the Soviet Union at this moment, and what are they likely to be two years hence? Decisions on international matters based upon, and referring to, the power relations between the United States and the Soviet Union cannot wait for measurements of power every two years. They must be made every day. And everyday changes, however small and imperceptible at first, in the factors making for national power add an ounce of strength to this side and take a grain of might away from the other.

On the relatively stable foundation of geography the pyramid of national power rises through different gradations of instability to its peak in the fleeting element of national morale. All the factors we have mentioned, with the exception of geography, are in constant flux, influencing one another and influenced in turn by the unforeseeable intervention of nature and man. Together they form the stream of national power, rising slowly and then flowing on a high level for centuries, as in Great Britain, or rising steeply and falling sharply from its crest, as was the case in Germany; or, as in the United States and the Soviet Union, rising steeply and facing the uncertainties of the future. To chart the course of the stream and of the different currents that compose it, and to anticipate the changes in their direction and speed, is the ideal task of the observer of international politics.

It is an ideal task and, hence, incapable of achievement. Even if those responsible for the foreign policy of a nation were endowed with superior wisdom and unfailing judgment, and could draw upon the most complete and reliable sources of information, there would be unknown factors to spoil their calculations. They could not foresee such natural catastrophes as famines and epidemics, such man-made catastrophes as wars and revolutions, as well as inventions and discoveries, the rise and disappearance of intellectual, military, and political leaders, the thoughts and actions of such leaders, not to speak of the imponderables of national morale. In short, even the wisest and best informed of men would still have to face all the contingencies of history and of nature. Actually, however, the assumed perfection in intellect and information is never available. Not all the men who inform those who make decisions in foreign affairs are well informed, and not all the men who make decisions are wise. Thus the task of assessing the relative power of nations for the present and for the future resolves itself into a series of hunches, of which some will certainly turn out to be wrong while others may be proved by subsequent events to have been correct. The success or failure of a foreign policy, insofar as it depends upon such power calculations, is determined by the relative importance of the right and wrong hunches of those responsible for a particular foreign policy of a particular nation, as well as those who conduct the foreign affairs of other nations. Sometimes the mistakes in the assessment of power relations committed by one nation are compensated for by the mistakes committed by another. Thus the success of the foreign policy of a nation may be due less to the accuracy of its own calculations than to the greater errors of the other side.

TYPICAL ERRORS OF EVALUATION

Of all the errors that nations can commit in evaluating their own power and the power of other nations, three types are so frequent and illustrate so well the intellectual pitfalls and practical risks inherent in such evaluations that they deserve some further discussion. The first disregards the relativity of power by erecting the power of one particular nation into an absolute. The second takes for granted the permanency of a certain factor that has in the past played a decisive role, thus overlooking the dynamic change to which most power factors are subject. The third attributes to one single factor a decisive importance, to the neglect of all the others. In other words, the first error consists in not correlating the power of one nation to the power of other nations, the second consists in not correlating actual power at one time to possible power at some future time, and the third consists in not correlating one power factor to others of the same nation.

The Absolute Character of Power

When we refer to the power of a nation by saying that this nation is very powerful and that nation is weak, we always imply a comparison. In other words, the concept of power is always a relative one. When we say that the United States is at present one of the two most powerful nations on earth, what we are actually saying is that if we compare the power of the United States with the power of all other nations, as they exist at present, we find that the United States is more powerful than all others save one.

It is one of the most elemental and frequent errors in international politics to neglect this relative character of power and to deal instead with the power of a nation as though it were an absolute. The evaluation of the power of France in the period between the two world wars is a case in point. At the conclusion of the First World War, France was the most powerful nation on earth from a military point of view. France was so regarded up to the very moment in 1940 when its actual military weakness became obvious in a crushing defeat. The newspaper headlines from the beginning of the Second World War in September 1939 to the defeat of France in the summer of 1940 tell most eloquently the story of that misjudgment of French military power. During that period of the so-called phony war, the German armies were supposed not to dare to attack the French because of the latter's superior strength, and on numerous occasions the French were reported to have broken through the German lines. At the root of that misjudgment there was the misconception that the military power of France was not relative to the military power of other nations, but something absolute. French military strength, taken by itself, was at least as great in 1939 as it was in 1919; France was therefore believed to be as strong a nation in 1939 as it had been in 1919.

The fatal error of that evaluation lies in the unawareness of the fact that in 1919 France was the strongest military power on earth only in comparison with other nations, of which its closest competitor, Germany, was defeated and disarmed. The supremacy of France as a military power was, in other words, not an intrinsic quality of the French nation that might be ascertained in the same way in which one might detect the national characteristics of the French people, their geographic location, and natural resources. That supremacy was, on the contrary, the result of a peculiar power configuration—that is, of the comparative superiority of France as a military power over the other nations. The quality of the French army as such had indeed not decreased between 1919 and 1939. Measured in numbers and quality of troops, artillery, airplanes, and staff work, French military power had not deteriorated. Thus even so keen an expert on international affairs as Sir Winston Churchill, comparing the French army of the late thirties with the French army of 1919, could declare in 1937 that the French army was the only guarantee of international peace.

He and most of his contemporaries compared the French army of 1937 with the French army of 1919, which had gained its reputation from comparison with the German army of the same year, instead of comparing the French army of 1937 with the German army of the same year. Such a comparison would have shown that the power configuration of 1919 was reversed in the late thirties. While the French military establishment still was essentially as good as it had been in 1919, Germany's armed forces were now vastly superior to the French. What exclusive concern with French armed might—as if it were an absolute quality—could not reveal, a comparison of the relative military strength of France and Germany might have indicated, and grave errors in political and military judgment might thus have been avoided.

A nation that at a particular moment in history finds itself at the peak of its power is particularly exposed to the temptation to forget that all power is relative. It is likely to believe that the superiority it has achieved is an absolute quality to be lost only through stupidity or neglect of duty. A foreign policy based on such assumptions runs grave risks, for it overlooks the fact that the superior power of that nation is only in part the outgrowth of its own qualities, while it is in part the result of the qualities of other nations compared with its own.

The predominance of Great Britain from the end of the Napoleonic Wars to the beginning of the Second World War was due mainly to its insular protection from attack and its quasi-monopolistic control of the main sea lanes of the world. In other words, Great Britain during that period of history had in comparison with other nations two advantages no other nation possessed. Great Britain's insular location has not changed, and its navy is still one of the most powerful in the world. But other nations have acquired weapons, such as nuclear bombs and guided missiles, that obviate to a considerable extent the two advantages from which the power of Great Britain grew. This change in the power position of Great Britain sheds light upon the tragic dilemma that confronted Neville Chamberlain in the years before the Second World War. Chamberlain understood the relativity of Britain's power. He knew that not even victory in war could stop its decline. It was Chamberlain's ironic fate that his attempts to avoid war at any price made war inevitable, and that he was forced to declare the war he dreaded as the destroyer of British power. It is, however, a testimony to the wisdom of British statecraft that, since the end of the Second World War, British foreign policy has by and large been conscious of the decline of British power relative to the power of other nations. British statesmen have been aware of the fact that, while the British navy, taken by itself, may be as strong as it was ten years ago and the Channel is as broad and unruly as it always was, other nations have increased their power to such an extent as to deprive those two British assets of much of their effectiveness.

The Permanent Character of Power

The second typical error impairing the evaluation of national power is related to the first one but proceeds from a different intellectual operation. While it may be well aware of the relativity of power, it singles out a particular power factor or power relation, basing the estimate upon the assumption that this factor or relation is immune to change.

We have already had occasion to refer to the miscalculation that up to 1940 saw in France the first military power on earth. Those who held this view erected French power as they had experienced it at the end of the First World War into a permanent quality of France that seemed impervious to historical change, forgetting that the eminence of that power in the twenties was the result of comparison and that it would have to be tested by comparison in order to ascertain its quality in 1940. Conversely, when the actual weakness of France revealed itself in military defeat, there developed a tendency in France and elsewhere to expect that weakness to endure. France was treated with neglect and disdain as though it were bound to be weak forever.

The evaluation of Russian power has followed a similar pattern, but in reverse historical order. From 1917 to the battle of Stalingrad in 1943, the Soviet Union was treated as if its weakness at the beginning of the twenties was bound to persist whatever change might occur in other fields. Thus the British military mission that was sent to Moscow in the summer of 1939 to conclude a military alliance with the Soviet Union, in anticipation of the approaching war with Germany, conceived its task with a view of Russian power that might have been justified ten or twenty years before. This miscalculation was an important element in the mission's failure. On the other hand, immediately after the victory of Stalingrad and under the impact of the Soviet Union's aggressive foreign policy, the belief in the permanent invincibility of the Soviet Union and in the permanency of its predominance in Europe was widely held as a dogma.

There is a seemingly ineradicable inclination in our attitude toward the Latin American countries to assume that the unchallengeable superiority of the colossus of the North, which has existed since the nations of the Western Hemisphere won their independence, was almost a law of nature that population trends, industrialization, and political and military developments might modify but could not basically alter. Similarly, since for centuries the political history of the world has been determined by members of the white races, while the colored races were in the main the objects of that history, it is difficult for members of all races alike to visualize a situation where the political supremacy of the white races might no longer exist—where, indeed, the relation between the races might even be reversed. It is especially the demonstration of seemingly irresistible military power that exerts a strange fascination over the minds of those who are given to hasty prophecies rather than to cautious analysis. It makes them believe that history has come to a standstill, as it were, and that today's holders of unchallengeable power cannot fail to enjoy this power tomorrow and the day after. Thus, when in 1940 and 1941 the power of Germany was at its peak, it was widely believed that German domination of Europe was established forever. When the hidden strength of the Soviet Union startled the world in 1943, Stalin was saluted as the future master of Europe and Asia. In the postwar years the American monopoly of the atomic bomb gave rise to the conception of the "American Century," a world dominion based upon unchallengeable American power.[1]

The root of all those tendencies to believe in the absolute character of power or to take the permanency of a particular power configuration for granted lies in the contrast between the dynamic, ever-changing character of the power relations among nations, on the one hand, and the human intellect's thirst for certainty and security in the form of definite answers, on the other. Confronted with the contingencies, ambiguities, and uncertainties of the international situation, we search for a definite comprehension of the power factors upon which our foreign policy is based. We all find ourselves in the position of Queen Victoria, who after dismissing Palmerston, whose unpredictable moves on the international scene had exasperated her, asked her new prime minister, John Russell, for "a regular programme embracing these different relations with other powers." The answers we receive are not always so wise as the one John Russell gave Queen Victoria. "It is very difficult," he replied, "to lay down any principles from which deviations may not frequently be made."[2] Yet a misguided public opinion is only too prone to blame statesmen for such deviations, deeming compliance with principles, without regard for the distribution of power, to be a virtue rather than a vice.

---

[1]The most spectacular contemporary victim of the fallacy of the permanent character of power is James Burnham. See George Orwell, "Second Thoughts on James Burnham," *Polemic*, No. 3 (May 1946), pp. 13 ff; "James Burnham Rides Again," *Antioch Review*, Vol. 7, No. 2 (Summer 1947), pp. 315 ff.
[2]Robert W. Seton Watson, *Britain in Europe, 1789–1914* (New York: Macmillan, 1937), p. 53.

What the observer of international politics needs in order to reduce to a minimum the unavoidable errors in the calculations of power is a creative imagination, immune from the fascination that the preponderant power of the moment so easily imparts, able to detach itself from the superstition of an inevitable trend in history, open to the possibilities for change that the dynamics of history entail. A creative imagination of this kind would be capable of that supreme intellectual achievement of detecting under the surface of present power relations the germinal developments of the future, combining the knowledge of what is with the hunch as to what might be, and condensing all these facts, symptoms, and unknowns into a chart of probable future trends that is not too much at variance with what actually will happen.

The Fallacy of the Single Factor

The third typical error in assessing the power of different nations—attributing to a single factor an overriding importance, to the detriment of all the others—can best be illustrated in three of its manifestations most consequential in modern times: geopolitics, nationalism, and militarism.

Geopolitics

Geopolitics is a pseudoscience erecting the factor of geography into an absolute that is supposed to determine the power, and hence the fate, of nations. Its basic conception is space. Yet, while space is static, the peoples living within the spaces of the earth are dynamic. According to geopolitics, it is a law of history that peoples must expand by "conquering space," or perish, and that the relative power of nations is determined by the mutual relation of the conquered spaces. This basic conception of geopolitics was first expressed in a paper by Sir Halford Mackinder, "The Geographical Pivot of History," read before the Royal Geographical Society in London in 1904. "As we consider this rapid review of the broader currents of history, does not a certain persistence of geographical relationship become evident? Is not the pivot region of the world's politics that vast area of Euro-Asia which is inaccessible to ships, but in antiquity lay open to the horse-riding nomads, and is today to be covered with a network of railways?" This is the "Heartland" of the world that stretches from the Volga to the Yangtze and from the Himalayas to the Arctic Ocean. "Outside the pivot area, in a great inner crescent, are Germany, Austria, Turkey, India and China, and in an outer crescent, Britain, South Africa, Australia, the United States, Canada and Japan." The "World-Island" is composed of the continents of Europe, Asia, and Africa, around which the lesser land areas of the world are grouped. From this geographical structure of the world, geopolitics draws the conclusion that "Who rules east Europe commands the Heartland; who rules the Heartland commands the World-Island; who rules the World-Island commands the World."[3]

---

[3]Sir Halford J. Mackinder, *Democratic Ideals and Reality* (New York: Henry Holt, 1919), p. 150.

Mackinder, on the basis of this analysis, foresaw the emergence of Russia, or whatever nation would control the territory described above, as the dominating world power. The German geopoliticians, under the leadership of General Haushofer, who exerted an important influence upon the power calculations and foreign policies of the Nazi regime, were more specific. They postulated an alliance with the Soviet Union or else the conquest of Eastern Europe by Germany in order to make Germany the predominant power on earth. It is obvious that this postulate cannot be directly inferred from the geopolitical premise. Geopolitics tells us only what space is destined, because of its location relative to other spaces, to harbor the master of the world. It does not tell us to what particular nation that mastery will fall. Thus the German school of geopolitics, eager to demonstrate that it was the mission of the German people to conquer the "Heartland," the geographical seat of world dominion, combined the geopolitical doctrine with the argument of population pressure. The Germans were a "people without space," and the "living space" that they must have in order to live beckoned to be conquered in the empty plains of Eastern Europe.

Geopolitics, as presented in the writings of Mackinder and Fairgrieve, had given a valid picture of one aspect of the reality of national power, a picture seen from the exclusive, and therefore distorting, angle of geography. In the hands of Haushofer and his disciples, geopolitics was transformed into a kind of political metaphysics to be used as an ideological weapon in the service of the national aspirations of Germany.[4]

Nationalism

Geopolitics is the attempt to understand the problem of national power exclusively in terms of geography, and it degenerates in the process into a political metaphysics couched in a pseudoscientific jargon. Nationalism tries to explain national power exclusively or at least predominantly in terms of national character, and it degenerates in the process into the political metaphysics of racism. As geographical location is for geopolitics the one determinant of national power, so membership in a nation is for nationalism a similar determinant. Membership in a nation may be defined in terms of language, culture, common origin, or race, or in the decision of the individual to belong to the nation. But no matter how it is defined, the membership always entails as its essence partaking in certain qualities, called the national character, that the members of a particular nation have in common and by which they are differentiated from the members of other nations. The preservation of the national character and, more particularly, the development of its creative faculties are the supreme task of the nation. In order to fulfill this

---

[4]The ideological connotations of isolationism and the solidarity of the Western Hemisphere are akin to geopolitics in that they derive a conception of foreign policy from distorted or fictional geographical factors. The distortion of isolationism has already been pointed out in the text; as to the fictional character of the geographical unity of the Western Hemisphere, see Eugene Staley, "The Myth of the Continents," in *Compass of the World*, edited by Hans W. Weigert and Vilhjalmur Stefansson (New York: Macmillan, 1944), pp. 89–108.

task, the nation needs power that will protect it against other nations and will stimulate its own development. In other words, the nation needs a state. "One nation—one state" is thus the political postulate of nationalism; the nation-state is its ideal.

But though the nation needs the power of the state for the sake of its preservation and development, the state needs the national community in order to maintain and increase its power. Particularly in the nationalistic philosophy of Germany—in the writings of Fichte and Hegel, for instance—the national character or spirit appears as the soul, and the political organization of the state as the body, of the national community, which needs both in order to fulfill its mission among the other national communities. The feeling of affinity, the participation in a common culture and tradition, the awareness of a common destiny, which are of the essence of national sentiment and patriotism, are transformed by nationalism into a political mysticism in which the national community and the state become superhuman entities, apart from and superior to their individual members, entitled to absolute loyalty and, like the idols of old, deserving of the sacrifice of men and goods.

This mysticism reaches its apogee in the racist worship of the national character. The nation is here identified with a biological entity, the race, which, so long as it remains pure, produces the national character in all its strength and splendor. The dilution of the race through the admixture of alien elements corrupts the character of the nation and thus weakens the power of the state. The homogeneity of the nation and the purity of the race thus appear as the very essence of national power, and for the latter's sake national minorities must either be absorbed or ejected. In the end, the national character of one's own nation comes to be regarded as the repository of all those qualities—courage, loyalty, discipline, industry, endurance, intelligence, and faculty for leadership—the possession of which justifies the exercise of supreme power over other nations and at the same time makes the exercise of such power possible. The overestimation of the qualities of one's own nation, which is characteristic of all nationalism, leads in the concept of the master race to the very idolatry of the national character. The master race is, by virtue of the superior quality of its national character, destined to rule the world. It has by virtue of these qualities the potential power to exercise worldwide dominion, and it is the task of statesmanship and of military conquest to transform those slumbering potentialities into the actualities of world empire.

The intellectual and political excesses of nationalism and of its degenerate offspring, racism, have shocked and repelled the nonnationalistic mind to a much greater degree than have the excesses of geopolitics. The latter have in the main been limited to Germany and were perpetrated in an esoteric language. The excesses of nationalism, on the other hand, are the logical outgrowth of a secular religion that has engulfed in the fanaticism of holy wars of extermination, enslavement, and world conquest only certain countries, yet has left its mark on many everywhere. Since nationalism has singled out the national character as the pivot of its political philosophy, program, and action, critical observers have frequently tended to go to the other extreme and have denied the existence of a national character altogether. Intent upon demonstrating the mythical and subjective essence of nationalism, they have been anxious to show that its alleged empirical basis, the national character, is also nothing but a myth.

One can readily agree with the critics of nationalism and racism that the allegedly inevitable determination of the national character by the "blood"—that is, the common biological characteristics of the members of a certain group—is a political fabrication without any basis in fact. One can also agree that the absolute constancy of the national character, deriving from the immutability of the qualities of a pure race, belongs in the realm of political mythology. The existence of the United States as a nation and its assimilative powers offer convincing proof of the fallacy of both assertions. On the other hand, to deny altogether the existence of the national character and its bearing upon national power runs counter to the facts of experience, of which we have given a few samples above.[5] Such denial would be an error no less detrimental to a correct assessment of the power of a nation in relation to others than the nationalistic deification of the national character has proved to be.

Militarism

Militarism commits the same type of error with respect to military preparedness that geopolitics and nationalism commit with regard to geography and national character. Militarism is the conception that the power of a nation consists primarily, if not exclusively, in its military strength, conceived especially in quantitative terms. The largest army, the biggest navy, the biggest and fastest air force in the world, and superiority in numbers of nuclear weapons become the predominant, if not the exclusive, symbols of national power.

Nations whose military strength lies in navies rather than in large standing armies are wont to point with abhorrence to the militarism of Germany, France, or the Soviet Union without recognizing that they have developed their peculiar brand of militarism. Influenced by writers such as Mahan, they have emphasized out of all proportion the importance of the size and quality of their navies for national power. In the United States there is a widespread tendency to overemphasize the technological aspects of military preparedness, such as the speed and the range of airplanes and the uniqueness of nuclear weapons. The average German was misled by masses of goose-stepping soldiers. The average Russian experiences the supremacy of Soviet power, derived from space and population, in the throngs filling the vastness of Red Square on May Day. The typical Englishman used to lose his sense of proportion in the presence of the gigantic form of a dreadnought. Many Americans succumbed to the fascination that emanated from the "secret" of the atomic bomb. All these attitudes toward military preparedness have in common the mistaken belief that all that counts,

---

[5]See pages 140 ff.

or at least what counts most for the power of a nation, is the military factor conceived in terms of numbers and quality of men and weapons.[6]

From the militaristic error follows inevitably the equation of national power with material force. To speak loudly and carry a big stick, to rephrase Theodore Roosevelt's famous dictum, is indeed the preferred method of militaristic diplomacy. The proponents of this method are unaware that it is sometimes wise to speak softly and carry a big stick, that it is sometimes even wiser to leave the big stick at home where it is available when needed. In its exclusive concern with military strength, militarism is contemptuous of the intangibles of power. Without them a powerful nation may frighten other nations into submission or it may conquer by sheer overwhelming force, but it cannot rule what it has conquered; for it cannot gain voluntary acceptance for its rule. In the end, the power of militarism must yield to a power tempered with self-restraint that seeks the effectiveness of national power in the infrequency of its military use. The failures of Spartan, German, and Japanese militarism, compared with the triumphs of the Roman and British policies of empire building, show the disastrous practical results of that intellectual error which we call militarism.

Thus the error of militarism gives new sharpness to the structure and contours of national power. Militarism—and here is the essence of its error—is unable to understand the paradox that a maximum of material power does not necessarily mean a maximum of overall national power. A nation that throws into the scale of international politics the maximum of material power it is capable of mustering will find itself confronted with the maximum effort of all its competitors to equal or surpass its power. It will find that it has no friends but only vassals and enemies. Since the emergence of the modern state system in the fifteenth century, no single nation has succeeded in imposing its will for any length of time upon the rest of the world by sheer material force alone. No nation that has tried the ways of militarism has been strong enough to withstand the other nations' combined resistance, which the fear of its superior material power had called into being.

The only nation that in modern times could maintain a continuous position of preponderance owed that position to a rare combination of potential superior

---

[6]This aspect of militarism is impressively described by R. H. Tawney, *The Acquisitive Society* (New York: Harcourt, Brace, 1920), p. 44: "Militarism is the characteristic, not of an army, but of a society. Its essence is not any particular quality or scale of military preparation, but a state of mind, which, in its concentration on one particular element in social life, ends finally by exalting it until it becomes the arbiter of all the rest. The purpose for which military forces exist is forgotten. They are thought to stand by their own right and to need no justification. Instead of being regarded as an instrument which is necessary in an imperfect world, they are elevated into an object of superstitious veneration, as though the world would be a poor insipid place without them, so that political institutions and social arrangements and intellect and morality and religion are crushed into a mold made to fit one activity, which in a sane society is a subordinate activity, like the police, or the maintenance of prisons, or the cleansing of sewers, but which in a militarist state is a kind of mystical epitome of society itself.

"Militarism . . . is fetish worship. It is the prostration of men's souls before, and the laceration of their bodies to appease an idol." (Reprinted by permission of the publisher.)

power, a reputation for superior power, and the infrequent use of that superior power. Thus Great Britain was able, on the one hand, to overcome all serious challenges to its superiority because its self-restraint gained powerful allies and, hence, made it actually superior. On the other hand, it could minimize the incentive to challenge it because its superiority did not threaten the existence of other nations. When Great Britain stood at the threshold of its greatest power, it heeded the warning of its greatest political thinker—a warning as timely today as when first uttered in 1793:

> Among precautions against ambition, it may not be amiss to take one precaution against our *own*. I must fairly say, I dread our *own* power and our *own* ambition; I dread our being too much dreaded. It is ridiculous to say we are not men, and that, as men, we shall never wish to aggrandize ourselves in some way or other. Can we say that even at this very hour we are not invidiously aggrandized? We are already in possession of almost all the commerce of the world. Our empire in India is an awful thing. If we should come to be in a condition not only to have all this ascendant in commerce, but to be absolutely able, without the least control, to hold the commerce of all other nations totally dependent upon our good pleasure, we may say that we shall not abuse this astonishing and hitherto unheard-of power. But every other nation will think we shall abuse it. It is impossible but that, sooner or later, this state of things must produce a combination against us which may end in our ruin.[7]

---

[7]Edmund Burke, "Remarks on the Policy of the Allies with Respect to France," *Works*, Vol. IV (Boston: Little, Brown, 1899), p. 457.

PART FOUR

LIMITATIONS OF NATIONAL POWER
The Balance of Power

11

The Balance of Power

The aspiration for power on the part of several nations, each trying either to maintain or overthrow the status quo, leads of necessity to a configuration that is called the balance of power[1] and to policies that aim at preserving it. We say "of necessity" advisedly. For here again we are confronted with the basic misconception that has impeded the understanding of international politics and has made us the prey of illusions. This misconception asserts that men have a choice between power politics and its necessary outgrowth, the balance of power, on the one hand, and a different, better kind of international relations, on the other. It insists that a foreign policy based on the balance of power is one among several possible foreign policies and that only stupid and evil men will choose the former and reject the latter.

It will be shown in the following pages that the international balance of power is only a particular manifestation of a general social principle to which all societies composed of a number of autonomous units owe the autonomy of their component parts; that the balance of power and policies aiming at its preservation are not only inevitable but are an essential stabilizing factor in a society of sovereign nations; and that the instability of the international balance of power is due not to the faultiness of the principle but to the particular conditions under which the principle must operate in a society of sovereign nations.

SOCIAL EQUILIBRIUM

Balance of Power as Universal Concept

The concept of "equilibrium" as a synonym for "balance" is commonly employed in many sciences—physics, biology, economics, sociology, and political science.

---

[1]The term "balance of power" is used in the text with four different meanings: (1) as a policy aimed at a certain state of affairs, (2) as an actual state of affairs, (3) as an approximately equal distribution of power, or (4) as any distribution of power. Whenever the term is used without qualification, it refers to an actual state of affairs in which power is distributed among several nations with approximate equality. For the term referring to any distribution of power, see pages 222 ff.

It signifies stability within a system composed of a number of autonomous forces. Whenever the equilibrium is disturbed either by an outside force or by a change in one or the other elements composing the system, the system shows a tendency to reestablish either the original or a new equilibrium. Thus equilibrium exists in the human body. While the human body changes in the process of growth, the equilibrium persists as long as the changes occurring in the different organs of the body do not disturb the body's stability. This is especially so if the quantitative and qualitative changes in the different organs are proportionate to each other. When, however, the body suffers a wound or loss of one of its organs through outside interference, or experiences a malignant growth in or a pathological transformation of one of its organs, the equilibrium is disturbed, and the body tries to overcome the disturbance by reestablishing the equilibrium either on the same or a different level from the one that obtained before the disturbance occurred.[2]

The same concept of equilibrium is used in a social science, such as economics, with reference to the relations between the different elements of the economic system, for instance, between savings and investments, exports and imports, supply and demand, or costs and prices. Contemporary capitalism itself has been described as a system of "countervailing power."[3] It also applies to society as a whole. Thus we search for a proper balance between different geographical regions, such as the East and the West, and the North and the South; between different kinds of activities, such as agriculture and industry, heavy and light industries, big and small businesses, producers and consumers, and management and labor; and between different functional groups, such as city and country, the old, the middle-aged, and the young, the economic and the political sphere, and the middle classes and the upper and lower classes.

---

[2]Cf., for instance, the impressive analogy between the equilibrium in the human body and in society in Walter B. Cannon, *The Wisdom of the Body* (New York: W. W. Norton, 1932), pp. 293–94: "At the outset it is noteworthy that the body politic itself exhibits some indications of crude automatic stabilizing processes. In the previous chapter I expressed the postulate that a certain degree of constancy in a complex system is itself evidence that agencies are acting or are ready to act to maintain that constancy. And moreover, that when a system remains steady it does so because any tendency towards change is met by increased effectiveness of the factor or factors which resist the change. Many familiar facts prove that these statements are to some degree true for society even in its present unstabilized condition. A display of conservatism excites a radical revolt and that in turn is followed by a return to conservatism. Loose government and its consequences bring the reformers into power, but their tight reins soon provoke restiveness and the desire for release. The noble enthusiasms and sacrifices of war are succeeded by moral apathy and orgies of self-indulgence. Hardly any strong tendency in a nation continues to the stage of disaster; before that extreme is reached corrective forces arise which check the tendency and they commonly prevail to such an excessive degree as themselves to cause a reaction. A study of the nature of these social swings and their reversal might lead to valuable understanding and possibly to means of more narrowly limiting the disturbances. At this point, however, we merely note that the disturbances are roughly limited, and that this limitation suggests, perhaps, the early stages of social homeostasis." (Reprinted by permission of the publisher. Copyright 1932, 1939, by Walter B. Cannon.)

[3]John K. Galbraith, *American Capitalism, the Concept of Countervailing Power* (Boston: Houghton Mifflin, 1952).

Two assumptions are at the foundation of all such equilibriums: first, that the elements to be balanced are necessary for society or are entitled to exist and, second, that without a state of equilibrium among them one element will gain ascendancy over the others, encroach upon their interests and rights, and may ultimately destroy them. Consequently, it is the purpose of all such equilibriums to maintain the stability of the system without destroying the multiplicity of the elements composing it. If the goal were stability alone, it could be achieved by allowing one element to destroy or overwhelm the others and take their place. Since the goal is stability plus the preservation of all the elements of the system, the equilibrium must aim at preventing any element from gaining ascendancy over the others. The means employed to maintain the equilibrium consist in allowing the different elements to pursue their opposing tendencies up to the point where the tendency of one is not so strong as to overcome the tendency of the others but strong enough to prevent the others from overcoming its own. In the words of Robert Bridges:

> Our stability is but balance; and wisdom lies
> In masterful administration of the unforeseen.

Nowhere have the mechanics of social equilibrium been described more brilliantly and at the same time more simply than in *The Federalist*. Concerning the system of checks and balances of the American government, No. 51 of *The Federalist* says:

> This policy of supplying, by opposite and rival interests, the defect of better motives, might be traced to the whole system of human affairs, private as well as public. We see it particularly displayed in all the subordinate distributions of power, where the constant aim is to divide and arrange the several offices in such a manner as that each may be a check on the other—that the private inter-ests of every individual may be a sentinel over the public rights. These inven-tions of prudence cannot be less requisite in the distribution of the supreme powers of the state.

In the words of John Randolph, "You may cover whole skins of parchment with limitations, but power alone can limit power."[4]

Balance of Power in Domestic Politics

The concept of equilibrium or balance has indeed found its most important application, outside the international field, in the sphere of domestic government

---

[4]Quoted after William Cabell Bruce, *John Randolph of Roanoke* (New York and London: G. P. Putnam's Sons, 1922), Vol. II, p. 211.

and politics.[5] Parliamentary bodies have frequently developed within themselves a balance of power. A multiparty system lends itself particularly to such a development. Here two groups, each representing a minority of the legislative body, often oppose each other, and the formation of a majority depends upon the votes of a third group. The third group will tend to join the potentially or actually weaker of the two, thus imposing a check upon the stronger one. Even the two-party system of the United States Congress displayed the typical configuration of this checking-and-balancing process when, in the last years of Franklin D. Roosevelt's administration and during most of Truman's, the Southern Democrats constituted themselves a third party, voting on many issues with the Republican minority. They thus checked not only the Democratic majority in Congress but also the executive branch, which was also controlled by the Democratic party.[6]

---

[5]It hardly needs to be pointed out that, while the balance of power is a universal social phenomenon, its functions and results are different in domestic and international politics. The balance of power operates in domestic politics within a relatively stable framework of an integrated society, kept together by a strong consensus and the normally unchallengeable power of a central government. On the international scene, where consensus is weak and a central authority does not exist, the stability of society and the freedom of its component parts depend to a much greater extent upon the operations of the balance of power. More concerning this will be said in Chapter 14.

Cf. also J. Allen Smith, *The Growth and Decadence of Constitutional Government* (New York: Henry Holt, 1930), pp. 241, 242: "In the absence of any common and impartial agency to interpret international law and supervise international relations, every state is anxious not only to increase its own authority but to prevent, if possible, any increase in the authority of rival states. The instinct of self-preservation, in a world made up of independent nations, operates to make each desire power in order to secure itself against the danger of external aggression. The fact that no country alone is sufficiently strong to feel secure against any possible combination of opposing states makes necessary the formation of alliances and counteralliances through which each state seeks to ensure the needed support in case its safety is menaced from without. This is usually referred to as the struggle to maintain the balance of power. It is merely an application of the check and balance theory of the state to international politics. It is assumed, and rightly so, that if any state should acquire a predominant position in international affairs, it would be a distinct menace to the interests and well-being of the rest of the world. Power, even though it may have been acquired as a means of protection, becomes a menace to international peace as soon as the country possessing it comes to feel stronger than any possible foe. It is no less necessary to maintain the balance of power in international politics than it is to prevent some special interest from gaining the ascendancy in the state. But since this balance of power idea is based on the fear of attack and assumes that every nation should be prepared for war, it can not be regarded as in any real sense a guaranty of international peace." (Reprinted by permission of the publisher.) Cf. also *The Cambridge Modern History* (New York: Macmillan, 1908), Vol. V, p. 276.

[6]Cf. the illuminating discussion of the general problem in John Stuart Mill, *Considerations on Representative Government* (New York: Henry Holt, 1882), p. 142: "In a state of society thus composed, if the representative system could be made ideally perfect, and if it were possible to maintain it in that state, its organization must be such that these two classes, manual laborers and their affinities on one side, employers of labor and their affinities on the other, should be, in the arrangement of the representative system, equally balanced, each influencing about an equal number of votes in Parliament; since, assuming that the majority of each class, in any difference between them, would be mainly governed by their class interests, there would be a minority of each in whom the consideration would be subordinate to reason, justice, and the good of the whole; and this minority of either, joining with the whole of the other, would turn the scale against any demands of their own majority which were not such as ought to prevail." See also page 147 and, concerning the balance of power within federal states, pages 9 and 191.

The American government is the outstanding modern example of a governmental system whose stability is maintained by an equilibrium among its component parts. In the words of Lord Bryce:

> The Constitution was avowedly created as an instrument of checks and balances. Each branch of the government was to restrain the others, and maintain the equipoise of the whole. The legislature was to balance the executive, and the judiciary both. The two houses of the legislature were to balance one another. The national government, taking all its branches together, was balanced against the State governments. As the equilibrium was placed under the protection of a document, unchangeable save by the people themselves, no one of the branches of the national government has been able to absorb or override the others . . . each branch maintains its independence and can, within certain limits, defy the others.
>
> But there is among political bodies and offices (i.e. the persons who from time to time fill the same office) of necessity a constant strife, a struggle for existence similar to that which Mr. Darwin has shown to exist among plants and animals; and as in the case of plants and animals so also in the political sphere this struggle stimulates each body or office to exert its utmost force for its own preservation, and to develop its aptitudes in any direction where development is possible. Each branch of the American government has striven to extend its range and its powers; each has advanced in certain directions, but in others has been restrained by the equal or stronger pressure of other branches.[7]

No. 51 of *The Federalist* has laid bare the power structure of this "dynamic equilibrium" or "moving parallelogram of force," as it was called by Charles A. Beard:[8] ". . . the defect must be supplied, by so contriving the interior structure of the government as that its several constitutional parts may, by their mutual relations, be the means of keeping each other in their proper places. . . . But the great security against a gradual concentration of the several powers in the same department, consists in giving to those who administer each department the necessary constitutional means and personal motives to resist the encroachment of others. . . . The provision for defense must in this, as in all other cases, be made commensurate to the danger of attack. Ambition must be made to counteract ambition. The interest of the man must be connected with the constitutional rights of the place. . . ." The aim of these constitutional arrangements is "to guard one part of the society against the injustices of the other part. Different interests necessarily exist in different classes of citizens. If a majority be reunited by a common interest, the rights of the minority will be insecure."

---

[7] *The American Commonwealth* (New York: Macmillan, 1891), Vol. I, pp. 390–91.
[8] *The Republic* (New York: Viking Press, 1944), pp. 190–91.

The author, Madison, expected to safeguard the rights of the minority "by comprehending in the society so many separate descriptions of citizens as will render an unjust combination of a majority of the whole very improbable, if not impracticable. . . . The society itself will be broken into so many parts, interests, and classes of citizens, that the rights of individuals, or of the minority, will be in little danger from interested combinations of the majority." Security will lie "in the multiplicity of interests," and the degree of security "will depend on the number of interests." And Charles A. Beard thus summarizes the philosophy of the American government: "The Framers understood that government in action is power. They tried to pit the ambitions, interests, and forces of human beings in the three departments against one another in such a way as to prevent any one set of agents from seizing all power, from becoming dangerously powerful."[9]

One needs only to substitute the terminology of international politics for the concepts used by *The Federalist*, Lord Bryce, and Charles A. Beard in their analysis of the structure and dynamics of the American government, and there emerge the main elements common to both the system of checks and balances of the American Constitution and the international balance of power. In other words, the same motive forces have given rise to the American system of checks and balances and to the international system of the balance of power. Both systems seek to fulfill the same functions for their own stability and the autonomy of their constituent elements, however much they may differ in the means they employ and in the degree to which they realize their aim. Both are subject to the same dynamic processes of change, disequilibrium, and the establishment of a new balance on a different level.

Which are the main patterns of the international balance of power? What are the typical situations out of which it arises and within which it operates? What functions does it fulfill? And to what transformations has it been subjected in recent history?

TWO MAIN PATTERNS OF THE BALANCE OF POWER

Two factors are at the basis of international society: one is the multiplicity and the other is the antagonism of its elements, the individual nations. The aspirations for power of the individual nations can come into conflict with one another—and some, if not most of them, do at any particular moment in history—in two different ways. In other words, the struggle for power on the international scene can be carried on in two typical patterns.

The Pattern of Direct Opposition

Nation A may embark upon an imperialistic policy with regard to Nation B, and Nation B may counter that policy with a policy of the status quo or with an

---

[9]Ibid. Cf. also John C. Calhoun, "A Disquisition on Government," in *The Works of John C. Calhoun* (Columbia: A. S. Johnston, 1851), Vol. I, pp. 35–36, 38–39.

imperialistic policy of its own. France and its allies opposing Russia in 1812, Japan opposing China from 1931 to 1941, and the Allied nations versus the Axis from 1941 on correspond to that pattern. The pattern is one of direct opposition between the nation that wants to establish its power over another nation and the latter, which refuses to yield.

Nation A may also pursue an imperialistic policy toward Nation C, which may either resist or acquiesce in that policy, while Nation B follows with regard to Nation C either a policy of imperialism or one of the status quo. In this case the domination of C is a goal of A's policy. B, on the other hand, is opposed to A's policy because it either wants to preserve the status quo with respect to C or wants the domination of C for itself. The pattern of the struggle for power between A and B is here not one of direct opposition but of competition, the object of which is the domination of C, and it is only through the intermediary of that competition that the contest for power between A and B takes place. This pattern is visible, for instance, in the competition between Great Britain and Russia for the domination of Iran, in which the struggle for power between the two countries has repeatedly manifested itself during the last hundred years. It is also clear in the competition for dominant influence in Germany that in the aftermath of the Second World War has marked the relations between France, Great Britain, the Soviet Union, and the United States. The competition between the United States and China or between the Soviet Union and China for control of the countries of Southeast Asia offers another example of the same pattern.

It is in situations such as these that the balance of power operates and fulfills its typical functions. In the pattern of direct opposition, the balance of power results directly from the desire of either nation to see its policies prevail over the policies of the other. A tries to increase its power in relation to B to such an extent that it can control the decisions of B and thus lead its imperialistic policy to success. B, on the other hand, will try to increase its power to such an extent that it can resist A's pressure and thus frustrate A's policy or else embark upon an imperialistic policy of its own with a chance for success. In the latter case, A must, in turn, increase its power in order to be able to resist B's imperialistic policy and to pursue its own with a chance for success. This balancing of opposing forces will go on, the increase in the power of one nation calling forth an at least proportionate increase in the power of the other, until the nations concerned change the objectives of their imperialistic policies—if they do not give them up altogether—or until one nation gains or believes it has gained a decisive advantage over the other. Then either the weaker yields to the stronger or war decides the issue.

So long as the balance of power operates successfully in such a situation, it fulfills two functions. It creates a precarious stability in the relations between the respective nations, a stability that is always in danger of being disturbed and, therefore, is always in need of being restored. This is, however, the only stability obtainable under the assumed conditions of the power pattern. For we are here in the presence of an inevitable inner contradiction of the balance of power. One of the two functions the balance of power is supposed to fulfill is stability in the power relations among nations; yet these relations are, as we have seen, by their very nature subject to continuous change. They are essentially unstable. Since the weights that determine the relative position of the scales have a tendency to change continuously by growing either heavier or lighter, whatever stability the balance of power may achieve must be precarious and subject to perpetual adjustments in conformity with intervening changes. The other function that a successful balance of power fulfills under these conditions is to insure the freedom of one nation from domination by the other.

Owing to the essentially unstable and dynamic character of the balance, which is not unstable and dynamic by accident or only part of the time, but by nature and always, the independence of the nations concerned is also essentially precarious and in danger. Here again, however, it must be said that, given the conditions of the power pattern, the independence of the respective nations can rest on no other foundation than the power of each individual nation to prevent the power of the other nations from encroaching upon its freedom. The following diagram illustrates this situation:

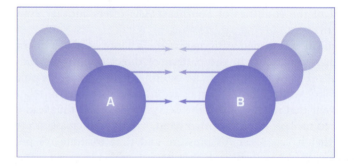

The Pattern of Competition

In the other pattern, the pattern of competition, the mechanics of the balance of power are identical with those discussed. The power of A necessary to dominate C in the face of B's opposition is balanced, if not outweighed, by B's power, while, in turn, B's power to gain dominion over C is balanced, if not outweighed, by the power of A. The additional function, however, that the balance fulfills here, aside from creating a precarious stability and security in the relations between A and B, consists in safeguarding the independence of C against encroachments by A or B. The independence of C is a mere function of the power relations existing between A and B:

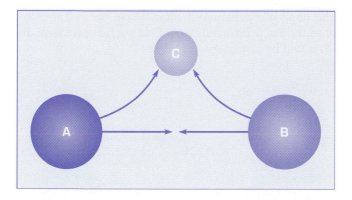

If these relations take a decisive turn in favor of the imperialistic nation—that is, A—the independence of C will at once be in jeopardy:

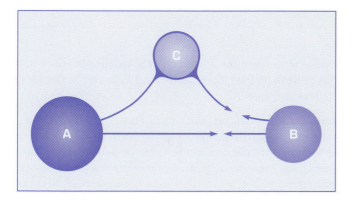

If the status quo nation—that is, B—should gain a decisive and permanent advantage, C's freedom will be more secure in the measure of that advantage:

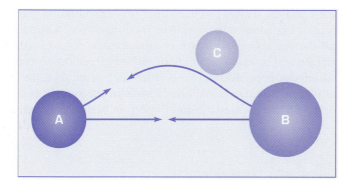

If, finally, the imperialistic nation—A—should give up its imperialistic policies altogether or shift them permanently from C to another objective—that is, D—the freedom of C would be permanently secured:

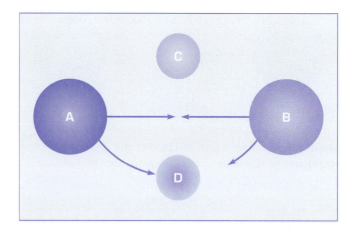

No one has recognized this function of the balance of power to preserve the independence of weak nations more clearly than Edmund Burke. He said in 1791 in his "Thoughts on French Affairs":

> As long as those two princes [the king of Prussia and the German emperor], are at variance, so long the liberties of Germany are safe. But if ever they should so far understand one another as to be persuaded that they have a more direct and more certainly defined interest in a proportioned mutual aggrandizement than in a reciprocal reduction, that is, if they come to think that they are more likely to be enriched by a division of spoil than to be rendered secure by keeping to the old policy of preventing others from being spoiled by either of them, from that moment the liberties of Germany are no more.[10]

Small nations have always owed their independence either to the balance of power (Belgium and the Balkan countries until the Second World War), or to the preponderance of one protecting power (the small nations of Central and South America, and Portugal), or to their lack of attractiveness for imperialistic aspirations (Switzerland and Spain). The ability of such small nations to maintain their neutrality has always been due to one or the other or all of these factors, for instance, the Netherlands, Denmark, and Norway in the First, in contrast to the Second, World War, and Switzerland and Sweden in both world wars.

---

[10] *Works* (Boston: Little, Brown, 1889), Vol. IV, p. 331.

The same factors are responsible for the existence of so-called buffer states—weak states located close to powerful ones and serving their military security. The outstanding example of a buffer state owing its existence to the balance of power is Belgium from the beginning of its history as an independent state in 1831 to the Second World War. The nations belonging to the so-called Russian security belt, which stretches along the western and southwestern frontiers of the Soviet Union from Finland to Bulgaria, exist by leave of their preponderant neighbor, whose military and economic interests they serve.

Korea and the Balance of Power

All these different factors have brought to bear successively upon the fate of Korea. Because of its geographic location in the proximity of China, it has existed as an autonomous state for most of its long history by virtue of the control or intervention of its powerful neighbor. Whenever the power of China was not sufficient to protect the autonomy of Korea, another nation, generally Japan, would try to gain a foothold on the Korean peninsula. Since the first century B.C.E., the international status of Korea has by and large been determined either by Chinese supremacy or by rivalry between China and Japan.

The very unification of Korea in the seventh century was a result of Chinese intervention. From the thirteenth century to the decline of Chinese power in the nineteenth century, Korea stood in a relationship of subservience to China as its suzerain and accepted Chinese leadership in politics and culture. From the end of the sixteenth century, Japan, after it had invaded Korea without lasting success, opposed to the claim of China its own claim to control of the country. Japan was able to make good that claim as a result of its victory in the Sino-Japanese War of 1894–95. Then Japan was challenged in its control of Korea by Russia, and from 1896 on the influence of Russia became dominant. The rivalry between Japan and Russia for control of Korea ended with the defeat of Russia in the Russo-Japanese War of 1904–05. Japanese control of Korea, thus firmly established, was terminated with the defeat of Japan in the Second World War. From then on, the United States replaced Japan as a check upon Russian ambitions in Korea. China, by intervening in the Korean War, resumed its traditional interest in the control of Korea. Thus for more than two thousand years the fate of Korea has been a function either of the predominance of one nation controlling Korea or of a balance of power between two nations competing for that control.

12 Different Methods of the Balance of Power

The balancing process can be carried on either by diminishing the weight of the heavier scale or by increasing the weight of the lighter one.

DIVIDE AND RULE

The former method has found its classic manifestation, aside from the imposition of onerous conditions in peace treaties and the incitement to treason and revolution, in the maxim "divide and rule." It has been resorted to by nations who tried to make or keep their competitors weak by dividing them or keeping them divided. The most consistent and important policies of this kind in modern times are the policy of France with respect to Germany and the policy of the Soviet Union with respect to the rest of Europe. From the seventeenth century to the end of the Second World War, it has been an unvarying principle of French foreign policy either to favor the division of the German Empire into a number of small, independent states or to prevent the coalescence of such states into one unified nation. The support of the Protestant princes of Germany by Richelieu, of the Rhinebund by Napoleon I, of the princes of southern Germany by Napoleon III, and of the abortive separatist movements after the First World War, and the opposition to the unification of Germany after the Second World War—all have their common denominator in considerations of the balance of power in Europe, which France found threatened by a strong German state. Similarly, the Soviet Union from the twenties to the present has consistently opposed all plans for the unification of Europe, on the assumption that the pooling of the divided strength of the European nations into a "Western bloc" would give the enemies of the Soviet Union such power as to threaten the latter's security.

The other method of balancing the power of several nations consists in adding to the strength of the weaker nation. This method can be carried out by two different means: Either B can increase its power sufficiently to offset, if not surpass, the power of A, and vice versa; or B can pool its power with the power of all the other nations that pursue identical policies with regard to A, in which case A will pool its power with all the nations pursuing identical policies with respect to B. The former alternative is exemplified by the policy of compensations and the armament race as well as by disarmament; the latter, by the policy of alliances.

COMPENSATIONS

Compensations of a territorial nature were a common device in the eighteenth and nineteenth centuries for maintaining a balance of power that had been, or was to be, disturbed by the territorial acquisitions of one nation. The Treaty of Utrecht of 1713, which terminated the War of the Spanish Succession, recognized for the first time expressly the principle of the balance of power by way of territorial compensations. It provided for the division of most of the Spanish possessions, European and colonial, between the Hapsburgs and the Bourbons *"ad conservandum in Europa equilibrium,"* as the treaty put it.

The three partitions of Poland in 1772, 1793, and 1795, which in a sense mark the end of the classic period of the balance of power, for reasons we shall discuss later,[1] reaffirm its essence by proceeding under the guidance of the principle of compensations. Since territorial acquisitions at the expense of Poland by any one of the interested nations—Austria, Prussia, and Russia—to the exclusion of the others would have upset the balance of power, the three nations agreed to divide Polish territory in such a way that the distribution of power among themselves would be approximately the same after the partitions as it had been before. In the treaty of 1772 between Austria and Russia, it was even stipulated that "the acquisitions . . . shall be completely equal, the portion of one cannot exceed the portion of the other."

Fertility of the soil and number and quality of the populations concerned were used as objective standards by which to determine the increase in power that the individual nations received through the acquisition of territory. While in the eighteenth century this standard was rather crudely applied, the Congress of Vienna refined the policy of compensations by appointing in 1815 a statistical commission charged with evaluating territories by the standard of number, quality, and type of population.

In the latter part of the nineteenth and the beginning of the twentieth centuries the principle of compensations was again deliberately applied to the distribution of colonial territories and the delimitation of colonial or semicolonial spheres of influence. Africa, in particular, was during that period the object of numerous treaties delimiting spheres of influence for the major colonial powers. Thus the competition between France, Great Britain, and Italy for the domination of Ethiopia was provisionally resolved, after the model of the partitions of Poland, by the treaty of 1906, which divided the country into three spheres of influence

---

[1]See page 213.

for the purpose of establishing in that region a balance of power among the nations concerned. Similarly, the rivalry between Great Britain and Russia with respect to Iran led to the Anglo-Russian treaty of 1907, which established spheres of influence for the contracting parties and a neutral sphere under the exclusive domination of Iran. The compensation consists here not in the outright cession of territorial sovereignty but rather in the reservation, to the exclusive benefit of a particular nation, of certain territories for commercial exploitation, political and military penetration, and eventual establishment of sovereignty. In other words, the particular nation has the right, without having full title to the territory concerned, to operate within its sphere of influence without competition or opposition from another nation. The other nation, in turn, has the right to claim for its own sphere of influence the same abstinence on the part of the former.

Even where the principle of compensations is not deliberately applied, however, as it was in the aforementioned treaties, it is nowhere absent from political arrangements, territorial or other, made within a balance-of-power system. For, given such a system, no nation will agree to concede political advantages to another nation without the expectation, which may or may not be well founded, of receiving proportionate advantages in return. The bargaining of diplomatic negotiations, issuing in political compromise, is but the principle of compensations in its most general from, and as such it is organically connected with the balance of power.

ARMAMENTS

The principal means, however, by which a nation endeavors with the power at its disposal to maintain or reestablish the balance of power are armaments. The armaments race in which Nation A tries to keep up with, and then to outdo, the armaments of Nation B, and vice versa, is the typical instrumentality of an unstable, dynamic balance of power. The necessary corollary of the armaments race is a constantly increasing burden of military preparations devouring an ever greater portion of the national budget and making for ever deepening fears, suspicions, and insecurity. The situation preceding the First World War, with the naval competition between Germany and Great Britain and the rivalry of the French and German armies, illustrates this point.

It is in recognition of situations such as these that, since the end of the Napoleonic Wars, repeated attempts have been made to create a stable balance of power, if not to establish permanent peace, by means of the proportionate disarmament of competing nations. The technique of stabilizing the balance of power by means of a proportionate reduction of armaments is somewhat similar to the technique of territorial compensations. For both techniques require a quantitative evaluation of the influence that the arrangement is likely to exert on the respective power of the individual nations. The difficulties in making such a quantitative evaluation—in correlating, for instance, the military strength of the French army of 1932 with the military power represented by the industrial potential of Germany–have greatly contributed to the failure of most attempts at creating a stable balance of power by means of disarmament. The only outstanding success of this kind was the Washington Naval Treaty of 1922, in which Great Britain, the United States, Japan, France, and Italy agreed to a proportionate reduction and limitation of naval armaments. Yet it must be noted that this treaty was part of an overall political and territorial settlement in the Pacific that sought to stabilize the power relations in that region on the foundation of Anglo-American predominance.[2]

ALLIANCES

The historically most important manifestation of the balance of power, however, is to be found not in the equilibrium of two isolated nations but in the relations between one nation or alliance of nations and another alliance.

The General Nature of Alliances

Alliances are a necessary function of the balance of power operating within a multiple-state system. Nations A and B, competing with each other, have three choices in order to maintain and improve their relative power positions. They can increase their own power, they can add to their own power the power of other nations, or they can withhold the power of other nations from the adversary. When they make the first choice, they embark upon an armaments race. When they choose the second and third alternatives, they pursue a policy of alliances.

Whether a nation shall pursue a policy of alliances is, then, a matter not of principle but of expediency. A nation will shun alliances if it believes that it is strong enough to hold its own unaided or that the burden of the commitments resulting from the alliance is likely to outweigh the advantages to be expected. It is for one or the other or both of these reasons that, throughout the better part of their history, Great Britain and the United States have refrained from entering into peacetime alliances with other nations.

Yet Great Britain and the United States have also refrained from concluding an alliance with each other even though, from the proclamation of the Monroe Doctrine in 1823 to the attack on Pearl Harbor in 1941, they have acted, at least in relation to the other European nations, as if they were allied. Their relationship during that period provides another instance of a situation in which nations dispense with an alliance. It occurs when their interests so obviously call for concerted policies and actions that an explicit formulation of these interests, policies, and actions in the form of a treaty of alliance appears to be redundant.

With regard to the continent of Europe, the United States and Great Britain have had one interest in common: the preservation of the European balance of

---

[2]The problem of disarmament will be discussed in greater detail in Chapter 23.

power. In consequence of this identity of interests, they have found themselves by virtual necessity in the camp opposed to a nation that happened to threaten that balance. And when Great Britain went to war in 1914 and 1939 in order to protect the European balance of power, the United States first supported Great Britain with a conspicuous lack of that impartiality befitting a neutral and then joined her on the battlefield. Had in 1914 and 1939 the United States been tied to Great Britain by a formal treaty of alliance, it might have declared war earlier, but its general policies and concrete actions would not have been materially different than they actually were.

Not every community of interests, calling for common policies and actions, also calls for legal codification in an explicit alliance. Yet, on the other hand, an alliance requires of necessity a community of interests for its foundation.[3] Under what conditions, then, does an existing community of interests require the explicit formulation of an alliance? What is it that an alliance adds to the existing community of interests?

An alliance adds precision, especially in the form of limitation, to an existing community of interests and to the general policies and concrete measures serving them.[4] The interests nations have in common are not typically so precise and limited as to geographic region, objective, and appropriate policies as has been the American and British interest in the preservation of the European balance of power. Nor are they so incapable of precision and limitation as concerns the prospective common enemy. For, while a typical alliance is directed against a specific nation or group of nations, the enemy of the Anglo-American community of interests could in the nature of things not be specified beforehand, since whoever threatens the European balance of power is the enemy. As Jefferson shifted his sympathies back and forth between Napoleon and Great Britain according to who seemed to threaten the balance of power at the time, so during the century following the Napoleonic Wars, Great Britain and the United States had to decide in the light of circumstances ever liable to change who posed at the moment the greatest threat to the balance of power. This blanket character of the enemy, determined not individually but by the function he performs, brings to mind a similar characteristic of collective security, which is directed against the abstractly designed aggressor, whoever he may be.

The typical interests that unite two nations against a third are both more definite as concerns the determination of the enemy and less precise as concerns the objectives to be sought and the policies to be pursued. In the last decades of the nineteenth century, France was opposed to Germany, and Russia was opposed to Austria, while Austria was allied with Germany against France and Russia. How could the interests of France and Russia be brought upon a common denominator, determining policy and guiding action? How could, in other

---

[3]See the quotations from Thucydides and Lord Salisbury, page 10.
[4]Glancing through the treaties of alliance of the seventeenth and eighteenth centuries, one is struck by the meticulous precision with which obligations to furnish troops, equipment, logistic support, food, money, and the like were defined.

words, the *casus foederis* be defined so that both friend and foe would know what to expect in certain contingencies affecting their respective interest? It was for the treaty of alliance of 1894 to perform these functions. Had the objectives and policies of the Franco-Russian alliance of 1894 been as clear as were the objectives and policies of Anglo-American cooperation in Europe, no alliance treaty would have been necessary. Had the enemy been as indeterminate, no alliance treaty would have been feasible.

Not every community of interests calling for cooperation between two or more nations, then, requires that the terms of this cooperation be specified through the legal stipulations of a treaty of alliance. It is only when the common interests are inchoate in terms of policy and action that a treaty of alliance is required to make them explicit and operative. These interests, as well as the alliances expressing them and the policies serving them, can be distinguished in five different ways: according to their intrinsic nature and relationship, the distribution of benefits and power, their coverage in relation to the total interests of the nations concerned, their coverage in terms of time, and their effectiveness in terms of common policies and actions. In consequence, we can distinguish alliances serving identical, complementary, and ideological interests and policies. We can further distinguish mutual and one-sided, general and limited, temporary and permanent, and operative and inoperative alliances.

The Anglo-American alliance with regard to Europe provides the classic example of an alliance serving identical interests; the objective of one partner—the preservation of the balance of power in Europe—is also the objective of the other. The alliance between the United States and Pakistan is one of many contemporary instances of an alliance serving complementary interests. For the United States it serves the primary purpose of expanding the scope of the policy of containment; for Pakistan it serves primarily the purpose of increasing her political, military, and economic potential vis-à-vis her neighbors.

The pure type of an ideological alliance is presented by the Treaty of the Holy Alliance of 1815 and the Atlantic Charter of 1941. Both documents laid down general moral principles to which the signatories pledged their adherence, and general objectives whose realization they pledged themselves to seek. The Treaty of the Arab League of 1945 provides an example of an alliance, expressing, since the war against Israel of 1948, primarily ideological solidarity.

Much more typical is the addition of ideological commitments to material ones in one and the same treaty of alliance.[5] Thus the Three Emperors' League of 1873 provided for military assistance among Austria, Germany, and Russia in case of attack on any of them and, at the same time, emphasized the solidarity of the three monarchies against republican subversion. In our times the ideological commitment against Communist subversion, inserted in treaties of alliance, performs a similar function. The ideological factor also manifests itself in the official interpretation of an alliance, based upon material interests, in terms of an ideological

---

[5]It ought to be pointed out that the Holy Alliance and the Atlantic Charter usually supplement material commitments contained in separate legal instruments.

solidarity transcending the limitations of material interests. The conception of the Anglo-American alliance, common before the British invasion of Egypt in 1956, as all-inclusive and world-embracing, based upon common culture, political institutions, and ideals, is a case in point.

As concerns the political effect of this ideological factor upon an alliance, three possibilities must be distinguished. A purely ideological alliance, unrelated to material interests, cannot but be stillborn; it is unable to determine policies or guide actions and misleads by presenting the appearance of political solidarity where there is none. The ideological factor, when it is superimposed upon an actual community of interests, can lend strength to the alliance by marshaling moral convictions and emotional preferences to its support. It can also weaken it by obscuring the nature and limits of the common interests that the alliance was supposed to make precise and by raising expectations, bound to be disappointed, for the extent of concerted policies and actions. For both these possibilities the Anglo-American alliance can again serve as an example.

The distribution of benefits within an alliance should ideally be one of complete mutuality; here the services performed by the parties for each other are commensurate with the benefits received. This ideal is more likely to be approximated in an alliance concluded among equals in power and serving identical interests; here the equal resources of all, responding to equal incentives, serve one single interest. The other extreme in the distribution of benefits is one-sidedness, a *societas leonia* in which one party receives the lion's share of benefits while the other bears the main bulk of burdens. Insofar as the object of such an alliance is the preservation of the territorial and political integrity of the receiving party, such an alliance is indistinguishable from a treaty of guarantee. Complementry interests lend themselves most easily to this kind of disproportion, since they are by definition different in substance and their comparative assessment is likely to be distorted by subjective interpretation. A marked superiority in power is bound to add weight to such interpretations.

The distribution of benefits is thus likely to reflect the distribution of power within an alliance, as is the determination of policies. A great power has a good chance to have its way with a weak ally as concerns benefits and policies, and it is for this reason that Machiavelli warned weak nations against making alliances with strong ones except by necessity.[6] The relationship between the United States and South Korea exemplifies this situation.

However, this correlation between benefits, policies, and power is by no means inevitable. A weak nation may well possess an asset that is of such great value for its strong ally as to be irreplaceable. Here the unique benefit the former is able to grant or withhold may give it within the alliance a status completely out of keeping with the actual distribution of material power. In recent history the relationships between the United States and Spain with regard to bases and between the United States and Saudi Arabia with regard to oil come to mind.

---

[6]*The Prince*, Chapter 21.

The misinterpretation of the Anglo-American alliance, mentioned before, also illustrates the confusion between limited and general alliances. In the age of total war, wartime alliances tend to be general in that they comprise the total interests of the contracting parties both with regard to the waging of the war and the peace settlement. On the other hand, peacetime alliances tend to be limited to a fraction of the total interests and objectives of the signatories. A nation will conclude a multitude of alliances with different nations that may overlap and contradict one another on specific points.

A typical alliance attempts to transform a small fraction of the total interests of the contracting parties into common policies and measures. Some of these interests are irrelevant to the purposes of the alliance, others support them, others diverge from them, and still others are incompatible with them. Thus a typical alliance is imbedded in a dynamic field of diverse interests and purposes. Whether and for how long it will be operative depends upon the strength of the interests underlying it as over against the strength of the other interests of the nations concerned. The value and the chances of an alliance, however limited in scope, must be considered in the context of the overall policies within which it is expected to operate.

General alliances are typically of temporary duration and most prevalent in wartime; for the overriding common interest in winning the war and securing through the peace settlement the interests for which the war was waged is bound to yield, once victory is won and the peace treaties are signed, to the traditionally separate and frequently incompatible interests of the individual nations. On the other hand, there exists a correlation between the permanency of an alliance and the limited character of the interests it serves; for only such a specific, limited interest is likely to last long enough to provide the foundation for a durable alliance.[7] The alliance between Great Britain and Portugal, concluded in 1703, has survived the centuries because Portugal's interest in the protection of her ports by the British fleet and the British interest in the control of Atlantic approaches to Portugal have endured. Yet it can be stated as a general historical observation that, while alliance treaties have frequently assumed permanent validity by being concluded "in perpetuity" or for periods of ten or twenty years, they could not have been more durable than the generally precarious and fleeting configurations of common interests that they were intended to serve. As a rule, they have been short-lived.

The dependence of alliances upon the underlying community of interests also accounts for the distinction between operative and inoperative alliances. For an alliance to be operative—that is, able to coordinate the general policies and concrete measures of its members—those members must agree not only on general objectives but on policies and measures as well. Many alliances have remained scraps of paper because no such agreement was forthcoming, and it was not forthcoming because the community of interests did not extend beyond general objectives

---

[7]This correlation, however, cannot be reversed. Especially in the seventeenth and eighteenth centuries, limited alliances were frequently concluded *ad hoc*—that is, to counter an attack, to engage in one, or to embark upon a particular expedition. With the passing of the specific occasion in view of which the alliance was concluded, the alliance itself lost its object and came to an end.

to concrete policies and measures. The classic case of an inoperative alliance is that of the United States and France, made inoperable by Washington's Neutrality Proclamation of 1793 after the War of the First Coalition had broken out between France and the monarchies of Europe. Hamilton justified that proclamation with an argument of general applicability: "There would be no proportion between the mischiefs and perils to which the United States would expose themselves, by embarking in the war, and the benefit which the nature of their stipulation aims at securing to France, or that which it would be in their power actually to render her by becoming a party." The Franco-Russian alliances of 1935 and 1944 and the Anglo-Russian alliance of 1942 are other cases in point. The legal validity of a treaty of alliance and its propagandistic invocation can easily deceive the observer about its actual operational value. The correct assessment of this value requires examination of the concrete policies and measures that the contracting parties have taken in implementation of the alliance.

These considerations are particularly relevant for alliances between a nuclear power (A) and a nonnuclear power (B), directed against another nuclear power (C). Will A risk nuclear destruction at the hands of C in order to honor the alliance with B? The extremity of the risk involved casts doubt upon the operational quality of such an alliance. This doubt, first explicitly raised by de Gaulle, has weakened the alliances between the United States and some of its major allies.

Alliances vs. World Domination

While the balance of power as a natural and inevitable outgrowth of the struggle for power is as old as political history itself, systematic theoretic reflections, starting in the sixteenth century and reaching their culmination in the eighteenth and nineteenth centuries, have conceived the balance of power generally as a protective device of an alliance of nations, anxious for their independence, against another nation's designs for world domination, then called universal monarchy. B, directly threatened by A, joins with C, D, and E, potentially threatened by A, to foil A's designs. Polybius has pointed to the essence of this configuration in his analysis of the relations between the Romans, the Carthaginians, and Hiero of Syracuse:

> The Carthaginians, being shut in on all sides, were obliged to resort to an appeal to the states in alliance with them. Hiero during the whole of the present war had been most prompt in meeting their requests, and was now more complaisant than ever, being convinced that it was in his own interest for securing both its Sicilian dominions and his friendship with the Romans, that Carthage should be preserved, and that the stronger Power should not be able to attain its ultimate object entirely without effort. In this he reasoned very wisely and sensibly, for such matters should never be neglected, and we should never contribute to the attainment by one state of a power so preponderant, that none dare dispute with it even for their acknowledged rights.[8]

---

[8]Polybius I, 83.

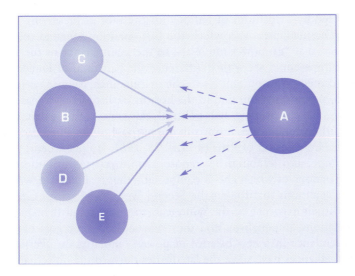

In modern times, Francis Bacon was, after the Florentine statesmen and historians Rucellai and Guicciardini, the first to recognize the essence of the balance of power by way of alliances. In his essay *Of Empire* he says:

> First, for their neighbors, there can no general rule be given (the occasions are so variable), save one which ever holdeth—which is, that princes do keep due sentinel, that none of their neighbors do overgrow so (by increase of territory, by embracing of trade, by approaches, or the like,) as they become more able to annoy them than they were. . . . During that triumvirate of kings, King Henry VIII of England, Francis I, king of France, and Charles V, emperor, there was such a watch kept that none of the three could win a palm of ground, but the other two would straightways balance it, either by confederation, or, if need were, by a war, and would not in any wise take peace at interest; and the like was done by that League (which Guicciardine saith was the security of Italy,) made between Ferdinando, kind of Naples, Lorenzius Medices, and Ludovicus Sforsa, potentates, the one of Florence, the other of Milan.

The alliances France I concluded with Henry VIII and the Turks in order to prevent Charles V of Hapsburg from stabilizing and expanding his empire are the first modern example on a grand scale of the balance of power operating between an alliance and one nation intent upon establishing a universal monarchy. In the second half of the seventeenth century, Louis XIV of France took over the role of the Hapsburgs and called forth a similar reaction among the European nations. Alliances were formed around England and the Netherlands with the purpose of protecting the European nations from French domination and establishing a new balance of power between France and the rest of Europe.

The wars against the France of 1789 and against Napoleon show the same configuration of one preponderant nation aiming at world domination and being opposed by a coalition of nations for the sake of preserving their independence. The manifesto with which the first coalition initiated these wars in 1792 declared that "no power interested in the maintenance of the balance of power in Europe could see with indifference the Kingdom of France, which at one time formed so important a weight in this great balance, delivered any longer to domestic agitations and to the horrors of disorder and anarchy which, so to speak, have destroyed her political existence." And when these wars approached their conclusion, it was still the purpose of the allied powers, in the words of the Convention of Paris of April 23, 1814, "to put an end to the miseries of Europe, and to found her repose upon a just redistribution of forces among the nations of which she is composed"—that is, upon a new balance of power. The coalitions that fought the Second World War against Germany and Japan owed their existence to the same fear, common to all their members, of the latter nations' imperialism, and they pursued the same goal of preserving their independence in a new balance of power. Similarly, the Western bi- and multilateral alliances have since the late forties pursued the objective of putting a halt to the imperialistic expansion of the Soviet Union through the creation of a new world balance of power.

Alliances vs. Counteralliances

The struggle between an alliance of nations defending their independence against one potential conqueror is the most spectacular of the configurations to which the balance of power gives rise. The opposition of two alliances, one or both pursuing imperialistic goals and defending the independence of their members against the imperialistic aspirations of the other coalition, is the most frequent configuration within a balance-of-power system.

To mention only a few of the more important examples: The coalitions that fought the Thirty Years' War under the leadership of France and Sweden, on the one hand, and of Austria, on the other, sought to promote the imperialistic ambitions, especially of Sweden and Austria, and, at the same time, to keep the ambitions of the other side in check. The several treaties settling the affairs of Europe after the Thirty Years' War tried to establish a balance of power serving the latter end. The many coalition wars that filled the period between the Treaty of Utrecht of 1713 and the first partition of Poland of 1772 all attempted to maintain the balance that the Treaty of Utrecht had established and that the decline of Swedish power and the rise of Prussian, Russian, and British strength tended to disturb. The frequent changes in the alignments, even while war was in progress, have startled the historians and have made the eighteenth century appear to be particularly unprincipled and devoid of moral consideration. It was against that kind of foreign policy that Washington's Farewell Address warned the American people.

Yet the period in which that foreign policy flourished was the golden age of the balance of power in theory as well as in practice. It was during that period that most of the literature on the balance of power was published and that the princes of Europe looked to the balance of power as the supreme principle to guide their conduct in foreign affairs. As Frederick the Great wrote:

> It is easy to see that the political body of Europe finds itself in a violent condition: it has, so to speak, lost its equilibrium and is in a state where it cannot remain for long without risking much. It is with it as it is with the human body which subsists only through the mixture of equal quantities of acids and alkalies; when either of the two substances predominates, the body resents it and its health is considerably affected. And when this substance increases still more, it can cause the total destruction of the machine. Thus when the policy and the prudence of the princes of Europe lose sight of the maintenance of a just balance among the dominant powers, the constitution of the whole body politic resents it: violence is found on one side, weakness on the other; in one, the desire to invade everything, in the other impossibility to prevent it; the most powerful imposes laws, the weakest is compelled to subscribe to them; finally, everything concurs in augmenting the disorder and the confusion; the most powerful, like an impetuous torrent, overflows its banks, carries everything with it, and exposes this unfortunate body to the most disastrous revolutions.[9]

It is true that the princes allowed themselves to be guided by the balance of power in order to further their own interests. By doing so, it was inevitable that they would change sides, desert old alliances, and form new ones whenever it seemed to them that the balance of power had been disturbed and that a realignment of forces was needed to restore it. In that period foreign policy was indeed a sport of kings, not to be taken more seriously than games and gambles, played for strictly limited stakes, and utterly devoid of transcendent principles of any kind. Since such was the nature of international politics, what looks in retrospect like treachery and immorality was then little more than an elegant maneuver, a daring piece of strategy, or a finely contrived tactical movement, all executed according to the rules of the game, which all players recognized as binding. The balance of power of that period was amoral rather than immoral. The technical rules of the art of politics were its only standard. Its flexibility, which was its peculiar merit from the technical point of view, was the result of imperviousness to moral considerations, such as good faith and loyalty, a moral deficiency that to us seems deserving of reproach.

From the beginning of the modern state system at the turn of the fifteenth century to the end of the Napoleonic Wars in 1815, European nations were the active elements in the balance of power. Turkey was the one notable exception. Alliances and counteralliances were formed in order to maintain the balance or to restore it. The century from 1815 to the outbreak of the First World War saw the gradual extension of the European balance of power into a worldwide system. One might say that this epoch started with President Monroe's message to Congress in 1823, stating what

---

[9]Frederick the Great, "Considerations on the Present State of the Political Body of Europe," *Oeuvres de Frédéric le Grand,* (Berlin: Rudolph Decker, 1848), Vol. VIII, p. 24. I have supplied the translation from the French.

is known as the Monroe Doctrine. By declaring the mutual political independence of Europe and the Western Hemisphere and thus dividing the world, as it were, into two political systems, Monroe laid the groundwork for the subsequent transformation of the European into a worldwide balance-of-power system.

This transformation was for the first time clearly envisaged and formulated in the speech George Canning made as British foreign secretary to the House of Commons on December 12, 1826. Canning had been criticized for not having gone to war with France in order to restore the balance of power that had been disturbed by the French invasion of Spain. In order to disarm his critics, he formulated a new theory of the balance of power. Through the instrumentality of British recognition of their independence, he included the newly freed Latin American republics as active elements in the balance. He reasoned thus:

> But were there no other means than war for restoring the balance of power?– Is the balance of power a fixed and unalterable standard? Or is it not a standard perpetually varying, as civilization advances, and as new nations spring up, and take their place among established political communities? The balance of power a century and a half ago was to be adjusted between France and Spain, the Netherlands, Austria, and England. Some years after, Russia assumed her high station in European politics. Some years after that again, Prussia became not only a substantive, but a preponderating monarchy.–Thus, while the balance of power continued in principle the same, the means of adjusting it became more varied and enlarged. They became enlarged, in proportion to the increased number of considerable states–in proportion, I may say, to the number of weights which might be shifted into the one or the other scale. . . . Was there no other mode of resistance, than by a direct attack upon France– or by a war to be undertaken on the soil of Spain? What, if the possession of Spain might be rendered harmless in rival hands–harmless as regarded us– and valueless to the possessors? Might not compensation for disparagement be obtained . . . by means better adapted to the present time? If France occupied Spain, was it necessary, in order to avoid the consequences of that occupation–that we should blockade Cadiz? No. I looked another way–I saw materials for compensation in another hemisphere. Contemplating Spain, such as our ancestors had known her, I resolved that if France had Spain, it should not be Spain *"with the Indies."* I called the New World into existence, to redress the balance of the Old.[10]

This development toward a worldwide balance of power operating by means of alliances and counteralliances was consummated in the course of the First World War, in which practically all nations of the world participated actively on one or the other side. The very designation of that war as a "world" war points to the consummation of the development.

In contrast to the Second World War, however, the First World War had its origins exclusively in the fear of a disturbance of the European balance of power,

---

[10]*Speeches of the Right Honourable George Canning* (London, 1836), Vol. VI, pp. 109–11.

which was threatened in two regions: Belgium and the Balkans. Belgium, located at the northeastern frontier of France and guarding the eastern approaches to the English Channel, found itself a focal point of great power competition, without being strong enough to participate actively in that competition. That the independence of Belgium was necessary for the balance of power in Europe was axiomatic. Its annexation by any of the great European nations would of necessity make that nation too powerful for the security of the others. This was recognized from the very moment when Belgium gained its independence with the active support of Great Britain, Austria, Russia, Prussia, and France. These nations, assembled at a conference in London, declared on February 19, 1831, that "they had the right, and the events imposed upon them the duty to see to it that the Belgian provinces, after they had become independent, did not jeopardize the general security and the European balance of power."[11]

In furtherance of that aim, in 1839 the five nations concerned concluded a treaty in which they declared Belgium to be "an independent and perpetually neutral state" under the collective guaranty of the five signatories. This declaration sought to prevent Belgium forever from participating, on one or the other side, in the European balance of power. It was the German violation of Belgium's neutrality which in 1914 crystallized the threat to the balance of power emanating from Germany and enabled Great Britain to justify its participation in the war on the side of France, Russia, and their allies.

The concern of Austria, Great Britain, and Russia in the preservation of the balance of power in the Balkans was concomitant with the weakening of Turkish power in that region. The Crimean War of 1854–56 was fought by an alliance of France, Great Britain, and Turkey against Russia for the purpose of maintaining the balance of power in the Balkans. The alliance treaty of March 13, 1854, declared "that the existence of the Ottoman Empire in its present extent, is of essential importance to the balance of power among the states of Europe." The subsequent rivalries and wars, especially the events that led to the Congress of Berlin of 1878 and the Balkan Wars of 1912 and 1913, are all overshadowed by the fear that one of the nations mainly interested in the Balkans might gain an increase in that region out of proportion to the power of the other nations concerned.

In the years immediately preceding the First World War, the balance of power in the Balkans increased in importance; for, since the Triple Alliance between Austria, Germany, and Italy seemed approximately to balance the Triple Entente between France, Russia, and Great Britain, the power combination that gained a decisive advantage in the Balkans might easily gain a decisive advantage in the overall European balance of power. It was this fear that motivated Austria in July 1914 to try to settle its accounts with Serbia once and for all and that induced Germany to support Austria unconditionally. It was the same fear that brought Russia to the support of Serbia, and France to the support of Russia. In his telegraphic message of August 2, 1914, to George V of England, the Russian czar summed the situation up well when he said that the effect of the predominance of

[11]*Protocols of Conferences in London Relative to the Affairs of Belgium* (1830–31), p. 60.

Austria over Serbia "would have been to upset balance of power in Balkans, which is of such vital interest to my Empire as well as to those Powers who desire maintenance of balance of power in Europe. . . . I trust your country will not fail to support France and Russia in fighting to maintain balance of power in Europe."[12]

After the First World War, France maintained permanent alliances with Poland, Czechoslovakia, Yugoslavia, and Rumania and, in 1935, concluded an alliance—which was, however, not implemented—with the Soviet Union. This policy can be understood as a kind of preventive balance-of-power policy that anticipated Germany's comeback and attempted to maintain the status quo of Versailles in the face of such an eventuality. On the other hand, the formation in 1936 of an alliance between Germany, Italy, and Japan, called the Axis, was intended as a counterweight against the alliance between France and the Eastern European nations, which would at the same time neutralize the Soviet Union.

Thus the period between the two world wars stands in fact under the sign of the balance of power by alliances and counteralliances, although in theory the principle of the balance of power was supposed to have been superseded by the League of Nations principle of collective security. Yet, actually, collective security, as will be shown later in greater detail,[13] did not abolish the balance of power. Rather, it reaffirmed it in the form of a universal alliance against any potential aggressor, the presumption being that such an alliance would always outweigh the aggressor. Collective security differs, however, from the balance of power in the principle of association by virtue of which the alliance is formed. Balance-of-power alliances are formed by certain individual nations against other individual nations or an alliance of them on the basis of what those individual nations regard as their separate national interests. The organizing principle of collective security is the respect for the moral and legal obligation to consider an attack by any nation upon any member of the alliance as an attack upon all members of the alliance. Consequently, collective security is supposed to operate automatically; that is, aggression calls the counteralliance into operation at once and, therefore, protects peace and security with the greatest possible efficiency. Alliances within a balance-of-power system, on the other hand, are frequently uncertain in actual operation, since they are dependent upon political considerations of the individual nations. The defection of Italy from the Triple Alliance in 1915 and the disintegration of the French system of alliances between 1935 and 1939 illustrate this weakness of the balance of power.

THE "HOLDER" OF THE BALANCE

Whenever the balance of power is to be realized by means of an alliance—and this has been generally so throughout the history of the Western world—two possible variations of this pattern have to be distinguished. To use the metaphor of the balance,

---

[12]*British Documents on the Origins of the War, 1898–1914* (London: His Majesty's Stationery Office, 1926), Vol. XI, p. 276.
[13]See Chapter 24.

the system may consist of two scales, in each of which are to be found the nation or nations identified with the same policy of the status quo or of imperialism. The continental nations of Europe have generally operated the balance of power in this way.

The system may, however, consist of two scales plus a third element, the "holder" of the balance or the "balancer." The balancer is not permanently identified with the policies of either nation or group of nations. Its only objective within the system is the maintenance of the balance, regardless of the concrete policies the balance will serve. In consequence, the holder of the balance will throw its weight at one time in this scale, at another time in the other scale, guided by only one consideration—the relative position of the scales. Thus it will put its weight always in the scale that seems to be higher than the other because it is lighter. The balancer may become in a relatively short span of history consecutively the friend and the foe of all major powers, provided they all consecutively threaten the balance by approaching predominance over the others and are in turn threatened by others about to gain such predominance. To paraphrase a statement of Palmerston: While the holder of the balance has no permanent friends, it has no permanent enemies either; it has only the permanent interest of maintaining the balance of power itself.

The balancer is in a position of "splendid isolation." It is isolated by its own choice; for, while the two scales of the balance must vie with each other to add its weight to theirs in order to gain the overweight necessary for success, it must refuse to enter into permanent ties with either side. The holder of the balance waits in the middle in watchful detachment to see which scale is likely to sink. Its isolation is "splendid"; for, since its support or lack of support is the decisive factor in the struggle for power, its foreign policy, if cleverly managed, is able to extract the highest price from those whom it supports. But since this support, regardless of the price paid for it, is always uncertain and shifts from one side to the other in accordance with the movements of the balance, its policies are resented and subject to condemnation on moral grounds. Thus it has been said of the outstanding balancer in modern times, Great Britain, that it lets others fight its wars, that it keeps Europe divided in order to dominate the Continent, and that the fickleness of its policies is such as to make alliances with Great Britain impossible. "Perfidious Albion" has become a byword in the mouths of those who either were unable to gain Great Britain's support, however hard they tried, or else lost it after they had paid what seemed to them too high a price.

The holder of the balance occupies the key position in the balance-of-power system, since its position determines the outcome of the struggle for power. It has, therefore, been called the "arbiter" of the system, deciding who will win and who will lose. By making it impossible for any nation or combination of nations to gain predominance over the others, it preserves its own independence, as well as the independence of all the other nations, and is thus a most powerful factor in international politics.

The holder of the balance can use this power in three different ways. It can make its joining one or the other nation or alliance dependent upon certain conditions favorable to the maintenance or restoration of the balance. It can make its support of the peace settlement dependent upon similar conditions. It can, finally, in either situation see to it that the objectives of its own national policy, apart from the maintenance of the balance of power, are realized in the process of balancing the power of others.

France under Louis XIV and Italy in the decade before the First World War attempted to play this role of arbiter of the European balance of power. But France was too deeply involved in the struggle for power on the European continent, too much a part of its balance of power, and too much lacking in the commanding superiority to play that role successfully. Italy, on the other hand, had not enough weight to throw around to give it the key position in the balance of power. For this reason it earned only the moral condemnation, but not the respect, that similar policies had brought Great Britain. Only Venice in the sixteenth century and Great Britain since the reign of Henry VIII were able to make the holding of the balance between other nations one of the cornerstones of their foreign policies, using the three methods mentioned above either severally or jointly.

The idea appeared for the first time with reference to the Venetians in a letter written in 1553 by Queen Mary of Hungary to the imperial ambassador in England. She pointed out that the Italians had good reason to oppose France; but, she continued: "You know how they fear the power of the one and of the other of the two princes [Charles V and Francis I] and how they are concerned to balance their power."[14] In the following years, on the occasion of Venice's refusals of French offers of alliance, French statesmen characterized the foreign policy of Venice in similar terms, with special reference to the aspects of isolation and detachment from alliances with either side. In 1554, for instance, Henry II of France was reported by a Venetian ambassador to have explained such refusals by the fear of Venice that, in the event of the death of Charles V, Spain might become inferior to France; Venice, however, tried to "keep things in balance *(tener le cose in equale stato)*." Another Venetian ambassador reported in 1558 that the French explained the foreign policy of Venice by its suspicion of the increase in power of France and Spain. Venice wanted to prevent "that the balance tip to either side *(que la bilancia non pendesse da alcuna parte)*." The ambassador added that "this policy is being praised and even admired by intelligent people; in these turbulent times the weak find protection nowhere but in the Republic of Venice and therefore all Italians in particular, desire her independence and welcome her armaments."[15]

The classic example of the balancer has, however, been provided by Great Britain. To Henry VIII is attributed the maxim *cui adhaero praeest* (he whom I support will prevail). He is reported to have had himself painted holding in his right hand a pair of scales in perfect balance, one of them occupied by France, the other

[14]*Papiers d'état du Cardinal de Granvelle* (Paris, 1843), Vol. IV, p. 121.
[15]Eugeno Albéri, *Le Relazioni degli Ambiasciatori Veneti al Senato*, Series I (Firenze, 1862), Vol. II, pp. 287, 464.

by Austria, and holding in his left hand a weight ready to be dropped in either scale. Of England under Elizabeth I it was said "that France and Spain are as it were the Scales in the Balance of Europe and England the Tongue or the Holder of the Balance."[16] In 1624 a French pamphlet invited King Jacob to follow the glorious example of Elizabeth and Henry VIII, "who played his role so well between the Emperor Charles V and King Francis by making himself feared and flattered by both and by holding, as it were, the balance between them."

With the appearance of Louis XIV as a new aspirant for the universal monarchy, it became more and more common, in England and elsewhere, to consider it the English mission to act as "arbiter of Europe" by keeping the Hapsburgs and France in balance. This same standard was applied critically to the foreign policies of Charles II and James II, who made common cause with Louis XIV, the strongest rival of British power, against the Netherlands, and in support of the anti-French policies of William III. With the War of the Spanish Succession, that standard was erected into a dogma, especially in England. It remained, as applied to ever new combinations of powers, practically unchallenged until the Manchester liberals after the middle of the nineteenth century advocated complete and permanent detachment from the affairs of the European continent—that is, isolationism—as the principle of British foreign policy. As the tradition and practice of British diplomacy, this variety of the balance of power seems to have disappeared only in recent years with the decline of British, and the growth of American and Russian, power.[17] When that tradition and practice were about to disappear, Sir Winston Churchill summarized it most eloquently in a speech to the Conservative Members Committee on Foreign Affairs in March 1936:

> For four hundred years the foreign policy of England has been to oppose the strongest, most aggressive, most dominating Power on the Continent, and particularly to prevent the Low Countries falling into the hands of such a Power. Viewed in the light of history these four centuries of consistent purpose amid so many changes of names and facts, of circumstances and conditions, must rank as one of the most remarkable episodes which the records of any race, nation, state or people can show. Moreover, on all occasions England took the more difficult course. Faced by Philip II of Spain, against Louis XIV under William III and Marlborough, against Napoleon, against William II of Germany, it would have been easy and must have been very tempting to join with the stronger and share the fruits of his conquest. However, we always took the harder course, joined with the less strong Powers, made a combination among them, and thus defeated and frustrated the Continental military tyrant whoever he was, whatever nation he led. Thus we preserved the liberties of Europe, protected the growth of its vivacious and

---

[16]William Camden, *Annales of the History of the Most Renowned and Victorious Princess Elizabeth, Late Queen of England* (London, 1635), p. 196.
[17]On this point see the detailed discussion in Chapter 21.

varied society, and emerged after four terrible struggles with an ever-growing fame and widening Empire, and with the Low Countries safely protected in their independence. Here is the wonderful unconscious tradition of British foreign policy. All our thoughts rest in that tradition today. I know of nothing which has occurred to alter or weaken the justice, wisdom, valour and prudence upon which our ancestors acted. I know of nothing that has happened to human nature which in the slightest degree alters the validity of their conclusions. I know of nothing in military, political, economic, or scientific fact which makes me feel that we are less capable. I know of nothing which makes me feel that we might not, or cannot, march along the same road. I venture to put this very general proposition before you because it seems to me that if it is accepted everything else becomes much more simple.

Observe that the policy of England takes no account of which nation it is that seeks the overlordship of Europe. The question is not whether it is Spain, or the French Monarchy, or the French Empire, or the German Empire, or the Hitler regime. It has nothing to do with rulers or nations; it is concerned solely with whoever is the strongest or the potentially dominating tyrant. Therefore we should not be afraid of being accused of being pro-French or anti-German. If the circumstances were reversed, we could equally be pro-German and anti-French. It is a law of public policy which we are following, and not a mere expedient dictated by accidental circumstances, or likes and dislikes, or any other sentiment.[18]

---

[18]Winston S., Churchill, *The Second World War*, Vol. I, *The Gathering Storm* (Boston: Houghton Mifflin, 1948), pp. 207–8. (Reprinted by permission of the publisher.)

13 The Structure of the Balance of Power

DOMINANT AND DEPENDENT SYSTEMS

We have spoken thus far of the balance of power as if it were one single system comprehending all nations actively engaged in international politics. Closer observation, however, reveals that such a system is frequently composed of a number of subsystems that are interrelated with one another but that maintain within themselves a balance of power of their own. The interrelationship between the different systems is generally one of subordination, in the sense that one dominates because of the relatively great weight accumulated in its scales, while the others are, as it were, attached to the scales of that dominant system.

Thus in the sixteenth century the dominant balance of power operated between France and the Hapsburgs, while at the same time an autonomous system kept the Italian states in equilibrium. In the latter part of the seventeenth century, a separate balance of power developed in Northern Europe out of the challenge with which the rise of Swedish power confronted the nations adjacent to the Baltic Sea. The transformation of Prussia into a first-rate power in the eighteenth century brought about a particular German balance of power, the other scale of which had Austria as its main weight. This autonomous system, "a little Europe within the great," was dissolved only in 1866 with the expulsion of Austria from the Germanic Confederation as a consequence of the Prusso-Austrian War of the same year. The eighteenth century saw also the development of an Eastern balance of power occasioned by the ascendancy of Russia. The partitions of Poland, by virtue of the principle of compensations, between Russia, Prussia, and Austria are the first spectacular manifestations of that new system.

Throughout the nineteenth century until the present day, the balance of power in the Balkans has been of concern to the nations of Europe. As early as 1790, Turkey concluded a treaty with Prussia in which the latter promised to go to war with Austria and Russia "because of the prejudice which the enemies, in crossing the Danube, have brought to the desirable and necessary balance of power."

In the latter part of the nineteenth century, one began to speak of an African balance of power with reference to a certain equilibrium among the colonial acquisitions of the great powers. Later on, the balance of power in the Western Hemisphere, in the Pacific, and in the Far and Near East was added to the diplomatic vocabulary. One even spoke of an "Austrian equilibrium"; and of the Austrian monarchy with its antagonistic nationalities it was said that it "is constrained to apply to itself the rules of conduct which the powers of Europe with their perpetual rivalries follow with regard to each other."[1]

It is not by accident that the autonomy of such local balance-of-power systems is the greater and their subordination to a dominant system the less noticeable, the more removed they are physically from the center of the struggle for power—the more they operate at the periphery of the dominant system, out of reach of the dominant nations. Thus an Italian balance of power could develop during the fifteenth century in relative autonomy, while the great nations of Europe were occupied in other regions. For the better part of the history of Western civilization, the different balance-of-power systems of Asia, Africa, and America were entirely independent of the configurations of the European nations, to the point of being hardly known to them.

The balance of power in the Western Hemisphere up to the Second World War and in Eastern Europe until the end of the eighteenth century owe their relatively autonomous development to their location at the periphery of the power centers of the time. The partitions of Poland that were intended to preserve the balance of power in Eastern Europe were executed by the directly interested nations without interference of any other nation. The alliance concluded in 1851 between Brazil and Uruguay against Argentina for the purpose of maintaining the balance of power in South America had only a very remote connection with the European balance of power. On the other hand, it has now become possible to speak of an autonomous African balance of power. Since the indigenous peoples of Africa have started to compete for power with one another and with non-African nations, Africa is no longer solely an object of the struggle for power centered elsewhere.

The more intimately a local balance of power is connected with the dominant one, the less opportunity it has to operate autonomously and the more it tends to become merely a localized manifestation of the dominant balance of power. The balance of power within the German Confederation from Frederick the Great to the War of 1866 presents an intermediate situation between full autonomy and complete integration. It combines a certain degree of autonomy with integration into the dominant system. While the equilibrium between Prussia and Austria was, as we have seen,[2] a precondition for the preservation of the liberties of the members of the Germanic Confederation, this equilibrium was also indispensable for the maintenance of the European balance of power as a whole.

---

[1] Albert Sorel, *L'Europe et la révolution française* (Paris: E. Plon, 1885), Vol. I, p. 443.
[2] See page 188.

The German balance thus fulfilled a dual function: one within its own framework, and another for the general system of which it was a part. Conversely, the fusion of Prussia and Austria or the domination of one by the other would not only have been destructive of the independence of the individual German states but would as well have threatened the freedom of the other European nations. "If Europe," as Edmund Burke put it, "does not conceive the independence and the equilibrium of the empire to be in the very essence of the system of balance of power in Europe . . . all the politics of Europe for more than two centuries have been miserably erroneous."[3] The perpetuation of the balance between Prussia and Austria was, therefore, in the interest not only of the other members of the Germanic Confederation but of all European nations.

When, as a consequence of the war of 1866, Prussia and later Germany gained a permanent advantage over Austria, which destroyed the balance between the two nations and made Germany predominant in Europe, it became one of the functions of the European balance of power to preserve at least the independence of Austria against infringement by its stronger neighbor. It was in consequence of that permanent European interest that after the First World War the victorious Allies sought by legal, economic, and political measures to prevent the fusion of Austria with Germany. Moreover, it was within the logic of this situation that Hitler regarded the annexation of Austria as a necessary stepping-stone on the road toward the overthrow of the European balance of power.

The balance of power in the Balkans has fulfilled a similar function since the last decades of the nineteenth century. Here, too, the maintenance of a balance of power among the Balkan nations has been regarded as a prerequisite for the maintenance of the European balance. Whenever the local balance was threatened, the great nations of Europe intervened in order to restore it. The statement of the Russian czar at the beginning of the First World War, quoted above,[4] clearly illustrates that connection.

STRUCTURAL CHANGES IN THE BALANCE OF POWER[5]

In recent times the relations between the dominant balance of power and the local systems have shown an ever increasing tendency to change to the detriment of the autonomy of the local systems. The reasons for this development lie in the structural changes that the dominant balance of power has undergone since the First World War and that became manifest in the Second. We have already indicated the gradual expansion of the dominant balance-of-power system from Western and Central Europe to the rest of the continent, and from there to other continents, until finally the First World War saw all the nations of the earth actively participating in a worldwide balance of power.

---

[3] *Works*, (Boston: Little, Brown, 1889), Vol. IV, p. 330.
[4] See page 204.
[5] For other structural changes, see pages 000 ff. and Chapter 21.

Hand in hand with the consummation of this expansion went a shift of the main weights of the balance from Europe to other continents. At the outbreak of the First World War in 1914, the main weights in the balance were predominantly European: Great Britain, France, and Russia in one scale, and Germany and Austria in the other. At the end of the Second World War, the principal weights in each scale were either entirely non-European, as in the case of the United States, or predominantly non-European, as in the case of the Soviet Union. In consequence, the whole structure of the world balance of power changed. At the end of the First World War, and even at the beginning of the Second, the two scales of the balance, so to speak, were still in Europe; only the weights of the scales came from all over the earth. The main protagonists of the power contest and the principal stakes for which it was fought were still predominantly European. To paraphrase the words of George Canning, already quoted, non-European powers were called in only for the purpose of redressing the balance of power of Europe. In Churchill's words of 1940, "The New World, with all its power and might, steps forth to the rescue and the liberation of the Old."

Today the balance of power of Europe is no longer the center of world politics around which local balances would group themselves, either in intimate connection or in lesser or greater autonomy. Today the European balance of power has become a mere function of the worldwide balance of which the United States and the Soviet Union are the main weights, placed on opposite scales. The distribution of power in Europe is only one of the concrete issues over which the power contests between the United States and the Soviet Union is being waged.

What is true of the formerly dominant system is true of all the traditional local systems as well. The balance of power in the Balkans, no less than the balances in the Near and Far East, have shared the fate of the general European system. They have become mere functions of the new worldwide balance, mere "theaters" where the power contest between the two great protagonists is fought out. One might say that of all the local balance-of-power systems only the South American system has retained a certain measure of autonomy, protected as it is by the predominance of the United States.[6]

---

[6]For the causes responsible for the destruction of most of those autonomous systems, see Chapter 21.

14 Evaluation of the Balance of Power

Considering especially its changed structure, how are we to evaluate the balance of power and to assess its future usefulness for the preservation of peace and security in the modern world?

In explaining its nature and operation, we have stressed its inevitable connection with, and protective function for, a multiple-state system. Throughout its history of more than four hundred years, the policy of the balance of power succeeded in preventing any one state from gaining universal dominion. It also succeeded in preserving the existence of all members of the modern state system from the conclusion of the Thirty Years' War in 1648 and to the partitions of Poland at the end of the eighteenth century. Yet universal dominion by any one state was prevented only at the price of warfare, which from 1648 to 1815 was virtually continuous and in the twentieth century has twice engulfed practically the whole world. And the two periods of stability, one starting in 1648 and the other in 1815, were preceded by the wholesale elimination of small states and were interspersed, starting with the destruction of Poland, by a great number of isolated acts of a similar nature.

What is important for our discussion is the fact that these acts were accomplished in the name of the very principle of the balance of power whose chief claim to serve as the fundamental principle of the modern state system had been that it was indispensable for the preservation of the independence of the individual states. Not only did the balance of power fail to protect the independence of Poland, but the very principle of territorial compensation to each member for the territorial aggrandizement of any other member brought about the destruction of the Polish state. The destruction of Poland in the name of the balance of power was but the first and most spectacular instance of a series of partitions, annexations, and destructions of independent states that, from 1815 to the present, have all been accomplished in application of that same principle. Failure to fulfill its function for individual states and failure to fulfill it for the state system as a whole by any means other than actual or potential warfare points up the three main weaknesses of the balance of power as the guiding principle of international politics: its uncertainty, its unreality, and its inadequacy.

THE UNCERTAINTY OF THE BALANCE OF POWER

The idea of a balance among a number of nations for the purpose of preventing any one of them from becoming strong enough to threaten the independence of the others is a metaphor taken from the field of mechanics. It was appropriate to the way of thinking of the sixteenth, seventeenth, and eighteenth centuries, which liked to picture society and the whole universe as a gigantic mechanism, a machine or a clockwork, created and kept in motion by the divine watchmaker. Within that mechanism, and within the smaller mechanisms composing it, the mutual relations of the individual parts could be, it was believed, exactly determined by means of mechanical calculations and their actions and reactions accurately foreseen. The metaphor of two scales kept in balance by an equal distribution of weights on either side, providing the mechanism for the maintenance of stability and order on the international scene, has its origin in this mechanistic philosophy. It was applied to the practical affairs of international politics in the spirit of that philosophy.

The balance of power, mechanically conceived, is in need of an easily recognizable quantitative criterion by which the relative power of a number of nations can be measured and compared. For it is only by means of such a criterion, comparable to the pounds and ounces of a real pair of scales, that one can say with any degree of assurance that a certain nation tends to become more powerful than another or that both tend to maintain a balance of power between them. Furthermore, it is only by means of such a criterion that variations in power can be converted into quantitative units to be transferred from one scale to the other in order to restore the balance. The theory and practice of the balance of power found such a criterion, as we have seen, in territory, population, and armaments. The policies of compensations and of competitive armaments have served throughout the history of the modern state system as the practical application of that criterion.

But does the power of a nation actually repose in the extension of its territory? Is a nation the more powerful the more territory it possesses? Our examination of the factors that make for the power of a nation has shown that the answer can be in the affirmative only with qualifications so far-reaching as almost to nullify the affirmative character of the answer. The size of French territory was greater at the end of Louis XIV's reign than it had been at its beginning, but France was weaker at the end of the reign than it had been at its beginning. The same inverse relation of size of territory and national power is revealed by a comparison of Prussian territory and power at the death of Frederick the Great in 1786 with the same factors ten years later. Until the beginning of the nineteenth century, Spain and Turkey possessed vast territories exceeding in size the territories of any of the major nations of Europe. But they were counted among the weakest nations actively engaged in international politics. While geography, of which territorial expansion is a part, is indeed a factor that goes into the making of national power, it is but one among other factors. Even if one takes into consideration, after the model of the compensations at the turn of the eighteenth century, the quality of the territory and the quality and quantity of the population within it, one still deals with fewer than all the factors of which the power of a nation is composed. The same holds true if one makes the quantity and quality of armaments the standard of comparison.

National character and, above all, national morale and the quality of government, especially in the conduct of foreign affairs, are the most important, but also the most elusive, components of national power. It is impossible for the observer of the contemporary scene or the explorer of future trends to assess even with approximate accuracy the relative contributions these elements may make to the power of different nations. Furthermore, the quality of these contributions is subject to incessant change, unnoticeable at the moment the change actually takes place and revealed only in the actual test of crisis and war. Rational calculation of the relative strength of several nations, which is the very lifeblood of the balance of power, becomes a series of guesses the correctness of which can be ascertained only in retrospect.[1] As Bolingbroke, one of the great practitioners of the balance of power, put it:

> The precise point at which the scales of power turn, like that of the solstice in either tropic, is imperceptible to common observation; and, in one case as in the other, some progress must be made in the new direction, before the change is perceived. They who are in the sinking scale, for in the political balance of power, unlike to all others, the scale that is empty sinks, and that which is full rises; they who are in the sinking scale do not easily come off from the habitual prejudices of superior wealth, or power, or skill, or courage, nor from the confidence that these prejudices inspire. They who are in the rising scale do not immediately feel their strength, nor assume that confidence in it which successful experience gives them afterwards. They who are the most concerned to watch the variations of this balance, misjudge often in the same manner, and from the same prejudices. They continue to dread a power no longer able to hurt them, or they continue to have no apprehensions of a power that grows daily more formidable.[2]

An eighteenth-century opponent of the balance of power tried to demonstrate the absurdity of the calculations common at the time by asking which of two princes was more powerful: one who possessed three pounds of military strength, four pounds of statesmanship, five pounds of zeal, and two pounds of ambition, or one who had twelve pounds of military strength but only one pound

---

[1]See the extensive discussion of this problem in Chapter 10.
[2]"On the Study and Use of History," *The Works of Lord Bolingbroke* (Philadelphia: Carey and Hart, 1841), Vol. II, p. 258.

of all the other qualities? The author gives the advantage to the former prince, but whether his answer will be correct under all circumstances is certainly open to question, even under the assumption—patently hypothetical—that the quantitative determination of the relative weight of these different qualities were possible.

This uncertainty of power calculations is inherent in the nature of national power itself. It will therefore come into play even in the most simple pattern of the balance of power—that is, when one nation opposes another. This uncertainty is, however, immeasurably magnified when the weights in one or the other or in both scales are composed not of single units but of alliances. Then it becomes necessary not only to compute one's own and the opponent's national power and to correlate one with the other but to perform the same operation on the national power of one's allies and those of the opponent. The risk of guessing is greatly aggravated when one must assess the power of nations belonging to a different civilization from one's own. It is difficult enough to evaluate the power of Great Britain or of France. It is much more difficult to make a correct assessment of the power of China, Japan, or even the Soviet Union. The crowning uncertainty, however, lies in the fact that one cannot always be sure who are one's own allies and who are the opponent's. Alignments by virtue of alliance treaties are not always identical with the alliances that oppose each other in the actual contest of war.

One of the masters of the balance of power, Frederick the Great, made wise by sad experiences, called the attention of his successor to this problem. He said in his Political Testament of 1768:

> A frequently deceptive art of conjecture serves as foundation for most of the great political designs. One takes as one's point of departure the most certain factor one knows of, combines it, as well as one can, with other factors, but imperfectly known, and draws therefrom the most correct conclusions possible. In order to make that clearer, I shall give an example. Russia seeks to gain the support of the King of Denmark. She promises him the duchy of Holstein-Gottorp, which belongs to the Russian Grand Duke, and hopes in this way to gain his support forever. But the King of Denmark is fickle. How can one foresee all the ideas that might pass through that young head? The favorites, mistresses and ministers, who will take hold of his mind and offer him advantages from another power which appear to him to be greater than those offered by Russia, are they not going to make him change sides as an ally? A similar uncertainty, although every time in another form, dominates all operations of foreign policy so that great alliances have often a result contrary to the one planned by their members.[3]

These words, written when the classical period of the balance of power was drawing to a close, lose nothing of their poignancy when tested by the events of recent history. The composition of the alliances and counteralliances that one might have foreseen in August 1938, immediately before the denouement of the

---

[3]*Die politischen Testamente Friedrichs des Grossen* (Berlin, 1920), p. 192.

Czechoslovakian crisis, was certainly quite different from that which came to pass a year later, at the outbreak of the Second World War, and from that which developed more than two years later in consequence of the attack upon Pearl Harbor. No statesman, however great his knowledge, wisdom, and foresight, could have anticipated all these developments and based his balance-of-power policies upon them.

Immediately before the outbreak of the First World War in July 1914, it was by no means certain whether Italy would fulfill its obligations under the Treaty of the Triple Alliance and join Germany and Austria in a war against France, Great Britain, and Russia; whether it would remain neutral; or whether it would join the other side. Nor were the responsible statesmen of Germany and Austria certain, as late as July 30, 1914, that Russia would oppose Austria in order to maintain the balance of power in the Balkans. On that day the British ambassador to Germany reported to his government as the opinion held by these statesmen "that a general war was out of the question as Russia neither could, nor wanted to, go to war."[4] According to the reports of the British ambassador, the same belief was held at Vienna.

Nor was it evident to everybody concerned that Great Britain would enter the First World War on the side of France and Russia. As late as June 1, 1914, the British secretary of foreign affairs declared in the House of Commons, confirming a declaration of the prime minister made the previous year, that Great Britain was bound by no obligation, unknown to Parliament and to the public, that might lead it into war. The British government was convinced that the secret exchange of letters between the secretary of foreign affairs and the French ambassador, which had taken place in November 1912, did not affect its freedom of action in case of a continental war. The French and Russian governments relied upon British intervention without being certain of it.[5] The British ambassador reported

---

[4]*British Documents, on the Origins of the War, 1898–1914* (London: His Majesty's Stationery Office, 1926), Vol. XI, p. 361.

[5]How ambiguous the situation was that this exchange of letters created is evident from the text of the letter that Sir Edward Grey, British foreign secretary, wrote on November 22, 1912, to Mr. Paul Cambon, the French ambassador to Great Britain, and that is substantially reiterated by the French ambassador's reply of the next day.

"From time to time in recent years the French and British naval and military experts have consulted together. It has always been understood that such consultation does not restrict the freedom of either Government to decide at any future time whether or not to assist the other by armed force. We have agreed that consultation between experts is not, and ought not to be regarded as, an engagement that commits either Government to action in a contingency that has not arisen and may never arise. The disposition, for instance, of the French and British fleets respectively at the present moment is not based upon an engagement to co-operate in war.

"You have, however, pointed out that, if either Government had grave reason to expect an unprovoked attack by a third Power, it might become essential to know whether it could in that event depend upon the armed assistance of the other.

"I agree that, if either Government had grave reason to expect an unprovoked attack by a third Power, or something that threatened the general peace, it should immediately discuss with the other whether both Governments should act together to prevent aggression and to preserve peace, and, if so, what measures they would be prepared to take in common. If these measures involved action, the plans of the General Staffs would at once be taken into consideration, and the Governments would then decide what effect should be given to them." *Collected Diplomatic Documents Relating to the Outbreak of the European War* (London: His Majesty's Stationery Office, 1915), p. 80.

The ambiguity of the situation is also well illustrated by the czar's telegram quoted on page 204.

from Berlin on July 30, 1914, that the French ambassador "is continuously scolding me about England keeping her intentions so dark and says that the only way by which a general war can be prevented is by . . . stating . . . that England will fight on the side of France and Russia."[6] The governments of the Central Powers were altogether ignorant of this exchange of letters until after the First World War had actually broken out. Thus they assumed that Great Britain would remain neutral; "up to the last moment," reports the British ambassador to Berlin, "they thought England would not come in."[7] Therefore, they concluded that the balance of power favored them. France and Russia started with the opposite assumption and arrived at the opposite conclusion.

The British policy of secrecy about Britain's commitments toward France has been widely criticized on the ground that Germany would never have gone to war against France and Russia if it had known in advance that Great Britain would join the latter powers—that is, if it had been able to make its balance-of-power calculations in knowledge of the Anglo-French agreement of November 1912. However, neither the British nor the French and Russian governments were themselves entirely sure beforehand what this agreement would mean for the balance of power in August 1914. Therefore, even if the German government had known about the agreement it could not have been certain what the actual distribution of power would be on the eve of the First World War. It is in this condition of extreme uncertainty, inherent in any balance-of-power system composed of alliances, that one must seek the reasons for the failure of the balance of power to prevent the First World War. The German undersecretary for foreign affairs expressed spontaneously the insecurity to which the system of alliance and counteralliances had led when he said to the British ambassador on August 1, 1914, that Germany, France, "and perhaps England" had been drawn into the war, "None of whom wanted war in the least and . . . that it came from 'this d——d system of alliances'" which were the curse of modern times."[8]

THE UNREALITY OF THE BALANCE OF POWER

This uncertainty of all power calculations not only makes the balance of power incapable of practical application but leads also to its very negation in practice. Since no nation can be sure that its calculation of the distribution of power at any particular moment in history is correct, it must at least make sure that its errors, whatever they may be, will not put the nation at a disadvantage in the contest for power. In other words, the nation must try to have at least a margin of safety that will allow it to make erroneous calculations and still maintain the balance of power. To that effect, all nations actively engaged in the struggle for power must actually aim not at a balance—that is, equality—of power but at superiority of

---

[6]*British Documents*, p. 361.
[7]Ibid., p. 363.
[8]Ibid., p. 284.

power in their own behalf. And since no nation can foresee how large its miscalculations will turn out to be, all nations must ultimately seek the maximum of power obtainable under the circumstances. Only thus can they hope to attain the maximum margin of safety commensurate with the maximum of errors they might commit. The limitless aspiration for power, potentially always present, as we have seen,[9] in the power drives of nations, finds in the balance of power a mighty incentive to transform itself into an actuality.

Since the desire to attain a maximum of power is universal, all nations must always be afraid that their own miscalculations and the power increases of other nations might add up to an inferiority for themselves that they must at all costs try to avoid. Hence all nations who have gained an apparent edge over their competitors tend to consolidate that advantage and use it for changing the distribution of power permanently in their favor. This can be done through diplomatic pressure by bringing the full weight of that advantage to bear upon the other nations, compelling them to make the concessions that will consolidate the temporary advantage into a permanent superiority. It can also be done by war. Since in a balance-of-power system all nations live in constant fear lest their rivals deprive them, at the first opportune moment, of their power position, all nations have a vital interest in anticipating such a development and doing unto the others what they do not want the others to do unto them. To quote Bolingbroke again:

> The scales of the balance of power will never be exactly poised, nor is the precise point of equality either discernible nor necessary to be discerned. It is sufficient in this, as in other human affairs, that the deviation be not too great. Some there will always be. A constant attention to these deviations is therefore necessary. When they are little, their increase may be easily prevented by early care and the precautions that good policy suggests. But when they become great for want of this care and these precautions, or by the force of unforeseen events, more vigor is to be exerted, and greater efforts to be made. But even in such cases, much reflection is necessary on all the circumstances that form the conjuncture; lest, by attacking with ill success, the deviation be confirmed, and the power that is deemed already exorbitant become more so; and lest, by attacking with good success, whilst one scale is pillaged, too much weight of power be thrown into the other. In such cases, he who has considered, in the histories of former ages, the strange revolutions that time produces, and the perpetual flux and reflux of public as well as private fortunes, of kingdoms and states as well as of those who govern or are governed in them, will incline to think, that if the scales can be brought back by a war, nearly, though not exactly, to the point they were at before this great deviation from it, the rest may be left to accidents, and to the use that good policy is able to make of them.[10]

---

[9] See pages 67 and 79 ff.
[10] "On the Study and Use of History" p. 291.

Preventive war, however abhorred in diplomatic language and abhorrent to democratic public opinion, is in fact a natural outgrowth of the balance of power. Here again, the events leading to the outbreak of the First World War are instructive; for it was on that occasion that foreign affairs were conducted for the last time according to the classical rules of the balance of power. Austria was resolved to change the balance of power in the Balkans in its favor once and for all. It believed that, although Russia was not yet ready to strike, its power was on the increase and that, therefore, postponement of decisive action would make the distribution of power less favorable to itself. Similar calculations were made in Berlin with respect to the distribution of power between Germany and Russia. Russia, on the other hand, was resolved not to permit Austria to change the distribution of power in its favor by crushing Serbia. Russia calculated that such an instant increase in the power of its prospective enemy might more than outweigh any probable future increase in its own power. It was partly in consideration of these Russian calculations that Great Britain refused until the last moment to declare openly its support of the Franco-Russian alliance. As the British ambassador to Germany put it on July 30, 1914: "A statement to that effect at the present stage, while it might cause Germany to hesitate, might equally urge Russia on; and if Russia attacked Austria, Germany would have to come in whether she feared the British fleet or not."[11] The Grand General Staff of Germany, in a memorandum to the imperial chancellor, on July 29, 1914, analyzed the mechanics of the balance of power with unusual clarity: Russia

> announces that she intends to mobilize when Austria advances into Serbia, as she cannot permit the destruction of Serbia by Austria, though Austria has explained that she intends nothing of the sort.
>
> What must and will the further consequences be? If Austria advances into Serbia she will have to face not only the Serbian army but also the vastly superior strength of Russia; thus she can not enter upon a war with Serbia without securing herself against an attack by Russia. That means that she will be forced to mobilize the other half of her Army, for she can not possibly surrender at discretion to a Russia all prepared for war. At the moment, however, in which Austria mobilizes her whole Army, the collision between herself and Russia will become inevitable. But that, for Germany, is the *casus foederis*. If Germany is not to be false to her word and permit her ally to suffer annihilation at the hands of Russian superiority, she, too, must mobilize. And that would bring about the mobilization of the rest of Russia's military districts as a result. But then Russia will be able to say: I am being attacked by Germany. She will then assure herself of the support of France, which, according to the compact of alliance, is obliged to take part in the war, should her ally, Russia, be attacked. Thus the Franco-Russian alliance, so often held up to praise as a purely defensive compact, created only in order to meet the aggressive plans of Germany, will become active, and the mutual butchery of the civilized nations of Europe will begin.[12]

---

[11]*British Documents*, p. 361.
[12]Max Montgelas and Walther Schuecking, editors, *Outbreak of the World War: German Documents Collected by Karl Kautsky* (New York: Oxford University Press, 1924), p. 307.

It will forever be impossible to prove or disprove the claim that by its stabilizing influence the balance of power has aided in avoiding many wars. One cannot retrace the course of history, taking a hypothetical situation as one's point of departure. But, while nobody can tell how many wars there would have been without the balance of power, it is not hard to see that most of the wars that have been fought since the beginning of the modern state system have their origin in the balance of power. Three types of wars are intimately connected with the mechanics of the balance of power: preventive war, already referred to, where normally both sides pursue imperialistic aims; anti-imperialistic war; and imperialistic war itself.

The opposition, under the conditions of the balance of power, between one status quo nation or an alliance of them and one imperialistic power or a group of them is very likely to lead to war. In most instances, from Charles V to Hitler and Hirohito, they actually did lead to war. The status quo nations, which by definition are dedicated to peaceful pursuits and want only to hold what they have, will hardly be able to keep pace with the dynamic and rapid increase in power characteristic of a nation bent upon imperialistic expansion.

The relative increases in the power of Great Britain and France, on the one hand, and of Germany, on the other, from 1933 to the outbreak of the Second World War in 1939 illustrate vividly the different pace and dynamics in the power increases of status quo and imperialistic nations. In such an armaments race the status quo nations are bound to lose, and their relative position cannot fail to deteriorate at an accelerated pace the longer the race lasts. Time is on the side of the imperialistic nations, and as time goes on, their scale sinks lower and lower under the ever-increasing weight of their power, while the scale of the status quo nations rises ever higher. Thus it becomes more and more difficult for the latter to redress the balance, and they cannot fail to realize that, if the trend is not forcibly reversed, the position of the imperialistic nations must become well-nigh unassailable, while their own chances for redressing the balance will be irretrievably lost. This was the situation in which Great Britain and France found themselves in September 1939. In such a situation, war, with its incalculable possibilities, seems to be the only alternative to an inglorious absorption into the power orbit of the imperialistic nation. The dynamics of international politics, as they play between status quo and imperialistic nations, lead of necessity to such a disturbance of the balance of power that war appears as the only policy that offers the status quo nations at least a chance to redress the balance of power in their favor.

Yet the very act of redressing the balance carries within itself the elements of a new disturbance. The dynamics of power politics as outlined previously make this development inevitable. Yesterday's defender of the status quo is transformed by victory into the imperialist of today, against whom yesterday's vanquished will seek revenge tomorrow. The ambition of the victor who took up arms in order to restore the balance, as well as the resentment of the loser who could not overthrow it, tend to make the new balance a virtually invisible point of transition from one disturbance to the next. Thus the balancing process has frequently led to the substitution of one predominant power, disturbing the balance, for another one.

Charles V of Hapsburg was thwarted in his aspirations for a universal monarchy by France, only to be succeeded by Louis XIV of France, whose similar aspirations united all of Europe against him. Once the balance had been restored against Louis XIV, a new disturbing factor arose in Frederick the Great of Prussia. The bid for world domination by France under Napoleon I was followed by a similar bid on the part of the Holy Alliance under the leadership of the most potent of Napoleon's former enemies, Austria and Russia. The defeat of the latter brought in its wake the rise of Prussia to dominance in Germany and of Germany in Europe. Twenty years after its defeat in the First World War, Germany was again the predominant nation in Europe, while Japan had risen to a similar position in Asia. The very moment these two nations were removed as active factors in the balance of power, a new power contest took shape between the United States, on the one hand, and the Soviet Union and Communist China, on the other. With the breakup of the Sino-Soviet bloc, China drew closer to the United States and the West while retaining its independence, thus contributing to a more complex balance of power.

The Balance of Power as Ideology

Our discussion has thus far proceeded on the assumption that the balance of power is a device for the self-defense of nations whose independence and existence are threatened by a disproportionate increase in the power of other nations. What we have said of the balance of power is true only under the assumption that the balance of power is used genuinely for its avowed purposes of self-protection. Yet we have already seen how the power drives of nations take hold of ideal principles and transform them into ideologies in order to disguise, rationalize, and justify themselves. They have done this with the balance of power. What we have said above about the popularity of anti-imperialistic ideologies in general applies to the balance of power.

A nation seeking empire has often claimed that all it wanted was equilibrium. A nation seeking only to maintain the status quo has often tried to give a change in the status quo the appearance of an attack upon the balance of power. When, at the outbreak of the Seven Years' War in 1756, England and France found themselves at war, British writers justified the policy of their country in terms of the necessities of the European balance of power, while French publicists claimed that France was compelled to oppose English supremacy on the sea and in North America in order to restore the "balance of commerce."

When the allied powers in 1813 submitted their conditions of peace to Napoleon, they invoked the principle of the balance of power. When Napoleon rejected these conditions, he, too, invoked "the equilibrium of rights and interests." When, early in 1814, the allies confronted the representative of Napoleon with an ultimatum demanding that France, in the name of the balance of power, give up all conquests made since 1792, the French representative replied: "Did the allied sovereigns not . . . want to establish a just equilibrium in Europe? Do they not declare that they want it still today? To maintain the same relative power which she always has had is also the sole actual desire of France. But Europe is no longer what it was twenty years ago." And he arrived at the conclusion that in the light of geography and strategy even the retention by France of the left bank of the Rhine would hardly be sufficient to restore the balance of power in Europe. The allied representatives declared in reply: "France, by retreating into the dimensions of 1792, remains one of the strongest powers on the continent by virtue of her central position, her population, the riches of her soil, the nature of her frontiers, the number and distribution of her strong points." Thus both sides tried to apply the principle of the balance of power to the same situation and arrived at irreconcilable results with the effect that the efforts to end the war failed.

A similar situation occurred forty years later for similar reasons. At the Conference of Vienna, which in 1855 tried to end the Crimean War, Russia agreed with its opponents to make the maintenance of the balance of power in the Black Sea the basis of the settlement. Yet, while Russia declared that "the preponderance of Russia in the Black Sea . . . is absolutely necessary for the European equilibrium," its adversaries sought to put an end to that preponderance and declared that the Russian navy was "still too strong in comparison to the Turkish fleet." Peace was concluded in 1856 on the latter terms.

The difficulties in assessing correctly the relative power positions of nations have made the invocation of the balance of power one of the favored ideologies of international politics. Thus it has come about that the term is being used in a very loose and unprecise manner. When a nation would like to justify one of its steps on the international scene, it is likely to refer to it as serving the maintenance or restoration of the balance of power. When a nation would like to discredit certain policies pursued by another nation, it is likely to condemn them as a threat to, or a disturbance of, the balance of power. Since it is the inherent tendency of the balance of power in the proper meaning of the term to preserve the status quo, the term has, in the vocabulary of status quo nations, become a synonym for the status quo and for any distribution of power existing at any particular moment. Any change in the existing distribution of power is therefore opposed as disturbing the balance of power. In this way a nation interested in the preservation of a certain distribution of power tries to make its interest appear to be the outgrowth of the fundamental, universally accepted principle of the modern state system and, hence, to be identical with an interest common to all nations. The nation itself, far from defending a selfish, particular concern, poses as the guardian of that general principle—that is, as the agent of the international community.

In this sense one speaks, for instance, of the balance of power in the Western Hemisphere that might be disturbed by the policies of non-American nations, or of the balance of power in the Mediterranean that must be defended against Russian intrusion. Yet what one means to defend in either case is not the balance of power but a particular distribution of power regarded as favorable to a particular nation or group of nations. The *New York Times* wrote in one of its reports on the Foreign Ministers' Conference in Moscow in 1947: "The new unity of France, Britain and the United States . . . may be only temporary but it does alter the balance of power perceptibly."[13] What was actually meant was not that the balance of power in the proper meaning of the term had been altered but that the distribution of power that existed after the conference was more favorable to the Western powers than the one that existed before.

The use of the balance of power as an ideology accentuates difficulties inherent in the mechanics of the balance of power. Yet it must be noted that the ready use as an ideology to which the balance of power lends itself is not an accident. It is a potentiality inherent in its very essence. The contrast between pretended precision and the actual lack of it, between the pretended aspiration for balance and the actual aim of predominance—this contrast, which, as we have seen, is of the very essence of the balance of power, makes the latter in a certain measure an ideology to begin with. The balance of power thus assumes a reality and a function that it actually does not have and therefore tends to disguise, rationalize, and justify international politics as it actually is.

THE INADEQUACY OF THE BALANCE OF POWER

We have recognized the actual contribution that the balance of power, during the period of its flowering in the seventeenth, eighteenth, and nineteenth centuries, has made to the stability of the modern state system and to the preservation of the independence of its members. Yet was it the balance of power alone that attained these beneficial results, or was, during that period of history, another actor in operation without which the balance of power could not have attained them?

Restraining Influence of a Moral Consensus

Edward Gibbon pointed to such a factor in 1781 at a moment when his country was fighting a losing war with its American Colonies, France, Spain, and Holland. He then proposed

> to consider Europe as one great republic, whose various inhabitants have attained almost the same level of politeness and cultivation. The balance of power will continue to fluctuate, and the prosperity of our own or the neighboring kingdoms may be alternately exalted or depressed; but these events cannot essentially injure our general state of happiness, the system of arts, and laws, and manners, which so advantageously distinguish, above the rest of mankind, the Europeans and their colonies . . . . The abuses of tyranny are restrained by the mutual influence of fear and shame; republics have acquired order and stability; monarchies have imbibed the principles of freedom, or, at least, of moderation; and some sense of honour and justice is introduced into the most defective constitutions by the general manners of the times. In peace,

---

[13]April 27, 1947, p. E3.

the progress of knowledge and industry is accelerated by the emulation of so many active rivals: in war, the European forces are exercised by temperate and undecisive contests.[14]

Comments Professor Toynbee on this passage:

And yet Gibbon's confidence was justified in the event by the peace settlement of A.D. 1783. In the American Revolutionary War Great Britain was eventually defeated by an overwhelming coalition of opposing forces; but her opponents did not think of crushing her. They had been fighting for the limited and precise objective of establishing the insurgent colonies' independence of the British Crown—the colonists because, for them, this independence was an end in itself, and the colonists' French allies because, in the estimation of a refined French statesmanship, the secession of the thirteen American colonies from the British Empire would just suffice to restore a Balance of Power which had been unduly inclined in Great Britain's favour by the cumulative effect of successive British victories in three previous wars. In A.D. 1783, when the victory was once more with the French for the first time in nearly a hundred years, French statesmanship was content to attain a minimum objective with a maximum economy of means. No rancorous memory of previous reverses tempted the French Government to seize this opportunity for paying off old scores. They were not even tempted to fight on for the disannexation of Canada, the principal American dominion of the French Crown, which had been conquered by the British Crown during the Seven Years' War and had been officially ceded by King Louis to King George in the peace settlement of A.D. 1763, only twenty years back. In the peace settlement of A.D. 1783 Canada was left in the British Crown's possession by a victorious France; and Great Britain, let off with the loss of her thirteen colonies, could congratulate herself, in Gibbonian language, upon having survived, without shipwreck, a fluctuation in the Balance of Power in which her turn had come to see her prosperity depressed, but in which no

---

[14] *The Decline and Fall of the Roman Empire* (Modern Library Edition), Vol. II, pp. 93–95. A similarly brilliant account of the beneficial results of the balance of power is found in an anonymous contribution to the *Edinburgh Review,* Vol. I (January 1803), p. 348: "But had it not been for that wholesome jealousy of rival neighbours, which modern politicians have learned to cherish, how many conquests and changes of dominion would have taken place, instead of wars, in which a few useless lives were lost, and some superfluous millions were squandered? How many fair portions of the globe might have been deluged in blood, instead of some hundreds of sailors fighting harmlessly on the barren plains of the ocean, and some thousands of soldiers carrying on a scientific, and regular, and quiet, system of warfare, in countries set apart for the purpose, and resorted to as the arena where the disputes of nations may be determined? We may indeed look to the history of the last century as the proudest area in the annals of the species; the period most distinguished for learning, and skill, and industry; for the milder virtues, and for common sense; for refinement in government, and an equal diffusion of liberty; above all, for that perfect knowledge of the arts of administration, which has established certain general rules of conduct among nations; has prevented the overthrow of empires, and the absorption of weak states into the bodies of devouring neighbours; has set bounds to the march of conquest, and rendered the unsheathing of the sword a measure of the last adoption; whereas, in other times, it was always resorted to in the first instance."

essential injury had been done to the general state of happiness of a polite society which was the common spiritual home of the subjects of King George and the subjects of King Louis.[15]

The great political writers of that age were aware of this intellectual and moral unity, upon whose foundations the balance of power reposes and which makes its beneficial operations possible. We shall mention only three of these writer: Fénelon, Rousseau, and Vattel.

Fénelon, the great philosopher of the reign of Louis XIV and mentor of the latter's grandson, wrote in the *Supplement to the Examination of Conscience about the Duties of Royalty:*

> This attention for the maintenance of a kind of equality and of equilibrium among neighboring nations assures tranquility for all. In this respect, all nations which are neighbors and have commercial relations form a great body and a kind of community. For instance, Christendom forms a kind of general republic which has its common interests, fears, and precautions. All members which compose this great body owe it to each other for the common good, and owe it also to themselves, in the interest of national security, to forestall any step on the part of any member which might overturn the equilibrium and bring about the inevitable ruin of all the other members of the same body. Whatever changes or impairs this general system of Europe is too dangerous and brings in its train infinite evils.[16]

Rousseau took up the same theme by stating, "The nations of Europe form among themselves an invisible nation . . . . The actual system of Europe has exactly that degree of solidity which maintains it in a state of perpetual agitation without overturning it."[17] And, according to Vattel, the most influential of the eighteenth-century writers on international law:

> Europe forms a political system, a body where the whole is connected by the relations and different interests of nations inhabiting this part of the world. It is not as anciently a confused heap of detached pieces, each of which thought itself very little concerned in the fate of others, and seldom regarded things which did not immediately relate to it. The confined attention of sovereigns . . . makes Europe a kind of republic, the members of which, thought independent, unite, through the ties of common interest, for the maintenance of order and liberty. Hence arose that famous scheme of the political equilibrium or balance of power; by which is understood such a disposition of things as no power is able absolutely to predominate, or to prescribe laws to others.[18]

---

[15]Arnold Toynbee, *A Study of History* (London: Oxford University Press, 1939), Vol. IV, p. 149. (Reprinted by permission of the publisher.)
[16]*Oeuvres* (Paris, 1870), Vol. III, pp. 349, 350.
[17]*Oeuvres completes* (Brussels: Th. Lejeune, 1827), Vol. 10, pp. 172, 179.
[18]*The Law of Nations* (Philadelphia, 1829), Book III, Chapter III, pp. 377–378.

The statements of the writers are echoed in the declarations of the statesmen. From 1648 to the French Revolution of 1789, the princes and their advisors took the moral and political unity of Europe for granted and referred as a matter of course to the "republic of Europe," "the community of Christian princes," or "the political system of Europe." But the challenge of the Napoleonic Empire forced them to make explicit the moral and intellectual foundations upon which the old balance of power had reposed. The Holy Alliance and the Concert of Europe, both of which shall be dealt with later in detail,[19] are attempts at giving institutionalized direction to these moral and intellectual forces that had been the lifeblood of the balance of power.

The Treaty of the Holy Alliance of September 26, 1815, obligated its signatories—all the sovereigns of Europe except three—to nothing more than to act in relation to each other and to their subjects in accordance with Christian principles. Yet the other treaties of the same year, which tried to reconstitute the European political system and which are popularly known by the name of the Holy Alliance, were directed against the recurrence of revolution anywhere, especially, of course, in France. Since the French Revolution had been the great dynamic force that destroyed the balance of power, it was believed that any revolution would carry with it a similar threat. Thus the principle of legitimacy and the inviolability of the frontiers of 1815 became the foundation stones upon which at least Austria, Prussia, and Russia tried to re-erect the political structure of Europe.

As late as 1860, when France obtained the cession of Savoy and Nice as compensation for the increase of territory obtained by Sardinia in Italy, England intervened by invoking one of the principles of 1815. "Her Majesty's Government," Earl Russell, the British foreign secretary, wrote to the British ambassador to France, "must be allowed to remark that a demand for cession of a neighbor's territory, made by a State so powerful as France, and whose former and not very remote policy of territorial aggrandizement brought countless calamities upon Europe, cannot well fail to give umbrage to every State interested in the Balance of Power and in the maintenance of the general peace."

The Concert of Europe—diplomacy by conferences among the great powers that would meet all threats to the political system by concerted action—became the instrument by which first the principles of the Holy Alliance and then, after the latter's disintegration culminating in the liberal revolutions of 1848, the common interests of Europe were to be realized. The Concert of Europe functioned on many occasions during the century from its inception in 1814 to the outbreak of the First World War in 1914. The conception underlying it—that is, the political unity of Europe or, in the words of the British statesman Castlereagh, "the general system of Europe"—was referred to in many official declarations. Thus the allied powers declared toward the end of 1813 that they "shall not lay down their arms . . . before the political status of Europe has been anew reaffirmed and before immutable principles have taken their rights over vain pretentions in order

---

[19]See Chapter 27.

to assure Europe a real peace." In the declaration of February 5, 1814, from which the Concert of Europe is generally dated, the representatives of Austria, Great Britain, Prussia, and Russia stated that they did not speak solely in the name of their respective countries "but in the name of Europe which forms but a single whole."

The same nations, joined by France, established in Protocol 19 of the 1831 Conference of London the independence of Belgium and, in the interest of the balance of power, put its neutrality under their joint guaranty. In justification, they declared: "Every nation has its laws, but Europe, too, has her law; the social order has given it to her." During the Franco-Prussian War of 1870, the French minister Thiers, searching in vain for aid from the other European nations in order to prevent the overthrow of the balance of power by Germany, complained that "Europe was not to be found." In that phrase he paid his respects to the same principle of European unity that since 1648 has been the lifeblood of the balance of power. It was to the same principle that British foreign secretary Sir Edward Grey appealed in vain when on the eve of the First World War he invited the nations of Europe to a conference in order to settle their differences. One might even say that British prime minister Neville Chamberlain, when in 1938 he forced Czechoslovakia to cede the Sudetenland to Nazi Germany, acted under the mistaken assumption that the moral, intellectual, and political unity of Europe still existed and that Nazi Germany formed an integral part of it.

Moral Consensus of the Modern State System

The confidence in the stability of the modern state system that emanates from all these declarations and actions derives, it will be noted, not from the balance of power but from a number of elements, intellectual and moral in nature, upon which both the balance of power and the stability of the modern state system repose. "In politics as in mechanics," as John Stuart Mill put it, "the power which is to keep the engine going must be sought for *outside* the machinery; and if it is not forthcoming, or is insufficient to surmount the obstacles which may reasonably be expected, the contrivance will fail."[20] What, for instance, Gibbon has

---

[20]*Considerations on Representative Government* (New York: Henry Holt, 1882), p. 21. Cf. also the penetrating remarks on pp. 235–236 on the importance of the moral factor for the maintenance of the balance of power in domestic politics: "When it is said that the question is only one of political morality, this does not extenuate its importance. Questions of constitutional morality are of no less practical moment than those relating to the constitution itself. The very existence of some governments, and all that renders others endurable, rests on the practical observance of doctrines of constitutional morality; traditional notions in the minds of the several constituted authorities, which modify the use that might otherwise be made of their powers. In unbalanced governments—pure monarchy, pure aristocracy, pure democracy—such maxims are the only barrier which restrains the government from the utmost excess in the direction of its characteristic tendency. In imperfectly balanced governments, where some attempt is made to set constitutional limits to the impulses of the strongest power, but where that power is strong enough to overstep them with at least temporary impunity, it is only by

pointed to with particular eloquence and insight as the fuel that keeps the motor of the balance of power moving is the intellectual and moral foundation of Western civilization, the intellectual and moral climate within which the protagonists of eighteenth-century society moved and that permeated all their thoughts and actions. These men knew Europe as "one great republic" with common standards of "politeness and cultivation" and a common "system of arts, and laws, and manners." The common awareness of these common standards restrained their ambitions "by the mutual influence of fear and shame," imposed "moderations" upon their actions, and instilled in all of them "some sense of honour and justice." In consequence, the struggle for power on the international scene was in the nature of "temperature and undecisive contests."

Of the temperateness and indecisiveness of the political contests, from 1648 to the Napoleonic Wars and then again from 1815 to 1914, the balance of power is not only the cause but also the metaphorical and symbolic expression as well as the technique of realization. Before the balance of power could impose its restraints upon the power aspirations of nations through the mechanical interplay of opposing forces, the competing nations had first to restrain themselves by accepting the system of the balance of power as the common framework of their

---

doctrines of constitutional morality, recognized and sustained by opinion, that any regard at all is preserved for the checks and limitations of the constitution. In well-balanced governments, in which the supreme power is divided, and each sharer is protected against the usurpations of the others in the only manner possible, namely, by being armed for defense with weapons as strong as the others can wield for attack, the government can only be carried on by forbearance on all sides to exercise those extreme powers, unless provoked by conduct equally extreme on the part of some other sharer of power; and in this case we may say that only by the regard paid to maxims of constitutional morality is the constitution kept in existence."

Cf. on this point also the analogy between industrial warfare and the international balance of power in R. H. Tawney, *The Acquisitive Society* (New York: Harcourt, Brace, 1920), pp. 40–41: "That motive produces industrial warfare, not as a regrettable incident, but as an inevitable result. It produces industrial war, because its teaching is that each individual or group has a right to what they can get, and denies that there is any principle, other than the mechanism of the market, which determines what they ought to get. For, since the income available for distribution is limited, and since, therefore, when certain limits have been passed, what one group gains another group must lose, it is evident that if the relative incomes of different groups are not to be determined by their functions, there is no method other than mutual self-assertion which is left to determine them. Self-interest, indeed, may cause them to refrain from using their full strength to enforce their claims, and, in so far as this happens, peace is secured in industry, as men have attempted to secure it in international affairs, by a balance of power. But the maintenance of such a peace is contingent upon the estimate of the parties to it that they have more to lose than to gain by an overt struggle, and is not the result of their acceptance of any standard of remuneration as an equitable settlement of their claims. Hence it is precarious, insincere and short. It is without finality, because there can be no finality in the mere addition of increments of income, any more than in the gratification of any other desire for material goods. When demands are conceded the old struggle recommences upon a new level, and will always recommence as long as men seek to end it merely by increasing remuneration, not by finding a principle upon which all remuneration, whether large or small, should be based."

See also p. 50: "But the balance, whether in international politics or in industry, is unstable, because it reposes not on the common recognition of a principle by which the claims of nations and individuals are limited, but on an attempt to find an equipoise which may avoid a conflict without adjuring the assertion of unlimited claims. No such equipoise can be found, because, in a world where the possibilities of increasing military or industrial power are illimitable, no such equipoise can exist." (Reprinted by permission of the publisher.)

endeavors. However much they desired to alter the distribution of the weights in the two scales, they had to agree in a silent compact, as it were, that, whatever the outcome of the contest, the two scales would still be there at the end of it. They had to agree that, however high one might have risen and however low the other might have sunk, the scales would still be joined together as a pair, hanging from the same beam and, hence, able to rise and fall again as the future distribution of weights would determine. Whatever changes nations might seek in the status quo, they all had at least to recognize as unchangeable one factor: the existence of a pair of scales, the "status quo" of the balance of power itself. And whenever a nation might tend to forget that indispensable precondition of independence and stability, as Austria did in 1756 with regard to Prussia, or France in 1919–23 with regard to Germany, the consensus of all the other nations would not allow it to forget for long.

This consensus grew in the intellectual and moral climate of the age and drew its strength from the actual power relations, which under normal conditions made an attempt at overthrowing the system of the balance of power itself a hopeless undertaking. This consensus, in turn, as an intellectual and moral force, reacted upon the intellectual and moral climate and upon the power relations, strengthening the tendencies toward moderation and equilibrium. As Quincy Wright put it:

> The States were so bounded and organized that aggression could not succeed unless it was so moderated and so directed that the prevailing opinion of the Powers approved it. Such approval was generally given to the Balkan revolts which gradually disintegrated the Ottoman Empire, to the Belgian revolt which separated that country from the Netherlands, to Prussian and Sardinian aggressions which united modern Germany and Italy, and to numerous aggressions in Africa, Asia, and the Pacific which increased European empires, and extended European civilization to these areas.[21]

It is this consensus—both child and father, as it were, of common moral standards and a common civilization, as well as of common interests—that kept in check the limitless desire for power, potentially inherent, as we know, in all imperialisms, and prevented it from becoming a political actuality. Where such a consensus no longer exists or has become weak and is no longer sure of itself, as in the period starting with the partitions of Poland and ending with the Napoleonic Wars, the balance of power is incapable of fulfilling its function for international stability and national independence.

Such a consensus prevailed from 1648 to 1772 and from 1815 to 1933. In the former period, the state system resembled nothing so much as a competitive society of princes, each of whom accepted the reason of state—that is, the rational pursuit, within certain moral limitations, of the power objectives of the individual

---

[21]"The Balance of Power," in *Compass of the World,* edited by Hans Weigert and Vilhjalmur Stefansson (New York: Macmillan, 1944), pp. 53–54.

state—as the ultimate standard of the behavior of states. Each expected, and was justified in expecting, everybody else to share this standard. The passions of the religious wars yielded to the rationalism and the skeptical moderation of the Enlightenment. In that tolerant atmosphere national hatreds and collective enmities, nourished by principles of any kind, could hardly flourish. Everybody took it for granted that the egotistical motives that animated his own actions drove all others to similar actions. It was then a matter of skill and luck as to who would come out on top. International politics became indeed an aristocratic pastime, a sport for princes, all recognizing the same rules of the game and playing for the same limited stakes.

After the interlude of the Napoleonic Wars, the dual fear of revolution and of a renewal of French imperialism called into being the morality of the Holy Alliance, with its blend of Christian, monarchical, and European principles. The Concert of Europe in the latter part of the nineteenth century, and the League of Nations after the First World War, added to this heritage the idea of the nation-state. This idea became, as a principle of national self-determination, one of the cornerstones upon which successive generations, from the liberal revolutions of 1848 to the outbreak of the Second World War, tried to erect a stable political structure. What the French foreign minister De la Valette wrote in 1866 to a French diplomatic representative became one of the basic convictions of this period of history—proclaimed again by Woodrow Wilson and made one of the standards of the Peace Treaties of 1919: "The emperor . . . sees a real equilibrium only in the satisfied wishes of the nations of Europe."[22]

What is left of this heritage today? What kind of consensus unites the nations of the world in the period following the Second World War? Upon the examination of the component elements of this consensus will depend the estimate of the role that the balance of power can be expected to play today for the freedom and stability of the community of nations.

---

[22]The importance of the moral factor for the preservation of the independence of small nations is well pointed out by Alfred Cobban, *National Self-Determination* (Chicago: University of Chicago Press, 1948), pp. 170–71: "But even the policies of great empires are influenced by the climate of opinion, and there has for long been a prejudice in favour of the rights of small independent states. With the sources of this prejudice we need not concern ourselves, but its existence is a fact which the student of international affairs cannot ignore. The various factors we have mentioned all undoubtedly have their importance, but in our opinion it was not the strength of national feeling in the smaller states, or even the effects of the balance of power, so much as the general recognition that the destruction of an independent sovereignty was an exceptional, and normally an unjustifiable, act which ultimately protected many of the small states of Europe, some no larger than a single city, from absorption by the greater powers. Even in the eighteenth century, when the power of the larger states was increasing rapidly, contemporary opinion, influenced by the classical city-state ideal, held up the smaller states for admiration and believed in their independence. During the nineteenth century the growth of the nationalist ideal did much to undermine this view, but in 1919, as we have seen, it still exercised considerable influence." (Reprinted by permission of the University of Chicago Press.)

LIMITATIONS OF NATIONAL POWER

International Morality and World Public Opinion

15 Morality, Mores, and Law as Restraints on Power

We have seen in the preceding chapter that power is a crude and unreliable method of limiting the aspirations for power on the international scene. If the motivations behind the struggle for power and the mechanisms through which it operates were all that needed to be known about international politics, the international scene would indeed resemble the state of nature described by Hobbes as a "war of every man against every man."[1] International politics would be governed exclusively by those considerations of political expediency of which Machiavelli has given the most acute and candid account. In such a world the weak would be at the mercy of the strong. Might would indeed make right.

Actually, however, the very threat of a world where power reigns not only supreme but without rival engenders that revolt against power that is as universal as the aspiration for power itself. To stave off this revolt, to pacify the resentment and opposition that arise when the drive for power is recognized for what it is, those who seek power employ, as we have seen, ideologies for the concealment of their aims. What is actually aspiration for power, then, appears to be something different, something that is in harmony with the demands of reason, morality, and justice. The substance, of which the ideologies of international politics are but the reflection, is to be found in the normative orders of morality, mores, and law.

From the Bible to the ethics and constitutional arrangements of modern democracy, the main function of these normative systems has been to keep aspirations for power within socially tolerable bounds. All ethics, mores, and legal systems dominant in Western civilization recognize the ubiquity of power drives and condemn them. Conversely, such political philosophies as Machiavelli's and Hobbes's, which regard the ubiquity of power drives as an ultimate fact of social life, to be accepted rather than condemned and restrained, have met with the disapproval of prevailing opinion. They have lacked the intellectual and practical

---

[1] *Leviathan*, Chapter XIII.

influence that has made such political philosophies as Saint Augustine's and Locke's potent forces in Western civilization.

On the other hand, that very tradition of Western civilization which attempts to restrain the power of the strong for the sake of the weak has been opposed as effeminate, sentimental, and decadent. The opponents have been those who, like Nietzsche, Mussolini, and Hitler, not only accept the will to power and the struggle for power as elemental social facts but glorify their unrestrained manifestations and postulate this absence of restraint as an ideal of society and a rule of conduct for the individual. But in the long run philosophies and political systems that have made the lust and the struggle for power their mainstays have proved impotent and self-destructive. Their weakness demonstrates the strength of the Western tradition that seeks, if not to eliminate, at least to regulate and restrain the power drives that otherwise would either tear society apart or deliver the life and happiness of the weak to the arbitrary will of the powerful.

It is at these two points that morality, mores, and law intervene in order to protect society against disruption and the individual against enslavement and extinction. When a society or certain of its members are unable to protect themselves with their own strength against the power drives of others—when, in other words, the mechanics of power politics are found wanting, as sooner or later they must be—these normative systems try to supplement power politics with their own rules of conduct. This is the message the normative systems give to strong and weak alike: superior power gives no right, either moral or legal, to do with that power all that it is physically capable of doing. Power is subject to limitations, in the interest of society as a whole and in the interest of its individual members, that are not the result of the mechanics of the struggle for power but are superimposed upon that struggle in the form of norms or rules of conduct by the will of the members of society themselves.

Three types of norms or rules of conduct operate in all higher societies: ethics, mores, and law. Their distinctive characteristics have been much debated in the literature of philosophy and jurisprudence. For the purpose of this study it is sufficient to point out that every rule of conduct has two elements: the command and the sanction. No particular command is peculiar to any particular type of norm—"thou shalt not kill" can be a command of ethics, mores, or law. It is the sanction that differentiates these three different types of rules of conduct.

"Thou shalt not kill" is a command of ethics, mores, or law according to whether, in case of its violation, a sanction peculiar to ethics or to mores or to law is applied to punish the violator and prevent further violations. If A kills B and afterward feels pangs of conscience or of remorse, we are in the presence of a sanction peculiar to ethics and, hence, of an ethical norm. If A kills B and unorganized society reacts with spontaneous demonstrations of disapproval, such as business boycott, social ostracism, and the like, we have to do with a sanction peculiar to the mores, and, hence, to a norm of the mores. If, finally, A kills B and organized society reacts in the form of a rational procedure with predetermined police action, indictment, trial, verdict, and punishment, the sanction is of a legal nature, and the norm, therefore, belongs in the category of law.

All domestic societies are regulated by an intricate maze of rules of conduct of this kind, supporting or contradicting one another or operating independently. The more important a society considers those interests and values that it tries to safeguard by rules of conduct, the stronger are the sanctions with which it threatens an infraction of its rules. Society exerts its greatest pressure, and therefore has the best chance of enforcing its rules of conduct against its recalcitrant members, when it brings all the different kinds of sanctions at its disposal simultaneously to bear upon the infractor of its rules. It is weakest, and therefore its sanctions are most likely to be ineffective, when only one type of sanction supports its interests and values. When one rule of conduct requires an action that another rule of conduct condemns, the fate of the interest or value concerned depends upon the relative strength of the sanctions supporting the contradictory commands.

Against a threat to its own existence by treason or by revolution, or a threat to the existence of its individual members by murder, society marshals all three types of sanction. Thus morality, mores, and law, reinforcing one another, give threefold protection to the life of society and to the lives of the individuals who compose it. The would-be traitor or killer faces the pangs of his conscience, the spontaneous reactions of society in the form, for instance, of ostracism, and the punishment of the law. The same situation prevails where not the existence of society or of its individual members but their property is at stake. Property, too, is surrounded by the triple wall of morality, mores, and law. Between the would-be thief and cheat and the property he covets, society interposes all the sanctions it is able to employ.

Where less highly priced interests and values are at stake, society may call upon only one type of sanction. Thus certain kinds of competitive practices in business and politics, such as lying, are opposed only by morality. The mores will come into play only under extreme conditions—if, for instance, the amount and degree of lying exceed the measure society regards as tolerable. The law will remain silent in the case of ordinary lying, if for no other reason than that no law prohibiting it can be enforced. It will speak only in case of qualified lying, such as perjury and cheating, where the lie threatens interests and values beyond mere truth. The rules of fashion, on the other hand, are enforced exclusively by the mores, for the issues involved are not important enough for morality and law to be concerned about them. It is, finally, the law alone that takes cognizance of violations of traffic regulations. Morality and mores do not participate in their enforcement, for the sanctions of the law are generally sufficient to establish some kind of mechanical order in the realm of traffic.

The problem of the relative strength of different injunctions becomes acute when there is conflict between different rules of conduct. The classic example, much discussed in the literature of jurisprudence, of a conflict between two rules of the same legal system is the prohibition of dueling in the criminal codes of certain European countries, while the military codes of the same countries require officers to settle certain disputes by way of duels. A system of ethics that commands us to obey God rather than man and at the same time to give unto Caesar what is Caesar's presents a similar conflict when a law of the state contradicts one of God's commandments. Conflicts of this kind are particularly frequent in the political sphere. Rival governments—a revolutionary government and a legitimate government, a government in exile and a quisling government—demand obedience from the same group of people. The rules of conduct with which a politician is expected to comply are often at odds with the norms that address all members of society. The ethics and mores of politics are generally considered to permit greater leeway than do the general ethics and mores of society in certain actions, such as "campaign oratory" and promises in general.

Conflicts between different rules of conduct are decided by the relative pressure the sanctions of the conflicting rules are able to exert upon the will of the individual. Unable to comply with all the norms addressed to him at the same time, he must choose the one to obey and violate the others. The relative strength of these pressures is, in turn, the expression of the relative strength of the social forces that support one set of values and interests against another. The normative order of society whose purpose is to keep the power aspirations of its individual members within socially tolerable bounds is itself in a certain measure the result of social forces contending with one another for the domination of society through their influence, say, on legislation or court decisions.

Social life consists overwhelmingly of continuous reactions, which have become largely automatic, to the pressures society exerts upon its members through its rules of conduct. These rules of conduct watch over the individual from morning till night, molding his actions into conformity with the standards of society. One might even say that society as a dynamic force is nothing but the sum total of its rules of conduct imposing patterns of action upon its members. What we call civilization is in a sense nothing but the automatic reactions of the members of a society to the rules of conduct by which that society endeavors to make its members conform to certain objective standards, to restrain their aspirations for power, and to domesticate and pacify them in all socially important respects. The civilization with which we are here of course mainly concerned—Western civilization—has been to a large extent successful in this endeavor. Western civilization has not, however, as many nineteenth- and twentieth-century writers believed, altogether banished the struggle for power from the domestic scene and replaced it with something different and better, such as cooperation, harmony, and permanent peace, nor is it on its way to doing so. This misconception of the role that the aspirations and the struggle for power play in politics has been treated in the third chapter of this book.

The best that Western civilization has been able to achieve—which is, as far as we can see, the best that any civilization can achieve—has been to mitigate the struggle for power on the domestic scene, to civilize its means, and to direct it toward objectives that, if attained, minimize the extent to which life, liberty, and the pursuit of happiness of the individual members of society are involved in the struggle for power. More particularly, the crude methods of personal combat have been replaced by the refined instruments of social, commercial, and professional competition. The struggle for power is being fought not with deadly weapons but with competitive examinations, with competition for social distinctions, with periodical elections for public and private offices, and, above all, with competition for the possession of money and of things measurable in money.

In the domestic societies of Western civilization, the possession of money has become the outstanding symbol of the possession of power. Through the competition for the acquisition of money, the power aspirations of the individual find a civilized outlet in harmony with the rules of conduct laid down by society. The different normative injunctions against homicide and against individual and collective violence of any kind seek to create the normative preconditions for such a civilized redirection of the struggle for power. All the social instrumentalities and institutions relevant to the different competitive devices of society serve the purpose, not of eliminating the struggle for power, but of creating civilized substitutes for the brutality and crudeness of an unlimited and unregulated struggle for power.

Such is, in brief and sketchy outline, the way ethics, mores, and law limit the struggle for power in the domestic societies of Western civilization. And what of international society? What rules of morality, mores, and law are effective on the international scene? What functions do they fulfill for international society? What kind of international ethics, international mores in the form of world public opinion, and international law is there to delimit, regulate, and civilize the struggle for power among nations in the same way the domestic normative systems affect the struggle for power among the members of a domestic society?

16 International Morality

A discussion of international morality must guard against the two extremes of either overrating the influence of ethics upon international politics or underestimating it by denying that statesmen and diplomats are moved by anything but considerations of material power.

On the one hand, there is the dual error of confounding the moral rules people actually observe with those they pretend to observe, as well as with those that writers declare they ought to observe. "On no subject of human interest, except theology," said Professor John Chipman Gray, "has there been so much loose writing and nebulous speculation as on international law."[1] The same must be said of international morality. Writers have put forward moral precepts that statesmen and diplomats ought to take to heart in order to make relations between nations more peaceful and less anarchic, such as the keeping of promises, trust in the other's word, fair dealing, respect for international law, protection of minorities, and repudiation of war as an instrument of national policy. But they have rarely asked themselves whether and to what extent such precepts, however desirable in themselves, actually determine the actions of men. Furthermore, since statesmen and diplomats are wont to justify their actions and objectives in moral terms, regardless of their actual motives, it would be equally erroneous to take those protestations of selfless and peaceful intentions, of humanitarian purposes, and international ideals at their face value. It is pertinent to ask whether they are mere ideologies concealing the true motives of action or whether they express a genuine concern for the compliance of international policies with ethical standards.

On the other hand, there is the misconception, usually associated with the general depreciation and moral condemnation of power politics, discussed earlier,[2] that international politics is so thoroughly evil that it is no use looking for moral

---

[1]*Nature and Sources of the Law* (New York: Macmillan, 1927), p. 127.
[2]See pages 35 ff.

limitations of the aspirations for power on the international scene. Yet, if we ask ourselves what statesmen and diplomats are capable of doing to further the power objectives of their respective nations and what they actually do, we realize that they do less than they probably could and less than they actually did in other periods of history. They refuse to consider certain ends and to use certain means, either altogether or under certain conditions, not because in the light of expediency they appear impractical or unwise but because certain moral rules interpose an absolute barrier. Moral rules do not permit certain policies to be considered at all from the point of view of expediency. Certain things are not being done on moral grounds, even though it would be expedient to do them. Such ethical inhibitions operate in our time on different levels with different effectiveness. Their restraining function is most obvious and most effective in affirming the sacredness of human life in times of peace.

THE PROTECTION OF HUMAN LIFE

Protection of Human Life in Peace

International politics can be defined, as we have seen, as a continuing effort to maintain and to increase the power of one's own nation and to keep in check or reduce the power of other nations. The relative power of nations depends, however, as we have also pointed out,[3] upon the quantity and quality of human beings in terms of size and quality of population, size and quality of military establishment, quality of government, and, more particularly, of diplomacy. Viewed as a series of technical tasks into which moral considerations do not enter, international politics would have to consider as one of its legitimate purposes the drastic reduction or even the elimination of the population of a rival nation, of its most prominent military and political leaders, and of its ablest diplomats. And when international politics was considered exclusively as a technique, without moral significance, for the purpose of maintaining and gaining power, such methods were used without moral scruples and as a matter of course.

According to its official records, the Republic of Venice, from 1415 to 1525, planned or attempted about two hundred assassinations for purposes of its foreign policy. Among the prospective victims were two emperors, two kings of France, and three sultans. The documents record virtually no offer of assassination to have been rejected by the Venetian government. From 1456 to 1472, it accepted twenty offers to kill Sultan Mahomet II, the main antagonist of Venice during that period. In 1514, John of Ragusa offered to poison anybody selected by the government of Venice for an annual salary of fifteen hundred ducats. The Venetian government hired the man "on trial," as we would say today, and asked him to show what he could do with Emperor Maximilian. In the same period the cardinals brought their own butlers and wine to a papal coronation dinner for fear they might

---

[3]See pages 131 ff.

otherwise be poisoned; this custom is reported to have been general in Rome, without the host's taking offense.

Such methods to attain political ends are no longer widely practiced today. Yet the political motives for employing them exist today as they did when practices of this kind actually prevailed. It is not a matter of indifference for the nations engaged in the competition for power whether or not their competitor can avail itself of the services of outstanding military and political leaders. Thus they may hope that an outstanding leader or governing group will be compelled to give up the reins of power, either through a political upheaval or through infirmity and death. We know now that during the Second World War speculations as to how long Hitler and Mussolini would stay alive, or at least in power, formed an important part of the power calculations of the antifascist alliance and that the news of President Roosevelt's death revived Hitler's hopes of victory. During the Cold War one factor in American policy toward the Soviet Union had been the expectation that the Soviet regime might disintegrate from within because of the inability of its rulers to keep themselves in power. The technical difficulties of engineering such removals from power by violent means are not greater today than they were in previous periods of history. Such removals are still as desirable and feasible as they always were. What has changed is the influence of civilization, which makes some desirable and feasible policies morally reprehensible and, hence, normally impossible of execution.

The existence and effectiveness of moral restraints became manifest in the reactions to the assassination plots engendered by the Central Intelligence Agency (CIA) of the United States. What the predominant segment of American public opinion objected to was not the lack of success of those attempts but their violation of moral restraints. That such attempts were made at all points to a weakening of moral restraint in a small number of public officials operating in secret. That such moral transgressions met with overwhelming disapproval on moral grounds testifies to the continued validity of such moral norms.

Moral limitations of the same kind protect in times of peace the lives not only of outstanding individuals but also of large groups, even of whole nations whose destruction would be both politically desirable and feasible. In the problem of Germany, as seen both by the Germans and by the rest of the world, modern history provides a striking illustration of the influence of ethics upon international politics. The fundamental fact of international politics from the German point of view has been from Bismarck to Hitler the "encirclement" of Germany by powerful nations to the east and the west. Bismarck, however ruthless and immoral his particular moves on the chessboard of international politics may have been, rarely deviated from the basic rules of the game that had prevailed in the society of Christian princes of the eighteenth century. It was a fraudulent and treacherous game, but there were a few things no member of that aristocratic society would stoop to do. Thus, confronted with the proximity of Russia and France as a condition of Germany's political existence, Bismarck accepted the inevitability of that fact and tried to turn it to Germany's advantage by maintaining close relations with Russia and by isolating France.

Hitler, on the other hand, did not recognize the social framework within whose limitations international politics had operated from the end of the Thirty Years' War virtually to his own ascent to power. He was free of the moral scruples that had compelled Bismarck to accept the existence of France and Russia as the inescapable fact upon which to build a German foreign policy. Hitler undertook to change that fact by physically destroying Germany's eastern and western neighbors. Considered as a mere problem of political technique devoid of ethical significance, Hitler's solution was much more thorough and politically expedient than Bismarck's, for it promised to solve the problem of Germany's international position once and for all as far as the eastern and western neighbors of Germany were concerned. Furthermore, in itself Hitler's solution proved to be as feasible as it would have been in Bismarck's time. It might have succeeded had it not been for certain political and military errors that carried Hitler and his policies to destruction and that the political genius of Bismarck might well have avoided.

The German problem, as it presents itself to the non-German world, and especially to the nations threatened with German hegemony, was formulated with brutal frankness by the French statesman Clemenceau when he declared on the occasion of the First World War that there were 20 million Germans too many. This statement points to the inescapable fact, which has confronted Europe and the world since the Franco-German War of 1870, that Germany is by virtue of size and quality of population the most powerful nation of Europe. To reconcile this fact with the security of the other European nations and of the rest of the world was the task of political reconstruction that faced the world after the First World War and that confronted it again after the Second. That, since Clemenceau, the German problem has always been posed in terms that take the existence of "20 million Germans too many" for granted reveals the same moral limitations on the pursuit of power that we found in Bismarck's foreign policy and that we did not find in Hitler's. For there are two ways of dealing with a problem of international politics such as the German.

One is the method by which the Romans irrevocably solved the Carthaginian problem. It is the method of solving a technical political problem by the appropriate means without regard for any transcendent moral considerations. Since, from the point of view of the power aspirations of Rome, there were too many Carthaginians, Cato would end his every speech by proclaiming: *"Ceterum censeo Carthaginem esse delendam"* ("As for the rest, I am of the opinion that Carthage must be destroyed"). With its destruction the Carthaginian problem, as seen by Rome, was solved forever. No threat to Rome's security and ambition was ever again to rise from the desolate place that once was Carthage. Similarly, if the Germans had been successful in their overall plans and if their firing squads and extermination camps could have finished their tasks, the "nightmare of coalitions" would have been forever banished from the minds of German statesmen.

A foreign policy that does not permit mass extermination as a means to its end does not impose this limitation upon itself because of considerations of political expediency. On the contrary, expediency would counsel such a thorough and effective operation. The limitation derives from an absolute moral principle, which must be obeyed regardless of considerations of national advantage. A foreign policy of this kind, therefore, actually sacrifices the national interest where its consistent pursuit would necessitate the violation of a moral principle, such as the prohibition of mass killings in times of peace. This point cannot be too strongly made; for frequently the opinion is advanced that this respect for human life is the outgrowth of "the obligation not to inflict *unnecessary* death or suffering on other human beings, i.e., death or suffering not necessary for the attainment of some higher purpose which is held, rightly or wrongly, to justify a derogation from the general obligation."[4] On the contrary, the fact of the matter is that nations recognize a moral obligation to refrain from the infliction of death and suffering under certain conditions despite the possibility of justifying such conduct in the light of a "higher purpose," such as the national interest.

The fundamental conflict between these two conceptions of international politics, one operating within a framework of morality, the other outside it, is graphically illustrated by an episode Sir Winston Churchill reports in his memoirs. At the Teheran Conference, Stalin raised the issue of the punishment to be inflicted upon the Germans after the war:

> The German General Staff, he said, must be liquidated. The whole force of Hitler's mighty armies depended upon about fifty thousand officers and technicians. If these were rounded up and shot at the end of the war, German military strength would be extirpated. On this I thought it right to say: "The British Parliament and public will never tolerate mass executions. Even if in war passion they allowed them to begin, they would turn violently against those responsible after the first butchery had taken place. The Soviets must be under no delusion on this point."
>
> Stalin however, perhaps only in mischief, pursued the subject. "Fifty thousand," he said, "must be shot." I was deeply angered. "I would rather," I said, "be taken out into the garden here and now and be shot myself than sully my own and my country's honour by such infamy."[5]

Protection of Human Life in War

Similar moral limitations are placed upon international policies in times of war. They concern civilians and combatants unable or unwilling to fight. From the beginning of history through the better part of the Middle Ages, belligerents were held to be free, according to ethics as well as law, to kill all enemies whether or not they were members of the armed forces, or else to treat them in any way they saw fit. Men, women, and children were often put to the sword or sold into slavery by the victor without any adverse moral reactions taking place. In Chapter IV

---

[4]E. H. Carr, *The Twenty Years' Crisis, 1919–1939* (London: Macmillan, 1939), p. 196.
[5]Winston S. Churchill, *The Second World War,* Vol. V, *Closing the Ring* (Boston: Houghton Mifflin, 1951), pp. 373–74. (Reprinted by permission of the publisher.)

of Book III of *On the Law of War and Peace,* under the heading "On the Right of Killing Enemies in a Public War and on Other Violence Against the Person," Hugo Grotius presents an impressive catalogue of acts of violence committed in ancient history against enemy persons without discrimination. Grotius himself, writing in the third decade of the seventeenth century, still regarded most of them as justified in law and ethics, provided the war was waged for a just cause.[6]

This absence of moral restraints upon killing in war resulted from the nature of war itself. In those times war was considered a contest between all the inhabitants of the territories of the belligerent states. The enemy to be fought was the total number of individuals owing allegiance to a certain lord or living within a certain territory rather than the armed forces of the legal abstraction called a *state* in the modern sense. Thus every individual citizen of the enemy state became an enemy of every individual citizen of the other side.

Since the end of the Thirty Years' War, the conception has become prevalent that war is not a contest between whole populations but only between the armies of the belligerent states. In consequence, the distinction between combatants and noncombatants has become one of the fundamental legal and moral principles governing the actions of belligerents. War is considered to be a contest between the armed forces of the belligerent states, and, since the civilian populations do not participate actively in the armed contest, they are not to be made its object. Consequently, it is considered to be a moral and legal duty not to attack, wound, or kill noncombatant civilians purposely. Injuries and death suffered by them as incidents of military operations, such as the bombardment of a town or a battle taking place in an inhabited area, are regretted as sometimes unavoidable concomitants of war. However, to avoid them to the utmost is again considered a moral and legal duty. The Hague Conventions with respect to the Laws and Customs of War on Land of 1899 and 1907, and the Geneva Convention of 1949, gave express and virtually universal legal sanction to that principle.

A corresponding development has taken place with regard to members of the armed forces unwilling or unable to fight. It follows from the conception of war prevailing in antiquity and in the better part of the Middle Ages that no exception to the moral and legal right to kill all enemies could be made for certain categories of disabled combatants. Thus Grotius could still state as the prevailing moral and legal conviction of his time: "The right to inflict injury extends even over captives, and without limitation of time. . . . The right to inflict injury extends even over those who wish to surrender, but whose surrender is not accepted."[7]

Yet, as the logical outgrowth of the conception of war as a contest between armed forces, the idea developed that only those who are actually able and willing to participate actively in warfare ought to be the object of deliberate armed action. Those who were no longer engaged in actual warfare because of sickness, wounds, or because they had been made prisoners or were willing to be made prisoners ought not to be harmed. This tendency toward the humanization of warfare

---

[6]See especially § III.
[7]Ibid., § X, XI.

started in the sixteenth century and culminated in the great multilateral treaties of the nineteenth and early twentieth centuries. Practically all civilized nations have adhered to these treaties. Between 1581 and 1864, 291 international agreements were concluded for the purpose of protecting the lives of the wounded and sick. The Geneva Convention of 1864, superseded by those of 1906, 1929, and 1949, translated into concrete and detailed legal obligations the moral convictions of the age as to the treatment to be accorded to the wounded, the sick, and the medical persons in charge of them. The International Red Cross is both the symbol and the outstanding institutional realization of those moral convictions.

As concerns prisoners of war, their lot was still miserable even in the eighteenth century, although they were as a rule no longer killed but were treated as criminals and used as objects of exploitation by being released only for ransom. Article 24 of the Treaty of Friendship, concluded in 1785 between the United States and Prussia, for the first time clearly indicated a change in the moral convictions on that matter. It prohibited the confinement of prisoners of war in convict prisons, as well as the use of irons, and stipulated their treatment as military personnel. The Hague Conventions of 1899 and 1907, as well as the Geneva Conventions of 1929 and 1949, laid down a detailed system of legal rules intended to assure humane treatment of prisoners of war.

From the same humanitarian concern for the life and sufferings of human beings exposed to the destructiveness of war emanate all the international treaties concluded since the mid-nineteenth century for the purpose of humanizing warfare. They prohibit the use of certain weapons, limit the use of others, define the rights and duties of neutrals—in short, they try to infuse into warfare a spirit of decency and of respect for the common humanity of all its prospective victims and to restrict violence to the minimum compatible with the goal of war—that is, breaking the enemy's will to resist. The Declaration of Paris of 1856 limited maritime warfare. The Declaration of St. Petersburg of 1868 prohibited the use of lightweight projectiles charged with explosives or inflammable substances. The Hague Declaration of 1899 prohibited the use of expanding (dum-dum) bullets. A number of international conventions prohibited gas, chemical, and bacteriological warfare. The Hague Conventions of 1899 and 1907 codified the laws of war on land and sea and the rights and duties of neutrals. The London Protocol of 1936 limited the use of submarines against merchant vessels. And, in our times, attempts are being made to limit nuclear warfare. All these efforts bear witness to the virtually universal growth of a moral reluctance to use unlimited violence as an instrument of foreign policy.

There may be legal arguments against the validity or effectiveness of these international treaties, derived from the wholesale disregard or violations of their prohibitions. Yet this is no argument against the existence of a moral conscience that feels ill at ease in the presence of violence, or at least certain kinds of violence, on the international scene. The existence of such a conscience is attested to by the attempts to bring the practice of states into harmony with moral principles through international agreements. It reveals itself also in the general justifications and excuses defending alleged violations of these agreements in moral terms. Most nations suscribe to legal agreements of this kind and try to live up to them, at least in a certain measure. Therefore, the protestations of innocence or of moral justification with which accusations in such matters are uniformly met are more than mere ideologies. They are the indirect recognition of certain moral limitations, which nations at times completely disregard and frequently violate. Finally, the moral conscience of large groups within a warring nation may revolt against undeniable and flagrant violations of moral and legal limitations upon the conduct of war. Such groups may demonstrate against the war and refuse to support it, thereby testifying to the existence of a moral conscience aware of moral limitations.

Moral Condemnation of War

Finally, since the turn of the century, the attitude toward war itself has reflected an ever-increasing awareness on the part of most statesmen that certain moral limitations restrict the use of war as an instrument of foreign policy. Statesmen have decried the ravages of war and have since the beginning of history justified their own participation in them in terms of self-defense or religious duty. The avoidance of war itself—that is, of any war—has become an aim of statecraft only since the turn of the century. The two Hague Peace Conferences of 1899 and 1907, the League of Nations of 1919, the Briand-Kellogg Pact of 1928 outlawing aggressive war, and the United Nations in our day all have the avoidance of war itself as their ultimate objective.

At the foundation of these and other legal instruments and organizations, of which Part Eight of this book will treat in detail, there is the conviction that war, and especially modern war, is not only a terrible thing to be avoided for reasons of expediency but also an evil thing to be shunned on moral grounds. The student of the different collections of diplomatic documents concerning the origins of the First World War is struck by the hesitancy on the part of almost all responsible statesmen, with the exception perhaps of those of Vienna and St. Petersburg, to take steps that might irrevocably lead to war. This hesitancy and the almost general dismay among the statesmen when war finally proved to be inevitable contrasts sharply with the deliberate care with which, as late as the nineteenth century, wars were planned and incidents fabricated for the purpose of making war inevitable and placing the blame for starting it on the other side.

In the years preceding the Second World War, the policies of the Western powers were animated, to their great political and military disadvantage, by the desire to avoid war at any price. This desire overrode all other considerations of national policy. Similarly, the anxiety of all the great powers without exception to limit the Korean War to the Korean peninsula and thus prevent it from developing into a third world war, and the self-restraint practiced by all of them during the many international crises that have arisen since the end of the Second World War, are striking illustrations of a fundamental change in the attitude toward war. It is especially in the refusal to consider seriously the possibility of preventive war, regardless of its expediency in view of the national interest, that the moral condemnation of war as such has manifested itself in recent times in the Western world. When war comes, it must come as a natural catastrophe or as the evil deed of another nation, not as a foreseen and planned culmination of one's own foreign policy. Only thus might the moral scruples, rising from the violated moral norm that there ought to be no war at all, be stilled, if they can be stilled at all.

International Morality and Total War

Thus, in contrast to antiquity and the better part of the Middle Ages, the modern age places moral limitations upon the conduct of foreign affairs insofar as they might affect the lives of individuals or groups of individuals. However, certain important factors in the present condition of mankind point toward a definite weakening of those moral limitations. Let us remember that the absence of moral limitations with regard to the destruction of life was concomitant with the total character of warfare in which whole populations faced each other as personal enemies. Let us remember, too, that the gradual limitation of killing in war, and its subjection to certain conditions, coincided with the gradual development of limited war in which only armies faced each other as active opponents. With war taking on in recent times, to an ever greater degree and in different respects, a total character, the moral limitations upon killing are observed to an ever-lessening degree. Indeed, their very existence in the consciences of political and military leaders, as well as of the common people, becomes ever more precarious and is threatened with extinction.

War in our time has become total in four different respects: (1) with regard to the fraction of the population engaged in activities essential for the conduct of the war, (2) with regard to the fraction of the population affected by the conduct of the war, (3) with respect to the fraction of the population completely identified in its convictions and emotions with the conduct of the war, and (4) with respect to the objective of the war.

Mass armies supported by the productive effort of the majority of the civilian population have replaced the relatively small armies of previous centuries, which consumed only a small portion of the national product. The success of the civilian population in keeping the armed forces supplied may be as important for the outcome of the war as the military effort itself. Therefore, the defeat of the civilian population (the breaking of its ability and will to produce) may be as important as the defeat of the armed forces (the breaking of their ability and will to resist). Thus the character of modern war, drawing its weapons from a vast industrial machine, blurs the distinction between soldier and civilian. The worker, the engineer, and the scientist are not innocent bystanders cheering on the armed forces from the sidelines. They are as intrinsic and indispensable a part of the military organization as are the soldiers, sailors, and airmen. Thus a modern nation at war must seek to disrupt and destroy the productive processes of its enemy, and the modern technology of war provides the means for the realization of that aim. The importance of civilian production for modern war and the interest in injuring enemy production were already generally recognized in the First World War.

Then, however, the technological means of affecting the civilian productive processes directly were but in their infancy. The belligerents had to resort to indirect means, such as blockades and submarine warfare. They attempted to interfere directly with civilian life through air attacks and long-range bombardment only sporadically and with indifferent results.

The Second World War has made the latter methods of direct interference the most effective instrument for the destruction of a nation's productive capacity and ability to resist. The interest in the mass destruction of civilian life and property coincided with the ability to carry such mass destruction through, and this combination has been too strong for the moral convictions of the modern world to resist. Voicing the moral convictions of the first decades of the century, Secretary of State Cordell Hull declared on June 11, 1938, with reference to the bombardment of Canton by Japan, that the administration disapproved of the sale of aircraft and aircraft armaments to countries that had engaged in the bombing of civilian populations. In his speech of December 2, 1939, President Roosevelt declared a similar moral embargo against the Soviet Union in view of its military operations against Finnish civilians. Only a few years later all belligerents engaged in practices of this kind on a scale dwarfing those that American statesmen had condemned on moral grounds. Warsaw and Rotterdam, London and Coventry, Cologne and Nuremberg, and Hiroshima and Nagasaki are stepping-stones, not only in the development of the modern technology of war but also in the development of the modern morality of warfare. The Indochina War for all practical purposes obliterated the distinction between combatants and the civilian population.

The national interest in the destruction of enemy productivity and his will to resist, as created by the character of modern war, and the opportunity the modern technology of warfare presents of satisfying that interest, have had a deteriorating effect upon international morality. This deterioration is further accentuated by the emotional involvement of the great masses of the warring populations in modern war. As the religious wars of the sixteenth and seventeenth centuries were followed by the dynastic wars of the later seventeenth and eighteenth centuries, and as the latter yielded to the national wars of the nineteenth and the early twentieth centuries, so war in our time tends to revert to the religious type by becoming ideological in character. The citizen of a modern warring nation, in contrast to his ancestors of the eighteenth and nineteenth centuries, does not fight for the glory of his prince or the unity and greatness of his nation, but he "crusades" for an "ideal," a set of "principles," a "way of life," for which he claims a monopoly of truth and virtue. In consequence, he fights to the death or to "unconditional surrender" all those who adhere to another, a false and evil, "ideal" and "way of life." Since it is this "ideal" and "way of life" that he fights in whatever persons they manifest themselves, the distinctions between fighting and disabled soldiers, combatants and civilians—if they are not eliminated altogether—are subordinated to the one distinction that really matters: the distinction between the representatives of the right and the wrong philosophy and way of life. The moral duty to spare the wounded, the sick, and the surrendering and unarmed enemy, and to respect him as a human being who was an enemy only by virtue of being found on the other side of the fence, is superseded by the moral duty to punish and to wipe off the face of the earth the professors and practitioners of evil.

These tendencies destructive of moral limitations have been powerfully strengthened by the impersonal nature of modern war. Throughout history until the First World War, soldiers met face to face in combat. These deadly encounters were not devoid of a human element: men looked each other in the eye, trying to kill and avoid being killed. These encounters had room for human emotions, virtues, and vices, demonstrated and perceived by men. After Achilles has fatally wounded Lykaos, Homer has him bend over the doomed adversary and say, "Die, friend."

Modern war is in large measure push-button war, anonymously fought by people who have never seen their enemy alive or dead and who will never know whom they have killed. Nor will the victims ever see the face of the enemy. The only connection between the enemies is the machinery with which they try to kill each other. Such a technologically dehumanized war is bound to be morally dehumanized as well. For the operator of the machinery, the experience of target practice is hardly different from that of a real attack, and an attack upon a military installation is for him indistinguishable from that upon a civilian target. As a pilot who flew bombing missions in Vietnam put it: "It's like being trained to fix TVs, like being a technician." Thus the technology of modern war drastically weakens, if it does not destroy altogether, the ability to make those factual distinctions without which it is impossible to discriminate between moral and immoral acts of war.

Under the impact of this fundamental change in the conception of warfare, not only were the moral limitations upon killing in war, to which we have referred above, extensively violated during the Second World War, but belligerents have tended to justify on moral grounds the refusal to take prisoners, the killing of prisoners, and the indiscriminate killing of members of the armed forces and of civilians, and thus to assuage their moral scruples, if not to shake them off altogether. Thus, while the moral limitations upon killing in times of peace remain intact, the moral limitations upon killing in war have proved to be largely ineffective. What is by and large more important for the purposes of this discussion, they have shown a tendency under the impact of a fundamentally altered conception of war to weaken and disappear altogether as rules of conduct.

More than a half-century ago, in an era of general optimism, a great scholar clearly foresaw the possibility of this development and analyzed its elements. John Westlake, Whewell Professor of International Law at the University of Cambridge, wrote in 1894:

> It is almost a truism to say that the mitigation of war must depend on the parties to it feeling that they belong to a larger whole than their respective tribes or states, a whole in which the enemy too is comprised, so that duties arising out of that larger citizenship are owed even to him. This sentiment has never been wholly wanting in Europe since the commencement of historical times, but there have been great variations in the nature and extent of the

whole to which the wider attachment was felt. . . . In our own time there is a cosmopolitan sentiment, a belief in a commonwealth of mankind similar to that of the Stoics, but stronger because the soil has been prepared by Christianity, and by the mutual respect which great states tolerably equal in power and similar in civilization cannot help feeling for one another. . . . There have been periods during which the level has fallen, and one such period it belongs to our subject to notice. The wars of religion which followed the Reformation were among the most terrible in which the beast in man ever broke loose, and yet they occurred in an age of comparative enlightenment. Zeal for a cause, however worthy the cause may be, is one of the strongest and most dangerous irritants to which human passion is subject; and the tie of Protestant to Protestant and of Catholic to Catholic, cutting across the state tie instead of embracing it unweakened in a more comprehensive one, enfeebled the ordinary checks to passion when they were most wanted. Such a degradation of war would tend to recur if socialism attained to the consistency and power of a militant creed, and met the present idea of the state on the field of battle. It is possible that we might then see in war a license equal to that which anarchism shows us in peace![8]

UNIVERSAL MORALITY VS. NATIONALISTIC UNIVERSALISM

The deterioration of international morality that has occurred in recent years with regard to the protection of life is only a special instance of a general and, for the purposes of this discussion, much more far-reaching dissolution of an ethical system that in the past imposed its restraints upon the day-by-day operations of foreign policy but does so no longer. Two factors have brought about this dissolution: the substitution of democratic for aristocratic responsibility in foreign affairs and the substitution of nationalistic standards of action for universal ones.

Personal Ethics of the Aristocratic International

In the seventeenth and eighteenth centuries, and to a lessening degree up to the First World War, international morality was the concern of a personal sovereign–that is, a certain individual prince and his successors–and of a relatively small, cohesive, and homogeneous group of aristocratic rulers. The prince and the aristocratic rulers of a particular nation were in constant, intimate contact with the princes and aristocratic rulers of other nations. They were joined together by family ties, a common language (French), common cultural values, a common style of life, and common moral convictions about what a gentleman was and was not allowed to do in his relations with another gentleman, whether of his own or of a foreign nation. The princes competing for power considered themselves to be competitors in a game

---

[8]*Chapters on the Principles of International Law* (Cambridge: Cambridge University Press, 1894), pp. 267 ff.

whose rules were accepted by all the other competitors. The members of their diplomatic and military services looked upon themselves as employees who served their employer either by virtue of the accident of birth (reinforced often, but by no means always, by a sense of personal loyalty to the monarch) or because of the promise of pay, influence, and glory he held out to them.

The desire for material gain especially provided for this aristocratic society a common bond that was stronger than the ties of dynastic or national loyalty. Thus it was proper and common for a government to pay the foreign minister or diplomat of another country a pension, that is, a bribe. Lord Robert Cecil, the minister of Elizabeth, received one from Spain. Sir Henry Wotton, British ambassador to Venice in the seventeenth century, accepted one from Savoy while applying for one from Spain. The documents that the French revolutionary government published in 1793 show that France subsidized Austrian statesmen between 1757 and 1769 to the tune of 82,652,479 livres, with the Austrian chancellor Kaunitz receiving 100,000. Nor was it regarded any less proper or less usual for a government to compensate foreign statesmen for their cooperation in the conclusion of treaties. In 1716, French cardinal Dubois offered British minister Stanhope 600,000 livres for an alliance with France. He reported that, while not accepting the proposition at that time, Stanhope "listened graciously without being displeased." After the conclusion of the Treaty of Basel of 1795, by which Prussia withdrew from the war against France, Prussian minister Hardenberg received from the French government valuables worth 30,000 francs and complained of the insignificance of the gift. In 1801 the Margrave of Baden spent 500,000 francs in the form of "diplomatic presents," of which French foreign minister Talleyrand received 150,000. It was generally intended to give him only 100,000, but the amount was increased after it had become known that he had received from Prussia a snuffbox worth 66,000 francs as well as 100,000 francs in cash.

The Prussian ambassador in Paris summed up well the main rule of this game when he reported to his government in 1802: "Experience has taught everybody who is here on diplomatic business that one ought never to give anything before the deal is definitely closed, but it has also proved that the allurement of gain will often work wonders."

Statesmen who participated in transactions of this kind could hardly be expected to be passionately devoted to the cause of the countries whose interests were in their care. Obviously, they had loyalties besides and above the one to the country that employed them. Furthermore, the expectation of material gain at the conclusion of a treaty could not fail to act as a powerful incentive for expediting the negotiations. Stalemates, adjournments sine die, and long-drawn-out wars were not likely to find favor with statesmen who had a very personal stake in the conclusion of treaties. In these two respects the commercialization of statecraft in the seventeenth and eighteenth centuries was bound to blunt the edge of international controversies and confine the aspirations for power of individual nations within relatively narrow limits.

In that period of history the Austrian ambassador to France felt more at home at the court of Versailles than among his own nonaristocratic compatriots.

He had closer social and moral ties with the members of the French aristocracy and the other aristocratic members of the diplomatic corps than with the Austrians of humble origin. In 1757 the Comte de Stainville was Austrian minister in Paris, while his son, later (as Duc de Choiseul) prime minister of Louis XV, was French ambassador at the Court of Vienna. At the same time, another son was major of a Croat regiment in Hungary. It was not surprising that in such circumstances the diplomatic and military personnel fluctuated to a not inconsiderable degree from one monarchical employer to another. It was not rare that a French diplomat or officer, for some reason of self-interest, would enter the services of the king of Prussia and would further the aims of Prussia, or fight in the Prussian army, against France. Louis XIV refused a commission to Prince Eugene of Savoy, son of Mazarin's niece, whereupon the prince entered the Austrian service and became the greatest of Austrian generals, ending the French dream of dominating Italy. During the eighteenth century a great number of Germans entered all branches of the Russian government; many of them were later dismissed in a kind of purge and returned to their countries of origin.

In 1756, shortly before the outbreak of the Seven Years' War, Frederick the Great sent the Scottish earl Marischall as his ambassador to Spain in order to get information about the Spanish intentions. The Scottish ambassador to Prussia had a friend in Spain, an Irishman by the name of Wall, who happened to be Spanish foreign minister and who told him what he wanted to know. The Scot transmitted this information to the British prime minister who, in turn, passed it on to the king of Prussia. As late as 1792, shortly before the outbreak of the War of the First Coalition against France, the French government offered the supreme command of the French forces to the Duke of Brunswick who, however, decided to accept an offer from the king of Prussia to lead the Prussian army against France. As late as 1815, at the Congress of Vienna, Alexander I of Russia had as ministers and advisors in foreign affairs two Germans, one Greek, one Corsican, one Swiss, one Pole—and one Russian. Even at the end of the nineteenth century, it was still possible for Prince Chlodwig zu Hohenlohe-Schillingsfuerst to be German chancellor, for one of his brothers to be a cardinal of the Roman curia, for one of his nephews to be an Austrian minister, and for another to be an Austrian general and diplomat who later on became ambassador in Berlin. Thus Guizot, a former prime minister of France, could write in the middle of the nineteenth century:

> The professional diplomats form, within the European community, a society of their own which lives by its own principles, customs, lights, and aspirations, and which amid differences and even conflicts between States, preserves a quiet and permanent unity of its own. Moved by the divergent interests of nations, but not by their prejudices or momentary passions, that small diplomatic world may well recognize the general interest of the great European community with sufficient clearness and fill it with sufficient strength, to make it triumph over differences, and cause men, who have long upheld very different policies without ever quarrelling among themselves, and who have

almost always shared the same atmosphere and horizons, to work sincerely for the success of the same policy.[9]

Bismarck's experience in 1862, on the occasion of his recall as Prussian ambassador to Russia, is significant for the persistence of this international cohesion of the aristocracy. When he expressed to the czar his regret at the necessity of leaving St. Petersburg, the czar, misunderstanding this remark, asked Bismarck whether he was inclined to enter the Russian diplomatic service. Bismarck reported in his memoirs that he declined the offer "courteously."[10] What is important and significant for the purposes of our discussion is not that Bismarck declined the offer—many such offers had certainly been declined before and perhaps even a few have been since—but that he did so "courteously" and that even his report, written more than thirty years after the event, showed no trace of moral indignation. Only a little more than half a century ago the offer to an ambassador, who had just been appointed prime minister, to transfer his loyalties from one country to another was considered by the recipient as a sort of business proposition that did not at all insinuate the violation of moral standards.

Let us imagine that a similar offer had been made in our time by a Russian prime minister to the American ambassador or by the American president to any diplomat accredited in Washington, and visualize the private embarrassment of the individual concerned and the public indignation following the incident, and we have the measure of the profundity of the change that has transformed the ethics of foreign policy in recent times. Today such an offer would be regarded as an invitation to treason, that is, the violation of the most fundamental of all moral obligations in international affairs—loyalty to one's own country. When it was made and even when it was reported, shortly before the close of the nineteenth century, it was a proposition to be accepted or rejected on its merits without any lack of moral propriety attaching to it.

The moral standards of conduct with which the international aristocracy complied were of necessity of a supranational character. They applied not to all Prussians, Austrians, or Frenchmen but to all men who by virtue of their birth and education were able to comprehend them and to act in accordance with them. It was in the concept and the rules of natural law that this cosmopolitan society found the source of its precepts of morality. The individual members of this society, therefore, felt themselves to be personally responsible for compliance with those moral rules of conduct; for it was to them as rational human beings, as individuals, that this moral code was addressed. When it was suggested to Louis XV that he counterfeit the bills of the Bank of England, the king rejected such a proposition, which "could be considered here only with all the indignation and all the horror which it deserves." When a similar proposition was made in 1792 with respect to the French currency in order to save Louis XVI, the Austrian emperor Francis II declared that "such an infamous project is not to be accepted."

---

[9]*Mémoires* (Brussels, 1858–67), Vol. II, pp. 266–67.
[10]*Bismarck, the Man and Statesman, Being the Reflections and Reminiscences of Otto, Prince von Bismarck* (New York and London: Harper and Brothers, 1899), Vol. I, p. 341.

This sense of a highly personal moral obligation to be met by those in charge of foreign policy with regard to their colleagues in other countries explains the emphasis with which the writers of the seventeenth and eighteenth centuries counseled the monarch to safeguard his "honor" and his "reputation" as his most precious possessions. Any action Louis XV undertook on the international scene was his personal act in which his personal sense of moral obligation revealed itself and in which, therefore, his personal honor was engaged. A violation of his moral obligations, as they were recognized by his fellow monarchs for themselves, would set in motion not only his conscience but also the spontaneous reactions of the supranational aristocratic society, which would make him pay for the violation of its mores with a loss of prestige, that is, a loss of power.

Destruction of International Morality

When in the course of the nineteenth century democratic selection and responsibility of government officials replaced government by the aristocracy, the structure of international society and, with it, of international morality underwent a fundamental change. Until virtually the end of the nineteenth century, aristocratic rulers were responsible for the conduct of foreign affairs in most countries. In the new age their place has been taken by officials elected or appointed regardless of class distinctions. These officials are legally and morally responsible for their official acts, not to a monarch (that is, a specific individual), but to a collectivity (that is, a parliamentary majority or the people as a whole). An important shift in public opinion may easily call for a change in the personnel conducting foreign policy. They will be replaced by another group of individuals taken from whatever group of the population prevails at the moment.

Government officials are no longer exclusively recruited from the aristocratic groups but from virtually the whole population within which members of the "establishment" occupy a privileged position. This has, of course, been the tradition in the United States, yet it is unprecedented in such countries as Great Britain and the Soviet Union. Mr. Bevin, former general secretary of the Transport and General Workers Union, became in 1945 British secretary of state for foreign affairs. Mr. Molotov, a former professional revolutionary, was for many years responsible for Russian foreign policy.

In such countries as Great Britain, France, and Italy, where the government needs the support of a majority of parliament for its continuation in office, any change in the parliamentary majority necessitates a change in the composition of the government. Even in such a country as the United States, where not Congress but only general elections can put an administration into office or remove it, the turnover of the policymakers in the State Department can be considerable. Within eighteen months, from July 1945 to January 1947, the United States had three secretaries of state. Of all the policymaking officials of the State Department–that is, the undersecretary and assistant secretaries–who held office in October 1945, none was still in office two years later. In the Reagan administration, a tendency that began in the Carter administration resulted in political appointments being made across the board in the Department of State down to the level of deputy assistant secretary positions. The fluctuation of the policymakers in international affairs and their responsibility to an amorphous collective entity has far-reaching consequences for the effectiveness, even for the very existence, of an international moral order.

This transformation within the individual nations changed international morality as a system of moral restraints from a reality into a mere figure of speech. When we say that George III of England was subject to certain moral restraints in his dealings with Louis XVI of France or Catherine the Great of Russia, we are referring to something real, something that can be identified with the conscience and the actions of certain specific individuals. When we say that the British Commonwealth of Nations, or even Great Britain alone, has moral obligations toward the United States or France, we are making use of a fiction. By virtue of this fiction international law deals with nations as though they were individual persons, but nothing in the sphere of moral obligations corresponds to this legal concept. Whatever the conscience of the monarch as the constitutional head of the British Commonwealth and of Great Britain demands of the conduct of the foreign affairs of Great Britain and of the Commonwealth is irrelevant for the actual conduct of those affairs; for the monarch is not responsible for those affairs and has no actual influence upon them. What of the prime ministers and the secretaries of state for foreign affairs of Great Britain and of the Dominions? They are but members of the cabinet, which as a collective body determines foreign policy, as any other policy, by majority decision. The cabinet as a whole is politically responsible to the majority party, whose political preferences it is supposed to translate into political action. It is legally responsible to Parliament, of which it is, constitutionally speaking, only a committee. Parliament, however, is responsible to the electorate, from which it has received the mandate to govern and from which its individual members hope to receive another mandate at the next general election.

The individual members of the electorate, finally, may have no moral convictions of a supranational character at all that determine their actions on election day and in between, or, if they have such convictions, they will be most heterogeneous in content. In other words, there will be those who act according to the moral maxim "Right or wrong—my country." There will be those who apply to their own actions with regard to international affairs as well as to the actions of the government the standard of Christian ethics. There will be those who apply the standard of the United Nations or of world government or of humanitarian ethics. The fluctuating members of the policymaking group or of the permanent bureaucracy of the Foreign Office may or may not reflect these and similar divisions of opinion. In any case, the reference to a moral rule of conduct requires an individual conscience from which it emanates, and there is no individual conscience from which what we call the international morality of Great Britain or of any other nation could emanate.

An individual statesman may follow the dictates of his own conscience in his conduct of foreign policy. If he does, it is to him as an individual that these moral convictions are attributed, not to the nation to which he belongs and in whose name he may even actually speak. Thus, when Lord Morley and John Burns felt that the participation of Great Britain in the First World War was incompatible with their moral convictions, they resigned from the British cabinet. This was their personal act and those were their personal convictions. When at the same moment the German chancellor admitted as head of the German government the illegality and immorality of the violation of Belgium's neutrality, justified only by a state of necessity, he spoke for himself only. The voice of his conscience could not be and was not identified with the conscience of the collectivity called Germany. The moral principles that guided Laval as minister of foreign affairs and prime minister of the pro-German Vichy regime during the Second World War were his, not those of France, and nobody pretended that the latter was the case.

Moral rules operate within the consciences of individual men. Government by clearly identifiable men, who can be held personally accountable for their acts, is therefore the precondition for the existence of an effective system of international ethics. Where responsibility for government is widely distributed among a great number of individuals with different conceptions as to what is morally required in international affairs, or with no such conceptions at all, international morality as an effective system of restraints upon international policy becomes impossible. It is for this reason that Dean Roscoe Pound could say as far back as 1923: "It might be maintained plausibly, that a moral . . . order among states was nearer attainment in the middle of the eighteenth century than it is today."[11]

Destruction of International Society

While the democratic selection and responsibility of government officials destroyed international morality as an effective system of restraints, nationalism destroyed the international society itself within which that morality had operated. The French Revolution of 1789 marks the beginning of the new epoch of history that witnesses the gradual decline of the cosmopolitan aristocratic society and of the restraining influence of its morality upon foreign policy. Professor G. P. Gooch wrote:

> While patriotism is as old as the instinct of human association, nationalism as an articulate creed issued from the volcanic fires of the French Revolution. The tide of battle turned at Valmy; and on the evening after the skirmish Goethe . . . replied to a request for his opinion in the historic words, "From to-day begins a new era, and you will be able to say that you were present at its birth."[12]

It was a slow process of corrosion, with the old order resisting valiantly, as illustrated by the Holy Alliance and such incidents as the one, discussed above, when as late as 1862 the Russian czar invited Bismarck to enter the Russian diplomatic service.[13] Yet the decline of the international society and its morality, which had united the monarchs and the nobility of Christendom, is unmistakable toward the end of the nineteenth century. This decline has nowhere become more painfully

---

[11]"Philosophical Theory and International Law," *Bibliotheca Visseriana*, Vol. I (Leyden, 1923), p. 74.
[12]*Studies in Diplomacy and Statecraft* (London, New York, Toronto: Longmans, Green, 1942), pp. 300, 301.
[13]See page 254.

patent than in the theatrical hollowness of William II's verbal attempts at arresting it. He wrote to the Russian czar in 1895, with regard to the French:

> The Republicans are revolutionists *de natura*. The blood of Their Majesties is still on that country. Has it since then ever been happy or quiet again? Has it not staggered from bloodshed to bloodshed? Nicky, take my word on it, the curse of God has stricken that people forever. We Christian Kings and Emperors have one holy duty imposed on us by Heaven, that is to uphold the principle of By the Grace of God.

And the anachronism of Wilhelm II's stillborn plan, conceived on the eve of the Spanish-American War, to unite the European powers in support of the Spanish monarchy against the American republic, dismayed his advisors.

But even in 1914, on the eve of the First World War, there is in many of the statements and dispatches of statesmen and diplomats a melancholy undertone of regret that individuals who had so much in common should now be compelled to part and identify themselves with the warring groups on the different sides of the frontiers. Even the Grand General Staff of Germany, in the memorandum quoted above, refers to the impending First World War as "the mutual butchery of the civilized nations of Europe" and continues on this note of anxiety and foreboding: "After this fashion things must and will develop, unless, one might say, a miracle happens to prevent at the last moment a war which will annihilate for decades the civilization of almost all Europe."[14] This, however, was only a feeble reminiscence that no longer had the power to influence the actions of men. By then, these men had naturally less in common with one another than they had with the respective peoples from whom they had risen to the heights of power and whose will and interests they represented in their relations with other nations. What separated the French foreign minister from his opposite number in Berlin was much more important than what united them. Conversely, what united the French foreign minister with the French nation was much more important than anything that might set him apart from it. The place of the one international society to which all members of the different governing groups belonged and that provided a common framework for the different national societies had been taken by the national societies themselves. The national societies now gave to their representatives on the international scene the standards of conduct that the international society had formerly supplied.

When, in the course of the nineteenth century, this fragmentation of the aristocratic international society into its national segments was well on its way to consummation, the protagonists of nationalism were convinced that this development would strengthen the bonds of international morality rather than weaken them. For they believed that once the national aspirations of the liberated peoples were satisfied and aristocratic rule replaced by popular government, nothing could divide the nations of the earth. Conscious of being members of the same humanity and inspired by the same ideals of freedom, tolerance, and peace, they would

---

[14]See page 297.

pursue their national destinies in harmony. Actually, the spirit of nationalism, once it had materialized in nation-states, proved to be not universalistic and humanitarian, but particularistic and exclusive. When the international society of the seventeenth and eighteenth centuries was destroyed, it became obvious that there was nothing to take the place of that unifying and restraining element which had been a real society superimposed upon the particular national societies. The international solidarity of the working class under the banner of socialism proved to be an illusion. Organized religion tended to identify itself with the national state rather than to transcend it. Thus the nation became the ultimate point of reference for the allegiance of the individual, and the members of the different nations all had their own particular object of allegiance.

We have in Lord Keynes's portrait of Clemenceau a vivid sketch of this new morality of nationalism:

> He felt about France what Pericles felt of Athens—unique value in her, nothing else mattering. . . . He had one illusion—France; and one disillusion—mankind, including Frenchmen, and his colleagues not least. . . . Nations are real things, of whom you love one and feel for the rest indifference—or hatred. The glory of the nation you love is a desirable end—but generally to be obtained at your neighbor's expense. Prudence required some measure of lip-service to the "deals" of foolish Americans and hypocritical Englishmen, but it would be stupid to believe that there is much room in the world, as it really is, for such affairs as the League of Nations, or any sense in the principle of self-determination except as an ingenious formula for rearranging the balance of power in one's own interests.[15]

This fragmentation of a formerly cohesive international society into a multiplicity of morally self-sufficient national communities, which have ceased to operate within a common framework of moral precepts, is but the outward symptom of the profound change that in recent times has transformed the relations between universal moral precepts and the particular systems of national ethics. The transformation has proceeded in two different ways. It has weakened, to the point of ineffectiveness, the universal, supranational moral rules of conduct, which before the age of nationalism had imposed a system—however precarious and wide-meshed—of limitations upon the foreign policies of individual nations. Conversely, it has greatly strengthened the tendency of individual nations to endow their particular national systems of ethics with universal validity.

Victory of Nationalism over Internationalism

The vitality of a moral system is put to its crucial test when its control of the consciences and actions of men is challenged by another system of morality. Thus the relative strength of the ethics of humility and self-denial of the Sermon on the

---

[15]*The Economic Consequences of the Peace* (New York: Harcourt, Brace, 1920), pp. 32, 33.1

Mount and of the ethics of self-advancement and power of modern Western society is determined by the extent to which either system of morality is able to mold the actions or at least the consciences of men in accordance with its precepts. Every human being, insofar as he is responsive to ethical appeals at all, is from time to time confronted with such a conflict of conscience, which tests the relative strength of conflicting moral commands. A similar test must determine the respective strength, with regard to the conduct of foreign policy, of supranational ethics and the ethics of nationalism. To supranational ethics, composed of Christian, cosmopolitan, and humanitarian elements, the diplomatic language of the time pays its tribute, and many individual writers postulate it. But the ethics of nationalism has been on the ascendancy throughout the world for the last century and a half.

It is indeed true that, even before that ascendancy of the ethics of nationalism, national ethics, as formulated, for instance, in the philosophy of reason of state of the seventeenth and eighteenth centuries, has in most conflict situations proved itself to be superior to universal moral rules of conduct. This is obvious from a consideration of the most elemental and also the most important conflict situation of this kind, the one between the universal ethical precept "Thou shalt not kill" and the command of a particular national ethics "Thou shalt kill under certain conditions the enemies of thy country." The individual to whom these two moral rules of conduct are addressed is confronted with a conflict between his allegiance to humanity as a whole, manifesting itself in the respect for human life as such, irrespective of nationality or any other particular characteristic, and his loyalty to a particular nation whose interests he is called upon to promote at the price of the lives of the members of another nation. In the words of Pascal:

> Why do you kill me? What! do you not live on the other side of the water? If you lived on this side, my friend, I should be an assassin, and it would be unjust to slay you in this manner. But since you live on the other side, I am a hero, and it is just. . . . Three degrees of latitude reverse all jurisprudence; a meridian decides the truth. . . . A strange justice that is bounded by a river! Truth on this side of the Pyrenées, error on the other side.[16]

Most individuals today and during all of modern history have resolved this conflict between supranational and national ethics in favor of loyalty to the nation. In this respect, however, three factors distinguish the present age from previous ones.

First, there is the enormously increased ability of the nation-state to exert moral compulsion upon its members. This ability is the result partly of the almost divine prestige the nation enjoys in our time and partly of the control over the instruments molding public opinion that economic and technological developments have put at the disposal of the state.

Second, there is the extent to which loyalty to the nation requires the individual to disregard universal moral rules of conduct. The modern technology of war has given the individual opportunities for mass destruction unknown to previous ages.

---

[16]*Pensées,* translated by W. F. Trotter, Modern Library (New York: Random House, 1941), Section V. (Reprinted by permission of the publisher.)

Today a nation may ask one single individual to destroy the lives of hundreds of thousands of people by firing one missile with a nuclear warhead. The compliance with a demand of such enormous consequences demonstrates the weakness of supranational ethics more impressively than do the limited violations of universal moral standards of conduct that were committed in preatomic times.

Finally, there is today, in consequence of the two other factors, much less chance for the individual to be loyal to supranational ethics when they are in conflict with the moral demands of the nation. The individual, faced with the enormity of the deeds he is asked to commit in the name of the nation, and with the overwhelming weight of moral pressure that the nation exerts upon him, would require extraordinary moral strength to resist those demands. The magnitude of the infractions of universal ethics committed on behalf of the nation, and of the moral compulsion exerted in favor of them, affects the qualitative relationship of the two systems of ethics. It puts in bold relief the desperate weakness of universal ethics in its conflict with the morality of the nation and decides the conflict in favor of the nation before it has really started.

Transformation of Nationalism

It is at this point that the impotence of universal ethics becomes an important factor in bringing about a significant and far-reaching change in the relations between supranational and national systems of morality. It is one of the factors that lead to the identification of both.[17] The individual comes to realize that the flouting of universal standards of morality is not the handiwork of a few wicked men but the inevitable outgrowth of the conditions under which nations exist and pursue their aims. He experiences in his own conscience the feebleness of universal standards and the preponderance of national morality as forces motivating the actions of men on the international scene, and his conscience does not cease to be ill at ease.

On the one hand, the continuous discomfort of a perpetually uneasy conscience is too much for him to bear; on the other, he is too strongly attached to the concept of universal ethics to give it up altogether. Two possibilities to resolve that conflict are open to him. He can sacrifice the moral demands of his nation for the sake of universal ethics. It is indeed the starkness of the contemporary conflict that has driven a minority to make that sacrifice by refusing to support certain foreign policies of their respective nations in the name of a higher universal morality. The majority, however, in order to overcome that conflict identifies the morality of a particular nation with the commands of supranational ethics. It pours, as it were, the contents of a particular national morality into the now almost empty bottle of universal ethics. So each nation comes to know again a universal morality–that is, its own national morality–which is taken to be the one that all the other nations ought to accept as their own. The universality of an ethics to which all nations adhere is replaced by the particularity of national ethics that claims the right to,

---

[17]For other factors, see Chapter 20.

and aspires toward, universal recognition. There are then potentially as many ethical codes claiming universality as there are politically dynamic nations.

Nations no longer oppose one another, as they did from the Treaty of Westphalia to the Napoleonic Wars, and then again from the end of the latter to the First World War, within a framework of shared beliefs and common values, which imposes effective limitations upon the ends and means of their struggle for power. They oppose one another now as the standard-bearers of ethical systems, each of them of national origin and each of them claiming and aspiring to provide a supranational framework of moral standards that all the other nations ought to accept and within which their foreign policies ought to operate. The moral code of one nation flings the challenge of its universal claim with messianic fervor into the face of another, which reciprocates in kind. Compromise, the virtue of the old diplomacy, becomes the treason of the new; for the mutual accommodation of conflicting claims, possible or legitimate within a common framework of moral standards, amounts to surrender when the moral standards themselves are the stakes of the conflict. Thus the stage is set for a contest among nations whose stakes are no longer their relative positions within a political and moral system accepted by all but the ability to impose upon the other contestants a new universal political and moral system re-created in the image of the victorious nation's political and moral convictions.

The first inkling of this development from one genuinely universal system to a multiplicity of particular moral systems claiming, and competing for, universality can be detected in the contest between Napoleon and the nations allied against him. On both sides the contest was fought in the name of particular principles claiming universal validity: here the principles of the French Revolution, there the principle of legitimacy. But with the defeat of Napoleon and the failure of the Holy Alliance to uphold its principles in competition with the rising movement of nationalism, this attempt at erecting a particular code of ethics into a universal one came to an end and thus remained a mere historical interlude.

The present period of history in which generally and, as it seems, permanently universal moral rules of conduct are replaced by particular ones claiming universality was ushered in by Woodrow Wilson's war "to make the world safe for democracy." It is not by accident and it has deep significance that those who shared Wilson's philosophy thought of that war as a "crusade" for democracy. The First World War, as seen from Wilson's perspective, has indeed this in common with the Crusades of the Middle Ages—it was waged for the purpose of making one moral system, held by one group, prevail in the rest of the world. In the words of Robert C. Binkley:

> The World War not only brought to the top statesmen who were philosophers; it also brought the professional philosophers down from their intellectual pedestals. In every country these men used their high talents to give to the "issues" of the war a cosmic significance. They proved that the iniquities of the adversary had been present all along as implications of a national philosophy and culture, and that the triumph of their own party was necessary in the ethical scheme of the universe. Immediately upon the outbreak of

hostilities, Bergson discovered that the war was a conflict between "life" and "matter," with the Entente Powers ranged on the side of life and the Central Powers defending matter. Scheler proclaimed that English philosophy and character were alike manifestations of cant; Santayana wrote of "egotism in German philosophy"; and the gentle Josiah Royce, himself deeply in the debt of Hegel, reached the conclusion that "Germany is the willful and deliberate enemy of the human race; it is open to any man to be a pro-German who shares this enmity." The philosophers were making a Great Schism out of a mere political conflict. Then, as if to make a permanent record of the prostitution of the philosophic art, the victorious governments issued to each soldier in their armies a bronze medal with the inscription, "Great War for Civilization."[18]

A few months after the democratic crusade had gotten underway, in October 1917, the foundations were laid in Russia for another moral and political structure that on its part, while accepted only by a fraction of humanity, was claimed to provide the common roof under which all humankind would eventually live together in justice and in peace. While, in the twenties, this latter claim was supported by insufficient power and, hence, was little more than a theoretical postulate, democratic universalism retired from the scene of active politics, and isolationism took its place. It was only in the theoretical challenge that the priests of the new Marxian universalism flung in the face of the democratic world and in the moral, political, and economic ostracism with which the latter met the challenge that the conflict between the two universalisms made itself felt at that time in the field of international politics.

In the thirties the philosophy of National Socialism, grown in the soil of a particular nation, was proclaimed as the new moral code that would replace the vicious creed of bolshevism and the decadent morality of democracy and would impose itself upon mankind. The Second World War, viewed in the light of our present discussion, tested in the form of an armed conflict the validity of this claim to universality, and National Socialism lost the test. Yet, in the minds of many on the side of the United Nations, the principles of the Atlantic Charter and of the Yalta Agreement made the Second World War also a contest for universal democracy, and democracy, too, lost the test. Since the end of the Second World War the two remaining moral and political systems claiming universal validity, democracy and Communism, have entered into active competition for the dominion of the world, and that is the situation in which we find ourselves today.

It would be the most dangerous of illusions to overlook or even to belittle the depth of the difference that exists between this situation and the condition of the modern state system from the end of the religious wars to the entrance of the United States into the First World War. One needs only to pick at random any conflict which occurred in that latter period, with the exception of the Napoleonic Wars, and compare it with the conflicts that have torn the world apart in the last three decades in order to realize the importance of that difference.

---

[18] *Selected Papers of Robert C. Binkley*, edited by Max H. Fish (Cambridge: Harvard University Press, 1948), p. 328.

Let us compare with the international issues of our time the issues that brought France and the Hapsburgs into almost continual conflict from the beginning of the sixteenth to the middle of the eighteenth century, or that pitted Great Britain and Prussia against France in the eighteenth century. These issues were territorial aggrandizement and dynastic competition. What was then at stake was an increase or decrease of glory, wealth, and power. Neither the Austrian nor the British nor the French nor the Prussian "way of life"—that is, their system of beliefs and ethical convictions—was at stake. This is exactly what is at stake today. In the seventeenth and eighteenth centuries, none of the contestants on the international scene aspired to impose its own particular system of ethics, provided it had one, upon the others. The very possibility of such an aspiration never occurred to them, since they were aware only of one universal moral code to which they all gave unquestioning allegiance.

That common "system of arts, and laws, and manners," "the same level of politeness and cultivation," and the "sense of honour and justice," which Gibbon had detected in "the general manners of the times," which for Fénelon, Rousseau, and Vattel were a lived and living reality and whose political results Arnold Toynbee has noted,[19] have today in the main become a historical reminiscence, lingering on in learned treatises, utopian tracts, and diplomatic documents, but no longer capable of moving men to action. Only shreds and fragments survive of this system of supranational ethics that exerts its restraining influence upon international politics, as we have seen, only in isolated instances, such as killing in peacetime and preventive war. As for the influence of that system of supranational ethics upon the conscience of the actors on the international scene, it is rather like the feeble rays, barely visible above the horizon of consciousness, of a sun that has already set. Since the First World War, with ever-increasing intensity and generality, each of the contestants in the international arena claims in its "way of life" to possess the whole truth of morality and politics, which the others may reject only at their peril. With fierce exclusiveness, all contestants equate their national conceptions of morality with what all mankind must and will ultimately accept and live by. In this, the ethics of international politics reverts to the politics and morality of tribalism, of the Crusades, and of the religious wars.[20]

---

[19]See pages 234–35.

[20] To what extent the profession of universalistic principles of morality can go hand in hand with utter depravity in action is clearly demonstrated in the case of Timur, the Mongol would-be conqueror of the world, who in the fourteenth century conquered and destroyed southern Asia and Asia Minor. After having killed hundreds of thousands of people—on December 12, 1398, he massacred one hundred thousand Hindu prisoners before Delhi—for the glory of God and of Mohammedanism, he said to a representative of conquered Aleppo: "I am not a man of blood; and God is my witness that in all my wars I have never been the aggressor, and that my enemies have always been the authors of their own calamity."

Gibbon, who reports this statement, adds: "During this peaceful conversation the streets of Aleppo streamed with blood, and re-echoed with the cries of mothers and children, with the shrieks of violated virgins. The rich plunder that was abandoned to his soldiers might stimulate their avarice; but their cruelty was enforced by the peremptory command of producing an adequate number of heads, which, according to his custom, were curiously piled in columns and pyramids." *The Decline and Fall of the Roman Empire* (Modern Library Edition), Vol. II, p. 1243.

However much the content and objectives of today's ethics of nationalistic universalism may differ from those of primitive tribes or of the Thirty Years' War, they do not differ in the function they fulfill for international politics and in the moral climate they create. The morality of the particular group, far from limiting the struggle for power on the international scene, gives the struggle a ferocity and intensity not known to other ages. For the claim to universality that inspires the moral code of one particular group is incompatible with the identical claim of another group; the world has room for only one, and the other must yield or be destroyed. Thus, carrying their idols before them, the nationalistic masses of our time meet in the international arena, each group convinced that it executes the mandate of history, that it does for humanity what it seems to do for itself, and that it fulfills a sacred mission ordained by Providence, however defined. Little do they know that they meet under an empty sky from which the gods have departed.

Human Rights and International Morality

We have seen that the conduct of foreign policy is not an enterprise devoid of moral significance; it is always subject to judgment, by the actor, those acted upon, and those who merely witness. To conclude from the omnipresence of the moral element in foreign policy that a country has a mission to apply its own moral principles to the rest of humanity or to certain segments of humanity is something quite different. For there is an enormous gap between the judgment we apply to ourselves and our own actions, and the universal application of our own standards of action to others. Take so elemental and obvious a principle of action as respect for human life and the refusal to take human life except under the most extraordinary, exculpating circumstances. There are obviously civilizations and even groups within Western civilization that have a much less strict conception of the sanctity of human life, that give much less heed to spending the lives of others than we would under similar circumstances.

So there exists of necessity a certain relativism in the relation between moral principles and foreign policy; one cannot overlook this if one wants to do justice to the principles of morality in international politics. The relativism is twofold. It is a relativism in time; certain principles are applicable in one period of history and not applicable in another. It is also a relativism in terms of culture—of contemporaneous culture—in that certain principles are obeyed by some nations, some political civilizations, but are not obeyed by others.

In recent years the relationship of foreign policy and international morality has often been discussed under the rubric of human rights. The problem at the heart of this issue is the extent to which it is both morally just and intellectually tenable to apply liberal democratic principles to states that, for a number of reasons, are impervious to them. It is obvious that the attempt to impose so-called human rights upon others or to punish them for not observing human rights assumes that human rights are of universal validity—that, in other words, all nations or all peoples living in different nations would respect human rights if they knew they existed and that in any event they are as inalienable for all men as the Declaration of Independence declares them to be for Americans.

It is unnecessary to enter into a discussion of the theological or strictly philosophic nature of human rights here. It suffices to say that whatever one's conception of their theological or philosophical nature, human rights as perceived by individuals are inevitably filtered through historical and social circumstances leading to different results in different times and under different circumstances. One need only look at the unique character of the American polity and at the very special, nowhere-else-to-be-found characteristics of human rights protection within the confines of the United States. There is, after all, an almost complete lack of respect for human rights in many nations, or even in most nations: consider that only a few countries in Africa, for example, possess a pluralist political system; all others are dictatorships of one sort or another. Such reflection helps us realize how daring—or how ignorant if you will, which can also be daring—it is to try to impose upon the rest of the world our own respect for human rights, or in particular to punish other nations for not showing respect for those rights. What we see here is an abstract principle we happen to hold dear, which we happen to a considerable extent to have put into practice, presented to the rest of mankind not for imitation but for mandatory acceptance.

It is quite wrong to assume that this has long been the American tradition. It has not been the American tradition at all. John Quincy Adams argued that it was not for the United States to impose its own principles of government upon the rest of mankind but rather to attract the rest of mankind through the example of the United States. Indeed this has been the principle the United States has usually followed. The American Revolution, to quote Thomas Paine, "was not made for America alone, but for mankind"; nevertheless, American policy has been that those universal principles the United States had put into practice were not to be exported by fire and sword but presented to the rest of the world through successful example. This has been the great difference between the early conception of America and its relations to the rest of the world, on the one hand, and what might be called the Wilsonian conception, on the other.

Woodrow Wilson wanted to make the world safe for democracy; he wanted to transform the world through the will of the United States. The Founding Fathers wanted to present an example of what man can do to the nations of the world, calling upon them to go and do likewise. So there is a fundamental difference, both philosophic and political, between contemporary agitation in favor of human rights as a universal principle and the longer-lived American tradition in this matter.

Two other objections can be made to the Wilsonian conception. One is the impossibility of enforcing the universal application of human rights. We can tell the Soviet Union—and we should from time to time—that its treatment of minorities is incompatible with our conception of human rights. But once we have said this we will find that there is very little more we can do to change matters. History has shown that the Soviet Union may yield under certain conditions to private pressure. There are examples where private pressure—for example, the shaming of high officials in the Soviet Union—has had an obvious result. But it is inconceivable on general grounds that such pressure should be effective when exerted publicly. More particularly, in view of the nature of the Soviet Union's government—which uses every sign of external pressure to justify repression at home—American agitation for human rights has no chance of being effective. So there is a considerable confusion in our theory and practice of human rights, especially vis-à-vis other nations.

There is a second weakness of the Wilsonian approach. The United States is a great power with manifold interests throughout the world—of which human rights is only one—and not the most important one at that. Thus the United States cannot consistently follow the path of the defense of human rights without maneuvering itself into a quixotic position. This is obvious in our different treatment of South Korea, China, and the Soviet Union. The United States dares to criticize and affront the Soviet Union because relations, in spite of periods of détente, are not particularly friendly. The United States has an interest in continuing the normalization of relations with mainland China and for this reason seeks not to hurt Chinese feelings: little was heard in the Carter or Reagan administrations about China's human rights record. South Korea is an ally of the United States; it has achieved considerable military importance for American policymakers, so American policy will do nothing to harm its relations with that state.

In other words, the defense of human rights cannot be consistently applied in foreign policy because it can and must come in conflict with other interests that may be more important in a particular instance. To say that the defense of human rights must be woven into the fabric of American foreign policy is merely to conceal the necessary inconsistencies of any such effort.

Thus there are two basic hindrances to a foreign policy integrally committed to the defense of human rights. On the one hand, consistency in such defense is impossible, since it is not the prime business of a state, interacting as it must with other states, to defend human rights. On the other hand, it is not feasible to pursue human rights without taking into consideration other aspects of relations with other nations, which may be more important than those connected with human rights.

A further aspect of the role of human rights in foreign policy concerns the notion of responsibility for the human rights violations of others. The Cambodian genocide carried out by the Khmer Rouge in the late 1970s and early 1980s raised this question in a particularly acute fashion. The chain of events that culminated in the destruction of Cambodian society started with the American extension of the Vietnam War into Cambodia through the massive bombing of Cambodian territory. It was the policy of the Cambodian ruler, Prince Sihanouk, to keep Cambodia out of the armed conflict between the United States and North Vietnam. It was United States policy to involve Cambodia in active military operations in order to facilitate victory in the Vietnam War. There existed a causal nexus between American policy with regard to Cambodia and the catastrophe that befell that country. In other words, if the United States had not made Cambodia an active participant in the Vietnam War, Cambodia would, in all likelihood, have been spared catastrophe. This is not to say that the United States bore a direct moral responsibility for what happened in Cambodia but rather to demonstrate the continuous moral responsibility statesmen bear for the unforeseen and unforeseeable consequences of their actions. It would be quite another matter to assume that because of this causal nexus the United States had a moral obligation to prevent what happened in Cambodia or to alleviate the sufferings of the Cambodian people. Rather, as we have seen, moral as well as legal obligations are subject to the qualification that is expressed in the principle of Roman law that nobody is obligated beyond his capacity (*ultra vires nemo obligatur*). Thus, even if the United States were held morally responsible for what happened in Cambodia, it could not be held responsible to carry out any particular policy implementing that moral obligation. Even if the United States resolved to act, it would be unable to do so without disproportionate risks and losses.

The "hawk" faction held that Cambodia would never have suffered such misery and destruction had the United States maintained its resolve to "stay the course" and win the war in Southeast Asia. But aside from the impossibility of foreseeing all the consequences of the loss of the Vietnam War, to forestall all possible consequences of the loss by winning it at whatever price would have violated the basic principle of foreign and military policy: that the risks taken and losses incurred in a particular action must be proportionate to the chances for the success of that action.

In this consideration of the relations of foreign policy and morality, we are in the presence not of a peculiar, extraordinary situation but of a particular manifestation of the general human condition. We are all moral beings to some degree, simply because we are human. We all try to a greater or lesser extent to realize the moral principles with which we identify. Again and again we find ourselves faced with contradictions and difficulties. Perhaps the best we can do is to act upon what Abraham Lincoln proposed as the basis of political morality.

He warned against the exaggeration of moral virtue we claim for ourselves and outlined the limits within which man can act morally and at the same time have a chance for success. Lincoln's statement was made during the Civil War and was a reply to a petition by a delegation of Presbyterian ministers who asked him to emancipate all slaves forthwith:

> In great contests each party claims to act in accordance with the will of God. Both *may* be, and one *must* be wrong. God can not be *for*, and *against* the same thing at the same time. . . .
>
> I am approached with the most opposite opinions and advice, and that by religious men, who are equally certain that they represent the Divine will. I am sure that either the one or the other class is mistaken in that belief, and perhaps in some respects both. I hope it will not be irreverent for me to say that if it is probable that God would reveal his will to others, on a point so

connected with my duty, it might be supposed that he would reveal it directly to me; for, unless I am more deceived in myself than I often am, it is my earnest desire to know the will of Providence in this matter. *And if I can learn what it is I will do it!* These are not, however, the days of miracles, and I suppose it will be granted that I am not to expect a direct revelation. I must study the plain physical facts of the case, ascertain what is possible and learn what appears to be wise and right.[21]

---

[21] *The Collected Works of Abraham Lincoln,* edited by Roy P. Basler (New Brunswick: Rutgers University Press), Vol. V, pp. 403 ff, 419 ff.

17 World Public Opinion

Little need be said about world public opinion that is not already implicit in the discussion of the preceding chapter. Yet the warning with which we started the discussion of international morality must be repeated here with special emphasis. We are concerned with the actuality of world public opinion. We want to know of what it consists, how it manifests itself, what functions it fulfills for international politics, and, more particularly, in what ways it imposes restraints upon the struggle for power on the international scene. But there is hardly a concept in the modern literature of international affairs that in the last four decades has been employed by statesmen and writers with greater effusiveness and less analytical precision than the concept of world public opinion.

World public opinion was supposed to be the foundation for the League of Nations. It was to be the enforcement agency for the Briand-Kellogg Pact, the decisions of the Permanent Court of International Justice, and international law in general. "The great weapon we rely upon," declared Lord Robert Cecil in the House of Commons on July 21, 1919, "is public opinion . . . and if we are wrong about it, then the whole thing is wrong."[1] As late as April 17, 1939, less than five months before the outbreak of the Second World War, Cordell Hull, then American secretary of state, maintained that "a public opinion, the most potent of all forces for peace, is more strongly developing throughout the world."[2] Today we hear that world public opinion will use the United Nations as its instrument, or vice versa. The General Assembly of the United Nations, in particular, is declared to be "the open conscience of the world."[3] *The New York Times* goes so far as to state as a matter of fact that the Assembly of the United Nations "has considerable reserve powers under the Charter . . . at least to the

---

[1] *The Parliamentary Debates:* Official Report. Fifth Series. Vol. 118. House of Commons, p. 992.
[2] *The New York Times*, April 18, 1939, p. 2.
[3] Leland M. Goodrich and Edward Hambro, *Charter of the United Nations* (Boston: World Peace Foundation, 1949), p. 151.

extent of mobilizing world opinion, which, in the last analysis, determines the international balance of power."[4]

Two all-important questions must be answered before the possible meaning of these and innumerable similar assertions and appeals can be ascertained: what do we mean when we speak of world public opinion, and how does this world public opinion manifest itself under the moral and social conditions of the late twentieth century?

World public opinion is obviously a public opinion that transcends national boundaries and that unites members of different nations in a consensus with regard to at least certain fundamental international issues. This consensus makes itself felt in spontaneous reactions throughout the world against whatever move on the chessboard of international politics is disapproved by that consensus. Whenever the government of any nation proclaims a certain policy or takes a certain action on the international scene that contravenes the opinion of mankind, humanity will rise, regardless of national affiliations, and at least try to impose its will through spontaneous sanctions upon the recalcitrant government. The latter, then, finds itself in about the same position as an individual or a group of individuals who has violated the mores of their national society or of one of its subdivisions. Society will either compel them to conform with its standards or ostracize them for their lack of conformity.

If such is the meaning of the common references to world public opinion, does such a world public opinion exist at present, and does it exert a restraining influence upon the foreign policies of national governments? The answer is bound to be in the negative. Modern history has not recorded an instance of a government having been deterred from some foreign policy by the spontaneous reaction of a supranational public opinion. There have been attempts in recent history at mobilizing world public opinion against the foreign policy of a certain government—the Japanese aggressions against China in the thirties, the German foreign policies since 1935, the Italian attack against Ethiopia in 1936, the Russian suppression of the Hungarian revolution in 1956. Yet, even if one supposed for the sake of argument that these attempts were successful in a certain measure and that a world public opinion actually existed in those instances, it certainly had no restraining effect upon the policies it opposed. But the supposition itself, as we shall see, is not supported by facts.

Why, then, is it that an affirmative answer is being given so often to these questions? The reason is to be found in the misinterpretation of two factors in the international situation that point to the possible development of a world public opinion and in the neglect of a third one that at present makes such a development impossible. The two factors from which the mistaken belief in the existence of a world public opinion originates are the common experience of certain psychological traits and elemental aspirations that unite all mankind, and the technological unification of the world. What has been neglected is the fact that, everywhere in the

---

[4]November 15, 1947, p. 16.

world, public opinion with regard to international affairs is molded by the agencies of national policies. These agencies, as pointed out previously,[5] tend to claim for their national conceptions of morality supranational—that is, universal—recognition.

PSYCHOLOGICAL UNITY OF THE WORLD

There is at the bottom of all political contentions and conflicts an irreducible minimum of psychological traits and aspirations that are the common possession of all mankind. All human beings want to live and, hence, want the things necessary for life. All human beings want to be free and, hence, want to have those opportunities for self-expression and self-development that their particular culture considers to be desirable. All human beings seek power and, hence, seek social distinctions, again varying with the particular pattern of their culture, that put them ahead of and above their fellow men.

Upon this psychological foundation, the same for all men, rises an edifice of philosophical convictions, ethical postulates, and political aspirations. These, too, might be shared by all men under certain conditions, but actually they are not. They might be shared by all if the conditions under which men can satisfy their desire to live, to be free, and to have power were similar all over the world and if the conditions under which such satisfaction is withheld and must be striven for were also similar everywhere. If this were so, the experience, common to all men, of what men seek, of what they are able to obtain, of what they are denied, and of what they must struggle for would indeed create a community of convictions, postulates, and aspirations that would provide the common standards of evaluation for world public opinion. Any violation of the standards of this world public opinion, against and by whomever committed, would call forth spontaneous reactions on the part of humanity; for, in view of the hypothetical similarity of all conditions, all men would fear that what happens to one group might happen to any group.

But reality does not correspond to our assumption of similarity of conditions throughout the world. The variations in the standard of living range from mass starvation to abundance; the variations in freedom, from tyranny to democracy, from economic slavery to equality; the variations in power, from extreme inequalities and unbridled one-man rule to wide distribution of power subject to constitutional limitations. This nation enjoys freedom, yet starves; that nation is well fed, but longs for freedom; still another enjoys security of life and individual freedom, but smarts under the rule of an autocratic government. In consequence, while philosophically the similarities of standards are considerable throughout the world—most political philosophies agree in their evaluation of the common good, of law, peace, and order, of life, liberty, and the pursuit of happiness—moral judgments and political evaluations show wide divergencies.

---

[5]See pages 259 ff.

The same moral and political concepts take on different meanings in different environments. Justice and democracy came to mean one thing here, something quite different there. A move on the international scene decried by one group as immoral and unjust is praised by another as the opposite. Thus the contrast between the community of psychological traits and elemental aspirations, on the one hand, and the absence of shared experiences, universal moral convictions, and common political aspirations, on the other, far from providing evidence for the existence of a world public opinion rather demonstrates its impossibility, as humanity is constituted in our age.

AMBIGUITY OF TECHNOLOGICAL UNIFICATION

That same age, however, witnesses a development that seems to have brought a world public opinion close to realization, if it has not actually created it—the technological unification of the world. When we say that this is "One World," we mean not only that the modern development of communications has virtually obliterated geographical distances with regard to physical contacts and exchange of information and ideas among the members of the human race. We mean also that this virtually unlimited opportunity for physical and intellectual communication has created that community of experience, embracing all humanity, from which a world public opinion can grow. Yet that conclusion is not borne out by the facts. Two considerations show that nothing in the moral and political spheres corresponds to the technological unification of the world, that, quite the contrary, the world is today further removed from moral and political unification than it was under much less favorable technological conditions.

First of all, modern technology, while enormously facilitating communications among different countries, has also given their governments and private agencies unprecedented power to make such communications impossible. Two hundred years ago, it was easier for a literate Russian to learn about French political thought and action than it is today. An Englishman who wanted to spread his political ideas among the French had then a better chance than he has today. It was then simpler for a Spaniard to migrate or even to travel to the North American continent than it is today. For modern technology has not only made it technologically possible for the individual to communicate with other individuals regardless of geographical distances, it has also made it technologically possible for governments and private agencies of communication to cut off such communications altogether if they see fit to do so. And while the communications between individuals have remained largely in the realm of technical possibility, government and private controls have become a technical and political actuality.

Fifty years ago, the American citizen who wanted to visit a foreign country needed only to command the means of transportation in order to go there. Today, the "One World" of technology will avail him nothing if he lacks one of those governmental papers without which no human being is able to cross a frontier. Yet, only in 1914, the stigma of backwardness and almost of barbarism attached to

Russia and Turkey as the only two major countries that required a passport for leaving or entering the national territory. We ought not to forget that it is modern technology that has made totalitarian governments possible by enabling them to put their citizens on a moral and intellectual diet, feeding them certain ideas and information and cutting them off from others. It is also modern technology that has made the collection and dissemination of news and of ideas a big business requiring considerable accumulations of capital.

In the technologically primitive age, when printing was done by hand, any man of moderate means could reach the public ear by having a book, pamphlet, or newspaper printed and distributed at his own expense. Today the great mass of the people everywhere have no influence upon the mouthpieces of public opinion. With few exceptions, only men and organizations of considerable means and those who hold opinions approved by them can make themselves heard in the arena of public opinion. In virtually all countries the overwhelming weight of these opinions supports what the respective governments consider in their relations with foreign governments to be the national interest. Little information and few ideas unfavorable to the national point of view are allowed to reach the public. These assertions are too obvious to require elaboration. This is indeed "One World" technologically, but it is not for this reason that it is or will become "One World" morally and politically. The technological universe that is technically possible has no counterpart in the actual conditions under which information and ideas are exchanged among the members of different nations.

Yet, even if information and ideas were allowed to move freely over the globe, the existence of a world public opinion would by no means be assured. Those who believe that world public opinion is the direct result of the free flow of news and of ideas fail to distinguish between the technical process of transmission and the thing to be transmitted. They deal only with the former and disregard the latter. The information and ideas to be transmitted are the reflection of the experiences that have molded the philosophies, ethics, and political conceptions of different peoples. Were those experiences and their intellectual derivatives identical throughout humanity, the free flow of information and of ideas would indeed create by itself a world public opinion. Actually, as we have seen, there is no identity of experience uniting mankind above the elemental aspirations common to all men. Since this is so, the American, Indian, and Russian will each consider the same news item from his particular philosophic, moral, and political perspective, and the different perspectives will give the news a different color. The same report on the Vietnam War or the revolution of 1968 will have a different weight as a newsworthy item, aside from any opinion to be formed about it, in the eyes of different observers.

Not only will the different perspectives color the same piece of information, but they will also affect the selection of what is newsworthy from among the infinite number of daily occurrences throughout the world. "All the News That's Fit to Print" means one thing for *The New York Times,* another thing for *Pravda,* and another thing for the *Hindustan Times.* A comparison of the actual content of those different newspapers on any particular day bears out that contention. When it comes to the interpretation of the news in the light of philosophy, morality, and politics, the cleavages that separate the members of different nations from each other become fully manifest. The same item of information and the same idea mean something different to an American, a Russian, and an Indian; for that item of information and that idea are perceived by, assimilated to, and filtered through minds conditioned by different experiences and molded by different conceptions of what is true, good, and politically desirable and expedient.

Thus, even if we lived in a world actually unified by modern technology, with men, news, and ideas moving freely regardless of national boundaries, we would not have a world public opinion. For if the minds of men were capable of communicating with one another without political impediments, they still would not meet. Even if the American, Russian, and Indian could speak to one another, they would speak with different tongues, and if they uttered the same words, those words would signify different objects, values, and aspirations to each of them. So it is with concepts such as democracy, freedom, and security. The disillusion of differently constituted minds communicating the same words, which embody their most firmly held convictions, deepest emotions, and most ardent aspirations, without finding the expected sympathetic response, has driven the members of different nations further apart rather than uniting them. It has hardened the core of the different national public opinions and strengthened their claims for exclusiveness rather than merged them into a public opinion of the world.

THE BARRIER OF NATIONALISM

In order to illustrate the importance of this last observation, let us consider Woodrow Wilson's Fourteen Points. During the last months of the First World War, the Fourteen Points were accepted by so substantial a portion of humanity, regardless of national boundaries and of allegiance to one or the other of the belligerent camps, as principles for a just and enduring peace settlement that there indeed seemed to exist a world public opinion in support of them. Yet, as Mr. Walter Lippmann's brilliant analysis of the public opinion supporting the Fourteen Points has made clear:

> It would be a mistake to suppose that the apparently unanimous enthusiasm which greeted the Fourteen Points represented agreement on a program. Everyone seemed to find something that he liked and stressed this aspect and that detail. But no one risked a discussion. The phrases, so pregnant with the underlying conflicts of the civilized world, were accepted. They stood for opposing ideas, but they evoked a common emotion. And to that extent they played a part in rallying the western peoples for the desperate ten months of war which they had still to endure.
>
> As long as the Fourteen Points dealt with that hazy and happy future when the agony was to be over, the real conflicts of interpretation were not made manifest. They were plans for the settlement of a wholly invisible environment,

and because these plans inspired all groups each with its own private hope, all hopes ran together as a public hope. . . . As you ascend the hierarchy in order to include more and more factions you may for a time preserve the emotional connection though you lose the intellectual. But even the emotion becomes thinner. As you go further away from experience, you go higher into generalization or subtlety. As you go up in the balloon you throw more and more concrete objects overboard, and when you have reached the top with some phrase like the Rights of Humanity or the World Made Safe for Democracy, you see far and wide, but you see very little. Yet the people whose emotions are entrained do not remain passive. As the public appeal becomes more and more all things to all men, as the emotion is stirred while the meaning is dispersed, their very private meanings are given a universal application. Whatever you want badly is the Rights of Humanity. For the phrase, ever more vacant, capable of meaning almost anything, soon comes to mean pretty nearly everything. Mr. Wilson's phrases were understood in endlessly different ways in every corner of the earth. . . . And so, when the day of settlement came, everybody expected everything. The European authors of the treaty had a large choice, and they chose to realize those expectations which were held by those of their countrymen who wielded the most power at home.

They came down the hierarchy from the Rights of Humanity to the Rights of France, Britain and Italy. They did not abandon the use of symbols. They abandoned only those which after the war had no permanent roots in the imagination of their constituents. They preserved the unity of France by the use of symbolism, but they would not risk anything for the unity of Europe. The symbol France was deeply attached, the symbol Europe had only a recent history.[6]

Mr. Lippman's analysis of the apparent world public opinion supporting Wilson's Fourteen Points lays bare the crux of the problem—the interposition of nationalism with all its intellectual, moral, and political concomitants between the convictions and aspirations of humanity and the worldwide issues that face men everywhere. While men everywhere subscribed to the words of the Fourteen Points, it was the particular nationalisms, molding and directing the minds of men, that infused their particular meanings into these words, painted them with their particular color, and made them symbols of their particular aspirations.

Yet nationalism has the same effect upon issues with regard to which humanity had developed not only common verbal expressions, such as the Fourteen Points, democracy, freedom, and security, but also an actual consensus bearing upon the substance of the case. In contemporary international politics there is no opinion more widely held anywhere in the world than the abhorrence of war, the opposition to it, and the desire to avoid it. When they think and speak of war in this context, the men in the streets of Washington, Moscow, Peking,

---

[6]Walter Lippmann, *Public Opinion*, pp. 214 ff. Copyright 1922, by The Macmillan Company and used with their permission.

New Delhi, London, Paris, and Madrid have pretty much the same thing in mind—that is, war waged with the modern means of mass destruction. There appears to exist a genuine world public opinion with respect to war. But here again the appearances are deceptive. Humanity is united in its opposition to war insofar as that opposition manifests itself in philosophic terms, moral postulates, and abstract political aspirations—that is, with regard to war as such, war in the abstract. But humanity thus united reveals its impotence, and the apparent world public opinion splits into its national components, when the issue is no longer war as such, in the abstract, but a particular war, this particular war; not any war, but war here and now.

When actual war threatens in our time, as it did in the recurring crises over Berlin at the beginning of the sixties, humanity remains united in its horror of war as such, and in opposition to it. But men are incapable of translating this abstract opposition to war as such into concrete action against this particular war. While most members of the human race, qua members of the human race, consider war under the conditions of the twentieth century an evil that will make the winner only slightly less miserable than the loser, most members of the human race, qua Americans, Chinese, Englishmen, and Russians, look at a particular war, as they have always done, from the point of view of their particular nations. They oppose wars that do not affect what they regard as their national interest, such as Italy's war against Ethiopia, yet they are unwilling to take or to support any action that might be effective in preventing or putting an end to the war. For, if it is to be effective, such action must be drastic, involving certain disadvantages and risks for what is considered to be the national interest. Even the risk of war for other than national objectives might have to be faced, and those national objectives themselves might thus be jeopardized.

The sanctions against Italy, after it had attacked Ethiopia in 1935, are the classic example of this general condemnation of war by so-called world public opinion and of its unwillingness to take effective action seemingly not required by what is considered to be the national interest. Churchill trenchantly formulated this dilemma between condemnation of war in the abstract and the unwillingness to act effectively in a concrete situation, when he said of the representative of the British sector of that world public opinion: "First the Prime Minister had declared that sanctions meant war; secondly, he was resolved that there must be no war; and thirdly, he decided upon sanctions. It was evidently impossible to comply with these three conditions."[7]

World public opinion, however, ceases to operate at all as one united force whenever a war threatens or breaks out that affects the interests of a number of nations. Under such circumstances the universal condemnation of war undergoes a significant change in focus. The opposition to war as such is transformed into opposition to the nation that threatens to start, or actually has started, a particular war, and it so happens that this nation is always identical with the national

---

[7] *London Evening Standard*, June 26, 1936.

enemy whose belligerent attitude threatens the national interest and, therefore, must be opposed as a war monger. In other words, out of the common soil of the universal condemnation of war grow specific acts of condemnation directed against whoever threatens through war the interests of particular nations. There will then be as many warmongers condemned by national public opinions as there are nations threatening the interests of others through war.

The situation throughout the world from 1938 on is instructive in this respect. During that period of history all nations have uniformly been opposed to war in general. Yet, when it came to the formation of an active public opinion that would take action in order to prevent or oppose a particular war, the lines were drawn according to the national interest involved in the particular situation. Thus the public opinion of Great Britain and France, throughout that period, condemned Germany as a potential or actual agent of war, yet it condemned the Soviet Union on that count only from August 1939 to June 1941, that is, during the operation of the Russo-German pact. Since the end of 1945, public opinion in these two countries has again been opposed to the foreign policies of the Soviet Union as a threat to world peace.

Russian public opinion, on the other hand, opposed Germany as the main threat to peace until the signing of the pact with Germany in August 1939. From then until the German attack against the Soviet Union in June 1941, the Western democracies were regarded as warmongers. Germany's attack swung Russian opinion against it, and until about the end of 1945, Germany held its former place in the Russian public mind as a threat to peace. Since the end of 1945, with ever-increasing emphasis, Russian public opinion has come to consider the United States as the main threat to peace. American public opinion coincided in different degrees of intensity with the British and French point of view up to the end of 1945. Then, returning the Russian compliment, it started to regard the Soviet Union as the main menace to peace. The intensity of this opinion in the United States has mounted at a rate paralleling the rising intensity of opinion in the Soviet Union.

The attitude of the different nations to the Korean War bears out this analysis. The Korean War was universally condemned by "world public opinion." Yet, while the Soviet Union and its supporters blamed the United States and its allies for it, the latter regarded North Korea and China as the aggressors, supported by the Soviet Union, and the "neutrals," such as India, divided the blame between the two camps. The actual participation of the different nations in this war was similarly determined by their conceptions of the national interest. Nations such as China and the United States, whose interests were directly affected by the war and who had the power to protect them, bore the war's main burden. Others such as France, with only limited interests and resources, took a correspondingly limited part in the war. Others, such as Denmark, without interests or resources, and India, with a positive interest in abstention, took no active part at all.

Thus, whenever a concrete threat to peace develops, war is opposed not by a world public opinion but by the public opinions of those nations whose interests are threatened by that war. It follows that it is obviously futile to base one's hopes for the preservation of peace in the world, as it is presently constituted, upon a world public opinion that exists only as a general sentiment but not as a source of action capable of preventing a threatening war.

Wherever one probes beneath the surface of popular phraseology, one finds that a world public opinion restraining the foreign policies of national governments does not exist. A final general consideration of the nature of public opinion, as it becomes active in the mores of society, will show that under present world conditions this cannot be otherwise. While one can visualize a society without an active public opinion, and while there have doubtless existed and still exist authoritarian societies whose public opinion does not operate as an active force in international politics, obviously no public opinion can exist without a society. Society, however, means consensus concerning certain basic moral and social issues. This consensus is predominantly moral in character when the mores of society deal with political issues. In other words, when public opinion in the form of the mores becomes operative with regard to a political problem, the people generally try to bring their moral standards to bear upon that problem and to have it solved in accordance with those standards. A public opinion capable of exerting a restraining influence upon political action presupposes a society and a common morality from which it receives its standards of action, and a world public opinion of this kind requires a world society and a morality by which humanity as a whole judges political actions on the international scene.[8]

As we have seen, such a world society and such a universal morality do not exist. Between the elemental aspirations for life, freedom, and power, which unite mankind and which could provide the roots for a world society and universal morality, and the political philosophies, ethics, and objectives actually held by the members of the human race, there intervenes the nation. The nation fills the minds and hearts of men everywhere with particular experiences and, derived from them, with particular concepts of political philosophy, particular standards of political morality, and particular goals of political action. Inevitably, then, the members of the human race live and act politically, not as members of one world society applying standards of universal ethics but as members of their respective national societies, guided by their national standards of morality. In politics the nation and not humanity is the ultimate fact. "Nations have affections for themselves, though they have none for one another," wrote an Irish pamphleteer in 1779; "the body politic has no heart . . . There is no such thing as political humanity. . . ."[9] Inevitably, then, what is real are national public opinions fashioned in the image of the political philosophies, ethics, and aspirations of the respective nations. A world public opinion restraining the international

---

[8]When governments are concerned about the distribution of votes in the United Nations General Assembly, as the former colonial powers regularly are, what they are really concerned about is not a nonexistent world public opinion but their prestige with other governments, which might be affected by an adverse vote showing how few supporters such a former colonial power has.

[9]*Considerations on the Expediency, etc.* (Dublin, 1779), quoted after L. B. Namier, *England in the Age of the American Revolution* (London: Macmillan, 1930), p. 42.

policies of national governments is a mere postulate; the reality of international affairs shows as yet hardly a trace of it.

When a nation invokes "world public opinion" or "the conscience of mankind" in order to assure itself, as well as other nations, that its foreign policies conform to the standards shared by men everywhere, it appeals to nothing real. It only yields to the general tendency, with which we have dealt before, to raise a particular national conception of morality to the dignity of universal laws binding upon all mankind. The confidence with which all the antagonists in the international arena believe themselves to be supported by world public opinion with respect to one and the same issue serves only to underline the irrationality of the appeal. In our century, as we have seen, people want to believe that they champion not only, and perhaps not even primarily, their own national interests but the ideas of humanity as well. For a scientific civilization that receives most of its information about what people think from public opinion polls, world public opinion becomes the mythical arbiter who can be counted upon to support one's own, as well as everybody else's, aspirations and actions. For those more philosophically inclined, the "judgment of history" fulfills a similar function. For the religious, there is the "will of God" to support their cause, and believers witness the strange and singularly blasphemous spectacle of one and the same God blessing through his ministers the arms on either side of the battleline and leading both armies either to deserved victory or to undeserved defeat.

PART SIX

LIMITATIONS OF NATIONAL POWER

International Law

18 The Main Problems of International Law

THE GENERAL NATURE OF INTERNATIONAL LAW

The same warning against extremes with which we started the discussion of international morality and of world public opinion must apply also to the discussion of international law. An increasing number of writers express the opinion that there is no such thing as international law. A diminishing number of observers hold that international law, if duly codified and extended to regulate the political relations of states, could becomes through its own inner force, if not a substitute for, at least a restraining influence upon, the struggle for power on the international scene. As J. L. Brierly put it:

> Too many people assume, generally without having given any serious thought to its character or its history, that international law is and always has been a sham. Others seem to think that it is a force with inherent strength of its own, and that if only we had the sense to set the lawyers to work to draft a comprehensive code for the nations, we might live together in peace and all would be well with the world. Whether the cynic or the sciolist is the less helpful is hard to say, but both of them make the same mistake. They both assume that international law is a subject on which anyone can form his opinions intuitively, without taking the trouble, as one has to do with other subjects, to inquire into the relevant facts.[1]

The modern system of international law is the result of the great political transformation that marked the transition from the Middle Ages to the modern period of history. It can be summed up as the transformation of the feudal system into the territorial state. The main characteristic of the latter, distinguishing it from its predecessor, was the assumption by the government of the supreme authority

---

[1]J. L. Brierly, *The Outlook for International Law* (Oxford: Clarendon Press, 1944), pp. 1, 2. (Reprinted by permission of the publisher.)

within the territory of the state. The monarch no longer shared authority with the feudal lords within the state territory of which he had been in a large measure the nominal rather than the actual head. Nor did he share it with the Church, which throughout the Middle Ages had claimed in certain respects supreme authority within Christendom. When this transformation had been consummated in the sixteenth century, the political world consisted of a number of states that within their respective territories were, legally speaking, completely independent of one another, recognizing no secular authority above themselves. In one word, they were sovereign.

If there was to be at least a certain measure of peace and order in the relations among such entities endowed with supreme authority within their territories and having continuous contact with one another, it was inevitable that certain rules of law should govern these relations. That is to say, there must be certain rules of conduct defined beforehand, whose violation would normally call forth certain sanctions, also defined beforehand as to their nature and the conditions and mode of their application. States must, for instance, know where the frontiers of their territory are on land and on sea. They must know under what conditions they can acquire a valid title to territory either owned by no one at all (as in the case of discovery), or by another state (as in the case of cession or annexation). They must know what authority they have over citizens of other states living in their territory and over their citizens living abroad. When a merchant vessel flying the flag of State A enters a port of State B, what are the rights of State B with regard to that vessel? And what if the vessel is a warship? What are the rights of diplomatic representatives accredited to a foreign government, and what are the rights of the head of the state on foreign soil? What is a state allowed and obligated to do in times of war with respect to combatants, civilians, prisoners, and neutrals, on sea and on land? Under what conditions is a treaty between two or more states binding, and under what conditions does it lose its binding force? And if a treaty or another rule of international law is claimed to have been violated, who has the right to ascertain the violation, and who has the right to take what kind of enforcement measures and under what conditions? These and many other issues of a similar nature rise of necessity from the relations among sovereign states, and if anarchy and violence are not to be the order of the day, legal rules must determine the mutual rights and obligations in such situations.

A core of rules of international law laying down the rights and duties of states in relation to one another developed in the fifteenth and sixteenth centuries. These rules of international law were securely established in 1648, when the Treaty of Westphalia brought the religious wars to an end and made the territorial state the cornerstone of the modern state system. Hugo Grotius's *On the Law of War and Peace,* published in 1628, is the classic codification of that early system of international law. On its foundation the eighteenth and, more particularly, the nineteenth and twentieth centuries built an imposing edifice, consisting of thousands of treaties, hundreds of decisions of international tribunals, and innumerable decisions of domestic courts. These treaties and decisions regulate, often in minute detail, the relations among nations arising from the multiplicity and variety of international contacts, which are the result of modern communications, international exchange of goods and services, and the great number of international organizations in which most nations have cooperated for the furtherance of their common interests. Such organizations include the International Red Cross, the International Court of Justice, Specialized Agencies of the United Nations such as the International Labor Organization (ILO), the World Health Organization (WHO), the United Nations Economic, Scientific and Cultural Organization (UNESCO), the Universal Postal Union, the International Monetary Fund, and many others.

It is also worth mentioning, in view of a widespread misconception in this respect, that during the four hundred years of its existence international law has in most instances been scrupulously observed. When one of its rules was violated, it was, however, not always enforced and, when action to enforce it was actually taken, it was not always effective. Yet to deny that international law exists at all as a system of binding legal rules flies in the face of all the evidence. This misconception as to the existence of international law is at least in part the result of the disproportionate attention that public opinion has paid in recent times to a small fraction of international law while neglecting the main body of it. Public opinion has been concerned mainly with such spectacular instruments of international law as the Briand-Kellogg Pact, the Covenant of the League of Nations, and the Charter of the United Nations. These instruments are indeed of doubtful efficacy (that is, they are frequently violated) and sometimes even of doubtful validity (that is, they are often not enforced in case of violation). They are, however, not typical of the traditional rules of international law concerning, for instance, the limits of territorial jurisdiction, the rights of vessels in foreign waters, and the status of diplomatic representatives.

To recognize that international law exists is, however, not tantamount to asserting that it is as effective a legal system as the national legal systems are and that, more particularly, it is effective in regulating and restraining the struggle for power on the international scene. International law is a primitive type of law resembling the kind of law that prevails in certain preliterate societies, such as the Australian aborigines and the Yurok of northern California.[2] It is a primitive type of law primarily because it is almost completely decentralized law.

The decentralized nature of international law is the inevitable result of the decentralized structure of international society. Domestic law can be imposed by the group that holds the monopoly of organized force—that is, the officials of the state. It is an essential characteristic of international society, composed of sovereign states, which by definition are the supreme legal authorities within their respective territories, that no such central lawgiving and law-enforcing authority can exist there. International law owes its existence and operation to two factors, both decentralized in character: identical or complementary interests of individual states and the distribution of power among them. Where there

---

[2]See A. R. Radcliffe-Brown, "Primitive Law," *Encyclopedia of the Social Sciences,* Vol. IX, pp. 203–4; for literature see p. 262.

is neither community of interest nor balance of power, there is no international law. Whereas domestic law may originate in, and be enforced by, the arbitrary will of the agencies of the state, international law is overwhelmingly the result of objective social forces.

That the balance of power is such a social force was recognized by one of the foremost modern teachers of international law. L. Oppenheim calls the balance of power "an indispensable condition of the very existence of International Law."[3] "Six morals," he states,

> can be said to be deduced from the history of the development of the Law of Nations:
>
> (1) The first and principal moral is that a Law of Nations can exist only if there be an equilibrium, a balance of power, between the members of the Family of Nations. If the Powers cannot keep one another in check, no rules of law will have any force, since an overpowerful State will naturally try to act according to discretion and disobey the law. As there is not and never can be a central political authority above the Sovereign States that could enforce the rules of the Law of Nations, a balance of power must prevent any member of the Family of Nations from becoming omnipotent.[4]

The balance of power operates as a decentralizing force only in the form of a general deterrent against violations of international law and in the exceptional cases when a violation of international law calls for a law enforcement action. On the other hand, identical and complementary interests as decentralizing agents are continuously at work; they are the very lifeblood of international law. They exert their decentralizing influence upon three basic functions that any legal system must fulfill: legislation, adjudication, and enforcement.

THE LEGISLATIVE FUNCTION IN INTERNATIONAL LAW

Its Decentralized Character

In our contemporary domestic societies, the most important rules of law are created by legislators and courts; that is to say, by centralized agencies that create law either for all members of the national community, as do Congress and the Supreme Court of the United States, or for certain regional groups, as do state legislatures, city councils, and regional and local courts. In the international sphere there are but two forces creating law: necessity and mutual consent. International law contains a small number of rules concerning, for instance, the limits of national sovereignty, the interpretation of its own rules, and the like,

---

[3]L. Oppenheim, *International Law*, 2nd ed. (London: Longmans, Green, 1912) Vol, 1, p. 193. It is interesting to note that this and the following reference to the balance of power were eliminated by the editor from the later editions.
[4]Ibid., p. 80.

which are binding upon individual states regardless of their consent; for without these rules there could be no legal order at all, or at least no legal order regulating a multiple-state system. Aside from this small number of rules of what one might call common or necessary international law, the main bulk of rules of international law owe their existence to the mutual consent of the individual subjects of international law themselves—the individual nations. Each nation is bound only by those rules of international law to which it has consented.

The main instrumentality by which international law is created is the international treaty. An international treaty creates international law only for those nations that are a party to it. A treaty concluded among the American nations binds only them and no other nation. A treaty concluded between the Soviet Union and Iran has usually no legal effect for any third nation. Hence, the conditions under which the legislative function operates in the field of international law are similar to what would exist on the domestic scene if the legislative function within the United States were to be performed by the individual citizens themselves in the form of private contracts, instead of by legislatures and courts operating under the rule of *stare decisis*—that is, bound by precedents. Instead of a municipal law regulating sewage disposal or zoning in a certain municipality, these issues would be taken care of by a number of private agreements concluded among the residents of the different streets. The municipality, then, would have as many regulations as there are streets. The inevitable result of such a system of legislation would be, on the one hand, lack of legal regulation altogether whenever the unanimous consent of all those concerned was not forthcoming. On the other hand, there would be uncertainty about what the law actually was in a particular case, and there would be contradictions among the different sets of rules regulating the same situations with regard to different individuals. That is the situation that exists in international law, mitigated only by the relatively small number—about 160 sovereign nations—of subjects that might create international law by concluding treaties among themselves.

From this decentralized character of the legislative function two consequences follow for international law. On the one hand, many matters bearing upon international relations, such as immigration and many aspects of economic policies, are not regulated by international law. The interests of the different nations in these matters are so divergent that they are unable to agree upon legal rules. On the other hand, in those matters with regard to which agreement was possible, insecurity and confusion frequently reign. If one wants to know which rules of international law the United States considers to be binding upon itself, one must consult all the treaties ever concluded by the United States, after determining which are still in force at the moment of investigation. Then one must examine the decisions of international tribunals in cases to which the United States has been a party, and the decisions of American courts applying rules of international law. Finally, one must study the diplomatic documents in which the representatives of the United States in international negotiations have acknowledged certain rules of international law as binding upon the conduct of the United States in international affairs. The sum total of all these rules is what Charles C. Hyde has called *International Law Chiefly as Interpreted and Applied by the United States.*[5]

By a similarly tedious process the rules of international law recognized by other nations have also been compiled. In order to know the sum total of the rules of international law binding in a particular period of history throughout the world, it would be theoretically necessary to make similar compilations with regard to all nations of the world. If such a task were actually undertaken, its results would show considerable divergencies with regard to general principles as well as particular rules. Worldwide compilations in limited fields of international law illustrate this lack of agreement. Many writers refer to continental law in contrast to Anglo-American international law, to the international law of the Americas, and to the Russian conception of international law.[6]

To take as a specific example the breadth of the maritime belt–that is, the question as to how far into the sea the territorial jurisdiction of the adjacent state extends–the rules of international law recognized by different nations in this field differ sharply. While a number of nations adhere to the principle of the 3-mile limit, Finland and Norway–over the objections of other states–claim a breadth of 4 miles for the maritime belt. Italy, Spain, Yugoslavia, India, Mexico, Iceland, Indonesia, the Soviet Union, Egypt, France, and Poland, for another instance, claim 12 miles. Albania claims 15; Ecuador 200 miles. Other nations, such as Germany, Belgium, and Great Britain, claim only 3 miles; but Britain claims a so-called contiguous zone beyond the territorial waters proper. Other nations, while rejecting the claim of these nations to a contiguous zone, recognize that under certain circumstances a nation has the right to extend its jurisdiction beyond the 3-mile limit and to submit the merchant vessels of foreign nations to some measure of control. Part II, Section 2, Article 3 of the Law of the Sea Treaty of 1982 calls for a 12-mile limit by states ratifying the treaty unless otherwise provided, but the question remains whether states with differing jurisdictional limits will ratify this provision and whether those who ratify it will at some point renounce such provisions.

This lack of precision, resulting from the confusing multitude of unilateral claims, permeates to a greater or lesser degree most branches of the law of nations, by virtue of the decentralized character of the legislative function. Governments, however, are always anxious to shake off the restraining influence that international law might have upon their foreign policies, to use international law instead for the promotion of their national interests, and to evade legal obligations that might be harmful to them. They have used the imprecision of international law as a ready-made tool for furthering their ends. They have done so by advancing unsupported legal claims and by misinterpreting

[5]2 vols. (Boston: Little, Brown, 1946).
[6]On these different conceptions of international law and the literature concerning them, cf. L. Oppenheim and H. Lauterpacht, *International Law,* 8th ed. (London: Longmans, Green, 1955), Vol. I, pp. 48 ff.

the meaning of generally recognized rules of international law. Thus the lack of precision inherent in the decentralized nature of international law is breeding ever more lack of precision, and the debilitating vice that was present at its birth continues to sap its strength.

Only those branches of international law, generally of a technical or humanitarian nature, that have been codified in general agreements, escape in a certain measure this weakness.[7] For a codification of international law is in its legal effects the equivalent of a genuine piece of international legislation in that it binds all or virtually all subjects of international law. It is only the requirement of the consent of all those who are to be bound by it—in contrast to the majority rule required by the democratic process of legislation—that sets codification of international law apart from genuine legislation.

Interpretation and Binding Force

The need to substitute the unanimous consent of all subjects of international law for genuine international legislation gives rise to yet another type of complication peculiar to international law. This is the problem of ascertaining the meaning of the provisions of international treaties, of the rights they confer, and of the obligations they impose. In the domestic sphere this problem is solved by the legislative bodies themselves, which generally try to make the legal rules they enact as precise as possible; by the courts, which are continually engaged in the task of interpreting the laws by applying them to concrete cases; and by the executive and administrative agencies, which issue orders performing the same function. International legal documents, such as the Charter of the United Nations, as well as many others of a purely technical character, are vague and ambiguous, not by accident or, like the American Constitution, for particular and exceptional reasons, but regularly and of necessity. For such documents, in order to obtain the approval of all subjects of the law, necessary for their acquiring legal force, must take cognizance of all the divergent national interests that will or might be affected by the rules to be enacted. In order to find a common basis on which all those different national interests can meet in harmony, rules of international law embodied in general treaties must often be vague and ambiguous, allowing all the signatories to read the recognition of their own national interests into the legal text agreed upon. If this should happen in the domestic sphere, as it has actually happened to a considerable extent with regard to the Constitution of the United States, some authoritative decision—whether of the Supreme Court as in the United States, or of Parliament as in Great Britain—would give concrete meaning to the vague and ambiguous provisions of the law.

---

[7]Examples are the codifications in the field of communications, such as the General Postal Convention of 1874, the Convention on International Civil Aviation of 1944, and many others, as well as the general international agreements referred to on pages 235 ff; which seek the humanization of warfare.

In the international field it is the subjects of the law themselves that not only legislate for themselves but are also the supreme authority for interpreting and giving concrete meaning to their own legislative enactments. They will naturally interpret and apply the provisions of international law in the light of their particular and divergent conceptions of the national interest. They will naturally marshal them to the support of their particular international policies and will thus destroy whatever restraining power, applicable to all, these rules of international law, despite their vagueness and ambiguity, might have possessed. Mr. Jean Ray well analyzed this situation when he said with regard to the Covenant of the League of Nations: "But the danger is obvious. If the members of the League as individuals have ultimate authority in matters of interpretation, divergent interpretations, all equally authoritative, are going to perpetuate themselves; and when an ambiguous text is being invoked in a conflict between two nations, there will be an impasse."[8] This has happened time and again in the history of the League of Nations, and the history of the United Nations has given us a number of instances of a similar nature.[9]

There is, finally, another difficulty that contributes to the weakness of international law from the legislative point of view, and that is the uncertainty as to whether a certain international treaty, duly signed and ratified, contains actually, in whole or in part, valid rules of international law binding upon the signatories. Such a question could hardly arise with regard to a piece of domestic legislation in the United States. For a federal law has either been passed by Congress and signed by the president in conformity with the constitutional requirements or it has not, and it has either been invalidated by the Supreme Court or it has not. There may be uncertainty as to its constitutionality or interpretation until the Supreme Court has spoken with final authority, but not as to its very existence as a valid rule of law. It is this uncertainty as to the existence of certain fundamental rules, duly signed and ratified by virtually all members of the international community, that shakes the very foundation of international law.

Let us consider the most spectacular example of this type of international law, the Briand-Kellogg Pact of 1928, in which virtually all nations agreed "to renounce war as an instrument of national policy in their relations with one another." Has this agreement been from the beginning a rule of international law binding upon all signatories, or is it merely a statement of moral principle without legal effect? Has the international law of the Nuremberg Trials, according to which the preparation for, and the waging of, aggressive war is an international

---

[8]*Commentaire du Pacte de la Sociéte des Nations* (Paris: Sirey, 1930), p. 44.
[9]In order to remedy this situation, the General Assembly of the United Nations passed in its Second Session, on November 14, 1947, a resolution declaring it to be of paramount importance that the interpretation of the Charter and of the constitutions of the specialized agencies be based on recognized principles of international law. The resolution called specifically upon the agencies of the United Nations to seek advisory opinions from the International Court of Justice on points of law that have arisen in the course of their activities (*United Nations Documents*, A/459). Upon the request of the General Assembly, the Court has rendered a number of advisory opinions concerning the interpretation of the Charter and other international treaties.

crime, applied the already existing law of the Briand-Kellogg Pact, or has it created international law that did not exist before?[10] And has it done the one or the other only for the specific cases decided in Nuremberg, or for any similar cases that might occur in the future? Different schools of thought have answered these questions differently, and this is not the place to settle the controversy. What is important to note in the context of this discussion is the weakness of a legal system that is incapable of giving a precise answer to so fundamental a question as to whether it forbids collective acts of violence for certain purposes. Thus there is today no way of stating with any degree of authority whether any nation that went to war after 1929 in pursuance of its national policies has violated a rule of international law and is liable before international law for its violation; or whether only those individuals responsible for preparing and starting the Second World War are liable in this way; or whether all nations and individuals that will prepare for, and wage, aggressive war in the future will thus be liable.

What about the legal validity of the Convention with Respect to the Laws and Customs of War on Land of 1899 and 1907, and its binding force upon its signatories in the Second World War and in a future war? This convention, which was fairly well observed during the First World War and whose violations were then pointed out regularly, was, as we have seen,[11] violated regularly and on a mass scale by all belligerents during the Second World War. Have these violations, unprotested and unpunished, put an end to the binding force of this convention, or has the convention survived the Second World War as a legal instrument that can be invoked, enforced, and made the standard of action in a future war? And what about similar questions with respect to the rules of maritime warfare that were also generally violated in the Second World War with hardly an attempt at enforcement being made? The Axis sank enemy ships indiscriminately and without warning, as did the Allies, and both sides bombed civilians, justifying these violations of the rules of war with military necessity. If rules of international law are consistently violated and the violations are accepted as a matter of course by all subjects of the law—if, therefore, the legal rules are treated by those who ought to enforce them as though they did not exist—the question arises: do they still exist as binding legal rules? No precise answer can be given to these questions at the moment. But, in view of the probable development of the technology of war and of international morality, the odds are against survival of these rules.

In 1936 the League of Nations sanctions against Italy failed, and in the following years the wholesale violations of the most important provisions of the Covenant were treated with indifference by all governments concerned. Then similar questions were raised with respect to the Covenant of the League of Nations as a whole and to certain of its provisions. Governments acted as though those provisions had lost their binding force, but did they actually lose it, or did their legal validity survive the crisis of the late thirties and of the Second World

---

[10]Cf. Hans J. Morgenthau, Erich Hula, and Moorhouse F. X. Millar, in *America*, Vol. 76, No. 10 (December 7, 1946), pp. 266–68.
[11]See pages 248 ff.

War to expire only with the formal dissolution of the League in 1946? No unequivocal and precise answer to these questions was forthcoming when they were first raised, nor is there an answer now. There can be little doubt that the transformation of the United Nations from what the Charter intended it to be into something quite different, with the concomitant disregard of legal rules, confronts the observer with similar questions and that his answers can be only uncertain, ambiguous, and tentative. The deficient character of the answers to so important and fundamental questions is again the measure of the deficiency of international law from the legislative point of view.

THE JUDICIAL FUNCTION IN INTERNATIONAL LAW

Despite these deficiencies resulting from the decentralized character of the legislative function, a legal system might still be capable of holding in check the power aspirations of its subjects if there existed judicial agencies that could speak with authority whenever a dissension occurred with regard to the existence or the import of a legal rule. Thus the ambiguities and generalities of the American Constitution have been made largely innocuous through the compulsory jurisdiction of the Supreme Court in matters of constitutional interpretation. More particularly, the English common law has been given certainty and precision primarily by the decisions of courts, and to only a small extent by formal legislative enactments. A hierarchy of judicial agencies performs in all developed legal systems the task of determining authoritatively and with finality the rights and duties of the subjects of the law.

If an individual citizen of the United States maintains against another American citizen that a federal statute does not apply to him either because of constitutional defects or in view of the meaning of the statute itself, either citizen can under certain procedural conditions submit his claim for an authoritative decision of the issue to a federal court. The jurisdiction of the court is established when the claim is made by either party; it is not dependent upon the consent of the other party. In other words, an American citizen can summon another citizen before a court of law to have their legal relations authoritatively determined, and is thus able to establish the jurisdiction of the court by his own unilateral action. The party that is dissatisfied with the decision can appeal to a higher court, until, as the court of last resort, the Supreme Court will say with finality what the law is in the case. That decision has, by virtue of the rule of *stare decisis,* the quality of a legislative action in that it creates law not only between the parties and with respect to the particular case but with regard to all future persons and situations to which the rationale of the decision applies.

International law is deficient in all three fundamentals of an efficient judicial system: compulsory jurisdiction, hierarchy of judicial decisions, and the application of the rule of *stare decisis* at least to the decisions of the highest court.

Compulsory Jurisdiction

The sole source for the jurisdiction of international courts is the will of the states submitting disputes for adjudication. It is axiomatic in international law that no state can be compelled against its will to submit a dispute with another state to an international tribunal. In other words, no international court can take jurisdiction over international disputes without the consent of the states concerned. "It is well established in international law," the Permanent Court of International Justice said in the *Eastern Carelia Case,* "that no state can, without its consent, be compelled to submit its disputes with other states either to mediation or to arbitration, or to any other kind of pacific settlement. Such consent can be given once and for all in the form of an obligation freely undertaken, but it can, on the contrary, also be given in a special case apart from any existing obligation."[12]

In the case of so-called isolated arbitration[13]—that is, when the parties agree to submit one individual dispute, after it has occurred, to the jurisdiction of an international tribunal—this principle manifests itself simply in the requirement of a contractual obligation between the parties establishing the jurisdiction of the court. Thus, when the United States and Great Britain were unable to settle the *Alabama* claims growing out of the Civil War by diplomatic negotiations, they agreed in a treaty to submit the dispute to an international tribunal. After the tribunal had rendered its judgment in this particular case, it disbanded; for its jurisdiction, derived from the treaty between the United States and Great Britain, was exhausted with the decision of this single case. If another dispute arose between the United States and Great Britain to be settled by international adjudication, another treaty would have to be concluded, and a similar procedure followed. If no agreement could be reached between the parties as to the definition of the dispute, the composition and the procedure of the tribunal, and the legal rules to be applied, no judicial settlement would be possible.

In the case of so-called institutional arbitration—that is, when a whole class of disputes (for example, those of a legal character or those arising from a peace or commercial treaty) are submitted in advance of their occurrence to international adjudication by a general agreement—the consent of the parties is generally required for two different stages in the proceedings. First, it is required for the general agreement to submit certain classes of disputes to the jurisdiction of an international court. Second, it is required for the particular agreement—concluded after a particular dispute has arisen—in which the parties declare that this particular dispute belongs to the class for which the general agreement provides international adjudication. When, for instance, an arbitration treaty between two nations provides that all legal disputes arising between them in the future shall be submitted

---

[12]P. C.I.J. Series B, No. 5, p. 27.

[13]We are using the terms "arbitration" and "adjudication" indiscriminately. While the former term is being used primarily for the judicial agencies that, prior to the establishment of the Permanent Court of International Justice, were created by bilateral agreements, the term "adjudication" is now generally used for all judicial agencies of an international character, regardless of the mode of their establishment.

to an international tribunal, neither state has as a rule the right to establish the jurisdiction of the court unilaterally, by simply submitting a particular legal dispute for adjudication. A special agreement relative to this particular dispute is necessary to establish the jurisdiction of the court.

The care with which states generally guard the contractual character of the jurisdiction of international courts is illustrated by Sir H. Lauterpacht:

> . . . the majority of the judgments given by the Permanent Court of International Justice has been concerned with so-called "pleas to the jurisdiction," i.e., with the refusal of one party, supported by a rigid and ingenious interpretation of relevant arbitration agreements, to accord to the other party the right, which Hobbes regarded as elementary even in a state of nature, of impartial adjudication. This has been done, as a rule, not for the reason that another international agency was competent to decide the issue, but on the ground that the state in question was not bound by any commitment to have recourse to judicial settlement.

The author adds that "even when the elementary duty of submission to adjudication is accepted [that is, in a general agreement], it is in practice often attended by elaborate reservations which reduce it to a mere formula devoid of any legal obligation."[14]

The Optional Clause

It is obvious that under such circumstances it is hardly possible to speak of a general obligation on the part of nations to submit disputes to judicial settlement in advance of their occurrence. The requirement of a special agreement concerning the particular dispute to be adjudicated and the qualification of the general agreement by reservations virtually preclude compulsory litigation. They allow a nation to preserve its freedom of action in all stages of the preliminary proceedings if it so wishes. It is for the purpose of assimilating the international judicial function, at least with regard to certain classes of disputes, to the strict compulsion of domestic litigation that Article 36 of the Statute of the Permanent Court of International Justice has created the so-called optional clause. This ingenious device is incorporated without change in Article 36 of the Statute of the new International Court of Justice. The provision gives the signatories of the Statute the opportunity to "recognize as compulsory *ipso facto* and without special agreement, in relation to any other state accepting the same obligation, the jurisdiction of the Court in all legal disputes."

Under the regime of the old Court, the clause was binding, at one time or another, for close to fifty states. Under the new Statute the number of signatories amounts to forty-five. Very few nations, however, have signed without reservations.

---

[14]H. Lauterpacht, *The Function of Law in the International Community* (Oxford: Clarendon Press, 1933), p. 427. (Reprinted by permission of the publisher.)

The declaration of the United States of August 14, 1946, accepting the compulsory jurisdiction of the International Court of Justice is the prototype of an acceptance so weakened by far-reaching reservations as to reduce the strict legal obligation to the vanishing point. According to its terms:

> . . . this declaration shall not apply to
>   *a.* disputes the solution of which the parties shall entrust to other tribunals by virtue of agreements already in existence or which may be concluded in the future; or
>   *b.* disputes with regard to matters which are essentially within the domestic jurisdiction of the United States of America as determined by the United States of America; or
>   *c.* disputes arising under a multilateral treaty, unless (1) all parties to the treaty affected by the decision are also parties to the case before the Court, or (2) the United States of America specially agrees to jurisdiction. . . .[15]

While reservation *a* is of minor importance, it is hard to visualize an international dispute that might not be interpreted so as to be covered by either reservation *b* or *c*. There are few matters liable to become the object of an international dispute on which the domestic jurisdiction of the countries concerned would not have some bearing. Does a trade agreement concluded between the United States and a foreign country remove the subjects that it regulates from the category of matters that are "essentially within the domestic jurisdiction of the United States"? What about international treaties concerning immigration, foreign loans, or limitation of armaments? Matters thus dealt with by international law are surely no longer "exclusively" within the domestic jurisdiction of the United States. But when do they cease to be "essentially" within that jurisdiction? Obviously, when the United States is no longer interested in preserving its freedom from judicial control with regard to such matters. Since what is and what is not "essentially" within the domestic jurisdiction of the United States is thus a matter of political opinion, and since according to reservation *b* the opinion of the United States will decide this issue without appeal, the United States will be able, if it so wishes, by virtue of reservation *b* alone to exclude from the jurisdiction of the Court most disputes to which it might be a party. Even if the opinion of the United States in this respect were clearly arbitrary and without factual foundation, the terms of the declaration make the United States the final judge in the matter. In April of 1984, the Reagan administration announced that for a period of two years it would not accept the jurisdiction of the Court on any matter involving Central America. Thus not only has the United States invoked the question of domestic jurisdiction, but it has also extended it to the region immediately south of it.

Reservation *c* takes care of whatever reservation *b* might have left to the compulsory jurisdiction of the Court. In modern times many of the more important

---

[15]Document United States/International Court of Justice/5, *Department of State Bulletin,* Vol. 15, No. 375 (September 8, 1946), p. 452.

international treaties, especially in view of their bearing on international politics, are multilateral, such as the Pan-American Treaties, the Charter of the United Nations, and the peace treaties terminating the Second World War. Considering the limited number of adherences to the optional clause and considering the possibilities of evasion with the aid of reservations, it is not likely that in the case of a dispute arising under such a treaty all the signatories of the treaty, numbering often more than a score or two of states, can simultaneously be made parties before the Court. The United States, then, is likely to retain its freedom of action in most cases where its acceptance of the compulsory jurisdiction of the Court with regard to multilateral treaties is involved.

Thus, in the end, the development of compulsory jurisdiction under the optional clause reverts to where it started from: the preservation, in a large measure and for the most important disputes, of national freedom of action with regard to the jurisdiction of international courts. The legal instrumentalities designed to preserve that freedom have become more refined under the regime of the optional clause. Instead of frankly exempting from adjudication the most important classes of disputes, they now serve primarily the purpose of smoothing over and concealing the contrast between verbal adherence to compulsory jurisdiction and actual unwillingness to accept it. It is, therefore, not surprising that the Permanent Court of International Justice was in the main concerned, not with the limitation of the struggle for power on the international scene but with the preliminary question of whether the parties were at all under obligation to submit the case to the jurisdiction of the Court. Only once did the Permanent Court of International Justice have to face squarely the problem of limiting a state's aspirations for power. That was in the case of the German-Austrian Customs Union of 1931,[16] and there the jurisdiction of the Court was founded not upon an agreement freely entered into by the parties but upon Article 14 of the Covenant of the League of Nations, authorizing the Council of the League to request advisory opinions from the Court. It is also worthy of note that, although the community of nations since the end of the Second World War has been rent apart by many disputes of different kinds, the International Court of Justice has decided only twenty-nine cases during the first thirty-five years of its existence.

All theoretical and practical considerations point to the conclusion that the optional clause has left the substance of the problem of compulsory jurisdiction where it found it. In the field of adjudication only slightly less than in the field of legislation, it is still the will of the individual nations that is decisive in all stages of the proceedings. Hence, international adjudication is unable to impose effective restraints upon the struggle for power on the international scene. Loose and ambiguous formulations of the general duty to submit to litigation and, in particular, a great variety of indefinite and sweeping reservations protect all states against the risk of having to submit any specific dispute to international litigation against their will. Hence, with regard at least to compulsory jurisdiction over

---

[16]P.C.I.J. Series A/B, No. 41.

important disputes, the decentralization of the judicial function is complete, barely disguised by legal formulae that, in turn, are rendered meaningless by reservations. As Secretary-General Hammarskjold put it in his Report of 1957: ". . . I cannot fail to express my own concern over the possibility that the present trend, if not soon halted, may render the whole system of compulsory jurisdiction virtually illusory."

International Courts

Since no legal system can be effective in limiting the activities of its subjects without compulsory jurisdiction over their disputes, the two other fundamental problems of adjudication—the organization of the judicial agencies and the effects of their decisions—are of subordinate importance. The establishment of the Permanent Court of International Justice and of its successor, the International Court of Justice, marks an important step, perhaps the most important of all, toward the centralization of functions in the field of international law. Up to the establishment of the Permanent Court in 1920, judicial organization in the international sphere was completely decentralized. That is to say, whenever two states agreed upon the judicial settlement of a specific dispute, they also agreed upon a particular person, such as the pope, a prince, a famous international lawyer, or a group of persons to function as a tribunal for the decision of this particular case. With the settlement of this dispute, the judicial function of this tribunal was automatically at an end. The judicial settlement of another dispute required the establishment of another tribunal. The Tribunal of Geneva, which in 1871 decided the *Alabama* case referred to above,[17] illustrates this situation.

The Hague Conventions for the Pacific Settlement of International Disputes in 1899 and 1907 tried to overcome this decentralization of the judicial organization by creating the so-called Permanent Court of Arbitration. The latter consists only of a panel of some 120 judges appointed by the different signatories to the convention. From this panel the parties to a specific dispute can select the members of a tribunal to be constituted for the adjudication of this specific dispute. It might, therefore, well be said that this institution is neither permanent nor a court. The so-called Court does not exist as a body; as such it does not fulfill judicial or any other functions. It is actually nothing more than a list of individuals "of recognized competence in questions of International Law, enjoying the highest moral reputation."[18] It facilitates the selection of judges for one of the special tribunals to be organized for the adjudication of a specific dispute. The so-called Permanent Court of Arbitration has never decided a case; only individual members of the panel have. It perpetuates the decentralization of judicial organization in the international field, while at the same time recognizing in the pretense of its name the need for a centralized judicial authority.

---

[17]See page 292.
[18]Article 44 of the Convention.

The main stumbling block for the establishment of a really permanent international court was the composition of the court. Nations were as anxious to preserve their freedom of action with respect to the selection of judges for each specific case as they were anxious to preserve their freedom of action with regard to the submission of each specific dispute to adjudication. More particularly, nations were reluctant to allow a dispute to be decided by an international tribunal of which neither one of their nationals nor a representative of their point of view was a member. No permanent international court with jurisdiction over more than a limited number of nations could meet the letter of such a requirement; for the number of nations subject to the jurisdiction of a world court would of necessity exceed the number of judges. The small nations, especially, feared that under these conditions most of them would be permanently deprived of representation in such a court, which might thus easily become an instrument of the great powers.

The Statute of the Permanent Court of International Justice and of its successor has solved this problem. The Court is composed of fifteen members, no two of whom may be nationals of the same state (Article 3). On the other hand, "The electors shall bear in mind . . . that in the body as a whole the representation of the main forms of civilization and of the principal legal systems of the world should be assured" (Article 19). The members of the Court are nominated and elected through a number of ingenious devices designed to insure high professional standards as well as compliance with the requirement of Article 19 of the Statute. The nominations are made by the members of the Permanent Court of Arbitration, organized into national groups, or by national groups appointed by their respective governments (Articles 4–6). The election is by absolute majority of the votes of the General Assembly and the Security Council of the United Nations, each body voting independently of the other (Articles 8–12). Article 31 of the Statute makes the additional concession of providing for special national judges who may be chosen by parties whose nationality is not represented among the members of the Court.

This Court, a truly centralized judicial agency, fulfills through its very existence two important functions for the international community. On the one hand, the Court, through being established in permanence and regardless of any dispute awaiting adjudication, is always available to nations that want to settle their differences by means of adjudication. Whatever else may stand in the way of a judicial settlement of their disputes, the problems of establishing a tribunal, selecting its members, providing for its procedure and substantive law have been solved for them once and for all by the Statute of the Court. The difficulties to which these problems, to be solved anew for each individual case of adjudication, may have given rise before 1920 no longer stand in the way of effective administration of international justice.

The International Court of Justice, whose members are elected for a period of nine years and may be reelected, provides for continuity in the performance of its judicial task. This quality is necessarily absent in a tribunal convened for the settlement of a specific dispute and terminating its existence with the rendering of the judgment. A court whose membership is bound to remain approximately identical for many years—the judges being elected for nine-year terms—cannot fail to develop a tradition of its own that it transmits to its successive members and upon the continuance of which the prospective parties can rely. This element of calculability and stability that is thus introduced into the operations of an international tribunal is in sharp contrast to the haphazard proceedings typical of the arbitration courts before the First World War.

The Effect of Judicial Decisions

This stability and calculability are the psychological result of a permanent organization rather than the legal effect of the judicial operations of the Court. Indeed, concerning the legal effect of the judicial decisions of the Court, the Statute pays tribute to the principle of decentralization by providing in Article 59 that "the decision of the Court has no binding force except between the parties and in respect of that particular case." Although the social fact of the continuing operation of the same persons within one organization is conducive to the development of uniformity and of a tradition in the jurisprudence of the Court, the latter is under no legal duty, as the Anglo-American courts are, to follow the rule of *stare decisis* and to justify its decisions in the light of precedent. Nevertheless, because of the social pressure for uniformity discussed above, the jurisprudence of the Court during the first three decades of its existence would hardly have been different if the Court actually had been bound by the rule of *stare decisis*. Nevertheless, the Court was and remains free to disregard its previous decisions should it so choose. Situations may arise where a court bound by the rule of *stare decisis* would hesitate to disregard its previous decisions, while the International Court of Justice might not.

This element of uncertainty within the jurisprudence of the International Court of Justice itself is, however, small in comparison with the one that, by virtue of Article 59 of the Statute, affects the relations between the jurisprudence of the Court and the many and heterogeneous other judicial agencies operating in the international field. The strength of the national systems of adjudication as a means of putting effective restraints upon the actions of the individual citizens derives in large part from the hierarchical nature of that system. Whatever act the individual citizen may perform, a court stands ready to say whether or not the act meets the requirements of the law. When these courts have spoken, a higher court can be appealed to in order to approve or disapprove the decision of the lower court. And, finally, a supreme court will state with ultimate authority the law in the case. Since all these courts operate under the rule of *stare decisis,* their decisions are logically consistent with one another not only within the same court but also within the whole system of courts. The hierarchical character of their relations guarantees the uniformity of the decisions throughout the system.[19] The combination of

[19]This is true only ideally; it suffers exceptions in the actual operation of the domestic judicial systems. In the federal judicial system, for example, logical consistency of the decisions of the different federal courts is assured only insofar as the Supreme Court has and takes jurisdiction as the highest court of appeals. Where, either by law or because the Supreme Court refuses to hear an appeal, the several Circuit Courts of Appeals decide similar cases without recourse to a higher tribunal, the legal rules applied by them to similar cases may, and frequently do, differ from one another. To this extent, then, there exists within the federal judicial system an exceptional situation that is rather normal in the realm of international adjudication.

hierarchical organization and of the rule of *stare decisis,* then, produces one system of jurisprudence throughout the judicial system, one body of coherent law ever ready to go into action at the request of whoever claims the protection of the law.

Nothing in the international sphere even remotely resembles this situation. The International Court of Justice is the one court that has potentially worldwide jurisdiction. But the multitude of other courts, created by special treaties for particular parties, for special types of disputes, or for specific single cases, have no legal connection at all either with each other or with the International Court of Justice. The International Court of Justice is in no sense a supreme court of the world that may decide, with final authority, appeals from the decisions of other international tribunals. It is but one international court among many others, outstanding through the permanency of its organization, the potential reach of its jurisdiction, and the generally high legal quality of its decisions. Yet in no sense is it hierarchically superimposed upon the other international courts. The decisions of the International Court of Justice may, by virtue of their professional excellence, put their imprint upon the decisions of other international courts. But, since they are not bound by the rule of *stare decisis,* other international courts are no more under the legal obligation to make their decisions consistent with the decisions of the International Court of Justice than they are to make their own decisions consistent with one another. Here again, decentralization is the earmark of the judicial function.

THE ENFORCEMENT OF INTERNATIONAL LAW

Its Decentralized Character

What for the legislative and judicial functions required elaborate proof is clear for all to see in the case of the executive function: its complete and unqualified decentralization. International law does not even provide for agencies and instrumentalities for the purpose of its enforcement apart from the agencies and instrumentalities of the national governments. Brierly describes the situation thus:

> The international system has no central organ for the enforcement of international legal rights as such, and the creation of any such general scheme of sanctions is for the present a very distant prospect. . . . This absence of an executive power means that each state remains free . . . to take such action as it thinks fit to enforce its own rights. This does not mean that international law has no sanction, if that word is used in its proper sense of means for securing the observance of the law; but it is true that the sanctions which it possesses are not systematic or centrally directed, and that accordingly they are precarious in their operation. This lack of system is obviously unsatisfactory, particularly to those states which are less able than others to assert their own rights effectively.[20]

[20]*The Law of Nations,* pp. 92, 93. (Reprinted by permission of The Clarendon Press, Oxford.)

In the same sense in which the individual nation is its own legislator and the creator of its own tribunals and of their jurisdiction, it is also its own sheriff and policeman. When individual A violates the rights of individual B within the national community, the law enforcement agencies of this state will intervene and protect B against A and compel A to give B satisfaction according to the law. Nothing of the kind exists in the international sphere. If State A violates the rights of State B, no enforcement agency will come to the support of B. B has the right to help itself if it can—that is to say, if it is strong enough in comparison with A to meet the infringement of its rights with enforcement actions of its own. Only under very exceptional and narrow conditions, in the forms of self-help and self-defense, does domestic law give the victim of a violation of the law the right to take the law into his own hands and enforce it against the violator. What is a narrowly circumscribed exception in domestic law is the principle of law enforcement in international law. According to this principle, the victim, and nobody but the victim, of a violation of the law has the *right* to enforce the law against the violator. Nobody at all has the *obligation* to enforce it.

There can be no more primitive and no weaker system of law enforcement than this; for it delivers the enforcement of the law to the vicissitudes of the distribution of power between the violator of the law and the victim of the violation. It makes it easy for the strong both to violate the law and to enforce it, and consequently puts the rights of the weak in jeopardy. A great power can violate the rights of a small nation without having to fear effective sanctions on the latter's part. It can afford to proceed against the small nation with measures of enforcement under the pretext of a violation of its rights, regardless of whether the alleged infraction of international law has actually occurred or whether its seriousness justifies the severity of the measures taken.

The small nation must look for the protection of its rights to the assistance of powerful friends; only thus can it hope to oppose with a chance of success an attempt to violate its rights. Whether such assistance will be forthcoming is a matter not of international law, but of the national interest as conceived by the individual nations, which must decide whether or not to come to the support of the weak member of the international community. In other words, whether or not an attempt will be made to enforce international law and whether or not the attempt will be successful do not depend primarily upon legal considerations and the disinterested operation of law-enforcing mechanisms. Both attempt and success depend upon political considerations and the actual distribution of power in a particular case. The protection of the rights of a weak nation that is threatened by a strong one is then determined by the balance of power as it operates in that particular situation. Thus the rights of Belgium were safeguarded in 1914 against their violation by Germany, for it so happened that the protection of those rights seemed to be required by the national interests of powerful neighbors. Similarly, when in 1950 South Korea was attacked by North Korea, their concern with the maintenance of the balance of power in the Far East and of territorial stability throughout Asia prompted the United States and some of its allies, such as France and Great Britain, to come to the aid of South Korea.

On the other hand, the rights of Colombia, when the United States supported the revolution in 1903 that led to the establishment of the Republic of Panama, and the rights of Finland, when attacked by the Soviet Union in 1939, were violated either with impunity or, as in the case of Finland, without the intervention of effective sanctions. There was no balance of power that could have protected these nations.

It must be pointed out, however, that the actual situation is much less dismal than the foregoing analysis might suggest. The great majority of the rules of international law are generally observed by all nations without actual compulsion, for it is generally in the interest of all nations concerned to honor their obligations under international law. A nation will hesitate to infringe upon the rights of foreign diplomats residing in its capital; for it has an interest, identical with the interests of all other nations, in the universal observance of the rules of international law that extend their protection to its own diplomatic representatives in foreign capitals as well as the foreign diplomats in its own capital. A nation will likewise be reluctant to disregard its obligations under a commercial treaty, since the benefits that it expects from the execution of the treaty by the other contracting parties are complementary to those anticipated by the latter. It may thus stand to lose more than it would gain by not fulfilling its part of the bargain. This is particularly so in the long run, since a nation that has the reputation of reneging on its commercial obligations will find it hard to conclude commercial treaties beneficial to itself.

Most rules of international law formulate in legal terms such identical or complementary interests. It is for this reason that they generally enforce themselves, as it were, and that there is generally no need for a specific enforcement action. In most cases in which such rules of international law are actually violated despite the underlying community of interests, satisfaction is given to the wronged party either voluntarily or in consequence of adjudication. And it is worthy of note that of the thousands of such judicial decisions that have been rendered in the last century and a half, voluntary execution was refused by the losing party in fewer than ten cases.

Thus the great majority of rules of international law are generally unaffected by the weakness of its system of enforcement, for voluntary compliance prevents the problem of enforcement from arising altogether. The problem of enforcement becomes acute, however, in that minority of important and generally spectacular cases, particularly important in the context of our discussion, in which compliance with international law and its enforcement have a direct bearing upon the relative power of the nations concerned. In those cases, as we have seen, considerations of power rather than of law determine compliance and enforcement. Two attempts have been made to remedy this situation and to give the executive function in international law at least a semblance of objectivity and centralization. Both attempts have failed, and for the same reason. One attempt, in the form of treaties of guaranty, can be traced to the beginning of the modern state system; the other, collective security, was first undertaken by the Covenant of the League of Nations.

Treaties of Guaranty

Taught by sad experience that the sacred and inviolable duty of fidelity to treaties is not always a safe assurance that they will be observed, men have sought to obtain securities against perfidy, means for enforcing observance independently of the good faith of the contracting parties. A guaranty is one of these means. When those who conclude a treaty of peace, or any other treaty, are not absolutely confident of its observance, they ask to have it guaranteed by a powerful sovereign. The guarantor promises to uphold the terms of the treaty and to procure their observance. As he may find himself obliged to use force, if either of the contracting parties should try to avoid the fulfillment of its promises, the position of guarantor is one which no sovereign will assume lightly or without good reasons. Princes seldom do so unless they have an indirect interest in the observance of the treaty or are induced by motives of friendship.[21]

This statement by Vattel, the greatest eighteenth-century authority on international law, defines well the motives and the legal content of treaties of guaranty, and does not fail to allude to their problematical nature as substitutes for a truly centralized organization of international law enforcement.

The simplest type of a treaty of guaranty is exemplified by what is generally considered to be the earliest such treaty in modern history: the Treaty of Blois of 1505 between France and Aragon, guaranteed by England. This guarantee signified that England took upon itself the legal obligation to perform the task of the policeman with regard to the execution of this treaty, promising to see that both parties remained faithful to it.

A more advanced type of international guarantee is to be found, for instance, in the guaranty of the territorial integrity of Turkey by the signatories of the Treaty of Paris of 1856 and of the Treaty of Berlin of 1878, and in the guaranty of the neutrality of Belgium and Luxembourg by the signatories of the treaties of 1831 and 1839, and 1867, respectively. In the Treaty of Mutual Guarantee of October 16, 1925, which forms part of the so-called Locarno Pact, Great Britain, Belgium, France, Germany, and Italy "collectively and severally guarantee . . . the maintenance of the *status quo* resulting from the frontiers between Germany and Belgium, and between Germany and France, and the inviolability of the said frontiers." In this type of treaty of guaranty, not one but a group of nations—generally most, if not all, of the great powers—pledge themselves, either severally or collectively, to enforce the legal provisions they have guaranteed against any violator, regardless of who he is.

In order to be able to fulfill their function as a substitute for centralized executive agencies, both types of treaties must meet two prerequisites: they must be effective in their execution, and the execution must be automatic. The effectiveness

---

[21]Emmerich de Vattel, *The Law of Nations* (Washington, DC: Carnegie Institution, 1916), Book II, § 235, p. 193.

of the execution, however, is again a function of the balance of power; that is to say, it depends upon the distribution of power between the guarantor nations and the lawbreaker. The distribution of power may favor the guarantor nations, especially in the case of collective guaranty, but not necessarily so. Particularly under modern conditions of warfare, situations can easily be visualized in which one lawbreaking great power will be able to withstand the united pressure of a great number of law-abiding guarantor nations.

Yet it is the uncertainty in applying the guaranty that vitiates its effectiveness altogether. One of the authoritative textbooks of international law has aptly pointed to the many loopholes through which a guarantor is able to evade the execution of the treaty without violating it. We read in Oppenheim-Lauterpacht:

> But the duty of the guarantors to render . . . the promised assistance to the guaranteed State depends upon many conditions and circumstances. Thus, first, the guaranteed State must request the guarantor to render assistance. Thus, secondly, the guarantor must at the critical time be able to render the required assistance. When, for instance, its hands are tied through waging war against a third State, or when it is so weak through internal troubles or other factors that its interference would expose it to serious danger, it is not bound to fulfil the request for assistance. So too, when the guaranteed State has not complied with previous advice given by the guarantor as to the line of its behaviour, it is not the guarantor's duty to render assistance.[22]

In other words, the obligation to guarantee compliance with international law through enforcement actions is no more stringent—and, if possible, rather less so—than the obligation to submit disputes to adjudication by an international court. In both cases the obligation is rendered virtually valueless by qualifications, reservations, and exceptions, covering all possible contingencies. Treaties of guaranty leave the executive function in the international field, for all practical purposes, as decentralized as it would be without them.

Collective Security

Collective security is the most far-reaching attempt on record to overcome the deficiencies of a completely decentralized system of law enforcement. While traditional international law leaves the enforcement of its rules to the injured nation, collective security envisages the enforcement of the rules of international law by all the members of the community of nations, whether or not they have suffered injury in the particular case. The prospective law-breaker, then, must always expect to face a common front of all nations, automatically taking collective action in defense of international law. As an ideal, collective security is without flaws; it presents indeed the ideal solution of the problem of law enforcement in a community of sovereign nations. But the two attempts that have been made to

---

[22]*International Law,* Vol. I, p. 966. (Reprinted by permission of Longmans, Green & Co., Inc.)

put the idea of collective security into practice—Article 16 of the Covenant of the League of Nations and Chapter VII of the Charter of the United Nations—fall far short of the ideal. In turn, the actual practice of the members of these two organizations has fallen far short of the collective measures authorized by these two documents.

Article 16 of the Covenant of the League of Nations

While the Covenant of the League of Nations today has only historical interest, the first three paragraphs of its Article 16[23] remain the pioneering attempt at putting a system of collective security into effect. The system of collective security provided for in these three paragraphs is from the outset limited to one type of violation of international law—that is, resort to war in violation of the provisions for the peaceful settlement of international disputes laid down in Articles 12, 13, and 15 of the Covenant.[24]

---

[23]Article 16 of the Covenant of the League of Nations reads:

1. Should any Member of the League resort to war in disregard of its covenants under Articles 12, 13 or 15, it shall *ipso facto* be deemed to have committed an act of war against all other Members of the League, which hereby undertake immediately to subject it to the severance of all trade or financial relations, the prohibition of all intercourse between their nationals and the nationals of the covenant-breaking State, and the prevention of all financial, commercial or personal intercourse between the nationals of the covenant-breaking State and the nationals of any other State, whether a Member of the League or not.

2. It shall be the duty of the Council in such case to recommend to the several Governments concerned what effective military, naval or air force the Members of the League shall severally contribute to the armed forces to be used to protect the covenants of the League.

3. The Members of the League agree, further, that they will mutually support one another in the financial and economic measures which are taken under this Article, in order to minimise the loss and inconvenience resulting from the above measures, and that they will mutually support one another in resisting any special measures aimed at one of their number by the covenant-breaking State, and that they will take the necessary steps to afford passage through their territory to the forces of any of the Members of the League which are cooperating to protect the covenants of the League.

4. Any Member of the League which has violated any covenant of the League may be declared to be no longer a Member of the League by a vote of the Council concurred in by the Representatives of all the other Members of the League represented thereon.

[24]Articles 12, 13, and 15 read:

Article 12

1. The Members of the League agree that if there should arise between them any dispute likely to lead to a rupture they will submit the matter either to arbitration or judicial settlement or to enquiry by the Council, and they agree in no case to resort to war until three months after the award by the arbitrators or the judicial decision or the report by the Council.

2. In any case under this Article the award of the arbitrators or the judicial decision shall be made within a reasonable time, and the report of the Council shall be made within six months after the submission of the dispute.

Article 13

1. The Members of the League agree that whenever any dispute shall arise between them which they recognise to be suitable for submission to arbitration or judicial settlement, and which cannot be satisfactorily settled by diplomacy, they will submit the whole subject-matter to arbitration or judicial settlement.

2. Disputes as to the interpretation of a treaty, as to any question of international law, as to the existence of any fact which, if established, would constitute a breach of any international obligation,

For all other violations of international law only the individualized, decentralized system of enforcement provided for by general international law is available.

The violations of international law that put the first three paragraphs of Article 16 into operation create the following four legal effects: (1) The lawbreaking nation "is deemed to have committed an act of war against all other members of the League." (2) The latter are under the legal obligation to isolate the lawbreaking nation, through a complete boycott, from any kind of intercourse with any other

---

or as to the extent and nature of the reparation to be made for any such breach, are declared to be among those which are generally suitable for submission to arbitration or judicial settlement.

3. For the consideration of any such dispute, the court to which the case is referred shall be the Permanent Court of International Justice, established in accordance with Article 14, or any tribunal agreed on by the parties to the dispute or stipulated in any convention existing between them.

4. The members of the League agree that they will carry out in full good faith any award or decision that may be rendered, and that they will not resort to war against a Member of the League which complies therewith. In the event of any failure to carry out such an award or decision, the Council shall propose what steps should be taken to give effect thereto.

Article 15

1. If there should arise between Members of the League any dispute likely to lead to a rupture, which is not submitted to arbitration or judicial settlement in accordance with Article 13, the Members of the League agree that they will submit the matter to the Council. Any party to the dispute may effect such submission by giving notice of the existence of the dispute to the Secretary-General, who will make all necessary arrangements for a full investigation and consideration thereof.

2. For this purpose, the parties to the dispute will communicate to the Secretary-General, as promptly as possible, statements of their case with all the relevant facts and papers, and the Council may forthwith direct the publication thereof.

3. The Council shall endeavor to effect a settlement of the dispute, and if such efforts are successful, a statement shall be made public giving such facts and explanations regarding the dispute and the terms of settlement thereof as the Council may deem appropriate.

4. If the dispute is not thus settled, the Council either unanimously or by a majority vote shall make and publish a report containing a statement of the facts of the dispute and the recommendations which are deemed just and proper in regard thereto.

5. Any Member of the League represented on the Council may make public a statement of the facts of the dispute and of its conclusions regarding the same.

6. If a report by the Council is unanimously agreed to by the members thereof other than the Representatives of one or more of the parties to the dispute, the Members of the League agree that they will not go to war with any party to the dispute which complies with the recommendations of the report.

7. If the Council fails to reach a report which is unanimously agreed to by the members thereof, other than the Representatives of one or more of the parties to the dispute, the Members of the League reserve to themselves the right to take such action as they shall consider necessary for the maintenance of right and justice.

8. If the dispute between the parties is claimed by one of them, and is found by the Council, to arise out of a matter which by international law is solely within the domestic jurisdiction of that party, the Council shall so report, and shall make no recommendation as to its settlement.

9. The Council may in any case under this Article refer the dispute to the Assembly. The dispute shall be so referred at the request of either party to the dispute provided that such request be made within fourteen days after the submission of the dispute to the Council.

10. In any case referred to the Assembly, all the provisions of this Article and of Article 12 relating to the action and powers of the Council shall apply to the action and powers of the Assembly, provided that a report made by the Assembly, if concurred in by the Representatives of those Members of the League represented on the Council and of a majority of the other Members of the League, exclusive in each case of the Representatives of the parties to the dispute, shall have the same force as a report by the Council concurred in by all the members thereof other than the Representatives of one or more of the parties to the dispute.

member of the community of nations. (3) The Council of the League is under the legal obligation to recommend to the member nations the military contribution to be made by them for the defense of the violated provisions of the Covenant. (4) The members of the League are under the legal obligation to give each other all economic and military assistance in the execution of the collective action.

The literal text of these provisions seems to create automatic obligations of a collective character with respect to points (1), (2), and (4). But with regard to point (3), which obviously is the most important, it limits itself to a recommendation the member nations must be free either to accept or to reject at their discretion. The appearances of point (1), (2), and (4) are, however, deceptive. The interpretative Resolutions, accepted by the Assembly of the League in 1921 and generally considered to be authoritative in fact, if not in law, have virtually eliminated the compulsory and automatic elements of Article 16 and have reduced the apparent obligations of the text to mere recommendations supported by nothing but the moral authority of the Council of the League.[25]

---

[25]The relevant Resolutions read as follows:

3. The unilateral action of the defaulting State cannot create a state of war: it merely entitles the other Members of the League to resort to acts of war or to declare themselves in a state of war with the covenant-breaking State; but it is in accordance with the spirit of the Covenant that the League of Nations should attempt, at least at the outset, to avoid war, and to restore peace by economic pressure.

4. It is the duty of each Member of the League to decide for itself whether a breach of the Covenant has been committed. The fulfilment of their duties under Article 16 is required from Members of the League by the express terms of the Covenant, and they cannot neglect them without breach of their Treaty obligations.

9. All States must be treated alike as regards the application of the measures of economic pressure, with the following reservations:

(a) It may be necessary to recommend the execution of special measures by certain states.

(b) If it is thought desirable to postpone, wholly or partially, in the case of certain States, the effective application of the economic sanctions laid down in Article 16, such postponement shall not be permitted except in so far as it is desirable for the success of the common plan of action, or reduces to a minimum the losses and embarrassments which may be entailed in the case of certain Members of the League by the application of the sanctions.

10. It is not possible to decide beforehand, and in detail, the various measures of an economic, commercial and financial nature to be taken in each case where economic pressure is to be applied. When the case arises, the Council shall recommend to the Members of the League a plan for joint action.

11. The interruption of diplomatic relations may, in the first place, be limited to the withdrawal of the heads of Missions.

12. Consular relations may possibly be maintained.

13. For the purposes of the severance of relations between persons belonging to the covenant-breaking State and persons belonging to other States Members of the League, the test shall be residence and not nationality.

14. In cases of prolonged application of economic pressure, measures of increasing stringency may be taken. The cutting off of the food supplies of the civil population of the defaulting State shall be regarded as an extremely drastic measure which shall only be applied if the other measures available are clearly inadequate.

15. Correspondence and all other methods of communications shall be subjected to special regulations. Humanitarian relations shall be continued.

16. Humanitarian relations shall be continued.

For the complete text, see League of Nations *Official Journal*, Special Supplement No. 6 (October 1921), pp. 24 ff.

First of all, the Resolutions, in contrast to the apparent purport of Article 16, establish the individualized, decentralized character of the League sanctions by declaring it to be the duty of each individual member nation to decide for itself whether a violation of international law has been committed and whether, therefore, Article 16 ought to apply at all. Furthermore, as interpreted by the Resolutions, point (1) authorizes the members of the League to resort to war with the law-breaking state, but does not create, as the literal meaning would indicate, a legal obligation in this respect. As regards points (2) and (4), the Resolutions leave to the individual nations the decision as to what measures they want to take against the lawbreaker and in support of one another. The Council acts as a mere coordinating agency with the power to make recommendations as to what measures ought to be taken, at what time, and by what nations, but without authority to bind the individual members against their will.

In sum, while the obligation to take action under Article 16 remains decentralized, the actions decided upon by the individual nations are to be executed under the centralized direction of the Council of the League. The Resolutions take a forward step in centralizing the technique of enforcement action decided upon by a number of individual nations. But, with respect to the compulsory and automatic character of the enforcement action, they fulfill the same function that reservations perform for compulsory adjudication and that exceptions and qualifications perform for treaties of guaranty—they reduce to the vanishing point the compulsory character of what purports to be a legal obligation.

The reformulation of Article 16 by the Assembly Resolutions amounts to the reaffirmation of the decentralized character of law enforcement. The practice of the League of Nations demonstrates the reluctance of the member nations to avail themselves of even the limited opportunities for the centralized execution of sanctions that the reformulated Article 16 offers. Collective measures of enforcement under Article 16 were applied in only one of the five cases in which undoubtedly a member of the League resorted to war in violation of the Covenant. With regard to the Sino-Japanese conflict that started in 1931, the Assembly of the League of Nations found unanimously that "without any declaration of war, part of the Chinese territory has been forcibly seized and occupied by the Japanese troops"[26] and that far-flung hostilities, initiated by Japan, had taken place between troops of the Chinese and Japanese governments. Yet the Assembly found also that Japan had not resorted to war in violation of the Covenant and that, therefore, Article 16 did not apply.

In 1934, during the Chaco War of 1932–35, when Paraguay continued hostilities against Bolivia in violation of the Covenant, many members of the League limited the arms embargo, originally imposed upon both belligerents, to Paraguay. This was a discriminatory measure falling far short of the spirit and the letter of the first paragraph of Article 16. When Japan, which by then had

---

[26]"League of Nations Assembly Report on the Sino-Japanese Dispute," *American Journal of International Law*, Vol. 27 (1933), Supplement, p. 146.

resigned from the League, invaded China in 1937, the Assembly found that Japan had violated the Nine Power Treaty of 1922 and the Briand-Kellogg Pact, that Article 16 was applicable, and that the members of the League had the right to take enforcement measures individually under that provision. No such measures were ever taken. When the Soviet Union went to war with Finland in 1939, it was expelled from the League by virtue of Article 16, paragraph 4, but no collective action of enforcement was taken against it.

In contrast to these cases, the Assembly found in 1935 that the invasion of Ethiopia by Italy constituted resort to war within the meaning and in violation of the Covenant and that, therefore, Article 16, paragraph 1, was to apply. In consequence, collective economic sanctions against Italy were decided upon and applied. Yet the two measures, provided for by Article 16, paragraph 1, that offered the best chance of making international law prevail under the circumstances and that in all probability would have compelled Italy to desist from its attack upon Ethiopia—namely, an embargo on oil shipments to Italy and the closure of the Suez Canal—were not taken. "However," as Sir H. Lauterpacht puts it, "although the sanctions of Article 16, paragraph 1, were formally put into operation and although an elaborate machinery was set up with a view to their successive and gradual enforcement, the nature of the action taken was such as to suggest that the repressive measures were being adopted as a manifestation of moral reprobation rather than as an effective means of coercion."[27]

One can, therefore, sum up the attempts at establishing a centralized system of law enforcement under Article 16 of the Covenant by saying that in most of the cases that would have justified the application of sanctions, sanctions were not applied at all. In the sole case in which they were applied, they were applied in such an ineffective fashion as virtually to assure both their failure and the success of the recalcitrant state.

Chapter VII of the Charter of the United Nations

Chapter VII of the Charter of the United Nations, comprising Articles 39–51, constitutes the counterpart to Article 16 of the Covenant of the League of Nations as the attempt to overcome the weakness of a decentralized system of international law enforcement. As such, it takes a long step toward the establishment of a centralized law enforcement agency. Articles 39, 41, and 42 of the Charter, which are the heart of the United Nations system of law enforcement, go far beyond anything that either the Covenant of the League of Nations or any other provision of international law has contemplated. They are, however, subject to three important qualifications and exceptions that, as we shall see, limit and under certain conditions even nullify the centralization of law enforcement for which the text of those articles provides.

---

[27]Oppenheim-Lauterpacht, *International Law* (6th ed., 1944), Vol. II, pp. 139–40. (Reprinted by permission of Longmans, Green & Co., Inc.)

The Covenant of the League of Nations leaves it to the individual nations to decide whether the Covenant has been violated. Resolution 4, interpreting Article 16 of the Covenant, reads: "It is the duty of each member of the League to decide for himself whether a breach of the Covenant has been committed." According to Resolution 6 the Council of the League renders no decision in this matter but only a recommendation with nothing more than moral authority. In contrast, Article 39 of the Charter of the United Nations reads: "The Security Council shall determine the existence of any threat to the peace, breach of the peace, or act of aggression and shall . . . decide what measures shall be taken in accordance with Articles 41 and 42 to maintain or restore international peace and security." It is the Security Council, and not the individual member states, that decides authoritatively in what situations measures of enforcement are to be taken. Such a decision is not a recommendation whose execution depends upon the discretion of the individual member states but is binding upon the latter, which in Article 25 of the Charter "agree to accept and carry out the decisions of the Security Council in accordance with the present Charter."

The same kind of binding, authoritative decision on the part of the Security Council determines the enforcement action to be applied in a particular case, and here again the discretion of the individual member states does not enter into the picture at all. With respect to economic sanctions dealt with in Article 41, the Security Council may "decide" and "call upon" the members to comply with its decisions. With respect to military sanctions, provided for in Article 42, the Security Council "may take . . . action." In order to make military action on the part of the Security Council possible, Article 43 imposes upon the member states the obligation "to make available to the Security Council . . . armed forces, assistance, and facilities . . . necessary for the purpose of maintaining international peace and security," and Article 45 emphasizes this obligation especially with respect to air force contingents "for combined international enforcement action." These obligations are to be discharged by way of agreements between the member states and the Security Council. The agreements shall determine "the numbers and types of forces, their degree of readiness and general location, and the nature of the facilities and assistance to be provided."

These agreements present the sole decentralized element in the enforcement scheme of Chapter VII of the Charter; for, by refusing to agree to more than a modest contribution to the military effort of the Security Council, a nation is in a position to limit correspondingly its subsequent obligations under the decisions of the Security Council. Or by withholding agreement altogether, it may evade completely the obligation to partake in military enforcement actions decided upon by the Security Council. In other words, the military factor of the enforcement mechanism of Chapter VII can be put into existence and operation only on condition that the individual member states agree individually to allow it to exist and operate. Once the military contingents have been created by individual agreements, the Security Council reigns supreme, and the discretionary power of the contracting nations has come to an end, at least within the limits of the law of the Charter.

Actually, the member states are still able, even after the conclusion of the agreements, to refuse, in violation of their obligation under Article 43, to heed the "call" of the Security Council and to make available to it the contingents and military facilities agreed upon. They can thus make the Security Council powerless to act. This, however, would be a kind of "mutiny" and as such an illegal act, the possibility of which all military establishments must take into account. Unlike other military establishments, however, the military establishment of the United Nations faces the possibility of not coming into existence at all if the subjects of the law do not take it upon themselves through voluntary agreements to bring it into existence.

The provisions of the Charter relative to military measures of law enforcement have thus far remained a dead letter, since no agreement under Article 43 has been concluded. In consequence, Article 106 of the Charter applies. This article provides that in the absence of such agreements the United States, Great Britain, the Soviet Union, China, and France shall "consult with one another and as occasion requires with other members of the United Nations with a view to such joint action on behalf of the organization as may be necessary for the purpose of maintaining international peace and security." With this the Charter of the United Nations reverts to the decentralization of the use of force to be found in Article 16 of the Covenant of the League of Nations and in common international law. Thus the will of the individual states—that is, decentralization—which we found at the foundation of international law with regard to legislation and adjudication, is at present still of the essence of law enforcement, insofar as the existence of the military establishment of the United Nations and, in its absence, the use of force in defense of the Charter are concerned.

This qualification of the enforcement system of Chapter VII of the Charter of the United Nations is not necessarily of an organic nature, for it will automatically become immaterial if and when the agreements of which Article 43 speaks will have been concluded. The Charter contains, however, two provisions of a different character. Their operation is not dependent upon a contingency such as the one envisaged by Article 106. They limit the operation of the enforcement system of Chapter VII necessarily and permanently. One is Article 51, and the other is to be found in Article 27, paragraph 3.

Article 51 stipulates that "nothing in the present Charter shall impair the inherent right of individual or collective self-defense if an armed attack occurs against a member of the United Nations." Individual self-defense as the right, in the absence of the law enforcement agent of the state, to meet an attack with commensurate force is an exception to centralized law enforcement, inherent in all legal systems, domestic or international. It would limit the law enforcement mechanism of the United Nations even though it were not expressly recognized by Article 51. Collective self-defense, on the other hand, is a newcomer to legal terminology and might even be considered a contradiction in terms. What Article 51 obviously aims at is the recognition of the right of any nation, whether directly attacked or not, to come to the aid of any nation that has been so attacked. This is, however, tantamount to the reaffirmation of the traditional principle of common international law: it is for the injured nation to enforce international law against the lawbreaker, and that nation can rely only upon the voluntary cooperation of other nations to make international law prevail. Insofar as a violation of international law takes the form of an armed attack, Article 51 reaffirms the decentralization of law enforcement, not only for the immediately injured nation but for all other nations as well.

It is true that Article 51 subjects this reaffirmation to three qualifications. They are, however, of a verbal rather than a substantive nature. First, the right of collective self-defense shall remain unimpaired only "until the Security Council has taken the measures necessary to maintain international peace and security." Second, measures taken in collective self-defense have to be reported immediately to the Security Council. And, third, such measures shall not affect the authority and responsibility of the Security Council to take appropriate action itself.

While the second qualification is obviously redundant, since it will duplicate the information that the Security Council must have already received through press, radio, and ordinary diplomatic channels, the other two qualifications are, in view of the situations likely to occur, virtually devoid of practical importance. An armed attack of A against B, to whose assistance C, D, and E come with their air, land, and naval forces, confronts the Security Council, especially under the conditions of modern warfare, with an accomplished fact to which it must adapt its enforcement measures. Air attacks will have been executed, battles will have been fought, territories will have been occupied, that is to say, a full-fledged war will have started by virtue of the right of collective self-defense. The Security Council, far from being able to stop that war and substitute for it its own enforcement measures, can only participate in it on terms that will necessarily be subordinated to the strategy of the individual belligerent states already engaged in full-scale hostilities. Once started as a measure of collective self-defense, a coalition war may receive the legal and political blessings and the active support of the United Nations. But it will hardly lose its initial character and be transformed into an enforcement action under the actual guidance of the Security Council.

The Veto

The real crux of the enforcement system of the United Nations, affecting every action to be taken by the Security Council under the provisions of Chapter VII, is Article 27, paragraph 3, of the Charter. It stipulates that "decisions of the Security Council . . . shall be made by an affirmative vote of nine members including the concurring votes of the permanent members." The permanent members, according to Article 23, are China, France, Great Britain, the Soviet Union, and the United States. This means that the consent of all five permanent members is needed for putting the enforcement machinery of Chapter VII into effect. Dissent by one of the permanent members is sufficient to make the execution of any enforcement measure impossible even when all the other fourteen members of the Security Council have consented. In other words, each of the permanent members has a veto with regard to any enforcement measure to be taken in pursuance of Chapter VII of the Charter.

Thus the veto reintroduces into the system of law enforcement of the United Nations the principle of decentralization by making the operation of the system dependent upon the will of each of the permanent members. The provisions of Chapter VII, which, as we have seen, constitute in themselves an important step toward the centralization of law enforcement, must be read in the light of Article 27, paragraph 3, which deprives them of much of their centralizing effect. More particularly, it incapacitates them for the performance of the function that concerns us here above all—namely, the imposition of effective restraints upon the struggle for power on the international scene. Three consequences of the veto are in this respect especially worthy of note.

First of all, the veto eliminates any possibility of centralized measures of law enforcement being applied against any of the permanent members. A permanent member as the prospective victim of such enforcement measures would simply veto the determination, required of the Security Council by Article 39, that "any threat to the peace, breach of the peace, or act of aggression" exists and that, therefore, any legal grounds exist for the application of enforcement measures. Even the raising of the issue of such measures would thus be precluded.

Second, if in view of Article 27, paragraph 3, the Security Council is capable at all of putting the enforcement machinery of the Charter into operation, it can do so only with regard to small and medium powers, that is, those that are not among the permanent members of the Security Council and, hence, cannot make centralized enforcement measures impossible through the veto. Yet, in view of the veto of the great powers, such measures will be applied even against the small and medium powers only under extraordinary circumstances. As international politics is constituted today, many of the small and medium powers are intimately aligned with one or the other of the great powers that dominate the international scene. They are unlikely to commit a breach of international law calling for enforcement measures under Chapter VII of the Charter without the encouragement or, at least, the approval of the great power with which they are aligned. Even without such alignment, any change in the status quo between two small nations anywhere in the world will have direct repercussions upon the relative power positions of the great powers that are the permanent members of the Security Council. The global political and military strategy of our time makes this inevitable.

Whether or not these permanent members will give their unanimous consent to enforcement measures against a medium or small nation will depend, therefore, not so much upon questions of international law as upon the power relations among the permanent members. If the latter are not pitted against one another in actual power contests, they might agree upon centralized enforcement measures. For, then, they can envisage with relative equanimity any future change in the power relations between the two quarreling nations. Whenever, on the other hand, two or more permanent members are actively engaged in the competition for power and, hence, when such enforcement measures will have a direct bearing upon their power positions, the unanimous consent of the permanent members will be impossible to obtain. By consenting to enforcement measures, at least one permanent member will weaken its own power position by weakening that of its friend and ally—that is, the prospective object of enforcement measures. That permanent member would have to take a stand against what it considers its own national interest. Such an eventuality must, of course, be discounted. In any event, putting into operation the centralized enforcement measures of Chapter VII depends upon the discretion of the permanent members of the Security Council, acting as individuals. The centralization of law enforcement, in large measure achieved by Chapter VII, is, therefore, largely nullified by Article 27, paragraph 3.

Finally, the veto eliminates for all practical purposes the qualifications by which Article 51 endeavors to subordinate the right of collective self-defense to the centralized enforcement system of Chapter VII. For it is hard to envisage a case of collective military action by a number of nations in which not at least one of the permanent members of the Security Council is involved on one or the other side. Under such circumstances, however, the requirement of unanimity of the permanent members according to Article 27, paragraph 3, either prevents the Security Council from taking any action, in which case the decentralized measures of self-defense will prevail as though the United Nations did not exist, or else vouchsafes the approval by the Security Council of the decentralized measures taken. In either case, the threat or the actuality of the veto will make it impossible for the Security Council to take centralized enforcement measures independently in the presence of decentralized measures already taken.

The picture that the Charter of the United Nations presents is, therefore, different from common international law only in its legal potentialities, hardly to be realized under present world conditions, but not in the actual operation of its system of law enforcement. The most important task of any such system is the imposition of effective restraints upon the struggle for power. This task the United Nations is incapable of performing at all where the need for its performance is greatest—that is, with respect to the great powers. For Article 27, paragraph 3, of the Charter puts the great powers beyond the reach of any enforcement action to be taken under the Charter. Insofar as the other nations are concerned, Articles 51 and 106 of the Charter operate as far-reaching reservations upon the general obligations under Articles 39, 41, and 42. The general political situation, as it affects the relations among the permanent members of the Security Council, in conjunction with Article 27, paragraph 3, militates against the latter's taking effective action in the field of law enforcement.

The "Uniting for Peace" Resolution

These weaknesses of the United Nations system of collective security were made obvious by their application to the aggression of North Korea against South Korea in June 1950. The Security Council was able to apply the collective security provisions of the Charter against North Korea only by virtue of the fact that the Soviet Union had absented itself temporarily from that body and, hence, could not veto the relevant resolutions. With the return of the Soviet Union to the Security Council, the General Assembly was called upon to carry the burden of organizing the collective action of the United Nations. The functions of the General Assembly with regard to measures of collective security are limited by Articles 10 and 18 of the Charter to making recommendations to the member states by a two-thirds majority. It is the nature of a recommendation to leave it to the discretion of the addressee whether or not he wishes to follow it. Hence, measures of collective security, taken by virtue of such recommendations, are completely decentralized.

The experience of the Korean War made most members of the United Nations aware of the impotence of the Security Council—permanent under present world conditions—to discharge its functions as an agency of collective security. Whatever measures of collective security the United Nations would be able to take in the future would have to be taken by the General Assembly. In consequence, in November 1950, the General Assembly passed the so-called Uniting for Peace Resolution, which attempts to strengthen the General Assembly as the principal agency for the organization of collective security. Its five main features are these:

1. A provision that the General Assembly can meet in twenty-four hours if the Security Council is prevented by the veto from exercising its primary responsibility for international peace and security.

2. A provision that in such cases the General Assembly can make recommendations to member states for collective measures, including the use of armed forces.

3. A recommendation that each member state maintain within its national armed forces elements that could promptly be made available for possible service as United Nations units.

4. The establishment of a Peace Observation Commission to observe and report in any area where international tension exists.

5. The creation of the Collective Measures Committee to study and report on the ways and means to strengthen international peace and security in accordance with the Charter of the United Nations.

The Collective Measures Committee has periodically reported to the General Assembly, which in turn has passed resolutions approving the work of the Committee and calling the attention of the member states to it.

In view of the fact that the General Assembly has the right only to recommend, but not to order, action on the part of the member states, the "Uniting for Peace" Resolution and the work of the Collective Measures Committee can have the purpose only of strengthening the willingness and ability of the member states to take speedy and effective action, in case the General Assembly should recommend such action. Thus it is natural that the Collective Measures Committee has concerned itself primarily with the stimulation of measures by the individual member states, the coordination of such measures, and their support with advice and supplementary measures by the Specialized Agencies of the United Nations.

The "Uniting for Peace" Resolution and the Collective Measures Committee, then, in view of the constitutional limitation under which they operate, cannot attempt to modify the decentralized character of the law enforcement measures the General Assembly may recommend to the member states. The member states remain as free as they ever were to comply or not to comply with these recommendations as they see fit. That decentralization forms the very constitutional foundation upon which the "Uniting for Peace" Resolution is based and upon which the Collective Measures Committee operates. The Resolution and the Committee ratify, as it were, that decentralization and endeavor to make decentralized enforcement actions as effective as such decentralized actions can be.[28]

In actuality the enforcement of international law remains, therefore, just as decentralized under the Charter of the United Nations as we found it to be under the Covenant of the League of Nations and in common international law. Wherever an attempt has been made to give international law the effectiveness of a centralized legal system, reservations, qualifications, and the general political conditions under which nations must act in the modern state system have nullified the legal obligations entered into for the purpose of establishing centralized functions.

No concerted efforts have been made to reform the legislative function of international law. But successive attempts have been made to reform the judicial and executive function. Against each such attempt the decentralized character of international law has reasserted itself. Decentralization, then, seems to be of the essence of international law itself. And the basic principle that makes decentralization inevitable is to be found in the principle of sovereignty.

---

[28]See, however, on the political transformation mitigating decentralization, pages 488 ff.

19 Sovereignty

THE GENERAL NATURE OF SOVEREIGNTY

Denunciation of the principle of sovereignty by those who realize the intimate connection between that principle and the weakness of a decentralized system of international law occurs much more frequently than does a serious endeavor to comprehend its nature and the function it performs for the modern state system. In consequence, despite the brilliant efforts of a few outstanding scholars, there is much confusion about the meaning of the term, and about what is and what is not compatible with the sovereignty of a particular nation.

The modern conception of sovereignty was first formulated in the latter part of the sixteenth century with reference to the new phenomenon of the territorial state. It referred in legal terms to the elemental political fact of that age—the appearance of a centralized power that exercised its lawmaking and law-enforcing authority within a certain territory. This power, vested at that time primarily, but not necessarily, in an absolute monarch, was superior to the other forces that made themselves felt in that territory. In the span of a century, it became unchallengeable either from within the territory or from without. In other words, it had become supreme.

By the end of the Thirty Years' War, sovereignty as supreme power over a certain territory was a political fact, signifying the victory of the territorial princes over the universal authority of emperor and pope, on the one hand, and over the particularistic aspirations of the feudal barons, on the other. The inhabitant of France found that nobody but the royal power could give him orders and enforce them. This experience of the individual French citizen was duplicated by the experience of the king of England or the king of Spain; that is to say, the supreme authority of the French king within French territory precluded them from exerting any authority of their own within that territory save by leave of the French king himself or by defeating him in war. But if the king of England and the king of Spain had no power in France, they had exclusive power in their own territories.

These political facts, present in the experience of the contemporaries, could not be explained by the medieval theory of the state. The doctrine of sovereignty elevated these political facts into a legal theory and thus gave them both moral approbation and the appearance of legal necessity. The monarch was now supreme within his territory not only as a matter of political fact but also as a matter of law. He was the sole source of manmade law—that is, of all positive law—but he was not himself subject to it. He was above the law, *legibus solutus*. His powers were, however, not limitless, for he remained bound by the divine law as it revealed itself in his conscience and as it was manifested in human reason as natural law.

The doctrine of sovereignty has retained its importance throughout the modern period of history, and in the conception of popular sovereignty it has provided the national democratic state with a potent political weapon. Yet it has also been subject to reinterpretations, revisions, and attacks, especially in the field of international law. The source of these doubts and difficulties lies in the apparent logical incompatibility of two assumptions that are of the essence of modern international law: the assumption that international law imposes legal restraints upon the individual nations and the assumption that these very same nations are sovereign—that is, the supreme law-creating and law-enforcing authorities—but not themselves subject to legal restraints. In truth, however, sovereignty is incompatible only with a strong and effective, because centralized, system of international law. It is not at all inconsistent with a decentralized, and hence weak and ineffective, international legal order. For national sovereignty is the very source of that decentralization, weakness, and ineffectiveness.

International law is a decentralized legal order in a dual sense. In the first place, its rules are, as a matter of principle, binding upon only those nations that have consented to them. In the second place, many of the rules that are binding by virtue of the consent given are so vague and ambiguous and so qualified by conditions and reservations as to allow the individual nations a very great degree of freedom of action whenever they are called upon to comply with a rule of international law. While the latter type of decentralization puts its imprint upon the judicial and executive functions of international law, the former is of paramount importance in the field of legislation.

Only a relatively small number of rules of international law do not owe their existence to the consent of the members of the international community. They are either the logical precondition for the existence of any legal system, such as rules of interpretation and rules providing sanctions, or they are the logical precondition for the existence of a multiple-state system, such as the rules delimiting the jurisdiction of individual states. Rules of this kind are binding upon all states, regardless of their consent, and might be called the common or necessary international law, the *jus necessarium* of the modern state system. Their binding force does not affect the sovereignty of the individual nations. Indeed, it makes sovereignty as a legal concept possible. For without the mutual respect for the territorial jurisdiction of the individual nation, and without the legal enforcement of that respect, international law and a state system based on it could obviously not exist.

Aside from these few common and necessary rules of international law, each individual nation is the highest lawgiving authority, insofar as the rules of international law binding upon it are concerned. No rules of international law are binding upon it but those it has created for itself through its consent. There is no lawgiving authority above it, for there is no state or group of states that can legislate for it. The decentralization of the legislative function in international law is, therefore, nothing but the principle of sovereignty as applied to the problem of legislation.

What holds true for the legislative function, with the sole qualification just mentioned, applies absolutely to the judicial and executive functions. The individual nation remains the supreme authority for deciding whether and under what conditions to submit a dispute to international adjudication, and no other nation can summon it before an international court without its consent. Where such consent is given in a general form, reservations make it generally possible to evade the jurisdiction of an international court in a concrete case without violating international law. Here again, decentralization of international adjudication is but another term for national sovereignty in respect to the judicial function.

In discussing sovereignty in the field of law enforcement, two situations must be distinguished. The sovereignty of the nation as law-enforcing agent is identical with sovereignty in the judicial field; that is, the ultimate decision as to whether and how to engage in a law-enforcing action lies with the individual nation. On the other hand, the sovereignty of the nation as the intended object of a law-enforcing action manifests itself in what is called the "impenetrability" of the nation. This is another way of saying that on a given territory only one nation can have sovereignty—supreme authority—and that no other state has the right to perform governmental acts on its territory without its consent. In consequence, all enforcement actions provided for by international law, short of war, are limited to the exercise of pressure upon the recalcitrant government—such as diplomatic protests, intervention, reprisal, and blockade—all of which leave intact the territorial sovereignty of the lawbreaking nation. War as the extreme form of law enforcement under international law is the only exception to that rule; for it is of the very essence of war to penetrate the territory of the enemy while safeguarding the "impenetrability" of one's own, and international law allows the occupying nation to exercise sovereign rights in the foreign territory occupied by its military force.

As the complete decentralization of the legislative, judicial, and executive functions is but so many manifestations of sovereignty, so are three other principles of international law synonymous with the concept of sovereignty and, indeed, the outgrowth of that concept. These principles are independence, equality, and unanimity.

SYNONYMS OF SOVEREIGNTY: INDEPENDENCE, EQUALITY, UNANIMITY

Independence signifies the particular aspect of the supreme authority of the individual nation that consists in the exclusion of the authority of any other nation. The statement that the nation is the supreme authority—that is, sovereign within a certain territory—logically implies that it is independent and that there is no authority above it. Consequently, each nation is free to manage its internal and external affairs according to its discretion, insofar as it is not limited by treaty or what we have earlier called common or necessary international law. The individual nation has the right to give itself any constitution it pleases, to enact whatever laws it wishes regardless of their effects upon its own citizens, and to choose any system of administration. It is free to have whatever kind of military establishment it deems necessary for the purposes of its foreign policy—which, in turn, it is free to determine as it sees fit.

As independence is, in the absence of treaty stipulations to the contrary, a necessary quality of all nations, so the duty to respect that independence is a necessary rule of international law. Unless it is abrogated by treaties, this rule prohibiting intervention is addressed to all nations. In 1931 the League of Nations intervened against a treaty between Germany and Austria establishing a customs union. This intervention could be justified only by certain treaty stipulations in which Austria had taken it upon itself to do nothing that might jeopardize its independence. In the absence of such special obligations by which Austria itself had limited its freedom of action, it would have been free to conclude whatever treaties it pleased with whatever parties it chose. In view of the purposes of our discussion, it is important to recognize not only the absence, in common international law, of any limitations upon the foreign policies of individual nations, but the positive duty, imposed upon all nations by common international law, not to interfere in the conduct of the foreign affairs of all other nations.

Equality, too, is nothing but a synonym for sovereignty, pointing to a particular aspect of sovereignty. If all nations have supreme authority within their territories, none can be subordinated to any other in the exercise of that authority. No nation has the right, in the absence of treaty obligations to the contrary, to tell any other nation what laws it should enact and enforce, let alone to enact and enforce them on the latter's territory. Being sovereign, nations cannot be subject to a lawgiving or law-enforcing power operating directly on their territory. International law is a law among coordinated, not subordinated, entities. Nations are subordinated to international law, but not to one another; that is to say, they are equal. When, therefore, Article 2 of the Charter of the United Nations declares that "the Organization is based on the principle of the sovereign equality of all its members," its redundant language emphasizes the importance it attributes to the principle of sovereignty and its logical corollary, the principle of equality.

From the principle of equality a fundamental rule of international law is derived that is responsible for the decentralization of the legislative and, in a certain measure, of the law-enforcing function: the rule of unanimity. It signifies that with reference to the legislative function all nations are equal, regardless of their size, population, and power. In any international conference creating new law for the international community, the vote of Panama counts as much as the vote of the United States, and the votes of both are required to make the new rules of international law binding for both. Were it otherwise, a large and powerful nation might be able to use its actual preponderance in representation to impose legal obligations upon a weak and small nation without the latter's consent. The powerful nation would thus make its own authority supreme within the territory of the small nation, destroying the latter's sovereignty. Under all circumstances the rule of unanimity gives each nation participating in the deliberations the right to decide for itself whether it wants to be bound by the decision. Whenever the consent of all participating nations is required in order to give legal validity to the decision, each nation has a right to veto the decision altogether by voting against the decision or withholding its consent.

The veto, then, in contrast to the strict rule of unanimity, has the effect of not only freeing the dissenting nation from any legal obligation under the decision but of stopping the lawgiving or law-enforcing process altogether. While the rule of unanimity is a logical consequence of sovereignty, this cannot be said of the veto. The rule of unanimity declares: without my consent your decision does not bind me. The veto declares: without my consent there is no decision at all. The veto, in other words, confronts the nations participating in the deliberations with the alternative of either agreeing upon a collective decision adhered to by all or of having no decision at all. With respect to this dual function, at once destructive and creative, the veto is more than a mere manifestation of sovereignty. Of this more will be said later.[1]

WHAT SOVEREIGNTY IS NOT

After having learned what sovereignty is, we now turn to the discussion of what sovereignty is not but is often believed to be.

1. Sovereignty is not freedom from legal restraint. The quantity of legal obligations by which the nation limits its freedom of action does not, as such, affect its sovereignty. The often-heard argument that a certain treaty would impose upon a nation obligations so onerous as to destroy its sovereignty is, therefore, meaningless. It is not the quantity of legal restraints that affects sovereignty but their quality. A nation can take upon itself any quantity of legal retraints and still remain sovereign, provided those legal restraints do not affect its quality as the supreme lawgiving and law-enforcing authority. But one single legal stipulation affecting that authority is in itself sufficient to destroy the sovereignty of the nation.

2. Sovereignty is not freedom from regulation by international law of all those matters that are traditionally left to the discretion of the individual nations or, as Article 15, paragraph 8, of the Covenant of the League of Nations[2] and Article 2, paragraph 7, of the Charter of the United Nations put it, are within the domestic jurisdiction of the individual nations. The relation between the matters international law regulates and those with which it does not concern itself is fluid. It depends upon the policies pursued by individual nations and upon the development of international law. Therefore, it is misleading to assert, for instance, that the international regulation of the immigration policies of individual nations would be incompatible with their sovereignty. This would hold true only for international

---

[1]See Chapters 27, 30.
[2]For the text see pages 305–07, note 24.

regulations to which the nations concerned had not consented beforehand. The conclusion of international treaties concerning matters of immigration would not affect the sovereignty of the contracting nations.

3. Sovereignty is not equality of rights and obligations under international law. Great inequalities in these respects can go hand in hand with sovereignty. Peace treaties frequently impose heavy disabilities upon the vanquished with regard to size and quality of the military establishment, armaments, fortifications, reparations, economic policies, and the conduct of foreign affairs in general. The defeated nation is not thereby deprived of its sovereignty. Germany, Austria, Hungary, and Bulgaria remained sovereign states despite the one-sided legal obligations with which the peace treaties of 1919 burdened them. The same peace treaties singled out other nations, such as Czechoslovakia, Poland, and Rumania, for special obligations concerning the treatment of certain racial and religious minorities among their own subjects. Rumania, together with Bulgaria, Montenegro, and Serbia, was subjected to such international obligations by the very treaty that in 1878 recognized it as a sovereign nation. Frequently, nations, having to comply with legal obligations of which other nations were free, have invoked the principles of sovereignty and equality in order to justify their demands for removal of those legal burdens. The issue in such cases has always been revision of treaties, not sovereignty.

4. Sovereignty is not actual independence in political, military, economic, or technological matters. The actual interdependence of nations in those matters and the actual political, military, and economic dependence of certain nations upon others may make it difficult or impossible for certain nations to pursue independent domestic and foreign policies, but it does not normally affect their supreme lawgiving and law-enforcing authority within their own territories—that is, their sovereignty.[3] They may be unable, because of prevailing actual conditions, to enact and enforce the kinds of laws that they would wish and that more powerful nations are able to enact and enforce. But the authority, within the limits of their obligations under international law, to enact and enforce the laws they please is not thereby abrogated. The actual inequality of nations and their dependence upon each other have no relevance for the legal status called sovereignty. Panama is as sovereign a nation as the United States, although in the choice of its policies and laws it is much more limited than the United States.

HOW SOVEREIGNTY IS LOST

Under what conditions, then, does a nation lose its sovereignty? What rules of international law and what kinds of international institutions created by them are actually incompatible with sovereignty? Where is the line to be drawn between legal and actual inequalities that leave sovereignty intact and that impairment of a nation's authority that destroys its independence?

[3]On the extreme situation in which sovereignty is thus lost, see pages 326 ff.

In theoretical terms the answer to these questions presents no difficulty. Sovereignty is the supreme legal authority of the nation to give and enforce the law within a certain territory and, in consequence, independence from the authority of any other nation and equality with it under international law. Hence, the nation loses its sovereignty when it is placed under the authority of another nation, so that it is the latter that exercises supreme authority to give and enforce the laws within the former's territory. Sovereignty can thus be lost in two different ways.

A nation may take upon itself legal obligations that give another nation final authority over its lawgiving and law-enforcing activities. Nation A will lose its sovereignty by conceding to Nation B the right to veto any piece of legislation enacted by its own constitutional authorities or any act of law enforcement to be performed by its own executive agencies. In this case the government of A remains the only lawgiving and law-enforcing authority actually functioning within the territory of A, but it is no longer supreme, since it is, in turn, subject to the control of the government of B. Through the exercise of that control, the government of B becomes the supreme authority and, hence, sovereign within the territory of A.

The other way in which sovereignty can be lost consists in the loss of what we have called the "impenetrability" of a nation's territory. Here the government of A is superseded as the lawgiving and law-enforcing authority by the government of B, which, through its own agents, performs the lawgiving and law-enforcing functions within the territory of A. The government of A, having lost authority altogether within the territory of A, survives in name and in appearances only, while the actual functions of government are performed by the agents of B.

Great difficulties, however, beset the application of these abstract standards to actual situations and concrete issues. At the root of the perplexities that attend the problem of the loss of sovereignty there is the divorce, in contemporary legal and political theory, of the concept of sovereignty from the political reality to which that concept is supposed to give legal expression.

Today, no less than when it was first developed in the sixteenth century, sovereignty points to a political fact. That fact is the existence of a person or a group of persons who, within the limits of a given territory, are more powerful than any competing person or group of persons and whose power, institutionalized as it must be in order to last, manifests itself as the supreme authority to enact and enforce legal rules within that territory. Thus the absolute monarch of the sixteenth and the following centuries was the supreme authority—that is, he was sovereign—within his territory, not as a matter of theoretical speculation or legal interpretation but as a political fact. He was more powerful than pope and emperor, on the one hand, and the feudal barons, on the other, and therefore he was able to give and enforce laws without interference from either.

Similarly, the federal government is today sovereign within the territory of the United States; for there is no supranational authority that could challenge its power, nor are there sectional or functional authorities within its territory that could think of doing so. This sovereignty, no less than the sovereignty of the French monarchy in the sixteenth century, is the result of the actual distribution of power in the state. It is, therefore, primarily the result of the Union's victory over the Confederacy in the Civil War. If the supreme authority of the federal government within the territory of the United States were to be whittled down by political or economic organizations strong enough to legislate for themselves and enforce their laws without effective control on the part of the federal government, a situation might arise similar to the one that confronted the emperor of the Holy Roman Empire when at the end of the Middle Ages the territorial states substituted their own supreme authority for his. The United States would then split into a number of territorial or functional units that would be actually sovereign although the federal government might still for a time, like the emperor, retain the legal attributes and the prestige of the sovereign power.

Four conclusions follow from the preceding discussion:

1. The location of sovereignty depends upon a dual test: (a) In what respects is the government of the state legally controlled by another government? and (b) Which government actually performs governmental functions within the territory of the state?

2. The location of sovereignty is a matter of political judgment as well as of legal interpretation.[4]

3. The location of sovereignty may be in temporary suspense if the actual distribution of power within a territory remains unsettled.

4. Sovereignty over the same territory cannot reside simultaneously in two different authorities; that is, sovereignty is indivisible.

The analysis, in the light of these four conclusions, of a number of historical situations will provide a test for the usefulness of the concept of sovereignty developed in these pages in view of the all-important question as to which international obligations are compatible with sovereignty, and which are not.

1. Before the declaration of Indian independence in 1947, the relations between the Indian states and Great Britain were regulated by treaties. While guaranteeing the internal independence of these states, these treaties gave to Great Britain the right to protect them against aggression, the administration of their foreign affairs, and the general supervision of their internal administration. Although most of these governments had virtually complete control within their territories, they were, in turn, completely controlled by the British government and, therefore, they were not sovereign. Both British and Indian courts have so decided.

2. It is instructive to contrast this situation with the so-called Platt Amendment, incorporated into the Treaty of Havana of 1901 between the United States and Cuba. The amendment obligated Cuba not to enter into any international treaty impairing its independence or giving control over any portion of Cuban territory to any foreign power. Cuba was not to contract any public debts

---

[4]Cf. Mr. Justice Holmes in *American Banana Co. vs. United Fruit Co.*, 213 U.S. 347 at 358 (1909): ". . . sovereignty is pure fact"; and in *The Western Maid*, 257 U.S. 419 at 432 (1921): "Sovereignty is a question of power, and no human power is unlimited."

that could not be taken care of by its ordinary revenue. It was to provide for the sanitation of its cities in order to prevent the recurrence of epidemic and infectious diseases. And it was to sell or lease to the United States lands necessary for coaling or naval stations at points to be agreed upon with the president of the United States. These provisions restricted to an unusual degree the discretion of the Cuban government in foreign and domestic affairs and even obligated it to surrender its sovereignty over certain parts of Cuban territory. But, since they did not substitute the American for the Cuban government as the supreme lawgiving and law-enforcing authority within the remainder of Cuban territory, these provisions did not affect the sovereignty of Cuba as such.

The situation is not so simple with regard to Article 3 of the Treaty of Havana, which reads that ". . . the government of Cuba consents that the United States may exercise the right to intervene for the preservation of Cuban independence, the maintenance of a government adequate for the protection of life, property, and individual liberty. . . ." This provision gave the government of the United States the right to take over the government of Cuba and thus to destroy Cuban sovereignty under conditions so general as to leave the discretion of the United States in this respect virtually without limits. Had the government of the United States chosen to avail itself of this right to the fullest extent and to establish its control permanently over the government of Cuba, Cuba would have been no more a sovereign state than were the Indian states under British domination. Had the United States, on the other hand, never made use of the right stipulated in Article 3 of the Treaty of Havana, the sovereignty of Cuba would have remained intact; for then the government of Cuba, in its actual lawgiving and law-enforcing operations, would have been permanently free from foreign control. It would have remained the supreme authority within the national territory, regardless of the legal possibility of foreign control.

Actually, however, the United States availed itself of the right under Article 3 of the Treaty of Havana and subjected the Cuban territory to military occupation from 1906 to 1909. During that period supreme authority within the Cuban territory was exercised by the armed forces of the United States, not by the government of Cuba. The government of Cuba, therefore, was no longer sovereign. Whether or not the government of Cuba regained sovereignty immediately after the evacuation of the American troops in 1909 is a question the answer to which depended upon the evaluation of the future political intentions of the United States with respect to Cuba. It could be answered unqualifiedly in the affirmative only if the government of the United States had made it clear in 1909 that it would abstain in the future from making use of Article 3 of the Treaty of Havana. In the absence of such a clarification of future intentions, the answer to our question could in 1909 be derived only from hunches as to what the policy of the United States was likely to be. Was the United States likely to pursue a policy of abstention in spite of its contractual right to intervene in Cuban affairs? Then sovereignty would have reverted to the government of Cuba. Was the United States, on the other hand, to be expected to resort to Article 3 of the Treaty of Havana in order to decide at least all important differences between itself and Cuba in its favor? Then supreme authority within the territory of Cuba would have passed to the United States. The question was answered definitely only in the Treaty of May 31, 1934, which abrogated Article 3 of the Treaty of Havana and reestablished without equivocation the sovereignty of the government of Cuba.

Thus the exercise of sovereignty is a political fact, defined and circumscribed in legal terms. Its determination may well depend upon gradual shifts in the exercise of political power from one government to another. It is to be detected through the appraisal of the political situation rather than through the interpretation of legal texts.[5]

3. We have pointed out above that the quantity of legal obligations by which a nation binds itself in its relations with other nations cannot, as such, affect its sovereignty. This statement requires elaboration in the light of the foregoing discussion. While it is true that a nation cannot lose its sovereignty by limiting its freedom of action through the conclusion of a great number of international treaties, it will have lost its sovereignty if its freedom of action no longer extends to those fundamental lawgiving and law-enforcing functions without which no government can under contemporary conditions maintain its authority within the national territory. In other words, it is not the quantity of legal commitments but their influence upon the quality of the government's political control that determines the issue of sovereignty.

Effective international control of atomic energy, in view of its actual military and prospective economic and social importance, would make the power of the agency exercising the control paramount within the territory of its operation. As a matter of political fact, such an agency would exercise supreme authority within the territory concerned; its control would be supranational rather than international. The national governments, however great their autonomy might be in all fields other than atomic energy, would have lost their sovereignty.

Two historical examples will make that issue clear: the relation between the permanent members of the Security Council and the other member states of the United Nations, and the position of the individual nations with regard to deviations from the principle of unanimity in international organizations other than the Security Council.

Majority Vote in International Organizations

It has been said frequently—in view of Article 27, paragraph 3, of the Charter of the United Nations—that while the permanent members of the Security Council have retained their sovereignty, the other members of the United Nations have lost theirs. The text of Article 27, paragraph 3, lends itself to such an interpretation; for, insofar as the relations between the permanent and the nonpermanent members of the Security Council and between the members of the Security Council and the other members of the United Nations are concerned, the majority

---

[5]The value of the criterion developed in the text might well be tested by the analysis of the status of such countries as the British Dominions, Egypt, and the Philippines in different periods of history.

principle replaces the principle of unanimity. In other words, "an affirmative vote of nine members including the concurring votes of the permanent members" of the Security Council binds all members of the Security Council, as well as all members of the United Nations. If such a majority vote could put the instrumentalities of law enforcement of the individual states at the disposal of the United Nations to be applied against any recalcitrant members, then the Security Council would indeed have supreme authority over the member states that are not permanent members of the Security Council. It, instead of the governments of those states, would be sovereign. While this result is legally possible by virtue of Article 27, paragraph 3, in conjunction with Articles 39, 41, and 42 of the Charter,[6] its actual realization depends upon three political conditions; none of these exists at present, and all three are not likely to exist simultaneously in the foreseeable future.

First, there must be unanimity as the legal manifestation of political harmony among the five permanent members of the Security Council in order that the Security Council exist at all as an operating law-enforcing agency. Second, the military forces that the member states agree, according to Articles 43 ff, to put at the disposal of the Security Council must be substantial enough to give the forces of the United Nations that would be available at any particular point unquestioned superiority over the forces of lawlessness. The military forces of the world, in other words, must be so distributed as to make the forces of the United Nations stronger than the national forces of any single nation or any likely combination of nations. Third, each member state must execute its obligations under the Charter, and especially under the military agreements, in good faith. It must sacrifice its national interests to the common good of the United Nations as defined by the Security Council. If these conditions were realized today or were capable of realization in the foreseeable future, one could indeed say that the Charter of the United Nations had eliminated, or was on its way to eliminating, the national sovereignty of those member states that are not permanent members of the Security Council.

Similarly, the contention is frequently advanced that unequal representation and majority decision in international agencies are incompatible with the sovereignty of the nations concerned. It was this argument that defeated all proposals for the establishment of a genuine international court at the two Hague Peace Conferences. It was widely used against the United States's joining the League of Nations and the Permanent Court of International Justice. Here again so sweeping an assertion needs to be qualified by political distinctions. In the light of these distinctions, unequal representation and majority rule may or may not be compatible with sovereignty. The answer would depend on whether or not this deviation from the rule of unanimity transfers supreme authority from the national governments to an international agency.

Aside from the International Court of Justice, where, as we have seen, the principle of unanimity is impossible of realization, a considerable number of

---

[6]For the text of these provisions, see pages 633–35.

international agencies, performing legislative, administrative, and executive functions, deviate from the principle of equal representation and unanimity. The European Communities have provided for unequal representation and also in large measure for different kinds of majority votes. Many international organizations determine the voting strength of their members on the basis of their financial contribution. On that basis the convention establishing the International Institute of Agriculture gave Great Britain twenty-two votes, the United States twenty-one, France nineteen, and so on. The international agreements creating the International Monetary Fund and the International Bank for Reconstruction and Development correlate voting strength to financial contribution. As a result, the United States has in both organizations more than a hundred times as many votes as the state with the lowest voting strength. Outright provision for majority rule is found in the Universal Postal Union, the International Danube Commission, the Food and Agricultural Organization, the International Civil Aviation Organization, the Economic and Social Council, and the Trusteeship Council of the United Nations. According to Article 18 of the Charter of the United Nations, each member of the General Assembly shall have one vote, and decisions shall be made by a majority of the members present and voting. Decisions on what Article 18, paragraph 2, calls "important questions" require a two-thirds majority.

The Security Council, in its composition as well as in its voting procedure, marks a departure from the principle of equal representation. According to Article 27, each member of the Security Council shall have one vote, and its decisions on procedural matters shall be made by an affirmative vote of nine out of the fifteen members. But their permanent representation, according to Article 23, gives China, France, Great Britain, the Soviet Union, and the United States an automatic preponderance in the decisions of the Security Council over the ten nonpermanent members elected periodically by the General Assembly. This preponderance is considerably enhanced by the right of the permanent members to veto the nonprocedural decisions of the Security Council according to Article 27, paragraph 3.

Evaluation of the bearing that these departures from the principle of equal representation have upon the sovereignty of the nations concerned must again be guided by the criterion of where, in consequence of these departures, the supreme lawgiving and law-enforcing authority within the territories of these nations is located. What is decisive in this respect is again not how and in how many different matters and organizations a nation is outvoted by others but in what kinds of matters. Here, too, the test is qualitative, not quantitative. The fact that a nation is under legal obligation to execute the majority decision of an international organization with regard to the postage on letters in international traffic does not affect its quality as the supreme lawgiving authority within the national territory. The nation has consented to forgo freedom of action where, by virtue of its sovereignty, freedom of action would exist in the absence of such consent. But it has not renounced its sovereignty.

The nation would have renounced its sovereignty if it had consented to submit to the majority vote of an operating international agency such matters as amendments to the constitution, declaration of war and conclusion of peace, size, composition, and activities of the armed forces, composition of the government, and financial policies. Then, by virtue of the international agreement establishing majority rule, the decisive political power would have shifted from the national government to the international agency. It would no longer be the national government but the international agency that would hold supreme power and, hence, exercise supreme lawgiving and law-enforcing authority within the national territory.

It must be obvious from what has been said that nowhere on the contemporary international scene do deviations from the rule of unanimity affect the sovereignty of the individual state. International adjudication is surrounded by elaborate safeguards that prevent matters of political importance from being decided by the majority vote of an international court. The majority vote in international administrative organizations is able to dispose of technical matters only, matters that have no significance for the distribution of power among national governments or between national governments and international agencies. The majority vote in the General Assembly of the United Nations is in the nature of a recommendation and, hence, is not binding upon the members. The strict majority decision of the Security Council, according to Article 27, paragraph 2, of the Charter, deals only with procedural matters that can have no bearing upon the supreme authority of the member states within their territories. The potentialities for superseding the national sovereignties with the sovereignty of the Security Council, which are legally implicit in Article 27, paragraph 3, are, as has been shown, incapable of realization at present or in the foreseeable future.

IS SOVEREIGNTY DIVISIBLE?

Our discussion has brought us to the last and perhaps the most important of the misunderstandings that have obscured the problem of sovereignty in the modern world—the belief that sovereignty is divisible. Elucidation of this misunderstanding may aid us in assessing the role of sovereignty, and of international law in general, in contemporary international politics. We have heard it said time and again that we must "surrender part of our sovereignty" to an international organization for the sake of world peace, that we must "share" our sovereignty with such an organization, that the latter would have "limited sovereignty" while we would keep the substance of it, or vice versa, that there are "quasi-sovereign" and "half-sovereign" states. We shall endeavor to show that the conception of a divisible sovereignty is contrary to logic and politically unfeasible, but that it is a significant symptom of the discrepancy between the actual and pretended relations existing between international law and international politics in the modern state system.

If sovereignty means supreme authority, it stands to reason that two or more entities—persons, groups of persons, or agencies—cannot be sovereign within the same time and space. He who is supreme is by logical necessity superior to everybody else; he can have no superior above him or equals beside him. If the president of the United States is the commander-in-chief of the armed forces, it is logically absurd to assert that somebody else, say, the secretary of defense, shares with him supreme authority over the armed forces. The Constitution might have divided this supreme authority between the two officials along functional lines, just as, according to medieval doctrine, supreme authority was divided between emperor and pope; the president might, then, have supreme authority over the organization and supply of the armed forces, and the secretary of defense over their military operations. If this were the actual division of authority and the actual distribution of functions, nobody would be commander-in-chief because nobody would have supreme overall authority over the armed forces. The office of commander-in-chief could not logically exist. Either the president commands the armed forces with ultimate authority, or somebody else does, or nobody does. These alternatives are logically conceivable, although not all of them, as we shall see, are politically feasible. But that the president as well as somebody else commands the armed forces with ultimate authority at the same time is both logically untenable and politically unfeasible.

A consideration of the actual political functions fulfilled by the sovereign authority within the state will make it clear that sovereignty cannot be divided in political actuality. Sovereignty signifies supreme lawgiving and law-enforcing authority. In other words, that authority within the state is sovereign which, in case of dissension among the different lawmaking factors, has the responsibility for making the final binding decision and which, in a crisis of law enforcement, such as revolution or civil war, has the ultimate responsibility for enforcing the laws of the land. That responsibility must rest somewhere—or nowhere. But it cannot be here and there at the same time. As Mr. Justice Sutherland said in *United States vs. Curtiss Wright Export Corporation*: "A political sovereignty cannot endure without a supreme will somewhere. Sovereignty is nowhere held in suspense."[7] If it rests nowhere—and there are constitutions, such as the Constitution of the Fourth French Republic, which seemed to assign no place to it—in times of constitutional crisis one of the constitutional authorities will usurp that responsibility, as did the French army in 1958, or else revolution will invest somebody, a Napoleon or a Council of People's Commissars, with supreme authority to make an end to chaos and establish order and peace. If the location of sovereignty seems to be held in abeyance because the constitution lends itself to different interpretations on that point, a struggle, political or military, between the pretenders to supreme authority will decide the question one way or the other. The struggle between our federal government and the states, issuing in a civil war that decided the question in favor of the federal government, is a classic example of this situation.

The simple truth that a divided sovereignty is logically absurd and politically unfeasible was never doubted by the members of the Constitutional Convention

---

[7]299 U.S. 304 at 316, 317 (1936).

of 1787, save one.[8] Those who believed that sovereignty ought to be vested in the states, as well as those who wanted it to be located in a central government, were convinced that it must reside either here or there but could not be divided between both. "I hold it for a fundamental point," wrote Madison to Randolph on April 8, 1787, "that an individual independence of the states is utterly irreconcilable with the idea of an aggregate sovereignty."[9] "We have been told," declared James Wilson on the floor of the Convention, "that, each state being sovereign, all are equal. So each man is actually a sovereign over himself, and all men are therefore naturally equal. Can he retain his equality when he becomes a member of a civil government? He cannot. As little can a sovereign state, when it becomes a member of a federal government. If New Jersey will not part with her sovereignty, it is vain to talk of government."[10] In the words of Hamilton: "Two sovereignties cannot co-exist within the same limits."[11] The same point was made later by John C. Calhoun in defense of the sovereignty of the states. "But how sovereignty itself–the supreme power–can be divided–how the people of the several States can be partly sovereign and partly *not* sovereign–partly supreme, and partly *not* supreme, it is impossible to conceive. Sovereignty is an entire thing;–to divide, is,–to destroy it."[12] "In spite of all that has been said, I maintain that sovereignty is in its nature indivisible. It is the supreme power in a State, and we might just as well speak of half a square or half of a triangle, as of half a sovereignty. It is a gross error to confound the exercise of sovereign powers with sovereignty itself, or the delegation of such powers with surrender of them."[13]

It was Madison, however, who put his finger on the qualitative element of political authority, in contrast to the "more or less" of treaty obligations, as the distinctive characteristic of the sovereignty of a government and, as such, incompatible with the sovereignty of those subordinate to it. Madison declared on June 28, 1787, on the floor of the Convention:

> This fallacy of the reasoning drawn from the equality of sovereign states, in the formation of compacts, lay in confounding mere treaties, in which were specified certain duties to which the parties were to be bound and certain rules by which their subjects were to be reciprocally governed in their intercourse, with a compact by which an authority was created paramount to the parties, and making laws for the government of them. If France, England, and Spain were to enter into a treaty for the regulation of commerce, &c., with the Prince of Monaco, and four or five other of the smallest sovereigns of Europe, they would not hesitate to treat as equals, and to make the regulations perfectly

---

[8]The exception is Dr. William S. Johnson. See *Debates on the Adoption of the Federal Constitution*, Vol. V of Elliot's *Debates* (Washington, 1845), p. 221.

[9]Ibid., p. 107.

[10]Ibid., p. 177.

[11]Ibid., p. 202; cf. also p. 199. The same point is made by Dr. Johnson, who said, in contrast to his remarks referred to in note 8, that sovereignty "can be but one in the same community" (Ibid., p. 448).

[12]*The Works*, Vol. I (The General Assembly of the State of South Carolina, 1851), p. 146.

[13]*The Works*, Vol. II (The General Assembly of the State of South Carolina, 1853), p. 233.

reciprocal. Would the case be the same if a council were to be formed of deputies from each, with authority and discretion to raise money, levy troops, determine the value of coin, &c.?[14]

Democratic constitutions, especially those consisting of a system of checks and balances, have purposely obscured the problem of sovereignty and glossed over the need for a definite location of the sovereign power. For while it is the main concern of these constitutions to create devices for the limitation and control of personal power, the clearest case of a definitely located sovereignty is the unfettered authority of Hobbes's *Leviathan*, the source not only of law but of ethics and mores as well. Thus the popular constitutional doctrines, rightly fearful of the unlimited power of absolute monarchy and of the risks of personal government, confounded the subjection of the sovereign authority to legal controls and political restraints with its elimination. In their endeavor to make democracy "a government of laws and not of men," they forgot that in any state, democratic or otherwise, there must be a man or a group of men ultimately responsible for the exercise of political authority. Since in a democracy that responsibility lies dormant in normal times, barely visible through the network of constitutional arrangements and legal rules, it is widely believed that it does not exist and that the supreme lawgiving and law-enforcing authority, which was formerly the responsibility of one man, the monarch, is now distributed among the different coordinate agencies of the government and that, in consequence, no one of them is supreme. Or else that authority is supposed to be vested in the people as a whole, who, of course, as such cannot act. Yet in times of crisis and war that ultimate responsibility asserts itself, as it did under the presidencies of Lincoln, Wilson, and the two Roosevelts, and leaves to constitutional theories the arduous task of arguing it away after the event.

In federal states, monarchical or democratic, ideological satisfaction must be given to the individual states that, once having been sovereign, are so no longer, yet are loath to admit it. To that end political practice develops a whole system of constitutional flatteries that bestows upon the officials and symbols of the individual states the honors due the officials and symbols of the sovereign states and that makes use of concepts and constitutional devices that have meaning only with reference to sovereign states.[15] Since it is constitutionally and politically impossible to deny that the federal government is sovereign, and since it is psychologically impossible to admit that the individual states are no longer sovereign, constitutional theory simply divides sovereignty between the federal government and the states, thus trying to reconcile political realities with political preferences. So it came about that Hamilton and Madison, who had emphatically proclaimed the indivisibility of sovereignty on the floor of the Convention of 1787, were just as emphatic in their insistence upon the divisibility of sovereignty when a year later

---

[14]Ibid., p. 250; cf. also Patterson, ibid., p. 194.
[15]The constitutional practices of the United States, of the Soviet Union, and of Germany under the Constitution of 1871 illustrate this point.

in *The Federalist* they endeavored to persuade the states that they could keep their sovereignty even though they endowed the federal government with the sovereign powers provided for in the new Constitution.[16]

Because of a similar need for building an ideological bridge between political realities and political preferences, the doctrine of divided sovereignty has gained wide acceptance in the field of international relations. On the one hand, the nation-state is to a higher degree than ever before the predominant source of the individual's moral and legal valuations and the ultimate point of reference for his secular loyalties. Consequently, its power among the other nations and the preservation of its sovereignty are the individual's foremost political concerns in international affairs. On the other hand, it is that very power and sovereignty, clashing under the conditions of modern civilization with the power and sovereignty of other nations, which imperils the existence of that civilization and, with it, of the nation-states themselves.

Thus, since the end of the Napoleonic Wars, humanitarians and statesmen have with ever-increasing frequency and intensity searched for means to avoid the self-destructive wars to which the struggle for power among modern nation-states gives rise. It has, however, become more and more obvious, especially in recent years, that the main stumbling block that thus far has vitiated all attempts at restraining the struggle for power on the international scene is national sovereignty itself. As long as the supreme lawgiving and law-enforcing authority remains vested in the national governments, the threat of war, especially under the moral, political, and technological conditions of our age, may be said to be unavoidable. Thus the political reality of the likelihood of self-destructive war confronts the political preference for the preservation of national sovereignty. While people everywhere are anxious to free themselves from the threat of war, they are also anxious to preserve the sovereignty of their respective nations. Yet, if the price of peace were only a slice of sovereignty and not the whole of it, if in order to lessen the likelihood of war it were necessary for the nation-state only to share sovereignty with an international organization and not to give it up altogether, one might have peace and national sovereignty at the same time.

In a public opinion poll taken in the spring of 1947, 75 percent of the people answered in the affirmative the question: "Would you like to see the United States join in a movement to establish an international police force to maintain world peace?" However, only 15 percent of the total population and 17 percent of those in favor of an international police force were willing to consent to the United States armed forces being smaller than the international police force.

---

[16]Cf. C. E. Merriam, *History of the Theory of Sovereignty Since Rousseau* (New York: Columbia University Press, 1900), p. 161: "The constitution reflected, therefore, the political facts and the political theory of the time in its peculiar division of powers between local and central governments, and in its failure to define clearly and explicitly the ultimate source of sovereign power."

For the general phenomenon of the discrepancy between theories of sovereignty and the political reality of sovereignty, see also Ernest Barker, *Essays on Government* (Oxford: Oxford University Press, 1945), pp. 88, 89.

"Only 13 percent of all the people want the United States to join in an international police force and are also willing to have the police force outnumber the armed forces of this country."[17] In other words, while a considerable majority of the American people favored an international organization capable of preventing war, only a small minority of those favoring such an organization (as well as of the people as a whole) were willing to transfer supreme law-enforcing authority—that is, sovereignty—from the United States to an international organization. The majority wanted to have it both ways; they wanted to "divide" sovereignty. It is significant in this respect that while 32 percent of those favoring an international police force wanted the American forces to be larger than the international police force, 41 percent, by far the largest of the groups expressing an opinion on the matter, wanted them to be of equal size. They want to "divide" sovereignty fairly and equitably by leaving 50 percent with the United States and giving 50 percent to an international organization.

The belief in a divisible sovereignty is the ideological manifestation of this contradiction between political reality and political preference. The doctrine of the divisibility of sovereignty makes it intellectually feasible to reconcile not only what logic proves to be incompatible—to give up sovereignty while retaining it—but also what experience shows to be irreconcilable under the conditions of modern civilization—national sovereignty and international order. Far from expressing a theoretical truth or reflecting the actuality of political experience, the advice to give up "a part of national sovereignty" for the sake of the preservation of peace is tantamount to the advice to close one's eyes and dream that one can eat one's cake and have it, too.

---

[17]*UNESCO and Public Opinion Today* (Chicago: National Opinion Research Center, 1947), Report No. 35, pp. 12 ff. A number of other polls, taken after the Second World War in this country and in Great Britain, have had similar contradictory results. Cf. particularly *Peace and the Public: A Study by Mass-Observation* (London, New York, Toronto: Longmans, Green, 1947).

PART SEVEN

INTERNATIONAL POLITICS IN THE CONTEMPORARY WORLD

20 The New Moral Force of Nationalistic Universalism

NATIONALISM, OLD AND NEW[1]

We should now be able to answer the question we asked when we pointed to the intellectual and moral tradition of the Western world as the force that through the instrumentality of the balance of power kept the modern state system together from the end of the religious wars to the First World War. What is left of this heritage today? we asked then. What kind of consensus unites the nations of the world in the period following the Second World War?[2]

The answer can be only that the moral limitations upon the struggle for power on the international scene are weaker today than they have been at any time in the history of the modern state system. The one international society of the seventeenth and eighteenth centuries has been replaced by a number of national societies that provide for their members the highest measure of social integration. In consequence, the international morality that in past centuries kept the aspirations for power of the individual nations within certain bounds has, except for certain fragmentary restraints, given way to the morality of individual nations. This morality not only does not recognize any moral obligations above and apart from it but even claims universal recognition from all the world. World public opinion is but an ideological shadow without even that substance of common valuations and reactions that in other times at least the international aristocracy shared. The main bulk of the rules of international law owes its existence to the sovereignty of the individual nations. To surround that sovereignty with legal safeguards is one of the main tasks of the rules of international law. Far from restraining the aspirations for power of individual nations, they see to it that the power position of individual nations is not adversely affected by whatever legal obligations they take upon

---

[1]This part reformulates the discussion, on pages 231 ff, of the problem of nationalism and nationalistic universalism.
[2]See page 231.

themselves in their relations with other nations. What national morality is in the field of ethics, what national public opinion is in the domain of the mores, sovereignty is for international law. Sovereignty refers in legal terms to the nation as the recipient of the individual's ultimate secular loyalties, as the mightiest social force, as the supreme authority giving and enforcing laws for the individual citizen.

The supranational forces, such as universal religions, humanitarianism, cosmopolitanism, and all the other personal ties, institutions, and organizations that bind individuals together across national boundaries, are infinitely weaker today than the forces that unite peoples within a particular national boundary and separate them from the rest of humanity. This weakening of the supranational forces, which must be strong in order to impose effective restraints upon the foreign policies of nations, is but the negative by-product of the great positive force that shapes the political face of our age—nationalism. Nationalism, identified as it is with the foreign policies of individual nations, cannot restrain these policies; it is itself in need of restraint. Not only has it fatally weakened, if not destroyed, the restraints that have come down to us from previous ages, it has also supplied the power aspirations of individual nations with a good conscience and a messianic fervor. It has inspired them with a thirst and a strength for universal dominion of which the nationalism of the nineteenth century knew nothing.

The nationalism of the late twentieth century is essentially different from what traditionally goes by that name and what culminated in the national movements and the nation-state of the nineteenth century. Traditional nationalism sought to free the nation from alien domination and give it a state of its own. This goal was considered to be a rightful one not for one nation only, but for all nations. Once a nation had united its members in one state, national aspirations were satisfied, and there was room for as many nationalisms as there were satisfied, and there was room for as many nationalisms as there were nations that wanted to establish or preserve a state of their own.

The international conflicts in which the nationalism of the nineteenth century was involved were, therefore, essentially of two kinds: the conflicts between a nationality and an alien master—the Balkan nations and Turkey, the Slav nations of the Danube basin and the Austro-Hungarian monarchy, the Poles and Russia—and the conflicts between different nationalities over the delimitation of their respective spheres of dominion, such as the struggle between the Germans, on the one hand, and the Poles and the French, on the other. International conflicts in the nineteenth century grew out of either different interpretations of the national principle or the refusal to accept it at all. It was hoped as late as the aftermath of the First World War that, once the aspirations of all nations for nation-states of their own were fulfilled, a society of satisfied nations would find in the legal and moral principles of national self-determination the means for its own preservation.

To call by the same name what inspired the oppressed and competing nationalities of the nineteenth century and what drives the superpowers of the late twentieth century into deadly combat is to obscure the fundamental change that separates our age from the preceding one. The nationalism of today, which is really a nationalistic universalism, has only one thing in common with the nationalism of the nineteenth century—the nation as the ultimate point of reference for political loyalties and actions. But here the similarity ends. For the nationalism of the nineteenth century, the nation is the ultimate goal of political action, the end-point of the political development beyond which there are other nationalisms with similar and equally justifiable goals. For the nationalistic universalism of the late twentieth century, the nation is but the starting point of a universal mission whose ultimate goal reaches to the confines of the political world. While nationalism wants one nation in one state and nothing else, the nationalistic universalism of our age claims for one nation and one state the right to impose its own valuations and standards of action upon all the other nations.

This evil would not necessarily be mitigated, but might be aggravated, by the fusion of a number of nations into a supranational union. The nations of Western Europe, for instance, are too weak to make themselves singly the effective spear-heads of the new nationalistic universalism. The time has passed when the French or the Germans could dream of making the world over in their own image. Yet if the nations of Western Europe were able to unite and form a new political and military unit of considerable potentialities, they would then have acquired the power basis for a new crusading spirit, common to all of Western Europe, to compete with the nationalistic universalism of other nations. That the traditional nation-state is obsolescent in view of the technological and military conditions of the contemporary world is obvious. Yet, while trying to replace it with a larger unit, better attuned to these conditions, it is well to take care that it not be replaced simply by a more efficient vehicle for the crusading nationalism of our age.

It is one of the characteristics of nationalistic universalism, stemming from its universalistic character and aspirations, that, although it is connected with a nation, it is not connected with any particular one. The Soviet Union has indeed been the vehicle on which Communism has tried to transform the world. But who can say that in this respect China or some other nation will not tomorrow take the place of the Soviet Union, at least in Asia? The nationalism of the nineteenth century grew indeed from the peculiar character and aspirations of a particular nation and could not be divorced from it without losing its meaning and functions. The nationalistic universalism of our age is different in these respects. It is a secular religion, universal in its interpretation of the nature and destiny of man and in its messianic promise of salvation for all mankind. A particular nation will bear its torch at any particular time, but in principle any nation can. Thus the claims to universal dominion in the name of the new crusading nationalism may shift from nation to nation according to the conditions of spirit and power.

THE STRUGGLE FOR THE MINDS OF MEN[3]

This new moral force of nationalistic universalism has added a new dimension to the structure of international politics: that of psychological warfare or propaganda. There is, of course, nothing new in the use of propaganda for purposes of foreign

[3]See also pages 161–62.

policy; it has been sporadically used for such purposes on a small scale since time immemorial. The dominant factions in the Greek and Italian city-states tried to win their politial battle by enlisting for their foreign policies the support of the foreigners sympathetic to their political philosophies and by winning converts among them. In the religious conflicts of the sixteenth and seventeenth centuries and in the wars of revolutionary France, the exploitation of religious and philosophic sympathies and the recruitment of religious and philosophic sympathizers among foreigners was developed into a potent weapon of political and military warfare. The Protestant prince who was able to convert the population of his Catholic opponent to his faith or to exploit the religious sympathies of the Protestant minority for his political and military purposes might win a battle, if not the war, without firing a shot. The convert to the ideas of the French Revolution was likely to be an active supporter of the foreign policies of revolutionary France.

Contemporary propaganda is quantitatively and qualitatively different from that of previous ages. Because of modern technology, its range and effectiveness have increased enormously since the Second World War. It has become an autonomous instrument of foreign policy, coordinated with the traditional instruments of diplomacy and military force. Thus during the monolithic period of Communism, Communists anywhere supported the foreign policies of the Soviet Union, and adherents of democracy at least opposed the foreign policies of the Soviet Union, if they were not active champions of those of the United States. The more Communists there were, the stronger was the support for the foreign policies of the Soviet Union; and the success of the foreign policies of the United States in large measure depended upon the strength and spread of anti-Communist convictions throughout the world. The outcome of an election or a civil war would determine the future course of a nation's foreign policy. If the Communist Party won, the country might align itself with the Soviet Union; if the democratic parties won, it might either remain uncommitted or support the United States. To forestall such adverse developments in the domestic distribution of power in other nations, and to promote favorable ones, becomes of vital concern to the contestants in the struggle of political philosophies for the allegiance of men.

Psychological warfare or propaganda joins diplomacy and military force as the third instrument by which foreign policy tries to achieve its aims. Regardless of the instrument employed, the ultimate aim of foreign policy is always the same: to promote one's interests by changing the mind of the opponent. To that end, diplomacy uses the persuasiveness of promises and threats in terms of the satisfaction or the denial of interests; military force, the physical impact of actual violence upon the opponent's ability to pursue certain interests; and propaganda, the use and creation of intellectual convictions, moral valuations, and emotional preferences in support of one's own interests. All foreign policy, then, is a struggle for the minds of men; but propaganda is so in the specific sense that it endeavors to mold the minds of men directly rather than through the intermediary of the manipulation of interests or physical violence.

Diplomacy and warfare look back upon a long and continuous history; hence, the theoretical comprehension of their principles is far advanced. Propaganda as an autonomous instrument of foreign policy is a novelty; its theory and practice bear the marks of inexperience.

THREE PRINCIPLES OF PROPAGANDA

What are the fundamental principles that must guide the struggle for the minds of men, fought with the weapons of propaganda? Three problems, frequently obscured in theory and mismanaged in practice, need elucidation: first, the relation between the content of propaganda and its effectiveness; second, the relation between propaganda and the life experiences and interests of those whom propaganda tries to reach; third, the relation between propaganda and the foreign policy as whose instrument propaganda serves.

1. The great philosophies of the past that captured the imagination of men and moved them to political action, such as the ideas of the American and French revolutions and the slogans of bolshevism and fascism, were successful, not because they were true but because they were believed to be true, because they gave the people to whom they appealed what they were waiting for, both in terms of knowledge and in terms of action. That the National Socialist race theories are totally false no one can doubt; yet the arguments of reputable anthropologists were completely wasted in their struggle with those theories for dominance over the popular mind. The economic interpretation of imperialism and war is obviously at odds with all the known facts; yet the popular belief in it is well-nigh ineradicable.

The patent falsity of these theories was irrelevant to their success or failure. What was decisive for their success was their ability to give satisfaction to deeply felt intellectual and political needs. The frustrated authoritarianism of the German people seized upon the race theories as a tool with which to prove to themselves, in spite of all appearances to the contrary, that by nature they were really superior to everybody else and, given the right policies, they would also become superior in fact. In anticipation of that ascendancy of Germany, the race theories made it virtually imperative for the German people to try their superiority out on the minorities within their borders, and the inevitable success of the trial seemed to provide experimental proof for the truth of the race theories themselves.

Similarly, the economic interpretation of imperialism and war satisfies deeply felt intellectual and political needs. The popular mind, baffled by the bewildering complexity of international relations in our time, longs for an explanation that is both simple and plausible. The economic interpretation, by providing it, puts the popular mind at rest. It fulfills for political action a function similar to those performed by the race theories. It provides in the "warmongers of Wall Street" or the "munitions makers" an easily accessible symbol that political action can use, as it were, for purposes of target practice. In accordance with the theory, measures can be taken "to take the profits out of war" or to restrict commerce with belligerents. With these measures accomplished, imperialism and war seem to have lost their threat, and the popular mind can rest doubly content, knowing what international politics is all about and conscious of having acted in accordance with this knowledge.

No exact correlation exists between the truth of a political philosophy and its effectiveness as political propaganda. Sometimes a political philosophy, false in its assumptions and conclusions, captures the minds of large masses of men, and a political philosophy cannot rely alone upon the inner force of its truths to win the struggle for the minds of men. Rather, it must seek to establish a peculiar connection between its truths and the human minds it seeks to influence. That connection is provided by the life experiences and interests that determine the receptiveness of men to political ideas.

2. Political philosophies claim the possession of truths valid everywhere and at all times, yet men are receptive only to certain ideas at particular times according to the circumstances under which they live. These circumstances, as we have seen,[4] vary greatly not only in time but also with regard to different types of people in one and the same period of history.

Communism has been successful wherever its tenets of social, economic, and political equality appeal to people for whom the removal of inequality has been the most urgent aspiration. Western philosophy has succeeded wherever in popular aspirations political liberty has taken precedence over all other needs. Thus Communism has largely lost the struggle for the minds of men in Central and Eastern Europe, and democracy has by and large been defeated in Asia. In Central and Eastern Europe the Communist promises of equality could not prevail against the life experiences the peoples of Central and Eastern Europe had with the tyranny of the Red Army and the Russian secret police. In those regions Communism has succeeded only with the segments of the population in whose life experiences the longing for equality, especially in the economic sphere, has taken precedence over the concern with liberty.

On the other hand, where democracy lost out in Asia it did so because its appeal was largely divorced from the life experiences and interests of the peoples of Asia. What the peoples of Asia wanted above everything else was freedom from Western colonialism. What chance was there for democracy to succeed in the struggle of ideas as long as democratic philosophy was contradicted by the life experiences of the peoples of Asia? The importance of political propaganda divorced from the life experiences of the common man is strikingly revealed in a report that appeared on September 30, 1950, in the *Chicago Daily News* under the byline of Fred Sparks:

> The other day I visited a small farmer near Saigon. . . .
>
> Through my interpreter I asked him to tell me what he thought of the Americans coming to Indochina. He said:
>
> "White men help white men. You give guns to help the French kill my people. We want to be rid of all foreigners and the Viet Minh . . . was slowly putting out the French."

---

[4]See pages 272–73.

I said: "Don't you know there is a white man behind the Viet Minh? Don't you know that Ho Chi Minh takes Russian orders?"

He said: "In Saigon I have seen Americans and I have seen Frenchmen. I have never heard of any white men being with the Viet Minh."

What makes this episode significant is the fact that to a large extent it is representative of Asia's reaction to Western ideas. Nowhere has this reaction been more drastic and more pregnant with dire consequences for the West than in China; for nowhere has the contrast between philosophy and the life experiences of the people been more drastic. The century-old anti-imperialistic record of the United States and the good will it had created in China for the United States were wiped out with one stroke when American weapons were used to kill Chinese and when American planes dropped bombs on the coastal cities of China. As a report in the London *Economist* put it with reference to the Nationalist air raids on Shanghai:

> In the press these raids were represented as being quite as much the work of the "American imperialists" as that of the "reactionary, remnant lackeys" of Taiwan, and while the raids drove out any faith in Chiang which might remain amongst the less educated they no less effectively drove out any faith in America in quarters where it was still harboured.

Here again, the inherent qualities of American ideas in terms of their truth and of the good they contain were entirely irrelevant for success or failure in the warfare of ideas. What decided the issue was the apparent irrelevance of democratic propaganda in the light of the experiences of the common man. The policies that the United States supported or seemed to support made success in the war of ideas impossible.

3. Political policy must fulfill three functions for psychological warfare. First, it must define clearly its objectives and the methods through which it proposes to attain them. Second, it must determine the popular aspirations of those to whom the propaganda appeal is to be made, with regard to its objectives and methods. Third, it must determine to what extent psychological warfare is capable of supporting political policy.

The psychological weakness of the West in Asia, aside from the other reasons already mentioned, results from the weakness of its political policies. Since the West has not been sure of its objectives and of the methods to reach them, its psychological policies have been only too prone to seek refuge from the uncertainties of policy in democratic generalities. Thus Western propaganda has been inclined to stress the virtues and truths of democracy and the vices and falsehoods of bolshevism.

The same propensity for such moral and philosophic abstractions has impeded the objective investigation of what other people want. Assured as we are, by and large, of the protection of our lives from the vicissitudes of death through violence or lack of food and shelter, we are taking the satisfaction of these biological needs for granted. Having taken care in good measure of the protection of life, we concentrate our thoughts and efforts upon the preservation of liberty and the pursuit of happiness. This being naturally so with us, we erect this limited experience, subject to the conditions of time and space, into a universal principle that claims to be valid everywhere and at all times. Thus we tend to assume, at least by implication, that what we are allowed to take for granted all men can take for granted, and that what we are striving for is the object of the aspirations of all mankind. Yet it has already been shown how the different life experiences of men have built, on the foundation of common psychological traits, a structure of different political aspirations.

The ability of Western democracy to speak effectively to the peoples of Europe and Asia, then, is dependent upon its ability to establish two different relationships: one between the aspirations of those peoples and the political policies of the West, the other between those policies and their verbal propagation. There are situations in which concordance among these three factors can be brought about with relative ease. The waging of political warfare against National Socialist Germany in occupied Europe during the Second World War was a relatively simple matter. Popular aspirations were clearly defined, and so were the policies pursued by the United Nations. Both sought the destruction of National Socialism, and it was easy to put that aim into words. Similarly, the political and military policies aimed at maintaining the territorial status quo in Europe against Soviet expansion express the aspirations of the people of Western Europe and lend themselves to verbal formulation in terms of the Truman Doctrine, the Marshall Plan, and the Atlantic Alliance. Neither in Eastern Europe nor in Asia nor in the Soviet Union itself is the task of psychological warfare so simple. Two basic dilemmas confront it. One concerns the incompatibility of a certain political policy pursued in one region with the kind of psychological warfare waged in another. The other dilemma arises from the impossibility of supporting a given political policy solely by means of psychological warfare.

The first dilemma is illustrated by the relations between what used to be considered the objective of American policy in Eastern Europe and the objective of our psychological warfare with regard to the Soviet Union. The objective of our policy in Eastern Europe was in the fifties defined as the liberation of the people of Eastern Europe from Russian domination. The objective of our political warfare with regard to the Soviet Union was then to appeal to the Russian people over the head of the Soviet government in terms of our real objectives and thus to force a revision of Soviet policies through the pressure of Russian public opinion. Yet the objective of the liberation of Eastern Europe, especially insofar as Poland and the Baltic states are concerned, runs counter to the centuries-old national aspirations of Russia, regarding which no cleavage between government and people has ever existed. A policy in Eastern Europe that sought to thwart the aspirations of both the Russian government and the Russian people was bound to cancel out the chances, whatever they might have been, of separating the Russian people from the Soviet government by means of psychological warfare. In situations such as these it is the task of overall policy to establish a priority of objectives and either to subordinate the objectives of political warfare to those of political policy, or vice versa.

A striking illustration of the other dilemma is provided by the propaganda effect of the American intervention in Indochina. The immediate psychological effects of that intervention were unfavorable to the United States. What the Indochinese peasant said to Mr. Sparks found a widespread echo. What is important in the context of this discussion was the inability of the United States to counteract the psychological liability of that intervention with immediate psychological countermeasures. The psychological effects of white intervention in the affairs of Asia in the traditional manner of Western imperialism can be refuted, not by means of political warfare but only by political, military, and economic policies, which will contradict the Indochinese experiences of white intervention. In situations such as these, the immediate answer to the psychological liability of a given political or military policy is not propaganda but policies that will establish the psychological preconditions for successful propaganda.

In this context, economic and technical aid for underdeveloped areas takes on a special importance. For such aid differs from mere propaganda exactly in that it is a deed rather than a promise. Rather than telling other peoples what could be done, or what is being done elsewhere, it makes the promises of propaganda good here and now. Yet in order to be fully effective as a weapon of propaganda, economic and technical aid must meet two requirements.

First, it must benefit the people to whom it is given not only in the long run but immediately and in a manner intelligible to them. Too often, foreign aid fails to meet that requirement; for it is up against political and cultural resistance to economic development. Economic underdevelopment is frequently not the result of natural causes but of a political system that has a stake in the perpetuation of backwardness. For instance, a political system deriving its power from the absentee ownership of land is not likely to destroy itself by embarking upon a program of land reform. Foreign aid, by being absorbed by the social groups opposed to economic development, may here actually strengthen the forces of the status quo and increase the cleavage between rich and poor. Economic backwardness may also be due to cultural factors, such as disbelief in the possibility of progress or the utility of saving, which are impervious to the transfer of money and technical know-how through foreign aid.[5]

Second, the foreign source of the aid must be apparent to the recipients. Here propaganda, properly speaking, comes into play again, giving credit to the foreign agency from which the aid has come and connecting that aid and its benefits with the general philosophy, character, and policies of the foreign agency.

The struggle for the minds of men, then, is a task of infinite subtlety and complexity. Nothing is easier, more certain of popular support in one's own country, and also more certain of failure than to approach so intricate a task in the spirit and with the techniques of a Fourth-of-July oration. The simple philosophy and techniques of the moral crusade are useful and even indispensable for the

---

[5]See for a systematic discussion Hans J. Morgenthau, *A New Foreign Policy for the United States* (New York: Frederick A. Praeger, 1969), pp. 88 ff.

domestic task of marshaling public opinion behind a given policy; they are but blunt weapons in the struggle of nations for dominance over the minds of men. Propaganda is not only a struggle between good and evil, truth and falsehood, but also of power with power. In such a struggle virtue and truth do not prevail simply upon being communicated. They must be carried upon the steady stream of political policy that makes them both relevant and plausible. To conceive of the psychological task of democracy in the struggle with bolshevism primarily in terms of the technological problem of piercing the Iron Curtain and communicating the eternal verities of democracy to all the world is in large measure to miss the point. Political warfare is but the reflection, in the realm of ideas, of the political and military policies it seeks to support. It can be worse than these policies, but it can never be better. From the qualities of these policies it draws its strength. With them it wins or fails. The call for victory in the struggle for the minds of men, to be effective, must be conceived primarily as a call for political and military policies that have the makings of victory. Here, too, deeds speak louder than words.

This struggle for the minds of men, advancing rival claims to universal dominion on the part of different nations, has dealt the final, fatal blow to that social system of international intercourse within which for almost three centuries nations lived together in constant rivalry, yet under the common roof of shared values and universal standards of action. The collapse of that roof has destroyed the common habitat of the nations of the world, and the most powerful of them each assert the right to build it anew after their own pattern. Beneath the ruins of that roof lies buried the mechanism that kept the walls of that house of nations standing: the balance of power.

21 The New Balance of Power

The destruction of that intellectual and moral consensus which restrained the struggle for power for almost three centuries deprived the balance of power of the vital energy that made it a living principle of international politics. Concomitant with the ebbing away of that vital energy, the system of the balance of power has undergone three structural changes that considerably impair its operations.[1]

INFLEXIBILITY OF THE NEW BALANCE OF POWER

Numerical Reduction of Great Powers

The most obvious of these structural changes that impairs the operation of the balance of power is to be found in the drastic numerical reduction of the players in the game. At the end of the Thirty Years' War, for instance, the German Empire was composed of 900 sovereign states, which the Treaty of Westphalia in 1648 reduced to 355. The Napoleonic interventions, of which the most notable is the dictated reforms of the Diet of Regensburg of 1803, eliminated more than 200 of the sovereign German states. When the Germanic Confederation was founded in 1815, only thirty-six sovereign states were left to join it. The unification of Italy in 1859 eliminated seven sovereign states; the unification of Germany in 1871, twenty-four. In 1815, at the end of the Napoleonic Wars, eight nations—Austria, France, Great Britain, Portugal, Russia, Prussia, Spain, and Sweden—had the diplomatic rank of great powers. With Portugal, Spain, and Sweden granted such rank only out of traditional courtesy and soon to lose that undeserved status altogether, the number of actually great powers was reduced to five. In the sixties, Italy and the United States joined them, followed toward the end of the century by Japan.

At the outbreak of the First World War, there were then again eight great powers, of which for the first time two were located totally outside Europe—Austria,

---

[1] See pages 195 ff, 211–12 for other changes that occurred earlier in the century.

France, Germany, Great Britain, Italy, Japan, Russia, and the United States. The end of the First World War found Austria definitely, and Germany and Russia temporarily, removed from that list. Two decades later, at the outbreak of the Second World War, one could count seven great powers, Germany and the Soviet Union having again become first-rate powers and the others having retained their status. The end of the Second World War saw this number reduced to three—Great Britain, the Soviet Union, and the United States—while China and France, in view of their past or their potentialities, were treated in negotiations and organizations as though they were great powers. British power, however, had declined to such an extent as to be distinctly inferior to that of the United States and the Soviet Union, which, in view of their enormous superiority over the power next in rank, deserved to be called superpowers.

This reduction in the number of nations that are able to play a major role in international politics has had a deteriorating effect upon the operation of the balance of power. This effect was increased by the reduction in the absolute number of states through the consolidations of 1648 and 1803 and the national unifications of the nineteenth century. These reductions were only temporarily offset in 1919 by the creation of new nations in Eastern and Central Europe; for these nations have in the meantime either disappeared as such—for example, the Baltic states—or, in any case, have ceased to be independent factors on the international scene. These developments deprived the balance of power of much of its flexibility and uncertainty and, in consequence, of its restraining effect upon the nations actively engaged in the struggle for power.

In former times, as we have seen, the balance of power operated in the main by way of coalitions among a number of nations. The principal nations, while differing in power, were still of the same order of magnitude. In the eighteenth century, for instance, Austria, France, Great Britain, Prussia, Russia, and Sweden belonged in the same class, insofar as their relative power was concerned. Fluctuations in their power would affect their respective positions in the hierarchy of powers but not their position as great powers. Similarly, in the period from 1870 to 1914, the game of power politics was played by eight players of the first rank, of which six, those of Europe, kept at the game constantly. Under such circumstances, no player could go very far in his aspirations for power unless he were sure of the support of at least one or the other of his coplayers, and nobody could generally be too sure of that support. There was virtually no nation in the eighteenth and nineteenth centuries that was not compelled to retreat from an advanced position and retrace its steps because it did not receive the diplomatic or military support it had counted upon from other nations. This was especially true of Russia in the nineteenth century. On the other hand, if Germany, in violation of the rules of the game, had not in 1914 given Austria a free hand in its dealings with Serbia, there is little doubt that Austria would not have dared to go as far as it did, and that the First World War might have been avoided.

The greater the number of active players, the greater the number of possible combinations and the greater also the uncertainty as to the combinations that will actually oppose one another and as to the role the individual players will actually perform in them. Both William II in 1914 and Hitler in 1939 refused to believe that Great Britain, and ultimately the United States too, would join the rank of their enemies, and both misjudged the effect of American intervention. It is obvious that these miscalculations as to who would fight against whom meant for Germany the difference between victory and defeat. Whenever coalitions of nations comparable in power confront each other, calculations of this kind will of necessity be close, since the defection of one prospective member or the addition of an unexpected one cannot fail to affect the balance of power considerably, if not decisively. Thus, in the eighteenth century, when princes used to change their alignments with the greatest of ease, such calculations were frequently almost indistinguishable from wild guesses. In consequence, the extreme flexibility of the balance of power resulting from the utter unreliability of alliances made it imperative for all players to be cautious in their moves on the chessboard of international politics and, since risks were hard to calculate, compelled them to take as small risks as possible. In the First World War, it was still of very great importance, bearing upon the ultimate outcome of the conflict, whether Italy would remain neutral or enter the war on the side of the Allies. It was in recognition of that importance that both sides made great efforts, by competing in promises of territorial aggrandizement, to influence Italy's decision. The same situation then prevailed, to a lesser degree, even with respect to so relatively weak a power as Greece.

The Bipolarity of Power

This aspect of the balance of power has undergone a radical transformation in recent years. In the Second World War the decisions of such countries as Italy, Spain, or Turkey, or even France, to join or not to join one or the other side were mere episodes, welcomed or feared, to be sure, by the belligerents but in no way even remotely capable of transforming victory into defeat, or vice versa. The disparity in the power of nations of the first rank, such as the United States, the Soviet Union, Great Britain, Japan, and Germany, on the one hand, and all the remaining nations, on the other, was then already so great that the defection of one ally or the addition of another could no longer overturn the balance of power and thus materially affect the ultimate outcome of the struggle. Under the influence of changes in alignments, one scale might rise somewhat and the other sink still more under a heavier weight. Yet these changes could not reverse the relation of the scales, which was determined by the preponderant weights of the first-rate powers. It was only the position of the major countries—the United States, the Soviet Union, and Great Britain, on the one hand, and Germany and Japan, on the other—that really mattered. This situation, first noticeable in the Second World War, is now accentuated in the polarity between the United States and the Soviet Union and has become the paramount feature of international politics. The power of the United States and of the Soviet Union in comparison with the power of their actual or prospective allies has become so overwhelming that through their own preponderant weight they determine the balance of power between them. That balance cannot at present be decisively affected at least in the short run by changes in the alignments of one or the other of their allies. The balance of power has been transformed from a multipolar into a bipolar one.

The Tendency Toward a Two-Bloc System

As a result, the flexibility of the balance of power and, with it, its restraining influence upon the power aspirations of the main protagonists on the international scene have disappeared. Two superpowers, each incomparably stronger than any other power or possible combination of other powers, oppose each other. The disparity in strength between major and minor powers is so great that the minor powers in the shadow of the superpowers have not only lost their ability to tip the scales, but they have also to a considerable extent lost that freedom of movement that in former times enabled them to play so important and often decisive a role in the balance of power. What was formerly true only of a relatively small number of nations, such as certain Latin American countries in their relations with the United States and Portugal in its relations with Great Britain, is true now of many nations: they are in the orbit of one or the other of the two giants whose political, military, and economic preponderance can hold them there even against their will. Thus it is not by accident that we speak of "satellites" when we refer to the unwilling and impotent allies of the other side.

Today neither the United States nor the Soviet Union need look over its shoulder, as they still did during the Second World War, lest the defection of one major ally upset the balance of power. Gone is the era of ever shifting alliances and new combinations demanding constant vigilance, circumspection, and caution, which reached its culmination in the eighteenth century and came to an end only with the Second World War.

Yet this development does not mean that the superpowers have nothing at all to fear from their allies. Even if those allies do not leave their respective orbits at their own volition, they can stay there either as willing and effective supporters of the policies of the superpowers or as balky and unreliable captives. They may at best be able to move from the center of the orbit to its periphery, thereby loosening the control the superpower exerts within its orbit and impairing their own usefulness within it.

Within an inflexible balance of power, insofar as the alignments on either side are concerned, the superpowers can find in their allies a source of weakness or of strength. Before the Second World War, one of the principal questions before the great powers was "How can we keep the allies we have?" In contrast, the main question that faces the superpowers today with regard to their allies is "How can we make and keep them willing and efficient participants in our policies?" This concern requires flexible and accommodating policies on the part of the superpowers. Their power is overwhelming vis-à-vis their allies, but it is not without limits. They are, it is true, to an unprecedented degree masters of their own policies and of their own fate; but they are not complete masters. Within certain limits, they must adapt their policies to the wishes of their allies if they want to draw the maximum of strength from their support.

With the committed nations firmly in their respective orbits, the main element of flexibility for the balance of power is provided by the prospective moves of the uncommitted nations. To which side if either are, for instance, the nations of Africa and Latin America finally going to turn? The development of the world balance of power in the immediate future will largely depend upon the course these and other uncommitted nations will take. Only in the more distant future will the question be answered as to whether political and technological conditions, such as the acquisition of nuclear weapons of their own, will lead to the development of new centers of power that can again move independently from one side to the other. These new centers of power could arise from within or without the two blocs. France has aspired to such a position of independent power within the loose framework of a traditional alliance with the United States; and so does China in competition with, and opposition to, the Soviet Union. Were such a development to come to pass, the present bipolar system of world politics would have reverted to the traditional multipolar one.

DISAPPEARANCE OF THE BALANCER[2]

The second change in the structure of the balance of power, which we are witnessing today, is but the inevitable result of the change just discussed. It is the disappearance of the balancer, the "holder" of the balance. Both naval supremacy and virtual immunity from foreign attack for more than three centuries enabled Great Britain to perform this function for the balance of power. Today Great Britain is no longer capable of performing it, for the modern technology of war has deprived navies of uncontested mastery of the seas. Air power has not only put an end to the invulnerability of the British Isles but has also transformed from an advantage into a liability the concentration of population and industries on a relatively small territory in close proximity to a continent.

In the great contest between France and the Hapsburgs, around which the modern state system evolved (at least until the "diplomatic revolution" of 1756, when France allied itself with the Hapsburgs against Prussia), Great Britain was able to play the controlling and restraining role of the balancer because it was strong enough in comparison with the two contenders and their allies to make likely the victory of whichever side it joined. This was again true in the Napoleonic Wars and throughout the nineteenth and the early twentieth centuries. Today Great Britain no longer holds so decisive a position. Its role as the "holder" of the balance has come to an end, leaving the modern state system without the benefits of restraint and pacification that it bestowed upon that system in former times. Even as late as the Second World War, the neutrality of Great Britain or its alignment with Germany and Japan instead of with the United Nations might easily have meant for the latter the difference between victory and defeat.

---

[2]See also the discussion of the "holder" of the balance on pages 204 ff.

Now, in view of the probable trends in the technology of warfare and the distribution of power between the United States and the Soviet Union, it may well be that the attitude of Great Britain in an armed conflict between these two powers would not decisively affect the ultimate outcome.

It follows from what has been said above that the decline of the relative power of Great Britain and its resultant inability to keep its key position in the balance of power is not an isolated occurrence solely attributable to Great Britain. It is rather the consequence of a structural change that affects the functioning of the balance of power in all its manifestations. It is, therefore, impossible that the privileged and dominating place Great Britain has held for so long could at present be inherited by another nation. It is not so much that the power of the traditional holder of the place has declined, incapacitating it for its traditional role, as that the place itself no longer exists. With two giants strong enough to determine the position of the scales with their own weight alone, there can be no chance for a third power or a third force to exert a decisive influence. It is, therefore, futile at the present moment to hope that another nation or group of nations will take the place vacated by Great Britain.

The Problem of a "Third Force"

Such hopes have been entertained at times by a number of nations or groups of nations that have not committed themselves definitely or completely to the Western or Eastern bloc. Such nations may indeed be able to hold the position of a "Third Force" by standing aside from the main political and military contests between East and West and continuing not to commit themselves completely or definitely. In view of the disparity of power between them and the two superpowers, it is hard to see at present how they can hope for more. While it would certainly be presumptuous to suggest that their hopes to play a decisive role as a "Third Force" in the world balance of power can never be fulfilled, especially in view of unforeseeable technological changes, it is safe to say that they are bound to be disappointed in the foreseeable future. General de Gaulle, for instance, advocated in a number of penetrating and eloquent speeches that a united Europe should perform as a "Third Force" the pacifying and restraining task of the "holder" of the balance between the colossus of the East and the colossus of the West. He said on July 28, 1946, what he repeated in many subsequent statements, especially after his return to power in 1958:

> It is certain indeed that, with respect to what it was before this thirty-year war the face of the world has altered in every way. A third of a century ago we were living in a universe where six or eight great nations, apparently equal in strength, each by differing and subtle accords associating others with it, managed to establish a balance everywhere in which the less powerful found themselves relatively guaranteed and where international law was recognized, since a violator would have faced a coalition of moral or material interests, and where, in the last analysis, strategy conceived and prepared with a view to future conflicts involved only rapid and limited destruction.

But a cyclone has passed. An inventory can be made. When we take into account the collapse of Germany and Japan and the weakening of Europe, Soviet Russia and the United States are now alone in holding the first rank. It seems as if the destiny of the world, which in modern times has in turn smiled on the Holy Roman Empire, Spain, France, Britain and the German Reich, conferring on each in turn a kind of preeminence, has now decided to divide its favor in two. From this decision arises a factor of division that has been substituted for the balance of yore.

After referring to the anxieties caused by the expansionist tendencies of the United States and the Soviet Union, de Gaulle raised the question of restoring a stable balance of power.

Who then can re-establish the equilibrium, if not the old world, between the two new ones? Old Europe, which, during so many centuries was the guide of the universe, is in a position to constitute in the heart of a world that tends to divide itself into two, the necessary element of compensation and understanding.

The nations of the ancient west have for their vital arteries the North Sea, the Mediterranean, the Rhine; they are geographically situated between the two new masses. Resolved to conserve an independence that would be gravely exposed in the event of a conflagration, they are physically and morally drawn together by the massive effort of the Russians as well as by the liberal advance of the Americans. Of global strength because of their own resources and those of the vast territories that are linked to them by destiny, spreading afar their influences and their activities, what will be their weight if they manage to combine their policies in spite of the difficulties among them from age to age![3]

But it is not only the weakness of the nations of Europe in comparison with the United States and the Soviet Union that incapacitates them to perform that task. Above all, General de Gaulle's argument leaves out of account the decisive fact that Great Britain was capable of making its beneficial contributions to peace and stability only because it was geographically remote from the centers of friction and conflict, because it had no vital interests in the stakes of these conflicts as such, because it had the opportunity of satisfying its aspirations for power in areas beyond the seas that generally were beyond the reach of the main contenders for power.

It was that threefold aloofness, together with its resources of power, that enabled Great Britain to play its role as "holder" of the balance. In none of these three respects are the nations of Europe aloof from the centers of conflict. Quite the contrary, they are deeply implicated in them in all three respects. For they are at once the battlefield and the prize of victory in the contest between the United States and the Soviet Union. They are permanently and vitally interested in the victory of one or the other side. And they are unable to seek satisfaction for their

---

[3] *The New York Times,* July 29, 1946, p. 1; cf. for later speeches, ibid., June 30, 1947; p. 1; July 10, 1947, p. 3; press conference of July 23, 1964, and address in Strasbourg on November 22, 1964.

vital political interests anywhere but on the European continent itself. It is for these reasons that the nations of Europe could not enjoy that aloofness and freedom of maneuver without which there can be no "Third Force" either as an uncommitted bystander or as the "holder" of the balance of power.

DISAPPEARANCE OF THE COLONIAL FRONTIER

With this discussion we are broaching a third change in the structure of the balance of power, namely, the disappearance of the colonial frontier. The balance of power owed the moderating and restraining influence it exerted in its classical period not only to the moral climate within which it operated and to its own mechanics but also in good measure to the circumstance that the nations participating in it rarely needed to put all their national energies into the political and military struggles in which they were engaged with one another. Nations in that period sought power through the acquisition of territory, then considered the symbol and substance of national power. Taking land away from a powerful neighbor was one method of gaining power. There was, however, a much less risky opportunity for achieving that end. That opportunity was provided by the wide expanses of three continents: Africa, the Americas, and the part of Asia bordering on the Eastern oceans.

Throughout the history of the balance of power, Great Britain found in this opportunity the main source of its power and of its detachment from the issues that involved the other nations in continuous conflict. Spain dissipated its strength in exploiting that opportunity and thus eliminated itself as a force to be reckoned with in the struggle for power. What for Great Britain and Spain was a constant and major concern attracted the energies of the other nations to a lesser degree or only sporadically. French policies in the eighteenth century present instructive examples of the reciprocal effect of colonial expansion and imperialistic attacks upon the existing balance of power; the more intense French imperialism was, the less attention France paid to colonial expansion, and vice versa. The United States and Russia were for long stages of their history absorbed by the task of pushing their frontiers forward into the politically empty spaces of their continents, and during those periods they did not take a very active part in the balance of power. The Austrian monarchy was too much concerned, especially during the nineteenth century, with maintaining its control over the restive non-German nationalities of Central and Southeastern Europe, which made up the bulk of its empire, to be capable of more than limited excursions into power politics. Furthermore, until deep into the eighteenth century, the threat of Turkish aggression limited Austria's freedom of movement on the chessboard of international politics. Prussia, finally, as the latecomer to the circle of the great powers, had to be satisfied with defending and securing its position as a great power. Besides, it was too weak internally and in too unfavorable a geographical position to think of a program of unlimited expansion. Even after Bismarck had made Prussian power predominant in Germany and German power predominant in Europe, his policy was aimed at preserving, not at expanding, that power.

In the period between 1870 and 1914, the stability of the status quo in Europe was the direct result, on the one hand, of the risks implicit in even the smallest move at the frontiers of the great powers themselves and, on the other, of the opportunity of changing the status quo in outlying regions without incurring the danger of a general conflagration. As Arnold Toynbee observes:

> At the center [of the group of states forming the balance of power], every move that any one state makes with a view to its own aggrandizement is jealously watched and adroitly countered by all its neighbors, and the sovereignty over a few square feet of territory and a few hundred "souls" becomes a subject for the bitterest and stubbornest contention. . . . In the easy circumstances of the periphery, quite a mediocre political talent is often able to work wonders. . . . The domain of the United States can be expanded unobtrusively right across North America from the Atlantic to the Pacific, the domain of Russia right across Asia from Baltic to Pacific, in an age when the best statesmanship of France or Germany cannot avail to obtain unchallenged possession of an Alsace or a Posen.[4]

With the unification of Germany in 1870, the consolidation of the great nation states was consummated, and territorial gains in Europe could henceforth be made only at the expense of the great powers or their allies. Thereafter, for more than four decades, the great issues of world politics were connected with African names, such as Egypt, Tunis, Morocco, the Congo, and South Africa, and with the decrepit Asiatic empires of China and Persia. Local wars arose as a result of these issues: the Boer War of 1899–1902 between Great Britain and the Boer Republics, the Russo-Japanese War of 1904–05, and the Russo-Turkish and Italo-Turkish Wars of 1877 and 1911–12, respectively. But it should be noted that in all these wars one of the great powers fought against what might be called a "peripheral" power, a power that was either the designated object of the former's expansion or, as in the exceptional case of Japan, an outside competitor. In no case was it necessary for a great power to take up arms against another great power in order to expand into the politically empty spaces of Africa and Asia.

The policy of compensations could here operate with a maximum of success, for there was so much political no-man's-land with which to compensate oneself and allow others to do the same. There was always the possibility of compromise without compromising one's vital interests, of retreating while saving one's face, of sidestepping and postponing. The period from 1870 to 1914, then, was a period of diplomatic bargains and horse-trading for other people's lands, of postponed conflicts and sidestepped issues, and it was also the period of continuous peace among the great powers.

It is significant that the most persistent and the most explosive of the great issues of that period, while still located at the periphery of the circle of the great powers, was closer to it geographically and weighed more directly

---

[4]Arnold Toynbee, *A Study of History* (London, New York, Toronto: Oxford University Press, 1934), Vol. III, p. 302. (Reprinted by permission of the publisher.)

upon the distribution of political and military power within it than any other of the great issues of that epoch. That issue (also called the Eastern or the Balkan Question) was how to distribute the inheritance of the European part of the Turkish Empire. Out of this issue arose the conflagration of the First World War. The Balkan Question more than any other issue of that period was likely to lead to open conflict among the great powers—especially since the vital interests of one of them, Austria, were directly affected by the national aspirations of Serbia. It is, however, doubtful that this outcome was inevitable. One might even plausibly maintain that if the other great powers, especially Germany, had dealt with the Balkan Question in 1914, as they had done successfully at the Congress of Berlin in 1878—that is, in recognition of its peripheral character—the First World War might well have been avoided.

When Bismarck declared in 1876[5] that, as far as the interests of Germany were concerned, the Balkans were not worth "the good bones of one single Pomeranian musketeer," he affirmed emphatically the peripheral character of the Balkan Question in relation to the political and military interests of Germany. When the German government in July 1914 promised to support whatever steps Austria decided to take against Serbia, it took the exact opposite of Bismarck's position, and for no good reason. Germany identified itself with the Austrian interest in the prostration of Serbia as though it was its own, while Russia identified itself with Serbia's defense of its independence. Thus a conflict at the periphery of the European state system transformed itself into a struggle that threatened to affect the overall distribution of power within that system.

Bargaining had become impossible if it was not to be the bargaining away of one's own vital interests. Concessions at somebody else's expense could no longer be made, because identification of one's own interests with the interests of the smaller nations involved had turned concessions at the apparent expense of others into concessions at one's own expense. The conflict could not be postponed because, as we have seen, most of the great powers feared that postponement would strengthen the other side for an armed conflict that was considered to be inevitable. For, once the issues had been brought from the periphery into the center of the circle of the great powers, there was no way of sidestepping them; there was, as it were, no empty space into which to step in order to evade the issue. Russia had to face the Austro-German determination to settle the Serbian problem on Austria's terms. In consequence, France had to face the invocation of the Franco-Russian alliance by Russia, Germany had to face the activation of that alliance, and Great Britain had to face the threat to Belgium. There was no sidestepping these issues except at the price of yielding what each nation regarded as its vital interests.

What came about in July 1914, at least in part by blundering diplomacy, has today become the ineluctable result of structural changes in the balance of power. In the period preceding the First World War it was possible for the great powers to deflect their rivalries from their own mutual frontiers to the periphery and into

---

[5]In the session of the German Reichstag of December 5, 1876.

politically empty spaces, because, as we have seen, virtually all the active participants in the balance of power were European nations and, furthermore, the main
weights of the balance were located in Europe. To say that during that period there
was a periphery of politically empty spaces is simply a negative way of saying that
during that period the balance of power was quantitatively and qualitatively circumscribed by geographical limits. As the balance of power—with its main weight
now in three different continents—becomes worldwide, the dichotomy between
the circle of the great powers and its center, on the one hand, and its periphery
and the empty spaces beyond, on the other, must of necessity disappear. The
periphery of the balance of power now coincides with the confines of the earth.

THE COLONIAL REVOLUTION

Thus what was formerly the periphery of world politics now tends to become one
of its centers—one of the main theaters where the struggle between the two superpowers is being fought out in terms of the control of territory and men's minds.
Two factors are responsible for this shift: the revolution of the colonial and semicolonial countries of the earth against their former masters, and the tendency
inherent in a bipolar system to transform itself into a two-bloc system.

The disappearance of the colonial frontier—that is, the consummation of
colonial expansion—is immediately followed by, and in large measure coincides
with, a reverse movement in which the objects of colonial expansion try to regain
their independence and achieve a fundamental change in the relations between
the white and colored races. As high tide is, at the same time, the end stage of the
ocean's forward surge and the beginning stage of its retreat, so does the consummation of colonial expansion signify the beginning of the end of colonialism
itself. For when the great colonial powers reached the limits of their expansion,
they happened to reach also the limits of their supreme power in the world. More
particularly, the political and military decline of the nations of Europe was the
cause, and later largely the result, of the colonial revolution.

If the disappearance of the colonial frontier had not coincided with the
decline of Europe as the power center of the world, what now, as the colonial revolution, has become one of the great turning points in the history of the world
would appear in retrospect as a series of colonial revolts, unsuccessful like so many
of their predecessors. Yet the obvious decline of the main European powers, especially as demonstrated by their defeats at the hands of Japan in the Second World
War, invited the colonial revolution and either made it successful or makes its success in the foreseeable future inevitable. Thus what seemed to be almost inconceivable at the end of the Second World War had become an accomplished fact
only twenty years later: the voluntary retreat of Great Britain from Burma,
Ceylon, India, Pakistan, Malaya, Singapore, and Egypt and its expulsion from
Iran, Iraq, and Jordan; the enforced retreat of the Netherlands from Indonesia; the
expulsion of France from Indochina; and the dissolution of the Belgian, British,
French, and Portuguese empires in Africa into independent nations.

One can see now in retrospect that this colonial revolution in the aftermath of the Second World War was but the concluding chapter in as well as the culmination of a process of decolonization that started with the American Revolution against Great Britain in the eighteenth century, continued with the revolutions of Latin America against Spain and Portugal, and of its European possessions against Turkey at the beginning of the nineteenth century, and took a giant step forward after the First World War with the dissolution of the Austrian-Hungarian Empire, the European part of the Russian Empire, and the Arab components of Turkey. The last phase of the colonial revolution, born of the weakness of Europe, has in turn made Europe weaker still. The political preeminence of Europe throughout modern times was primarily the result of its predominance over the colored races. It was the technological, economic, and military differential between the white man of Europe and the colored man of Africa and Asia that allowed Europe to acquire and keep its dominion over the world. Its disappearance has dried up the main source of strength—military, economic, political—upon which the European nations could draw in order to make up for their inferiority in numbers, space, and natural resources.

Yet while the decline of European power gave the colonial revolution its chance to succeed, it did not give it its impetus. Like all genuine revolutions, the colonial revolution sprang from a moral challenge to the world as it was. This is true particularly of its most mature manifestation, the revolution of Asia.

The moral challenge emanating from Asia is in its essence a triumph of the moral ideas of the West. It is carried forward under the banner of two moral principles: national self-determination and social justice. These are the ideas that for more than a century have in the West either guided policies, domestic and international, or have at least been appealed to as justifications for political action. In the wake of its conquests, the West brought to Asia not only its technology and political institutions but also its principles of political morality. The nations of the West taught the peoples of Asia by their own example that the full development of the individual's faculties depends upon the ability of the nation to which he belongs to determine of its own free will its political and cultural destinies, and that this national freedom is worth fighting for; and the people of Asia learned that lesson. The West taught the people of Asia also that poverty and misery are not God-given curses that man must passively accept but that they are largely man-made and can be remedied by man; and most of the peoples of Asia learned that lesson too. It is these principles of national self-determination and social justice that Asia today hurls against the West, condemning and revolting against Western political and economic policies in the name of the West's own moral standards.

THE DECLINE OF THE WEST

Present concern with the decline of the West is also caused by the obvious decline of American power. The defeat suffered by United States policy in Indochina was not only total but ignominious. Even if defeat seven thousand miles from American shores had to be anticipated as inevitable, there was nothing inevitable about the American inability to retreat from an untenable position with at least a modicum of poise. The natural concern with the decline of American power obscures the relationship between it and the decline of the West in general. More particularly, it has obscured the fact that the United States owes its rise to predominance after the Second World War to the selfsame decline of the West of which it now appears as the prime example. In other words, the decline of the West was preceded by the decline of the traditional nation-states of Western Europe, of which the United States was, briefly, the main beneficiary.

The outcome of the Second World War was decided by nations either completely or largely outside Europe. The material productivity and technical ingenuity of the United States, undamaged—in contrast to all the other combatants' systems—but greatly stimulated by the war, was a decisive factor in victory and reconstruction. Thus, the conjunction of the decline of the traditional nation-states of the West and the ascendancy of the United States—both in consequence of two world wars—accounts for the rise of the United States in the context of the West's decline.

A similar shift from the traditional nation-states of the West to the United States can be observed on the moral plane. The First World War brought to the fore two challenges to the traditional moral order: communism and fascism. Faced with the choice, many of the ruling elites chose fascism as protection against communism or even radical reform. They chose fascism even if it meant opening the gates to the enemy of the nation. "Rather Hitler than Blum" became the slogan of the French right, and the Vichy regime became the political manifestation of that moral preference.

The United States has never had to choose between fascism and Communism, for both threats to American democracy were always remote—however much the aberration of McCarthyism made it temporarily appear that communism was the main danger to America at home and abroad. Thus, while the nations of Western Europe risked national disintegration in the struggle between democracy and the two totalitarianisms, America was able to present a united national front against the two enemies from without—first against the totalitarianism of fascism, then against that of communism. The simplistic moral stance of Secretary of State John Foster Dulles, which divided the world into good nations, evil nations, and the morally tainted neutral nations, expressed on the moral plane the political and military confrontation of the Cold War. Thus the United States became the "leader of the free world," both by dint of the actual distribution of political power and of the simple moral position it could afford to take vis-à-vis the enemies of the "free world." That ascendancy of the United States to seemingly unchallengeable leadership, not only in the "free world" but in the world at large, effectively concealed the actual decline of the collectivity called the Western world and the trends toward deterioration within the United States itself. That trend toward Western decline and disarray was made manifest in the ideological crusade of the Reagan administration against "the evil empire" of Soviet Communism, often without regard for the unity of the already weakened North Atlantic community.

What sapped the moral strength of the United States was not the contradiction between national interest and class interest (as in Europe) but, on the one hand, the reduction of complex political issues to a simple moral juxtaposition with communism and, on the other, spectacular demonstrations of moral obtuseness at home and abroad. What confronted the nations of Western Europe in the aftermath of the Second World War—both as a threat and a challenge—was the military presence of the Red Army 100 kilometers east of the Rhine, the political presence of large communist parties within their borders, and political, economic, and social structures and policies creating and maintaining the cleavages on which communism thrives.

Simplistic American anticommunism was adequate to counter the Soviet military threat through the policy of containment. But the countersubversive programs America operated in the democratic countries of the West remained not only by and large ineffective but also counterproductive. What was difficult for the countersubversive technicians of the American secret services to understand was that the hold which communism had over many among Western peoples was not primarily, let alone exclusively, the result of the machinations of foreign communist governments but of indigenous conditions exploited—but not created—from abroad. Thus rigid ideological commitment to a dogmatic anticommunism, reducing a complex reality to a simple juxtaposition between good and evil, has proven untenable on philosophical and historical grounds—nothing short of a political and moral disaster.

Committed to a precarious if not doomed status quo in a largely revolutionary or prerevolutionary world, the United States was forced by the very logic of its commitment to support or create the kind of government whose antagonistic rhetoric left nothing to be desired and that was willing to fight communism by all means fair or foul. Thus the United States found itself supported by, and supporting, governments throughout the world whose political philosophy and practice were completely at odds with American principles of government. The protection of the "free world" from communism became the main purpose of American foreign policy whether in Europe or Asia and Central America. In its name, or its alias, national security policies were pursued and outrages committed that defied the moral standards by which government theory and practice had traditionally been judged.

American moral and political commitment to anticommunism succeeded only where the military and economic power of the United States could be effectively brought into play. It failed when its pure moral force was appealed to. Paradoxically, it failed not because the peoples whose freedom was at stake were not willing to listen to its message but because America, the bearer of the message, did not know how to live up to it. The fear of communism blocked the road to freedom. In the contest between the colonial powers of Europe and their colonies, the United States frequently took the side of the former, not because it was in favor of colonialism but because it was afraid that communism might be the alternative to colonialism. The champion of freedom became the defender and restorer of the colonial status quo. Making common cause with the colonial powers, it came to share with them the moral taint of colonialism. Thus America lost the peculiar moral aura that it thought had set it apart from all other nations.

Yet while America's indiscriminate, dogmatic opposition to communism, or to what looked like communism, compelled it to join forces with the status quo, its libertarianism and anticolonialist tradition evoked its sympathies with the aspirations of the Third World. That world had painted a picture of its condition flattering to itself and disparaging to its former colonial masters and the industrial nations at large. Its miseries and failures are presented as the responsibility of the developed nations, which have the moral obligation to right the wrong they have done. This moral dichotomy between the "good" members of the Third World and the "evil" colonial exploiters cut across the American dichotomy between "good" democratic capitalists and "evil" communists. For many of the nations of the "free world" are sympathetic to one or another brand of communism—or at least to some brand of authoritarianism that bears the name of "communism" or "socialism."

What occurred on the moral plane, then, was the opposite of what took place in the arena of power. In the latter, the United States benefited at the expense of its associates. On the former, it profited from their disrepute. Perhaps not surprisingly—considering the resentment that unchallengeable power evokes—the unprecedented power of the United States has not been matched by a reputation for benevolent use of that power. That discrepancy produced the undoing of America's moral position. The Third World attacked the United States with the same arguments that America used to argue against the colonialism, racism, and exploitation perpetuated by its friends. Arguing within its traditional moral framework, the United States had no answer when its own arguments were turned against it. It had spoken as the champion of the downtrodden and the exploited in the name of equality and freedom, and now defended in its deeds the status quo of colonialism and exploitation in the name of anticommunism.

This moral disarmament by an adversary invoking the other side's moral arguments for his own purposes is no novelty; it was used brilliantly by Hitler in the Czechoslovakian crisis of 1938.[6]

The United States—threatened materially and weakened morally by its association with the traditional nation-states of the West—finds itself in the end weakened by the very magnitude of its material power. It is one of the paradoxes of the nuclear age that, in contrast to the experience of all previous history, an increase in military power is no longer necessarily tantamount to an increase in political power.[7] The unprecedented power that modern technology has put into the hands of Western nations is useful only under extraordinarily limiting conditions. Under most possible and actual circumstances, that power is an empty threat and is readily disregarded by nations much inferior in material power. Thus the power that really counts, a few extreme exceptions to the contrary notwithstanding, is conventional power, and here the gap between the

[6]See page 106.
[7]See pages 31–32, 135.

United States and the other Western nations, on the one hand, and the non-Western nations, on the other hand, is of course by no means as wide as it is if one puts nuclear power into the scales. Consequently, when one compares the conventional power of the West with the conventional power of the non-Western world, one notices that the nations of the West are much less powerful than they previously appeared to be. That impression is strengthened when one examines the moral principles on behalf of which the Western nations may be willing to use conventional power and with a chance for success. The defeat of the United States in Indochina illustrates vividly the decline of Western power—material and moral.

It is one of the great ironies of contemporary history that the moral and material decline of the West has in good measure been accomplished through the moral and material triumphs of the West. The Third World has shaken off the Western yoke by invoking the principles of self-determination and social justice that the West had proclaimed and endeavored to put into practice. That, in the process, national self-determination was to become the ideology of new imperialisms and social justice the ideological disguise of servitudes new and old was to be expected. What points to the moral exhaustion of the West is its inability to stipulate moral principles with which to justify its positions and interests against its enemies and detractors.

This moral helplessness whenever the West had to contend with the use of its moral principles on behalf of its enemies—dramatically revealed in the Czechoslovakian crisis of 1938—has been one of the main sources of its weakness in action. It is simple and convenient to identify this weakness with one particular man acting in a particular episode and thus isolate the "spirit of Munich" from the Western moral stance in foreign policy. It is equally simple and convenient to decry any kind of accommodation and compromise in foreign policy as "appeasement," relying instead upon the uncompromising containment of the enemy. Lacking credible moral standards that could guide his action, the statesman is reduced to either denying the moral issue altogether or universalizing it to the point of irrelevance.

As we have seen, on the material plane the West has become vulnerable to the use of oil as a political weapon.[8] This vulnerability of highly developed Western industrial nations is a function of their industrial advancement. The shift of power from the oil-consuming to the oil-producing nations is a by-product of the former's industrial power. Industrial development has widened the gap between the advanced and backward nations in favor of the former, but it has supplied some of the latter with a new weapon: a quasi-monopoly of oil. Ironically, it is a weapon some backward nations have used against other backward states, illustrating the crazy-quilt patterns of international politics.

That weapon can be deadly, but it resembles nuclear power in that it is purely destructive. An oil-producing nation can bring an oil-consuming one to its knees,

[8]See page 127–28.

but it cannot govern it by virtue of its oil monopoly. Thus the potency of the oil weapon demonstrates dramatically the decline of Western power. Yet it indicates no substitute for that declining power—except the power of destruction.

The moral and material decline of the West is an observable fact. What is not observable is the kind of order that could take the place of the fading one created and maintained by the power of the West. Instead of the outlines of a new order created and supported by a new center of power, what appears on the horizon of the civilized world is the specter of anarchy, with legal arrangements, institutions, and procedures utterly out of tune with the objective technological conditions of the age.

POTENTIALITIES OF THE BIPOLAR SYSTEM

The colonial revolution has profoundly altered the moral, military, and political relationships between Africa, Asia, and Latin America, on the one hand, and the rest of the world, on the other. Seen in terms of the bipolarity of contemporary world politics, it has created, as it were, a moral, military, and political no-man's-land, neither completely nor irrevocably committed to either side. Will these new nations embrace communism or democracy; and will they align themselves politically and militarily with Moscow, Beijing, or Washington? This, then, is the challenge that the uncommitted nations throughout the world present to the two superpowers.

The latter have not been slow in taking up that challenge, for a bipolar political system has an inherent tendency to transform itself into a two-bloc system. With the flexibility of the multipolar system gone and their allies firmly within their respective orbits, the two superpowers can increase their strength in terms of prestige, territory, population, and natural resources only by drawing the uncommitted nations into their orbits. Their flexibility is limited to those regions that have not yet irrevocably joined one or the other orbit, or have joined only under the compulsion of military occupation. Here the superpowers can still advance and retreat, bargain and maneuver. Here are still opportunities for conquest—moral, military, political. The Soviet Union if it could draw India into its orbit would gain an important victory in the struggle between East and West. Thus the two superpowers have poured into the uncommitted spaces the resources of their strength—moral, economic, military, political—trying to transform these spaces into two gigantic blocs that border on each other and oppose each other at the four corners of the earth.

The Possibility of Its Breakup

Yet the very prospects that make the transformation of the bipolar into a two-bloc system attractive to the superpowers make it repulsive to the uncommitted nations and to those nations who have been committed to one or the other bloc by force of circumstance and who seek to restore their freedom of action. The opposition to this transformation, inherent as a potentiality in a bipolar system, thus calls into being another potentiality.

In this scheme of things the revolution of the nations of Asia and, more particularly, of China may well in the long run carry the gravest implications for the rest of the world. It is here that nations with space, natural resources, and great masses of men are just beginning to use political power, modern technology, and modern moral ideas for their ends. More than a billion and a half people, not counting close to one billion Chinese, who thus far have been the objects of the policies of others have now entered world politics as active participants. One may well anticipate that these awakening masses will sooner or later come into full possession of those instruments of modern technology, especially in the nuclear field, which until recently have been a virtual monopoly of the West.

Such a development, amounting to a drastic shift in the distribution of power, would be more important for the future of the world than all other factors thus far mentioned. It might well mean the end of the bipolarity centered in Washington and Moscow, which now puts its imprint upon world politics. After all, the Soviet Union is no longer uncontested in the political, technological, and moral leadership of world communism; and in terms of numbers and power potential, China, not the Soviet Union, is the leading communist country in the world.

The possibility of the breakup of the bipolar system in the long run is also suggested by a potentiality inherent in the system itself. The opposition of the uncommitted and unwillingly committed nations to the attraction of the two political poles, Washington and Moscow, runs in the same direction: to overcome that attraction if they could. The formation, from among these nations, of independent power centers, armed with nuclear weapons, might sound the death knell of the bipolar system itself.

The bipolar system, then, contains within itself two contradictory potentialities: the tendency to expand into a two-bloc system by absorbing the uncommitted nations of the world, and the tendency to disintegrate under the pull of centrifugal forces from within and the attraction of new power centers from within or without.

Continuation of the Cold War

Turning from long-run possibilities to short-run probabilities, we find it likely that two power blocs centered on two superpowers will continue to dominate the arena of world politics. From the aftermath of the Second World War onward, these two blocs have faced each other like two fighters in a short and narrow lane. They have tended to advance and meet in what was likely to be combat, or retreat and allow the other side to advance into what to them is precious ground. Those manifold and variegated maneuvers through which the masters of the balance of power tried either to stave off armed conflicts altogether or at least to make them brief and decisive yet limited in scope—the alliances and counteralliances, the shifting of alliances according to whence the greater threat or the better opportunity might come, the sidestepping and postponement of issues, the deflection of rivalries from the exposed front yard into the colonial back yard—have been difficult to maintain. With them have gone into oblivion the peculiar finesse and subtlety of mind, the calculating and versatile intelligence and bold yet circumspect decisions, that were required from the players in that game. And with those modes of action and intellectual attitudes there has disappeared that self-regulating flexibility, that automatic tendency, of which we have spoken before,[9] of disturbed power relations either to revert to their old equilibrium or to establish a new one.

For the two giants that today determine the course of world affairs only one policy has seemed to be left—that is, to increase their own strength and that of their allies. Most of the players that count have taken sides, and in the immediate future no major switch from one side to the other is likely to take place. Since the issues everywhere boil down to retreat from, or advance into, areas that both sides regard as of vital interest to themselves, positions must be held, and the give-and-take of compromise becomes a weakness each side seeks to avoid.

While formerly war was regarded, according to the classic definition of the German philosopher of war, von Clausewitz, as the continuation of diplomacy by other means, the art of diplomacy is now transformed into a variety of the art of warfare. That is to say, we have lived in the period of Cold War where the aims of warfare were being pursued, for the time being, with other than violent means. In such a situation the peculiar qualities of the diplomatic mind are disparaged, for they have nothing to operate with and are consequently superseded by the military type of thinking. The balance of power, once disturbed, can be restored only, if at all, by an increase in the weaker side's military strength. Yet, since no important variables in the picture are recognized aside from the inherent strength of the two giants themselves, either side must fear that the temporarily stronger contestant will use its superiority to eliminate the threat from the other side by shattering military and economic pressure or by a war of annihilation.

Thus the international situation is reduced to the primitive spectacle of two giants eying each other with watchful suspicion. They bend every effort to increase their military potential to the utmost, since this is all they have to count on. Both prepare to strike the first decisive blow, for if one does not strike it the other might. Thus, contain or be contained, conquer or be conquered, destroy or be destroyed, become the watchwords of Cold War diplomacy.

That such has been the political state of the world does not of necessity result from the mechanics of the new balance of power. The changed structure of the balance of power has made the hostile opposition of two gigantic power blocs possible, but it has not made it inevitable. Quite the contrary, the new balance of power is a mechanism that contains in itself the potentialities for unheard-of good as well as for unprecedented evil. Which of these potentialities will be realized depends not upon the mechanics of the balance of power, but upon moral and material forces that use that mechanism for the realization of their ends.

[9]See pages 347–49.

The New Diplomacy of Movement

Comparing today's world politics with what it was as recently as the late 1960s, one is impressed both by the drastic changes that have occurred, and by the continuities that have survived. The degree to which many of these changes were unplanned and even unanticipated by the most powerful nations is striking. The political world today is much less manageable—and, hence, much more dangerous—than the world that, roughly speaking, ended with Richard M. Nixon's accession to power in 1969.

The configuration into which the political world congealed in the aftermath of the Second World War was relatively simple and fairly easily managed. There were two power blocs, defined in ideological terms and rigidly grouped around two superpowers, which restrained each other through the mutual threat of atomic destruction; these groupings competed rather harmlessly and ineffectually for the allegiance of the nations of the so-called Third World—that is, those who had not joined one or the other of the power blocs. The main issue that pitted the two power blocs against each other was the territorial settlement of the Second World War, especially in Central Europe; and it was from that unresolved issue that the Cold War arose.

That issue was virtually liquidated by the *Ostpolitik* of the Federal Republic of Germany. The achievements of that policy were ratified in the treaties of 1970 and 1972, which recognized the territorial status quo in Central Europe and renounced the "Hallstein Doctrine," which claimed that the Federal Republic was the sole representative of all Germany, East and West, which would one day be united under its control. That settlement was almost, but not quite complete for two reasons; one existential, the other a direct descendant of the central issue of the Cold War. No agreement, however generously worded and faithfully executed, can change the fact that West Berlin is an enclave surrounded by the territory of a hostile state. That geopolitical situation gives the GDR (East Germany) a power for good or ill that the Western nations cannot match. It is this condition that can become—especially in conjunction with wider issues—a potent source of conflict, as past Berlin crises have shown.

On the other hand, while the Federal Republic has given up the unrealistic positions of the Cold War, it still holds to the proposition that Germany East and West forms one nation—"one nation in two states"—to be united one day, however remote. The genuine yet qualified détente within the area from which the Cold War arose was accompanied and strengthened for a time by an ideological thawing-out of East-West relations. Rigidity of alignments, which had been characteristic of the Cold War, was a function not only of the intractability of substantive political issues but also of the irreconcilable nature of ideological positions. The partial liberation of foreign policy from its ideological orientation cleared the road for a new diplomacy of movement that replaced the rigidities of the earlier Cold War polemics for a time.

The new diplomacy offered the politically active nations new opportunities and confronted them with new risks—more often than not in international politics one nation's opportunity turns out to be another nation's risk. Thus the settlement of old issues gives rise to new ones, and advantage will accrue to the nation that recognizes the new issues and chooses the policies appropriate to them. Europe and, more particularly, the Atlantic Alliance provided empirical illustrations of these general propositions.

The accompanying tendencies toward disintegration within the Atlantic Alliance are, of course, of long standing. Doubts about the stability of the American nuclear deterrent, changing perceptions of the Soviet military threat, concern about the American approach to negotiations on arms control, the economic revival of Western Europe, and divergent national interests are all responsible. A survey of the international issues confronting the members of the alliance in the early 1960s and again in the 1970s and 1980s did not uncover a single one on which all the allies saw eye to eye. The leadership of and close cooperation with the United States—accepted in the late 1940s not as a matter of choice but as the condition of survival—are now widely experienced on both sides of the Atlantic as a burden to be lightened by the pursuit of particular national interests.

In the measure that the cohesion of the Atlantic Alliance is loosened and American power and influence within it decline, the power and influence of the Soviet Union are likely to loom larger in the affairs of Western Europe. The Soviet Union, although no longer perceived as the threat it was during the 1940s and 1950s, still is objectively the colossus bestriding the Eurasian land mass, against whom a viable European balance of power can be maintained only through the permanent military presence in Europe of the United States cooperating with the nations of Western Europe. In other words, the Atlantic Alliance has been the instrument through which the United States and the nations of Western Europe first restored and then maintained the European balance of power.

The decline of American power and influence, therefore, tilts the balance of power in favor of the Soviet Union and, in consequence, increases the insecurity of Western Europe. Talk by American policymakers of withdrawing from Europe if differences persist adds to the anxiety. These nations—ambivalent toward the United States, whose support they need but resent—may then perceive themselves as having been abandoned by the United States and having to face the Soviet Union alone, unchallengeable in its military power. It is this state of mind that would give the Soviet Union its long-sought opportunity to stabilize what it calls "European" security, which is in truth a euphemism for its own. Seen from the vantage point of the Kremlin, European security requires the reduction, if not the elimination, of American power on the Continent, the resultant emasculation of NATO, and the consequent isolation of the Federal Republic of Germany. The nations of Western Europe, cut loose from one another and from the United States, would then no longer be able to maintain a viable balance of power vis-à-vis the Soviet Union and would have to accommodate themselves to the Soviet hegemony over the Eurasian land mass.

This accommodation—were the Federal Republic of Germany to join in it—would signify a drastic change in the distribution of world power. The Western orientation of the FRG has been derived from calculations of comparative political, military, and economic advantage. The vote of November 21, 1983, by a substantial majority of the Social Democratic Party against deployment of cruise and Pershing II missiles suggests, however, that that orientation has not remained unchallenged from within the *Bundesrepublik,* even while rational calculation argued in its favor. If the development described above were to come to pass, rational arguments would be made in support of an Eastern orientation. Traditionally fearful of the "Russian bear," a West Germany deprived of assured American protection would be driven into a neutral, if not friendly, political and military position with respect to its towering neighbor to the east. That position would be greatly strengthened by the complementary relationship of the West German and Soviet economies. As the European pipeline dispute in the early 1980s made clear, the Soviet Union has obviously decided to supplement its own efforts at industrial modernization with a massive influx of Western technology. The Federal Republic is one of the most highly developed industrial nations, dependent on large-scale exports for its prosperity. Once the political, military, and economic ties among the Western European nations and between them and the United States were loosened, the Soviet Union could offer a profitable alternative.

Such a development would also greatly relieve Soviet anxieties over the Chinese threat, which—at the very least in the short run—have influenced the Soviet stance in world politics. The so-called policy of détente with the United States owed its existence not only to economic considerations and the desire to destroy the Atlantic Alliance as the foundation stone of the European balance of power, but also to the fear of being caught in a confrontation on both the eastern and western frontiers of the Soviet Union. Insofar as the Soviet Union has become convinced that reconciliation with China is impossible—and, in consequence, that war with China is possible if not probable—it must seek to relieve the pressure that the Atlantic Alliance has exerted upon its western frontiers through the policy of "containment."

In that search, the new American policy toward China presents both an opportunity and a risk. It hardly needs to be said that the normalization of relations between the United States and China was twenty years overdue when the first steps toward it were taken in 1971. These steps meant little for the bilateral relations between the United States and China as long as the United States continued to recognize the government of Taiwan and to stress in word and deed the validity of its commitment to that government. But they can mean a great deal for the new three-cornered relations among the United States, China, and the Soviet Union. The United States enjoys a certain freedom of maneuver between the two other powers, which allows it to take advantage of the implacable hostility between them. Both must compete for American support against each other, or at least prevent American support from going to the other side. These interests dictate self-restraint within rather narrow limits in the pursuit of policies that the United States might oppose (viz., military support of North Vietnam and of "wars of national liberation" in general) and readiness for accommodation, again within rather narrow limits, to American preferences. The United States, in turn, while it has by no means the freedom of action Great Britain enjoyed from Henry VIII to Sir Edward Grey as the "holder" of European balance of power, is at liberty to make at least small changes in its position between the two other powers in order to encourage policies favorable to its interests.

China is the country that has benefited most from normalization of relations. It has done so in two major respects. Its admission to the family of nations and, in particular, to the United Nations has given it a new opportunity to seek the leadership of the so-called Third World of under-developed nations against the two superpowers. While since 1917 the Soviet Union has identified itself with "the world revolution of the have-nots," against imperialism both on the national and class level, China puts the two superpowers into the same leaking imperialist boat and takes over the traditional position that (at least in Chinese rhetoric) the Soviet Union has vacated. Furthermore, the new American attitude toward China has freed Japan from the onerous restraints that formerly made its dealings with China so difficult due to the close coordination of its foreign policies with those of the United States. While Japan could not afford to strike out on its own in normalizing its relations with China, once the United States started to do so, Japan followed suit. Weighing the potentialities of this new relationship between Japan and China, one discovers complementary interests not dissimilar to those making possible closer West German–Soviet ties. Japan is a highly developed modern industrial nation that must export on a large scale in order to live. China presents especially in the long run an immense underdeveloped market for industrial machinery and products. In combination, the two countries could indeed dominate Asia economically, politically, and militarily. Such a combination would resemble the "Asian Coprosperity Sphere" that Japan tried in vain to establish by way of conquest, but would now be based upon the mutual recognition of complementary interests.

The new mobility Japan enjoys as a by-product of the American initiative is not limited to its relations with China. As the United States can now maneuver within narrow limits between the Soviet Union and China, so can Japan. For the Soviet need of foreign participation in its industrial and technological development is a standing invitation to Japan, just as it is to West Germany.

The new diplomacy of movement characterizes not only direct relations among the great powers but also their indirect relations through the smaller powers. The most striking example of this is the Middle East. Until the October war of 1973, the Arab nations of the Middle East were lined up against Israel, each side supplied and supported by one of the superpowers. The rigidity of that alignment has now made way for an unprecedented flexibility of American policy. Not only has the United States facilitated and supported the Israeli-Egyptian peace accords reached at Camp David, it has also provided aid to Jordan and Saudi Arabia and shown a readiness to do the same for Syria, should the latter prove receptive. American policy obviously aims at the limitation, if not expulsion, of Soviet power and influence in the Middle East, just as Soviet policy seeks the limitation, if not expulsion, of American power and influence in Western Europe. If the Soviet Union might emerge from such changes as the predominant power in all of Europe, so might the United States attain a similar position in the Middle East.

These opportunities for diplomatic maneuver were once the main stakes of foreign policy. Their judicious use was once the main instrument, short of war, by which nations tried to achieve their ends. Their usefulness has by no means been eliminated altogether; for it is still necessary for nations to compete for power and other advantages, to accommodate and reconcile divergent interests, to settle conflicts peacefully. But that usefulness has been qualified by two factors that have no precedent in recorded history: (1) the divorce of military power from economic and political power insofar as the latter is derived from the former; and (2) the availability of nuclear weapons, transforming war from part of the rational continuum of foreign policy into an instrument for the enemy's total destruction.

The military impotence of well-armed and otherwise strong powers vis-à-vis nations weak in every respect but two (the quasi-monopolistic control of oil and the enormous financial resources they make available) points up the basic defect of contemporary world politics, the main source of global disorder, and the principal threat to the survival of civilization. It is the incompatibility of the nation-state as the basic unit of political organization with the social forces at work in the technology of transportation, communication, and warfare, and with the quasi-monopolistic control, by relatively few nations, of the products of nature necessary to maintain civilization and life itself.

International disorder and its possible denouement in nuclear catastrophe is a genuine if dramatic potential in contemporary world politics. Until recently, this situation has been glossed over by the relative coherence of the two blocs dominated by the superpowers, on the one hand, and, on the other, by the weakness of the Third World nations. It is exactly the new diplomacy of movement that threatens to bring these hidden tendencies toward anarchy and nuclear destruction to the fore. To create out of these disintegrative and destructive tendencies a "structure of peace" will test the ability of even the greatest of statesmen.

Détente and Peaceful Coexistence

Political ideas are especially susceptible to the dangers of misunderstanding and abuse when it is attempted to move from theory to practice. In the 1970s, President Richard M. Nixon sought to bring about the relaxation of tensions between the superpowers through a foreign policy of détente. In 1976, President Jimmy Carter sought to redefine the meaning and content of détente. A debate ensued between the critics and defenders of détente. The fog of that debate—the product partly of genuine confusion, partly of purposeful obfuscation—continues to blur distinctions vital to an adequate understanding of foreign policy.

Two examples illustrate the difficulty. (1) President Nixon returned from Moscow in 1972 to declare that the United States and the Soviet Union had taken an "irreversible" step toward building a "structure of peace." Yet the first lesson one learns when studying international relations is the reversibility of everything: of friendships, enmities, alignments, interests, means, and ends. A cursory look at the history of Soviet-American relations (before and after 1972) and the relations between the Soviet Union, on the one hand, and Germany and China, on the other, provides vivid illustrations of that statement. As concerns a "structure" of peace, in contrast to peace pure and simple, where is it? Where are the institutions and procedures that have made peace more secure than it was before détente became the watchword of the day? Peace between the two superpowers has been preserved not through détente but through the nuclear balance of terror. That balance has imposed effective restraints upon the foreign policies of both superpowers: Take, for instance, the American abstention during the Hungarian Revolution of 1956 and the Soviet occupation of Czechoslovakia in 1968, or the Soviet retreats on the occasions of the Cuban missile crisis of 1962 and the Middle Eastern war of 1973. Hence it is not far-fetched to suggest that the possibility of détente, too, results from that balance. Thus it is not détente that makes for peace, but it is the nuclear balance that makes both for détente and peace.

(2) The late Senator Henry Jackson once suggested that the United States ought to work for an accommodation with China rather than with the Soviet Union, since that would be much easier to achieve. Underlying this suggestion is an essentially mechanistic conception of international relations. It assumes that one can interchange one power for another as friend or enemy, like pawns on a chessboard. If détente with the Soviet Union does not work, simply substitute China for the Soviet Union and all will be well. By virtue of the military weakness of China and the absence of acute points of friction, tensions between the United States and China are low; hence, their abatement or elimination would indeed be easy. But it is exactly because it *was* easy—for in a sense it was already an accomplished fact—that détente between China and the United States is not an urgent task for American foreign policy. Conversely, it is exactly because it *is* difficult that détente between the Soviet Union and the United States is urgent; for wherever the two superpowers confront each other directly or vicariously in hostile alignments, mutual nuclear deterrence is put to the test. Should deterrence fail that test even once, the result might bring into play mutually assured destruction, or MAD, as the strategists have dubbed it.

In order to gain perspective it may not be superfluous to remind oneself of the literal meaning of détente. The word refers to the previous existence of tension which has been abated or eliminated. Since there have been many tensions between the United States and the Soviet Union on different levels of social interaction and in different geographical locations, it is futile to raise the question whether or not détente as an abstract, comprehensive concept has worked. It makes sense only to ask whether or not previously existing specific tensions have been abated or eliminated by Soviet and American policies. When posed in such concrete, specific terms, the question deserves a positive answer—at least until the late 1970s—with regard to three kinds of tensions that had formerly poisoned relations between the superpowers.

One manifestation of such détente was the removal from overall Soviet-American relations of the crusading ideological fervor that during the early Cold War—and again in the 1980s—transformed every contest into a Manichean conflict between good and evil, making negotiated settlements difficult if not impossible. Such ideological decontamination improved the international political atmosphere during part of the 1960s and the 1970s, an improvement that in an intangible fashion improved the chances for the negotiated settlement of substantive issues. Another manifestation of détente was the substantial settlement of the German question through West German recognition of the territorial status quo in Central Europe and, more particularly, of the East German state, and through agreement on the international status of West Berlin. Finally, the SALT I agreements, regulating the competition for offensive nuclear weapons and virtually eliminating it for defensive ones, the tacit observance of the moribund SALT II treaty, and continuing nuclear arms negotiations—all these at least partially reduced the tensions concomitant with an unregulated nuclear arms race.

The short list of détente's successes is counterbalanced by a long list of issues that remained unaffected by it; many have even been aggravated by its partial achievement. That is particularly true of Europe, where the conferences on European security and mutual, balanced reduction of forces remain deadlocked. In those instances the very fact of détente in Central Europe and the apparent overall lessening of frictions between the United States and the Soviet Union accentuated the disintegrative tendencies within NATO. In the Middle East the two superpowers compete for power and influence, as they do in the countries bordering on the Indian Ocean. Soviet expansion, thrusting from the eastern Mediterranean through the Middle East to South Asia and supported by rapidly increasing naval and military power, seems intended to move into the "empty" spaces left by the liquidation of the colonial empires; hence the USSR's foreign policy has continued to create new points of tension. More recently, the Soviet departure from the START talks further illustrates the deteriorating of Soviet-American relations to the lowest point since the late 1940s.

As an abstraction, détente partakes of the same universal psychological appeal of concepts previously launched by the Soviet Union, such as peace fostered by peace congresses, general and complete disarmament, relaxation of tensions, and collective security. No right-thinking person can oppose such concepts when presented in the form of abstract goals. Nobody in his senses will come out in favor of war, the arms race, more and better tensions, or greater insecurity. Yet while Americans tend to take these abstractions at their face value, the Soviets have launched successful propaganda campaigns on behalf of them in the service of concrete political interests and goals. They have not suddenly discovered the virtues and benefits of détente as a universal abstraction. What they discovered was that the burden of sustaining great military pressures on both their eastern and western frontiers and of simultaneously competing with the United States for nuclear and general technological parity was too heavy to bear. Hence they were receptive to West Germany's recognition of the territorial status quo in Central Europe, which created genuine détente at the very heart of the Cold War. They sought successfully the same recognition on the part of the other European nations, as well as the non-European members of NATO, through the instrumentality of the European Security Conference, again using the abstraction of European security as a cover for policies serving their own security. Finally and most importantly, they sought a massive infusion of Western technology and industry into the lagging Soviet economic system.

The invocation of détente as a kind of disembodied spirit, permeating and thereby transforming the overall relations of formerly hostile nations, has become a substitute for detached examination of the objective factors of interests and power. Even so astute a statesman as Secretary of State Henry Kissinger was not immune to that fallacy. Mr. Kissinger expected the Soviet Union to act before, during, and at the conclusion of the Yom Kippur War of 1973 "in the spirit of détente"–but it did nothing of the kind. It acted in accordance with its conception of its national interest. It aided and abetted Arab preparations for the war, it did not inform the United States of the imminence of the conflict, and it called upon all Arab governments to participate in the war, in violation of the agreements of the 1973 summit. It opposed the termination of the war as long as the Arabs were winning, and it urged immediate cessation of hostilities when they were losing. It threatened and prepared for direct military intervention as an alternative to such cessation. It was not the "spirit of détente" that prevented a direct military confrontation between the United States and the Soviet Union but the alertness of the American strategic forces at a crucial point in the struggle. It was the threat and counterthreat of military force that preserved the peace between the United States and the Soviet Union, as it had during the Cuban missile crisis of 1962.

Two factors are bound to throw into question the few alleged instances of real achievement through détente: the largely unsuccessful record in arms control negotiations since 1972, and the American reaction to certain domestic policies of the Soviet Union. The rekindled nuclear arms race has created tensions wiping out many of the limited gains made possible by détente. Since each side suspects the other of seeking a first-strike capability, the current arms race introduces new instability into the present balance of terror, and as we have seen, it is this balance– and not détente–that has actually prevented the outbreak of nuclear war so far.

The negative impact of the domestic policies of the Soviet Union upon détente is another observable fact. Since Woodrow Wilson's time, the relevance of the domestic policies of a nation (particularly the character of its government) to the kind of foreign policy it pursues has been a question of intense debate in the United States. Two different answers have been given to this question. One is the Wilsonian and general liberal assertion that only democracies can be trusted to keep their commitments and pursue peaceful policies, for autocracies are inherently untrustworthy and prone to deflect domestic discontent to foreign adventures and war. Consequently, it is the mission of the United States to support democratic governments and to oppose and reform autocratic governments throughout the world. Underlying this view is the philosophic assumption, advanced most effectively by Rousseau, that "the people" are good and peaceful by nature, so democratic control of foreign policy tends toward decent and peaceful international relations. Thus one cannot do business with dictators, but one can deal with democracies. (It should be noted in passing that Bismarck thought Prussia could not do business with England because the foreign policy of a parliamentary government was inherently unreliable.)

The second answer holds that, regardless of their domestic politics or the character of their governments, nations try to pursue their interests in a rational manner, and in any event foreign policy has its own laws that are essentially unaffected by domestic circumstances. Hence, a democratic country such as the United States has to deal with all kinds of governments, even those whose character and policies it morally condemns, and must take as the yardstick for its policies the interests and power of the nations concerned. It cannot afford to jeopardize its own interests by indulging its domestic political preferences and moral judgments of other nations. It should make a pact with the devil himself, to paraphrase Churchill, if it is in the national interest to do so. No doubt this is the correct answer. Nations have in fact consistently taken this position, since a rational foreign policy is otherwise impossible. Yet, while the answer appears to be right, and the practice derived from it sound, the story does not end there.

International peace and order are a function of the balance of power—that is, of an approximately equal distribution of power among several nations or a combination of nations, preventing any one of them from gaining the upper hand over the others. It is this approximate, tenuous equilibrium that provides whatever peace and order exist in the world of nation-states.

But the equilibrium does not operate mechanically, as the "balance" metaphor would seem to indicate. Rather, it requires a consensus among the nations involved in favor of the maintenance—or, if it should be disturbed, of the restoration—of the balance of power. In other words, the dynamics of the arrangement are embedded in a moral framework without which, in the long run, it cannot operate. The participants must give their moral approval, in theory and more importantly in practice, to the principles of the balance of power itself in order to make it work. The eighteenth century was one of the classic balance-of-power periods precisely because a strong moral consensus supported the concept as a political mechanism.

The practical question demanding an answer today is: does a common morality, similar to that of the eighteenth century, unite the nations of the world—or at least the United States and the Soviet Union? Who can give a positive response to this question? The superpowers are united not by a common morality, but only by the fear of nuclear war that might destroy them both. By seeking a second-strike capability so strong as to approach the level of a first strike, even this elemental striving for self-preservation is qualified by the implicit effort to gain a decisive advantage ensuring one's survival at the expense of the other's demise.

There is no escaping the conclusion that in the Soviet Union, and to a lesser degree in the United States, in place of the common morality that is indispensable for a viable balance of power and genuine détente, we have a national morality resting on the belief that the government has a monopoly of truth and virtue and that the people are merely children who must be guided, if not coerced, to do the government's bidding. The Soviet Union, moreover, has added to the traditional practices of czarist despotism the devices of modern totalitarianism. These devices keep virtually the whole population in ignorance about what is happening in their own country and the rest of the world, and reduce to a minimum physical and intellectual contacts with the outside world.

For reality they substitute a patchwork of metaphysical notions called—quite unfairly to Marx and Lenin—Marxism-Leninism.

A government that cuts itself and its people off from objective contact with the outside world becomes the prisoner of its own propaganda; it cannot pursue a foreign policy capable of recognizing, let alone respecting, those self-imposed moral limitations that are the basis of a viable balance of power policy. It does not follow that a relaxation of domestic totalitarianism would automatically call forth a more rational foreign policy. It would, however, remove an important obstacle to such a policy by making possible the beginnings of a dialogue among different schools of thought within the Soviet Union—after the model of the great debates that preceded and followed great decisions in American foreign policy. Such a dialogue would at least have a chance of clarifying positions and contributing to the slow and painful growth of a political and moral consensus more in keeping with that of the rest of the world.

What makes the character and domestic policies of Soviet government of vital concern to the outside world is its refusal to become part of a "system of arts, and laws, and manners" that is the lifeblood for the balance of power and would make genuine détente possible. Were the Soviet Union part of such a system, one would indeed not need to care on *political* grounds about how autocratic and despotic its government might be. But as long as the Soviet Union remains outside such a system, at best indifferent and at worst hostile to it, the rest of the world has a vital interest in the character of the Soviet government and of its domestic policies. If the Kremlin abated its present totalitarian practices by allowing its people a modicum of freedom of expression and movement, it would be taking the first step toward joining and in a sense re-creating a system that would itself be a manifestation of détente and provide the moral framework for the balance of power.

Thus serious interest in the totalitarian excesses of the Soviet government is not simply unwarranted meddling in the affairs of another sovereign nation in a misguided spirit of liberal reform. Nor does it solely express humanitarian concern or serve to placate public opinion at home. Foremost, it is at the service of that basic interest which the United States and the Soviet Union have in common: survival in the nuclear age through a viable balance of power and genuine détente.

The French philosopher Fénelon, in his advice to the grandson of Louis XIV, from which we have quoted before,[10] gave an account of the different types of the balance of power. In assessing their respective advantages and weaknesses, he bestowed the highest praise upon the opposition between two equally strong states as the perfect type of the balance of power. He said:

> The fourth system is that of a power which is about equal with another and
> which holds the latter in equilibrium for the sake of the public security. To
> be in such a situation and to have no ambition which would make you
> desirous to give it up, this is indeed the wisest and happiest situation for a

---

[10]See page 226.

state. You are the common arbiter; all your neighbors are your friends, and those that are not make themselves by that very fact suspicious to all the others. You do nothing that does not appear to have been done for your neighbors as well as for your people. You get stronger every day; and if you succeed, as it is almost inevitable in the long run by virtue of wise policies, to have more inner strength and more alliances than the power jealous of you, you ought to adhere more and more to that wise moderation which has limited you to maintaining the equilibrium and the common security. One ought always to remember the evils with which the state has to pay within and without for its great conquests, the fact that these conquests bear no fruit, the risk which one runs in undertaking them, and, finally, how vain, how useless, how short-lived great empires are and what ravages they cause in falling.

Yet since one cannot hope that a power which is superior to all others will not before long abuse that superiority, a wise and just prince should never wish to leave to his successors, who by all appearances are less moderate than he, the continuous and violent temptation of too pronounced a superiority. For the very good of his successors and his people, he should confine himself to a kind of equality.[11]

The distribution of power which Fénelon envisaged distinctly resembles the distribution of power that exists between the United States and the Soviet Union. The potentially beneficial results of an equilibrium between two independent powers, maintaining that equilibrium through moderate competition, were impressed upon the French philosopher by the contemplation of history, and they have been impressed upon us by contemporary experience. Yet the relationship between bipolarity of power and political stability is not a modern discovery. The ancients knew of it and tried to create it through the artifice of constitutional arrangements. Thus Sparta was governed by two kings, and the Roman Republic by two consuls, of equal power. A similar relationship existed between the two military leaders of the Iroquois Confederation and the two civil heads of the medieval city of Augsburg.[12]

Such an equilibrium is always threatened by its inherent instability. This instability is the result of the dynamics of the struggle for power. It is this threat to which the bipolar equilibrium between the United States and the Soviet Union is constantly exposed. That threat is magnified by the character of modern war, which, under the impact of nationalistic universalism and modern technology, has undergone truly revolutionary changes. It is here that we find the last of the fundamental changes that distinguish contemporary world politics from the international politics of previous ages.

---

[11]*Oeuvres* (Paris, 1870), Vol. III, pp. 349–50.
[12]Cf. Kurt H. Wolff, editor, *The Sociology of Georg Simmel* (Glencoe: Free Press, 1950), pp. 138 ff. The terms "relaxation of tensions" and "détente" are really synonyms of "peaceful coexistence," used to refer to the peculiar relationship between two superpowers of approximately equal strength.

22 Total War

We have already pointed out that war in our time has become total in four different respects: with respect to (1) the fraction of the population completely identified in its emotions and convictions with the wars of its nation, (2) the fraction of the population participating in war, (3) the fraction of the population affected by war, and (4) the objective pursued by war. When Fénelon wrote at the beginning of the eighteenth century, war was limited in all these respects and had been so limited since the beginning of the modern state system.

Let us take as an extreme example of this type of limited warfare the Italian wars of the fourteeth and fifteenth centuries. These wars were fought primarily by mercenaries who, their interests being in the main financial, were not eager to die in battle or to invite that risk by killing too many of their enemies. Furthermore, the *condottieri*—the leaders of the contending armies—were not interested in sacrificing their soldiers, for the soldiers constituted their working capital. They had invested money in their armies and they wanted them to remain going concerns. Nor did the *condottieri* want to kill many enemy soldiers, for as prisoners they could be sold for ransom or hired as soldiers for their own armies, but they could not be put to financial gain after they had been slain. The *condottieri* were not interested in decisive battles and wars of annihilation, for without a war and without an enemy there was no job. In consequence, these Italian wars consisted in good measure in skilled maneuvers and tactical artifices to compel the enemy to give up his positions and retreat, losing prisoners rather than wounded or dead.[1]

---

[1] See the description by Sir Charles Oman, *A History of the Art of War in the Middle Ages* (London: Methuen, 1924), Vol. II, p. 304: "For the combatants had no national or religious hatred for each other, and generally not even personal hatred, though some *condottieri* were jealous of others, or had old grudges of treachery or insult against them. But the men-at-arms of each host had probably served half a dozen times side by side with their enemies of the moment, since the bands were always passing into the pay of new employers. They might often be old friends of the particular squad against whom they were tilting. And even if this were not the case, all mercenaries were more or less brothers in arms, and despised the tyrant or the *bourgeoisie* which paid them. Moreover, a prisoner was worth to his captor not only the value of his horse and armour, but also a ransom, while a dead man could pay nothing. Hence victories became ridiculous—a tactically beaten corps made no great effort to escape, because surrender meant no more than pecuniary loss. And there was a possibility that the victor might offer them the chance of enlisting in his ranks—in which case the captive would not even lose horse and arms."

Thus Machiavelli can report a number of fifteenth-century battles, some of great historical significance, in which either nobody at all or only one man was killed, and he not by enemy action but by falling from his horse.

Machiavelli's account may be exaggerated, but there can be no doubt that those wars[2] were the manifestations of a type of limited war that prevailed, with the sole significant exceptions of the Wars of Religion and the Napoleonic Wars, throughout modern history up to the First World War. One of the great military leaders of the eighteenth century, the Marshal of Saxe, proclaimed the very same principle of warfare that guided the *condottieri* of the fourteenth and fifteenth centuries, when he said: "I am not at all in favor of battles, especially at the beginning of a war. I am even persuaded that an able general can wage war all his life without being compelled to give battle." At the turn of that century, Daniel Defoe observed: "Now it is frequent to have armies of fifty thousand men of a side at bay within view of one another, and spend a whole campaign in dodging, or, as it is genteelly called, observing one another, and then march off into winter quarters."[3] On January 12, 1757, in a letter to his son, the Earl of Chesterfield described the wars of his times in these terms:

> . . . even war is pusillanimously carried on in this degenerate age; quarter is given; towns are taken, and the people spared: even in a storm, a woman can hardly hope for the benefit of a rape.[4]

On the other hand, when that epoch of limited war had come to a close, Marshal Foch, in lectures given in 1917 at the French War College, summed up the old and the new—total—type of war:

> Truly a new era had begun, that of national wars which were to absorb into the struggle all the resources of the nation, which were to be aimed not at dynastic interests, not at the conquest or possession of a province, but at the defense or spread of philosophic ideas first, of principles of independence, unity, immaterial advantages of various kinds afterwards. They were destined to bring out the interest and faculties of each soldier, to take advantage of sentiments and passions never before recognized as elements of strength. . . . On one side, intensive use of human masses fired by strong feelings, absorbing every activity of society and conforming to their needs the material parts of the system, such as fortifications, supplies, use of ground, armament, encampments, etc.
>
> On the other side, the 18th century side: regular and methodical use of these material parts which become the foundation of various systems, differing of course with time but aiming always to control the use of troops, in order to

[2]Contemporaries distinguished between "good" and "bad" wars, the former corresponding to the type of war discussed in the text, the latter referring to the ferocity of the Swiss, especially in their encounters with German *Landsknechts*, who reciprocated in kind.

[3]Quoted after John U. Nef, "Limited Warfare and the Progress of European Civilization, 1640–1740," *The Review of Politics*, Vol. 6 (July 1944), p. 277.

[4]Charles Strachey, editor, *The Letters of the Earl of Chesterfield to His Son* (New York: G. P. Putnam's Sons, 1901), Vol. II, p. 321.

preserve the army, property of the sovereign, indifferent to the cause for which it fights but not without some professional qualities, especially as regards military spirit and tradition.[5]

It is significant in this context that the phrase Fénelon used in the early eighteenth century to characterize the battles of the religious wars—"Either you are vanquisher or vanquished"—reappears in Foch's characterization of the new world wars of the twentieth century:

> If the defeated side only comes to terms when it has no means left of discussion, the aim must be to destroy its means of discussion. A decision by arms, that is, the only judgment that counts because it is the only one that makes a victor or a vanquished; it alone can alter the respective situations of the opponents, the one becoming master of his actions while the other continues subject to the will of his adversary.[6]

WAR OF TOTAL POPULATIONS

That in the new age of warfare the masses of individual citizens identify themselves fully with the wars in which their country is engaged is strikingly illustrated by two factors, one moral, the other empirical.

The moral factor is the revival, in the twentieth century, of the doctrine of just war—that is to say, of the distinction between belligerents whose participation in war is justified in ethics and law, and those who are not considered to have the legal and moral right to take up arms. This doctrine dominated the Middle Ages, but with the ascendancy of the modern state system it was watered down to the vanishing point. As Professor Ballis has pointed out in reference to the development of the doctrine in the sixteenth century: "The notion of the mediaeval schoolmen on a just war—guilt on one side and righteousness on the other—practically vanished. There came in its place the idea that the Sovereign was to make war as an accuser and as a judge." As a result, the new doctrine "widened by casuistry the chances for making virtually any kind of war just."[7]

Throughout the period of limited warfare, the distinction between just and unjust war remained at best ambiguous and was finally abandoned in the nineteenth century when war was considered to be a mere fact, the conduct of which was subject to certain moral and legal rules, but of which all states had a legal and moral right to avail themselves at their discretion. In this view, war was an instrument of national and, more particularly, of dynastic policy to be used alternately or simultaneously with diplomacy, as the government saw fit.

---

[5]Ferdinand Foch, *The Principles of War*, translated by J. de Morinni (New York: H. K. Fly, 1918), pp. 31–32.
[6]Ibid., pp. 39, 42–43.
[7]William Ballis, *The Legal Position of War: Changes in Its Practice and Theory from Plato to Vattel* (The Hague: Nijhoff, 1937), pp. 102–03.

For the masses of a people to identify themselves wholly with such a war was obviously impossible. For such an identification, a moral issue was needed for whose defense or attainment war was to be waged. In other words, war had to be just on one's own side and unjust on the side of the enemy in order to evoke moral enthusiasm in support of one's own cause and hostile passion against the enemy. Perhaps soldiers of fortune and professionals would be willing to lay down their lives without this justification, but not citizens-in-arms. Nationalism in the Napoleonic Wars and in the German and Italian wars of national unification in the nineteenth century, and nationalistic universalism in the two world wars of the twentieth, have supplied that principle of justice and, with it, that passion and enthusiasm which have restored to masses of fighting men the willingness to conquer and die for an idea.

The vehicle upon which the ideas of nationalism and nationalistic universalism rode to victory was universal military service through conscription. Neither mercenaries nor the riffraff pressed into military service nor the good people kidnapped into it, all of which made up the rank and file of armies in the period of limited warfare before the nineteenth century, could be expected to be inspired by moral and ideal considerations. Their main interest to avoid battle and stay alive coincided with the desire of their leaders to keep the financial investment and the risks low by trying to win wars through maneuvering rather than fighting. Under Frederick the Great, two-thirds of the Prussian Army were recruited from foreign mercenaries. One-third of the Prussian Army that opposed the armies of the French Revolution in 1792 still consisted of mercenaries, and its inept maneuvering, aimed primarily at the avoidance of battle, expressed well the spirit of its soldiers, who did not know for or against what they fought. "The French system of conscription," said the Duke of Wellington, referring to the French and English armies of that period, "brings together a fine specimen of all classes; our army is composed of the scum of the earth—the mere scum of the earth."

During the period of limited warfare, desertions not only of individuals but of whole units were common. A mercenary, or an army of mercenaries, would serve one employer in the spring and another in the fall, according to the benefits to be expected. If his contract was only for one fighting season, this procedure was perfectly regular; yet he would not hesitate to follow it regardless of contractual obligations if he was dissatisfied with the wages and working conditions under his old master.

It was especially effective in labor disputes of this kind for a contingent of mercenaries to look for another employer immediately before a battle or during a siege. Thus in 1521, at the siege of Parma, three thousand Italians deserted the French Army and went over to the other side. In October 1521, the Swiss contingent of the French Army in Italy was within a few weeks reduced through desertion from twenty thousand to six thousand men. The following spring, the new contingent of Swiss went on strike the day before the battle of Bicocca, virtually dictating the French battle plan, with the result that the Swiss attack was beaten back and the battle lost. In the opposing camp during the same battle, the German contingent is reported to have demanded double pay for staging a counterattack, neither of which was forthcoming. A few days before the battle of Pavia in 1525, six thousand Swiss and two thousand Italians left the French Army, although they had received their full pay. Their desertion reduced the strength of the French Army by almost one-third.

During the religious wars of the sixteenth and seventeenth centuries, whole armies changed sides time and again. In the eighteenth century, the losses armies suffered from desertion exceeded the losses in battle, and the practice was so widespread that it was inadvisable for armies to camp or maneuver in poorly visible terrain and in other than close formation. To keep enough men in the field, Frederick the Great was forced to pay rewards to deserters who returned to their units within six months.

Military service was widely used as alternative punishment for crimes. The Landgrave of Hesse, for instance, who was opposed to capital punishment, used to send criminals under sentence of death to his regiment, and it was general practice to give insolvent debtors the alternative between serving their sentence or enlisting in the army. The general contempt in which armies of this kind were held was commensurate with their morale. They were, as a contemporary of Frederick the Great put it, "animated neither by a spirit of patriotism nor by loyalty to their prince." They were kept together only by iron discipline and the prospect of rewards; and in view of their social origin, their social prestige, and the character of the wars fought by them, this could not have been otherwise.[8]

In order to have an army that was capable of identifying itself wholly with the cause of a war, it was necessary to have a cause that could unite a large mass of men behind it and an army that was homogeneous in terms of that cause. When Protestants and Catholics fought each other over the issue of whose religion should prevail, the unifying cause and the mass of men capable of being unified under that cause had materialized. When, in the period of limited warfare, wars were fought for the succession to a throne, the possession of a province or town, or the glory of the monarch, the two prerequisites were present for that fraction of the nobility which considered military service for the monarch as its hereditary privilege, but for nobody else. With the defense by the French nation-in-arms of the revolutionary freedoms against foreign aggression, a homogeneous army again had a cause to which it could be loyal and for which it was willing to die.

---

[8]Another variety of a limited war, of which the British were masters, has been well described by an anonymous author in the *Edinburgh Review*, Vol. I (January 1803), p. 357: "Those states, which are the most injured by the operations of war, are also the richest in superfluous stock. They have contrived a species of pecuniary commutation of war, similar to the commutation of military service, which paved the way for the introduction of standing armies: they have managed to turn off the battle from their gates, by paying less wealthy allies for fighting in their cause at a safe distance. The operations of war are in this manner rendered very harmless, and a foundation is laid for their gradual disuse. A few useless millions, and a few still more useless lives are sacrificed; the arts of peace continue to flourish, sometimes with increased prosperity; and the policy of preferring to purchase defeat at a distance, rather than victory at home—of paying allies for being vanquished, rather than gain the most splendid triumphs on their own ground—has been amply rewarded by the safety, increased resources, and real addition of power, which results from an enjoyment of all the substantial blessings of peace, with the only real advantages of necessary warfare."

The French law of 1793, making military service compulsory for all able-bodied men between the ages of eighteen and twenty-five, was the first legislative recognition of the new character of war.

While even an army originating in universal military service might fail to identify itself wholly with the cause of the war it is fighting, it can safely be said that as a rule only an army so constituted will be fully capable of that identification. Thus it is not by accident that the period of limited warfare coincides in the main with a morally indifferent conception of war fought by heterogeneous armies whose main cohesive force was compulsion and the love of adventure and money. On the other hand, total war is coeval with the nation-in-arms imbued with the conviction of the justice of the war it is fighting.

Thus it was only consistent that, with the termination of the Napoleonic period and the restoration of the Bourbons and their dynastic foreign policies, conscription was abolished in France, to be reestablished only by the Third Republic. What the law of 1793 was for France, the laws of 1807 and of the following years were for Prussia. They abolished the hiring of mercenaries, prohibited the enlistment of foreigners, and culminated in the law of 1814 proclaiming the duty of every citizen to defend his country. Both the France of the revolution and the Prussia of the War of Liberation used conscription as an instrument of the national spirit against foreign aggression, the former against the Prussia of the *ancien régime*, the latter against the France of Napoleonic imperialism.

WAR BY TOTAL POPULATIONS

When in the twentieth century the character of war again changes and its purpose transforms itself from national liberation and unification into nationalistic universalism, the participation of the population in war is correspondingly enlarged. Now not only able-bodied men are conscripted, but, in totalitarian countries, women and children as well. In the nontotalitarian countries the auxiliary services of women—Wacs, Waves, and the like—are requested on a voluntary basis. Everywhere, however, all the productive forces of the nation are harnessed to the purposes of warfare. Whereas, in the period of limited warfare, war was of little concern to the population at large, which was primarily affected by it through increased taxation, the wars of the twentieth century have become everybody's business, in the sense not only of nationalistic identification but also of military or economic participation.

Two factors are responsible for this development: the increase in the size of armies and the mechanization of warfare. The size of armies has increased enormously in the twentieth century, both absolutely and relative to the total population. In the sixteenth, seventeenth, and eighteenth centuries, the size of armies, while steadily increasing, was counted in the tens of thousands. In the Napoleonic Wars some armies reached a number of several hundred thousand men. In the First World War armies for the first time passed the million mark, and the Second World War saw military establishments in excess of 10 million men.

The proportion of the population engaged in military service in the different periods of modern history roughly corresponds to these absolute figures. To mobilize 1 percent of the population for military services in the seventeenth and eighteenth centuries was an enormous undertaking that was rarely achieved; on an average no more than one-third of 1 percent of the population was mobilized during that period. In the First World War the great European powers called 14 percent of their populations to arms. In the Second World War the corresponding figure for the main belligerents was somewhat lower. It exceeded 10 percent probably only in the case of the United States, the Soviet Union, and Germany. This decrease is accounted for by the enormously increased mechanization of warfare.

Mechanization in weapons, supplies, transportation, and communications, together with the increase in size (which even at 10 percent of the population is still ten times more than the maximum attained in previous centuries) requires the productive effort of virtually the total working population if the military establishment is to be kept fit for war. It has been estimated that the productive efforts of at least a dozen men are needed to keep one man in the battle line. In the Second World War the armed forces of the great military powers, such as Germany, the Soviet Union, and the United States, exceeded 10 million. Even if one takes into account that only a fraction of these forces were actually combatants and that the majority were service troops, the numbers of the civilian population supplying all of them with weapons, transportation, communications, clothing, and nourishment must have constituted the overwhelming majority of the working population. Thus modern war has indeed become war by total populations.

WAR AGAINST TOTAL POPULATIONS

War has become total not only in the sense of everybody being a prospective participant in war but also in the sense of everybody being a prospective victim of warfare. The comparative figures of losses in war, unreliable though they are in detail, are eloquent on that point. To take France as the nation that in modern history has been regularly engaged in the great wars of the epoch, and to take as an example the percentage, computed by decades, of the French population killed or wounded in war from 1630 to 1919, we find that from 1630 to 1789, the outbreak of the French Revolution, the maximum is 0.58, the minimum 0.01 percent. In the period from 1790 to 1819, which is roughly the period of the Napoleonic Wars, the figure rises steeply to 1.48, 1.19, and 1.54 percent, respectively, while it sinks in the period from 1820 to 1829, coincident with the revival of dynastic foreign policies, to the low of 0.001. While the figures for the remainder of the nineteenth century fit closely into the general picture presented by the whole period, the figure for the second decade of the twentieth century, the period of the First World War, rises to the all-time high of close to 15 percent. It is also significant that while the whole period from 1630 to 1829 shows for only one decade, 1720–29, no war losses at all, there are five such decades in the nineteenth century alone, the century of colonial expansion.

The picture is similar when we consider the figures for deaths in military service by centuries. The figures for Great Britain show the typical curve, slumping in the nineteenth century and rising steeply in the twentieth. Great Britain had 15 deaths in military service per 1,000 deaths for the total population in the seventeenth century, 14 in the eighteenth, 6 in the nineteenth, and 48 in the twentieth up to 1930. The corresponding figures for France show a considerable rise in the eighteenth and no slump in the nineteenth century because of the interruption of the period of limited warfare by the Napoleonic Wars. The figures are 11 for the seventeenth century, 27 for the eighteenth, 30 for the nineteenth, and 63 for the twentieth up to 1930. The destructiveness of modern war, expressed in these figures, is still more strikingly revealed by the fact that in the preceding centuries far more military losses were caused by disease than by armed action. In consequence, losses through military action have increased relatively and absolutely to an enormous extent in the twentieth century.

Unprecedented since the end of the religious wars are the losses the civilian populations have suffered through military action in the wars of the twentieth century. There can be little doubt that the total civilian losses due to military action in the Second World War surpass the total military losses. The number of civilians killed by the Germans through measures of deliberate extermination alone is estimated at close to 12 million. While the French record of close to 15 percent of the total population killed or wounded in the First World War has not even been approximated by France in the Second World War, the share of the civilian population in the total losses has greatly increased. The same is true of the Soviet Union, which must have lost during the Second World War in killed and wounded close to 10 percent of the total population.[9] Thus, as regards civilians, the trend toward an enormous increase in the destructiveness of modern war has continued. The invention of new destructive methods of warfare, either not used at all in the preceding world wars, such as bacteriological warfare, or used only on a small scale, such as poison gas and nuclear weapons, ensures a continuation and further acceleration of that trend for both civilians and military personnel.

THE MECHANIZATION OF WARFARE

The enormously increased destructiveness of twentieth-century warfare, for combatants and civilians alike, is the result of the mechanization of warfare. Its effects in this respect are twofold: the ability to eliminate an unprecedented number of enemies through one single operation or the accelerated multiple operation of a weapon, and the ability to do so over long distances. Both developments started

[9]As to the contradictory figures of the Russian losses, see Dudley Kirk, *Europe's Population in the Interwar Years* (Series of League of Nations Publications. II. Economic and Financial. 1946. II. A. 8), p. 69, note 24, p. 70, note 28; *The World Almanac* (1946), p. 44; (1947), p. 521; (1948), p. 552; (1949), p. 326. The estimate in the text is derived from the preponderant estimates in these sources.

in the fourteenth century with the invention of gunpowder and its use for artillery. But it was only in the late nineteenth century that these developments were speeded up to a considerable extent, and only our time has witnessed such an enormous acceleration of these trends as to amount to a revolution in the technology of war.

The Mechanization of Weapons

The extreme slowness of these developments in the first six centuries of their history and the extreme rapidity in the seventh is illustrated by the history of artillery. The guns with which the Turks besieged Constantinople in 1453 could fire cannon balls weighing eight hundred pounds at a range of a mile, their rate of fire being seven rounds per day and one per night. In 1650 a cannon carrying a nine-pound shot had a point-blank range of 175 yards, while two hundred years later the same range of an English nine-pounder smoothbore was 300 yards. As Cervantes put it when artillery had just been invented:

> Happy the blest ages that knew not the dread fury of those devilish engines of artillery, whose inventor I am persuaded is in hell receiving the reward of his diabolical invention, by which he made it easy for a base and cowardly arm to take the life of a gallant gentleman; and that, when he knows not how or whence, in the height of the ardor and enthusiasm that fire and animate brave hearts, there should come some random bullet, discharged perhaps by one who fled in terror at the flash when he fired off his accursed machine, which in an instant puts an end to the projects and cuts off the life of one who deserves to live for ages to come.[10]

At the end of the eighteenth century, artillery was still regarded in most countries, with the one notable exception of France, as a subordinate and somewhat unbecoming weapon with which a gentleman would rather have nothing to do. Even Frederick the Great asked contemptuously what was valuable about artillery, and what art there was in shooting well. Yet, only a few decades later, Napoleon could say: "It is with the artillery that war is made," and it has been estimated that in the century following this remark the efficiency of artillery increased ten times.

The low esteem of the most potent and, together with the musket, lone representative of the mechanization of warfare remained traditional in the Prussian Army. In the eighteenth century this contempt may not have been altogether without justification in view of the extreme slowness of loading, the inaccuracy of the aim, and the limited range (a maximum of 2,000 yards). But the nineteenth century witnessed a progress in the rapidity of fire and the range of firearms that foreshadowed the revolution of the twentieth. While, for instance, in 1850 the number of bullets fired by a smooth-bore muzzle loader by a thousand men in one minute was 500 and their range about the same as it had been for the musket of the sixteenth, seventeenth, and eighteenth centuries—that is, close to 300 yards—the

---

[10]Miguel de Cervantes, *The History of Don Quixote de la Mancha*, Part I, Chapter 38.

corresponding figures for the needle gun are 1,000 rounds and 2,200 yards; for the 1866 model, 2,000 rounds and 2,700 yards; for the 1886 model, 6,000 rounds and 3,800 yards; and for the repeating rifle with charger in 1913, 10,000 rounds and 4,400 yards. Between 1850 and 1913, the rapidity of fire had increased twentyfold, and the range expanded sixteen times. Yet today we have machine guns that fire 1,000 rounds a minute, making 1,000,000 for a thousand men where there were only 10,000 in 1913, and even semiautomatic shoulder rifles, such as the Garand, are able to fire 100 aimed rounds per minute—that is, ten times more than the fastest small arms in 1913.[11]

How great the progress made in this respect was between 1850 and 1913, and how overwhelming between 1913 and 1938, becomes apparent from a comparison with the slow progress made between 1550 and 1850. In the mid-sixteenth century, the range of the hand cannon was about one hundred yards, and one round in two minutes was about the best rate of fire attainable. In the First World War the maximum range of heavy artillery—with great inaccuracy in aim and excessive wear on the gun, which was worn out after a maximum of thirty rounds—did not exceed 76 miles (attained only by the German 18.4-inch guns). By contrast, today guided missiles—that is, containers of explosives traveling under their own power—have, for practical purposes, unlimited range. The range of a fully loaded bomber capable of returning to its base after the execution of its mission was in the neighborhood of 1,500 miles at the end of the Second World War and has since been increased to exceed considerably 6,000 miles. Thus, while at the turn of the century the maximum distance within which a nation could attack a point in enemy territory was a few miles, it had increased in the First World War to 76 miles for artillery and a few hundred miles for—ineffective and lightly loaded—aircraft, and in the Second World War to about 1,500 miles; it has now become unlimited. Warfare in the second half of the twentieth century, then, has become total in that virtually the whole earth is apt to be made the theater of operations by any country fully equipped with the technological instruments of the age.

The extension of the range of instruments of war to the whole earth can mean much or little for the character of modern war and its bearing upon contemporary world politics, according to whether or not the increase in the destructiveness of war has kept pace with the increase in the range of its weapons. Through the enormous increase in destructiveness that has actually occurred during this century, and more particularly since the Second World War, modern war has transformed the potentialities of the total range of its weapons into the actuality of total war.

Until the invention of artillery, and aside from naval warfare, one military operation by one single man was as a matter of principle capable of eliminating no more than one single enemy. One strike with a sword, one thrust with a spear

---

[11]These figures are theoretical in that they refer to the optimum attainable under ideal conditions. It goes without saying that under actual battle conditions these figures are considerably less; yet their relationship will remain approximately what it is under theoretical conditions.

or a pike, one shot from a musket would at best yield one disabled enemy. The first step toward mechanization taken at the end of the Middle Ages when gunpowder was used in warfare did not at first increase the ratio of one to one between military operation and eliminated enemy. Rather, the reverse was the case. The loading and firing of an early musket, for instance, required as many as sixty different motions, executed generally by more than one man, and then the aim was so poor that only a small percentage of the shots fired would hit the target, eliminating one man. As for cannon, a considerable number of men were needed to bring it into position and load it, and the inaccuracy of the aim vitiated much of that collective effort. When a shot hit the target, the victims of one shot were at best counted by hardly more than the score.

The situation changed rapidly only with the invention of the improved machine gun in the latter part of the nineteenth century. With this weapon one man in one operation could fire hundreds of rounds with the optimum effect, never attained under actual battle conditions, of eliminating in one operation nearly as many enemies as there were shots fired. The radical improvement of artillery, starting in about the same period, and succeeding developments in the fields of air and gas warfare, brought about a considerable increase in the number of enemies who could be eliminated in one operation by one or very few men. The number was certainly still to be counted by the hundreds in the First World War, whose staggering losses are in the main accounted for by the machine gun mowing down charging infantry. Even during virtually the whole of the Second World War, the number of victims of one direct hit by a blockbuster could hardly have exceeded the thousand mark, and it has been estimated that the total number of bombs dropped approximately equaled the total number of lives lost by bombardment from the air.

Nuclear warfare and, as a potentiality, bacteriological warfare have wrought in this respect a revolution similar to, yet far exceeding in magnitude, the one that the machine gun achieved a few decades earlier. A few men dropping one atomic bomb at the end of the Second World War disabled well over a hundred thousand of the enemy. With atomic bombs increasing drastically in potency, and the defense remaining as powerless as it is now, the number of the prospective victims of one nuclear bomb, dropped over a densely populated region, will be counted in the millions. The destructive power of a few of the most potent nuclear bombs equals that of all the bombs dropped during the Second World War. The potentialities for mass destruction inherent in bacteriological warfare exceed even those of the most potent nuclear bomb, in that one or a few strategically placed units of bacteriological material can easily create epidemics affecting an unlimited number of people.

But weapons capable of destroying millions of people anywhere on earth can do no more than that and are to that extent a mere negative element in the scheme of things military and political. They may be able to break the will of the enemy to resist; but by themselves they cannot conquer and keep what has been conquered. Reaping the fruits of total war and transforming them into permanent political gains require the mechanization of transportation and communications.

The Mechanization of Transportation and Communications

Nowhere, indeed, has mechanical progress in the last decades been more staggering than with regard to the ease and speed of transportation and communications. It can safely be said that the progress achieved in this respect during the first half of the twentieth century is greater than the progress in all of previous history. It has been remarked that the thirteen days it took Sir Robert Peel in 1834 to hurry from Rome to London in order to be present at a cabinet meeting were exactly identical with the travel time allowed a Roman official for the same journey seventeen centuries earlier. The best travel speed on land and sea throughout recorded history until nearly the middle of the nineteenth century was 10 miles an hour, a speed rarely attained on land. In the early twentieth century, railroads had increased the speed of travel by land to 65 miles an hour on the fastest train, six and a half times what it had been throughout history. Steamships had speeded up travel by sea to 36 miles an hour, three and a half times the previous maximum. Today the maximum speed of a passenger plane exceeds 600 miles per hour—that is, ten and twenty times, respectively, more than the best travel speed about four decades ago. The supersonic passenger plane more than doubles these figures.

In 1790 it took four days in the best season to go from Boston to New York, a distance somewhat exceeding two hundred miles. Today the same time is sufficient for circling the globe, regardless of season. In terms of travel speed, Moscow is today as close to New York as Philadelphia was a century and a half ago, and the whole earth is considerably smaller than were the combined territories of the thirteen states that founded the United States of America. How rapid this development has been, especially in the last few years, leaving far behind the expectations even of expert observers, is strikingly illustrated by the question Professor Staley asked in 1939, while discussing the problems with which we are here concerned: "Is three hundred miles an hour an impossible passenger transport speed within twenty-five years?"[12] In 1960 the cruising speed of the fastest passenger plane was more than double what Professor Staley expected it to be in 1964. General Motors predicted in 1939 that, by 1960, 38 million cars would be on the roads; that number was actually more than doubled in 1960.

The significance of mechanical progress for passenger travel is virtually identical with its significance for transportation of goods, because the mechanical means in both cases are virtually identical. The only difference might be found in the even greater rapidity of the mechanical development of the land transport of goods because of its lower starting point. While today goods can be as speedily transported as persons, with the exception of the heaviest goods at maximum speeds, before the invention of the railroad the limitations of space and of power imposed greater limitations upon the speed of the land transport of goods than of persons. The introduction of railroads in Germany before the middle of the nineteenth century increased the speed of the transportation of goods eight times, while the corresponding increase for persons was hardly more than fivefold.

---

[12]Eugene Staley, *World Economy in Transition* (New York: Council on Foreign Relations, 1939), p. 13.

The corresponding development is, however, incomparably more rapid in the field of oral and written communications. Here mechanical progress has far outstripped that in transportation of persons and goods. Before the invention in the nineteenth century of the telegraph, the telephone, and the undersea cable, the speed of the transmission of oral or written communications was identical with the speed of travel. That is to say, the only way to transmit such communications, aside from visible signals, was by the usual means of transportation. The nineteenth-century inventions reduced the speed needed for the transmission of such communications from what had formerly been days and weeks to hours. Radio and television have made the transmission instantaneous with the utterance.

WAR FOR TOTAL STAKES

These mechanical developments make the conquest of the world technically possible, and they make it technically possible to keep the world in that conquered state. It is true that there have been great empires before. The Macedonian Empire stretched from the Adriatic to the Indus, the Roman Empire from the British Isles to the Caucasus, and Napoleon's conquests from the borders of Gibraltar to Moscow. Yet these great empires either did not last, or they lasted only because of an overwhelming differential in civilization, technical and otherwise, in favor of the ruling power over the subject peoples. The expansion of the Roman Empire illustrates this point. Many of its moves resemble colonial expansion into politically empty spaces rather than the overpowering of first-rank competitors. The other empires, however, could not last and fell far short of conquering all of the known political world because they were lacking in those technological resources necessary for the subjugation and permanent control of great masses of people dispersed over wide expanses of territory.

The technological prerequisites for a stable worldwide empire are essentially three in number: (1) enforced social integration through centralized control over the minds of the subjects of the empire, (2) superior organized force at any point of possible disintegration within the empire, and (3) permanency and ubiquity of these means of control and enforcement throughout the empire. None of these three military and political prerequisites has been achieved in the past, yet they are within the reach of our time.

Then the means of communication were nonmechanical or, where mechanical, they were strictly individualized and, hence, decentralized. News and ideas could be transmitted only by word of mouth, by letters, or through the printing press that one individual could operate in his home. In this field, then, the would-be conqueror of the world had to compete on an approximately equal footing with an unlimited number of rivals. He could put his rivals into prison or condemn them to death if he was able to identify and apprehend them. But he could not smother their voices through a monopoly or near-monopoly of the collection and dissemination of news, of press, radio, and moving pictures. Nineteen centuries ago, Saint Paul could go from city to city and write letters to the Corinthians and

Romans, spreading the Gospel, which was about all that the representatives of the official polytheistic religion of the Roman Empire could do, and when he was executed he left thousands of disciples doing what he had done in ever more effective and widespread competition with the representatives of the state. What could Saint Paul do in the world empire of tomorrow without a newspaper or magazine to print his messages, without a radio network to carry his sermons, without newsreel and television to keep his likeness before the public, probably without a post office to transmit his letters, and certainly without a permit to cross national frontiers?

The means of violence, as we have already pointed out, were in former times largely nonmechanical and always individualized and decentralized. Here, too, the would-be founder of a world empire met his future subjects, barring superior organization and training, on a footing of approximate equality. Either side had virtually the same weapons with which to cut, to thrust, and to shoot. The conqueror, in order to maintain his empire, would have had to achieve the impossible by establishing everywhere actual superiority of organized force against all possible opponents. Thus the inhabitants of Madrid could on May 3, 1808, raise against the French conqueror the same arms that the latter had at his disposal and drive him from the city. Today the government of a world empire, apprised of a similar situation by radio, would send within a few hours a squadron of bombers and a score of transports loaded with parachutists, mortars, and tanks—weapons of which it would have a monopoly or near-monopoly—to the insurgent city and squelch the revolt with ease. The very threat of the intervention of such overwhelming force, ready to strike at any place at a moment's notice, would discourage the mere thought of revolt.

Finally, the mechanization of transportation has relieved the would-be founder of a world empire from that dependency upon favorable climate and geographical location which proved the undoing of Napoleon and prevented less dynamic and less tempted leaders from even conceiving the idea of world conquest. The one great impediment to world conquest in this respect was the necessity, lasting well into the nineteenth century, to stop fighting during the late fall, winter, and early spring; for it was impossible to protect the army in the field against the weather and supply it with the necessities of life and the implements of war. Thus the enemy, if he was not overpowered beyond the hope of recovery in one campaign, was given a chance to prepare himself for a new campaign in the next fighting season. War, then, resembled a boxing match in which the intermissions after each round were long enough virtually to assure the comeback of the weaker opponent, provided he was not knocked unconscious. Under such circumstances, to think of world conquest would have been sheer folly, for the work of conquest done in one fighting season had to be largely redone in the next. Since victory was less the result of conquest and annihilation than of the comparatively greater exhaustion of the vanquished, even the victor would have been far from possessing the resources necessary to take on new enemies every spring until he had conquered the world.

Yet, even if he had been brazen enough to start on the road to world conquest, he could not have gone far. Incapable of maintaining actual superiority of armed strength throughout the conquered territories, he would have been constantly faced with the likelihood of revolts prepared and executed without his being able to meet them in time. The slowness of communications and the technical difficulties of transportation would have made it impossible for the would-be conqueror of the world to consolidate whatever permanent conquests he might have been able to make. The further he extended the limits of his empire, the greater would be the probability of his downfall. When Napoleon's empire had reached the zenith of its power in 1812, it was also closer to its disintegration than ever before. For while Napoleon was fighting at the fringes of his domain, pushing them ever farther away from the French sources of his power, the victims of his conquest could prepare behind his back for liberation. When they struck, aided by the largely uncommitted and unconquered resources of Great Britain and Russia, the main bulk of Napoleon's forces was far away and had to be brought back to the scene of revolt in defiance of the winter season and with tremendous losses, to be beaten at the spot that not the conqueror but the conquered had chosen.

Today the prospective conqueror of the world has technical means at his disposal for stabilizing beyond recall gains once made, for within the conquered territory the superiority of organized force, of which we have spoken above, is at his disposal everywhere and at all times, regardless of season and distance. An incipient revolt occurring a thousand miles from the next concentration of his air force takes place in a distance of about five miles in terms of the Napoleonic technology of transportation, and happens just around the corner in terms of the Napoleonic technology of communications. In other words, the conqueror is in a position to put all the modern techniques of mass propaganda into operation almost instantaneously in order to dissuade the disaffected from their undertaking. Within the span of a few hours, he can bring his superiority in organized force to bear upon the revolutionaries.[13]

Thus a conquest once made is made for good, from the point of view of the technological possibilities and barring, of course, blunders by the government, outside intervention, or political and military contingencies from within the empire. With these qualifications a people once conquered will stay conquered, for it has no longer the means to revolt, and the chances are that the conqueror, through his monopolistic control of the means of communications, will have deprived it of the will to revolt as well. For as Edmund Burke has said: "Let us only suffer any person to tell us his story, morning and evening, but for one twelve-month, and he will become our master."[14]

Today no technological obstacle stands in the way of a worldwide empire if the ruling nation is able to keep its superiority in the technological means of domination.

---

[13]The failure of the plot against Hitler in 1944 well illustrates this enormous superiority of the government in the face of an attempted revolt, even if staged by part of the armed forces. It shows, in particular, the decisive importance of modern mass communications, controlled by the government; for it was for all practical purposes the voice of Hitler, speaking over the radio to the people and to some of the leaders of the revolt, which decided the issue in favor of the government. Cf. the excellent account in Allen W. Dulles, *Germany's Underground* (New York: Macmillan, 1947).

[14]"Thoughts on French Affairs," *Works*, Vol. IV (Boston: Little, Brown, 1889), p. 328.

A nation that has a monopoly of nuclear weapons and of the principal means of transportation and communications can conquer the world and keep it conquered, provided it is capable of keeping that monopoly and control. First of all, it will be able to mold the minds of the citizens of its world empire into a uniformity of submissiveness, of which the totalitarian societies of the recent past and present have given us fair samples. On the assumption of a reasonably effective government, the will to revolt will at best be scattered and, in any case, will lack political and military significance. Second, any attempt at revolt will meet with the speedy reaction of superior power and is thus doomed to failure from the outset. Finally, modern technology makes it possible to extend the control of mind and action to every corner of the globe regardless of geography and season.

TOTAL MECHANIZATION, TOTAL WAR, AND TOTAL DOMINION

This analysis of the mechanization of modern war and of its military and political implications would not be complete if it did not consider the overall mechanization of Western culture, of which the mechanization of warfare is but a particular manifestation. For without that overall mechanization the modern nations would never have been able to put mass armies into the field and keep them supplied with provisions and arms. Total war presupposes total mechanization, and war can be total only to the degree to which the mechanization of nations waging it is total.

From the beginning of history to the American Civil War and the Franco-Prussian War of 1870, all military movements were executed by muscular power. Men would carry themselves and the implements of war either with their own muscles or with those of animals. All military movements, as well as the size and quality of arms and armies, were limited by the natural quantity and quality of the available muscular power of men and beasts. It was the German army that in 1870 for the first time used railroads systematically as a means of transportation, after they had been used sporadically during the Civil War. The Germans thus gained a considerable strategic and tactical advantage over the French.

As late as 1899, during the Boer War, as many as thirty-two oxen were used for drawing one five-inch gun. The slowness of the movement, the natural limitations of numbers that no human effort could overcome, and the requirements for the procurement and the transport of fodder made a war thus waged slow and cumbersome. It was the energy supplied not by muscle but by coal, water, and oil, in the form of the steam engine, the turbine, the electric motor, and the internal combustion engine, that multiplied by many times the productivity of men in peace and war. Professor James Fairgrieve, speaking primarily of Great Britain, vividly describes the contribution of coal to this development:

> Then into this world of agriculture and pasture and little market towns with a few ports and governmental cities there came, a little more than a century and a half ago, the beginnings of the Industrial Revolution. Coal, which up til then

had been used here and there merely for domestic purposes, came to be used to drive machines which would do far more work than the individual man or animal, or even a number of men or animals could do. Man harnessed energy outside himself to do the things which before then he had to do himself with his own hands. Here was a tremendous new store of energy, not food energy at all, by which things could be done which could not be done before. Man has been able to use energy on a far vaster scale. . . . A man's clothing is prepared for him to the last stitch, so that there is very little clothes-making in the home. His food is to a very great extent made ready for his table, with the result that even in his home there is far less preparation of it, and in great cities food preparation on a large scale is such an industry that he may at almost any hour of the day or night obtain such a meal as suits his pocket or his palate. . . .

It has been calculated that the coal used in our factories alone, all other uses whatsoever being excluded, gives the equivalent of the energy of 175,000,000 hard-working men, and in such a useful form as men could never supply. The power of Greece, whereby she achieved such great things in all directions of human progress, was largely based in the first instance on the work done by the servile class. On the average each Greek freeman, each Greek family, had five [slaves] whom we think of not at all when we speak of the Greeks, and yet these were the men who supplied a great part of Greek energy. In Britain, we may say, every family has more than twenty [slaves] to supply energy, requiring no food and feeling nothing of the wear and tear and hopelessness of a servile life. With a population of 45 million men, women and children, Britain's factories are worked by 175 million manpower more. In comparison with the energy supplied by machines in which things are made to move by purely mechanical means, the physical energy supplied by the fewer than 20 million men and women scarcely counts. We have become a nation of engineers, pressing buttons and pulling levers, oiling and packing, so that the great social machine will work smoothly and as easily as possible. The inanimate helots grind our corn, make our clothes, fetch our food from the ends of the earth, carry us hither and thither to work and play, print our news and our books of wisdom, and perform numberless services of which the Greeks never dreamed. . . . There are fifty inanimate slaves of the furnace for every man, woman and child in the United States. . . .[15]

The savings in labor by virtue of this mechanization are enormous. To quote Professor Fairgrieve again: "Between 1855 and 1894 the time of human labour required to produce one bushel of Indian corn on an average was reduced from four and a half hours to under three-quarters of an hour. Between 1830 and 1896 the time of human labour required to produce a bushel of wheat was reduced from three hours to ten minutes."[16] American farm production in 1952 was the

---

[15]*Geography and World Power*, 8th ed. (London: University of London Press, 1941), pp. 314–17, 326. (Reprinted by permission of the publisher.)
[16]Ibid., pp. 323–24.

largest in history, while in the same year the number of people employed in agriculture was the lowest for more than eighty years. While in technologically backward countries up to 90 percent of the population is engaged in agriculture, the percentage of the total population working in agriculture in the United States declined from 50 percent in 1870 to less than 20 percent in 1940. And while from 1910 to 1914 approximately one-third of the population of the United States was engaged in farming, producing 12.4 percent of the national income, the corresponding figures were 22.7 percent of the population and 7.8 percent of the national income in 1941, 15.9 percent of the population and 6.4 percent of the national income in 1952, 6.8 percent of the population and 2.5 percent of the national income in 1964, and 3.1 percent of the population and 2.8 percent of the national income in 1981.

Professor Hornell Hart reports the following examples illustrating the same trend in industry:

> Until 1730 spinning, for example, was all done by hand: the spinner slowly and laboriously drew out one strand at a time. During the past 200 years machinery has so revolutionized the process that one operative takes care of 125 spindles, all turning at a speed of 10,000 revolutions per minute. In the Philippines, where industry is still in the ancient man-power stage, a cargo of copra is loaded by 200 to 300 coolies, in San Francisco, with its Machine-Age economy, 16 men unload the ship in one quarter of the time required to load it. The efficiency of the men working with power-machinery is fifty times that of the man-power loaders. One steam shovel does the work of 200 unskilled men; a glass blowing machine takes the place of 600 skilled workers; one automatic electric bulb machine produces as much as 2300 workers could formerly.[17]

In the middle of the nineteenth century, 22 percent of the physical work in the United States was done by men, 51 percent by animals, and 27 percent by mechanical devices. In 1900 the corresponding figures were 15, 33, and 48 percent. In 1948 men did 4 percent of the physical work, animals did 2 percent, and 94 percent was performed by mechanical devices. As a result of this mechanical revolution, the output of goods per man-hour of work increased more than fivefold during that period. In 1966, one man-hour of farm labor produced more than five times as much food as it did in 1920, and one farm worker fed thirty-two people, whereas in 1945 he fed only twelve.

A number of industrial processes have virtually eliminated human labor altogether; mechanization has here become automation. This is true particularly in the production of hydroelectric power, which takes place without the presence of a single worker and is controlled by automatic electric signals. The production of pulp paper is entirely automatic from the feeding of the fluid pulp into the machinery to the emergence of the rolled paper. The same is true of the printing of newspapers from the feeding of the empty pulp into the machine to the emergence

---

[17] *The Technique of Social Progress* (New York: Henry Holt, 1931), p. 134. (Reprinted by permission of the publisher.)

of the folded end product. The manufacture of rayon and silk, of steel and auto-
mobiles, and the production and canning of food, especially the processing of
flour, have been mechanized with similar effects upon the increase in productivity
and the displacement of muscular labor. While, owing to the small degree of
mechanization in many productive processes, the overall results of mechanization
are considerably less impressive than these most spectacular examples would indicate, the trend is so general and so radical in some of the most important fields of
production as to amount to a revolution—the greatest in recorded history—of the
productive processes of mankind.

It is this revolution in the productive processes of the modern age that has
made total war and worldwide dominion possible. Before its advent war was
bound to be limited in its technological aspects. The productivity of a nation was
not sufficient to feed, clothe, and house its members and to keep large armies supplied with the implements of war for any length of time. More particularly, national
economies operated on so narrow a margin above the mere subsistence level that
it was impossible to increase to any appreciable extent the share of the armed
forces in the national product without endangering the very existence of the
nation. In the seventeenth and eighteenth centuries, it was not at all unusual for
a government to spend as much as, or more than, two-thirds of the national budget
for military purposes. A few times during that period military expenses consumed
more than 90 percent of the total outlay of the government; for military expenditures had, of course, precedence over all others, and the national product was
too small to be taxed extensively for other purposes. Thus it was not by accident
that before the nineteenth century all attempts at universal military service failed;
for, in the interest of keeping national production going, the productive classes of
the population had to be exempt from military service. Only the scum that was
unable to engage in productive enterprises and the nobility that was unwilling to
engage in them could safely be conscripted.

The Industrial Revolution and, more particularly, the mechanization of agricultural and industrial processes in the twentieth century have had a triple effect
upon the character of war and of international politics. They have increased enormously the total productivity of the great industrial nations. They have, furthermore, reduced drastically the relative share of human labor in the productive
processes. They have, finally, together with the new techniques in medicine and
hygiene, brought about an unprecedented increase in the population of all
nations. The increase in productivity thus achieved exceeds by far the increased
demands upon the national product caused by the higher standard of living and
the greater number of consumers. Excess in productivity is now available for new
purposes, and it can be guided into the channels of total war. The new energy created by the machine, and much of the human energy that a century and a half ago
was still absorbed in the business of keeping alive, can now be employed for military purposes, either directly by way of military service or indirectly through
industrial production.

The human energy now available for war is not muscular energy only. The
machine age has lightened immensely the intellectual and moral burden of keeping

oneself and one's dependents fed, clothed, and protected from the elements and from disease—which endeavors a century and a half ago still absorbed most of the vital energies of most men. Moreover, the machine age has provided most men with an amount of leisure that only few men have ever had before. Yet, paradoxically enough, by doing so it has freed tremendous intellectual and moral energies that have gone into the building of a better world, but that have also gone into the preparation and the waging of total war. This concatenation of human and material forces, freed and created by the age of the machine, has given war its total character.

It has also given total war that terrifying, world-embracing impetus which seems to be satisfied with nothing short of world dominion. With his intellectual and moral energies no longer primarily concerned about this life, nor any more able to be deflected toward concern with the life thereafter, modern man looks for conquests, conquest of nature and conquest of other men. The age of the machine, which has sprung from man's self-sufficient mind, has instilled in modern man the confidence that he can save himself by his own unaided efforts here and now. Thus the traditional religions, negating that confidence and relying upon divine intervention, have become bloodless images of themselves. The intellectual and moral lifeblood of modern man streams into the political religions that promise salvation through science, revolution, or the holy war of nationalism. The machine age begets its own triumphs, each forward step calling forth two more on the road of technological progress. It also begets its own victories, military and political; for with the ability to conquer the world and keep it conquered, it creates the will to conquer it.

Yet it may also beget its own destruction. Total war waged by total populations for total stakes under the conditions of the contemporary balance of power may end in world dominion or in world destruction or in both. For either one of the two contenders for world dominion may conquer with relatively small losses to itself; or they may destroy each other, neither being able to conquer; or the least weakened may conquer, presiding over universal devastation. Such are the prospects that overshadow world politics in the second half of the twentieth century.

Thus we have gone full circle. We recognized the driving element of contemporary world politics in the new moral force of nationalistic universalism. We found a simplified balance of power, operating between two inflexible blocs, to be the harbinger of great good or great evil. We discovered the menace of evil in the potentialities of total war. Yet the element that makes total war possible—the mechanization of modern life—makes possible also the moral force that, through the instrumentality of total war, aims at total dominion. The three great revolutions of our age—the moral, political, and technical—have this in common: They support and strengthen each other and move in the same direction—that of a global conflagration. Their coincidence in time and their parallel development aggravate the threat to the survival of Western civilization, which each of them carries independently.

The concatenation of these revolutions has had three important results: the permanent decline of Europe as the center of the political world, the rise of two superpowers to unchallenged prominence, and the emergence of Asia as an independent political and moral factor. Just as the political emancipation of Asia from Europe coincides with its assumption of moral opposition to the West, so does the rise of Washington and Moscow as political centers of the world coincide with their transformation into the seats of universal political religions. The decline of Europe as the political, moral, and technological center of the world is a mere by-product of the destruction, through its worldwide expansion, of the delicate social mechanism of the modern state system, of the spread of modern technology from Europe to the four corners of the earth, of the triumph of Europe's moral ideas in Asia. Europe has given to the world its political, technological, and moral achievements, and the world has used them to put an end to the preeminence of Europe.

Against this somber picture of contemporary world politics and its potentialities, we must examine the foremost problem of our time: the problem of peace.

PART EIGHT

THE PROBLEM
OF PEACE

Peace Through

Limitation

23 Disarmament

THE PROBLEM OF PEACE IN OUR TIME

Two world wars within a generation and the potentialities of nuclear warfare have made the establishment of international order and the preservation of international peace the paramount concern of Western civilization. War has always been abhorred as a scourge. As the rise of the territorial state transformed the Holy Roman Empire from the actual political organization of Christendom into an empty shell and a legal fiction, writers and statesmen reflected more and more on substitutes for the lost political unity of the Western world. Erasmus in the sixteenth century; Sully, Éméric Crucé, Hugo Grotius, and William Penn in the seventeenth; and the Abbé de Saint-Pierre, Rousseau, Bentham, and Kant in the eighteenth were the great intellectual forerunners of the practical attempts undertaken in the nineteenth and twentieth centuries to solve the problems of international order and peace.

Of these attempts, the Holy Alliance, the Hague Peace Conferences of 1899 and 1907, the League of Nations, and the United Nations are the outstanding examples. These organizations and conferences, together with other less spectacular endeavors to shape a peaceful world, were made possible by four factors—spiritual, moral, intellectual, and political—that started to converge at the beginning of the nineteenth century and culminated in the theory and practice of international affairs prevalent in the period between the two world wars.

Since the time of the Stoics and the early Christians, there has been alive in Western civilization a feeling for the moral unity of mankind, which strives to find a political organization commensurate with it. The Roman Empire was such a political organization of universal scope. After its downfall the Roman Empire remained throughout the ages a symbolic reminder of the unity of the Western world, and the ultimate goal and standard that inspired Charlemagne no less than Napoleon and determined the policies of the Holy Roman Empire until the beginning of the religious wars. It is not by accident that the dissolution of the

Holy Roman Empire in 1806 coincided with Napoleon's attempt to revive it and antedates by little less than a decade the beginning of that period of modern history which has made the restoration of international order one of its major objectives.

The moral root of these attempts to establish a stable and peaceful international order is to be found in the increase in the humaneness and civilized character of human relations that the last centuries have witnessed in the Western world. The philosophy of the Enlightenment and the political theory of liberalism postulated respect for human life and the promotion of human welfare. The great political and social reforms of the nineteenth and twentieth centuries drew their inspiration from these postulates. To extend the reign of law, peace, and order to the international sphere was then the great humanitarian task that the modern age had to solve.

The intellectual factor promoting this development is connected with the rise of the commercial classes first to social and then to political importance. With them rose to prominence the commercial and scientific spirit that dreaded war and international anarchy as irrational disturbances of the calculable operations of the market. "A war in the midst of different trading nations," the French philosopher Diderot noticed, "is a fire disadvantageous to all. It is a process which threatens the fortune of a great merchant and makes his debtors turn pale."[1] According to Kant, "the commercial spirit cannot coexist with war."[2] Thus, toward the end of the eighteenth century, it had become the conviction of many that war was obsolete or in any case an atavism that a concerted rational effort of humanity could banish from the earth with relative ease.

It was, however, the cataclysm of the Napoleonic Wars that demonstrated the need for supplementing with practical measures the theoretical quest for the solution of the problem of international order and peace. The importance of the Napoleonic Wars in this respect is twofold. They destroyed the balance of power and threatened temporarily to replace it with a universal empire. While this factor passed with the definitive defeat of Napoleon in 1815, the other element has threatened the stability of the modern state system for a century and a half and has not yet spent its force. This other element is nationalism. The idea of nationalism, evoked by the French Revolution and carried by the Napoleonic conquests through Europe, challenged the principle of dynastic legitimacy, which had been the organizing principle of the modern state system and was still the foundation of the peace settlements of 1815.

The convergence of these four experiences at the beginning of the nineteenth century and their dynamic release into the political arena through the shock of the Napoleonic Wars provided the intellectual and moral energy that has sustained for the last century and a half the search for alternatives to war and international anarchy. This search, insofar as it has left the realm of mere ideas, hopes,

---

[1]"Fragments politiques," *Œuvres complètes*, Vol. IV (Paris: Garnier Frères, 1875), p. 42.
[2]*Perpetual Peace* (New York: Macmillan, 1917), p. 157.

and admonitions and has materialized in actual measures and institutions of an international character (it is with the latter that we are here alone concerned), has been carried on through three different media: (1) limitation of the destructive and anarchical tendencies of international politics, (2) transformation of international politics by eliminating its destructive and anarchical tendencies altogether, and (3) accommodation of divergent interests by depriving the destructive and anarchical tendencies of international politics of their rational objectives.

Of the attempts to achieve peace through limitation, the most persistent has been that of disarmament.

THE HISTORY OF DISARMAMENT

Disarmament is the reduction or elimination of certain or all armaments for the purpose of ending the armaments race. It is believed that, by doing away with one of the typical manifestations of the struggle for power on the international scene, one can do away with the typical effects of that struggle: international anarchy and war.

Four basic distinctions must be kept in mind: between disarmament and arms control, between general and local disarmament, between quantitative and qualitative disarmament, and between conventional and nuclear disarmament. While disarmament is the reduction or elimination of armaments, arms control is concerned with regulating the armaments race for the purpose of creating a measure of military stability. When we speak of general disarmament, we refer to a kind of disarmament in which all the nations concerned participate. Examples are the Washington Treaty for the Limitation of Naval Armaments of 1922, signed by all major naval powers, and the World Disarmament Conference of 1932, at which practically all members of the community of nations were represented. We speak of local disarmament when only a limited number of nations are involved. The Rush-Bagot Agreement of 1817 between the United States and Canada is an example of this type. Quantitative disarmament aims at an overall reduction of armaments of most or all types. This was the goal of most nations represented at the World Disarmament Conference of 1932. Qualitative disarmament envisages the reduction or abolition of only certain special types of armaments, such as the aggressive weapons Great Britain tried to have outlawed by the World Disarmament Conference of 1932, or nuclear weapons, the abolition and control of which were discussed by the Atomic Energy Commission of the United Nations and were the object of the so-called SALT Agreements (Strategic Arms Limitation Treaty) and START (Strategic Arms Reduction Talks) between the United States and the Soviet Union. The distinction between nuclear and conventional weapons bears upon the political and military preconditions for arms control and disarmament.

The history of the attempts at disarmament is a story of many failures and few successes. Both failures and successes point up the fundamental problems raised by disarmament as a device to insure international order and peace.

The Failures

The first practical step in favor of disarmament as a measure of general pacification[3] coincides with the beginning of that period of international relations in which statesmen to an ever increasing extent have dedicated their efforts to the establishment of international peace and order. In 1816 the czar of Russia proposed to the British government the "simultaneous reduction of the armed forces of every kind." The British monarch replied by suggesting the implementation of the Russian proposal in the form of an international conference where the military representatives of all powers should determine the respective strength of the armies of each power. Austria and France expressed their sympathies with the proposal, which, however, was not seriously considered by any of the governments and thus remained without any practical results. In 1831 the French government made similar proposals to the representatives of the great powers. These proposals were favorably received, but nothing more was heard of them. The same must be said of the proposals Napoleon III made in 1863, 1867, and 1869 for a general reduction of armaments. In 1870, immediately before the outbreak of the Franco-Prussian War, Great Britain, at the instigation of France, twice approached the Prussian government on the question of the reduction of armaments, but without success. Another such approach, this time undertaken by Italy in 1877, was similarly rejected by Germany. The First Hague Peace Conference of 1899 had as one of its main purposes the limitation of armaments and of military budgets. It was attended by the representatives of twenty-eight nations, among them all the major powers. The results of the deliberations of the conference with regard to disarmament are embodied in two resolutions that speak for themselves. The committee in which these deliberations took place declared that it was "of the opinion that the restriction of military charges, which are at present a heavy burden on the world, is extremely desirable for the increase of the material and moral welfare of mankind."[4] The full conference, in adopting this resolution, expressed "the wish that the governments taking into consideration the proposals made at the conference may examine the possibility of an agreement as to the limitation of armed forces by land and sea, and of war budgets."

The Second Hague Peace Conference of 1907, attended by forty-four nations, confirmed "the resolution adopted by the Conference of 1899 in regard to the limitation of military expenditure; and inasmuch as military expenditure has considerably increased in almost every country since that time, the Conference declares that it is eminently desirable that the governments should resume the serious examination of this question."[5] The president of the conference, the Russian delegate, summed up the efforts of both conferences with regard to

---

[3]There were a few steps toward local disarmament in the eighteenth century.
[4]James Brown Scott, *The Proceedings of The Hague Peace Conference. The Conference of 1899* (New York: Oxford University Press, 1920), p. 390.
[5]Ibid., *The Conference of 1907*, Vol. I, pp. 89, 90.

disarmament by thus commenting on this resolution: "If the question was not ripe in 1899, it is not any more so in 1907. It has not been possible to do anything on these lines, and the Conference today finds itself as little prepared to enter upon them as in 1899."[6]

The Treaty of Versailles took another step toward disarmament as a means of general pacification by stipulating the drastic limitation of German armaments "in order to render possible the initiation of a general limitation of the armaments of all nations."[7] Article 8 of the Covenant of the League of Nations more specifically declared "that the maintenance of peace requires the reduction of national armaments to the lowest point consistent with national safety and the enforcement by common action of international obligations." It charged the Council of the League of Nations with the formulation of plans for such reduction. In pursuance of these stipulations, the Council established in 1925 a Preparatory Commission for a Disarmament Conference. Its tentative and incomplete conclusions were submitted to a World Disarmament Conference, which convened at Geneva in 1932. With the withdrawal of Germany in October 1933, the conference became moribund. Its general commission met for the last time in 1934. The World Disarmament Conference was an unmitigated failure, unable to reach formal agreements of any kind.

These efforts at general disarmament were interrupted by the Second World War. The Charter of the United Nations took up where the Covenant of the League of Nations had left off. According to Article 11, paragraph 1, of the Charter, "The General Assembly may consider the general principles of cooperation in the maintenance of international peace and security, including the principles governing disarmament and the regulation of armaments, and may make recommendations with regard to such principles to the Members or to the Security Council or to both." Article 26 of the Charter provides that "in order to promote the establishment and maintenance of international peace and security with the least diversion for armaments of the world's human and economic resources, the Security Council shall be responsible for formulating . . . plans to be submitted to the Members of the United Nations for the establishment of a system for the regulation of armaments."

In pursuance of these provisions of the Charter, the General Assembly created, through its resolution of January 24, 1946, an Atomic Energy Commission to make specific proposals "for control of atomic energy to the extent necessary to insure its use only for peaceful purposes; for the elimination from national armaments of atomic weapons and of all other major weapons adaptable to mass destruction."[8] With regard to so-called conventional armaments, the General Assembly passed on December 14, 1946, a resolution on

---

[6]Ibid., p. 92.
[7]Introduction to Part V of the Treaty of Versailles.
[8]Resolution of the General Assembly, *Atomic Energy Commission Official Records, Supplement No. 1*; also *U.N. doc. A/64*, p. 9.

"Principles Governing the General Regulation and Reduction of Armaments."[9] In it the General Assembly recognized "the necessity of an early general regulation and reduction of armaments and armed forces," and called upon the Security Council to consider promptly the practical means necessary to that effect. Consequently, on February 13, 1947, the Security Council passed a resolution establishing a Commission for Conventional Armaments. The purpose of this commission was the preparation of "proposals (a) for the general regulation and reduction of armaments and armed forces, and (b) for practical and effective safeguards in connection with the general regulation and reduction of armaments."[10]

In making this distinction between atomic and conventional weapons, the United Nations was moved by the hope that progress in atomic disarmament, separately achieved, would stimulate progress with regard to disarmament in conventional weapons. Neither the Commission for Conventional Armaments nor the Atomic Energy Commission succeeded in reaching agreement of any kind on the substantive problems before them. Thus the General Assembly resolved on January 11, 1952, to combine the work of the two commissions and establish a new Disarmament Commission, composed of the members of the Security Council and Canada. Unable to reach agreement, it was replaced by a subcommittee composed of China, France, Great Britain, the Soviet Union, and the United States in pursuance of a General Assembly resolution of November 28, 1953, calling for negotiations by "the powers principally involved." This subcommittee, with the Soviet Union opposed, submitted on August 29, 1957, a draft for a disarmament agreement, which the General Assembly accepted on November 14, 1957. The Soviet Union refused to participate in any further negotiations of the Disarmament Commission or its subcommittee and called for a Disarmament Commission composed of all members of the United Nations. As a compromise move, the General Assembly expanded on November 19, 1957, the membership of the commission to 25. The new commission remained inoperative; and since the beginning of 1958, disarmament negotiations—dealing primarily with the suspension of nuclear tests and the prevention of surprise attacks—were carried on outside the United Nations by Albania, Canada, Czechoslovakia, France, Great Britain, Italy, Poland, Rumania, the Soviet Union, and the United States. In 1959 these same nations established a new disarmament commission outside the United Nations to consider the overall problem of disarmament and, with Bulgaria replacing Albania, met in conference in March 1960. After continuing deadlock, the Soviet bloc withdrew from the conference in June of that year. In March 1962 a general disarmament conference with a membership of eighteen nations was convoked under the auspices of the United Nations. It was from the outset boycotted by France and has met periodically without achieving any results.

[9]*Journal of the United Nations*, No. 75, Supp. A-64, add. 1, p. 827.
[10]*U.N. doc.* S/P.V. 105.

The Successes

The only successful disarmament provisions of the nineteenth century are found in the Rush-Bagot Agreement of 1817 concerning the frontier between the United States and Canada. It limits the naval forces on the Great Lakes to three vessels of equal tonnage and armament for each nation. Revised early in the Second World War in order to allow Canada to construct vessels on the Great Lakes for use against the Axis, it has remained in force to this day.[11]

The outstanding example of a venture in disarmament compounded of success and failure is the Washington treaty of 1922 for the Limitation of Naval Armaments. This treaty established approximate equality in capital ships between the United States and the British Empire, with Japan, France, and Italy trailing the English-speaking countries in this order. In consequence, the British Empire, the United States, and Japan scrapped about 40 percent of their strength in capital ships. Furthermore, it was stipulated that replacements, to begin in 1931, should establish by 1942 a 5:5:3:1.67:1.67 ratio for the capital ships of the British Empire, the United States, Japan, France, and Italy. The Washington conference, however, failed to produce agreement with regard to any naval craft other than capital ships, such as cruisers, destroyers, and submarines.

The Geneva Naval Conference of 1927, attended only by Great Britain, Japan, and the United States, likewise failed to reach agreement on this issue. Finally, at the London Naval Conference of 1930, the United States, Great Britain, and Japan agreed upon parity between the United States and Great Britain for cruisers, destroyers, and submarines, with Japan limited to approximately two-thirds of the American and British strength in these categories. France and Italy did not accede to the treaty, since Italy demanded parity with France, which France refused to concede.

In December 1934, Japan served formal notice of its intention to terminate the Washington Treaty of 1922. It submitted to the London Naval Conferencee of 1935–36 a demand for parity in all categories of naval armament. This demand was rejected by the United States and Great Britain. In consequence Japan resumed its freedom of action. The only result of the conference that had any bearing upon the size of naval armaments was an agreement among the United States, Great Britain, and France, adhered to by Germany and the Soviet Union in 1937, which limited the maximum size of naval vessels, provided that no other nation exceeded that maximum. A separate Anglo-German agreement, concluded in 1935, limited German total naval strength to 35 percent of the British and allowed Germany a strength in submarines equal to that of the British Empire, provided that the total submarine tonnage of Germany remained within the 35 percent limit.

---

[11]For its persistent violations, see James Eayrs, "Arms Control on the Great Lakes," *Disarmament and Arms Control*, Vol. II, No. 4 (Autumn 1964), pp. 372 ff.

In the field of nuclear disarmament and arms control, the SALT Agreements of 1972 and 1975 constitute a success. The Treaty to Limit ABMs (antiballistic missiles) provides for genuine disarmament. It prohibits the deployment of ABM systems for the defense of the territory of the United States and the Soviet Union. It limits the deployment of ABMs to 100 each for two areas of a 150-kilometer radius, one being the respective capitals of the two nations. The Interim Agreement on Offensive Missiles is a measure of arms control in that it provides for numerical limitations on different types of strategic offensive nuclear arms. It limits the number of intercontinental ballistic missiles (ICBMs) to those deployed or under construction at the conclusion of the agreement. It permits the construction of a certain number of additional submarines and sub-marine-launched ICBMs if an equal number of older land-based ICBMs or older submarine and submarine missile launchers are dismantled. While the SALT II Treaty signed by President Carter and Premier Brezhnev in 1979 was not ratified by the Senate, both superpowers, by tacit consent, were abiding by its terms in 1984.

FOUR PROBLEMS OF DISARMAMENT

This record, long in failures and short in successes, raises four fundamental questions. Success or failure of any particular attempt at disarmament depends upon the answers that can be given to these questions:

1. What should be the ratio among the armaments of different nations?

2. What is the standard according to which, within this ratio, different types and quantities of armaments are to be allocated to different nations?

3. Once these two questions have been answered, what is the actual effect of the answers in view of the intended reduction of armaments?

4. What is the bearing of disarmament upon the issues of international order and peace?

The Ratio

Armaments and the armaments race are a manifestation—and one of the most important manifestations—of the struggle for power on the international scene. From this fundamental fact all the technical arguments, proposals, counterpro-posals, and disagreements with regard to disarmament receive their significance. Nations arm either because they want to defend themselves against other nations or because they want to attack them. All politically active nations are by defini-tion engaged in a competition for power of which armaments are an indispensa-ble element. Thus all politically active nations must be intent upon acquiring as much power as they can—that is, among other things, upon being as well armed as they can. Nation A, which feels inferior in armaments to nation B, must seek to become at least the equal of B and if possible to surpass B. On the other hand, nation B must seek at least to keep its advantage over A, if not to increase it. Such are, as we have seen,[12] the inevitable effects of the balance of power in the field of armaments.

What is at stake in the armaments race between A and B is the ratio of the armaments of both nations. Shall A and B be equal in armaments, or shall A be superior to B, or vice versa, and if so, to what extent? This question is necessarily first on the agenda of disarmament commissions and conferences. It can find a satisfactory answer only under three alternative conditions: (a) The nations concerned do not engage in competition for power with other nations; (b) a nation or group of nations have such a preponderance over another nation or group of nations that they are able to impose upon the latter a ratio favorable to themselves; (c) two or more nations find it advantageous for the time being to engage in regulated rather than free competition for power and to enter into an armaments race within agreed-upon limits rather than into a wild scramble for increases in military strength.

It is obvious that these alternatives are likely to materialize only under the conditions of local disarmament. For only under such conditions is the competition for power likely either to be eliminated altogether or to be transformed into a regulated, relatively stable pattern that is reflected in the ratio of armaments. The few successful ventures into disarmament have actually all been of the local kind.

The Rush-Bagot Agreement, the Washington Treaty, and the Anglo-German Naval Agreement

The classic example of pattern (a) is the Rush-Bagot Agreement between the United States and Canada. In the relations of the two countries there is virtually no chance for a competition for power that might transform itself into an armed quest for each other's territory. This absence of the possibility of armed conflict has made the thirty-eight hundred miles of Canadian-American frontier the longest unarmed frontier of the world. It also constitutes the political precondition for the permanent success of naval disarmament on the Great Lakes.

The Washington Treaty of 1922 provides an example of pattern (a) with respect to the relations between the United States and Great Britain, and of pattern (b) with regard to the relations between the United States and Great Britain, on the one hand, and Japan, on the other.

The United States sought parity with Great Britain in battleship strength. It was bound to achieve that parity because of its superior and militarily uncommitted industrial resources. The only question was whether it would achieve parity by way of bitter and costly competition or by way of mutual agreement. Since there was no political conflict between the two countries that would have justified such competition, the two countries agreed upon a practically identical maximum tonnage for the battleships of both.

---

[12]See pages 192–93.

Furthermore, the First World War had made Japan the preponderant naval power in the Far East, thus threatening the interests of the United States and Great Britain in that region and inviting them to a naval armaments race. But the United States, for financial and psychological reasons, was anxious to avoid such a race. Great Britain, on the other hand, was tied to Japan by a military alliance. More particularly, the British dominions dreaded the possibility of finding themselves on the Japanese side in the event of a conflict between Japan and the United States. Thus Great Britain and the United States not only had no political conflicts with each other that might lead to war; they had also an identical interest in avoiding an armaments race with Japan. By dissolving the alliance with Japan and agreeing to parity with the United States on a level it could afford, Great Britain solved its politico-military problems in the field of naval armaments. By separating Great Britain from Japan and reaching parity with Great Britain cheaply, the United States, too, obtained what it wanted in that field.

This understanding between the United States and Great Britain not only isolated Japan but placed it at the same time in a position of hopeless inferiority with regard to heavy naval armaments. Instead of embarking upon a ruinous armaments race it had no chance of winning, Japan made the best of an unfavorable and humiliating situation: it accepted its status of inferiority for the time being and agreed upon stabilizing this inferiority at the ratio mentioned above. When the Anglo-American reaction to Japan's invasion of China at the beginning of the thirties showed that the united front of Great Britain and the United States with regard to the Far East, which had made the Washington Treaty of 1922 possible, no longer existed, Japan at once freed itself from the shackles of that treaty. As far as the Japanese position vis-à-vis the Anglo-American naval supremacy was concerned, the disarmament provisions of the Washington Treaty were the product of a peculiar political situation. These provisions could not survive the political conditions that had created them.

Of pattern (c), the Anglo-German Naval Agreement of 1935 is a typical instance. At that time, the breakdown of the World Disarmament Conference and the policies of the German government demonstrated the unshakable resolve of the latter to rearm in order to attain what it called "equality" with the other major military powers. In relation to Great Britain, rearmament could only mean sufficient strength in smaller craft to meet British superiority in capital ships. On the other hand, the British government was as firmly resolved not to engage in policies that were calculated to maintain the status quo with regard to Germany's naval armaments. For such policies would involve the risk of war or at least of an uncontrolled armaments race with Germany and would in any case strengthen French and Russian influence in Europe at the expense of Germany. In such circumstances the question before the British government was not how to prevent the naval rearmament of Germany, but how to preserve British naval supremacy in the face of it, without imposing upon Great Britain an expensive rearmament program.

The Anglo-German Naval Agreement of 1935 was the codification of these complementary interests of Great Britain and Germany. Great Britain held German naval strength, in terms of tonnage, at a safe distance. In case of need it could even have increased that distance by increasing its own tonnage to such an extent and at such speed as to make it impossible for Germany with its belated start and committed resources ever to reach the agreed-upon maximum of 35 percent of the British tonnage. Germany received the recognition of its right to rearm within limits that, in view of its resources and other military commitments, it would in no event have been able to exceed in the immediate future. More particularly, the agreement gave Germany parity in submarines, the one naval weapon that, in view of Germany's strategic position, was the natural means of attack and defense against a navy whose superiority in overall tonnage and battleship strength was beyond challenge. In the spring of 1939, it had become unmistakably clear that Great Britain and Germany had entered upon an out-and-out armaments race in preparation for an inevitably approaching war. It was only in keeping with this change in the political situation that Germany, in April 1939, denounced the Agreement of 1935 and resumed in law the freedom of action that its political objectives had already compelled it to resume in fact.

The SALT Agreements are also an example of pattern (c). They derive from the recognition of two basic facts that distinguish nuclear from conventional weapons: the dubious efficacy of defensive systems, whose deployment, however, would greatly stimulate the competition in strategic offensive weapons, and the sufficiency for assured destruction of the prospective enemy, attained by both superpowers. In view of the recognition of the first fact, the Treaty to Limit ABMs, rather than abolishing them altogether, appears to be in the nature of a face-saving device. Unwilling to admit that it was a mistake to deploy ABMs, it pays tribute to the idea by allowing each nation two token systems.

It will be noted that in all these cases disarmament was agreed upon by two nations or a limited number of nations and was, therefore, of a local character. It will also be noted that the agreed-upon ratio reflected either the absence of competition for power or the preponderance, unchallengeable for the time being, of one or more nations over another, or a temporary preference on either side for regulated rather than unregulated competition for power in the form of competition for armaments.

What, then, are the chances for agreement upon a ratio of armaments to be reached when most or all the major powers are seeking general disarmament, while at the same time pursuing their contests of power? To put it bluntly, the chances are nil. All attempts at general disarmament, such as the two Hague Conferences, the Geneva Conference of 1932, and the disarmament commissions of the United Nations, as well as most of the local undertakings of the last century and a half, have not failed primarily because of shortcomings in preparation and personnel or of bad luck. They could not have succeeded even under the most favorable circumstances; for the continuation of the contest for power among the nations concerned made agreement upon the ratio of armaments impossible. Two examples will serve to illustrate this statement: the controversies between France and Germany at the World Disarmament Conference of 1932 and the conflict between the United States and the Soviet Union in the United Nations Atomic Energy Commission.

The World Disarmament Conference

The First World War made France the preponderant military power in Europe and in the world. It left Germany so thoroughly disarmed as to incapacitate it for war with any first-rate military power, let alone with France. This distribution of power persisted in principle, however modified by the secret rearmament of Germany and the increasing technological and strategic obsolescence of the French military establishment, when the World Disarmament Conference met in 1932. Germany's avowed purpose at the conference was to change that distribution of power. France's avowed purpose was to maintain it. Germany tried to attain its goal by obtaining recognition of "equality of right" between France and itself, to be transformed gradually—that is, within the span of a number of years—into actual equality of armaments. France, on the other hand, tried to realize its objectives by countering the German principle of equality with the principle of security. The French conception of security meant in practice that any increase in German military strength would be matched by an increase in French power. France, however, was already close to having exhausted its own military potentialities, while Germany had not even begun to tap its resources in population and industrial potential, to mention only its two most spectacular and portentous military assets in view of its relations with France.

Under such circumstances, France, in order to be "secure" in its relations with a Germany of potentially superior power, had to look beyond its own borders for additions to its strength. France found these additions in three factors: in military alliances with Poland and the nations of the Little Entente—Czechoslovakia, Yugoslavia, and Rumania; in new collective guarantees of the territorial status quo of the Treaty of Versailles; and in the compulsory judicial settlement of all international disputes on the basis of the international law of the Treaty of Versailles. If the French proposals had been adopted by the conference, any increase in German military strength would have been neutralized and deprived of all political effects favorable to Germany. This would have been accomplished by judicial decisions upholding the status quo of Versailles and calling to its defense the combined might of virtually all the other nations of the globe. It is for this reason that the French proposals had no chance of being adopted. On the other hand, if the German plan had been adopted by the conference, the international order of Versailles and the status quo established by the victory of the Allies in the First World War would have gradually, but inextricably, crumbled away until Germany, by virtue of its superior military potential, would have transformed itself from the vanquished into the victor.

Hence, the controversy between France and Germany as to the ratio of their respective armaments was in its essence a conflict over the distribution of power. Behind what the delegates to the conference expressed in the ideological terms of security versus equality, retrospective analysis discovers the moving force of international politics: the desire to maintain the existing distribution of power, manifesting itself in a policy of the status quo, on the one hand, and the desire to overthrow the existing distribution of power, expressing itself in a policy of imperialism, on the other. To expect, then, that France and Germany could agree upon the ratio of their respective armaments was tantamount to expecting that they could agree upon the distribution of power between them. Agreement on the latter issue in the form of a compromise between actual French preponderance and potential German preponderance might perhaps—and the doubt looms large—have been possible in the twenties. It was out of the question on the eve of Hitler's ascent to power, and thus agreement on the ratio of armaments was likewise out of the question.

For Germany to give up the demand for equality in armaments would have meant to accept its inferiority in power as permanent and legitimate and to renounce all aspirations to become again the predominant power in Europe. For France to give up its demands for security would have meant to relinquish its position of preponderance and to acquiesce in the comeback of Germany as a first-rate power. The impasse between France and Germany with respect to the ratio of their respective armaments was, therefore, incapable of solution in terms of disarmament. Since it was a manifestation of the struggle for predominance between the two countries, this impasse could have been solved only in terms of the general distribution of power between them, if it could have been solved at all.

Disarmament Negotiations Since the Second World War

The disarmament negotiations, of which the several United Nations commissions and their successors outside the United Nations have been the scene, have reenacted in a new and greatly simplified setting the basic plot of the World Disarmament Conference of 1932. Either side—that is, principally the United States and the Soviet Union—has advanced proposals that either would have stabilized the distribution of military power insofar as it was favorable to that side or else would have changed it in its favor. In the field of conventional armaments, the Soviet Union proposed a proportional reduction, that would have left its superiority intact, while the Western powers advanced proposals that would have eliminated or at least drastically reduced that superiority.

In the field of nuclear armaments, the issue has consistently centered upon the relationship between prohibition and control and the character of the latter. The Soviet Union has defended the priority of prohibition over control and, in one way or other, national sovereignty with regard to control. This plan was bound to improve the military position of the Soviet Union and for this reason alone could not be accepted by the Western allies. For the prohibition of nuclear weapons, faithfully executed by all nations concerned, would have deprived the Western allies of their sole effective counterweight to the Russian superiority in conventional arms. The control system, whose operations or results would in the last instance be controlled by the Soviet Union itself, would have preserved that secrecy upon which Russian governments have insisted for centuries; and undetected nuclear armaments could have given the Soviet Union a decisive military advantage, which the Western allies, in view of the democratic character of their governments and societies, would have found it hard to match.

On the other hand, the Western allies have refused to consider nuclear disarmament without an effective—that is, truly supranational—system of control. Such a system, opening up the secret installations and operations of the Soviet Union to the scrutiny of foreign observers, would have given the Western allies a great military advantage. This advantage might have been decisive during the first stages of gradual nuclear disarmament, when the control system would have been in full operation while the Western allies were still in possession of nuclear weapons and delivery systems.

The conflict between the United States and the Soviet Union, like that between France and Germany of the early thirties, then, is being fought on two levels: on the superficial level of disarmament and on the fundamental level of the struggle for power. On the level of disarmament, the conflict resolves itself into a controversy between two theoretical conceptions: security first, disarmament later versus disarmament first, security later. On the level of the struggle for power, the conflict is posed in terms of competition for military advantage, each side trying, at worst, to maintain the existing distribution of power and, at best, to change it in its favor. Throughout the early 1980s, the Reagan administration proposed that the Soviet Union dismantle all or most of its large land-based SS-20 missiles in Europe in exchange for the United States's not deploying cruise and Pershing missiles. The Soviets in turn made proposals that would have preserved its superiority in Europe in such missiles while allowing for quite limited American deployment. As relations further deteriorated, each side proclaimed its stand in public announcements and televised statements more often than in hard bargaining in private negotiations. Of this competition, the controversy about nuclear disarmament is merely an outward expression, following the contours of the conflict as the cast of clay follows the shape of the form into which it is molded. As the cast can only be changed by changing the mold, so the problem of nuclear disarmament can only be solved through a settlement of the power conflict from which it has arisen.

Standards of Allocation

The ratio among the armaments of different nations is the most important problem an attempt at disarmament must solve. Once it is solved, another question must be answered. It is less fundamental than the problem of the ratio but full of practical difficulties in which the power relations of the nations concerned are again reflected. This question concerns the standards according to which different types and quantities of armaments are to be allocated to different nations within the agreed ratio. The Preparatory and World Disarmament Conferences of Geneva had to face that question innumerable times. The voluminous literature these conferences have left is in its futility and inconclusiveness a monument to the hopelessness of the task in view of the conditions under which it was undertaken.

At the World Disarmament Conference, Germany, as we have seen, demanded equality in armaments with France. France agreed to that ratio as an abstract principle, provided the problem of security could be solved to its satisfaction.

However, once the ratio was agreed upon in the abstract, what did equality mean in the concrete with respect, let us say, to armed effectives, trained reserves, heavy artillery, total number and types of aircraft, and so forth?

The standard to be employed was obviously sought in the military needs of the two countries. These military needs were defined in terms of defense. Defense against whom? The answer given implicitly and explicitly was: defense primarily against each other. It was the inevitable result of this definition that the military needs of the two countries could not be identical. The different strategic positions of the two countries—to mention, at this point, only one factor among many—required defensive armaments different in quality and quantity. Equality in armaments, then, could not mean mathematical equality in the sense that France and Germany should have armed effectives, trained reserves, artillery, and air forces absolutely equal in quality and quantity. Equality could only mean equality in the defensive position of each country against foreign attack.

It was, then, incumbent upon the World Disarmament Conference to evaluate, first, the risks of foreign attack against each country; second, the means of defense other than armaments, such as geographical location, self-sufficiency in food and raw materials, industrial capacity, and number and quality of population; and third, the need for armaments in view of the other two factors. This threefold task confronted the conference with three difficulties that proved to be insuperable.

First, that task could not be accomplished without the evaluation of the power of one nation in comparison with the power of their nations. We have tried to show earlier in this book[13] how difficult, speculative, and, in certain areas, almost impossible such a comparative evaluation is. If the data of such an evaluation go into the standards for the allocation of armaments, these standards must become highly subjective and, hence, make for controversy rather than agreement.

Second, that task requires the assessment of the political intentions of the governments concerned. All nations habitually protest their peaceful intentions. Yet all nations declare that they must be able to defend themselves against attack, thus imputing aggressive intentions to some other nation. To reach agreement among the nations concerned as to who must defend himself against whom is obviously made impossible by the very nature of the controversy.

Finally, and most importantly, the controversies that are bound to ensue on the issues thus raised will inevitably reflect the actual and anticipated policies of the nations concerned. The nation that has aggressive tendencies against another or fears aggressive tendencies on the part of another—and all nations are in the latter category—is compelled by considerations of self-interest to keep the estimate of its own defensive needs as high as possible and to reduce those of its rivals to the lowest possible point. In other words, what the different nations want to achieve through their foreign policies—the retention and aggrandizement of their own

[13]See Chapter 10.

power and the containment and reduction of that of their rivals—is expressed in numerical terms in the evaluation of their own and other nations' military needs. The standards they apply are determined by their political aims and not by anything remotely resembling objective criteria. Therefore, these standards can be determined through free agreement of the nations concerned only after they have agreed on a settlement of the political issues dividing them. The problem of the standards for the allocation of armaments, then, presents itself in the same terms as the problem of the ratio: Political settlement must precede disarmament. Without political settlement, disarmament has no chance for success.

The most striking illustration of this relation between political settlement and agreement on the standards for the allocation of armaments is again provided by the conflict between France and Germany at the World Disarmament Conference. In view of their unsettled conflict over the status quo of Versailles, France translated the abstract ratio of equality into standards of actual armaments that were likely to perpetuate France's preponderance. On the other hand, Germany transformed the same ratio into concrete standards that, if effectuated, would have carried it to preponderance over France. Thus France insisted upon its need for a larger army than Germany's because of the larger German population and its greater rate of increase. Germany countered by pointing to the superiority of France in trained reserves and to the large reserves of manpower and raw materials in the French colonial empire. Germany demanded a certain amount of artillery and airplanes because of its geographical position in the midst of potentially hostile nations. France denied that need by reminding the conference of its own special defense needs in view of its lack of natural strategic frontiers with Germany and of the fact that thrice within a century France had become the victim of German invasion. One could write the history of the World Disarmament Conference in terms of that conflict for power between France and Germany, a conflict that precluded even agreement on small technical details. The contradictory claims for power of the competing nations were reflected in their contradictory claims for arms.

Aside from the political issues that stood between France and Germany, the problem of comparative evaluation presented a formidable obstacle with which the World Disarmament Conference wrangled in vain. What was the value of 100,000 trained French reserves in terms of a corresponding number of effectives of the German Army? Was it 50,000, 60,000, 80,000, 100,000, or perhaps 120,000? What was the margin by which German industrial capacity was superior to that of France defined in numbers of French tanks, artillery, and aircraft? How many Germans in excess of the French population were equal to how many French colonials? Or, to use a contemporary example, how many divisions of Russian infantry equal how many American guided missiles? Or how many Soviet land-based missiles equal how many American airplanes and submarines from which missiles can be launched? Obviously, there can be no answer to such questions in the terms of mathematical exactitude in which the World Disarmament Conference conceived of them. What answers there are to such questions must be sought by means of political bargaining and diplomatic compromise. In the historical instance we have been considering, the employment of such methods presupposed the settlement of the political conflict. The continuance of that conflict made it impossible for France and Germany to agree on standards for the allocation of different quantities and types of arms through the techniques of accommodating diplomacy.

Thus, whether the issue is one of the overall ratio of the armaments of different nations or whether the issue is the standard for allocating different types and quantities of arms, these issues are incapable of solution in their own terms, so long as the conflicts of power from which they have arisen remain unsolved.

Does Disarmament Mean Reduction of Armaments?

In view of the few instances in which these issues were actually solved and agreement on the ratio and allocation of armaments was reached, let us ask ourselves what was the effect of these agreements on the quality and quantity of armaments of the nations concerned. Three treaties need to be considered: the Washington Treaty of 1922, the London Treaty of 1930, and the Anglo-German Agreement of 1935.

By virtue of the Washington Treaty, the American, British, and Japanese strength in capital ships was reduced by about 40 percent. A total of seventy ships were scrapped by the signatories. To that extent the Washington Treaty provided for a general reduction of armaments. Two factors must, however, be noted. On the one hand, the reduction was to be only temporary. The treaty stipulated that the five signatories could in 1931 start to build replacements that by 1942 would have established the ratio of 5:5:3:1.67:1.67. In 1931 the period of the reduction of armaments with regard to capital ships came to an end and was replaced by a period of regulated competition for armaments.

On the other hand, because of the rapid development of the technology of war, especially with regard to firepower and aircraft, the kind of capital ships in use during the First World War tended to become obsolete at a faster rate than any other type of weapon with the exception of airplanes. Mindful of the lessons of the First World War, an increasing number of experts believed that the battleship as such had become outmoded, that at best it was a waste of money, and that the future use of naval power lay in light and speedy vessels with high firepower. If it is assumed that such considerations had weight with the signatories of the Washington Treaty, the reduction in battleship strength would then appear as recognition of the decline of the battleship as a weapon. Since the signatories would in any event have scrapped a considerable number of their battleships, they might as well do it in concert and according to plan as by unregulated competition.

As if to support that assumption, the Washington Treaty was the signal for an armaments race among the signatories in all vessels not covered by the treaty, especially in cruisers, destroyers, and submarines. Those were, as we have seen, the vessels most important for the kind of naval war then contemplated. At least in its effects, therefore, the Washington Treaty neutralized competition in that sphere of naval armaments where competition was not likely to be keen. By the same token, it freed energies and material resources and thereby stimulated competition in those branches of naval armaments in which the naval powers were most likely to compete.

Whatever the motives of the signatories and whatever its effects, the Washington Treaty actually limited certain naval armaments. The same cannot be said of either the London Treaty of 1930 or of the Anglo-German Agreement of 1935. The main achievement of the London Treaty was agreement among the United States, Great Britain, and Japan with regard to the tonnage of cruisers, destroyers, and submarines. The London Treaty purported to provide for the limitation of the naval strength of the respective nations in these categories of vessels. In actuality, however, it provided for the rearmament of the United States and Japan within the limits established by the maximum strength of the British Navy in these categories.

The treaty gave parity to the United States and Great Britain, with Japan trailing at about two-thirds of the maximum. By doing so, however, the treaty simply recognized as legitimate the existing naval supremacy of Great Britain, especially in cruisers, and perpetuated this supremacy for all practical purposes. For the tonnage allocated by the treaty was so high as to be out of reach for Japan and to be attainable by the United States at a cost (a billion dollars over five years) then considered by American public opinion as unbearable. In other words, the treaty allowed the United States to bring its naval strength in the three categories up to Great Britain's if it wanted to spend the money, which obviously the United States did not.[14] The treaty allowed Japan to have about two-thirds of the tonnage of the United States and Great Britain if it could afford to build this fleet, which obviously Japan could not. The only contribution the London Treaty made to the limitation of naval armaments, then, consisted in the establishment of a maximum that no signatory was allowed to exceed and that the United States and Japan were unlikely even to reach. Thus, far from reducing armaments, the treaty allowed for their increase within certain limits.

Furthermore, even this agreement as to maximum tonnage was in its very existence qualified by the continuing freedom of France and Italy, which did not sign the treaty, to increase at will their armaments in the respective categories. In order to meet a possible threat from this quarter to the interests of any of the signatories, especially of Great Britain in the Mediterranean, the treaty restored complete freedom of action to any signatory if in its opinion new construction by a nonsignatory adversely affected its national security. In case a signatory increased its tonnage on these grounds beyond the limits of the treaty, the two other nations were allowed to increase their own naval strength in proportion. What would have remained of the London Treaty in such an exigency would have amounted to nothing more than an armaments race whose pace would follow a certain rhythm determined by one or the other of the great naval powers.

---

[14]The United States spent for the construction of ships of all kinds in the fiscal years 1931–35 a total of somewhat more than 324 million—that is, less than a third of a billion—dollars. (*The World Almanac* for 1947, p. 812.)

Not more than a word need be said about the Angle-German Naval Agreement of 1935. This agreement, couched in the terminology of limitation, had nothing to do with disarmament. It provided frankly for the naval rearmament of Germany within limits that Germany could not and did not want to exceed at that time and that, short of war, Great Britain could not prevent Germany from reaching.

Does Disarmament Mean Peace?

Disarmament has been realized only under extraordinary conditions. Even when it seemed to have been realized, more often than not disarmament meant increase in armaments rather than reduction. These considerations, however, are but preliminary to the question that is decisive in the context of our discussion: what is the bearing of disarmament upon the issues of international order and peace? Provided the nations of the earth could agree upon quantitative or qualitative disarmament and would actually disarm in accordance with the agreement, how would such reduction of all, or elimination of certain, armaments affect international order and peace?

The modern philosophy of disarmament proceeds from the assumption that men fight because they have arms. From this assumption the conclusion follows logically that if men would give up all arms, all fighting would become impossible. In international politics only the Soviet Union has taken this conclusion seriously—and it is questionable whether it was very serious after all—by submitting to the World Disarmament Conference of 1932 and in 1959 to the United Nations proposals for complete, universal disarmament (with the exception of light arms for police functions). The contemporary Russian attitude with respect to atomic disarmament is somewhat in keeping with that position. So is the philosophy of disarmament expressed in the report to the president by the United States deputy representative to the United Nations Disarmament Commission of January 12, 1953, as follows:

> The objective of a disarmament program must be to prevent war, not to regulate the armaments used in war. We have tried to make clear that the United States does not accept war as inevitable; that the job is to reduce the likelihood of war by ensuring that no nation possesses the means to commit a successful act of armed aggression. The aim is to reduce the likelihood of war by reducing the possibility of war and armed aggression.

But even where less extreme conclusions are drawn, the proposition is tacitly admitted that there exists a direct relation between the possession of arms, or at least of certain kinds and quantities of arms, and the issue of war and peace.

Such a relation does indeed exist, but it is the reverse of that which the advocates of disarmament assume it to be. Men do not fight because they have arms. They have arms because they deem it necessary to fight. Take away their arms, and they will either fight with their bare fists or get themselves new arms with which to fight. What makes for war are the conditions in the minds of men that make war appear the lesser of two evils. In those conditions must be sought the disease of which the desire for, and possession of, arms is but a symptom. So long as men seek to dominate one another and to take away one another's possessions, and so long as they fear and hate one another, they will try to satisfy their desires and to put their emotions to rest. Where an authority exists strong enough to direct the manifestations of those desires and emotions into nonviolent channels, men will seek only nonviolent instruments for the achievement of their ends. In a society of sovereign nations, however, which by definition constitute the highest authority within the respective national territories, the satisfaction of those desires and the release of those emotions will be sought by all the means the technology of the moment provides and the prevailing rules of conduct permit. These means may be, in different periods of history, arrows and swords, guns and bombs, gas and guided missiles, bacteria and nuclear weapons.

Reducing the quantity of weapons actually or potentially available at any particular time could have no influence upon the incidence of war; it could conceivably affect its conduct. Nations limited in the quantity of arms and men would concentrate all their energies upon the improvement of the quality of such arms and men as they possess. They would, furthermore, search for new weapons that might compensate them for the loss in quantity and assure them an advantage over their competitors.

The elimination of certain types of weapons altogether would have a bearing upon the technology of warfare and, through it, upon the conduct of hostilities. It is hard to see how it could influence the frequency of war or do away with war altogether. Let us suppose that it were possible, for instance, to outlaw the manufacture and the use of nuclear weapons. What would be the effect of such a prohibition, provided it were universally observed? It would simply reduce the technology of war in this particular to the level of the morning of July 16, 1945, before the first atomic bomb was exploded in New Mexico. The nations adhering to the prohibition would employ their human and material resources for the development and discovery of weapons other than nuclear ones, which might be more or less destructive. The technology of warfare would change, but not the incidence of war. Yet it could be plausibly argued that the threat of all-out nuclear war has actually been the most important single factor that has prevented the outbreak of general war in the atomic age. The removal of that threat through nuclear disarmament might increase the danger of war without assuring, as we shall see, that the belligerents, using nonnuclear weapons at the start, would not resort to such weapons in the course of the war.

The abortive attempts of Great Britain to have the World Disarmament Conference outlaw aggressive, in contrast to defensive, weapons illustrate the impossibility of solving the problem by way of qualitative disarmament. Great Britain assumed that the ability to wage aggressive war was the result of the possession of aggressive weapons. The conclusion followed that without aggressive weapons there could be no aggressive war. The conclusion falls with the assumption. Weapons are not aggressive or defensive by nature, but are made so by the purpose they serve. A sword, no less than a machine gun or a tank, is an instrument of attack or defense according to the intentions of its user. A knife can be used for carving meat, for performing a surgical operation, for holding an attacker at bay, or for stabbing somebody in the back. An airplane can serve the purpose of carrying passengers and freight, of reconnoitering enemy positions, of attacking undefended cities, or of dispersing enemy concentrations poised for attack.

The British proposals really amounted to an attempt to make the status quo secure from attack by outlawing the weapons most likely to be used for overthrowing it. They tried to solve the political problem by manipulating some of the instruments that might serve its solution by violent means. Even if it were possible to agree on the characteristics of aggressive weapons, the political problem would have reasserted itself in the use of whatever weapons remained available. Actually, however, agreement on that point was out of the question. For the weapons Great Britain deemed to be aggressive happened to be identical with those upon which the anti–status quo nations placed their main reliance for achieving their political ends. For instance, Great Britain thought that battleships were defensive and submarines offensive weapons, while nations with small navies put it the other way around. As part of an enterprise generally beset by contradictions and doomed to futility, the British proposals for qualitative disarmament bear to a peculiar degree the mark of that political obtuseness which brought the World Disarmament Conference to an inglorious end.

Let us finally assume that standing armies or nuclear weapons were completely outlawed and would in consequence disappear. The only probable effect of such a prohibition on war would be the limited and primitive character of its beginning. The armaments race among hostile nations would simply be postponed to the beginning of hostilities instead of preceding and culminating in it. The declaration of war would then be the signal for the warring nations to marshal their human and material resources and, more particularly, their technological skills for the speedy manufacture of all the implements of war their technological ability made feasible. It is indeed possible to outlaw nuclear weapons, but it is not possible to outlaw the technological knowledge and ability to make them. It is for this obvious reason that the prohibition of particular weapons has generally not been effective in war. This prohibition has failed, for instance, when applied to lightweight projectiles charged with explosives or inflammable substances, the bombing of civilians from airplanes, and unlimited submarine warfare.[15]

Victory is the paramount concern of warring nations. They may observe certain rules of conduct with regard to the victims of warfare; they will not forgo the use of all the weapons their technology is able to produce. The observance of the prohibition of the use of poison gas in the Second World War is but an apparent exception. All the major belligerents manufactured poison gas; they trained troops in its use and in defenses against it and were prepared to use it if such use would seem to be advantageous. Only considerations of military expediency deterred all

---

[15]For the respective international treaties, see page 246.

belligerents from making use of a weapon of which they had all availed themselves with the intention of using it if necessary.

That quantitative and qualitative disarmament affects the technology and strategy, but not the incidence, of war is clearly demonstrated by the results of the disarmament imposed upon Germany by the Treaty of Versailles. This disarmament was quantitative as well as qualitative and so thorough as to make it impossible for Germany to wage again a war similar in kind to the First World War. If this was the purpose, it was fully realized. If the purpose, however, was to incapacitate Germany forever to wage war of any kind—and this was the actual purpose—the disarmament provisions of the Treaty of Versailles were a spectacular failure. They forced the German General Staff to part with the methods of warfare prevalent in the First World War and to turn their ingenuity to new methods not prohibited by the Treaty of Versailles because they were not widely used or not used at all during the First World War. Thus the Treaty of Versailles—far from depriving Germany of the ability to wage war again—virtually compelled Germany to prepare for the Second World War instead of, like France, for a repetition of the First. Disarmament in terms of the technology and strategy of the First World War, then, was for Germany actually a blessing in disguise. Disarmament made it virtually inevitable for Germany to refashion its military policy along the lines of the future rather than of the past.

It has been suggested that, while disarmament could not by itself abolish war, it could to a great degree lessen the political tensions that might easily lead to war. More particularly, the unregulated armaments race—which generates, and feeds on, fear and imposes ever increasing financial burdens—may lead to so intolerable a situation that all or some parties to the race will prefer its termination by whatever means, even at the risk of war, to its indefinite continuation.

Disarmament or at least regulation of armaments is an indispensable step in a general settlement of international conflicts. It can, however, not be the first step. Competition for armaments reflects, and is an instrument of, competition for power. So long as nations advance contradictory claims in the contest for power, they are forced by the very logic of the power contest to advance contradictory claims for armaments. Therefore, a mutually satisfactory settlement of the power contest is a precondition for disarmament. Once the nations concerned have agreed upon a mutually satisfactory distribution of power among themselves, they can then afford to reduce and limit their armaments. Disarmament, in turn, will contribute greatly to the general pacification. For the degree to which the nations are able to settle the issue of disarmament will be the measure of the political understanding they were able to achieve.

Disarmament, no less than the armaments race, is the reflection of the power relations among the nations concerned. Disarmament, no less than the armaments race, reacts upon the power relations from which it arose. As the armaments race aggravates the struggle for power through the fear it generates and the burdens it imposes, so disarmament contributes to the improvement of the political situation by lessening political tensions and by creating confidence in the purposes of the respective nations. Such is the contribution disarmament can make to the establishment of international order and the preservation of international peace. It is an important contribution, but it is obviously not the solution to the problem of international order and peace.

ARMS CONTROL IN THE NUCLEAR AGE

Why has arms control, the effort to strengthen international peace by increasing military stability, been only moderately successful in the nuclear field and failed altogether with regard to conventional arms? As concerns the latter, the reasons for failure are identical with those for the failure of disarmament. The quantity and disposition of conventional weapons have a direct bearing upon the distribution of military power. Since the nations concerned compete for military advantage, an agreement on the control of conventional weapons would signify the end of competition. The termination of military competition, however, depends upon the settlement of the outstanding political issues.

The control of nuclear weapons is made possible in theory at least by the ability of major nuclear powers to reach that optimum of assured destruction beyond which it is irrational to go. This measure can be defined as the availability of the number of nuclear warheads and invulnerable delivery systems necessary to destroy the military installations and industrial and population centers of a prospective enemy. A nation that possesses this capability has realized its maximum military potential both in terms of deterrence and of the actual waging of nuclear war. The acquisition of additional warheads and delivery vehicles is wasteful because it adds nothing to the military power of the nation concerned. Consequently, the conventional conceptions of military superiority and inferiority here become within certain limits meaningless. A nation that is capable of inflicting unacceptable damage on its prospective enemy ten times over under the worst of circumstances gains nothing militarily by increasing its already abundant nuclear capability, and its prospective enemy, capable of inflicting unacceptable damage upon the other nation "only" six times over is not militarily inferior to the latter and gains no additional military power by increasing its nuclear capability. Once the two nations have reached this optimum of assured destruction, they are equal in usable nuclear capabilities; within certain limits quantitative differences do not affect that qualitative equilibrium. These limits would be left behind if one nation gained so great an advantage that it would be capable of destroying the retaliatory capability of the other nation in a first strike.

Mindful that disparity must remain within these limits, the United States and the Soviet Union have a common interest in stabilizing the nuclear arms race by regulating it. They can do so in three different ways. First, they can limit the production of nuclear weapons and delivery vehicles by unilateral action, based upon their own judgment of what is enough in terms of deterrence and actual nuclear war. The United States has done this by cutting back or discontinuing the production of certain types of missiles and airplanes, and it can be assumed that the Soviet Union has done the same.

Second, nations can control their armaments by tacit agreement, one side's action or omission being predicated upon the other side's example, and vice versa. On that basis, the United States and the Soviet Union refrained from testing nuclear weapons in the atmosphere from 1958 to 1961; in 1964 they announced a cutback in the manufacture of fissionable materials.

Third, nations can control their armaments by formal agreement. The partial test ban treaty, concluded in 1963 by Great Britain, the Soviet Union, and the United States, is a case in point. It prohibits the testing of nuclear devices above ground and under water but permits the continuation of underground tests. It thereby stabilizes the technology of nuclear weapons insofar as their development depends upon atmospheric or underwater tests. The Interim Agreement on Offensive Missiles (SALT I) draws from the unique nature of nuclear weapons the most far-reaching consequences for arms control thus far. It roughly stabilizes the quantity of nuclear weapons but allows for their qualitative improvement. More particularly, by providing for moderate increases in the number of submarines and submarine-based missiles, it takes account of the technological shift away from land-based missiles, which have become vulnerable to quantitatively and qualitatively improved offensive missiles.

Arms control can also take the form of excluding certain types or all kinds of weapons from certain geographical regions or groups of nations. The Antarctic Treaty of 1961, the Outer Space Treaty of 1967, the Latin American Nuclear Free Zone Treaty of 1967, the Nonproliferation Treaty of 1970, the Seabed Treaty of 1971, and the convention on the Prohibition of the Development, Production, and Stockpiling of Bacteriological (Biological) and Toxic Weapons of 1972 all fall into this category. It must, however, be pointed out that most of these treaties do nothing more than ratify through legal stipulations what the nations concerned would have been unwilling or unable to do anyhow. With continuing poor relations between countries such as the United States and the Soviet Union and Iraq and Iran, progress in certain areas appeared threatened by reversals.

The nuclear debate has raised a number of seemingly vital issues, including the military balance of power between the United States and the Soviet Union at present and in the future, the potentialities of certain weapons systems, and the possibility of verifying Soviet compliance with arms treaties. Yet the debate has also brought to the fore an element that the various camps share and that in the long run is likely to prove more important for the future of the United States than all the scenarios, details, and technicalities upon which our attention has been focused so far: the *obsolescence* of our modes of thought and action with regard to nuclear weapons. What Einstein said half a century ago is still true today: "The unleashed power of the atom has changed everything except our way of thinking." In other words, the unleashed atom presents us with problems of unprecedented novelty, requiring for their solution modes of thought and action of similar novelty. However, many parties on both sides continue to think and act largely as though the atomic revolution of 1945 had not occurred.

The availability of nuclear weapons has fundamentally altered the traditional relationship between political aims and physical violence. Down to 1945 a great power, such as the United States, had a rational choice between violence and non-violence in achieving its ends vis-à-vis other nations. If it wanted a certain result badly enough, and could not achieve it by peaceful means, it might well resort to violence, provided a calculus of risk and advantage favored such a resort. Such a calculus a priori counsels against the use of nuclear weapons since their very destructiveness, in both the short and long terms, eliminates all possible advantage. The use of nuclear weapons, even initially on a limited scale, is an unmitigated disaster, which in the end can only lead to the destruction of both sides.

Thus even our conventional use of language, dealing with nuclear phenomena in terms of "weapons" and "war," shows a certain atavistic inadequacy. For terms such as "weapons" and "war" imply a rational relationship between those concepts and certain human objectives. A "weapon" traditionally serves a certain rational purpose, and "war" is traditionally undertaken for such a rational purpose; both are absent in the nuclear relations between two nuclear powers. Thus use of conventional language, when dealing with nuclear weapons and nuclear war, conceals the new reality for whose novelty appropriate words have not been found.

Use of conventional words for novel phenomena not only tends to hide the truth, it also suggests that the truth is to be found in the conventional meaning of conventional words. Since these words have over long stretches of history accumulated a network of associations, assumptions, and conclusions, the uncritical application of such words to nuclear phenomena precludes adequate understanding and successful action. Thus it is fatal to the cause of nuclear arms control and disarmament to deal with nuclear weapons and nuclear war as though they were but a quantitative extension of conventional weapons and war. In truth, they are different in kind because they are instruments of total destruction, spatially and temporally; therefore they are incapable of performing the functions that history has taught us to assign to weapons and war.

In recognition of irrationality, the superpowers have tried to control the nuclear arms race, such control issuing ultimately—it is hoped—in nuclear disarmament. In the process they have shown alarmingly the extent to which they are in practice oblivious to the distinction between conventional and nuclear arms control and disarmament. They have bargained and haggled for years over issues that might be relevant for conventional weapons but that are, in most cases, irrelevant to the nuclear field. What does it mean, for instance, that certain Russian missiles are allowed to carry only a specified number of independently targetable warheads? What would happen if they were to carry more, either by mutual consent or in violation of the treaty? As long as the number of warheads does not affect the principle of mutually assured destruction, the quality and quantity of the mutual means of destruction are irrelevant. To use a conventional metaphor: as long as my enemy has one gun with which to kill me it is irrelevant for our mutual relations that he has also the finest collection of guns in town. To repeat, *the strategic nuclear balance between the United States and the Soviet Union, which must indeed be maintained, rests upon the mutual ability of utter destruction, which, in turn, rests not upon equality of numbers and performance but exclusively upon the ability to destroy the enemy regardless of the quality and quantity of nuclear weapons he may have.*

Comparable military strength is but one concept among many, hallowed by tradition, that have been rendered obsolete by the nuclear revolution. Defense, limited war, victory, alliances, verification, and the distinction between combatants and noncombatants are other familiar concepts similarly invalidated by the availability of nuclear weapons. What is disquieting and ominous is the reluctance of most of those who do our thinking in these matters to desist from applying obsolete modes of thought and action to the novel conditions of the times. The confused and confusing debate on SALT II and the halting and unsuccessful character of subsequent negotiations are prime examples of the operation of a cultural lag, one that leads us to attempt to solve issues of the nuclear age with the modes of thought and action of a bygone age.

In a fundamental way, this cultural lag has dominated the theory and practice of nuclear weapons since 1945. The history of nuclear military doctrine and practice is the story of a succession of futile attempts to assimilate nuclear weapons to the traditional purposes of the nation-state. For more than three decades—from the so-called clean H-bomb to the counterforce strategy—we have tried to make it appear that nuclear weapons are just conventional weapons writ large, to be manipulated in a conventional way.

The heart of that debate is the issue of strategic superiority between the United States and the Soviet Union. Both sides in the debate recognize in the abstract the irrelevance of the concept when applied to nuclear weapons. Henry Kissinger gave vent to that irrelevance when, during a press conference in July 1974, he declared: "What in the name of God is strategic superiority? What is the significance of it . . . at these levels of numbers? What do you do with it?" Yet in his statement to the Senate Foreign Relations Committee on July 31, 1979, he voiced for whatever reasons his regret at having intimated in 1974 that strategic superiority had become a meaningless concept:

> My statement reflected fatigue and exasperation, not analysis. If both sides maintain the balance, then indeed the race becomes futile and SALT has its place in strengthening stability. But if we opt out of the race unilaterally, we will probably be faced eventually with a younger group of Soviet leaders who will figure out what can be done with strategic superiority.

It hardly needs to be pointed out that this is a less-than-convincing argument in favor of strategic superiority.

Kissinger and others have admitted the meaninglessness of the concept of superiority in the conventional military sense while endeavoring to give it a new political meaning. Once a nation has attained the nuclear optimum in terms of assured destruction, so the argument runs, additional nuclear weapons can add significantly to its political power, if what counts in the power calculus is not only the actual power available but the perception, by other nations, of the power available. That is to say, if the Soviet Union possesses more warheads than the United States, it does not thereby become militarily more powerful than the United States, but it increases its political power vis-à-vis the United States because people perceive it—falsely—to have become more powerful militarily.

The argument, left at this point, is incomplete: it lacks a qualification centered on the people who are doing the perceiving. To be frank, the argument assumes those doing the perceiving are ignorant. For only ignorant people, unaware of the distinction between conventional and nuclear weapons, will attribute significance—military or political—to the possession of nuclear weapons in excess of the military optimum.

The defenders of the intellectual status quo have also advanced a political and military argument that is a typical example of obsolete thinking. The strategy of mutual assured destruction, so the argument runs, limits drastically the options of the president of the United States. The government of the United States is faced with two equally unacceptable choices: the slaughter of tens of millions of civilians or, if it is repelled by this barbarous alternative, appeasement. Nuclear arms beyond the optimum for assured destruction make it possible to wage limited nuclear war, that is, a kind of atomic warfare that leaves in its wake "merely" the kind of limited destruction with which modern conventional war has acquainted us.

This search for a way of dealing with nuclear weapons in a conventional manner has been, in different guises, a *leitmotif* of nuclear strategy since 1945. An enumeration of the different attempts at a new strategy, which would allow us to use nuclear weapons without the universal, uncontrolled destructive effects that, in theory, we correctly associate with nuclear weapons is instructive. Take the so-called clean H-bomb, which made its appearance at the beginning of the 1950s—that is, an H-bomb that would not have the devastating, indiscriminate effects that even the kiloton bombs dropped on Hiroshima and Nagasaki had. It was a bomb that would have little or no fallout and whose effects would be those of a gigantic conventional bomb. In the words of a former chief of staff of the American Air Force, General Curtis LeMay, the nuclear bomb is "just another bomb." The U.S. Atomic Energy Commission made short shrift of this idea in *The Effects of Nuclear Weapons*, published in 1962. The commission said that there is no such thing as a clean H-bomb, and that all H-bombs are more or less "unclean"—even though the distribution of blast, fire, and radiation may be different in different designs of the bomb. The idea that it is possible to devise an H-bomb that is not essentially different from a conventional bomb is utterly mistaken.

Consider, as another example, the conception of "graduated deterrence." This is a method of waging nuclear war that does not escalate almost immediately into all-out war. Instead—in a rational, almost predetermined way similar to a chess game—one side makes a move by, say, "taking out" one city, and the other side makes another move, "taking out" a city of its opponent. Thus each side, in a perfectly detached, rational way, inflicts a certain degree of damage upon the other. This idea has gained wide acceptance in certain so-called think tanks, where playing games with survival issues is highly developed. An argument can be made in favor of reviewing the hypothetical possibilities that exist. However, in practical terms, it is inconceivable that living human beings, with the ideological conceptions and values that the policymakers in the Soviet Union, the United States, and China possess, would look at, say, the destruction of Chicago by the Soviet Union or at the destruction of Minsk by the United States with the same detachment with which chess players look at the exchange of pawns. They would quickly arrive at a point where—quite aside from the aroused emotions that make calculation difficult—one side or the other would feel that in any rational simulation of a chess game one side would take advantage of the other. The equivalence theoretically assumed between Minsk and Chicago would not be self-evident to the players of the game under such circumstances. The Soviet Union will inevitably find that Minsk is more important than Chicago—and the United States will find that Chicago is more important than Minsk. They will find that this type of graduated deterrence is really not deterrence at all, because it leads inevitably by its own dynamism to escalation and to an all-out strategic war, which it was the purpose of the enterprise to avoid in the first place. Once the United States has arrived at the conclusion that Chicago is more important than Minsk, it will take out two Soviet cities, which are regarded as the equivalent of another American city, whereupon the Soviet Union will take out two American cities, which are regarded as the equivalent of one Soviet city. Furthermore, we have to reckon with the passions of the people at large and those of the policymakers, for in such an undertaking, started in a rational way, enormous powers of passion come into play on both sides. The population of the United States will not look with equanimity at the successive, however rational, elimination or partial destruction of American cities and their inhabitants; neither will the people and the government of the Soviet Union. Once again, we have a force that almost inevitably will lead to escalation and to the various effects that the graduated deterrence was intended to avoid. Since we are confronted with the possibility of nuclear war, we want to make nuclear war as painless as possible, as limited as possible, one might even say, if so grotesque a juxtaposition is allowed, as humane as possible. On the other hand, the official military doctrine of the Soviet Union has never accepted those distinctions. Soviet doctrine assumes that a war, especially a European war, which starts as a conventional or limited nuclear war and whose stakes the belligerents regard as of prime importance, is bound to escalate into all-out nuclear war. Thus the idea of the fire break—the pause between either conventional war or limited nuclear war, on the one hand, and all-out nuclear war, on the other—is alien to the military doctrine of the Soviet Union.

The strategy of counterforce, first enunciated by Secretary of Defense Robert S. McNamara in 1962, was another example of a fundamental misunderstanding of nuclear war. It was an attempt to limit nuclear war, thus making it acceptable as an instrument of national policy. The counterforce strategy was simple; it assumed that a nuclear war could be waged and ought to be waged not against population and industrial centers, but against strictly military objectives. The revival of this doctrine in recent times rests on the same assumption, fortified by the increase in the sophistication of nuclear weapons. In 1962 one could well make the case that it was impossible, in view of the character of nuclear weapons, to distinguish in practice strictly between military and civilian objectives, that the indiscriminate and widespread destructiveness of nuclear weapons was so enormous that a nuclear weapon aimed at a military objective was bound to destroy, by virtue of the mere proximity of civilian objectives, the latter as well. That argument is still valid. If the Soviet Union tries to take out the missile sites near Phoenix and Cheyenne, to give only two examples, the Soviet missiles are not likely to be so accurate as to destroy the missile sites without any negative effect upon the adjacent population and industrial centers. Recent increases in accuracy may have improved the situation somewhat, and there may be a grain more merit in the revival of the counterforce strategy than in its original formulation.

A more profound question about the counterforce strategy can be asked, however, namely, the question as to its ultimate military purpose. In the case of the American version of the counterforce strategy, which has been the most familiar one, the United States will not initiate a nuclear war by a first strike. It will wait until the other side has initiated a nuclear war by a first strike; only then will it attack military targets, which the other side presents not merely in the form of missile sites but also of the missiles themselves. But the first strike would already have emptied of meaning the distinction between missile sites that still contain their missiles and other missile sites from which the missiles have already departed.

But let us suppose that this distinction can nevertheless be made, and that this exchange operates as intended. This of course presupposes that the enemy who started the war has not destroyed all its own missile sites and that it has a sufficient number of missiles left with which to destroy enemy missile sites that still contain missiles. Accept all of this and assume that the two belligerents knock out their land-based missiles reciprocally; what have they gained? They are in the same position that they were originally, except that now they have to rely exclusively upon the seaborne deterrent and perhaps upon the airborne deterrent. So one would have the same distribution of destructive power with the same deterrent effect one had at the beginning of the war with only the difference that the mechanics would have changed from land-based to sea-based missiles. Some authorities argue that land-based missiles are obsolete anyhow and that they should be phased out through arms control negotiations between the United States and the Soviet Union. If this position is correct, then in the projected counterforce exchange we would simply have engaged in a mutual disarmament enterprise by knocking out each other's land-based missiles. We would then be in the same position as we were before—that is to say, there would be no victor and no vanquished.

This leads to another point—the basic distinction between victory and defeat in war—which is again a distinction that is deeply ingrained in consciousness because it has been derived from millennia of historical experience. Thus the military, in particular, have found it unacceptable both in Korea and Vietnam that a conventional war should not end in the clear-cut victory of that side whose cause is regarded to be just—which is of course one's own side. The same reluctance to give up the distinction between victory and defeat is apparent in thinking on nuclear war. The idea that a nuclear war should necessarily end in a stalemate or in the mutual destruction of the belligerents is unacceptable to those who have made it their profession to prepare for victorious wars. They are in the position of a businessman whose main purpose in life is to make a profit for his company; then he is suddenly faced with the assertion that the best he can hope for is to break even. He will never make a profit, never again pay a dividend; obviously, such an idea goes against his nature. As far as nuclear war is concerned, however, this is the sort of situation we face, a situation utterly different from any in the past: war itself becomes a completely senseless, irrational enterprise. Even if one can keep it limited (counterforce strategy), it will simply end in the same kind of equilibrium with which it started, except the composition of forces making up the equilibrium will be different.

Or take the concept of defense. It has been axiomatic throughout history that any new weapon will sooner or later call forth a counterweapon, a defense against it. Let us assume that this axiom is borne out by historical experience. Yet the destructiveness of nuclear weapons is so enormous that it is inconceivable—in view of present technology, and in particular of costs that were blithely overlooked by some in the Reagan administration—that an effective defense against nuclear weapons can be devised. Thus the abolition, for all practical purposes, of antiballistic missiles (ABMs) by the two SALT negotiations was a recognition of objective facts of the nuclear age. Once we have a defense against nuclear weapons, we have removed the main deterrent against nuclear war. It is this reality that proposals for star wars defenses overlooks. If mankind expects to survive a nuclear war, then to wage or not to wage nuclear war involves an approach similar to that of conventional war, a pragmatic calculation of expedience.

A tactical nuclear war strategy is another attempt to make possible a nuclear war that will not lead to the destruction of both sides, but that can lead to the victory of one side. The conception of tactical nuclear war—that is to say, of the battlefield use of nuclear weapons—faces a number of practical and theoretical difficulties. First, there is the impossibility of drawing an objective, generally recognized and recognizable line between tactics and strategy in general. Military schools of thought in all countries have debated this question without arriving at a definitive conclusion. The distinction is not so much in the objective situation on the battlefield as in the minds of the military planner or director of military operations. The fact that the Hiroshima and Nagasaki bombs today are classified as tactical nuclear weapons shows how far tactics can be stretched to cover what generally would be regarded as strategy. What might be intended by one side as a tactical maneuver may thus be interpreted by the other side as a strategic move, and the reply of the other side may be interpreted in either tactical or strategic terms by the first side. Since in such situations both sides are inclined to use a worst-case approach to the problems—that is, to assume the worst in terms of the intentions of the enemy—the distinction is bound to break down very quickly. While this is true of conventional as well as nuclear war, the problem is aggravated by the nature of the latter.

Assume for a moment that a conventional war breaks out in Central Europe involving both the United States and the Soviet Union. The United States, which has about 9,000 so-called tactical nuclear warheads in Europe, first uses some of them against Soviet military targets: bridges, military concentrations, ammunition dumps, and logistics installations. But even that limited a use of nuclear weapons leads to the destruction of, say, certain cities in White Russia. The Soviet Union replies in the same tactical spirit by attacking the Channel ports of Brest, Cherbourg, Le Havre, and so forth, in order to inflict upon the Western armies the same tactical disadvantages the Americans have inflicted upon the Soviet Union. But since the tactical targets are different in nature, asymmetric in the extreme on both sides, when they see Le Havre, Brest, and Cherbourg going up in flames, the Americans will ask themselves, what are the Soviets after? Is this tactical or is it strategic? Applying the worst-case interpretation, the Americans take out some Russian cities as a response. The Soviets then reply in kind: if the Americans take out some of our cities, we take out some of theirs. Both sides find themselves engaged in an all-out strategic war, not because either side wanted it, but because the objective dynamism of the initial act leaves neither side a choice. Leon Wieseltier explains it thus:

> If the United States ever fights a nuclear war with the Soviet Union, it will almost certainly not be because the Soviet Union attacked the United States. It will be because the Soviet Union attacked an ally of the United States. The war will not begin with a strategic nuclear exchange, but it will probably escalate to it. The defense policy of the Atlantic alliance is based upon the inexorability of escalation. The official metaphors for escalation are "chain of deterrence," "web of deterrence," "continuum of deterrence"; the new missiles will be installed to complete this chain, this web, this continuum.[16]

Deterrence must hold at all levels if the worst nuclear fear of the age is not to come to pass. Thus conventional warfare must be abjured, lest tactical theater nuclear weapons be used; tactical nuclear weapons must be abjured, lest strategic nuclear weapons be used; and strategic nuclear weapons must be abjured at virtually all costs. The promise of escalation is what stays everybody's hand. When there is peace, it is a promise of good. But when there is war, it is a promise of evil. The metaphors of deterrence are, after all, metaphors of entanglement. When deterrence fails, it may fail at all its levels. That is its dark side. The United States has repeatedly declared its intention, in its famous policy of "first use," to rescue Europe's armies by the use of nuclear weapons—that is, to "upgrade" a conventional war into a nuclear war. And the Soviet Union has declared its intention to interpret any nuclear attack by NATO as an attack by the United States—that is, to interpret a theater nuclear war as a strategic nuclear war, and to act accordingly.

But it is not only doctrine that will make escalation inexorable. It is the real situation on the ground. The single most decisive fact about that situation is the inadequacy of our allies' conventional defenses. NATO and the Warsaw Pact are roughly equal in manpower, but the Warsaw Pact has particularly large advantages in tanks (2.64 to 1), artillery pieces (2.07 to 1), land-based bombers (4.83 to 1), fighters (5.07 to 1), and interceptors (7.14 to 1); and its supply lines are less of a

---

[16] *Nuclear War, Nuclear Peace* (New York: Holt, Rinehart and Winston, 1983), pp. 65–66.

problem than NATO's. If a conventional war goes badly for these reasons, there will almost certainly be escalation into nuclear exchange. A "first use" then is really a last resort. In order to make a nuclear defense more credible (not least to the citizens of the democracies to be defended), the destructive consequences of first use were concealed for a time behind the doctrine of "flexible response," according to which the most horrible nuclear strikes would be averted, or in any case saved for last. The deficiencies in the doctrine of flexible response, however, have been amply illustrated. The less horrible strikes are pretty horrible. And the nuclear strikes would have to begin at once.[17]

Instead of adapting our thinking to the phenomenon of nuclear weapons, we have tried to adapt the proposed use of nuclear weapons to our conventional way of thinking. But as more than three decades of debate have shown, it cannot be done. Limited nuclear war with limited damage is conceivable only on the premise that the stakes of the war are equally limited. Yet it is difficult to imagine a rational resort to nuclear weapons on behalf of interests that are not of the first magnitude, justifying—initially or through escalation—unlimited nuclear commitment and potentially unlimited damage. This is the main reason nuclear weapons have not been used since 1945. Their limited application is a contradiction in terms: nuclear weapons are instruments of uncontrollable and potentially unlimited destruction, coordinated to interests of the first rank. Thus Soviet military doctrine stipulates that nuclear war on behalf of limited interests, while possible in the initial stages of a nuclear war, is likely to escalate into all-out nuclear war. If they are used on behalf of first-rank interests, such as in Europe, they will be used as instruments of total war.

The conventional modes of thought that have dominated the nuclear debate thus far are not accidental. They are the symptoms of a pervasive unwillingness to part with conventions hallowed by all of history and of a determination to apply to nuclear weapons the modes of thought and action appropriate to bygone eras. The issue of nuclear arms control is a literally vital issue, not only for the superpowers, not only for their allies, but for all of humanity. For with proliferation now underway in earnest, there is little doubt that a nuclear arms race—no longer limited to two superpowers with cautious governments that are mortally afraid of each other—but spreading over the whole globe, is bound, sooner or later, to lead to an unspeakable catastrophe. For history shows, if history shows anything, that all nations have been governed at times by fools and knaves, and even a combination of both. That was bad enough before nuclear weapons existed. But imagine a fool or knave or a combination of both in the possession of nuclear weapons, and nuclear war becomes unavoidable. So it is the almost inevitable danger of actual nuclear war, inherent in the dynamism of a generalized unlimited nuclear arms race, that makes nuclear arms control and in the end nuclear disarmament a question of life or death for all mankind.

---

[17]Ibid., pp. 63–65.

Yet what is theoretically required is particularly difficult to obtain. The control of nuclear weapons is made possible by the ability of major nuclear powers to reach that optimum of assured destruction beyond which it is irrational to go. But in practice it is predicated upon the stability of nuclear technology; for it is only on that assumption that the nations concerned can afford to desist from competition. Thus the major nuclear powers could agree upon the cessation of atmospheric and underwater tests since for the time being no technological progress can be expected from testing in these media. Yet they continue to test underground and in outer space and to engage in research and experimentation, searching for opportunities of improving existing weapons technologies and discovering new ones. Nuclear arms control, in view of its dependence upon technological stability, is likely to remain both limited and temporary. As long as with respect to conventional arms the political incentive to military competition persists and the basic distinction between conventional and nuclear weapons is not consistently recognized, disarmament is impossible and arms control at best precarious.

24 Security

The more thoughtful observers have realized that the solution for the problem of disarmament does not lie within disarmament itself. They have found it in security. Armaments are the result of certain psychological factors. So long as these factors persist, the resolution of nations to arm themselves will also persist, and that resolution will make disarmament impossible. The generally professed and most frequent actual motive for armaments is fear of attack, that is, a feeling of insecurity. Hence, it has been argued that what is needed is to make nations actually secure from attack by some new device and thus to give them a feeling of security. The motive force and the actual need for armaments would then disappear; for nations would find in that new device the security they had formerly sought in armaments. Since the end of the First World War, all politically active nations of the world have been, at one time or another, legally committed to two such devices: collective security and an international police force.

COLLECTIVE SECURITY

We have already discussed the legal aspects of the problem of collective security as it has presented itself in Article 16 of the Covenant of the League of Nations, in Chapter VII of the Charter of the United Nations, and in the "Uniting for Peace" Resolution of the United Nations General Assembly.[1] It remains to consider the political problems that collective security poses, with special reference to the problem of international order and peace.

In a working system of collective security, the problem of security is no longer the concern of the individual nation, to be taken care of by armaments and other elements of national power. Security becomes the concern of all

---

[1]See pages 304 ff.

nations, which will take care collectively of the security of each of them as though their own security were at stake. If A threatens B's security, C, D, E, F, G, H, I, J, and K will take measures on behalf of B and against A as though A threatened them as well as B, and vice versa.[2] One for all and all for one is the watchword of collective security. As Bismarck put it to the British ambassador Lord Loftus on April 12, 1869, according to the latter's report to the British foreign secretary, the Earl of Clarendon, on April 17, 1869: "If you would only declare that whatever Power should willfully break the Peace of Europe, would be looked upon by you as a common enemy—we will readily adhere to, and join you in that declaration—and such a course, if supported by other Powers, would be the surest guarantee for the Peace of Europe."

We have already pointed out that the logic of collective security is flawless, provided it can be made to work under the conditions prevailing on the international scene.[3] For collective security to operate as a device for the prevention of war, three assumptions must be fulfilled: (1) The collective system must be able to muster at all times such overwhelming strength against any potential aggressor or coalition of aggressors that the latter would never dare to challenge the order defended by the collective system; (2) at least those nations whose combined strength would meet the requirement under (1) must have the same conception of security that they are supposed to defend; (3) those nations must be willing to subordinate their conflicting political interests to the common good defined in terms of the collective defense of all member states.

It is conceivable that all these assumptions may be realized in a particular situation. The odds, however, are strongly against such a possibility. There is nothing in past experience and in the general nature of international politics to suggest that such a situation is likely to occur. It is indeed true that, under present conditions of warfare no less than under those of the past, no single nation is strong enough to defy a combination of all the other nations with any chance for success. Yet it is extremely unlikely that in an actual situation only one single nation would be found in the position of the aggressor. Generally, more than one nation will actively oppose the order collective security tries to defend, and other nations will be in sympathy with that opposition.

The reason for this situation lies in the character of the order defended by collective security. That order is of necessity the status quo as it exists at a particular moment. Thus the collective security of the League of Nations sought the preservation of the territorial status quo as it existed when the League of Nations was established in 1919. But in 1919 a number of nations were already strongly opposed to that territorial status quo—the nations defeated in the First World War, as well as Italy, which felt itself despoiled of some of the promised fruits of victory. Other nations, such as the United States and the Soviet Union, were at best indifferent toward the status quo. For France and its allies, who were the main beneficiaries of the status quo of 1919 and most anxious to defend it by means of

---

[2]See the diagram on page 438.
[3]See pages 304–05.

collective security, security meant the defense of the frontiers as they had been established by the peace treaties of 1919 and the perpetuation of their predominance on the continent of Europe. Security for the dissatisfied nations meant the exact opposite: the rectification of those frontiers and a general increase in their power relative to France and its allies.

This grouping of nations into those in favor of the status quo and those opposed to it is not at all peculiar to the period following the First World War. It is, as we know, the elemental pattern of international politics. As such, it recurs in all periods of history. Through the antagonism between status quo and imperialistic nations, it provides the dynamics of the historical process. This antagonism is resolved either in compromise or in war. Only on the assumption that the struggle for power as the moving force of international politics might subside or be superseded by a higher principle can collective security have a chance for success. Since, however, nothing in the reality of international affairs corresponds to that assumption, the attempt to freeze the particular status quo by means of collective security is in the long run doomed to failure. In the short run, collective security may succeed in safeguarding a particular status quo because of the temporary weakness of the opponents. Its failure to succeed in the long run is due to the absence of the third assumption upon which we have predicated the success of collective security. In the early 1980s, Britain and Argentina clashed over the Falkland Islands, Israel invaded Lebanon, and the United States sent troops into Grenada. Whatever resolutions the United Nations passed, neither it nor its members were able to turn back the states engaged in these actions.

In the light of historical experience and the actual nature of international politics, we must assume that conflicts of interest will continue on the international scene. No nation or combination of nations, however strong and devoted to international law, can afford to oppose by means of collective security all aggression at all times, regardless of by whom and against whom it may be committed. The United States and the United Nations came to the aid of South Korea when it was attacked in 1950 because they had the strength and interest to do so. Would they make themselves again the champions of collective security if tomorrow Indonesia should be the victim of aggression, or Chile, or Egypt? What would the United States and the United Nations do if two different aggressors should start marching at the same time? Would they oppose these two aggressors indiscriminately, without regard for the interests involved and the power available, and would they refuse to violate the principles of collective security and refrain from taking on only the one who was either more dangerous or easier to handle? And if tomorrow South Korea should turn the tables and commit an act of aggression against North Korea or China, would the United States and the United Nations then turn around and fight South Korea?

The answer is bound to be either "No," as in the last-mentioned hypothetical case, or a question mark. Yet according to the principles of collective security, the answer ought to be an unqualified "Yes." These principles require collective measures against all aggression, regardless of circumstances of power and interest. The principles of foreign policy require discrimination among different kinds of aggressions and aggressors, according to the circumstances of power and interest. Collective security as an ideal is directed against all aggression in the abstract; foreign policy can operate only against a particular concrete aggressor. The only question collective security is allowed to ask is, "Who has committed aggression?" Foreign policy cannot help asking, "What interest do I have in opposing this particular aggressor and what power with which to oppose him?"

Collective security, then, can succeed only on the further assumption that all or virtually all nations will come to the defense of the status quo, threatened in the security of a particular nation, even at the risk of war, regardless of whether they could justify such a policy in view of their own individual interests. In other words, what collective security demands of the individual nations is to forsake national egotisms and the national policies serving them. Collective security expects the policies of the individual nations to be inspired by the ideal of mutual assistance and a spirit of self-sacrifice that will not shrink even from the supreme sacrifice of war should it be required by that ideal.

This third assumption is really tantamount to the assumption of a moral revolution infinitely more fundamental than any moral change that has occurred in the history of Western civilization. It is a moral revolution not only in the actions of statesmen representing their countries but also in the actions of plain citizens. Not only are the latter expected to support national policies that are at times bound to run counter to the interests of the nation, they are also expected to be ready to lay down their lives and risk total destruction in a nuclear war for the security of any nation anywhere on the globe. It can be maintained that, if men everywhere would feel and act that way, the lives of all men would be forever secure. The truth of the conclusion is as much beyond dispute as the hypothetical character of the premise.

Men generally do not feel and act, whether as individuals among themselves or as members of their nations with regard to other nations, as they ought to feel and act if collective security is to succeed. And there is, as we have tried to show,[4] less chance today than there has been at any time in modern history that they would act in conformity with moral precepts of a supranational character if such action might be detrimental to the interests of their respective nations. There is no law-enforcing agency above the individual nations, and there are no overwhelming moral and social pressures to which they could be subjected. Thus they are bound always to pursue what they regard to be their own national interests. Conflicts between national and supranational interests and morality are inevitable, at least for some nations, under any conceivable conditions that might call for the realization of collective security. Those nations cannot help resolving such a conflict in favor of their own individual interests and thus paralyzing the operations of the collective system.

In the light of this discussion, we must conclude that collective security cannot be made to work in the contemporary world as it must work according to its ideal assumptions. Yet it is the supreme paradox of collective security that any

---

[4]See pages 251 ff.

attempt to make it work with less than ideal perfection will have the opposite effect from what it is supposed to achieve. It is the purpose of collective security to make war impossible by marshaling in defense of the status quo such overwhelming strength that no nation will dare to resort to force in order to change the status quo. But the less ideal are the conditions for making collective security work, the less formidable will be the combined strength of the nations willing to defend the status quo. If an appreciable number of nations are opposed to the status quo and if they are unwilling to give the common good, as defined in terms of collective security, precedence over their opposition, the distribution of power between the status quo and antistatus quo nations will no longer be overwhelmingly in favor of the former. Rather, the distribution of power will take on the aspects of a balance of power that may still favor the status quo nations, but no longer to such an extent as to operate as an absolute deterrent upon those opposed to the status quo.

The attempt to put collective security into effect under such conditions—which are, as we know, the only conditions under which it can be put into effect—will not preserve peace but will make war inevitable. And not only will it make war inevitable, it will also make localized wars impossible and thus make war universal. For, under the regime of collective security as it actually would work under contemporary conditions, if A attacks B, then C, D, E, and F might honor their collective obligations and come to the aid of B, while G and H might try to stand aside and I, J, and K might support A's aggression. Were there no system of collective security, A might attack B with whatever consequences that might have for A and B, with no other nations being involved in the war. Under a system of collective security operating under less than ideal conditions, war between A and B, or between any other two nations

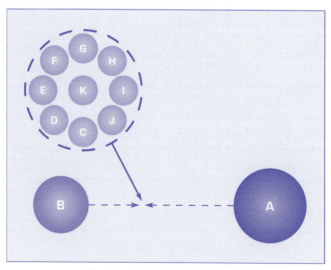

The Ideal of Collective Security

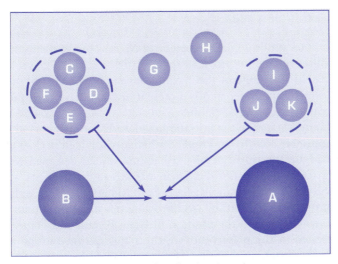

The Reality of Collective Security

anywhere in the world, of necessity evokes the risk of war among all or at best most nations of the world.

From the beginning of the modern state system to the First World War, it was the main concern of diplomacy to localize an actual or threatened conflict between two nations, in order to prevent it from spreading to other nations. The efforts of British diplomacy in the summer of 1914 to limit the conflict between Austria and Serbia to those two nations are an impressive, however unsuccessful, example. By the very logic of its assumptions, the diplomacy of collective security must aim at transforming all local conflicts into world conflicts. If this cannot be one world of peace, it cannot help being one world of war. Since peace is supposed to be indivisible, it follows that war is indivisible, too. Under the assumptions of collective security, any war anywhere in the world, then, is potentially a world war. Thus a device intent upon making war impossible ends by making war universal. Instead of preserving peace between two nations, collective security, as it must actually operate in the contemporary world, is bound to destroy peace among all nations.[5]

These comments on collective security as a practical device for preserving peace are borne out by the experience of the two attempts to apply collective security in a concrete case—the League of Nations' sanctions against Italy in 1935–36 and the United Nations' intervention in defense of the territorial integrity of South Korea from 1950 to 1953.

---

[5]How collective security might operate successfully on the regional level—that is, in the shadow of a great power—has been indicated above, pages 186 ff; see also pages 530 ff.

The Italo-Ethiopian War

After Italy's attack on Ethiopia, the League of Nations put into motion the mechanism of collective security provided for in Article 16 of the Covenant. It soon became apparent that none of the assumptions upon whose realization the success of collective security depends was present or could have been present under the actual conditions of world politics.

The United States, Germany, and Japan were not members of the League system of collective security and were, furthermore, divided in their sympathies. Germany had already openly embarked upon policies designed to overthrow the existing status quo in Europe. Japan was already well on its way to overthrowing the status quo in the Far East. Both, therefore, could only look with favor on an undertaking that, by overthrowing the status quo in an out-of-the-way region, would weaken the position of Great Britain and France, who were vitally interested in the preservation of the status quo in Europe and the Far East. The United States, on the other hand, approved of the attempts to strengthen the defense of the status quo, while the temper of public opinion in the country prevented it from taking an active part in such attempts. The nations that were prepared to do everything they could for the success of the League experiment were either too weak to do much of consequence—such as the Scandinavian countries—or—as in the case of the Soviet Union—their ulterior motives were suspect. Furthermore, the Soviet Union was lacking in naval strength, indispensable under the circumstances, and had no access to the theater of decisive operations without the cooperation of the geographically intervening nations, which was not forthcoming.

Thus the case of collective security versus Italy was in essence the case of Great Britain and France versus Italy. This was a far cry from the ideal prerequisite of a concentration of overwhelming power that no prospective lawbreaker would dare to challenge. It is of course true that the combined strength of Great Britain and France would have sufficed to crush Italy. Yet Great Britain and France were not only members of the League system of collective security; they had other moral, legal, and political commitments. Nor were they engaged in defending the status quo against Italy alone. They were involved in a worldwide struggle for power, of which the conflict with Italy was only one—and not the most important—segment. While they were opposing Italy's attack upon the status quo, they could not overlook the progressing attack of Japan, nor could they be oblivious to the preparations for attack going on east of the Rhine. Nor, finally, were they able to divorce from their policies toward the Soviet Union their fear of communism as a revolutionary movement threatening the domestic status quo. What Great Britain and France conceived as their national interests contradicted what collective security required them to do. More particularly, they were resolved and made their resolution known not to go so far in defense of Ethiopia as to risk war with Italy. In the already quoted words of Sir Winston Churchill: "First, the Prime Minister had declared that sanctions meant war; secondly, he was resolved that there must be no war; and thirdly, he decided upon sanctions. It was evidently impossible to comply with these three conditions."[6]

Unwilling to subordinate their national interests to the requirements of collective security, Great Britain and France were also unwilling to pursue their national interests without regard to collective security. This was the fatal error of British and French foreign policy. By pursuing either cause halfheartedly and without consistency, they failed in both. Not only did they not save the status quo in East Africa, but they also pushed Italy into the arms of Germany. They destroyed the collective system of the League of Nations as well as their own prestige as defenders of the status quo. Among the causes for the increasing boldness of the anti–status quo nations in the late thirties, culminating in a war of aggression, this loss of prestige holds a prominent place.

The debacle of collective security, as applied to the Italian aggression against Ethiopia, conveys two important lessons. It shows the contradiction between an ideally perfect scheme of reform and a political reality that lacks all the elements upon which the success of the scheme was predicated. It shows also the fatal weakness of a foreign policy that is incapable of deciding whether to be guided by the national interest, however defined, or by a supranational principle embodying what is considered to be the common good of the community of nations.

The Korean War

The lessons that could have been learned from the theoretical analysis of collective security, and that were borne out by the experience of the Italo-Ethiopian War, were fully confirmed by the experience of the Korean War.

The attack of North Korea against South Korea on June 25, 1950, joined by China in November of the same year, was as clear-cut a case of aggression as one can imagine. In the absence of even the slightest doubt as to the legal merits of the case, collective security would have required that all members of the United Nations come to the aid of South Korea, the victim of aggression. In view of the nature and the military consequences of the aggression, this aid, to be effective, could only have taken the form of the dispatch of armed forces to the battlefront. Yet of the sixty members of the United Nations, only sixteen sent armed forces of any kind, and of these only the United States, Canada, Great Britain, and Turkey can be said to have contributed more than token forces. South Korea, the country immediately concerned, and the United States provided about 90 percent of the armed forces that fought in Korea. In the course of the war, one great power, China, joined the aggressor as an active participant in the aggression itself. Other members of the United Nations with military capabilities, such as Argentina, Brazil, Czechoslovakia, India, Mexico, and Poland, remained on the sidelines, taking no active part in the military operations on either side. Thus the reality of collective

---

[6]*London Evening Standard,* June 26, 1936.

security, as applied in the Korean War, corresponds exactly to the pattern outlined above. Given the conditions of contemporary world politics, it could not have been otherwise.

In order to understand the different attitudes taken by different nations with regard to the Korean War, it is neither sufficient nor necessary to consult the legal texts concerning the obligations imposed upon the member states by a system of collective security. It is, however, sufficient and indeed indispensable to consult their interests and the power available to them in support of those interests.

As was shown above,[7] the very existence of Korea as an autonomous state has been for more than two thousand years a function of the balance of power in the Far East, either in terms of the supremacy of one power that controlled and protected Korea or in terms of rival imperialisms meeting on the Korean peninsula and establishing there a very unstable equilibrium of generally short duration. The controlling and protecting power was traditionally China, challenged from time to time with varying success by Japan. Toward the end of the nineteenth century, Russia replaced China as the competitor of Japan for the control of Korea. At the end of the Second World War, with China and Japan too weak to perform their historical function with regard to Korea, the United States and the Soviet Union took over that function, the United States, as it were, taking the place of Japan and the Soviet Union that of China. Neither the United States nor the Soviet Union could allow the other power to control all of Korea. As seen from the vantage point of Japan, whose protection is a vital interest of the United States, Korea in the hands of a potentially hostile power is like a drawn dagger, and so it is as seen from the vantage point of Russia and, more particularly, China. Thus the division of Korea into an American and Russian zone at the end of the Second World War was the expression both of the interests of the two nations concerned and of the power available to them, since at that time neither was in a position to risk a major conflict over the control of all of Korea.

This issue of the control of all of Korea was reopened when South Korea was attacked by North Korea, supported by the Soviet Union. The all-out support of the United States for South Korea was justified by its interest in the security of Japan and the overall stability of the Far East. It was that latter interest that justified the substantial support of Canada and Great Britain. The token contributions of other nations, such as Australia, Belgium, Colombia, France, Luxembourg, and Turkey, can be explained either by the same interest or by their special dependence upon the good will of the United States. And the failure of most nations to contribute anything derives from lack of interest or lack of power, or from both.

But even this support, slight when compared with the total military strength of the members of the United Nations, would have been ample for the repulsion of the North Korean aggression, short of a major war. In other words, collective security could have operated successfully even under the less than ideal conditions

---

[7]See page 189.

that prevailed before the intervention of China. That intervention transformed completely the character of the Korean War. Before it, the war could still be called a collective security war or a police action by virtue of the preponderant military force opposing the aggressor. With that intervention the conflict took on the character of a traditional war in which the approximately equal forces of two coalitions oppose each other. Short of a general conflagration, there was no possibility for either side to defeat the other, as South Korea would have been able to defeat North Korea with the assistance of the United Nations forces. From the moment a great power joined the aggressor, only a collective security effort commensurate with the magnitude of the aggression—that is, all-out war against a great power— could have defeated the aggressors. In short, collective security, conceived as an instrument for the protection of the status quo by peaceful means, defeats its avowed purpose and becomes an instrument of all-out war if the aggressor is a great power.

The Korean War did not put collective security to the full test of this paradox, for the interests of the great powers involved in it limited the war to the Korean peninsula. China intervened against the United Nations advance into North Korea for the same reasons that had led to the intervention of the United States against the North Korean advance into South Korea: the fear of a united Korea in potentially hostile hands. Collective security would have required not only the momentary repulsion of aggression but also the establishment of security for the future, an objective to be achieved only by the defeat of China in an all-out war. Similarly, the restoration of traditional Chinese control over the Korean peninsula would have required the defeat of the United States in an all-out war. Neither the United States nor China was willing to take upon itself the burden and risks demanded by such an enterprise. Thus both nations were satisfied with a temporary continuation of the division, however precarious and unstable, of Korea into two spheres of influence, reflecting the balance of power in the Far East.

In this respect, as in the others discussed before, the dilemmas and contradictions to which the Korean War, considered as a collective security action, has given rise stem from the contradictions inherent in the very idea of collective security when it is put into practice under the political conditions of the contemporary world.

AN INTERNATIONAL POLICE FORCE

The idea of an international police force goes a step beyond collective security in that the application of collective force against an actual or prospective lawbreaker no longer lies within the control of the individual nations. The international police would operate under the command of an international agency, which would decide when and how to employ it. No such police force has ever operated as a permanent international organization. The members of the United Nations are, however, obligated by Articles 42 ff of the Charter to create such a force in the form of a United Nations Armed Force. No progress has yet been made in executing that obligation.

The hopes for the preservation of peace that have been connected with an international police force since the end of the First World War are derived from an analogy with the peace-preserving functions the police perform in domestic societies. This analogy is, however, misleading on three grounds.

Domestic societies are composed of millions of members of which at any one time normally only a very small fraction is engaged in violating the law. The spread of power among members of domestic societies is extreme, since there are very powerful and very weak members; yet the combined power of law-abiding citizens will normally be far superior to any combination of even the most powerful lawbreakers. The police as the organized agency of the law-abiding majority do not need to exceed relatively small proportions in order to be able to cope with any foreseeable threat to law and order.

In these three respects the international situation is significantly different. International society is composed of a relatively small number of members, amounting to more than 150 sovereign states. Among these there are giants, such as the United States and the Soviet Union, and pygmies, such as Luxembourg and Nicaragua. What is more important, the power of any one of the giants constitutes a very considerable fraction of the total power of the community of nations. A giant in combination with one or two second-rate nations or a few small ones may easily exceed the strength of all the other nations combined. In view of such a formidable potential opposition, a police force of truly gigantic dimensions would obviously be needed if it should be able to squelch an infringement of law and order without transforming every police action into full-scale war. This would still be true, only on a proportionately smaller scale, if general disarmament should reduce drastically the armed forces of the individual nations. For the international police would still have to constitute a counterweight of overwhelming superiority to the military spirit and training, industrial capacity, and strategic advantages—in short, the power potential of the great powers—which in case of conflict could easily be transformed into actual military strength.

On the assumption, then—which is indeed merely hypothetical—that nations would be willing to surrender the instruments for the protection and furtherance of their own interests to an international police force, how is such an international police force to be composed? The nature of international society as it actually is allows no satisfactory answer to that question.

In domestic societies the police force is naturally composed of members who are fully identified with the existing law and order. But let us assume that among them there are some opposed to the existing law and order and that their number is proportionate to the segment of the total population opposed to it; the number of the disaffected would be so small as to be virtually negligible and unable to affect the striking power of the police. An international police force would necessarily have to be composed of a proportionate or equal number of citizens of the different nations. These nations, however, as we have seen, are virtually always divided into defenders and opponents of the existing status quo—that is, of the existing law and order. Their citizens as members of the international police force could not but share the national preferences in this respect.

Would they be expected to fight against their own nations in defense of a status quo to which they, as members of their nations, must be opposed? Given the relative strength of national and international loyalties in the contemporary world, in case of conflict the national loyalties could not but attract the respective members of the international police force like so many magnets, thus dissolving the international police force before it could ever meet a challenge to the existing law and order.

These general considerations, applying to international society as a whole and more particularly to its most powerful members, are of course not invalidated by the exceptional possibility for an international police force to prevent strictly circumscribed local breaches of the law, provided all the nations directly concerned have an interest in that prevention. The classic example of this possibility is the United Nations Emergency Force, established after the Suez invasion of 1956 to protect the frontiers between Egypt and Israel around the Gaza Strip and to enforce the demilitarization of the Straits of Tiran. The example of UNEF is also illustrative of the limitations created by the opposing states when one recalls the immediate compliance with Egypt's request to withdraw the force in 1967.

An international police force in a society of sovereign states is a contradiction in terms. In the larger context of the world state we will meet this problem again. The problem of an international police force, to be solved at all, must be solved within the framework of a world society that commands the ultimate secular loyalty of its individual members and has developed a conception of justice by which the individual nations composing it are willing to test the legitimacy of their individual claims.[8]

---

[8]Cf. in greater detail, Hans J. Morgenthau, "The Political Conditions for an International Police Force," *International Organization*, Vol. XVII, No. 2 (Spring 1963), pp. 393 ff; and "The Impartiality of the International Police," in Salo Engel and B. A. Métall, *Law, State, and International Legal Order: Essays in Honor of Hans Kelsen* (Knoxville: University of Tennessee Press, 1964), pp. 209 ff.

25 Judicial Settlement

THE NATURE OF THE JUDICIAL FUNCTION

The existence of conflicts among nations makes the realization of international peace through disarmament, collective security, and an international police force impossible. Nation A wants something of Nation B that Nation B is not willing to concede. In consequence, an armed contest between A and B is always possible. If there were a way acceptable to A and B of settling that conflict peaceably, it would make war superfluous as the supreme arbiter of conflicts among nations. And here again the analogy with domestic society is tempting.

In primitive societies individuals often settle their conflicting claims through fighting. They abstain from seeking a decision by violent means only when in the appeal to the authoritative decision of impartial judges they find a substitute for their appeal to arms. It seems obvious to conclude that, if such impartial judges were only available for the authoritative decision of international disputes, the main cause of war would be removed.

Such is indeed the conclusion many humanitarians and statesmen have drawn with increasing frequency and intensity since the middle of the nineteenth century. Toward the end of that century, the so-called Arbitration Movement, whose main tenet was the compulsory settlement of all international disputes by international tribunals, could boast considerable mass support and enthusiastic loyalties. Its public influence was comparable to that of the mass movements that later pinned their hopes on the League of Nations, the United Nations, and a world state. We have already traced the history of the unsuccessful attempts to establish compulsory jurisdiction of international courts for the peaceful settlement of international disputes that otherwise might lead to war.[1] It remains to examine the reasons for the failure of most nations, particularly the great powers,

---

[1]See pages 293 ff.

to accept the compulsory jurisdiction of international courts. It is not the stupidity or wickedness of statesmen or nations that must be held responsible for this failure but the nature of international politics and of the society within which it operates.

The analogy between the pacifying influence of domestic courts and the anticipated similar effect of international courts is mistaken. Courts decide disputes on the basis of the law as it is. The law as it is provides the common ground on which the plaintiff and the defendant meet. Both claim that the law as it is supports their cause, that it is on their side, and they ask the court to decide the case on that ground. The disputes they ask the court to decide—aside from questions of fact—concern the bearing of the existing law, differently interpreted by plaintiff and defendant, on their respective claims.

Such is the fundamental issue with which courts, domestic and international, must deal, and such is the nature of virtually all cases with which international courts have actually dealt. But those are not the issues which set nation against nation in deadly conflict and entail the risk of war. What is at stake in those international conflicts that are rightly called "political" and that have caused all major wars is not what the law is but what it ought to be. The issue is here not the interpretation of the existing law recognized as legitimate by both sides, at least for the purposes of the lawsuit, but the legitimacy of the existing law in the face of the demand for change.

To cite only a few recent examples: everybody knew in 1938 what the legal situation was with regard to Czechoslovakia. Nobody had any doubts in 1939 what international law said with regard to the status of Danzig and the German-Polish frontier. There is no disagreement today concerning the rules of international law that apply to the rights and the obligations of the Soviet Union and Turkey with reference to the Dardanelles. What was or is at issue in all these controversies evoking the specter of war is not the application and interpretation of international law as it is, but the legitimacy of the existing legal order and the justification of the demand for its change. What Germany was opposed to in regard to Czechoslovakia, Danzig, and Poland, and what the Soviet Union opposes with respect to the Dardanelles, is not a particular interpretation of international law concerning these matters but the existing legal order as such. What Germany wanted and what the Soviet Union wants is a new legal order to replace the old. It is this demand that was resisted by Great Britain and France in the case of Germany. The incompatibility between the demand for a new legal order and the defense of the old brought on the Second World War. And it is the same demand on the part of the Soviet Union, in the form of wars of national liberation, and the resistance to it by the Western powers, that poisons the international atmosphere today.

In political terms, such clashes between the existing legal order and the demand for its change are but another manifestation of the antagonism between the status quo and imperialism. Any particular distribution of power, once it has reached some degree of stability, is hardened into a legal order. This legal order not only provides the new status quo with ideological disguises and moral justifications; it also surrounds the new status quo with a bulwark of legal safeguards, the violation of which will put into motion the enforcement mechanisms of the law. The function of the courts is to put the enforcement action into motion by determining whether the concrete case under consideration justifies such action according to the existing rules of law. Thus any system of existing law is of necessity an ally of the status quo, and the courts cannot fail to be its custodians. This is so in the international sphere no less than on the domestic scene.

Whenever the issue is one of determination of rights or of accommodation of interests within the generally accepted framework of the status quo, the courts will find for the plaintiff or the defendant, as the case may be. Whenever the issue is one of preservation or fundamental change of the status quo, the answer of the courts is ready before a question is even asked: they must decide in favor of the existing status quo and refuse the demand for change. The courts of France in 1790 could no more have abolished the feudalistic monarchy and transformed France into a middle-class republic than an international court in 1800 could have given Napoleon predominance over Europe. It is not open to doubt that an international court would have rendered judgment in 1938 for Czechoslovakia, in 1939 for Danzig and Poland, and in 1950 for South Korea, against Germany and North Korea, respectively. Since it is in its essence the status quo couched in legal terms, existing law favors the status quo, and the courts can only apply the existing law to the case in hand.

To invoke international law and international courts in a crisis where not the determination of rights and the accommodation of interests within the status quo but the very survival of the status quo is at stake is a favorite device of status quo nations. International law and international courts are their natural allies. Imperialistic nations are inevitably opposed to the existing status quo and its legal order and will not think of submitting the controversy to the authoritative decision of an international court. For the court cannot grant their demands without destroying the very foundation on which its authority rests.

THE NATURE OF INTERNATIONAL CONFLICTS: TENSIONS AND DISPUTES

Not only will controversies about changing the status quo not be submitted to courts, but they will generally not even be formulated in legal terms, the only terms of which courts can take cognizance. In September 1938 the real issue between Germany and Czechoslovakia was not sovereignty over the Sudetenland but the military and political domination of Central Europe. The dispute over the Sudetenland was only one symptom of this issue among several. Of these symptoms the outstanding were the dispute with Austria culminating in the annexation of Austria by Germany in March 1938 and the dispute with Czechoslovakia in March 1939 resulting in the establishment of a German protectorate over that country.

The one cause underlying all these symptoms was a conflict whose stakes were not territorial concessions and legal adjustments within the framework of a recognized status quo but the survival of the status quo itself, the overall distribution of power, the all or nothing of supremacy in Central Europe. The disputes symptomatic of the power conflict could be formulated in the legal terms of claims, counterclaims, and denials and as such be admitted and rejected by a court of law. The underlying cause was incapable even of formulation in legal terms, for the legal order whose survival was threatened by the claim for change had no legal concepts to express that claim, let alone a legal remedy to satisfy it.

At the bottom of disputes that entail the risk of war there is a tension between the desire to preserve the existing distribution of power and the desire to overthrow it. These conflicting desires, for reasons already discussed,[2] are rarely expressed in their own terms—terms of power—but are couched in moral and legal terms. What the representatives of nations talk about are moral principles and legal claims. What their talk refers to are conflicts of power. We propose to refer to the unformulated conflicts of power as "tensions" and call the conflicts formulated in legal terms "disputes." A discussion of the typical relations between tensions and disputes will make clear the function international courts are able to fulfill for the preservation of international peace. Three such typical relations can be distinguished.

Pure Disputes

Between two nations there is sometimes no tension at all, yet there are disputes. Or sometimes, despite the existence of a tension, the dispute has no relation to the tension. In this case we speak of "pure disputes."

Let us suppose that the United States and the Soviet Union are involved in a dispute over the exchange rate between dollars and rubles for the diplomatic personnel of the two countries. Despite the tension that exists between the United States and the Soviet Union, it is conceivable that such a dispute be submitted by the two parties to an international court for authoritative decision. Pure disputes, then, are susceptible to judicial decision.

Disputes with the Substance of a Tension

A relation may, however, exist between a tension and a dispute. Such a relation can be of two different kinds. The subject matter of the dispute may be identical with a certain segment of the subject matter of the tension. The tension may be compared to an iceberg, the main part of which is submerged while the top stands out above the surface of the ocean. That small segment of the tension can be defined in legal terms and made the subject of a dispute. We call this type "disputes with the substance of a tension."

---

[2]See Chapter 7.

One of the main issues of the tension between the United States and the Soviet Union is the distribution of power in Europe. The Potsdam Agreement is a legal document that endeavored to settle the aspects of that issue connected with the occupation and administration of Germany by the Allies. The subject matter of the Potsdam Agreement, then, was identical with a segment of the issue that constituted the subject matter of the tension between the United States and the Soviet Union. A dispute over the interpretation of the Potsdam Agreement had a direct bearing upon the overall power relations between the United States and the Soviet Union. An interpretation favorable to one nation will add so much power to one side and deduct that much power from the other side, since the issue is one upon which the power contest between the two countries had seized as one of its main stakes.

To accept beforehand the authoritative decision of such a dispute by an international court, whatever it might be, is tantamount to surrendering control over the outcome of the power contest itself. No nation has been willing to go so far. Since a court of law cannot help being a defender of the status quo formulated in legal terms, its decision is most likely to support the interpretation of a legal document that favors the status quo. By doing this, the court may meet the point of the dispute, but it misses the point of the tension. With respect to the tension, the interpretation of a legal document, such as the Potsdam Agreement, is but a phase in a contest whose issue is not the interpretation of the law as it is, but the justice of its existence.

A court, the product and the mouthpiece of the law as it is, has no way of deciding the real issue of a dispute whose subject matter is also the subject matter of a tension. A court is, in a sense, a party to such a dispute. A court, identified as it is with the status quo and the law representing it, has no standard of judgment transcending the conflict between the defense of the status quo and the demand for change. It cannot settle that conflict. It can only take sides. In the guise of an impartial settlement of the real issue, a court is almost bound to decide the apparent issue in favor of the status quo. In this inability of a court to transcend the limitations of its origin and functions lies the real cause of its inability to decide between the relative merits of the status quo and a new distribution of power.

Disputes Representing a Tension

The other type of dispute that stands in relation to a tension is the most important one in view of this discussion. We call disputes of this kind "disputes representing a tension." On the surface, disputes of this kind resemble pure disputes. As a matter of fact, pure disputes often transform themselves into disputes representing a tension, and vice versa. The subject matter of such a dispute has no relation at all to the subject matter of the tension. It is in the representative and symbolic function alone that the relation between tension and dispute consists.

Let us consider again the example of a dispute between the United States and the Soviet Union concerning the exchange rate of dollars and rubles for the diplomatic representatives of both countries. This dispute may, as we have seen, lack any relation to the tension that exists between the United States and the Soviet Union. Yet it may also be that the two nations, engaged as they are in a contest over the general distribution of power, will seize upon this dispute and make it the concrete issue by which to test their respective strength.

The fundamental issue that separates the United States and the Soviet Union—the overall distribution of power in the world—is for the moral and ideological reasons already mentioned[3] incapable of rational formulation in terms of claims and counterclaims. To use a term of modern psychology, it is "repressed." Conveying, as it were, the unsettled foundation of the relations between the two countries, the tension may communicate its turbulent agitation to any dispute of whatever kind and of whatever intrinsic importance. Once this has happened, the dispute takes the place of the tension in the relations between the two countries. All the intensity of feeling and the uncompromising harshness of the rivalry for power, with which the nations consider the tension in peace and act upon it in war, is released into the dispute.

What in times of peace the nations cannot do with regard to the tension, they do now with regard to the dispute. The dispute becomes a test case in which claim and counterclaim represent and symbolize the respective power positions of the nations. Concessions are out of the question. For the claimant to concede, let us say, one-tenth of the object of the dispute would be tantamount to revealing a proportionate weakness in its overall power position. For the other side to lose out altogether is unthinkable. The loss of the object of the dispute would be the symbolic equivalent of the loss of a decisive battle or of a war. It would signify defeat in the overall struggle for power, insofar as that struggle is brought out on the level of disputes. Thus each nation will fight on a matter of procedure or prestige with uncompromising tenacity, as though the national existence itself were at stake. And in a symbolic sense it actually is at stake.

> Rightly to be great,
> Is not to stir without great argument,
> But greatly to find quarrel in a straw
> When honor's at the stake.[4]

Whenever a dispute stands in such a representative relation to a tension, a settlement in terms of the dispute becomes obviously impossible. This is true of a settlement by diplomatic negotiations, which of necessity must proceed through the give-and-take of compromise. By the same token, this is true of a settlement by authoritative judicial decision. What has been said in this respect of disputes with the subject matter of a tension applies to this category of disputes. Disputes representing a tension are looked upon by the nations concerned as though they were the tension itself. Similarly, the judicial decision of such a dispute will be evaluated in terms of its bearing upon the tension. No nation, and especially no

---

[3]See Chapter 7.
[4]*Hamlet*, Act IV, Scene iv.

antistatus quo nation, for reasons already discussed, will take the risk of submitting a dispute of this kind, and through it the issue of the tension itself, to the authoritative decision of a court.

LIMITATIONS OF THE JUDICIAL FUNCTION

We arrive, then, at the conclusion that political disputes—disputes that stand in relation to a tension and in which, therefore, the overall distribution of power between two nations is at stake—cannot be settled by judicial methods. This conclusion, arrived at by way of analysis, is borne out by the actual behavior of nations. We have already pointed to the extreme care with which nations are wont to define and qualify their obligation to submit disputes to international courts.[5] They do this in order to retain the ultimate control over the kind of settlement to be applied to their disputes. As the late Prime Minister Nehru of India put it, when he rejected a resolution of the United Nations Security Council calling for arbitration of the India-Pakistan dispute over Kashmir: "Great political questions—and this is a great political question—are not handed over in this way to arbitrators from foreign countries or any country."[6]

It is significant that the nations that have concluded arbitration treaties without any qualification, thus submitting all disputes of any kind to the judicial process, are those between whom conflicts over the overall distribution of power, and hence political disputes, are virtually impossible. Such treaties have been concluded, for instance, between Colombia and El Salvador, Peru and Bolivia, Denmark and The Netherlands, Denmark and Italy, Denmark and Portugal, The Netherlands and China, The Netherlands and Italy, Austria and Hungary, France and Luxembourg, Belgium and Sweden, and Italy and Switzerland. No two states that had the slightest reason to anticipate the possibility of a political conflict with each other in the not-too-distant future have entered into legal obligations requiring either side to submit political disputes to judicial settlement.

Furthermore, among the twenty decisions rendered by the Permanent Court of Arbitration, there is none that can be called political in the sense in which we are using the term. Among the thirty judgments and twenty-seven advisory opinions rendered by the Permanent Court of International Justice,[7] there is one that can be called political: the advisory opinion in the case of the Austro-German Customs Union. We have already pointed to the fact that the jurisdiction of the court in this case was based upon Article 14 of the Covenant of the League of Nations authorizing the Council of the League to request advisory opinions from the Court.[8] Being advisory, the opinion did not bind the council but left it free

---

[5]See pages 293 ff.
[6]*London Times,* August 8, 1952, p. 4.
[7]Different authors use different figures. We follow Oppenheim-Lauterpacht, op. cit. (7th ed., 1952), Vol. II, pp. 80–88.
[8]See pages 296–97.

to take whatever measures it saw fit in the light of its own legal and political evaluation of the case. The council of the League of Nations in this case acted as an
organ of the status quo. It was inevitable that the council should play such a role,
in view both of its composition and the function it was supposed to fulfill as the
political executive of the League of Nations.

This request for an advisory opinion drew the court into a confusion that
led to the greatest intellectual debacle in the history of that judicial agency. The
fact that there were four different opinions—and that, out of fifteen judges, seven
felt the need to identify themselves with the two concurring opinions, and seven
signed a dissenting opinion—illustrates the extent of the confusion. The measure
of the intellectual debacle can only be conveyed by a perusal of the opinions
themselves. The inability of so highly competent a tribunal to cope adequately
with the case of the Austro-German Customs Union was the inevitable result of
the nature of the case.

With the proposed Customs Union, Germany and Austria challenged the
status quo of 1919. The Permanent Court of International Justice was intellectually
prepared to deal with any case arising within the framework of the existing status
quo. The legal order of that status quo furnished it with the intellectual instruments to perform that task. Confronted with a challenge to that status quo, the
court was thrown off balance by its inability to find grounds above the contentions of the parties from which to judge the claims and counterclaims. Being
an organ of the status quo and performing functions that had to take the legitimacy of that status quo for granted, the court found itself faced with a task no
court of law is capable of performing: to pass judgment on the legitimacy of the
status quo itself by finding upon the legality of the projected Austro-German
Customs Union.

Judge Anzilotti, in his brilliant and profound concurring opinion, put his
finger on the essentially political problem that faced the court and that it could
not meet with the judicial means at its disposal. "Everything points to the fact that
the answer depends upon considerations which are for the most part, if not entirely,
of a political and economic kind. It may therefore be asked whether the Council
really wished to obtain the Court's opinion on this aspect of the question and
whether the Court ought to deal with it. . . . I grant that the Court may refuse to
give an opinion which would compel it to depart from the essential rules governing
its activity as a tribunal."[9] The court did not refuse to give an opinion and, by trying to decide a conflict between the status quo and the desire for change, departed
"from the essential rules governing its activity as a tribunal."

The International Court of Justice avoided this pitfall in which the
Permanent Court of International Justice had fallen. When in 1951 Great Britain
submitted to it the case of the Anglo-Iranian Oil Company, it refused to take jurisdiction. The Iranian government had nationalized the property of the Anglo-
Iranian Oil Company in obvious violation of the existing treaties. The dispute

---

[9]*P.C.I.J.* Series A/B, No. 41, pp. 68, 69.

between Iran and Great Britain did not concern the applicability of existing law; it rather concerned the legitimacy of the status quo, codified in the existing law, opposed to the legitimacy of a new legal order. A court, as we have seen, must assume the legitimacy of the existing legal order and defend it by its judgments. Hence, it was perfectly logical that Great Britain, interested in the preservation of the status quo, would appeal to the International Court of Justice, while Iran, interested in the change of the status quo, denied the court's jurisdiction. By taking jurisdiction, the court could have sided only with Great Britain without considering the real issue of the case. By declining jurisdiction on technical grounds, it recognized implicitly the limitation of the judicial function with which we are dealing here.

Finally, perhaps the most impressive empirical evidence for the analysis offered above is presented by the relations between the United States and the Soviet Union as they have developed since the end of the Second World War. It has been a matter of much comment that it is extremely difficult to define the fundamental issue that has separated the United States and the Soviet Union. It is not Germany, or Cuba, or Korea, or Vietnam. Nor is it the sum of all these single issues. Nor can the fundamental issue be defined in terms of the conflict between two antagonistic philosophies and systems of government, for that conflict existed for twenty-five years without having the kind of repercussions on the international scene that we are witnessing today. The issues mentioned, either singly or combined, cannot account for the depth and the bitterness of the conflicts that engulf the United States and the Soviet Union wherever they meet, and for the stalemates that attend their every effort at settling those conflicts by peaceful means.

The existence of a tension embracing the whole globe can explain these peculiarities of the individual conflicts. That tension provides the lifeblood that pulsates in all the issues, small and large, standing between the United States and the Soviet Union, and imparts to them the same color, the same temperature, and the same peculiarities. It is indeed the fundamental issue of which all the single issues mentioned above are but ramifications or symbolic representations. The discord between the United States and the Soviet Union over the distribution of power throughout the world precludes the solution on its own merits of any single dispute pending between the two countries. By the same token, it precludes also the judicial settlement of such disputes.

Through analytical and empirical considerations, we have arrived at the conclusion that the disputes that are most likely to lead to war cannot be settled by judicial methods. Since they are the ramifications or symbolic representations of a tension, their real issue is the maintenance of the status quo versus its overthrow. No court, domestic or international, is equipped to settle this issue. The consideration of the question of how this issue is normally settled in the domestic sphere shows from yet another angle the fallacy of the analogy between the pacifying function of domestic and international courts.

26 Peaceful Change

PEACEFUL CHANGE WITHIN THE STATE

Tensions are a universal phenomenon of social life. They occur in the domestic no less than in the international sphere. In the domestic sphere, too, a given status quo is stabilized and perpetuated in a legal system. Social forces hostile to this status quo arise and try to overthrow it by changing the legal system. It is not the courts that decide the issue. The courts must act as agents of the status quo. In the struggle between the desire for change and the status quo, the cause of change is upheld, if at all, by legislatures, and sometimes by the executive power. Thus the tension between the status quo and the demand for change frequently resolves itself in the domestic sphere into a conflict between the courts as the defenders of the status quo and the legislature as the champion of change.

This is true of many of the great controversies of modern history in which tensions manifested themselves. Thus the tension between the status quo of feudalism and the desire for change for the middle classes expressed itself in the rivalry between courts and Parliament in nineteenth-century Britain. In the intellectual realm this rivalry was foreshadowed in the polemic of Bentham, the apostle of reform through legislation, against Blackstone, the conservative defender of the common law and of its courts. A similar conflict arose in the United States in the first decades of the twentieth century when the doctrine of laissez faire economics was protected by the courts against social and regulatory legislation. In both cases change won out, and the courts became the defenders of the new status quo.

Three factors made this peaceful transformation possible: (1) the ability of public opinion to express itself freely, (2) the ability of social and political institutions to absorb the pressure of public opinion, and (3) the ability of the state to protect the new status quo against violent change.

In both nineteenth-century England and twentieth-century America, public opinion expressed the desire for change through the spoken and printed word, through organized efforts and spontaneous reactions. Under the impact of these expressions, the moral climate of the community changed, putting the stamp of its approval upon the desire for change and depreciating the status quo and its defenders. No social or political agency could escape the all-pervading influence of this moral climate. In that intangible transformation of moral valuations we find the most potent force promoting the transformation of the status quo.

Public opinion not only had the opportunity to voice its desire for change; it also had the chance to compete with the defenders of the status quo in fashioning legal rules that would either support or change the status quo. This competition took the form either of elections to legislative bodies or of campaigns for certain pieces of legislation within these bodies. Thus the social forces demanding change were channeled into parliamentary institutions. There they met their opponents in a peaceful contest, which determined the winner according to the objective standards of the majority vote, accepted beforehand by all. In this way the status quo was transformed on those two spectacular occasions without disrupting the continuity of the legal processes and without endangering the peace and order of society.

Finally, the authority and power of the state stand ready to enforce whatever legal order has emerged from the contest between social groups and political factions, provided that legal order conforms to the minimum requirements of the moral consensus upon which the whole structure of public institutions is founded. This readiness of the state and its unchallengeable superiority to any possible opposition not only discourage minority groups from opposing a given status quo by violent means but also impose two important restraints upon public opinion. They restrain the influential sections of public opinion from advancing demands so extreme as to be unacceptable to any other influential section and, hence, to be enforceable by the state only at the risk of armed resistance. They act as powerful incentives for compromise in legislative bodies that are aware of the power of the state and of its limitations. For the state can and will enforce those laws that do not flout the minimum requirement of the moral order of the state itself. But the state cannot try to enforce laws that contravene those minimum requirements without risking the disintegration of its own fabric in anarchy or civil war.

Such is the normal process of social change in a free society. It is apparent that this process is not performed by any particular agency discharging its regular duties. Social forces, elevating their needs into principles of justice, capture public opinion. It is the all-pervading influence of public opinion that determines the moral valuations and legal decisions of legislative agencies, as it does in the long run of courts and of the executive power. Legislative, judicial, and executive agencies are instruments of public opinion. They all fulfill the same function for public opinion: to provide peaceful and orderly channels for the presentation and scrutiny of its demands, for their evaluation in the light of generally shared principles of justice, and for the transformation into reality of those that have been recognized as legitimate.

What the legislative bodies contribute to this process of change is primarily a forum for the public presentation of divergent views and of the ratification of a choice already made by unorganized society. It would be naïve to believe that the issue between the status quo and change, whenever it arises, needs only to be submitted to a legislative body that will settle the issue either by passing or refusing to pass a law. In this process of peaceful change legislatures play an indispensable yet secondary role.

Whatever contribution the courts may make to the process of a peaceful change from one status quo to another is governed by the moral climate that pervades the halls of justice no less than the chambers of Congress, the White House, and the homes of ordinary citizens. Since, as we have seen, the courts can only apply the law as it is, they cannot help but be instruments of the status quo. Once the legislature has passed a new law embodying a new status quo, however, the courts can accelerate and smooth the transition from one status quo to another, or they can retard it and endanger its peaceful and orderly progress. In other words, the courts can resist inevitable change, or they can contribute to its peaceful and orderly realization. Which of these roles the courts will play depends upon the strength and single-mindedness of public opinion, as well as upon the receptiveness of the courts to that public opinion.

The executive branch of the government in a democracy can influence and lead public opinion and bring its pressure to bear upon the other branches of the government. It cannot bring about major changes through its own independent efforts. Its main function is that of enforcing the decisions the other branches have made. In a dictatorship, however, all functions of the government are merged in the hands of the executive, who decides and enforces at the same time. Yet it would be a mistake to believe that the dictator can decide as he sees fit regardless of public opinion. He is indeed able to manipulate public opinion through effective use of the channels of communications over which he holds monopolistic control. But for his propaganda to be effective it must not be too much at variance with the life experiences of his subjects. The dictator, then, must either square these experiences with his propaganda or else adapt his propaganda to these experiences. In any case, even the dictator is exposed to pressures of public opinion that he can neither completely mold nor ignore.

Such are, in sketchy outline, the processes of peaceful change on the domestic scene. They make it possible for tensions to manifest themselves in public controversies, election campaigns, parliamentary debates, and governmental crises, instead of in violent conflagrations. If, however, those processes do not operate, or operate badly, the domestic situation that will arise resembles the conditions existing on the international scene. Demands for change, unable to assert themselves in the competition of the marketplace, in electoral and legislative contests, go underground, as it were. The controversy between the status quo and the demand for change becomes a tension with effects upon disputes similar to those that we have recognized in the international field. Domestic society, then, will enter a prerevolutionary or revolutionary stage. The groups of the population identified respectively with the status quo and the demand for change will oppose each other like two armed camps that, unable to appeal to the arbitrament of the majority vote or to common standards of justice, seek a decision in economic or military war.

Whether such a situation actually degenerates into revolution and civil war depends on the distribution of power within domestic society. We have already pointed out in another context that the modern technology of war and communications makes popular revolutions extremely unlikely.[1] The odds are very much in favor of violent changes in form of coups d'état. Instead of one fraction of the population rising against the government supported by another fraction of the population, it is more likely that one segment of the governmental machinery, especially of the armed forces, will try to gain control over the whole government.

What is important for our present discussion is to recognize that it is not the domestic courts that peacefully settle disputes that otherwise might lead to revolution and civil war. When in the Dred Scott case the issue of the territorial extension of slavery was before the Supreme Court of the United States, the Court decided in favor of the status quo. Yet that decision settled nothing. No court of law could have settled what was at stake in the Dred Scott case. Even society as a whole was unable to settle by peaceful means the conflict between the status quo and the desire for change. For that conflict not only challenged the existing distribution of power between North and South; in the issues of slavery and the relations between the federal and state governments, it also reopened the question of the content of the moral consensus upon which the political structure of the United States was built. That question was addressed not to a court or a legislature but to society as a whole. And American society gave two incompatible answers. Those answers made the conflict "irrepressible."

The vital function of peaceful change within the state is performed, not by any particular agency acting in isolation but by domestic society as an integrated whole. The moral consensus of society, supported by the authority and material power of the government, will avail itself of all social and political agencies to bring about a state of affairs in conformity with its conception of justice. For this process of peaceful change, legislative bodies play a particularly important role if, as in democratic societies, they are free agents. But legislatures, too, are only the agents of society as a whole. Without society's support their laws are impotent to bring about the desired change. The history of legislation is strewn with laws, such as the antitrust laws, that, while enacted by the legislature and remaining on the statute books, have failed to achieve their purpose because the moral consensus of society does not support them. Thus legislative bodies are no more capable than courts of peacefully changing an old status quo into a new one by merely performing their technical functions. In other words, legislation is no more sufficient than a judicial decision when society is confronted with its supreme challenge: to change the distribution of power inside society without jeopardizing the orderly and peaceful processes upon which the welfare of society depends.

---

[1] See pages 389 ff.

PEACEFUL CHANGE IN INTERNATIONAL AFFAIRS

An important lesson can be learned from the analogy between the legal processes of domestic and international societies. But it is not the lesson the advocates of the judicial settlement of international disputes have drawn. Domestic courts do not and cannot fulfill the function that advocates of judicial settlement ascribed to them. They do not and cannot peacefully settle disputes that otherwise would lead to violent conflagrations. The forces and institutions that fulfill this function for domestic society do not exist at all on the international scene.

As we have seen,[2] there is no longer an international moral consensus from which quarreling nations can receive a common standard of justice for the settlement of their disputes. This lack of a moral consensus has prevented the realization of the provisions, found in many arbitration treaties and also in the Statute of the International Court of Justice, which under certain conditions allow international courts to decide not according to strict international law but *ex aequo et bono,* that is, according to the general principles of equity and justice. Provisions of this kind are sound in that they recognize the existence of disputes not susceptible to judicial settlement on the basis of the existing rules of international law. Such provisions are, however, unsound in that they assume that the problem posed by the latter category of disputes can be solved simply by authorizing courts to depart from the existing rules of international law and to invoke some general principles of equity and justice. International courts can invoke such principles only if these principles exist. They cannot invent them or appeal to them as to a *deus ex machina,* standing ready to intervene whenever an international court is caught between the status quo and the desire for change. International society is in want of generally accepted standards of justice through which the respective merits of the defense of, and the attack upon, the status quo could be determined. To empower a court to use such standards is of little help if the standards to be used do not exist.

International society also lacks legislative bodies that could fulfill the functions in the process of peaceful change similar to the functions legislative agencies perform for domestic society. Article 19 of the Covenant of the League of Nations and Articles 10 and 14 of the Charter of the United Nations have endeavored to supply an instrumentality of peaceful change. Article 19 of the Covenant reads: "The Assembly may from time to time advise the reconsideration by Members of the League of treaties which have become inapplicable and the consideration of international conditions whose continuance might endanger the peace of the world." Article 10 of the Charter states that "the General Assembly may discuss any question or any matters within the scope of the present Charter . . . and . . . may make recommendations to the Members of the United Nations or to the Security Council or to both on any such questions or matters." Article 14 of the Charter refers more specifically to "the peaceful adjustment of any situation, regardless of origin, which it [*the General Assembly*] deems likely to impair the general welfare or friendly relations among nations."

---

[2]See pages 260 ff.

Article 19 of the Covenant of the League of Nations

Concerning Article 19 of the Covenant of the League of Nations, Frederick S. Dunn has rightly stated that it "has been a dead letter from the beginning."[3] Article 19 was formally invoked only once, by Bolivia against Chile in 1920. In view of an unfavorable report by a committee of jurists appointed by the Assembly of the League of Nations, Bolivia retracted its request and up to 1929 refused to participate any further in the work of the League.

In its report the committee of jurists made two important points: one obvious, the other seriously limiting the applicability of Article 19. The report declared what the text of Article 19 obviously suggests—that the Assembly had no authority to modify treaties with binding effect, that such modification was within the exclusive competence of the contracting parties, and that it could only give advice to the members of the League. The condition for giving such advice with regard to treaties, however, was their inapplicability. And the committee defined inapplicability of treaties as the intervention of such radical material and moral changes "that their application has ceased to be reasonably possible."[4] A situation where the perpetuation of the status quo is so obviously outrageous as to meet these requirements would be rare indeed.

Let us, however, assume that the Assembly had advised the members concerned to reconsider a treaty or to consider a situation that threatened the peace. The parties were free to accept or reject this advice. If they accepted the advice voluntarily, it would be safe to surmise that the interests at stake were not vital and that any kind of outside pressure, encouragement, or face-saving device would probably have induced them to agree on reconsideration of the treaty or consideration of the situation. Yet consideration does not mean agreement. The parties concerned might have considered the treaty or the situation and thereby complied with the advice of the Assembly. They might still not have agreed upon a solution, and Article 19 vested no authority in the Assembly to impose a solution upon them.

It is an open question whether the Assembly could have given advice in pursuance of Article 19 only by unanimous vote or whether a majority vote would have been sufficient. If one assumes that unanimity was required, the Assembly would have been unable to give advice if even one nation was opposed. And the nation whose interests would have been adversely affected by a change in the status quo would most likely have been opposed. If, on the other hand, the parties concerned were already agreed upon reconsideration of the status quo, they were not in need of advice to that effect, and the proceedings by virtue of Article 19 were without purpose.

If one assumes, however, that only a majority vote was required, the situation was similar to the one that we found to vitiate the practical operation of collective

---

[3] *Peaceful Change* (New York: Council on Foreign Relations, 1937), p. 111.
[4] *Journal of the Second Assembly of the League of Nations*, 1921, p. 218.

security.[5] In any situation where the perpetuation of the status quo is at stake, it is probable that the community of nations will be divided into two hostile camps. One group will favor the perpetuation of the status quo; the other will demand its overthrow. Which group has a numerical majority is obviously an irrelevant question. What solely counts in a society of sovereign nations is where the preponderance of power resides. A minority of great powers will assuredly disregard the advice of a majority of weak and medium powers; the advice of a majority ready to use overwhelming strength will be heeded by the minority. Actually, however, it is much more likely that two camps of not too disproportionate strength will oppose each other. In such a contingency the issue would not have been decided by the advice of the antistatus-quo nations that might have had a majority in the Assembly of the League of Nations.

The Charter of the United Nations

These considerations, merely speculative with respect to Article 19 of the Covenant of the League of Nations, have been tested by the actual performance of the organs of the United Nations. Article 18, paragraph 2, of the Charter provides that the General Assembly of the United Nations can make recommendations, by virtue of Articles 10 and 14, by a two-thirds majority of the members present and voting. While broader and less specific in their wording than Article 19 of the Covenant, Articles 10 and 14 are intended to perform for the United Nations the same function Article 19 was supposed to perform for the League: that of opening a legal avenue for peaceful change. The General Assembly of the United Nations has availed itself with remarkable frequency of this power to make recommendations. Many of these recommendations either had no relevance for the problem of peaceful change or aimed at the maintenance of the status quo through the preservation or restoration of peace. A number of cases that came before the General Assembly, however, raised the issue of peaceful change. These cases were Palestine, Korea, Germany, Austria, Hungary, Tunisia, Morocco, Algeria, West Irian, Cyprus, Formosa, the Suez Canal, Jordan, Lebanon, and the former Italian colonies. The overall record has been negative, as it was bound to be.

On the other hand, a recommendation to change the status quo that is acceptable to all parties concerned is superfluous; its acceptance shows that whatever disagreements there might have been among the parties did not affect the overall distribution of power among them but affected only adjustments within an overall distribution of power upon which all parties concerned were agreed. On the other hand, a recommendation to change the status quo that is opposed by one of the parties concerned will either remain a dead letter or must be enforced. Hence the recommendation, to be effective, must become a decision backed by force. It was the purpose of the requests of the General Assembly that

---

[5]See Chapter 24.

this transformation of recommendation into decision be brought about by the only agency of the United Nations that the Charter has given the power to use force: the Security Council. Since the Security Council was unable to use force, the recommendations of the General Assembly remained a dead letter.

If the parties concerned do not agree, peaceful change is possible only under the ideal conditions of collective security where overwhelming force is marshaled against the dissenting party. Since, as we have seen, the realization of these conditions is very unlikely, the mechanisms for peaceful change provided by modern international organizations are bound to be generally unworkable. If they are put into operation at all there will either be no change, or what change there is will not be peaceful. In other words, either the recommendations for change will not be enforced, or war between the nations favoring and those opposing change will decide the issue. This cannot be otherwise in a society of sovereign nations. For sovereign nations are moved to action by what they regard as their national interests rather than by the allegiance to a common good that, as a common standard of justice, does not exist in the society of nations.

27 International Government

The remedies for international anarchy and war that have been discussed thus far are all specific remedies. They attack a particular problem in which the lack of international order and the tendency toward war are manifest, and they endeavor to solve the general problem of international order and peace through a solution of the particular problem. International government owes its existence to the recognition that peace and order are the products, not of a specific device meeting a particular problem, but of the common bond that unites an integrated society under a common authority and a common conception of justice. How to found such an authority in a society of sovereign states and to create such a conception of justice is, then, the task any attempt at international government must try to solve.

Each of the three world wars of the last century and a half was followed by an attempt to establish an international government. The total failure to keep international order and peace called forth an overall effort to make international order and peace secure. The Holy Alliance followed the Napoleonic Wars; the League of Nations, the First World War; the United Nations, the Second World War. With regard to each of these attempts at international government, three questions must be asked: (1) Where is the authority to govern vested, or who is to govern? (2) By what principle of justice is the government to be guided, or what is the conception of the common good to be realized by the government? (3) To what extent has the government been able to maintain order and peace?

THE HOLY ALLIANCE

History

The international government commonly called the Holy Alliance was based upon three treaties: the Treaty of Chaumont of March 9, 1814; the Quadruple Alliance signed at Paris on November 20, 1815; and the Treaty of the Holy

463

Alliance of September 26, 1815. In the Treaty of Chaumont, Austria, Great Britain, Prussia, and Russia concluded an alliance for twenty years, for the purposes of preventing the Napoleonic dynasty from returning to France and of guaranteeing the territorial settlement to be made at the end of the war against Napoleon. The Quadruple Alliance reaffirmed the provisions of the Treaty of Chaumont and in its Article VI laid down the principles of what is known as "congressional government" or "diplomacy by conference."[1]

In contrast to the Quadruple Alliance—which presented, as it were, the constitutional law of the international government of the Holy Alliance—the Treaty of the Holy Alliance itself, from which the international government received its name, contained no principles of government at all. It proclaimed the adherence of all rulers to the principles of Christianity, with God as the actual sovereign of the world. It is replete with phrases such as "reciprocal service," "unalterable good will," "mutual affection," "Christian charity," and "indissoluble fraternity." Originally signed by the rulers of Austria, Prussia, and Russia, the Holy Alliance was adhered to by all European rulers, with the exception of the pope and the sultan.[2] Obviously inspired by Czar Alexander I of Russia, it reaffirmed the moral unity of Europe. That reaffirmation of a moral consensus among the nations is the main function the Treaty of the Holy Alliance actually fulfilled.

The Treaty of the Holy Alliance was of no significance for the actual operations of the international government that bore its name. Its principles were invoked from time to time by the czar, affirmed in words and rejected in action by the other powers. Castlereagh, British foreign minister at the time of its conclusion, called it "a piece of sublime mysticism and nonsense," and the Austrian chancellor Metternich made vulgar jokes at its expense. Yet it served as moral justification for the principles of justice that the three original signatories of the treaty propounded and for the policies by which they endeavored to realize these principles. Thus the Treaty of the Holy Alliance also fulfilled an ideological function and became the symbol of this whole era of international relations.

In 1818 the four signatories of the Quadruple Alliance admitted France as a fifth member to take part in all further meetings to be held by virtue of Article VI of that treaty. In a circular signed in 1820 at the Congress of Troppau, Austria, Prussia, and Russia pledged themselves never to recognize the right of any people to circumscribe the power of their king. This compact is known as the Neo-Holy

---

[1]Article VI reads as follows: "To assure and facilitate the execution of the present Treaty, and to consolidate the intimate relations which to-day unite the 4 Sovereigns for the good of the world, the High Contracting Parties have agreed to renew, at fixed periods, whether under the immediate auspices of the Sovereigns, or by their respective Ministers, reunions devoted to the great common interests and to the examination of the measures which, at any of these periods, shall be judged most salutary for the repose and prosperity of the peoples, and for the maintenance of the peace of the State."

[2]The British monarch, for constitutional reasons, could not formally adhere; the prime minister acceded informally.

Alliance. Castlereagh, in two dispatches of the same year, refused to have any part in policies whose purpose was to interfere by force in the internal affairs of other countries. His successor, George Canning, maintained this principle at the Congress of Verona in 1822, the last of the congresses Great Britain attended.

When the news of the failure of the Congress of Verona reached him, Canning, in a letter to the British diplomat Bagot of January 3, 1823, hailed the end of international government by congresses and the beginning of a new era, as far as Great Britain was concerned, by invoking the religious principle of the Holy Alliance with a vengeance: "Every nation for itself, and God for us all!" International government by conference as a going concern did not survive the British defection. After two more abortive attempts—one with reference to the Spanish colonies, the other concerning Greece and Turkey—it came to an end in 1825.

The system of an overall international government instituted by Article VI of the Quadruple Alliance of November 20, 1815, did not last even a decade. The lifetime of the system of ambassadorial conferences for the settlement of special problems was even shorter. It, too, was established by the treaties of 1815 and consisted of three agencies: the ambassadors to France of Austria, Great Britain, Prussia, and Russia, dealing mainly with the problems raised by the peace treaties with France, yet acting in a general way as the paramount executive organ of the Quadruple Alliance; the ambassadors of the great powers meeting in London to organize the abolition of the slave trade; and the ambassadorial conference at Frankfort for the discussion of German problems. All these agencies had disappeared by 1818.

Government by the Great Powers

The international government of the Holy Alliance was government by the great powers. The Austrian statesman and writer Friedrich Gentz described its general character thus:

> The system which has been established in Europe since 1814 and 1815 is a phenomenon unheard-of in the history of the world. The principle of equilibrium or, to put it better, of counterweights formed by particular alliances, a principle which has governed and too often also troubled and covered Europe with blood for three centuries, has been superseded by a principle of a general union, uniting the sum total of states in a federation under the direction of the major powers. . . . The second-, third-, and fourth-rate states submit in silence and without any previous stipulation to the decisions jointly taken by the preponderant powers; and Europe seems to form finally a great political family, united under the auspices of an areopagus of its own creation.[3]

---

[3] *Dépêches Inédites du Chevalier de Gentz aux Hospodors de Valachie* (Paris: E. Plon, 1876), Vol. 1, p. 354. The English translation has been supplied by the author.

The distinction between great and small powers as a political fact pointing to the extreme differences in power among nations is of course one of the elemental experiences of international politics. As an institution of international politics and organization, carrying differences in legal status, it sprang from the brain of Castlereagh and became the very foundation of the scheme adopted in 1815. It is true that the protocol of the Congress of Aix-la-Chapelle of November 15, 1818, providing for future meetings of the five great powers, also stipulated "that in the case of these meetings having for their object affairs specially connected with the interests of the other States of Europe, they shall only take place in pursuance of a formal invitation on the part of such of those States as the said affairs may concern, and under the express reservation of their right of direct participation therein, either directly or by their Plenipotentiaries." Yet this stipulation remained without appreciable influence upon the policies of the Holy and, more particularly, of the Neo-Holy Alliance.

Dual Meaning of the Status Quo

To the question as to what principle of justice guided the Holy Alliance, the answer seems to be clear: the maintenance of peace on the basis of the status quo. This principle was never more clearly stated than in the declaration of the five great powers signed at Aix-la-Chapelle on November 15, 1818: "The object of this Union is as simple as it is great and salutary. It does not tend to any new political combination—to any change in the Relations sanctioned by existing Treaties. Calm and consistent in its proceedings, it has no other object than the maintenance of Peace, and the guarantee of those transactions on which the Peace was founded and consolidated."

This answer, however, becomes highly ambiguous if one raises the further question as to what was meant by the status quo. What Great Britain meant from the very beginning was not at all what Russia meant, and the conception of the status quo that guided the policies of the Neo-Holy Alliance was diametrically opposed to the conception behind the policies of Castlereagh and Canning. The status quo that Great Britain tried to preserve through the instrumentality of the Holy Alliance was strictly limited to the political situation that existed at the end of the Napoleonic Wars with regard to France. To the British statesmen, the mortal peril into which Napoleon had put the British Isles was identical with the threat to the European balance of power that had emanated from the Napoleonic Empire. Great Britain was willing to support an international government whose purpose was to forestall the rise of a new conqueror from French soil and to that end to enforce the peace settlement of 1815 against France. The British conception of the status quo was limited to the territorial settlement of 1815 and the exclusion of a member of the Napoleonic family from the French throne. In this respect there was no difference between the foreign policies of Castlereagh and Canning.

The conception of the status quo that determined the policies of Russia from the outset, and those of Austria, Prussia, and France from the end of the second decade of the nineteenth century, was unlimited territorially and as to subject matter. According to that conception, formulated in more uncompromising terms than the actual political conditions permitted to realize, it was the purpose of the international government of the Holy Alliance to maintain everywhere in the world the territorial status quo of 1815 and the constitutional status quo of the absolute monarchy. The instrument of the realization of the latter purpose was bound to be intervention into the internal affairs of all nations where the institution of the absolute monarchy seemed to be in danger.

The inevitable by-product of such intervention was an increase in the power of the intervening nations. The more widespread national and liberal movements became, the greater was the chance for the intervening nation or group of nations to increase their strength and expand and thus disturb the balance of power again. The main beneficiary of such a development was bound to be Russia. At this point Great Britain and Russia parted company.

Great Britain had not, for almost a quarter of a century, fought the Napoleonic Empire, nourished by the dynamism of the French Revolution, to exchange it for a Russian empire, inspired by the religious mysticism of universal brotherhood and of absolute government. In the measure that the spread of national and liberal movements gave the Neo-Holy Alliance an opportunity to test its principles of general intervention, Great Britain held aloof from it and opposed its policies. When in 1818 Russia proposed to send an allied army to aid Spain in the war against its American colonies, Great Britain prevented the execution of the plan. Yet, when in 1820 revolutions broke out in Naples, Piedmont, and Portugal, Austria, in the name of the Neo-Holy Alliance, restored the absolute monarchies of Naples and Piedmont to their thrones by force of arms. In 1820 a revolution broke out in Spain. Against the constitutional regime installed by it, France intervened by force of arms in 1823, acting on its own behalf, but with the moral support of Austria, Prussia, and Russia.

Peace, Order, and the National Interest

These actions of the Holy Alliance reveal two facts. One is the absence of a serious threat of war in any of these situations. The disparity of power between the intervening state and the object of intervention—the revolutionary group that had to contend not only with its own antirevolutionary compatriots but also with a foreign army—was such as to give the intervention the character of a punitive expedition rather than of a war.

The other fact is the determination of the policies of all nations by their national interests, however much the language of diplomacy of the period made concessions to the mystical predilections of the Russian czar. This is most obvious in the actions of Great Britain. Neither Castlereagh nor Canning—who was particularly frank and eloquent in this respect—took pains to hide the fact that he was guided by the traditional interests of Great Britain, limited only by the general interest in peace and security. Both the Austrian intervention in Italy and the French intervention in Spain were dictated by traditional national interests. This connection is demonstrated by the very fact that the policy of interventions on the part of Austria and France in the affairs of their neighbors to the south survived the Holy Alliance by almost half a century.

More important still in view of our discussion is the victory the particular national interests gained over the general principles of the Holy Alliance whenever both came into conflict. This happened twice, in 1820 and in 1822. In both cases Russia proposed a collective intervention on the part of all the members of the alliance and to that end offered to send a large Russian army into Central and Western Europe. That Great Britain would have opposed such a proposal is obvious from what has already been said of the British return to its traditional balance-of-power policy. That Great Britain should have been joined in this opposition by Austria, the other pillar of the Neo-Holy Alliance, demonstrates the ideological character of the principles of the Holy Alliance. These principles were invoked when they seemed to be able to give moral justification to policies dictated by the national interest. They were discarded when nothing was to be gained for the national interest by invoking them.

The attitude of the powers when in 1821 the Greeks revolted against the Turks is instructive in this respect. This is also the only situation arising during the era of the Holy Alliance that contained the germs of a general war and that in the century following it led time and again to the actual outbreak of war. The principles of the Neo-Holy Alliance allowed of only one attitude to be taken vis-à-vis a national revolt against a legitimate government: the legitimate government must be given active support. Yet this was not the answer the national interest of the most affected power demanded.

Russia had been the traditional protector of the subjects of the Ottoman Empire who were of the Orthodox Christian faith. The possession of Constantinople was a centuries-old dream of the rulers of Moscow. Thus, when the Greek revolt broke out, the Russian czar was inclined, in complete disregard of the principles of the Neo-Holy Alliance, to declare war against Turkey. Austria and Great Britain, on the other hand, could see only with misgivings, felt before and for almost a century afterward, the extension of Russian power in the Balkans and Russia's advance toward the Mediterranean. Thus Castlereagh, the opponent of the Neo-Holy Alliance, and the Austrian chancellor Metternich, its ardent supporter, joined hands in order to dissuade Russia from taking active steps in support of the Greek insurgents. That they made successful use of the principles of the Neo-Holy Alliance against their author is an ironic comment on the difficulties facing a foreign policy based upon abstract principles rather than upon a clear recognition of the national interest. As Castlereagh wisely put it: It is difficult enough in international affairs to hold the balance "between conflicting nations"; it is still more difficult to hold the balance "between conflicting principles."

When, finally, in 1826 the danger of war between Russia and Turkey became acute, it was not the defunct Holy Alliance that averted it but Canning's audacious move of entering into an agreement with Russia for the purpose of forcing Turkey to make concessions to the Greeks, without Russia's gaining immediate advantages from such internal reforms. After Canning's death, the event occurred that Canning had been successful in preventing: in 1828, Russia alone declared war on Turkey, thus having the latter at its mercy. The outbreak of this war may have been partly due to the decline of British statesmanship after Canning's death. It certainly was not at all due to the absence of the international government of the Holy Alliance.

The Holy Alliance, then, was a short-lived experiment that contributed nothing to the maintenance of international peace. As an international government imposing its rule upon its sphere of domination, it was successful for hardly more than half a decade. At the very hour of its ascendancy, in 1818, Friedrich Gentz, one of its architects and its outstanding philosopher, put his finger on its congenital weakness:

> The strongest objection to the present system is the obvious difficulty to maintain for long the combination of heterogeneous elements of which it is composed. The most divergent interests, the most antagonistic tendencies, the most contradictory predictions, views, and secret thoughts are for the moment encompassed and submerged in the common action of a league which resembles much more a coalition, created for an extraordinary purpose, than a genuine alliance based upon distinct and permanent interests. Unique circumstances were needed to bring about such a league; it would be against human nature and the nature of things for it to take for any length of time the place of that opposition and strife to which the diversity of situations, interests, and opinions always leads a number of independent nations, each of necessity with its own particular character and plan of action.[4]

Two congenital infirmities made the early demise of the Holy Alliance inevitable. One was the diametrical opposition between the two main members of the alliance as to what the defense of the status quo—upon which they had all agreed as the guiding principle of justice in the abstract—meant in concrete political terms. That meaning was determined by the national interests of the individual members. If those interests happened to coincide, the alliance could act in unison as one collective body. If those interests diverged, as they were bound to do from time to time and as they did permanently in the case of Great Britain and Russia, the alliance ceased to operate.

The other infirmity from which the Holy Alliance suffered was the contrast between the principle of justice upon which the governments of Russia, Prussia, and Austria agreed as a guide to concrete political action, and the conception of justice adhered to by the majority of the individuals living under the rule of the Holy Alliance. The conflict between the principles of legitimate government and the principles of liberalism and nationalism made the operation of an international government inspired by the former dependent upon the continuous use of armed force in order to protect and restore absolute monarchies and their possessions throughout the world.

---

[4]Ibid., p. 355.

It is a matter for conjecture how long an international government could have performed such a task had all its members shared the convictions and the zeal of Alexander I of Russia. The Holy Alliance could not prevail against the opposition of some of its members and of the peoples subject to its rule. In the era of Castlereagh, that dual opposition moved without contact on parallel lines, Castlereagh abstaining from active cooperation with the policies of the Neo-Holy Alliance. It was Canning's great innovation, favored by the increasing strength of the national and liberal movements and later perfected by his successor, Palmerston, to use those movements in support of British purposes—that is, as weights in the scales of the balance of power. With that innovation, Canning ushered in the British policy toward the continent of Europe that was to remain dominant throughout the nineteenth century.

The international government of the Holy Alliance lacked any kind of permanent organization and consisted, aside from the ephemeral ambassadorial committees mentioned above, of nothing but a number of international congresses for the purpose of settling current international affairs. Nevertheless, the Holy Alliance was an international government in the true sense of the term. An incomplete list of the issues on the agenda of the Congress of Aix-la-Chapelle will illustrate the range of its governmental activities: the claims of the German mediatized princes against the abuses of their new sovereigns, the petition of the Elector of Hesse to exchange his title for that of king, the request by Napoleon's mother for the release of her son, the grievances of the people of Monaco against their prince, the claims of Bavaria and the House of Hochberg to the succession in Baden, a dispute between the Duke of Oldenburg and Count Bentinck about the lordship of Knupenhaussen, the situation of the Jews in Prussia and Austria, the rank of diplomatic representatives, the suppression of the slave trade and of the Barbary pirates, and the question of the Spanish colonies.

The Concert of Europe

In comparison with these widespread governmental activities of the Holy Alliance, the subsequent century was retrogressive. The spectacle of a government of great powers sitting in judgment over the affairs of the world did not reappear until in 1919 the Council of the League of Nations reenacted the role that the Holy Alliance had played. Yet the era between the Holy Alliance and the League of Nations was not devoid of ad hoc attempts at settling international problems through the concerted action of the great powers. After the demise of the Holy Alliance, the great powers continued to assume responsibility for the settlement of political issues that without such settlement might have led to war. That responsibility was realized in a number of conferences dealing with problems endangering the peace, such as the Belgian question at the beginning of the 1830s, the Eastern question at the beginning of the 1850s and again in 1878, and the problems of Africa at the beginning of the twentieth century. It was to that responsibility of the great powers for the peace of the world, operating through ad hoc conferences and generally known as the Concert of Europe, that Sir Edward Grey appealed in vain on the eve of the First World War.

The Concert of Europe differed from a genuine international government in two respects. On the one hand, it was not institutionalized. There was no agreement among the great powers to meet regularly or to meet at all. The great powers met whenever the international situation seemed to demand concerted action. On the other hand, the Concert of Europe was no longer animated, as has already been noted,[5] by a strong moral consensus that could have neutralized conflicts and supplied standards for common judgments and actions. The cleavage between nationalism and legitimacy that the French Revolution had opened remained open throughout the nineteenth century. It might at times narrow or widen, but it did not close. Only at the end of the First World War did the national principle triumph, carrying to their doom the monarchies of Central and Eastern Europe.

Yet, despite the lack of a strong moral consensus, of an institutionalized government by conferences, let alone of an organized one, the Concert of Europe was most successful in preserving general peace during the ninety years of its existence. The only major international war the world experienced during that period, the Crimean War of 1854–56, was due to a series of accidents. Had any one of these accidents failed to materialize, the war might well have been avoided. The Concert of Europe had already agreed upon the formula for peace, but a delay of twenty-four hours in the transmission of the formula changed the picture.

What accounted for the success of the Concert of Europe in preventing general wars? Three factors must be mentioned. In that period of history the moral consensus of the European community lived on as a feeble echo, strengthened, however, by the humanitarian moral climate of the times. The political configuration, as we have seen,[6] favored expansion into politically empty spaces with accommodation of conflicting interests. Finally and most importantly, however, that period of history saw a succession of brilliant diplomatists and statesmen who knew how to make peace, how to preserve peace, and how to keep wars short and limited in scope. The portentous lesson their work conveys to our age will be pondered later in this book.

THE LEAGUE OF NATIONS

With the end of the First World War, a new epoch began in the history of international government. The League of Nations showed in its functions a great deal of similarity with the Holy Alliance. In its organization, however, it constituted a radical departure from the experiment that had preceded it a century before.

---

[5]See pages 255 ff.
[6]See pages 351 ff.

Organization

The League of Nations, in contrast to the Holy Alliance, was a real organization with a legal personality, agents, and agencies of its own. Its political agencies were the Assembly, the Council, and the Permanent Secretariat. The Assembly was composed of representatives of all the member states. In the Assembly, as well as in the Council, each state had one vote, and unanimity of all members present was required for all political decisions, including those that concerned the prevention of war.[7] The main exceptions were Article 15, paragraph 10,[8] and the rule that in decisions concerning the settlement of international disputes the votes of the parties to the dispute were not to be counted.

The Council consisted of two types of members: permanent and nonpermanent. All great powers belonging at a particular time to the League were permanent members—for example, originally France, Great Britain, Italy, and Japan, to which were later added Germany and the Soviet Union. The nonpermanent members numbered originally four. Their numbers were increased successively until in 1936 the Council comprised eleven nonpermanent members. Thus originally permanent and nonpermanent members were equal in numbers. From 1922 on, the nonpermanent members had an ever-increasing majority over the permanent ones. In 1939, after Germany, Italy, and Japan had resigned and the Soviet Union had been expelled, the Council comprised two permanent (France and Great Britain) and eleven nonpermanent members.

What is important in view of the distribution of power between great and small nations is not their numerical relationship but the permanent membership of the great powers in the Council. By virtue of this permanent membership, in conjunction with the rule of unanimity, the great powers could be sure that the Council could make no decisions without the consent of all of them. Furthermore, the distribution of voting strength in an international agency never tells the whole story. No great power will ever be alone in voting in favor of or against a certain measure if it does not want to be alone, nor need any group of great powers ever run the risk of being outvoted if it is anxious not to be in the minority on a particular question. Most small and medium powers depend economically, militarily, and politically upon the support of a great power.

---

[7] Cf. the emphasis the Permanent Court of International Justice placed upon the principles of unanimity in the Advisory Opinion concerning Article 3, paragraph 2, of the Treaty of Lausanne (frontier between Turkey and Iraq): "In a body . . . whose mission is to deal with any matter 'within the sphere of action of the League or affecting the peace of the world,' observance of the rule of unanimity is naturally and even necessarily indicated. Only if the decisions of the Council have the support of the unanimous consent of the Powers composing it, will they possess the degree of authority which they must have: the very prestige of the League might be imperilled if it were admitted, in the absence of an express provision to that effect, that decisions on important questions could be taken by a majority. Moreover, it is hardly conceivable that resolutions on questions affecting the peace of the world could be adopted against the will of those amongst the Members of the Council who, although in a minority, would, by reason of their political position, have to bear the larger share of the responsibilities and consequences ensuing there from." (*P.C.I.J.* Series B, No. 12, p. 29.)

[8] For the text, see page 473, note 9.

Such a nation will hardly cast its vote against a great power that has intimated that the smaller nation is expected to heed its advice. Thus every great power controlled a number of votes of the small and medium members of the League. On any important issue France could be certain of the votes of Belgium, Czechoslovakia, Yugoslavia, Rumania, and—for more than a decade—Poland. Great Britain could count upon the votes of the dominions, the Scandinavian countries, and Portugal.

This controlling influence of the great powers, regardless of the legal structure of the organization, operated in the League of Nations side by side with the brilliant intellectual leadership of the representatives of a number of small and medium nations. These representatives exerted an influence upon the work of the League of Nations out of all proportion to, and irrespective of, the power of their particular countries. The scene of that leadership was primarily the Assembly. The Assembly of the League of Nations, in contrast to the General Assembly of the United Nations, had the authority to render binding decisions not only with regard to routine matters or questions of secondary importance but also concerning political problems, such as peace-preserving measures.[9] To that extent the Assembly of the League of Nations played the role of a real parliament where leadership fell many times to the best-qualified representative, regardless of the power and sometimes even of the interests of his country.

But that leadership stopped at the line where the vital interests of the great powers began. In the great crises of the League, the leadership of the great powers asserted itself. When in a conflict of first-rate political importance, such as the Italo-Ethiopian War or the Spanish Civil War, the attitude of some of the small and great powers diverged, the policies of the great powers were bound to win. For the preponderance of the great powers on the international scene is a fact, as the preponderance of great economic organizations is a fact, in domestic society. No legal arrangement nor organizational device, short of destroying that preponderance of power itself, can undo the political consequences of that disparity of power. Thus in the League the small nations enjoyed a greater opportunity for influence and independent action than they ever did before or since in modern times. Yet the international government of the League of Nations, at least in the sphere of high politics, was a government of the great powers.

---

[9]See Article 3, paragraph 3, of the Covenant: "The Assembly may deal at its meetings with any matter within the sphere of action of the League or affecting the peace of the world." See also Article 15, paragraphs 9, 10: "The Council may in any case under this Article refer the dispute to the Assembly. The dispute shall be so referred at the request of either party to the dispute provided that such request be made within fourteen days after the submission of the dispute to the Council.

"In any case referred to the Assembly, all the provisions of this Article and of Article 12 relating to the action and powers of the Council shall apply to the action and powers of the Assembly, provided that a report made by the Assembly, if concurred in by the Representatives of those members of the League represented on the Council and of a majority of the other members of the League, . . . shall have the same force as a report by the Council concurred in by all the Members thereof. . . ."

Dual Meaning of the Status Quo: France vs. Great Britain

What were the principles of justice that the international government of the League of Nations was to realize? That question has found a symbolic answer in the fact that the twenty-six articles of the Convenant of the League of Nations are identical with the first twenty-six articles of the peace treaties that settled the issues of the First World War. The intimate connection between the League of Nations and the status quo of 1919 was thus made obvious from the very outset. The provisions of the Covenant put that connection in explicit legal terms. The Preamble refers to "international law as the actual rule of conduct among governments" and to "a scrupulous respect for all treaty obligations." Article 10 makes the League of Nations the defender of the territorial status quo of 1919 by establishing the legal obligation of the members "to respect and preserve as against external aggression the territorial integrity and existing independence of all members of the League." All provisions of the subsequent articles concerning the settlement of disputes and its enforcement must be read in the light of this provision of Article 10. This provision lays down the standard by which the agencies of the League were to be guided in evaluating the claims and actions of nations and in devising methods to meet a threat to the peace.

It is true that the framers of the Covenant tried to relieve the League from the stigma of being completely identified with the status quo of 1919. To that end, they provided in Article 19 for peaceful change. We have already pointed to the intrinsic weakness of that provision, which remained a dead letter from the beginning. But aside from its intrinsic defects, Article 19 pales into insignificance if seen in its orphanlike isolation within the structure of the Covenant and if compared with the organic connection in which Article 10 stands to the peace treaties of 1919, on the one hand, and to the peace-preserving and law-enforcing provisions of Articles 11–16 of the Covenant, on the other. Article 19, then, was little more than a verbal concession to the undeniable fact of change. Its fundamental law no less than its origin, identical with the peace treaties of 1919, made it inevitable that the League as a working organization of international government should judge and act as the defender of the status quo.

Two principles were at the foundation of the status quo of 1919: the permanent inability of Germany to wage war and the principle of national self-determination. Yet, from the very outset, the two nations mainly responsible for the policies of the League, Great Britain and France, interpreted these two principles in distinctly different ways and tried to shape the policies of the League according to these different interpretations. For France, Germany's permanent inability to wage war was synonymous with the permanent preponderance of France on the continent of Europe. For Great Britain, Germany's permanent inability to wage war was not incompatible with the comeback of Germany as a great power within controlled limits so that at least the semblance of a balance of power would again exist on the continent of Europe.

France looked to the League of Nations primarily as a kind of collective sheriff that would add its strength to the military might of France for the defense of the status quo of 1919. Great Britain considered the League of Nations primarily a kind of clearinghouse where the statesmen of the world would meet to discuss their common problems and seek agreement by way of compromise. Finally, France used the principle of national self-determination as a political weapon with which to strengthen its allies in Eastern Europe against Germany. Great Britain saw in it a principle capable of universal application, at least on the European continent, which one might well use to strengthen Germany at the expense of the allies of France.

At the bottom of these divergent interpretations of standards of justice and of political principles we find again the basic pattern of international politics. France subordinated all its policies as one of the leading members of the international government of the League of Nations to its overriding desire to maintain the status quo of 1919. This status quo was identical with France's hegemony on the European continent. Great Britain thought it could regain the controlling influence it had exerted over the affairs of Europe during the nineteenth century. To that end, it tried to restore the power configuration that had existed during that period: a balance of power on the European continent with Great Britain as its "holder." Thus its policies as the other leading member of the international government of the League were all directed toward undermining the status quo of 1919—within manageable limits, which Great Britain thought it could determine at will. This goal of British foreign policy could only be attained by weakening France.

This conflict between the British and French conceptions and policies did not, however, wreck the League of Nations, as the conflict between Great Britain and Russia had the Holy Alliance. It rather led to a creeping paralysis in the political activities of the League and to its inability to take determined action against threats to international order and peace. It culminated in the triumph of the British over the French conception. The distribution of power between Great Britain and France was in the main responsible for this development.

The margin of French superiority started to shrink in the mid-twenties in proportion to the growth of German strength, first slowly and imperceptibly, and then—following Hitler's ascent to power—with ever-increasing speed. In 1919, France sought the separation of the left bank of the Rhine from Germany and treaties of alliance with Great Britain and the United States. France received neither. It was able to make only two additions to its own military strength, which barely concealed its intrinsic weakness in comparison with the potentialities of German power. One addition was the alliances with Poland, Czechoslovakia, and Rumania, and the treaty of friendship with Yugoslavia. These allies, however, were at best medium states. Some, if not all of them, were militarily overrated and could not be relied upon to act always in unison. The other addition was the Locarno Treaties of 1925, putting the Franco-German frontier under the joint guarantee of Great Britain and Italy. Yet France was unable to obtain a similar guarantee for the German-Polish frontier, nor was it able to gain British support for an automatic system of collective security that would have closed certain loopholes left open by the Covenant of the League of Nations.[10]

---

[10]See pages 478–79.

Under such conditions of hegemonial power in the short run and incurable weakness in the long run, France started in the mid-twenties to follow the British lead in its policies within the League of Nations, at first hesitatingly, and in the thirties without alternative.[11] For by then, due to its own indecision and now apparent weakness, France was no longer able to seek on its own account the implementation of those provisions of the Covenant through which the League could have played the role of an international government for the maintenance of international order and the prevention of war. France by itself did not have the power to make the League play that role. Great Britain had no interest in making the League play it. For the performance of that role would have meant the perpetuation of unchallenged French supremacy on the European continent—a supremacy that Great Britain was resolved to bring to an end. Thus the British conceptions and policies put their imprint upon the governmental activities of the League of Nations.

Three Weaknesses of the League of Nations

This is not to say that the League of Nations did not exercise important governmental functions. The League of Nations governed two territories: the Saar Basin and the city of Danzig. It governed indirectly—according to the text of Article 22 of the Covenant—rather than in actuality the mandated territories.[12] Yet, when it came to the maintenance of international order and the preservation or restoration of peace, it governed only in the rare instances when either the interests of the great powers among its members were not affected or the common interests of the most influential among them seemed to require it.

---

[11]This trend was interrupted only for a short while in 1934 when French Foreign Minister Barthou prepared the ground for a military alliance with the Soviet Union, which, however, none of his successors dared to implement. The foreign policy of Laval in that period, while strongly anti-British in intent and favoring an understanding with the Axis powers, was identical with that of Great Britain in undermining the status quo of 1919.

[12]Cf. the following provisions of Article 22: "To those colonies and territories which as a consequence of the late war have ceased to be under the sovereignty of the States which formerly governed them and which are inhabited by peoples not yet able to stand by themselves under the strenuous conditions of the modern world, there should be applied the principle that the well-being and development of such peoples form a sacred trust of civilisation and that securities for the performance of this trust should be embodied in this Covenant.

"The best method of giving practical effect to this principle is that the tutelage of such peoples should be entrusted to advanced nations who, by reason of their resources, their experience or their geographical position, can best undertake this responsibility, and who are willing to accept it, and that this tutelage should be exercised by them as Mandatories on behalf of the League. . . .

"In every case of mandate, the Mandatory shall render to the Council an annual report in reference to the territory committed to its charge.

"The degree of authority, control or administration to be exercised by the Mandatory shall, if not previously agreed upon by the Members of the League, be explicitly defined in each case by the Council.

"A permanent Commission shall be constituted to receive and examine the annual reports of the Mandatories and to advise the Council on all matters relating to the observance of the mandates."

The League of Nations did not act as an international government when in 1920 Poland seized Vilna, the old Lithuanian capital; for that violation of international law was committed by the strongest ally of France, and the intervention of the League was opposed by the Soviet Union. But in 1925 incipient war between Bulgaria and Greece was easily stopped by the president of the Council of the League, who sent a telegram to the parties demanding immediate cessation of hostilities. He was actively supported by France and Great Britain, which acted on this occasion in unison and used their influence in particular to deter Greece from offensive action.

The League of Nations refused to act when in 1923 Italy occupied the Greek island of Corfu. It did nothing even approaching the nature of enforcement action after Japan invaded Manchuria in 1931 and after it invaded China proper in 1937. The League did nothing to prevent or stop the Chaco War between Bolivia and Paraguay in 1932–35, except to recommend an arms embargo. From 1935 on the League did nothing effective to maintain its authority within the territory of Danzig, and it did nothing in the face of the continuous violations of the Treaty of Versailles by Germany. What the League did in 1935–36 with respect to Italy's attack upon Ethiopia could not, as we have seen,[13] have been different had it been calculated to be ineffective. In 1936–39 the League did nothing to control the international effects of the Spanish Civil War. In December 1939, however, the League expelled the Soviet Union because of its attack against Finland. It was the last and—aside from the sanctions against Italy—the most drastic of the League's political actions.

The League of Nations prevented no major war, and it was ineffective in maintaining international order. The reasons for this failure, aside from the prevalence of the British conception over the French, are threefold: constitutional, structural, and political.

Constitutional Weakness

The Covenant of the League of Nations did not outlaw war as such. The members of the League were not allowed to go to war under certain conditions. By the same token, they were allowed to go to war in the absence of those conditions. Thus the Preamble to the Covenant stipulated "the acceptance of obligations[14] not to resort to war." Article 12 provided that the members should not "resort to war until three months after the award by the arbitrators." By virtue of Article 13, paragraph 4, the members agreed "that they will not resort to war against a member of the League which complies" with the judicial decision of a dispute. Finally, according to Article 15, paragraph 6, "If a report by the Council is unanimously agreed to by the members thereof other than the Representatives of one

---

[13]See pages 440–41.
[14]In contradistinction to "the obligation." The French text (*"certaines obligations"*) is more emphatic on that score.

or more of the parties to the dispute, the Members of the League agree that they will not go to war with any party to the dispute which complies with the recommendations of the report."

Only the two latter provisions contain an outright prohibition to go to war. As Jean Ray put it: "We are convinced that this timidity of the authors of the Covenant has serious consequences and puts in jeopardy the new system which they tried to erect. As a matter of fact, since the contrary opinion was not clearly expressed, it remained tacitly admitted that war is a solution, the normal solution, of international conflicts. These obligations, as a matter of law, are presented only as exceptions; the implicit rule is the recourse to war."[15] Even if the members had lived up to the provisions of the Covenant, they would have found in the fundamental law of the League an instrument for the prevention of some wars and for the legalization of others.

Structural Weakness

This constitutional weakness, however, did not affect the actual operations of the League, for the League did not live up to its constitution. On the other hand, the structural weakness of the League had a direct bearing upon its failure to prevent the wars that occurred under its jurisdiction. That weakness consisted in the contrast between the distribution of power within it and the distribution of power in the world at large.

The structure of the League was predominantly European in a period when the main factors of international politics were no longer predominantly European. Both great powers that in turn dominated it, France and Great Britain, were European powers. The only non-European great power that was a member of the League was Japan. Of the two nations that in the twenties were already potentially the two most powerful nations on earth, the United States was never a member, and the Soviet Union only during the League's declining years, from 1934 to 1939.

It is, of course, true that of the thirty-one original members only ten were European and of the thirteen nations that joined it later only seven were. But here again numbers do not tell the story. An international organization whose main purpose is the maintenance of international order and peace does not need to be universal in the sense that all nations of the world belong to it. It must, however, be universal in the sense that all powerful nations, which are most likely to disturb the peace of the world, are under its jurisdiction.

Article 17 of the Covenant, therefore, attempted to make the jurisdiction of the League universal regardless of membership. It gave the League authority in case of a dispute between two states, one or both of which were not members of the League, to invite the nonmembers "to accept the obligations of membership in the League for the purposes of such disputes, upon such conditions as the

---

[15] *Commentaire du Pacte de la Société des Nations* (Paris: Sirey, 1930), pp. 73–74.

Council may deem just. . . . If a state so invited shall refuse to accept the obligations of membership and shall resort to war against a member of the League," the sanctions of Article 16 shall be applicable against such a state. "If both parties to the dispute . . . refuse to accept the obligations of membership . . . the Council may take such measures, and make recommendations as will prevent hostilities and will result in the settlement of the dispute."

This last paragraph of Article 17 endeavored to make the League of Nations a world government for the purpose of preserving peace. The feasibility of such a government must again depend upon the distribution of power between the members of the League acting in unison and those states over which the governmental functions are to be exercised. The League would have had no difficulty in making its will prevail over two small or medium states. Let us suppose, however, that a dispute had broken out between a member of the League, on the one hand, and the United States or the Soviet Union or both, on the other; or between the two latter powers any time between 1919 and 1934, when neither country was a member of the League. Under such circumstances, the attempt to impose the League's will upon the United States or the Soviet Union or both would have amounted to a world war between the members of the League and either one or two of the potentially most powerful nations on earth, with a number of nonmember nations either joining the latter or remaining neutral. The attempt to preserve peace on a universal scale would have led to war on a universal scale.[16] Thus the membership of some great powers and the nonmembership of other great powers rendered the League powerless to preserve peace on a worldwide scale.

This lack of universality in the membership of the great powers also indicates the fundamental reason for the failure of British and French policies in the period between the two world wars. The policies of both countries were anachronistic. The policies of France might perhaps have succeeded in the age of Louis XIV. Then the main weights of the balance of power were located in Central and Western Europe, and such a preponderance as France gained in 1919 would have given it a real chance to establish its permanent hegemony over the continent. Yet, after Russia had become one of the main factors in the balance of power, Napoleon had to learn that a hegemony over the European continent meant little, with the resources of Eastern Europe and of the better part of Asia either uncommitted or hostile. This lesson was heeded by the brilliant French diplomatists who in the two decades preceding the First World War founded French foreign policy upon close ties with Russia. Their successors in the period between the two world wars based their hopes upon a system of alliances with the balkanized countries of Eastern and Southeastern Europe, a poor substitute for the "grand alliance" with Russia. Obsessed with the fear of revolution, very much like the French aristocrats in the years after 1789, they were ready to commit national suicide rather than yield to the logic of a new international configuration.

---

[16]The reader will remember that this situation is identical with the one that results from the consistent application of collective security; see pages 437–39.

British foreign policy in that period was as anachronistic as the French. Great Britain was intrinsically as weak with regard to the continent of Europe as France was with regard to Germany. The role that Russia played in relation to France was similar to the one the United States and, to a much lesser degree, Japan played in relation to Great Britain. A policy that was still successful in the age of Disraeli was doomed to failure in the age of Stanley Baldwin. Throughout the nineteenth century, Great Britain's back yard, as it were, had been secure; the British navy controlled the seas without challenge. In the thirties, other great naval powers had arisen, one of them potentially the most powerful nation on earth. Furthermore, the airplane brought the British Isles closer to the Continent than ever before. Such conditions allowed British foreign policy but two alternatives. It could place its weight permanently in that scale of the European balance of power where British interests in the long run seemed to be most secure. Or it could make itself the spearhead of American policy in Europe.[17] What British policy could not do was to continue the policy of "splendid isolation." And this is what it did.

It will remain forever a moot question whether or not France and Great Britain had any real choice in the face of the policies actually pursued by the Soviet Union and the United States. It is, however, beyond doubt that an international government never had a chance whose leading members, either by choice or by necessity, followed policies so completely at odds with the actual distribution of power in the world.

Political Weakness

This would have been true even on the assumption that the League of Nations had been able to act as a unit in the face of a threatening war of major proportions. Actually, this assumption was never realized. Divergent national interests pursued by the great powers prevailed over the principles of justice defined by the League of Nations in terms of the status quo. In 1921, immediately after the First World War, the four permanent members of the Council of the League were still able to act in unison with respect to relatively important political issues, such as the fortification of the Aaland Islands involving Finland and Sweden and the partition of Upper Silesia, which was a bone of contention between Germany and Poland. After these promising beginnings, it was not only the conflict between France and Great Britain that incapacitated the League for collective action on matters of major importance but the separate and generally antagonistic policies of the great powers.

When Germany joined the League in 1925, it pursued a policy of undermining the status quo of Versailles, mainly using the principle of national self-determination as the dynamite with which to crack the foundations of the territorial status quo. This policy was at odds with the policies of France and its Eastern allies

---

[17]It is worthy of note that since the end of the Second World War Great Britain has pursued these two foreign policies simultaneously.

and was aimed, first surreptitiously and later openly, at the termination of their preponderance on the continent of Europe. In addition to the principle of national self-determination, Germany used the dual fear of bolshevist revolution and Russian imperialism, which obsessed the Western powers, as a weapon with which to strengthen its own position. While alternately offering itself as a bulwark against bolshevism and threatening to ally itself with the Soviet Union, Germany was able to wring concessions from the Western powers, to isolate Poland from France, and to paralyze the League.

Italy, on its part, pursued in the twenties a policy somewhat similar to the one pursued by Great Britain. Italy welcomed the comeback of Germany within certain limits as a means to weaken France and its Eastern allies, especially Yugoslavia. When in the thirties the impotence of the League had become obvious, Italy used Germany as Germany was using the Soviet Union, alternately as common menace and as a silent partner, and made an open bid against Great Britain and France for domination of the Mediterranean.

The Soviet Union was as isolated within the League as it had been without. Its potential strength as a nation and its sponsorship of world revolution made it a dual menace to the Western powers. It proved to be impossible for France, Great Britain, and the Soviet Union to unite for common action in any of the great crises from 1934 to 1939, with the exception of the sanctions against Italy. In all those crises the Western powers and the Soviet Union found themselves in opposite camps. Even when in 1939 Germany threatened both the Soviet Union and the Western powers with war, they were unable to agree upon common preventive action. Instead, each side tried to deflect the threatening stroke of lightning to the other side. It was only Hitler's folly in waging war against both at the same time that made them allies despite themselves.

Finally, Japan, smarting under the inferiority that the treaties of 1922 had imposed upon it, prepared for the moment when it could establish its own hegemony in the Far East. Japan could do so only by dislodging Great Britain and the United States from their positions in the Far East and by "closing the door" to China that, as a matter of traditional policy, Great Britain and the United States had insisted upon keeping open for all nations. Thus, when Japan took the first step toward establishing its Far Eastern empire by invading Manchuria in 1931, it could not help coming into conflict with France and Great Britain, the leading members of the League of Nations. It is not without ironic significance that Japan, in establishing its dominion, made use of the same principle of national self-determination that had carried France and Great Britain to dominance in the League. Now it was employed to rally the colored races of the Far East against the colonialism of the leaders of the League. Yet neither while Japan remained a member of the League nor after its resignation in 1932 did Great Britain feel strong enough to lead the League in effective collective action in order to stop Japan's attack against China.

The ability of the League of Nations to prevent war was predicated upon the unity of its members, and especially of the great powers. By virtue of the principle of unanimity, any member of the League, except parties to a dispute, could veto a decision by voting against a motion to take action. Given the antagonistic policies pursued by the leading members of the League, the very likelihood of a veto impeded even attempts at decisive collective action. Only an overriding principle of justice could have made such action possible. As we have seen, such principles of justice did exist in the abstract as collective defense of the status quo against the nations vanquished in the First World War and as national self-determination.

Confronted with a political situation demanding concrete action, these abstract principles transformed themselves into ideological justifications for the separate policies pursued by the individual nations. Thus these abstract principles of justice, far from providing common standards of judgment and guides for common action, actually strengthened international anarchy by strengthening the antagonistic policies of individual nations. The inability of the League of Nations to maintain international order and peace, then, was the inevitable result of the ascendancy that the ethics and policies of sovereign nations were able to maintain over the moral and political objectives of the international government of the League of Nations.

28 International Government: The United Nations

In order to understand the constitutional functions and actual operations of the United Nations, it is necessary to distinguish sharply between the constitutional provisions of the Charter and the manner in which the agencies of the United Nations, under the pressure of unforeseen political circumstances, have actually performed their functions under the Charter. The government of the United Nations, like the government of the United States, can be understood only by confronting the provisions of the constitution with the realities of political practice. Such a separate analysis of constitutional function and actual performance points up a series of significant transformations not only in the particular political functions performed by the agencies of the United Nations but in the very character of the United Nations as an international organization.

THE UNITED NATIONS ACCORDING TO THE CHARTER

Government by Superpowers

In its constitutional organization the United Nations resembles the League of Nations. It, too, has three political agencies: the General Assembly composed of all members of the United Nations, the Security Council as the political executive of the organization, and the Secretariat. The distribution of functions between the General Assembly and the Security Council, however, differs distinctly from that between the Council and the Assembly of the League of Nations. The tendency toward government by the great powers, which was already unmistakable in the League of Nations, completely dominates the distribution of functions in the United Nations. This tendency manifests itself in three constitutional devices of the Charter: the inability of the General Assembly to make decisions in political matters, the limitation of the requirement of unanimity to the permanent members of the Security Council, and the right of parties to disputes to veto any enforcement measures against themselves.

The Assembly of the League of Nations was, as we have seen, a real international parliament, which could take action in political matters alone or in competition with the Council of the League. The General Assembly of the United Nations, according to Articles 10–14 of the Charter, has only the power to make recommendations in political matters either to the parties concerned or to the Security Council. With regard to the maintenance of international peace and security, it can debate, investigate, and recommend, but it cannot act. Even those modest functions are qualified by Article 12 of the Charter, which precludes the General Assembly from making even recommendations on matters that are on the agenda of the Security Council. Thus the concurrent jurisdiction of a deciding Council and a deciding Assembly, which was a distinguishing feature of the League of Nations, is replaced by the alternate jurisdiction of a deciding Security Council and a recommending General Assembly. When the Security Council concerns itself with a matter, the General Assembly may still debate, but it can no longer even recommend.

This device enables the Security Council to control indirectly the functions of the General Assembly in matters of political importance. By simply putting a matter on its agenda, the Security Council can transform the General Assembly into a debating society without even the right to express its collective opinion on the matter.

This limitation of the functions of the General Assembly has endowed the United Nations with a split personality. The General Assembly may with a two-thirds majority recommend to the Security Council a solution to an international problem, which the Security Council may disregard at its discretion. This discretion of the Security Council would be no serious matter if the General Assembly were an advisory body of limited membership, and not the representative body of virtually all the nations of the world. As it is, the distribution of functions between the Security Council and the General Assembly is a constitutional monstrosity. The United Nations may speak with respect to the same issue with two voices—the General Assembly's and the Security Council's—and between these two voices there is no organic connection. Two-thirds or more of the total membership of the United Nations may recommend one thing, and nine of the fifteen members of the Security Council may disregard the recommendation and decide something else.

The vice of this constitutional arrangement does not lie in the predominance of the great powers, which we found to exist in the Holy Alliance and the League of Nations as well. The vice lies rather in the opportunity for the General Assembly to demonstrate its impotence. The Holy Alliance was frankly an international government of the great powers. The League of Nations was an international government of the great powers with the advice and consent of all member nations, each of which, by virtue of the principle of unanimity and save for Article 15, paragraph 10, of the Covenant,[1] could stop the international government from

---

[1]For the text see page 306.

acting. The United Nations is an international government of the great powers that resembles in its constitutional arrangements the Holy Alliance and in its pretense the League of Nations. It is the contrast between pretense and constitutional actuality, between the democratic expectations roused by the words of the Charter and the autocratic performance envisaged by the actual distribution of functions, which characterizes the constitutional provisions of the United Nations.

The international government of the United Nations, then, is identical with the international government of the Security Council. The Security Council appears, as it were, as the Holy Alliance of our time. The predominance of the Security Council having thus been established, the Charter proceeds to establish the predominance of the great powers within the Security Council. For in actuality it is the five permanent members that are supposed to perform the governmental functions. We have seen that the principle of unanimity has been abrogated with respect to all decisions of the Security Council and has been replaced with regard to substantive decisions by the requirement of nine affirmative votes in which the votes of the five permanent members must be included. Given the preponderant influence of some of the five permanent members (China, France, Great Britain, the Soviet Union, the United States), their unanimous decision is expected to attract at least four more votes of other members of the Security Council.

The United Nations, then, is predicated upon the continuing unity of the permanent members of the Security Council. In the scheme of the Charter, these five members are, as it were, the nucleus of a world federation, a Holy Alliance within a Holy Alliance. By limiting the principle of unanimity to them, the Charter makes them the international government of the United Nations. It follows that with but one permanent member dissenting there can be no international government of the United Nations.

This great-power monopoly of governmental action is still further enhanced by Article 27, paragraph 3, according to which a party to a dispute is prevented from voting only with regard to the pacific settlement of disputes under Chapter VI of the Charter. In other words, the great-power veto applies to the enforcement measures under Chapter VII. When a great power is a party to a dispute, the Security Council can render a decision by virtue of Article 27, paragraph 3, regardless of the attitude of that great power. If the Security Council should try to enforce that decision, the dissent of any of the great powers, although a party to the dispute, would erect a legal barrier to enforcement action. In such a contingency the decision of the Security Council would remain a dead letter.

Actually, however, the international government of the United Nations is government of the great powers to a still greater degree than the foregoing analysis would indicate. Of the five permanent members of the Security Council, only two, the United States and the Soviet Union, are really great powers. Great Britain and France are medium powers; China is only potentially a great power. Under present conditions of world politics, most members of the Security Council, the permanent members included, can be prevailed upon, if need be, to support the position taken by the United States, China, and the

Soviet Union. The international government of the United Nations, stripped of its legal trimmings, then, is really the international government of the United States, China, and the Soviet Union acting in unison. At best—if they are united—they can govern the rest of the world for the purpose of maintaining order and of preventing war. At worst—if they are disunited—there will be no international government at all.

Ideally, the United Nations is an instrument for governing the world through the combined power of the United States, China, and the Soviet Union. The Charter of the United Nations, however, does not envisage the possibility that the United Nations operate as an international government for the purpose of establishing or maintaining order in the relations among the United States, China, and the Soviet Union or of preventing war among them. The device of the veto excludes the purpose of subjecting the United States, China, and the Soviet Union to an international government against their will.

Undefined Principles of Justice

The standards of justice that shall guide the judgment and actions of the agencies of the United Nations are found in three places: in the Preamble, in Chapter 1 dealing with Purposes and Principles, and interspersed through the Charter. Yet, in contrast to the basic principles of the Holy Alliance and of the League of Nations, the principles of justice upon which the United Nations is founded are beset by two kinds of inner contradictions: one concerning the mode of actions to be performed by the United Nations, the other concerning the purposes for which the actions are to be performed.

The Preamble reaffirms "faith . . . in the equal rights . . . of nations large and small," and Article 2, paragraph 1, declares that "the Organization is based on the principle of sovereign equality of all its Members." That principle is strengthened by Article 2, paragraph 7, which exempts "matters which are essentially within the domestic jurisdiction of any state" from the jurisdiction of the United Nations, except insofar as enforcement measures under Chapter VII are concerned.[2] Yet the whole structure of the United Nations, as laid out in the main body of the Charter, is based upon what one might call paradoxically the "sovereign inequality" of its members. We have already pointed to the fact that, if the United Nations were to operate as provided for in its Charter, all its members who are not members of the Security Council would lose their sovereignty and would remain sovereign in name and form only.[3] Thus the principle of sovereign equality proclaimed by the Charter in its introductory provisions is contradicted by the actual distribution of functions that the Charter itself provides.

[2]See what was said earlier about the destructive effect the reservation of domestic jurisdiction has upon international obligations, pages 294–96.
[3]See pages 326 ff.

The Preamble and Chapter 1 formulate five political purposes of action: (1) maintenance of international peace and security, (2) collective security, (3) prohibition of the use of force "against the territorial integrity or political independence of any state" and reservation of its use for "the common interest" as defined in the Charter, (4) maintenance of "justice and respect for the obligations arising from treaties and other sources of international law," and (5) national self-determination.

Of these five purposes, the first two are general and of an instrumental nature. They tell us that whatever the United Nations does it should do peacefully and according to the principle of collective security. The other three principles are specific and concrete. They tell us what the United Nations should or should not do in concrete situations. It should use force under certain conditions and not use it under others; it should act justly and in harmony with the rules of international law and with the principle of national self-determination.

It is significant that the Charter is most explicit in elaborating and implementing the first two purposes (cf. particularly Chapters VI and VII) and that it is virtually silent with regard to the remaining three. Article 11, paragraph 1, and Article 24, paragraph 2, refer the General Assembly and the Security Council in general terms to the Purposes and Principles as guides for their deliberations and actions. But the concrete meaning of such concepts as justice, respect for international law, and national self-determination is not self-evident, nor is it the same everywhere and at all times. In the abstract, most men may be able to agree upon a definition of those terms. It is the concrete political situation that gives these abstract terms a concrete meaning and enables them to guide the judgment and actions of men. Nowhere in the main body of the Charter is there a definition of, or reference to, a substantive principle of justice. Nor are there any other sources that would give unequivocal content to these abstractions.

THE UNITED NATIONS—POLITICAL REALITY

The Rise and Decline of the General Assembly

The constitutional scheme of the United Nations was built upon three political assumptions. First, the great powers, acting in unison, would deal with any threat to peace and security, regardless of its source. Second, their combined wisdom and strength would be sufficient to meet all such threats without resort to war. Third, no such threat would emanate from one of the great powers themselves. These assumptions have not stood the test of experience. The great powers have not been able to act in unison when their divergent interests were at stake, which is another way of saying that they have been able to act in unison only in rare and exceptional circumstances. And the main threat to the peace and security of the world emanates from the great powers themselves. Thus the constitutional scheme of the Charter has been defied by the political reality of the postwar world.

The contrast between constitutional intentions and political reality has transformed the United Nations into something different from what it was intended to be. In view of the dynamic changes in the relations between the two, one can distinguish three stages in that transformation. The first decade, roughly speaking, witnesses the decline of the Security Council and the ascendancy of the General Assembly. The second decade, again roughly speaking, is characterized by the ascendancy of the secretary general, acting under the delegated authority of the Security Council and the General Assembly. The constitutional crisis of 1964, resulting from the conflict over the financing of peacekeeping operations, made manifest the decline in the powers of the General Assembly and of the secretary general, and in consequence the Security Council began to reassert its constitutional authority.

These changes in the relative importance of the Security Council and the General Assembly are graphically illustrated by the quantitative changes in the activities of the two agencies. Judged by the number of political issues dealt with, the Security Council began, in accordance with the intentions of the Charter, as the leading political organ of the United Nations. Yet from July 1, 1948, onward, its activities, while fluctuating in absolute terms, have been consistently inferior to those of the General Assembly.

The conflict between the United States and the Soviet Union and the absence of Communist China prevented the United Nations from becoming the international government of the great powers that the Charter intended it to be. That conflict has paralyzed the Security Council as an agency of international government. In the few instances when it has been able to act as such an agency, it has been able to do so either, as at the beginning of the Korean War, by the accidental and temporary absence of the Soviet Union or, as in the Indonesian, Kashmir, Middle East, and Suez issues, by a fortuitous and exceptional coincidence of interests.

The changes in the number of meetings of the Security Council similarly illustrate the changes in its importance as the leading political organ of the United Nations.

The worldwide interests and commitments of the United States and the Soviet Union make it inevitable that in almost every issue that has come, or might come, before the Security Council the interests and commitments of the two superpowers are somehow involved. This involvement has made agreement generally impossible, and the voting in the Security Council has generally found the Soviet Union on one side of the issue and the majority on the other. It is then through the instrumentality of the veto that the minority great power registers its dissent from the majority and protects its interests from being adversely affected by a hostile majority.

The rise of the General Assembly to its eminence as the most active branch of the international government of the United Nations is due to two factors: the use of five constitutional devices by the majority of the General Assembly and the character of contemporary world politics.

POLITICAL ISSUES CONSIDERED BY GENERAL ASSEMBLY AND SECURITY COUNCIL JANUARY 1, 1946, TO JUNE 30, 1964

Period	General Assembly	Security Council
January 1, 1946–June 30, 1946	2	8
July 1,1946–June 30, 1947	6	8
July 1,1947–June 30, 1948	9	14
July 1,1948–June 30, 1949	15	10
July 1,1949–June 30, 1950	13	12
July 1,1950–June 30, 1951	24	12
July 1,1951–June 30, 1952	17	9
July 1,1952–June 30, 1953	18	5
July 1,1953–June 30, 1954	12	8
July 1,1954–June 30, 1955	18	4
July 1,1955–June 30, 1956	13	4
July 1,1956–June 30, 1957	19	11
July 1,1957–June 30, 1958	22	9
July 1,1958–June 30, 1959	15	6
July 1,1959–June 30, 1960	14	2
July 1,1960–June 30, 1961	20	6
July 1,1961–June 30, 1962	24	8
July 1,1962–June 30, 1963	15	4
July 1,1963–June 30, 1964	11	8
Total	286	147

NUMBER OF MEETINGS OF THE SECURITY COUNCIL

1946	88	1956	51
1947	137	1957	48
1948	168	1958	36
1949	62	1959	5
1950	73	1960	71
1951	39	1961	68
1952	42	1962	38
1953	43	1963	58
1954	32	1964	86
1955	23		

The constitutional practices the General Assembly has followed in its activities as an agency of international government have tended to diminish the authority of the Security Council and increase that of the General Assembly. First of all, the control over the activities of the General Assembly, which Article 12, paragraph 1, of the Charter gives to the Security Council, has been circumvented by two constitutional devices. A number of cases have been removed from a deadlocked Security Council to the General Assembly by a simple majority vote, on the assumption that such removal is a procedural matter that does not require the unanimous vote of all the permanent members according to Article 27, paragraph 3, of the Charter. In other words, the Security Council has proceeded on the assumption that the veto does not apply to a majority decision to remove an issue from the Security Council to the General Assembly.

Furthermore, the General Assembly has interpreted Article 12, paragraph 1, liberally and has made recommendations with regard to issues that were at the same time on the agenda of the Security Council. This happened in the cases of Palestine and Korea. The procedure has been justified by the legal argument that the General Assembly was dealing with an aspect of the same issue different from that with which the Security Council was concerned. It is obvious that this argument tends to emasculate Article 12, paragraph 1, and, in consequence, opens the door wide for the General Assembly's assumption of unlimited jurisdiction over virtually any issue submitted to it.

The General Assembly went further by assuming in a positive way primary and specific responsibility for the preservation of peace and security—for which, according to Article 24, paragraph 1, the Security Council is primarily responsible. The General Assembly achieved this result through the Uniting for Peace Resolution,[4] which established the Collective Measures Committee and gave it broad advisory functions for the maintenance of peace and security. When the Soviet Union declared this resolution to be illegal, it went too far; when it alleged that the Collective Measures Committee was designed to "circumvent" the Security Council, it was not far off the mark. For the Collective Measures Committee owes its existence to the demonstrated inability of the Security Council to act as an agency of international government on any issue in which divergent interests of the great powers are involved.

In view of the text of the Charter, the General Assembly should never have been able to supersede the Security Council in any respect. For the Charter erects a seemingly insurmountable obstacle to any such usurpation by giving only the Security Council the power to make legally binding decisions and by allowing the General Assembly to do no more than recommend. The ever-more-marked inability of the Security Council to decide brought about a subtle change in the relative powers of the two agencies. This change endowed the recommendations of the General Assembly, at least in certain matters and within certain limits,[5] with an authority akin to that of a legally binding decision. A substantial majority of the

---

[4]For its contents, see pages 314–16.
[5]The nature of these qualifications will be discussed on pages 498 ff.

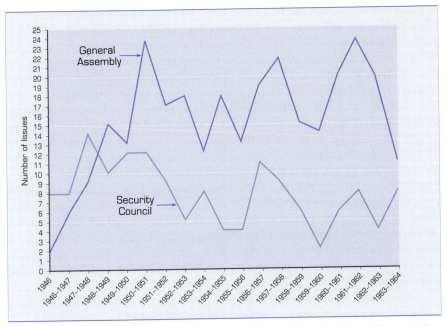

Political Issues Considered by General Assembly and Security Council, 1946–64

members of the United Nations obviously felt that the United Nations ought to take action with regard to certain matters and that, in the absence of a Security Council able to act, the General Assembly ought to act in the manner the Security Council would have acted were it able to do so. Thus, while technically speaking the General Assembly can only recommend, a substantial majority of the members showed a tendency, with regard to certain matters and within certain limits, to act upon these recommendations as though they were legally binding decisions.[6]

This transformation of the General Assembly into the politically dominant agency of the United Nations was possible only because at least two-thirds of the member states favored it. For if at least a two-thirds majority had not voted for the recommendations submitted to the General Assembly, that transformation would not have taken place. This two-thirds majority was the instrument that brought this transformation into being, that gave the transformation life as long as it supported it, and that determined its content and its strength. And it is upon the composition of that majority that the character of the transformation depended.

The composition of the majority supporting the recommendations of the General Assembly underwent a drastic change with the admission of twenty new members in 1955–56. This date constitutes a turning point in the history of the United Nations, closing one phase and ushering in a new one. It can even be said that the United Nations that existed before that date was a different instrument

[6]It is worth recalling in this connection that in one isolated and in certain respects unique instance–the case of the Italian colonies–France, Great Britain, the Soviet Union, and the United States agreed beforehand to accept the decision of the General Assembly as binding.

of international government from the United Nations that existed afterward, capable of performing different functions from those that the United Nations is able to perform today. The transformation the United Nations underwent did not stop with the shifting of the center of political decision from the Security Council to the General Assembly. It created within the General Assembly itself two different types of international organization, built upon two different kinds of majorities.

The majority that carried the recommendations of the General Assembly until the end of 1956 had as its nucleus the United States, the nations of Western Europe, most members of the British Commonwealth, and the Latin American nations, amounting to thirty-nine votes. Around this nucleus other nations grouped themselves in ever changing configurations—sometimes voting with the majority, sometimes against it, sometimes abstaining. Permanently excluded from it was the Soviet bloc, numbering five votes. Not only was this United Nations an international government conducted without the participation of the Soviet bloc, it was also an international government that opposed the Soviet bloc as the latter opposed it. It owed its very existence, and found its main political and military purpose, in the opposition it offered to the Soviet bloc. In its purpose it could well be called a grand alliance directed against the Soviet bloc.

Conceived as an instrument of great-power government against aggression, whatever its source, the United Nations became, by dint of political necessity, an instrument of many powers, great and small, against the aggression, actual and potential, emanating from an identified source. According to its Charter, the United Nations was to be a weapon against aggression in the abstract—any aggression, anywhere. By the logic of political interest, it became a weapon against certain individual aggressors, identified as such by their deeds. Thus, when in March 1953 the Russian delegate to the General Assembly, during the discussion of the report of the Collective Measures Committee, declared that the Uniting for Peace Resolution and the work of the committee were a plot fostered by the United States against the Soviet Union, he pointed in demagogic language to the fundamental change in the structure and purpose of the United Nations. And when the American delegate replied that the resolution and the work of the committee were not directed against "anyone," but against aggression, he paid verbal tribute to the spirit of the Charter rather than to political reality, using the Charter as an ideological disguise for the reality of international politics.

The increase in the membership of the United Nations from the original fifty to the present 158 members drastically changed the distribution of voting power in the General Assembly and, with it, the political functions the United Nations is able to perform through the General Assembly. The increase in membership led to three politically significant changes in the distribution of votes. The Western bloc lost its ability to marshal regularly a two-thirds majority in support of resolutions directed against the Soviet bloc. The best the United States can hope for is to impose a veto upon objectionable resolutions by withholding the vote of its supporters from them. At best, the United States can still perform a negative task: prevent the use of the United Nations against its interests. But it can no longer count upon using the United Nations for the positive task of promoting its interests.

While the influence of the United States within the United Nations has thus drastically declined, that of the Soviet bloc has increased. During the first postwar decade, the Soviet Union was in a virtually hopeless minority in both the Security Council and the General Assembly. In the Security Council it has been able, as we have seen, to protect itself against the consequences of being regularly outvoted through the use of the veto. In the General Assembly it was unable as a rule to prevent resolutions objectionable to it from passing because it could count upon less than one-third of the members to support its position. Now the Soviet Union has a good chance to add to the votes of the members of its bloc the votes of a number of other nations, which votes together would amount to more than one-third of the membership and would thus place the Soviet Union in a position to prevent resolutions objectionable to it from being passed. The representation of mainland China in the United Nations has not materially affected that chance since it and its supporters, while likely to take positions antagonistic to the Soviet Union, at present control but a few votes.

This shift in the distribution of voting strength results from the fact that the massive increase in the membership of the United Nations primarily benefited nations belonging to the so-called Afro-Asian bloc. The Afro-Asian bloc comprises more than one-third of the membership of the United Nations. Thus, if it were to vote in unison, it could either exercise a veto on any resolution adverse to its interests or else, by joining either the American or the Soviet bloc, become the core of a working two-thirds majority. In reality, however, the Afro-Asian bloc has but rarely voted as a unit; its vote has typically been split, with some members voting with the American, others with the Soviet bloc, and a very considerable number abstaining. Consequently, as concerns the ability of the United Nations to function politically through the General Assembly, the Afro-Asian bloc has thus far performed a negative function. By splintering its vote between them, it has strengthened the power of the American and Soviet blocs to oppose the will of a simple majority with the veto of more than one-third of the membership. As a result, the General Assembly has found it difficult to pass resolutions calling for substantive policies more specific than opposition to the remnants of colonialism and racial discrimination, invitations to warring parties to cease firing and negotiate a settlement, and authorizations to the secretary general to investigate, observe, report, use his good offices, organize peacekeeping forces, and do what he deems necessary to restore peace and order. Thus the difficulty of two-thirds of the General Assembly to agree upon specific substantive policies resulted in the ascendancy of the secretary general to the temporary eminence of chief executive officer of the United Nations.

The Charter intends the secretary general to be "the chief administrative officer of the organization." He "may bring to the attention of the Security Council any matter which in his opinion may threaten the maintenance of international peace and security." And he "shall perform such other functions as are entrusted to him by (the) organs" of the United Nations. It is from this provision of the Charter that the new functions of the secretary general as the apparent chief political agent of the United Nations derive.

The new functions are intimately related to the impotence of the General Assembly, as the responsibility for action that the General Assembly has taken on is intimately related to the impotence of the Security Council. And one can go one step further and say that the responsibility for the settlement of political issues with which the United Nations as a whole has been burdened is a by-product of the inability of the nations directly concerned, especially the great powers, to settle outstanding political issues among themselves. So they charge the United Nations with finding a settlement. The members of the General Assembly, taking the place of the paralyzed Security Council, are no more able to agree on a settlement collectively than they were when acting as individual nations. So they charged the secretary general with finding a solution.

Thus the secretary general became a kind of prime minister of the United Nations. By virtue of delegations of power, generally vague, by the Security Council or the General Assembly, his office took over political functions that the Security Council and the General Assembly themselves should have performed but were unable to. This transformation of the office owes much to the initiative and skill of Dag Hammarskjöld, who was secretary general from 1953 to 1961. He transformed the United Nations, to use his own words, into "a dynamic instrument of governments." He set out, to quote him again, "to create a new executive responsibility somewhere . . ." and "to help fill any vacuum that may appear in the systems which the Charter and traditional diplomacy provide for the safeguarding of peace and security." Hammarskjöld even went beyond interpreting broadly the mandate he had received from the General Assembly or the Security Council and acted at times without any mandate at all and in the face of the explicit opposition of a member of the United Nations. Thus he established in 1959 a United Nations presence in Laos even though the Soviet Union had declared beforehand that it was opposed to his visit and specifically to his leaving a United Nations representative behind. Thus he decided in 1958 to enlarge the United Nations observer corps in Lebanon even though the Soviet Union had already vetoed an American proposal to enlarge it as well as a Japanese proposal that he should be given a free hand.

This enlargement of the secretary general's office into something approaching a supranational political agency was bound not only to evoke the opposition of particular nations to particular measures taken by the secretary general but also to pose in acute form the inner contradiction that has paralyzed all political international organizations: the contradiction between national sovereignty and the effectiveness of an international organization. The Soviet Union has consistently defended national sovereignty against encroachments by international treaties and organizations, and it has consistently opposed the stewardship of Hammarskjöld and his predecessor, Trygve Lie, as the embodiment of the supranational aspirations of the United Nations. When Charles de Gaulle came to power in 1958, the Soviet Union was joined by France. The Soviet Union tried to destroy the power of the secretary general through the so-called troika proposal, which would have replaced a single secretary general with three officials of equal power acting in unison, one each representing the uncommitted nations, the Soviet, and the

Western blocs. Had this proposal succeeded, the office of the secretary general would have been subjected to the veto and would have been paralyzed by it as the veto has paralyzed the Security Council. When it failed, both the Soviet Union and France and the nations supporting them found another instrument to halt and reverse the supranational trend of the United Nations. They found it in the issue of financial support for the peacekeeping measures recommended by the General Assembly.

Article 19 of the Charter provides that "a member of the United Nations which is in arrears in the payment of its financial contributions to the organization shall have no vote in the General Assembly if the amount of its arrears equals or exceeds the amount of the contributions due from it for the preceding two full years." The Soviet Union was in that position on December 1, 1964; France and a number of small nations were in it on January 1, 1965. The Soviet Union and France maintained, despite a contrary advisory opinion of the International Court of Justice, that they were not obligated to pay for peacekeeping measures that the General Assembly had voted. They argued that only the Security Council, in which the great-power veto protects them from being outvoted, was competent to order peacekeeping measures, such as those in the Gaza Strip and the Congo, which were authorized by a two-thirds majority of the General Assembly.

If the provisions of the Charter had been applied, the Soviet Union would have been automatically deprived of its vote at the beginning of the 1964 session, and France and the other delinquent nations after January 1, 1965. The United Nations would thus have asserted its authority even against great powers among its members. By doing so, it would have risked an open split within its ranks or even defections from them.

A number of member states were unwilling to take this risk, and even the United States, while emphatic in words about its resolution to apply Article 19, was unwilling to bring the issue ito the open by asserting the authority of the United Nations. Instead of voting, the General Assembly operated through "unanimous consensus"; that is, it transacted only that kind of business for which there was unanimous consent, and that consent was established not through formal votes in the Assembly hall but through informal agreements in the lobby. And when, on the last day of the session, Albania tried to bring the issue into the open by moving that the General Assembly resume its ordinary voting procedure, that motion was voted down. In this vote the delinquent members participated—on the legally untenable ground that Article 19 covers only substantive but not procedural votes.

These legal positions and arguments are the mere surface manifestations of a conflict inherent in the very structure of the United Nations. It is the conflict between national sovereignty and effective international organization. These two concepts, as we have seen,[7] are irreconcilable in theory and practice. In the measure that an international organization is effective, it is bound to impair the freedom

[7]See pages 326 ff.

of action of its members, and in the measure that the member states assert their freedom of action, they impair the effectiveness of the international organization. The Charter itself testifies to that unresolved conflict by stressing, on the one hand, the "sovereign equality" of all member states and, on the other, assigning to the permanent members of the Security Council a privileged position amounting to a limited world government.

The defenders of national sovereignty and opponents of a strong United Nations won a definitive victory when in 1965 the General Assembly decided to forgo the enforcement of Article 19 of the Charter and to accept the principle of voluntary contributions to peacekeeping measures of the United Nations. This victory amounts to a veritable counterrevolution against the United Nations as it had developed by virtue of the extraconstitutional developments outlined above. This decision nullified these extraconstitutional developments of almost two decades. It returned the United Nations to the original intentions of the Charter.

That means in practice that the Security Council becomes again the chief executive organ, still threatened with paralysis by the veto and by the expansion of its membership from eleven to fifteen, that the General Assembly is reduced essentially to a debating society debilitated by the massive influx of ministates whose collective voting strength is out of proportion to their actual power, and that the secretary general is stripped of the executive power that the General Assembly had bestowed upon him. That is to say, the Security Council is powerless, the General Assembly is powerless, and the secretary general is powerless. The United Nations has ceased to be an effective international organization. As Secretary General U Thant put it in a speech on March 22, 1965:

> We are witnessing today, I feel, a definite reversal of the slow progress the United Nations has made toward stability and world peace. A further drift in this direction, if not arrested in time, will mark the close of a chapter of great expectations and the heralding of a new chapter in which the world organization will provide merely a debating forum and nothing else.

Only the future can tell whether there exist now sufficient communities of interest among the permanent members of the Security Council to allow it to operate according to the intentions of the Charter and whether there exists now among the members of the General Assembly a sufficient awareness of their interest in a strong United Nations to restore to the General Assembly the power it once possessed.

The decline of the powers of the secretary general is the result not only of the opposition from within the United Nations to which we have referred but also of the congenital weakness of his office. Parties to a political conflict can be induced by outsiders to agree on a peaceful settlement by four methods, employed alternately or simultaneously: They can be threatened with disadvantages expected to outweigh the advantages to be gained from continuing the conflict; they can be promised advantages greater than those to be expected from seeing the conflict through to a successful conclusion; they can be persuaded by rational arguments pointing to the advantages and disadvantages to be expected and to the intentions and capabilities of the other side and of interested third parties; or they can be helped in taking the last small step toward the consummation of a settlement already achieved in substance through the elaboration of a face-saving and technically satisfactory formula. Of these four devices, the first two tower in importance over the two others, which perform essentially subsidiary functions. It is the measure of the weakness of the secretary general's position as a political agent that he is almost completely deprived of the two most potent instruments of conciliation, threat and promise, and limited to the use of rational persuasion and formulation of agreements already substantially attained.

The weakness of the General Assembly, as presently composed, then, is reflected in the weakness of the secretary general. Both can talk, explain, and formulate, but neither can at present put a hand on that lever of threats and promises which is the very soul of political action. The temporary eminence of the secretary general was but a function of his personality and of the General Assembly's embarrassment at being called upon to act without being able to. When Secretary General Kurt Waldheim sought to free the hostages in Iran, he was met first by hostility from their captors and thereafter by criticism from Americans for his failure. And a call to action addressed to the General Assembly is in turn but the great powers' cry of despair at being unable to settle among themselves issues that, as long as they remain unsettled, carry within themselves the threat of war. Thus the actions of the secretary general, like the resolutions of the General Assembly, are not so much harbingers of recovery, let alone a cure for the disease, as symptoms of its intractability. Yet they can also have the effect of sedatives for jangled nerves and of medication that prevents existing wounds from opening still wider. This is indeed the contribution that the United Nations is at present able to make to the peaceful settlement of international disputes.

The General Assembly is, at any rate for the time being, in the position in which the Security Council found itself from the very beginning: It is unable to act for the reason that the majority required by the Charter is lacking. Yet, while the Security Council was paralyzed from the outset by the foreseeable and almost automatic use of the veto by the Soviet Union, the paralysis of the General Assembly has been the result of a dynamic process that can be broken down into three phases: disintegration of the two-thirds majority led by the United States, the vain attempt by the two superpowers to fashion a two-thirds majority in support of their respective policies, and the attempt by the two superpowers to minimize the voting support of the other side, an action that U.N. Ambassador Jeane Kirkpatrick in the Reagan administration described as primarily one of forestalling action by others. This continual search for votes, or at least abstentions, has become one of the main preoccupations of the great powers in the General Assembly. Out of it, a new diplomatic procedure has developed, the significance of which is twofold. It forces the great powers to defer, at least in the formulation of their policies, to the preferences of the small member nations and thereby blunts the sharp edges of international conflict. It provides the nations concerned with an opportunity to shift the apparent responsibility for unpleasant decisions to the United Nations and thereby acts as a face-saving and shock-absorbing device. The exceptions have been the tenures of Ambassadors Kirkpatrick and Moynihan, both of whom chose to formulate and defend American policy in the United Nations in confrontational terms.

New Procedures

The powerful nation that needs for the successful execution of its policies the support of small nations can follow one of two courses of action. It can resort to the traditional method of diplomacy and bring its superior power directly to bear upon the weaker nations. In this way dependencies are established and alliances are formed. However, a powerful nation that tries to gain support for its policies through the United Nations General Assembly cannot rely upon its superior power alone. Superior power avails it nothing if it is unable to attract the number of votes sufficient for the purposes of its policy. Thus it must pursue a different course of action, which is determined by the procedures of the General Assembly. These procedures and the new United Nations diplomacy that has developed from them tend to diminish the distinction between great and small nations, since all of them have but one vote.

If a great power had only the task of fashioning an alliance with the techniques of traditional diplomacy, it would select the members of that alliance primarily in view of the power they could add to it. Yet the task of the new United Nations diplomacy is not so much to build an alliance with a maximum of political and military power as to form a majority with a maximum of voting strength. In the General Assembly, India's vote counts for as much as Iceland's, and Qatar's is as valuable as Great Britain's. The most powerful member of an alliance can afford to disregard the preferences of small states whose power counts for nothing, making concessions only to those whose power counts. The most powerful member of a majority in the process of formation must heed the wishes of even the weakest nation whose vote is needed. For this reason, some U.N. ambassadors of the United States, including Adlai Stevenson, Charles Yost, William Scranton, and Donald McHenry, are best remembered for their patient efforts in the corridors and cloakrooms seeking support for U.S. policies.

It stands to reason that the power of the big nation is still felt, as is the weakness of the small one; for the former speaks in the persuasive voice of power to which the latter can reply only in the whisper of weakness. Yet, while power and weakness still count in the new United Nations diplomacy, they do not count for as much as they do in the traditional one. Here lies the important distinction between the techniques of traditional and United Nations diplomacy: the latter is compelled to persuade where the former could afford not to care. Thus a great power must present the issues to be voted on in terms acceptable to the members whose votes are needed. This necessity involves a dual transformation of the measure from what it would be were it to serve exclusively the purposes of the great power.

First of all, the measure must be presented in language reflecting the common interests of the prospective members of the two-thirds majority rather than the interests of a particular nation or more limited group of nations. The linguistic transformation may frequently amount to no more than the ideological justification and rationalization of national policies in terms of supranational ones. Yet the constant use of a certain terminology, not only for purposes of propaganda but in the give-and-take of political transactions, may well exert a subtle influence upon the substance of the transactions themselves. For the language constantly used will create in the participants to the transaction expectations to which the transaction somehow must conform or from which, at the very least, it cannot completely deviate.

Thus a foreign policy with which a certain nation or limited group of nations is completely identified and for which the broad support of two-thirds of the General Assembly is sought may well undergo a subtle change if, for the purpose of gaining such broad support, it is constantly presented in supranational terms. Such a change would hardly ever go so far as to run counter to the objectives and methods envisaged by the original national policy. Yet it may well result in the blunting of the sharp edges of a national policy, its retreat from an advanced position, and its reformulation and adaptation in the light of the supranational principles embodied in the language of the resolution. The more experienced U.N. diplomats have gained recognition for their skill in drawing other nations to their side by trimming and adjusting their own policies to accord with those of an emerging majority of states.

The same result will be directly and almost inevitably achieved in the course of the negotiations by which a two-thirds majority in support of the resolution is formed. The divergence of interests, capabilities, and points of view among the members whose support is sought necessitates a search for a common denominator, which is bound to be below the maximum desired by the originator of the national policy. How far below that maximum the measure enacted by the General Assembly is going to be will depend in part upon the skill with which different nations make use of the new methods of United Nations diplomacy. In large measure, however, the distribution of material power between the nations seeking support for a policy and the nations whose support is sought will decide the extent to which the former must give way in order to gain that support. For the nations that can afford to do so will use their power as a lever through which to gain concessions and avoid making them. It is here that old and new diplomacy merge.

Yet the United Nations presents two great inducements for making concessions, at least in the formulation of policies: It is at present powerless to act, and it speaks with a voice that pretends and appears to be, and within certain limits actually is, different from that of the great powers. Thus nations in conflict with each other can afford to do vis-à-vis the United Nations what they think they cannot afford to do in their relations with each other—make concessions in the formulation, if not the substance, of their policies without fear of losing face. This is particularly so if the face-saving formula is proposed by a "neutral" nation or group of nations. For then the parties to the dispute appear to make concessions, not to each other but to the majority of the General Assembly in whose name the "neutral" nation appears to speak. Conversely, the refusal to make concessions appears in the circumstances not so much as defense of one's own rightful position against the enemy but rather as defiance of the "political voice of mankind itself." However intangible and imponderable these influences are that the General Assembly is able to bring to bear by virtue of its very existence as an operating agency, they do exist and are being taken into account by the nations concerned.

The secretary general, as designer of the face-saving formula, personifies both the "neutral" nations and the "political voice of mankind," and partakes of the influences they exert in the General Assembly. However, he has at his disposal two more devices that enable him under favorable circumstances to mitigate international conflicts. One is a function of his office and the sole means of real pressure at his disposal. He can warn a reluctant party that he will bring the situation to the attention of the General Assembly as a threat to international peace and security, and in terms that place the blame where the secretary general thinks it belongs. By doing this, he threatens to bring those influences into motion that enable the General Assembly to play the mediating and mitigating role to which we have referred.

The other instrument at the disposal of the secretary general is a function of his personality and lies purely in the realm of persuasion. The late Mr. Hammarskjöld's tenure of office shows impressively how dependent the peace-promoting functions of the secretary general are upon the intellectual and moral qualities of the holder of that office. Only a man of Hammarskjöld's personality could have tried to do what he did in this respect and have achieved what he achieved.

In view of the magnitude of the unsettled issues, it is fair to say that what he achieved is little enough, and this judgment must be extended to the United Nations as a whole. But in view of the enormity of the consequences with which these unsettled issues threaten not only individual nations but civilization itself, it must also be said that the little that has been achieved by the United Nations is better than nothing.

THE UNITED NATIONS AND THE PROBLEM OF PEACE

The United Nations, as envisaged by the Charter, takes unity among the great powers for granted and concerns itself with the preservation of peace among the medium and small powers through the instrumentality of great-power government. The new United Nations takes disunity between the two superpowers for granted and concerns itself with the coordination of resources and policies among its members for the purpose of the efficient support of their respective policies. The United Nations of the Charter was born of the illusion that peace among the great powers was assured; the new United Nations owes its existence to the reality of the conflicts among them.

The contribution the new United Nations is able to make to the preservation of peace is, then, bound to be radically different from that which the United Nations of the Charter was supposed to make. There is no evidence to show that the United Nations has prevented any war. There is, however, unmistakable evidence to show that it has materially contributed to the shortening of five wars: in Indonesia in 1949, in Palestine in 1949, in Egypt in 1956 and 1973, and in Kashmir in 1965. It has been able to achieve these results because, as envisaged by the Charter, the great powers had a common interest in shortening these wars, or at least none of them had an interest in prolonging them. In similar circumstances the United Nations might be able to perform again a similar function of shortening the duration of a war.

The very fact that the Western alliance still dwells together with the Soviet bloc in the virtually empty frame devised by the Charter is not without significance for the ability of the United Nations to contribute to the preservation of peace. For as long as the two blocs coexist within the same international organization, with uncommitted nations floating back and forth between them, the claim of the United Nations of the Charter to universality and the maintenance of peace among all nations, great and small, is still alive. And there persists also the opportunity of personal contacts between representatives of East and West, which can be used unobtrusively for the mitigation or settlement of conflicts. In the 1960s and the latter part of the 1970s, the United States, because of the policies of given administrations and the personalities of the ambassadors, was rather successful in its use of informal channels of diplomacy. At other times, including the early 1980s, American representatives have used the United Nations more as a sounding board for proclaiming American foreign policies. In one exchange, the American representative invited members who differed with the United States to leave and "to sail off into the sunset."

The contribution the United Nations can make to the preservation of peace, notwithstanding the harsh rhetoric by American, Soviet, and Third World representatives, would appear to lie in taking advantage of the opportunity that the coexistence of the two blocs in the same international organization provides for the unobtrusive use of the techniques of traditional diplomacy. The United Nations would then become, so to speak, the new setting for the old techniques of diplomacy. As the secretary general put it in his Annual Report of 1955:

> We have only begun to make use of the real possibilities of the United Nations as the most representative instrument for the relaxation of tensions, for the lessening of distrust and misunderstanding, and for the discovery and delineation of new areas of common ground and interest. . . . Conference diplomacy may usefully be supplemented by more quiet diplomacy within the United Nations, whether directly between representatives of Member Governments or in contacts between the Secretary-General and Member Governments. . . . Within the framework of the Charter there are many possibilities, as yet largely unexplored, for variation of practices. . . . It is my hope that solid progress can be made in the coming years in developing new forms of contact, new methods

of deliberation and new techniques of reconciliation. With only slight adjustments, discussions of major issues of a kind that have occurred outside the United Nations could often be fitted into its framework, thus at the same time adding to the strength of the world organization and drawing strength from it.

"The greatest need," to quote the introduction to the secretary general's Annual Report of 1957,

> . . . today is to blunt the edges of conflict among the nations, not to sharpen them. If properly used, the United Nations can serve a diplomacy of reconciliation better than other instruments available to the member states. All the varied interests and aspirations of the world meet in its precincts upon the common ground of the Charter. Conflicts may persist for long periods without an agreed solution and groups of states may actively defend special and regional interests. Nevertheless, and in spite of temporary developments in the opposite direction under the influence of acute tension, the tendency in the United Nations is to wear away, or break down, differences, thus helping toward solutions which approach the common interest and application of the principles of the Charter.

The new United Nations is a child of the Cold War, born of the conflict between East and West. The United Nations of the Charter is a ruin, rent asunder by the conflict between East and West. Like the conflict between Great Britain and Russia within the Holy Alliance, like the conflict between Great Britain and France within the League of Nations, so the conflict between the United States and the Soviet Union within the United Nations resolves itself into diametrically opposed standards of judgment and action, which virtually incapacitate the international organization to act at all in political matters.

Experience has shown that the attempt to use the United Nations for the purpose of forcing agreement upon either of the superpowers is futile and only aggravates the disagreement. The Charter enables the United Nations—that is, the United States and the Soviet Union acting in unison—to prevent wars among the other nations. Built upon the foundation of the United States and the Soviet Union acting as one, the United Nations of the Charter is constitutionally unable to prevent a war between them, and the new United Nations can at best make only a modest contribution to its prevention. Yet such a war threatens the United States, the Soviet Union, and all mankind. For its prevention we must look elsewhere than to the United Nations.

PART NINE

THE PROBLEM
OF PEACE

Peace Through

Transformation

29 The World State

Our investigation of the problem of international peace has left us with two conclusions: No attempt to solve the problem of international peace by limiting the national aspirations for power has succeeded, and none could have succeeded under the conditions of the modern state system. What, then, accounts for the instability of peace and order in the relations among states, and what accounts for their relative stability within states? In other words, what factor making for peace and order exists within national societies that is lacking on the international scene? The answer seems obvious—it is the state itself.

National societies owe their peace and order to the existence of a state that, endowed with supreme power within the national territory, keeps peace and order. This was indeed the doctrine of Hobbes, who argued that without such a state national societies would resemble the international scene and the war "of every man against every man"[1] would be the universal condition of mankind. From this premise it was logically inevitable to conclude that peace and order among nations would be secure only within a world state comprising all the nations of the earth. Since the breakdown of the universal order of the Middle Ages, this conclusion has been advanced from time to time.[2]

The experience of two world wars within a quarter of a century and the prospects of a third one to be fought with nuclear weapons have imparted to the idea of a world state an unprecedented urgency. What is needed, so the argument runs, in order to save the world from self-destruction is not limitation of the exercise of national sovereignty through international obligations and institutions but the transference of the sovereignties of individual nations to a world authority, which would be as sovereign over the individual nations as the individual nations are sovereign within their respective territories. Reforms within the international society have failed and were bound to fail. What is needed, then, is a radical

---

[1] *Leviathan,* Chapter XIII.
[2] See the references on pages 401 ff.

transformation of the existing international society of sovereign nations into a supranational community of individuals.

The argument rests upon an analogy with national societies. It is, therefore, our first task to find out how peace and order are preserved in national societies.

CONDITIONS OF DOMESTIC PEACE

Peace among social groups within the nation reposes upon a dual foundation: the disinclination of the members of society to break the peace and their inability to break the peace if they should be so inclined. Individuals will be unable to break the peace if overwhelming power makes an attempt to break it a hopeless undertaking. They will be disinclined to break the peace under two conditions. On the one hand, they must feel loyalties to society as a whole that surpass their loyalties to any part of it. On the other hand, they must be able to expect from society at least an approximation of justice through a modicum of satisfaction for their demands. The presence of these three conditions—overwhelming force, suprasectional loyalties, and expectation of justice—makes peace possible within nations. The absence of these conditions on the international scene evokes the danger of war.

What are the factors that make for the presence of these conditions? And what is the role the state plays in this respect? A closer consideration of the interplay of social forces that make for peace within the nation will help us to answer these questions.

Suprasectional Loyalties

National societies are composed of a multiplicity of social groups. Some of these are antagonistic to one another in the sense that their respective claims are mutually exclusive. That mutual exclusiveness of opposing claims is particularly obvious in the economic sphere, where one group may demand a share in the economic product that another group refuses to grant. This problem of the distribution of the economic product is only a spectacular instance of a ubiquitous social phenomenon. Political parties, religious denominations, racial groups, regions, and localities meet in similar contests. How are those conflicts being prevented from degenerating into violence?

First of all, citizen A, who as a member of economic group E1 opposes citizen B as a member of another economic group E2, is unable to identify himself completely with E1 and give it his undivided loyalties. He is unable to do so for three reasons.

A is not only a member of E1 but also of the religious group R, the political group P, and the ethnic and cultural group C. All these groups make demands on his allegiance; and if he wants to do justice to all of them, he cannot identify himself completely with any. While he acts as a member of E1, he cannot forget that he also has responsibilities to R. While he throws himself into the struggle for the objectives of P, he cannot help being mindful of what he owes to C. This pluralism of domestic groupings and conflicts, then, tends to impress upon the participants the relativity of their interests and loyalties and thus to mitigate the clashes of different groups. This pluralism brings about, as it were, an economy in the intensity of identification, which must be spread wide in order to give every group and conflict its share.

Furthermore, while A as a member of E1 opposes B as a member of E2, he might find himself in another respect on the same side of the fence with B, both being members of P. In other words, A and B are enemies in the economic sphere, yet they are friends in politics. They are opposed to each other economically, yet they are united politically. A and B are also members of religious, ethnic, and regional groups, and so forth, and both of them may have similar relations of conflict and association with any number of members of these groups. A, then, is not only at the same time identified with a plurality of different social groups, but he is also, as a member of these different groups, simultaneously the friend and foe of any number of his fellows, insofar as they belong to different groups of which he is either a member or an opponent.

This plural role of friend and opponent that A plays with regard to a number of his fellows imposes restraints upon him as both a friend and a foe. He cannot identify himself completely with his political friends who are also his economic opponents without the risk of losing the struggle for economic advantage. He cannot push the struggle for economic advantage to extremes without losing the political support he needs as a member of the political group. If A wants to be economic opponent and political friend at the same time, he must take care to be both within such limits that one does not get in the way of the other. Thus the overlapping of social roles played by different members of society tends to neutralize conflicts and to restrain them within such limits as to enable the members of society to play their different roles at the same time.

Finally, A and B are not only members of contending economic groups and have not only identical political affiliations, not to speak of all the other social groupings to which they belong, but by definition they are also members of the same national society. They partake of the same language, the same customs, the same historical recollections, the same fundamental social and political philosophy, and the same national symbols. They read the same newspapers, listen to the same radio programs, observe the same holidays, and worship the same heroes. Above all, they compare their own nation with other nations and realize how much more they have in common with each other than with members of the other nations. More particularly, they are convinced that the national characteristics they have in common are superior in all important respects, especially those of morality, to the qualities of those who belong to a different nation. Thus A and B come to feel not only that they belong to the same national family, but also that because of that family relation they have something very precious in common, something that enhances their worth and makes them "better" men in every important respect in comparison with outsiders.

The self-respect of A and B, as well as the esteem in which they hold each other, is intimately connected with their membership in the same national community.

Their intellectual convictions and moral valuations derive from that membership. How that membership gives vicarious satisfaction to their power drives has already been related in detail.[3] The loyalties with which they cling to the nation are more than the mere repayment of a debt of gratitude for benefits received. They are the very conditions of those benefits. It is only by being faithful to the nation, by adhering to it as to the fountainhead of all earthly goods, by identifying oneself with it that one will experience as one's own the security of belonging, the exultation of national pride, the triumphs of the Fatherland in the competition with other nations. Thus protection of the nation against destruction from without and disruption from within is the overriding concern of all citizens. Likewise, loyalty to the nation is a paramount commitment of all citizens. Nothing can be tolerated that might threaten the coherence of the nation. Interests, ideas, and loyalties that might not be compatible with the concern for the unity of the nation must yield to that concern.

This concern imposes an ever-present limitation upon the kind of issues that will be allowed to separate A and B and places ever present restraints upon the methods by which A and B fight these issues out. Whatever the stakes of their conflicts, they will not raise the issue of national unity itself. Whatever methods A and B may employ in order to settle the conflict on their own terms, they will not resort to measures that might put the coherence of the nation itself in jeopardy. All conflicts within a nation are thus limited as to objectives pursued and means employed. They are, as it were, embedded within the densely woven fabric of the national community that keeps them within bounds. In conjunction with the pluralism and overlapping of sectional loyalties, it is the limiting and restraining influence of national loyalties that constitutes the first of the three factors that make for peace within the nation.

Expectation of Justice

How do national societies create the expectation on the part of hostile social groups that none of their claims will be completely ignored but that all have a chance for at least partial satisfaction? How are all contending groups enabled to expect at least an approximation of justice from the national society to which they belong?

In national societies the problem of justice is posed on two levels. One is the level of general principles shared by society as a whole; the other is the level of specific claims advanced by particular groups. On the level of general principles no threat to the peace arises, for all are agreed upon the general principles by which the common good of society is defined. Principles such as democracy, social justice, equality, and freedom of speech do not give rise to conflicts endangering the peace of society so long as they remain in the realm of abstractions defining the ultimate goal of society's collective endeavors.

These abstractions, however, become potent weapons in social conflicts when seized upon by social groups that advance their conflicting claims in the

---

[3]See pages 113 ff.

name of these principles. These claims confront society with its supreme challenge. Society may be able to disregard the claims of small and weak groups without endangering its peace. Its social cohesion and monopoly of organized violence are strong enough to keep the resentment and disaffection of such small and weak groups from turning openly against the social order. Yet society cannot afford to remain deaf to the claims for justice of large and potentially powerful groups without inviting the risk of revolution and civil war—that is, without endangering its peace and its very survival as an integrated whole.

It is here that the intricate mechanism of peaceful change comes into play, giving all groups a chance to submit their claims for justice to the arbitrament of public opinion, of elections, of parliamentary votes, of examination boards, and the like. We have already sketched the workings of these mechanisms in another context and refer the reader to it.[4] These mechanisms guide the conflicting claims of social groups into peaceful channels by giving them a chance to make themselves heard and to compete with each other for recognition according to rules binding upon all. Under the conditions of these contests, no group can be sure to prevail in the long run, but all groups can rely upon the chance of taking at one time or another some forward steps toward the attainment of justice.

Overwhelming Power

The third factor in preserving peace within national societies is the overwhelming power with which society can nip in the bud all attempts at disturbing the peace. This overwhelming power manifests itself in two different ways: in the form of material force as a monopoly of organized violence, and in the form of irresistible social pressure.

The power that is at the disposal of society in the form of a monopoly of organized violence is set apart by two characteristics from any other form of violence, especially the one we encounter in the international sphere.

The organized violence of national societies is in some measure neutral with regard to the conflicting claims of social groups so long as they remain within the limits of the law and avail themselves of peaceful means. The liberal doctrine of the nineteenth century held that the organized violence of society was completely neutral, standing above the turmoil of conflicting interests, ready to enforce the law against whoever had violated it. Against that doctrine Marxism claims that the organized violence of society is nothing but the weapon with which the ruling class maintains its rule over the exploited masses. Actually, the compulsory organization of society cannot be completely neutral, for, as we have seen,[5] the legal order it enforces is not completely neutral and cannot help favoring the status quo to which it owes its existence. If challenged, the status quo can count upon the support of the compulsory organization of society.

---

[4]See Chapter 26.
[5]See pages 455 (see Chapter 20).

It is, however, the peculiar characteristic of the compulsory organization of society that it has a bias in favor of the status quo but in large measure not a bias in favor of any particular status quo. The compulsory organization of American society has defended the status quo of 1800, of 1900, of 1932, and of 1940. The compulsory organization of British society has supported in succession the status quo of feudalism, capitalism, and socialism. Yet it may be that a particular status quo is offensive to the fundamental moral convictions and the vital interests of a considerable portion of the population and that a considerable fraction of the enforcement agents sympathize with their uncompromising opposition to the status quo. In such a case, the legal order embodying the status quo will not be enforced. In the United States the constitutional background of the Civil War and the fate of Prohibition illustrate that case.

The other characteristic peculiar to the compulsory organization of national societies is the scarcity of its collective action. As a rule, the compulsory organization of national societies maintains peace and order only against individual lawbreakers. It is a rare exception for it to oppose as a collective force another collectivity that threatens to disturb the peace. The use of force in labor disputes is the outstanding example of this kind. Normally, the very existence, in the hands of society, of a monopoly of organized violence, ready to intervene in case of need, deters collective disturbances of domestic peace. The very fact of its existence makes it unnecessary for the compulsory organization of society to act.

Aside from this factor and probably surpassing it in importance is the enormous unorganized pressure society exerts upon its members to keep the peace. A group, in order to be able to escape that pressure, would have to erect within the very framework of the national society a social structure of its own, more integrated, more compelling, and commanding higher loyalties than the national society in whose midst it dwells. In our times, the intensity of nationalism, its transformation into the political religion of nationalistic universalism, the ubiquity of the modern mass media of communications, and their control by a small and relatively homogeneous group have multiplied and magnified the social pressures that in national societies tend to keep dissenting groups within the bounds of law and peace.

The Role of the State

What is the contribution of the state to the maintenance of domestic peace? "State" is but another name for the compulsory organization of society–for the legal order that determines the conditions under which society may employ its monopoly of organized violence for the preservation of order and peace. When we have spoken in the preceding pages of the compulsory organization and of the legal order of society, we have really spoken of the state. Its functions for the maintenance of domestic peace are threefold: (1) The state provides the legal continuity of the national society. It thus enables the individual to experience the nation as a continuum in time and space, as a personality in whose name men act, who demands and receives services and bestows benefits, to whom one can feel personal loyalties that are felt toward few other social groups except the family and the church. (2) The state provides most of the institutionalized agencies and processes of social change. (3) The state provides the agencies for the enforcement of its laws.

It remains for us to determine how important the state's contribution to domestic peace is. The answer to this question is twofold. The state's contribution to domestic peace is indispensable, but it is not in itself sufficient. Without the state's contribution there can be no domestic peace, but with nothing but the state's contribution there can be no domestic peace either.

That there can be no domestic peace without the state is already implicit in what we have said about the problems of power, of the balance of power, and of sovereignty. Hostile social groups will use whatever means are at their disposal for the purpose of gaining the objectives they consider vital to themselves. If such social groups control the means of physical violence, as sovereign states do in their mutual relations, they will use them in two different ways. They will either exert pressure upon their opponents by displaying what they consider to be their superiority, or they will employ them for the destruction of the opponent's means of physical violence. In either alternative the purpose of physical violence is the breaking of the opponent's will to resist the demands of the other side.

The history of national societies shows that no political, religious, economic, or regional group has been able to withstand for long the temptation to advance its claims by violent means if it thought it could do so without too great a risk. However strongly the other social factors might have supported the cause of peace, their effectiveness did not long survive the promise of a speedy and definitive victory that violence holds out to its possessor. Thus national societies have disintegrated and have split into a number of smaller units, either temporarily or permanently, whenever the state was incapable of maintaining its monopoly of organized violence and of using effectively whatever means of violence it retained for the purpose of maintaining peace and securing its own survival.

Since whoever is able to use violence will use it if the stakes seem to justify its use, a social agency is needed strong enough to prevent that use. Society might find substitutes for the legal unity the state conveys to it in time and space and for the agencies for social change through which the state regulates the dynamics of the social processes. Society has no substitute for the power of the Leviathan whose very presence, towering above contending groups, keeps their conflicts within peaceful bounds.

The state is indispensable for the maintenance of domestic peace; such is the true message of Hobbes's philosophy. Yet the state by itself cannot maintain domestic peace; such is the great omission of Hobbes's philosophy. That the power of the state is essential, but not sufficient, to keep the peace of national societies is demonstrated by the historical experience of civil wars. If there had been only few of them over a long period of history, they might be disregarded as exceptions to the rule. However, of a total of two hundred and seventy-eight wars fought between 1480 and 1941, seventy-eight—28 percent of the total—were civil wars. In the period from 1840 to 1941, the ratio between civil and international wars was, with eighteen of the former and sixty of the latter, approximately one to three. For the period between 1800 and 1941, the figures are twenty-eight civil and eighty-five international wars, the ratio being almost exactly one to three.[6] Concerning the costliness of civil wars, Quincy Wright observes: "Civil wars such as the French Huguenot wars of the sixteenth century, the British War of the Roses of the fifteenth century and the Civil War of the seventeenth century, the Thirty Years' War from the standpoint of Germany, the Peninsula War from the standpoint of Spain, the American Civil War, and the Chinese Taiping Rebellion were costly both in lives and in economic losses far in excess of contemporary international wars."[7]

The frequency and destructiveness of civil wars demonstrate that the existence of the state does not assure the preservation of domestic peace. The reason lies in the nature of the state itself. The state is not the artificial creation of a constitutional convention, conceived in the image of some abstract principles of government and superimposed upon whatever society might exist. On the contrary, the state is part of the society from which it has sprung, and prospers and decays as society prospers and decays. The state, far from being a thing apart from society, is created by society.

The peace of a society whose intergroup conflicts are no longer limited, restrained, and neutralized by overriding loyalties, whose processes of social change no longer sustain the expectation of justice in all the major groups; and whose unorganized forces of compulsion are no longer sufficient to impose conformity upon these groups—the peace of such a society cannot be saved by the state, however strong. The forces of destruction arising within society in the form of class, racial, religious, regional, or purely political struggles will erupt in revolutions, coups d'état, and civil wars. The state does not stand apart from these conflagrations as a fire department stands apart from fires, ready to extinguish them when they break out. The state is inevitably involved in these conflagrations in a dual sense. On the one hand, the state is the prime target of revolution, against which it must defend itself through the use of force. On the other hand, the dissensions that disrupt society also split its compulsory organization, the state. The state, then, will either cease to operate as one body, its discordant parts will join the warring groups in society at large, and the unity of the state will dissolve in civil war, or else—and this is more likely in our time in view of the monopoly of effective power that modern technology gives to the state—the issues that divide the people will be fought out not by the people at large, but through internecine struggles within the organization of the state in the form of coups d'état, conspiracies, and purges.[8]

THE PROBLEM OF THE WORLD STATE

Our analysis of the problem of domestic peace has shown that the argument of the advocates of the world state is unanswerable: there can be no permanent international peace without a state coextensive with the confines of the political

---

[6]Quincy Wright, *A Study of War* (Chicago: University of Chicago Press, 1942), Vol. I, p. 651.
[7]Ibid., p. 247.
[8]On the obsolescence of popular revolutions in our times, see pages 389 ff.

world. The question to which we now must direct our attention concerns the manner in which a world state can be created.

Two Schools of Thought

In the first chapter of his *Considerations on Representative Government*, John Stuart Mill faced the same problem with respect to particular forms of government. The two "conflicting conceptions of what political institutions are" that Mill found to be at the basis of all discussions of his problem determine also the discussions of how to create a world state. By one school of thought,

> government is conceived as strictly a practical art, giving rise to no questions but those of means and an end. Forms of government are assimilated to any other expedients for the attainment of human objects. They are regarded as wholly an affair of invention and contrivance. Being made by man, it is assumed that man has the choice either to make them or not, and how or on what pattern they shall be made. . . . To find the best form of government; to persuade others that it is the best; and having done so, to stir them up to insist on having it, is the order of ideas in the minds of those who adopt this view of political philosophy. They look upon a constitution in the same light (difference of scale being allowed for) as they would upon a steam plough, or a threshing machine.

The other school of thought regards government

> as a sort of spontaneous product, and the science of government as a branch (so to speak) of natural history. According to them, forms of government are not a matter of choice. We must take them, in the main, as we find them. Governments cannot be constructed by premeditated design. They "are not made, but grow." . . . The fundamental political institutions of a people are considered by this school as a sort of organic growth from the nature and life of that people: a product of their habits, instincts, and unconscious wants and desires, scarcely at all of their deliberate purposes. Their will has had no part in the matter but that of meeting the necessities of the moment by the contrivances of the moment, which contrivances, if in sufficient conformity to the national feelings and character, commonly last, and by successive aggregation constitute a polity, suited to the people who possess it, but which it would be vain to attempt to superduce upon any people whose nature and circumstances had not spontaneously evolved it.

Mill took his stand between the extremes of these two doctrines, availing himself "of the amount of truth which exists in either." On the one hand,

> political institutions . . . are the work of men; owe their origin and their whole existence to human will. . . .
> On the other hand, it is also to be borne in mind that political machinery does not act of itself. As it is first made, so it has to be worked, by men, and even by ordinary men. It needs not their simple acquiescence, but their active participation; and must be adjusted to the capacities and qualities of such men

as are available. This implies three conditions. The people for whom the form of government is intended must be willing to accept it; or at least not so unwilling as to oppose an insurmountable obstacle to its establishment. They must be willing and able to do what is necessary to keep it standing. And they must be willing and able to do what it requires of them to enable it to fulfill its purposes. . . . They must be capable of fulfilling the conditions of action, and the conditions of self-restraint, which are necessary either for keeping the established polity in existence, or for enabling it to achieve the ends, its conduciveness to which forms its recommendation.

The failure of any of these conditions renders a form of government, whatever favourable promise it may otherwise hold out, unsuitable to the particular case.

The Triple Test of Popular Support

This triple test devised for specific forms of government may well be applied to the world state. Are the peoples of the world willing to accept world government, or are they at least not so unwilling as to erect an insurmountable obstacle to its establishment? Would they be willing and able to do what is necessary to keep world government standing? Would they be willing and able to do or refrain from doing what world government requires of them so that it may fulfill its purposes? The answers to these questions are implicit in what has been said above in connection with the problems of nationalism, nationalistic universalism, international morality, and world public opinion.[9] The answers are also implicit in what has been said about the conditions for the maintenance of domestic peace. The answers are bound to be in the negative.

No society exists coextensive with the presumed range of a world state. What exists is an international society of sovereign nations. There does not exist a supranational society that comprises all individual members of all nations and, hence, is identical with humanity politically organized. The most extensive society in which most men live and act in our times is the national society. The nation is, as we have seen, the recipient of man's highest secular loyalties. Beyond it there are other nations, but no community for which man would be willing to act regardless of what he understands the interests of his own nation to be. Men are willing to give food, clothing, and money to the needy regardless of nationality. But they prefer to keep the needy where they are rather than to allow them to go where they please and thus become useful citizens again. For, while international relief is regarded as compatible with the national interest, freedom of immigration is not. Under the present moral conditions of mankind, few men would act on behalf of a world government if the interests of their own nation, as they understand them, required a different course of action. On the contrary, the overwhelming majority would put what they regard as the welfare of their own nation above everything else, the interests of a world state included. In other words, the peoples of the

---

[9]See especially Chapter 17.

world are not willing to accept world government, and their overriding loyalty to the nation erects an insurmountable obstacle to its establishment.

Nor are the peoples of the world willing and able to do what is necessary to keep world government standing. For they are not prepared to perform that revaluation of all values, that unprecedented moral and political revolution, which would force the nation from its throne and put the political organization of humanity on it. They are willing and able to sacrifice and die so that national governments may be kept standing.

The odds are so much in favor of the nation that men who might be willing and able to sacrifice and die that the world state be kept standing do not even have the opportunity to do so in the world as it is constituted today. The man who would want to oppose the interests and policy of his own nation for the sake of humanity and its state would by that act of opposition (weakening his own nation) strengthen the nation with which his own government might be engaged in deadly combat. At best he might make himself the martyr of his convictions by inviting the punishment that the nation metes out to traitors. Nothing shows more strikingly the absence of the social and moral preconditions for anything resembling a world state than the moral paradox that a man who would want to act as a citizen of the world would by the conditions of the world be forced to act as partisan of another nation and as traitor to his own. For above one's own nation there is nothing political on behalf of which a man could act. There are only other nations besides one's own.

Finally, the peoples of the world are not willing and able to do what the world state requires of them so that it may fulfill its purposes. The prime purpose of a world state would be to maintain the peace of the world. To that end, the world state would have to perform three functions: (1) It would give humanity a legal personality that would keep the unity of mankind before its eyes; (2) it would create and keep in motion agencies for worldwide social change that might allow all groups of mankind to expect at least some satisfaction for their conflicting claims; (3) it would establish enforcement agencies that would meet any threat to the peace with overwhelming strength. One might concede the possibility, for which there is support in the public opinion polls referred to above,[10] that the peoples of the world would support the world state in the performance of function (1). Enough has already been said to the absence of support for function (3).[11] Let us, then, briefly examine the chances of the peoples of the world supporting the world state in the performance of function (2), which, as we know, is the very heart of the peace-preserving functions of any state.

We shall not dwell upon the problem of how the different peoples of the world shall be represented in legislative agencies for social change. Numerical representation would obviously be unacceptable to the white races, since it would put the world under the domination of the colored ones. Any type of representation that in violation of the majority principle would tend to stabilize white supremacy

---

[10]See page 334, note 17.
[11]See pages 333–34.

in the world would meet with the opposition of the colored races, who would thus be held in a permanent state of inferiority. Nor shall we dwell upon the obvious impossibility of putting such legislative agencies in operation, even if it were possible to establish them. A parliament representing peoples of such different moral convictions, political interests, and abilities for self-government as the Americans, the Chinese, the Indians, and the Russians would hardly be able to create out of these differences an operating whole. None of its constituent groups would willingly submit to the majority vote of a legislative assembly thus constituted. The threat and the actuality of civil war would hang over such institutions, which would have to substitute compulsion for the lacking moral and political consensus.

Let us consider two concrete issues with regard to which the claims of different nations traditionally collide: immigration and trade. A world state, like any other federal state, could not leave the regulation of interstate migration and interstate trade to the discretion of its component parts. It would itself have to regulate these issues. Even if the authority of the world state in these two respects were strictly circumscribed by the world constitution, is there any chance that the American people would be prepared to give a world government powers to open the borders of the United States for the annual immigration of, say, 100,000 Russians, 250,000 Chinese, and 200,000 Indians? And is it likely that the Soviet government would be inclined to allow the annual emigration of 10,600 Russians to the United States? Would the American people allow the import of any quantity of foreign agricultural products that might compete with domestic ones on equal terms? Is there any likelihood that the Russians would allow cheap consumer goods to be imported that might upset their planned economy and undermine confidence in their political system as well? If these questions must be answered in the negative, as obviously they must, how is a world state expected to govern at all? How is a world state expected to be able to resolve peacefully the tensions between nations that threaten the peace of the world?

There is no shirking the conclusion that international peace cannot be permanent without a world state and that a world state cannot be established under the present moral, social, and political conditions of the world. In the light of what has been said thus far in this book, there is also no shirking the further conclusion that in no period of modern history was civilization more in need of permanent peace and, hence, of a world state, and that in no period of modern history were the moral, social, and political conditions of the world less favorable for the establishment of a world state. There is, finally, no shirking the conclusion that, as there can be no state without a society willing and able to support it, there can be no world state without a world community willing and able to support it.

TWO FALSE SOLUTIONS

How, then, can a world state be created? Two solutions have been offered: world conquest and the examples of Switzerland and of the creation of the United States by the Constitutional Convention of 1787.

World Conquest

All historical political structures that have come close to being world states have had one thing in common: one powerful state created them by conquering the other members of what was then the known political world. Most of these world states have another thing in common: they hardly ever survived the lifetime of the founder.

In Western civilization the sole exception to that rule is the Roman Empire. This world state owed its unique longevity to two unusual transformations. The Roman conquerors transformed the conquered into Romans either by receiving them into the dominant civilization as Roman citizens or by uprooting them from their native civilizations and making them into slaves. Yet in the process of conquest, especially of the Hellenistic world, the Roman conqueror transformed himself by remaking his own civilization in the image of the civilizations of the conquered. Through this dual process of amalgamation, Rome created a new moral and political community coextensive with its conquests and capable of lending stability to the new state. To these two transformations must be added the further circumstance that after the conquest of the Mediterranean world the Roman Empire expanded into politically empty spaces, settled by barbarians whose loosely organized civilizations disintegrated under the impact of the superior and attractive civilization of the conqueror.

Most of the other world states disintegrated as soon as conquest had built them. For, beneath the political and military superstructure erected by force, the national societies lived on, each with its separate moral values and political interests and each trying to shake off the conqueror's yoke. These world states were not the natural outgrowth of a world community coextensive with them but a creation of force artificially superimposed upon a multiplicity of unwilling national societies. It is of course true that, for instance, Napoleon's would-be world state was destroyed by the untapped reserves of Great Britain and Russia. Yet, when in 1812 that empire for the first time showed its military weakness by failing in a major task of expansion, the national societies of which it was composed reasserted themselves and joined Great Britain and Russia in putting an end to it.

Conquests on a smaller scale, which are unable to unite the conquering and conquered populations in a new community, face the smaller risk of revolt and irredentist separatism. The relations between Ireland and Great Britain and between the nations of Eastern Europe and Russia are cases in point. If the conqueror can muster overwhelming strength, no danger to the peace may arise from the conflict of two national societies living within the same state. If, however, the strength of the conquered people is not out of all proportion to the conqueror's, a potential state of civil war between the conqueror and the conquered will sap the strength of the state, even though under the modern conditions of warfare it may not endanger its existence.[12]

---

[12]See, on this point, pages 389 ff.

Such are the likely consequences of limited conquests that are unable to create a new community coextensive with themselves. It follows that a world state created by conquest and lacking the support of a world community has a chance to maintain peace within its borders only if it can create and maintain complete discipline and loyalty among the millions of soldiers and policemen needed to enforce its rule over an unwilling humanity. Such a world state would be a totalitarian monster resting on feet of clay, the very thought of which startles the imagination.

The Examples of Switzerland and the United States

What the world state is expected to bring about, Switzerland seems to have already achieved—the creation of a new federal state out of a number of sovereign nations with language, culture, history, loyalties, and policies of their own. Switzerland has been able to unite twenty-two sovereign states, speaking four different languages, in one political organization. Why should the 150-odd nations of the world not be able to do the same? Let them adopt a federal constitution as the Swiss have done, let them act toward one another as the Swiss states do, and the problem of the world state will be solved. The argument seems to be persuasive and is considered frequently in popular discussions. It dissolves, however, when confronted with the facts of Swiss history.

First of all, the unified Swiss state dates from 1848. Before then the Swiss states formed a confederation that resembled more a successful League of Nations or United Nations than a single state. That confederation grew from a number of permanent alliances concluded among the so-called Forest Cantons and some of the City Cantons in the course of the fourteenth century. These alliances were the result of certain identical and complementary interests that drew these states together in defense against common dangers. Why did these alliances survive the special occasions from which they arose and even harden into the close ties of a confederation with common agencies of government? The answer to that question will provide the explanation to the phenomenon of Switzerland.

(1) The thirteen members of the original confederation, occupying a contiguous territory, were united in a common opposition to the German Empire and the Hapsburgs, of whom they had all been subjects, from whom they had liberated themselves in common efforts, and who remained the common enemies of the liberties of all of them. (2) The famous victories of the Swiss armies over the knights in the fourteenth and fifteenth centuries had a dual effect. They established for centuries the reputation of the Swiss as the most redoubtable soldiers in Europe, and they proved the virtual immunity from foreign attack of the mountain valleys that were the core of the original confederation. (3) Compared with these military risks that an attack upon the Swiss entailed, the attractions of victory were small. In view of the poverty of these valleys in natural resources, these attractions were exclusively strategic—that is, the control of some of the Alpine passes joining Italy with the north of Europe. Yet for four centuries, with the one significant exception of the Napoleonic Wars, the great rival powers adjacent to

Switzerland found it more advantageous to have the Swiss defend the Alpine passes against all warring nations than to try to capture them from the Swiss. It is, however, significant that the balance of power exerted this protective influence only as long as the rivalry among Switzerland's powerful neighbors lasted. The Napoleonic victories in Italy at once destroyed that protection, and from 1798 on Switzerland was the hapless prey of contending armies. It is also worth remembering that while Austria, Germany, and Italy were joined in the Triple Alliance the Italian general staff proposed six times to the German general staff to march through Switzerland in a joint campaign against France.

Thus it was not merely an act of will expressing itself in a constitutional arrangement but a number of peculiar and, in their combination, unique circumstances that made it possible for Switzerland to be born and survive. While these circumstances allowed Switzerland to survive in the midst of powerful neighbors, they did not permit it to maintain peace among its component states. Within the span of little more than 300 years, the Swiss states fought among themselves numerous minor wars and five religious wars involving all or virtually all of them, the last as late as 1847. A great number of revolutions and coups d'état round out the picture of civil strife.

What light, then, does the history of Switzerland shed upon the problem of the world state? We can subscribe to Rappard's conclusions that Switzerland as a confederation had limited national security only "by virtue of special circumstances alien to this regime itself. . . . In so far as the Swiss experience of five centuries of collective security can suggest a lesson to the present generation, this lesson is clearly negative. It confirms at the same time the observations drawn from the most recent past and the teachings of simple common sense. As long as the security of the international society depends only upon the free cooperation of fully sovereign states, it remains necessarily fragile."[13] Thus the Swiss experience confirms our own conclusions concerning the fragility of peace by limitation, while it emphasizes both the need and the difficulty of establishing a state above the national states.

The example of the way in which the United States was created is often cited as proof of the feasibility of creating a world state here and now by way of a constitutional convention. Actually, the example of the United States proves only the dependence upon a preexisting moral and political community of any state that can be expected to endure.

When the Constitutional Convention met in 1787, the thirteen states were sovereign in name rather than in political actuality. They did not constitute thirteen separate sovereignties about to merge into a single one. After they had declared their independence from Britain in 1776, sovereignty remained in suspense. By establishing the United States, they exchanged one sovereignty—that of the British Crown—for another. And they exchanged one common loyalty for another common loyalty. All the while they retained the same language, the same culture, the

[13]William E. Rappard, *Cinq siècles de sécurité collective (1291–1798)* (Paris: Librairie du Recueil Sirey, 1945), p. 594.

same national heritage, the same moral convictions, and the same political interests that had just been tested in a revolutionary war fought in unison under a single command. The thirteen colonies formed a moral and political community under the British Crown, they tested it and became fully aware of it in their common struggle against Britain, and they retained that community after they had won their independence. As John Jay put it in No. 2 of *The Federalist:*

> Providence has been pleased to give this one connected country to one united people; a people descended from the same ancestors, speaking the same language, professing the same religion, attached to the same principles of government, very similar in their manners and customs, and who, by their joint counsels, arms and efforts, fighting side by side throughout a long and bloody war, have nobly established their general liberty and independence. . . .
>
> Similar sentiments have hitherto prevailed among all orders and denominations of men among us. To all general purposes, we have uniformly been one people. Each individual citizen everywhere enjoying the same national rights, privileges, and protection. As a nation, we have made peace and war: as a nation, we have vanquished our common enemies: as a nation, we have formed alliances and made treaties, and entered into various compacts and conventions with foreign states.

What the convention of Philadelphia did was to replace one constitution, one sovereignty, and one state with another one, both resting upon the same preexisting community. The convention did not create one state where before there had been thirteen separate ones. Far from proving that a state can be created by agreement on the text of a constitution, the creation of the United States proves the truth of the two propositions advanced earlier: wars can occur within states as well as among states, and the United States was founded upon a moral and political community the Constitution did not create but found already in existence. The community of the American people antedated the American state, as a world community must antedate a world state.

30 The World Community

This last conclusion—that a world community must antedate a world state—has given birth to two efforts to create a world community: the United Nations Educational, Scientific, and Cultural Organization, known as UNESCO, and the other specialized agencies of the United Nations.[1]

THE CULTURAL APPROACH: UNESCO

According to Article 1 of the Constitution of UNESCO,

The purpose of the Organization is to contribute to peace and security by promoting collaboration among the nations through education, science, and culture in order to further universal respect for justice, for the rule of law, and for the human rights and fundamental freedoms which are affirmed for the peoples of the world, without distinction of race, sex, language, or religion, by the Charter of the United Nations.

   To realize this purpose the Organization will:

(a) collaborate in the work of advancing the mutual knowledge and understanding of peoples, through all means of mass communication and to that end recommend such international agreements as may be necessary to promote the free flow of ideas by word and image;

(b) give fresh impulse to popular education and to the spread of culture;

   by collaborating with Members, at their request, in the development of educational activities;

   by instituting collaboration among the nations to advance the ideal of equality of educational opportunity without regard to race, sex or any distinctions, economic or social;

---

[1]See, in connection with this chapter, what has been said above in Chapter 7 about world public opinion.

by suggesting educational methods best suited to prepare the children of the world for the responsibilities of freedom;

(c) maintain, increase, and diffuse knowledge;

by assuring the conservation and protection of the world's inheritance of books, works of art, and monuments of history and science, and recommending to the nations concerned the necessary international conventions;

by encouraging cooperation among the nations in all branches of intellectual activity, including the international exchange of persons active in the fields of education, science, and culture and the exchange of publications, objects of artistic and scientific interest, and other materials of information;

by initiating methods of international cooperation calculated to give the people of all countries access to the printed and published materials produced by any of them.

In order to evaluate the contribution UNESCO is able to make for the preservation of international peace, three distinctions must be made: (1) We are here not concerned with the contribution UNESCO is able to make to the dissemination and improvement of culture and education as ends in themselves. (2) We are here not concerned with the contribution UNESCO is able to make to the preservation of international peace through the very fact of international cooperation; this aspect of the problem will be dealt with in the last section of this chapter. (3) We are here concerned only with the question of what UNESCO can do for the preservation of international peace by promoting international understanding, education, and general cultural activities.

What the Carnegie Endowment for International Peace declared in its appraisal of UNESCO's program for 1948—"Above all else its individual items were not always clearly and obviously related to the safeguarding of peace and security,"[2]—is true of all activities of UNESCO, however meritorious they may be intrinsically. This defect is not an accidental quality of certain programs undertaken by UNESCO, which only need to be revised and tightened in order to fulfill their peace-preserving function. On the contrary, the defect is congenital, growing from the very philosophy that is at the foundation of the agency and permeates all its activities. Thus, summing up on November 17, 1952, the discussions of the General Conference of UNESCO, Mr. Jaime Torres Bodet, its outgoing director-general, warned "that the greatest danger UNESCO has to guard against is dissipation of its efforts."

The philosophy of UNESCO assumes that education (especially when it aims at international understanding), cultural exchange, and, in general, all activities that tend to increase contacts among members of different nations and make them understand one another contribute necessarily to the creation of an international community and the maintenance of peace. Implicit in this assumption is the supposition that nations are nationalistic and go to war with one another because they do not know one another well enough and because they operate on different levels of education and culture. Both assumptions are erroneous.

---

[2]*International Conciliation*, No. 438 (February 1948), p. 77.

Cultural Development and Peace

There are primitive peoples, completely lacking in institutionalized education, who are generally peace-loving and receptive to the influence of foreign cultures to the point of suicide. There are other peoples, highly educated and steeped in classical culture, such as the Germans, who throughout most of their history have been nationalistic and warlike. The Athenians under Pericles and the Italians of the Renaissance created cultures not equaled in the history of Western civilization, and both were at least as nationalistic and warlike in that period of their history as at any time before or after.

Furthermore, in the history of some nations, such as the British and the French, periods of nationalistic exclusiveness and warlike policies alternate with cosmopolitan and peaceful ones, and no correlation exists between these changes and the development of education and culture. The Chinese people have a tradition of respect for learning superior to that of any other people, and they can look back upon a history of cultural attainments longer than any other and at least as creative. These high qualities of education and culture have made the Chinese look with contempt on the profession of the soldier, as well as upon all other nations, which at the beginning of the nineteenth century were still regarded as barbarian vassals of the Chinese emperor. Yet all this has not made the Chinese people less nationalistic and more peaceful. Russian education in our time has reached a higher level of achievement than ever before, especially in the fields of literacy and technical education. Its excellence has had no influence upon the receptiveness of the Russian people to foreign ideas or upon the foreign policies of the Russian government.

These examples, taken at random, show that the quantity and quality of education and culture as such is obviously irrelevant to the issue of a world community. That issue hinges, not upon knowledge and the creation and appreciation of cultural values, but upon a moral and political transformation of unprecedented dimensions.

Cultural Unity and Peace

What has been said of education and culture as such holds true also of educational and cultural activities aiming at the interchange of the products of different national cultures. The existence of a multitude of interpersonal relations transcending national boundaries is no answer to our problem. More particularly, the existence of intellectual and esthetic ties across national boundaries proves nothing in favor of a world community. A world community with political potentialities is a community of moral standards and political action, not of intellect and sentiments. That an intellectual elite in the United States enjoys Russian music and literature and that Shakespeare has not been banned from the Russian stage has no relevance at all for the problem with which we are concerned. This sharing of the same intellectual and esthetic experiences by members of different nations does not create a society, for it does not create morally and politically relevant actions on the part of the members of different nations with respect to each other that they would not have undertaken had they not shared in those experiences.

It should be remembered that on a much higher plane than the intellectual and esthetic, and with the objective of clearly defined action, the nations of the West, Russia included, have shared the same experiences for more than a thousand years. They have prayed to the same God, have held the same fundamental religious beliefs, have been bound by the same moral laws, and have had the same ritual symbols in common. That community of religious experiences, much more intimately related to the whole personality of the individual and to his actions than anything that supranational intellectual and esthetic experiences have to offer, has been able to create an international community of sorts but not an international community sufficiently integrated to make a world state possible. How, then, can we expect that the melodies of Tchaikovsky, the profundities of Dostoevsky, the insights of *The Federalist,* and the imagery of *Moby Dick,* which might be shared by all Americans and Russians alike, could create not only a fleeting community of feeling but a community of moral valuations and political actions shunting aside old loyalties and establishing new ones?

History has given an unmistakable answer to that question. Cultural unity, much closer than anything UNESCO can plan and achieve, has coexisted with war in all periods of history. We are not speaking here of civil wars, which by definition are fought by members of the same national culture. The wars among the Greek city-states, the European wars of the Middle Ages, the Italian wars of the Renaissance, the religious wars of the sixteenth and seventeenth centuries, even the wars of the eighteenth century insofar as the elite was concerned, were fought within the framework of a homogeneous culture. These cultures had all essentials in common: language, religion, education, literature, art. Yet these cultures did not create a community, coextensive with themselves, that could have kept disruptive tendencies in check and channeled them into peaceful outlets. How, then, can one expect that such a community will be created through interchange among cultures so diverse in all the respects in which those historical ones were homogeneous?

International Understanding and Peace

It is in the third purpose of UNESCO, international understanding, that the basic fallacy of UNESCO's conception of international affairs comes to the fore. International conflicts, it is believed, are the result of an intellectual deficiency, of ignorance and lack of judgment as to the qualities of other peoples. If Americans could only come to understand the Russians, and vice versa, they would realize how much they are alike, how much they have in common, and how little they have to fight about. The argument is fallacious on two counts.

Individual experience, which anybody can duplicate at will, shows that increased friendship is not necessarily a concomitant of increased understanding. There are, of course, numerous instances in which A has misunderstood the character and the motives of B and in which clarification of the facts will remove the source of conflict. Such is not the case when A and B are engaged in a conflict in which their vital interests are at stake. A does not fight B for economic advantage because he misunderstands the intentions of B; it is rather because he understands them only too well. Many an American GI went to France full of sentimental friendship for the French people whom he did not know. His friendly feelings did not survive the shock of understanding. The similar experiences of many friendly visitors to Russia are too typical to need elaboration.

Among those who from the beginning were most firmly opposed to the foreign objectives of the National Socialist regime, even at the risk of war, were some who had a profound understanding of German culture. It was exactly that understanding that made them implacable enemies of the National Socialist regime. Similarly, the students of Russian history and culture, those who really understand Russia and the Russians, have as a rule been equally unaffected by the pro- and anti-Russian hysteria. They have known the traditional objectives of Russian expansionism, as well as the traditional methods of Russian diplomacy. If their understanding had had an influence upon the conduct of foreign affairs in the Western democracies, that conduct would certainly have been more intelligent and successful than it actually was. Whether or not such understanding would have made for better relations with the Soviet Union is an open question. An intelligent and successful foreign policy depends upon the Americans' and the Russians' understanding what both nations are and want. Peace between the United States and the Soviet Union depends in the last analysis upon whether what one of them is and wants is compatible with what the other one is and wants.

This observation points up the other fallacy in UNESCO's conception of international affairs. The conception that international conflicts can be eliminated through international understanding rests on the implicit assumption that the issues of international conflicts, born as they are of misunderstandings, are but imaginary and that actually no issue worth fighting about stands between nation and nation. Nothing could be farther from the truth. All the great wars that decided the course of history and changed the political face of the earth were fought for real stakes, not for imaginary ones. The issue in those great convulsions was invariably: Who shall rule and who shall be ruled? Who shall be free, and who slave?

Was misunderstanding at the root of the issue between the Greeks and the Persians, between the Athenians and the Macedonians, between the Jews and the Romans, between emperor and pope, between the English and the French in the late Middle Ages, between the Turks and the Austrians, between Napoleon and Europe, between Hitler and the world? Was misunderstanding of the other side's culture, character, and intentions the issue, so that those wars were fought over no real issue at all? Or could it not rather be maintained that in many of these conflicts it was exactly the misunderstanding of the would-be conqueror's culture, character, and intentions that preserved peace for a while, whereas the understanding of these factors made war inevitable? So long as the Athenians refused to heed the warnings of Demosthenes, the threat of war remained remote. It was only when, too late for their salvation, they understood the nature of the Macedonian Empire and of its policies that war became inevitable. That correlation between understanding and the inevitability of conflict is one of the melancholy lessons history conveys to posterity: The more thoroughly one understands the other side's position, character, and intentions, the more inevitable the conflict often appears to be.

Irrespective of its great intrinsic merits, the program of UNESCO is irrelevant to the problem of world community because its diagnosis of the bars to world community so completely misses the point. The problem of world community is a moral and political, and not an intellectual and esthetic, one. The world community is a community of moral judgments and political actions, not of intellectual endowments and esthetic appreciation. Let us suppose that American and Russian education and culture could be brought to the same level of excellence or completely amalgamated and that Russians would take to Mark Twain as Americans would take to Gogol. If that were the case, the problem of who shall control the Middle East would still stand between the United States and the Soviet Union, as it does today. So long as men continue to judge and act in accordance with national rather than supranational standards and loyalties, the world community remains a postulate that still awaits its realization.

THE FUNCTIONAL APPROACH

The Specialized Agencies of the United Nations

How is such a transformation of standards and loyalties to be brought about? The specialized agencies of the United Nations have pointed a way. They are autonomous organizations, owing their existence to particular agreements among a number of states whose identity differs from agency to agency. They have their own constitutions, their own budgets, and their own policymaking and administrative bodies, and each agency has a membership of its own. The names of some of these agencies are indicative of the functions they fulfill: International Labor Organization, Food and Agriculture Organization, International Bank for Reconstruction and Development, International Monetary Fund, International Telecommunication Union, Universal Postal Union, International Civil Aviation Organization, UNESCO, World Heath Organization.

Chapters IX and X of the Charter of the United Nations provide for organizational and functional relations between the specialized agencies and the United Nations. The Charter stresses to a degree unknown in the history of international organization the responsibility of the United Nations for the rights and the well-being of the individual regardless of national affiliation. It has created in the Economic and Social Council a special organ for the discharge of that responsibility. The Economic and Social Council has the authority to conclude agreements—and has done so in a number of instances—with the specialized agencies, "defining the terms on which the agency concerned shall be brought into relationship with the United Nations."[3] The United Nations may "make recommendations for the coordination of the policies and activities of the specialized agencies."[4] The Economic and Social Council may take steps to receive regular and special reports from the specialized agencies and may perform services at the request of members of the United Nations and of specialized agencies.[5]

What is the philosophy underlying the social and economic activities the specialized agencies are undertaking with the cooperation of the United Nations? What is the relevance of that philosophy for the problem of the international community? This question has been answered with great brilliance and persuasiveness by Professor Mitrany:

> If the evil of conflict and war springs from the division of the world into detached and competing political units, will it be exorcised simply by changing or reducing the lines of division? Any political reorganization into separate units must, sooner or later, produce the same effects; any international system that is to usher in a new world must produce the opposite effect of subduing political division. As far as one can see, there are only two ways of achieving that end. One would be through a world state which would wipe out political divisions forcibly; the other is the way discussed in these pages, which would rather overlay political divisions with a spreading web of international activities and agencies, in which and through which the interests and life of all the nations would be gradually integrated. That is the fundamental change to which any effective international system must aspire and contribute: to make international government co-extensive with international activities. . . . It must care as much as possible for common needs that are evident, while presuming as little as possible upon a social unity which is still only latent and unrecognized. . . . [In that way] The community itself will acquire a living body not through a written act of faith but through active organic development. . . . That trend is to organize government along the lines of specific ends and needs, and according to the condition of their time and place, in lieu of the traditional organization on the basis of a set constitutional division of jurisdiction of rights and powers. . . . The functional approach . . . would help the growth of such positive and constructive common work, of common habits and interests, making frontier lines meaningless by overlaying them with a natural growth of common activities and common administrative agencies.[6]

This is indeed the way in which communities grow and in which governments grow out of communities. We have already noted that sovereignty was a fact before it was a theory and that the American people formed a community before they created a state. How, then, can a community be created where none exists?

---

[3] Article 63, paragraph 1.
[4] Article 58; cf. also Articles 62, 63, paragraph 2.
[5] Articles 64, 66, paragraph 2.
[6] David Mitrany, *A Working Peace System*, 4th ed. (London: National Peace Council, 1946), pp. 14, 15, 18, 28, 34, 35. (Reprinted by permission of the author.)

According to Professor Mitrany, an international community must grow from the satisfaction of common needs shared by members of different nations. The specialized agencies of the United Nations, serving peoples all over the world regardless of national boundaries, could create by the very fact of their existence and performance a community of interests, valuations, and actions. Ultimately, if such international agencies were numerous enough and served the most important wants of most peoples of the earth, the loyalties to these institutions and to the international community of which they would be the agencies would supersede the loyalties to the separate national societies and their institutions. For proof that such a development is feasible under present world conditions, Professor Mitrany relies in the main upon the experiences the Allies had during the Second World War with functional international agencies, such as the Anglo-American Raw Materials Board and the Middle East Supply Centre. These examples put in sharp focus the problem raised by the functional approach.

In war the loyalties to the common cause and the common interest in victory over the common enemy overrode separate national loyalties and made possible the successful operation of international functional agencies of major importance. In peace, what the nation has to offer the individual seems to outweigh by far the benefits to be derived from the international functional agencies, although it is ever more widely recognized that the citizens of different nations have certain interests in common, such as physical survival through avoidance of nuclear war and nonproliferation of nuclear weapons, protection of the natural environment, and economic well-being through the control of international trade, the monetary system, and global corporations, that can be satisfied only a supranational basis. More particularly, the conflicts of power that separate nations and the insecurity they create make identification with the nation the overriding concern of most members of all nations. The nation offers the individual protection, vicarious gratification of power drives, and immediate satisfaction of material needs. With few sporadic exceptions, such as the assistance of the World Health Organization in combating an epidemic, the specialized agencies of the United Nations offer hopes and satisfactions far removed from the direct experiences of ordinary people and that may make themselves felt only through the intermediary of a number of national agencies, so that its international origins are hard to trace. When mailing a letter to a foreign country, who would think of giving thanks to the Universal Postal Union for the contribution that international agency is making to the operation?

Thus the contributions international functional agencies make to the well-being of members of all nations fade into the background. What stands before the eyes of all are the immense political conflicts that divide the great nations of the earth and threaten the well-being of the loser, if not his very existence. This is not primarily a matter of false emphasis born of ignorance. It is rather the recognition of the undeniable fact that, from a functional point of view, what the national government does or does not do is much more important for the satisfaction of individual wants than what an international functional agency does or does not do. More important than anything else is the ability of the national government

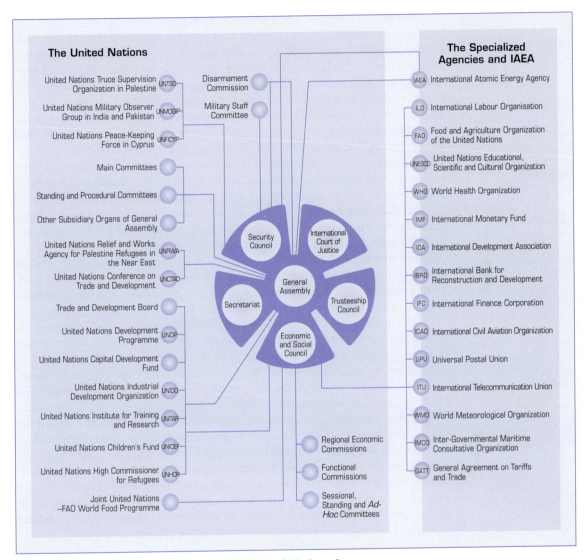

The United Nations System

to defend its territory and citizens against foreign aggression and within its territory to maintain peace and keep in operation the processes of social change. The neglect with which the public treats international functional agencies is but the exaggerated reflection of the minor role these agencies play for the solution of important international issues.

This is true when no conflict exists between the national interests of a particular nation and the objectives and operations of an international functional agency. In case of such conflict, the national interest wins out over the international objective. Thus it is deeply significant that, of the two great antagonists on the scene of contemporary world politics, one, the Soviet Union, traditionally fearful of foreign intervention and jealous of the integrity of its political and economic system, has joined only three of the new specialized agencies—the International Labor Organization, UNESCO, and the World Meteorological Organization—is collaborating with one—the World Health Organization—and is a member of the two that have existed for the better part of a century and are the most unpolitical in character—the Universal Postal Union, established in 1874, and the International Telecommunication Union, which replaced the International Telegraph and Radiotelegraph Unions of 1865 and 1912, respectively.

The answer to the question of how a world community can be created by way of the functional approach, then, lies in the sphere of international politics. This is borne out by the analysis of the role three different kinds of functional agencies play and are able to play in this respect: the North Atlantic Treaty Organization, the European Communities, and the agencies for economic and technical assistance. All these agencies have this in common: they try to solve a common problem, which none of the participants could have solved by its own efforts, through the coordination of technical functions on a supranational level. To that end they use and develop the novel procedures of international government, to which we have referred above.[7]

These procedures are novel in two different respects. They combine, following the model of the new United Nations, central direction in the execution of policies with negotiated agreement as to the nature of the policies to be pursued. In this fashion they combine the factual superiority of power and resources, which resides either in one of the participants or in the agency itself, with the legal claim of all the participants to equality.

These procedures are novel also—and in this respect they go beyond the model of the new United Nations—in that they tend to obliterate the time-honored distinction between international and domestic affairs and, with it, the equally time-honored principle of nonintervention in the domestic affairs of other nations. For it is of the very essence of these new procedures that they transform into a matter of international concern such issues as military preparations, industrial productivity, and prices and tariffs, which have traditionally been considered to fall in the exclusive domestic jurisdiction of the individual nations.

The North Atlantic Treaty Organization (NATO)

The treaty establishing NATO was signed on April 4, 1949, by Belgium, Canada, Denmark, France, Great Britain, Iceland, Italy, Luxembourg, The Netherlands, Norway, Portugal, and the United States; Greece and Turkey joined the organization in 1952, Germany in 1955. The treaty establishes the principle of collective security for its members. According to Article 5, "an armed attack against one or more of them in Europe or North America shall be considered an attack against them all . . . ," to be resisted by all. This general purpose does not distinguish NATO from a traditional

---

[7]See pages 498 ff.

alliance, nor does the immediate objective of increasing the military strength of the members. Yet NATO has as further objectives the maintenance of economic and political stability among its members and the establishment of closer ties among them in general and endeavors to achieve these objectives through an intricate multinational organization. The purpose of this organization is to give central direction to the military and economic policies of the members on the basis of negotiated agreements among them. In its comprehensive objectives and the techniques used to accomplish them, NATO indeed moves beyond the limits of a traditional alliance toward a novel type of functional organization.

The organization of NATO is headed by the North Atlantic Council, composed of cabinet officers of each member state. The council is the supreme governing body of NATO; it lays down production schedules for the individual members, budgetary requirements, the quality and quantity of military contributions, and the like. The council is assisted by an international staff under a secretary general, which is a truly international body working exclusively for the organization; it is the permanent civilian bureaucracy of NATO.

Under the council operate a number of civilian and military agencies. The military organization of NATO is headed by the Military Committee, composed of the chiefs of staff of the member nations. It advises the council on military matters, plans military measures for the common defense, and is assisted by the International Military Staff. It is responsible for the general strategy of the North Atlantic defense and gives military guidance and instructions to the various NATO commands. Of these commands, Supreme Headquarters, Allied Powers, Europe (SHAPE), is the most important. Under the supreme allied commander in Europe, it directs the integrated forces in Western Europe. SHAPE, too, is a truly international agency, composed as it is of high officers of the different member nations. The supreme commander receives his orders from the Military Committee but has direct access to the chiefs of staff and other high officers of any of the member nations.

NATO is in its scope—comprising the military, economic, and financial policies of the member nations—the most ambitious of the new functional agencies that try to bring the new procedures of international government to bear on a specific technical field for a common purpose. The relative strength and relationship of three factors will decide whether or not NATO will achieve its immediate military objective and its broader and more remote political and social goals. How urgent will the members of NATO consider the establishment of a unified defense system? How important will their separate national interests appear to them in comparison with the urgency of that common military task? Finally, how will American power influence the relationships that the policies of the member nations will establish between that common military task and these separate interests? In other words, to which of the two will the policies of the member nations give priority over the other?

This interplay between a common supranational interest, separate national interests, and American power will determine whether or not NATO will accomplish what it has set out to do. The interplay of the first two factors is decisive not only for the future of NATO but for the success or failure of the other designs, in the form of the European Communities, to unite the nations of Europe on a functional basis.

The European Communities

The European Communities consist of the European Coal and Steel Community, the European Economic Community (Common Market), and the European Atomic Energy Community (Euratom). The European Coal and Steel Community came into effect on July 25, 1952, while the other two communities started to operate on January 1, 1958. Their membership is identical, consisting of Belgium, France, West Germany, Italy, Luxembourg, and The Netherlands. Their organs, originally similar but separate, were merged in 1967. In consequence, the communities operate now under a common executive authority called the European Commission, a common parliament called the Assembly, and a common Court of Justice; a Council of Ministers and an Economic and Social Committee round out the organs. Since the common institutions are patterned after those of the European Steel and Coal Community, an analysis of the latter will serve to elucidate the governmental structure.

The European Coal and Steel Community was established for the purpose of creating a single market for the coal and steel production of its members. The High Authority, predecessor of the European Commission, was the executive organ of the community. Supposed to act "in complete independence, in the general interest of the community" without instructions from any government, it was a truly supranational agency. It had the power to make binding decisions with regard to prices for coal and steel, taxation, fines for violations of its orders, the direction of investments, and borrowing and lending. The Common Assembly was composed of 78 members chosen either by the national parliaments or popular election. It had to approve the annual report of the High Authority and could, by a two-thirds vote, force its members to resign. The Council of Ministers, composed of one representative from each member state, served as the link between the High Authority and the member states and also as a check upon the High Authority, since for the most far-reaching decisions of the latter the concurrence of the council was required. The Court of Justice decided appeals from decisions of the High Authority and annulled unconstitutional acts of the Common Assembly and the Council of Ministers.

The importance of all the European Communities as functional organizations comes to the fore in the political purpose they are intended to serve. Aside from trying to compensate, through united effort, for the loss of power of the individual European nations, the European Communities are a revolutionary attempt at solving an age-old political problem. That problem is characterized by two basic facts. One is the natural superiority of Germany among the nations of Europe; the other is the unwillingness of the other European nations to accept that natural superiority. Since 1870 the great convulsions on the European continent, and the diplomatic moves preceding those convulsions, have all been dominated by those two facts.

Before and after the First World War, France tried to deal with those two facts by using the methods suggested by the balance of power as it had been practiced in previous centuries. It tried to make up for its own inherent weakness by a system of alliances that would counterbalance that natural superiority of Germany. In those attempts France failed. In both world wars, France was saved neither by its own strength nor by the strength of its continental allies but by the intervention of Great Britain and, more particularly, of the United States. This failure is another fact that we must keep in mind in assessing the chances of the European Communities.

These communities constitute a revolutionary departure from the traditional methods by which inferior powers have tried to counter a superior one. For instead of countering that potentially superior power by a system of alliances, the other nations of Western Europe are trying to draw, as it were, Germany into their arms in order to disarm it and to make the superior strength of Germany innocuous. The European Communities are, in other words, an attempt at fusing a superior power with an inferior one for the purpose of creating a common control of their pooled strength. Thus Western Europe hopes to be able to forestall the use of that superior German power for hostile purposes, especially for the creation of a new German hegemony on the European continent.

The European Communities are equally revolutionary in the manner in which they try to realize this objective. In former times, and especially in the interwar period, the unification of Europe was attempted, as it were, from the top. That is to say, an all-comprehensive legal organization was proposed or established; a legal framework for an overall government was the goal of those attempts. The Council of Europe, composed of a Committee of Ministers and a Consultative Assembly of national delegates, today moves in that tradition. The European Communities start, as it were, from the opposite end of the envisaged structure. They start from the bottom rather than from the top. They try to create a functional unity within a limited sphere of action, expecting that the operation of that unity within that limited sphere will lead, first of all, to a community of interests within that particular sphere, and that this example will then spread to other functional fields, such as agriculture, transport, electricity, and military forces. Finally, it is hoped that out of this series of functional units political unity will grow organically. Once all the functional organizations have been established as going concerns, sovereignty will have been transferred in fact to a common European government by gradual steps, without the individual nations really being aware of it.

The success of this design depends upon three fundamental factors, all having to do with the national interests of the individual nations and with the distribution of power among them. The first question one must ask in this respect is, What is the internal distribution of power within and among the different agencies of the European Communities? What, for instance, is the composition of the European Commission? Is it composed of technicians following an independent course of action on the basis of their technical convictions about the best techniques of, say, coal and steel production and distribution, or is it composed of representatives of the member governments, perhaps not taking orders from them, but being unable to banish from their minds the national interests of the member nations and their own dedication to them?

What is the relation between the European Commission and the assembly, the pseudoparliamentary representation of the member nations? And what of the relations between the commission and the council, the representatives of the governments concerned? What kind of use does the court make of its enormous powers, at least on paper, with regard to the activities of the commission, the assembly, and the council?

Second, what is the distribution of power between the agencies of the communities and the member governments? According to the statute, the High Authority as the executive organ of the Coal and Steel Community, for instance, has primarily investigative and indirect powers. It has almost no direct administrative powers within the territories of the constituent nations. Its main power lies in the field of investment, and here its power is primarily the negative one of withholding investments, loans, and guarantees for loans from recalcitrant member nations. But what if those recalcitrant member nations do not need those loans, or can get them elsewhere?

Third, what is the degree of unity among the member nations in the economic, military, and political fields? In other words, what is the relationship between the hoped-for community of interests in the spheres of coal and steel, atomic energy, and trade and the actual economic, military, and political interests of the individual member nations? To what extent will, for instance, the unfulfilled aspirations of all Germans for the reunification of their country or those of France for a dominant national position get in the way of the operations of the communities? Are the economic interests of France and Germany in the communities strong enough to counteract and even to transcend their unfulfilled national aspirations?

Agencies for Economic and Technical Assistance

Both NATO and the European Communities are relatively advanced functional agencies in purpose, subject matter, and procedures. Yet they are much inferior to many functional agencies, less advanced in these respects, in that they are of a regional character. If they succeed, they will have overcome the obsolescent separatism of the nation state. Their contribution to a world community will still be a moot question, to be answered by the policies the new supranational, regional units will pursue toward the rest of the world.[8] Under the conditions of contemporary world politics, functional agencies of a regional nature cannot help being drawn into the unsettled political conflicts on one or the other side. Thus, while they exert a unifying influence vis-à-vis the nation-state, in view of the ultimate goal of a world community they are bound, at least in the short run, to strengthen the divisive forces.

---

[8]See, on the ambivalence of overcoming nationalism by regionalism, page 339.

The agencies for economic and technical assistance avoid in good measure the ambivalence of regionalism, for the assistance most of them provide is, at least potentially, worldwide in scope. Yet they are amorphous in subject matter, purpose, and procedure. Hence, their influence upon the unification of the world on a functional basis is bound, in any case in the short run, to be intangible, vague, and politically ineffective. This is true of the three main groups of agencies of this type: the United Nations specialized agencies and Technical Assistance Board, those established unilaterally by the United States and the Soviet Union, and those provided for by the British Commonwealth of Nations under the Colombo Plan. These agencies have been politically most effective when they have been closely tied to the political interests of a particular nation, such as the Soviet Union, thus negating, at least in the short run, the ideal of a world community.

Aside from its obvious humanitarian aspects, the purpose of such a program of economic and technical assistance has less obvious political implications. For the politically most important underdeveloped areas of the world are the uncommitted nations for whose allegiance East and West compete. In that competition the promise of a better life is an important weapon, and the actual provision of a better life is more important still.[9]

Yet it is not aid as such or its beneficial results that creates political loyalties on the part of the recipients, but the positive relationship that the mind of the recipient establishes between the aid and its beneficial results, on the one hand, and the political philosophy, the political system, and the political objectives of the giver, on the other. That is to say, if the recipient continues to disapprove of the political philosophy, system, and objectives of the giver, despite the aid he has received, the political effects of the aid are lost. The same is true if he remains unconvinced that the aid received is but a natural, if not inevitable, manifestation of the political philosophy, system, and objectives of the giver. Economic and technical aid remains politically ineffectual as long as the recipient says either "Aid is good, but the politics of the giver are bad" or "Aid is good, but the politics of the giver good, bad, or indifferent have nothing to do with it."[10]

In order to be effective for the establishment of a community between giver and recipient, the procedures through which aid is given, and the subject matter to which it is applied, must lend themselves to the creation of a connection between aid and the politics of the giver that reflects credit upon the latter. In the rare instances in which such a connection has been established through the foreign-aid policies of the United Nations or Western agencies, it has been by accident rather than by design; for neither the subject matter nor the procedures, as they exist at present, can by themselves be conducive to the establishment of such a connection.

---

[9]See what has been said about this aspect of the struggle for the minds of men on pages 339 ff.
[10]We assume here, in order to simplify and limit the argument to the essentials of its political aspects, that economic and technical aid will necessarily be welcomed as "good" by the recipient. Actually, such assistance may well create great psychological tensions and social dislocations, raise in the short run more problems than it solves, and be resented rather than welcomed.

The subject matter of economic and technical aid covers the whole range of personal and social needs from education and health to public administration and hydroelectric power. This proliferation of effort is enormous, not only with regard to the subject matter to which it is applied but also with regard to the source from which it emanates in the form of different national and international agencies. It makes it hard for the recipients to attribute the benefits they receive to a particular supranational source and to transform that source into a symbol of benevolence in which they have a higher stake than in their national governments—and to which, therefore, they must transfer their loyalties.

This transfer of national loyalties is made even more difficult by the standard procedures these agencies follow. They give aid generally only upon the request of individual governments. Furthermore, purpose, kind of aid, and the modalities of its execution are subject to agreement between the agency and the recipient government. Under such conditions, the agency is likely to appear to the individual recipients as the agent of their respective governments, assisting them on their initiative and according to their plan. This appearance will tend to strengthen their national loyalties and will, by the same token, impede that transfer of loyalties to a supranational symbol upon which we found the development of a world community to depend. Thus economic and technical assistance, as it is presently conceived, is at best likely to leave the problem of international peace where it found it, and at worst to contribute to making international conflicts more intractable by strengthening the national loyalties of individuals throughout the underdeveloped areas of the world.

We proposed that the first step toward the peaceful settlement of the international conflicts that might lead to war was the creation of an international community as foundation for a world state. We find that the creation of an international community presupposes at least the mitigation and minimization of international conflicts so that the interests uniting members of different nations may outweigh the interests separating them. How can international conflicts be mitigated and minimized? This is the final question that calls for examination.

PART TEN

THE PROBLEM OF PEACE

Peace Through Accommodation

31 Diplomacy

We have seen that international peace cannot be preserved through the limitation of national sovereignty, and we found the reasons for this failure in the very nature of the relations among nations. We concluded that international peace through the transformation of the present society of sovereign nations into a world state is unattainable under the moral, social, and political conditions prevailing in the world in our time. If the world state is unattainable in our world, yet indispensable for the survival of that world, it is necessary to create the conditions under which it will not be impossible from the outset to establish a world state. As the prime requisite for the creation of such conditions, we suggested the mitigation and minimization of those political conflicts that in our time pit the two superpowers against each other and evoke the specter of a cataclysmic war. This method of establishing the preconditions for permanent peace we call peace through accommodation. Its instrument is diplomacy.

FOUR TASKS OF DIPLOMACY

We have already had occasion to emphasize the paramount importance of diplomacy as an element of national power. The importance of diplomacy for the preservation of international peace is but a particular aspect of that general function. For a diplomacy that ends in war has failed in its primary objective: the promotion of the national interest by peaceful means. This has always been so and is particularly so in view of the destructive potentialities of total war.

Taken in its widest meaning, comprising the whole range of foreign policy, the task of diplomacy is fourfold: (1) Diplomacy must determine its objectives in the light of the power actually and potentially available for the pursuit of these objectives; (2) diplomacy must assess the objectives of other nations and the power actually and potentially available for the pursuit of these objectives; (3) diplomacy must determine to what extent these different objectives are compatible with one another; and (4) diplomacy must employ the means suited to the pursuit of its objectives.

Failure in any one of these tasks may jeopardize the success of foreign policy, and with it the peace of the world.

A nation that sets itself goals it has not the power to attain may have to face the risk of war on two counts. Such a nation is likely to dissipate its strength and not to be strong enough at all points of friction to deter a hostile nation from challenging it beyond endurance. The failure of its foreign policy may force the nation to retrace its steps and to redefine its objectives in view of its actual strength. Yet it is more likely that, under the pressure of an inflamed public opinion, such a nation will go forward on the road toward an unattainable goal, strain all its resources to achieve it, and, finally, confounding the national interest with that goal, seek in war the solution to a problem that cannot be solved by peaceful means.

A nation will also invite war if its diplomacy wrongly assesses the objectives of other nations and the power at their disposal. We have already pointed to the error of mistaking a policy of the status quo for a policy of imperialism, and vice versa, and of confounding one kind of imperialism with another.[1] A nation that mistakes a policy of imperialism for a policy of the status quo will be unprepared to meet the threat to its own existence that the other nation's policy entails. Its weakness will invite attack and may make war inevitable. A nation that mistakes a policy of the status quo for a policy of imperialism will evoke through its disproportionate reaction the very danger of war that it is trying to avoid. For as A mistakes B's policy for imperialism, so B might mistake A's defensive reaction for imperialism. Thus both nations, each intent upon forestalling imaginary aggression from the other side, will rush to arms. Similarly, the confusion of one type of imperialism with another may call for disproportionate reaction and thus evoke the risk of war.

As for the assessment of the power of other nations, either to overrate or to underrate it may be equally fatal to the cause of peace. By overrating the power of B, A may prefer to yield to B's demands until, finally, A is forced to fight for its very existence under the most unfavorable conditions. By underrating the power of B, A may become overconfident in its assumed superiority. A may advance demands and impose conditions upon B that the latter is supposedly too weak to resist. Not suspecting B's actual power of resistance, A may be faced with the alternative of either retreating and conceding defeat or of advancing and risking war.

A nation that seeks to pursue an intelligent and peaceful foreign policy cannot cease comparing its own objectives and the objectives of other nations in the light of their compatibility. If they are compatible, no problem arises. If they are not compatible, A must determine whether its objectives are so vital to itself that they must be pursued despite that incompatibility with the objectives of B. If it is found that A's vital interests can be safeguarded without the attainment of these objectives, they ought to be abandoned. On the other hand, if A finds that these objectives are essential for its vital interests, A must then ask itself whether B's objectives, incompatible with its own, are essential for B's vital interests. If the answer seems to be in

---

[1]See pages 75 ff, 102 ff.

the negative, A must try to induce B to abandon its objectives, offering B equivalents not vital to A. In other words, through diplomatic bargaining, the give-and-take of compromise, a way must be sought by which the interests of A and B can be reconciled.

Finally, if the incompatible objectives of A and B should prove to be vital to either side, a way might still be sought in which the vital interests of A and B might be redefined and reconciled, and their objectives thus made compatible with each other. Here, however—even provided that both sides pursue intelligent and peaceful policies—A and B are moving dangerously close to the brink of war.

It is the final task of an intelligent diplomacy, intent upon preserving peace, to choose the appropriate means for pursuing its objectives. The means at the disposal of diplomacy are three: persuasion, compromise, and threat of force. No diplomacy relying only upon the threat of force can claim to be both intelligent and peaceful. No diplomacy that would stake everything on persuasion and compromise deserves to be called intelligent. Rarely, if ever, in the conduct of the foreign policy of a great power is there justification for using only one method to the exclusion of the others. Generally, the diplomatic representative of a great power, in order to be able to serve both the interests of his country and the interests of peace, must at the same time use persuasion, hold out the advantages of a compromise, and impress the other side with the military strength of his country.

The art of diplomacy consists in putting the right emphasis at any particular moment on each of these three means at its disposal. A diplomacy that has successfully discharged its other functions may well fail in advancing the national interest and preserving peace if it stresses persuasion when the give-and-take of compromise is primarily required by the circumstances of the case. A diplomacy that puts most of its eggs in the basket of compromise when the military might of the nation should be predominantly displayed, or stresses military might when the political situation calls for persuasion and compromise, will likewise fail.

INSTRUMENTS OF DIPLOMACY

These four tasks of diplomacy are the basic elements of which foreign policy consists everywhere and at all times. One might say that the chieftain of a primitive tribe maintaining political relations with a neighboring tribe will have to perform these four functions in order to be successful and preserve peace. The need for the performance of these functions is as old and as widespread as international politics itself. Only the performance of these functions by organized agencies is of relatively recent origin.

The organized instruments of diplomacy are two: the foreign offices in the capitals of the respective nations and the diplomatic representatives sent by the foreign offices to the capitals of foreign nations. The foreign office is the policy-forming agency, the brains of foreign policy where the impressions from the outside world are gathered and evaluated, where foreign policy is formulated, and where the impulses emanate that the diplomatic representatives transform into actual foreign policy. While the foreign office is the brains of foreign policy, the diplomatic representatives are its eyes, ears, and mouth; its fingertips; and, as it were, its itinerant incarnations. The diplomat fulfills three basic functions for his government—symbolic, legal, and political.

Symbolic Representation

The diplomat is first of all the symbolic representative of his country. As such, he must continuously perform symbolic functions and expose himself to symbolic functions on the part of other diplomats and of the foreign government to which he is accredited. These functions serve to test, on the one hand, the prestige in which his nation is held abroad and, on the other, the prestige with which his own nation regards the country to whose government he is accredited. The American ambassador in London will, for instance, represent the president of the United States at the official functions to which he is invited and at those that he gives himself, such as state dinners, receptions, and the like. He extends and receives congratulations and condolences upon occasions joyful or sad for the nations concerned. He performs the symbolic functions of the diplomatic ceremonial.[2]

As a significant example of the symbolic function of diplomacy, mention has been made of the lavish entertainment most diplomatic missions feel constrained to offer to the members of the government to which they are accredited, to their fellow diplomats, and to the high society of the capital where they reside. This custom, which has been the object of much adverse comment in democratic countries, is not primarily the expression of a love for luxury on the part of the individual diplomats, but fulfills a special function in the scheme of diplomatic representation.

While entertaining, the diplomat does not act for himself as an individual but as the symbolic representative of his country. It is the Soviet ambassador as such who invites guests to a reception in commemoration of the October Revolution of 1917. Through him (his identity is irrelevant for this symbolic purpose), it is the Soviet Union that entertains, celebrates, and tries to impress its guests—as well as those who pointedly have not been invited—with its wealth and generosity. It is not by accident that in the thirties, after the Soviet Union had regained an important, yet suspect position in the society of nations, the parties given by the Soviet embassies throughout the world were famed for their lavishness and for the quantity and quality of food and drink. The purpose of this extravagance was not to show the bourgeois inhabitants of the Western world how well off the Russian people were. The purpose was rather to compensate for the political inferiority from which the Soviet Union had just barely escaped and into which it feared it might sink again. By instructing its diplomatic representatives to act in matters of entertainment as the equals, if not the betters, of their colleagues in foreign capitals, the Soviet Union—not unlike an upstart who has just crashed

---

[2]See pages 84 ff.

society—endeavored to demonstrate symbolically that it was at least as good a nation as any other.

Legal Representation

The diplomat also acts as the legal representative of his government. He is the legal agent of his government in the same sense in which a domestic corporation with its seat in Wilmington, Delaware, is represented by legal agents in other states and cities. These agents act in the name of that legal fiction which we call a corporation, make declarations binding upon it, sign contracts obligating it, and act within the limits of the corporate charter as though they were the corporation. Similarly, the American ambassador in London performs in the name of the government of the United States the legal functions that the Constitution, the laws of the United States, and the orders of the government allow him to perform. He may be authorized to sign a treaty or to transmit and receive ratification documents by which a treaty already signed is brought into force. He gives legal protection to American citizens abroad. He may represent the United States at an international conference or in the agencies of the United Nations and cast his vote in the name, and according to the instructions, of his government.

Political Representation

The diplomat, together with the foreign office, shapes the foreign policy of his country. This is by far his most important function. As the foreign office is the nerve center of foreign policy, so are the diplomatic representatives its outlying fibers maintaining the two-way traffic between the center and the outside world.

Upon the diplomats' shoulders lie the main burden of discharging at least one of the four tasks of diplomacy discussed above: they must assess the objectives of other nations and the power actually and potentially available for the pursuit of these objectives. To that end, they must inform themselves of the plans of the government to which they are accredited, through direct interrogation of government officials and political leaders, and through canvasing the press and other mouthpieces of public opinion. Furthermore, they must evaluate the potential influence upon government policies of opposing trends within the government, political parties, and public opinion.

A foreign diplomat in Washington must keep his government informed about the present and probable future attitude of the different branches of the United States government with regard to current problems of international affairs. He must appraise the importance for the development of foreign policy of different personalities in the government and the political parties. What stands are different presidential candidates likely to take, in the event of their election, on the pending issues of foreign policy? What is the influence of a certain columnist or commentator upon official policy and public opinion, and how representative of official thinking and of the trends in public opinion are his views? Such are some of the questions the diplomat must try to answer. Upon the reliability of his reports and the soundness of his judgment the success or failure of the foreign policy of his government and its ability to preserve peace may well depend.

When it comes to evaluating the actual and potential power of a nation, the diplomatic mission takes on the aspects of a high-class and sub rosa spy organization. High-ranking members of the armed services are delegated to the different diplomatic missions where, as military, naval, and air attachés, they are responsible for accumulating, by whatever means are available, information about actual and planned armaments, new weapons, military potential, military organization, and war plans of the countries concerned. Their services are supplemented by the commercial attachés, who collect information about economic trends, industrial developments, and the location of industries, especially with regard to their bearing upon military preparedness. In this and many other respects too numerous to mention, the accuracy and soundness of the reports a government receives from its diplomatic missions abroad are indispensable for the soundness of its own decisions.

In this function of gathering information, especially secret information upon which the foreign policies of one's own nation could be founded, lies the root of modern diplomacy. In the Middle Ages it was taken for granted that the special envoy of a prince traveling in a foreign country was a spy. When in the course of the fifteenth century the small Italian states started to make use of permanent diplomatic representatives in their relations with stronger states, they did so primarily for the purpose of receiving timely information of aggressive intentions on the part of the latter. Even when in the sixteenth century permanent diplomatic missions had become general, diplomats were widely regarded as a nuisance and a liability for the receiving state. At the beginning of the seventeenth century, Hugo Grotius, the founder of modern international law, went so far as to advocate their abolition.

Diplomatic representatives are not merely the eyes and the ears that report the events of the outside world to the nerve center of foreign policy as the raw material for its decisions. Diplomatic representatives are also the mouth and the hands through which the impulses emanating from the nerve center are transformed into words and actions. They must make the people among whom they live, and especially the mouthpieces of their public opinion and their political leaders, understand and, if possible, approve the foreign policy they represent. For this task of "selling" a foreign policy, the personal appeal of the diplomat and his understanding of the psychology of the foreign people are essential prerequisites.

In the performance of the peace-preserving functions of persuasion, negotiation, and threat of force, the diplomatic representative plays an outstanding part. His foreign office can give him instructions concerning the objectives pursued and the means to be employed. Yet for the execution of these instructions it must rely upon the judgment and the skill of the diplomatic representative himself. The foreign office can tell its representative to use persuasion or to threaten force or to avail himself of both tactics simultaneously but must leave to the representative's discretion how and when to make use of those techniques. How persuasive an argument will be, what advantages a negotiated agreement will yield, what impression the threat of force will make, how effectively emphasis is placed upon one or the other of these techniques—all this lies in the hands of the diplomat, who has it in his power to bungle a good, and avoid the worst consequences of a bad, foreign policy. We have mentioned the spectacular contributions great diplomatists have made to the power of their nations.[3] Their contributions to the cause of peace are no less important.

THE DECLINE OF DIPLOMACY

Today diplomacy no longer performs the role, often spectacular and brilliant and always important, that it performed from the end of the Thirty Years' War to the beginning of the First World War. The decline of diplomacy set in with the end of the First World War. In the twenties a few outstanding diplomatists were still able to make important contributions to the foreign policies of their countries. In the decade preceding the Second World War, the part diplomatists took in shaping foreign policy became even smaller, and the decline of diplomacy as a technique of conducting foreign affairs became more and more patent. Since the end of the Second World War, diplomacy has lost its vitality, and its functions have withered away to such an extent as is without precedent in the history of the modern state system. Five factors account for that decline.

The Development of Communications

The most obvious of these factors is the development of modern communications. Diplomacy owes its rise in part to the absence of speedy communications in a period when the governments of the new territorial states maintained continuous political relations with one another. Diplomacy owes its decline in part to the development of speedy and regular communications in the form of the satellite, the airplane, the radio, the telegraph, the teletype, and the long-distance telephone.

When at any time before the First World War the governments of the United States and of Great Britain wanted to enter into negotiations, it was indispensable for them to have permanent representatives, endowed with a great deal of discretion, in London and Washington to carry on the negotiations. These permanent representatives were necessary because the facilities for transmitting rapidly and continuously detailed messages were cumbersome and, more particularly, because the time consumed by travel made personal consultations impossible without disrupting the negotiations. Today an official of the State Department needs only to converse over the transatlantic telephone with his counterpart in the British Foreign Office or with the American ambassador in London, or to board a transatlantic plane in the evening to start negotiations in London the next morning. Whenever direct consultations with his government become necessary, a day is all he needs to cross and recross the Atlantic, inform his government of the latest developments, and receive its instructions.

---

[3]See pages 153 ff.

Only a quarter of a century ago, it would have been unthinkable for the secretary of state to absent himself from Washington for weeks in order to participate in an international conference or visit foreign capitals. Now, when he is absent from the capital he remains in continuous contact with the State Department through telephone and radio, and an overnight trip will bring him back to Washington on a moment's notice. Thus as a rule important negotiations are carried on, not by diplomatic representatives but by special delegates who may be the foreign ministers themselves or high officials of the foreign offices or technical experts. The modern technology of communications has made "shuttle diplomacy" possible.

The Depreciation of Diplomacy

These technological developments are, however, not solely responsible for the discard into which the traditional methods of diplomacy have fallen. To the technological ability to part with the services of diplomacy must be added the conviction that those services ought to be parted with because they not only contribute nothing to the cause of peace, but actually endanger it. This conviction grew in the same soil that nourished the conception of power politics as an accident of history to be eliminated at will.[4]

That conviction and this conception both recognize the intimate relation between power politics and the functions of diplomacy, and in this they are right. The emergence of diplomacy as an institution coincides with the rise of the nation state and, hence, with the appearance of international relations in the modern sense. The contemporary emergence of diplomacy and the modern state system is, however, more than a mere coincidence. If there is to be intercourse at all among sovereign nations with the goal of creating and maintaining at least a modicum of order and peace in international affairs, that intercourse must be carried on by permanent agents. The opposition to, and depreciation of, diplomacy is then but a peculiar manifestation of hostility to the modern state system and the kind of international politics it has produced.

It is indeed true that the diplomat has been held morally in low esteem throughout modern history, and not only by those who thought that there was an easy way of eliminating the struggle for power from the international scene. The diplomat's reputation for deviousness and dishonesty is as old as diplomacy itself. Well known is the definition of a diplomat, attributed to Sir Henry Wotton, an English ambassador at the beginning of the seventeenth century, as "an honest man sent abroad to lie for his country." When Metternich was informed of the death of the Russian ambassador at the Congress of Vienna, he is reported to have exclaimed: "Ah, is that true? What may have been his motive?"

The modern version of that depreciation of diplomacy attaches special importance to one particular aspect of the diplomatic technique—its secrecy. During and after the First World War, wide currency was given to the opinion that the secret machinations of diplomats shared a great deal, if not the major portion,

---

[4]See pages 35 ff.

of responsibility for that war, that the secrecy of diplomatic negotiations was an atavistic and dangerous residue from the aristocratic past, and that international negotiations carried on and concluded under the watchful eyes of a peace-loving public opinion could not but further the cause of peace.

Woodrow Wilson was the most eloquent spokesman of this new philosophy of international affairs. The Preamble to and the first of his Fourteen Points are the classic statement of the new philosophy. The Preamble to the Fourteen Points states:

> It will be our wish and purpose that the processes of peace, when they are begun, shall be absolutely open, and that they shall involve and permit henceforth no secret understandings of any kind. The day of conquest and aggrandizement is gone by; so is also the day of secret covenants entered into in the interest of particular governments, and likely at some unlooked-for moment to upset the peace of the world. It is this happy fact, now clear to the view of every public man whose thoughts do not still linger in an age that is dead and gone, which makes it possible for every nation whose purposes are consistent with justice and the peace of the world to avow, now or at any other time, the objects it has in view. The first point reads: "Open covenants of peace, openly arrived at, after which there shall be no private international understandings of any kind, but diplomacy shall proceed always frankly and in the public view."[5]

Diplomacy by Parliamentary Procedures

It was in deference to this new philosophy that after the First World War the statesmen of the world began to depart from the established pattern of diplomacy. They created in the League of Nations and later in the United Nations a new type of diplomatic intercourse: diplomacy by parliamentary procedure. International problems requiring solution are put on the agenda of the deliberative bodies of these organizations. The delegates of the different governments discuss the merits of the problem in public debate. A vote taken in accordance with the constitution of the organization disposes of the matter.

This method has been employed before by special conferences, such as the Hague Peace Conferences of 1899 and 1907. As an overall method of dealing with international problems, it was employed for the first time by the League of Nations. Its use by that organization was, however, apparent rather than real. The public discussions of the Council and the Assembly of the League were as a rule carefully rehearsed, especially when political matters were under consideration. A solution to which all could agree was generally sought and often found by the traditional means of secret negotiations, preceding the public meetings. The latter, then, simply gave the delegates of the nations concerned an opportunity of restating their positions for public consumption and of ratifying, in compliance with the provisions of the Covenant, the agreement secretly reached.

---

[5] *Selected Addresses and Public Papers of Woodrow Wilson*, edited by Albert Bushnell Hart (New York: Boni and Liveright, 1918), pp. 247–88.

The United Nations, on the contrary, has taken seriously the parliamentary methods of transacting the business of diplomacy. It has developed the new methods of United Nations diplomacy, whose purpose it is to re-create for every issue coming to a vote in the General Assembly the two-thirds majority required by the Charter.[6] Generally speaking, the aim of the new diplomacy of the United Nations is not the settlement of an issue dividing the members but the line-up of a two-thirds majority to outvote the other side. It is a vote at which its processes aim and in which they culminate.

The trend toward public parliamentary procedures instead of traditional diplomatic negotiations, of which the operations of the General Assembly of the United Nations are typical, has also affected the postwar international conferences, which by composition, issues, and objectives most closely resemble the diplomatic gatherings of the nineteenth and early twentieth centuries. The Paris Peace Conference of 1946, attended by twenty-one nations, operated in the full light of publicity and duplicated in its procedures the pattern established by the deliberative agencies of the United Nations. The Foreign Ministers' Conferences, composed of the foreign ministers of France, Great Britain, the Soviet Union, and the United States, which tried to dispose of the legacy of the Second World War, have debated and voted either in full public view or behind the transparent screen of semisecrecy that allowed the public to follow the main phases of the debate as reported by the different delegations to the correspondents of the press.

However, the ease of communications, the condemnation of secret diplomacy, and the new parliamentary diplomacy cannot fully account for this overall disintegration of diplomacy. Two additional factors must share responsibility for the decline: the peculiarly untraditional approach of the two superpowers to the issues of international politics, and the very nature of world politics in the second half of the twentieth century.

The Superpowers: Newcomers to Diplomacy

In its formative years the United States benefited from the services of an unusually brilliant diplomacy. From the Jacksonian era on, the eminent qualities of American diplomacy disappeared as the need for them seemed to disappear. When the need for an active American foreign policy became manifest in the late 1930s there was nothing to build on but a mediocre foreign service, the condemnation of power politics and of secret diplomacy transformed into moral indignation at "aggressor nations," and the tradition of the big stick, which had worked so well in the Western Hemisphere. Thus it was the improvisations of Franklin D. Roosevelt alone, guided at times by an intuitive grasp of the international realities, that kept American foreign policy in tune with American interests.

In that decisive period neither the secretary of state nor the permanent staff of the State Department nor the diplomatic representatives abroad exerted more than a subordinate influence upon the conduct of American foreign policy.

---

[6]See the discussion of United Nations diplomacy on pages 459 ff.

When Roosevelt, who for twelve years had almost single-handedly made American foreign policy, left the scene, there was no man or group of men capable of creating and operating that intricate and subtle machinery by which traditional diplomacy had given peaceful protection and furtherance to the national interest. Nor could that small group of able and devoted public servants who knew what foreign policy was all about rely upon the public understanding of, and popular support for, the rational and intricate processes of foreign policy, without which foreign policy in a democracy cannot be successfully conducted.

For quite different reasons the Soviet Union has found it difficult to develop adequate instruments for diplomatic intercourse. The Bolshevist Revolution of 1917 destroyed the Russian diplomatic service, which could look back upon a long tradition and had a number of brilliant achievements to its credit. The few old-school diplomats who were retained in office after the revolution and the new diplomats of talent who rose from the ranks of the revolutionaries had little opportunity to prove themselves. The hostility between the Soviet Union and most other nations and the resulting isolation of the Soviet Union prevented the conduct of normal diplomatic relations.

Furthermore, the Russian diplomat is the emissary of a totalitarian government that punishes failure, or even too much discretion in interpreting official orders, at least with loss of office. In consequence, postrevolutionary Russian diplomats have traditionally—and more than ever since the conclusion of the Second World War—conceived of their task as the transmission of the proposals of their governments, which other governments might accept or reject as they see fit. Counterproposals and other new elements in the negotiations call for new instruments from the foreign office. The content of these new instruments is again submitted to the other governments, which may take it or leave it, and so forth, until the patience of one or the other or of all parties is exhausted. Such a procedure destroys all the virtues of diplomatic negotiations, such as quick adaptation to new situations, clever use of a psychological opening, retreat and advance as the situation may require, persuasion, the quid pro quo of bargaining, and the like. Diplomatic intercourse, as practiced by the new Russian diplomacy, resembles nothing so much as a series of military orders relayed from the high command—the foreign office—to the field commanders—the diplomatic representatives—who in turn communicate the terms of agreement to the enemy.

A diplomat whose main concern must be to retain the approval of his superiors is usually only too eager to report what the latter would like to hear, regardless of whether the report is true. This tendency to bend the truth to the wishes of the foreign office and to paint the facts in favorable colors is found in all diplomatic services; for compliance enhances security in office and increases the chance for advancement.

The Nature of Contemporary World Politics

What is lacking in this explanation of the decline of diplomacy in our time is supplied by the very nature of contemporary world politics. Imbued with the crusading spirit of the new moral force of nationalistic universalism, and both tempted and frightened by the potentialities of total war, two superpowers, the centers of two gigantic power blocs, have faced each other in inflexible opposition. They could not retreat without giving up what they considered vital to them. They could not advance without risking combat. Persuasion, then, was tantamount to trickery, compromise meant treason, and the threat of force spelled war.

Given the nature of the power relations between the United States and the Soviet Union, and given the states of mind these two superpowers used to bring to bear upon their mutual relations, diplomacy had little with which to operate and tended to become obsolete. Under such moral and political conditions, it was not the sensible, flexible, and versatile mind of the diplomat, but the rigid, relentless, and one-track mind of the crusader that guided the destiny of nations. The crusading mind knows nothing of persuasion and compromise. It knows only of victory and of defeat.

The moralistic fanaticism that has thus been injected into the conduct of foreign policy would endanger the national interests, rationally understood, of the nations concerned under any circumstances. The religious wars of the sixteenth and seventeenth centuries, the Napoleonic wars of the turn of the eighteenth century, and the Cold War following the Second World War are cases in point. That fanaticism has become particularly absurd and self-destructive in our period of history. That period is distinguished from preceding history by the need for a reformulation of the national interest in transcendent rather than exclusive terms. Traditionally and in considerable measure still today, satisfaction of the national interest of A is tantamount to the dissatisfaction of the national interest of B. Hence, the national interest of A can be promoted only at the risk of conflict with B. Modern technological developments have brought about a fundamental change in that relationship. To an ever greater extent, certain national interests of A must not be pursued at the expense of B, but, quite to the contrary, their satisfaction will benefit B as well. Take, as spectacular examples, the control of peaceful nuclear power, the nonproliferation of nuclear weapons, the avoidance of nuclear war, the production and distribution of technologically essential natural resources, the adequate production and distribution of food, the control of population growth, and the preservation of the natural environment. The satisfaction of the national interests of A is, first of all, possible only through cooperation with B and, second, A's benefits are dependent not upon B's disadvantages but upon B's benefits as well. In other words, A's national interests can be satisfied only through the simultaneous satisfaction of B's national interests. In order to be satisfied they must transcend A's exclusivity and comprise B's interests as well.

Thus diplomacy has here the new task of creating and maintaining new institutions and procedures through which the new common interests of nations can be pursued. If the task were hopeless and if war were inevitable, this book might end here. If war is not inevitable, the conditions for the revival of diplomacy and for its successful operation in the service of peace remain to be considered.

32 The Future of Diplomacy

HOW CAN DIPLOMACY BE REVIVED?

The revival of diplomacy requires the elimination of the factors, or at least of some of their consequences, responsible for the decline of the traditional diplomatic practices. Priority in this respect belongs to the depreciation of diplomacy and its corollary: diplomacy by parliamentary procedures. Insofar as that depreciation is only the result of the depreciation of power politics, what we have said about the latter should suffice for the former.[1] Diplomacy, however morally unattractive its business may seem to many, is nothing but a symptom of the struggle for power among sovereign nations, which try to maintain orderly and peaceful relations among themselves. If there were a way of banning the struggle for power from the international scene, diplomacy would disappear of itself. If order and anarchy, peace and war, were matters of no concern to the nations of the world, they could dispense with diplomacy, prepare for war, and hope for the best. If nations who are sovereign, who are supreme within their territories with no superior above them, want to preserve peace and order in their relations, they must try to persuade, negotiate, and exert pressure upon one another. That is to say, they must engage in, cultivate, and rely upon diplomatic procedures.

The new parliamentary diplomacy is no substitute for these procedures. On the contrary, it tends to aggravate rather than mitigate international conflicts and leaves the prospect for peace dimmed rather than brightened. Three essential qualities of the new diplomacy are responsible for these unfortunate results: its publicity, its major votes, and its fragmentation of international issues.

The Vice of Publicity

Much of the confusion attending discussion of the problem of secret diplomacy results from the failure to distinguish between two separate aspects of the problem:

---

[1]See pages 35 ff.

between "open covenants" and "covenants openly arrived at," between publicity for the results of diplomatic negotiations and publicity for the diplomatic negotiations themselves. Disclosure of the results of diplomatic negotiations is required by the principles of democracy, for without it there can be no democratic control of foreign policy. Yet publicity for the negotiations themselves is not required by democracy and runs counter to the requirements of common sense. It takes only common sense derived from daily experience to realize that it is impossible to negotiate in public on anything in which parties other than the negotiators are interested. This impossibility derives from the very nature of negotiation and from the social context in which negotiations generally operate.

It is a common characteristic of negotiations that they are started by each side with maximum demands, which are whittled down in a process of persuasion, bargaining, and pressures until both sides meet on a level below the one from which they started. The saving grace of negotiations is the result that satisfies the demands of either side, at least up to a point, and tends to strengthen amity between the parties by demonstrating in the act of agreement the existence of identical or complementary interests binding them together. On the other hand, the process leading up to the result reveals the parties in roles in which they would rather not be remembered by their fellows. There are more edifying spectacles than the bluffing, blustering, haggling, and deceiving, the real weakness and pretended strength, that go with horse-trading and the drive for a bargain. To publicize such negotiations is tantamount to destroying, or at least impairing, the bargaining position of the parties in any further negotiations in which they might be engaged with other parties.

Not only will their bargaining positions suffer. Their social status, their prestige, and their power will face irreparable damage if publicity attends these negotiations, uncovering their weakness and unmasking their pretenses. Competitors for the gains the negotiators seek will take advantage of what the public negotiations have revealed to them. They will do so not only in further negotiations with the parties, but also in their overall calculations, plans, and dispositions, which take into account the qualities and potentialities of all participants in the competition.

It is for these reasons that in a free market no seller will carry on public negotiations with a buyer, no landlord with a tenant, no institution of higher learning with its staff. No candidate for office will negotiate in public with his backers, no public official with his colleagues, no politician with his fellow politicians. How then, are we to expect that nations are able and willing to do what no private individual would think of doing?

The disadvantage to which nations would be put by the publicity of their negotiations is further increased by the fact that the audience witnessing the spectacle of public international negotiations comprises not only a limited number of interested parties but the whole world. More particularly, the governments concerned negotiate under the watchful eyes of their own peoples and, especially when they are democratically elected, in full view of the oposition. No government that wants to stay in power or simply retain the respect of its people can afford to give up publicly part of what it had declared at the outset to be just and necessary, to retreat from a position initially held, to concede at least the partial justice of the other side's claims. Heroes, not horse traders, are the idols of public opinion. Public opinion, while dreading war, demands that its diplomats act as heroes who do not yield in the face of the enemy, even at the risk of war, and condemns as weaklings and traitors those who yield, albeit only halfway, for the sake of peace.

Furthermore, traditional diplomacy used to transact the business of state in a language and with manners well fitted for its purpose. The aim of diplomacy then was to promote the national interest with moderation and leave the door open for compromise in the form of a negotiated settlement. Measured words and formalized phrases, used in those transactions, committed the speaker to nothing or to just as much as he was willing to make good. These phrases and formalities are empty of, or in any case vague in, meaning and hence are susceptible to all kinds of interpretations in support of whatever policy or settlement seems to be advantageous in the end. They are also polite and, hence, make it easy for those who use them to get along with each other, however grave the issues may be that separate nations. In sum, they are the perfect instrument of the subtle, cautious, moderate, conciliatory negotiator.

Public diplomacy and its advocates can have nothing but contempt for such an instrument, which, so they think, belongs to a bygone age of aristocratic snobbery and moral indifference. Crusaders for the right—and that is what public diplomats are supposed to be—do not speak like that. Seated on a stage with the world as their audience, the public diplomats speak to the world rather than to one another. Their aim is not to persuade one another that they could find common ground for agreement but to persuade the world and especially their own nations that they are right and the other side is wrong and that they are and always will remain staunch defenders of the right.

No man who has taken such a stand before the attentive eyes and ears of the world can in full public view agree to a compromise without looking like a fool and a knave. He must take himself at his public word and must stand unyieldingly "on principle," the favored phrase of public diplomacy, rather than on negotiation and compromise. He must defend the position initially taken, and so must the other side. Neither side being able to retreat or advance, a "phony war" of positions ensues. Both sides oppose each other inflexibly, each side knowing that the other will not and cannot move. To offer the public some semblance of activity, they fire into the air the empty shells of words, which explode noisily and, as everybody knows, are aimed at nothing. It is only in mutual vituperation that the minds of the delegates meet. When the delegates finally part, embittered and frustrated, they reach, however indignantly, an agreement of sorts at least on one point: The other side has engaged in propaganda. It so happens that on this point both sides are right.

This degeneration of diplomatic intercourse into a propaganda match is, then, the inevitable concomitant of the publicity of the new diplomacy. Not only is a publicly conducted diplomacy unable to reach agreement or even to negotiate for the purpose of reaching agreement, but each public meeting leaves international matters in a worse state than before. For each propaganda match strengthens the conviction of the different delegates and of their nations that they are absolutely right and that the other side is absolutely wrong and that the gap separating them is too deep and wide to be bridged by the traditional methods of diplomacy. There is much wisdom in the plea that the secretary general of the United Nations made in his report of 1956, elaborated in the report of 1959, to "give greater emphasis to the United Nations as an instrument for negotiation of settlements, as distinct from the mere debate of issues."

The Vice of Majority Decision

The evil wrought by the public conduct of diplomacy is compounded by the attempt to decide issues by majority vote. In the General Assembly of the United Nations, this method has developed into the pattern of at least two-thirds of the members trying to vote down the rest. That this method of conducting the business of diplomacy has made no direct contribution to the peaceful settlement of a single outstanding issue is obvious from the results. For instance, the Soviet bloc was voted down time and again on the Korean issue. Yet the voting in the General Assembly was relevant for the settlement of the Korean issue only insofar as it demonstrated the voting strength, and thereby enhanced the political strength, of the Western bloc and enabled the nations supporting the United Nations action in Korea to act in unison vis-à-vis the Soviet bloc. Beyond that indirect contribution in terms of increasing the strength of one side, the voting contributed nothing to the settlement of the Korean issue. That issue was settled on the battlefield and in diplomatic negotiations between East and West, not in the chamber of the General Assembly. The reason the outvoting of an opponent in a deliberative international body is a useless and may even be a mischievous undertaking, aside from its occasional use for strengthening a particular group, is to be found in the very nature of international society in contrast to national societies.

When the Congress of the United States votes down a minority, it actually decides the issue for the time being. It is able to do so for four reasons, all of which are absent on the international scene.

1. The parliamentary majority vote is an integral part of a whole system of devices for peaceful change, each being able to operate in supplementation or support of, or as a corrective upon, the others, and all limited and coordinated by the Constitution. The minority and the majority in Congress make up an integrated society. Aside from deliberative bodies deciding by majority vote, the national society has created a series of devices, such as the presidential veto and judicial review, by which the majority vote can be overridden and the minority can be protected against unconstitutional use and arbitrary misuse of the majority vote. Behind a majority decision, as well as behind the defeated minority, stands the whole moral and political power of the national community, ready to enforce a decision of the majority and to protect the minority against injustice and abuse.

2. The instrumentalities of peaceful change that operate within the national community give the minority a chance to become a majority sometime in the future. That chance is inherent in the device of periodical elections and in the dynamics of the social process, which produce ever new alignments and distributions of power. These dynamics also see to it that a minority in a deliberative assembly is never a minority in all the respects important to it. A group may be a religious minority, outvoted in issues of this kind, but may be part of the economic majority determining economic legislation, and so forth.[2]

3. The numerical relation between minority and majority is at least an approximation to the actual distribution of power and interests within the whole population. When the House of Representatives votes a motion down—say, 270 to 60—it is generally safe to assume that only a relatively small minority of the American people is identified with the defeated measure.

4. While in Congress each vote cast counts for one, it is of course true, politically speaking, that all votes are not of equal weight. The negative vote of a powerful committee chairman, industrialist, farmer, or labor leader with respect to a piece of legislation affecting the interests of his respective group may well have a bearing upon the political, economic, or social consequences that the majority intended the piece of legislation to have. Yet even the most powerful single vote in Congress represents but a small fraction of the total power of the American people.

None of these four factors that make possible the contribution of the majority vote to domestic peaceful change operates on the international scene.

1. The majority vote is the sole device for compulsory peaceful change within the framework of the United Nations. There is no constitution, no presidential veto, no compulsory judicial review, and no bill of rights imposing substantive and procedural restraints upon the majority and protecting the minority against injustice and abuse. Nor is there a community imposing moral restraints upon majority and minority alike and able to enforce the decision of the majority against a recalcitrant minority. The majority can outvote the minority as often as it wants to and on any issue it chooses, and the minority can protect itself with the veto and its power against any majority decision it wants to annual.

2. A minority in the United Nations is likely, especially under present political conditions, to be a permanent one. For the same reason, its minority status is bound to extend to certain questions of major importance. The two-bloc system, modified by the independent position of China and the Third World nations, that dominates contemporary world politics leads to permanant alignments on either side of the divide. The tension between the two blocs transforms the majority of issues into political ones. When such

---

[2]See also the general discussion of peaceful change, Chapter 26.

issues come to a vote, the adherents of the two blocs are likely to split along the line separating the blocs.

3. The numerical relation between a minority and a two-thirds majority in the General Assembly obviously does not of necessity correspond to the actual distribution of power and interests among the members of the United Nations, nor does the vote of the most powerful members of the General Assembly represent a relatively small fraction of the total power of the community of nations. An overwhelming majority composed of all the small nations of Africa, Asia, Europe, and Latin America means little in terms of power as compared with the one vote of the United States or the Soviet Union.

To outvote habitually a powerful minority in a deliberative international agency, while it may have been a potent weapon in the Cold War, does not contribute to the preservation of peace. For the minority cannot accept the decision of the majority, and the majority cannot enforce its decision short of war. At best, parliamentary procedures transferred to the international scene leave things as they are; they leave problems unsolved and issues unsettled. At worst, however, these procedures poison the international climate and aggravate the conflicts that carry the seeds of war. They provide a majority with an opportunity to humiliate the minority in public and as often as it wishes. In the form of the veto, the corollary of the majority vote in a society of sovereign nations, these procedures provide the minority with a weapon with which to obstruct the will of the majority and to prevent the international agency from functioning at all. Neither the majority nor the minority needs to use self-restraint or be aware of its responsibility to the international organization or to humanity, since what either side votes for or against cannot, as such, influence the course of events. For one group of sovereign nations to vote down habitually another group of sovereign nations is, then, to engage in a puerile game that can accomplish nothing for the peaceful settlement of international conflicts, but may well carry mankind further down the road to war.

The Vice of Fragmentation

The decision by majority vote implies the third of the vices that stand in the way of a revival of the traditional diplomatic practices: the fragmentation of international issues. By its very nature, the majority vote is concerned with an isolated case. The facts of life to be dealt with by the majority decision are artificially separated from the facts that precede, accompany, and follow them, and are transformed into a legal "case" or a political "issue" to be disposed of as such by the majority decision. In the domestic field, this procedure is not necessarily harmful. Here the majority decision of a deliberative body operates within the context of an intricate system of devices for peaceful change, supplementing, supporting, or checking each other, as the case may be, but in any case attuned to each other in a certain measure and thus giving the individual decisions coherence with each other and with the whole social system.

On the international scene, no such system of integrating factors exists. Consequently, it is particularly inadequate here to take up one "case" or "issue" after the other and to try to dispose of them by a succession of majority votes. A case or issue, such as the Middle East or Berlin, is always a particular phase and manifestation of a much larger situation. Such a case or issue is rooted in the historical past and extends its ramifications beyond its particular locale and into the future. Our discussion of the relations between disputes and tensions has given us an indication of the intimate relations that exist between the surface phenomena of international conflicts and those large and undefined problems that are buried deep under the surface of the daily occurrences of international life.[3] To deal with cases and issues as they arise, and to try to dispose of them according to international law or political expediency, is to deal with surface phenomena and leave the underlying problems unconsidered and unsolved. The League of Nations fell victim to that vice, and the United Nations has been heedless of the League's experience.

For instance, there is no doubt that the League of Nations was right, according to international law, in expelling the Soviet Union in 1939 because of its attack upon Finland. But the political and military problems with which the Soviet Union confronted the world neither began with its attack on Finland nor ended there; it was unwise for the League to pretend that such was the case and to decide the issue on that pretense. History has proved the unwisdom of that pretense, for only Sweden's refusal to allow British and French troops to pass through Swedish territory in order to come to the aid of Finland saved Great Britain and France from being at war with Germany and the Soviet Union at the same time. Whenever the League of Nations endeavored to deal with political situations presented as legal issues, it could deal with them only as isolated cases according to the applicable rules of international law, not as particular phases of an overall political situation that required an overall solution according to the rules of the political art. Hence, political problems were never solved, but only tossed about and finally shelved according to the rules of the legal game.

What was true of the League of Nations has already proved to be true of the United Nations. In its approach to many of the issues brought before its political agencies, the United Nations has remained faithful to the tradition established by the League of Nations. These cases have provided opportunities for exercise in parliamentary procedure and just that chicanery for which traditional diplomacy has so often been reproached, but only on rare occasions has even an attempt been made to face the political issues of which these situations are the surface manifestations.

The special political conferences of the postwar period have repeated the pattern of fragmentation established by the League of Nations and the United Nations. They have dealt, for instance, with Korea, German unification, or disarmament. None of these conferences has faced the problem of which all these issues are particular phases and manifestations and upon whose solution the settlement

---

[3]See pages 448 ff.

of these issues depends: the problem of the overall relations between the United States and the Soviet Union. Since they were unwilling to come to grips with the fundamental problem of international politics, they were unable to settle any of the particular issues on which they concentrated their attention.

This failure of contemporary diplomacy even to see the problem upon whose solution the preservation of peace depends, let alone to try to solve it, is the inevitable result of the methods it has employed. A diplomacy that, instead of speaking in conciliatory terms to the other side, addresses the world for purposes of propaganda; that, instead of negotiating with compromise as its goal, strives for the cheap triumphs of futile majority decisions and of obstructive vetoes; that, instead of facing the primary problem, is satisfied with manipulating the secondary ones—such a diplomacy is a liability rather than an asset for the cause of peace.

These three essential vices of contemporary diplomacy are aggravated by the misuse of modern communications. The conquest of time and space by modern technology has inevitably reduced the importance of diplomatic representation. Yet it has by no means made necessary the confusion of function between the foreign office and diplomatic representation that is characteristic of contemporary diplomacy. A secretary of state or foreign minister is physically able to converse with any foreign capital within a few minutes' time by way of modern communications and to reach it in person within a few days at the most. Thus the tendency has grown for the men responsible for the conduct of foreign affairs to assume the role of roving ambassadors, hurrying from one conference to another, stopping in between conferences for a short while at the foreign office, and using their time there in preparation for the next meeting. The men who are supposed to be the brains of diplomacy, its nerve center, fulfill at best the functions of the nerve ends. In consequence, there is a void at the center. There is nobody who faces the overall problem of international politics and sees all the particular issues as phases and manifestations of the whole. Instead, each specialist in the foreign office deals with the particular problems belonging to his specialty, and the fragmentation of the conduct of foreign affairs to which the techniques of contemporary diplomacy lend themselves is powerfully supported by the lack of overall direction of foreign affairs.

THE PROMISE OF DIPLOMACY: ITS NINE RULES[4]

Diplomacy could revive if it would part with these vices, which in recent years have well-nigh destroyed its usefulness, and if it would restore the techniques that have controlled the mutual relations of nations since time immemorial. By doing so, diplomacy would realize only one of the preconditions for the preservation of peace. The contribution of a revived diplomacy to the cause of peace would depend upon the methods and purposes of its use. The discussion of these uses is the last task we have set ourselves in this book.

---

[4]We by no means intend to give here an exhaustive account of rules of diplomacy. We propose to discuss only those that seem to have a special bearing upon the contemporary situation.

We have already formulated the four main tasks with which a foreign policy must cope successfully in order to be able to promote the national interest and preserve peace. It remains for us now to reformulate those tasks in the light of the special problems with which contemporary world politics confronts diplomacy. We have seen that the bipolar system, which is the dominant and distinctive element of contemporary world politics, carries with it potentialities for enormous evil and enormous good. We have quoted the French philosopher Fénelon to the effect that the opposition of two approximately equal nations constitutes the ideal system of the balance of power. We found that the beneficial results Fénelon expected from the bipolar system have failed to attend the opposition between the United States and the Soviet Union.[5]

Finally, we saw the main reason for this threatening aspect of contemporary world politics in the character of modern war, which has changed profoundly under the impact of nationalistic universalism and modern technology. The effects of modern technology cannot be undone. The only variable that remains subject to deliberate manipulation is the new moral force of nationalistic universalism. The attempt to reverse the trend toward war through the techniques of a revived diplomacy must start with this phenomenon. That means, in negative terms, that a revived diplomacy will have a chance to preserve peace only when it is not used as the instrument of a political religion aiming at universal dominion.

Four Fundamental Rules

1. Diplomacy must be divested of the crusading spirit. This is the first of the rules that diplomacy can neglect only at the risk of war. In the words of William Graham Sumner:

> If you want war, nourish a doctrine. Doctrines are the most frightful tyrants to which men ever are subject, because doctrines get inside of a man's own reason and betray him against himself. Civilized men have done their fiercest fighting for doctrines. The reconquest of the Holy Sepulcher, "the balance of power," "no universal dominion," "trade follows the flag," "he who holds the land will hold the sea," "the throne and the altar," the revolution, the faith—these are the things for which men have given their lives. . . . Now when any doctrine arrives at that degree of authority, the name of it is a club which any demagogue may swing over you at any time and apropos of anything. In order to describe a doctrine, we must have recourse to theological language. A doctrine is an article of faith. It is something which you are bound to believe, not because you have some rational grounds for believing it is true, but because you belong to such and such a church or demonination. . . . A policy in a state we can understand; for instance, it was the policy of the United States at the end of the eighteenth century to get the free navigation of the Mississippi to its mouth, even at the expense of

---

[5] See pages 370–71.

war with Spain. That policy had reason and justice in it; it was founded in our interests; it had positive form and definite scope. A doctrine is an abstract principle; it is necessarily absolute in its scope and abstruse in its terms; it is a metaphysical assertion. It is never true, because it is absolute and the affairs of men are all conditioned and relative. . . . Now to turn back to politics, just think what an abomination in statecraft an abstract doctrine must be. Any politician or editor can, at any moment, put a new extension on it. The people acquiesce in the doctrine and applaud it because they hear the politicians and editors repeat it, and the politicians and editors repeat it because they think it is popular. So it grows. . . . It may mean anything or nothing, at any moment, and no one knows how it will be. You accede to it now, within the vague limits of what you suppose it to be; therefore, you will have to accede to it tomorrow when the same name is made to cover something which you never have heard or thought of. If you allow a political catchword to go on and grow, you will awaken some day to find it standing over you, the arbiter of your destiny, against which you are powerless, as men are powerless against delusions. . . . What can be more contrary to sound statesmanship and common sense than to put forth an abstract assertion which has no definite relation to any interest of ours now at stake, but which has in it any number of possibilities of producing complications which we cannot foresee, but which are sure to be embarrassing when they arise![6]

At the very beginning of colonial history, this conflict between self-interest and the crusading spirit was clearly recognized and decided in favor of the former by John Winthrop, the first governor of Massachusetts. In the words of Professor Edmund S. Morgan:

Winthrop had many more occasions to notice how self-righteousness extinguished charity. It also blinded men to realities. He knew that New England depended on the outside world in its new economy, and his heart was gladdened every time another ship splashed off the ways at Boston to carry New England codfish to markets where idolatrous Roman Catholics paid good money for them. He also knew, what a good foreign minister had to know, that righteousness endangered his community when it produced a blind and undiscriminating defiance to surrounding evils. Thus, when his colleagues refused to aid Rhode Island against the Indians, he remarked that it was an error in state policy, for though the Rhode Islanders were "desperately erroneous and in such distraction among themselves as portended their ruin, yet if the Indians should prevail against them, it would be a great advantage to the Indians, and danger to the whole country by the arms, etc., that would there be had, and by the loss of so many persons and so much cattle and other substance belonging to above 120 families. Or, if they should be forced to seek

---

[6]"War," *Essays of William Graham Sumner* (New Haven, CT: Yale University Press, 1934), Vol. 1, pp. 169 ff.

protection from the Dutch, who would be ready to accept them, it would be a great inconvenience to all the English to have so considerable a place in the power of strangers so potent as they are."[7]

The Wars of Religion have shown that the attempt to impose one's own religion as the only true one upon the rest of the world is as futile as it is costly. A century of almost unprecedented bloodshed, devastation, and barbarization was needed to convince the contestants that the two religions could live together in mutual toleration. The two political religions of our time have taken the place of the two great Christian denominations of the sixteenth and seventeenth centuries. Will the political religions of our time need the lesson of the Thirty Years' War, or will they rid themselves in time of the universalistic aspirations that inevitably issue in inconclusive war?

Upon the answer to that question depends the cause of peace. For only if it is answered in the affirmative can a moral consensus, emerging from shared convictions and common values, develop—a moral consensus within which a peace-preserving diplomacy will have a chance to grow. Only then will diplomacy have a chance to face the concrete political problems that require peaceful solution. If the objectives of foreign policy are not to be defined in terms of a world-embracing political religion, how are they to be defined? This is the fundamental problem to be solved once the crusading aspirations of nationalistic universalism have been discarded.

2. The objectives of foreign policy must be defined in terms of the national interest and must be supported with adequate power. This is the second rule of a peace-preserving diplomacy. The national interest of a peace-loving nation can be defined only in terms of national security, and national security must be defined as integrity of the national territory and of its institutions.[8] National security, then, is the irreducible minimum that diplomacy must defend with adequate power without compromise. But diplomacy must ever be alive to the radical transformation that national security has undergone under the impact of the nuclear age. Until the advent of that age, a nation could use its diplomacy to purchase its security at the expense of another nation. Today, short of a radical change in the atomic balance of power in favor of a particular nation, diplomacy, in order to make one nation secure from nuclear destruction, must make them all secure. With the national interest defined in such restrictive and transcendent terms, diplomacy must observe the third of its rules.

3. Diplomacy must look at the political scene from the point of view of other nations. "Nothing is so fatal to a nation as an extreme of self-partiality, and the total want of consideration of what others will naturally hope or fear."[9] What are the national interests of other nations in terms of national security, and are

---

[7]Edmund S. Morgan, *The Puritan Dilemma: The Story of John Winthrop* (Boston: Little, Brown, 1958), pp. 189, 190.
[8]For a more extensive discussion of the relevant problems, see Chapter 24.
[9]Edmund Burke, "Remarks on the Policy of the Allies with Respect to France" (1793), *Works* (Boston: Little, Brown, 1889), Vol. IV, p. 447.

they compatible with one's own? The definition of the national interest in terms of national security is easier, and the interests of the two opposing nations are more likely to be compatible, in a bipolar system than in any other system of the balance of power. The bipolar system, as we have seen, is more unsafe from the point of view of peace than any other, when both blocs are in competitive contact throughout the world and the ambition of both is fired by the crusading zeal of a universal mission. "Vicinity, or nearness of situation, constitutes nations' natural enemies."[10]

Yet once they have defined their national interests in terms of national security, they can draw back from their outlying positions, located close to, or within, the sphere of national security of the other side, and retreat into their respective spheres, each self-contained within its orbit. Those outlying positions add nothing to national security; they are but liabilities, positions that cannot be held in case of war. Each bloc will be the more secure the wider it makes the distance that separates both spheres of national security. Each side can draw a line far distant from each other, making it understood that to touch or even to approach it means war. What, then, about the interjacent spaces, stretching between the two lines of demarcation? Here the fourth rule of diplomacy applies.

4. Nations must be willing to compromise on all issues that are not vital to them.

> All government, indeed every human benefit and enjoyment, every virtue and every prudent act, is founded on compromise and barter. We balance inconveniences; we give and take; we remit some rights, that we may enjoy others; and we choose rather to be happy citizens than subtle disputants. As we must give away some natural liberty, to enjoy civil advantages, so we must sacrifice some civil liberties, for the advantages to be derived from the communion and fellowship of a great empire. But, in all fair dealings, the thing bought must bear some proportion to the purchase paid. None will barter away the immediate jewel of his soul.[11]

Here diplomacy meets its most difficult task. For minds not beclouded by the crusading zeal of a political religion and capable of viewing the national interests of both sides with objectivity, the delimitation of these vital interests should not prove too difficult. Compromise on secondary issues is a different matter. Here the task is not to separate and define interests that by their very nature already tend toward separation and definition but to keep in balance interests that touch one another at many points and may be intertwined beyond the possibility of separation. It is an immense task to allow the other side a certain influence in those interjacent spaces without allowing them to be absorbed into the orbit of the other side. It is hardly a less immense task to keep the other side's influence as small as possible in the regions close to one's own security zone without absorbing those regions

---

[10]*The Federalist*, No. 6.
[11]Edmund Burke, "Speech on the Conciliation with America," *Works*, Vol. II, p. 169.

into one's own orbit. For the performance of these tasks, no formula stands ready for automatic application. It is only through a continuous process of adaptation, supported both by firmness and self-restraint, that compromise on secondary issues can be made to work. It is, however, possible to indicate a priori what approaches will facilitate or hamper the success of policies of compromise.

First of all, it is worth noting to what extent the success of compromise—that is, compliance with the fourth rule—depends upon compliance with the other three rules, which in turn are similarly interdependent. As the compliance with the second rule depends upon the realization of the first, so the third rule must await its realization from compliance with the second. A nation can take a rational view of its national interests only after it has parted company with the crusading spirit of a political creed. A nation is able to consider the national interests of the other side with objectivity only after it has become secure in what it considers its own national interests. Compromise on any issue, however minor, is impossible so long as both sides are not secure in their national interests. Thus nations cannot hope to comply with the fourth rule if they are not willing to comply with the other three. Both morality and expediency require compliance with these four fundamental rules.

Compliance makes compromise possible, but it does not assure its success. To give compromise, made possible through compliance with the first three rules, a chance to succeed, five other rules must be observed.

Five Prerequisites of Compromise

1. Give up the shadow of worthless rights for the substance of real advantage. A diplomacy that thinks in legalistic and propagandistic terms is particularly tempted to insist upon the letter of the law, as it interprets the law, and to lose sight of the consequences such insistence may have for its own nation and for humanity. Since there are rights to be defended, this kind of diplomacy thinks that the issue cannot be compromised. Yet the choice that confronts the diplomat is not between legality and illegality but between political wisdom and political folly. "The question with me," said Edmund Burke, "is not whether you have a right to render your people miserable, but whether it is not your interest to make them happy. It is not what a lawyer tells me I *may* do, but what humanity, reason and justice tell me I ought to do."[12]

2. Never put yourself in a position from which you cannot retreat without losing face and from which you cannot advance without grave risks. The violation of this rule often results from disregard for the preceding one. A diplomacy that confounds the shadow of legal right with the actuality of political advantage is likely to find itself in a position where it may have a legal right, but no political business, to be. In other words, a nation may identify itself with a position, which it may or may not have a right to hold, regardless of the political consequences.

---

[12]"Speech on Conciliation with the Colonies" (1775), *The Works of Edmund Burke* (Boston: Little, Brown, 1865), Vol. II, p. 140.

And again compromise becomes a difficult matter. A nation cannot retreat from that position without incurring a serious loss of prestige. It cannot advance from that position without exposing itself to political risks, perhaps even the risk of war. That heedless rush into untenable positions and, more particularly, the stubborn refusal to extricate oneself from them in time is the earmark of incompetent diplomacy. Its classic examples are the policy of Napoleon III on the eve of the Franco-Prussian War of 1870 and the policies of Austria and Germany on the eve of the First World War. Its outstanding contemporary example is the American involvement in Indochina. These examples also show how closely the risk of war is allied with the violation of this rule.

3. Never allow a weak ally to make decisions for you. Strong nations that are oblivious to the preceding rules are particularly susceptible to violating this one. They lose their freedom of action by identifying their own national interests completely with those of the weak ally. Secure in the support of its powerful friend, the weak ally can choose the objectives and methods of its foreign policy to suit itself. The powerful nation then finds that it must support interests not its own and that it is unable to compromise on issues that are vital not to itself, but only to its ally.

The classic example of the violation of this rule is to be found in the way in which Turkey forced the hand of Great Britain and France on the eve of the Crimean War in 1853. The Concert of Europe had virtually agreed upon a compromise settling the conflict between Russia and Turkey, when Turkey, knowing that the Western powers would support it in a war with Russia, did its best to provoke that war and thus involved Great Britain and France in it against their will. Thus Turkey went far in deciding the issue of war and peace for Great Britain and France according to its own national interests. Great Britain and France had to accept that decision even though their national interests did not require war with Russia and they had almost succeeded in preventing its outbreak. They had surrendered their freedom of action to a weak ally, which used its control over their policies for its own purposes.

4. The armed forces are the instrument of foreign policy, not its master. No successful and no peaceful foreign policy is possible without observance of this rule. No nation can pursue a policy of compromise with the military determining the ends and means of foreign policy. The armed forces are instruments of war; foreign policy is an instrument of peace. It is true that the ultimate objectives of the conduct of war and of the conduct of foreign policy are identical: both serve the national interest. Both, however, differ fundamentally in their immediate objective, in the means they employ, and in the modes of thought they bring to bear upon their respective tasks.

The objective of war is simple and unconditional: to break the will of the enemy. Its methods are equally simple and unconditional: to bring the greatest amount of violence to bear upon the most vulnerable spot in the enemy's armor. Consequently, the military leader must think in absolute terms. He lives in the present and in the immediate future. The sole question before him is how to win victories as cheaply and quickly as possible and how to avoid defeat.

The objective of foreign policy is relative and conditional: to bend, not to break, the will of the other side as far as necessary in order to safeguard one's own vital interests without hurting those of the other side. The methods of foreign policy are relative and conditional: not to advance by destroying the obstacles in one's way but to retreat before them, to circumvent them, to maneuver around them, to soften and dissolve them slowly by means of persuasion, negotiation, and pressure. In consequence, the mind of the diplomat is complicated and subtle. It sees the issue in hand as a moment in history, and beyond the victory of tomorrow it anticipates the incalculable possibilities of the future. In the words of Bolingbroke:

> Here let me only say, that the glory of taking towns, and winning battles, is to be measured by the utility that results from those victories. Victories, that bring honour to the arms, may bring shame to the councils, of a nation. To win a battle, to take a town, is the glory of a general, and of an army. . . . But the glory of a nation is to proportion the ends she proposes, to her interest and her strength; the means she employs to the ends she proposes, and the vigour she exerts to both.[13]

To surrender the conduct of foreign affairs to the military, then, is to destroy the possibility of compromise and thus surrender the cause of peace. The military mind knows how to operate between the absolutes of victory and defeat. It knows nothing of that patient, intricate, and subtle maneuvering of diplomacy, whose main purpose is to avoid the absolutes of victory and defeat and meet the other side on the middle ground of negotiated compromise. A foreign policy conducted by military men according to the rules of the military art can only end in war, for "what we prepare for is what we shall get."[14]

For nations conscious of the potentialities of modern war, peace must be the goal of their foreign policies. Foreign policy must be conducted in such a way as to make the preservation of peace possible and not make the outbreak of war inevitable. In a society of sovereign nations, military force is a necessary instrument of foreign policy. Yet the instrument of foreign policy should not become the master of foreign policy. As war is fought in order to make peace possible, foreign policy should be conducted in order to make peace permanent. For the performance of both tasks, the subordination of the military under the civilian authorities that are constitutionally responsible for the conduct of foreign affairs is an indispensable prerequisite.

5. The government is the leader of public opinion, not its slave. Those responsible for the conduct of foreign policy will not be able to comply with the foregoing principles of diplomacy if they do not keep this principle constantly in mind. As has been pointed out above in greater detail,[15] the rational requirements of good foreign policy cannot from the outset count upon the support of a public

---

[13]*Bolingbroke's Defence of the Treaty of Utrecht* (Cambridge, UK: Cambridge University Press, 1932), p. 95.
[14]William Graham Sumner, *Essays*, p. 173.
[15]See pages 158 ff.

opinion whose preferences are emotional rather than rational. This is bound to be particularly true of a foreign policy whose goal is compromise and which, therefore, must concede some of the objectives of the other side and give up some of its own. Especially when foreign policy is conducted under conditions of democratic control and is inspired by the crusading zeal of a political religion, statesmen are always tempted to sacrifice the requirements of good foreign policy to the applause of the masses. On the other hand, the statesman who would defend the integrity of these requirements against even the slightest contamination with popular passion would seal his own doom as a political leader and, with it, the doom of his foreign policy, for he would lose the popular support that put and keeps him in power.

The statesman, then, is allowed neither to surrender to popular passions nor disregard them. He must strike a prudent balance between adapting himself to them and marshaling them to the support of his policies. In one word, he must lead. He must perform that highest feat of statesmanship: trimming his sails to the winds of popular passion while using them to carry the ship of state to the port of good foreign policy, on however roundabout and zigzag a course.

CONCLUSION

The road to international peace that we have outlined cannot compete in inspirational qualities with the simple and fascinating formulae that for a century and a half have fired the imagination of a war-weary world. There is something spectacular in the radical simplicity of a formula that with one sweep seems to dispose of the problem of war once and for all. This has been the promise of such solutions as free trade, arbitration, disarmament, collective security, universal socialism, international government, and the world state. There is nothing spectacular, fascinating, or inspiring, at least for the people at large, in the business of diplomacy.

We have made the point, however, that these solutions, insofar as they deal with the real problem and not merely with some of its symptoms, presuppose the existence of an integrated international society, which actually does not exist. To bring into existence such an international society and keep it in being, the accommodating techniques of diplomacy are required. As the integration of domestic society and its peace develop from the unspectacular and almost unnoticed day-by-day operations of the techniques of accommodation and change, so the ultimate ideal of international life—that is, to transcend itself in a supranational society—must await its realization from the techniques of persuasion, negotiation, and pressure, which are the traditional instruments of diplomacy.

The reader who has followed us to this point may well ask: but has not diplomacy failed in preventing war in the past? To that legitimate question two answers can be given.

Diplomacy has failed many times, and it has succeeded many times, in its peace-preserving task. It has failed sometimes because nobody wanted it to succeed. We have seen how different in their objectives and methods the limited wars of the past have been from the total war of our time. When war was the normal activity of kings, the task of diplomacy was not to prevent it but to bring it about at the most propitious moment.

On the other hand, when nations have used diplomacy for the purpose of preventing war, they have often succeeded. The outstanding example of a successful war-preventing diplomacy in modern times is the Congress of Berlin of 1878. By the peaceful means of an accommodating diplomacy, that congress settled, or at least made susceptible of settlement, the issues that had separated Great Britain and Russia since the end of the Napoleonic Wars. During the better part of the nineteenth century, the conflict between Great Britain and Russia over the Balkans, the Dardanelles, and the eastern Mediterranean hung like a suspended sword over the peace of the world. Yet, during the fifty years following the Crimean War, though hostilities between Great Britain and Russia threatened to break out time and again, they never actually did break out. The main credit for the preservation of peace must go to the techniques of an accommodating diplomacy that culminated in the Congress of Berlin. When British prime minister Disraeli returned from that congress to London, he declared with pride that he was bringing home "peace . . . with honor." In fact, he had brought peace for later generations, too; for a century there has been no war between Great Britain and Russia.

We have, however, recognized the precariousness of peace in a society of sovereign nations. The continuing success of diplomacy in preserving peace depends, as we have seen, upon extraordinary moral and intellectual qualities that all the leading participants must possess. A mistake in the evaluation of one of the elements of national power, made by one or the other of the leading statesmen, may spell the difference between peace and war. So may an accident spoiling a plan or a power calculation.[16]

Diplomacy is the best means of preserving peace that a society of sovereign nations has to offer, but, especially under the conditions of contemporary world politics and of contemporary war, it is not good enough. It is only when nations have surrendered to a higher authority the means of destruction that modern technology has put in their hands—when they have given up their sovereignty—that international peace can be made as secure as domestic peace. Diplomacy can make peace more secure than it is today, and the world state can make peace more secure than it would be if nations were to abide by the rules of diplomacy. Yet, as there can be no permanent peace without a world state, there can be no world state without the peace-preserving and community-building processes of diplomacy. For the world state to be more than a dim vision, the accommodating processes of diplomacy, mitigating and minimizing conflicts, must be revived. Whatever one's conception of the ultimate state of international affairs may be, in the recognition of that need and in the demand that it be met, all men of good will can join.

If authority were needed in support of the conception of international peace presented in these pages, it can be found in the counsel of a man who committed

---

[16] See pages 166 ff, 214 ff.

fewer errors in foreign policy than any of his contemporaries—Sir Winston Churchill. Viewing with concern the contemporary scene in his speech to the House of Commons of January 23, 1948, and asking himself, "Will there be war?" Mr. Churchill called for peace through accommodation—as he had done in almost fifty speeches since the outbreak of the Cold War—when he said:

> I will only venture now to say that there seems to me to be very real danger in going on drifting too long. I believe that the best chance of preventing a war is to bring matters to a head and come to a settlement with the Soviet Government before it is too late. This would imply that the Western democracies, who should, of course, seek unity among themselves at the earliest moment, would take the initiative in asking the Soviet for a settlement.
>
> It is idle to reason or argue with the Communists. It is, however, possible to deal with them on a fair, realistic basis, and, in my experience, they will keep their bargains as long as it is in their interest to do so, which might, in this grave matter, be a long time, once things are settled. . . .
>
> There are very grave dangers—that is all I am going to say today—in letting everything run on and pile up until something happens, and it passes, all of a sudden, out of your control.
>
> With all consideration of the facts, I believe it right to say today that the best chance of avoiding war is, in accord with the other Western democracies, to bring matters to a head with the Soviet Government, and, by formal diplomatic processes, with all their privacy and gravity, to arrive at a lasting settlement. There is certainly enough for the interests of all if such a settlement could be reached. Even this method, I must say, however, would not guarantee that war would not come. But I believe it would give the best chance of coming out of it alive.[17]

---

[17] *Parliamentary Debates (Hansard), House of Commons,* Vol. 446, No. 48, pp. 562–63.

Appendix A Updating Realism for the Twenty-First Century

THE FALSE PROMISE OF INTERNATIONAL INSTITUTIONS

John J. Mearsheimer

This article examines the claim that institutions push states away from war and promote peace. I concentrate on assessing the major international relations theories that employ institutions as a core concept; liberal institutionalism, collective security, and critical theory.[1] I begin, however, with a brief review of realism, because the "institutionalist" theories are largely a response to realism, and each directly challenges realism's underlying logic.[2] Realists and institutionalists particularly disagree about whether institutions markedly affect the prospects for international stability. Realists say no; institutionalists say yes. Realists maintain that institutions are basically a reflection of the distribution of power in the world. They are based on the self-interested calculations of the great powers, and they have no independent effect on state behavior. Realists therefore believe that institutions are not an important cause of peace. They matter only on the margins. Institutionalists directly challenge this view of institutions, arguing instead that institutions can alter state preferences and therefore change state behavior. Institutions can discourage states from calculating self-interest on the basis of how every move affects their relative power positions. Institutions are independent variables, and they have the capability to move states away from war.

Although institutionalists are united in their opposition to realist claims about institutions, each institutionalist theory makes a different argument about how institutions work to alter state behavior. My goal is to evaluate these three theories to determine whether the claim that institutions cause

John J. Mearsheimer is a professor in the Political Science Department at the University of Chicago.

International Security, Vol. 19, No. 31 (Winter 1994–95), pp. 5–49
© 1995 by the President and Fellows of Harvard College and the Massachusetts Institute of Technology.

This article emerged from a working paper written for "The Changing Security Environment and American National Interests," a project of the John M. Olin Institute for Strategic Studies at Harvard University. I am grateful to Robert Art, Benjamin Frankel, Markus Fischer, Charles Glaser, Hein Goemans, Joseph Grieco, Robert Jervis, Christopher Layne, Eric Lopez, Robert Pape, Ashley Tellis, Bradley Thayer, Ivan Toft, Stephen Van Evera, Stephen Walt, and especially Michael Desch for their most helpful comments.

[1] Prescriptions about how best to maintain peace should rest on general theories about the causes of war and peace. This point is true for both academics and policymakers. Although policymakers are seldom self-conscious in their use of theory, their views about institutions are nevertheless shaped by their implicit preferences for one theory of international relations over another.

[2] Keohane, for example, writes, "Institutionalist thinking has focused its critical fire on realism." Robert O. Keohane, "Institutional Theory and the Realist Challenge After the Cold War," in *Neorealism and Neoliberalism The Contemporary Debate*, David A. Baedwin, ed. (New York: Columbia University Press, 1993), p. 271.

peace is persuasive. That task involves answering four questions: (1) What are institutions? (2) How do they work to cause peace? Specifically, what is the causal logic that underpins each theory? (3) Are these different logics that explain how institutions work compelling? (4) Does the evidence support these theories?

My central conclusion is that institutions have minimal influence on state behavior and thus hold little promise for promoting stability in the post–Cold War world. The three theories on which the case for institutions is based are all flawed. Each has problems in its causal logic, and all three institutionalist theories find little support in the historical record.

The remainder of this article is organized as follows. I begin with a brief definition of institutions and a discussion of realism, because each of the institutionalist theories takes its bearings from realism. In the main body of the article, I describe and evaluate liberal institutionalism, collective security, and critical theory. The concluding section considers why institutions are so highly regarded by policymakers and academics, when there is so little evidence that they are an important cause of peace.

What Are Institutions?

There is no widely agreed-upon definition of institutions in the international relations literature.[3] The concept is sometimes defined so broadly as to encompass all of international relations, which gives it little analytical bite.[4] For example, defining institutions as "recognized patterns of behavior or practice around which expectations converge" allows the concept to cover almost every regularized pattern of activity between states, from war to tariff bindings negotiated under the General Agreement on Tariffs and Trade (GATT), thus rendering it largely meaningless.[5] Still, it is possible to devise a useful definition that: is consistent with how most institutionalist scholars employ the concept.

I define institutions as a set of rules that stipulate the ways in which states should cooperate and compete with each other.[6] They prescribe acceptable forms of state behavior and proscribe unacceptable kinds of behavior. These rules are negotiated by states, and according to many prominent theorists, they entail the mutual acceptance of higher norms, which are "standards of behavior defined in terms of rights and obligations."[7] These rules are typically

---

[3]Regimes and institutions are treated as synonymous concepts in this article. They are also used interchangeably in the institutionalist literature. See Robert O. Keohane, "International Institutions: Two Approaches," *International Studies Quarterly*, Vol. 32, No. 4 (December, 1988), p. 384; Robert O. Keohane, *International Institutions and State Power: Essays in International Relations Theory* (Boulder, CO: Westview Press, 1989), pp. 3–4; and Oran R. Young. *International Cooperation: Building Regimes for Natural Resources and the Environment* (Ithaca, NY: Cornell University Press, 1989), Chaps. 1 and 8. The term "multilateralism" is also virtually synonymous with institutions. To quote John Ruggie, "the term 'multilateral' is an adjective that modifies the noun 'institution.' Thus, multilateralism depicts a *generic institutional form* in international relations. . . . [Specifically,] multilateralism is an institutional form which coordinates relations among three or more states on the basis of 'generalized' principles of conduct." Ruggis, "Multilateralism," pp. 570–71.

[4]For discussion of this point, see Arthur A. Stein, *Why Nations Cooperate: Circumstance and Choice in International Relations* (Ithaca, NY: Cornell University Press, 1990), pp. 25–27. Also see Susan Strange. "*Cazel Hic Dragones:* A Critique of Regime Analysis," in *International Regimes*, edited by Stephen D. Krasner, special issue of *International Organisation*, Vol. 36, No. 2 (Spring, 1982), pp. 479–96.
[5]Oran R. Young, "Regime Dynamics: The Rise and Fall of International Regimes," In Krasner, *International Regimes*, p. 277.
[6]See Douglans C. North and Robert P. Thomas, "An Economic Theory of the Growth of the Western World," *The Economic History Review*, 2nd series, Vol. 23, No. 1 (April 1970), p. 5.
[7]Krasner, *International Regimes*, p. 186. Nonrealist institutions are often based on higher norms, while few, if any, realist institutions are based on norms. The dividing line between norms and rules is not sharply defined in the institutionalist literature. See Robert O. Keohane, *After Hegemony: Cooperation and Discord in the World Political Economy* (Princeton, NJ: Princeton University Press, 1984), pp. 57–58. For example, one might argue that rules, not just norms, are concerned with rights and obligations. The key point, however, is that for many institutionalists, norms, which are core beliefs about standards of appropriate state behavior, are the foundation on which more specific rules are constructed. This distinction between norms and rules applies in a rather straightforward way in the subsequent discussion. Both collective security and critical theory challenge the realist belief that states behave in a self-interested way, and argue instead for developing norms that require states to act more altruistically. Liberal institutionalism, on the other hand, accepts the realist view that states act on the basis of self-interest, and concentrates on devising rules that facilitate cooperation among states.

formalized in international agreements, and are usually embodied in organizations with their own personnel and budgets.[8] Although rules are usually incorporated into a formal international organization, it is not the organization per se that compels states to obey the rules. Institutions are not a form of world government. States themselves must choose to obey the rules they created. Institutions, in short, call for the "decentralized cooperation of individual sovereign states, without any effective mechanism of command."[9]

To answer the three remaining questions about how institutions do or do not work, we must examine the different institutionalist theories separately. However, a brief discussion of realism is in order first.

Realism

Realism paints a rather grim picture of world politics.[10] The international system is portrayed as a brutal arena where states look for opportunities to take advantage of each other and therefore have little reason to trust each other.[11] Daily life is essentially a struggle for power, where each state strives not only to be the most powerful actor in the system but also to ensure that no other state achieves that lofty position.

International relations is not a constant state of war, but it is a state of relentless security competition, with the possibility of war always in the background. The intensity of that competition varies from case to case. Although it might seem counterintuitive, states do frequently cooperate in this competitive world. Nevertheless, cooperation among states has its limits, mainly because it is constrained by the dominating logic of security competition, which no amount of cooperation can eliminate. Genuine peace, or a world where states do not compete for power, is not likely, according to realism.

This pessimistic view of how the world works can be derived from realism's five assumptions about the international system. The first is that the international system is anarchic. This does not mean that it is chaotic or riven by disorder.[12] It is easy to draw that conclusion, since realism depicts a world characterized by security competition and war. However, "anarchy" as employed by realists has nothing to do with conflict; rather, it is an ordering principle, which says that the system comprises independent political units (states) that have no central authority above them. Sovereignty, in other words, inheres in states, because there is no higher ruling body in the international system. There is no "government over governments."[13]

The second assumption is that states inherently possess some offensive military capability, which

---

[8]International organizations are public agencies established through the cooperative efforts of two or more states. These administrative structures have their own budget, personnel, and buildings. John Ruggie defines them as "palpable entities with headquarters and letterheads, voting procedures, and generous pension plans." Ruggie, "Multilateralism," p. 573. Once rules are incorporated into an international organization, "they may seem almost coterminous," even though they are "distinguishable analytically." Keohane, *International Institutions and State Power,* p. 5.

[9]Charles Lipson, "Is the Future of Collective Security Like the Past?" in *Collective Security Beyond the Cold War,* George W. Downs, ed. (Ann Arbor, MI: University of Michigan Press), p. 114.

[10]Although realist scholars agree about many aspects of international politics, there are important intellectual disagreements among them. Consider Hans Morgenthau and Kenneth Waltz, probably the two most influential realists over the past fifty years: Morgenthau maintains that states have a will to power, while Waltz begins his theory with the assumption that states merely want to survive and are therefore driven to maximize security. See Hans J. Morgenthau, *Politics Among Nations: The Struggle for Power and Peace,* 5th ed. (New York: Knopf, 1973); and Kenneth N. Waltz, *Theory of International Politics* (Reading, MA: Addison-Wesley, 1979). The discussion in this section is based on my own thinking about realism, which is closer to Waltz than to Morgenthau.

[11]See Stephen Van Evera, "The Hard Realities of International Politics," *Boston Review,* Vol. 17, No. 6 (November/December 1992), p. 19.

[12]See Waltz, *Theory of International Politics,* pp. 88–93. Also see Robert J. Art and Robert Jervis, editors, *International Politics: Anarchy, Force, Imperialism* (Boston: Little, Brown, 1973), Part 1; and Helen Milner, "International Theories of Cooperation Among Nations: Strengths and Weaknesses," *World Politics,* Vol. 44, No. 3 (April 1992), p. 468.

[13]Inis L. Claude, Jr., *Swords into Plowshares: The Problems and Progress of International Organization,* 4th ed. (New York: Random House, 1971), p. 14.

gives them the wherewithal to hurt and possibly to destroy each other. States are potentially dangerous to each other. A state's military power is usually identified with the particular weaponry at its disposal, although even if there were no weapons, the individuals of a state could still use their feet and hands to attack the population of another state.

The third assumption is that states can never be certain about the intentions of other states. Specifically, no state can be certain another state will not use its offensive military capability against the first. This is not to say that states necessarily have malign intentions. Another state may be reliably benign, but it is impossible to be certain of that judgment because intentions are impossible to divine with 100 percent certainty. There are many possible causes of aggression, and no state can be sure that another state is not motivated by one of them. Furthermore, intentions can change quickly, so a state's intentions can be benign one day and malign the next. Uncertainty is unavoidable when assessing intentions, which simply means that states can never be sure that other states do not have offensive intentions to go with their offensive military capability.

The fourth assumption is that the most basic motive driving states is survival. States want to maintain their sovereignty. The fifth assumption is that states think strategically about how to survive in the international system. States are instrumentally rational. Nevertheless, they may miscalculate from time to time because they operate in a world of imperfect information, where potential adversaries have incentives to misrepresent their own strength or weakness and to conceal their true aims.

None of these assumptions alone mandates that states will behave competitively. In fact, the fundamental assumption dealing with motives says that states merely aim to survive, which is a defensive goal.[14] When taken together, however, these five assumptions can create incentives for states to think and sometimes to behave aggressively. Specifically, three main patterns of behavior result.

First, states in the international system fear each other. They regard each other with suspicion, and they worry that war might be in the offing. They anticipate danger. There is little room for trust among states. Although the level of fear varies across time and space, it can never be reduced to a trivial level.[15] The basis of this fear is that in a world where states have the capability to offend against each other, and might have the motive to do so, any state bent on survival must be at least suspicious of other states and reluctant to trust them. Add to this the assumption that there is no central authority that a threatened state can turn to for help, and states have even greater incentive to fear each other. Moreover, there is no mechanism—other than the possible self-interest of third parties—for punishing an aggressor. Because it is often difficult to deter potential aggressors, states have ample reason to take steps to be prepared for war.

The possible consequences of falling victim to aggression further illustrate why fear is a potent force in world politics. States do not compete with each other as if international politics were simply an economic marketplace. Political competition among states is a much more dangerous business than economic intercourse; it can lead to war, and war often means mass killing on the battlefield and even mass murder of civilians. In extreme cases, war can even lead to the total destruction of a state. The horrible consequences of war sometimes cause

---

[14]Morgenthau, as emphasized, maintains that states have an innate will to power, and are therefore inherently offensive in their outlook. The argument here is that states begin with a defensive motive but are forced to think and sometimes act offensively because of the structure of the international system.

[15]This point is illustrated by the reaction of Britain and France to German reunification at the end of the Cold War. Despite the fact that these three states had been close allies for almost forty-five years, both Britain and France immediately began thinking about the dangers of a united Germany. See David Garnham, "European Defense Cooperation: The 1990s and Beyond," in *The 1992 Project and the Future of Integration in Europe*, Dale L. Smith and James Lee Ray, eds. (Armonk, NY: M. E. Sharpe, 1993), pp. 203–5; and Margaret Thatcher, *The Downing Street Years* (New York: HarperCollins, 1993), Chaps. 25–26.

states to view each other not just as competitors but as potentially deadly enemies.

Second, each state in the international system aims to guarantee its own survival. Because other states are potential threats, and because there is no higher authority to rescue them when danger arises, states cannot depend on others for their security. Each state tends to see itself as vulnerable and alone, and therefore it aims to provide for its own survival. As Kenneth Waltz puts it, states operate in a "self-help" system. This emphasis on self-help does not preclude states from forming alliances.[16] But alliances are only temporary marriages of convenience, where today's alliance partner might be tomorrow's enemy, and today's enemy might be tomorrow's alliance partner. States operating in a self-help world should always act according to their own self-interest, because it pays to be selfish in a self-help world. This is true in the short term as well as the long term, because if a state loses in the short run, it may not be around for the long haul.

Third, states in the international system aim to maximize their relative power positions over other states.[17] The reason is simple: the greater the military advantage one state has over other states, the more secure it is. Every state would like to be the most formidable military power in the system because this is the best way to guarantee survival in a world that can be very dangerous. This logic creates strong incentives for states to take advantage of one another, including going to war if the circumstances are right and victory seems likely. The aim is to acquire more military power at the expense of potential rivals. The ideal outcome would be to end up as the hegemon in the system. Survival would then be almost guaranteed.

All states are influenced by this logic, which means not only that they look for opportunities to take advantage of one another but also that they work to insure that other states do not take advantage of them.[18] States are, in other words, both offensively oriented and defensively oriented. They think about conquest themselves, and they balance against aggressors; this inexorably leads to a world of constant security competition, with the possibility of war always in the background. Peace, if one defines that concept as a state of tranquility or mutual concord, is not likely to break out in this world.

Cooperation in a Realist World

Although realism envisions a world that is fundamentally competitive, cooperation between states does occur. It is sometimes difficult to achieve, however, and always difficult to sustain. Two factors inhibit cooperation: relative-gains considerations, and concern about cheating.[19]

States contemplating cooperation must consider how the profits or gains will be distributed among them. They can think about the division in two different ways. They can think in terms of absolute gains, which means each side focuses on maximizing its own profit and cares little about how much the other side gains or loses in the deal. Each side cares about the other only to the extent that the other side's behavior affects its own prospects for achieving maximum profits. Alternately, states can think in terms of relative gains, which means each side considers not only its individual gain but also how well it does compared to the other side.

---

[16]See Stephen M. Walt, *The Origins of Alliances* (Ithaca, NY: Cornell University Press, 1987).

[17]There is disagreement among realists on this point. Some realists argue that states are principally interested in maintaining the existing balance of power, not maximizing relative power. For examples of this "defensive realism," which contrasts with my "offensive realism," see Joseph M. Grieco, "Anarchy and the Limits of Cooperation: A Realist Critique of the Newest Liberal Institutionalism," *International Organization*, Vol. 42, No. 3 (Summer 1988), pp. 498–500; Jack L. Snyder, *Myths of Empire: Domestic Politics and International Ambition* (Ithaca, NY: Cornell University Press, 1991), pp. 10–13; and Waltz, *Theory of International Politics*, pp. 126–27. Also see Fareed Zakaria, "Realism and Domestic Politics: A Review Essay," *International Security*, Vol. 17, No. 1 (Summer 1992), pp. 190–96. Morgenthau is also an offensive realist. This disagreement notwithstanding, all realists do believe that states care greatly about the relative balance of power.

[18]See Walt, *Origins of Alliances.*

[19]See Grieco, "Anarchy and the Limits of Cooperation."

Because states in a realist world are concerned about the balance of power, they must be motivated primarily by relative gains concerns when considering cooperation. While each state wants to maximize its absolute gains, it is more important to make sure that it does better, or at least no worse, than the other state in any agreement. However, cooperation is more difficult to achieve when states are attuned to relative-gains logic, rather than absolute-gains logic. This is because states concerned about absolute gains need only make sure that the pie is expanding and that they are getting at least some portion of the increase, while states that worry about relative gains must care also about how the pie is divided, which complicates cooperative efforts.

Concerns about cheating also hinder cooperation. States are often reluctant to enter into cooperative agreements for fear that the other side will cheat on the agreement and gain a relative advantage. There is a "special peril of defection" in the military realm, because the nature of military weaponry allows for rapid shifts in the balance of power. Such a development could create a window of opportunity for the cheating state to inflict a decisive defeat on the victim state.[20]

These barriers to cooperation notwithstanding, states do cooperate in a realist world. For example, balance-of-power logic often causes states to form alliances and cooperate against common enemies. States sometimes cooperate to gang up on a third state, as the Germans and the Soviets did against Poland in 1939.[21] Rivals as well as allies cooperate. After all, deals can be struck that roughly reflect the distribution of power and satisfy concerns about cheating. The various arms control agreements signed by the superpowers during the Cold War illustrate this point.

The bottom line, however, is that cooperation takes place in a world that is competitive at its core—one where states have powerful incentives to take advantage of other states. This point is graphically highlighted by European politics in the forty years before World War I. There was much cooperation among the great powers during this period, but that did not stop them from going to war in 1914.[22]

Institutions in a Realist World

Realists also recognize that states sometimes operate through institutions. However, they believe that those rules reflect state calculations of self-interest based primarily on the international distribution of power. The most powerful states in the system create and shape institutions so that they can maintain their share of world power, or even increase it. In this view, institutions are essentially "arenas for acting out power relationships."[23] For realists, the causes of war and peace are mainly a function of the balance of power, and institutions largely mirror the distribution of power in the system. In short, the balance of power is the independent variable that explains war; institutions are merely an intervening variable in the process.

NATO provides a good example of realist thinking about institutions. NATO is an institution, and it certainly played a role in preventing World War III and helping the West win the Cold War. Nevertheless, NATO was basically a

---

[20]Lipson, "International Cooperation," p. 14.
[21]Randall L. Schweller, "Bandwagoning for Profit: Bringing the Revisionist State Back In," *International Security*, Vol. 19, No. 1 (Summer 1994), pp. 72–107.

[22]See John Maynard Keynes, *The Economic Consequences of the Peace* (New York: Penguin Books, 1988), Chap. 2; and J. M. Roberts, *Europe, 1880–1945* (London: Longman, 1970), pp. 239–41. There was also significant cooperation between the United States and the Soviet Union during World War II, but that cooperation did not prevent the outbreak of the Cold War shortly after Germany and Japan were defeated.
[23]Tony Evans and Peter Wilson, "Regime Theory and the English School of International Relations: A Comparison," *Millennium: Journal of International Studies*, Vol. 21, No. 3 (Winter 1992), p. 330.

manifestation of the bipolar distribution of power in Europe during the Cold War, and it was that balance of power, not NATO per se, that provided the key to maintaining stability on the continent. NATO was essentially an American tool for managing power in the face of the Soviet threat. Now, with the collapse of the Soviet Union, realists argue that NATO must either disappear or reconstitute itself on the basis of the new distribution of power in Europe.[24] NATO cannot remain as it was during the Cold War.

Varieties of Institutionalist Theories

There are three institutionalist theories, and each offers a different argument about how institutions push states away from war and help foster stability.[25] Liberal institutionalism is the least ambitious of the three theories. It does not directly address the important question of how to prevent war but focuses instead on explaining why economic and environmental cooperation among states is more likely than realists recognize. Increased cooperation in those realms is presumed to reduce the likelihood of war, although liberal institutionalists do not explain how. The theory is predicated on the belief that cheating is the main inhibitor of international cooperation and that institutions provide the key to overcoming that problem. The aim is to create rules that constrain states, but not to challenge the fundamental realist claim that states are self-interested actors.

Collective security directly confronts the issue of how to prevent war. The theory starts with the assumption that force will continue to matter in world politics, and that states will have to guard against potential aggressors. However, the threat of war can be greatly reduced, according to the theory, by challenging realist thinking about state behavior, and substituting in its place three antirealist norms. First, states should reject the idea of using force to change the status quo. Second, to deal with states that violate that norm and threaten (or start) a war, responsible states must not act on the basis of their own narrow self-interest. Rather, they must suppress the temptation to respond in whatever way would maximize their individual gains, and instead automatically join together to present the aggressor with the threat of overwhelming force. Third, states must trust each other to renounce aggression and to mean that renunciation. They must also be confident that other states will come to their rescue, should they become the target of aggression.

Critical theory is the most ambitious of the theories, as its ultimate aim is to transform the fundamental nature of international politics and to create a world where there is not just increased cooperation among states, but the possibility of genuine peace. Like collective security, but unlike liberal institutionalism, critical theory directly challenges realist thinking about the self-interested behavior of states. The theory is predicated on the assumption that ideas and discourse—how we think and talk about international politics—are the driving forces behind state behavior. It utterly rejects realism's claim that state behavior is largely a function of the given structure of the external world. For critical theorists, ideas shape the material world in important ways, and thus the way to revolutionize international politics is to change drastically the way individuals think and talk about world politics. Intellectuals, especially the critical theorists themselves, are believed to play a key role in that process. . . .

---

[24]See Gunther Hellmann and Reinhard Wolf, "Neorealism, Neoliberal Institutionalism, and the Future of NATO," *Security Studies,* Vol. 3, No. 1 (Autumn 1993), pp. 3–43.

[25]Despite these differences among institutionalist theories, proponents of each theory occasionally make favorable reference to the other theories and thus seem to recognize that all three theories are part of an institutionalist body of literature that takes antirealism as its main point of reference. See, for example: Charles A. Kupchan and Clifford A. Kupchan, "Concerts, Collective Security, and the Future of Europe," *International Security,* Vol. 16, No. 1 (Summer 1991), pp. 114–61; and Ruggie, "Multilateralism," pp. 561–98.

Flaws in the Causal Logic

There is an important theoretical failing in the liberal institutionalist logic, even as it applies to economic issues. The theory is correct as far as it goes: cheating can be a serious barrier to cooperation. It ignores, however, the other major obstacle to cooperation: relative-gains concerns. As Joseph Grieco has shown, liberal institutionalists assume that states are not concerned about relative gains but focus exclusively on absolute gains.[26] Keohane acknowledged this problem in 1993: "Grieco has made a significant contribution by focusing attention on the issue of relative gains, a subject that has been underemphasized, especially by liberal or neoliberal commentators on the world economy."[27]

This oversight is revealed by the assumed order of preference in the Prisoners' Dilemma game: each state cares about how its opponent's strategy will affect its own (absolute) gains but not about how much one side gains relative to the other. In other words, each side simply wants to get the best deal for itself and does not pay attention to how well the other side fares in the process.[28] Nevertheless, liberal institutionalists cannot ignore relative-gains considerations, because they assume that states are self-interested actors in an anarchic system, and they recognize that military power matters to states. A theory that explicitly accepts realism's core assumptions—and liberal institutionalism does that—must confront the issue of relative gains if it hopes to develop a sound explanation for why states cooperate.

One might expect liberal institutionalists to offer the counterargument that relative-gains logic applies only to the security realm, while absolute-gains logic applies to the economic realm. Given that they are mainly concerned with explaining economic and environmental cooperation, leaving relative-gains concerns out of the theory does not matter.

There are two problems with this argument. First, if cheating were the only significant obstacle to cooperation, liberal institutionalists could argue that their theory applies to the economic, but not the military, realm. In fact, they do make that argument. However, once relative-gains considerations are factored into the equation, it becomes impossible to maintain the neat dividing line between economic and military issues, mainly because military might is significantly dependent on economic might. The relative size of a state's economy has profound consequences for its standing in the international balance of military

---

[26] See Grieco, "Anarchy and the Limits of Cooperation." Other works by Grieco bearing on the subject include: Joseph M. Grieco, "Realist Theory and the Problem of International Cooperation: Analysis with an Amended Prisoner's Dilemma Model," *The Journal of Politics*, Vol. 50, No. 3 (August 1988), pp. 600–624; Grieco, *Cooperation Among Nations: Europe, America, and Non-Tariff Barriers to Trade* (Ithaca, NY: Cornell University Press, 1990); and Grieco, "Understanding the Problem of International Cooperation: The Limits of Neoliberal Institutionalism and the Future of Realist Theory," in Baldwin, *Neorealism and Neoliberalism*, pp. 301–38. The telling effect of Grieco's criticism is reflected in ibid., which is essentially organized around the relative-gains versus absolute-gains debate, an issue given little attention before Grieco raised it in his widely cited 1988 article. The matter was briefly discussed by two other scholars before Grieco. See Joanne Gowa, "Anarchy, Egoism, and Third Images: *The Evolution of Cooperation* and International Relations," *International Organization*, Vol. 40, No. 1 (Winter 1986), pp. 172–79; and Oran R. Young, "International Regimes: Toward a New Theory of Institutions," *World Politics*, Vol. 39, No. 1 (October 1986), pp. 118–19.

[27] Robert O. Keohane, "Institutional Theory and the Realist Challenge," in Baldwin, *Neorealism and Neoliberalism*, p. 283. When liberal institutionalists developed their theory in the mid-1980s, they did not explicitly assume that states pursue absolute gains. There is actually little evidence that they thought much about the distinction between relative gains and absolute gains. However, the assumption that states pursue absolute but not relative gains is implicit in their writings.

[28] Lipson writes: "The Prisoner's Dilemma, in its simplest form, involves two players. Each is assumed to be a self-interested, self-reliant maximizer of his own utility, an assumption that clearly parallels the Realist conception of sovereign states in international politics." Lipson, "International Cooperation," p. 2. Realists, however, do not accept this conception of international politics and, not surprisingly, have questioned the relevance of the prisoners' dilemma (at least in its common form) for explaining much of international relations. See Gowa, "Anarchy, Egoism, and Third Images"; Grieco, "Realist Theory and the Problem of International Cooperation"; and Stephen D. Krasner, "Global Communications and National Power: Life on the Pareto Frontier," *World Politics*, Vol. 43, No. 3 (April 1991), pp. 336–66.

power. Therefore, relative-gains concerns must be taken into account for security reasons when looking at the economic as well as military domain. The neat dividing line that liberal institutionalists employ to specify when their theory applies has little utility when one accepts that states worry about relative gains.[29]

Second, there are nonrealist (i.e., nonsecurity) logics that might explain why states worry about relative gains. Strategic trade theory, for example, provides a straightforward economic logic for why states should care about relative gains.[30] It argues that states should help their own firms gain comparative advantage over the firms of rival states, because that is the best way to insure national economic prosperity. There is also a psychological logic, which portrays individuals as caring about how well they do (or their state does) in a cooperative agreement, not for material reasons, but because it is human nature to compare one's progress with that of others.[31]

Another possible liberal institutionalist counterargument is that solving the cheating problem renders the relative-gains problem irrelevant. If states cannot cheat each other, they need not fear each other, and therefore, states would not have to worry about relative power. The problem with this argument, however, is that even if the cheating problem were solved, states would still have to worry about relative gains because gaps in gains can be translated into military advantage that can be used for coercion or aggression. And in the international system, states sometimes have conflicting interests that lead to aggression.

There is also empirical evidence that relative-gains considerations mattered during the Cold War even in economic relations among the advanced industrialized democracies in the Organization for Economic Cooperation and Development (OECD). One would not expect realist logic about relative gains to be influential in this case: The United States was a superpower with little to fear militarily from the other OECD states, and those states were unlikely to use a relative-gains advantage to threaten the United States.[32] Furthermore, the OECD states were important American allies during the Cold War, and thus the United States benefited strategically when they gained substantially in size and strength.

Nonetheless, relative gains appear to have mattered in economic relations among the advanced industrial states. Consider three prominent studies. Stephen Krasner considered efforts at cooperation in different sectors of the international communications industry. He found that states were remarkably unconcerned about cheating but deeply worried about relative gains, which led him to conclude that liberal institutionalism "is not relevant for global communications." Grieco examined American and EC efforts to implement, under the auspices of GATT, a number of agreements relating to nontariff barriers to trade. He found that the level of success was not a function of concerns about cheating but was influenced

---

[29]My thinking on this matter has been markedly influenced by Sean Lynn-Jones, in his June 19, 1994, correspondence with me.

[30]For a short discussion of strategic trade theory, see Robert Gilpin, *The Political Economy of International Relations* (Princeton, NJ: Princeton University Press, 1987), pp. 215–21. The most commonly cited reference on the subject is Paul R. Krugman, editor, *Strategic Trade Policy and the New International Economics* (Cambridge, MA: MIT Press, 1986).

[31]See Robert Axelrod, *The Evolution of Cooperation* (New York: Basic Books, 1984), pp. 110–13.

[32]Grieco maintains in *Cooperation Among Nations* that realist logic should apply here. Robert Powell, however, points out that "in the context of negotiations between the European Community and the United States . . . it is difficult to attribute any concern for relative gains to the effects that a relative loss may have on the probability of survival." Robert Powell, "Absolute and Relative Gains in International Relations Theory," *American Political Science Review*, Vol. 85, No. 4 (December 1991), p. 1319, note 26. I agree with Powell. It is clear from Grieco's response to Powell that Grieco includes nonmilitary logics like strategic trade theory in the realist tent, whereas Powell and I do not. See Grieco's contribution to "The Relative-Gains Problem for International Relations," *American Political Science Review*, Vol. 87, No. 3 (September 1993), pp. 733–35.

primarily by concern about the distribution of gains. Similarly, Michael Mastanduno found that concern about relative gains, not about cheating, was an important factor in shaping American policy toward Japan in three cases: the FSX fighter aircraft, satellites, and high-definition television.[33]

I am not suggesting that relative-gains considerations make cooperation impossible; my point is simply that they can pose a serious impediment to cooperation and must therefore be taken into account when developing a theory of cooperation among states. This point is apparently now recognized by liberal institutionalists. Keohane, for example, acknowledges that he "did make a major mistake by underemphasizing distributive issues and the complexities they create for international cooperation."[34]

Can Liberal Institutionalism Be Repaired?

Liberal institutionalists must address two questions if they are to repair their theory. First, can institutions facilitate cooperation when states seriously care about relative gains, or do institutions matter only when states can ignore relative-gains considerations and focus instead on absolute gains? I find no evidence that liberal institutionalists believe that institutions facilitate cooperation when states care deeply about relative gains. They apparently concede that their theory applies only when relative-gains considerations matter little or hardly at all.[35]

Thus the second question: when do states not worry about relative gains? The answer to this question would ultimately define the realm in which liberal institutionalism applies.

Liberal institutionalists have not addressed this important question in a systematic fashion, so any assessment of their efforts to repair the theory must be preliminary. What exists are a lengthy response by Keohane to Grieco's original work on relative gains and two studies responding to Grieco's writings by Robert Powell and Duncan Snidal, which Keohane and other liberal institutionalists point to as exemplars of how to think about the relative-gains problem.[36]

Powell and Snidal offer different arguments about when relative-gains considerations are slight. Nevertheless, both are essentially realist arguments.[37] Neither study discusses how institutions might facilitate cooperation, and both explanations are built around familiar realist concepts.

At the root of Powell's argument is the well-known offense-defense balance made famous by Robert Jervis, George Quester, Jack Snyder, and Stephen Van Evera.[38] Powell maintains that

---

[33]Krasner, "Global Communications and National Power," pp. 336–66; Grieco, *Cooperation Among Nations;* and Michael Mastanduno, "Do Relative Gains Matter? America's Response to Japanese Industrial Policy," *International Security*, Vol. 16, No. 1 (Summer 1991), pp. 73–113. Also see Jonathan B. Tucker, "Partners and Rivals: A Model of International Collaboration in Advanced Technology," *International Organization*, Vol. 45, No. 1 (Winter 1991), pp. 83–120.

[34]Keohane, "Institutional Theory and the Realist Challenge," p. 292.

[35]For example, Keohane wrote after becoming aware of Grieco's argument about relative gains: "Under specified conditions—where mutual interests are low and relative gains are therefore particularly important to states—neoliberal theory expects neorealism to explain elements of state behavior." Keohane, *International Institutions and State Power*, pp. 15–16.

[36]Keohane, "Institutional Theory and the Realist Challenge," pp. 269–300; Powell, "Absolute and Relative Gains," pp. 1303–20; and Duncan Snidal, "Relative Gains and the Pattern of International Cooperation," *American Political Science Review*, Vol. 85, No. 3 (September 1991), pp. 701–26. Also see Powell, "Anarchy in International Relations Theory: The Neorealist-Neoliberal Debate," *International Organization*, Vol. 48, No. 2 (Spring 1994), pp. 313–44; Snidal, "International Cooperation Among Relative Gains Maximizers," *International Studies Quarterly*, Vol. 35, No. 4 (December 1991), pp. 387–402; and Powell and Snidal's contributions to "The Relative-Gains Problem for International Cooperation," pp. 735–42.

[37]On this point, see Sean Lynn-Jones, "Comments on Grieco, 'Realist Theory and the Relative Gains Problem for International Cooperation: Developments in the Debate and the Prospects for Future Research'," unpublished memorandum, December 10, 1992.

[38]Robert Jervis, "Cooperation Under the Security Dilemma," *World Politics*, Vol. 30, No. 2 (January 1978), pp. 167–214; George H. Quester, *Offense and Defense in the International System* (New York: John Wiley, 1977); Jack Snyder, *The Ideology of the Offensive: Military Decision Making and the Disasters of 1914* (Ithaca, NY: Cornell University Press, 1984); and Stephen Van Evera, "The Cult of the Offensive and the Origins of the First World War," *International Security*, Vol. 9, No. 1 (Summer 1984), pp. 58–107.

relative-gains considerations matter little and that states act in accordance with liberal institutionalism when the threat of aggressive war is low and "the use of force is no longer at issue."[39] That situation obtains when the cost of aggression is high, which is, in turn, a function of the "constraints imposed by the underlying technology of war."[40] In other words, when the prevailing military weaponry favors the offense, then the cost of war is low, and relative-gains considerations will be intense. Institutions can do little to facilitate cooperation in such circumstances. However, when defensive technology dominates, the cost of initiating aggression is high and the relative-gains problem is subdued, which allows institutions to cause cooperation.

Snidal maintains that relative-gains concerns might not matter much to states even if they face a serious threat of war. The root concept in his argument is the distribution of power in the international system.[41] Specifically, he maintains that in a multipolar system where more than a small number of states have roughly equal power, states will not worry much about relative gains. Increasing the number of states in the system decreases concern for relative gains. "The reason is that more actors enhance the possibilities of protecting oneself through forming coalitions; and, generally, the less well united one's potential enemies, the safer one is."[42] However, he concedes that "the relative gains hypothesis . . . has important consequences for

two-actor situations and, where there are small numbers or important asymmetries among larger numbers, it may modify conclusions obtained from the absolute gains model."[43]

I draw three conclusions from this discussion of the liberal institutionalists' efforts to deal with the relative-gains problem. First, even if one accepts Powell and Snidal's arguments about when states largely ignore relative-gains concerns, those conditions are rather uncommon in the real world. Powell would look for a world where defensive military technologies dominate. However, it is very difficult to distinguish between offensive and defensive weapons, and Powell provides no help on this point.[44] Nuclear weapons are an exception; they are defensive weapons in situations of mutual assured destruction.[45] Still, the presence of massive numbers of nuclear weapons in the arsenals of the superpowers during the Cold War did not stop them from engaging in an intense security competition where relative-gains considerations mattered greatly. Very importantly, Powell provides no historical examples to illustrate his central argument. Snidal would look for a multipolar world with large numbers of roughly equal-sized great powers. However, historically we find multipolar systems

---

[39]Powell, "Absolute and Relative Gains," p. 1314; also see p. 1311.

[40]Ibid., p. 1312. Powell does not use the term "offense-defense" balance in his article.

[41]Although Snidal's basic arguments about distribution of power fit squarely in the realist tradition (in fact, Grieco made them in abbreviated form in "Anarchy and the Limits of Cooperation," p. 506), the formal model he develops rests on the nonrealist assumption that "gains from cooperation are proportional to the size of the involved states and are shared equally between them." Snidal, "Relative Gains," p. 715. This assumption essentially eliminates the possibility of gaps in gains and thus erases the relative-gains problem. For discussion of this matter, see Grieco's contribution to "The Relative-Gains Problem for International Cooperation," pp. 729–33.

[42]Snidal, "Relative Gains," p. 716.

[43]Ibid., p. 702.

[44]There is general agreement that defensive weapons make conquest difficult and costly, while offensive weapons make conquest cheap and easy. However, there is no recognized set of criteria for assigning specific weapons either offensive or defensive status. See Marion Boggs, *Attempts to Define and Limit "Aggressive" Armament in Diplomacy and Strategy* (Columbia, MO: University of Missouri, 1941); Jack Levy, "The Offensive/Defensive Balance of Military Technology: A Theoretical and Historical Analysis," *International Studies Quarterly*, Vol. 28, No. 2 (June 1984), pp. 219–38; John J. Mearsheimer, *Conventional Deterrence* (Ithaca, NY: Cornell University Press, 1983), pp. 25–27; and Jonathan Shimshoni, "Technology, Military Advantage, and World War I: A Case for Military Entrepreneurship," *International Security*, Vol. 15, No. 3 (Winter 1990/1991), pp. 187–215.

[45]See Shai Feldman, *Israeli Nuclear Deterrence: A Strategy for the 1980s* (New York: Columbia University Press, 1982), pp. 45–49; Charles L. Glaser, *Analyzing Strategic Nuclear Policy* (Princeton, NJ: Princeton University Press, 1990); Jervis, "Cooperation Under the Security Dilemma"; and Stephen Van Evera, *Causes of War*, Vol. II: *National Misperception and the Origins of War*, forthcoming), Chap. 13.

with small numbers of great powers—usually five or six—and very often significant power asymmetries within them. Snidal offers no historical examples of multipolar systems in which the great powers largely ignored relative-gains considerations.[46]

Second, liberal institutionalism itself has little new to say about when states worry about relative gains. Proponents of the theory have instead chosen to rely on two realist explanations to answer that question: the offense-defense balance and the distribution of power in the system. Thus, liberal institutionalism can hardly be called a theoretical alternative to realism, but instead should be seen as subordinate to it.[47]

Third, even in circumstances where realist logic about relative gains does not apply, nonmilitary logics like strategic trade theory might cause states to think in terms of relative gains. Liberal institutionalist theory should directly confront those logics.

Flaws in the Causal Logic

There are two major flaws in collective security theory, and both concern the all-important component of trust. Collective security is an incomplete theory because it does not provide a satisfactory explanation for how states overcome their fears and learn to trust one another. Realists maintain that states fear one another because they operate in an anarchic world, have offensive military capabilities, and can never be certain about other states' intentions. Collective security is largely silent about the first two realist assumptions, as the theory says little about either anarchy or offensive capability.[48] However, it has something to say about intentions, because the theory's first two norms call for states not to aggress but only to defend. States, in other words, should have only benign intentions when contemplating the use of military force.

However, the theory recognizes that one or more states might reject the norms that underpin collective security and behave aggressively. The very purpose of a collective security system, after all, is to deal with states that have aggressive intentions. In effect, collective security admits that no state can ever be completely certain about another state's intentions, which brings us back to a realist world where states have little choice but to fear each other.

There is a second reason states are not likely to place their trust in a collective security system: it has a set of demanding requirements—I count nine—that are likely to thwart efforts to confront an aggressor with preponderant power. Collective security, as Claude notes, "assumes the satisfaction of an extraordinarily complex network of requirements."[49]

First, for collective security to work, states must be able to distinguish clearly between aggressor and victim, and then move against the aggressor. However, it is sometimes difficult in a crisis to determine who is the troublemaker and who is the victim.[50] Debates still rage about which European great power, if any, bears responsibility for starting World War I. Similar disputes have followed most other wars.

---

[46]Keohane actually discusses the prospects for stability in post–Cold War Europe in his response to Grieco; see Keohane, "Institutional Theory and the Realist Challenge," pp. 284–91. Surprisingly, his optimistic assessment pays no attention to either Powell or Snidal's arguments, although earlier in that response, he relies on their arguments to "delimit the scope of both realist and institutionalist arguments." See ibid., p. 276.

[47]Liberal institutionalists have not always been clear about the relationship between their theory and realism. For example, Keohane makes the modest claim in *After Hegemony* (p. 14) that his theory is a "modification of Realism. Realist theories . . . need to be supplemented, though not replaced." He made a somewhat bolder claim a few years later, writing that, "despite [certain] affinities with neorealism, neoliberal institutionalism should be regarded as a distinct school of thought." Keohane, *International Institutions and State Power,* p. 8. In that same piece, however, he makes the very bold argument that "we must understand that neoliberal institutionalism is not simply an alternative to neorealism but, in fact, claims to subsume it." Ibid., p. 15.

[48]Advocates of collective security usually favor widespread arms reductions, but they also recognize that states must maintain a significant offensive capability so that they can challenge an aggressor. For this reason, some scholars suggest that collective security might undermine stability. See Glaser, "Why NATO Is Still Best," pp. 30–33.

[49]Claude, *Swords into Plowshares,* p. 250.

[50]See Bourquin, *Collective Security,* pp. 295–338.

Second, the theory assumes that all aggression is wrong. But there are occasionally cases where conquest is probably warranted. For example, there are good reasons to applaud the 1979 Vietnamese invasion of Cambodia, since it drove the murderous Pol Pot from power.

Third, some states are especially friendly for historical or ideological reasons. Should a state with close friends be labeled an aggressor in a collective security system, its friends are probably going to be reluctant to join the coalition against it. For example, it is difficult to imagine the United States using military force against Britain or Israel, even if they were branded aggressors by the international community.

Fourth, historical enmity between states can also complicate collective security efforts. Consider that a European collective security system would have to depend heavily on Germany and Russia, the two most powerful states on the continent, to maintain order. However, the idea of Germany, which wrought murder and destruction across Europe in 1939–45, and Russia, which was the core of the Soviet empire, maintaining order in Europe is sure to meet significant resistance from other European states.

Fifth, even if states agree to act automatically and collectively to meet aggression, there would surely be difficulty determining how to distribute the burden. States will have strong incentives to pass the buck and get other states to pay the heavy price of confronting an aggressor.[51] During World War I, for example, Britain, France, and Russia each tried to get its allies to pay the blood price of defeating Germany on the battlefield.[52] Rampant buck-passing might undermine efforts to produce the preponderant military power necessary to make collective security work.

Sixth, it is difficult to guarantee a rapid response to aggression in a collective security system. Planning beforehand is problematic because "it is impossible to know what the alignment of states will be if there is an armed conflict."[53] There are also significant coordination problems associated with assembling a large coalition of states to fight a war. Rapid response becomes even more problematic if the responsible states must deal with more than one aggressor. It took more than six months for the United States to put together a coalition to liberate Kuwait from Saddam Hussein. As impressive as the American effort was, threatened states are not likely to have much faith in a security system that tells them help is likely to come but will arrive only months after they have been conquered.

Seventh, states are likely to be reluctant to join a collective security effort because the system effectively transforms every local conflict into an international conflict. States that see conflict around the globe will surely be tempted to cordon off the troubled area and prevent further escalation, as the West has done in the former Yugoslavia.[54] Collective security, however, calls for escalation, even though it is intended for peaceful purposes.

Eighth, the notion that states must automatically respond to aggression impinges in fundamental ways on state sovereignty and will therefore be difficult to sell. States, especially democracies, are likely to guard jealously their freedom to debate whether or not to fight an aggressor. War is a deadly business, especially if great powers are involved, and few countries want to commit themselves in advance to paying a huge blood price when their own self-interests are not directly involved.

---

[51]See Mancur Olson, Jr., and Richard Zeckhauser, "An Economic Theory of Alliances," *Review of Economics and Statistics,* Vol. 48, No. 3 (August 1966), pp. 266–79; and Barry R. Posen, *The Sources of Military Doctrine: France, Britain, and Germany Between the World Wars* (Ithaca, NY: Cornell University Press, 1984).
[52]David French, *British Strategy and War Aims, 1914–1916* (London: Allen and Unwin, 1986).

[53]G. F. Hudson, "Collective Security and Military Alliances," in *Diplomatic Investigations: Essays in the Theory of International Politics,* Herbert Butterfield and Martin Wight, eds. (Cambridge, MA: Harvard University Press, 1966), p. 177.
[54]For an example of this line of thinking, see Stephen M. Walt, "Collective Security and Revolutionary Change: Promoting Peace in the Former Soviet Union," in Downs, *Collective Security Beyond the Cold War,* pp. 169–95.

Ninth, there is some contradiction concerning attitudes toward force that raises doubts about whether responsible states would actually come to the rescue of a threatened state. Collective security theory is predicated on the belief that war is a truly horrible enterprise, and therefore states should renounce aggression. At the same time, the theory mandates that states must be ready and willing to use force to thwart troublemakers. However, responsible states find war so repellent that they would renounce it; this raises doubts about their willingness to go to war to stop aggression. Indeed, most advocates of collective security prefer "creative diplomacy and economic sanctions" to military force when dealing with an aggressor state.[55]

In sum, states have abundant reasons to doubt that collective security will work as advertised when the chips are down and aggression seems likely. Should it fail, potential victims are likely to be in deep trouble if they have ignored balance-of-power considerations and placed their faith in collective security. Recognizing this, states are not likely to place their fate in the hands of other states, but will prefer instead the realist logic of self-help. . . .

Critical Theory

Critical theorists[56] directly address the question of how to bring about peace, and they make bold claims about the prospects for changing state behavior.[57] Specifically, they aim to transform the international system into a "world society," where states are guided by "norms of trust and sharing." Their goal is to relegate security competition and war to the scrap heap of history, and create instead a genuine "peace system."[58]

Critical theorists take ideas very seriously. In fact, they believe that discourse, or how we think and talk about the world, largely shapes practice.

[55]Robert C. Johansen, "Lessons for Collective Security," *World Policy Journal*, Vol. 8, No. 3 (Summer 1991), p. 562.

[56]Critical theory is an approach to studying the human condition that is not tied to a particular discipline. In fact, critical theory was well developed and employed widely in other disciplines before it began to penetrate the international relations field in the early 1980s. This article does not focus on critical theory per se but examines the scholarly literature where critical theory is applied to international relations. I treat those works as a coherent whole, although there are differences, especially of emphasis, among them. For a general discussion of critical theory, see David Held, *Introduction to Critical Theory: Horkheimer to Habermas* (Berkeley: University of California Press, 1980); and Pauline M. Rosenau, *Post-Modernism and the Social Sciences: Insights, Inroads, and Intrusions* (Princeton, NJ: Princeton University Press, 1992). Also see Pauline Rosenau, "Once Again into the Fray: International Relations Confronts the Humanities," *Millennium: Journal of International Studies*, Vol. 19, No. 1 (Spring 1990), pp. 83–110.

[57]Among the key works applying critical theory to international relations are Richard K. Ashley, "The Poverty of Neorealism," *International Organization*, Vol. 38, No. 2 (Spring 1984), pp. 225–86; Ashley, "The Geopolitics of Geopolitical Space: Toward a Critical Social Theory of International Politics," *Alternatives*, Vol. 12, No. 4 (October 1987), pp. 403–34; Robert W. Cox, "Gramsci, Hegemony and International Relations: An Essay in Method," *Millennium: Journal of International Studies*, Vol. 12, No. 2 (Summer 1983), pp. 162–75; Cox, "Social Forces, States and World Orders: Beyond International Relations Theory," *Millennium: Journal of International Studies*, Vol. 10, No. 2 (Summer 1981), pp. 126–55; Cox, "Towards A Post-Hegemonic Conceptualization of World Order: Reflections on the Relevancy of Ibn Khaldun," in *Governance Without Government: Order and Change in World Politics*, James N. Rosenau, and Ernst-Otto Czempiel, eds. (New York: Cambridge University Press, 1992), pp. 132–59; Rey Koslowski and Friedrich V. Kratochwil, "Understanding Change in International Politics: The Soviet Empire's Demise and the International System," *International Organization*, Vol. 48, No. 2 (Spring 1994), pp. 215–47; Friedrich Kratochwil and John G. Ruggie, "International Organization: A State of the Art on an Art of the State," *International Organization*, Vol. 40, No. 4 (Autumn 1986), pp. 753–75; Ruggie, "Continuity and Transformation in the World Polity: Toward a Neorealist Synthesis," *World Politics*, Vol. 35, No. 2 (January 1983), pp. 261–85; Ruggie, "Territoriality and Beyond: Problematizing Modernity in International Relations," *International Organization*, Vol. 47, No. 1 (Winter 1993), pp. 139–74; Alexander Wendt, "The Agent-Structure Problem in International Relations Theory," *International Organization*, Vol. 41, No. 3 (Summer 1987), pp. 335–70; Wendt, "Anarchy Is What States Make of It: The Social Construction of Power Politics," *International Organization*, Vol. 46, No. 2 (Spring 1992), pp. 391–425; and Wendt, "Collective Identity Formation and the International State," *American Political Science Review*, Vol. 88, No. 2 (June 1994), pp. 384–96. I use the label "critical theory" to describe this body of literature; other labels are sometimes used, among them constructivism, reflectivism, postmodernism, and poststructuralism.

[58]The quotations in this paragraph are from Ashley, "Poverty of Neorealism," p. 285; and Wendt, "Anarchy Is What States Make of It," p. 431.

Roughly put, ideas are the driving force of history. Furthermore, they recognize that realism has long been the dominant theory of international politics and, therefore, according to their account of reality, has had substantial influence on state behavior. But critical theorists intend to change that situation by challenging realism and undermining it. Richard Ashley graphically describes their intentions: "Let us then play havoc with neorealist concepts and claims. Let us neither admire nor ignore the orrery of errors, but let us instead fracture the orbs, crack them open, crack them and see what possibilities they have enclosed. And then, when we are done, let us not cast away the residue. Let us instead sweep it into a jar, shine up the glass, and place it high on the bookshelf with other specimens of past mistakes."[59] With realism shattered, the way would presumably be open to a more peaceful world.

Critical theory is well-suited for challenging realism because critical theory is, by its very nature, concerned with criticizing "hegemonic" ideas like realism, not laying out alternative futures. The central aim is "to seek out the contradictions within the existing order, since it is from these contradictions that change could emerge."[60] It is called "critical" theory for good reason. Very significantly, however, critical theory per se has little to say about the future shape of international politics. In fact, critical theory emphasizes that "it is impossible to predict the future."[61] Robert Cox explains this point: "Critical awareness of potentiality for change must be distinguished from utopian planning, i.e., the laying out of the design of a future society that is to be the end goal of change. Critical understanding focuses on the process of change rather than on its ends; it concentrates on the possibilities of launching a social movement rather than on what that movement might achieve."[62]

Nevertheless, international relations scholars who use critical theory to challenge and subvert realism certainly expect to create a more harmonious and peaceful international system. But the theory itself says little about either the desirability or feasibility of achieving that particular end. . . .

Flaws in the Causal Logic

The main goal of critical theorists is to change state behavior in fundamental ways, to move beyond a world of security competition and war and establish a pluralistic security community. However, their explanation of how change occurs is at best incomplete and, at worst, internally contradictory.[63]

Critical theory maintains that state behavior changes when discourse changes. But that argument leaves open the obvious and crucially important question: What determines why some discourses become dominant and others lose out in the marketplace of ideas? What is the mechanism that governs the rise and fall of discourses? This general question, in turn, leads to three more specific questions: (1) Why has realism been the hegemonic discourse in world politics for so long? (2) Why is the time ripe for its unseating? (3) Why is realism likely to be replaced by a more peaceful communitarian discourse?

Critical theory provides few insights on why discourses rise and fall. Thomas Risse-Kappen

---

[59]Ashley, "Poverty of Neorealism," p. 286.
[60]Robert W. Cox, *Production, Power, and World Order: Social Forces in the Making of World History* (New York: Columbia University Press, 1987), p. 393.
[61]Cox, "Post-Hegemonic Conceptualization," p. 139.

[62]Cox, *Production, Power, and World Order*, p. 393. The young Karl Marx summed up this approach in 1844: "The advantage of the new trend [is] that we do not attempt dogmatically to prefigure the future, but want to find the new world only through criticism of the old." Karl Marx, "For a Ruthless Criticism of Everything Existing," in *The Marx-Engels Reader*, 2nd ed., Robert C. Tucker, ed. (New York: Norton, 1978), p. 13. Marx's early writings have markedly influenced critical theory. See, for example, Ashley, "Poverty of Neorealism," pp. 226–30; and Cox, "Social Forces," p. 133. Critical theorists, however, disparage Marx's later writings, which lay out a structural theory of politics that has much in common with realism.
[63]My thinking on this matter has been markedly influenced by Hein Goemans.

writes, "Research on . . . 'epistemic communities' of knowledge-based transnational networks has failed so far to specify the conditions under which specific ideas are selected and influence policies while others fall by the wayside."[64] Not surprisingly, critical theorists say little about why realism has been the dominant discourse and why its foundations are now so shaky. They certainly do not offer a well-defined argument that deals with this important issue. Therefore, it is difficult to judge the fate of realism through the lens of critical theory.

Nevertheless, critical theorists occasionally point to particular factors that might lead to changes in international relations discourse. In such cases, however, they usually end up arguing that changes in the material world drive changes in discourse. For example, when Ashley makes surmises about the future of realism, he claims that "a crucial issue is whether or not changing historical conditions have disabled longstanding realist rituals of power." Specifically, he asks whether "developments in late capitalist society," such as the "fiscal crisis of the state," and the "internationalization of capital," coupled with "the presence of vastly destructive and highly automated nuclear arsenals, [have] deprived statesmen of the latitude for competent performance of realist rituals of power."[65] Similarly, Cox argues that fundamental change occurs when there is a "disjuncture" between "the stock of ideas people have about the nature of the world and the practical problems that challenge them." He then writes, "some of us think the erstwhile dominant mental construct of neorealism is inadequate to confront the challenges of global politics today."[66]

It would be understandable if realists made such arguments, since they believe there is an objective reality that largely determines which discourse will be dominant. Critical theorists, however, emphasize that the world is socially constructed and not shaped in fundamental ways by objective factors. Anarchy, after all, is what we make of it. Yet when critical theorists attempt to explain why realism may be losing its hegemonic position, they too point to objective factors as the ultimate cause of change. Discourse, so it appears, turns out not to be determinative but mainly a reflection of developments in the objective world. In short, it seems that when critical theorists who study international politics offer glimpses of their thinking about the causes of change in the real world, they make arguments that directly contradict their own theory but that appear to be compatible with the theory they are challenging.[67]

There is another problem with the application of critical theory to international relations. Although critical theorists hope to replace realism with a discourse that emphasizes harmony and peace, critical theory per se emphasizes that it is impossible to know the future. Critical theory, according to its own logic, can be used to undermine realism and produce change, but it cannot serve as the basis for predicting which discourse will replace realism,

---

[64]Thomas Risse-Kappen, "Ideas Do Not Float Freely: Transnational Coalitions, Domestic Structures, and the End of the Cold War," *International Organization*, Vol. 48, No. 2 (Spring 1994), p. 187. Also see Koslowski and Kratochwil, "Understanding Change," p. 225.

[65]Ashley, "Geopolitics of Geopolitical Space," pp. 426–27.

[66]Cox, "Post-Hegemonic Conceptualization," p. 138. Also see Cox, "Social Forces," pp. 138–49. For other examples, see Ruggie, "Continuity and Transformation," pp. 281–86; and Wendt, "Collective Identity Formation," pp. 389–90.

[67]Cox is apparently aware of this problem. After spending eleven pages outlining various objective factors that might shape a new world order, he notes, "It would, of course, be *logically inadmissible*, as well as imprudent, to base predictions of future world order upon the foregoing considerations." Cox, "Social Forces," p. 149, emphasis added. Nevertheless, he then emphasizes in the next few sentences how important those objective considerations are for understanding future world order prospects. He writes: "Their utility is rather in drawing attention to factors which could incline an emerging world order in one direction or another. The social forces generated by changing production processes are the starting point for thinking about possible futures. These forces may combine in different configurations, and as an exercise one could consider the hypothetical configurations most likely to lead to three different outcomes as to the future of the state system. The focus on these three outcomes is not, of course, to imply that no other outcomes or configurations of social forces are possible." In other words, Cox does rely heavily on objective factors to explain possible future world orders.

because the theory says little about the direction change takes. In fact, Cox argues that although "utopian expectations may be an element in stimulating people to act . . . such expectations are almost never realized in practice."[68] Thus, in a sense, the communitarian discourse championed by critical theorists is wishful thinking, not an outcome linked to the theory itself. Indeed, critical theory cannot guarantee that the new discourse will not be more malignant than the discourse it replaces. Nothing in the theory guarantees, for example, that a fascist discourse far more violent *than realism will not emerge as the new hegemonic discourse.*

[68]Cox, *Production, Power, and World Order,* p. 393.

REALIST CONSTRUCTIVISM

J. Samuel Barkin

Constructivism appears to have taken a place in the literature on international relations (IR) theory in direct opposition to realism. Examples of this opposition can be found in a number of places. Constructivist theory came into the IR mainstream as a critique of a variant of realism: structural realism (Wendt 1987a; Dessler 1989; Onuf and Klink 1989). Self-proclaimed constructivists often have (or at least are seen to have) worldviews that fall within liberalism, broadly defined and often accept that categorization. Moreover, some recent constructivist theorizing argues explicitly that constructivism and realism are logically incompatible (for

example, Wendt 1999; Patomäki and Wight 2000) or, at least, antagonistic (Lebow 2001). International relations pedagogy is also increasingly defining realism and constructivism as being categorically distinct, as witnessed by the increasing tendency in IR textbooks, even at the introductory level, to define realism and constructivism as two of three or more distinct paradigms in the field (for example, Hughes 2000; Kegley and Wittkopf 2001; Lieber 2001).

To claim that constructivism is an IR paradigm in the way that realism or liberalism [is] is misleading, and the tendency to do so in textbooks is rarely mirrored in the scholarly literature. In the latter, constructivism is usually identified as an ontology, epistemology, or methodology. As such, it is usually defined as being distinct from either materialism or rationalism. Recent state-of-the-field exercises (Katzenstein, Keohane, and Krasner 1998; Ruggie 1998), in fact, identified the rationalism–constructivism controversy as the central debate in contemporary IR theory. Constructivists who claim their methodology is incompatible with realism focus on the association between realism and both materialism and rationalism. Realists who claim their paradigm is incompatible with constructivism focus for the most part not on the methodology per se but on a perceived tendency for constructivists to be idealists or utopians.

Neither argument, however, holds up to careful scrutiny. Claims by constructivists that realist theory is incompatible with intersubjective epistemologies and methodologies are based on either caricatures or very narrow understandings

J. Samuel Barkin is a professor in the Department of Political Science, University of Florida.

© 2003 International Studies Review, Vol. 5, pp. 325–42.

Constructivism appears to have taken a place in the literature on international relations (IR) theory in direct opposition to realism. Constructivists who claim their methodology is incompatible with realism focus on the association between realism and both materialism and rationalism. Realists who claim their paradigm is incompatible with constructivism focus for the most part on a perceived tendency for constructivists to be idealists or utopians. Neither argument, however, holds up. This essay examines constructivist epistemology and classical realist theory, contending that they are, in fact, compatible; not that constructivism is necessarily realist but that constructivist research is as compatible with a realist worldview as with any other. Having a realist constructivism could prove useful in IR theory beyond clarifying methodological debates, including helping to specify the relationship between the study of power in international politics and the study of international relations as a social construction.

of realism. And realist critics of constructivism are similarly guilty of inferring from the world-views of some (perhaps many) practicing constructivists that the methodology is inherently biased toward liberalism. An examination of constructivist epistemology and classical realist theory suggests that they are, in fact, compatible; not, of course, that good constructivism is necessarily realist but that constructivist research is as compatible with a realist worldview as with any other.

The purpose of this essay is to conduct such an examination. The first step in doing so is to define terms and to clear up some of the terminological confusion surrounding the discourse connecting constructivism and realism. The second step is to make the argument that a realist constructivism (or, for that matter, a constructivist realism) is epistemologically, methodologically, and paradigmatically viable. The final step is to discuss what a realist constructivism might look like and where it fits in the study of international relations more broadly. Having such an approach could, among other things, fulfill several useful functions. One function is to clear up a number of debates in the field in which the protagonists speak past, rather than to, each other. Another function is to clarify the relationship between, on the one hand, the study of power and the study of ideals in international relations and, on the other, the study of the social construction of international politics. A final function is to act as a bridge between mainstream approaches to international relations and critical and postmodern approaches that view both constructivism and realism as problematic, albeit for different reasons.

Definitions

Part of the reason so many scholars in the field talk past each other when discussing issues of paradigm and epistemology is terminological confusion. Scholars tend to redefine terms frequently, creating a situation in which the same term is used by different authors with very different meanings. This observation holds for most of the key terms in this essay—and certainly for the two main concepts: realism and constructivism. The confusion is exacerbated by individual authors who provide different definitions for the same words. For example, Alexander Wendt (1999) speaks of both political and scientific realism, arguing that the two are incompatible. He also provides two definitions of idealism, as the "ism" of ideas and the "ism" of ideals—two quite different concepts. We will address idealism and scientific realism shortly. The first step, however, is to define the two terms most central to this essay—constructivism and realism (political)—and to specify how they will be used here. Both terms are defined in a way that includes as many scholars in the self-defined constructivist and realist research communities as possible.

Constructivism is the easier of the two terms to define inclusively. Most (possibly all) self-described constructivists would agree that the defining feature of this approach is a focus on the social construction of international politics. Constructivists see the facts of international politics as not reflective of an objective, material reality but an intersubjective, or social, reality (Onuf 1989). In other words, what actors do in international relations, the interests they hold, and the structures within which they operate are defined by social norms and ideas rather than by objective or material conditions.

Within this broad definition, constructivists differ considerably. One plane on which they differ is the extent to which there is an empirically identifiable reality to be identified and studied. Opinions tend to coalesce into one of two epistemologies: One argues that an identifiable reality exists out there and can be accessed through empirical research; the other contends that we can never know for sure if what we observe really exists independently of our observation of it and, therefore, no true reality exists for empirical research to find. These two epistemologies are known variously as "neoclassical" and "postmodernist" constructivism (see Ruggie 1998) as well as "thin" and "thick" constructivism (see Wendt 1999). The case for a realist constructivism will be made in this essay by focusing on the neoclassical variant of constructivism because it is the more difficult case to make. Postmodern constructivism is generally more accepting of the centrality of power in politics, and power, as is argued below, is the core concept of realism. The postmodernist response, that realism is inherently foundationalist, will be addressed later in this section and in the next.

The harder to define of the two basic terms is realism because so many definitions abound that seem, on their face, to be mutually incompatible. To get to the point, the common feature of realism—that is, the concept that is to realism as intersubjectivity is to constructivism—is power. This observation may seem to some readers obvious to the point of banality. But many contemporary definitions of realism give power little prominence and fail to indicate the extent to which they ultimately rely on it (for example, Mearsheimer 1994/1995; Jervis 1998; Legro and Moravcsik 1999). Power, to other readers, may seem too broad a category to be particularly useful in the analysis of international relations; this criticism will be addressed below. To make the case that power is the core concept of realism, we must look at the range of definitions of realism that exist, noting the extent to which they are ultimately derived from propositions about the centrality of power in international relations.

The term *realism* came into the IR discourse in reference to the need to study international politics as they are, not as we feel they should be (see Schuman 1933; Kirk 1947; Morgenthau 1948; Carr 1964; Rommen 1994). The logic behind this need centered [on] power. We cannot, by wishing politics were different, make them so because we do not have the power; therefore, we must work within the existing power structure (Lasswell 1935; Wight 1946; Morgenthau 1948; Carr 1964). The seminal works developing realist theory in the United States explicitly defined realism as being about power. Hans Morgenthau (1985:31–32), for example, made all the study of international politics about power by definitional fiat. He defined political science as the social science

concerned with power. If we were to study some element of international relations that did not revolve around power, we would be studying international economics, or international law, or international sociology rather than international politics. In taking this stance, Morgenthau (1948:15) was not arguing that international law, economics, or sociology are irrelevant. What he was saying, however, is that, in the international domain, politics defined as power is important and merits study in its own right.

In the more than half a century since *Politics Among Nations* (Morgenthau 1948) was first published, this original kernel of the definition has occasionally gotten lost. Beyond power, contemporary definitions of realism usually contain some combination of the following: the analytic centrality of states, their interest in survival, the primacy of material capabilities, and rationality (for a review of definitions of realism, see Donnelly 2000). Together these elements show a clear lineage from the core realist concept of power, but often with little recognition of how they relate to the ideas from which they descend. Looking at these concepts one at a time allows us to reconnect them.

Many contemporary definitions of realism assume that the state is the central actor in international politics. For early realists, this premise was more a matter of observation than of deduction. The major political events during the first half of the twentieth century were the two world wars, and these wars were fought by and between states. States were the organizations in international politics with power. Indeed, no other organizations had much effective power internationally; therefore, states mattered. But E. H. Carr (1964:224–35) concluded that though states were currently the locus of power in global politics, they need not necessarily remain the central actor. Since then, however, states have, almost by habit among realists, been presented as a definitional element of realism in their own right (see, for example, Jervis 1998). One effect of this removal of states from observational to definitional centrality is the argument, advanced by both critics of realism and some neorealists, that what happens within states does not matter to realists. But few realist theorists (and few seminal neorealist theorists, for that matter) make this argument. In realist theory, what goes on within the state both determines the extent to which states are powerful and defines what their goals for that power are.[1] Classical realist theory is, in fact, very much a first-image theory, which was Kenneth Waltz's (1959, 1979) critique of it. Attempts by IR theorists, such as Jeffrey Legro and Andrew Moravcsik (1999), to draw the distinction between realist and liberal theory by proposing that the former was a third-image theory and the latter combined both first- and second-image theories are, thus, misplaced. In realism, states matter because they have power; people and domestic institutions matter because they determine how much power states will have, and how that power will be used.

The assumption that states share an interest in survival flows from the just discussed premise of state centrality. For realist theory, assuming an interest in survival is a generalization rather than a categorical rule: states that are not interested in their own survival are not likely to last in an anarchical world. Therefore, we can assume that those states that have lasted and populate our contemporary world are those with an interest in survival (Morgenthau 1948:13; Waltz 1979:74–77; Jervis 1998:980–81). Survival need not be the only, or even the key, motivator of state behavior; however, in situations in which survival is relevant, states are likely to take to into account. Some critics of realism contend that the assumption that states value survival borders on the trivial, and, therefore, there must be some further implicit assumptions in realism about state preferences (see, for example, Legro and Moravcsik 1999:14; Wendt 1999:235). But the triviality of this assumption is precisely the point. In a world in which power matters, states need only have in common a basic concern for survival to think in terms of relative power (see, for example, Waltz 1979; Grieco 1997; Schweller 1998).

The third concept that often appears in contemporary definitions of realism is rationality. To many, perhaps most, current students of political science, the term rationality invokes rational choice theory (see Kahler 1998; Katzenstein, Keohane, and Krasner 1998). This approach to the study of politics begins with the premise that we can usefully study political actors, given their exogenously defined preferences, as if they were instrumentally rational. The use of rationality in the context of realist theory, however, does not invoke the assumptions of rational choice theory. Two elements concerning rationality arise in classical realism. The first is that we, as scholars, should be rational, which is to say ordered and "scientific" in a loose usage of that term, in our study of politics. In other words, we should look for general patterns of behavior, an admonition accepted by a wide range of (though certainly not by all) social scientists.[2] The second way in which rationality is discussed in realism is more prescriptive than predictive—not that statespeople necessarily *will* behave rationally, but that in order to pursue the interests of their states they *should*. That is, if national policymakers want to make a difference rather than just a statement in international politics, they must rationally marshal their power resources. In Morgenthau's (1985:10) words, "foreign policy ought to be rational in view of its own moral and practical purposes." Thus, what is often read as an assumption of rationality is, in point of fact, a prescription for rationality based on an assumption of the centrality of power.

---

[1]Note that Kenneth Waltz (1979:121–22) refers to this sort of thing as the study of foreign policy as distinct from the systemic study of international politics and argues that it can be done only in a reductionist way. But he never dismisses it as unimportant.

[2]This admonition, however, does not imply a commitment to a pure deductive model of social science, the model ascribed to rationalists by constructivists such as Ruggie (1998:880) and Wendt (1999:48). Morgenthau (1946), in fact, used the term "scientific man"—one who would deduce solutions to the problems of international politics from first principles—as his polemical foil to realists in the same way that Carr (1964) used "utopians."

The fourth concept, the assumption of the primacy of material capabilities, is something more often ascribed to realist theory by its critics than claimed by realists themselves (see, for example, Kratochwil 1984:310; Wendt 1999:30). Realists, it is true, often focus more on military power than on other forms of power, whether economic, organizational, or moral (for example, Mearsheimer 1994/1995). This predisposition can be attributed to the assumption that the military power of an adversary can threaten the very existence of a state, whereas other forms of power cannot. (Of course, whether or not this assumption is valid is open to debate.) It can also be ascribed to the context in which much of the seminal realist work took place, the Cold War (see Oren 2000) or to the ease with which the tools of military power can be counted. But in situations in which no imminent military threat exists, as is currently the case among many of the world's major powers, no a priori reason exists within realist theory to privilege military power over other forms of power. During the Cold War, there was a cottage industry in counting up military manpower and hardware that owed more to the behavioral revolution than to realist theory, and it is, perhaps, from this development that realism has come to be associated with material capabilities.[3] But few realist theorists subscribe to such an assumption, and many argue explicitly that the sources of power are nonmaterial (see, for example, Waltz 1979:131; Morgenthau 1985:34–36).

When the assumption of materialism is ascribed to realism by its critics, then, one has to wonder why this particular straw man is being created. One reason might be to make realism more compatible with rational choice theory. It can, in fact, allow us to treat power the way that formal theorists treat preferences. For classical realist theory, however, power is at least partially endogenous: One cannot

know how much power one has without knowing how it is being used. The materialization of power resources has the effect, though, of making power an exogenous variable; it becomes something that is out there, measurable and independent from immediate political activity. Formal theory must similarly take the preferences of actors as exogenous to the game being played. So through the materialization of power, realism becomes "rationalized" both for rationalists and their critics (for example, Legro and Moravcsik 1999 and Wendt 1999, respectively).

The previous discussion implies that power is the core, and common, element of realist theory. Of the four concepts imbedded in contemporary definitions of realism, the analytic centrality of states and an interest in survival are descended from the original realist focus on power; the third concept, rationality, when used in the realist rather than the rational choice manner, suggests a focus on power as well. The fourth, the primacy of material capabilities, is more an effect of the behavioral turn in political science research during the mid–Cold War period and its rationalist turn in the late–Cold War period than an expression of a core realist idea. And, yet, it is this fourth feature, rather than a focus on power, that is most often invoked to argue that constructivism and realism are incompatible.

Realism and Constructivism

Many constructivists explicitly accept that power matters in international relations. Wendt (1999:13–14), for example, notes that to the extent realism is about power, he too is a realist. He and other constructivist theorists often part company with realists because of the belief that, at its core, realist theory sees politics as having "a material rather than a social basis" (Wendt 1999:13–14). This charge has three parts: that realist theory (1) focuses on material capabilities, (2) views human nature as materialistic, and (3) emphasizes empiricism. These three charges are distinct from one another, and, if any of them were to hold, it

---

[3] It is important to note, however, that the most dedicated of the counters of material capabilities, such as those involved in the Correlates of War project, described themselves as peace theorists or conflict resolution theorists and as antirealist (see, for example, Singer 1990; Vasquez 1998).

would indicate an incompatibility between realism and constructivism. But, under scrutiny, none of them are sustainable.

The first of these charges, that the realist understanding of power favors a focus on material capabilities, has already been alluded to above. It is certainly true that many self-described realist researchers have attempted to reduce the idea of power to quantitative measures. But no reason exists to believe that such a procedure is inherent to realist theory. Indeed, the behavioral, and thus quantitative, turn in IR is generally considered to have happened decades after the realist turn, suggesting that the latter cannot be inherent to the former (Bull 1972; Vasquez 1983; Holsti 1985). Many seminal realist theorists, furthermore, have argued explicitly that nonmaterial factors are central to a complete understanding of power in international relations (see, for example, Morgenthau 1948; Wolfers 1962; Carr 1964; Waltz 1979; Gilpin 1981; Strange 1987). Moreover, students of power analysis, some of them self-described realists, have pointed out how complex and multifaceted power analysis can be (see, for example, Lasswell and Kaplan 1950; Bachrach and Baratz 1962; Baldwin 1989; Hall 1997). Even studies of military issues conducted by those calling themselves realists after the behavioralist turn often focused on such nonmaterial elements as doctrines (see, for example, Mearsheimer 1983; Posen 1984). The fact that some realist researchers use quantitative measures of brute material capabilities should, therefore, not be interpreted to mean that this sort of materialism is inherent in realism.

The second charge is that realist logic requires certain materialist assumptions about human nature and human needs that govern the behavior of actors in international politics (Wendt 1999:30, 131–33). The particular assumptions ascribed to realist understandings of human nature often include the presence of insecurity and fear (Waltz 1959; Wendt 1999). It is true that realists must begin with some theory of human nature. Indeed, as Wendt (1999:131) has observed, all social theory must begin with some theory of human nature,

even if it is that human nature is infinitely malleable. There exist theories of human nature that are incompatible with political realism, including those that argue that human nature is infinitely malleable or ultimately perfectible. But we can also identify a broad range of theories of human nature that are compatible with both realist and constructivist theory, including those that suggest that individuals differ. (For a general discussion of this literature, see Sterling-Folker 2000.) Realist logic does not require that all individuals be aggressive or self-interested, simply that some of them are. In other words, the theory requires that all individuals cannot be nonaggressive and other-oriented. As long as some people will try to accumulate power, and no countervailing power stops them, other people face insecurity. This logic is, for example, the heart of Randall Schweller's (1998) distinction between status quo and revisionist states. Critics might respond that, phrased as such, realist logic is sufficiently broad and obvious as to be banal; this criticism will be addressed below.

The third charge is that political realism is, variously, "positivist" or "empiricist" and, as a result, incompatible with constructivist methodology (see, for example, Pettman 2000 and Wendt 1999, respectively). This charge seems on its face to be methodological, but a number of constructivist theorists have recently taken to making it at the ontological level. This criticism is made via a reference to "scientific" (Wendt 1999) or "critical" (Patomäki and Wight 2000) realism, a concept in the philosophy of science that bears no relationship to "political" realism. The essence of scientific realism as applied in the social sciences is the idea that real social structures exist out there, independent of our observation of them. In short, the view is that a "there" actually exists out there (see Hellman 1983; Leplin 1984; Bhaskar 1986; Archer et al. 1998). This perspective contrasts with the logical positivist-empiricist notion that we can only know what we observe (for example, Ayer 1959; Lapid 1989) and the postmodern-deconstructivist notion that, because all social knowledge is discursively created, no social structures can exist out there independent of our discourses about them (for example, George 1994). Both the logical positivist and deconstructivist positions share the premise that there can be no knowledge of social phenomena separate from the observer, whereas the scientific realist position is that social phenomena can exist apart from the observer and can be adduced even when not directly observed (Patomäki and Wight 2000). The constructivist critique political realist ontology associates with these antiscientific realist positions.

This last charge has evolved over time. Postpositivists (for example, Ashley and Walker 1990a) in the positivist-postpositivist debate often dismiss realism as positivist and, as a result, incompatible with new trends in thinking about IR. But, from a constructivist perspective, such a dismissal is problematic because any definition of positivism broad enough to capture the range of realist thinking (as in, for example, Walt 1987; Snyder 1988) is broad enough to capture much of contemporary constructivist thinking as well. Many critics of realism also conflate it with neorealism, understandable given the prominence of Waltz's (1979) work in the last two decades of the last century, but problematic given that his work is itself an explicit critique of classical realism.[4]

Heikki Patomäki and Colin Wight (2000) argue that political realism is too close to both the logical positivist position and the deconstructivist position, in that all share an anthropocentric view of knowledge that is incompatible with the scientific realism that they argue should underlie constructivism. They (Patomäki and Wight 2000:219–23) trace this anthropocentrism back through the seminal realists of the middle of the twentieth century, all the way back to the ontological writings of Hume and Kant in the eighteenth century.[5] In

doing so, they associate the development of political realism and its introduction into IR within the United States by Morgenthau both with the empiricism of Hume and the postmodernism of Nietzsche. The point of this genealogy is to posit a sharp disjuncture in realist thought between the realms of the empirically observable and of moral thought. In a sense, it provides a way of restating the charge that political realism is positivist and of arguing that positivism understood narrowly is incompatible with scientific realism.

Morgenthau's writing on the "science" of political science can, indeed, seem confusing at first reading. In *Scientific Man Versus Power Politics*, he (Morgenthau 1946) argues that "scientific man," who would solve the problems of politics through the application of reason, is incapable of successfully addressing those problems. In contrast, in *Politics Among Nations*, Morgenthau (1985:5) speaks of political realism as "believing . . . in the objectivity of the laws of politics" and "the possibility of developing a rational theory that reflects" those laws. Some constructivist critics of political realism posit that Morgenthau underwent a radical change of mind in the period between writing the two books. Patomäki and Wight (2000:222), for example, interpret the earlier work as an expression of skepticism that we can find scientific knowledge about the world, an interpretation that seems irreconcilable with the Morgenthau of *Politics Among Nations*.

But to make this claim is to confuse predictive with prescriptive rationality, as was discussed above. What Morgenthau (1946:122–31) is arguing against in *Scientific Man* is the attempt to understand the world as a rational place rather than to rationally understand the world. What he (Morgenthau 1948:3–5) is contending in *Politics Among Nations* is that there is a problem in attempting to rationally understand the world, when the world is not, in fact, a rational place. In other words, both books are arguing the same point but coming at it from different directions. This interpretation does suggest an incompatibility between classical realism and rational choice theory, or what Ruggie (1998) calls

---

[4]On the "rationalization" of realism suggested by neorealism, see Spegele (1996), who speaks of "commonsense" and "concessionary" realism rather than classical and neorealism.

[5]This genealogy is contestable; in some places Morgenthau seems quite dismissive of the phenomenal-noumenal distinction that they accuse him of implicitly sharing (see, for example, Morgenthau 1946:170–71).

neo-utilitarianism.[6] It also, however, suggests a compatibility between classical realism and neoclassical, or thin, constructivism. The antipathy to "scientific man," the acceptance of the importance of ideas, and the insistence that historical context matters found in the works of Morgenthau (see 1946:130 for a discussion of "social causation") fit quite well into a statement of constructivist epistemology, whether neoclassical or postmodern. And the ontology of classical realism, accepting a reality separate from subjective opinion but not, as a result, denying the role of unobservables such as morality, is hardly the sort of brute materialism that constructivist critics sometimes associate with realism.

All of this leaves us having dealt with the proposed incompatibilities between constructivism and political realism, the latter being defined as the study of IR that focuses on power relations in the international sphere. Many readers, no doubt, will have begun to wonder by this point, so what? Has realism been made compatible with constructivism by defining the concept so broadly that it fails to exclude anyone. To answer this question, we return to an earlier observation about the terminological confusion in the field. Recall, we noted that Wendt (1999) uses the terms *realism* and *idealism* in two different ways. The distinction between realisms, political and scientific, was the subject of this section. The distinction between idealisms, a focus on ideas versus a focus on ideals, is the subject of the next.

Ideas, Utopias, and Liberals

"Ever since Carr's devastating critique, 'idealist' has functioned in IR primarily as an epithet for naivete" (Wendt 1999:33). Wendt makes this point after distinguishing between idealism as a theory of social politics and Idealism (which he capitalizes) as a theory of IR. The first idealism refers to social theory that looks at the importance of ideas, whereas the second refers to a theory of IR based on ideals rather than on realism. Wendt makes the claim that he is involved in doing the former, not the latter. This claim is disputed below. Interestingly, in *The Twenty Years' Crisis,* Carr (1964) does not use the term *idealism* at all; instead, he discusses utopianism. Similarly, Moravcsik (1997:514) tries explicitly to distance himself from "liberalism's historical role as an ideology" in his redefinition of liberal theory in IR. Liberalism is the foil to realism in Morgenthau's (1946) *Scientific Man Versus Power Politics.* Both Wendt (1999:39) and Moravcsik (1997:514) share in common a desire to liberate the label each applies to himself, idealist and liberal, respectively, from normative associations in an attempt to create "scientific" and, presumably therefore, value-free, social science.

Both these scholars are, in fact, trying to rehabilitate the terms *idealism* and *liberalism* (although in very different ways) from the charge that these concepts reflect a normative approach to social science: an ideology. The goal in this section is to rehabilitate the normative approach to IR from which both Moravcsik and Wendt are striving to distance themselves. As rhetorical foils to realism, Carr (1964) used "utopianism" and Morgenthau (1946) used "liberalism" and "scientific man." Although the terms that Carr and Morgenthau employed seem quite different, both were, in fact, referring to the sort of liberal idealism and scientific humanism often associated with political scientists in the tradition of Woodrow Wilson (see Kegley 1993; Schmidt 1998). The essence of this school of thought is that people have consistent and reasonable (or at least predictable) preferences, which they pursue rationally.[7] As a result, well-designed political institutions within

---

[6]This observation speaks to some recent attempts, such as that by Jeffrey Legro and Andrew Moravcsik (1999), to redefine realism in rationalist terms. Such attempts can be seen in the context of this essay more as entries in the rationalist-constructivist debate than as entries in interparadigmatic debates. In effect, redefining classical realism in rational choice terms can be viewed as a way of associating the traditional approach to postwar IR with rational choice, thereby increasing the marginalization of critics of rationalist approaches.

[7]A key difference between this school of thought and contemporary rationalist approaches in the study of IR is that in the latter the assumption of reasonableness falls out. People are assumed to be instrumentally rational, but are not necessarily assumed to respect the rights and well-being of others when to do so would not be demonstrably instrumentally rational.

which people can rationally pursue their preferences in a way that interferes as little as possible with the abilities of others to do so will appeal sufficiently to people's reasonableness as to obviate any necessity for power politics. In other words, for the liberal idealist the right political structure can, indeed, insure perpetual peace, to use Immanuel Kant's phrase (1957).

The classical realist response is that no ultimate solutions are available. "Peace is subject to the conditions of time and space and must be established and maintained by different methods and under different conditions of urgency in the every-day relations of concrete nations. The problem of international peace as such exists only for the philosopher" (Morgenthau 1946:217). That is, the right institutions can deal successfully with particular political problems at a particular time and place, but this nexus of problem, time, and place is historically unique; there will inevitably be other problems in other times and places. To the extent that many, if not most, international political problems have at least some distributional ramifications, the relative gains or preferential distributions in the solutions to new problems, or problems in different times and places, will likely reflect the interests of the actors best able to stake their claim to those gains, that is, the actors with the greater power. As such, no matter how well designed the structure of political institutions, power will always be the ultimate arbiter of outcomes in international politics.

So, then, is there ultimately nothing other than power that matters in international relations? Quite the contrary, for Morgenthau (1946:177–78), people are inherently moral as well as political animals; all political acts have ethical significance. For Carr (1964:235), "it is an unreal kind of realism which ignores the element of morality in any world order." In classical realism, moral theory in the absence of a recognition of power is a futile exercise as the use of power in the absence of morality is an empty exercise. The latter is the case for two reasons, one practical and one philosophical. The practical reason is that, because humans are moral beings, they will not accept power without

morality. Subjects of political domination will recognize the distinction we are trying to make here—between power used for good and power used for evil—and will support the former and oppose the latter (see, for example, Morgenthau 1946:176–78 and the discussion of Thucydides in Johnson Bagby 1994). The Philosophical reason is that power for its own sake is hollow; it gets you nowhere without some notion as to what to do with it. Indeed, "the characteristic vice of the utopian is naivete; of the realist, sterility" (Carr 1964:12). Classical realism, thus, views the art of international politics as the practical balancing of the demands of power on the one hand and morality on the other—as a dialectic between power and morality (see Kubálková 1998).

In short, from its inception realism has been viewed as a necessary corrective to idealism, but *not* as a replacement. Idealism, for the classical realist, is necessary to inform but actions and underlie our interests in the pursuit of international politics, but realism will always remain a necessary part of relations among states. Herein lies the difference between realists and "utopians" or "scientific men." Whereas the latter believe that we can ultimately build a world politics not based on power, the realist believes that we cannot. For realism, however well designed our international institutions, however well aligned our national interests, and however well intentioned our ideas, power will remain the ultimate arbiter (note, not the ultimate source) of outcomes. Because neither human nature nor human institutions [is] ultimately perfectible, we will always have to remain diligent both in identifying those who would subvert the system to their own ends and in dealing with them effectively.

Well and good, but does anyone actually disagree with the realist premise stated in this way? "The proposition that the nature of international politics is shaped by power relations invariably is listed as one of the defining characteristics of Realism. This cannot be a *uniquely* Realist claim, however, since then every student of international politics would be a Realist" (Wendt 1999:96–97). With this statement, Wendt would seem to preempt the usefulness of the broad definition of realism being used in this essay. But it can be argued that many members of the groups that Wendt identifies as accepting the centrality of power, including both neoliberals and himself, in the end do not. Moravcsik (1997:531), for example, includes in his list of scientific approaches to liberal theory proponents of the idea of a democratic peace.[8] The logical conclusion of the presence of a democratic peace is that if all countries were to become democratic, there would be no more war. Universalizing the right domestic political structures, in other words, would eliminate the threat posed by military power. This idealist conclusion is, as the terms are defined here, incompatible with realism. Neoliberal institutionalists argue that international cooperation in specific issue areas can happen given properly designed international institutions (see Keohane and Nye 1977; Keohane 1984; Haas, Keohane, and Levy 1993; Keohane and Martin 1995).[9] Once these institutions are in place, power is no longer an issue. Thus, at least in reference to particular issue areas, neoliberal institutionalists are idealists; they claim that perfecting institutions can obviate the need for national power.

All of which is to say that there are still idealists; there are still liberals by the old normative or ideological definition. Not every student of international politics is a realist. But what of constructivists? Despite the quotation by Wendt in the previous paragraph, an argument can be made that most current constructivist theorists working in the United States are, in fact, liberal idealists. Support for this argument can be presented in two ways: through what might be called the macroperspective and through the microperspective.

The former examines the way in which constructivism is, and has been, characterized as a general approach; the latter looks specifically at the work of leading constructivist theorists.

Using a macroperspective, reviews of constructivism by both practitioners and critics tend to characterize it, either explicitly or implicitly, as liberal-idealist. Moreover, such characterizations are rarely, if ever, disputed. A recent review of the study of norms in IR (Finnemore and Sikkink 1998:916), for example, once again explicitly distances the contemporary study of norms from Carr's utopianism, but it argues that a fundamental part of the reintroduction of the study of norms is "aimed precisely at showing how the 'ought' becomes the 'is.'" The claim of distance from Carr's utopianism is based on the improved standards of empirical research employed by today's scholars, making constructivist work an exercise in the systematic use of empirical evidence rather than an exercise in political theory (Finnemore and Sikkink 1998:890). In essence, what Finnemore and Sikkink are contending is that Carr's utopians failed in methodology, not in worldview. They clearly imply that the study of norms and ideas in IR theory, the hallmarks of constructivism, involves examining the ways in which these two phenomena independently make the world better. Another recent review of constructivism by one of its originators, Nicholas Onuf (2001), clearly identifies it politically with liberal institutionalism (see also Sterling-Folker 2000).

Critics of constructivism, from both the neorealist and postmodernist directions, also associate constructivism with a liberal idealism that is not sufficiently cognizant of the role of power in international relations. For example, in a recent review of the relationship between postmodernism and feminism, Birgit Locher and Elisabeth Prügl (2001) compliment constructivism for its "transformational" characteristics but criticize it for not accepting the central role of power in the construction of international politics. This observation sounds very much like the classical realist critique of liberal idealism, that it puts too much

---

[8]He calls this variant more broadly "republican liberalism." On the idealist nature of republican liberalism as the route to peace more generally, see Doyle (1983a, 1983b) and Kant (1957).

[9]None of these scholars makes a universal idealist claim; but they do claim a limited, and increasing, scope for the cooperative effects of international institutions. This school of thought seems recently to have lost the "neoliberal" part of its label, being more often referred to simply as "institutionalists."

stock in the ability of ideals alone, without power, to change the world.

Neorealist criticism of constructivism is remarkably similar. In "The False Promise of International Institutions," for instance, John Mearsheimer (1994/1995:37–47) characterizes critical theory, in which he includes constructivism, as focusing on the transformation of world politics without addressing the role of power in creating and disseminating ideas and modes of discourse. Mearsheimer's missive resulted in a set of responses in a later issue of the same journal, two of them by self-described constructivists. In one, Ruggie (1995) argues from a traditionally liberal perspective that the right international institutions do, in fact, make the world a better place, aside from considerations of power politics. In the other, Wendt (1995) corrected Mearsheimer's polemical portrayal of constructivism, but in doing so he showed the sensitivity to being branded a utopian that we have already seen.

Which brings us to the microperspective approach to showing that constructivist theorists are, in fact, predominantly liberal idealists. A complete review of the constructivist literature is, of course, impossible here. Instead, the focus here will be on two specific tendencies toward liberal idealism in the work of self-described contemporary constructivists.[10] The first tendency involves choosing to study issue areas compatible with liberal idealism in relatively noncritical ways. The second is to use as philosophical touchstones theorists of a liberal-idealist bent.

We cannot, of course, reasonably ascribe a normative bias to a methodological approach based on the topical foci of some of its practitioners. However, we can note a tendency to approach certain types of issues in a non-self-critical fashion. The fact that many of the well-known mainstream constructivists focus on issues such as human rights (Sikkink 1993; Klotz 1995; Keck and Sikkink 1998; Risse, Ropp, and Sikkink 1999; Burgerman 2001), security communities (Adler and Barnett 1998), or multilateralism (Ruggie 1993) does not make them liberal idealists. Rather, it is the way in which they focus on such issues that makes them so. Illustrating with the first of these issues, constructivists who write about human rights generally look at the role of international civil society, however understood,[11] as changing the behavior of states for the better. This work is applied constructivism—intersubjective norms affect definitions of interest. But it is also liberal-idealist, in the sense that these norms are accepted largely uncritically as good ones, as are the elements of international civil society involved in spreading these norms.

Similarly, we cannot reasonably ascribe a normative bias to a methodological approach based on the theoretical antecedents upon which some of its practitioners draw. But to the extent that constructivists in the United States draw on the work of political theorists (as opposed to the social theorists upon which they draw methodologically and epistemologically), these theorists often have liberal-idealist leanings. A good example is Wendt. He claims to accept the role of power in international relations and, thus, the basic realist premise as defined here. But he also argues, with reference to Kant, that the endogenous dynamic of international anarchy is progressive. In other words, absent exogenous shock, the culture of anarchy will tend to evolve from the Hobbesian world of enemies to the Lockean world of rivals and, ultimately, to the Kantian world of friends (Wendt 1999:308–12). Once we have arrived in the Kantian "role relationship" (Wendt 1999:309) of friend, international politics is unlikely to regress.

---

[10]The purpose of this discussion is not to imply that those included are more important or central to constructivist theory than those not included—the selection is, in this sense, not systematic.

[11]Sikkink (1993) speaks of principled issue-networks, Keck and Sikkink (1998) of advocacy networks, and Burgerman (2001) simply of activists. None would likely object to having what they are studying characterized as an element of global civil society. Burgerman speaks uncritically both of the activist community and of multilateralism.

Changing the social construction of anarchy can thereby obviate the worry that our neighbors will become enemies or rivals.

Another example involves constructivist research that draws on the work of Jürgen Habermas (for example, Linklater 1990, 1998; Lynch 1999; Risse 2000). Using ideas such as communicative rationality, Habermas argues that communicative action and a well-structured public sphere can be an emancipatory force. He is generally identified as a critical theorist, but in certain respects he is a liberal idealist. Idealist in the sense that he has a clear notion of what constitutes political progress and the political good life, and liberal in the sense that this notion of the political good life is based on individual self-expression and a form of rationality (albeit not an instrumental rationality). Constructivist research that draws on Habermasian theory cannot easily separate the social theory (public spheres matter) from the normative theory (public spheres are good).

To be sure, neither of these tendencies—to choose particular issue areas or to rely on philosophical touchstones sympathetic to the liberal-idealist project—is universal. For example, Rodney Bruce Hall (1997) speaks explicitly of legitimacy as power; Martha Finnemore (1996) takes liberal theory to task for its ideological commitments. Perhaps, more telling, all of the constructivists discussed above work in the United States; it is probably both fairer and more accurate to ascribe the liberal-idealist tendency only to U.S. constructivism, not constructivism more broadly. Indeed, for surveys of constructivist theory by scholars not working in the United States, see Ralph Pettman (2000) and Karen Fierke and Knud Erik Jørgensen (2001). The relationship between U.S. constructivism and liberal idealism itself is something that a realist constructivism might do well to examine.

Realist Constructivism

This discussion leaves us with the observation that constructivism as a methodology in the study of international relations need not be idealist, but

that in practice in the United States it tends to be liberal-idealist. Such a statement is in no way a derogation of either constructivism or liberal idealism. The classical realists argued quite explicitly that moral ideals are an integral and necessary part of the practice of international politics and that political realism in the absence of morality, in the absence of a vision of utopia, is both sterile and pointless. A realist constructivism would, thus, serve to help rehabilitate idealism by requiring as its corollary a self-consciously idealist constructivism and by contending that the study of ideals, as well as ideas, is integral to a full understanding of international politics. The original constructivist starting point was more a critique of the "structural" part of structural realism than of classical realism; the former allows much less scope for incorporating moral ideals than the latter. The classical realist argument is that to have an impact, any politics of moral ideals must be tempered by a politics of power.

A corollary of this argument is the observation that without addressing "the compromise between power and morality" (Carr 1964:210) we cannot successfully address the phenomenon of political change. Interestingly, this inability to account for change is one of the standard charges leveled against neorealism, particularly Waltz's (1979) variety (for example, Ruggie 1983b; Walker 1987). In this sense, Waltz has come full circle to meet the Wilsonian idealists who provided the foil for both Carr and Morgenthau. Waltz's theory of the structure of power, without scope for morality, becomes static in the same way that theories of the structure of morality without power do. Neither pure realism nor pure idealism can account for political change, only the interplay of the two, subject to the assumption that morality is contextual rather than universal.

Therefore, to the extent that constructivist methodology can illuminate the workings of international politics, both an idealist constructivism and a realist constructivism—distinct from, but in a dialectical relationship with, each other—are necessary to account for and explain change in the international system. The idealist constructivism would be freed from any perceived need to claim to study only ideas in an attempt to distance itself from the study of ideals. The realist constructivism would look at the way in which power structures affect patterns of normative change in international relations and, conversely, the way in which a particular set of norms affects power structures. Many of the theorists labeled above as idealist constructivists could respond that they already do one or the other of these things. Someone studying human rights networks in Latin America, for example, might respond that he or she is explicitly arguing that human rights norms are changing the power structure by empowering nongovernmental organizations at the expense of traditional governing elites. But underlying this research is inevitably a moral idealism that sees power in the hands of such organizations as better than power in the hands of the traditional elites. Therefore, the more power that flows from the latter to the former, the better.

We may well agree with this moral perspective. But the realist response is that power will ultimately be used by those who accrue it for a specific set of ends. Furthermore, not all ends toward which power can be invested, even if used in the interest of a moral ideal, will be compatible, because not all moral ideals are compatible. In other words, even once the human rights norms in question are generally accepted in the relations among countries, power will still matter. The specific groups that have been empowered by the norms will at some point find that their goals differ; at that time the relative power among them will begin to become important. Even if all actors in the international system at a given point in time accept the same basic set of normative structures, they will differ in their interpretations of those structures, whether for rationally self-interested reasons or for psychological reasons (see, for example, Jervis 1976; Rosati 2000; Shannon 2000). When interpretations differ, the power of the interpreter continues to matter. The role of a realist constructivism, then, is to examine, skeptically from a moral perspective the interrelationships between power and international norms (see Loriaux 1992).

In this moral skepticism lies a key difference between idealism and realism. Idealism recognizes a single ideal, a universal political morality toward which we should strive. Realism argues that no universal political morality exists and, therefore, if we want ours to triumph, we must arrange to have it do so through the application of power. But the classical realists, particularly Carr, warn us that the relationship can be used both ways: morality can also be used as a tool of power. So that when we apply power to promote our preferred political morality, others might see it as a use of power simply to promote our interests. Political psychology (see, for example, Jervis 1976) suggests, furthermore, that when we justify a use of power to ourselves as being for moral purposes, we may simply be fooling ourselves and rationalizing an action as moral that we want to take for other reasons. As such, even though power is hollow without political morality, the classical realist argument is that we must, nonetheless, apply to that morality, ours as well as others, a certain skepticism when it is used to justify power.

Stated as such, classical realism begins to sound much like certain kinds of critical theory as applied in IR (see, for example, Ashley 1984). Parts of *The Twenty Years' Crisis* (Carr 1964), in fact, sound like a Foucaultian critique of Wilsonian idealism (Foucault 1980; see also Ashley 1984; Der Derlan 1990 and Walker 1990b; Walker 1993). These sections include the argument that political actions in the international domain, even when motivated by the best of intentions, have ramifications on the distribution of power that can affect both the ultimate effectiveness of the actions and the way those actions are viewed by others. Thus, the League of Nations, even if it was created by the status quo powers to promote international peace, was viewed by others as an exercise in supporting the relative power of the states that created it. The tendency of U.S. constructivism toward liberal idealism can similarly be viewed from outside the central status quo power as an exercise in maintaining that status quo—and clearly has been by some postmodern critics of IR theory (see, for example, George 1994:127).

A realist constructivism could specifically address these sorts of issues. It could study the relationship between normative structures, the carriers of political morality, and uses of power. And, as a result, realist constructivism could address issues of change in international relations in a way that neither idealist constructivism (with its ultimately static view of political morality) nor positivist-materialist realism (with its dismissive view of political morality) can manage. In doing so, a realist constructivism could fill a gap in theorizing in IR between mainstream theorizing and critical theory.[12] It could do so by adopting the focus on power found in most critical theory without the negativity inherent in that theory's emancipatory project with its interest in emancipation "from" rather than "to" (see Spegele 1996; Wæver 1996; Patomäki and Wight 2000). Realist constructivism could also do so by including in any exploration of power not only postmodern theory's study of subjective text and positivist realism's study of objective phenomena but also constructivism's study of intersubjectivity—of norms and social rules.

What, in the end, does this line of argument have to say about the conduct of research and discourse in the field of IR? To constructivists, it suggests that constructivism—whether understood as a methodology, epistemology, or ontology—should not be understood as a paradigm in the way that realism and liberalism and, for that matter, Marxism are. By paradigm is meant here a set of assumptions about how politics works. Constructivism is a set of assumptions about how to study politics. As such, it is compatible (as are other sets of assumptions about how to study politics, such as rationalism) with a variety of paradigms, including realism. To idealist constructivists (idealism here referring to ideals rather than ideas), this line of argument suggests that a realist constructivism should be seen as an opportunity. By distinguishing questions

concerning the role of ideals from questions about the role of ideas, it allows idealists to focus on the ideals specifically and encourages them to be explicit about their idealism, to move beyond the stigma that has been associated with utopianism since *The Twenty Years' Crisis* (Carr 1964). In other words, it suggests that they not hide their ideals behind the claim of objective science. To realists, it says not only that constructivism can be a useful research methodology but that addressing constructivist epistemological and ontological premises can provide a useful corrective to the assumptions of individual rationalism and materialism that have been confusing definitions of realism for the past few decades.

References

ADLER, EMANUEL, AND MICHAEL BARNETT, eds. *Security Communities*. Cambridge, UK: Cambridge University Press, 1998.

ARCHER, MARGARET, et al., eds. *Critical Realism: Essential Readings*. London: Routledge, 1998.

ASHLEY, RICHARD. "The Poverty of Neorealism." *International Organization* (1994) 38:225–86.

ASHLEY, RICHARD, AND R.B.J. WALKER. "Reading Dissidence/Writing the Discipline: Crisis and the Question of Sovereignty in International Studies." *International Studies Quarterly* 34 (1990a):367–416.

———"Speaking and Language of Exile: Dissident Thought in International Studies." *International Studies Quarterly* 34 (1990b):259–68.

AYER. ALFRED JULES, ed. *Logical Positivism*. Glencoe, IL: Free Press, 1959.

BACHRACH, PETER, AND MORTON BARATZ. "Two faces of Power." *American Political Science Review*. 56 (1962):947–52.

BALDWIN, DAVID. *Paradoxes of Power*. New York: Blackwell, 1989.

BHASKAR, ROY. *Scientific Realism and Human Emancipation*. London: Verso, 1986.

BULL, HEDLEY. "The Theory of International Politics, 1919–1969." In *The Aberystwyth Papers: International Politics 1919–1969*, Brian Porter, ed. London: Oxford University Press, 1972.

BURGERMAN, SUSAN. *Moral Victories: How Activists Provoke Multilateral Action*. Ithaca, NY: Cornell University Press, 2001.

---

[12]The relationship between mainstream constructivism and critical theory is itself open to dispute. See, for example, Price and Reus-Smit (1998) and Kubálková, Onuf, and Kowert (1998) for different perspectives on this relationship.

CARR, EDWARD HALLETT. *The Twenty Years' Crisis, 1919–1939: An Introduction to the Study of International Relations.* Reprinted from the earlier edition. New York: Harper and Row, 1964.

DER DERLAN, JAMES. "The (S)pace of International Relations: Simulation, Surveillance, and Speed." *International Studies Quarterly* 34 (1990):295–310.

DESSLER, DAVID. "What's at Stake in the Agent-Structure Debate?" *International Organization* 43 (1989):441–73.

DONNELLY, JACK. *Realism and International Relations.* Cambridge, UK: Cambridge University Press, 2000.

DOYLE, MICHAEL. "Kant, Liberal Legacies, and Foreign Affairs: Part 1." *Philosophy and Public Affairs* 12 (1983a):205–35.

____ "Kant, Liberal Legacies, and Foreign Affairs: Part 2." *Philosophy and Public Affairs* 12 (1983b):323–53.

FIERKE, KAREN, AND KNUD ERIK JØRGENSEN, eds. *Constructing International Relations: The Next Generation.* Armonk, NY: M. E. Sharpe, 2001.

FINNEMORE, MARTHA. *National Interests in International Society.* Ithaca, NY: Cornell University Press, 1996.

FINNEMORE, MARTHA, AND KATHRYN SIKKINK. "International Norm Dynamics and Political Change." *International Organization* 52 (1998):887–917.

FOUCAULT, MICHAEL. *Power/Knowledge: Selected Interviews and Other Writings, 1972–1977,* Colin Gordon, ed. New York: Pantheon, 1980.

GEORGE, JIM. *Discourses of Global Politics: A Critical (Re)Introduction to International Relations.* Boulder, CO: Lynne Rienner, 1994.

GILPIN, ROBERT. *War and Change in World Politics.* Cambridge, UK: Cambridge University Press, 1981.

GRIECO, JOSEPH. "Realist International Theory and the Study of World Politics." In *New Thinking in International Relations Theory,* Michael Doyle and G. John Ikenberry, eds. Boulder, CO: Westview Press, 1997.

HAAS, PETER, ROBERT KEOHANE, AND MARC LEVY, eds. *Institutions for the Earth: Sources of Effective International Environmental Protection.* Cambridge, MA: MIT Press, 1993.

HALL, RODNEY BRUCE. "Moral Authority as a Power Resource." *International Organization* 51 (1997):555–89.

HELLMAN, GEOFFREY. "Realist Principles." *Philosophy of Science* 50 (1983):227–49.

HOLSTI, KALEVI J. *The Dividing Discipline: Hegemony and Diversity in International Theory.* Boston: Allen and Unwin, 1985.

HUGHES, BARRY. *Continuity and Change in World Politics: Competing Perspective,* 4th ed. Upper Saddle River, NJ: Prentice-Hall, 2000.

JERVIS, ROBERT. *Perceptions and Misperceptions in International Politics.* Princeton, NJ: Princeton University Press, 1976.

____ Realism in the Study of World Politics. *International Organization* 52 (1998):971–91.

JOHNSON BAGBY, LAURIE. "The Use and Abuse of Thucydides in International Relations." *International Organization* 48 (1994):131–53.

KAHLER, MILES. "Rationality in International Relations." *International Organization* 52 (1998):919–41.

KANT, IMMANUEL. *Perpetual Peace,* Lewis White Beck, ed. New York: Macmillan, 1957.

KATZENSTEIN, PETER, ROBERT KEOHANE, AND STEPHEN KRASNER. "International Organization and the Study of World Politics." *International Organization* 52 (1998):645–85.

KECK, MARGARET, AND KATHRYN SIKKINK. *Activists Beyond Borders: Advocacy Networks in International Politics.* Ithaca, NY: Cornell University Press, 1998.

KEGLEY, CHARLES. "The Neoidealist Moment in International Studies? Realist Myths and the New International Realities." *International Studies Quarterly* 37 (1993):131–47.

KEGLEY, CHARLES, AND EUGENE WITTKOPF. *World Politics: Trends and Transformations,* 8th ed. Boston: Bedford/St. Martin's, 2001.

KEOHANE, ROBERT. *After Hegemony: Cooperation and Discord in the World Political Economy.* Princeton, NJ: Princeton University Press, 1984.

KEOHANE, ROBERT, AND LISA MARTIN. "The Promise of Institutionalist Theory." *International Security* 20 (1995):39–51.

KEOHANE, ROBERT, AND JOSEPH NYE, JR. *Power and Interdependence: World Politics in Transition.* Boston: Little, Brown, 1977.

KIRK, GRAYSON. *The Study of International Relations in American Colleges and Universities.* New York: Council on Foreign Relations, 1947.

KLOTZ, AUDIE. *Norms in International Relations: The Struggle Against Apartheid.* Ithaca, NY: Cornell University Press, 1995.

KRATOCHWIL, FRIEDRICH. "Errors Have Their Advantages." *International Organization* 38 (1984):305–20.

KUBÁLKOVÁ, VENDULKA. "The Twenty Years' Catharsis: E. H. Carr and IR." In *International Relations in a Constructed World,* Vendulka Kubálková, Nicholas

Onuf, and Paul Kowert, eds. Armonk, NY: M. E. Sharpe, 1998.

KUBÁLKOVÁ, VENDULKA, NICHOLAS ONUF, AND PAUL KOWERT. "Constructing Constructivism." In *International Relations in a Constructed World,* Vendulka Kubálková, Nicholas Onuf, and Paul Kowert, eds. Armonk, NY: M. E. Sharpe, 1998.

LAPID, YOSEF. "The Third Debate: On the Prospects of International Theory in a Post-Positivist Era." *International Studies Quarterly* 33 (1989):235–54.

LASSWELL, HAROLD. *World Politics and Personal Insecurity.* New York: McGraw-Hill, 1935.

LASSWELL, HAROLD, AND ABRAHAM KAPLAN. *Power and Society: A Framework for Political Inquiry.* New Haven, CT: Yale University Press, 1950.

LEBOW, RICHARD NED. "Thucydides the Constructivist." *American Political Science Review* 95 (2001):547–60.

LEGRO, JEFFREY, AND ANDREW MORAVCSIK. "Is Anybody Still a Realist?" *International Security* 24 (1999):5–55.

LEPLIN, JARRETT, ed. *Scientific Realism.* Berkeley: University of California Press, 1984.

LIEBER, ROBERT. *No Common Power: Understanding International Relations,* 4th ed. Upper Saddle River, NJ: Prentice Hall, 2001.

LINKLATER, ANDREW. *Beyond Realism and Marxism: Critical Theory and International Relations.* London: Macmillan, 1990.

____ *The Transformation of Political Community: Ethical Foundations of the Post-Westphalian Era.* Columbia, SC: University of South Carolina Press, 1998.

LOCHER, BIRGIT, AND ELISABETH PRÜGL. "Feminism and Constructivism: Worlds Apart or Sharing the Middle Ground?" *International Studies Quarterly* 45 (2001):111–29.

LORIAUX, MICHAEL. "The Realists and St. Augustine: Skepticism, Psychology, and Moral Action in International Relations Thought." *International Studies Quarterly* 36 (1992):401–20.

LYNCH, MARK. *State Interests and Public Spheres: The International Politics of Jordan's Identity.* New York: Columbia University Press, 1999.

MEARSHEIMER, JOHN. *Conventional Deterrence.* Ithaca, NY: Cornell University Press, 1983.

____ "The False Promise of International Institutions." *International Security* 19 (1994/1995):5–49.

MORAVCSIK, ANDREW. "Taking Preferences Seriously: A Liberal Theory of International Politics." *International Organization* 51 (1997):513–53.

MORGENTHAU, HANS. *Scientific Man Versus Power Politics.* Chicago: University of Chicago Press, 1946.

____ *Politics Among Nations: The Struggle for Power and Peace.* New York: Knopf, 1948.

____ *Politics Among Nations: The Struggle for Power and Peace,* 6th ed. Revised by Kenneth Thompson. New York: McGraw-Hill, 1985.

ONUF, NICHOLAS. *World of Our Making.* Columbia, SC: University of South Carolina Press, 1989.

____ "The Politics of Constructivism." In *Constructing International Relations: The Next Generation,* Karen Fierke and Knud Eric Jørgensen, eds. Armonk, NY: M. E. Sharpe, 2001.

ONUF, NICHOLAS, AND FRANK KLINK. "Activity, Authority, Rule." *International Studies Quarterly* 33 (1989):149–74.

OREN, IDO. "Is Culture Independent of National Security? How America's National Security Concerns Shaped 'Political Culture' Research." *European Journal of International Relations* 6 (2000):543–73.

PATOMÄKI, HEIKKI, AND COLIN WIGHT. "After Postpositivism? The Promises of Critical Realism." *International Studies Quarterly* 44 (2000):213–37.

PETTMAN, RALPH. *Commonsense Constructivism: Or the Making of World Affairs.* Armonk, NY: M. E. Sharpe, 2000.

POSEN, BARRY. *The Sources of Military Doctrine: France, Britain, and Germany Between the World Wars.* Ithaca, NY: Cornell University Press, 1984.

PRICE, RICHARD, AND CHRISTIAN REUS-SMIT. "Dangerous Liaisons? Critical International Theory and Constructivism." *European Journal of International Relations* 4 (1998):259–94.

RISSE, THOMAS. 'Let's Argue!' Communicative Action in World Politics." *International Organization* 54 (2000):1–39.

RISSE, THOMAS, STEPHEN ROPP, AND KATHRYN SIKKINK, eds. *The Power of Human Rights: International Norms and Domestic Change.* Cambridge, UK: Cambridge University Press, 1999.

ROMMEN, HANS. "Realism and Utopianism in World Affairs." *Review of Politics* 6 (1994):193–215.

ROSATI, JEREL. "The Power of Human Cognition in the Study of World Politics." *International Studies Review* 2 (2000):45–75.

RUGGIE, JOHN GERARD. "Continuity and Transformation in the World Polity." *World Politics* 35 (1983):261–85.

___ ed. *Multilateralism Matters: The Theory and Praxis of an Institutional Form*. New York: Columbia University Press, 1993.

___ "The False Premise of Realism." *International Security* 20 (1995):62–70.

___ "What Makes the World Hang Together? Neo-Utilitarianism and the Social Constructivist Challenge." *International Organization* 52 (1998): 855–85.

SCHMIDT, BRIAN. *The Political Discourse of Anarchy: A Disciplinary History of International Relations*. Albany, NY: State University of New York Press, 1998.

SCHUMAN, FREDERICK. *International Politics: An Introduction to the Western State System*. New York: McGraw-Hill, 1933.

SCHWELLER, RANDALL. *Deadly Imbalances: Tripolarity and Hitler's Strategy of World Conquest*. New York: Columbia University Press, 1998.

SHANNON, VAUGHN. "Norms Are What States Make of Them: The Political Psychology of Norm Violation." *International Studies Quarterly* 44 (2000):293–316.

SIKKINK, KATHRYN. "Human Rights, Principled Issue-Networks, and Sovereignty in Latin America." *International Organization* 47 (1993):411–41.

SINGER, J. DAVID. *Models, Methods, and Progress in World Politics: A Peace Research Odyssey*. Boulder, CO: Westview Press, 1990.

SYNDER, JACK. "Science and Sovietology: Bridging the Methods Gap in Soviet Foreign Policy Studies." *World Politics* 40 (1988):169–193.

SPEGELE, ROGER. *Political Realism in International Theory*. Cambridge, UK: Cambridge University Press, 1996.

STERLING-FOLKER, JENNIFER. "Competing Paradigms or Birds of a Feather? Constructivism and Neoliberal Institutionalism Compared." *International Studies Quarterly* 44 (2000):97–119.

___ "Realism and the Constructivist Challenge: Rejecting, Reconstructing, or Rereading." *International Studies Review* 4 (2002):73–97.

STRANGE, SUSAN. "The Persistent Myth of Lost Hegemony." *International Organization* 41 (1987): 551–574.

VASQUEZ, JOHN. *The Power of Power Politics: A Critique*. New Brunswick, NJ: Rutgers University Press, 1983.

___ *The Power of Power Politics: From Classical Realism to Neotraditionalism*. Cambridge, UK: Cambridge University Press, 1998.

WÆVER, OLE. "The Rise and Fall of the Inter-Paradigm Debate." In *International Theory: Positivism and Beyond*, Steve Smith, Ken Booth and Marysia Zalewski, eds. Cambridge, UK: Cambridge University Press, 1996.

WALKER, R.B.J. "Realism, Change, and International Political Theory." *International Studies Quarterly* 31 (1987):65–86.

___ *Inside/Outside: International Relations as Political Theory*. Cambridge, UK: Cambridge University Press, 1993.

WALT, STEPHEN. *The Origins of Alliances*. Ithaca, NY: Cornell University Press, 1987.

WALTZ, KENNETH. *Man, the State, and War*. New York: Columbia University Press, 1959.

___ *Theory of International Politics*. Reading, MA: Addison-Wesley. 1979.

WENDT, ALEXANDER. "The Agent-Structure Problem in International Relations Theory." *International Organization* 41 (1987):335–70.

___ "Constructing International Politics." *International Security* 20 (1995):71–81.

___ *Social Theory of International Politics*. Cambridge, UK: Cambridge University Press, 1999.

WIGHT, MARTIN. *Power Politics*. London: Royal Institute of International Affairs, 1946.

WOLFERS, ARNOLD. *Discord and Collaboration: Essays on International Politics*. Baltimore, MD: Johns Hopkins University Press, 1962.

THE ENGLISH SCHOOL VS. AMERICAN REALISM: A MEETING OF MINDS OR DIVIDED BY A COMMON LANGUAGE?

Richard Little*

. . . I want to demonstrate that American realism and the English School share a common intellectual heritage that can be traced back to the classical realists who were developing their ideas in the middle of the twentieth century. What the modern

Review of International Studies 29 (2003):443–60.
Copyright British International Studies Association.

*Thanks to Theo Farrell for helpful comments on an earlier draft of this article.

American realists have done, however, is to take one strand of classical realist thinking and refine it on the basis of their positivist methodology. There would be no problem with this procedure, in principle, provided that they had self-consciously decided to make a break with the classical realists. But members of this school often associate themselves with the classical realist tradition without apparently being aware of what they have left behind.

Ironically, the reverse of this argument applies to the founding fathers of the English School. Bull, for example, explicitly dissociated himself from the classical realists and insisted that Morgenthau's work represented "an instructive failure" and reflected "the bankruptcy of a whole line of inquiry."[1] Nevertheless, Alderson and Hurrell acknowledge that the idea of international society grew out of a "critical engagement" with classical realism, which is seen to have underestimated "the social nature of international life."[2] In practice, however, the overlap is more significant than Alderson and Hurrell allow. A close reading reveals that the key concepts that lie at the heart of the English School approach—international system, international society, world society, and international justice—can all be clearly identified in the works of seminal theorists in classical realism such as Morgenthau.

What the English School does, therefore, is to clarify an approach that is more implicit than explicit in classical realism. By exploring these links between the English School and classical realism in the first part of this contribution, I hope to reveal what is distinctive about the English School orientation. I will also reveal why, from an English School perspective, there is certainly an important social element missing from modern American realism, which is present in classical realism. From the English School perspective, therefore, American realism presents a one-dimensional account that generates a distorted, or certainly incomplete, understanding of international relations. In the second part of the contribution I shall then try to show what this missing element adds to our understanding of contemporary international politics.

Finally, in the conclusion I will return to the main criticisms leveled at the English School by the American realists.

Classical Realism and the English School

There are significant links that can be established between classical realism and the English School. These can be highlighted by focusing on the central concepts that underpin English School thinking—international system, international society and world society, and international justice. What we see in this section is that although the English School highlighted these concepts, the antecedents of their thinking in each case can be traced back to the classical realists. Highlighting these links helps to reveal that the American realists have emphasised only one element of classical realism at the expense of thinking about the social dimension of international politics.

The International System

Conventional wisdom suggests that the dynamics of the international system, and, in particular, the dynamics associated with the balance of power, provide the main focal point for classical realists. In the case of Morgenthau, however, this assessment certainly requires some modification. For him, there is an implicit distinction drawn between how the balance of power operates in the international system and how it operates in an international society. Although there is not the clear-cut distinction drawn between international system and society that we find in the English School, there is the same presumption that they co-exist. A theory of the balance of power shorn of all normative implications, therefore, is distinctive to modern American realists.

An international system emerges for the English School when "states are in regular contact with each other and where in addition there is interaction between them, sufficient to make the behaviour of each a necessary element in the calculation of the other."[3] Classical realists subscribe to a similar position and Morgenthau accepts that there is an automatic law ensuring that if one state increases its power capabilities in order to pursue an imperial policy at the expense of a rival, then there will be a "proportionate increase in the power of the other."[4] A systematic balance of power, therefore, represents the default position in any anarchic arena. It is this kind of logic that underpins the American realist theory of international politics, and there is no doubt that the thinking has resulted in a much more coherent and comprehensive theory of a systemic balance of power than was advanced by the classical realists or the English School. But, as a consequence, the persistence of unipolarity in the post–Cold War world poses a much bigger anomaly for the American realists than for the other two schools, and there is no straightforward answer as to why the United States has not been confronted by a balancing alliance.

Classical realism, however, presupposes that the balance of power can work effectively only in the context of societal norms. If states refuse to accept the moral standing of each other then they will find that they engage in a struggle of unlimited "ferociousness and intensity."[5] A purely systemic balance is very different from a societal balance. It would resemble, Morgenthau argues, a Hobbesian "state of nature."[6] By contrast, although the English School acknowledges that classical realists have postulated an "automatic tendency" for a balance of power to emerge in the international system, they deny that there is an "inevitable tendency for a balance of

power to arise" because states do not always seek to maximize their relative power position, often preferring to devote their resources and energies to other ends.[7] As a consequence, Bull formulates the idea of a "fortuitous" balance of power that can emerge without "any conscïous effort" on the part of the members of the system.[8] This outcome is seen to be most likely in a situation where two dominant states are both striving to achieve hegemony within an international system. Because the outcome is independent of the objectives being pursued by the states, it is viewed as a product of the system. As Watson puts it, systemic pressures "act mechanically in the sense that they act outside of the will of the community concerned."[9] Bull, moreover, advances a similar image to Morgenthau, arguing that in a bipolar anomic world with the two dominant powers aiming at absolute aggrandizement we can only imagine the balance of power to be "a moment of deadlock in a struggle to death between two contending powers."[10]

The English School acknowledges, therefore, that a balance of power might fortuitously arise within the international system, but, like Morgenthau, the members do not consider that such a balance could provide the basis for a stable international order. As a consequence, Bull displays very little interest in a purely systemic balance of power and immediately turns his attention to a societal balance of power. The reluctance of the English School to accept that there is a logic to anarchy necessarily generating a balance of power could be a consequence of their presumption that anarchy is a very fragile structure and that, as Watson has put it, there has been a perennial pendulum swing in international relations between empire and anarchy, with the pull being toward empire rather than anarchy.[11]

[3]Hedley Bull, *The Anarchical Society: A Study of Order in World Politics* (New York: Columbia University Press, 1977), p. 10.
[4]Hans J. Morgenthau, *Politics Among Nations: The Struggle for Power and Peace*, 5th ed. (New York: Alfred A. Knopf, 1973), p. 174.
[5]Ibid., p. 256.
[6]Ibid., p. 225.

[7]Bull, *The Anarchical Society*, p. 107.
[8]Ibid., p. 100.
[9]Adam Watson, *The Evolution of International Society: A Comparative Historical Analysis* (London: Routledge, 1992), p. 311.
[10]Bull, *The Anarchical Society*.
[11]Watson, *The Evolution of International Society*.

Certainly the historical record indicates that it has been more difficult for anarchic systems to survive than the American realist's theory would suggest. For the American realists, the persistence of anarchy is not seen to be problematic, but from the English School perspective, this is itself a problem.

International Society

Although the English School makes the concept much more explicit, classical realists also subscribed to the idea of an international society. Both accept, in other words, that international behaviour has been regulated, on a habitual basis, by an established body of norms. Morgenthau, for example, goes to considerable pains to contest what he sees as the "widespread misconception" that there is no such thing as international law.[12] He asserts, to the contrary, that international law emerged over 400 years ago and that it has been "scrupulously observed" from the start.[13] At the beginning of the Cold War, however, Morgenthau feared that the international society of states was under grave threat. He observed an emerging international system characterised by a mutual struggle for survival between the two superpowers, and he argued that their policies were creating a "new balance of power"[14] that would deal the "final, fatal blow" to

a balance of power which had permitted the long-term survival of a society of states defined by "shared values and universal standards of action."[15] Morgenthau insisted that during the era of the European balance of power, imperial drives for power had been constrained by "moral limitations," accepted by states as the result of establishing "a silent compact" that all states had a right to survive.[16] States agreed, therefore, on an "ultimate standard" of behaviour reflecting a body of rules that all states were obliged to follow.[17] During this distinctive period of history every ruler "expected and was justified in expecting everybody else to share this standard."[18]

Morgenthau, therefore, established an intimate link between international society and the balance of power, and the English School travels along exactly the same route. Bull, for example, draws a sharp distinction between a "fortuitous" balance that sometimes operates within an international system, and a "contrived" balance that is seen to underpin any international society. A contrived balance is associated with any international setting where the Great Powers all accept the need to sustain a society of states. It follows that there is an intersubjective agreement, a "silent compact," to refrain from endeavouring to monopolise international power and to take the necessary steps to restrain any state that does pursue this strategy. So a "contrived" balance of power becomes synonymous with the survival of a society of states. The Great Powers engage in voluntary restraint because they know that any attempt to overthrow the balance will be a "hopeless undertaking."[19] Although this argument is not spelled out, it is also apparent that while the undertaking may eventually prove to be "hopeless," it could lead to the demise of the societal balance and the emergence of a systemic balance which both the English School and the

---

[12]Morgenthau, *Politics Among Nations*, p. 273.

[13]Ibid., p. 273. Where international law is seen to have failed is in the attempts to eliminate war from the international system and establish an element of international government. Morgenthau was extremely sceptical about the utility of using international law to try to make progress on these fronts because international law, like diplomacy, is an international institution that is designed to sustain a society of sovereign states. It is through international law and diplomacy that the society of states is constantly being reproduced. By contrast, a world with an effective international government that could police the system would no longer constitute a society of sovereign states. From a classical realist perspective, therefore, because diplomacy and international law are designed to protect the sovereign state, they are unlikely to be effective when it comes to introducing measures that are designed to undermine the sovereign state.

[14]Morgenthau, *Politics Among Nations*, ch. 21.

[15]Ibid., pp. 330–1.
[16]Ibid., p. 219.
[17]Ibid., p. 274.
[18]Ibid.
[19]Ibid., p. 219.

classical realists believe has the potential to turn into a "state of nature."[20]

Both the English School and the classical realists go further, however, and insist that there is a necessary relationship between international law and the societal balance of power. The logic underpinning this relationship, however, is never spelled out with anything like the precision that characterises the analyses offered by American realists. The argument seems to be that in the context of a societal balance of power each state will abide by international law because if it fails to do so, other states will sanction them. Reciprocity seems to lie at the heart of this process.[21] This procedure will prove effective, however, only provided that there is no state in the system that can ignore the sanctions of other states. There will be a tendency for states to voluntarily subscribe to international law, therefore, because infringements of international law pose a threat to the societal balance of power. But classical realists and the English School have failed to explore this idea in detail. To do so would require them to make more of the distinction between a systemic and a societal balance of power. The former acts as a counterfactual, deterring states from violating international law because of the fear of moving into a systemic balance of power, that operates in the absence of a normative framework.

This line of argument may still not seem sufficient to account for why states obey rules, when it is not in their immediate interests to do so. But as Hurrell has suggested, members of the English School have provided various reasons to account for the observation of international law. He suggests that norms are observed because of "power and coercion, self-interest and reciprocal benefits, institutionalised habit or inertia, the existence of a sense of community, procedural legitimacy of the process of rule creation, or the moral suasion that derives from a shared sense of justice." But Hurrell also acknowledges that the English School does no more than establish an aggregate list of factors "without providing any precise guide as to their relationship."[22] Thus it is not only American realists who find the arguments presented by the English School incomplete and inadequate.[23]

World Society

Although the idea of world society is most closely associated with the English School, the concept also plays a key role in Morgenthau's discussion of the formation of a world state. Although he accepted that international law and diplomacy are designed to maintain a society of states and are unlikely, as a consequence, to promote international government, he did not suggest that a world government is inconceivable or that the formation of a world government should be opposed on principle. On the contrary, he believed that, if we are to survive, then it is essential, in the long run, for a world government to be established, because only a world government can effectively eliminate war. A world government, however, presupposes

---

[20]Price argues that this is how Thucydides characterises the Peloponnesian War. See Jonathan J. Price, *Thucydides and Internal War* (Cambridge, UK: Cambridge University Press, 2001).

[21]See G. Schwarzenberger, *Power Politics*, 3rd ed. (London: Stevens, 1964), p. 203; and K. W. Thompson, *Political Reform and the Crisis of World Politics* (Princeton, NJ: Princeton University Press), p. 169.

[22]Andrew Hurrell, "International Society and the Study of Regimes: A Reflective Approach," in V. Rittberger, ed., *Regime Theory and International Relations* (Oxford: Clarendon Press, 1993), p. 55.

[23]See Ole Wæver, "Four Meanings of International Society: A Transatlantic Dialogue," in B. A. Roberson, ed., *International Society and the Development of International Relations Theory* (London and Washington: Pinter, 1998), p. 90, who argues, however, that the arguments enumerated by the English School have the potential to take us much further than the liberal institutionalists who investigate only one item on the list. Moreover they focus on individual rules. He goes on (p. 91), "Often the general interest in international society is important in explaining compliance with specific rules, while the specific rules add up to a general system of international law that is constitutive of the structure of the state-system itself. Because states come to believe that they have a long-term interest in this international legal system, the rules achieve obligation and normativity in a way which becomes more lawlike and where compliance is hard to calculate in terms of specific and calculable interests."

the existence of a world state and the demise of the society of sovereign states.[24]

Morgenthau is clear that such a development cannot be implemented from the top, either through world conquest, by an imperial state, or by some kind of constitutional confederation. Any successful movement away from a society of states must be preceded by a transformation at the level of the community. A necessary, if not sufficient, precondition for the establishment of a world state is that individuals must have shifted their primary allegiance from their local community to a world community. Morgenthau acknowledged, however, that it would be extremely difficult to establish a world community, although he was very enthusiastic about the functional theory associated with the writings of Mitrany and saw the special agencies associated with the United Nations as one way forward to promote the creation of a world community.[25]

The English School has a different and more complex take on this issue. Members of the school are divided on the significance of what they call world society for the existence of international society, with some arguing that an element of world society has to have emerged if a stable society of states is going to exist. Others are less certain. But there is considerable ambiguity surrounding the issue. For example, very much in line with Morgenthau, Bull argues at one point that an expansion of world society, by making individuals the subjects of international law, would undermine "the international order based on the society of states."[26] Later, however, he argues that the

"future of international society is likely to be determined, among other things, by the preservation and extension of a common culture."[27] Diez and Whitman come to the conclusion that this ambiguity is a feature of international politics, and we can establish substantial analytical purchase by making the ambiguity explicit and "treating it as an *inherent characteristic of the international.*"[28]

International Justice

Classical realists and the English School both draw a distinction between order and justice.[29] It is acknowledged, in other words, that there is no reason to suppose that a rule-governed society will necessarily be a just society. On the contrary, classical realists such as Morgenthau and Carr, both heavily influenced by Mannheim, the sociologist of knowledge, worked from the premise that those with power will use their power to promote their own interests, although often they will also rely heavily on a dominant ideology to obscure this ink between power and interest.

As Niebuhr notes, "the individual or group which organised any society, however social its intentions or pretentions, arrogates an inordinate portion of social privilege to itself."[30] A crucial task of the realist, according to both Morgenthau and Carr, is to expose the truth about where power exists and how it supports the *status quo*. As a consequence, the realist "cannot help being a subversive and revolutionary force with regard to certain vested interests."[31]

---

[24]Morgenthau, *Politics Among Nations*, ch. 29. Morgenthau refers to a world community rather than a world society. See Barry Buzan, "From International System to International Society: Structural Theory and Regime Theory Meet the English School," *International Organization*, 47 (3) (1993), pp. 327–52, who takes this distinction seriously. He is currently working on a book that uses this distinction to clarify English School thinking.
[25]Morgenthau, *Politics Among Nations*, ch. 30. See also David Mitrany, *The Functional Theory of Politics* (London: Robertson, 1975).
[26]Bull, *The Anarchical Society,* p. 152.

[27]Ibid., p. 317.
[28]Thomas Diez and Richard Whitman, "Analysing European Integration: Reflecting on the English School," *Journal of Common Market Studies*, 40(1) (2002), pp. 43–67, p. 49.
[29]In fact this issue is debated within the English School, because some argue that it is not possible to have a concept of order that makes no provision for justice. See Ian Harris, "Order and Justice in *The Anarchical Society,*" *International Affairs*, 69(4) (1993), pp. 725–41.
[30]R. Niebuhr, *Moral Man and Immoral Society* (London: SCM Press, 1963), pp. 6–7.
[31]Hans J. Morgenthau, "The Commitments of Political Science," in Hans J. Morgenthau, *Politics in the Twentieth Century,* abridged ed. (Chicago: Chicago University Press, 1971), p. 258.

The weakness of realism, argues Carr, is that it then fails to acknowledge that there is an independent role for ideas in international politics. Carr acknowledges, therefore, that it is not only possible to envisage a transformed world but also to turn this vision into a reality. Whenever any vision is realised, however, then some parties will benefit from the new system more than others [will], and they will turn these benefits into power, which will then be used to maintain the system. The perennial task of the realist is to expose this axiomatic link between power and interest. From Carr's perspective, therefore, both the realist emphasis on material forces and the utopian preoccupation with transformative ideas have an essential role to play in any understanding of world politics. Armed with this understanding, Carr concludes, as a consequence, that it is obvious why satisfied states that wish to preserve an established system should ensure that they offer significant concessions to those who benefit least from the system, to ensure that their position is made bearable.[32]

The English School has also thought hard about the role of justice in international relations and are clear that there are ideas about what constitutes justice in international relations and that these ideas "play a role in the course of events."[33] Bull goes on to draw a distinction between justice at the level of the state and justice at the level of the individual. Justice at the level of the state requires international society to ensure, for example, that the sovereign rights of states are observed. But this tells us nothing about human justice. In other words, just as in any society, it is inevitable that those states with power will use their power to ensure that the interests of these states are served at the expense of the remaining states in the system. With the consolidation of the state, therefore, the idea of human rights has gone "underground" and indeed can now be seen to be potentially "subversive of international society itself."[34] Despite the obvious moral ambiguity attached to this position, Bull was clear that it was essential for order to take priority over justice. However, toward the end of his life, he began to reconsider this position and recognized that there was a need to rectify the imbalance between the rich and the poor states within the system. Justice demands, Bull argued, that the West abandon "position of undue privilege."[35] . . .

---

[34]Ibid., p. 183.
[35]"Justice in International Relations: The 1983 Hogey Lectures," in Alderson and Hurrell, *Hedley Bull on International Society*, p. 244.

MORGENTHAU: POLITICS AS THE STRUGGLE FOR POWER

Ashley Tellis

Perhaps the most distinguished and articulate exponent of political realism in the twentieth century, Hans Morgenthau sought to provide a comprehensive philosophical understanding of politics. Politics was conceived essentially as a struggle for power, and philosophy, "primarily an unusually stubborn attempt to think clearly,"[1] was intended to illumine those fundamental principles

---

[32]E. H. Carr, *The Twenty Years' Crisis, 1919–1939: An Introduction to the Study of International Relations*, with new introduction by Michael Cox, ed. (New York: Palgrave, 2001). See also Bull's assessment, "The Twenty Years' Crisis Thirty Years on," in Alderson and Hurrell, *Hedley Bull on International Society*, pp. 125–38. For a different reading of Carr than given here, see Charles A. Jones, "Carr, Mannheim and a Post-Positivist Science of International Relations," *Political Studies*, 45(1) (1997), pp. 232–46. For perceptive essays on Carr, see Michael Cox ed., *E. H. Carr: A Critical Reappraisal* (London: Palgrave, 2000).
[33]Bull, *The Anarchical Society*, p. 78.

In Benjamin Frankel, ed., *Roots of Realism* (London: Frank Cas, 1996).

---

[1]William James's phrase cited in Kenneth Thompson, "Philosophy and Politics: The Two Commitments of Hans J. Morgenthau," in *Truth and Tragedy*, augmented edition, Kenneth Thompson and Robert J. Myers, eds. (New Brunswick, NJ: Transaction, 1984), 28.

which could guide statesmen in their understanding of political realities. Morgenthau's arrival on the American scene, part of the great European intellectual migration to the United States prior to the Second World War, immediately entangled him with the great debate then prevailing among scholars and practitioners of foreign policy.

The legalist tradition had sought to define the goals of American foreign policy in terms of creating a harmonious international society based on the search for and acceptance of universal moral principles.[2] At the heart of this objective lay the liberal philosophy of the Enlightenment with its belief

> that a rational and moral political order, derived from universally valid abstract principles, [could] be achieved here and now. It assume[d] the essential goodness and infinite malleability of human nature and attribute[d] the failure of the social order to measure up to rational standards to lack of knowledge and understanding, obsolescent social institutions, or the depravity of certain isolated individuals or groups.[3]

Thanks to this presumption of an eternal harmony of interests, the legalist tradition perceived international conflict to be a product of political misperceptions and unintended mistakes. Accordingly, Reason, embodied in "education, reform, and the sporadic use of force,"[4] was held out as the solution through which human beings could realize the authentic truth of their common estate. Thus,

> if all men followed reason, the conflicts which separate them would disappear or, at worst, be resolved

in compromise; the wants from which they suffer would be satisfied; the fears which destroy their lives would be dispelled; and harmony, welfare, and happiness would reign.[5]

The institutions of law, education, and trade were thus envisaged as the main instruments by which individuals could be brought to the recognition of their mutual interdependence and harmonious interests. It was hoped that such recognition would result in the establishment of an international society, in a manner analogous to the establishment of the state. With these premises and beliefs, the objectives of American foreign policy were defined to be the creation of those international institutions which could sustain a new universal moral order based on and nourished by Reason.

Rejecting the optimistic premises underlying such proposals, Morgenthau argued that political life, far from presupposing an eternal harmony of interests, is "rooted in the lust for power which is common to all men, [and] is for this reason inseparable from social life itself."[6] Based on an Augustinian understanding of the fallen nature of man, Morgenthau, quoting Martin Luther, suggested that "concupiscence is insuperable" and, therefore, the lustful craving for power, being ubiquitous to the human condition, must be recognized as "the element of corruption and sin which injects even into the best intentions at least a drop of evil and thus spoils it."[7] In the final analysis, all politics is therefore evil if for no other reason than it represents an activity conducted by evil men.

Elaborating further on the nature of political activity, Morgenthau argued that its diabolic character is rooted in two human drives. On one hand, it derives from an elementary egoism which arises from the competition for those scarce material

[2]See, by way of example, Frank Tannenbaum, "The Balance of Power versus the Coordinate State," *Political Science Quarterly* 47 (June 1952): 173–97, and Thomas I. Cook and Malcolm Moos, *Power through Purpose: The Realism of Idealism as a Basis for Foreign Policy* (Baltimore, MD: Johns Hopkins University Press, 1954).
[3]Hans J. Morgenthau, "Another Great Debate: The National Interest of the United States," *American Political Science Review* 46 (1952): 961–62.
[4]Ibid.

[5]Hans J. Morgenthau, *Scientific Man vs. Power Politics* (Chicago: University of Chicago Press, 1974), 14.
[6]Ibid., 9.
[7]Ibid., 194–95.

and ideational goods that enable individual human beings to survive. These goods "such as money, jobs, marriage, and the like, have an objective relation to the vital needs of the individual" and, therefore, the selfishness of humans in this regard may be construed as having "limits."[8] In contrast to such demands emanating from the requirements of physical survival, Morgenthau saw, on the other hand, the *animus dominandi*—"the desire to maintain the range of one's own person with regard to others, to increase it, or to demonstrate it"[9]—as a human will to power that has no constitutive limits. He explained the boundlessness of this latter drive explicitly in theological terms: "For while man's vital needs are capable of satisfaction, his lust for power would be satisfied only if the last man became an object of his domination, there being nobody above or beside him, that is, if he became like God."[10] The distinction between these two drives is rooted in the fact that while "there is in selfishness an element of rationality presented by the natural limitation of the end" (since human beings presumably need only a relatively finite amount of material goods to survive), both finitude and rationality are "lacking in the will to power."[11]

It thus appears as if Morgenthau is asserting that the evil of politics is derived from two ontologically distinct drives: in a selfishness which originates in necessity provoked by the demands of survival, and in an aggrandizement which originates in the choices of individuals who seek the exhilaration of conquest and mastery. Quickly disposing off what seems like an ontological distinction, he argues that these contrasts, if they exist at all, are merely phenomenological, that is, merely different facets of the same uniformly evil nature of man:

> By setting in this way the desire for power apart from selfishness, on the one hand, and from the other transcendent urges, on the other, one is already doing violence to the actual nature of that desire; for actually it is present whenever man intends to act with regard to other men. One may separate it conceptually from the other ingredients of social action; actually there is no social action which does not contain at least a trace of this desire to make one's own person prevail against others. It is this ubiquity of the desire for power which, besides and beyond any particular selfishness or other evilness of purpose, constitutes the ubiquity of evil in human action.[12]

Consequently, the very fact that egoist human beings exist among one another is sufficient for the *animus dominandi* to assert itself, and in it can be found the causes of all social strife. The heart of Morgenthau's understanding of politics is centered, therefore, on an explicit first-image explanation of conflict: strife is caused by the evil and egoistic nature of man. Such egoism, essentially taking the form of each man placing his own interests before the interests of all others, results in a scramble for power because "what the one wants for himself, the other already possesses or wants, too."[13] As a result, politics is transformed into an arena of evil where individuals have no choice but to partake of selfishness even if they otherwise seek to comport with the moral obligation to be unselfish toward others.[14]

If evil and disordered individuals are thus understood, as Thucydides and Machiavelli did, to be the true units of political life, the question of how political order can be constructed immediately becomes a pressing issue. Thucydides avoided answering this question directly, but Machiavelli, recognizing the salience of the subject, provided an explicit answer inductively garnered from history: states are created by force, principally through crimes of great magnitude carried out by individuals of exemplary *virtu*. Morgenthau, in

---

[8]Ibid., 193.
[9]Ibid., 192.
[10]Ibid., 193.
[11]Ibid., 193–94.

[12]Ibid., 194.
[13]Ibid., 192.
[14]Ibid.

contrast, is generally silent about how political order is created. He admits that "it is always the individual who acts" and that "the action of society, of the nation, or of any other collectivity, political or otherwise, as such has no empirical existence at all,"[15] but he does not provide any generative understanding of how egoist individuals come to be ordered into those minimally cohesive aggregations called "states" which he treats as the analytic units of international politics. Instead, he resolves this issue descriptively by treating all macroscopic social entities as unadulterated collections of egoistic individuals. Morgenthau, then, resembles Thucydides at least in this respect. The narcissistic quest for power, considered the defining characteristic of human beings, is treated as an operative mechanism visible at all levels of social life, but neither theorist utilizes it for the causal explanation of either the origins or the structure of macroscopic entities like the state despite the fact that both assign theoretical primacy to individuals and analytical primacy to states in their explanatory systems.[16]

This lack of generative mechanism is self-evident in Morgenthau's discussion of the relationship between domestic and international politics:

> Regardless of particular social conditions, the decisive argument against the opinion that the struggle for power on the international scene is a mere historical accident must be derived from the nature of domestic politics. The essence of international politics is identical with its domestic counterpart. Both domestic and international politics are a struggle for power, modified only by the different conditions under which this struggle takes place in the domestic and in the international spheres.

The tendency to dominate, in particular, is an element of all human associations, from the family through fraternal and professional associations and local political organizations to the state. On the family level, the typical conflict between the mother-in-law and her child's spouse is in essence a struggle for power, the defense of an established power position against the attempt to establish a new one. As such it foreshadows the conflict on the international scene between the policies of the status quo and the policies of imperialism. Social clubs, fraternities, faculties, and business organizations are scenes of continuous struggles for power between groups that either want to keep what power they already have or seek to attain greater power. Competitive contests between business enterprises as well as labor disputes between employers and employees are frequently fought not only, and sometimes not even primarily, for economic advantages, but for influence over each other and over others; that is, for power. Finally, the whole political life of a nation, particularly of a democratic nation, from the local to the national level, is a continuous struggle for power. In periodic elections, in voting in legislative assemblies, in lawsuits before courts, in administrative decisions and executive measures—in all these activities men try to maintain or to establish their power over other men . . . In view of this ubiquity of the struggle for power in all social relations and on all levels of social organization, is it surprising that international relations is of necessity power politics? And would it not be rather surprising if the struggle for power were but an accidental and ephemeral attribute of international politics when it is a permanent and necessary element of all branches of domestic politics?[17]

The similarity of domestic and international politics is therefore established by inductive analogies rather than by logical demonstration. States are described as entities composed of power-seeking individuals, and international politics is then

---

[15]Ibid., 187.

[16]Thucydides no doubt speaks to the issue of state structure. His teaching on the question, however, is made manifest only implicitly through his description of the processes of political decay. He does not provide causal explanation of how state structures come to be (either through his own comments or through the speeches) in a way that he does when the issues of imperialism and systemic war are discussed.

[17]Morgenthau, *Politics Among Nations*, 31–33.

described as little other than domestic politics writ large. This approach to understanding international politics may therefore be seen as assimilating the core argument offered by previous realists, namely that the egoistic nature of man is the cause of all political strife. Unlike one previous realist, however—Machiavelli—who offered a detailed explanation about how domestic and external political order are linked in causal terms, Morgenthau's interest shifts quickly from the domestic realm to international politics proper. Hence, after briefly asserting that the nature of the international system and the nature of the state, third-image and second-image realities respectively, share certain characteristic similarities with their first-image constituent, man with his lust for power, the theoretical primacy of individuals drops out of the analysis altogether and Morgenthau's magnum opus, *Politics Among Nations,* proceeds briskly to its chief objective: the description of international politics as the struggle for power among analytically primal units called states.

As might be expected, Morgenthau begins with a brief analysis of the nature of power but, unlike Machiavelli, who parsimoniously described power as the coercive capability flowing from "good arms," Morgenthau defines power as a "psychological relation" between unequals flowing from "the expectation of benefits, the fear of disadvantages, [and] the respect or love for men or institutions."[18] Thus, threats, orders, persuasion, [and] charisma are all avenues through which power is exercised, and the "tendency to reduce political power to the actual application of force or at least to equate it with successful threats of force" is explicitly rejected on the grounds that it neglects the role of prestige in politics.[19] Later on in the work the nature of national power is elaborated in copious detail with an elaborate typology that includes every conceivable component from geography at one end through natural resources, military

preparedness, and population all the way to national character, morale, and quality of diplomacy and government at the other end.[20] The discussion about power concludes with a revealing section titled "The Fallacy of the Single Factor," in which Morgenthau discusses the fallacy of monocausal explanations, be they based on geography, military power, or national ethos.[21]

The discussion of power in *Politics Among Nations* is fascinating for the light it sheds on Morgenthau's attitude toward the possibility of a political science. While both Thucydides and Machiavelli sought in different ways to provide some kind of scientific formulation of political realism, Morgenthau is conspicuous for his heated polemical rejection of the possibility of political "science." Thus, while claiming on one hand that "politics, like society in general, is governed by objective laws that have their roots in human nature,"[22] he energetically rejects on the other hand the notion that these objective laws could be divined by the abstract and deductive methods of rationalist inquiry. Believing that rationalism was defined by the claim that control and change were automatically predicated by a scientific understanding, Morgenthau rejected political "science" on the grounds that it harbored the illusion of being able to transform the reality of human evil. His sweeping denunciation of all rationalized political science thus derived from the erroneous perception that all "scientific approaches to politics" necessarily proffered the false promise of eradicating human asociality by scientifically engineered solutions. His refusal to countenance the absurdity of some rationalisms, especially those of the liberal-legalist kind he encountered in the great debate, blinded him to the possibility that an alternative rationalism based on the permanent premise of human asociality could in fact be created. Such a rationalism would not only be able to

---

[18]Ibid., 27.
[19]Ibid.

[20]Ibid., 97–144.
[21]Ibid., 153–60.
[22]Ibid., 4.

provide logical and deductive realist formulations of greater testability and expanded explanatory power but would readily admit its inability to provide scientific solutions that could decisively abolish evil in history.

Given Morgenthau's inability to envisage the possibility of such a rationalist political realism, he rejected abstract deductive systematization altogether in favor of understanding "the principles of international politics" as gleaned from inductivist "comparisons between [various] events."[23] History, in other words, was to be the essential, if not the exclusive, foundation for the study of international politics, and the latter discipline, in turn, was tasked with the intellectual objective of "distinguishing the specific from the general and dealing meaningfully with both."[24] With this conception of the foundations of international politics, it is no surprise that the substantive portions of *Politics Among Nations* are concerned primarily with providing "a map of the political scene." Obviously, "such a map does not provide a complete description of the political landscape as it is in any particular period of history" but rather describes "the timeless features of its geography distinct from their ever changing historical setting."[25]

This attempt at surveying the timeless features of international politics becomes conspicuous in Morgenthau's analysis of international politics as the struggle for power. The key category of analysis here is defined as the "national interest," which, in turn, is composed of permanent "minimum requirements" relating to the survival of the state as well as a "whole gamut of other [variable and supernumerary] meanings that are logically compatible with it."[26] Since state behavior always seeks to promote the national interest, the struggle for power in history is seen to conform to three basic patterns:

the policy of the "status quo" aimed at keeping one's power; the policy of "imperialism" aimed at increasing one's power; and the policy of "prestige" aimed at acquiring reputation and demonstrating one's power. Why does a state choose one policy rather than another? Morgenthau's answer is set out in empirical rather than in logical terms. Thus, for example, the incentive to choose imperial policies is provided either by "victorious wars," "lost wars," or "weakness," with each of these explanations derived from historical events. Similarly, history provides the basis for the claim that not all imperialisms are alike and, therefore, Morgenthau proceeds to distinguish them both by the nature of their goals—"world empire," "continental empire," and "local preponderance"—and the character of the methods—"military," "economic," and "cultural"—used to attain them.

This discussion of national power as gleaned from the historical record is complemented by analysis of the various limitations besetting it, and here again Morgenthau's objective consists of providing a comprehensive catalog of the numerous features of the political landscape. Thus, the "balance of power," "international morality," and "international law," are duly recognized as limiting forces, albeit of varying intensity, on the drive to power.[27] Clearly, the balance of power is held to be the most important limitation on the untrammeled exercise of a state's power and "the aspiration for power on the part of several nations, each trying either to maintain or overthrow the status quo, leads of necessity to a configuration . . . called the balance of power and to policies aimed at preserving it."[28] While such an explanation appears to be rationalist in form, in that it looks like an explanation derived deductively from the logic of a given situation, it is in fact induced from the historical experience of European statecraft, an inescapable conclusion given Morgenthau's description of the six conditions associated with the classic balance of

[23]Ibid., 17.
[24]Norman A. Graebner, "Morgenthau as Historian," in Thompson and Myers, *Truth and Tragedy*, 67.
[25]Hans J. Morgenthau, *Dilemmas of Politics* (Chicago: University of Chicago Press, 1958), 39.
[26]Ibid., 65.

[27]Morgenthau, *Politics Among Nations,* 161–296.
[28]Morgenthau, *Dilemmas of Politics,* 41, 258.

power: the presence of a large number of independent states; the common European culture; the geographical constriction of the international system; the absence of weapons of mass destruction; the freedom of elites to make policy; and, the presence of a "balancer."[29] Given the postwar changes in international relations, Morgenthau concludes this discussion of the balance of power on a pessimistic note since most of the classic six conditions for successful balancing have been all but obliterated. In fact, given his detailed inductive reading of the European balance, it is not even certain—in terms of his own descriptions—whether the concept of the balance is at all a meaningful one because in some instances states are seen to seek equality of countervailing power and in others, a clear margin of superiority.[30] For this reason perhaps, he concluded elsewhere that "the character of imperialism as a universal phenomenon of international politics must be maintained."[31]

Morgenthau's *Politics Among Nations* represents the summation of the inductivist construction of the realist program because it is such a detailed inventory of the complex and often divergent behaviors that are manifested in international politics. While these behaviors share a common thread, in that they represent state actions related to increasing security through power maximization, no attempt at parsimonious ordering is either attempted or achieved in his work. In fact, the exhaustive depiction of political facts, even if appearing contradictory at times, was deemed desirable precisely because a rational-theoretical understanding of political life falsely ordered a reality which was, and could be, only chaotic. Warning, in Montaigne's words, against the "wrested, forced, and biased interpretation"[32] of politics when filtered through rationalist constructions, Morgenthau

held out a philosophically conditioned empiricism as the ideal methodology for the study of international relations and the appropriate alternative to rationalist science.

The first lesson which the student of international politics must learn and never forget is that the complexities of international affairs make simple solutions and trustworthy prophecies impossible. It is here that the scholar and the charlatan part company. Knowledge of the forces which determine politics among nations, and knowledge of the ways by which their political relations proceed, reveals the ambiguity of the facts of international politics. In every political situation contradictory tendencies are at play. One of these tendencies is more likely to prevail under certain conditions than others. But which tendency will actually prevail is anybody's guess. The best the scholar can do, then, is to trace the different tendencies which, as potentialities, are inherent in a certain international situation. He can point out the different conditions which make it more likely for one tendency to prevail than for another and, finally, assess the probabilities for the different conditions and tendencies to prevail in actuality.[33]

With this approach, *Politics Among Nations* represents the denial of the efficacy and value of all rationalist-scientific methods of understanding politics. There could be no rationalized study of international political behavior, only expository reflections that aid various prudential forms of statecraft. The "science" of politics is, therefore, nothing other than *episteme politike*, a practical science that requires both commitment and distance. It involves distance in that the statesman has to stand back as it were and use his philosophically conditioned but inductively generated store of knowledge to arrive at an assessment of the many reasonable and prudential political choices; but it also requires commitment in that the best political

---

[29]Morgenthau, *Politics Among Nations*, 167–95.
[30]Ibid., 196–223.
[31]Hans J. Morgenthau and Kenneth W. Thompson, eds., *Principles and Problems of International Politics* (New York: Knopf, 1950), 61.
[32]Morgenthau, *Politics Among Nations*, 17.

[33]Ibid., 19.

choice can be discerned only from within the context of the alternatives facing a particular statesman and his particular state.

In attempting to illuminate the practical truths required for such successful choices in the world of power, Morgenthau's objective, as incarnated in his work, represents a significant shift in emphasis from that of Machiavelli's: whereas the latter was more interested in prescribing techniques for successful politics and in understanding politics primarily as a means to that goal, Morgenthau appears more interested in understanding politics, its character and its limitations, for its own sake. While a normative policy interest certainly exists at a subsidiary level in all his work, Morgenthau's distinctive contribution to the evolution of the realist program consists of his systematic, empiricist exposition of international political practice. This exposition was no doubt conditioned by a distinctive view of human nature and human destiny, but, in the final analysis, it was aimed largely at creating a framework which "imposes intellectual discipline upon the observer, infuses rational order into the subject matter of politics, and thus makes the theoretical understanding of politics possible."[34]

With this objective, traditional realism could be said to have reached its high point in the long march toward scientific theory. In the work of Thucydides, it began as a metaphysical research program which, in bearing a fertile world view, gave birth to a new tradition of viewing politics. This understanding of politics over time gave rise to a desire for practical control and, not surprisingly in the work of Machiavelli, the realist program evolves into a search for practical generalizations aimed at manipulating political outcomes. In the final stage, the realist program comes to embody a desire that transcends mere technological control, and, consequently, in the work of Morgenthau, it takes the form of producing a systematized body of empirical information which, while partly intended

to help make good policy, is now fundamentally aimed at creating objective knowledge for its own sake. To the degree that Morgenthau's work represents the latter aspiration, it could justifiably be considered the epitome of the empiricist approaches characterizing traditional realism.

Traditional Realism: The Logic of Domination, the Primacy of Individuals, Austere Inductivism

The tradition of political realism examined thus far through the approaches of three practitioners—one ancient, the other premodern, and the third modern—suggests that the realist research program could be summarized in the following way.

At the level of substantive claims, all three theorists are engaged by the problem of order and all explain the reality of conflict and strife in terms of the logic of domination engendered by necessity. Each theorist asserts either explicitly or implicitly that all political entities—even if they seek only security *ex ante*—are forced by the demands of competition to embark on a course of action which ultimately involves control, conquest, and domination. Only Machiavelli, however, utilizes this logic explicitly to explain how order is produced. Both Thucydides and Morgenthau recognize the importance of the question, but neither addresses it explicitly or in causal form. Machiavelli alone systematically describes both the processes through which individuals interact to constitute order-producing entities called "states" and how these constituted states thereafter behave in a world of interstate politics. Consequently, Machiavelli can lay claim to being called the "compleat realist": his work exhibits a clarity and consistency of argument and a fullness of explanatory scope which neither Thucydides nor Morgenthau can rival. Despite the limitations of the latter, however, it is important to recognize that all three theorists acknowledge that security competition ends in a struggle for domination, and it is this substantive claim which, more than any other, unifies the traditional realist teaching on politics in the earthly city.

---

[34]Hans J. Morgenthau, *Politics Among Nations*, 5th ed. (New York: Knopf, 1978), 4–5.

At the level of units of analysis and logic of causation, all three theorists share important similarities again. Despite operating within the premises of the state-system, Thucydides focuses on the character of "men in their national entities" in an attempt to discover the egoism which is distinctively human. Machiavelli bases his reading of politics on the nature of the individual as well. Similarly, Morgenthau focuses on the evil in human nature to explain behavior at all three levels of political aggregation, even if only in a metaphorical way. Therefore, in terms of the units of analysis, all three theorists assign theoretical primacy to individuals in their explanatory systems. They do not differ in their emphasis on what is most significant for the successful explanation of politics, namely, egoist individuals and their self-regarding nature. They do differ, however, in their utilization of human nature for purposes of causal explanation. Machiavelli uses human nature most coherently and explicitly both to constitute macroscopic political entities and to explain their behavior. Thucydides uses human nature to explain the behavior of macroscopic political entities, but only implicitly: he does not explain their generation except by insinuation, but concentrates instead on their decay and breakdown. Morgenthau also does not use human nature explicitly in his causal explanations of international politics. The evil in human nature remains the backdrop, but it is not used causally to explain either how macroscopic political entities are constituted or how they behave. The traditional realist emphasis on human nature, while laudable in a Popperian sense, is therefore marred by the inability to incorporate it explicitly in causal systems of explanation which describe both the constitution and behavior of macroscopic political entities as outcomes of interindividual action. Machiavelli is certainly the exception here, but his contribution, too, remains stymied because his explanatory system is historically derived and inductively justified and as such lacks the absolute necessity that derives only from a system of formal (deductive) logic.

Finally, at the level of methodological form, all three traditional realists are unified by their reliance on empiricist-inductivism (which, with the exception of Thucydides, is concerned, in some degree or another, with solving the practical problems of statecraft). This concern with collating empirical generalizations on the basis of an austere perception of visible phenomena is perhaps the earliest method of acquiring knowledge, and the empiricist tradition has been distinguished by its effort at creating universal generalizations, both practical and theoretical, through the inductive technique of iterating and comparing singular observation statements. All three traditional realists conduct their political analysis based on such collected singular observation statements about political life. Using Einstein's words, it may be said that their epistemological presumption is that "experience is the alpha and omega of all our knowledge of reality."[35] In none of the traditional realists does the emphasis on postulating theoretical categories, internally related to each other by deductive generation with a high degree of predictable content, become manifest. In the great dialectic between "empirical" and "rational" knowledge which Einstein often spoke about, the traditional realists are firmly wedded to the methodology of the former.[36] Since the need for determinacy, predictability, and logical systematization via deductively generated explanations was explicitly eschewed by at least one of them (and, perhaps implicitly, by both others), the idea of a purely rational construction in which every generalization "proceed[s] from step to step with such precision that every single one of its propositions [becomes] absolutely indubitable"[37] is not yet salient.

From the perspective of the critical rationalist methodology of science, all traditional realist approaches must therefore be found wanting. Their emphasis on individuals as the appropriate units of

---

[35]Albert Einstein, "On the Method of Theoretical Physics," in *Ideas and Opinions*, trans. and rev. Sonja Bargmann (New York: Crown, 1954), 271.
[36]For an excellent discussion of Einstein's method and the distinction between rationalist and empiricist approaches to science, see Gerald Holton, "Thematic Presuppositions and the Direction of Scientific Advance," in *Scientific Explanation*, A. F. Heath, ed. (Oxford: Clarendon Press, 1981), 1–27.
[37]Einstein, "On the Method," 271

analysis and as the efficient causes of all political action is commendable and comports perfectly with the critical rationalist stipulation of methodological individualism. Their reliance on induction for purposes of justifying their insights, however, remains problematic, and their failure to order their causal explanations in systematic, deductive form deprives them of the possibility of demonstrating that their conclusions hold not merely [owing] to the exigencies of chance but by sheer logical and theoretical necessity. To that degree, traditional realism lacks the fundamental ingredient which makes the scientific method so useful and attractive, and, consequently, it is no surprise that the first modification contributed by its successors, the scientific realists, was not so much substantive as methodological: the shift from a historically based and inductively justified set of explanations to a more abstract and deductively systematized body of causal hypotheses. Such an effort, which is peculiar to modern social science, first becomes evident in the pathbreaking work of Morton Kaplan, and it is his approach and, later on, that of Waltz, which must be now reviewed.

AN IRAQ RETROSPECT

Admiral William J. Crowe, Jr.

The Iraqi intervention may have a deeper impact on our republic than the September 11 attacks. All of our services have derived a host of professional lessons from the campaign, but I don't intend to go into them. Instead, I want to address what I

Admiral Crowe, former chairman of the Joint Chiefs of Staff, has been professor of geopolitics at the University of Oklahoma, counsel at the Institute of Strategic and International Studies Center at Georgetown University in Washington, DC., and U.S. ambassador to the United Kingdom. More recently, he was chairman of the President's Foreign Intelligence Advisory Board and chairman of the Board of Advisors of Global Options and International Relations Institution based in Washington. The following paper was delivered at the Miller Center in Charlottesville, VA, in April 2004.

consider to be some of the larger lessons that citizens should be aware of as we face future Third World challenges. There's some indication that we're going to face a number of challenges particularly [owing] to our new policy of preemption, which calls on the government to anticipate new threats and take prompt military action against them.

The rapid victory in Iraq once again demonstrated the remarkable ability, flexibility, and technical superiority of America's military. And that came as no surprise at least to the professionals. At the same time, to put things in perspective, it should be understood that Saddam Hussein's forces were especially inept. He failed to take advantage of the time before the invasion, and his army proved to be incapable of participating in a war maneuver. The victory, of course, has demonstrated once again (and I'm not so sure the lesson has seeped into the Third World) the futility of a Third World force confronting the United States directly in the field. It is this very fact that turns our opponents toward terrorism or, as some of the professors of terrorism put it, toward asymmetrical warfare.

The quick capitulation, however, papered over some misjudgments and flawed assumptions that are relatively important. The Pentagon predicted that the occupation would come at little financial cost and that the Iraqi population would welcome the victors as liberators. Both were wide of the mark, although the Department of Defense has yet to admit any mistake. While peace and democracy may come to Iraq, there are some signs, at least in the early going, that these goals are by no means assured. The population did welcome us initially, which is not unusual in an oppressed country, but the celebrations eroded quickly, and our troops are being treated more and more as colonial occupiers, not liberators. The Pentagon's intention was to withdraw the bulk of forces after the Iraqi army collapsed, and this has certainly proved impossible. Incidentally, there were Arabists in our country, many in the State Department, who predicted these problems and made thoughtful recommendations, but these were essentially ignored by the leadership.

The situation was exacerbated by the failure to field larger numbers of troops. The chief of staff of the U.S. Army at the time, General Eric Shinseki, testified before Congress that more troops would be required than we had planned in the pacification and reconstruction phase. But the Pentagon's leadership publicly derided his testimony, and he was soon retired with little fanfare. There is little question that having more units, particularly with special expertise, to protect our logistic lines and to move into rather than bypass communities, would have attenuated some of the subsequent chaos and security problems. More importantly, the chairman of the Joint Chiefs of Staff, General Richard Meyers, had previously made the point that our troops were not trained for a policing and nation-building mission, and time has certainly proved him right.

Now, both the (U.S.) Army and the Marines have made dramatic changes in their training programs and are engaged in a frantic effort to correct this deficiency. In turn, a spirited argument has sprung up between the (U.S.) Army and Marines as to the best tactics for conducting a prolonged pacification program. The aftermath proved even worse than the math.

We're putting this argument between the (U.S.) Army and Marines to the test. Now, we will retaliate, against aggressors, but we will not do so quickly or hastily. We will do so in a deliberate and thoughtful fashion. This brings up one of the more disturbing unintended consequences of the occupation. Having to keep large forces in Iraq for a protracted period has stretched the (U.S.) Army and the Marines thin. For example, to maintain a 120,000-troop strength means that ground troopers will serve one year in every three either in country or in support billets in the Gulf. Our ability to maintain other overseas commitments has been seriously threatened or at least put on hold. For example, until we free up some of those Iraqi units, we cannot mount a similar attack on Iran, and being able to fight in Korea at this point is problematic.

The unanticipated wear and tear on equipment in the desert environment has also heavily impacted the military budget, as well as overall readiness. The divisions returning to the United States are below the minimum readiness standard and will take some time to reconstitute. Moreover, the National Guard and Reserves have been stretched very thin, with unexpectedly long overseas deployments. When the dust settles, Congress likely will conduct a major overhaul of the National Guard and Reserves structure.

Also, there's some sentiment building in Congress for larger standing forces, which the Pentagon leadership opposes for unknown reasons. U.S. troops and civilians in Iraq are inviting targets for mischief makers of all stripes: Baathists, nationalists, criminals, and imported anti-Americans. Incidentally, according to on-scene intelligence—mainly Army intelligence—most of the opposition is internal, rather than inspired by foreigners, although this may be contrary to reports in the media. Unfortunately, the shaky security situation lessens the likelihood of our allies joining our efforts, which, in turn, shatters another crucial assumption: that once we conquered Iraq serious terrorist resistance in the Arab world would crumble. It is difficult to believe that more sophisticated individuals actually subscribed to that view.

In a similar vein, it is not clear why an early attack on Iraq was so necessary. Our military capabilities were improving daily, much more so than Saddam Hussein's. With our marked superiority, weather or even surprise were no longer important considerations. A more measured approach would have given arms inspectors time to complete their search, the Turkish government time to change its mind about our use of Turkish military bases, and our diplomats time to attract allied units. We undersold our own capability and, in turn, our flexibility, which gave us less room to maneuver.

In retrospect, the civilian leadership made some positive contributions to our combat operations, closely overseen and reviewed by the Pentagon. But the civilian leadership gave too little attention to the follow-up conditions. A chief of staff of the (U.S.) Army used to say, "When they get mixed up with military ops they all want to go to the front and tell the platoons how to maneuver; they don't want to deal with other issues." The leadership failed to gauge not only popular attitudes and Arab politics but also the extremely complicated economic situation in that part of the world.

It is fascinating to recall some of the original projections. In April 2003, AID estimated the cost of rebuilding Iraq at $1.7 billion. OMB (Office of Management and Budget) grandly announced that Iraq would not require sustained aid. Deputy Secretary of State Paul Wolfowitz ignored the Pentagon staffers who were putting the cost at $60 billion during the first year, a relatively accurate estimate. Wolfowitz then went on to say that Iraq could finance its own reconstruction. There was similar optimism about Iraqi oil production; it now appears that it will be three to five years, barring further destruction, before the petroleum infrastructures is fully functional. The administration has already sought for this one year more than $150 billion; this does not include the $4 billion a month for the military and the additional $25 billion as a supplement to cover the expenses for fighting in Fallujah in the spring of 2004.

Civilian control of the military is a two-way street. One of the most important functions of a civilian leadership is to address the diplomatic and political environment that will attend and follow victory. Likewise, involving all government agencies in postwar planning before combat operations commence is a civilian responsibility, and the leadership failed in this regard. Only a segment of the government's total expertise was brought to bear on the problem beforehand. This was, of course, related to some of the administration's assumptions, which were flawed and simplistic. If we are serious about countering terrorism and supporting a preemptive military policy, then the challenges of "nation building," a term earlier rejected by President Bush, become as important as, or perhaps more so than, the military operations. They must be planned with equal vigor and with the entire government participating. In essence, you may win some battles, but you don't win the war if you don't win the peace. This is the number-one lesson for our bureaucracy.

Now let me turn to coalition politics, a highly controversial issue. On the political side, the failure to involve our major allies, particularly in Western Europe, was crucial. Despite Defense Secretary Donald Rumsfeld's chatter about the "new Europe," we need our old friends for the same old reasons. "Old Europe" was in the habit of cooperating with the United States. The latest poll by the PEW Institute reported that opposition to U.S. policy has reached record levels in most European nations and in all countries in the Middle East. Even in Great Britain a large majority oppose U.S. policy. A few days after the railroad bombing in Spain, the new Spanish government announced that it would withdraw its small military unit from Iraq. This was the first crack in the present coalition. And Poland has also expressed disillusionment with Washington that some of the promises that were made to Poland, such as on contracts and on weapons of mass destruction, have not materialized. There are now some serious doubts about Poland staying in the coalition. These are only initial steps, but they will have a heavy psychological impact. The European continent is suspicious of the emerging tendency for Washington to go it alone, not only in counterterrorism but on many other foreign policy issues.

This is not necessarily to suggest that European views are justified. The point is, the Europeans believe they are justified, so we should seek some understanding of their views even if we don't agree with them. Western Europe has been plagued with terrorism since the 1950s; many Europeans looked at the events of September 11 as having introduced America to the real world after being naively sheltered for several decades. Some Europeans also see the "war on terrorism" as an overreaction used more for domestic political purposes. And they are skeptical of the administration's changing rationales: first al-Qaeda, then WMDs, Saddam's brutality, regional stability, and so on. In essence, Europeans are afraid that the United States will involve them in ways they don't control or want. The *Economist* magazine asked what is more important to Bush: America's unfettered freedom of action or the Atlantic Alliance. The U.S. government has yet to deliver a clear answer. In any case, we are paying a price for our failure to make serious attempts to understand the point of view of our major allies and to reach some accommodation with them. In fact, these disagreements remind me of something I was told when I was in Great Britain, something that applies to all major disagreements between countries. "If you understand the Irish problem, it hasn't been explained to you right."

Part of this calculus, of course, involves the United Nations. The Bush administration itself was divided on the approach to take. In the end, the president would have preferred to have a UN stamp of approval, but only on his terms. The other members of the UN have some grounds for being confused. (Incidentally, Israel has ignored more UN resolutions, and on frequent occasions as well, and the United States has done so occasionally. This has drawn little fire.) Shortly after the truce, the UN was eager to share in the restoring of Iraq, but Washington refused the offer. *Time* magazine recently quoted a high-level American official as saying that since then the administration has become desperate for the UN to take on some of the responsibilities of rebuilding, but the United Nations has largely backed off. The simple truth is, we need friends and we need to do more to keep them. A coalition, if it is to hang together, must be constant and collegial, not selective. To paraphrase Churchill: the only thing worse than having allies is fighting without allies. And that goes for military as well as political contexts. For several decades following World War II, multilateralism was a pillar of our foreign policy, but recently, it's been given short shrift. The pendulum seems to be slowly returning to the center, but it is a bit iffy as of yet, and our tardiness has caused some pain and money.

Turning to domestic politics, the burning question for the American public today is how deeply and for how long we should involve ourselves in Iraq. This is not a theoretical problem concerning grand visions; it's a specific problem, for voters and

for the U.S. government. The president is buffeted by many considerations. All along he has stated: "We will stay as long as necessary." What it means to say that we will remain until we get Iraq "squared away" is not clear to me. Bush has now set June 30 as the date for turning over in some fashion some measure of sovereignty to the Iraqis or to an Iraqi council. On June 30 over 100,000 U.S. troops will remain, and the U.S. embassy of over 3,000 people will assume many of Paul Bremer's duties. This suggests that the administration plans to keep pulling the important strings—and this may not be all bad. Unfortunately, the Iraqis themselves are not of one mind with regard to having U.S. troops on the ground. But most believe that for a new government to take root it is necessary for the United States to retain its presence for months, if not years, to come. Senator John McCain has said that he sees our presence in Iraq lasting several years. Some influential Iraqis question the June 30th deadline, arguing that even a modest drawdown will invite more killing and chaos. They can take little comfort from the hastily trained Iraqi police force. Even U.S. commanders have expressed doubts about the locals taking over responsibility for several months. These questions can't be dismissed easily. Without security democracy is academic. But for the U.S. electorate the political challenge is far from academic. There are two sides to this issue, and both have legitimate arguments, so let me start with the early-turnover group.

Granted, turning over control to the Iraqis and bringing our troops home has great appeal, especially to prevent the killing and wounding of our own and the Iraqi people. It was this desire, no doubt, that inspired the gesture of setting a June 30th deadline. These Iraqis argue that there are too many unknowns and that the progress in Iraq, no matter how long we stay, will be modest. More importantly, they believe that an early withdrawal will deprive Arab terrorists of a host of U.S. targets in Iraq—which certainly would be a positive development. In their eyes, no one knows if we can genuinely democratize that country and how quickly we can do it. This group believes that the responsibility should rest with the Iraqis themselves, or even the United Nations, but not with Washington. It's interesting to note that the British governed Iraq for thirty-two years and tried desperately to put a parliamentary system into effect but never succeeded. Likewise, the early-turnover group contends that it is a fantasy that a democratic Iraq would bring representative government to the rest of the Gulf region. They cite, of course, the Israeli-Palestine conundrum, which has worsened, not moderated, as a result of Iraq. In their minds, our military victory has not muted opposition in the Arab world; if anything, it has fanned the flames. (Polls suggest that anti-Americanism has escalated in every Muslim country, even in alleged allied nations such as Bahrain, Pakistan, and Saudi Arabia.) Moreover, they insist that an early withdrawal would not be disastrous to the United States, and cite Vietnam, from which we withdrew without victory. Despite some temporary difficulties our prestige suffered no permanent damage. This group does not see our presence in Iraq as part of the counterterrorism effort and would like to focus our military forces on confronting al-Qaeda.

Two comments must be made about those who don't want to stay long. First, they are not proposing a different approach to managing Iraq; they are not dealing with nuances. In essence, given the absence of WMDs, they don't believe we should be there at all. Second, the number of people who hold this opinion has grown steadily, and if we don't solve the security problem and stop the killing, these numbers will continue to grow. As Vietnam demonstrated, you don't have to have a decided majority to exert terrific pressure on the White House.

The long-haul advocates likewise field strong arguments. Many Americans and many members of the administration want to remain until we have made demonstrable progress in democratizing Iraq. The June 30th turnover will not meet their goals, and to them it sounds as if the original game plan has been abandoned. They ignore escalating costs and say that the WMDs furor is irrelevant.

Improving the quality of Iraqi life is to them a worthwhile and sufficient objective in itself, although rather idealistic. They are willing to stay as long as needed and to invest whatever it takes. In turn, they believe, the worldwide U.S. image will be enhanced if they do—and they may well be right. In their view, a hasty turnover to a rather indecisive Iraqi council or government will hardly ensure the kind of democratic outcome that we want. More alarmingly, they argue, it will run a serious risk of provoking a civil war, an argument the Iraqis themselves frequently make. They expand their vision and contend that a truly democratic Iraq will have a moderating influence throughout the Muslim world, though I'm not sure history supports that conclusion. Needless to say, the proponents of these arguments are very skeptical of more UN involvement. It is difficult to envision grand outcomes in Iraq without a genuinely secure environment, and that means a protracted American occupation and perhaps lots more U.S. troops. This approach has strong appeal for some in our republic. Americans are basically optimistic: we have a tendency to believe that every problem can be solved with persistence. Moreover, some contend that our fundamental mission as a country is to spread democracy globally, and even impose it if necessary.

Despite our optimism and our belief we can solve problems, we Americans also consider ourselves to be practical. No matter how idealistic we are, we cannot ignore real-world considerations. The dilemma is not just a choice between good and evil, but a choice between worthwhile but uncertain gains and what is considered a reasonable expenditure of lives, people, resources, and energy. And no decision can be made about Iraq isolated from its impact at home. [Editor's note: Our stay is not made any easier by developments involving the mistreatment of Iraqi prisoners of war.]

Every such step should be weighed against its impact on our fundamental values, our image overseas, our other global policies, and, of course, our domestic fiscal health. In a sense these kinds of decisions are a zero-sum game; when you improve one side you take something away from the other. Our voters supported the president's request for $87 billion this year for Iraq. I'm not confident that this translates into a blank check over an extended time; our resources are not unlimited. It is impossible, however, to overemphasize the significance of this issue for our republic. It has already injected itself into the presidential election, it will remain salient for some time, and it does involve the quality of our life and the future of our republic. WMDs have been a frontburner issue raising serious concerns about our intelligence community, which we thus far have conveniently danced around. On the foreign policy front, our relationships with Iran, Saudi Arabia, and Pakistan have all been placed in a new light by this crisis. Both Riyadh and Islamabad, for example, have in some fashion supported terrorists at some time. Each of these countries is going to present. Washington with complex new dilemmas.

As a genuine superpower, America has every right to be proud of what it has achieved in the nearly 230 years of its existence. But every now and then, it is appropriate to step back, take account of how we're using our power, and reappraise how we can employ it more effectively. We have the strength to withstand criticism and to put up with disagreement without responding in a hasty or less-than-thoughtful fashion. To do that requires a careful balance between our military capability, global diplomacy, and financial policies. We should do more listening and should recognize that we don't have all the answers, that we can't do everything alone, and that some problems can't be solved, particularly by force. A few weeks ago John Whitehead, who was deputy secretary of state under President Reagan, told an audience that we tend sometimes to be prouder of the wars we've won with the use of our military power than of the wars we have avoided through patient diplomacy. He was, of course, talking about the Cold War, during which we faced down the Soviet Union, but he was also saying that he had concerns about what he perceived as a shift toward using our military as the

primary problem solver. He went on to say that as a superpower that has become more powerful in every way, we can afford to risk working the diplomatic course a little harder and a little longer. This seems to me to be good advice. I have a friend who insists that war is God's way of teaching Americans geography. I hope that we'll learn a little more than geography from our intervention in Iraq.

NEW DEPARTURES IN THE PHILOSOPHIES OF INTERNATIONAL POLITICS

General Brent Scowcroft

The approach of the current administration to the situation in the Middle East has led, perhaps in part inadvertently, to a new conceptual framework through which to view international politics. Philosophical approaches to international politics first (at least for me) became enshrined in Hans Morgenthau's *Politics Among Nations*. He divided approaches to international politics into two schools: realists and idealists. During the Cold War, a new categorization appeared—hawks and doves—designed to differentiate between approaches to dealing with the Soviet Union. A similar analogy in domestic political terms is generally considered to be conservatives and liberals. Of late, under the pressures of terrorism and Middle East turmoil, and in the context of the contemporary dominant position of the United States in the world, there

Lt. General Scowcroft was the national security advisor in the George H. W. Bush administration and served in the Ford administration. A former member of the Miller Center Governing Council, Scowcroft served as chair of the President's Foreign Intelligence Advisory Board and headed the commission that prepared a widely read report on U.S. intelligence in 2002. This essay encapsulates views Scowcroft expressed in a forum on U.S. foreign policy with former Secretary of State Lawrence S. Eagleburger at the Miller Center in June 2004.

has developed a philosophical differentiation between what I would call traditionalists and transformationalists.

Traditionalists believe that we should approach foreign policy issues in the tradition of the United States over the past half century or so—that is, in close coordination and cooperation with our friends, our allies, and the United Nations. Conversely, transformationalists argue that the world situation is deteriorating too rapidly for such a business-as-usual approach. Forty years of business as usual, they claim, is what has led to the distressing state of the Middle East today. We must take bold action. We know what needs to be done and we have the power to do it. We cannot permit others to act as a brake on our doing what is required. After we have accomplished our goals, the world will see that we were right and applaud our actions. What is it, according to the transformationalists, that needs to be done? Our goal must be a democratized Middle East. Beginning with Iraq as the core, we must insist on the triumph of democracy throughout the region as the only sure route to a peaceful and stable region.

One of the unusual aspects of this new philosophical approach (transformationalism) is that it cuts across the more conventional pairings. That is, transformationalists are—using conventional terminology—idealistic (Wilsonian) hawks. This is a new pattern of thinking in the contemporary world, and it has engendered much confusion. There is much to admire in the views of the transformationalists. But in setting such lofty goals, we must never lose sight of our multiple national interests. In fact, we have multiple interests in the Middle East, interests that must be balanced in full awareness of the intimate interrelationship of the key issues in the region. If we can do that, keeping foremost our transcendent priority of counterterrorism, we can maximize our potential for success across the entire range of our security interests. Even the transformationalists must pay heed to our multiple interests in the real world.

DID THE UNITED STATES WIN THE COLD WAR?

By Ambassador David D. Newsom

At the beginning of the twenty-first century, the United States faces threats of terrorism, antagonism in the Muslim world, and suspicions of its motives throughout much of Asia, Africa, and Latin America. Many of the roots of such problems lie in U.S. actions and policies of the last half of the twentieth century—in the unintended consequences of the Cold War.

Conventional wisdom holds that the United States won the Cold War. With the collapse of the Soviet Union, international Communism ceased to be a threat, and the United States became the "world's only superpower."

But accompanying that "wisdom" is an uncertainty about the global future and, in the United States, questions about why a nation so powerful and "good" has such difficulty in wielding its worldwide influence.

In light of current challenges to U.S. interests, could it be that the presumed success in the Cold War was a Pyrrhic victory? Did the unintended consequences of anti-Soviet efforts contribute to problems Washington faces today?

The confrontation with the Soviet Union was fought most actively in the arena of Asian and African states emerging from colonialism and in Latin American countries resisting oligarchs. U.S. policies pursued much that was positive in these areas, supporting economic development, human rights, conflict resolution, and multilateral cooperation. Since the fall of the Berlin Wall in 1989, the future of the options taken looks brighter than we first imagined it was. Nevertheless, in regions

Ambassador Newsom is former U.S. ambassador to Libya, Indonesia, and the Philippines and retired professor of international relations at the University of Virginia. This essay was written in reaction to a presentation on post–Cold War policy at the Miller Center in June 2004 by Lawrence Eagleburger and Brent Scowcroft.

important to American interests, the United States was often perceived as an instrument of neocolonialism rather than as a defender of the free world. In regions where emotions lie in history and memories are long, the effects of such views continue.

In the immediate post–World War II period, Communist parties in Western Europe, backed by a nuclear and ambitious Soviet Union, did represent both a political and military threat. The Soviet takeover of Eastern Europe had a profound effect on public opinion in the United States. No administration could have failed to respond. Actions of the countries of the Atlantic Alliance in initiating and supporting anti-Soviet policies were justified and understandable.

The Korean War gave further impetus to the fears of Communist ambitions. The leftist rhetoric of leaders of newly independent countries and Soviet aid to these nations were seen as evidence of a continuing Communist advance; in the views of Americans, nationalism became fused with Soviet ambitions. To meet this perceived threat in the 1950s, the containment philosophy of the North Atlantic Treaty and the Truman Doctrine was extended eastward into Asia and southward to Africa and Latin America. Encirclement became the objective of global policy. For strategic thinkers at the time, the world became a giant game of Risk, with scant appreciation of the game board on which they were playing. The results still haunt us today.

The first manifestation of this approach appeared in 1953 in Iran. Alarmed by the growth of the leftist Tudeh Party's influence under Prime Minister Mohammad Mossadeq, the Eisenhower administration cooperated with the British to overthrow the prime minister and restore the shah to power. Subsequent U.S. administrations built up the shah as a U.S. anti-Communist surrogate in the region. Such support was of little avail when, in 1978, Islamic militants overthrew the shah and took 53 American diplomats hostage. The earlier U.S. overthrow of Mossadeq figured prominently in the anti-American rhetoric of the Iranian revolution and is still recalled in Iranian politics today.

In the wake of the Korean War and the Mossadeq experience in Iran, Secretary of State John Foster Dulles in 1954 began the effort to create a series of treaties that would contain the Soviet Union in Asia. Beginning with the signing of the Southeast Asia Treaty Organization (SEATO) in 1954, the pacts were intended to close the circle between NATO and the U.S. strategic position in Japan. "Nonalignment," popular among the newly independent nations, was not, for Secretary Dulles, an option for free nations.

In the mid-1950s, the United States faced two serious threats to its perceived interests in the region: more aggressive Soviet moves and strong Arab nationalist influences emanating from Egypt's Gemal Abdul Nasser. The two were intertwined. Two U.S. initiatives intended to counter both led to failures and further deterioration in the U.S. position in the region. The U.S. opposition to the French, British, and Israeli attack on Suez in October 1956 only temporarily reversed this trend.

In 1955, Washington stimulated the organization of the Baghdad Pact to include the United Kingdom, Iraq, Turkey, Pakistan, and Iran. Secretary Dulles saw the pact not only as a way to contain the Soviets but also as an effort to divert Arab, and especially Iraqi, attention away from Israel and toward the Communist menace. Iraq, on the contrary, saw adherence as a possible way to gain greater American support for the Arab position. The United States did not formally join the pact, but supported it financially and militarily. The pact was attacked by Arab nationalists as an effort to continue the "colonial" domination of the period of the earlier British and French mandates.

The pact had two serious consequences for U.S. policy. Because of the continuing dispute with India over Kashmir, the adherence of Pakistan raised suspicions in New Delhi of U.S. motives, suspicions that lasted well into the 1970s and the prime ministership of Indira Gandhi.

In Baghdad the act met with strong opposition from Arab nationalists and was seen as a continuation of the unpopular alliance with Britain. The decision of Iraq's strongman, Prime Minister Nuri al Said, to join the pact was at least one of the factors that undermined the Hashemite monarchy and led to the revolution of 1958 in Baghdad. The series of military coups that followed led ultimately to the rule of Saddam Hussein, with consequences clearly visible today.

Seeking greater flexibility in the administration of economic and military aid to confront the perceived Communist threat in the Middle East, the U.S. Congress in 1957 passed a Middle East Resolution that promulgated what became the Eisenhower Doctrine. Two hundred million dollars in aid was offered to those countries that would commit themselves to opposing international Communism. The administration basically wanted a means of circumventing strict congressional limits on the management of aid funds; it was true throughout the Cold War that, to be successful in Congress, any initiative on aid had to be set in an anti-Soviet context. A retired member of Congress, James P. Richards, was sent to the Middle East to "sell" the doctrine and obtain commitments. Middle Eastern nations, however, did not wish to "stand up and be counted," particularly in the wake of U.S. support for the establishment of the state of Israel seven years earlier. Only two countries, Iraq and Lebanon, endorsed the doctrine. The Iraq revolution occurred a year later. Lebanon was saved from chaos only by the intervention of U.S. marines.

Across Asia in Indochina, the French lost their position in Vietnam; at the Geneva Conference in 1954, Vietnam was divided between North and South. The Kennedy administration saw the growing threat of North Vietnam to the anti-Communist South as a wider threat to the nations of the region. Fearful of "dominoes" falling, the administration began a U.S. involvement that escalated eventually into a full-scale war. The U.S. intervention in Vietnam was perceived in Washington as an essential move in the battle to prevent the fall of Asian dominoes to the Communists. But in much of Asia it was viewed as an effort to perpetuate French colonialism.

One of the dominoes of concern to Washington was Indonesia. The Eisenhower administration and, especially, Secretary of State John Foster Dulles and his brother, CIA chief Allen Dulles, were troubled by the policies of President Sukarno. They looked for dissident activities in the outer islands that might be supported to weaken or remove the Sukarno regime. The opportunity came in 1957 when dissident colonels in Sumatra organized a rebellion and received arms from the CIA. But the uprising collapsed and the CIA role was subsequently revealed, further tarnishing the image of the United States in Indonesia and the region. Paul Gardner writes of the aftermath of this episode in *Shared Hopes, Separate Fears:* "Although the U.S. denial of involvement in the PRRI/Permesta rebellion averted a situation in which the Indonesian government would have felt compelled to break diplomatic relations, it also caused Indonesians to dismiss denials of later reports of U.S. complicity in anti-Indonesian activities."[1]

Throughout the 1960s, Washington was obsessed with perceived Soviet and Chinese threats to the emerging independent states of Africa. Through both covert actions and proxy wars, the United States opposed groups seen by Washington as pro-Communist but by many Africans as proindependence. The murder of Patrice Lumumba in 1960, a nationalist hero in the Congo, is still blamed on the Americans. The accession of Mobutu Sese-Seko to power in Kinshasha became a prime example of America's willingness to support corrupt and undemocratic autocrats in the name of fighting Communism.

U.S. resistance to independence for the Portuguese colonies in Africa was viewed as an effort to perpetuate colonialism. U.S. covert support for Joseph Savimbi's UNITA movement in Angola and the long civil war that followed in the

---

[1]*Shared Hopes, Separate Fears: Fifty Years of U.S.-Indonesian Relations* (Boulder, CO: Westview Press, 1997), p. 162.

name of fighting communism devastated a significant part of Africa.

Throughout this period the U.S. image suffered due to the positions taken in the United Nations General Assembly (UNGA) on such issues as colonialism, apartheid, and Palestine. Although the UNGA positions were not binding, the posture of the United States was frequently seen in Africa and Asia as reflecting opposition to basic nationalistic and racial attitudes in these newly emerging nations. The Reagan administration made matters worse by seeking to tie aid levels to favorable votes by African and Asian countries on these issues.

The reaction to perceived communist threats was not confined to Asia and Africa. In 1954, alarmed by the leftist tendencies of Guatemalan president Jacobo Arbenz Guzman, the United States assisted in the overthrow of his government. In 1973 the U.S. involvement was suspected in the overthrow and death of Chilean president Salvador Allende Gossens, another left-leaning Latin American leader. The Reagan administration saw a communist threat to the United States in the growing leftist movements in Central America and undertook to support anti-communist elements in El Salvador, Honduras, and Guatemala. To many in the poorer countries of Latin America, such activities were further evidence of "gringo" manifest destiny.

Undoubtedly the most damaging of the unintended consequences of the Cold War resulted from support for the *mujahadin,* Muslim fighters resisting the Soviet forces in Afghanistan after the invasion of 1978. The Soviet invasion created alarms in the Carter administration that the Soviets were about to realize their dream of gaining access to the Persian Gulf. The United States saw an opportunity to make the Soviets pay a heavy price for the invasion by providing arms and assistance, in cooperation with Saudi Arabia and Pakistan, to the resistance. Muslim fighters from Arab countries and other Islamic regions were accepted and trained for *jihad* against the infidel invader. Islamic militantism was mobilized to fight the Soviets, but, after the Soviets left in 1989, the militants looked for new targets. Out of that effort to train and encourage militant Muslim forces to fight the Soviets–with extensive CIA help–grew the influence of Osama Bin Laden and the al-Qaeda movement, arguably one of the most serious of the unintended consequences of the Cold War period.[2]

The Cold War fears of Communist advances were replaced in the 1990s by concern over the threat of Saddam Hussein to dominate the oil-rich Persian Gulf region. But a consequence of the first Gulf War was the strengthening of al-Qaeda, fed by resentment over the presence of U.S. forces in Saudi Arabia.

Opposition in the Middle East to the U.S. invasion of Iraq is undoubtedly a reflection of beliefs fostered during the Cold War that America was anti-Muslim and sought to dominate the oil-rich region for its own purposes. No blame should be assigned to those who framed the policies that led to the unintended consequences of the Cold War. In the main, policymakers were responding to fears in the public, the media, and Congress that overwhelmed contrary views, which were brushed aside.

Throughout the period a constant dichotomy appeared between a view of the world held by many top policymakers and in Congress and the views of many with experience in the regions involved, whether diplomats, scholars, journalists, or foreign observers. Officers in the embassy in Baghdad in 1955 raised questions about the wisdom of pressuring the Iraqi government into an anti-communist pact. Those serving in Tehran in later years expressed their doubts about the stability of Iran under the shah. But these views were unwelcome to decision makers in Washington unwilling to hear challenges to established policy.

The debate over Vietnam policy is well documented. In a recent biography of Ellsworth Bunker,

---

[2]For a full account of the role of the CIA in Afghanistan, see Steve Coll, *Ghost Wars* (New York: Penguin Press, 2004).

who served as U.S. ambassador to Vietnam from 1967 to 1973, Howard Schaffer writes:

> As he settled into a steady, mutually confident relationship with [President] Thieu in the Nixon-Kissinger years, his messages presented a picture of sustained if uneven advance toward stability, security, and a measure of prosperity for South Vietnam.
>
> Some on the embassy staff differed sharply with his assessments, especially officers in the political section but others, mostly younger officers, as well. These negative views about Vietnam's prospects were shared by many American correspondents, with whom they regularly compared notes. This pattern, senior officials taking an optimistic view of developments, more junior ones and media representatives more skeptical, was not uncommon throughout the war.[3]

Foreign observers were equally skeptical. Indonesians were part of an international commission in Vietnam and traveled throughout the country. In January 1975 (four months before the fall of Saigon), Graham Martin, the U.S. ambassador to Saigon, came to Jakarta to brief the Indonesians. He painted a rosy picture of progress and denigrated U.S. critics of the war. One of the Indonesian observers later said to an American embassy officer, "We were most interested in what Ambassador Martin had to say. He must be working in a different country than we are."

Regarding the growth of al-Qaeda in Afghanistan, there is little evidence that doubts were raised about the possible long-term risks of assisting militant Islamic groups in opposing the Soviets. Debates during the *mujahadin* period seemed to revolve mostly around doubts about the wisdom of collaborating with Pakistani intelligence and with various possible radical elements among the Afghan warlords. It was only after three major terrorist attacks on U.S. targets—the World Trade Center in New York in 1993, the U.S. embassies in Nairobi and Dar Es Salaam in 1998, and the *U.S.S. Cole* in 2000—that the full extent of bin Laden's role and of the al-Qaeda threat became known. But, even then, the worst of the unintended consequences of the U.S. war against the Soviets in Afghanistan still lay ahead.

This pattern of U.S. ambassadors faithfully pursuing policies devised in the political and strategic arena of Washington in the face of contrary assessments by others has been repeated in every one of the U.S. Cold War crises in Asia, Africa, and Latin America.

Should the United States, then, have been inactive in the face of threats to pro-Western, anticommunist governments outside of Europe? Would the U.S. position be better today if it had not intervened in the countries of the Middle East and in Indonesia, Vietnam, Angola, and Nicaragua?

Certainly, many of the long-range assessments that drove U.S. policy were off the mark. The dominoes did not fall in Southeast Asia. The United States today has friendly relations with Vietnam. Indonesia is having its first democratic election. Information on the origins of the Soviet invasion of Afghanistan suggest that the action was less part of a drive to gain a foothold in the oil-rich Gulf than an effort to curb the influence of Islamic militants in Soviet Central Asia. Would the Soviet Union have been any more successful at bringing stability to Afghanistan than the British before them or the Americans today?

It is difficult to predict what might have happened in Iran and Iraq. It is hard to imagine that, under a continuation of the Mossadeq government in Tehran, the U.S. position today would be any worse. Clearly, the end result of the expenditure of U.S. lives and resources in Iraq is yet to be determined, but the American dream of a pro-American, democratic Iraq is still far from realization.

The fall of the Soviet Union demonstrated the inherent weakness of that nation and certainly raises questions about its long-range capacity to alter societies in Asia, Africa, and Latin America. The endless hours spent by U.S. officials seeking to counter Soviet and Chinese offers of aid to

---

[3]Howard Schaffer, *Ellsworth Bunker: A Biography* (Chapel Hill, NC: University of North Carolina Press, 2003).

these continents seemed essential at the time, but in retrospect seem less justified.

U.S. interventions beyond Europe during the Cold War did not create the current terrorist threat. They did create fears of Western intervention and antipathy toward the West in areas that had experienced colonialism and European domination in other forms. Such fears of renewed occupation lie dormant throughout the region, subject to exploitation by demagogues and autocrats. In the Middle East the continuing U.S. identification with the unresolved Israeli-Palestinian issue makes the exploitation possibility especially real.

The clash between Washington's perceptions of an issue, created by the inevitable interplay of politics, pressures, and interests that characterize U.S. foreign policymaking, and the different reality seen by observers on the ground will never end. The results of Cold War policies cannot be reversed, but setting forth the consequences can, perhaps, lead to a better understanding of the limitations of a superpower's ability to control global events. That understanding can also demonstrate how difficult it is, under the pressures of immediate action, to foresee the longer-term consequences of that action.

Appendix B Charter of the United Nations

We the peoples of the United Nations determined

> to save succeeding generations from the scourge of war, which twice in our lifetime has brought untold sorrow to mankind, and

> to reaffirm faith in fundamental human rights, in the dignity and worth of the human person, in the equal rights of men and women and of nations large and small, and

> to establish conditions under which justice and respect for the obligations arising from treaties and other sources of international law can be maintained,

> and to promote social progress and better standards of life in larger freedom,

and for these ends

> to practice tolerance and live together in peace with one another as good neighbors, and

> to unite our strength to maintain international peace and security, and

> to ensure, by the acceptance of principles and the institution of methods, that armed force shall not be used, save in the common interest, and

> to employ international machinery for the promotion of the economic and social advancement of all peoples,

have resolved to combine our efforts to accomplish these aims.

> Accordingly, our respective Governments, through representatives assembled in the city of San Francisco, who have exhibited their full powers found to be in good and due form, have agreed to the present Charter of the United Nations and do hereby establish an international organization to be known as the United Nations.

Chapter 1 PURPOSES AND PRINCIPLES

Article 1

The Purposes of the United Nations are:

1. To maintain international peace and security, and to that end: to take effective collective measures for the prevention and removal of threats to the peace, and for the suppression of acts of aggression or other breaches of the peace, and to bring about by peaceful means, and in conformity with the principles of justice and international law, adjustment or settlement of international disputes or situations which might lead to a breach of the peace;

2. To develop friendly relations among nations based on respect for the principle of equal rights and self-determination of peoples, and to take other appropriate measures to strengthen universal peace;

3. To achieve international cooperation in solving international problems of an economic, social, cultural, or humanitarian character, and in promoting and encouraging respect for human rights and for fundamental freedoms for all without distinction as to race, sex, language, or religion; and

4. To be a center for harmonizing the actions of nations in the attainment of these common ends.

Article 2

The Organization and its Members, in pursuit of the Purposes stated in Article 1, shall act in accordance with the following Principles.

1. The Organization is based on the principle of the sovereign equality of all its Members.

2. All Members, in order to ensure to all of them the rights and benefits resulting from membership, shall fulfil in good faith the obligations assumed by them in accordance with the present Charter.

3. All Members shall settle their international disputes by peaceful means in such a manner that international peace and security, and justice, are not endangered.

4. All Members shall refrain in their international relations from the threat or use of force against the territorial integrity or political independence of any state, or in any other manner inconsistent with the Purposes of the United Nations.

5. All Members shall give the United Nations every assistance in any action it takes in accordance with the present Charter, and shall refrain from giving assistance to any state against which the United Nations is taking preventive or enforcement action.

6. The Organization shall ensure that states which are not Members of the United Nations act in accordance with these Principles so far as may be necessary for the maintenance of international peace and security.

7. Nothing contained in the present Charter shall authorize the United Nations to intervene in matters which are essentially within the domestic jurisdiction of any state or shall require the Members to submit such matters to settlement under the present Charter; but this principle shall not prejudice the application of enforcement measures under Chapter 7.

Chapter 2 MEMBERSHIP

Article 3

The original Members of the United Nations shall be the states which, having participated in the United Nations Conference on International Organization at San Francisco, or having previously signed the Declaration by United Nations of January 1, 1942, sign the present Charter and ratify it in accordance with Article 110.

Article 4

1. Membership in the United Nations is open to all other peace-loving states which accept the obligations contained in the present Charter and, in the judgment of the Organization, are able and willing to carry out these obligations.

2. The admission of any such state to membership in the United Nations will be effected by a decision of the General Assembly upon the recommendation of the Security Council.

Article 5

A Member of the United Nations against which preventive or enforcement action has been taken by the Security Council may be suspended from the exercise of the rights and privileges of membership by the General Assembly upon the recommendation of the Security Council. The exercise of these rights and privileges may be restored by the Security Council.

Article 6

A Member of the United Nations which has persistently violated the Principles contained in the present Charter may be expelled from the Organization by the General Assembly upon the recommendation of the Security Council.

Chapter 3 ORGANS

Article 7

1. There are established as the principal organs of the United Nations: a General Assembly, a Security Council, an Economic and Social Council, a Trusteeship Council, an International Court of Justice, and a Secretariat.

2. Such subsidiary organs as may be found necessary may be established in accordance with the present Charter.

Article 8

The United Nations shall place no restrictions on the eligibility of men and women to participate in any capacity and under conditions of equality in its principal and subsidiary organs.

Chapter 4 THE GENERAL ASSEMBLY

Composition

Article 9

1. The General Assembly shall consist of all the Members of the United Nations.

2. Each Member shall have not more than five representatives in the General Assembly.

Functions and Powers

Article 10

The General Assembly may discuss any questions or any matters within the scope of the present Charter or relating to the powers and functions of any organs provided for in the present Charter, and except as provided in Article 12, may make recommendations to the Members of the United Nations or to the Security Council or to both on any such questions or matters.

Article 11

1. The General Assembly may consider the general principles of cooperation in the maintenance of international peace and security, including the principles governing disarmament and the regulation of armaments, and may make recommendations with regard to such principles to the Members or to the Security Council or to both.

2. The General Assembly may discuss any questions relating to the maintenance of international peace and security brought before it by any Member of the United Nations, or by the Security Council, or by a state which is not a Member of the United Nations in accordance with Article 35, paragraph 2, and, except as provided in Article 12, may make recommendations with regard to any such questions to the state or states concerned or to the Security Council or to both. Any such question on which action is necessary shall be referred to the Security Council by the General Assembly either before or after discussion.

3. The General Assembly may call the attention of the Security Council to situations which are likely to endanger international peace and security.

4. The powers of the General Assembly set forth in this Article shall not limit the general scope of Article 10.

Article 12

1. While the Security Council is exercising in respect of any dispute or situation the functions assigned to it in the present Charter, the General Assembly shall not make any recommendation with regard to that dispute or situation unless the Security Council so requests.

2. The Secretary General, with the consent of the Security Council, shall notify the General Assembly at each session of any matters relative to the maintenance of international peace and security which are being dealt with by the Security Council and shall similarly notify the General Assembly, or the Members of the United Nations if the General Assembly is not in session, immediately the Security Council ceases to deal with such matters.

Article 13

1. The General Assembly shall initiate studies and make recommendations for the purpose of:

a. promoting international cooperation in the political field and encouraging the progressive development of international law and its codification;

b. promoting international cooperation in the economic, social, cultural, educational, and health fields, and assisting in the realization of human rights and fundamental freedoms for all without distinction as to race, sex, language, or religion.

2. The further responsibilities, functions, and powers of the General Assembly with respect to matters mentioned in paragraph 1 (b) above are set forth in Chapters 9 and 10.

Article 14

Subject to the provisions of Article 12, the General Assembly may recommend measures for the peaceful adjustment of any situation, regardless of origin, which it deems likely to impair the general welfare or friendly relations among nations, including situations resulting from a violation of the provisions of the present Charter setting forth the Purposes and Principles of the United Nations.

Article 15

1. The General Assembly shall receive and consider annual and special reports from the Security Council; these reports shall include an account of the measures that the Security Council has decided upon or taken to maintain international peace and security.

2. The General Assembly shall receive and consider reports from the other organs of the United Nations.

Article 16

The General Assembly shall perform such functions with respect to the international trusteeship system as are assigned to it under Chapters 12 and 13, including the approval of the trusteeship agreements for areas not designated as strategic.

Article 17

1. The General Assembly shall consider and approve the budget of the Organization.

2. The expenses of the Organization shall be borne by the Members as apportioned by the General Assembly.

3. The General Assembly shall consider and approve any financial and budgetary arrangements with specialized agencies referred to in Article 57 and shall examine the administrative budgets of such specialized agencies with a view to making recommendations to the agencies concerned.

Voting

Article 18

1. Each member of the General Assembly shall have one vote.

2. Decisions of the General Assembly on important questions shall be made by a two-thirds majority of the members present and voting. These questions shall include: recommendations with respect to the maintenance of international peace and security, the election of the non-permanent members of the Security Council, the election of the members of the Economic and Social Council, election of members of the Trusteeship Council in accordance with paragraph 1 (c) of Article 86, the admission of new Members to the United Nations, the suspension of the rights and privileges of membership, the expulsion of Members, questions relating to the operation of the trusteeship system, and budgetary questions.

3. Decisions on other questions, including the determination of additional categories of questions to be decided by a two-thirds majority, shall be made by a majority of the members present and voting.

Article 19

A Member of the United Nations which is in arrears in the payment of its financial contribution to the Organization shall have no vote in the General Assembly if the amount of its arrears equals or exceeds the amount of the contributions due from it for the preceding two full years. The General Assembly may, nevertheless, permit such a Member to vote if it is satisfied that the failure to pay is due to conditions beyond the control of the Member.

Procedure

Article 20

The General Assembly shall meet in regular annual sessions and in such special sessions as occasion may require. Special sessions shall be convoked by the Secretary General at the request of the Security Council or of a majority of the Members of the United Nations.

Article 21

The General Assembly shall adopt its own rules of procedure. It shall elect its President for each session.

Article 22

The General Assembly may establish such subsidiary organs as it deems necessary for the performance of its functions.

Chapter 5   THE SECURITY COUNCIL

Composition

Article 23

1. The Security Council shall consist of fifteen Members of the United Nations. The Republic of China, France, the Union of Soviet Socialist Republics, the United Kingdom of Great Britain and Northern Ireland, and the United States of America shall be permanent members of the Security Council. The General Assembly shall elect ten other Members of the United Nations to be non-permanent members of the Security Council, due regard being specially paid, in the first instance to the contribution of Members of the United Nations to the maintenance of international peace and security and to the other purposes of the Organization, and also to equitable geographical distribution.

2. The non-permanent members of the Security Council shall be elected for a term of two years. In the first election of the non-permanent members after the increase of the membership of the Security Council from eleven to fifteen, two of the four additional members shall be chosen for a term of one year. A retiring member shall not be eligible for immediate reelection.

3. Each member of the Security Council shall have one representative.

Functions and Powers

Article 24

1. In order to ensure prompt and effective action by the United Nations, its Members confer on the Security Council primary responsibility for the maintenance of international peace and security, and agree that in carrying out its duties under this responsibility the Security Council acts on their behalf.

2. In discharging these duties the Security Council shall act in accordance with the Purposes and Principles of the United Nations. The specific powers granted to the Security Council for the discharge of these duties are laid down in Chapters 6, 7, 8, and 12.

3. The Security Council shall submit annual and, when necessary, special reports to the General Assembly for its consideration.

Article 25

The Members of the United Nations agree to accept and carry out the decisions of the Security Council in accordance with the present Charter.

Article 26

In order to promote the establishment and maintenance of international peace and security with the least diversion for armaments of the world's human and economic resources, the Security Council shall be responsible for formulating, with the assistance of the Military Staff Committee referred to in Article 47, plans to be submitted to the Members of the United Nations for the establishment of a system for the regulations of armaments.

Voting

Article 27

1. Each member of the Security Council shall have one vote.

2. Decisions of the Security Council on procedural matters shall be made by an affirmative vote of nine members.

3. Decisions of the Security Council on all other matters shall be made by an affirmative vote of nine members including the concurring votes of the permanent members; provided that, in decisions under Chapter 6, and under paragraph 3 of Article 52, a party to a dispute shall abstain from voting.

Procedure

Article 28

1. The Security Council shall be so organized as to be able to function continuously. Each member of the Security Council shall for this purpose be represented at all times at the seat of the Organization.

2. The Security Council shall hold periodic meetings at which each of its members may, if it so desires, be represented by a member of the government or by some other specially designated representative.

3. The Security Council may hold meetings at such places other than the seat of the Organization as in its judgment will best facilitate its work.

Article 29

The Security Council may establish such subsidiary organs as it deems necessary for the performance of its functions.

Article 30

The Security Council shall adopt its own rules of procedure, including the method of selecting its President.

Article 31

Any member of the United Nations which is not a member of the Security Council may participate, without vote, in the discussion of any question brought before the Security Council whenever the latter considers that the interests of that Member are specially affected.

Article 32

Any Member of the United Nations which is not a member of the Security Council or any state which is not a Member of the United Nations, if it is a party to a dispute under consideration by the Security Council shall be invited to participate, without vote, in the discussion relating to the dispute. The Security Council shall lay down such conditions as it deems just for the participation of a state which is not a Member of the United Nations.

Chapter 6 PACIFIC SETTLEMENT OF DISPUTES

Article 33

1. The parties to any dispute, the continuance of which is likely to endanger the maintenance of international peace and security, shall, first of all, seek a solution by negotiation, enquiry, mediation, conciliation, arbitration, judicial settlement, resort to regional agencies or arrangements, or other peaceful means of their own choice.

2. The Security Council shall, when it deems necessary, call upon the parties to settle their dispute by such means.

Article 34

The Security Council may investigate any dispute, or any situation which might lead to international friction or give rise to a dispute, in order to determine whether the continuance of the dispute or situation is likely to endanger the maintenance of international peace and security.

Article 35

1. Any Member of the United Nations may bring any dispute, or any situation of the nature referred to in Article 34, to the attention of the Security Council or of the General Assembly.

2. A state which is not a Member of the United Nations may bring to the attention of the Security Council or of the General Assembly any dispute to which it is a party if it accepts in advance, for the purposes of the dispute, the obligations of pacific settlement provided in the present Charter.

3. The proceedings of the General Assembly in respect of matters brought to its attention under this Article will be subject to the provisions of Articles 11 and 12.

Article 36

1. The Security Council may, at any stage of a dispute of the nature referred to in Article 33 or of a situation of like nature, recommend appropriate procedures or methods of adjustment.

2. The Security Council should take into consideration any procedures for the settlement of the dispute which have already been adopted by the parties.

3. In making recommendations under this Article the Security Council should also take into consideration that legal disputes should as a general rule be referred by the parties to the International Court of Justice in accordance with the provisions of the Statute of the Court.

Article 37

1. Should the parties to a dispute of the nature referred to in Article 33 fail to settle it by the means indicated in that Article, they shall refer it to the Security Council.

2. If the Security Council deems that the continuance of the dispute is in fact likely to endanger the maintenance of international peace and security, it shall decide whether to take action under Article 36 or to recommend such terms of settlement as it may consider appropriate.

Article 38

Without prejudice to the provisions of Articles 33 to 37, the Security Council may, if all the parties to any dispute so request, make recommendations to the parties with a view to a pacific settlement of the dispute.

Chapter 7 ACTION WITH RESPECT TO THREATS TO THE PEACE, BREACHES OF THE PEACE, AND ACTS OF AGGRESSION

Article 39

The Security Council shall determine the existence of any threat to the peace, breach of the peace, or act of aggression and shall make recommendations, or decide what measures shall be taken in accordance with Articles 41 and 42, to maintain or restore international peace and security.

Article 40

In order to prevent an aggravation of the situation, the Security Council may, before making the recommendations or deciding upon the measures provided for in Article 39, call upon the parties concerned to comply with such provisional measures as it deems necessary or desirable. Such provisional measures shall be without prejudice to the rights, claims, or position of the parties concerned. The Security Council shall duly take account of failure to comply with such provisional measures.

Article 41

The Security Council may decide what measures not involving the use of armed force are to be employed to give effect to its decisions, and it may call upon the Members of the United Nations to apply such measures. These may include complete or partial interruption of economic relations and of rail, sea, air, postal, telegraphic, radio, and other means of communication, and the severance of diplomatic relations.

Article 42

Should the Security Council consider that measures provided for in Article 41 would be inadequate or have proved to be inadequate, it may take such action by air, sea, or land forces as may be necessary to maintain or restore international peace and security. Such action may include demonstrations, blockade, and other operations by air, sea, or land forces of Members of the United Nations.

Article 43

1. All Members of the United Nations, in order to contribute to the maintenance of international peace and security, undertake to make available to the Security Council, on its call and in accordance with a special agreement or agreements, armed forces, assistance, and facilities, including rights of passage, necessary for the purpose of maintaining international peace and security.

2. Such agreement or agreements shall govern the numbers and types of forces, their degree of readiness and general location, and the nature of the facilities and assistance to be provided.

3. The agreement or agreements shall be negotiated as soon as possible on the initiative of the Security Council. They shall be concluded between the Security Council and Members or between the Security Council and groups of Members and shall be subject to ratification by the signatory states in accordance with their respective constitutional processes.

Article 44

When the Security Council has decided to use force it shall, before calling upon a Member not represented on it to provide armed forces in fulfillment of the obligations assumed under Article 43, invite that Member, if the Member so desires, to participate in the decisions of the Security Council concerning the employment of contingents of that Member's armed forces.

Article 45

In order to enable the United Nations to take urgent military measures, Members shall hold immediately available national air-force contingents for combined international enforcement action. The strength and degree of readiness of these contingents and plans for their combined action shall be determined, within the limits laid down in the special agreement or agreements referred to in Article 43, by the Security Council with the assistance of the Military Staff Committee.

Article 46

Plans for the application of armed force shall be made by the Security Council with the assistance of the Military Staff Committee.

Article 47

1. There shall be established a Military Staff Committee to advise and assist the Security Council on all questions relating to the Security Council's military requirements for the maintenance of international peace and security, the employment and command of forces placed at its disposal, the regulation of armaments, and possible disarmament.

2. The Military Staff Committee shall consist of the Chiefs of Staff of the permanent members of the Security Council or their representatives. Any Member of the United Nations not permanently represented on the Committee shall be invited by the Committee shall be invited by the Committee to be associated with it when the efficient discharge of the Committee's responsibilities requires the participation of that Member in its work.

3. The Military Staff Committee shall be responsible under the Security Council for the strategic direction of any armed forces placed at the disposal of the Security Council. Questions relating to the command of such forces shall be worked out subsequently.

4. The Military Staff Committee, with the authorization of the Security Council and after consultation with appropriate regional agencies, may establish regional subcommittees.

Article 48

1. The action required to carry out the decisions of the Security Council for the maintenance of international peace and security shall be taken by all the Members of the United Nations or by some of them, as the Security Council may determine.

2. Such decisions shall be carried out by the Members of the United Nations directly and through their action in the appropriate international agencies of which they are members.

Article 49

The members of the United Nations shall join in affording mutual assistance in carrying out the measures decided upon by the Security Council.

Article 50

If preventive or enforcement measures against any state are taken by the Security Council, any other state, whether a Member of the United Nations or not, which finds itself confronted with special economic problems arising from the carrying out of those measures shall have the right to consult the Security Council with regard to a solution of those problems.

Article 51

Nothing in the present Charter shall impair the inherent right of individual or collective self-defense if an armed attack occurs against a Member of the United Nations, until the Security Council has taken the measures necessary to maintain international peace and security. Measures taken by Members in the exercise of this right of self-defense shall be immediately reported to the Security Council and shall not in any way affect the authority and responsibility of the Security Council under the present Charter to take at any time such action as it deems necessary in order to maintain or restore international peace and security.

Chapter 8 REGIONAL ARRANGEMENTS

Article 52

1. Nothing in the present Charter precludes the existence of regional arrangements or agencies for dealing with such matters relating to the maintenance of international peace and security as are appropriate for regional action, provided that such arrangements or agencies and their activities are consistent with the Purposes and Principles of the United Nations.

2. The Members of the United Nations entering into such arrangements or constituting such agencies shall make every effort to achieve pacific settlement of local disputes through such regional arrangements or by such regional agencies before referring them to the Security Council.

3. The Security Council shall encourage the development of pacific settlement of local disputes through such regional arrangements or by such regional agencies either on the initiative of the states concerned or by reference from the Security Council.

4. This Article in no way impairs the application of Articles 34 and 35.

Article 53

1. The Security Council shall, where appropriate, utilize such regional arrangements or agencies for enforcement action under its authority. But no enforcement action shall be taken under regional arrangements or by regional agencies without the authorization of the Security Council, with the exception of measures against any enemy state, as defined in paragraph 2 of this Article, provided for pursuant to Article 107 or in regional arrangements directed against renewal of aggressive policy on the part of any such state, until such time as the

Organization may, on request of the Governments concerned, be charged with the responsibility for preventing further aggression by such a state.

2. The term enemy state as used in paragraph 1 of this Article applies to any state which during the Second World War has been an enemy of any signatory of the present Charter.

Article 54

The Security Council shall at all times be kept fully informed of activities undertaken or in contemplation under regional arrangements or by regional agencies for the maintenance of international peace and security.

Chapter 9 INTERNATIONAL ECONOMIC AND SOCIAL COOPERATION

Article 55

With a view to the creation of conditions of stability and well-being which are necessary for peaceful and friendly relations among nations based on respect for the principle of equal rights and self-determination of peoples, the United Nations shall promote:

   a. higher standards of living, full employment, and conditions of economic and social progress and development;

   b. solutions of international economic, social, health, and related problems; and international cultural and educational cooperation; and

   c. universal respect for, and observance of, human rights and fundamental freedoms for all without distinction as to race, sex, language, or religion.

Article 56

All members pledge themselves to take joint and separate action in cooperation with the Organization for the achievement of the purposes set forth in Article 55.

Article 57

1. The various specialized agencies, established by intergovernmental agreement and having wide international responsibilities, as defined in their basic instruments, in economic, social, cultural, educational, health, and related fields, shall be brought into relationship with the United Nations in accordance with the provisions of Article 63.

2. Such agencies thus brought into relationship with the United Nations are hereinafter referred to as specialized agencies.

Article 58

The Organization shall make recommendations for the coordination of the policies and activities of the specialized agencies.

Article 59

The Organization shall, where appropriate, initiate negotiations among the states concerned for the creation of any new specialized agencies required for the accomplishment of the purposes set forth in Article 55.

Article 60

Responsibility for the discharge of the functions of the Organization set forth in this Chapter shall be vested in the General Assembly and, under the authority of the General Assembly, in the Economic and Social Council, which shall have for this purpose the powers set forth in Chapter 10.

Chapter 10 THE ECONOMIC AND SOCIAL COUNCIL

Composition

Article 61

1. The Economic and Social Council shall consist of twenty-seven Members of the United Nations elected by the General Assembly.

2. Subject to the provisions of paragraph 3, nine members of the Economic and Social Council shall be elected each year for a term of three years. A retiring member shall be eligible for immediate re-election.

3. At the first election after the increase in the membership of the Economic and Social Council from eighteen to twenty-seven members, in addition to the members elected in place of the six members whose term of office expires at the end of that year, nine additional members shall be elected. Of these nine additional members, the term of office of three members so elected shall expire at the end of one year, and of three other members at the end of two years, in accordance with arrangements made by the General Assembly.

4. Each member of the Economic and Social Council shall have one representative.

Functions and Powers

Article 62

1. The Economic and Social Council may make or initiate studies and reports with respect to international economic, social, cultural, educational, health, and related matters and may make recommendations with respect to any such matters to the General Assembly, to the Members of the United Nations, and to the specialized agencies concerned.

2. It may make recommendations for the purpose of promoting respect for, and observance of, human rights and fundamental freedoms for all.

3. It may prepare draft conventions for submission to the General Assembly, with respect to matters falling within its competence.

4. It may call, in accordance with the rules prescribed by the United Nations, international conferences on matters falling within its competence.

Article 63

1. The Economic and Social Council may enter into agreements with any of the agencies referred to in Article 57, defining the terms on which the agen-

cy concerned shall be brought into relationship with the United Nations. Such agreements shall be subject to approval by the General Assembly.

2. It may coordinate the activities of the specialized agencies through consultation with and recommendations to such agencies and through recommendations to the General Assembly and to the Members of the United Nations.

Article 64

1. The Economic and Social Council may take appropriate steps to obtain regular reports from the specialized agencies. It may make arrangements with the Members of the United Nations and with the specialized agencies to obtain reports on the steps taken to give effect to its own recommendations and to recommendations on matters falling within its competence made by the General Assembly.

2. It may communicate its observations on these reports to the General Assembly.

Article 65

The Economic and Social Council may furnish information to the Security Council and shall assist the Security Council upon its request.

Article 66

1. The Economic and Social Council shall perform such functions as fall within its competence in connection with the carrying out of the recommendations of the General Assembly.

2. It may, with the approval of the General Assembly, perform services at the request of Members of the United Nations and at the request of specialized agencies.

3. It shall perform such other functions as are specified elsewhere in the present Charter or as may be assigned to it by the General Assembly.

Voting

Article 67

1. Each member of the Economic and Social Council shall have one vote.

2. Decisions of the Economic and Social Council shall be made by a majority of the members present and voting.

Procedure

Article 68

The Economic and Social Council shall set up commissions in economic and social fields and for the promotion of human rights, and such other commissions as may be required for the performance of its functions.

Article 69

The Economic and Social Council shall invite any Member of the United Nations to participate, without vote, in its deliberations on any matter of particular concern to that Member.

Article 70

The Economic and Social Council may make arrangements for representatives of the specialized agencies to participate, without vote, in its deliberations and in those of the commissions established by it, and for its representatives to participate in the deliberations of the specialized agencies.

Article 71

The Economic and Social Council may make suitable arrangements for consultation with nongovernmental organizations which are concerned with matters within its competence. Such arrangements may be made with international organizations and, where appropriate, with national organizations after consultation with the Member of the United Nations concerned.

Article 72

1. The Economic and Social Council shall adopt its own rules of procedure, including the method of selecting its President.

2. The Economic and Social Council shall meet as required in accordance with its rules, which shall include provision for the convening of meetings on the request of a majority of its members.

Chapter 11 DECLARATION REGARDING NON-SELF-GOVERNING TERRITORIES

Article 73

Members of the United Nations which have or assume responsibilities for the administration of territories whose peoples have not yet attained a full measure of self-government recognize the principle that the interests of the inhabitants of these territories are paramount, and accept as a sacred trust the obligation to promote to the utmost, within the system of international peace and security established by the present Charter, the well-being of the inhabitants of these territories, and, to this end:

a. to ensure, with due respect for the culture of the peoples concerned, their political, economic, social, and educational advancement, their just treatment, and their protection against abuses;

b. to develop self-government, to take due account of the political aspirations of the peoples, and to assist them in the progressive development of their free political institutions, according to the particular circumstances of each territory and its peoples and their varying stages of advancement;

c. to further international peace and security;

d. to promote constructive measures of development, to encourage research, and to cooperate with one another and, when and where appropriate, with specialized international bodies with a view to the practical achievement of the social, economic, and scientific purposes set forth in this Article; and

e. to transmit regularly to the Secretary General for information purposes, subject to such limitation as security and constitutional considerations may require, statistical and other information of a technical nature relating to economic, social, and educational conditions in the territories for which they are respectively responsible other than those territories to which Chapters 12 and 13 apply.

Article 74

Members of the United Nations also agree that their policy in respect of the territories to which this Chapter applies, no less than in respect of their metropolitan areas, must be based on the general principle of good-neighborliness, due account being taken of the interests and well-being of the rest of the world, in social, economic, and commercial matters.

Chapter 12 INTERNATIONAL TRUSTEESHIP SYSTEM

Article 75

The United Nations shall establish under its authority an international trusteeship system for the administration and supervision of such territories as may be placed thereunder by subsequent individual agreements. These territories are hereinafter referred to as trust territories.

Article 76

The basic objectives of the trusteeship system, in accordance with the Purposes of the United Nations laid down in Article 1 of the present Charter, shall be:

a. to further international peace and security;

b. to promote the political, economic, social, and educational advancement of the inhabitants of the trust territories, and their progressive development towards self-government or independence as may be appropriate to the particular circumstances of each territory and its peoples and the freely expressed wishes of the peoples concerned, and as may be provided by the terms of each trusteeship agreement;

c. to encourage respect for human rights and for fundamental freedoms for all without distinction as to race, sex, language, or religion, and to encourage recognition of the interdependence of the peoples of the world; and

d. to ensure equal treatment in social, economic, and commercial matters for all Members of the United Nations and their nationals, and also equal treatment for the latter in the administration of justice, without prejudice to the attainment of the foregoing objectives and subject to the provisions of Article 80.

Article 77

1. The trusteeship system shall apply to such territories in the following categories as may be placed thereunder by means of trusteeship agreements:

a. territories now held under mandate;

b. territories which may be detached from enemy states as a result of the Second World War; and

c. territories voluntarily placed under the system by states responsible for their administration.

2. It will be a matter for subsequent agreement as to which territories in the foregoing categories will be brought under the trusteeship system and upon what terms.

Article 78

The trusteeship system shall not apply to territories which have become Members of the United Nations, relationship among which shall be based on respect for the principle of sovereign equality.

Article 79

The terms of trusteeship for each territory to be placed under the trusteeship system, including any alteration or amendment, shall be agreed upon by the states directly concerned, including the mandatory power in the case of territories held under mandate by a Member of the United Nations, and shall be approved as provided for in Articles 83 and 85.

Article 80

1. Except as may be agreed upon in individual trusteeship agreements, made under Articles 77, 79, and 81, placing each territory under the trusteeship system, and until such agreements have been concluded, nothing in this Chapter shall be construed in or of itself to alter in any manner the rights whatsoever of any states or any peoples or the terms of existing international instruments to which Members of the United Nations may respectively be parties.

2. Paragraph 1 of this Article shall not be interpreted as giving grounds for delay or postponement of the negotiation and conclusion of agreements for placing mandated and other territories under the trusteeship system as provided for in Article 77.

Article 81

The trusteeship agreement shall in each case include the terms under which the trust territory will be administered and designated the authority which will exercise the administration of the trust territory. Such authority, hereinafter called the administering authority, may be one or more states or the Organization itself.

Article 82

There may be designated, in any trusteeship agreement, a strategic area or areas which may include part or all of the trust territory to which the agreement applies, without prejudice to any special agreement or agreements made under Article 43.

Article 83

1. All functions of the United Nations relating to strategic areas, including the approval of the terms of the trusteeship agreements and of their alteration or amendment, shall be exercised by the Security Council.

2. The basic objectives set forth in Article 76 shall be applicable to the people of each strategic area.

3. The Security Council shall, subject to the provisions of the trusteeship agreements and without prejudice to security considerations, avail itself of the assistance of the Trusteeship Council to perform those functions of the United Nations under the trusteeship system relating to political, economic, social, and educational matters in the strategic areas.

Article 84

It shall be the duty of the administering authority to ensure that the trust territory shall play its part in the maintenance of international peace and security. To this end the administering authority may make use of volunteer forces, facilities, and assistance from the trust territory in carrying out the obligations towards the Security Council undertaken in this regard by the administering authority, as well as for local defense and the maintenance of law and order within the trust territory.

Article 85

1. The functions of the United Nations with regard to trusteeship agreements of all areas not designated as strategic, including the approval of the terms of the trusteeship agreements and of their alteration or amendment, shall be exercised by the General Assembly.

2. The Trusteeship Council, operating under the authority of the General Assembly, shall assist the General Assembly in carrying out these functions.

Chapter 13 THE TRUSTEESHIP COUNCIL

Composition

Article 86

1. The Trusteeship Council shall consist of the following Members of the United Nations:

a. those Members administering trust territories;

b. such of those Members mentioned by name in Article 23 as are not administering trust territories; and

c. as many other Members elected for three-year terms by the General Assembly as may be necessary to ensure that the total number of members of the Trusteeship Council is equally divided between those Members of the United Nations which administer trust territories and those which do not.

2. Each member of the Trusteeship Council shall designate one specially qualified person to represent it therein.

Functions and Powers

Article 87

The General Assembly and, under its authority, the Trusteeship Council, in carrying out their functions, may:

a. consider reports submitted by the administering authority;

b. accept petitions and examine them in consultation with the administering authority;

c. provide for periodic visits to the respective trust territories at times agreed upon with the administering authority; and

d. take these and other actions in conformity with the terms of the trusteeship agreements.

Article 88

The Trusteeship Council shall formulate a questionnaire on the political, economic, social, and educational advancement of the inhabitants of each trust territory, and the administering authority for each trust territory within the competence of the General Assembly shall make an annual report to the General Assembly upon the basis of such questionnaire.

Voting

Article 89

1. Each member of the Trusteeship Council shall have one vote.

2. Decisions of the Trusteeship Council shall be made by a majority of the members present and voting.

Procedure

Article 90

1. The Trusteeship Council shall adopt its own rules of procedure, including the method of selecting its President.

2. The Trusteeship Council shall meet as required in accordance with its rules, which shall include provision for the convening of meetings on the request of a majority of its members.

Article 91

The Trusteeship Council shall, when appropriate, avail itself of the assistance of the Economic and Social Council and of the specialized agencies in regard to matters with which they are respectively concerned.

Chapter 14 THE INTERNATIONAL COURT OF JUSTICE

Article 92

The International Court of Justice shall be the principal judicial organ of the United Nations. It shall function in accordance with the annexed Statute, which is based upon the Statute of the Permanent Court of International Justice and forms an integral part of the present Charter.

Article 93

1. All Members of the United Nations are *ipso facto* parties to the Statute of the International Court of Justice.

2. A state which is not a Member of the United Nations may become a party to the Statute of the International Court of Justice on conditions to be determined in each case by the General Assembly upon the recommendation of the Security Council.

Article 94

1. Each member of the United Nations undertakes to comply with the decision of the International Court of Justice in any case to which it is a party.

2. If any party to a case fails to perform the obligations incumbent upon it under a judgment rendered by the Court, the other party may have recourse to the Security Council, which may, if it deems necessary, make recommendations or decide upon measures to be taken to give effect to the judgment.

Article 95

Nothing in the present Charter shall prevent Members of the United Nations from entrusting the solution of their differences to other tribunals by virtue of agreements already in existence or which may be concluded in the future.

Article 96

1. The General Assembly or the Security Council may request the International Court of Justice to give an advisory opinion on any legal question.

2. Other organs of the United Nations and specialized agencies, which may at any time be so authorized by the General Assembly, may also request advisory opinions of the Court on legal questions arising within the scope of their activities.

Chapter 15 THE SECRETARIAT

Article 97

The Secretariat shall comprise a Secretary General and such staff as the Organization may require. The Secretary General shall be appointed by the General Assembly upon the recommendation of the Security Council. He shall be the chief administrative officer of the Organization.

Article 98

The Secretary General shall act in that capacity in all meetings of the General Assembly, of the Security Council, of the Economic and Social Council, and of the Trusteeship Council, and shall perform such other functions as are entrusted to him by these organs. The Secretary General shall make an annual report to the General Assembly on the work of the Organization.

Article 99

The Secretary General may bring to the attention of the Security Council any matter which in his opinion may threaten the maintenance of international peace and security.

Article 100

1. In the performance of their duties the Secretary General and the staff shall not seek or receive instructions from any government or from any other authority external to the Organization. They shall refrain from any action which might reflect on their position as international officials responsible only to the Organization.

2. Each Member of the United Nations undertakes to respect the exclusively international character of the responsibilities of the Secretary General and the staff are not to seek to influence them in the discharge of their responsibilities.

Article 101

1. The staff shall be appointed by the Secretary General under regulations established by the General Assembly.

2. Appropriate staffs shall be permanently assigned to the Economic and Social Council, the Trusteeship Council, and, as required, to other organs of the United Nations. These staffs shall form a part of the Secretariat.

3. The paramount consideration in the employment of the staff and in the determination of the conditions of service shall be the necessity of securing the highest standards of efficiency,

competence, and integrity. Due regard shall be paid to the importance of recruiting the staff on as wide a geographical basis as possible.

Chapter 16 MISCELLANEOUS PROVISIONS

Article 102

1. Every treaty and every international agreement entered into by any Member of the United Nations after the present Charter comes into force shall as soon as possible be registered with the Secretariat and published by it.

2. No party to any such treaty or international agreement which has not been registered in accordance with the provisions of paragraph 1 of this Article may invoke that treaty or agreement before any organ of the United Nations.

Article 103

In the event of a conflict between the obligations of the Members of the United Nations under the present Charter and their obligations under any other international agreement, their obligations under the present Charter shall prevail.

Article 104

The Organization shall enjoy in the territory of each of its Members such legal capacity as may be necessary for the exercise of its functions and the fulfillment of its purposes.

Article 105

1. The Organization shall enjoy in the territory of each of its Members such privileges and immunities as are necessary for the fulfillment of its purposes.

2. Representatives of the Members of the United Nations and officials of the Organization shall similarly enjoy such privileges and immunities as are

necessary for the independent exercise of their functions in connection with the Organization.

3. The General Assembly may make recommendations with a view to determining the details of the application of paragraphs 1 and 2 of this Article or may propose conventions to the Members of the United Nations for this purpose.

Chapter 17 TRANSITIONAL SECURITY ARRANGEMENTS

Article 106

Pending the coming into force of such special agreements referred to in Article 43 as in the opinion of the Security Council enable it to begin the exercise of its responsibilities under Article 42, the parties to the Four-Nation Declaration, signed at Moscow, October 30, 1943, and France, shall, in accordance with the provisions of paragraph 5 of that Declaration, consult with one another and as occasion requires with other Members of the United Nations with a view to such joint action on behalf of the Organization as may be necessary for the purpose of maintaining international peace and security.

Article 107

Nothing in the present Charter shall invalidate or preclude action, in relation to any state which during the Second World War has been an enemy of any signatory to the present Charter, taken or authorized as a result of that war by the Governments having responsibility for such action.

Chapter 18 AMENDMENTS

Article 108

Amendments to the present Charter shall come into force for all Members of the United Nations when they have been adopted by a vote of two thirds of the members of the General Assembly and ratified in accordance with their respective constitutional processes by two thirds of the Members of the United Nations, including all the permanent members of the Security Council.

Article 109

1. A General Conference of the Members of the United Nations for the purpose of reviewing the present Charter may be held at a date and place to be fixed by a two-thirds vote of the members of the General Assembly and by a vote of any seven members of the Security Council. Each Member of the United Nations shall have one vote in the conference.

2. Any alteration of the present Charter recommended by a two-thirds vote of the conference shall take effect when ratified in accordance with their respective constitutional processes by two thirds of the Members of the United Nations including all the permanent members of the Security Council.

3. If such a conference has not been held before the tenth annual session of the General Assembly following the coming into force of the present Charter, the proposal to call such a conference shall be placed on the agenda of that session of the General Assembly, and the conference shall be held if so decided by a majority vote of the members of the General Assembly and by a vote of any seven members of the Security Council.

Chapter 19 RATIFICATION AND SIGNATURE

Article 110

1. The Present Charter shall be ratified by the signatory states in accordance with their respective constitutional processes.

2. The ratifications shall be deposited with the Government of the United States of America, which shall notify all the signatory states of each deposit as well as the Secretary General of the Organization when he has been appointed.

3. The present Charter shall come into force upon the deposit of ratifications by the Republic of China, France, the Union of Soviet Socialist Republics, the United Kingdom of Great Britain and Northern Ireland, and the United States of America, and by a majority of the other signatory states. A protocol of the ratifications deposited shall thereupon be drawn up by the Government of the United States of America which shall communicate copies thereof to all the signatory states.

4. The states signatory to the present Charter which ratify it after it has come into force will become original Members of the United Nations on the date of the deposit of their respective ratifications.

Article 111

The present Charter, of which the Chinese, French, Russian, English, and Spanish texts are equally authentic, shall remain deposited in the archives of the Government of the United States of America. Duly certified copies thereof shall be transmitted by that Government to the Governments of the other signatory states.

IN FAITH WHEREOF the representatives of the Governments of the United Nations have signed the present Charter.

DONE at the city of San Francisco the twenty-sixth day of June, one thousand nine hundred and forty-five.

MEMBER STATES OF THE UNITED NATIONS, 1985

The 157 Member States of the United Nations, with the dates on which they became Members, are listed below:

Member	Date of Admission
Afghanistan	Nov. 19, 1946
Albania	Dec. 14, 1955
Algeria	Oct. 8, 1962
Angola	Dec. 1, 1976
Antigua	Nov. 11, 1981
Argentina	Oct. 24, 1945
Australia	Nov. 1, 1945
Austria	Dec. 14, 1955
Bahamas	Sept. 18, 1973
Bahrain	Sept. 21, 1971
Bangladesh	Sept. 17, 1974
Barbados	Dec. 9, 1966
Belgium	Dec. 27, 1945
Belize	Sept. 25, 1981
Benin*	Sept. 20, 1960
Bhutan	Sept. 21, 1971
Bolivia	Nov. 14, 1945
Botswana	Oct. 17, 1966
Brazil	Oct. 24, 1945
Bulgaria	Dec. 14, 1955
Burma	Apr. 19, 1948
Burundi	Sept. 18, 1962
Byelorussia	Oct. 24, 1945
Canada	Nov. 9, 1945
Cape Verde	Sept. 16, 1975
Central African Empire	Sept. 20, 1960
Chad	Sept. 20, 1960
Chile	Oct. 24, 1945
China	Oct. 24, 1945
Colombia	Nov. 5, 1945
Comoros	Nov. 12, 1975
Congo	Sept. 20, 1960
Costa Rica	Nov. 2, 1945
Cuba	Oct. 24, 1945
Cyprus	Sept. 20, 1960
Czechoslovakia	Oct. 24, 1945
Democratic Kampuchea[†]	Dec. 14, 1955
Democratic Yemen	Dec. 14, 1967
Denmark	Oct. 24, 1945
Djibouti	Sept. 20, 1977

Member	Date of Admission
Dominican Republic	Oct. 24, 1945
Ecuador	Dec. 21, 1945
Egypt[‡]	Oct. 24, 1945
El Salvador	Oct. 24, 1945
Equatorial Guinea	Nov. 12, 1968
Ethiopia	Nov. 13, 1945
Fiji	Oct. 13, 1970
Finland	Dec. 14, 1955
France	Oct. 24, 1945
Gabon	Sept. 20, 1960
Gambia	Sept. 21, 1965
German Democratic Republic	Sept. 18, 1973
Germany, Federal Republic of	Sept. 18, 1973
Ghana	Mar. 8, 1957
Greece	Oct. 25, 1945
Grenada	Sept. 17, 1974
Guatemala	Nov. 21, 1945
Guinea	Dec. 12, 1958
Guinea-Bissau	Sept. 17, 1974
Guyana	Sept. 20, 1966
Haiti	Oct. 24, 1945
Honduras	Dec. 17, 1945
Hungary	Dec. 14, 1955
Iceland	Dec. 19, 1946
India	Oct. 30, 1945
Indonesia[§]	Sept. 28, 1950
Iran	Oct. 24, 1945
Iraq	Dec. 21, 1945

[‡]Egypt and Syria were original members of the United Nations from October 24, 1945. Following a plebiscite on February 21, 1958, the United Arab Republic was established by a union of Egypt and Syria and continued as a single member. On October 13, 1961, Syria, having resumed its status as an independent state, resumed its separate membership in the United Nations.

[§]By letter of January 20, 1965, Indonesia announced its decision to withdraw from the United Nations "at this stage and under the present circumstances." By telegram of September 19, 1966, it announced its decision "to resume full co-operation with the United Nations and to resume participation in its activities." On September 28, 1966, the General Assembly took note of this decision, and the president invited representatives of Indonesia to take seats in the Assembly.

* Formerly Dahomey.
[†] Formerly Cambodia.

Member	Date of Admission
Ireland	Dec. 14, 1955
Israel	May 11, 1949
Italy	Dec. 14, 1955
Ivory Coast	Sept. 20, 1960
Jamaica	Sept. 18, 1962
Japan	Dec. 18, 1956
Jordan	Dec. 14, 1955
Kenya	Dec. 16, 1963
Kuwait	May 14, 1963
Lao People's Democratic Republic*	Dec. 14, 1955
Lebanon	Oct. 24, 1945
Lesotho	Oct. 17, 1966
Liberia	Nov. 2, 1945
Libya	Dec. 14, 1955
Luxembourg	Oct. 24, 1945
Madagascar	Sept. 20, 1960
Malawi	Dec. 1, 1964
Malaysia†	Sept. 17, 1957
Maldives	Sept. 21, 1965
Mali	Sept. 28, 1960
Malta	Dec. 1, 1964
Mauritania	Oct. 27, 1961
Mauritius	Apr. 24, 1968
Mexico	Nov. 7, 1945
Mongolia	Oct. 27, 1961
Morocco	Nov. 12, 1956
Mozambique	Sept. 16, 1975
Nepal	Dec. 14, 1955
Netherlands	Dec. 10, 1945
New Zealand	Oct. 24, 1945
Nicaragua	Oct. 24, 1945
Niger	Sept. 20, 1960
Nigeria	Oct. 7, 1960
Norway	Nov. 27, 1945
Oman	Oct. 7, 1971
Pakistan	Sept. 30, 1947

Member	Date of Admission
Panama	Nov. 13, 1945
Papua New Guinea	Oct. 10, 1975
Paraguay	Oct. 24, 1945
Peru	Oct. 31, 1945
Philippines	Oct. 24, 1945
Poland	Oct. 24, 1945
Portugal	Dec. 14, 1955
Qatar	Sept. 21, 1971
Romania	Dec. 14, 1955
Rwanda	Sept. 18, 1962
St. Kitts	Sept. 23, 1983
St. Lucia	Sept. 12, 1979
St. Vincent and Grenadines	Sept. 16, 1980
Samoa	Dec. 15, 1976
Sao Tome and Principe	Sept. 16, 1975
Saudi Arabia	Oct. 24, 1945
Senegal	Sept. 28, 1960
Seychelles	Sept. 21, 1976
Sierra Leone	Sept. 27, 1961
Singapore	Sept. 21, 1965
Solomon Islands	Sept. 19, 1978
Somalia	Sept. 20, 1960
South Africa	Nov. 7, 1945
Spain	Dec. 14, 1955
Sri Lanka	Dec. 14, 1955
Sudan	Nov. 12, 1956
Surinam	Dec. 4, 1975
Swaziland	Sept. 24, 1968
Sweden	Nov. 19, 1946
Syria‡	Oct. 24, 1945 (resumed Oct. 13, 1961)
Thailand	Dec. 16, 1946
Togo	Sept. 20, 1960
Trinidad and Tobago	Sept. 18, 1962
Tunisia	Nov. 12, 1956

*Formerly Laos.

†The Federation of Malaya joined the United Nations on September 17, 1957. On September 16, 1963, its name was changed to Malaysia, following the admission to the new federation of Singapore, Sabah (North Borneo), and Sarawak. Singapore became an independent state on August 9, 1965, and a member of the United Nations on September 21, 1965.

‡Egypt and Syria were original members of the United Nations from October 24, 1945. Following a plebiscite on February 21, 1958, the United Arab Republic was established by a union of Egypt and Syria and continued as a single member. On October 13, 1961, Syria, having resumed its status as an independent state, resumed its separate membership in the United Nations.

Member	Date of Admission
Turkey	Oct. 24, 1945
Uganda	Oct. 25, 1962
Ukraine	Oct. 24, 1945
Union of Soviet Socialist Republics	Oct. 24, 1945
United Arab Emirates	Dec. 9, 1971
United Kingdom	Oct. 24, 1945
United Republic of Cameroon	Sept. 20, 1960
United Republic of Tanzania*	Dec. 14, 1961
United States	Oct. 24, 1945

Member	Date of Admission
Upper Volta	Sept. 20, 1960
Uruguay	Dec. 18, 1945
Vanuata	Jul. 8, 1981
Venezuela	Nov. 15, 1945
Viet Nam, Socialist Republic of	Sept. 20, 1977
Yemen	Sept. 30, 1947
Yugoslavia	Oct. 24, 1945
Zaire	Sept. 20, 1960
Zambia	Dec. 1, 1964
Zimbabwe	Aug. 25, 1980

*Tanganyika was a member of the United Nations from December 14, 1961, and Zanzibar was a member from December 16, 1963. Following the ratification on April 26, 1964, of Articles of Union between Tanganyika and Zanzibar, the United Republic of Tanganyika and Zanzibar continued as a single member, changing its name to United Republic of Tanzania on November 1, 1964.

Bibliography

The purpose of this bibliography is to direct the reader to the most important and most accessible literature on the general problems of international politics. Three limitations follow from this purpose. First, the bibliography is of necessity selective. Second, the voluminous literature dealing with special problems, especially of a particular nation or region, has not been considered. Third, the main emphasis is placed upon publications in the English language.

PART ONE

On political realism, see:

Berlin, Isaiah. "Realism in Politics." *The Spectator* 193 (December 17, 1954): 774–76.

Bozeman, Adda B. *Politics and Culture in International History*. Princeton, NJ: Princeton University Press, 1960.

Butterfield, Herbert. *Christianity and History*. New York: Charles Scribner's Sons, 1950.

____. *History and Human Relations*. London: Collins Press, 1951; Scribner Library, 1961.

____. "The Scientific vs. the Moralistic Approach in International Affairs." *International Affairs* 27, no. 4 (October 1951): 411–22.

____. *Christianity, Diplomacy and War*. London: Epworth Press, 1953.

Butterfield, Herbert, and Wight, Martin, eds. *Diplomatic Investigations*. Cambridge, MA: Harvard University Press, 1966.

Carleton, William G. "Wanted: Wiser Power Politics." *The Yale Review* 41, no. 2 (Winter 1952): 194–206.

Carr, Edward Hallett. *The Twenty Years' Crisis, 1919–1939*. London: Macmillan, 1946; New York: Harper Torchbooks, 1946.

Cook, Thomas I., and Moos, Malcolm. *Power Through Purpose: The Realism of Idealism as a Basis for Foreign Policy*. Baltimore, MD: Johns Hopkins University Press, 1954.

Frankel, Joseph. *National Interest*. New York: Praeger, 1970.

Greenstein, Fred I. *Personality and Politics*. New York: W. W. Norton, 1969.

Greenstein, Fred I., and Polsby, Nelson, eds. *Handbook of Political Science*. Vol. 8, *International Politics*. Reading, MA: Addison-Wesley, 1975.

Halle, Louis. *Men and Nations*. Princeton, NJ: Princeton University Press, 1962.

Halperin, Morton H. *Bureaucratic Politics and Foreign Policy*. Washington, DC: The Brookings Institution, 1974.

Herz, John H. *Political Realism and Political Idealism.* Chicago: University of Chicago Press, 1951.

Hinsley, F. H. *Power and the Pursuit of Peace: Theory and Practice in the History of Relations Between States.* Cambridge, UK: Cambridge University Press, 1963.

Hoffman, Stanley H., ed. *Contemporary Theory in International Relations.* Englewood Cliffs, NJ: Prentice Hall, 1960.

____. "An American Social Science: International Relations." *Daedalus* I (Summer 1977): 41–60.

Kissinger, Henry. *White House Years.* Boston and Toronto: Little, Brown, 1979.

Leurdijk, J. Henk. "From International to Transnational Politics: A Change of Paradigms?" *International Social Science Journal* XXVI, no. 1 (1974): 53ff.

Manning, C.A.W. *The Nature of International Society.* London: G. Bell and Sons, 1962.

Morgenthau, Hans J. *Scientific Man vs. Power Politics.* Chicago: University of Chicago Press, 1946; Canaan: Phoenix Books, 1965.

____. *In Defense of the National Interest.* New York: Alfred A. Knopf, 1951; Washington, DC: University Press of America, 1982.

____. *Politics in the Twentieth Century.* 3 vols. Chicago: University of Chicago Press, 1962.

Morgenthau, Hans J., and Thompson, Kenneth W. *Principles and Problems of International Politics: Selected Readings.* New York: Alfred A. Knopf, 1951; Washington, DC: University Press of America, 1982.

Niebuhr, Reinhold. *The Children of Light and the Children of Darkness.* New York: Charles Scribner's Sons, 1944; reprint, Scribner Library.

____. *Christian Realism and Political Problems.* New York: Charles Scribner's Sons, 1953.

____. *Beyond Tragedy.* New York: Charles Scribner's Sons, 1955; reprint, Scribner Library.

Rommen, Hans. "Realism and Utopianism in World Affairs." *Review of Politics* 6, no. 2 (April 1944): 193–215.

Rosenau, James. *The Scientific Study of Foreign Policy.* New York: Free Press, 1971.

Said, Abdul, ed. *Theory of International Relations: The Crisis of Relevance.* Englewood Cliffs, NJ: Prentice Hall, 1968.

Schuman, Frederick L. "International Ideals and the National Interest." *The Annals of the American Academy of Political and Social Science* 280 (March 1952): 27–36.

Smith, Michael J. *Realism as an Approach to International Relations.* Ph.D. diss., Harvard University, 1982.

Thompson, Kenneth W. *Political Realism and the Crises of World Politics.* Princeton, NJ: Princeton University Press, 1960; Washington, DC: University Press of America, 1982.

____. *American Diplomacy and Emergent Patterns.* New York: New York University Press, 1962; Washington, DC: University Press of America, 1983.

____. *Ethics, Functionalism and Power in International Politics.* Baton Rouge, LA, and London: Louisiana State University Press, 1979.

____. *Cold War Theories: World Polarization, 1943–1953,* Vol. I. Baton Rouge, LA, and London: Louisiana State University Press, 1981.

____. *Winston Churchill's "Worldview": Statesmanship and Power.* Baton Rouge, LA, and London: Louisiana State University Press, 1983.

Wolfers, Arnold. *Discord and Collaboration: Essays on International Politics.* Baltimore, MD: Johns Hopkins University Press, 1962.

On the study of international politics, see:

Beitz, Charles. *Political Theory and International Relations.* Princeton, NJ: Princeton University Press, 1979.

Best Geoffrey. *Humanity in Warfare.* New York: Columbia University Press, 1980.

Booth, Ken, and Wright, Moorhead. *American Thinking About War and Peace.* New York: Barnes and Noble, 1978.

Bull, Hedley. *The Anarchical Society.* New York: Columbia University Press, 1977.

Corbett, Percy E. "Objectivity in the Study of International Affairs." *World Affairs* 4, no. 3 (July 1950): 257–63.

Deutsch, Karl. *The Analysis of International Relations.* Englewood Cliffs, NJ: Prentice Hall, 1967.

Dougherty, James E., and Pfalzgraff, Robert L., Jr. *Contending Theories of International Relations.* Philadelphia: J. B. Lippincott, 1971.

Dunn Frederick S. "The Present Course of International Relations Research." *World Politics,* 2, no. 1 (October 1949): 80–95.

Ferrell, Robert H. *American Diplomacy: A History.* New York: W. W. Norton, 1975.

Finnegan, Richard B. "International Relations: The Disputed Search for Method." *The Review of Politics* 34, no. 1 (January 1972): 40–66.

Fitzsimons, M. A. *The Foreign Policy of the British Labour Government.* Notre Dame, IN: University of Notre Dame Press, 1953.

Fox, W. T. R. *The American Study of International Relations.* New York: Columbia Institute of International Studies, 1968.

Frankel, Joseph. *Contemporary International Theory and the Behavior of States.* New York: Oxford University Press, 1973.

George, Alexander L. *Presidential Decisionmaking in Foreign Policy: The Effective Use of Information and Advice.* Boulder, CO: Westview Press, 1980.

Gurian, Waldemar. "The Study of International Relations." *Review of Politics* 8, no. 3 (July 1946): 275–82.

Harrison, Horace V., ed. *The Role of Theory in International Relations.* Princeton, Toronto, New York: D. Van Nostrand, 1964.

Herz, John H. "Relevancies and Irrelevancies in the Study of International Relations." *Polity* 4, no. 1 (Fall 1971): 25–47.

Jervis, Robert. *Perception and Misperception in International Politics.* Princeton, NJ: Princeton University Press, 1976.

Joynt, Carey B., and Corbett, Percy E. *Theory and Reality in World Politics.* Pittsburgh, PA: University of Pittsburgh Press, 1978.

Manning, C. A. W. "The Pretensions of International Relations." *Universities Quarterly* 7, no. 4 (August 1953): 361–71.

Mansback, Richard, Ferguson, Yale H., and Lampert, Donald. *The Web of World Politics: Nonstate Actors in the Global System.* Englewood Cliffs, NJ: Prentice-Hall, 1976.

May, Ernest R. *The "Lesson" of the Past: The Use and Misuse of History in American Foreign Policy.* New York: Oxford University Press, 1973.

Platig, E. Raymond. *International Relations Research: Problems of Evaluation and Advancement.* Santa Barbara, CA: Clio Press, 1967.

Rosenau, James N. *International Studies and the Social Sciences.* Beverly Hills and London: Sage, 1973.

Singer, J. David. "Theorizing About Theory in International Politics." *Journal of Conflict Resolution* IV, no. 4 (December 1960): 431–42.

Thompson, Kenneth W. "The Study of International Politics: A Survey of Trends and Developments." *Review of Politics* 14, no. 4 (October 1952): 433–67.

____. "The Empirical, Normative, and Theoretical Foundations of International Studies." *Review of Politics* 29, no. 2 (April 1967): 147–59.

____. "Neibuhr's Conception of Politics." *Interpretation* 6, no. 2 (May 1977): 124–31.

_____. *Masters of International Thought: Major Twentieth Century Theorists and the World Crisis.* Baton Rouge, LA, and London: Louisiana State University Press, 1980.

_____. "Power, Force and Diplomacy." *Review of Politics* 43, no. 3 (July 1981): 410–35.

_____. "The Cold War Legacy of Morgenthau's Approach." *Social Research* 48, no. 4 (Winter 1981): 660–67.

_____. "Foreign Policy Books from Theory to Practice." *Book Forum* 6. no. 4 (1984): 409–15.

Thompson, Kenneth, and Myers, Robert J. *Truth and Tragedy: A Tribute to Hans J. Morgenthau,* Washington, DC: New Republic, 1977; Rutgers: Transaction Books, 1984.

Waltz, Kenneth N. *Man, the State and War.* New York: Columbia University Press, 1954.

_____. *Theory of International Politics.* Reading, MA: Addison-Wesley, 1979.

Webster, C. K. *The Study of International Politics.* Cardiff, UK: University of Wales Press Board, 1923.

Woodward, E. L. *The Study of International Relations at a University.* Oxford: Clarendon Press, 1945.

Wright, Quincy. *The Study of International Relations.* New York: Appleton-Century-Crofts, 1955.

Zimmerman, William. *Soviet Perspectives on International Relations.* Princeton, NJ: Princeton University Press, 1969.

PART TWO

For the concept of political power, see:

Bryson, Lyman, Finkelstein, Louis, and MacIver, R. M., eds. *Conflicts of Power in Modern Culture.* New York: Harper & Brothers, 1947.

Clausewitz, Karl von. *War, Politics and Power: Selections.* Chicago: Henry Regnery, 1962.

Dunn, Frederick S. *Peaceful Change.* New York: Council on Foreign Relations, 1937.

Gerth, H. H., and Mills, C. Wright, eds. *From Max Weber: Essays in Sociology.* New York: Oxford University Press, 1946; San Francisco: Harbinger Books, 1958.

Hersh, Seymour M. *The Price of Power: Kissinger in the Nixon White House.* New York: Summit Books, 1983.

Katznelson, Ira, and Kesselman, Mark. *The Politics of Power.* New York: Harcourt Brace Jovanovich, 1975.

Keohane, Robert O., and Nye, Joseph S. *Power and Interdependence: World Politics in Transition.* Boston: Little, Brown, 1977.

Lasswell, Harold D. *Politics: Who Gets What, When, How.* New York: Whittlesey House, 1936; Silver Spring: Meridian Books, 1958.

Lorenz, Konrad. *On Aggression.* New York: Harcourt, Brace and World, 1966.

Mannheim, Karl. *Man and Society in an Age of Reconstruction.* New York: Harcourt, Brace, 1941.

Merriam, Charles E. *Political Power: Its Composition and Incidence.* New York: Whittlesey House, 1934; New York: Collier Books, 1964.

Miroff, Bruce. *Pragmatic Illusions: The Presidential Politics of John F. Kennedy.* New York: David McKay, 1976.

Parsons, Elsie Clouse. *Social Rule: A Study of the Will to Power.* New York: G. P. Putnam's Sons, 1915.

Parsons, Talcott. *The Structure of Social Action.* New York: McGraw-Hill, 1937.

____, ed. *Max Weber: The Theory of Social and Economic Organization.* New York: Oxford University Press, 1947.

Plamenatz, John. "Interests." *Political Studies* 2, no. 1 (February 1954): 1–8.

Russell, Bertrand. *Power.* New York: W. W. Norton, 1938; New York: Barnes and Noble, 1962.

Stillman, Edmund, and Pfaff, William. *Power and Impotence.* New York: Random House, 1966.

Concerning the depreciation of political power, see, in addition to the following books, those cited under Part One, on political realism:

Ash, Maurice A. "An Analysis of Power, with Special Reference to International Politics." *World Politics* 3, no. 2 (January 1951): 218–37.

Beard, Charles A. *A Foreign Policy for America.* New York: Alfred A. Knopf, 1940.

____. *The American Spirit: A Study of the Idea of Civilization in the United States.* New York: Macmillan, 1942.

Beard, Charles A., and Beard, Mary R. *The Rise of American Civilization* II. New York: Macmillan, 1927.

Becker, Carl L. *How New Will the Better World Be?* New York: Alfred A. Knopf, 1944.

Brucan, Silviu. *The Dissolution of Power.* New York: Alfred A. Knopf, 1971.

Curti, Merle. *The Growth of American Thought.* New York: Harper and Brothers, 1943.

Neibuhr, Reinhold. *The Irony of American History.* New York: Charles Scribner's Sons, 1952; New York: Scribner Library, 1962.

Osgood, Robert E. *Ideals and Self-Interest in America's Foreign Relations.* Chicago: University of Chicago Press, 1953; Canaan: Phoenix Books, 1964.

Temperley, Harold. *The Victorian Age in Politics, War and Diplomacy.* Cambridge, UK: Cambridge University Press, 1928.

Thompson, Kenneth W. "The Uses and Limits of Two Theories of International Relations." In *Isolation and Security*, Alexander De Conde, ed. Durham, NC: Duke University Press, 1957.

Vagts, Alfred. "The United States and the Balance of Power." *The Journal of Politics* 3, no. 4 (November 1941): 401–49.

For the general nature of international politics, see, in addition to the books cited under Part One:

Ferrero, Guglielmo. *The Principles of Power: The Great Political Crisis of History.* New York: G. P. Putnam's Sons, 1942.

Hammond, Paul Y. *Cold War and Detente.* New York: Harcourt Brace Jovanovich, 1975.

Lasswell, Harold D. *World Politics and Personal Insecurity.* New York: McGraw-Hill, 1953.

Morgenthau, Hans J. *Truth and Power.* New York: Praeger, 1970.

Niebuhr, Reinhold. *The Structure of Nations and Empires.* New York: Charles Scribner's Sons, 1949; London: Faber and Faber, 1960.

Spykman, Nicholas. *America's Strategy in World Politics: The United States and the Balance of Power.* New York: Harcourt, Brace, 1942.

Thompson, Kenneth W. "Toynbee and World Politics." *Diogena* (January 1956).

____. "Toynbee and World Politics: War and National Security." *World Politics* VIII (April 1956): 374–91.

____. "Theory and Practice in International Relations." *The Review of Politics* 44, no. 3 (July 1982): 328–41.

Wight, Martin. *Power Politics.* London: Royal Institute of International Affairs, 1946.

For the different aspects of imperialism, see:

Aaron, Raymond. "The Leninist Myth of Imperialism." *Partisan Review* 18, no. 6 (November–December, 1951): 646–62.

Beard, Charles A. *The Devil Theory of War.* New York: Vanguard Press, 1936.

Bukharin, Nikolai I. *Imperialism and World Economy.* New York: International Publishers, 1929.

Cohen, Benjamin J. *The Question of Imperialism: The Political Economy of Dominance and Dependence.* New York: Basic Books, 1973.

Delaisi, Francis. *Political Myths and Economic Realities.* New York: Viking Press, 1927.

Einzig, Paul. *Bloodless Invasion.* London: Duckworth, 1938.

____. *Appeasement Before, During and After the War.* London: Macmillan, 1941.

Feis, Herbert. *The Diplomacy of the Dollar.* Baltimore, MD: Johns Hopkins University Press, 1950.

Hallgarten, George W. F. *Imperialismus vor 1914.* 2 vols. Munich: C. H. Beck, 1951.

Handman, Max. "War, Economic Motives, and Economic Symbols." *The American Journal of Sociology* 44, no. 5 (March 1939): 629–48.

Heinmann, Eduard. "Schumpeter and the Problems of Imperialism." *Social Research* 19, no. 2 (June 1952): 177–97.

Hobson, John A. *Imperialism.* London: G. Allen and Unwin, 1938.

Hovde, Brynjolf J. "Socialist Theories of Imperialism Prior to the Great War." *Journal of Political Economy* 36, no. 5 (October 1928): 569–91.

Koebner, Richard, and Schmidt, Helmat Dan. *Imperialism: The Story and Significance of a Political Word, 1840–1960.* Cambridge, UK: Cambridge University Press, 1964.

Langer, William L. *The Diplomacy of Imperialism.* New York: Alfred A. Knopf, 1935.

Lichtheim, George. *Imperialism.* New York: Praeger, 1971.

Moon, Parker Thomas. *Imperialism and World Politics.* New York: Macmillan, 1926.

Nearing, Scott. *The Tragedy of Empire.* New York: Island Press, 1945.

Petras, James. *Critical Perspectives on Imperialism and Social Class in the Third World.* New York: Monthly Review Press, 1979.

Robbins, Lionel. *The Economic Causes of War: Some Reflections on Objectives and Mechanisms.* New York: Macmillan, 1948.

Rosen, Steven J., and Kurth, James R. *Testing Theories of Economic Imperialism.* Lexington, MA: Lexington Books, 1974.

Schumpeter, Joseph. *Imperialism and Social Classes.* New York: Augustus M. Kelley, 1951; Silver Spring: Meridian Books, 1960.

Seilliere, Ernest. *Introduction à la Philosophie de l'Imperialisme.* Paris: Felix Alcan, 1911.

Sulzbach, Walter. *"Capitalist Warmongers"–A Modern Superstition.* Chicago: University of Chicago Press, 1942.

Viner, Jacob. *International Economics.* Glencoe, IL: Free Press, 1951, pp. 49–85, 216–31.

Winslow, E. M. *The Pattern of Imperialism.* New York: Columbia University Press, 1948.

On the policy of prestige, see, in addition to the following book, the literature cited under Part Ten:

Nicolson, Harold. *The Meaning of Prestige.* Cambridge, UK: Cambridge University Press, 1947.

Two fundamental works on political ideologies are:

Mannheim, Karl. *Ideology and Utopia: An Introduction to the Sociology of Knowledge,* with a Preface by Louis Wirth. New York: Harcourt, Brace, 1936; New York: Harvest Books, 1955.

Ulam, Adam. *Ideologies and Illusions: Revolutionary Thought from Herzen to Solzhenitsyn.* Cambridge, MA: Harvard University Press, 1976.

See also:

Burks, Richard V. "A Conception of Ideology for Historians." *Journal of the History of Ideas* 10, no. 2 (April 1949): 183–98.

Roucek, Joseph S. "A History of the Concept of Ideology." *Journal of the History of Ideas* 5, no. 4 (October 1944): 479–88.

Thompson, Kenneth W. "Liberalism and Conservatism in American Statecraft." *Orbis* 2 (Winter 1959): 457–77.

PART THREE

On national power in general, see:

Baldwin, Hanson W. *The Price of Power.* New York: Harper and Brothers, 1948.

Beard, Charles A. *The Idea of National Interest.* New York: Macmillan, 1934.

Frankel, Joseph. *The Making of Foreign Policy.* London: Oxford University Press, 1963.

Hirschman, Nau. *National Power and the Structure of Foreign Trade.* Berkeley: University of California Press, 1981.

Strausz-Hupe, Robert. *The Balance of Tomorrow.* New York: G. P. Putnam's Sons, 1945.

Thompson, Kenneth W. "National Security in a Nuclear Age." *Social Research* 25 (Winter 1958): 439–48.

On nationalism, see:

Barker, Ernest. *Christianity and Nationality.* London: Oxford University Press, 1927.

Baron, Salo Wittmayer. *Modern Nationalism and Religion.* New York: Harper and Brothers, 1947.

Carr, Edward Hallett. *Nationalism and After.* New York: Macmillan, 1945.

Chadwick, H. Munro. *The Nationalities of Europe and the Growth of National Ideologies.* New York: Macmillan, 1946.

Coban, Alfred. *National Self-Determination,* rev. ed. Chicago: University of Chicago Press, 1948.

Deutsch, Karl W. *Nationalism and Socialism Communication.* New York: John Wiley and Sons, 1953.

____. *Nationalism and Its Alternatives.* New York: Alfred A. Knopf, 1969.

Friedmann, W. *The Crisis of the National State.* London: Macmillan, 1943.

Gooch, George P. *Nationalism.* New York: Harcourt, Brace, 1920.

Grodzins, Morton. *The Loyal and the Disloyal.* Chicago: University of Chicago Press, 1956.

Hayes, Carleton J. *The Historical Evolution of Modern Nationalism.* New York: R. R. Smith, 1931.

Hertz, Frederick. *Nationality in History and Politics.* New York: Oxford University Press, 1944.

Herz, John. *The Nation-State and the Crisis of World Politics.* New York: David McKay, 1976.

Hula, Erich. "National Self-Determination Reconsidered." *Social Research* 10, no. 1 (February 1943): 1–21.

____. *Nationalism and Internationalism.* Washington, DC: University Press of America, 1984.

Janowsky, Oscar I. *Nationalities and National Minorities.* New York: Macmillan, 1945.

Kohn, Hans. *The Idea of Nationalism.* New York: Macmillan Company, 1944, 1961.

Royal Institute of International Affairs. *Nationalism.* New York: Oxford University Press, 1946.

Shafer, Boyd C. *Faces of Nationalism: New Realities and Old Myths.* New York: Harcourt Brace Jovanovich, 1972.

Smith, Anthony D. *Theories of Nationalism.* New York: Harper and Row, 1971.

Sulzbach, Walter. *National Consciousness.* Washington, DC: American Council on Public Affairs, 1943.

West, Rebecca. *The Meaning of Treason.* New York: Viking Press, 1947.

Wirth, Louis. "Types of Nationalism." *The American Journal of Sociology* 41, no. 6 (May 1936): 723–37.

On the different elements of national power, see:

Allison, Graham, and Szanton, Peter. *Remaking Foreign Policy: The Organizational Connection.* New York: Basic Books, 1976.

Barker, Ernst. *National Character and the Factors of Its Formation.* London: Methuen, 1927.

Benedict, Ruth. *The Chrysanthemum and the Sword.* Boston: Houghton Mifflin, 1946.

Fairgrieve, James. *Geography and World Power,* 8th ed. London: University of London Press, 1941.

Ginsberg, Morris. *Reason and Unreason in Society.* Cambridge, MA: Harvard University Press, 1948, pp. 131–76.

Hartshorne, Richard. *The Nature of Geography.* Ann Arbor, MI: Edwards Brothers, 1946.

Hirschman, Albert O. *National Power and the Structure of Foreign Trade.* Berkeley: University of California Press, 1945.

Hume, David. "Of National Characters." *Essays, Moral, Political, and Literary,* Vol. 1. New edition. London: Longmans, Green, 1889.

Knorr, Klaus. *The Power of Nations.* New York: Basic Books, 1975.

Leith, C. K., Furness, J. W., and Lewis, Cleona. *World Minerals and World Peace.* Washington, DC: Brookings Institution, 1943.

Madariaga, Salvador. *Englishmen, Frenchmen, Spaniards,* 4th ed. London: Oxford University Press, 1937.

Mead, Margaret. "National Character." In *Anthropology Today,* A. L. Kroeber, ed. Chicago: University of Chicago Press, 1953.

Sprout, Harold, and Sprout, Margaret. *The Ecological Perspective on Human Affairs: with Special Reference to International Politics.* Princeton, NJ: Princeton University Press, 1965.

Thompson, Warren S., and Lewis, David T. *Population Problems,* 5th ed. New York: McGraw-Hill, 1965.

Whittlesey, Derwent. *The Earth and the State: A Study of Political Geography.* New York: Henry Holt, 1944.

Wriggins, W. Howard, and Guyot, James F. *Population, Politics, and the Future of Southern Asia.* New York and London: Columbia University Press, 1973.

On geopolitics, see:

Conant, Melvin, and Gold, Fern. *The Geopolitics of Energy.* Boulder, CO: Westview Press, 1978.

Mackinder, Sir Halford J. "The Geographical Pivot of History." *Geographical Journal* 23 (1904): 421–44.

____. *Democratic Ideals and Reality*. New York: Henry Holt, 1942.

Mattern, Johannes. *Geopolitik: Doctrine of National Self-Sufficiency and Empire*. Baltimore, MD: Johns Hopkins University Press, 1942.

Spykman, Nicholas J. *The Geography of the Peace*. New York: Harcourt, Brace, Company, 1944.

Strausz-Hupe, Robert. *Geopolitics*. New York: G. P. Putnam's Sons, 1942.

Weigert, Hans W. *German Geopolitics*. New York: Oxford University Press, 1941.

____. *Generals and Geographers*. New York: Oxford University Press, 1942.

PART FOUR

On the theory of the balance of power, see:

Carleton, William G. "Ideology of Balance of Power?" *Yale Review* 36, no. 4 (June 1947): 590–602.

Dehio, Ludwig. *The Precarious Balance*. New York: Alfred A. Knopf, 1962.

Elzbacher, O. "The Balance of Power in Europe." *The Nineteenth Century and After* 57 (May 1905): 787–804.

Gulick, Edward Vose. *Europe's Classical Balance of Power*. Ithaca, NY: Cornell University Press, 1955.

Hume, David. "Of the Balance of Power." *Essays Moral, Political, and Literary*, Vol. 1. New edition. London: Longmans, Green, 1889.

Liska, George. *Nations in Alliance: The Limits of Interdependence*. Baltimore, MD: Johns Hopkins University Press, 1962.

Newman, William J. *The Balance of Power in the Interwar Years, 1919–1939*. New York: Random House, 1968.

Phillimore, Sir Robert. *Commentaries upon International Law*, Vol. 1, 2nd ed. London: Butterworths, 1871.

Riker, William H. *The Theory of Political Coalitions*. New Haven, CT: Yale University Press, 1962.

Spykman, Nicholas. *America's Strategy in World Politics*. New York: Harcourt, Brace, 1942.

Tannenbaum, Frank. "The Balance of Power in Society." *Political Science Quarterly* 61, no. 4 (December 1946): 481–504.

Thompson, Kenneth W. "The Morality of Checks and Balances." In *The Search for Justice*, W. Lawson Taitte, ed. Dallas: University of Texas, 1983.

Toynbee, Arnold J. *A Study of History*, Vol. 3. New York: Oxford University Press, 1934; New York: Galaxy Books, 1962.

On the classic Indian theory of power politics and the balance of power, see:

Kautilya. *Arthasastra*. Translated by R. Shamasastry. Mysore: Wesleyan Mission Press, 1929.

Law, Narendra Nath. *Interstate Relations in Ancient India*. London: Luzac, 1920.

For the history of the balance of power, see:

Grant, A. J., and Temperley, Harold. *Europe in the Nineteenth and Twentieth Centuries (1789–1939)*. New York: Longmans, Green, 1940.

Hudson, G. F. *The Hard and Bitter Peace*. London: Pall Mall, 1966.

Langer, William L. *The Diplomacy of Imperialism.* New York: Alfred A. Knopf, 1935.

____. *European Alliances and Alignment, 1871–1890,* 2nd ed. New York: Alfred A. Knopf, 1950.

Petrie, Sir Charles. *Diplomatic History, 1713–1933.* London: Hollis and Carter, 1946.

Schmitt, Bernadotte E. *Triple Alliance and Triple Entente.* New York: Henry Holt, 1934.

Seton-Watson, Robert W. *Britain in Europe, 1789–1914.* New York: Macmillan, 1937.

Sontag, Raymond J. *European Diplomatic History, 1871–1932.* New York: Century, 1933.

Sorel, Albert. *Europe Under the Old Regime.* Los Angeles: Ward Ritchie Press, 1947; New York: Harper Torchbooks, 1964.

Temperley, Harold. *The Foreign Policy of Canning, 1822–1827: England, the Neo-Holy Alliance, and the New World.* London: G. Bell and Sons, 1925.

Vagts, Alfred. "The Balance of Power: Growth of an Idea." *World Politics* 1, no. 1 (October 1948): 82–101.

Webster, Charles K. *The Foreign Policy of Castlereagh, 1812–1815.* London: G. Bell and Sons, 1931.

Wolfers, Arnold. *Britain and France Between Two Wars.* New York: Harcourt, Brace, 1940.

PART FIVE

For the general problem of rules of conduct, see:

Timasheff, N. S. *An Introduction to the Sociology of Law.* Cambridge, MA: Harvard University Committee on Research in the Social Sciences, 1939.

On the problem of international morality, see:

Bennett, John C., ed. *Nuclear Weapons and the Conflict of Conscience.* New York: Charles Scribner's Sons, 1962.

Berger, Peter. *Pyramids of Sacrifice: Political Ethics and Social Change.* Garden City, NJ: Anchor Books, 1974.

Bosanquet, Bernard. *The Philosophical Theory of the State.* New York: Macmillan, 1899.

Cahn, Edmond. *The Moral Decision.* Bloomington, IN, and London: Indiana University Press, 1955.

____. *The Sense of Injustice.* Bloomington, IN, and London: Indiana University Press, 1975.

Canavan, Francis, ed. *The Ethical Dimension of Political Life.* Durham, NC: Duke University Press, 1983.

Carr, Edward Hallett. *Conditions of Peace.* New York: Macmillan, 1944.

Falk, Richard A. *Law, Morality and War in the Contemporary World.* New York: Praeger, 1963.

____. *Legal Order in a Violent World.* Princeton, NJ: Princeton University Press, 1968.

Freund, Paul A. *On Law and Justice.* Cambridge, MA: Harvard University Press, 1968.

Goulet, Denis, *A New Moral Order.* Ossining, NY: Orbis Books, 1974.

Hare, J. E., and Joynt, Carey B. *Ethics and International Affairs.* New York: St. Martin's Press, 1982.

Huizinga, J. H. "On the High Cost of International Moralizing." *The Fortnightly Review* 156, New Series (November 1944): 295–300.

Kennan, George F. "Morality, Politics and Foreign Policy." In *The Virginia Papers on the Presidency,* Kenneth W. Thompson, ed. Washington, DC: University Press of America, 1979, pp. 3–30.

Lindsay, A. D. *The Modern Democratic State*. New York: Oxford University Press, 1947; New York: Galaxy Books, 1962.

MacIntyre, Alasdair. *After Virtue*. Notre Dame, IN: University of Notre Dame Press, 1981.

May, Henry F. *The End of American Innocence*. Oxford and New York: Oxford University Press, 1959.

Morgenthau, Hans J., and Hein, David. *Essays on Lincoln's Faith and Politics*. Washington, DC: University Press of America, 1983.

Niebuhr, Reinhold. *Christianity and Power Politics*. New York: Charles Scribner's Sons, 1940.

–––. "Democracy as a Religion." *Christianity and Crisis* 7, no. 14 (August 1947): 1–2.

____. *Moral Man and Immoral Society: A Study in Ethics and Politics*. New York: Charles Scribner's Sons, 1932; New York: Scribner Library, 1960.

____. *Leaves from the Notebook of a Tamed Cynic*. Reprint. New York: Harper and Row, 1980.

Osgood, Robert E., and Tucker, Robert W. *Force: Order and Justice*. Baltimore, MD: Johns Hopkins University Press, 1967.

Petro, Nicolai N. *The Predicament of Human Rights*. Washington, DC: University Press of America, 1983.

Rajaee, Farhang. *Islamic Values and World View*. Washington, DC: University Press of America, 1983.

Ramsey, Paul. *War and the Christian Conscience*. Durham, NC: Duke University Press, 1961.

Rawls, John. *A Theory of Justice*. Cambridge, MA: Harvard University Press, 1971.

Thompson, J. W., and Padover, S. K. *Secret Diplomacy: A Record of Espionage and Double Dealings, 1500–1815*. London: Jarrolds, 1937.

Thompson, Kenneth W. *Christian Ethics and the Dilemmas of Foreign Policy*. Durham, NC: Duke University Press, 1959; Washington, DC: University Press of America, 1983.

____. *The Moral Issue in Statecraft*. Baton Rouge, CA: Louisiana State University Press, 1966.

____. "New Reflections on Ethics and Foreign Policy." *The Journal of Politics* 40, no. 4 (November 1978): 984–1010.

____. *The Moral Imperatives of Human Rights*. Washington, DC: University Press of America, 1980.

____. *Morality and Foreign Policy*. Baton Rouge, CA, and London: Louisiana State University Press, 1980.

____. *Political Traditions and Contemporary Problems*. Washington, DC: University Press of America, 1982.

____. *Diplomacy and Values*. Washington, DC: University Press of America, 1984.

____. *Ethics in Foreign Policy*. Rutgers, NJ: Transaction Books, 1984.

____. *Moralism and Morality*. Washington, DC: University Press of America, 1984.

____. *Traditions and Values*. Washington, DC: University Press of America, 1984.

Weldon, T. D. *States and Morals*. New York: McGraw-Hill, 1947.

See also the books by Carr, Morgenthau, and Thompson cited under Part One.

On Nationalistic universalism, consult the books in Part Three under nationalism.

On world public opinion, see:

Dicey, A. V. *Lectures on the Relation Between Law and Public Opinion in England During the Nineteenth Century*. London: Macmillan, 1914.

Ferrero, Guglielmo. *The Unity of the World*. London: Jonathan Cape, 1931.

Lasswell, Harold D. *World Politics and Personal Insecurity*. New York: Whittlesey House, 1935.

Lippmann, Walter. *Public Opinion*. New York: Macmillan, 1922, 1960.

Lowell, A. Lawrence. *Public Opinion and Public Government*. New York: Longmans, Green, 1914.

____. *Public Opinion in War and Peace*. Cambridge, MA: Harvard University Press, 1926.

Smith, Charles W. *Public Opinion in a Democracy*. New York: Prentice Hall, 1939.

Stratton, George Malcomb. *Social Psychology of International Conduct*. New York: D. Appleton, 1929.

PART SIX

For the general problems of international law, see:

Bailey, Sydney D. *Prohibitions and Restraints in War*. London and New York: Oxford University Press, 1972.

Bentwich, Norman. *International Law*. London: Royal Institute of International Affairs, 1945.

Brierly, J. L. *The Outlook for International Law*. Oxford: Clarendon Press, 1944.

____. *The Law of Nations*, 4th ed. Oxford: Clarendon Press, 1949.

____. *The Basis of Obligation in International Law*. London: Oxford University Press, 1958.

Coll, Alberto R. *The Western Heritage and American Values*. Washington, DC: University Press of America, 1982.

Corbett, Percy E. *Law and Society in the Relations of States*. New York: Harcourt, Brace, 1951.

____. *Law in Diplomacy*. Princeton, NJ: Princeton University Press, 1959.

Dickinson, Edwin D. *What Is Wrong with International Law?* Berkeley, CA: James J. Gillick, 1947.

Franck, Thomas M. *The Structure of Impartiality*. New York: Macmillan, 1968.

Friedmann, Wolfgang. *The Changing Structure of International Law*. New York: Columbia University Press, 1964.

Henkin, Louis. *How Nations Behave*. New York: Praeger, 1968.

Higham, Robin, ed. *Intervention or Abstention*. Lexington, KY: University Press of Kentucky, 1975.

Jessup, Philip C. *A Modern Law of Nations*. New York: Macmillan, 1948.

Kaplan, Morton A., and Katzenbach, Nicholas de B. *The Political Foundation of International Law*. New York: John Wiley and Sons, 1961.

Keeton, George W., and Schwarzenberger, Georg. *Making International Law Work*, 2nd ed. London: Stevens and Sons, 1946.

Kelsen, Hans. *Principles of International Law*. New York: Rinehart, Inc., 1952.

Lauterpacht, H. *The Function of Law in the International Community*. Oxford: Clarendon Press, 1933.

Levi, Werner. *Law and Politics in the International Society*. Beverly Hills, CA: Sage, 1976.

Moore, John Bassett. *International Law and Some Current Illusions*. New York: Macmillan, 1924.

Morgenthau, Hans J. "Positivism, Functionalism, and International Law." *American Journal of International Law* 34 (April 1940): 260–84.

O'Brien, William V. *The Conduct of Just and Limited War*. New York: Praeger, 1981.

Royal Institute of International Affairs. *International Sanctions*. London, New York, Toronto: Oxford University Press, 1938.

Schwarzenberger, Georg. *International Law and Order*. New York: Praeger, 1971.

Starke, J. G. *Introduction to International Law*. London: Butterworths, 1947.

Stone, Julius. *Legal Controls of International Conflict*. New York: Rinehart, 1954.

____. *Aggression and World Order*. Berkeley and Los Angeles: University of California Press, 1958.

Visscher, Charles de. *Theory and Reality in Public International Law*. Princeton, NJ: Princeton University Press, 1957.

Walzer, Michael. *Just and Unjust Wars*. New York: Basic Books, 1977.

Williams, Sir John Fischer. *Chapters on Current International Law and the League of Nations*. New York: Longmans, Green, 1929.

____. *Aspects of Modern International Law*. New York: Oxford University Press, 1939.

On special problems connected with the Covenant of the League of Nations and the Charter of the United Nations, see the books cited under Part Eight.

On sovereignty, see:

Chace, James. *Solvency: The Price of Survival*. New York: Random House, 1981.

Corwin, Edward S. *The President: Office and Powers*, 2nd ed. New York: New York University Press, 1941.

____. *Total War and the Constitution*. New York: Alfred A. Knopf, 1947.

Dickinson, Edwin D. *The Equality of States in International Law*. Cambridge, MA: Harvard University Press, 1920.

____. "A Working Theory of Sovereignty." *Political Science Quarterly* 42, no. 4 (December 1927): 524–48; 43, no. 1 (March 1928): 1–31.

Duguit, Leon. *Law in the Modern State*. New York: B. W. Huebsch, 1919.

Fromkin, David. *The Independence of Nations*. New York: Praeger, 1981.

Keeton, George W. *National Sovereignty and International Order*. London: Peace Book, 1939.

Kelsen, Hans. *Das Problem der Souveranität und die Theorie des Völkerrechts*. Tübingen: J.C.B. Mohr, 1920.

____. *General Theory of Law and State*. Cambridge, MA: Harvard University Press, 1945.

Koo, Wellington, Jr. *Voting Procedures in International Organizations*. New York: Columbia University Press, 1947.

Krabbe, H. *The Modern Idea of the State*. New York: D. Appleton, 1922.

Laski, Harold J. *Studies in the Problem of Sovereignty*. New Haven, CT: Yale University Press, 1917.

____. *Authority in the Modern State*. New Haven, CT: Yale University Press, 1919.

____. *The Foundations of Sovereignty and Other Essays*. London: G. Allen and Unwin, 1921.

Mattern, Johannes. *Concepts of State, Sovereignty and International Law*. Baltimore, MD: Johns Hopkins University Press, 1928.

Merriman, Charles E. *History of the Theory of Sovereignty Since Rousseau*. New York: Columbia University Press, 1900.

Riches, Cromwell A. *Majority Rule in International Organizations*. Baltimore, MD: Johns Hopkins University Press, 1940.

Vernon, Raymond. *Sovereignty at Bay*. New York: Basic Books, 1971.

Watkins, Frederick M. *The State as a Concept of a Political Science*. New York and London: Harper and Brothers, 1934.

PART SEVEN

On the general nature of contemporary world politics, see:

Ambrose, Stephen E. *Rise to Globalism,* 3rd ed. New York: Penguin Books, 1983.

Aron, Raymond. *The Century of Total War.* New York: Doubleday, 1954; Boston: Beacon Press, 1955.

____. *Peace and War.* Garden City, NJ: Doubleday, 1966.

____. *The Imperial Republic: The United States and the World.* Englewood Cliffs, NJ: Prentice Hall, 1974.

Banisadr, Abolhassan. *Islamic Government.* Translated by Mohammad R. Ghanoon-parvar. Lexington, MA: Mazda, 1981.

Beloff, Max. *New Dimensions in Foreign Policy.* New York: Macmillan, 1961.

Beres, Louis Rene. *Apocalypse: Nuclear Catastrophe in World Politics.* Chicago: University of Chicago Press, 1980.

Blake, David, and Walters, Robert. *The Politics of Global Economic Relations.* Englewood Cliffs, NJ: Prentice Hall, 1976.

Bozeman, Adda B. *Conflict in Africa.* Princeton, NJ: Princeton University Press, 1976.

Braestrup, Peter. *Vietnam as History.* Washington, DC: University Press of America, 1984.

Brown, Seyom. *New Forces in World Politics.* Washington, DC: Brookings Institution, 1974.

Calvocoressi, Peter. *World Order and the New States.* New York: Praeger, 1962.

____. *World Politics Since 1945,* 4th ed. London and New York: Longman, 1982.

Carr, Edward Hallett. *Conditions of Peace.* New York: Macmillan, 1944.

Chicago Council on Foreign Relations. *Detente and the Atlantic Nations.* Chicago Council on Foreign Relations, 1977.

Dunn, Frederick S. *War and the Minds of Men.* New York: Harper and Brothers, 1950.

Ellis, John. *The Social History of the Machine Gun.* New York: Pantheon Books, 1976.

Fischer, Eric. *The Passing of the European Age.* Cambridge, MA: Harvard University Press, 1943.

Fox, William T. R. *The Super-Powers.* New York: Harcourt, Brace, 1944.

Franck, Thomas M., and Weisband, Edward. *World Politics: Verbal Strategy Among the Superpowers.* New York: Oxford University Press, 1971.

Fromm, Erich. *May Man Prevail?* Garden City, NJ: Doubleday, 1961; New York: Anchor Books, 1961.

George, Alexander L., and Smoke, Richard. *Deterrence in American Foreign Policy: Theory and Practice.* New York: Columbia University Press, 1974.

Gilpin, Robert. *War and Change in World Politics.* Cambridge, UK: Cambridge University Press, 1981.

Gompert, David C., Mandelbaum, Michael, Garwin, Richard L., and Barton, John. *Nuclear Weapons and World Politics: Alternatives for the Future.* New York: McGraw-Hill, 1977.

Graebner, Norman A. *Cold War Diplomacy,* 2nd ed. New York: D. Van Nostrand, 1977.

____. *The Age of Global Power.* New York: John Wiley and Sons, 1979.

Harkavy, Robert. *The Arms Trade and International Systems.* Cambridge, MA: Ballinger, 1975.

Herz, John. *International Politics in the Atomic Age.* New York: Columbia University Press, 1959.

Hoffmann, Stanley. *The State of War.* New York: Praeger, 1966.

____. *Primacy or World Order.* New York: McGraw-Hill, 1978.

Jaspers, Karl. *The Future of Mankind.* Chicago: University of Chicago Press, 1961; Phoenix: Phoenix Books, 1963.

Jensen, Lloyd. *Return from the Nuclear Brink: National Interest and the Nuclear Nonproliferation Treaty.* Lexington, MA: Lexington Books, 1974.

Johnson, Harry G. *Technology and Economic Interdependence.* New York: St. Martin's Press, 1976.

Keegan, John. *The Face of Battle.* New York: Viking Press, 1976.

Kemp, Geoffrey, Pfalzgraff, Robert L., Jr., and Ra'anan, Uri. *The Superpowers in a Multinuclear World.* Lexington, MA: Lexington Books, 1974.

____, eds. *The Other Arms Race: New Technologies and Non-Nuclear Conflict.* Lexington, MA: Lexington Books, 1975.

Kennan, George F. *American Diplomacy, 1900–1950.* Chicago: University of Chicago Press, 1951; New York: Mentor Books, 1952.

Kinter, William R., and Sicherman, Harvey. *Technology and International Politics: The Crisis of Wishing.* Lexington, MA: Lexington Books, 1975.

Kissinger, Henry A. *Nuclear Weapons and Foreign Policy.* New York: Harper and Brothers, 1957; Garden City: Anchor Books, 1958.

LaFeber, Walter. *America, Russia and the Cold War, 1945–73,* 3rd ed. New York and London: John Wiley and Sons, 1976.

Lippmann, Walter. *U.S. Foreign Policy.* Boston: Little, Brown, 1943.

____. *U.S. War Aims.* Boston: Little, Brown, 1944.

____. *The Cold War.* New York: Harper and Brothers, 1947.

____. *Isolation and Alliances.* Boston: Little, Brown, 1952.

Martin, Laurence. *Arms and Strategy: The World Power Structure Today.* New York: David McKay, 1973.

Melanson, Richard. *Writing History and Making Policy.* Washington, DC: University Press of America, 1983.

Mikdashi, Zuhayr. *International Politics of National Resources.* Ithaca, NY, and London: Cornell University Press, 1976.

Morgenthau, Hans J. *In Defense of the National Interest.* New York: Alfred A. Knopf, 1960; Washington, DC: University Press of America, 1982.

____. *A New Foreign Policy for the United States.* New York: Praeger, 1969.

Morse, Edward L. *Modernization and the Transformation of International Relations.* New York: Free Press, 1976.

Nau Henry R. *National Politics and International Technology: Nuclear Reactor Development in Western Europe.* Baltimore, MD: Johns Hopkins University Press, 1974.

Niebuhr, Reinhold. *The Structure of Nations and Empires.* New York: Charles Scribner's Sons, 1959.

Osgood, Robert E., et al. *America and the World: From the Truman Doctrine to Vietnam.* Baltimore, MD: Johns Hopkins University Press, 1970.

Osgood, Robert E. *Limited War: The Challenge to American Strategy.* Chicago: University of Chicago Press, 1957.

Piscatori, James P. *Islam in the Political Process.* Cambridge, MA: Cambridge University Press, 1983.

Ramazani, R. K. *The United States and Iran.* New York: Praeger, 1982.

Schachter, Oscar. *Sharing the World's Resources.* New York: Columbia University Press, 1976.

Schulzinger, Robert D. *American Diplomacy in the Twentieth Century.* New York and Oxford: Oxford University Press, 1984.

Scott, Andrew M. *The Revolution in Statecraft.* New York: Random House, 1965.

Skolnikoff, Eugene B. *The International Imperatives of Technology.* Berkeley, CA: University of California Press, 1972.

Thompson, Kenneth W. *Understanding World Politics*. Notre Dame, IN: University of Notre Dame Press, 1975.

____. *Interpreters and Critics of the Cold War*. Washington, DC: University Press of America, 1978.

Ulam, Adam B. *The Rivals*. London: Allen Lane, 1973.

____. *Expansion and Coexistence: Soviet Foreign Policy*, 2nd ed. New York: Praeger, 1974.

____. *Dangerous Relations: The Soviet Union in World Politics, 1970–82*. New York and Oxford: Oxford University Press, 1983.

Vernon, Raymond. *Storm over the Multinationals: The Real Issues*. Cambridge, MA: Harvard University Press, 1977.

Viner, Jacob. "The Implications of the Atomic Bomb for International Relations." *Proceedings of the American Philosophical Society* 90, no. 1 (1946): 53–58.

Wall, David. *The Charity of Nations: The Political Economy of Foreign Aid*. New York: Basic Books, 1973.

Wheeler-Bennett, John, and Nicholls, Anthony. *The Semblance of Peace: The Political Settlement After the Second World War*. New York: St. Martin's Press, 1972.

On total war, see:

Aron, Raymond. *On War*. New York: W. W. Norton, 1968.

Brodie, Bernard. *See Power in the Machine Age*. Princeton, NJ: Princeton University Press. 1941.

____, ed. *The Absolute Weapon: Atomic Power and World Order*. New York: Harcourt, Brace, 1946.

____. *Escalation and the Nuclear Option*. Princeton, NJ: Princeton University Press, 1966.

____. *War and Politics*. New York: Macmillan, 1973.

Brown, Neville. *Nuclear War: The Impending Strategic Deadlock*. New York: Praeger, 1965.

Butterfield, Herbert. *International Conflict in the Twentieth Century*. New York: Harper and Brothers, 1960.

Clarkson, Jesse, and Cochran, Thomas C., eds. *War as a Social Institution*. New York: Columbia University Press, 1941.

Earle, Edward Mead, ed. *Makers of Modern Strategy*. Princeton, NJ: Princeton University Press, 1944.

Ferrero, Guglielmo. *Peace and War*. London: Macmillan, 1933.

Hart, B. H. Liddell. *The Revolution in Warfare*. London: Faber and Faber, 1946.

Howard, Michael. *The Causes of War*. Cambridge, MA: Harvard University Press, 1983.

Kahn, Herman. *On Thermonuclear War*. Princeton, NJ: Princeton University Press, 1960.

____. *Thinking About the Unthinkable*. New York: Horizon Press, 1962.

Mumford, Lewis. *Technics and Civilization*. New York: Harcourt, Brace, 1946; San Francisco: Harbinger Books, 1963.

Ogburn, William Fielding, ed. *Technology and International Relations*. Chicago: University of Chicago Press, 1949.

Oman, Sir Charles. *A History of the Art of War in the Sixteenth Century*. New York: E. P. Dutton, 1937.

Schelling, Thomas C. *Arms and Influence*. New Haven, CT, and London: Yale University Press, 1966.

Schultz, Theodore W. "Changes in the Economic Structure Affecting American Agriculture." *Journal of Farm Economics* 28, no. 1 (February 1946): 15–27.

Spaulding, O. L., Nickerson, Hoffman, and Wright, J. W. *Warfare*. New York: Harcourt, Brace, 1925.

Speier, Hans. *Social Order and the Risks of War,* Part III. New York: George W. Stewart, 1952.

Speier, Hans, and Kahler, Alfred, eds. *War in Our Time.* New York: W. W. Norton, 1939.

Tucker, Robert W. *Nation or Empire: The Debate over American Foreign Policy.* Baltimore, MD: Johns Hopkins University Press, 1968.

Vagts, Alfred. *A History of Militarism.* New York: W. W. Norton, 1937.

Wohlstetter, Albert. "Technology, Prediction, and Disorder." *Vanderbilt Law Review* 17, no. 1 (December 1963): 1–14.

Woolsey, R. James. *Nuclear Arms.* San Francisco, CA: Institute for Contemporary Studies, 1984.

PART EIGHT

On the history of peace plans, see:

Falk, Richard A. *A Study of Further Worlds.* New York: Free Press, 1975.

Hemleben, Sylvester John. *Plans for World Peace Through Six Centuries.* Chicago: University of Chicago Press, 1945.

Lance, Christian. *Histoire de l'Internationalisme.* New York: G. P. Putnam's Sons, 1919.

Marriott, J. A. R. *Commonwealth or Anarchy? A Survey of Projects of Peace from the Sixteenth to the Twentieth Century.* New York: Columbia University Press, 1939.

Paullin, Theodore. *Comparative Peace Plans.* Philadelphia: Pacifist Research Bureau, 1943.

Pragellis, Stanley, ed. "The Quest for Political Unity in World History." *Annual Report of the American Historical Association, 1942,* Vol. 3. United States Government Printing Office, 1944.

Souleyman, Elizabeth V. *The Vision of World Peace in Seventeenth- and Eighteenth-Century France.* New York: G. P. Putnam's Sons, 1941.

Wynner, Edith, and Lloyd, Georgia. *Searchlights on Peace Plans.* New York: E. P. Dutton, 1944.

On disarmament, see:

Barnet, Richard J. *Who Wants Disarmament?* Boston: Beacon Press, 1960.

Beckhoefer, Bernard J. *Postwar Negotiations for Arms Control.* Washington, DC: Brookings Institution, 1961.

Blackett, P.M.S. *Studies of War.* New York: Hill and Wang, 1962.

Brennan, Donald G., ed. *Arms Control, Disarmament, and National Security.* New York: George Braziller, 1961.

Buell, Raymond Leslie. *The Washington Conference.* New York: D. Appleton, 1922.

Bull, Hedley. *The Control of the Arms Race.* New York: Praeger, 1961.

Burton, John W. *Peace Theory: Precondition of Disarmament.* New York: Alfred A. Knopf, 1962.

Dougherty, James E. *How to Think About Arms Control and Disarmament.* New York: Cane, Russak, 1973.

Epstein, William. *Disarmament: 25 Years of Effort.* Toronto: Canadian Institute of International Affairs, 1971.

____. *The Last Chance: Nuclear Proliferation and Arms Control.* New York: Free Press, 1976.

Fallows, James. *National Defense.* New York: Random House/Vintage Books, 1982.

Forbes, Henry W. *The Strategy of Disarmament.* Washington, DC: Public Affairs Press, 1962.

Gray, Colin S. *The Soviet-American Arms Race.* Lexington, MA: Lexington Books, 1976.

Griswold, A. Whitney. *The Far Eastern Policy of the United States.* New York: Harcourt, Brace, 1938; New Haven, CT: Yale University Press, 1964.

Hadley, Arthur T. *The Nation's Safety and Arms Control.* New York: Viking Press, 1961.

Harvard Nuclear Study Group. *Living with Nuclear Weapons.* New York: Bantam Books, 1983.

Huntington, Samuel P. "Arms Races: Prerequisites and Results." *Public Policy,* Vol. 8. Cambridge: Harvard Graduate School of Public Administration, 1958, pp. 41–86.

Kennan, George F. *The Nuclear Delusion.* New York: Pantheon Books, 1982.

Levine, Robert A. *The Arms Debate.* Cambridge, MA: Harvard University Press, 1963.

Melman, Seymour, ed. *Inspection for Disarmament.* New York: Columbia University Press, 1958.

Morgan, Laura Puffer. *The Problem of Disarmament.* New York: Commission to Study the Organization of Peace, 1947.

Myrdal, Alva. *The Game of Disarmament: How the United States and Russia Run the Arms Race.* New York: Pantheon Books, 1977.

Nogee, Joseph L. *Soviet Policy Toward International Control of Atomic Energy.* Notre Dame, IN: University of Notre Dame Press, 1961.

Possony, Stefan T. "No Peace Without Arms." *The Review of Politics* 6, no. 2 (April 1944): 216–27.

Schelling, Thomas C., and Halperin, Morton H. *Strategy and Arms Control.* New York: Twentieth Century Fund, 1961.

Shils, Edward A. *Atomic Bombs in World Politics.* London: National Peace Council, 1948.

Singer, J. David. *Deterrence, Arms Control, and Disarmament: Toward a Synthesis in National Security Policy.* Columbus: Ohio State University Press, 1962.

Smith, Gerard. *Double-Talk: The Story of SALT I.* Garden City, NJ: Doubleday, 1980.

Spainer, John W., and Nogee, Joseph L. *The Politics of Disarmament: A Study of Soviet-American Gamesmanship.* New York: Praeger, 1962.

Stone, Jeremy J. *Strategic Persuasion: Arms Limitation Through Dialogue.* New York: Columbia University Press, 1967.

Tate, Merze. *The Disarmament Illusion.* New York: Macmillan, 1942.

____. *The United States and Armaments.* Cambridge, MA: Harvard University Press, 1948.

Thompson, Kenneth W. *The President and the Public Philosophy.* Baton Rogue, LA, and London: Louisiana State University Press, 1981.

Wheeler-Bennett, John. *The Pipe-Dream of Peace: The Story of the Collapse of Disarmament.* New York: William Morrow, 1935.

Wieseltier, Leon. *Nuclear War, Nuclear Peace.* New York: Holt, Rinehart and Winston, 1983.

Wolfers, Arnold, and Osgood, Robert, eds. *The United States in a Disarmed World.* Baltimore, MD: Johns Hopkins University Press, 1966.

Woodward, E. L. *Some Political Consequences of the Atomic Bomb.* New York: Oxford University Press, 1946.

Wright, Sir Michael. *Disarm and Verify.* New York: Praeger, 1964.

On security, see:

Beaton, Leonard. *The Reform of Power: A Proposal for an International Security System.* New York: Viking Press, 1972.

Brown, Harold. *National Security.* Boulder, CO: Westview Press, 1983.

Gaddis, John Lewis. *Strategies of Containment.* New York and Oxford: Oxford University Press, 1982.

Halle, Louis J. *The Elements of International Strategy*. Washington, DC: University Press of America, 1984.

Jessup, Philip C. *International Security*. New York: Council on Foreign Relations, 1935.

Mitrany, David. *The Problem of International Sanctions*. New York: Oxford University Press, 1925.

Royal Institute of International Affairs. *International Sanctions*. London: Oxford University Press, 1938.

Thompson, Kenneth W. "Collective Security." *International Encyclopedia of the Social Sciences*. New York: Macmillan/Free Press, 1968, pp. 565–67.

Wild, Payson S. *Sanctions and Treaty Enforcement*. Cambridge, MA: Harvard University Press, 1934.

On judicial settlement, see:

Kelsen, Hans. *Peace Through Law*. Chapel Hill, NC: University of North Carolina Press, 1944.

Lauterpacht, H. *The Function of Law in the International Community*. Oxford: Clarendon Press, 1933.

Lissitzyn, Oliver J. *The International Court of Justice*. New York: Carnegie Endowment for International Peace, 1951.

Morgenthau, Hans J. *La notion du "politique" et la theorie des differents internationaux*. Paris: Librairie du Recueil Sirey, 1933.

Rosenne, Shabtai. *The International Court of Justice*. Leyden: Sijthoff, 1957.

For peaceful change, see in addition the titles under international government:

Bloomfield, Lincoln P. *Evolution or Revolution? The United Nations and the Problem of Peaceful Territorial Change*. Cambridge, MA: Harvard University Press, 1957.

Cruttwell, C.R.M.F. *A History of Peaceful Change in the Modern World*. New York: Oxford University Press, 1937.

Dunn, Frederick S. *Peaceful Change*. New York: Council on Foreign Relations, 1937.

On international government in general, see:

Barker, Ernest. *The Confederation of Nations*. Oxford: Clarendon Press, 1918.

Briggs, Herbert W. "Power Politics and International Organization." *American Journal of International Law* 39, no. 4 (October 1945): 664–79.

Corbett, Percy E. *Post-War Worlds*. Los Angeles: Institute of Pacific Relations, 1942.

Davis, Harriet Eager, ed. *Pioneers in World Order*. New York: Columbia University Press, 1944.

Dell, Robert. *The Geneva Racket, 1920–1939*. London: Robert Hale, 1940.

Freeman, Harrop A. *Coercion of States in International Organizations*. Philadelphia: Pacifist Research Bureau, 1944.

Freeman, Harrop A., and Paullin, Theodore. *Coercion of States in Federal Unions*. Philadelphia: Pacifist Research Bureau, 1934.

Hankey, Lord Maurice P. *Diplomacy by Conference*. New York: G. P. Putnam's Sons, 1946.

Kissinger, Henry A. *A World Restored: Castlereagh, Metternich, and the Problem of Peace, 1812–22*. Boston: Houghton Mifflin, 1957.

Levi, Werner. *Fundamentals of World Organization*. Minneapolis: University of Minnesota Press, 1950.

McCallum, R. B. *Public Opinion and the Last Peace.* New York: Oxford University Press, 1944.

Mangone, Gerard J. *A Short History of International Organization.* New York: McGraw-Hill, 1954.

Nicolson, Harold. *The Congress of Vienna: A Study in Allied Unity, 1812–1822.* New York: Harcourt, Brace, 1946; London: Constable, 1946; Rochester, NY: Compass Books, 1961; New York: Harcourt Brace Jovanovich, 1970 (paperback), 1974 (hardcover).

Nys, M. Ernest. "Le Concert Européen et la notion du droit international." *Revue de droit international,* Deuxieme Serie, vol. 1 (1899): 273–313.

Oppenheim, L. *The League of Nations and Its Problems.* London: Longmans, Green, 1919.

Phillips, Walter Alison. *The Confederation of Europe.* London: Longmans, Green, 1914.

Ray, Jean. *Commentaire du Pacte de la Societe des Nations.* Paris: Recueil Sirey, 1930.

Schenk, H. G. *The Aftermath of the Napoleonic Years: The Concert of Europe—An Experiment.* New York: Oxford University Press, 1948.

Thompson, Kenneth W. *Institutions for Projecting American Values Abroad.* Washington, DC: University Press of America, 1983.

Walters, F.P.A. *A History of the League of Nations.* 2 vols. New York: Oxford University Press, 1952.

World Organization: A Balance Sheet of the First Great Experiment. Washington, DC: American Council on Public Affairs, 1942.

Zimmern, Sir Alfred E. *The League of Nations and the Rule of Law.* New York: Macmillan, 1939.

See also the books by Temperley, Webster, and Wolfers, cited under Part Four.

On the United Nations, see:

Alker, Chadwick F., and Russett, Bruce M. *World Politics in the General Assembly.* New Haven, CT: Yale University Press, 1965.

Bailey, Sidney D. *The General Assembly of the U.N.: A Study of Procedure and Practice.* New York: Praeger, 1960.

Bentwich, Norman, and Martin, Andrew. *A Commentary on the Charter of the United Nations.* London: Routledge and Kegan Paul, 1950.

Bloomfield, Lincoln P. *Evolution or Revolution?* Cambridge, MA: Harvard University Press, 1957.

____. *The U.N. and U.S. Foreign Policy.* Boston: Little, Brown, 1960.

Brierly, J. L. *The Covenant and the Charter.* Cambridge, UK: Cambridge University Press, 1947.

Claude, Inis L. *Swords into Plowshares,* 3rd ed. New York: Random House, 1964.

Cohen, Benjamin V. *The U.N.: Constitutional Developments, Growth, and Possibilities.* Cambridge, MA: Harvard University Press, 1961.

Cox, Robert W., and Jacobson, Harold K. *The Anatomy of Influence.* New Haven, CT, and London: Yale University Press, 1973.

Feller, A. H. *United Nations and World Community.* Boston: Little, Brown, 1952.

Goodrich, Leland M. *The United Nations.* New York: Thomas Y. Crowell, 1959.

____. *The United Nations in a Changing World.* New York: Columbia University Press, 1974.

Gross, Ernest A. *The U.N.: Structure for Peace.* New York: Harper and Row, 1962.

Hasluck, Paul. *Workshop of Security.* Melbourne: F. W. Chesire, 1948.

Haviland, H. Field, Jr. *The Political Role of the General Assembly.* New York: Carnegie Endowment for International Peace, 1951.

Hiscocks, Richard. *The Security Council: A Study in Adolescence.* New York: Free Press, 1974.

Hovet, Thomas, Jr. *Bloc Politics in the United Nations.* Cambridge, MA: Harvard University Press, 1960.

Jacobson, Harold Karan. "The Changing United Nations." In *Foreign Policy in the Sixties: The Issues and Instruments*, Roger Hilsman and Robert Good Baltimore, eds. Baltimore, MD: Johns Hopkins University Press, 1965.

Kelsen, Hans. *The Law of the United Nations*. New York: Praeger, 1950.

McDermott, Geoffrey. *The New Diplomacy and Its Apparatus*. London: Plume Press/Ward Lock, 1973.

Miller, Linda B. *World Order and Local Disorder: The United Nations and International Conflict*. Princeton, NJ: Princeton University Press, 1967.

Morgenthau, Hans J., ed. *Peace, Security, and the United Nations*. Chicago: University of Chicago Press, 1946.

Nicholas, Herbert. *The United Nations as a Political Institution*. New York: Oxford University Press, 1959.

Ross, Alf. *The United Nations: Peace and Progress*. Totowa, NJ: Bedminster Press, 1966.

Stoessinger, John. *The United Nations and the Superpowers*. New York: Random House, 1965.

Thompson, Kenneth W. "Collective Security Reexamined." *The American Political Science Review* 47 (September 1953): 753–72.

____. *Foreign Assistance*. Notre Dame, IN: University of Notre Dame Press, 1972; Washington, DC: University Press of America, 1983.

Wainhouse, David W. *Remnants of Empire: The United Nations and the End of Colonialism*. New York: Harper and Row, 1964.

PART NINE

On the problem of the world state, see:

Bibo, Istvan. *The Paralysis of International Institutions and the Remedies*. New York: Halsted Press, 1976.

Brinton, Crane. *From Many One: The Process of Political Integration: The Problem of World Government*. Cambridge, MA: Harvard University Press, 1948.

Ewing, Alfred C. *The Individual, the State, and World Government*. New York: Macmillan, 1947.

Hammond, Mason. *City-State and World State in Greek and Roman Political Thought Until Augustus*. Cambridge, MA: Harvard University Press, 1951.

Ionescu, Ghota, ed. *Between Sovereignty and Integration*. New York: Halsted Press, 1974.

Klein, Robert A. *Sovereign Equality Among States: The History of an Idea*. Toronto: University of Toronto Press, 1974.

Lewis, Edward R. "Are We Ready for a World State?" *The Yale Review* 35, no. 3 (March 1946): 491–501.

Mangone, Gerald J. *The Idea and Practice of World Government*. New York: Columbia University Press, 1951.

Marriott, T.A.R. *Federalism and the Problem of the Small State*. London: G. Allen and Unwin, 1943.

Martin, William. *A History of Switzerland*. London: Grant Richards, 1931.

Meyer, Cord. *Peace or Anarchy*. Boston: Little, Brown, 1947.

Näf, Werner. *Die Schweiz in Europa*. Bern: Herbert Lang, 1938.

Niebuhr, Reinhold. "The Illusion of World Government." *Foreign Affairs* 27, no. 3 (April 1947): 379–88.

Pelcovits, N. A. "World Government Now?" *Harper's* 193, no. 1156 (November 1946): 396–403.

Rappard, William E. *Cinq siècles de sécurité collective, 1291–1798.* Paris: Recueil Sirey, 1945.

Reves, Emery. *The Anatomy of Peace.* New York: Harper and Brother, 1946; Rochester, NY: Compass Books, 1963.

Rider, Fremont. *The Great Dilemma of World Organization.* New York: Reynal and Hitchcock, 1946.

Schuman, Frederick L. *The Commonwealth of Man.* New York: Alfred A. Knopf, 1952.

Sewell, James P. *UNESCO and World Politics: Engaging in International Relations.* Princeton, NJ: Princeton University Press, 1975.

On the problem of the world community, see:

Beloff, Max. "The 'Federal Solution' in Its Application to Europe, Asia, and Africa." *Political Studies* 1, no. 2 (June 1953): 114–31.

Buchan, Alastair. *NATO in the 1960s.* New York: Praeger, 1960.

———. *Europe's Futures, Europe's Choices.* New York: Columbia University Press, 1969.

Camps, Miriam. *European Unification in the Sixties.* New York: McGraw-Hill, 1966.

Denian, J. F. *The Common Market.* London: Barrie and Rockliff with Pall Mall Press, 1960.

Freeman, Harrop A., and Paullin, Theodore. *Road to Peace: A Study in Functional International Organization.* Ithaca, NY: Pacifist Research Bureau, 1947.

Haas, Ernest B. *The Uniting of Europe.* Stanford, CA: Stanford University Press, 1958.

Hallstein, Walter. *United Europe: Challenge and Opportunity.* Cambridge, MA: Harvard University Press, 1952.

Huxley, Julian. *UNESCO.* Washington, DC: Public Affairs Press, 1947.

James, William. *A Moral Equivalent for War.* New York: Carnegie Endowment for International Peace, 1926.

Kitzinger, U. W. *The Politics and Economics of European Integration.* New York: Praeger, 1963.

Lindberg, Leon N. *The Political Dynamics of European Economics Integration.* Stanford, CA: Stanford University Press, 1963.

Liska, George. *The New Statecraft: Foreign Aid in American Foreign Policy.* Chicago: University of Chicago Press, 1960.

———. *Europe Ascendant: The International Politics of Unification.* Baltimore, MD: Johns Hopkins University Press, 1964.

McMurry, Ruth Emily, and Lee, Muna. *The Cultural Approach: Another Way in International Relations.* Chapel Hill, NC: University of North Carolina Press, 1947.

Mason, Edward S. *Foreign Aid and Foreign Policy.* New York: Harper and Row, 1964; paperbound, 1964.

Mitrany, David. *A Working Peace System.* Chicago: Quadrangle Books, 1966.

Murphy, Gardner, ed. *The Moral Implications of Loyalty to the United Nations.* New Haven, CT: Edward W. Hazen Foundation, 1952.

Niebuhr, Reinhold. *Human Nature and Enduring Peace.* New Haven, CT: Edward W. Hazen Foundation, 1952.

Osgood, Robert E. *NATO: The Entangling Alliance.* Chicago: University of Chicago Press, 1962.

Patterson, Ernest Minor, ed. "NATO and World Peace." *The Annals of the American Academy of Political and Social Science* 288 (July 1953).

Sewell, James Patrick. *Functionalism and World Politics.* Princeton, NJ: Princeton University Press, 1966.

Shuster, George N. *Cultural Cooperation and the Peace.* Milwaukee, WI: Bruce, 1952.

Thompson, Kenneth W. *Ethics, Functionalism and Power in International Politics*. Baton Rouge, LA, and London: Louisiana State University Press, 1979.
Tucker, Robert W. *A New Isolationism*. Washington, DC: Potomac Associates, 1972.
West, Ranyard. *Psychology and World Order*. London: Penguin Books, 1945.

PART TEN

On the problems of diplomacy, see:

Beard, Charles A. *The Idea of National Interest*. New York: Macmillan, 1934.
Burton, J. W. *Systems, States, Diplomacy and Rules*. London and New York: Cambridge University Press, 1968.
Callieres, Francois de. *On the Manner of Negotiating with Princes*.
Cambon, Jules. *Le Diplomate*. Paris: Hachette, 1926.
Chamburn, Charles de. *L'Espirit de la diplomatie*. Paris: Editions Correa, 1944.
Craig, Gordon A., and Gilbert, Felix, eds. *The Diplomats, 1939*. Princeton, NJ: Princeton University Press, 1953; New York: Atheneum, 1963.
Craig, Gordon A., and George, Alexander L. *Force and Statecraft*. New York and Oxford: Oxford University Press, 1983.
Fisher, Roger, and Ury, William. *Getting to Yes: Negotiating Agreement Without Giving In*. Boston: Houghton Mifflin, 1981; New York: Penguin Books, 1983.
Foster, John W. *The Practice of Diplomacy*. New York: Houghton Mifflin, 1906.
Franck, Thomas M., and Weisband, Edward. *Secrecy*. New York: Oxford University Press, 1974.
Friedrich, Carl Joachim. *Diplomacy and the Study of International Relations*. Oxford: Clarendon Press, 1919.
Halle, Louis, and Thompson, Kenneth W. *Foreign Policy and the Democratic Process*. Washington, DC: University Press of America, 1978.
Ikle, Fred Charles. *How Nations Negotiate*. New York: Harper and Row, 1964.
Jackson, Elmore. *Meeting of Minds*. New York and Toronto: McGraw-Hill, 1952.
Jones, Joseph M. *A Modern Foreign Policy for the United States*. New York: Macmillan, 1944.
Jusserand, Jean A. *The School for Ambassadors and Other Essays*. New York: G. P. Putnam's Sons, 1925.
Kennan, George F. *The Cloud of Danger*. Boston and Toronto: Little, Brown, 1977.
Kertesz, Stephen D., ed. *American Diplomacy in a New Era*. Notre Dame, IN: University of Notre Dame Press, 1961.
____. *The Quest for Peace Through Diplomacy*. Englewood Cliffs, NJ: Prentice Hall, 1967.
____. *Between Russia and the West*. Notre Dame, IN: University of Notre Dame Press, 1984.
Lippmann, Walter. *The Stakes of Diplomacy*. New York: Henry Holt, 1917.
Mably, Abbé Gabriel Bonnet de. "Principes des négociations." *Collection complète des œuvres de l'Abbé de Mably* 5. Paris: 1794–95.
McGhee, George. *Envoy to the Middle World*. New York: Harper and Row, 1969.
McLachlan, Donald. "The Death of Diplomacy." *The Twentieth Century* 149, no. 889 (March 1951): 173–80.
Macomber, William. *The Angels' Game: A Handbook of Modern Diplomacy*. New York: Stein and Day, 1975.
Mattingly, Garrett. *Renaissance Diplomacy*. Boston: Houghton Mifflin, 1955; New York: Penguin Books, 1964.

Morley, John Viscount. *On Compromise*. London: Macmillan, 1923.

Mowrer, Paul Scott. *Our Foreign Affairs: A Study in National Interest and the New Diplomacy*. New York: E. P. Dutton, 1924.

Nicolson, Harold G. *Diplomacy*. London: T. Butterworth, 1939; New York: Galaxy Books, 1964.

_____. *The Evolution of Diplomatic Method*. London: Constable, 1954.

Oncken, Hermann. *Politik und Kriegsführung*. Munich: Max Huber, 1928.

Pearson, Lester B. *Diplomacy in the Nuclear Age*. Cambridge, MA: Harvard University Press, 1959.

Redlich, Marcellus D. *International Law as a Substitute for Diplomacy*. Chicago: Independent, 1928.

Reinsch, Paul S. *Secret Diplomacy*. New York: Harcourt, Brace, 1922.

Rock, Vincent P. *A Strategy of Interdependence*. New York: Charles Scribner's Sons, 1964.

Schelling, Thomas G. *The Strategy of Conflict*. Cambridge, MA: Harvard University Press, 1960; New York: Galaxy Books, 1963.

Spanier, John. *American Foreign Policy Since World War II*, 9th ed. New York: Holt, Rinehart and Winston, 1983.

Thayer, Charles W. *Diplomat*. New York: Harper and Brothers, 1959.

Thomson, David, Meyer, E., and Briggs, A. *Patterns of Peacemaking*. London: Kegan Paul, Trench, Trubner, 1945.

Watson, Adam. *Diplomacy*. New York: McGraw-Hill, 1983.

Wellesley, Sir Victor. *Diplomacy in Fetters*. London: Hutchinson, 1944.

Willits, Joseph H. "Social Adjustments to Atomic Energy." *Proceedings of the American Philosophical Society* 90, no. 1 (Philadelphia: 1946): 48–52.

Woodward, E. L. "The Old and the New Diplomacy." *The Yale Review* 36, no. 3 (Spring 1947): 405–22.

Yergin, Daniel. *Shattered Peace*. Boston: Houghton Mifflin, 1977.

Young, George. *Diplomacy Old and New*. London: Swarthmore Press, 1921.

Zartman, I. William, and Berman, Maureen R. *The Practical Negotiator*. New Haven, CT and London: Yale University Press, 1982.

Historical Glossary

Adams, John

1735–1826. Second president of the United States (1797–1801). Appointed one of the peace commissioners to France in 1777; one of the negotiators of the Treaty of Paris (1783) to end the American War of Independence; envoy to Great Britain (1785–88). As president, Adams prevented a war with France by a moderate, conciliatory policy.

Adams, John Quincy

1767–1848. Sixth president of the United States (1825–29). Minister to the Netherlands (1794–97) and to Prussia (1797–1801); U.S. senator (1803–8); minister to Russia (1809–14); helped draw up the Treaty of Ghent (1814), ending the War of 1812; minister to Great Britain (1815–17). As secretary of state (1817–25) he played a large role in the enunciation of the Monroe Doctrine.

Alabama Claims

United States claims against England resulting from damage inflicted during the Civil War upon northern ships by the Confederate cruiser *Alabama,* which had been built and fitted out in England. The claims were finally settled in 1871 by an arbitration tribunal meeting in Geneva.

Alexander I

Czar of Russia (1801–25). The failure of Napoleon's invasion left Alexander one of the most powerful rulers in Europe. Inspired by a strange combination of mysticism and reaction, he promoted the Holy Alliance.

Alexander the Great

King of Macedon, 336–23 B.C.E. Through the military conquest of Thrace, Illyria, and Egypt, and the invasion of Persia and northern India, Alexander became virtual master of the Mediterranean center of civilization.

Angell, Norman

1874–1967. British pacifist. He became famous through his popular book *The Great Illusion* (1910), which presented the thesis that wars do not pay and drew the inference that if nations would only realize this there would be no more wars.

Atlantic Charter

Statement of general principles, signed by President Roosevelt and Prime Minister Churchill in August 1941, setting forth the national policies of the United States and Great Britain with respect to the postwar world; included principles of national self-determination, opposition to aggression, disarmament, and equal access to trade and raw materials.

Augustus

Adopted son and heir of Julius Caesar. First Roman emperor (27 B.C.E.–C.E. 14); gained control of Italy, Africa, Sardinia, and Sicily; became sole ruler of the Roman world by defeating Anthony and Cleopatra at the battle of Actium (31 B.C.E.).

Austerlitz, Battle of

In 1805 at Austerlitz, in what is now Czechoslovakia, Napoleon I defeated the Russian and Austrian armies. Considered Napoleon's most brilliant victory, this battle marked the peak of Napoleon's fortunes.

Bacon, Francis (Viscount St. Albans)

1561–1626. English philosopher.

Baldwin, Stanley

1867–1947. British Conservative leader; chancellor of the Exchequer, 1922–23; prime minister, 1923–24, 1924–29, 1935–37.

Barbarossa, Frederick

Epithet of Frederick I, Holy Roman emperor and king of Germany, 1152–90.

Berrère, Camille E. P.

1851–1940. French ambassador to Italy (1897–1924).

Barthou, Jean Louis

1862–1934. French statesman. As foreign minister (1934) he sought to strengthen France's relations with Russia, Great Britain, and the Little Entente.

Bay of Pigs

A part of the Cuban coastline where in 1961 a group of Cuban refugees staged an invasion under American auspices and failed.

Beard, Charles A.

1874–1948. American historian and political scientist.

Beneš, Edvard

1887–1948. Czechoslovakian statesman. As foreign minister (1918–35) and premier (1921–22), he was largely responsible for the Little Entente and the Czech alliance with France. Elected president in 1935; went into exile after the Munich Pact (1938); headed provisional government during Second World War; reelected president in 1946; resigned shortly after communist coup of 1948.

Bentham, Jeremy

1748–1832. English philosopher and jurist; founder of the utilitarian school.

Berlin, Congress of

1878. Called by the signatories of the Treaty of Paris (1856), which ended the Crimean War, to reconsider the terms of the Treaty of San Stefano, forced on the Ottoman Empire by Russia earlier in 1878.

Beveridge, Albert J.

1862–1927. U.S. senator (1889–1911) and biographer of John Marshall. As a politician his fame rests upon his support of imperialism in international politics and the progressive movement in domestic politics.

Big Stick Policy

The characterization of a vigorous exercise of national power, derived from president Theodore Roosevelt's (1901–9) famous dictum: "Speak softly, but carry a big stick."

Bismarck, Otto von

1815–98. German statesman. Prussian premier (1862–71) and German chancellor (1871–90); he united Germany under Prussian leadership and made the German Empire one of the great powers.

Boer War
1899–1902. War between British and Dutch colonists (called Boers) in South Africa.

Bohlen, Charles E.
1904–1974. American diplomat. Ambassador to the Soviet Union (1953–57).

Bolingbroke, Henry St. John, 1ˢᵗ Viscount
1678–1751. English Tory statesman and writer.

Bose, Subhas Chandra
1897–1945. Indian nationalist, jailed by the British for his Axis sympathies during the Second World War. He escaped, fled to Germany, and headed Japanese-sponsored "provisional government of India."

Bourbons
Royal family, originally of France, with branches that ruled Spain, the Two Sicilies, and Parma; ruled France, except during the French Revolution and the Napoleonic era, from the end of the sixteenth century to 1848.

Boxer Rebellion
1900. Violent attacks on foreigners and Christians in China (especially Beijing), perpetrated by an antiforeign military organization known as the Boxers.

Briand-Kellogg Pact
A treaty, also called Pact of Paris, signed in 1928 by the United States and 43 other nations, pledging the signatories to renounce war as an instrument of national policy and to seek the settlement of international disputes by peaceful means only. Chiefly the work of United States secretary of state Kellogg and French foreign minister Briand.

Bright, John
1811–89. Member of British parliament. Liberal champion of the middle-class reform movement in England.

Bryce, James
1838–1922. English historian, statesman, diplomat, and jurist. Chiefly known in the United States for his classic study of American society and politics, *The American Commonwealth* (1888), and his ambassadorship to the United States (1907–13).

Bukharin, Nikolai I.
1888–1938. Russian communist; chief party theoretician after Lenin's death; member of Politburo; executed in 1938 purge.

Burke, Edmund
1729–97. British statesman and political philosopher of enlightened conservatism.

Burns, John
1858–1943. British socialist and member of Parliament (1892–1918).

Caesar, Julius
100–44 B.C.E. Roman statesman and general, who founded the Roman Empire.

Calhoun, John C.
1782–1850. American statesman and political philosopher. Defender of the interests of the Southern planter aristocracy and author of the constitutional theory of nullification. Secretary of war (1817–25); vice president (1825–29); secretary of state (1844–45).

Cambon, Jules M.
1845–1935. French diplomat; brother of Pierre Paul Cambon. ambassador to the United States during the Spanish-American War, to Spain (1902–7), and to Germany (1907–14).

Cambon, Pierre Paul

1843–1924. French diplomat; brother of Jules Cambon. As ambassador to England (1898–1920) he helped to create the Entente Cordiale (1904) and the Anglo-Russian Agreement of 1907, and he encouraged England to enter the First World War.

Canning, George

1770–1827. British statesman; prime minister (1827); foreign secretary (1807–9, 1822–27).

Carthaginian Peace

The destruction of Carthage effected by Rome in 146 B.C.E. at the end of the Third Punic War, 149–46 B.C.E.

Castlereagh, Robert Steward, Marquess of Londonderry, Viscount

1769–1822. British Tory statesman. secretary of war (1805, 1807–9); foreign secretary (1811–22).

Catherine the Great (Catherine II)

Czarina of Russia (1762–96). Expanded and strengthened the Russian Empire, chiefly at the expense of Turkey.

Cato (the Elder)

234–149 B.C.E. Roman statesman, implacable foe of Carthage; his influence helped to bring on the Third Punic War.

Cavour, Camillo B.

1810–61. Italian statesman, Premier of Sardinia (1852–59, 1860–61); achieved the political unification of Italy.

Chaco War

1932–35. War between Bolivia and Paraguay over possession of the Chaco territory.

Chamberlain, Joseph

1836–1914. British statesman. As colonial secretary (1895–1903) he advocated imperial expansion, consolidation, and reform.

Chamberlain, Neville

1869–1940. English statesman; son of Joseph Chamberlain. As prime minister (1937–40) he was the outstanding advocate of a policy of "appeasement" toward the Axis; forced to resign after British debacle in Norway (April 1940).

Charlemagne

Emperor of the West (800–814); king of the Franks (768–814).

Charles II

King of England, Scotland, Ireland (1660–85).

Charles V

Emperor of Holy Roman Empire (1519–58) and (as Charles I) king of Spain (1516–56).

Charles VIII

King of France (1483–98). Invaded Italy in 1494; forced to retreat by league comprising Ferdinand V of Spain, Emperor Maximilian I, Pope Alexander VI, and the rulers of Milan and Venice.

Chesterfield, Philip Dormer Stanhope, 4th Earl of

1694–1773. English statesman and author.

Churchill, Winston L. S.

1874–1965. British statesman and author. First lord of the admiralty (1911–15, 1939–40); held various cabinet posts before and after First World War; prime minister (1940–45, 1951–55).

Clausewitz, Karl von

1780–1831. Prussian general and writer on military strategy. His masterpiece, *On War*, has had an enormous influence on military strategy and tactics and the theory of war.

Clemenceau, Georges

1841–1929. French statesman, twice premier (1906–9, 1917–19). Chief antagonist of Woodrow Wilson at the Paris Peace Conference (1919).

Cobden, Richard

1804–65. English statesman, leader in the liberal reform movement; especially concerned with the promotion of free trade.

Colombo Plan

A British Commonwealth plan, established in 1951, for cooperative economic development in South and Southeast Asia.

Corneille, Pierre

1606–84. French dramatist.

Council of Europe

International body created in 1949 by representatives of Great Britain, France, Belgium, the Netherlands, Luxemburg, Norway, Sweden, Denmark, Ireland, and Italy; joined by Greece and Turkey in 1950. The council aims, through the work of its Committee of Ministers and Consultative Assembly, to achieve a European federation.

Covenant of the League of Nations

Constitution of the League of Nations.

Crimean War

1854–56. War in which France, Great Britain, and Turkey were allied against Russia. The Treaty of Paris (1856), ending the war, placed the Danubian principalities under the joint guaranty of the great powers, neutralized the Black Sea, and pledged the signatories to respect the independence and integrity of Turkey.

Crucé, Émeric

1590–1648. In *Le Nouveau Cynée* (1623) Crucé envisioned a council of ambassadors, representing all monarchs and sovereign republics, that would judge international disputes by majority vote and enforce its decisions.

Demosthenes

384–322 B.C.E. Greatest of Greek orators, he warned the Athenians in his *Philippics* (351, 344, 341 B.C.E.) about the threat of Philip II's Macedon, which conquered Greece in 338 B.C.E.

Descartes, René

1596–1650. French philosopher.

Diderot, Dénis

1713–84. French philosopher and man of letters.

Disraeli, Benjamin (Earl of Beaconsfield)

1804–81. British statesman and author; prime minister (1867–68, 1874–80). Revitalized the Tory Party with a twofold policy of imperialism and democratic reform.

Elizabeth I

Queen of England (1558–1603).

Erasmus, Desiderius

1469–1536. One of the great humanists of the Renaissance.

Eugene of Savoy

1663–1736. The greatest military leader of his time and a great statesman in the service of Austria.

European Defense Community

Abortive proposal agreed upon in 1952 by France, Germany, Italy, Belgium, the Netherlands, and Luxembourg, with the intention of creating a common defense force.

European Payments Union

Organization established in 1950 by members of the Organization for European Economic Cooperation (OEEC) in order to develop and liberalize inter-European exchanges. The union, now replaced by the European Monetary Agreement, enabled members to balance their accounts with the other member states by utilizing any foreign currency to settle debit balances with any country.

Farewell Address

1796. President George Washington's advice to his countrymen upon retiring from office at the end of his second administration.

Fénelon, François

1651–1715. French theologian and author; archbishop of Cambrai.

Fichte, Johann Gottlieb

1762–1814. German philosopher.

Foch, Ferdinand

1851–1929. Marshal of France; from March 1918 on, chief of the unified Allied command during the First World War.

Four Freedoms

In his message to Congress proposing Lend-Lease (January 6, 1941), President Franklin D. Roosevelt stated that four freedoms should prevail everywhere in the world—freedom of speech, freedom of worship, freedom from want, and freedom from fear.

Fourteen Points

President Woodrow Wilson's formulation of Allied war aims and of a general peace program, which he presented in an address to Congress, January 8, 1918.

Francis I

King of France (1515–47).

Francis II

Last emperor of the Holy Roman Empire (1792–1806); first emperor of Austria (as Francis I, 1804–35); king of Bohemia and Hungary (1792–1835).

Franklin, Benjamin

1706–90. American statesman, printer, scientist, and writer. One of the greatest diplomats of the American Revolution and the newborn nation; played a major role in gaining French recognition of the new republic (1778) and in negotiating peace with Great Britain in 1782.

Frederick II (Frederick the Great)

King of Prussia (1740–86). Through his brilliant military tactics, especially in the War of the Austrian Succession (1740–48) and the Seven Year's War (1756–63), be made Prussia the foremost military power in Europe.

Freeport, Sir Andrew

One of the characters invented by Richard Steele and Joseph Addison as mouthpieces for their views on current affairs in the English daily *Spectator,* published in the early eighteenth century.

de Gaulle, Charles

1890–1970. French general and statesman. In the Second World War he opposed the Franco-German armistice in 1940, fled to England, and became leader of the Fighting French and of the French provisional government. In postwar France he was the leader of the nationalist-rightist party, R.P.F. (*Rassemblement du Peuple Français*), and in 1958 was elected president of the Fifth Republic.

Genoa, Republic of

An Italian maritime power; reached the peak of its strength in the fourteenth century. Annexed to France in 1805 and united with the kingdom of Sardinia in 1815.

George III
King of Great Britain and Ireland (1760–1820).

George VI
King of Great Britain (1936–52).

Goethe, Johann Wolfgang von
1749–1832. German poet, dramatist, and novelist.

Gogol, Nikolai V.
1809–52. Russian novelist and playwright.

Good Neighbor policy
A phrase that President Franklin D. Roosevelt chose to characterize his policy, begun under President Hoover's administration, of eschewing armed intervention in Latin America in favor of a program of friendly cooperation.

Grey, Edward Grey, 1st Viscount
1862–1933. British statesman. As foreign secretary (1905–16) he played a major role in the formation of the Triple Entente.

Grotius, Hugo
1583–1645. Dutch jurist and humanist, the "father" of international law. Wrote the first systematic text on international law *(De jure belli ac pacis)*.

Guicciardini, Francesco
1483–1540. Italian historian and diplomat. A follower of Machiavelli, Guicciardini is chiefly known for his history of the period of the Italian Wars (1492–1534).

Guizot, François
1787–1874. French historian and liberal statesman.

Gustavus Adolphus
1594–1632. King of Sweden; leader of the Protestants in the Thirty Years' War.

Hague Conventions
Treaties, signed by the United States and other major powers, resulting from the Hague Peace Conferences of 1899 and 1907. Provided for a so-called Permanent Court of Arbitration, defined the laws and usages of land warfare, rights and obligations of neutrals, etc.

Hamilton, Alexander
1757–1804. American statesman. Delegate to the Federal Constitutional Convention, where he was a strong proponent of a centralized government; with Madison and Jay, author of *Federalist Papers*. As secretary of the Treasury and a leader of the Federalist Party during Washington's administration, Hamilton exercised great influence over foreign, as well as fiscal, affairs.

Hannibal
247–182 B.C.E. Carthaginian, general; invaded Italy by crossing the Alps in the Second Punic War (218–201 B.C.E.).

Hapsburg
Ruling house of Austria from 1282 to 1918; from it were chosen the emperors of the Holy Roman Empire from 1438 to 1806.

Hegel, Georg Wilhelm Friedrich
1770–1831. German philosopher.

Henry II
King of France (1547–59); continued the struggle of his father, Francis I, against Emperor Charles V and Charles's son, Philip II of Spain.

Henry VIII
King of England (1509–47).

Hilferding, Rudolph

1877–1941. German socialist and economist; finance minister (1923, 1928–29).

Hobbes, Thomas

1588–1679. English philosopher.

Hobson, John A.

1858–1940. English economist.

Holy Roman Empire

962–1806. A Western European political entity claiming to be the successor to the Roman Empire, which was suspended in 476. Remained until the sixteenth century a European commonwealth, though European nations did not recognize its suzerainty. It lost virtually all political importance as a result of the Thirty Years' War (1618–48) and was dissolved in 1806.

Hull, Cordell

1871–1955. U.S. secretary of state (1933–44).

International Bank for Reconstruction and Development

Autonomous institution affiliated with the United Nations. Its function is to make loans to member nations and foreign investors in order to facilitate productive investment, encourage foreign trade, and discharge international debts.

International Bureau of Weights and Measures

Intergovernmental organization established in 1875 to standardize weights and measures. Affiliated with the United Nations since 1949.

International Civil Aviation Organization

Affiliate of the United Nations, organized in 1947; designed to expand international air trade and make it safer and more economical.

International Danube Commission

Established by Treaty of Versailles (1919) to administer the internationalized section of the river; repudiated by Germany in 1936 and dissolved in 1940.

International Institute of Agriculture

Founded in 1905, with the object of collecting and disseminating knowledge relating to agriculture.

International Monetary Fund

Autonomous organization, affiliated since 1947 with the United Nations; cooperates closely with the International Bank for Reconstruction and Development; designed to facilitate international trade, reduce inequities in exchange, and stabilize currencies.

International Telecommunication Union

Designed to maintain and extend international cooperation for the improvement and rational use of all kinds of telecommunication. It was established in 1934 as an amalgamation of the International Telegraph Union, established in 1865, and the International Radiotelegraph Union, established in 1906.

International Telegraph Union

Established in 1865, this organization was the first important public international union. Became known as the Telecommunication Union in 1934; now a specialized agency of the United Nations.

James, William

1842–1910. American philosopher and psychologist.

Jay, John

1745–1829. President of the Continental Congress (1778); minister plenipotentiary to Spain on a mission to seek aid and recognition (1779); one of the commissioners to negotiate peace with Great Britain. Author, with Hamilton and Madison, of *Federalist Papers*.

Secretary of foreign affairs (1784–89); first chief justice of the Supreme Court (1789–95). Concluded (1794) Jay's Treaty with England, settling difficulties arising out of violations of the Treaty of Paris (1783).

Jefferson, Thomas

1743–1826. Third president of the United States (1801–9). Author of the Declaration of Independence; governor of Virginia; served in Continental Congress; succeeded Franklin as minister to France (1785); secretary of state (1790–93).

John of Salisbury

c. 1115–80. English scholastic philosopher.

Kant, Immanuel

1724–1804. German philosopher.

Kautsky, Karl Johann

1854–1938. Leading German-Austrian theoretician of socialism.

Kennan, George F.

1904–   American diplomat and historian. Ambassador to the Soviet Union (1952).

Korean War

Began with the attack by North Korea on South Korea (June 1950) across the 38th parallel of latitude, the postwar dividing line fixed by an agreement between Russia and the United States. South Korea was joined by United Nations forces, under United States command, after the United Nations passed a resolution (June 25) charging a breach of peace and demanding cessation of hostilities and withdrawal of North Korean forces. North Korea was joined by Chinese Communists in November 1950 when United Nations forces approached the Manchurian border. In 1951 the battle lines were again stabilized at the 38th parallel. An armistice was concluded in July 1953.

Laval, Pierre

1883–1945. French politician; premier (1931–32, 1935–36); virtual dictator of the Vichy government under Pétain (1942–45). After the Second World War he was executed for collaborating with the Germans.

Lenin, V. I.

1870–1924. Russian revolutionist and statesman; founder of bolshevism, the Third International, and the Soviet Union.

Leopold I

King of Belgium (1831–65).

Leopold II

King of Belgium (1865–1909).

Little Entente

Treaties of alliance concluded in 1920 and 1921 among Czechoslovakia, Rumania, and Yugoslavia for the common defense of the status quo of 1919.

Lloyd George, David (1st Earl of Dwyfor)

1863–1945. British statesman and prime minister during World War I.

Locarno Treaties

1925. Included a treaty of mutual guaranty of the Franco-German and Belgo-German frontiers (signed by Germany, France, Belgium, and by Great Britain and Italy as guarantors), various arbitration treaties, and a Franco-Polish and Franco-Czechoslovakian treaty for mutual assistance in case of attack by Germany. Created a brief period of international good feeling known as the "spirit of Locarno."

Locke, John

1632–1704. English philosopher.

Long, Huey
1893–1935. Governor of Louisiana (1928–31); U.S. senator (1931–35).

Louis XIV
King of France (1643–1715).

Louis XV
King of France (1715–74).

Louis XVI
King of France (1774–92).

Love, Alfred Henry
1830–1913. American pacifist.

Luxemburg, Rosa
1870–1919. German Marxist; founded Spartacus Party in the First World War and aided in its transformation into the German Communist Party.

Macedonian Empire
Reached peak of its power during the reign of Alexander the Great in the third century B.C.E.; defeated, divided, and annexed by Rome in the second and first centuries B.C.E.

Machiavelli, Niccolò
1469–1527. Italian political philosopher and statesman.

Madison, James
1751–1836. Author, with Hamilton and Jay, of *Federalist Papers;* secretary of state (1801–8) under Jefferson, whom he succeeded as president (1809–17).

Maginot Line
System of fortifications along the eastern frontier of France; named for André Maginot, French minister of war (1922–24, 1929–31), who began its construction. Considered impregnable, the whole line became useless when the Germans turned it by means of the breakthrough at Sedan, which initiated the invasion of France in 1940.

Mahan, Alfred Thayer
1840–1914. American historian, naval officer, and publicists; formulated a doctrine of sea power that exerted great influence in the United States, Great Britain, Germany, Japan, and Russia.

Mahomet II
1429–81. Ottoman sultan (1451–81); completed conquest of Byzantine Empire; founder of Ottoman Empire.

Maria Theresa
Empress of Austria-Hungary (1740–80).

Marx, Karl
1818–83. German economist and social philosopher, who laid the theoretical foundation of modern socialism.

Mazarin, Jules
1602–61. French statesman; cardinal of the Roman Catholic Church. Leading minister (1643–61) in the first period of Louis XIV's reign.

Mediatization
The act by which in the Holy Roman Empire the "immediate" relationship between a state and the Empire was transformed into a "mediate" one through the intercession of a superior state, which represented from then on the mediatized state in its relations with the Empire.

Metternich, Prince Klemens von
1773–1859. Austrian foreign minister (1809–21), chancellor (1821–48); took a major part in shaping the diplomacy of Europe during the Napoleonic Wars, and was the leading statesman of Europe from 1815 to 1848.

Mill, John Stuart
1806–73. English philosopher and economist.

Minorities Treaties
Treaties, concluded after the First World War, binding most of the states of Central and Eastern Europe to protect minorities within their borders by assuring them liberty to practice their religions, speak their own languages, and educate their children in the minority cultures. The League of Nations was responsible for enforcing these stipulations.

Morley, John, Viscount Morley of Blackburn
1838–1923. English liberal statesman and man of letters.

Munich settlement
September 1938. Marked the peak of the policy of "appeasement." England, represented by Neville Chamberlain, and France, represented by Édouard Daladier, surrendered to Hitler's demands and permitted Germany to occupy the Sudetenland in Czechoslovakia. Although France and Britain guaranteed the new boundaries, neither acted when Hitler took over all of Czechoslovakia in March 1939.

Napoleon I
1769–1821. Emperor of France (1804–15).

Napoleon III
1808–73. Emperor of France (1852–70); nephew of Napoleon I. As president of the Second Republic after the revolution of 1848, he made himself dictator and then emperor; abdicated after defeat in the Franco-Prussian War (1870–71).

Napoleonic Wars
1796–1815. Wars waged by France, under Napoleon I's military and political leadership, against England, Austria, Prussia, Russia, and most of the other countries of Europe at various times and in various combinations. Ended with Napoleon's defeat at Waterloo.

National Socialists
Members of the National Socialist German Workers Party (abbreviated to the term "Nazis"), founded after the First World War and led by Hitler.

Nehru, Jawaharlal
1889–1964. A leader of the Indian independence movement; president of the Indian National Congress since 1929; prime minister of independent India, 1947–1964.

Nietzsche, Friedrich Wilhelm
1844–1900. German philosopher.

Nine Power Treaty
1922. The United States, Great Britain, Japan, and six other members of the Washington Conference bound themselves to respect the "sovereignty, the independence, and the territorial and administrative integrity of China," and to uphold the principle of the Open Door.

North, Frederick North, 7th Baron
1732–92. English prime minister (1770–82).

Nuremberg Trials
1945–47. Trials of Nazis for "war crimes" by an International Military Tribunal sitting in Nuremberg, Germany.

Nye Committee
Senate committee (1934–36), headed by Senator Gerald P. Nye (North Dakota), formed to investigate the activities of bankers and munitions manufacturers in the First World War. It concerned itself chiefly with proving that war profiteers had been responsible for American intervention. The popularity of this thesis was reflected in the neutrality legislation of 1935–37.

Open Door

United States policy toward China, originally promulgated by Secretary of State John Hay in 1899 in the form of identical notes to the great powers calling for the observation of equal commercial rights in China and expanded by a similar note in 1900 upholding China's territorial integrity and political independence as well.

Paléologue, Maurice

1849–1944. French diplomat and writer; ambassador to Russia (1914–17).

Palmerston, Henry John Temple, 3rd Viscount

1784–1865. British foreign secretary (1830–41); prime minister (1855–58).

Paris, Treaty of

1856. See *Crimean War*.

Peel, Sir Robert

1788–1850. British home secretary (1822–27); prime minister (1834–35, 1841–46).

Penn, William

1644–1718. English Quaker; founder of Pennsylvania. In his *Essay Towards the Present and Future Peace of Europe* (1693), Penn put forth the idea of a league of nations whose disputes would be settled by an international court of arbitration.

Permanent Court of International Justice

Otherwise known as the World Court. Established in 1921, pursuant to the Covenant of the League of Nations; terminated in 1945 when its functions were transferred to the International Court of Justice provided by the Charter of the United Nations.

Peter the Great (Peter I)

Czar of Russia (1682–1725); founder of the modern Russian state.

Philip II

King of Spain, Naples, and Sicily (1556–98), and (as Philip I) King of Portugal (1580–98). Philip's foreign policy was directed toward preserving Spanish hegemony on the continent of Europe and securing the triumph of the Roman Catholic Church over heresy. Undertook disastrous expedition against England, which resulted in the defeat of the Spanish Armada in 1588.

Pitt (the Younger), William

1759–1806. English statesman; prime minister (1783–1801, 1804–6).

Potsdam Agreement

Result of a conference (1945) of the United States, the Soviet Union, and Great Britain at Potsdam, Germany. Transferred the chief authority in Germany to the American, Russian, British, and French occupation authorities and to a four-power Allied Control Council; laid down the terms of denazification, demilitarization, and democratization. Delivered, with the concurrence of China, a surrender ultimatum to Japan.

Proudhon, Pierre J.

1809–65. French social philosopher.

Punic Wars

Wars between Carthage (whose language was called "Punic"), which controlled Northwest Africa and the Western Mediterranean, and Rome. First Punic War, 264–241 B.C.E. Second Punic War, 218–201 B.C.E. Third Punic War, 149–146 B.C.E. Ended in the destruction of Carthage and the ascendance of Rome as the greatest power in the Western world.

quisling

Traitor or fifth columnist. The term is derived from Vidkun Quisling, a Norwegian fascist leader who helped Germany prepare the conquest of Norway in 1940 and was later made premier. Executed in 1945.

Racine, Jean
1639–99. French dramatist.

Radiotelegraph Union
Established in 1906; amalgamated with the International Telegraph Union to form the present International Telecommunication Union.

Reform Acts
Three bills (1832, 1867, 1884) that reformed the British electoral system and extended the franchise.

Regensburg, Diet of
A permanent congress of the envoys of the princes of the Holy Roman Empire (1663–1806).

Rhinebund
A league of German princes formed in 1806 under the leadership of Napoleon I.

Richelieu, Armand Jean du Plessis, Duc de
1585–1642. French statesman; controlled the government as minister (1624–42) of Louis XIII; cardinal of the Roman Catholic Church.

Robespierre, Maximilien Marie Isidore
1758–94. As head of the Jacobins, an extremist republican group, he instigated the Reign of Terror during the French Revolution and became virtual dictator of France, before he himself was executed.

Rousseau, Jean Jacques
1712–78. French philosopher.

Rucellai, Bernardo
1449–1514. Italian historian and diplomat.

Russo-Finnish War
1939–40. Began with a Russian attack on Finland (November 30, 1939); ended one hundred days later with the collapse of Finnish resistance. In the peace treaty of March 12, 1940, Finland ceded to the U.S.S.R. the Karelian Isthmus, the city of Viipuri, a naval base, and territories totaling 16, 173 square miles, with a population of 450,000.

Saint-Pierre, Charles I. C., Abbé de
1658–1743. French social philosopher. In his *Project of Perpetual Peace* (1713) he advocated an international court of arbitration, the renunciation of war, and a league of Christian states, bound together in a perpetual alliance for mutual security.

Salisbury, Robert Arthur Talbot Gascoyne-Cecil, 3rd Marquess of
1830–1903. British foreign secretary under Disraeli (1878–80); prime minister (1885, 1886–92, 1895–1902).

SALT
Strategic Arms Limitation Talks between the United States and the Soviet Union.

Seven Years' War
1756–63. Worldwide war fought in Europe, North America, and India between France, Austria, Russia, Saxony, Sweden, and (after 1762) Spain on one side and Prussia, Great Britain, and Hanover on the other; originated in the colonial rivalry between France and England and the struggle for supremacy in Germany between Austria and Prussia.

Sombart, Werner
1863–1941. German economist and sociologist who started out as a Marxist, then turned sharply against Marxism, and ended up as a supporter of National Socialism.

Spanish Succession, War of the
See *Utrecht, Treaty of.*

Spencer, Herbert

1820–1903. English philosopher.

stare decisis

The doctrine of adhering to precedents in applying the same principle of law to similar situations.

Sternberg, Fritz

1895–1963. Marxist writer.

Stoics

Adherents of the philosophy of stoicism, founded by Zeno at the beginning of the third century B.C.E.

Sully, Maximilien de Béthune

1560–1641. French statesman. His Grand Design was a plan for the federation of all Christian nations.

Sumner, William Graham

1840–1910. American sociologist and economist; professor of political and social science at Yale University.

Suzerainty

The political control of one state over another, which preserves all outward attributes of sovereignty.

Tacitus, Cornelius

c. 55–120. Roman historian.

Talleyrand, Charles Maurice de

1754–1838. French foreign minister (1797–99, 1800–7, 1814–15).

Teheran Conference

Meeting in 1943 of Roosevelt, Churchill, and Stalin at Teheran, Iran; reached agreement on scope and timing of the invasion of France and operations against Germany.

Thiers, Louis Adolphe

1797–1877. French statesman, journalist, and historian. Three times premier; first president of the Third Republic (1871–73).

Third Republic of France

Lasted from France's defeat in the Franco-Prussian War (1871) to the formation of the Vichy government under the German occupation in 1940.

Thirty Years' War

1618–48. A general European war, fought mainly in Germany; essentially a war of petty German princes and foreign powers–France, Sweden, Denmark, England–against the Holy Roman Empire, as represented by the Hapsburgs in Austria, Germany, Italy, the Netherlands, and Spain, as well as a religious war of Protestants against Catholics.

Thucydides

c. 460–400 B.C.E. Athenian historian.

Titulescu, Nicholas

1883–1941. Rumanian statesman. As foreign minister (1927–36) he championed the French-sponsored policy of collective security and was one of the architects of the Little Entente with Czechoslovakia and Yugoslavia.

Tocqueville, Alexis de

1805–59. French statesman, political theorist, and historian. After a visit to the United States in 1831, he wrote *Democracy in America* (1835–40), a penetrating analysis of the nature of American democracy and of democracy in general.

Trajan
Roman emperor (98–117).

Troppau, Congress of
1820. International conference called by Metternich, under the provisions of the Holy Alliance, to consider means of suppressing the liberal uprisings against the kings of Sicily and Spain.

Truman Doctrine
Outlined by President Truman in an address to Congress (March 1947) in support of the Greek-Turkish aid bill. The policy that came to be known as the Truman Doctrine calls, in effect, for the "containment" of communism by giving aid to governments seeking to repel "totalitarian aggression."

United Nations Economic and Social Council
Constituent organ of the United Nations with the function of investigating international economic and social questions and reporting to the General Assembly and other United Nations organs for action.

United Nations Food and Agriculture Organization
Established in 1946, with the object of bettering the conditions of rural life, improving agricultural production and distribution, and raising the level of nutrition.

United Nations Trusteeship Council
Supervises control of non-self-governing territories according to the Charter of the United Nations; consists of members administering trust territories, and an equal number of other member nations (including always the permanent members of the Security Council).

Universal Postal Union
Established in 1875 with headquarters in Bern, Switzerland; became a specialized agency of the United Nations in 1947.

UNRRA
United Nations Relief and Rehabilitation Administration, founded in 1943 to give aid to countries ravaged by the war; discontinued European operations in 1947; dissolved in 1949.

Urban II
Pope (1088–99).

Utrecht, Treaty of
Concluded the War of the Spanish Succession (1701–4) after the defeat of France by England and Holland.

Vattel, Eméric de
1714–67. Swiss philosopher and jurist; leading authority on international law.

Venice, Republic of
One of the great maritime powers of the fifteenth and sixteenth centuries, whose ambassadors developed diplomacy into a great art. Venice united with the kingdom of Italy in 1866.

Verona, Congress of
1822. Last conference under provisions of Quadruple Alliance; called to consider what to do about a revolution in Spain. The congress decided, against the opposition of the English foreign secretary, Canning, to send a French army to suppress this uprising.

Versailles, Treaty of
The principal treaty terminating the First World War.

Victoria

Queen of England (1837–1901) and Empress of India (1876–1901).

Vienna, Congress of

1814–15. Peace conference following the Napoleonic Wars, at which the great powers–Austria, Russia, Prussia, Great Britain, and France–agreed upon territorial and political terms of settlement.

Voltaire

1694–1778. French philosopher and author.

Wagram, Battle of

At Wagram, Austria, in 1809, Napoleon I won one of his most brilliant victories. Six days later Austria was forced to conclude an armistice.

Weber, Max

1864–1920. Most influential German sociologist.

Weimar, Republic of

1919–33. The German state that was established under a democratic federal constitution passed by a constitutional assembly in the city of Weimar.

Wellington, Arthur Wellesley, 1ˢᵗ Duke of

1769–1852. British soldier and statesman. Commander of British and allied armies in the wars against Napoleon (1808–15); won his most famous victory at Waterloo (1815); prime minister (1828–30); foreign secretary (1834–35).

Westphalia, Treaty of

1648. General settlement terminating the Thirty Years' War; ended the power of the Holy Roman Empire, with France emerging as the dominant European power.

William II

1859–1941. German emperor (1888–1918).

William III

1650–1702. King of England, Scotland, and Ireland (1689–1702).

William the Conqueror (William I)

1027–87. King of England (1066–87).

Wilson, Woodrow

1856–1924. Twenty-seventh president of the United States (1913–21).

Wolsey, Thomas

1472–1530. English statesman and cardinal of the Roman Catholic Church; privy councilor and lord chancellor of Henry VIII.

World Health Organization

United Nations specialized agency, established in 1948. Its object is "the attainment by all peoples of the highest level of health."

Yalta (or Crimea) Agreement

Result of a meeting (1945) of Roosevelt, Churchill, and Stalin at Yalta, Crimea, U.S.S.R.; complete text not disclosed until 1947. Set forth the terms for the occupation of Germany, pledged the establishment of a new Poland on a democratic basis, and bound the signatories to give joint assistance to countries liberated from Nazi domination, enabling them to establish, through "free elections," governments "responsive to the will of the people." Announced a formula for big-power voting in the United Nations, and committed the Soviet Union to enter the war against Japan in return for the restoration of certain territories lost in the Russo-Japanese War (1904–5), and joint Chinese-Soviet operation of the Chinese-Eastern railway.

Index